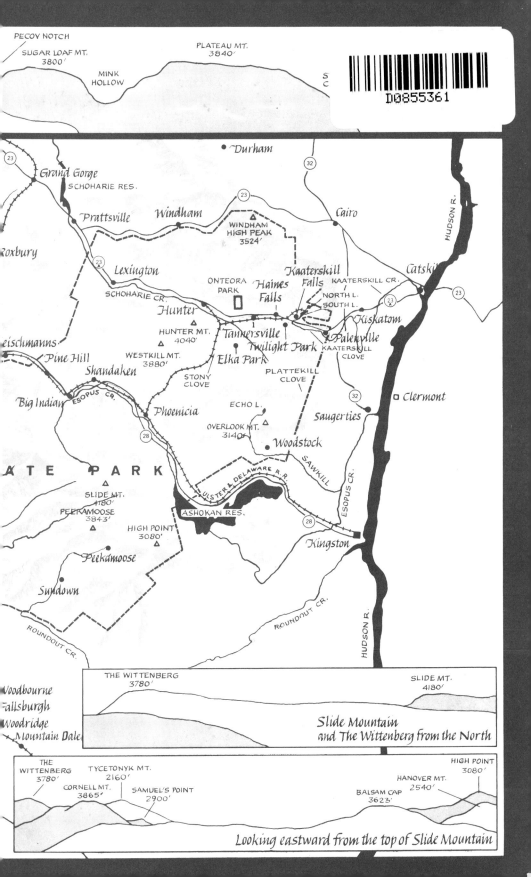

PECOY NOTCH

SUGAR LOAF MT.
3800'

PLATEAU MT.
3840'

MINK
HOLLOW

• Durham

(23)

Grand Gorge
SCHOHARIE RES.

(32)

(23)

Cairo

Prattsville   Windham

Roxbury

WINDHAM
HIGH PEAK
3524'

Catskill

(23)

Lexington

SCHOHARIE CR.

ONTEORA
PARK

Haines
Falls

Kaaterskill
Falls

KAATERSKILL CR.

NORTH L.

Hunter

HUNTER MT.
4040'

Tannersville

SOUTH L.

Kiskatom

(23)

eischmanns

Pine Hill

WESTKILL MT.
3880'

Twilight Park

Palenville

Shandaken

Elka Park

KAATERSKILL
CLOVE

Big Indian

ESOPUS CR.

STONY
CLOVE

PLATTEKILL
CLOVE

(28)

Phoenicia

ECHO L.

(32)

Clermont

OVERLOOK MT.
3140'

Saugerties

ATE   PARK

SLIDE MT.
4180'
PEEKAMOOSE
3843'

HIGH POINT
3080'

Woodstock

ULSTER & DELAWARE R.R.

ASHOKAN RES.

SAWKILL

(28)

ESOPUS CR.

Peekamoose

Kingston

Sundown

ROUNDOUT CR.

ROUNDOUT CR.

HUDSON R.

HUDSON R.

Woodbourne
Fallsburgh
Woodridge
Mountain Dale

THE WITTENBERG
3780'

SLIDE MT.
4180'

Slide Mountain
and The Wittenberg from the North

THE
WITTENBERG
3780'

TYCETONYK MT.
2160'

CORNELL MT.
3865'

SAMUEL'S POINT
2900'

BALSAM CAP
3623'

HANOVER MT.
2540'

HIGH POINT
3080'

Looking eastward from the top of Slide Mountain

THE CATSKILLS

From Wilderness to Woodstock

ALF EVERS

THE CATSKILLS
From Wilderness to Woodstock

Revised and Updated

✤ ✤ ✤ ✤ ✤

THE OVERLOOK PRESS

Woodstock, New York

First published by Overlook Press 1982
The Overlook Press
Lewis Hollow Road
Woodstock, New York 12498
Second Printing, 1985
Third Printing, 1986
Copyright © 1972 Alf Evers
Postscript Copyright © 1982 Alf Evers
First published by Doubleday & Company 1972

Library of Congress Cataloging in Publication Data

Evers, Alf.
The Catskills from wilderness to Woodstock.

Reprint. Originally published: Garden City,
N.Y.: Doubleday, 1972.
Bibliography: p.
Includes index.
1. Catskill Mountains (N.Y.)—History. I. Title.
F.127.C3E93   974.7′38   82-6495
ISBN 0-87951-162-1   AACR2

Printed in the USA

To Barbara Moncure

Acknowledgments

During the eight years which I have spent putting together this book, I have been given generous help by hundreds of people among the Catskills and elsewhere. These people deserve mention and thanks here because without their· help this book could never have been written. I wish that I could thank each one by name, but that is not possible. I can only express my gratitude to a representative sampling and trust that the others will believe that although I have not listed their names I am deeply grateful. On the official level, the members of the staffs of the County Clerks and Surrogates of Albany, Greene, Delaware and Sullivan counties have given me guidance in locating materials which I might not have found without their expert help. County Historians Mabel Parker Smith of Greene and Fletcher Davidson of Delaware opened up many sources of information and shared with me their own collections of local materials. Town Historians Harry Siemsen of Sawkill, Irma Mae Griffin of Roxbury, and the late Ralph M. Lord of Tannersville responded cheerfully and well to my many inquiries. Dewey Borden of Liberty, Helen Ham and Dorothy Ingalls of Hunter, John Kelly of Fleischmanns, Eva Trumpbour of Palenville, and E. C. Elmendorf of Coeymans were among the many who supplied information which cleared up my confusion on special aspects of Catskill history.

The New York State Library at Albany must come first among those to which I am grateful for help. Its librarians were uniformly courteous and generous with their time and skill; those of the library's manuscript room were especially imaginative and patient in their desire to be of help. The library of the New-York Historical Society with its vast and wideranging collections supplied much material on the Catskills' early history; its librarians like those at Albany often went far beyond the call of duty in giving me expert guidance. C. E. Dornbusch, formerly librarian of the Research Library of the Greene County Historical Society, and Raymond

Beecher, the Museum and Library director, helped me use their library's excellent collections to the best possible advantage. The libraries and librarians at Stamford, Monticello, Delhi, Fleischmanns, and Haines Falls were all of more than routine assistance.

Finally I want to say a word of appreciation to my sister Elisabeth for many acts of helpfulness and to Mari Bollman whose transformation on her typewriter of my much revised manuscript into legibility will always seem to me to verge on the miraculous.

Contents

Illustrations

THE CATSKILLS

From Wilderness to Woodstock

1

A Special Shade of Blue

❧ AFTER AN ELECTION in a Catskill Mountain town, an occasional gray-haired member of the losing side will indulge in an odd kind of grumbling. "What do you expect," he will ask, "of a part of the country which didn't even begin acting like it was in the United States until about a hundred years ago?" The man may go on to growl about something called the Hardenbergh Patent as being at the bottom of it all. This patent, he may explain, wasn't the kind a man gets when he's invented something. It was the document by which muddleheaded Queen Anne of England gave away a million and a half acres of the Catskills in the year 1708. And gave the land to a group of perfect strangers to Her Majesty, at that.[1]

In most parts of the United States the land patents which gave white men the right, in the eyes of their law, to take possession of the Indian's land are dead and buried. But it is not so among the Catskills. There the Hardenbergh Patent, in the shape of a lively ghost, continues to haunt the region. Some say it gives a special shade of blue to the mountains[2] as they seem to roll along the horizon like gigantic waves; it certainly turns up in remote hollows and valleys to give an unexpected turn to phrases falling from the lips of old-timers. Not too long ago people among the Catskills sometimes talked about living "on the Patent." One old lady, who lived within shouting distance of Yankeetown Pond in the town of Woodstock, went farther than that. In moments of deep feeling she would refer to the whole world as "God's Patent." "I've looked all over God's Patent for that thimble and I can't find it," she would say. Or, "You won't find a nicer woman—not if you look all over God's Patent."[3] Almost as if, back in 1708 Queen Anne, in an unusually absent-minded spell, had granted the whole earth to the Lord by means of a great parchment deed, rich in "whereases" and "therefores," and with a great royal seal attached.

A century and a half ago the Catskills were largely a region of absentee landlords and struggling tenants. While landlords sailed for Europe (landlord Robert R. Livingston took along his family coach lashed to the deck of the ship for the ladies of the party to use as a parlor in fine weather)[4] or while they collected paintings or raced fine horses as the Hunters were to do, or edited Shakespeare as did Gulian Verplanck,[5] their mountain tenants were very differently employed. In shadowy valleys beside cold and rushing streams, they entertained witches and repeated Old World lore while they fought the stubborn land with weapons not too different from those their ancestors had used in subduing the marshes and forests of northern Europe a thousand years before.

At the same time, and all unknown to the tenants, a way of looking at life called romanticism was taking hold of sophisticated Europeans and Americans. Before long the tenants and their land would become the prize romantic exhibit of America. From their mountains and waterfalls, and out of their toil and pain, paintings, a tale and a remarkable play, both called *Rip Van Winkle,* would be shaped to the delight of the whole world.

As a romantic glow began gathering around the summits of the Catskills, resentment against their landlords deepened among the mountain tenants. This resentment had exploded in murder even before the first painters set up easels on mountaintops and pioneer poets counted syllables beside waterfalls. As the Catskills became established as "a kind of wonderland"[6] and "a rallying point for romance and fable,"[7] landlords and tenants clashed in a mimic war that had something of the air of an operetta complete with music, dances, and elaborate costumes. No one realized it at the time, but even this struggle was in keeping with the personality of the Catskills. For among the mountains, two powerful sides of life have operated side by side and, by a thousand strokes, given the region its shape. One was the greed for land and wealth and the power over others, which both symbolize; the other was the free play of the imagination in the arts and in the exploration of nature. Sometimes the two forces worked together, more often they were locked in battle. The story of their relationship is, at the same time, the story of three centuries of the Catskills.

It is not easy to describe the boundaries of the Catskill Mountains. I once asked an old man who lived within the shadow of Plattekill Mountain just where the Catskills began. "You keep on going," he said, "until you get to where there's two stones to every dirt. Then, b' Jesus you're there."[8] It used to be said that you could tell where the Catskills' boundaries lay by the way the crows flew. You watched a flight of crows heading toward the mountains and when they turned aside that was where the Catskills began. The crows were too smart to fly over the Catskills—

they knew that the landlords had picked the place so clean that a crow would starve there.[9]

Mountain people used to define the Catskills in ways that showed the effects of farming on steeply tilted fields. "The trouble with the Catskills is they got too much land. Had to set it all on edge before they could put it on the map."[10] Some say that the resulting crookedness of the landscape is reflected in the character of its people.

> There is nothing on the level
> In the mountains it is said.
> The people are so crooked here
> They can't lay straight in bed.

So goes a set of verses which circulated in Tannersville forty years ago.[11] Everything in the mountains showed the effects of their steepness. "Take the bears, for instance. They've growed hind legs three times as long as their front legs. That means they can run uphill as fast as you or I can on level ground. Both their ends is on the level that way. Now if a bear should ever chase you in the Catskills, use your head. Don't try to run away from him by heading uphill or you'll be a goner. Go downhill. Then the bear's hind end will rise up so high he'll tip over and fall down. Many a bear has had his back broke that way, and many a man has saved his life by knowing how a bear in the mountains is constructed. It's only in the Catskills that bears is built that way."[12]

More reliable as guides to the Catskills' boundaries are the yellowed records filed in archives and the ancient legal documents stored in the cellars of county courthouses. These tell that the phrase "Catskill Mountains" was first applied some three centuries ago only to the part of the region visible from the point where the waters of the stream known as the Catskill joined the Hudson River. Slowly the name spread to the west and south. It hesitated for a long time at the brink of the Esopus Valley before engulfing the Shandaken Mountains. It marched on and annexed much of the valleys of the Rondout Creek and the upper Delaware River.

Only to the east and northeast do the Catskills have simple natural boundaries. There, a fortress-like wall rises between two and three thousand feet above the Hudson a few miles away. This wall is banded by horizontal rock ledges supporting hanging gardens of oak, pine, mountain laurel, wintergreen, and huckleberries. The great wall is almost entirely without human habitation; along it bear and deer wander, in some parts rattlesnakes abound. In only two places have roadmakers breached the wall and sent highways winding up the precipitous gorges known as the Kaaterskill and Plattekill cloves.

On their other sides the Catskills have no obvious boundaries. The mountains to the northwest and west merge into a high plateau presenting no natural feature that says, "Here the Catskills end." Common consent accepts the country around Stamford in Delaware County as forming the Catskills' northwest corner. From here the common-consent line runs southward through as lovely a farming region as the eye of man may rest upon. There the gurgling of brooks is everywhere, in early summer the air is heavy with the fragrance of wild strawberries, pasture after pasture soars upward toward forest-crowned hill or mountaintop. Cows outnumber humans.

The line moves down the Delaware Valley into lake-studded Sullivan County, where the hills become lower but not less lovely, where the valleys broaden, where huge modern resort hotels crown the hills like castles of old, and where, by summer at least, the cows are in the minority. Somewhere in southern Sullivan County—there is debate about just where—the common-consent line heads eastward until it reaches the foot of the Shawangunk Mountains. It then goes northeastward to the beginning of the eastern wall at Woodstock's Overlook Mountain.[13]

Anyone who thinks he has arrived at a working knowledge of the boundaries of the Catskills has only to speak to a geologist to come all undone. Geologists are a special breed of men. They deal with time in hundred-million-year chunks instead of in terms of fifteen-minute coffee breaks or forty-hour weeks. This gives them an air of remote but firmly founded authority. When a geologist is asked about the bounds of the Catskills he is likely to smile indulgently and state that there really aren't any Catskill Mountains—the whole thing is an illusion. What the layman refers to as the Catskill Mountains is merely a small part of the Allegheny Plateau which runs northeastward all the way from Tennessee to across the Canadian border. When a series of bucklings in the earth's surface some two hundred million years ago formed the Appalachian chain of mountains, what is now called the Catskills refused to go along. Its bedrock behaved in an ornery unco-operative fashion and simply would not buckle. Instead it rose up by easy stages from the shallow sea in which its rocks had been formed from the rubble of ancient mountains to the east.

Raised high in the air, the plateau became an easy prey to the cutting action of the streams which carried off the plateau's rain water. It was carved up like a Thanksgiving turkey. The tough parts remained while the more tender portions were quickly disposed of. What laymen call the Catskills, the geologists explain, is simply a tough part of the Allegheny Plateau turkey which the streams, even with the help of frost and gravity, have not yet cut down to size. In time, of course, they will do away with the whole thing and then no one will have to worry about where the boundaries of the Catskills are—there won't be any. In the meanwhile anyone who wants to do the right thing, scientifically speaking, should describe the Catskills as "a maturely dissected part of the Allegheny Plateau."[14] This is excellent advice, which no one living among the Catskills follows.

Squabbling over boundaries has eaten up an immense amount of human energy and put an end to countless lives ever since the curious concept of real estate crept into human minds. The Romans were lucky enough to have a god to help take care of boundary questions—his name was Terminus. If Roman sculptors are to be trusted, Terminus had a watchful eye and a body composed of a fence post. Lacking a similar god to help moderate passions, the people of the Catskills abandoned themselves to centuries of boundary disputing. At the foot of Overlook Mountain, two brothers who lived together are said to have stopped speaking to one another over a boundary question. For thirty years they lived in the same house without ever breaking their silence.[15] A man in one of the high mountain towns used to say that although he'd never left his birthplace he'd lived in two counties and three towns—in so brisk a way did even official boundaries jump around.[16]

Just as the cutting power of the stones and the sand rolled along by streams shaped a plateau into the Catskill Mountains, so ways in which land was held and the popularity of boundary disputing shaped the minds of the first white-skinned people who came to live among the Catskills. The date when this process began is hard to pin down exactly; it was a little before 1700. On the twentieth of April 1708, with the granting by Queen Anne of a million and a half acres, including nearly all the Catskills, to seven visible men and one invisible one, the process had its legal birth.

Behind the granting of what was to become famous as the Hardenbergh or the Great Patent, lies a long and complex snarl in which the clashings of power groups, simple greed, desires to raise social status by means of land ownership, the use of bribery and the misuse of official position all played their parts. It is unlikely that the snarl can ever be completely untangled. Key documents have vanished from archives and the trail has been deliberately confused by parties to struggles for power going back two and a half centuries.

It is a pleasant custom of human beings looking back at the origins of their people and of their way of life to see it all in a flattering light. The Catskill Mountains have a fine example of this custom in an old tradition of how and why the mountains within the limits of the Hardenbergh Patent came to be the property of eight men headed by Johannis Hardenbergh, a Kingston merchant and trader with the Indians.

Hardenbergh, the tradition goes, was so loyal a subject of Queen Anne that he traveled to England to offer his services as a soldier to Her Majesty who was then involved in the War of the Spanish Succession. He served under the great Duke of Marlborough at the Battle of Blenheim in August 1704. Such was Hardenbergh's valor on that eventful day, when the Duke and Prince Eugene led the attack that defeated the French and Bavarians, that the Queen knighted him. And the Queen's gratitude took a more tangible form. She granted Hardenbergh nearly all of the Catskills as a monument to his bravery. Hardenbergh, so the tradition goes, gratefully accepted the land, but was too modest to the end of his long life ever to sign his name as Sir Johannis Hardenbergh, Knt.[17]

This inspiring tale of modesty, courage, and royal gratitude has turned out to be no more than a charming fabrication. There is evidence to show that during the War of the Spanish Succession, Hardenbergh was busily tending his Kingston store and begetting a succession of children.[18] The way in which the ancient Indian owners lost and white men gained the Catskill Mountains was very different.

It was a way in which honor, courage, and gratitude played no part. It was, instead, what the mid-twentieth century knows as "a deal," but it was a remarkable deal.

2

The Indian Proprietors

❧ IN SEPTEMBER 1917, people of the hamlet of Woodstock at the foot of Overlook Mountain were not thinking about Johannis Hardenbergh. The United States had entered the war against Germany the previous April, and Woodstock boys had already left to serve in their country's armed forces. Everyone knew that Germany was a ruthless enemy and that she had hordes of spies hard at work all over the world. Every stranger coming to Woodstock was given a good looking over—the most plausible individual getting off the stage from the railroad station at West Hurley was not safe from suspicion until he had established his patriotism by a few disrespectful remarks about the Kaiser or by proof of a half-dozen generations of American ancestry. At this point, a man who gave his name as Professor Max Schrabisch arrived in Woodstock. He was equipped with a German accent. He carried a number of awkward-looking packs and had a slightly deformed shoulder.

How Schrabisch explained his presence in Woodstock has escaped recording. Whatever his explanation might have been it was quickly passed on in ever modified form until it became established as having something to do with weapons, or locating weapons previously concealed somewhere in the town. Schrabisch seemed to be bent on doing all a man could to solidify suspicion. After reconnoitering the lower slopes of Overlook Mountain, he took up a position at the base of a cliff commanding Woodstock and there he began digging.

Quickly two schools of thought arose. Schrabisch was a German spy who proposed gathering information in Woodstock and sending it to the Kaiser by means of a wireless station he was setting up, or Schrabisch was getting ready an emplacement for machine guns which would have Woodstock at their mercy. Soon Max Schrabisch found himself escorted to Kingston and making explanations. There he located an unimpeachable character witness in the form of Judge Alphonso Trumpbour Clearwater, once of the New York State Supreme Court, editor of a stout history of Ulster County, a trustee of Rutgers College in New Jersey, a man of might in his community. The judge accompanied Schrabisch to the office of the Ulster County Sheriff and vouched for the professor's loyalty to the United States Government. His own connection with Rutgers College, the judge stated, had made him acquainted with the professor's fame, his achievements, and his high standing in the world of science.[1]

The judge was right enough in one respect—Schrabisch was no German spy. He was an amateur archaeologist of talent but he was neither a professor nor New Jersey's State Archaeologist. He had excavated Indian rock shelters in southern New York, in New Jersey, and in Pennsylvania. His accounts of this work had been published by the American Museum of Natural History and the state of New Jersey. Apart from that he was—like his new friend the judge—a man whose enthusiasm often ran away with his judgment. In conversation he had a tendency to build himself up and to claim in advance honors which he hoped, honestly enough, would some day be his.

The Kingston *Freeman* made amends in its columns for the suspicions, which Judge Clearwater had so completely swept away, about Schrabisch's character. It printed a story headlined:

> HUNTER OF INDIAN ARROWS NOT A SPY. HE
> IS A GERMAN BUT NOT HUNTING FOR WEAP-
> ONS TO USE AGAINST HIS FELLOW-CITIZENS.[2]

A collection of objects dug up by Schrabisch in Indian rock shelters in Woodstock, in Sullivan County, and among the Shawangunk Mountains was later bought by the New York State Museum. With these went Schrabisch's report of his excavations complete with diagrams and photographs. Although the state bought Schrabisch's report with the intention of publishing it, this was never done. The professor lived at the end of an era of enthusiastic amateurs in archaeology, and his work did not measure up to the standards of the highly trained professionals who were taking over.[3] Toward the end of his life when he was living on relief in Paterson, New Jersey, Schrabisch bombarded the State Museum with pleas that his report be published. He stirred up the Paterson relief workers, who were his last contacts with officialdom, to back his letters with appeals of their own—but all was in vain. Today Schrabisch's unpublished report and a few of the arrow points, bones, potsherds, and implements he collected among the Catskills are neatly filed away in the New York State Museum. No one has followed up Schrabisch's work and made a study of Indian life in the eastern Catskills and it may be that no one ever will. For the professor dug with such passion and energy that he may have damaged any possibility of a future scientific study of the subject.

Once Judge Clearwater had cleared Schrabisch of all suspicion of spying, a fresh suspicion followed to add further confusion. Had the professor been digging for treasures hidden by the Indians of long ago? Had he been no academic naïf but a foxy treasure hunter masquerading as spy and professor? This theory has had its adherents and for many years every account of treasure unearthed in Asia Minor stimulated exploration of the sites so well stirred up by Schrabisch. Recently a Woodstock man was toying with the notion of using a bulldozer to push one of Schrabisch's major rock shelters apart in order, as he said with caution, "to see what there is in there."[4]

With so many more important scenes of Indian activity waiting to be studied, it is no wonder that modern archaeologists have kept away from the Catskills. The lower slopes of the outer Catskills were hunting grounds and not year-round residences through a thousand years and more of Indian life. Indians and whites alike live where food is easiest to get at. The chilly upper levels of the Catskills with their thick coat of evergreen trees are not regions of plenty for most animals including man. But some of the sunnier lower slopes were once covered with such nut-bearing trees as beeches, chestnuts, and various oaks; these attracted large numbers of deer, bear, wild turkeys, and other food animals each fall. Year after year, century after century, Indians of the Hudson and Esopus valleys came in hunting parties to rock shelters on these slopes. Later, when they felt the push of the white men, some lived the year round beneath rock ledges, enclosed with sheets of bark, and with good springs and cornfields close by. Then small groups of Indians uprooted from their old homes lived on the shores of the lakes scattered among the Catskills or on fertile fields in mountain valleys.[5]

The Indian's physical connection with the Catskills was never great, yet the mountains loomed large in Indian life. Early explorers and settlers around the perimeter of the Catskills had more profitable things to do than collecting and writing down the Indian lore of the mountains, yet we have a right to assume that this kind of lore existed.

Indians were animists—they believed that all parts of the universe and everything in it possessed souls. They were convinced that success in hunting, fishing, and all other phases of living depended on getting on good terms with the souls of animals, fish, trees, and the rain-bearing clouds. When their cornfields on the rich plains beneath the Catskill Mountains withered in the sun of a rainless August, did the Esopus Indians appeal for help to the clouds which then as today seem to be drawn together around the summits of the mountains? When floods poured down from the mountains and threatened their settlements of bark huts, did the Indians implore the mountains to have mercy? It is likely that they did, for they lived at a stage of human development in which man and nature are on intimate speaking terms, and a mountain may be a kindly mother or a relentless enemy—while still remaining a mountain.

No record remains of how the Catskills looked to the Indians or what part they played in the Indian understanding of life. We must trust to hints, analogies, and a piecing together of the few scraps of information to be found in old reports and in promotional writings aimed at attracting settlers to the New World. But we know beyond doubt of certain roles which the mountains played in the world of the Indians around them. Most important of these was the Catskills' role as a barrier first between groups of Indians differing in language and customs and later between groups of hostile whites, each with its bands of Indian allies. The mountains played a part, too, as a source of antagonisms between Indians and whites; these antagonisms have left an easily followed trail in ancient records and have only recently died away among the people of the modern Catskills.

The Indians who lived "under the Blew Mountains," as the old chroniclers phrase it, enter history in a mild and disarming way. Robert Juet, who was mate of the *Half Moon* when it sailed up the Hudson in 1609, had the first word. "At night," wrote Juet, "we came to other Mountaines which lie from the Rivers side. There we found very loving people and very old men; where we were well used."[6]

Juet's mountains were the Catskills. The loving people were probably a division of the Esopus or the Mahican Indians. The very old men are likely enough to have been taking care of the Indians' home camp while the younger people were hunting on the mountainside, for the month was September; chestnuts may have been tumbling from their prickly burs, beechnuts were ripe, and deer and wild turkeys were hastening to the feast.

The loving people whom Juet and the *Half Moon*'s master, Henry Hudson, met on their pioneer voyage of exploration were a totemic group whose emblem is most likely to have been the wolf. For many miles to the south other groups—each with its totemic emblem, its settlement, its storage pits for corn, and its tilled fields—were strung out. To the northwest and well hidden by the Catskills were groups who spoke a very different language from the Algonkian of the Esopus Indians—theirs was an Iroquois dialect. To the north of the Esopus Indians lived the speakers of an Algonkian dialect different from that of the Esopus people—they were called the Mahicans. On the western and southwestern borders of the mountains, still another Algonkian-speaking group was thinly settled on favorable spots in the Delaware Valley from the Minnisink country northward to present day Margaretville and Arkville.[7]

These then were "the Indian proprietors" (they were so called in old deeds) who ringed the Catskill Mountains in that pleasant hazy September of 1609. These Indians did not suspect that their way of life was nearing its end, that they would soon become an uprooted and bewildered people, and that their great-grandchildren would turn over the mountains to something that was neither a god nor a beast nor an Indian but a group of white men joined together in something they called "Johannis Hardenbergh and Company." But that day was ninety-nine years in the future.

3

Dreams of Gold and Silver

✤ THE CATSKILLS' layers of red shale might have been made of pure gold and its mighty gray-sandstone ledges of silver, and the Indians of 1609 would have left them undisturbed. For the Indians were living in a stone age and knew nothing of the uses to which Europeans put metals or the value they placed upon them. A little copper had been traded to them by earlier visitors than Henry Hudson or by copper-using Indians who lived far to the northwest—that was their sole relation with metals. The material side of their culture drew for raw materials on stone, skins, shells, wood, and bark. All the possibilities of metals were unsuspected by the Algonkian-speaking Indians who lived in the shadow of the Catskills.

This age of innocence did not last long. Hudson's mate, Robert Juet, made it plain as he sailed the "Great River of the Mountaynes" that he had an eye out for indications of metals. He noted some in the highlands just below Newburgh Bay. "The Mountaynes looked as if some metall or mineral were in them," he wrote, "for the trees that grow on them were all blasted and some of them barren with few or no leaves." Near the site of the Hoboken of today, Juet saw cliffs which seemed to glow with silver or copper "and I think it be one of them by the Trees that grow upon it. For they be all burned and the other places as greene as grass."[1]

In another two centuries blasted trees were to be hunted out by romantic painters and conspicuously placed in their Hudson River and Catskill Mountain landscapes; Juet's interest was more practical. He and Hudson had probably done some homework before embarking on their voyage which they hoped would discover a short cut by water to the Far East. They may well have read a translation of a book by a German named Agricola. It was called *De re metallica*. In this book Agricola brought together in one charming volume a vast amount of the mining lore of his and former times. He listed in detail the surface indications of underground veins of metals, he described favorable mountain locations in which mining could be carried on profitably, and he described mining techniques. Among the most prominent of the surface indications of the presence of metals in Agricola's book were blasted trees of the very kind Robert Juet set down with such relish.[2]

It would have been strange indeed if the four or five decades following Hudson's voyage had not seen the Catskills pretty thoroughly searched for metals. The Dutch West India Company, which controlled the colony of New Amsterdam, had a monopoly on all mines and mining, but it promised liberal rewards to those who discovered veins of metal and it granted mineral rights to individuals. Besides, there must have been, then as now, men who delighted in outwitting authority and making off with treasures under the very noses of the duly constituted rulers of the land—secret prospecting cannot be ruled out. We have in Agricola's book what amounts to a guide, which in our day might have been called *How to Get Rich by Doing Your Own Mining*. It can suggest to us some of the strange goings on which early prospectors among the Catskills might have indulged in. That they had book learning to help them is shown by the presence in Kingston at a sale in 1665 of the effects of Dr. Gysbert Van Imborch of a book or manuscript on *The gaining of land and the wonders of mountain-mining*. It was bought for seven guilders by a metalworker named Jan the Smith.[3]

Blasted or ailing trees, unusual plants or fungi growing in streaks on mountainsides, regions of uprooted trees, trees with leaden-colored leaves or trunks—all these and many more hints to the location of veins of minerals were explained in *De re metallica* and probably in Jan's book. Although Agricola was skeptical of the power of the dowsing rod, he gave instructions for its use. It requires little stretching of the imagination to see a Dutch prospector, looking much like the bearded one Agricola shows in a woodcut, clambering up Overlook Mountain's Minister's Face—a most likely place for metals according to ancient lore—with his dowsing rod clutched firmly in both hands.[4]

The most spectacular of all means of quickly discovering and collecting metals was through the use of forest fires. Ancient traditions of Greek and Roman days tell of this having been done around the Mediterranean. Agricola passed on the information but without recommending its use. He quotes the Roman Lucretius as writing that copper, gold, silver, iron, and lead were first discovered when accidental fires, caused by lightning, war, or the efforts of men to clear land for farming, swept up mountains. ". . . from whatever the cause the heat of flame had swallowed up the forests with a frightful crackling from their very roots, and had thoroughly baked the earth with fire, there would run from the boiling veins and collect into the hollows of the grounds a stream of silver and gold, as well as of copper and lead."[5]

The Indians of the Catskill Mountains region used fire in clearing land for their cornfields. Early chroniclers of the Hudson Valley say that the Indians set fires in spring and fall to sweep toward the Catskills to clear away trees and brush presumably to provide better living space for deer and other food animals.[6] White settlers made more lavish and careless use of fire in clearing valley lands and often set mountains ablaze deliberately. Did Jan the Smith, with visions of rivers of precious metals running down the sides of the Catskills, set off for the mountains with his seven-guilder bargain under his arm and some glowing coals in a pot and start flames roaring up Shokan Point or Tyce Teneyck Mountain? There is no evidence that he or anybody else did this—but then any such attempt would surely have been kept secret. It remains a possibility, for wonderful is the power of a chance at sudden riches upon the human mind and emotions.

During the 1640s a current of excited whispering and a good deal of scurrying here and there were set in motion by rumors of finds of precious metals in the Dutch colony of New Amsterdam. Adrian Van der Donck and Governor Kieft watched an Indian interpreter named Agheroense at Fort Orange—now Albany—painting his face with a shining substance. They bought some of the stuff and it proved to contain gold. The Indian later led the way to the secret source of his cosmetic. Dr. Johannes la Montagne assayed a bucketful of the ore and this too seemed to contain gold. The whole thing was hushed up. It was decided to send samples of the ore to Holland for more expert study than the limited skill and equipment of Dr. la Montagne could afford. No ship was sailing for Holland from New Amsterdam that bitter January. The ores in charge of a Delaware River trader named Arendt Corrsen were hurried to New Haven where a brand-new ship, known as "the great ship" because of her size, was about to set sail across the Atlantic from the icebound harbor.

The great ship got off with Corrsen and the ore aboard, thanks to much chopping of ice and a vast amount of effort on the part of New Haven's citizens—but that was all. It was never seen again, except in a rather odd form. The next June, as a violent thunderstorm ended, the great ship sailed into New Haven harbor, but as she neared the shore, she faded away. The awestruck beholders knew then that they had seen a specter ship. The New Haven clergy drew appropriate morals in the pulpits the next Sunday; Cotton Mather set down the details of the wonder in his *Magnalia*

Christi Americana. Later on, Henry Wadsworth Longfellow told the tale of the treasure ship in verse, concluding,

> And the masts, with all their rigging,
> Fell slowly, one by one,
> And the hulk dilated and vanished,
> As a sea-mist in the sun.[7]

In 1647 hard-boiled Governor Kieft set off for Holland himself on board the ship *Princess.* In the hold Kieft had loaded a substantial quantity of ores from various parts of the colony of New Amsterdam. As the *Princess* sailed up Bristol Channel to make her first port in Europe, she hit turbulent seas and piled up on a rock. After an agonizing few hours, the ship broke into pieces. Some of the passengers, including two bitter political enemies of Kieft, were saved. Kieft was drowned and his precious ores were scattered on the bottom of Bristol Channel. There, for all anyone knows, they still lie.[8]

Treasure seekers are not easily discouraged. Ghost ships, drowning, shipwrecks—these are all in the day's work for a true treasure man. In the Catskills people used to tell of a man named Hendrick Van Guilder who paid cash for the secret of a gold mine. When he was asked what he was up to, digging all alone by day and night, Hendrick would answer in a jumble of Dutch, German, and English: "Het koningrijk der hemelen or dis het my graf." (Either the kingdom of Heaven or my grave.) One day he was found dead in his pit, his spade still in his hand. In this posture and place he was buried. The kingdom of Heaven—his gold mine—had eluded Hendrick. He had settled for a grave.[9]

Between the lines of old accounts of the wreck of the two treasure ships, we can sense a decided uneasiness which suggests that people in the colony of New Amsterdam saw the twin disasters as a warning that the Lord would prefer having the treasures he had placed in the mountains of the colony remain where He had hidden them. Was there such a thing as being too greedy? Was man placed on this earth for better things than spending his life in the pursuit of riches? Such thoughts must have passed through many a New Amsterdam head—and quickly passed out again. By 1651 the pack of treasure hunters was once more hot on the trail. And this time their goal was no secret. It was a specific part of the Catskill Mountains where a find was reported to have been made by that most innocent of all creatures—a farmer's daughter who was to meet sudden and tragic death as her reward.

4

Treasure Hunters

✿ ON SPRING EVENINGS during my boyhood on an Ulster County farm, I sometimes gazed toward the Catskills lying blue and mysterious on the horizon, and I gazed with a purpose. Thin, old Charley Wood who helped on the farm had assured me that watching the mountains in the spring might pay off—so they said. For spring was the time when the secret silver mines of the Catskills and Shawangunks "blowed off." This blowing off made itself visible as a glow of phosphorescent light issuing from the mine—so they said. They said, too, Charley told me, that a vapor rose from the mountains' still undiscovered coal mines and that "you could light it with a match." When I saw what looked like a small forest fire on the Catskills some twenty miles away it might be nothing more than the lighted vapor from a coal mine. But you would never mistake the blowing-off of a silver mine for a forest fire, no sirree. The color was very different—it was pale and ghastly-looking. So they said, Charley added. Some said this blowing-off was the Lord's way of revealing the location of mines to people who'd obeyed His commandments. Charley didn't know about it himself. He went by what they said.[1]

Just how the young farmer's daughter of 1651 found the heavy stone believed by her betters to contain silver has not been recorded. Whether it was revealed by a blowoff or whether it was a simple, though everyday, accident remains obscure. What the legend does tell us is that once the stone had been found, the tale stirred a headstrong man named Brandt Van Schlechtenhorst to the very soles of his boots. Killian Van Rensselaer, the patroon of Rensselaerwyck on the upper Hudson, had died in 1646 without ever leaving the safety of Holland and visiting his vast New World possessions. Van Schlechtenhorst had come to New Amsterdam to manage the patroon's thriving colony for Van Rensselaer's son who was yet a minor. He enjoyed the title of Director.

Upon his arrival Van Schlechtenhorst found that the late patroon's wish to extend his holdings to include the fertile flatlands along the Catskill and Kaaterskill at the base of the mountains was being thwarted. Upon the patroon's death Governor Kieft had given lands there to a man named Cornelis Anthonisz Van Schlick as a reward for Van Schlick's clever dealing with Indians: he had helped end a war and had ransomed prisoners. Van Schlechtenhorst ignored Van Schlick's claim and the sputtering of Governor Peter Stuyvesant. He proceeded to buy the lands in question from the local Indians and to settle tenant farmers upon them. It was the daughter of one of these tenants who came upon the fateful heavy stone.

Between Director Van Schlechtenhorst and Governor Stuyvesant, a full-scale feud was soon raging. They quarreled over the sale of firearms to Indians, over land rights and water rights, over the levy the governor laid upon Rensselaerwyck to help pay the cost of holding back the New England Yankees from encroaching on lands claimed by New Amsterdam. In 1651 Stuyvesant threw Van Schlechtenhorst in jail and there he lay for four months. Then he escaped with the help of his jailer and fled to the security of Rensselaerwyck. It was at this unfortunate moment that the farmer's daughter discovered the stone.

Van Schlechtenhorst was in a pretty predicament. To leave Rensselaerwyck and go to Catskill would be to invite arrest by his enemy, the governor. To ignore the stone would mean that Stuyvesant or his agents might seize it and claim the mountainside mine from which a torrent had carried the stone to the lowlands. They might go on to claim everything else in sight.

In a fine display of good judgment, Van Schlechtenhorst dispatched his unarrestable son Gerrit to Catskill to handle the situation and perhaps explore and claim the Catskill Mountains.[2] Gerrit had hardly arrived at the farm when one of those sudden and violent rainstorms for which the Catskills are famous descended upon the region. The stream beside the farm rose mightily and burst its banks. The farmhouse, the farmer, the heavy stone, and the farmer's daughter were all swept away to destruction. Young Gerrit alone remained to tell of the tragedy. Once again Divine intervention seemed to have saved the secret mineral riches of the Catskills from grasping human hands. And once again treasure hunters mulled over the matter and, having recovered their breaths, decided to have another go at the Catskills.

That another go was undertaken is made plain in a letter which the directors of the West India Company wrote to Governor Stuyvesant on April 25, 1659. "Gerrit Jansen Kuiper and Abel de Wolfe," wrote the directors, "have also requested us that such lands and minerals may be granted to them (as we conceive situate near the Esopus Kil in and about the high Catskill Mountains.)"[3]

New Amsterdam officials expressed ignorance of Kuyper's and De Wolfe's activities and intentions but they promised that "In the Fall or early next Spring when the woods and hills are burned over and cleared of brushes, and if the good God gives us life, we shall not fail to make enquiries and send your Honors samples of the discovered minerals."[4]

From across the primeval Catskills came the voice of "an old and experienced inhabitant and Indian trader," Claes de Ruyter, to testify to the existence of mineral riches on the southern and western fringes of the mountains. A "crystal mountain was situate between that Colonie (on the South or Delaware River) and the Manhattans, whereof he himself had brought divers pieces and speciments; furthermore that the acknowledged gold mine was there, for he, having kept house with the Indians living high up the river and about Bachom's country had understood from them that quicksilver was to be found there—"[5] The crystal mountain was the Shawangunk range, Bachom's country lay in the Neversink Valley in present Sullivan County. De Ruyter denied the existence of a copper mine on the Delaware, but a hundred years later two such mines were being shown on maps close to the East Branch of the Delaware, in present-day Stamford and Roxbury.[6] In 1735 one mine was inspected on behalf of its rumored claimant, Governor William Cosby.[7]

Obviously a great deal of exploration and prospecting was going on through the 1650s and 1660s and it may well be that behind all this activity lay some sort of central direction. The most likely candidates for the post of codirectors are the Gerrit Jansen Kuyper, who asked for lands in the high Catskill Mountains, and Abel de Wolfe. These two were substantial traders of Amsterdam. Although they never, as far as is known, visited the New World, they had many commercial ties with its people. They may have made a deal with the West India Company to finance secret mineral prospecting and development. About this time, tradition says mining was begun along the Delaware River and in the Shawangunks, and a one-hundred-mile road linking Kingston and the Delaware was built. Did the two Amsterdam businessmen have a guiding hand in all this? There is, as yet, not enough evidence to justify a yes or no answer and the official records are silent.[8]

The sedimentary rocks of the Catskills are among the least likely places on this earth for precious metals to lurk. The Shawangunks' conglomerate, however, has been found in modern times to contain lead, silver, and gold, although never in paying quantities. Yet in both Catskills and Shawangunks, the same fever that may have sent Dutchmen scrambling through the underbrush and up precipitous cliffs with dowsing rods and mining manuals still hangs on.

When an undermined ledge on the Wittenberg at the end of Woodland Valley crashed down during a spell of heavy rain in the 1940s, local mountain people rushed to the scene.[9] Some came out of a natural curiosity. Yet many were responding to an ancient impulse. They wanted to see if the Lord was taking this way of revealing treasures of gold and silver which He had tucked away to reveal to the proper persons at the proper time.

During the last half century the attention of treasure hunters in the Catskills has turned to oil and natural gas. Oil and gas companies because of their favored position in our tax system can undertake exploration at little cost and they have taken full advantage of this. In recent years they have kept the Catskills in a tizzy. Many a head has been turned when the oil geologists arrive to be followed by options, the sale of shares, and the inevitable letdown as dreams of sudden wealth vanished from one part of the mountains to pop up in another. Yet the mountain people have not given up hope of becoming millionaires via the oil route. All they have to do is lick a villain named New York City.

A Chichester man[10] told me in a whisper that it is a well-known fact that "the Catskills are floating in oil. You know why no oil is being taken from the Catskills? Well, there's your answer—the Ashokan Reservoir"— the man pointed in the direction of the great reservoir in which New York stores rain water from the Catskills until it is wanted by the city. "Oil has been discovered in the Catskills over and over again. And every time that happens the city of New York gets busy and buys off the oil companies." I asked why.

"Do you like the taste of kerosene oil in your water?" the man asked. I said I didn't. "Well neither do the people of New York City. Once oil starts to flow in the Catskills nobody on God's earth can keep it from getting into the Ashokan Reservoir—and there'd be no way of stopping it from coming out of every faucet in New York City. The place would be finished. New York's goose would be cooked. That's why New York will spend any amount of money to keep oil from being found in the Catskills. We're sitting on millions of dollars right now. But we can't touch it. I tell you it's a funny world, isn't it?"

I said that it certainly was.

5

The Indian Traders

✢ A NEW FASHION in men's hats as well as the mineral mania had a great deal to do with what happened in the Catskills in the century following Henry Hudson's first voyage up the "River of the Mountains." Hats made of a felt derived from beaver fur had become symbols of a man's position and power in western Europe. A man who wanted to get on in the world had to buy as imposing and expensive a beaver hat as he could if he wanted to impress others.[1] The prices of beaverskins shot up. Very soon after 1609 it became apparent that the land seen by Hudson was a rich beaver mine—and this mine was at once worked.

Anyone who looks at a map of the Catskill Mountains can easily see that a vast system of streams spreads from the mountains toward the lowlands around. The Esopus, the Schoharie, the Rondout, and many tributaries of the Delaware have their birth among the Catskills. Beaver found conditions along the streams radiating from the Catskills to their liking. In 1609 beaver dams in countless numbers slowed the current of Catskill streams. The Indians of the country were fond of beaver fur. They were wise in the lore of beaver hunting and in the preparation of beaverskins. It did not take long for the whites to find this out and to take advantage of it.

When two ways of life come together neither will ever be the same again. It was this way with European and Indian cultures. Europeans absorbed Indian wood lore and smoked Indian tobacco. They ate Indian corn, Indian beans, and Indian pumpkins. They took Indian words into their language—woodchuck, wigwam, and squash are all Algonkian words which have become good English.

Because European culture was a seasoned thing, able to absorb and adapt new ways without losing its identity, the Europeans got the better of the bargain. The Indians with a long past of isolation were at first delighted and then destroyed as they struggled to mix European and Indian ways into a balanced cultural diet.

First of all it was the beaver hat that left its mark on the Indians. Even before Henry Hudson's arrival, fur traders may have anchored their boats in the mouths of streams flowing into the Hudson from the Catskills— the Rondout, the Catskill, the Esopus, and the Mohawk into which the Schoharie empties. The Indians were dazzled by European trade goods; by the mirrors, which were so much more effective than the surface of water; by the steel knives, which cut so much more easily than the Indian stone ones; by iron and brass kettles, which made cooking faster; by woolen cloth, iron nails, jews'-harps, and glass beads. The trader's rum had an almost mystical meaning for the Indians. For it seemed to open the door to another world in which the old became young, the sad became gay, and all troubles vanished. It was a world that had something in common with the afterlife in which Indians believed.

During the 1640s the whites left the water and established themselves on the banks of the Catskill. By the 1650s they were settled at Esopus. From these points they and their black slaves spread along the Hudson and across fertile valley flats toward the Catskills. In the 1660s Schenectady was established in the Mohawk Valley and, from this base, traders and settlers ascended the valley of the Schoharie and reached the mountains. In the Minisink country in what is now Sullivan County, a few farmer-traders took hold and made contact with the Indians scattered here and there along the upper Delaware. By the 1660s the Catskills were circled by a loosely fitting ring of Europeans and Africans.[2] The Indians were wearing trails along mountain streams as they searched for beaver and other fur bearers to take to the trading posts. But the mountains were on the verge of a much greater change than that.

The first settlements of the whites were based on a mutual misunderstanding. The whites believed they were buying the land on which they settled from the Indians, in accordance with European customs. The Indians who had no tradition of private ownership of lands believed they were merely giving permission for a friendly people to settle among them. In the past they had often given such permission to Algonkian groups driven from their home territories by hunger or war.[3]

Misunderstanding led to hostility, to murder, and to war. In 1665 Richard Nicolls, first English governor of New York, signed a peace treaty with the Esopus Indians.[4] This treaty made it plain that the beaver hat had been replaced by the white men's hunger for land as the central force in Indian-white relations in the region of the Catskill Mountains. A house for the Indians was to be built outside Esopus "where the Indians can lodge and leave their arms and sell and buy what they please from the Christians."[5] Apart from that they were to remain on their own lands—and these lands were shrinking. During the next half century the Indian lands were to shrink to nothing.[6]

Sound political reasoning led a succession of English governors to encourage settlement by whites in the Catskill Mountains region. The Canadians to the north were alert to take advantage of any weakness in New York's defenses. Their traders were luring New York Indians to Montreal and some were penetrating the Delaware Valley. More ominous than that, in an era of religious bitterness, the Canadians were Roman Catholics whose zealous Jesuit missionaries were active among the Indians of upper and western New York. Rumors of Papist plots were rife in New York and Albany; if Protestant settlers took the place of the unreliable Indians, the whole province would feel more secure.

Such reasoning was sound enough for its time and place. The Lords of Trade in faraway London urged New York's governors to spread the settlement of what was now called the Province of New York by making grants of land to important provincial men—men who had the means to carry out widespread schemes of settlement, and who would support the government in return for the grants.

The Lords of Trade were sensible men who must have known that in practice this program would not work. New York's governors with few exceptions were needy adventurers eager to extract the last possible farthing from their position of power. The important provincial leaders were shrewd, acquisitive men to whom the ownership of land was the most impressive of all status symbols. They were eager to accept grants of potentially valuable lands—having first made cash presents to the governor and to other officials. They were unwilling to venture upon the dubiously profitable task of settlement except in the most favorable locations, and the Catskill Mountains was not one of them.

Right and left, lands were granted by the royal governors, but the Catskill Mountains remained rejected and unwanted, a refuge for Indians and a source of furs but no fit object in which to invest money. If anyone had wanted the Catskills he, first of all, would have had to ask the governor's permission to buy them from the Indians who were becoming shrewder in such matters and were demanding bigger payments. Besides, there was some question about just which Indians were to be dealt with: several conflicting claimants might have to be bought off. The law was strict about this matter of purchasing from the Indians. It was not to ensure a fair deal to the Indians but in order to make sure that white owners had a clear title under English law. All land titles under English law, said the legal pundits, were first vested in the King. The Indians of New York held their lands under the King by reason of the treaties which they had signed. No European could properly own land in His Majesty's Province of New York unless he first "extinguished the Indian title."[7]

Extinguishing Indian titles, with the aid of rum and deception, went on at a merry pace. Governors returned to England with tidy fortunes, and ambitious New York tradesmen climbed into niches in the newborn provincial aristocracy with the aid of land grants. The Lords of Trade grumbled amid the fogs of London because the settlement of upriver New York was not taking place. Instead much of the land in the province had been given away by the Crown to men who were making no effort at all to put settlers on the land. The Lords revised the land-granting rules to make sure that settlement would follow granting. In Ulster County two shrewd traders were among the many who paid no attention at all to the new rules. They were Jacob Rutsen and Johannis Hardenbergh.

In the late 1680s a teen-ager named Johannis Hardenbergh set out from Albany to seek his fortune in the smaller settlement of Kingston. This cluster of stone houses with reed-thatched roofs had close ties with the central and southern Catskill Mountains. It stood on the Esopus Kill which rose among the highest peaks of the mountains. Overlook Mountain, later to become known as the cornerstone of the Catskills, dominated the skyline of the settlement to the northwest where it marked the point at which the mountains swung westward after twenty-five miles of facing the Hudson.

Beaver, otter, and deerskins from the Catskills were among the staple articles of trade in Kingston. Indian hunters and trappers from deep in the mountains converged on the place by following the winding of the Esopus and its branches. Kingston people relied on the Indians not only for furs but for the venison which made regular appearances on Kingston tables. The Catskills were still an unmapped wilderness, a source of furs and meat and trader's profits, but young Hardenbergh was to change all that. For he was shrewd, energetic, and above all ambitious to rise above the social level upon which he had been born. And that level was an ideal one from which to climb higher.

Young Hardenbergh came to Kingston at a time when a man who aspired to become accepted as a member of the upper classes of the Province of New York simply had to be a landowner on a large scale. Success in business was not enough. A few acres and a house, however elegant, were all very well, but unless thousands of acres of land were attached to his holdings, no climber could hope to reach anywhere near the peak of provincial society. Europe was still very close to the minds and emotions of all white-skinned New Yorkers. In Europe aristocratic families were landed families. That was why the transplanted Europeans of New York's early days dreamed first of acquiring wealth in trade and of then using the wealth to get hold of land and as they put it, "to found a family."[8] Once they had done that—and behaved themselves reasonably well for a generation or so—they were "in." European bluebloods might smile at their pretensions, yet in their own corner of the New World they might hold their heads high.

Dreams of climbing to the top never entered the heads of the tenant farmers, craftsmen, and laborers who made up the bulk of the population of the province as the seventeenth century neared its end. But to a man in the position of Johannis Hardenbergh—especially if he were personable, intelligent, and energetic—the top could often seem something well worth dreaming about. Hardenbergh's position as he took root in Kingston was good not so much for what it was but for the possibilities to which it might act as a springboard. It was Johannis' father, Holland-born Gerrit Janz Hardenbergh, who had created these possibilities. He had done well on a moderate scale in Albany. There he left marks in the land and trading records which suggest that he bought and sold goods and did well enough to invest in an occasional lot or house. Probably he bartered with the Indians, which was often a quick road to prosperity. He owned a sloop on the Hudson and had dealings in New York where he lived for part of his later life—one old record styles him "merchant of New York."[9]

A family on the way up had not only to acquire money and land, it also had to make the proper connections by marriage. Old Hardenbergh never managed to accumulate any startling amount of money or land yet he did have the knack of making useful matrimonial alliances for his children. In 1688 his first-born, Elisabeth, was married in New York to a man of standing, Leonard Lewis, at various times alderman of New York, member of the Colonial Assembly, colonel in the militia, judge of the Court of Common Pleas of Dutchess County, and a friend of New York's great in politics and business. At the time of his marriage the alderman was beginning to invest the profits made in trade in substantial tracts of land. When the time came for his brother-in-law, Johannis Hardenbergh, to use the Catskill Mountains for the purpose of social climbing, the alderman was to become an important member of the expedition.

Even more important than Leonard Lewis to Johannis Hardenbergh's ambitions was Colonel Jacob Rutsen of Ulster County who was to become Hardenbergh's father-in-law in 1699, when the up-and-coming young man married Rutsen's daughter Catherine. Rutsen was a mighty man in Ulster County—and no wonder, for it was whispered that he was the county's richest individual. Waiting on customers behind the counter of his Kingston shop, bargaining with Indian trappers, measuring out cloth and shipping wheat and furs to New York, Rutsen grew almost daily in wealth and respectability. Before long he began collecting land on an imposing scale.[10] By the time Hardenbergh first came to Kingston, Rutsen owned much of the fertile valley of the Rondout which rises in the Catskills and joins the Hudson near Kingston. He freely petitioned provincial governors for grants of land. And the grants were made, but with men close to the governor cut in as partners by way of part payment for the grants.

Barely a year after Hardenbergh's marriage, Rutsen turned over his Kingston store to his promising son-in-law and devoted the remainder of his days to leading the life of a landed gentleman. He left Kingston and took up residence on his own acres at Rosendale. In a country house modestly put together of local limestone and set beside a ford in the Rondout, he cared for his land, sat on the bench as a magistrate, and worked diligently as a member of the Colonial Assembly.

At Rutsen's old stand in Kingston, Hardenbergh carried on and followed closely in the footsteps of the older man. Like Rutsen, he dickered with farmers for wheat grown on the fat soil carried down from the Catskills by floods and deposited on the flats along the Esopus Creek. He shipped farm products to New York on chubby Hudson River sloops, and the sloops in return brought him tea and iron to sell.

The business of traders like Rutsen and Hardenbergh rested firmly on two commodities: wheat grown by Dutch-speaking farmers and furs trapped by Indians. A Kingston trader would not get very far if he simply sat in his shop and waited for the Indians to bring him the furs of beaver, otter, and mink. The business was too competitive for that. Traders from Albany and even from Canada found their way to Indian settlements behind the Catskills and along the fringes of the mountains and skimmed the cream from the trade. "Wood runners" was what these lively traders were called. Hardenbergh, like Rutsen before him, had to become a part-time wood runner himself.[11]

Taking to the wilderness to trade with the Indians had decided advantages. It helped a man make Indian friends, it forced him to learn Indian dialects. It made it possible for him to be more liberal with rum with no prying neighbors to report him—for using rum in trade was hemmed

about with government regulations. It fostered boldness, physical endurance, and ingenuity. Most useful of all, this roaming the Indian trails was
the best possible way for a man to get acquainted with the country. He
might see with his own eyes where regions of good farm soil were tucked
away among the mountains; he might locate stands of valuable white
pines or sites for sawmills; he might note that certain Indian trails could
be turned, some day, into wagon roads.

Some traders with the Indians were content to put their knowledge of
the wilderness at the service of big land jobbers for a fee or a favor.
Others, like Rutsen and Hardenbergh, kept their knowledge to themselves
and, when the time came, used it to their own advantage. In 1701 Hardenbergh began petitioning the governor of New York for grants of small
tracts of wilderness which could readily be turned into productive farms.
In 1702 he asked for permission to buy from the Indians two hundred and
fifty acres "called by ye Indians by ye names of Sakewaneeckock and Pog
Kanecook, lying to ye northwest of ye Town of Kingston . . . upon a
certain creek called Sawkill."[12] These two hundred and fifty acres lay not
far from the base of Overlook Mountain in what is now the town of
Woodstock. The petition marked an important turn in Hardenbergh's
career, for this small tract was to grow by leaps and bounds into the
million and a half acres of the Hardenbergh Patent.

It is unlikely that the Johannis Hardenbergh of 1702 had the slightest
ambition to invest in the Catskill Mountains. Half a century of prospecting
among the mountains had only brought disappointment to others; the
mountains had no cash value at all. They had tall timber aplenty yet they
were too far from the liquid highway of the Hudson to make harvesting
their timber anything but a losing game. Owning the mountains could
bring a man no high social status. If anyone were mad enough to invest
good money in the fees and bribes necessary to get the grant of the
mountains, his neighbors would laugh at him. They might derisively name
him the "Lord of the Catskills" and avoid him as they would a lunatic.
The people of the Province of New York formed a strongly commercial
society—they respected land that would earn a profit in money or status.
They had no use for impractical dreamers.

It was not the mountains of the Catskills that interested Hardenbergh;
it was only the low, flat valley lands that lay beneath their ridges. It was this
kind of land that Rutsen had collected along the Rondout and that was
already paying off in cash and public respect for its owner. Hardenbergh
probably hoped to follow Rutsen's example in and around the Catskills.
If he did he hastily gave up that plan in 1704. That was the year when a

group of farmers on the banks of the Esopus Creek sent a petition to the governor of New York.[18] All the petitioners wanted, they said, was pasture for their cattle and a supply of firewood. But Hardenbergh and Rutsen read between the lines of the modest petition a desire to lay hold of the entire region of the Catskills—rocks and precipices, waterfalls and flatlands, beech and hemlock trees. They took immediate action—action that would force Hardenbergh, whether he intended it or not, to become, for all practical purposes, the Lord of the Catskills.

How Hardenbergh took the steps that led to the granting of the Hardenbergh Patent can be traced in the yellowed papers filed away in official archives. But these steps left more lively traces elsewhere—in the lore that has been passed down from father to son among the Catskills and in all the region over which the mountains assert their power.

6

Queen Anne's Cousin Edward

✲ I WAS GETTING my breath after a square dance at Henry Wilgus' place about four miles from the foot of Overlook Mountain. A weather-beaten man leaned toward me from the next table and spoke. "I hear you live up to Lewis Hollow on the side of Overlook. Now there's this here about Overlook Mountain. Maybe you've never heard it before. . . ."[1] The man sipped his beer and then eyed me expectantly.

"That's possible," I admitted.

Thus encouraged the man went on. "I don't suppose you've ever noticed the direction the old stone walls run between the Hudson and the Catskills, hey?"

I hadn't and I freely admitted the fact.

"They run straight toward Overlook Mountain except the ones that goes to High Peak," the weather-beaten man said, "and now I'll tell you why." He hitched his chair closer to mine. "When they first come to this country it was all woods. But the Hudson River—that was the same as it is today. So they come up the river on this ship and there was this fellow sitting on the deck in his easy chair and he sings out, 'See that broken-down hickory tree standing on the bank? Take a line straight from there to the top of Overlook Mountain and that'll be Fred's line.' So the fellows took the line and they sailed up the river. Pretty soon the fellow in the chair sings out, 'See that big rock that lays on the bank? Well take a line from there to the top of Overlook, and that'll be Joe's line.' So the fellows took the line and they went on up the river laying out one line after another from the river to Overlook Mountain. After a while they come abreast of High Peak and from there on they took lines to it instead of Overlook."

The weather-beaten man eyed me fiercely and said he guessed I got what was going on. I answered that I wasn't sure.

"I'll tell ye," the man said. "The fellow in the easy chair—he was the governor of New York and all the fellows on the ship was his friends. He was dividing up the land among them. It was all done by the politicians of those times the same way such things are done by the politicians today. And that's how what they call the Hardenbergh Patent was laid out—by a bunch of politicians sailing up the Hudson."

"But what about the stone walls?" I asked. My informant said he was coming to that. "The reason all the old stone walls between the Hudson and the mountains point toward either Overlook or High Peak is because they're following the lines the fellows laid out—that's why. Every one of them is following the lines."

A few days later I tried to check the weather-beaten man's story about those walls. And I found that there weren't enough old stone walls left to prove or disprove his theory. Most were used up in foundations of the highways which were built following the advent of the automobile. Others were bulldozed into low spots to prepare the way for the industrial plants and housing developments which came to the Hudson Valley after the Second World War. The stone walls that had survived didn't agree. Some ran toward Overlook but the majority didn't. Yet in some respects the tale of the weather-beaten man agreed with the facts as set down in the records by ancient clerks. A royal governor had indeed presided over the granting of the Hardenbergh Patent; a good half of the patentees had been his cronies; and the governor had sailed up the Hudson not long before the patent was officially granted.[2]

Johannis Hardenbergh, however, was no crony of the governor. He and his family and friends were among the governor's political enemies. It is hard to believe that the governor with whom Hardenbergh had to deal in his quest for land was not invented by some writer with a romantic imagination. He was Edward, Viscount Cornbury—later to become the Earl of Clarendon. He was a cousin of Queen Anne and a grandson of a great Lord Chancellor. He was also a dissolute and debt-ridden cavalry officer who earned royal gratitude by deserting James II and leading his regiment to William of Orange when William invaded England in 1689. William rewarded Cornbury by appointing him governor of New York. When William died, Queen Anne renewed the appointment. With Daniel Honan at his elbow—Honan was the man who had engineered a dubious land grant in the Neversink Valley for Jacob Rutsen a few years before—Cornbury left for New York full of hope that he could squeeze enough money from the province to pay his debts and perhaps even set himself up for life.

New York greeted the new governor with an enthusiasm that quickly changed to contempt. The Lords of Trade who had kept a suspicious eye on the viscount all along ordered him to send his friend Honan packing and this Cornbury promised to do. Yet he kept Honan lurking in the shadows close to him ever ready to give advice on means of milking New York to the utmost. Cornbury chose as "his grand vizier"[3] an army friend named Peter Fauconnier, a clever and acquisitive Huguenot refugee, who turned out to be an artist at placating New Yorkers ruffled by the governor and a genius at extracting personal profit from the most unpromising situations.

Cornbury had one admirable trait: he was deeply devoted to his wife. But, New Yorkers asked, was Lady Katherine worth all this devotion? For she was as greedy as the viscount. When she was seen approaching a New York house with intent to pay a call, they said, a hasty scurrying about to conceal valuables would take place. The cry of "Hide this," or that, "her ladyship is coming," rang out. For Lady Katherine believed that if she coveted any possession of a New York subject of the Queen, it became the subject's duty to present it to her at once. She set up a little court with daughters of prominent New Yorkers as her ladies-in-waiting. The ladies found out very quickly that their positions were not merely honorary—they were expected to do the Cornbury housework, free.[4]

Upsetting as all this was to New Yorkers, Cornbury himself managed to upset them even more. At a regular hour each day it was his custom to dress himself with care in the silk and lace of a lady of fashion. With fan in hand he then strolled on the ramparts of Fort Anne, the most conspicuous spot in all of New York. Friends explained that his lordship did this in order to draw attention in a striking manner to the fact that he was the Queen's personal representative in New York and to emphasize in a pardonable display of vanity his own marked resemblance to his royal cousin.[5]

Cornbury began serving as governor in May 1702; it could not have taken many months for tales of his peculiarities to find their way up the Hudson to the ears of the people of Kingston and of all Ulster County. The people of Ulster had Dutch customs and spoke in Dutch even after many years of English rule. They could not have been happy at hearing that his lordship did not think much of the New York Dutch or of their Reformed Church. He didn't like Presbyterians either, for that matter, and he abominated the Quakers of New Jersey over which he was also governor. He detested Roman Catholics and Frenchmen with the exception of Fauconnier and a few other friends. Very quickly it became clear in

Ulster County and throughout the province that Cornbury's ideal of a perfect human being was a man of his own height and weight with all his prejudices and oddities intact—and like his cousin, the Queen, a zealous member of the Church of England and an enemy of all dissenters.

Ambitious Johannis Hardenbergh could not have been cheered when he learned what sort of man was to rule over New York on behalf of the Queen. Men in Hardenbergh's position needed to get along with the governor if they were to rise in wealth and social position. The alliance between business and government in Hardenbergh's day was close; government contracts, government grants of land, appointment to government posts with fat fees and commercial opportunities attached—all these were the means by which New Yorkers climbed into positions of power and wealth. Hardenbergh with his Dutch background and his membership in the Reformed Dutch Church was not the sort of man whom Cornbury would look upon with favor. What made his situation even worse was that the new governor seemed to sympathize with one of the province's two political parties. Hardenbergh with all his friends and relations was firmly committed to the opposing one.

Back in 1690 when he was twenty, Hardenbergh had been given a brief taste of political power. In that year Acting Governor Jacob Leisler, a champion of New York's malcontents, appointed him sheriff of Ulster County, an important post in a day when a sheriff had the power to influence the course of elections, act as a justice of the peace, collect many fees, and seize and prosecute violators of the law. Sheriff Hardenbergh served only briefly, for when Leisler was hanged as a traitor his term of office ended abruptly. Yet he remained a devoted Leislerite in the politically tumultuous years that followed. His father-in-law, Jacob Rutsen, was a Leislerite member of the Provincial Assembly; his brother-in-law, Leonard Lewis, was a Leislerite alderman of New York. Most of Hardenbergh's neighbors in Ulster County were Leislerites.[6] Their party was under the control of small merchants, men who felt that a fresh power deal would give them a better chance to rise. They wanted to see their governor's powers curbed by a strong Assembly.

Cornbury became an open anti-Leislerite. His was the party of the landed, the rich, of those who had arrived and wanted things to remain as they were without any such nonsense as letting the people have a larger share in their government.

In July 1702 Cornbury made a state voyage up the Hudson to have a talk with the Iroquois Indians. Former governors had made similar trips in a quiet way—but not Lord Cornbury. He was aware that the royal barges of British sovereigns were imposing sights on the river Thames, and now he proceeded up the Hudson on what amounted to a vice-regal barge of his own, newly painted and with its crew in smart new uniforms. Salutes were probably fired at the slightest excuse; Cornbury's fondness for this amusement was soon to draw a reprimand from the Lords of Trade. On board were a sufficient number of pipes of Madeira to cheer the governor and the friends who accompanied him. It was under these noble conditions that the people of Ulster County had their first chance to catch a glimpse of their governor. And it was on this trip that Cornbury first laid eyes on the Catskill Mountains.

What the white settlers, thinly strung out on the banks of the Hudson and "beneath the Blew Mountains," thought of the governor and what he thought of them are matters which no one considered worth recording. Nor did anyone on the glittering barge take down in writing the governor's opinion of the Catskills. This, it is likely, is no great loss. The day when travelers on the Hudson would describe the blue Catskills in ornate prose and poems, or would sketch their likeness with stormy clouds wreathing their summits, was a long time in the future. To Europeans and Americans alike, mountains were still without charm except for the minerals they might contain or the fertile valleys they might enclose.

Most Christians believed in that summer of 1702 that mountains were a symbol of God's wrath at mankind, created at the time He expelled Adam and Eve from the Garden of Eden. A mountain was something to glance at hastily, and perhaps to shiver at, before looking again at more pleasant parts of the earth's surface. Mountains were melancholy reminders of man's sinfulness and of his mortality.[7]

To Lord Cornbury the Catskills could have had only one practical interest or value. They were a part of his stock in trade as governor, and a rather minor part at that. He had come to New York to mend his battered fortunes, and the still ungranted lands of the province if properly managed might yield him a substantial sum. Earlier governors had granted away the most fertile acres and the lands most readily reached by water and had returned to England as rich men. The ungranted lands Cornbury could observe from his barge were rocky or mountainous. If anyone wanted them—and was willing to pay for them— even if he were a political enemy, a dissenter, and a Dutchman, all inside one skin, Cornbury was in no position to hesitate. He would simply make the best bargain he could.

It was this situation that made it possible for Johannis Hardenbergh to do business with Queen Anne's remarkable cousin.

7

The Great Hardenbergh Patent

✣ IN OCTOBER 1704 Lord Cornbury and his council met at Fort Anne
on the ramparts of which his lordship liked to display his skill as a female
impersonator. But for this occasion Cornbury appeared in male garb, for he
was to preside over a business meeting. Among the matters for deliberation
was a modest petition which was to set in motion the chain of events that
led to the granting of the Hardenbergh Patent.

The petition had an innocent enough sound. Cornelis Cool and a
group of neighbors who farmed on the rich lowlands along the Esopus
Creek in Hurley in Ulster County had a complaint to make. They were
being squeezed between the town of Marbletown to the west and the
Corporation of Kingston to the east. Hurley people didn't have enough
public pasture—"commonage for their cattel," Cool called it. They didn't
have a sufficient source of firewood. But it wasn't necessary, Cool implied,
for Hurley people to freeze through the winter or for their cows to
starve. The petitioners "are informed that between the north bounds of
Kingston and the great mountain commonly called the Blew Hills"—
these were the Catskills—"there is found vacant Land left unappropriated
fitt for Commonage and firewood but not for cultivation. But your
Petitioners cannot describe unto your Excellency the exact bounds and
limits thereof." Cool asked the governor to order his surveyor general to
survey the lands and then to grant them to the Hurley people.[1]

The governor and his council might have rejected the petition on
the ground that it was not properly drawn. The lands asked for were
still in the possession of the Indians. Permission to buy from them had
not been requested, and this was the first step required by law. Instead
Surveyor General Augustine Graham was ordered to make the survey.
Although the petitioners would have to pay Graham a fee for his work,

Graham acted as if he were in no hurry for his money. In fact he took his own good time.

The balance of 1704 went by and Graham did not carry out the order of the governor and his council. All twelve months of 1705 melted into the past, and still the surveyor general took his time. Finally in October 1706 he made a very perfunctory survey. Having accomplished this, Graham paused. On June 18, 1707 he finally presented his survey to the governor.[2] Graham's slowness, seen through the murk of two and a half centuries, has a decided charm to the people of an era of hurry and worry. It seems at first glance like part of a golden age when man savored life more thoroughly because he knew better than to taste it on the run. But any such conclusion would be a mistake. Graham, in fact, was hard at work during the three years following the presentation of Cool's petition—hard at work stalling Cool while he and Hardenbergh and half a dozen other people raced around at top speed making sure that the Catskills would go to the right people—and the right people in their view were not Cool and his friends.

On July 18, 1706 Lord Cornbury and his council again met at Fort Anne. They considered a neatly penned communication headed "The Petition of Johannis Hardenbergh and Comp:y." With a modesty rivaling that of Cornelis Cool and considerably less regard for grammar, the petitioners stated that they had "Discovered a small tract vacant and un-appropriated Land in the County of Ulster and desiring to settle and Improve the Same if your Excellency bee pleas:d to favor him and his company therein most humbly apply to your Excellency for a License to purchase the same. . . ."[3] His Excellency could not have been impressed by the self-deprecating tone of the petition for all the petitions he received were similarly phrased. Yet something must have impressed him for he at once granted the license even though the lands at stake were not described and might, for all he knew, have already been bought from the Indians by someone else. He and his council were not discouraged either by the fact that Hardenbergh's signature on the petition had not been written by Hardenbergh but by someone else who had only a moderate gift for signing other people's names. The signer had not even bothered to spell the name as it appeared in its correct form in the body of the petition but had changed the "i" in "Johannis" to an "e" and omitted the final "h" from "Hardenbergh."

With a speed which contrasted effectively with Graham's slowness, the license granted by Cornbury was at once put to use. By July 31 Jacob Rutsen had already talked business with an Indian named "Nisinos one of the Cheifs & sachims and Lawful Owners and Proprietors of several Tracts and parcels of Land in Ulster County." The two had reached the stage when understandings can be set down on paper before witnesses. Hardenbergh's Discovery, the "small tract vacant . . . Land," had grown in the thirteen days since he'd asked license to buy it to "Several Tracts and Parcels of Land." As described in the deed signed by Nisinos with a sketch of his totemic emblem of the turtle, the Discovery is no longer a thing of tracts and parcels but an imposing poem in Indian place names. In return for a payment of two hundred pounds, Nisinos sold to Rutsen lands "called or known by the Indian names of Mohogwagsinck, Kawinsinck, Pakataghkan, Menegherack being a great island, Natagherackaghkananteponck, and Passighkawanonck. . . ."[4] These were the lowlands along the east bank of the Delaware River from its source to the Minisink country far to the south. The deed (or more properly speaking the bond, for it includes a provision for renegotiation under certain conditions) was signed in the presence of William Nottingham, a justice of the peace of Ulster and a son-in-law of Rutsen.

If Jacob Rutsen tried to keep his dealings with Nisinos secret he failed, for before long a cry of anguish rose from the little settlement of Hurley on the winding Esopus Creek. The land Cool and his friends had asked for first was being snatched away from under their noses by somebody else. Cool retained Abram Gouverneur of New York, whom Cornbury heartily disliked, to enter a caveat aimed at preventing the granting of any Hardenbergh Patent.[5]

Hardenbergh countered by renewing his former petition with variations. The lands he and his company wanted, he explained, "were hilly and Rockey in Generale" yet he asked once again for a grant of these lands which he had already "Lawfully purchased" from the Indians. He and his company, he added, had heard of Cool's caveat which he assured His Excellency had been entered "against there obtaining a Grant for the same only to annoye them therein out of invy." He concluded with a request that a day be appointed for a hearing of the matter "in order that justice may be done to whom it belongs."[6] Whoever signed Hardenbergh's name—and he was neither Hardenbergh nor the man who had signed Hardenbergh's name earlier—did a fair job somewhat marred by an "e" which managed to slip once again into "Johannis."

Hardenbergh had already fortified himself by getting another deed from Nisinos whom he knew as Nonisinos. The description of Hardenbergh's Discovery this time abandoned all the Indian place names of Nisinos' former deed and blew up the claim to include a great deal more land than the earlier ones. The Discovery had matured to its full size of a million and a half acres with fantastic speed.[7]

The Hardenbergh Patent papers piled up in the office of the provincial secretary: the appointment of a committee to consider the Cool caveat; a withdrawal of the caveat; various attempts on the part of Hardenbergh and Company to prod the governor into speeding up the granting of their patent. From the point of view of Hardenbergh and Company, there was an excellent, even an urgent, reason for haste. The position of Lord Cornbury, with whom the members of the company had been dealing, was becoming more and more shaky. By the beginning of 1708 it was clear that Cornbury and his cronies were near the end of their New York adventure. The next governor might be harder to do business with— he might even be an honest man.

Complaints against the governor had been crossing the Atlantic on almost every outbound ship. Queen Anne and the Lords of Trade were sad. It was one thing for a royal governor to mismanage and graft in a gentlemanly way; it was quite another to carry things so far as to endanger the prestige of the Crown and to allow the Assembly, elected by the people, to threaten to control the province. On March 28, 1708 the Queen removed Cornbury from office and appointed Lord John Lovelace as his successor. The appointment was to become effective upon the arrival in New York of Lovelace. Thanks to red tape in London and foul weather on the Atlantic this did not happen until mid-December.

It was as what was later to be known as a lame duck governor that Cornbury presided over the granting of the Hardenbergh Patent on April 20, 1708. It was as a lame duck that he approved the recommendations of his committee on the Cool claim: that a patent for pasture and forest be given the inhabitants of Hurley to hold in common, and that the Hardenbergh patentees sell Cool and his friends for their personal use a little tract snipped from their roomy patent.[8]

Once Lovelace had taken office, Cornbury's numerous creditors fell upon him, seized his property and sent him to jail. There the viscount remained for most of the next year. Early in 1709 news of the death of his father, the Earl of Clarendon, reached New York. Cornbury returned to England, took his father's seat in the House of Lords, and accepted a pension which it was hoped—but in vain—would help keep the new earl out of mischief.

In New York the members of Hardenbergh and Company pondered their next move. Their company had been a device for evading the regulation which forbade any one man to be granted more than two thousand acres of land at a time.[9] It had served too as a handy means by which government officials might be quietly cut in on the deal in return for their influence or their misuse of their positions. The smart thing for such a company to do was to divide the spoils as quickly as possible after a patent was granted. Although one of Lord Cornbury's last acts as governor had been to approve a law making such divisions simpler, the Hardenbergh patentees were in no position to take advantage of it. To do so would have meant revealing a pair of very embarrassing secrets.

One secret was that two of the seven men to whom the patent was granted were mere dummies behind which lurked important government officials. One lurker was Thomas Wenham, member of the governor's council. The other was May Bickley, acting Attorney General of New York. The second secret was that the Hardenbergh Patent had a stowaway aboard. He was no less a personage than Surveyor General Augustine Graham.

Wenham and Bickley were tucked away with considerable skill. But so cleverly hidden was Graham that even the sharpest legal eye could never detect him among the resounding phrases by which the provincial secretary, George Clarke, conveyed the patent on behalf of "Anne by the Grace of God of England, Scotland, France and Ireland, Queen Defender of the Faith . . ." to "our loving subjects Johannis Hardenbergh, Leonard Lewis, Philip Rokeby, William Nottingham, Peter Fauconnier & Robert Lurting by their humble Petition Presented unto our Right Trusty and well beloved Counzin Edw:d Viscount Cornbury. . . ."[10]

There were compelling reasons why the dummies and the stowaway had become involved in what began as an attempt to prevent the Catskills from becoming the cow pasture and wood lot of the town of Hurley. Hardenbergh had been the initiator of the enterprise with help from Jacob Rutsen. Because of the two-thousand-acre restriction he had invited his in-laws Nottingham and Alderman Lewis into the picture, and Captain Benjamin Faneuil, a New York trader and distiller of rum, may have been brought in by Lewis. All the rest of the open and secret sharers in the patent were there by way of payment for their services in obtaining the patent, and a rumor which is still alive puts Lord Cornbury himself among them.[11]

Graham was specifically forbidden as surveyor general from being granted land. That was why he couldn't even risk having a dummy. Instead, each of the actual sharers, by a method known as lease and release, conveyed an equal share in the patent to him some months before it was granted. This method had the advantage of being valid without having been made a matter of public record. At the same time and in the same way, Dr. Philip Rokeby, son-in-law of New York's Mayor Ebenezer Wilson, conveyed his share to May Bickley who had been legal adviser and attorney to both sides in the patent deal. Robert Lurting, a rich New York merchant, turned over his share to Thomas Wenham his fellow warden of Trinity Church. Both Rokeby and Lurting declared that they had been acting in trust for the two officials.[12]

One government official saw no reason why his presence in the patent should be hidden. He was Peter Fauconnier, whose concern as receiver general was with customs duties and not with land deals. His part in obtaining the patent was that of "fixer"—a role which Fauconnier often played with skill.

Among Lord Cornbury's last official acts was his approval of a law aimed at making the division of the lands he had granted easier and to enable men like the Hardenbergh patentees to take advantage of the Queen by interpreting their vague boundaries to their own advantage.[13] But this law was of little use to the oddly assorted group of patentees burdened by their secret deals. The terms of their patent required them to make a beginning of settlement within five years. With the patent undivided this would be hard to do, for unanimous agreement on every step would be necessary. But how could they make the division before some nosy new governor might ferret out the sorry details of their land deal and demand that it be declared invalid? Dividing the patent seemed urgent, yet at the same time it was impossible.

Luckily for the Hardenbergh patentees, the new governor had other things besides land deals to occupy his mind. Queen Anne's War—the American phase of the War of the Spanish Succession—was still in progress and Lord Lovelace was deeply involved in the mounting of the Glorious Expedition which, it was hoped, would drive the French from the American continent. But Lovelace never recovered from the effects of his stormy voyage to New York; he died within a few months and the Glorious Expedition failed. For a time confusion and gloom took hold of New York. Large landholders wondered if all the effort they had put into acquiring their acres was to be wasted. The possibility that the French would conquer New York cast a shadow upon their world.

In the summer of 1710 an able governor arrived to brighten the prospects. He was Robert Hunter, a man whose twin aims were to deal a deathblow to French ambitions and to settle the New York frontiers with resolute pioneers to act as a bulwark against any future invasion. Hunter was willing to let bygones be bygones as far as political feuds and land deals were concerned. He quickly approved an act of the Assembly which provided that the titles to all the lands granted in Cornbury's term be declared good provided they had not already been questioned.[14] The law was a dubious affair, yet the Hardenbergh patentees could relax for the moment. Johannis Hardenbergh was now in a position to assert leadership in the affairs of the patent. For a long time he had been a mere "front man." The complicated series of dickers and deals leading to the granting of the patent had been managed by Bickley, Wenham, Graham, and Fauconnier—Hardenbergh hadn't even signed his own name to the long series of petitions and other documents. Probably he had often been unaware of what was going on behind the scenes in New York and had not been consulted on the various moves being made. But once the patent had been granted and seemed to have a fair chance of sticking, Hardenbergh came into his own.

The mountains and valleys of the Catskills were doomed to remain the tangled wilderness they had been for thousands of years until the patent could be divided. But before division could be thought of, the land had to be surveyed and its boundaries determined and defended against other claimants, Indian and white. Major Hardenbergh knew the country, its Indians, and its neighboring landowners.

For more than thirty years, in rain, snow, and heat, the major prowled the borders of his patent, cajoled Indian claimants in their bark huts, evicted squatters, pursued timber thieves, and stood up in court for what he considered the rights of his patent. He had found what he wanted— a position that commanded respect. But it was a position he could not maintain without struggle.[15]

8

Hardenbergh Lore and Legend

✤ JOHANNIS HARDENBERGH took his last look at the Catskills more than two centuries ago. Yet his ghost is often summoned back to the mountains —so often that Hardenbergh might be said to haunt the Catskills. And he not only haunts, he haunts doubly, for the ghost reveals itself in two very different forms. The first is the one that materializes as old ledgers are opened and dusty heaps of papers stirred. This ghost makes itself known to antiquarians and to elderly lawyers whose interest in odd corners of their business leads them into unprofitable rummaging among ancient papers. Because one ghost is a paper one, he is somewhat flat and considerably yellowed with age. He is made up of pounds, shillings, and pence, of so many hundredweight of salt fish or so many schepels of wheat, of deeds with their habendum and reddendum clauses and all the other trimmings dear to the hearts of colonial lawyers. He is given warmth only by the church records which show him to have become involved in such unbusinesslike ventures as birth and death.

The second ghost is very different, for, far from being flat, he is often a little too round and full for belief. He is the Hardenbergh ghost who materializes upon the lips of old men and women as they talk of old times. He is the Hardenbergh of legend and folklore who reflects the human need for beliefs that can give meaning to life, and is therefore a being of romance and imagination. Those who meet the paper ghost may feel repelled by his chilly precision of outline, but no one who becomes acquainted with the legendary ghost can fail to come to the conclusion that human life is a very remarkable and worthwhile thing indeed and is filled with wonders and marvels beyond counting.

The paper ghost has a good deal to communicate to those to whom he shows himself. For example, his upward progress through the society of his day can be traced by the way his name is set down by old clerks in the trail of documents he left behind. For in Hardenbergh's time a man's name and address were not enough to identify him; his occupation and social status also found their way into the records. Did a man cultivate a fair amount of land which he owned outright? Then he was "John Smith, yeoman." If he worked rented land he might be described as a "farmer." If he made shoes for a living he would be "John Smith, cordwainer"; if he operated a trading vessel on the seas he was "Captain John Smith, mariner." If he bought and sold goods for a living on any but the smallest scale, he was likely to be named "merchant" although this term, to fussy individuals, meant only a wholesaler or an importer and exporter. Johannis Hardenbergh from his earliest appearance in the records was a merchant. But this was but a beginning.[1]

It was the ambition of every aspiring merchant of Hardenbergh's time to become known by at least one of the titles of honor available in colonial New York. Once he became a justice of the peace—and this was no difficult achievement for a prosperous man who was not politically obnoxious to the governor—then he might have the pleasure of reading the abbreviation "Esq." after his name. If he preferred a military title, he might acquire one in the militia even though he took scant interest in military matters. Travelers in colonial America marveled at the abundance of military titles even in the most poverty-stricken settlements. Dr. Alexander Hamilton, a sharp-witted Scot, remarked in mid-eighteenth century that colonels abounded beyond any imaginable necessity in the Province of New York. They sold drinks over bars, ran roadside taverns, and obligingly cut the travelers' hair. Whimsical Dr. Hamilton explained that every man who had killed a rattlesnake was known thereafter as "colonel."[2] That was the origin of the pungent American phrase of "rattlesnake colonel."

A successful merchant often owned a number of titles of honor although he could seldom use them all at once. When he could, the effect was dazzling. Hardenbergh occasionally dazzles those who raise his ghost as the result of a paper chase. For while his Leislerian sympathies barred him from all official appointments while Cornbury was governor, once Hunter took over, things were different. Hunter in his intelligent and realistic way skillfully curbed the party squabbles which had disgraced previous administrations. He even made many appointments based on merit. Speedily Hardenbergh became once more sheriff of Ulster County and, by virtue of this office, a justice of the peace entitled to sit on the bench of the County Court of Sessions. The court records display him in all his official splendor as "Major Johannis Hardenbergh, Esq. High Sherriffe."[3]

The paper Hardenbergh arrived at a position of eminence in his adopted county at the age of forty or so, yet he had not reached his limit. Of all titles of honor within the reach of colonial merchants, that of "Gentleman" was the hardest to come by. The son of an old English landed family, a man who lived on wealth acquired by his ancestors, the relative of a peer—such fortunate beings make the records with the syllable "Gent." tailing their names. But a man might arrive at the state of gentleman by his own unaided efforts. A merchant nearing the end of a busy and acquisitive life and living in opulent retirement on his gains was often respectfully styled "Gent." It was as if he had become his own posterity, with his earlier identity as a striving, accumulating merchant serving as the mere dim shade of some remote ancestor. Hardenbergh, thanks to the patent which bore his name, was to claim this state as the finale to his career. He could not have more than briefly enjoyed it, for he made his only appearance as a paper gentleman on that most melancholy of documents, his last will and testament.[4]

The legendary Hardenbergh's ghost is restrained by no such bonds as those which confine his paper counterpart. He does not stop at becoming a mere gentleman. He advances into the ranks of the nobility; every imaginable human dignity short of a throne becomes his, and even a throne of modest size has been hinted at.

Part of the price which we humans pay for our exalted rank among living things is a lessened fertility. The dandelion, the guppy of the home aquarium, even the most lackadaisical bacterium are our masters when it comes to reproduction at a wholesale rate. Yet a pair of humans, given enough time, can make a respectable showing. Johannis and Catherine Hardenbergh have given rise to a small army of descendants. If the entire Hardenbergh Patent of 1708 were to be divided among them today, each one would probably receive far less than the two thousand acres per person allowable under Queen Anne; it would work out to no more than a few hundred acres apiece at best.

It is said by descendants of Johannis and Catherine that there is at least one descendant of the ancestral pair in each of the fifty states of the union. When groups of these descendants get together their talk gets around before long to Johannis and the patent, so a Hardenbergh-by-marriage told me. They discuss acreage and surveys; they speculate about lost deeds which, if found, might restore the patent to them; they show something of the same pride of family and the same passion for land that drove Johannis of long ago. They discuss the family lore and family legends which have grown up around Johannis until the old patentee seems almost to be present in the flesh among them.

The Hardenbergh of legend and folklore does not appear to his descendants alone. He has become a part of the lore of the Catskills and it does not take long for a man newly arrived among the mountains to feel his presence and even to feel a sort of pride in him. Much of the Hardenbergh legend and lore has its roots in a very widespread misunderstanding. Because the patent was known by Hardenbergh's name it is assumed that it was entirely his. The fact that the names of six other men are listed in the original grant is brushed aside with the statement that these fellows were "straw men" paid a small fee "to satisfy the requirements of the law."[5] At the proper time they turned over their shares to Johannis. Among the great landowners across the Hudson River— the Livingstons were among them—it was customary to refer to the Hardenbergh Patent as "The Great Patent." This referred to the patent's size, but it may have involved an attempt to exclude Hardenbergh from the great landowners club which tried to set itself up as a New World aristocracy and into which Hardenbergh was never invited.

In an attempt to explain exactly how one mere mortal managed to be granted a tract usually estimated as including two million acres, many varied legends have arisen. The belief that it was Hardenbergh's valor at Blenheim that caused Queen Anne not only to give him the land but also to knight him, still has some adherents. Another legend, once widely printed in family histories, holds that Hardenbergh was no descendant of simple Dutch ancestors but a scion of the noble German family of Von Hardenberg. It was only fitting that enough land to found a German principality should be granted to a man of such exalted social standing. Somehow Hardenbergh lost control of the situation and so the Catskills never became a principality with red-tiled schlosses on every peak, grapes growing contentedly on the mountains' natural terraces, smiling peasants tramping out the vintage with their bare feet—a region of clinking steins and dancing folk with Prince Johannis I reigning benignly over the Catskills.[6]

Another school of legend holds sway in the valley of the East Branch of the Delaware. There, near the point at which route 30 crosses from Roxbury into Prattsville, a roadside sign sponsored by the Department of Education of the State of New York proclaims that the imposing stone house above was "Hardenbergh Manor." The Hardenbergh Patent, some used to say, was in fact a manor with its rights of court-leet and court-baron and advowson, and all the other picturesque medieval survivals. The Hardenberghs had not been able to keep their vast lands because "squatters moved in" and refused to budge. All but a small part of the patent was seized by these violent and rude men who moved to the patent in such numbers that in spite of a determined Hardenbergh resistance, they won out and finally were judged to have a good title to their stolen lands because of "adverse possession."[7]

On a small remnant of their former manor lands surrounding the stone house, the Hardenberghs lived on in considerable splendor for many years. But the day came when a descendant of Johannis who lived there had to face the fact that he had only one daughter and no son to carry on after he was gone. The grant from Queen Anne had provided that as long as a Hardenbergh survived the land could not be sold under any circumstances—so local people like to say. The man consulted a lawyer and the lawyer made arrangements under which whoever married the man's daughter would assume the name of Hardenbergh and enable the land and manor house to continue in the family. But the daughter was not cooperative. She never married and in 1933 she died.[8]

A Margaretville man told me that he had known the "last of the Hardenberghs." "Knew her in school," he said slowly, "she was different—she was different. She was kinda dark and a lot like an old-time Dutch woman. Very Dutch—that's what she was. We all knew she was the last of the Hardenberghs—the kids used to talk about it. Well, she's gone now." The man shook his head solemnly. "Yes, she's gone—died a long time ago. She was the last of the Hardenberghs—the very last. It all came to an end with her. Then they had an antique shop in her house and now they say a dentist owns it. That's the way the world goes all right—changing all the time."

All the lore of Johannis Hardenbergh does not follow well-worn romantic trails. A good deal reflects the cynicism of people who get little from this world and resent those who get more. Much of this kind of lore has come down to the descendants of the tenant farmers who were to become the pioneers of the Catskill Mountains. "Hardenbergh wasn't too smart," a Sullivan County woman said. "He was a Dutchman but it wasn't the Dutch gave him the patent. It was the English. And those English knew what they were doing. They took the gold and silver and let Hardenbergh have what was left—a heap of stones called the Catskill Mountains."[9] The Hardenbergh Patent grant reserved gold and silver mines to the Crown, and the phrasing of the reserving clause could easily suggest to a hasty reader that mines had actually been in operation.

Some mountain people maintain that the Hardenbergh Patent owed its huge size "more to accident than to design," as the J. B. Beers *History of Greene County* put it in 1884. A man who sat next to me at a lunch counter in Catskill while we dealt with hamburgers and coffee put it less formally. "A fellow in those days was only allowed to have two thousand acres—no more. Well, that was what Hardenbergh asked for like anybody else—get me? Well you know London is a long ways from the Catskill Mountains. How could Queen Anne be expected to know that the Catskills go halfway to hell and back? She thought the Catskills were the same kind of iddy-biddy mountains they have over there in England. So she thought, when Hardenbergh asked for part of the Catskills, 'Hell, I might as well let him have the whole lot'—get me? Then the joke was on the Queen," the man concluded as he stared gloomily at his coffee.

A Margaretville man told the same tale with extra embellishments. "Hardenbergh asked for two thousand acres like he had a right to," the man explained. "But some dumb cluck of a clerk over there in England copied things wrong and made it two million instead—what the hell did he care, it wasn't his land. When Hardenbergh got his patent and saw it was for two million acres he was surprised. Well, there were smart people in those days the same as there are now. Hardenbergh kept his mouth shut and after twenty-one years the statute of limitations took holt and the mountains was his'n. Me, I ain't smart like that. If I was, for Christ's sake, what am I doing in Margaretville?"[10]

Hardenbergh's paper ghost and his legendary one speak of different aspects of the man whose passion for land was to leave its mark on the Catskills. No portrait of Hardenbergh has survived, if any was ever painted; no description of him, no intimate personal touch has been preserved in any letter, for he and his family seem not to have indulged in letter writing. What we know of him is in the records and in the minds of people of the Catskills who have interpreted his actions in the light of their own wishes and their own dreams.

9

The Lord of the Catskills

✤ THE AMERICA of Johannis Hardenbergh was a place in which land formed part of the dreams of almost everyone. Rich merchants dreamed of land as a hiding place for the profits of trade, since undeveloped lands were not taxed. Others dreamed of founding towns in the wilderness and seeing their wooded valleys converted into patchworks of productive fields and meadows. To some, land was a means of indulging in the excitement of speculation. Lands bought for a few hundred pounds might be worth thousands after the efforts of other people had brought settlers to the surrounding region. Land, many a speculator assured his friends, was bound to rise. All a land speculator had to do was to sit tight. And while he waited, a little effort at persuading settlers to clear the forest from his lands would pay off by giving the owner the appearance of a New World version of a European landed gentleman.

Poor men, too, dreamed of land but in a way of their own. In Europe they and their ancestors had been usually denied the right to own the land they tilled. They had to pay an annual rent in labor, grain, and farm animals to a rich landlord. In the New World, once the Indians had been pushed aside, there was such an abundance of land that it seemed clear that every man might have a farm of his own. He might enjoy the results of his own labor and of the bounty of nature and hand on his acres to his children. It was to make this dream a reality that the poor of Europe flocked to America.[1]

The Province of New York proved a disappointment to the land-hungry poor. Wages were good and unemployment was almost unknown. But when a man had worked at his trade long enough to have saved the price of a patch of wilderness which he might turn into a farm of his own, then he found that while unused land stretched to the horizons in limitless abundance, it was not for him. The ancient European system of landholding from which he had fled was being set up all over again in New York. If a man wanted the kind of independent self-reliant way of life which the New World promised, he would be unlikely to find it in New York. He would have to turn to Pennsylvania or parts of New Jersey where land was to be bought easily and cheaply. That was why the population of New York grew slowly. Its untilled lands were frozen in the grip of speculators or of landlords with Old World notions.[2] But this was not the only reason why lands like the Hardenbergh Patent were occupied only by primeval forest decade after decade while prospective settlers glanced at them and then turned away.

The Lords of Trade had over and over instructed governors to make sure that crown lands were surveyed before they were granted, for unless this were done no one could be sure just where his lands began or ended or how many acres were included. But this sensible order had been ignored partly through a desire to save trouble and expense but mostly in order to give landowners a chance to claim more than had actually been granted. It became the first duty of a newly created patentee to work the boundary game. If he played the game well, he might convert the modest, barren, and utterly useless trifle of land asked for in his original petition into a tract large and valuable enough to keep his descendants supplied with coaches, silver plate, and slaves for centuries to come.

Johannis Hardenbergh quickly found out that this boundary game was one at which a great many could play. Hardly had his patent been granted when Cornelis Cool and his Hurley neighbors got together and agreed to share the costs of defending their new territory against aggression from their neighbors.[3] The trustees of Kingston looked toward the Catskills and speculated as to whether it might not be possible to send their boundary line climbing up the mountains into the lands Hardenbergh claimed. Hardenbergh had been one of the Kingston trustees; he dropped out as his position on both sides of the fence became uncomfortable. Among the limestone ridges of Marbletown, on the rich creekside meadows of Rochester, men looked toward the Blew Hills and felt desire stirring in their souls. They examined old deeds, they questioned Indians, they asked their young men venturing into the wilderness of the Catskills as Indian traders to keep their eyes and ears open. Against all this effort and scheming, it became Johannis Hardenbergh's duty to fight and to wage aggressive war for the honorable goal of stretching his patent like a child's balloon until it stopped just short of bursting.

As difficulties multiplied, all thought of a quick division had to be given up. Annoying young government officials, eager to make names for themselves as friends of the Crown, yapped incessantly at the heels of Hardenbergh and Cornbury's other patentees. The viscount's land-granting efforts had been a smelly business, they proclaimed. Cornbury's patentees ought to be cut down to size—the grants ought to be revoked and each patentee given the mere two thousand acres to which he was entitled.[4] But Major Hardenbergh, burdened with his three secret partners, with his envious neighbors, and with critics of his honesty, had even more to contend with—an unbusinesslike adversary named death who seemed determined to break up Hardenbergh and Company.

Thomas Wenham was the first to go and he went like a gentleman. His will made no mention of his secret share in the patent—it had already been quietly transferred to his son John who lived in London. And thanks to his father's industry as an unsalaried councilman and a successful merchant, John was in no hurry to cash in on his share in the patent.

In 1719 death claimed both Augustine Graham and Captain Faneuil. Graham had made a reputation of an unusual kind as a surveyor who earned his fees by not surveying. It was only in keeping with this reluctance to do the usual thing that Graham should die without making a will. Yet so well had lawyer Bickley managed conveying Graham's share in the Hardenbergh Patent that even the settling of his estate did not reveal it. Faneuil left his "Indian boy Peter and my silver watch" to his eldest son and all his lands to his "beloved consort Anne during her widowhood."[5] Hardenbergh and Company was no longer an association of vigorous and alert men; it was becoming increasingly a thing of uncertain widows and distant and uninterested orphans. All this gave Major Hardenbergh, who was perpetually on the spot and in close touch with all developments, the dominating position in all patent affairs.

By 1721 pressure from neighboring landowners was becoming intense. May Bickley on behalf of Major Hardenbergh and Company took the bold step of petitioning Governor Burnet to order the surveyor general to survey, not their own boundaries, but those of their neighbors because "for want of a sufficient certainty"[6] of the neighbors' lines, those of the Hardenbergh Patent could not be ascertained. The governor ordered the survey to be made—there is nothing in the records to show that the order was ever carried out.

By the mid-1720s disputes over boundaries had become acute at a point which tradition places at the spot in the present town of Woodstock long known as Hardenbergh's Mill. Here a fine millsite and some excellent nearby flats were claimed by Hardenbergh under his grant of 1702. He had settled tenants on the land and perhaps set up a sawmill—it seems to have become part of the Great Patent after 1708. But the trustees of Kingston claimed the same land under the grant of 1687 which created Kingston Commons. On October 20, 1727 a group of Hardenbergh patentees complained that "Some persons belonging to the Corporation of Kingston . . . have lately arbitrarily pulled the fences of some [Hardenbergh] tenants and Discouraged Others by threats and imposing on them wrong Notions as to their Own boundaries and to those of the above said [Hardenbergh] Grant, whereby they have Induced Several to betray the trust reposed on them by the said Hardenbergh. . . ." The patentees stated their willingness to arbitrate the dispute which, they said, had worked toward "the Discredit . . . of their title and to the disturbance of the publick Peace. . . ."[7] Otherwise they made it plain they would go to court over the matter. The arbitration attempt failed and the Kingston trustees began suit. Then as now the law moved slowly. By 1729 four men described as Indian traders—two were in-laws of Major Hardenbergh—were making the first attempt to locate the northern and western bounds of the Hardenbergh Patent on behalf of the company. A crude map was one result of the traders' efforts.[8]

For more than fifteen years the lawsuit against Hardenbergh and Company raged and languished by turns. Indians and Indian traders were closely questioned by both sides as to the location of the points mentioned in the original description of the Hardenbergh Patent. Just where did the "Blew Hills" begin and end? In what direction did they "range?" Where were the sites of the great and the small "Yagh Houses," the shelters used by Indians on hunting trips?

Hardenbergh from the beginning must have felt a good deal of uneasiness over the deed which Nisinos had given him, and by the 1720s that uneasiness apparently increased. In 1726 he persuaded a group of Indians named Nawaquary, Nackepent, Quaquatenen, Abell, Amerkas, Masinenek, Wannoloues, Laemhalen, Tanehes, Laelhakenent, and Naimesightagken to sign a statement that "Johannis Hardenbergh of Kingston, Merchant" had made payments amounting to a total of one hundred and eleven pounds to them at various times since the early part of 1707 in return for the Indians' rights to the lands within the patent. The Indians furthermore agreed "to Free and Cleare the above granted premises of and from any and all demands and pretenses of other Indians what so ever."[9]

Hardenbergh was not alone in feeling that the foundations of his patent, now under so fierce an attack, needed shoring up. The growing number of widows and orphans who joined the ranks of Hardenbergh and

Company from time to time must have felt little confidence in their inherited shares in a tract of land which was coming more and more to be shadowed by suspicion and doubt. In 1721 the great bubble of the South Seas Company had burst; many New Yorkers as well as Londoners had lost heavily in the explosion. Even shrewd Peter Fauconnier was among the losers. Hardenbergh and Company was taking on more and more of the look of another bubble. The Catskills seen from the Hudson River, many a later traveler was to observe, had the look of a fairy castle seen in a dream; there was something insubstantial and magical about them. They seemed about to vanish at the waving of a wand in the hand of a knowledgeable magician. To the widows and orphans paying good money at frequent intervals to defend their shares in the patent, the whole thing must often have seemed a fantasy. Only the lawyers rubbed their hands and thanked God for the Catskill Mountains.

Among these lawyers, alas, "busy waspish"[10] May Bickley had no place. In 1724 he had pleaded mortality and died, disinheriting an ungrateful young man whom he had treated as a son, forbidding any and all pipe smoking at his funeral, and leaving his lands to his widow without mentioning his still secret share in the Catskills. One more recruit took her place among the Hardenbergh Patent widows. In 1729 Augustine Graham's son decided that since twenty-one years had elapsed since the granting of the Hardenbergh Patent, it was safe to step forward and claim his father's share. No one raised any objection.[11]

As the suit of the trustees of Kingston versus Major Hardenbergh wheezed on, the number of sharers in the patent increased. By the 1730s it required a fair head for mathematics to figure out just how to express the share of a new owner. Peter Fauconnier gave his granddaughter a one-eighth interest in his one-eighth share in the patent as a wedding present. Someone mislaid the fraction somewhere along the line and the land was never claimed.[12] Leonard Lewis left shares in his share in the patent to his eleven children and so gave a mighty boost to the membership of Hardenbergh and Company.

The company was becoming a large one but it was far from a merry one. The original expenses of obtaining the patent had been great; ever since the patentees had been spending money on lawyers' fees. The pressure to get the whole enterprise wound up and divided was becoming greater as widows and the guardians of orphans discovered that their shares in the fearfully snarled and obviously shaky patent were not easy to sell. If the Indians who were disputing among themselves over the mystery of just which Indians had owned just which part of the Catskills before 1708 ever had their way, the whole patent might go back to them. White men were keeping in touch with the quarrels of the Indians and wondering how they might turn all this hostility to their own profit.

The most potentially valuable part of the entire patent lay to the west and northwest where fertile plains and meadows stretched along the Schoharie Creek, and between the two branches of the upper Delaware River. The Mohawks claimed this land but so did the River Indians, a loose term which included the Esopus and Mahican groups. The Cochecton Indians who lived on the Delaware in present-day Sullivan County took a lesser part in the argument.

According to a note made by a lawyer for the Hardenbergh side at a later stage of the battle of the upper Delaware, Nisinos, the Esopus sachem, had a perfect right to sell the riverside lands to Hardenbergh in 1706. He was a son of "Dosto, an old squa"[13] who lived in the Rondout Valley near Wawarsing—her name appears in the old land records of Ulster County—so said the lawyer.[14] The Mohawks had given the Delaware River lands to her and to her descendants, and the Esopus Indians had had their hunting houses in this country without protest for many years. The argument was a slender one and it was incapable of proof, yet it seems to have been the best available to the Hardenbergh patentees.

The Mohawks denied that the River Indians had any right at all to a single acre of the western and northwestern slopes of the Catskills. River Indians' territory, they declared, came to an end at a line drawn along the edge of the high mountainous parts of the western Catskills. The hilly and valley lands beneath were the Mohawks'. If the River Indians ever tried to sell any of these lands to the whites, said the Mohawk chiefs, Seth and Hance Wey, the Mohawks "would hunt them like deer."[15]

In the same year the Mohawks complained to the governor about the land deals of the River Indians along the Schoharie. They asked "our Brother who is Sent here by our Father the Great King on the other side of the Great Lake" (this was George I) to protect them against the River Indians who were stealing land "which was possessed by us and our fathers Great Grand fathers Ever Since the Sun Shone." "They the River Indians Dare not look our Tribe in the face or dispute their right to the same or so much as show their faces to Challenge it (being conscious of their Guilt). . . . We know the River Indians are Thieves and will Steal any bodys Land they can." If the governor would not take action, the Mohawks declared, they would be forced to "do themselves Justice upon the River Indians."[16]

Thirty years passed after the Hardenbergh Patent was granted, and it

was still undivided and unsettled. Its boundaries on all sides were in
dispute. It threatened to become the cause of an Indian war. No wonder
that the land-hungry immigrants pouring from every ship that touched at
New York quickly learned that the valleys of the Catskills, thanks to the
greed of the politicians and businessmen who had grabbed them way back
in Cornbury's time, were useless to anybody. The Catskills had become
a great blue monument to the human capacity for messing things up.

Johannis Hardenbergh never faltered in his attempts to unravel the
snarl of his patent. When he was over seventy—that was in 1742—he
rode with a surveyor through seven stormy autumn days in an attempt
to define part of his patent's borders. The weather buffeted the two men
struggling through the wilderness, yet they worked on. They put up at
night in the cabins of frontiersmen, and dickered with the Indians for
venison to eat. On October 29 it "snowed, hailed & rained all day." By
November 1 the major was back at his home in Kingston, convinced that
he had located the two "Yagh Houses" over which dispute had raged for
so long.[17]

As middle age overtook Johannis Hardenbergh, he began signing
his name in a new way. Others had signed it for him back in the days
when the Hardenbergh Patent was still in the petitioning stage; he had
signed it himself early in life in a straightforward manner, forming the
letters according to the Dutch tradition in which he had been brought up.
After his patent became a central force in his life, Hardenbergh changed
his way of signing his name. No longer did he sign it in full—the
initial "J" of the first name was incorporated into the "H" of Hardenbergh
in a way that was not immediately obvious. Signing one's name in this
and similar ways was not uncommon during the eighteenth century. The
poor did not often do it, nor did those so highly placed in society as
to feel secure. But men struggling toward a higher status often evolved
signatures that suggested they were so busy and signed their names so often
that they found it advisable to use a shortened form. And this kind of
signature suggested something more. At first glance it resembled the
signatures of peers, fortunate people who signed documents with no more
than the names of their seignories. Lord Cornbury, for example, signed
official papers with "Cornbury." Years later as genealogists delved into
the background of the Hardenbergh family, they seized upon the major's
way of signing his name as evidence that he was a nobleman. And so the
major's little try at boosting his status by means of a signature had an
effect on his descendants that would surely have pleased him. It helped
give him, if only temporarily, the look of being the Lord of the Catskills.[18]

10

Robert Livingston
Invests in the Patent

✤ WHILE LORD CORNBURY and his friends were making the most of the granting of the Hardenbergh Patent back in the days of Queen Anne, a very engaging young New Yorker in his teens was struggling with the odes of Horace at a Latin school in Leith in Scotland. He was under the impression that he was preparing himself for a career as a lawyer. He was a younger son of Robert Livingston, who had become lord of the manor of Livingston on the east bank of the Hudson as the climax of a frenzy of acquisition. Trading with the Indians, clerking, taking shares in privateering and piratical ventures, marrying, moneylending, playing politics, doing favors to put government officials in his debt—all these and many more were the devices by which the elder Robert Livingston sought to appease his lust for the power symbolized by the possession of money and land.

Under the rule of primogeniture which then prevailed, Philip, the oldest son of the lord of Livingston Manor, would inherit his father's lands and the lion's share of his wealth. Younger children would be modestly provided for: Robert's European education capped, according to family tradition, by a study of law in London's Temple, would enable him to shine at the New York bar or to engage in politics with success. He was a handsome young man who liked "genteel" surroundings and possessions. He bubbled over with goodwill and optimism, had a quick mind, an explosive imagination, and something of his father's daring in business without the old man's cold, hard concentration on profits. It was this young man whose destiny would be to unlock the Catskill Mountains and allow a flood of settlers to pour into the wilderness long known only as the hunting grounds of the River Indians.

Seen from the Livingston Manor of young Robert's boyhood, the Catskills are an imposing sight; there is no ignoring them; they cannot be brushed aside as a mere useless rocky wall along the horizon; they insist on being taken into consideration. Yet there is nothing aggressive about the Catskills as they present themselves to Livingston Manor. To the manor's lord, to the members of his family, to his many Negroes, to the Dutch and German-speaking tenants of the manor farms, the mountains to the west were all persuasion. They were things of mystery, things which asserted their influence over the manor folks in subtle ways which were past puzzling out. Rainstorms and windstorms, for example, plainly formed about the heads of the mountains and from there swooped down to revive or destroy manor crops. In the fall the snow whitened the Catskills while summer still lingered on the manor as if to warn those below to get their pumpkins in and heap leaves and straw about the foundations of their houses in preparation for the coming winter. Every change in temperature or humidity brought a corresponding change in the look of the mountains. Sometimes they seemed to advance, at others to retreat; their deep blue color changed in a few moments to lavender or gray. On a summer afternoon they seemed soft and green, and in the winter when the foliage of their oaks and beeches fell, they displayed hard rocky faces capped by evergreens showing black against the snow. It would have been hard for imaginative young Robert to escape feeling the influence of the Catskills and carrying their image with him to Scotland, there to merge it with that of the Lothian Hills near Edinburgh among which his own ancestors had lived. The manor tenants' lives were narrowed and their imaginations checked by long and hard hours of toil; promising children quickly lost their eager curiosity and asked few questions about the world around them. They were there to work and not to wonder. To the son of the lord of the manor, wondering was part of the game, especially when he returned from Europe with his provincial roughness rubbed off and his head well furnished not only with Latin quotations appropriate for all occasions, but also with fresh ideas to feed that lively imagination of his.

Young Robert escaped the usual landless fate of a younger son by what Livingston family tradition remembers as a romantic incident. Some of the manor Negroes plotted an uprising—some say it was the Indians—and one hid himself in the chimney of the elder Livingston's house in readiness to creep out and slaughter the master. Young Robert glimpsed a pair of feet showing in a fireplace and pulled the owner down. His father, in gratitude for what may well have been an act which saved his life, cut thirteen thousand acres from his manor and gave them to

Robert. So by the accident of a pair of naked feet seen in a fireplace, Robert became the owner of a great property which he was to use as a base from which to invade the Catskills.[1]

Robert wanted to name his estate Callendar, for the Livingstons were proud of their descent from the Scottish earls of Callendar. His older brother Philip objected, Livingston tradition holds, on the ground that so glorious a name was not for a younger son to toss about. Robert then proposed Ancram, the name of the historic Scottish village where his clergyman grandfather had preached. This too, said the older brother, was too presumptuous. Young Robert then made do with Claremont, a name with no family associations at all.[2] It was probably borrowed from the English Claremont famous for its architectural and landscape splendor. It was also the subject of a well-known poem by Sir Samuel Garth and the home of the immensely rich landowning Whig statesman, the Duke of Newcastle, who was also the Earl of Clare. Later in the eighteenth century the Livingstons of Claremont, coming under French influence, would change the spelling to Clermont, the name of a famous and ancient French town.

Thirteen thousand acres of land and no money to speak of—that was a situation that called for action. Robert of Clermont quickly gave up any thought of a legal career and went into business in New York. He bought and sold, imported and exported, backed privateers engaged in raiding Britain's enemies and indulging in a little piracy on the side. By 1740 Livingston, at fifty-two, was able to turn his thoughts away from barrels of rum received from the West Indies and hundredweights of flour and pine planks shipped overseas, to make plans for settling down on his own acres at Clermont. From there in his increased leisure he could contemplate the Catskills once again. From the side of the Hudson opposite his mansion and a little below, Livingston could see the mouth of the Esopus Creek snaking its way down from the Shandaken Valley, which was the heart of the southern Catskills, as if heading toward his doorstep. Directly opposite stood the mountain known today as Overlook jutting out from the rest of the Catskills as if leading the whole mountain company toward Clermont. Would these mountains be worth adding to Clermont? Livingston's imagination took fire at the thought. He knew that all was not well with the Hardenbergh Patent which included most of the mountains visible from the riverside door of Clermont. Only two of the original band of eight acquisitive men, with whom Lord Cornbury had done business in 1708, survived. Peter Fauconnier down in New Jersey was a tottering old man; Johannis Hardenbergh alone still struggled stubbornly to make something of the patent. The rest of the owners were a mixed group of heirs, wealthy people, poor people, a baker, a blacksmith, a cooper, farmers, and businessmen. Many were eager to sell, if they could. But, alas, the "reputation" of the patent was not of the best as Livingston was to say some years later.[3] A share in the Catskills was not worth anything like the amount of money that had been sunk into it. The whole thing had been a bad speculation for all hands except for the old major doggedly fighting on.

Accident played a part in putting Robert Livingston into a position of power—if the tradition of the two feet in the fireplace is to be believed. However there was nothing accidental in the way Livingston added a vast territory in the Hardenbergh Patent to the thirteen thousand acres he owned at Clermont. As confidence in the Hardenbergh Patent sank, many a New York businessman must have wondered. At what point would the value of a share in the patent sink so low as to become a good speculation? That point was reached, decided Robert Livingston and his fellow merchant Gulian Verplanck, about the year 1740. That year the first survey of the patent was undertaken, and then or perhaps a year or two later, Robert Livingston himself ventured into the patent on an effort at exploration. Guided by woodsman Henry Bush who had settled close to the foot of the mountains in Shokan, Livingston and his son Robert R. followed the Esopus Creek to the Pine Hill, crossed the hill, and made their way to the bank of the East Branch of the Delaware at the site of what would become Margaretville.[4] In 1741 Livingston and Verplanck bought the share in the still undivided patent of James Graham of Morrisania in Westchester. (He was the son of Augustine Graham, the dilatory surveyor general.) They paid three hundred pounds for Graham's one-eighth share. This was in New York pounds worth a little more than half that much in pounds sterling.

In quick succession Livingston alone and in partnership with Verplanck bought out other shares in the patent. Aged Elizabeth Bickley, widow of the acting attorney general who had wanted no smoking at his funeral, had debts which Livingston paid. He then took the Bickley share valued at three hundred seventy-five pounds in settlement. Old Fauconnier sold at the same price, so did the impoverished heirs of William Nottingham.[5] By 1743 Livingston could look from the riverside door of his mansion at Clermont and reflect that he owned one third of the mountains rising across the river.

In 1739 an abortive attempt to divide the patent had been made. Announcements of the intended division had been posted on the doors of churches in New York and Albany, and the Assembly had been asked to allow the partition.[6] It had all come to nothing, for the difficulties were formidable. There were boundary disputes that still needed settling, and the Indians of the region were ever ready to raise a whoop of "Foul!" whenever any attempt was made to clear up the difficulties that lay in the way of putting the patent into the hands of individual white owners.

The energy and unflagging optimism of Livingston gave new life to the effort to untangle the patent mess. Old Hardenbergh fussed away with renewed zeal over disputed boundaries. He tackled the Indian problem and rounded up claimants who questioned the right of Nisinos to sell all or part of the patent. He agreed, probably at Livingston's urging, to allow settlement by arbitration of the lingering lawsuit of the Corporation of Kingston against Major Hardenbergh and Company.[7] He joined Livingston in paying off Indian claimants and putting a deed from them on file in the hope of clearing the patent's title. For three hundred pounds, Kakalarimne, Cacawalomin, alias Henry Hekan, "Moonhaw, the right Ancrop," and others sold the Hardenbergh Patent to white men all over again.[8]

Livingston had plainly become the driving power in the patent affairs. For thirty-five years Major Hardenbergh had been the undisputed front man of the patent. His trip to the patent's southern borders in the snow and rain of October 1742 was his last recorded effort on behalf of the region known by his name. By September 1743 old age or infirmity had caught up with him, for his son-in-law Charles Brodhead and his oldest son, Johannis, Jr., were acting for him in land and legal matters. In that month the old man severed his connection with the patent forever. His son and his son-in-law, acting for the major, conveyed to themselves his one-eighth share in the patent, and a few years later turned over a small share to another son, Abraham.[9]

That was why, when the old man died in 1748, he owned no part of the great mountain region for which he had struggled so hard for so many years. The desire for land had been a dominating force through his adult life. As death approached he may have realized the futility of such a motive, for he asked that all his lands down to the smallest bit be sold and the proceeds placed at interest for the benefit of his widow, Catherine. He had not, as might have been expected, left his share to his eldest son; he had made his exit from the patent in an ambiguous way, and his son-in-law and two of his sons had re-entered the patent almost as if they believed three men were required to take the old major's place.

Old Hardenbergh was gone, but he was not to be forgotten. Some fifteen years after his death, timber thieves crossed the patent line and made off with valuable trees. When Robert Livingston heard of this, he was moved to pay a tribute to the major's fierce devotion to the interests of his patent. "They durst not have done this in old Hardenbergh's time!" he exclaimed.[10]

Old Hardenbergh did more for the Catskills than serve as watchdog for a group of men who had acquired a shaky title to the region. He had held the whole creaking enterprise together for thirty-five years. That made it possible for a scheme which embodied the way of doing things in Lord Cornbury's day to survive into an era when such an enterprise had almost an air of antiquity. It was as a survival from the past that the Hardenbergh Patent was to be opened to settlement by the land-hungry poor on Old World terms. But before that could happen, the patent's boundaries had to be given some sort of firmness. In order to do this, Henry Wooster of Connecticut and, later on, his brother Ebeneezer were employed to make a survey of the entire perimeter of the patent.

This would have been a hard job under the best of conditions. The Woosters found it very discouraging indeed because the Indians were waiting for them in the woods. The Indians objected to the survey and they objected very strongly.

11

A Rough Game:
Surveyors and Indians

🌿 RULES FOR PLAYING the game of surveyors and Indians will not
be found in any cyclopedia of sports and pastimes. Yet the game was
once popular and no wonder, for it had something of the excitement of
football, hockey, or even of the ancient game called war. From 1740 to
1751, the Catskills were the playing field for as lively a game of surveyors
and Indians as any in the record books.[1]

The game originated in the Indians' observation that surveyors were
men of evil omen. When the Indians sold lands to white men it was in an
atmosphere of good fellowship rich with the fumes of rum and tobacco.
But convivial occasions like these had unpleasant consequences—not merely
the headache and regret of the day after but also the arrival of surveyors
in the wilderness. And behind the surveyors marched an army of settlers
with axes as weapons to help them destroy the forest and to drive the
Indians from their ancient hunting grounds. The surveyors tried to advance
and measure the land, the Indians tried to turn them back—that was how
the game was played.[2]

Many years after the surveyors and Indians had given up displaying
their skill against each other among the Catskills, aged trapper-hermits
and doddering Indian traders recalled the details of the classic series of
games played between 1740 and 1751. And each, as might be expected,
recalled the game in his own way and to his own glory or profit. The
leaders in the game on the surveyors' side were two Connecticut Yankee
brothers, Henry and Ebeneezer Wooster of Stamford. In old memories
the two often merged into a single heroic figure named "Wooster" who
combined the vigor and shrewdness of two men.

However confused the two brothers may have become in memory, there is no doubt about which one made the opening move. It was Henry who was summoned by Johannis Hardenbergh to the Shokan Mountains—an old name for the cluster of peaks which rises south of the Esopus Kill. Word spread among the Indians that Henry was beginning a survey and they watched his progress along the southern part of the Hardenbergh Patent's perimeter without missing a move. When Henry reached the Delaware River the Indians entered the game.

"As said Wooster was on the Survey Somewhere about Cushy tonk," says an old account, "the Savages took his Compass from him & carry'd it to Esopus, and the Patentees settled the affair with the Indians. . . ."[3]

The Indians at this point played the game strictly according to the rules. They did not injure Wooster or the Indian interpreter and the chain-men who made up his surveying party. They did not steal his compass—they took it only in order to return it to Major Hardenbergh. Before the game could be resumed, the Hardenbergh side had to negotiate two new Indian deeds and make a fresh payment to the Indians.[4] Henry Wooster probably got back to his survey after this penalty was levied but details of the game's second half are muddy. At some point, however, he managed to reach a swamp two miles long and a few rods wide in what was to become the town of Roxbury. On either side mountains rose sharply; from the swamp two little streams trickled. One made its way northward to the Schoharie, the other flowed southward—it was the source of the Pawpacktunk or East Branch of the Delaware. On the dividing line between the two watersheds, Wooster or one of his men swung an ax and marked a spruce tree with three X's. Then, if an account set down in 1769 is to be trusted, Henry proposed continuing from the marked tree to the West Branch of the Delaware—his instructions ordered him to do this, he told his Indian opponents. The Indians forbade him to go on and insisted that he had reached the northwestern corner of the patent. Whether or not Henry went on is in doubt, and on that note the game ended.[5]

There was much debate as to which side had won the game—Wooster claimed he had. The Indians disagreed. Many years later they were saying that Hardenbergh had made a dishonest deal with the leader of the Indian team. He was the gray-haired "Cheif Cheshan of the Dallaware and Esopus Indians"[6] whose name was Cacawlomin to Indians and Hendrick Heckan or Hegan to the whites. Heckan, they said, had quietly taken money from Hardenbergh in return for the land, which he didn't own,[7] between the two branches of the Delaware.

Hendrick Heckan was very different from the Indians whom Henry Hudson had met in the Hudson Valley in 1609. He had learned and put into practice many of the white man's ways. On his home acres at Papakunk, a few mines below Margaretville, he had planted and tended an apple orchard in which he took great pride. Here he made cider each fall. When Heckan met a white trader or hunter he often invited him to come to Papakunk and sample his cider.[8] Heckan learned more than the art of cider making from the whites: he caught on to the tricks of their land buyers and speculators and became shrewd enough to turn them now and then to his own profit.

A second game of surveyors and Indians began on April 7, 1749. Once more Heckan led the River Indians' side, but this time Henry Wooster had been taken out of the game, and his brother Ebeneezer was put in his place. Ebeneezer hoped to accomplish more than Henry had. His object was to make a more careful survey of the patent's boundaries and to divide the land into fifty-two "Great Lots" which would then be divided among the patent's shareholders. The principal object of the Indians was to prevent the survey from reaching the still-contested lands lying between the two branches of the upper Delaware.[9]

With the Indians watching to make sure that he didn't cheat, Wooster made his survey and placed monuments of heaped-up stones along the patent's perimeter. As he moved up the East Branch of the Delaware, the Indians who were following picked up some of his monuments and tossed them into the river.[10] As the survey came to this part of the patent, the Indians were playing not for fun but from fear. At various times powerful Iroquois tribes who claimed this region had accused the River Indians of selling land that was not theirs—they had been especially angry when River Indians sold the western parts of the Hardenbergh Patent. It was then that the Mohawks had stated in their petition to King George I that "we know the River Indians are thieves and will Steal any bodys land they can. . . ."[11]

As Ebeneezer reached the spruce tree marked by his brother some nine years earlier, his Indian opponents were on the alert to prevent him from turning to the left and heading for the West Branch of the Delaware which Wooster's employers claimed as their western boundary. Whether the Indians succeeded or not is by no means clear. In an affidavit made in 1785 in a case before New York State's Land Board, Wooster's Indian interpreter, Petrus P. Low, swore that a shortage of provisions caused the surveying party to hesitate for two days in the narrow clove in which the East Branch is born. Low then offered "to go himself for supplies to the settlement at Schoharie but it was objected lest they should be stopped"[12] by the Indians. Wooster then turned eastward—some say after getting fresh supplies from Kingston—and made his way to the patent's northeastern corner at the head of the Kaaterskill or Cartwright's Kill as the wording of the patent had it.

Low's account makes it seem that the Indians had scored a point. But Petrus Dumond, also testifying before the New York State Land Board in 1785, put on record hearsay evidence to prove the exact opposite. Dumond stated that Henry Bush who had been Robert Livingston's guide to Pakatakan in the early 1740s told him that he "had been out with Wooster the Surveyor . . . at the head of the East branch of Delaware River—that they from thence took a northerly course in search of another Branch of said River"[13] and so reached the West Branch. Low was almost certainly confusing the two Wooster brothers and the games they played. Henry Bush's own affidavit made in the same boundary case contradicts what Dumond reported he said about his experiences and those of his father, Jacob, with "one Worster, a Surveyor." Bush mentions no tangle with Indians although Dumond gives him as authority for one of the liveliest incidents of any game of surveyors and Indians ever played among the Catskills. This incident has been accepted by most connoisseurs of Hardenbergh Patent lore as having taken place during Ebeneezer Wooster's survey of 1749 and not during the earlier one by Henry.

Dumond stated that as Henry Bush and Wooster came to the West Branch of the Delaware they "either found or made a Cannoe in which they embarked with their Instruments for surveying, that in falling down said Stream they overset their Cannoe and wetted their Instruments, by which the Surveyor's chain became exceedingly rusty that they never the less pursued down the course of the said River to Cook house"—probably between present-day Walton and Deposit—"where they found many Indians who discovering that they had a surveyor as also Instruments for surveying Lands were much enraged and talked of killing the whole party as they the said Indians claimed the Lands as their property—that Wooster and his party diverted the Indians from their purpose by assuring them that they had not surveyed any of the Lands on that River and in proof there of shewed them the Rust on their Chain which satisfied the Indians that they had not used it."[14]

"Wooster the Surveyor" was telling the naked truth to the Indians when he said he had not surveyed the West Branch. The handsome map of the Hardenbergh Patent which Ebeneezer drew late in the fall of 1749 shows no survey beyond the East Branch although lines are protracted across the disputed lands to divide them into Great Lots. The West Branch would not become an officially surveyed and recorded boundary of a white man's grant until the Harper Grant—to the west of the West Branch—was made in 1769. The Wooster map was drawn on a great sheet of parchment in several colors and gave the Catskills the look of a mythical kingdom, perhaps on another planet. Wooster had tried to "give Sum Description of the Land and the form of the Mountains," he explained, "the green sheweth the Mountains and the yellow the Loe Land." Yet Wooster's rivers wander miles off their true courses, his mountains are mere blobs of green which show how very random indeed his own and his brother's exploration and survey of the patent had been.

It was on the basis of Ebeneezer Wooster's dreamy map that the patent was at last divided among the long-suffering widows and orphans and the two sharp bargain hunters, Robert Livingston and Gulian Verplanck. The land between the rivers, although it showed on the map, was not yet divided because its survey, said Wooster, had "been prevented by the Indians."[15]

The patent had hardly been carved up and served to its owners when old Hendrick, the cider-making sachem, died. His two sons and some twenty other Indians at once overcame their fear of Mohawk vengeance and sold to the Hardenbergh patentees their right to all the lands, about seventy thousand acres running to a point two miles above Lake Utsayantha, between the two branches of the Delaware—a right which they themselves would have been the first to admit they weren't quite sure they ever had. For this the Indians were paid one hundred seventy-five pounds and some shillings.[16] It is a safe bet that the Indians pocketed the cash in a cheerful mood; they had emerged from the game of surveyors and Indians with a very nice cash prize. If that didn't mean they had won, what would?

In 1751 the last of the Hardenbergh Patent lands between the two rivers were doled out among the patentees. That event marked the dissolution of Hardenbergh and Company and of its forty-three years of stalemate.[17] At long last the lands in and around the Catskills were ready to be put to whatever uses their owners wished. Miserly owners could hoard them, adventurous souls might speculate with them—they might even be sold to pioneer settlers eager to brave the dangers of the frontier for the sake of a farm of their own. The moment for decision had come.

At once the owners of the lands surrounding the patent sent up a cry of alarm. The Woosters had been faithful to their employers' interests. They had interpreted the language of the 1708 grant in the most liberal manner imaginable; they had bulged and pushed and expanded the patent's boundaries in the most laudable way. The next step would be for the owners of the fifty-two Great Lots to have their own surveys made and each one, of course, would make the most of any vagueness or ambiguity in his lot's boundaries. In the town of Rochester on the southeastern marches of the patent an eloquent voice was raised in warning.

"You have to do with witty people," wrote one Rochester landowner, amid the frost and snow of February 1750, "they [the owners of the Hardenbergh Patent] intend in ye Spring Early to begin their Surveys on the several allotments they will press in upon you and when you let them go on to Incrotch & take position, it will be harder to git them moved than now betimes to keep them out. . . . I would have you to consider not to Loose a Sheep for a penny worth of Tarr, as ye old saying is. I mean you should with the best Information & Instruction you could git Give a handsome Retaining fee to one or two lawyers before they are all in their hands. . . ."[18]

Once the Indians' prize money was safely in the pockets of tavernkeepers and Indian traders, a grim future faced the onetime owners of the Catskills. Up to 1751 they had been allowed to go on using the mountains as their hunting grounds. Now how long would it take for the whites to drive them out?

A lean future stared at the Indians, but upon another group of humans the whole Hardenbergh Patent situation turned the rosiest of smiles. Already, since May Bickley had pioneered the close relation of the legal profession to the patent, two generations of lawyers had done well by dealing with its intricate points, its subtle niceties. A third generation was preparing to take over, and this would be far from the last to find the vast patent and its troubles a comfortable and dependable source of income.

The lawyers this time were not alone in sniffing profits on the breezes that swept across the Hudson Valley from the Catskills. Businessmen, too, looked up with attention when they heard the phrase "Hardenbergh Patent" mentioned. The Catskill mountains began to beckon them, and they responded gladly.

12

Cornelius Tiebout
Tempts a Bishop

As THE EIGHTEENTH CENTURY reached its middle years, the Catskill Mountains seemed to many people to be awakening from a long sleep. Now that the million and a half acres of the Hardenbergh Patent were in individual hands the whole region seemed to be up and about and ready to face the world and do business with it. In a good many places there was talk about the Catskills.

In New York counting rooms, in merchants' warehouses among bales and barrels of cloth and sugar and rum, in candlelit city parlors, on isolated manors, men with an itch for speculation talked about the Catskills as they drank their Madeira or smoked their long clay pipes. Already surveyors had been commissioned to divide some of the patent's fifty-two Great Lots into smaller units, and much of the land would soon be on the market. Were the Catskills a good gamble for a man with more cash than he needed?

In cramped rooms on New York back streets, in the stinking holds of immigrant ships, in sunny hayfields and in stables, poor men wondered if at last the valleys of the Catskills would be open to settlement on New World terms. The answer was in the making. Soon it would be shouted from the mountaintops.

Over in London, John Wenham, son of Lord Cornbury's onetime councilor, heard of what was going on and bestirred himself. John Wenham was by this time a comfortable old man who had no desire to risk the dangers of a voyage across the Atlantic to take care of his one-eighth part of the Hardenbergh Patent. He authorized Jacob Franks, an able man who was prominent in Jewish life in New York, to sell his share in the patent at the best price he could get. A mixed group of men joined forces and did business with Franks. One was Robert Livingston of Clermont, still eager to add to his already huge holdings among the Catskills. Another was Captain Tingley—he was master of a ship—and his associate, David Cox, barber. More elevated socially were William Alexander, who was soon to claim the Scottish title of Earl of Stirling, and Philip Livingston of Livingston Manor. John Aspinwall and Cornelius Tiebout, both prosperous New York businessmen, joined in. Once Wenham's scattered tracts in the patent were bought they were quickly surveyed and divided.[1] The new owners then worked together to build up their backwoods acres into something with the look of a New World Garden of Eden—on paper at least.

In June 1752, a majority of the owners drew up and signed a document in which they made no statement which was altogether untrue, and yet managed to convey a decidedly false impression of their isolated and backcountry wilderness. They addressed their appeal to German immigrants who were then, thanks to a lull in Europe's almost continuous wars, able and eager to settle in America.

Their lands, the statement boasted, were "situated within a few miles of Several Setled Townships at Esopus near Hudson River in Ulster County in (the) Province of New York. To which a Good road is already made, and which are convenient to the Markets of either the City of New York or Philadelphia, they being within a hundred miles of both said Places and the greatest part of the way by Water Carriage, and as we are willing to encourage the speedy Setling the same, Therefore we do promise and hereby bind ourselves to let any number of families who shall come from Germany and apply to us for that purpose within three years after the Date hereof have any quantity of above mentioned lands in any part thereof at their own election, provided they take it in Lotts as it is divided which are from one thousand to fifteen hundred acres each at the rate of twenty-five pounds New York money for each Hundred acres, clear of any Quit rents whatever."[2]

There was no frenzied rush to buy—for a number of good reasons. The "Good road" did indeed enter the southeastern corner of the patent, but it soon fainted and then revived as a line of blazed trees and an old Indian trail. Part of the lands advertised were close to settlements near Kingston—these were the forbidding and unfarmable mountains facing the Hudson between Overlook Mountain and Plattekill Clove. One corner of the lands was within one hundred miles of New York. Another bit was not too much more than a hundred miles, in a straight line, from Philadelphia. The "Water Carriage" to Philadelphia was down the still unnavigable upper Delaware. The lands were isolated; they were encumbered with gigantic and unmarketable trees; and impenetrable thickets of laurel made even seeing the soil difficult. For such lands the price was exorbitantly high.

By the fall of 1752 a mere half-dozen Würtembergers and one German had taken the bait and were making clearings in the forest a little north of Monticello in Sullivan County. Each had given a bond of ten pounds to be forfeited if he became discouraged and ran out on his agreement.[3]

The mastermind of the land-selling scheme which had bagged the six pioneers was Cornelius Tiebout. Tiebout's portrait shows an elegantly dressed but paunchy figure and a complacent face which eyes modern man with a shrewdness bordering upon cunning. The Tiebout of the portrait does not look like a man who was easily discouraged, and the real Tiebout wasn't. Half a dozen Germans weren't enough; in April 1753 he tried a fresh gambit to entice Germans in the wholesale numbers he wanted. His bait was one which has become well known in our own day—it was nothing less than "an amazing free offer." The offer was not made to the public; it was open to only one man, Bishop August Gottlieb Spangenberg of the Moravian Church. It was an offer of four thousand acres of land in the Hardenbergh Patent—absolutely free. The bishop was amazed and incredulous. Or was this an answer to a prayer?[4]

The Moravians wanted land very much, but for reasons of their own. They wanted places upon which they could set up communities to carry on their own way of life without interference. These Moravians were industrious and God-fearing people. Yet they were absolutely incomprehensible to proper citizens of European and American countries. The Moravians didn't believe in war or military service; they wouldn't take oaths; they scorned all earthly governments; they regarded the buying and selling of goods as an unpleasant necessity to be avoided whenever possible. They were driven by an overpowering compulsion not to accumulate money but to convert the heathen to Christianity. And most disturbing of all, they regarded the heathen, whether they were Eskimos, Negroes, Ceylonese, Lapps, Tartars, or even American Indians, as brothers. Their world leader was a man who was able enough by the strictest standard but who was, to say the least, eccentric. He was Nicolaus Ludwig, Count of Zinzendorf and Pottendorf. The count was a mystic, a dreamer, a man of inspiration and emotion. Under his leadership the Moravian sect was brought back to vigorous life at a moment when it threatened to die out. Moravian missions spread out over the world from the count's estate at Berthelsdorf in Germany. Luckily for the movement, levelheaded, practical Bishop Spangenberg had the knack of turning the count's visions into hard realities and so keeping the whole movement from soaring right off the surface of the earth and vanishing among the stars.

When Tiebout's offer arrived, Spangenberg was waiting in New York for Captain Dean of the ship *John* to decide just when wind, tide, and consigners of cargo would combine to make it possible for him to set sail for London, where the bishop planned to attend a conference of the heads of his church. The bearer of the offer of land was no man to play a practical joke upon a bishop. He was Ludowick Bamper whose luxurious house and elegant garden were the talk of New York. Bamper was associated in two glassmaking ventures with Christian Hertell, who was Tiebout's brother-in-law and partner in speculations. The line of transmission of the offer was plausible enough to convince the bishop that it was seriously meant. Yet he remained skeptical.

Four thousand acres of land for absolutely nothing! That was a little hard to believe, especially when the offer came from so shrewd and self-seeking a man as Tiebout. Count Zinzendorf might have dreamed and prayed about the offer. Spangenberg wrote to Tiebout and bluntly asked exactly why he made it. Nothing could have been more convincing or more flattering than the answer. "Our intention in offering this land to the brethren," wrote Tiebout, "is, I have reason to believe, that by their settling on the same, the lands nearby, in which we are all concerned, may rise in value, which is the certain consequence of such a settlement, and especially if the inhabitants are a sober, orderly people, and industrious which character the brethren deservedly bear."[5] Four thousand acres would be given outright, Tiebout repeated, another seven thousand adjoining would be sold to the Moravians at five shillings per acre. Mr. Tiebout himself stood ready to serve as guide to a group of the brethren if they wished to take a look at the lands.

The bishop was delighted. The Moravian Brethren had thriving communities at Bethlehem and Nazareth in Pennsylvania and elsewhere, but they had lost their bridgehead to the Indians in the Province of New York under painful circumstances only a few years before. Then their village of Shekomoko, almost within sight of the Catskills in Dutchess County, had been destroyed and its Indian converts dispersed. The Moravian missionaries had been banished from the province. The reasons? Well, some said the Moravians were secret agents of the Pope, others believed they were Canadian Jesuits in disguise furthering the aims of the King of France. And anyway they had been teaching the Indian children to read and acting as if Indians were as good as anybody else, which, as any sensible New Yorker believed, they weren't.

The Moravians were outcasts in New York until good sense prevailed. Was Tiebout's offer a sign of the changing times? Only a few months before, Robert Livingston's clever brother William had written most approvingly of the Moravians in the new periodical called *The Independent Reflector*. "They are such a people as no Man can get any Thing by their Religion but internal Tranquillity. . . . They are a plain, open, inoffensive people: they profess universal Benevolence to all Men and are irreprehensible in their Lives and Conversations. . . . In regard to their religious Principles, it must be owned, they have their peculiar Sentiments. . . . But that is saying no more than that they think for themselves. . . ."[6] Were Tiebout the trader and young William Livingston messengers sent by the Lord to invite the Moravians to enter a Land of Canaan in New York? It could be—stranger things had been brought about by the decrees of Providence.

Hardly had Spangenberg digested Tiebout's message when an alternative offer arrived. If the Moravians would prefer, Tiebout wrote, he would be willing to let them have all his group's fifty thousand acres in the Catskills at four shillings per acre and on the easiest terms imaginable. The bishop replied that he would not "buy a cat in a bag. We must view the land."[7]

And view the land he did—by proxy—while the ship *John* pitched and rolled her way across the Atlantic. That May, three Moravian Brethren, A. A. Lawatsch, Owen Rice, and Jacob Loesch, explored the tracts owned by Tiebout and his associates. Their reports are still preserved in the archives of their church at Nazareth in Pennsylvania in all their factual sobriety with, here and there, an outburst of enthusiasm.

The explorers found that the four-thousand-acre gift and the seven thousand acres adjoining lay in the far southwestern corner of the patent near Cochecton where Henry Wooster had lost his compass to the Indians thirteen years before. Everywhere gigantic trees covered the land. They towered side by side in unbelievable closeness, and their roots intertwined and filled the soil. Brother Lawatsch saw white pines one hundred feet high and more with diameters of eight to ten feet—these would be suitable for ships' masts. It was cool country; no oaks grew there but many spruce, sugar maple, beech, and other trees which thrive in cool and moist soil. In many places mountain laurel bushes six to eight feet tall formed thickets impenetrable to man or beast. The forest was so dense that horses and cows would starve for lack of grass. The explorers brought food for their horses and had to hasten back to the settlements when this gave out. The soil, where it could be seen, was an unfamiliar red.

There were disadvantages: the isolation, the lack of a usable road, the unusual difficulty of clearing posed by the size and amazing quantity of the trees. Yet more than half the land offered was good and could produce excellent crops of grain when cleared. Brother Loesch felt "a little cautious." The water was red (it was spring and the streams were eroding their banks as they carried off the past winter's mountaintop snow).[8]

To balance all this, there were the Indians. Across the Delaware were groups of the Iroquois. (The Moravians had already sent solitary missionaries to settle among them, and Zinzendorf himself had lived with them.) Upstream was the settlement where Hendrick Heckan had made his cider; downstream in Pennsylvania were the Nanticokes and Shawnees. "We could visit the Indians,"[9] wrote Brother Lawatsch.

The report was speeded to Bishop Spangenberg and the conferees at Lindsay House in London. The conference considered the matter of the proposed settlement and gave its approval. Late that October the Moravians' famous convert, the Indian Shebosch, and another Moravian visited the proposed site to prepare the way for an official inspection tour by Bishop Peter Boehler. But rain descended. The gigantic trees stood up to their ankles in water, the laurel thickets were flooded. Red, red water covered the wilderness almost everywhere. There was nothing to do but to postpone the official visit until spring.

By March 1754 plans for the new community were well advanced. It was to be known as Zauchenthal—Count Zinzendorf himself chose the name. Bishop David Nitschman was to be *hausvater* at Zauchenthal with an assistant to help with clerical labors; tools, cattle, horses, and wagons would be brought from Bethlehem. A gristmill and a sawmill would be speedily built. So too would a smithy and a tannery. The first settlers were chosen —there would have to be a weaver, a cobbler, a millwright, a blacksmith, and other men with special skills. There would be no school for the children during the first busy years.

Zauchenthal seemed almost a reality. Henry Van Vleck of New York was given a power of attorney to arrange for the transfer of the property. The deeds were drawn up by the Tiebout group.[10] Then out of the wilderness of the Hardenbergh Patent came Owen Rice bearing doubts and dark second thoughts. The free lands were not as good as had seemed at first, he said; the only land suitable as a site for Zauchenthal lay to the east in the region a little north of the Monticello of later days, where the Concord and other great resort hotels of modern times were to rise.

The Tiebout group was willing to consider a change. But there were those half-dozen Würtembergers who had already been settled on parts of the lands Rice favored. Well, it didn't matter—things could be arranged.

With a little persuasion and shifting about of the Würtembergers, the Moravians might have the land they wanted. New agreements were signed and Henry Van Vleck set to work to arrange conveying the new site. Everybody concerned was aglow with enthusiasm. William Alexander had visited the Moravian town of Bethlehem and come back to New York raving about the Moravians' industry, neatness, honesty, and prosperity.

The Tiebout group "are all in high spirits about the Brethren going on the land yet this fall, and begin to raise the prices of land already,"[11] wrote Henry Van Vleck. One settler named Matthew Kolb was proving difficult: he was clearing land and building a cabin to the southwest of what is now known as Kiamesha Lake. But Kolb could be taken care of, Tiebout declared.

Over the issue of Matthew Kolb, Zauchenthal began to fall apart before ever it was built. Cornelius Tiebout, who had been all eagerness to deal with Kolb, began hedging and suggesting that the Moravians should dispossess the man and compensate him for his "improvements." Spangenberg became convinced that Tiebout did not mean to go through with the deal. He permitted himself to write that Tiebout had more land than he would ever want—his fussing over a few acres didn't make sense. Finally after a few evasive letters from Tiebout, Spangenberg instructed Van Vleck to pack up his papers relating to Zauchenthal, send them to Bethlehem, and forget the whole thing. Zauchenthal, it turned out, had only been a dream. All that remains of it are the ghostly papers filed away in the archives of the Moravian Church.

Robert Livingston had not been involved in the plan for luring the Moravian Church into serving as volunteer live bait for a land-development scheme. He had quickly sold his share in the lands offered to the Moravians and from that moment he merely watched the proceedings from the sidelines. He did not like or trust Tiebout, whom he once described as "an illiterate designing man."[12] Thanks to the acquisitive drive of his father, Livingston was now a member of the colonial aristocracy. He could look on with amusement at the sordid antics which men like Tiebout indulged in as they sought to climb upward to the exalted limb of the social tree on which the Livingstons now perched. What made Tiebout's goings-on all the more amusing was that, as everyone knew, the curse of sterility was upon the man—he had no children and could not hope to found a family. All his acquiring was to no long-range purpose; he was merely responding to the pressures of his society like a bee with one wing gathering nectar when it can never return to the pleasures of the hive.

Livingston was no mere objective spectator at the rise and fall of

Zauchenthal; he was watching with a purpose. Hardly had the Moravian dream been dissipated when he approached Bishop Spangenberg with an offer that, he suggested, might raise Zauchenthal from the dead. He would let the Moravians have twenty thousand acres of his own to the north in the valley of the Beaverkill. But there would be none of this Tiebout nonsense about free land. All Livingston expected was a straightforward rent of a hundred bushels of wheat per hundred acres—forever.[13]

The bishop received the offer in a cautious mood. He sent a party of explorers to take a look at Livingston's land. In the fall of 1755 the Moravian church leaders considered the explorers' report and Livingston's terms and turned down the offer. By that action they excluded the Moravian way of life from becoming a factor in the settlement of the Catskills. They also removed a possible obstacle to the domination of the region by the Livingston way.

Even as the Moravians and Tiebout were dickering in 1753, two new ways of dealing with the world were making their first contact with the mountains. These ways questioned the values which Livingston, Tiebout, and the Hardenbergh patentees held dear. They questioned the utility of the intoxicating mixture of pacifism, practicality, goodwill, and unreality which Count Zinzendorf had put together for the Moravians to drink. Of all methods by which humans have sought to assert power over their surroundings, these two were the farthest removed from the ways of life of our brother creatures, the lions and mice, the apes, the amoebas, and mosses. They were the methods of science and art brought to the Catskills in September 1753 by a man and a boy. The man was weakened by a raging fever; the boy had failed to take along the brand-new box of paints given to him by "a Switzer Gentleman" who had been impressed by his talent for drawing. The Catskill Mountains, thanks to these two, would never again leave quite the same impression on the human mind as they did in the innocent age of Johannis Hardenbergh. The man was John Bartram, botanist of Philadelphia. The boy was his son William, aged fourteen.

13

John Bartram Explores
a Shady Vale

✤ WHEN WILLIAM BARTRAM was a grown man his mind went back to the Catskills of 1753 and he wrote ". . . when in my youth, attending my father on a journey to the Catskill Mountains, in the government of New York, having nearly ascended the peak of Gilead, being youthful and vigorous in pursuit of botanical and novel objects, I had gained the summit of a steep rocky precipice, ahead of our guide, when, just entering a shady vale, I saw, at the foot of a small shrub, a singular and beautiful appearance, which I remember to have instantly apprehended to be a large kind of fungus. . . ."

The boy was about to kick the gray-and-yellow mass when his father recognized it for what it was. "A rattlesnake, my son," he cried. He seized the boy's shoulder and jerked him back. He "probably saved my life,"[1] William reflected years later. The incident saw print in William's account of his travels in the Carolinas, Georgia, and Florida, first published in 1791. The book was read and admired by William Wordsworth, by S. T. Coleridge, by Chateaubriand, and by Mrs. Felicia Hemans (whose boy stood on the burning deck), and left its mark on the work of all these writers. It still remains a landmark in American literature. In William Bartram's book, for the first time, the American landscape, American trees, American flowers, and American Indians were handled with conscious and sensitive literary art.

It was in this book, if only on a single page, that the Catskills made their first appearance in literature. There the spot where William's adventure with the rattler took place first stirred human imaginations through the medium of printed words. No more appropriate place could have been chosen at which to begin the process of transforming the Catskill Moun-

tains into one of the great romantic regions of the world. For William
Bartram's shady vale near the summit of the peak of Gilead was no ordinary hollow among the Catskills. In the minds of nineteenth-century men
and women, it was to become an enchanted spot about which romantic
legends crystallized and which lured painters, poets, and culture lovers by
the thousands each year. Seventy years after William met the rattlesnake in
the shady vale, pilgrims to the place found a hotel newly built nearby to
accommodate them in comfort. The same year William died, while digging
in his Philadelphia garden, unaware that he, his father, and a rattlesnake
had formed little links in a chain of events that was leading human beings
with irresistible force to the vale. The rolling ridges that enclosed the vale
on two sides; the rocky precipices that were its limits on two others; the
waterfalls that gracefully leaped down the precipices; the two lakes that
gleamed so unexpectedly within the vale—all these by the time William
died were in the process of being transformed in human eyes and minds
into things of magic.

In 1753, however, the shady vale held no hint of the enchantment
which was to hover about it in later years. It was instead an especially
undesirable piece of real estate of the kind beloved only by the Devil
and his regiments of evil spirits. Its thin soil, its isolation behind ridges and
precipices, its jagged rocks flung here and there as if to discourage human
penetration combined to make it scorned and unwanted. Smart speculators
asked for grants of land all around it; but no one was foolish enough to
ask for the shady vale which was to become—so great was the revolution
that took place in men's minds—the most valuable spot in the entire region
of the Catskill Mountains.

When Johannis Hardenbergh and Company petitioned Lord Cornbury
for nearly all the Catskills in 1706, they did their best to exclude the shady
vale. They might have had it for the asking but they knew better than to
include so useless a place in their request. Yet the vale had one thing
they wanted: it was the upper part of the stream which was born in the two
lakes and dashed down precipice after precipice as the Kaaterskill, until it
peacefully joined the Hudson River and there lost its identity. The stream
might some day be useful and profitable for it had the power to turn the
wheels of mills—so thought the members of Johannis Hardenbergh and
Company. More than that, it and its tributaries had succeeded in carving
into the rocks of the Catskills the only pass for many miles along the
mountain wall that led from the Hudson Valley to the great inner plateau
of the mountains. It was to make sure that the Kaaterskill and its Kaaterskill Clove were included in his grant that Hardenbergh and Company

gave as their northeast corner "ye head of a certain small river commonly known by ye name of Cartwright's Kill" (Lord Cornbury disliked everything Dutch, and this may have been a prudently Anglicized form of the Dutch Kaaterskill) "& soe by ye northerly side of ye said kill or river to ye northermost bounds of Kingstowne on said kill or river. . . ."[2]

By these words Hardenbergh and Company established as their corner the point at which the Kaaterskill emerges from the more southern of the two lakes, the one known today as South Lake. In later years as magic settled upon the shady vale of the two lakes, this point responded to the magic by moving about here and there. In the course of time the Hardenbergh Patent line followed the shore of South Lake. It changed from a straight line to one with all the serpentine grace of William Bartram's rattlesnake as it writhed and twisted in its effort to encompass the vale.

In the year 1706 the beauty and enchantment which were later to be seen so plainly in the shady vale and in the adjoining Kaaterskill Clove were invisible to Johannis Hardenbergh and most other adult Americans. As children these Americans had responded with wonder and interest to the natural world around them. They had explored this world with eyes and mouths and hands—until they had been taught better. The business of a man, their elders taught them, was to acquire property and status, to love one's mate and children and, by sharing the beliefs of other Christians and taking part in simple religious observances, to ensure a reserved seat in the world to come. For a child to delight in flowers or flowing water or white clouds floating across a summer sky or the fragrance of a meadow in July —this was understandable. For a man it was a nonsensical waste of time. And what was worse, it was without profit in pounds, shillings, and pence, or in earthly or heavenly status.

In Johannis Hardenbergh, the child he had once been lay dead beyond recall; he had responded well to the shaping forces of his society. With John Bartram it was otherwise. Society had failed to make of him the kind of man it wanted. Not that he was unacquisitive, not that he failed to support and love his wife and children, not that he was irreligious, but because the child he had been remained alive and active in him to the end of his days. Side by side with the successful farmer John Bartram walked another Bartram—a man who asked questions about how rocks and rivers came to be, who stared at flowers and birds, who pried into the secrets of wasp life and tree life, and so wasted time he should have spent in acquiring even more property than he needed to support himself and his family.

In spite of thousands of years of pressure to bring civilized man to conformity, failures like John Bartram have been not uncommon. Usually such men or women lead baffled and frustrated lives, but when they manage to come into communication with others in whom the wondering child lives on, then their lives may flower into prodigies of achievement. John Bartram happened to live at a time when a great surge of wondering and asking questions was beginning to pound at old social foundations. In England men who had the right combination of intelligence, money, and leisure—peers, businessmen, physicians, and clergymen—were studying the ways of life of worms and bees, staring at the moon, watching the goings-on in drops of ditch water through crude microscopes, and speculating endlessly about what makes the world go round. They wrote papers and sent them to the Royal Society of London; they performed chemical experiments; they spied upon nesting birds and observed the fertilization of flowers. Some discovered that an amateur scientist might easily work his way into exalted company in an age when an interest in science had become something of a passport to the most elevated social level. To wonder had become sophisticated and even fashionable. The age of the natural sciences was becoming firmly rooted in the Western world. In Holland, in the principalities of Germany, in Italy, in Sweden, and in Switzerland, amateur and professional natural scientists multiplied. They visited across national boundaries, they wrote endless letters back and forth, and they exchanged information and opinions. The world was being rediscovered and revalued. Human energy was being set to racing through new channels. The demands of war and money-making and national and religious prejudice might slow but they could not stop the process. The poor knew nothing of all this. They continued to cherish their ancient beliefs and to regard the interest in the natural world of their judge or landlord as merely another amusement of the rich to be discarded when time should turn it into a bore as time always did with such frivolities.[3]

Even in the cities and towns of British America, with the native Indians lurking in the surrounding forests, an occasional member of the upper classes became a "natural philosopher" and observed, experimented, and corresponded with European philosophers. In Philadelphia, James Logan took time from his duties as chief justice of Pennsylvania and president of the council to study and write about the sex life of Indian corn (and to translate Latin classics into limpid English). Logan met Bartram and encouraged him in his botanical efforts, as did a successful young printer named Benjamin Franklin. Through these and other Philadelphia friends, Bartram came into close relations with an English woolens merchant named Peter Collinson. It was Collinson who made it possible for Bartram to wander and to wonder for the rest of his life. It was Collinson who, from faraway London, guided Bartram to the Catskill Mountains and its shady vale.

Peter Collinson was born near the shores of Lake Windermere in the Lake District of northwestern England. His ancestors had done well as makers of "men's mercery"—woolens of which men's clothing were made. Young Collinson set up in business in London as an exporter of the kind of textiles that had made his family prosper. Before long he was exporting woolens to every seaport of British North America. But Collinson was not only an imaginative businessman, he was also a natural philosopher with a fascinated interest in the ways of the natural world. He encouraged his colonial customers to send him such strange wares as wasps' nests and butterfly cocoons. Botany too charmed Collinson, and the ships which took his woolens to New York and Philadelphia fetched back seeds and plants which the woolens merchant planted in a botanical garden of his own. When he discovered John Bartram he found a man after his own heart— a man who wanted only a little encouragement to send him into a perfect frenzy of botanizing. Collinson was an important part of the international club of natural philosophers, and he set Bartram to sending new plants and friendly letters to Charles Linnaeus, the great Swedish botanist, to the younger Gronovius of Leyden, to botanically minded peers, and even to royalty. All wrote back with enthusiasm and encouraged Bartram to further efforts.[4]

Collinson had an infinite capacity for rejoicing at the richness and variety of the world's living things. And to this was wedded a gift for acting as a clearinghouse which could put in touch people with similar tastes who needed each other's help. Bartram had an economic problem— he was not a rich man. Collinson put his mind to work on Bartram's case and came up with an answer in the shape of a method by which "friend John" might finance his botanical explorations. From now on he would act as a supplier of botanical materials to the nobility and gentry of Britain who were taking up the new and fascinating fad of landscape gardening.

Every further penetration into the mysteries of the universe stimulates human beings to freshly directed activity in many fields. Shortly after 1700 the new attitude toward science began to make itself felt in literature and in the arts. Soon some British poets and landscape painters were showing a new kind of feeling in their work. For want of a better term it is usually called romanticism. This romanticism was an expression of a heightened awareness, sometimes in a mystical way, of the closeness of man to the rest of the natural world and to his own unconscious self. It found in trees and mountains a kind of reflection of human emotion, and it went back for the enlightenment of grownups to the child's view of the world in which trees might talk if they chose and raindrops are the tears of the clouds. The first bold expression of romanticism in Britain took the form of a sweeping away of stiff old gardens with their clipped box hedges and their prim beds of tulips and the substitution of landscape gardens which aimed at imitating and improving upon nature. "All nature [is] a garden"[5]: this was a maxim which guided devotees of the new game of landscape gardening. To the Chinese this approach to garden design was an old story rich in intellectual and aesthetic meanings; in England it often became an extravagant fad in which snobs and social climbers competed to speak the latest word in eccentricity. Artificial caves and ponds, shells, turtles, mosses, and vines imported from far corners of the earth, found their way into English landscape gardens. Ruins were designed by architects to be set in landscapes; hermitages of rude construction were built on carefully designed cliffs or beside newly made waterfalls, and hermits were hired to inhabit them. "There are no people so obviously mad as the English,"[6] wrote Horace Walpole even before he built his mock-Gothic house on Strawberry Hill surrounded by his own landscape garden. Walpole was right in this matter at least: the landscape madness seized upon all those Britons who could afford it—and upon some unfortunates who discovered too late that they could not. But to Peter Collinson's sharp eyes, all this seemed to offer a vast opportunity to help his friend John. For landscape gardens consumed immense amounts of plant material, and they used not just the standard British oaks and beeches but also exotic plants from all over the globe. There must be plants to express sublimity, plants to suggest melancholy, plants to send shivers down the backs of spectators seeing them artfully planted in crevices of cliffs. In this kind of gardening the tree was king. There could not be enough trees to meet the demand, and there could not be a sufficiently great variety of trees to express all the emotion that was burning to be expressed.

    Peter Collinson arranged a sort of plant of the month club for Bartram. "I employed him," Collinson wrote of Bartram, "to collect seeds,—100 species in a box at five Guineas each from the year 1735 to this year 1760 about 20 boxes a year one with another which I have to oblige the curious in planting . . . among the Nobility and Gentry. . . ."[7] Thus financed, Bartram went forth to do battle with the American wilderness for the delight of his patrons to whom he sent, in the course of time, boxes, bales, and barrels of plants and seeds. The chief of his subscribers was the eighth Lord Petre, a young, handsome, kindly, generous man (so wrote Peter Collinson). He was the son of the seventh lord who had once snipped a lock of hair from the head of a reigning beauty, Miss Arabella Fermor, and so inspired Alexander Pope to write *The Rape of the Lock*. Glamorous and rich, Lord Robert Petre was a connoisseur of greens. His landscape gardens used the green leaves of trees with subtlety, "great art and skill being shown in consulting every one's particular growth and the well blending of the variety of greens. Dark green being a great foil to lighter ones . . . bluish greens to yellow ones . . ."[8] Lord Petre's garden was the greatest of its kind in all of Britain; he had, said Collinson, ten thousand American plants.

In October 1735 Judge Paul Dudley of Roxbury, Massachusetts, sent Collinson a list of the evergreens of New England. Collinson's attention was riveted by a tree called the balm of Gilead fir. Firs were in great demand by landscape gardeners. Some gave the right note of desolation to a newly built ruin, others had the kind of silvery needles that supplied a color and quality in short supply but which was being eagerly hunted for. Collinson began suggesting to Bartram, with ever-increasing firmness, that he go out after firs and especially after the balm of Gilead. The subscribers craved these trees, Collinson wrote. Dr. Cadwallader Colden who lived near the Catskill Mountains could show him where they were to be found. In frequent letters Collinson gave Bartram instructions in methods of collecting and shipping seeds and plants; he praised him, and answered his questions about plants, fossils, and insects. Over and over he kept returning to the wonderful balm of Gilead tree which was to be found high on the Catskill Mountains. "Pray go soon and look out sharp for the Balm of Gilead Fir, . . ." "We all hope thee has taken or will take a progress to Hudson's River to find the Balm of Gilead Fir. . . ."[9] (Collinson had not yet learned the name of the Catskill Mountains.) On September 1, 1741, in answer to a letter in which Bartram informed him that he was about to visit the Catskills, the London woolens merchant wrote happily, "I shall now wait with some impatience to hear from thee, and how thou fared in thy expedition to Hudson's River; what discoveries thou hast made, to tempt thy subscribers to continue their subscriptions."[10] From this expedition Bartram sent to England several bladders filled with the resinous exudation of the balm of Gilead. He was too late in the season to gather seeds from the trees he found growing in all their silvery beauty near the two lakes. The next September he returned.

On his way to the Catskills, Bartram stopped at Cadwallader Colden's house on his extensive estate of Coldenham. Collinson had laid great stress on the value of friendship with Colden, and Bartram found him to be a "facetious, agreeable gentleman."[11] He was a physician, surveyor general of the Province of New York, and an extraordinarily skilled botanist; he could be of great help to a man in Bartram's position. The doctor, alas, was not at home but his wife was and she sent Bartram off to the Catskills with a basket of food she packed for him. "Part of the bounty she [Mrs. Colden] was pleased to bestow upon me I enjoyed on ye top of ye Catts kill Mountains & part brought home for my wife to taste . . ."[12] Bartram wrote Colden. The botanist had eaten the first recorded picnic lunch consumed on the Catskills. He was in high spirits on that expedition, for Collinson's letters written just before he left glow with the possibilities that are to flow from Lord Petre's patronship.

Bartram had hardly returned from the Catskills when he received a mournful letter from his London friend. Lord Petre was dead. He had succumbed to smallpox at the age of thirty. Collinson added a brief cry from his heart. "All our schemes are broke."[13]

But the schemes of the two friends were only beginning to flower. Collinson would in time wangle for Bartram an appointment as Botanist to the King for Georgia and Florida, and he would help him gain many other honors. Heartbroken as he was at the death of Lord Petre, Collinson continued to prod his American friend into renewed botanical explorations. He urged him to return to the Catskills to hunt out the shy seeds of the balm of Gilead fir to send to the eagerly waiting landscape gardeners of Britain. Lord Petre was gone, but the whirlwind of scientific and aesthetic inquiry was raising more dust than ever in Europe and America, and the odd midget whirlwinds that appeared around its margin were increasing in number. Lord Petre was gone but the spirit that inspired him lived on.

14

The Balm of Gilead Tree

☘ IF THE PLACES where the balsam fir—known in John Bartram's day as the balm of Gilead fir—grows naturally were to be marked on a map of southern Canada and the eastern part of the United States, Canada would appear as the homeland or mainland of the tree. Broad capes would be seen projecting from the mainland far into New England and the Adirondacks. To the south the marked map would show a scattering archipelago stretching to Virginia—each island formed of a mountaintop or high ridge. Below Virginia a smaller but related fir would take over in high places. This is the Fraser fir, sometimes called the she-balsam.

The balsam fir and spruce islands of the Catskills are memorials to the process by which a coat of vegetation began clothing the Catskills after the retreat of the last ice sheet to cover the region some fifteen thousand years ago. The ice once extended well into Pennsylvania to the south. It scoured the land clean of living things. But as the edge of the ice sheet moved northward, plant life began to take over. It moved in from what is now the southeastern United States where, as in some natural Noah's ark, a vast company of living things had waited out the years of chill. From here arctic vegetation crept to the edge of the receding ice and became established well enough to prepare the soil, as the ice continued to retreat, for less hardy plants. Eventually the New England and New York of our day were ready for trees. These emerged from the Noah's ark with the balsam fir among the leaders and covered all the region except for the still-bald mountaintops.

The ice line moved northward, not steadily but in a series of spurts, and the climate of what is now the region of the Catskills grew milder. The time came when rivals of the balsam firs and spruce such as the hemlocks could emerge from the ark of the Appalachians and settle down in favorable valleys. Before long, they shot above the balsam firs and deprived them of light and food. And balsam firs and spruce vanished from the valleys. But by this time the higher elevations had acquired something of a coat of soil thanks to the work of the arctic plant pioneers, and the balsam firs and spruce found it possible to take over. There they have remained ever since. But the islands on which they and their companion trees live grow smaller and smaller. It is likely that some day the balsam fir will vanish from the Catskills to return only after another ice sheet has swept the land clean once again.[1]

The balsam fir, while it is young and vigorous, has a charm of its own to human eyes. In Canada, the Adirondack Mountains, and the state of Maine, it is too common to exert its charm to the full. Among the White Mountains of New Hampshire, it marks a level through which a climber must struggle on his way to his proper goal: the world of alpine plants and granite wastes above the timberline. But because the Catskills fall short of reaching the timberline by a thousand feet, the balsam fir islands of its summits become the most rewarding goals of a climber. On the mountain-top islands of the Catskills—Slide Island, Wittenberg Island, Indian Head Island, and many of the rest—balsam firs stand alone or beside the spruces which are their favorite companions and exhibit all their beauty. The young trees bearing their first crop of cones have an irresistible appeal. The lavender cones do not hang down as do those of the spruces, they stand erect and conspicuous on their extended branches in midsummer, each cone capped and sparkling with beads of crystal clear balsam. The heat of the sun releases the aromatic fragrance of the balsam until a climber mopping his forehead on a mountain trail cannot help thinking of an old-fashioned Christmas when balsam trees released the same fragrance in thousands of warm American parlors, and candles instead of lavender cones stood twinkling on their branches. It is only in sheltered spots that the balsam firs grow up with straight trunks and symmetrical branches— on the highest summits of the Catskills, they seem of a very different breed.

Early explorers found summits such as those of High Peak and Slide to be almost impenetrable jungles of balsam firs, crouching as if on their knees in their efforts to resist the gales that attacked them. It was necessary to hack a path through gnarled branches to reach many summits. Once there, no far-reaching view could be seen unless the explorers tumbled to the fact that, so dense had the balsam fir boughs become because of endless exercise in fighting wind and ice, a man might climb a tree and stand on its topmost branches as if on a green carpet. As recently as fifty years ago guides to Catskill peaks were leading their customers up balsam firs and inviting them to recline on the tops. In winter the dense upper boughs sometimes caught the snow and ice and formed solid roofs beneath which dark caves and alleys wound to the pleasure of the snowshoe hares and their enemies the wildcats, both of whom haunt Catskill summits. Old-time hunters caught in the mountains by nightfall sometimes took refuge in these tree-made caves, making sure that a bear had not thought of the same thing first. On lower levels benighted hunters fashioned beds of balsam fir boughs laid in overlapping rows like shingles and often constructed what they called a "wigwam" of boughs around their beds. Through the night the hunter would rest in soft comfort while inhaling the delicious fragrance from all around him, happy in the thought—if his lungs gave him trouble—that with each breath he was drawing in a healing balsamic vapor.[2]

The early explorers among the Catskills found one region in which the balsam fir flourished with a special splendor. This was on the shores of the twin lakes that ornamented William Bartram's shady vale. In this charmed and protected spot balsam firs reached a size and elegance unknown elsewhere in the mountains. As late as 1820 Henry E. Dwight, grandson of President Timothy Dwight of Yale College, reported that "Around the lakes, and for several miles west of them, a tree which is usually called the Silvery Fur, and sometimes the balsam, is very abundant. This tree is much admired for its beauty, and is often procured to adorn the grounds of the opulent. I have never observed any which had the rich silvery lustre, or grew to the same elevation, with those near these bodies of water. The soil appears peculiarly adapted to the growth of these trees, some of which are fifty feet in height."[3]

The balsam firs that stood on the shores of the two lakes were the closest of any to the Indians who lived in the Hudson Valley. It is likely enough that from time to time the Indians climbed the heights in search of the trees, for the sticky exudation of the balsam fir once had a valued place in the pharmacopeia of the Indians. On the trunks of the trees, blisters filled with a clear turpentine commonly called "balsam" appear. The Indians of New York, it is said, called the tree Cho-koh-tung, or blisters, because of this.

In many parts of the world people living close to the earth and its green children have observed that some trees produce a substance which is released when the tree is injured and which then acts as a dressing for the wounds of the tree's bark. Actually such substances do keep out bacteria and fungi and so promote healing. Men and women reasoned that if a tree was helped by the stuff, why would not a human be helped too? So a variety of balsams, as they were called, came to be widely used especially in treating infected wounds and cancers. Some were true resins, and some were turpentines, but all were wondrously aromatic and exceedingly sticky when fresh.

The white settlers around the Catskills regarded the native Indians as an inferior people. But in one way they respected them. The Indians seemed to the whites to have a knowledge of the land in which they lived and of its plant and animal beings that sometimes verged upon the magical. They knew that a remedy for every human ill could be found in the leaves or fruits or roots or other parts of plants. The wilderness which so terrified an ailing white was, to a plantwise Indian, a vast storeroom filled with medicine. Many a white groaning in pain or burning with a fever would reject the white doctor who tried to treat him and insist that his family send for an Indian. It did not take white settlers long to learn from the Indians the medicinal uses of the plants of the New World.[4] They merged this knowledge with their own European plant lore and with that of the Bible. For to these people, the Bible was more than a holy book—it was their university in which they learned statecraft, the art of war, practical psychology, and in which they might take courses in a dozen other subjects. Even if they could not read—and many of them could not—biblical knowledge thundered at them from the pulpit and painlessly infiltrated them through the words of the psalms they sang. They had all heard the prophet Jeremiah speaking of the precious balm or balsam which the ancient Israelites found upon Mount Gilead in the Holy Land. When the Indians told them of the healing substance placed high upon the Catskills by a kindly Creator, the white settlers quickly equated this balsam of the New World with that of Jeremiah. After that they looked upon the Blew Mountains with a dawning respect, for they had begun to take on in their minds a touch of biblical glamor. Some even called the part of the Catskills where the balsam firs grew most conveniently to the settlements, Mount Gilead. The tree that bore the fragrant aromatic medicine became generally known as the balm of Gilead tree, a common name it now shares with a poplar whose buds yield a sticky substance which more recently had a large place in American Negro folk medicine.

A century and a half ago faith in the virtue of balm of Gilead, or Canada balsam as it was known a little later, led people of the town of Catskill to gather it systematically upon their Mount Gilead and to ship it by Hudson River sloop to New York and other cities.[5] Today old Jeremiah's despairing question, "Is there no balm in Gilead?" must be answered in the negative. For in a society that places its confidence in laboratories and corporate research rather than in the rich if sometimes misleading distillations of folk wisdom, Canada balsam has vanished from the shelves of druggists and the black bags of physicians. Yet here and there among the Catskills and in the region around, an occasional old-timer still believes in the stuff with a stubbornness that cannot be talked down. Ralph M. Lord, for many years the druggist of Tannersville near the two lakes, remembers that he often gathered Canada balsam near the lakes to be sold for applying to infected wounds and cancers. He used a bottle equipped with a sharp metal beak which punctured the tree blister and allowed the balsam to trickle into the bottle; more than a hundred of the little blisters had to be pricked in order to yield a pint of liquid. Until recently the Indians of the Province of Quebec gathered Canada balsam by similar methods on a large scale, for it was once widely used not only in medicine but as an adhesive by makers of lenses and microscope slides. Today synthetic substitutes are pushing it out of the market as an adhesive for glass.

When John Bartram traveled to the Catskills in search of the seeds of the balsam fir, the relation of the tree and humans was close. Yet it was far from being as close as it was to become in later years. The gathering of balm of Gilead on a commercial scale was many years in the future; so too was the digging up of young balsam firs to "adorn the grounds of the opulent"[6] of America. The glamorous heyday of the man-balsam relation, when the young trees cut in the Catskills were to be sold in vast quantities as the first Christmas trees of the New World,[7] was as yet undreamed of. Bartram came to the Catskills four times in search of botanical knowledge. By gathering seeds of the balsam fir and other plants he merely hoped to finance his expeditions. On August 20, 1753 Bartram wrote to Peter Collinson and told him of his current botanical ambitions: "I am now very intent upon examining the true distinguishing characters of our forest trees, finding it a very difficult task—and can have no help from either ancient or modern authors, they having taken no particular observation worth notice. . . ."[8] His friend Benjamin Franklin had promised to give him specimens of the evergreens of New England; he himself would collect specimens of the evergreens of the "York government," would compare these with those of Pennsylvania, and put his findings in writing. This would mark a beginning. Next he would go on to study and compare "our Oaks and Hickories. . . ."

In the 1750s Bartram had two favorite places for studying plants and gathering their seeds. There was the valley of the Shenandoah for flowering herbs and there was the Catskill Mountains for trees. He wrote to Collinson of both. In the "spacious vale" of the Shenandoah "I have gathered my

finest autumnal flowers and where by report of the inhabitants it is like as
if Flora sported in solitary retirement as Sylva doth on the Katskill Mountains where there is the greatest variety of uncommon trees and shrubs that
I ever saw in such a compass of ground."[9] Bartram planned to go to the
Catskills to study its trees, but he did not forget his noble and gentle
British subscribers. "I design to set out with my little botanist ('Billy'),"
he wrote, "the first of September which is ten days sooner than usual,
hoping to gather the Balm of Gilead and Larix seed—which was generally
fallen before I got there . . . neither do I design to be in such a hurry as
I have been."[10] On Bartram's three previous trips to the Catskills he had
climbed the mountains and then hastily descended. He had never yet
spent a night high among the Catskills, and he hoped to do that this time.

As had often happened before when he planned to visit the Catskills,
fate seemed bent on keeping him at home. Bartram was feeling shaky
even as he wrote to Collinson. Soon he was wrestling with a high fever
and other unpleasant symptoms. He knew that if he did not go to the
Catskills early in September, he would have to wait a whole year before
he could gather the seeds of the balm of Gilead tree. For this tree handles
the distribution of its seeds in its own precipitate manner. Other cone-
bearing trees manage things more slowly and in a more guarded way.
But once the balsam fir seeds are ripe, they are thrown out into the world
without any dillydallying at all. While the seeds are immature the cones
within which they lie are protected against molestation by the sticky
balsam which glues the scales of the cones together and lies in glittering
drops on its surface. A seed-hungry chickadee or red squirrel tackling the
cone at this stage would be in for a messy time. But as the winged seeds
swell and mature, the cones which hold them tucked in pairs at the
bases of the scales lose their lavender color. They turn brown, and the
balsam they contain becomes less and less sticky by contact with the air
and at last turns brittle enough to allow the whole cone to fall apart. The
seeds are released and if all goes well the wind will scatter them. If the
seeds are fertile—and often enough they are not—a few will fall on favorable
ground and give rise to a younger generation of balsam firs.

There is a critical moment in all this. Once the cones lose their
stickiness and the scales begin to loosen, the cones are easy targets for
the birds and the small seed-eating mammals. And they appear to be tasty,
for a big proportion of each crop gets itself eaten. Even before the seeds
are entirely ripe and when they are beginning to lose their sticky protection, heaps of purplish scales may be seen lying beneath balsam trees,
showing that some red squirrel has jumped the gun and eaten a meal of

balsam fir seeds even before it was properly cooked. That is why anyone wanting to gather the seeds must act just before the scales begin to come apart. Gathered then, the nearly ripe cones placed in a dry place indoors will fall apart and release their seeds in safety. John Bartram had built ingenious cupboards beside his fireplaces for just such uses.

It had been an early ambition of John Bartram to become a physician. Throughout his long life he absorbed bits and pieces of information about the practice of medicine, especially when drugs derived from plants were involved. He often treated ailing neighbors who could not afford the services of a regular physician. As August of 1753 came to its end, John Bartram, the shrewd amateur physician, knew that he was in no shape to undertake his long trip on horseback to the Catskill Mountains. Yet undertake it he did, for the landscape gardeners of Britain who were his subscribers had to be served or else, as Collinson had hinted, they might not pay their subscriptions. The balsam firs of the shady vale in the Catskills were ready. If he delayed, Bartram might reach them to find their seeds dispersed and only the brown cores of their cones standing on the branches to mock him. As he left home on September first he recorded that he felt "pretty well recovered" but that a fever "still hanged upon me known by A very bad tast in my mouth my urin high colored & A weakness & dullness in stirring but hopeing this would wear off by traveling in change of air wee setout. . . ."[11]

15

"To Ye Cats Kill Mountains
with Billy"

✤ "A JOURNEY to ye Cats kill mountains with billy 1753"—that was
how John Bartram headed his account of his trip. And it was a good
heading, for Billy was taking his first expedition into the wilderness. Like
many another fourteen-year-old he was a source of mingled pride and
anxiety to his father. He showed great talent at drawing and painting and
he was a keen observer of the world of nature, but these were not
occupations at which a man might make a living. During the next few
years Bartram consulted his friends about possible occupations for Billy.
Benjamin Franklin suggested printing; Bartram himself thought surveying
might give the boy a chance to make a good living and at the same time
remain close to the plants and wild animals which he loved. He may
even have taken Billy on this expedition of 1753 in order to give him a
chance at winning the help of Dr. Cadwallader Colden, who managed to
study botany and physics while filling the post of surveyor general of New
York and, at the same time, enriching himself in land deals.[1]

The two started off with vigor and covered some ninety miles their
first two days. They crossed the Delaware into New Jersey probably in the
neighborhood of Easton, Pennsylvania. On the Jersey side Billy found a
rattlesnake which the two studied and allowed to go away unharmed after
they had observed his reactions to their presence, for John and William
had what a later generation was to call a "reverence for life" and did no
needless killing. As they jogged along, the Bartrams watched and wondered
endlessly. John noted the trees and other plants and the locations in which
they grew. He asked himself why it was that the soil in one place along
the Delaware was gravelly and in another filled with broken rock. How
had the broad and fertile plains of "ye menesink" been formed? What

power had caused the great Delaware Water Gap to be shaped? What kind of rock or soil lay far beneath the feet of his horse? He asked the settlers along the Delaware what they had struck when digging their wells and so found part of the answer to this last question. He then marshaled his observations on paper and from them drew a set of what he called "wandering conjectures" in which, despite the limitations of his power of expression, John conveys an awesome sense of the wearing away of mountains by the irresistible power of the Delaware River of ancient days as it pushed rock and earth aside, formed a vast lake, burst its boundaries, and gave the landscape of its valley the shape it now has. Peter Collinson would smile in the indulgent way of a man of superior education listening to the naïve cosmic conjectures of a simple backwoodsman when he read Bartram's wandering conjectures, but time would prove that here Bartram was a pioneer in understanding the part water plays in giving form to the surface of our earth.

The two went on. They spent one night in a rude tavern and another in a crowded and unclean settler's hut, ever wondering, ever observing, ever speculating. The excitement of the first days of the trip sustained John for a time, but then his fever returned in force; nothing he ate agreed with him; he felt weak. A double disappointment awaited the father and son at Dr. Colden's. The doctor was away from home. John could not get his help in conquering his illness, and William could not meet him. For two days the Bartrams botanized in the neighborhood of Coldenham. John's fever grew worse. High in the mountains the balm of Gilead cones continued maturing. Delay in the hope that the doctor might return was out of the question. Early one morning the Bartrams set off for the settlement of Catskill and by brisk riding reached there that evening. They lodged three miles "from ye foot of ye mountain," probably in the newly built Abeel house on the banks of the Kaaterskill. A guide was hired for four shillings a day and the next morning, laden with provisions and the heavy leather bags in which John stowed seeds and botanical specimens, the two men and the boy headed toward the Catskill Mountains.

The party followed the dry bed of Silver Brook which pointed up the wall of the Catskills directly at the exalted region of the two lakes. Wrote John: "I found it heavy climbing up with a strong feavor & heavy boots & great thirst most of ye springs was dryed up but when near half way up we found water where we rested a few minutes. . . ." The Bartrams had reached a long high ledge from which a spring issued. The spring came from a crack in the ledge and so suggested to a mind filled with biblical imagery the one Moses created with a blow of his staff in the desert of

Sinai to provide water for the children of Israel. The spot was to become the goal of semireverent vacationing pilgrims by the thousands during the nineteenth century when it was known as Moses Rock. In 1753 it was known only to Indian and white woodsmen and to the mice and deer and squirrels of the vicinity.

Up the successive precipices of the mountain they went with renewed energy. "We . . . set all our strength to climb makeing use of every bush in our way to pull ourselves up. . . ." But John was weak. His guide was kind enough to add Bartram's pack to his own, but even with this help it was a hard morning's work for John. By noon the climbers had reached the shore of North Lake where they sat down to eat lunch. William and the guide ate heartily. John was so ill that he "loathed food."

Twelve years before, in the late summer of 1741, John had come for the first time to this very spot. He had reported on it altogether too briefly to Collinson who inquired in reply, "Pray, did thee find no sort of shells on the verge of those lakes on the mountain?"[2] For the Quaker merchant was fascinated as were many curious-minded people of his day by the presence of marine shells on mountaintops. Were they vestiges of the great flood of Noah? Or were they disturbing hints of an incompleteness in the biblical account of the Creation? "Pray," asked Collinson again, "from what species of Fir, or Pine were those bladders gathered? Our own Balm of Gilead sweats out tears of balsam from the buds, in the summer months. . . ."[3] Collinson was referring to two ox bladders filled with the balsam of the balsam fir which Bartram had gathered near the lakes and which he had perhaps failed to label properly—or perhaps he had indeed made labels and the long winter voyage by sea had destroyed them. Collinson's "our own Balm of Gilead" was the European silver fir, similar to the balsam fir of America except in not producing blisters of balsam on its trunk.

"The bladders of balm which I sent thee," John replied, "I gathered on the Balm of Gilead Tree, on the Katskill Mountains—a delicate fragrant liquor as clear as water."[4] In the late summer of 1742 when John returned to the region of the lakes, he came home with his leather bags stuffed to overflowing with balsam fir cones. But, alas, the seeds proved infertile. Collinson had continued to urge Bartram to send him balm of Gilead seeds and the botanist deputed Colonel Salisbury of Old Catskill, near the present hamlet of Leeds, to gather some. The colonel went off to New York after instructing a servant to climb to the lakes at the proper time.

The servant reported that the birds had been ahead of him and had eaten all the seeds.[5]

The quest of the balm of Gilead seeds had proved difficult and disappointing. On that September noon in 1753, as John Bartram sat beside North Lake waiting for his son and the guide to finish their lunch, another chance to gather the shy seeds was at hand. Yet to this John gave no thought. Lightheaded with fever, shaky in his legs, uneasy in his stomach, he was intent on performing a fresh service to Collinson and his British subscribers. He had heard rumors of an amazing waterfall near the lakes. Bartram was determined, weak as he was, to see the waterfall and make a report on it.

The landscape gardeners of Britain were in the early, madly enthusiastic stages of a cult of the waterfall. A natural waterfall was a treasure, so artificial waterfalls were often being built at vast expense in places where waterfalls had no business being. Not long before, a waterfall had interest and value only in proportion to its usefulness in turning mill wheels. Johannis Hardenbergh, for example, had placed a high value on such waterfalls. But in Britain the waterfall had become as much an aesthetic object as a painting by Claude or Salvator Rosa; it was fashionable to be a connoisseur of waterfalls and to be conversant with their fine points. A few years later, the Reverend William Gilpin would analyze the aesthetics of waterfalls and come to the conclusion that a multiple fall was the finest and most meaningful.[6] Hidden in the wilderness near the lakes was a double fall. In 1742 Bartram had returned from an expedition to the Great Lakes and written Collinson an account of the falls of the Oswego River. He made a sketch of them which had aroused the enthusiasm of Collinson.[7] Now he was determined to report on the Great Falls of the Kaaterskill. To do this was even more important to him at the moment than to race the chickadees and squirrels for balsam seeds. The three set off. "My eager desire to see ye great falls three miles of [off] animated me to travail stoutly," Bartram wrote. The guide led the way "under ye spruice ballm of gilead & hemlock firs where ye sun hardly ever shines here was a large ledge of rock that projected over 5 foot above ye surface that above 100 men might have lodged dry in a shower of rain we left our baggage here while we went to ye falls. . . ." The Bartrams had come to the long ledge which runs along the southeastern shore of North Lake and under which hunters and fishermen, Indian, Negro, and white, have taken shelter from time immemorial. Here they proposed to return and spend the night. Free from the weight of their baggage they hastened toward the falls, following the shore of North Lake to its outlet, then moving along the watercourse which tied North and South lakes together, "good travelling under ye shade of lofty firs being pretty open. . . ." They rapidly passed South Lake and started down the infant Kaaterskill. "At last we came to ye great gulph that swallowed all down." They were standing on the rocky platform at the top of the falls. The falls were not at their best. It was a dry season in a dry year. "We throwed down stones to ye bottom could count 20 while going down. . . ." Bartram estimated the height of the upper section of the falls at one hundred feet. His account is hurried and sketchy—probably he described the falls at greater length in a letter to Collinson. There are suggestions in some of Collinson's letters that either John or young Billy sent a sketch across the Atlantic. In this way the Kaaterskill Falls, which were in time to become one of the wonders of the Catskills, were introduced to the world of European aesthetes.

The elder Bartram, eager for more waterfall wonders, insisted on exploring Spruce Creek which joins the Kaaterskill just above the great falls. But after a mile had been covered it became apparent that no more falls would be found. The party cut across the low base of a shoulder of North Mountain in the direction of North Lake. Before they reached the lake they met the rattlesnake of which Billy was to write. "Ye ground was pretty level and very shady being under large firs & beech very pleasant walking our guide going first billy next & I the last for two reasons one because I could not well keep up with them ye other for stairing round about to observe ye trees and plants." It was while John was "stairing" that Billy's sharp eyes found a "great black rattlensake quoiled up. . . ."

By the time the rattlesnake was disposed of by the determined guide and the baggage had been located under its rocky canopy, it was time to think of getting ready for the night—"came to our lodging kindled a fire & I being very weary tumbled down on ye moss that was spread on ye ground for our bed while my guide & son gathered wood to keep a good fire all night & a fine pleasant lodging we had a great rock between us & ye lake which served for a back to kindle ye fire against which reflected heat to ye under side of ye rock that projected over us A bright moonshine night & nothing wanting [to] render all agreable but ye abscence of my feavor. . . ."

Waterfalls, fever, and weariness—these had taken up most of John Bartram's first day in the region of the lakes. The next morning he got down to the business of collecting seeds for his subscribers and plant specimens for himself to use in his study of forest trees and shrubs. Here the guide who had been so kind the day before proved difficult. Bartram's fever had "rather increased in ye morning," yet he followed his usual method of shinnying up tall trees with an ax and lopping off branches which bore cones. The guide flatly refused to climb. He would cut down any tree, he said, but climb? No, that he would not do. The guide was a sensible man. To chop off branches while perched high in a tree is an easy way of damaging an arm or a leg or tumbling to the ground never to stir again. John Bartram at the age of fifty-four, burning with fever, weak from not eating, could chop away like a giant woodpecker in the treetops, but no four-shilling-a-day guide could be expected to follow him.

The guide was set to work cutting down trees; tall balsam firs, red spruce, white birches—these and more crashed to the floor of the shady vale to please the landscape garden devotees of Britain. White birches were in demand to use as accents; balsam firs and spruces were just the thing to give the proper note of gravity and melancholy to the path leading to a hermitage in which some hireling hermit-by-the-day sat telling his beads whenever a visitor to the garden hove in sight. But the trees of the vale were sacrificed in vain. The fallen evergreens did not yield "a hatful of cones." "I never saw seeds so scarce here before," Bartram lamented. "We fell several trees of ye paper birch but could not get a spoonful of seed. . . ." "Got home"—that is, to his lodging at Catskill—"about sun set & being much tired and loathing any food I went to bed without my supper." The next morning John and Billy rose early, mounted their horses and by nightfall of a day of heavy rain had covered fifty miles over as rough a road as was to be found in the settled parts of His Majesty's Province of New York.

Neither John nor William ever returned to the Catskills to pursue the quest of balm of Gilead seeds. And that was just as well for John's reputation as a purveyor of exotic seeds to the nobility and gentry of Britain. The balm of Gilead seeds gathered high among the Catskills proved reluctant to germinate in Britain even when given tender, almost maternal care. Those which did germinate produced spindly and uncertain seedlings which found it hard to survive the days of their infancy. A few did manage to achieve a precarious adulthood. Two or three of these unhappy exiles from the Catskills lingered on surrounded by other botanical debris of once ambitious landscaping projects and were pointed out to visiting tree lovers as nothing more than quaint American oddities. For growing far from home in a more relaxed climate they showed, even when young, little of the charm which would have been theirs at home. They grew into spindling and awkward adults. Proud Britains inspecting the trees could not help wondering what all the fuss had been about in the days of their first immigration and they inevitably came to the conclusion that their own unblistered British silver fir was far superior to its colonial cousin.[8]

When Billy was safely back home in Philadelphia in his father's fine stone house, which John had built with his own hands, he may have eagerly gotten out the paints and paper the Switzer gentleman had given him and proceeded to work up rough sketches made on his trip to the Catskills. This would have been in keeping with Billy's passion for drawing and painting. Whether he actually did or not can only be matter for conjecture. But before long his father sent Collinson a batch of Billy's drawings from nature (some of them may have been inspired by the Catskills) which aroused Collinson to superlatives. They are owned today by the British Museum.

We know beyond any doubt what the elder Bartram worked at upon his arrival home. He wrote his account of the Catskills trip and added to it his "Observations on ye Katts Kill Mountains" filling altogether nine crowded pages of a notebook. These pages constitute an important document in the story of the Catskills. They give the first account of the mountains from the point of view of a naturalist. They contain the earliest known attempt at understanding the structure of the mountains and the forces that gave them their shape. There is a not entirely complete list of the trees and shrubs of the Catskills, and some advice to future climbers: "the ascent indeed is tiresome enough to one that is used to walk on level ground & dangerous enough to a Careless heavy lubber who may have frequent opportunitys of breaking his neck but to a nimble careful person ye way is pleasant & safe. . . ."

To John Bartram, as to others of his age, the Catskills were an extension of the Appalachian Mountains which were long known as the Alleghenies. Seven great chains of the Appalachians running all the way from "ye back parts of Carolina," John explained, came together at the Catskills—almost as if tied there in a knot, he implies. Here Bartram's "wandering conjectures" wandered far from the mark but when he dealt with his notions about how the mountains had been shaped, his theories make sense to people of our own day. He saw the Catskills not only as an elevated mass of rock covered thinly with soil and vegetation, but as a system of watercourses which by devious ways conveyed the rain falling upon the mountains to the sea. The Catskills, Bartram wrote, contain "ye sources of ye branches or heads of ye adjacent rivers whose waters rusheth down ye declivities & perpendicular rocks in glistening cascades in as various forms and dementions as numbers . . . many of them united together hath worn and divided ye mountains into deep narrow valleys into many spireing ridges on all sides. . . ."

The surface of the soil coat of the Catskills, Bartram wrote, was composed of rotten wood, moss, and fallen leaves with few stones showing except on the mountaintops and along the watercourses "which is full of stones of all dimentions some places all solid rock at bottom which indicates to me that ye main body of these mountains is rock and that ye soil is very shallow."

Rain falling on the Catskills, Bartram decided, quickly passes "thro ye rotten mossy soil to ye rock which by its declivity guides it to ye gathering water courses. . . ." In some places such as, for example, the vale of the two lakes, the bedrock being concave "holds ye water like a bason."

In his pioneer account of the Catskills, Bartram makes what may look to a modern reader like an extraordinary omission. The father and son and their guide climbed the Catskills from a point directly below the ledge upon which the great Catskill Mountain House was to be built many years later. Their route can be easily traced today, for they followed the rocky hollow that ascends the mountain close to the scar left by the funicular railway sent soaring up the mountain in 1892. This route would have taken the Bartram party to the clifftop known as the Pine Orchard, which lies at the brink of the mountain a few minutes' walk southeast of the two lakes. To the Pine Orchard in another two generations men and women would be making pilgrimages each summer in order to experience the emotions aroused by the exciting view of "all creation" which, out of all places in the New World, could be had in its greatest intensity, many said, at this spot. At the Pine Orchard young ladies would some day faint away in sheer inability to cope with what they saw and be caught in the arms of their bearded escorts, while hard-bitten speculators would feel tears coming to their eyes, they knew not why, as they looked out across the Hudson Valley to the misty mountains of New England that lay beyond. Painters and poets would haunt this spot and industriously sketch and scribble. In 1828 an annual publication called the *Atlantic Souvenir* would relate how clergymen were inspired by what they saw from the Pine Orchard. "An aged minister of the gospel was gazing at the view by moonlight in company with a group of young people," said the *Atlantic Souvenir*. He felt, he said in a "clear though tremulous voice, as if we were in a mighty temple, upon the lofty dome of which is inscribed in characters, that all intelligent beings may read, worship the creator."[9]

John Bartram passed within a few feet of the spot which was destined to work with such power upon the feelings of people of the future. The weather was sunny, the view was there for him to see, yet if he saw it he did not think it important enough to deserve a single word in his notebook. Among his British subscribers a few advanced souls were beginning to become initiated into the meaning of a view from a mountaintop. The invention of the telescope and microscope; the work of such men as Galileo, Kepler, and Sir Isaac Newton; the speculations of churchmen like Thomas Burnet—all these were beginning to elevate views from mountaintops into symbols of infinity, of the vastness of the universe into which man was thrust, of the relationship of the human individual to the stars, to the daisies and the bright-eyed mice, and the things that the microscope showed to be wriggling in a drop of ditch water. In September of 1753 all these meanings had not yet crystallized in the unconscious minds of western Europeans to be ready to spring instantly into the consciousness when stimulated by an extensive view from a mountaintop.[10] If John Bartram glanced at the view from the Pine Orchard, he did no more than that and passed on. Another forty years would have to pass before the view from the cliff adjoining the vale of the twin lakes would be able to seize human minds and emotions with irresistible force.

16

"A Fatality Has Attended
Our Patent"

❦   "I AM AFRAID that that Fatality which has so long attended our patent will still do so. . . ."[1] It was Judge Robert R. Livingston of New York's Admiralty Court who wrote those words to his father, Robert Livingston of Clermont, in July 1760.

The judge was right. Many generations were to come and go before the Hardenbergh Patent would cease to be "a reproach and a byword"[2] and shake off what some may well have suspected was a curse laid upon it in the days of Lord Cornbury. The skirmishing of Cornelius Tiebout and then Robert Livingston with the unworldly Moravians had seemed like a hopeful prelude to a flood of settlers in the Catskills. Then "the Fatality" once again hovered over the mountains. Hardly had the last of the Moravian explorers faded from the mountains when war between the British and French made the entire region a possible battleground.

In New York and Albany a war boom got under way and the businessmen who made up the membership of the Provincial Assembly were kept busy handling their profits. New Englanders bitterly accused them of selling supplies to the enemy, and there is no doubt that some of them did. Speculation in lands on the frontiers ceased; the Catskills took on a new aspect. They became a great protective wall behind which the enemy might be kept at bay. But the Catskills unguarded and uninhabited could be a menace furnishing a thousand lurking places for Indians and Frenchmen, so it became necessary for armed bands of "Scouts and Rangers" to patrol the mountains by day and night. More than that, it became vital that the demoralized settlers on the borders of the mountains stay where they were. If they fled to the Hudson Valley settlements and left their pitiful farms untenanted, the enemy would flow in. Their presence alone had military value in keeping the frontier from being brought closer to the prosperous settlements in the Hudson Valley. These settlers on the frontier belonged to what the rich merchants and the great landowners called "the lower sort."[3] They were poor and usually illiterate, but they were brave. Many stayed at what their betters assured them were their posts of duty and died there. They were supported by a desire to protect their log barns and little haystacks and by a conviction widespread among the poor of New York that they were suffering in the cause of the only true religion in a war inspired by the Pope and his Jesuit missionaries among the Indians.

From 1755 to 1759, detachments from militia units in Ulster County followed old Indian trails along the dark valleys of the Catskills, studied the ground for signs of Indian war parties, filed through the Kaaterskill and Plattekill cloves, and camped on the banks of the Schoharie and upper Esopus.[4] These militiamen were young and adventurous. They had been brought up and their ways had been formed in a society which lived close to the soil with the wilderness ever beckoning a few miles away. Later most of them would become standardized members of their narrow world, but in the 1750s the imaginations of some were limber enough to leap at what they found in the wilderness of the Catskills. They marveled at the bottom lands, rich with the birth and decay of thousands of years of living things and snugly enclosed within mountain walls; at waterfalls able to turn the wheels of thousands of mills; at stands of tall straight pine trees, and wild cherry trees a yard in diameter; at groves of giant beeches to which wild pigeons flocked in such numbers as to shut out the light of the sun; at springs and crystal-clear streams everywhere, their water as cold as ice and so clear as to make the trout swimming at the bottom seem to be suspended in air. To these men the Catskills were a land of danger; they were also a land of wonders. Not many years later the memory of these wonders was to draw some of the militiamen back to the mountains.[5]

With the fall of Quebec in September 1759, French power in North America collapsed and although a peace treaty was not signed until 1763, the Catskills' role as a barrier against enemies came to an end. The fall of Quebec brought something else—the bursting of the war boom which had been so pleasant a feature of the decade to the merchants of the province. Robert Livingston of Clermont had done well dealing in foodstuffs and financing privateers which preyed on commerce. But he was caught in the deflation and saw his war profits slipping away. This was the time to see what could be made of his half million acres in the Catskills.[6]

Robert Livingston of Clermont liked to say that he had brought up his only son, the judge, "to keep an estate, not to get one."[7] He had devoted his life to piling up wealth in trade in order that his son might be able to live on his rents like an English gentleman. The son had been urged to cultivate his mind and to acquire social graces rather than money. Robert R. fell in with his father's plans; he sprinkled his letters with Latin tags and cultivated personal charm; and what was best of all, he married a great heiress, Margaret Beekman. His father-in-law, old Henry Beekman, regarded himself as the Livingstons' social inferior. He was a prominent man in the province but his manners were said to be uncouth and his intellect unpolished. But through the 1760s Beekman was still alive and vigorous and what was worse was still clinging to his money and his immense landholdings. Robert R., even after he advanced to a seat on the bench of the Provincial Supreme Court, was under the necessity of practicing law and picking up what he could on the side in trade.

To the old man—he was seventy-two in 1760—all this was at once a matter for pride and shame. He must have felt keenly his failure to do what he had promised for his clever son. He became filled with a determination to atone for his misdeeds by making something handsome for his son out of his Hardenbergh Patent holdings. He went at this in what seems to modern eyes a sensible and even a remarkably imaginative way.

First of all, old Livingston cultivated the society of frontiersmen, trappers, and Indian traders who knew the Catskills, and he talked to the militiamen who had been patrolling the region a few years before. He became an easy convert to their belief that there were wonders among the Catskills and that the whole region might with a little effort be made to send up a great fountain of gold. Livingston had some personal knowledge of the Catskills. He had begun acquiring it when twenty years before he and his son had followed Indian trails across the mountains to Pakatakan under the guidance of the Indian trader and frontiersman Henry Bush—or as the Dutch knew him, Hendrick Boss. That had been a prudent visit of inspection made before buying into the patent. Now vigorous old Livingston began exploring the Catskills by proxy with a view to development.[8]

Little by little a plan took form—and a most seductive form it was. The Catskills had four things to offer a man in search of money. They had abundant water power; they had, as John Bartram had observed, a remarkable variety of trees; they had a scattering of valley floors with enough fertile and tillable land to support thousands of farmers; and, finally, the mountains were close to cheap transportation on the Hudson River. Robert of Clermont had been educated in almost treeless Scotland

and in an England in which shipbuilding, ironmaking, and the use of wood for glassmaking and other industries as well as for fuel had deforested much of the countryside and made the British dependent on Baltic fir and other imported woods. In America the rapid growth of towns had skimmed the forests from the neighborhoods of population centers; already firewood was being brought by water from considerable distances to New York, Boston, and Philadelphia. At the same time timber was being exported to England and settlers were burning vast quantities merely to get rid of it.

The number of trees in the Catskills was immense but far more important than that, the quality of their timber was high. Pines fit for the finest ships' masts grew almost knot-free in valleys, and white ash which was ideally suited to becoming oars and tool handles grew on lower slopes—its wood was tough and light because the trees grew so fast. On warm southern slopes oaks grew all the bigger in a soil once ravaged by Indian fires. High in the mountains tall and straight spruces offered their light yet strong wood to builders, makers of musical instruments, and many others. Nowhere, the old-timers assured Livingston, did useful wood grow in such variety and of such quality. And there was one thing more. American gunsmiths had found curly maple from the Catskills to be among the very best of all woods for gunstocks. Not only was it light and tough when properly seasoned, it was also beautiful. Its grain rippled like the water along a honey-colored beach on a summer day. Even in England gunsmiths craved it.[9]

Very quickly Robert of Clermont built a dream castle among the Catskills. He would begin with building sawmills which would bring in cash. The valleys among the mountains would be surveyed into little farms, each with its lowland for raising grain and its upland for pasture and timber. Tenants would be forbidden to cut the most valuable trees. They would be forbidden to waste timber; for example, the use of "browse pastures" would be outlawed. These pastures were no more than areas in which trees were cut down in order that cattle in the grassless wilderness might feed on the tender buds and twigs. Cutting trees for tanbark or merely to make charcoal from their wood would also be forbidden. Each tenant located near a sawmill would be required as part of his rent to haul a specified quantity of boards or planks each year from a Livingston sawmill to the landing on the Hudson directly opposite the Livingston mansion at Clermont.[10]

In time, Livingston planned, he would set up works for making iron, using trip hammers operated by water power and charcoal made by his tenants. Some said there were deposits of iron among the mountains, some said not. Anyway across the Hudson there was plenty of iron ore, which it might pay to haul to the Catskills, perhaps in a crudely refined form. "Charcoal iron" was high in quality and much in demand. Perhaps if the Lords of Trade would relax their restrictions on American manufactures, such objects as iron kettles and axes might be made. Beech, which grew in vast numbers, was a favorite fuel of glassmakers. In time—who could tell?—glassmaking might become established on the Livingstons' domain among the Catskills. Tanneries, shops for making barrels or furniture—there was no end to the possibilities.

The glorious future Robert Livingston foresaw for the Catskills was a unified one. Tenants and artisans, woodsmen, charcoal burners, sawyers, each would fill a niche in a great overall plan for enabling the judge to live the life of a landed gentleman and send each one of his large brood of children into the world, when the time came, with money in his or her purse or pocket and an assured status on the upper level of provincial society.

The judge, busy in New York, viewed his father's bustling about among the Catskills with respectful and affectionate skepticism. He would have preferred selling part of the half million acres in the Catskills to embarking on any long-range plan of development. He located promoters who planned to bring large numbers of Irishmen or Scots to America and settle them somewhere in "a Township." He persuaded these men, for the judge was a most agreeable man, that the Catskills were just the place for their Irish or Scottish or German settlements. But a hurried inspection of the wilderness, without roads or clearings, without churches or neighbors within two days' journey, always brought emphatic rejection from the promoters.[11] It was the judge's hope that selling several strategically located large tracts upon which thriving settlements might be formed would raise the value of the remaining lands. This had been the notion of Cornelius Tiebout. He urged his father to sell, but the old man was impervious to argument.

By the end of 1762 Robert of Clermont had a sawmill completed at Waghkonk now known as Woodstock. He had a number of tenants established there and on the shores of the Cooper Lake of our own day. Others had agreed to take leases of lands surveyed by John Cantine of Marbletown along the Esopus in the present town of Shandaken. Some of these were Germans who, perhaps lured to the Catskills by Tiebout's advertising in 1752, were already established there. At Pakatakan (the flats between Margaretville and Arkville) a number of the militiamen who had patrolled the mountains earlier and close relatives of theirs were making up their minds to settle in the spring. Livingston found it necessary to sell some small farms outright in order to get settlement at Pakatakan started. Peter and Harmonus Dumond and Johannis Van Wagenen were among the pioneers. Robert Livingston was jubilant that year. "It is growing like a snoe ball," he wrote to Robert R. If God gave him another year of life he would "raise the reputation"[12] of the patent to a dizzy height.

It is doubtful if Robert R. knew an ash tree from a maple. He was largely an urban product to whom trees had value only as merchandise. He found it impossible to enter into the dream world in which his father was having so rollicking a time. Once the old man wrote of his chief adviser on Catskill Mountain matters, Sergeant Abram Post, who lived in what is now part of the town of Saugerties, "he is a great hunter and an intelligible man" who knew the Catskills "as well as you do the streets of New York."[13] A man who is as thoroughly at home as was Robert R. on the streets of New York is seldom able to understand the excitement of country people over such things as soil and trees. Robert R. never did. Yet he too dreamed of the Catskills—in his own way.

On Christmas Eve 1762, the judge sat down to write to his father at Clermont. He began prosaically enough by telling how a Mr. Howard whom he had sent to the Catskills in search of land for founding a township had come back and grumpily reported that the land "did not answer the description"[14] he had been given. Yet all hope of selling land to Howard was not gone if only Robert of Clermont would make up his mind to sell instead of trying to hang onto every acre.

Here the Christmas spirit descended upon Robert R. and his letter took an unexpected turn. He would be pleased, he wrote, if some three thousand pounds might be raised on the patent. "One thousand of this," he wrote, "I hope to have you lay out in a neat Chappell to serve (as) a Repository of the Dead of our Family, another to lay out in what might give you most pleasure. . . ." The third thousand would go to work up the business of the gristmill at Clermont. "To the Chappell," the judge continued, "a Chaplain might come in time to serve as a Tutor, but I would have him always dependent on the Owner of the Estate otherwise you may have an enemy in your Household"—here the the judge pulled up short— "excuse the Revery," he added and returned to business.

An ivy-covered private chapel with rows of ancestral tombs, a tutor who would instruct little Livingstons when not occupied in cringing before the master of Clermont—this was the Christmas Eve vision of Robert R. The old man at Clermont reading the letter must have felt his heart bound with pride. For Robert R. was fulfilling the destiny his father had planned for him. On Christmas Eve he had seen the kind of vision that could only have presented itself on such an occasion to an English gentleman.

That same Christmas Eve, amid the snow and bitter wind of the vast Hardenbergh Patent, a handful of representatives of the lower sort were huddled under bearskin covers in their drafty log shelters and wondering, we have a right to guess, if this game of pioneering was worth the candle.

17

"Beware of Tiebout!"

✿ ROBERT LIVINGSTON was getting old, and this was something he could not disguise. And like all aging people he was finding younger ones looking at him from time to time in a speculative way. If he repeated a story he had told a month before, if he fumbled for the name of a neighbor, if he forgot where he'd put his hat, younger people looked at him and wondered, Is he showing his age? Is his mind beginning to go?

Judge Livingston and his father regarded each other with deep affection. But as old Robert began romping through his seventies the son, who was of a cautious turn of mind, began to have doubts. Was it right for a man in his seventies to be so unbelievably optimistic, to have so volatile an imagination? It was true that the elder Livingston had by way of balance a little of the irritability and suspiciousness that are accepted as perfectly proper in old age. He hated Cornelius Tiebout, for example, and made no bones of his opinion that the fellow was a thoroughgoing rascal. He regarded his neighbors in the Hardenbergh Patent as little better than thieves determined to push in upon his boundaries and steal his land, but this was normal behavior for owners of tracts within the Great Patent. What was less understandable to the judge, pondering the letters his father pelted him with, was the old fellow's frolicking imagination and the youthful way he had of making exuberant plans for the future. Was he under the illusion that he was not an old man? Did he believe he was immortal? Such questions must have prompted the soothing replies the judge sent in answer to his father's jubilant reports of progress in settling the patent. And they may have inspired pious passages in which the judge respectfully hinted that it was about time his father began to give some thought to the life to come and to groom himself for the ordeal of meeting his Maker.[1]

One oddity of old Robert brought no protest from his son. This was his decision to change the name of the Catskill Mountains. The familiar

A layered sandstone ledge close to the summit of the Wittenberg. An anonymous photographer of the 1890s has caught the bold look of the higher levels of the mountains. (*Geroldseck-Schadle Collection.*)

Here the East Branch of the Delaware makes its winding way over rich farmlands and beneath wooded mountains. The time is about 1880, the place Roxbury, N.Y. From *History of Delaware County, 1797–1880,* W. Munsell, pub., Philadelphia. (*Courtesy of New York State Library.*)

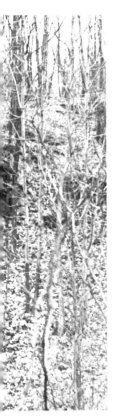

Above left, a large rock shelter long used by Indians who came to Overlook Mountain on hunting trips; excavated by Max Schrabisch, 1917. Photograph courtesy of the Historical Society of Woodstock, N.Y.

Above, early prospectors for gold and silver were strongly attracted by crumbling rocky outcroppings and cliffs like these near the entrance to the Kaaterskill Clove. Drawing by Harry Fenn for *Picturesque America*, W. C. Bryant, ed., 1879.

Left, the Hardenbergh milldam in what is now Zena on the eastern edge of Woodstock was desirable enough to cause many boundary disputes between the Trustees of Kingston and the Hardenbergh Patentees. The dam has been washed away in a flood since this photograph was taken by Harry Siemsen of Sawkill.

Edward Hyde, Lord Cornbury, shown here in woman's dress at about the time he granted the Hardenbergh Patent on behalf of his cousin, Queen Anne. (*Courtesy of the New-York Historical Society.*)

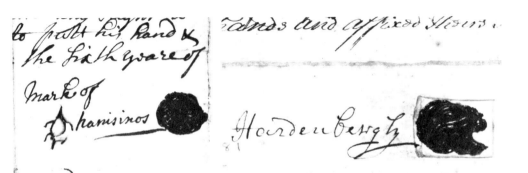

Above left, when Nisinos or Nanisinos, the Indian sachem, sold land to white men he signed the deeds with his totemic mark, the turtle.

Above right, the signature of Major Hardenbergh which led his descendants to suppose he was a nobleman. (*Courtesy of New York State Library.*)

Many maps were drawn to show the division of the Patent into individual holdings following the Wooster survey. None was entirely accurate, and this one does not show all the subdivisions made by 1795 when surveyor Cornelius C. Wynkoop drew it. (*Courtesy of New York State Library.*)

Cornelius Tiebout, New York merchant and speculator in lands among the Catskills. From a copy of a portrait by Lawrence Kilburn. (*Courtesy of the New-York Historical Society.*)

An early print of the Kaaterskill Falls from a sketch by Thomas Doughty, published in the *Atlantic Souvenir,* 1828. (*Courtesy of New York Public Library.*)

Cones like these stand in summer on balsam fir boughs high in the Catskills. From engraving in F. A. Michaux' *The North American Sylva,* Philadelphia, 1850.

Part of the shallow cave near North Lake in which John and William Bartram spent a night in September 1753. (Author's photograph.)

This detail from a William Cockburn map of 1765 shows Robert Livingston's mill around which the hamlet of Woodstock would form. (In Print Room, New-York Historical Society.)

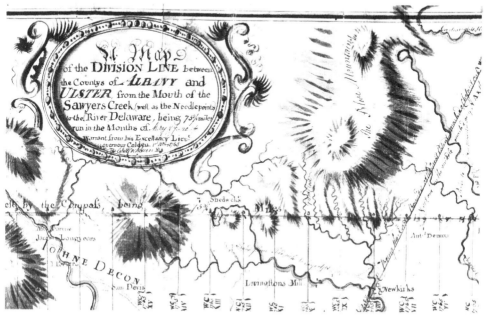

Dutch name, which was already in the 1760s of a respectable if not hoary antiquity, did not fit in with Robert's dreams. It would have to go, and in its place a new name redolent of the ancient Scottish background of the Livingstons would take its place. The mountains would hereafter be known as the Lothian Hills. They would be divided into the North Lothians, the West Lothians, the Midlothians, and the South Lothians[2]—all names of counties in the part of Scotland from which the Livingston family had sprung. The stream that was born behind Pine Hill and flowed into the Delaware at Pakatakan lost its Dutch name of the Bushkill at Robert's command and took on the Scottish one of the Tweed. Robert's father and his brother Philip had imposed Scottish names on places on Livingston Manor. Now Robert was asserting his right to take similar action. He had been denied the right to give his Clermont estate a Scottish name, they said. Here in the wild Catskills he was bestowing names as he pleased. He was no longer a mere younger son but the founder of a new and—he hoped—greater branch of the Livingston family. All this was of a piece with the judge's neat "Chappell," his moldering tombs, and the timid tutor. The judge did not object. It is likely enough that he approved.

What first roused the judge to treat his father with soothing words may have been merely a display of the old man's strong competitive instinct. He owned only one third of the Great Patent—there were other owners. A few years later it was stated by Robert Livingston's grandson that more than five hundred human beings owned large tracts, small tracts, and mere snippets of the patent.[3] Alderman Lewis and his children had wasted a substantial fortune in riotous reproduction; his descendants in a few decades were almost regimental in numbers, each one owning little besides a minute share in the patent. Benjamin Faneuil's share had been sold to a fellow Huguenot, Elias Desbrosses, a New York distiller and liquor dealer, from whom it descended to his nephew. Gulian Verplanck, who had been Robert Livingston's partner in buying into the patent, died in 1751 and his share was then scattered among his children.

When a shortage of cash brought gloom to hundreds of fractional heirs they often asked whether something might not be raised on the patent and the answer, until the dawning of what seemed to be going to be the peaceful sixties, was an emphatic "No." But once the sixties were under way, plans to do something with shares in the patent stirred in many a mind. In most the stirring was all that happened and the deed to the fraction was put back in its box. There it had a certain value—it was something to dream on. Gold might be discovered upon the land it represented, for, as old people sometimes wisely said then as now when the Catskills were mentioned, "God didn't put those mountains there for nothing."[4]

Robert Livingston made it plain in his letters to the judge that he believed he was struggling against fierce competitors in settling the patent. Colonel Johannis Hardenbergh, son of the old major, and his sister's children were trying to lure settlers to their lands. On April 17, 1762 Robert wrote to his son from Clermont ". . . you write that the Great Patent is under a cloud. However I must acquaint you that I have lett 8 farms of 100 acres to John Sheefer and Company at Wachkonk about the Lake (this was the present Cooper Lake in Woodstock) being 8 substantial persons for the 20th of all grain and each Farm to ride 50 bords from the Saw Mill. . . . I think this is much preferable to any proposal the Hardenberghs will make."[5] The Hardenberghs were openly and honestly competing for the Ulster County men and women willing to venture as tenant farmers into the wilds of the Hardenbergh Patent—so it appeared to old Livingston. Cornelius Tiebout of New York, however, was a very different kettle of flesh. The sinister figure of the portly Mr. Tiebout, now taking up again the pursuit of the unfortunate Moravians, now trying to cheat the Livingstons in a land deal, flits through the pages of the Robert–Robert R. letters. "Beware of Tiebout!" This warning rings out over and over again. Yet it was necessary to deal with Tiebout, evil as he was.

When Ebeneezer Wooster had cut up the patent into fifty-two Great Lots, he did so on the basis of an exceedingly limited acquaintance with the Catskills except for the perimeter of the patent. His lines ignored mountains and valleys and most other geographical features. Later these arbitrary lines would cause many a headache to road builders and town and county politicians. In the early 1760s some of them were maddening Robert Livingston.

By 1762 the outlines of Livingston's plans for his Catskill Mountain lands had taken quite firm shape. He would be willing to sell outright his more distant holdings in the western part of the patent. He would hang on at all costs to the lands that seemed to be an extension of Clermont and ran through Woodstock and Shandaken to the Delaware River. But here the northwestern line of his Great Lot Eight presented an annoying problem. It ran smack through the present town of Woodstock and cut the choicest part of the town in two. Here Livingston was setting up his first sawmill on an ideally perfect site from every point of view but one. On the other side of the Great Lot line only a few hundred yards away, his neighbor was none other than that rascal Tiebout. The sly merchant, had he trained down that bulge of his and built up his muscle, might almost have stood on his own land and tossed a stone on the roof of Livingston's mill. This was an intolerable situation. The Livingstons, father and son, put their combined ingenuity into trying to engineer a swap with Tiebout which would move him back and out of stoneshot of the heart of the sawmill settlement at Woodstock.

Never did opponent prove slyer, less reasonable, or more wily than Tiebout. The Livingstons hoped to persuade him to trade at least part of his land across the Great Lot Eight line for a tract of theirs far away in the southwestern corner of the patent in the region they called Kasighton, which is better known as Cochecton. Tiebout pronounced the land worthless; Robert instructed the judge to advertise it for sale in the New York papers in glowing terms. This would "put Tiebout to his Trumps[6] . . ." Robert predicted. But Tiebout did not have to play his trumps. As had so often happened in the past, Providence interfered on the side of the Livingstons. Tiebout sniffed a rumor of a mine newly discovered on, of all places, a tract of barren wilderness belonging to Robert Livingston which included parts of Plattekill and Overlook mountains.[7] The Livingstons regarded themselves as sophisticated and rational people to whom these ancient folk tales of mines were so much nonsense of the sort that circulated among the slaves and the lower classes. Quickly the trade was arranged and Robert made no secret of his belief that he had triumphed over credulous Cornelius Tiebout.

The father and son working together—by no means smoothly—were managing to make a decided dent in the Hardenbergh Patent. The Woodstock mill was completed, and close by rose a substantial building known as "the Mill House" which acted as Robert's Woodstock headquarters. There, surrounded by a retinue of hunters, surveyors, old settlers, tenants, and Indian traders, Robert had expert assistance in foreseeing a glorious future for the Catskills. A rough road was built to lead from the sawmill to the Hudson opposite Clermont, another wound up the Esopus Valley, across Pine Hill, and on to the settlement at Pakatakan.[8] Prospective tenants came to the Catskills, signed leases, and vanished never to be heard from again; few dreamed of paying any rent or of performing the services they had agreed to. Squatters moved in and refused to be converted into tenants. All this did not bother Robert. The patent was being settled. No matter how it was done, to get the mountains opened up was the important thing.

Down in New York, Robert R. was ably abetting the old man. He combined in one person the wisdom and authority of the bench, the shrewdness of the bar, the hard sense of a businessman, and the aura of respectability that flowed from his position as a member of the provincial aristocracy. By 1763 he had persuaded sixty men from Stamford, Connecticut, to buy a "Township" in the Livingstons' Great Lot 42 situated in the remote northwestern corner of the Great Patent. Ebeneezer Wooster, the surveyor, was among the sixty. Probably it was he who had carried back to his native Stamford tales of the charms of the upper Delaware Valley and set in motion the whole deal. By the mid-eighteenth century, population in New England was reaching the limits of the carrying capacity of much of its thin soil. The sixty men did not immediately settle their land but they were the advance guard of the torrent of hungry Yankees which was soon to push up every hollow in the Catskills.

As settlement proceeded, Robert grew ever more ebullient and the judge more and more disturbed. The judge had a good deal on his mind at the time besides the Hardenbergh Patent. As a member of the New York Assembly he was becoming deeply involved in the growing resistance to the tendency of the British Parliament toward curbing traditional English liberties in its colonies. The Sugar Act, the Stamp Act, these and other evidences of parliamentary tyranny found Robert and others of "the better sort" warily making common cause with the lower sort. Talk of imposing a tax by the acre on colonial lands was being revived in London. "The Ministry appears to have run mad . . ."[9] commented Robert R. The judge sent his father gloomy reports on the situation and at the same time did his best to curb the old man's fiery optimism about the prospects for his lands in the Catskills. "It is best not to raise our Expectations too high for by that means we avoid Disappointments,"[10] he cautioned in reply to a rosy report the old man sent from his Woodstock headquarters.

But Robert Livingston's expectations were not to be held down. In March of 1766, as the winter's snow still lingered among the Catskills, his expectations soared to a peak that sent the judge into action. It was a bad moment for aristocratic optimists like Robert. The lower sort were growing restless, a "levelling spirit" was abroad in the Hudson Valley, city people were rioting, and tenant farmers were rising in armed revolt at the urging of Yankee speculators who questioned the legality of Livingston Manor itself.[11] The old caste system of the Hudson Valley was threatening to fall apart, and the seedbed for the conviction that "all men are created equal" was being prepared. But to all this old Robert paid scant heed. He was now seventy-eight and full of vigor. A vision of a glorious future based on the development of the Catskills had him in its grip. His eyes were fixed on the delightful blue mountains to the west of Clermont, and he had eyes for nothing else.

The judge hastened to Clermont to study the situation at firsthand. On April 12 he wrote from New York, "When I was at the Manor [this was Clermont which, of course, was a manor only by courtesy] my Duty obliged me to write what I there heard. I did it with concern lest you should be offended, my regard for you however prevailed over my Interest in your Affections and I ventured to inform you of what I thought essential to your Happiness. . . ."[12] Robert's reply only increased the judge's apprehension. "It is impossible for me to dissemble the concern it [Robert's reply] gives me for it fully convinces me that you have a parcel of people about you who are endeavoring by the slyest and most cunning artifices leading you from one barren project to another to fatten themselves on your spoils, as soon as one thing miscarries they push you on to another. . . . My dear Father, you must forgive me, I must speak tho' ruin to myself should be the Consequence. Nothing can save you but the discharge of many of your People. . . .

"I remember the time well when being asked by your old Friends to what Business you intended to bring me up you used to say to keep an Estate not to get one for this I may say I was not ill qualified my thoughts were ever more turned to the improvement of my mind than my Fortune & through all my Life I never was addicted to any expensive Pleasures. By this time I thought your view in me would be answered. But God having thought proper to defeat these Earthly Designs It is high time for us both to look forward to a future State, . . . all I beg of God is that he will not suffer Your Earnestness to increase your Estate & the artifices of the —— who are with you to deprive my numerous Family of what would otherwise remain for their Support. . . ."

The judge then proceeded to pay his respects to his father's dreams of riches to be derived from the Catskills forests. "Your 1000 acres is not worth 30,000 pounds, if it was what a Rich Country would this be. . . . Lord Stirling has a Swamp of 4000 Acres as thick of all sorts of Timber as can well be imagined and the Distance from Water is but 15 miles. He is very far however from looking upon it in any other light than an incumbrance and actually gives away the Timber for the clearing. He that had the Consumate Impudence to tell you that you might make money by making Oars carried his abuse of the confidence you place in him to the greatest height. . . ."

Robert had picked up the notion that ash oars were worth one shilling per foot. The judge prowled the wharves of New York and learned that they were worth a mere tuppence per foot—and retail at that. "As to curl'd maple I know it has been hinted to you to build a mill for that purpose but I am sure it will answer no other purpose but to involve you in Troubles, 20 pounds worth I am sure will be more than can be sold to Gunsmiths in a year. I am convinced that nothing but pine boards will answer. I am convinced that they will not answer if the proper Season of cutting Logs sawing them and riding Boards be not embraced. This must be done by a few Hands if many be imployed they must be kept fed and paid. . . . The expense will be double the value of the Boards. . . ."

Having demolished Robert's sawmill in the Catskills the judge took care of his projected flyer in iron. "I know you have been told that an Iron Work may be carried out at a trifling Expense but the Active C——s[13] are ruined tho' they had a very good stock of their own and borrowed from & cheated everybody they could. I thank my God you are not engaged in one."

By May 14 the judge was in Woodstock making a personal inspection of his father's projects among the mountains.[14] He did more than inspect, he took over. From that day on the judge was at the helm in developing the Livingston's mountain lands. Old Robert, by what means we do not know, had been persuaded to curb his imagination and limit his activities to dignified retirement at Clermont. Time was to prove old Robert right in his belief that the forests of the Catskills were their greatest economic asset and that a combination of valley farming and mountainside lumbering would be the best way to squeeze the greatest possible income from the Catskills. His vision was realistic in every respect but one. The timber was there, so was the water power for sawing it, so too was the Hudson River for carrying finished timber to market. But where, in the 1760s, were the customers? That was the fatal flaw in Robert's scheme. The country was not yet sufficiently populous to buy what the Catskills had to offer in such quality and abundance. That time would come, in another half century, when another dreamer would found a fortune on one hundred thousand white ash oars shipped from the Catskills, and cabinetmakers and gunsmiths would eagerly buy the mountains' curly maple. Robert Livingston's imagination had carried him into a society that was not yet born and whose shape could be only dimly guessed at.

At Clermont old Robert rose at five each morning as had been his lifelong habit and he dressed with care in the fashion of his youth. As an old man he continued to take pride in having everything about him "genteel." His manners, much admired for their polish when he was young, remained with him, although now they appeared to a new generation to have a quaint old-fashioned air. As always old Livingston read widely. In his early eighties, he took up the study of the German language and mastered it. Cheerfully submitting to his son's decision to retire him from active duty, he lived on amid the troubled days that preceded the American Revolution relishing every moment of the fortunate life which was his.[15]

The settling of the Catskills proceeded in a new spirit. The judge in his cool and rational manner enticed tenants, signed leases, and continued the sawmill but on a much-reduced program. In 1769 he and all other promoters of settlements in the Catskills received a jolting blow. It was delivered by Lieutenant Colonel John Bradstreet of His Majesty's Army in America. The Hardenbergh Patent, the colonel claimed, had been conceived in sin and born in iniquity back in 1708. It was therefore invalid. It could be granted all over again. He asked King George to give him a fat slice of it as a reward for his military services to the Crown.

18

General Bradstreet Attacks the Patent

✠ IT HAD SEEMED like the sensible thing to do, back in the days when Lord Cornbury was amusing some New Yorkers and shocking others, to get all you could while you could, and to grab with both hands as fate propelled you through this brief life. Everybody was doing it—the rich and powerful in their way, the poor and humble in theirs. The Bible said this kind of thing was wrong. "Lay not treasures up on earth,"[1] the Bible spoke out plainly. But men and women during the reign of Queen Anne were living in a world in which an unwritten law ordered them to get all they could, to lay up treasures in land and houses, in silver plate and golden guineas, in the form of power over other humans; in the flesh of Negro slaves and Indians, in the sweat of ignorant and illiterate laborers, in the blood of soldiers who died to keep the wheels of commerce moving, in the breath of sailors who drowned for the same great cause. The eight men of the Hardenbergh Patent had been respected by their neighbors; they were envied and even admired. If they skated close to the law, so would anybody else who had the chance. If they violated the law (there was Augustine Graham stowed away for twenty-one years amid the verbiage of the patent), well, they got away with it. And who on this earth doesn't try to get away with this or that? Go to church on Sunday and be practical the rest of the week. What was wrong with that?

The eight men of the Hardenbergh Patent were all gone from this earth by the year 1769. If their churchgoing had paid off, they would be seated in heaven enjoying the songs of the angels. If not—well, it wouldn't do to think about such a dreadful possibility. Already the wigs they had worn, the slang terms they had used were forgotten. The portraits of some in their old-fashioned clothes stared down upon their grandchildren's dinner parties in disbelief at what the world was coming to.

By 1769 the eight men of the Hardenbergh Patent were very much gone, but the work they did was living on. They had acquired, while they lived, a vast amount of material things. Unfortunately they had not been able to take these things along with them to heaven. Some, like the Hardenbergh Patent, remained to plague their descendants, for they carried within them scars and imperfections caused by the ancient and musty greed of their former possessors. Judge Livingston had sensed a "Fatality" hanging over the Hardenbergh Patent. The Fatality was there right enough. It had not been born by chance. It had been created by the eight respectable men when they laid hands, which were not entirely clean—at least by biblical standards—upon a fair region of the earth, a region of mountains and sparkling streams, kept spotless by the winds and the rain and perfumed by the smell of balsam.

Many an eighteenth-century Hardenbergh Patent lawyer or landed proprietor never set foot on the Catskill Mountains. To these people the region was symbolized by the rolls of mildewed maps, the surveyors' field books, and the deeds taken out of their strongboxes and inspected whenever boundary disputes arose. These entombed papers and parchments when resurrected had an odd and by no means pleasant smell which they exhale to this very day. They smelled of old frauds and chicaneries. No rain falling on the Catskills could wash away that smell, nor could any wind however strong or sweet carry it away. Neither, as it turned out, could Lieutenant Colonel Bradstreet, although he blew hard enough. It may even be he helped blow himself into his grave in the attempt.

There was general agreement in the 1760s that Bradstreet deserved well of King and country. He had first come to notice at the siege of Fort Frontenac in 1758; had served as an officer of provincial units and units of the Royal Americans; had been adjutant general to General Shirley, lieutenant governor of St. John's, Newfoundland (the post was a sinecure); and quartermaster general (ever a place of opportunity).[2] In 1769 King and country were in a mood to reward the then lieutenant colonel with something more than words. Far back in the history of the Province of New York, soldiers had been rewarded upon retirement with tracts of land—the custom went back to the ancient world. It was not always the best land— that, of course, went to the best people. It was hoped this policy might settle men skilled in the arts of war on the frontiers where they would be able to help turn back enemies of the King. The old Romans, in their day, had entertained similar hopes for their own frontiers. On October 7, 1763 George the Third of England by Royal Proclamation following the ending of the Seven Years' War made grants of crown lands in America available to "reduced officers" and men who had served in the American phase of the war commonly called the French and Indian War. The proclamation soon had its effect upon the region of Catskills.

By 1767 the old soldiers were marching to the mountains. Not of course to the heart of the mountain region—that was already granted away. But to the mountains' fringes. Wherever a tract of promising land lay in a hollow scooped from the side of a mountain, wherever a few hundred level acres lay, as they often did, just beneath the ledge which seemed to serve as the base of a mountain, here the old soldiers came. Singly and in groups of two or three, by the half dozen or the dozen, they made their applications to the governor who was empowered to give away acres on behalf of His Majesty.

The veterans took up land in a great crescent beginning beneath the Catskills near Saugerties and extending along the base of the mountains through parts of present-day Catskill, Cairo, Windham, and Durham. Among them were George Butrick, "late Quarter-Master in His Majesty's 45th Regiment of Foot"; William Baker, late sergeant in the same regiment; corporals James Glassford and John Gillaspie of the 27th. Privates were usually given fifty acres, non-commissioned officers two hundred. A lieutenant colonel like Richard Maitland was considered to deserve five thousand; lieutenants—Walter Stewart was one of them—were given two thousand acres. George Sutherland and John Henry, "late privates," got one hundred acres between them "lying under the Blue Mountains." Sir Henry Seaton, Bart., of Scotland, was given a patent of three thousand acres in Durham. Page after page of the provincial land records were required to list these and many other examples of royal bounty between 1767 and 1772.[3]

Most of the reduced officers and men did not settle on their land. They held it for a rise in value or sold out to speculators. One purchaser was James Barker who set up as a New World version of an English landed gentleman at a place he named Woodstock. Barker's Woodstock was located in what is now the town of Cairo, some twenty-five miles north of the Woodstock which Robert Livingston had named a few years earlier.[4] Near Barker's clearing was an important road known as John Dies Road. It ran northwest from the Hudson at the mouth of the Catskill where mysterious John Dies had built a fine stone house and led to land grants and a rumored copper mine in which Dies had shares—one grant was long known in his honor as Dies Manor. John Dies Road forked near Barker's Woodstock. By turning right a traveler would be led along the base of the mountains westward, by turning left he would find himself being boldly lifted across the high rim of the Catskills and taken from the headwaters of the Batavia Kill to the stream's junction with the Schohary Kill near the Prattsville of later times. For a while this road did much to attract settlers to the northern Catskills. The Livingstons of Clermont used it as a selling point in trying to bring buyers and tenants to their holdings in the Hardenbergh Patent's Great Lot 23. And the road must have been moderately good, for in 1769 reduced officer Staats Long Morris and his wife, the dowager Duchess of Gordon, accompanied by two wagonloads of baggage, traveled it to reach their land grants in the Susquehanna Valley.[5]

While all the land granting was going on, Lieutenant Colonel John Bradstreet was not idle. His rank entitled him to a grant of five thousand acres. But to a man of the lieutenant colonel's large views, five thousand acres would be a mere dooryard. He put in a request for three hundred thousand, including all that part of the Hardenbergh Patent which lay between the two branches of the upper Delaware River. Behind this request lay careful planning, the spending of a considerable amount of money, and much dickering with the Indians who claimed to be the owners of the lands. In Bradstreet's corner was Sir William Johnson, Superintendent of Indian Affairs and a man of vast influence among both whites and Indians. It was Sir William who had made possible Bradstreet's request when he negotiated the Treaty of Fort Stanwix in 1768. Under that treaty the Iroquois or Six Nations agreed to cede to the Crown all the lands they claimed east and south of a line running irregularly from a little east of Lake Oneida to the Mississippi Valley. George III approved the treaty in December 1769, and the line of division laid down by the treaty came to be known as the Property Line or the Line of Property.[6]

To the old soldiers contemplating deployment among the northern Catskills the treaty was good news. Much of the land the King was so generously pledged to giving away was not really his under English law since it had not yet been given up by the Indians. An eager confusion of Indian claimants appeared. The Iroquois claimants at least were disposed of at one blow. The old soldiers rejoiced, but their rejoicing was as nothing compared to that which prevailed at more exalted social levels. The land-hungry among the rich and well-connected of the province saw in the Indian lands newly come within the clutch of the Crown a vast opportunity for increasing their riches and making themselves even better connected. Provincial officials began lining up with outstretched hands, for the mechanics of land deals had not changed much since the days of Johannis Hardenbergh.

Colonel Bradstreet's military career was in the making even before his birth, for he sprang from a line of military men. In 1735 he purchased an ensignship in an infantry regiment, and an infantry officer he remained. Moving men and equipment through the wilderness, transferring from wagons to batteaux on flood-swollen rivers, fighting mud and cold and the ravenous insects of the wilderness in an effort to get men and materials where they belonged on time was the kind of activity in which Bradstreet excelled. No one who knew him doubted his ambition, his determination, or his organizing ability, and when he set his heart on a vast land grant he put all these qualities to work toward this new goal. In the first place, like the good officer he was, he anticipated the actions of the enemy. Before the Fort Stanwix Treaty was drawn up he had made a deal with four Oquaga Indians for his three hundred thousand acres between the headwaters of the Delaware's East Branch and those of the Susquehanna River. Such direct dealing with the Indians had been outlawed by royal proclamation but this did not disturb Bradstreet; he was the kind of man who scorned such technicalities in his determination to get things done.

Part of the land which the colonel bought from the Indians—that which lay between the East and West branches of the upper Delaware—had been sold to the Hardenbergh patentees long before by Esopus Indians. Now, with Sir William Johnson's encouragement, Bradstreet declared that the Esopus Indians had never owned the land between the rivers and therefore could not legally sell it. More than that, he insisted, the whole Hardenbergh Patent was void because the original patentees had obtained it "by false suggestions and in dece[i]t of the Crown."[7] The patentees had violated the terms of their grant from the Crown by failing to put the stipulated number of settlers on their land within five years after the grant became final. The entire million and a half acres of the patent should rightfully be taken from its pretended proprietors and given to such deserving individuals as Lieutenant Colonel John Bradstreet.

By the time Bradstreet turned his heavy guns upon the Hardenbergh Patent it had been battered by the storms of more than half a century. It had a bad reputation, no one could deny that. Widows, orphans, and land jobbers had lost money among its peaks and forests. To the poor who wanted farms of their own in its sheltered valleys it had become the Land of the Forbidden Mountains, closed to them by the mysterious logic of the powerful of their province. Artfully enough, Robert Livingston had sold a few small farms outright to carefully selected settlers. To others he allowed a rent-free period of years while they were clearing their lands. These actions had done something to attract penniless men to the Catskills, and to suggest that if they were loyal to the Livingstons they might some day be rewarded by being permitted to buy the farms they had created from the wilderness. While Bradstreet's guns thundered away at the walls of the patent, a trickle of settlers continued to move in. To all but a few, a change of landlords would mean nothing: what did it matter to them to whom they paid their hard-earned rent?

In the larger world outside the mountains the Bradstreet campaign had immediate and startling effects. The possibility that the Hardenbergh Patent might be found invalid sent an additional body of reduced officers following Bradstreet into the Catskills. These men filed claim after claim to the rich farmlands lying along the Delaware and its tributaries. The lands, the officers recited in their petitions, "remain vested in the Crown notwithstanding the claims set up by those called the Proprietors of Hardenbergh's Patent."[8] The governor appointed a committee on the lands within the Hardenbergh Patent to which these petitions were referred. The committee, as is the way of committees, filed the petitions and then waited.

Colonel James Montresor, Director of Engineers in America, asked for ten thousand acres on the "south side of Pagkatghan Creek or River." Lieutenant John Montresor asked for two thousand nearby. Colonel Richard Maitland, this time on behalf of Captain David Skene, wanted three thousand "up Beaver Creek"—this was on Livingston land. John Carter, Assistant Surgeon to His Majesty's Hospital, and four others asked for ten thousand acres below Beaver Creek. Eight reduced officers got together and petitioned for twenty-four thousand acres of Livingston and Verplanck land a little below present-day Margaretville. To the more timid proprietors of lands within the patent it must have looked as if the vultures were moving in to the feast tricked out in gold braid and scarlet. Bolder proprietors, such as the Livingstons, insisted that all would be well and proceeded to engage lawyers to resist Bradstreet and the officers and men who were joining in the attack upon the Hardenbergh Patent.

Once again Esopus Indians were hunted out, flattered, dined and rummed, and paid cash for their autographs. Most of the Indians had left the Catskills neighborhood and were living as civilized Christians close to New England missionary Gideon Hawley on the banks of the Susquehanna. The Esopus Indians' part in the contest was vital. Sir William Johnson urged Bradstreet to get hold of them and take a look at the deeds they had. Bradstreet took this advice and soon had sworn statements from these Indians upholding his claim that the Hardenbergh Patent extended no farther west than Pakatakan. Jacob Heckan, son of cider-making Henry, swore that his father had deeded part of the patent to the Hardenbergh proprietors in an act of private enterprise without consulting his fellow sachems.[9]

Agents of both sides ransacked the public records; key papers vanished never to be seen again; lawyers on both sides wrangled bitterly over the custody of old Indian deeds. Many feelers about possible compromises were put out and rejected. Each side seemed determined to hold its ground. The governor's council after many postponements considered the matter in 1771 and made a surprising decision. Bradstreet was to be given twenty thousand acres at any place of his choosing between the two branches of the Delaware.[10] Under this decision Bradstreet could have thrown out the large group of Yankees from Stamford, Connecticut, who had bought land from Robert Livingston at what is now Stamford, New York, and he could have dispossessed the Scottish immigrants who were settling down nearby. He could have put an end to the settlement along the East Branch which was clustering around the three or four little farms which Robert Livingston had sold outright in order to create a nucleus for a "township" composed of tenants. (The nucleus was to expand into Margaretville.)

Governor Dunmore and his council did not try to justify their very odd decision in favor of Bradstreet by finding the Hardenbergh Patent invalid; they side-stepped the issue of validity entirely and stated that they were giving Bradstreet his twenty thousand acres merely "as compensation for the expense he has been at in endeavoring to prove the facts he of a battle between colonial power groups shines. In Bradstreet's corner, alledges."[11] But through the whimsicality of the official decision the glow beside Sir William Johnson, were his close friend Philip Schuyler of Albany and the landholding Van Rensselaers. In the Hardenbergh corner were a group of New York and Hudson Valley landowners who were powerful in the Provincial Assembly which seemed to take pleasure in opposing the governor's wishes and to assert the developing American spirit of independence. One element in the decision was certainly rooted in the power struggle going on between Crown and Assembly, but another was a desire to "pass the buck" as a later generation of politicians would have put it. For the governor must have been well aware that the Hardenbergh proprietors would not take his decision with placid resignation. Would they take the obvious step of carrying their case to the courts and trying for a decision which would upset the governor's and settle the question of the validity of their patent for good and all? The better sort of the province waited for an answer. Days and months went by. Governor Dunmore was replaced by Governor Tryon and no suit pitting the Hardenberghers against the Bradstreeters was initiated. In London, however, the news of the decision of the governor and his council had an immediate effect. It threw staid British officials into a state of irritated amazement. Not that the officials were at all hostile to Bradstreet or grudged him his acres—in fact they were very much on his side in their sympathies. What annoyed them was the cavalier way Governor Dunmore handled the matter. To reward a man for his efforts in trying to demonstrate that a royal grant of land had been obtained by deceitful and fraudulent means by giving him a part of the very grant and at the same time letting those claiming to be the proprietors keep the rest was contrary to all established precedent and was not to be tolerated. The Privy Council considered the matter and urgently recommended the King to veto the governor's action. King George did not hesitate. He commanded Governor Tryon "that you do not upon any pretence whatever sign any grant or patent for those lands."[12]

Bradstreet was not at all discouraged. When he learned of the decision of the governor and his council he continued to insist that he was entitled to all and not a mere twenty thousand acres of the lands between the branches of the Delaware. When the King's command reached him he redrew his original petition and made his claim on a somewhat different basis.

At about this time Bradstreet received a decided boost upward in colonial society. By sheer force of seniority in an army that was being sharply reduced, Bradstreet arrived at the rank of major general, and then retired. But he did not have long to enjoy his exalted status. Still fighting valiantly against the "pretended proprietors of the Hardenbergh Patent," the new general fell ill of the dropsy and died. With full honors of war, Bradstreet was buried from New York's Trinity Church. The funeral, an outstanding social event of the season, was attended by the mayor and the Corporation of New York plus a fine assortment of civilian and military dignitaries. The general's will, which had been drawn up by Judge William Smith, disclosed that Bradstreet had left his land claims to his daughters. Moreover the will itself excited favorable comment and added greatly to Bradstreet's posthumous fame. For clarity, succinctness, and style, it was hailed as a masterpiece. Among lawyers it was agreed that no other achievement of his distinguished career surpassed Bradstreet's will.[13]

Before Bradstreet died he had put in his claim for the five thousand acres of land to which he was indisputably entitled as a retired officer; a year after his death his daughters, Agatha and Martha, took action to have this land at Papakunk turned over to them. Would the two girls go on to revive their father's claim to the entire three hundred thousand acres for which he had asked? New Yorkers with sporting blood pondered this question and it may well be that bets were made upon it. But as the governor and his council considered the claim of the Misses Bradstreet in the fall of 1774 and the Misses Bradstreet gave no sign to the waiting public of what they proposed to do about the larger claim, the attention of New York's sporting set was diverted from the Bradstreet case to the remarkable doings of William Alexander, who insisted on being known as the Earl of Stirling. For Alexander was launching an illegal private lottery with an imposing array of prizes.

The largest of the earl's prizes was his New York town house, a large structure with elegant gardens. (It was leased at the time to General Gage.) Other prizes were numerous and scattered tracts of land, including a good many bits in the Hardenbergh Patent. Would Stirling be able to unload his unfortunate investments in the Catskill Mountains and elsewhere by means of his lottery? The sporting fraternity was divided in its opinion. But preparations for the lottery went forward relentlessly. For the truth was that Lord Stirling was exceedingly hard up, and if his lottery were to fail he would be sunk.

19

Lord Stirling's Lottery

✤ IN THE DAYS when the granting of the Hardenbergh Patent to eight men had been in progress, these men were kept in a state of pleasant excitement by the chancyness of their enterprise. At any moment the Lords of Trade might change the land-granting rules and someone else might treat the Esopus Indians to an especially delicious new brand of rum and get their signatures on deeds. Lord Cornbury might even trip on his skirts and crack his skull. In fact, the effort to get the patent had many of the elements of a gambling device. But as the years wore on, every hint of chance waned from the patent. If you put your money on the patent you lost it, it was as simple as that. That was one reason why when in 1772 broadsides advertising the "Scheme of the Delaware Lottery of Lord Stirling"[1] began decorating the walls of city and backwoods taverns, many people shook their heads. Lord Stirling himself was well aware that his holdings in the Hardenbergh Patent would have no appeal to ordinary lottery lovers. To them they were merely fillers in a long list of prizes or like bread crumbs in a family meat loaf, adding bulk and substance to an otherwise scanty dish. Yet to true lottery connoisseurs the crumbs themselves made a decided appeal.

Tavern idlers scanning the scheme and toying with the thought of raising the four pounds needed for taking a chance, hesitated at the thought that they might win one of his lordship's strips of mountain swamp. But sophisticated gamblers found pleasure in the knowledge that if they were paying their four pounds for a chance at Lord Stirling's fine town house in Broad Street, they were also laying themselves open to winning a Hardenbergh Patent tract that might eerily figure in future nightmares, for General Bradstreet's assault upon the validity of the patent was still in progress.

A gambling device that offers only rewards attracts the simple; one that offers both rewards and punishments is for the advanced amateur. That may have been one reason why Stirling's lottery made an instant appeal to one of America's most knowing connoisseurs of lotteries, a Virginia gentleman named George Washington. Washington was a fortunate as well as a great and noble man. But when he signed up for six tickets in the Stirling lottery he took the first step toward winning five hundred acres in the most remote corner of the entire Hardenbergh Patent. By this piece of bad luck, it may be, Fate tried to even the Washington account.

To his contemporaries, William Alexander, titular Earl of Stirling, was an imposing and admired figure. To begin with, once he claimed the title he began acquiring the look of a hero. A German colonel remarked toward the end of Stirling's life that his lordship looked as much like the Marquess of Granby as "one egg is like another."[2] The marquess, as everyone knew in the eighteenth century, was the military hero of the Seven Years' War, whose portrait decorated countless signboards of British inns. The ruddy, strong, and melancholy marquess swinging in the wind outside taverns was the best friend British brewers ever had; in thousands of minds he was the model of what a man at his very best should be. But Stirling was fortunate in his ancestry as well as in his Granbylike appearance. His father, James Alexander, they said, had fled Scotland after taking part in the doomed Jacobite uprising of 1715; he had become a rich and distinguished lawyer, government official, and speculator in lands. His mother, when James Alexander first met her, was the rich widow of a New York merchant (whether of "Ready Money David Provost," the smuggler, or his more plodding cousin, Samuel, authorities disagree). The mother was what we should call a successful businesswoman, for she managed a provisions business with profit throughout the childhood and adolescence of the Lord Stirling-to-be. But William's talents, by a not uncommon genetic quirk, were the reverse of those of his father and mother: they lay in distributing money rather than in acquiring it. This talent lay dormant while the elder Alexander lived. William clerked in his mother's shop, became a partner, helped engineer army contracts, and personally followed the contracts into the army by becoming first a commissary officer and then the aide-de-camp and secretary of Governor William Shirley.[3]

By 1760 William Alexander's parents were dead and he had assumed the title of Earl of Stirling to which he had indeed considerable right. An Edinburgh "Jury of Service"—a kind of official board in genealogical and armorial matters—had awarded it to him, but the British House of

Lords refused him a seat. This made Alexander all the more determined not only to assert his title but also to prove his right by acting and looking like a peer. "He is accused of liking the table and the bottle full as much as becomes a lord . . ."[4] remarked the Marquis de Chastellux. He lived in splendor on his estate at Basking Ridge in New Jersey; his house and its outbuildings were so very fine for that part of the world that they were known in the vicinity merely as "The Buildings" as if no others were worthy of being compared with them. "To blue and gold leather hangings for his Lordship's drawing room" reads a bill filed away in the library of the New Jersey Historical Society and, it may be, never paid. Stirling's coach, with his crest emblazoned on its doors, was described as magnificent.

The finest Madeira, the fastest horses, the most elegant furniture and upholstery, the services of modish tailors and wigmakers were set to work to enable Lord Stirling to convince the world that he was indeed the rightful Earl of Stirling. He had created a self-image to which he was committed to conforming, and conform he did. As a youth, his appearance—if surviving early portraits are to be trusted—was not particularly impressive. But after he had assumed his title his resemblance to the noble face on the tavern signboard grew ever more marked until the two seemed, to observers like the German officer, to coincide.

All this, of course, took money. Stirling had inherited a good deal but his inheritance was not enough to support his title. In an effort to increase his income he indulged in a great variety of what he mistook for speculations but which turned out to be no more than cruel traps lying in wait for wandering pounds, shillings, and pence. Mines, iron foundries, towns and cities beautifully laid out on paper and nowhere else, city lots, tracts of wilderness, and many similar projects siphoned off Stirling's inheritance. Prodigality in money matters was the very hallmark of a true peer. In this Stirling was so outstanding that fifteen years after his mother's death he was said to be in debt to the tune of eighty thousand pounds. Stirling did not give up, but planned instead to raise the sum of £49,100 by a method worthy of a peer: a lottery in which the cash of the lower and the better sorts would be accepted with equal grace, and which would give both sorts a sporting run for their money. The lottery, if you looked at it in that way, was actually a public benefaction.

By 1770 when Stirling first began thinking hopefully of the lottery solution to his difficulties, the kind he had in mind had one formidable hurdle to leap—it was illegal in nearly all the provinces of America and in England as well.[5] Delaware, however, was kindly disposed toward promoters of private lotteries and its Assembly approved Stirling's plan. As a first step his lordship decided upon the lands he wanted to throw into the lottery. The New York house with its elegant gardens, a few New York building lots, twenty Ulster County farms "situate on the west side of the Walkill, in Ulster County," and others near Newburgh, unimproved lands at Sharon in Connecticut, lands in Rockland County near Haverstraw, the Elizabeth-Town-Point ferry in New Jersey with "large commodious dwelling," stables and so on, building lots in Elizabeth Town, about twenty lots in the Hardenbergh Patent averaging about one thousand acres apiece, a lot in the Westenhook Patent on the east side of the Hudson, and numerous small cash prizes.

One of the Hardenbergh Patent lots lay between Kaaterskill and Plattekill cloves running back from the base of the Catskills and including the summit of High Peak, long known, with neighboring Round Top, as the highest of the Catskills. Another was not far from the Stamford of our day at what Stirling called "the head of Delaware,"[6] and two lay "near the Great Forks of the Delaware." The rest were scattered across present-day Sullivan County from Mountain Dale to near Cochecton Center. Each was only half of an already surveyed lot and his lordship hoped that some winner might attempt to settle his half and so raise the value of the half retained. The list of managers of the lottery was formidable. It was headed by two members of the New York governor's council, William Smith, lawyer and colonial historian, and Hugh Wallace, who had made a fortune as an importer of Irish merchandise. The rest of the managers were prosperous New York businessmen: Leonard Lispenard, William Bayard, John Harris Cruger, William MacAdam, Isaac Low, Charles MacEvers, and Anthony Van Dam.

Four experts were appointed as "apprizers" of the lands offered. They had little difficulty until they came to the Hardenbergh Patent. Stirling's land there, the men reported, were "wilde lands."[7] Some were so very wild that no amount of effort could locate them, and the weary apprizers had to give up. Their low opinion of the patent is reflected in the values they placed upon Stirling's patent lands—they were far lower per acre than any others in the lottery. Eight shillings an acre was the top, the least valuable in the judgment of the apprizers was the tract including the summit of High Peak at ninepence per acre.

Hardly had tickets and advertising broadsides been printed, when resistance developed. The New York Assembly in spite of the high standing of the lotteries managers passed an act which strengthened earlier anti-lottery legislation and seemed aimed directly at Lord Stirling. "Whereas the Laws now in being for the suppression of Private Lotteries have been found ineffectual . . . and whereas many mischievous consequences have been experienced from the Practice which has proved highly prejudicial to Trade, has occasioned Idleness and Inattention to Business, has been productive of Fraud and Imposition and has given Birth to a dangerous spirit of Gaming . . ."[8] therefore prizes in any lottery would be forfeited and any lands won within New York's boundaries could not be legally conveyed. The law with some of its loopholes plugged was re-enacted two years later. To all this legislation Lord Stirling seemed impervious and his ticket-selling campaign went on. For over half a century the Assembly had been grinding out anti-lottery laws; the King himself had issued a proclamation outlawing lotteries except for public purposes. Yet if a man had the right connections, evasion was not too difficult, and Stirling's connections were of the best.

Lady Stirling had been Sarah Livingston, daughter of Philip, second Lord of Livingston Manor, and a sister of Governor Livingston of New Jersey. The couple led an active social life and had vast numbers of friends. With their two charming daughters, Lady Kitty and Lady Mary, they visited in the various American colonies and were received with delight everywhere, for nowhere in the English-speaking world was there more reverence for a title. Their friends may have felt that the lottery was a dubious enterprise, yet it had decided snob appeal. They took some of the tickets Lord Stirling sent them and sold the balance among their friends. Lord Stirling had many acquaintances from his business and army days; he had made more when in London to help Governor Shirley defend his conduct during the Seven Years' War and to push his own claim to an earldom. To all his acquaintances went packages of lottery tickets, copies of the printed Scheme, and friendly personal appeals.

The response was not always encouraging. "My Lord," wrote Alexander Small of Villiers Street in London, "I was duly honored with your Lordships Letter containing the printed Schemes of the Lottery, and am very sorry the Lottery cannot be advertized here for fear of the Law. . . ." In addition, numerous recent business failures made purchasers hesitate. "Losses by the Hurricane in the West Indies has tied up every Mans Hands here in Money Matters."[9]

From Canada, from the West Indies, from a variety of American cities came similar excuses. An Annapolis man wrote that a local lottery for improving the docks in the city was offering strong competition. Besides "the Prizes, some few of the largest excepted, would not be worth looking after, as, from the Remoteness of their Situation, few would know how to dispose of them; this inconvenience has been severely felt by some who were lately fortunate in a similar Lottery drawn by Col Bird in Virginia."[10] Byrd had indeed unloaded some of his inaccessible lands in the backwoods of Virginia and the "Fortunate adventurers" who had won them had not yet cooled off. His lottery may have been the model that Stirling followed.

Lord Stirling had announced in his printed "Scheme" that all prizes unclaimed after three years would become the property of the newly organized "Society of the Hospital, in the City of New-York in America . . . a most benevolent institution lately established, for the relief and recovery of the poor, diseased and distressed of all denominations." He presented the Society with a dozen tickets as further mark of his goodwill and as what our generation knows as a public relations gesture.[11] Anyone who might have qualms of conscience about breaking the anti-lottery laws could feel at least that he was doing it in a good cause. If he won a lot in the Hardenbergh Patent he would simply turn it over to the Society of the Hospital which would surely be permitted to take title, if its managers wanted to. If he won a big prize—well, he could cross that bridge when he came to it.

Among those Americans who received a package and a letter from Lord Stirling in 1772 was Colonel George Washington of Mount Vernon.[12] Lotteries always appealed strongly to Washington. He had served as a manager of one and had signed the tickets for another. It was a rare lottery that did not claim him as an adventurer. He had invested fifty pounds in Colonel Byrd's venture and won a tract of land and had emerged a winner from others. In his delight in lotteries, raffles, and other gambling devices, Washington was acting as a normal member of the better sort of Virginia. He had been born and shaped in a society that regarded such upper-class amusements as riding to hounds and gambling as normal parts of a well-spent life. Of the eighteen tickets Washington received, he bought six; the rest he sold among friends in Virginia as a friendly gesture toward his lordship for whom Washington always showed great respect.

The drawing of prizes in the lottery was announced for May 1773. But the drawing was postponed. Another date was set and it in turn was postponed. The process was repeated a number of times. It was obvious that all was not going well with Stirling's lottery. The shady character of many previous private lotteries had given all such attempts at raising money a bad name, and anti-lottery laws of New York made many feel that if they won a prize they would never receive it. Stirling's financial problems were common knowledge and as he set the dates of lottery drawings, he was being badgered by sheriffs trying to collect old debts. Many of Stirling's friends, unwilling to offend even a dubious lord, kept their lottery tickets but did not pay for them, which made it hard to say just how many tickets had been bought and paid for. The lottery managers calculated that not enough money had been received to make it possible to pay the prizes—almost two thirds of the tickets remained on their hands. Lord Stirling in a gesture worthy of a lord, volunteered to make up any deficit out of his "other property" and the drawing finally took place on Burlington Island in the Delaware River on September 1, 1774.[13]

George Washington had been awaiting the outcome of the lottery with his usual interest in such matters. On January 20, 1775 he wrote to Stirling: "My Lord: Your Lordships favour of the 31st of October never came to my hands till a few days ago and then unaccompanied with any Printed Lists of the fortunate Prizes mentioned in your letter. Some time ago I came across one of these lists in a Genms. possession wch. I found that out of the Six Tickets wch. I kept on my own Acct. two of them were fortunate viz.

"One of 200 pounds no 58 in the division of Wenhams great Lot in the Hardenbergh Patent in Ulster County near Rochester

"The other (I think) of 6 pounds and numbered 347

"If your Lordship will be obliging enough to let me know what kind of Lotts these are, and what kind of use they can be put to, I shall thank you. not having a list about me (at the time I examined my own) of the remaining 12 tickets I could not tell whether any of them were fortunate or not, but have wrote to the purchasers for payment, and shall settle with Mr. Cock agreeable to your Lordships desire.

"In respect to my own Lotts you will please to do the needful in respect to the conveyancing of them. My respectful Compts. await Lady Sterling Lady Mary and Lady Kitty. . . ."[14]

As George Washington wrote asking to have his prize lots conveyed, Stirling was in no position to oblige. Creditors were pressing him hard, all the worthwhile prizes in his lottery were mortgaged to the hilt, the rest were not because they were so nearly valueless as to be absolutely unmortgageable. On April 5, 1775, the Pennsylvania *Gazette* reported that Lord Stirling had declared his lottery "null and void." He asked those who had actually paid for tickets to apply for repayment, not to him, but to those agents, like Washington, from whom they had bought the tickets. There is no evidence to show that any such repayments were ever made. Yet such was the power of a title and so great was the genuine regard in which Lord Stirling was held that no accusations of fraud have been recorded. As Stirling's creditors crouched for a final pounce upon his assets, a distraction appeared. The American Revolution began. Stirling was a friend of the governor of New Jersey and a member of the provinces' royal council. At a time like this what he did was a matter of widespread public concern. Stirling soon made his position clear: he was very much on the side of the Revolution.

Six months after Washington asked in vain for the delivery of his prizes, Stirling was commissioned a colonel in the New Jersey militia, a year later he was landing in the city of New York with six hundred Jerseymen under his command to begin fortifying the city against an expected British attack. He served bravely and well at the Battle of Long Island and elsewhere, and reached the rank of major general. As an intemperate, debt-ridden, and rheumatic man who began an active military career at the age of fifty, Stirling deserves admiration whether as a commander or as an officer gallantly leading his men in person against superior odds. He died in uniform as the war came to an end. He was said to have died like the Marquess of Granby, of gout. Like the marquess, he died heavily in debt.

Lord Stirling was not the only large landholder of the Catskills to serve on the American side during the Revolution; nearly all the large landholders, in one way or another, quickly staked everything they had on the success of the American rebels. But their tenants struggling for existence on the vast Hardenbergh Patent hesitated, changed their minds, listened to fresh rumors, and changed their minds again. Which side would they take, that of King or Congress? It was not an easy decision for a poor tenant to make.

20

Whig or Tory?

✤   "Our fathers struck their flints for the rights of man, and by the tender mercies of God, sparks, and the blaze of freedom flashed across the Atlantic and are spreading like the rays of the sun toward the Pacific."[1] In these words eccentric William Boyse, pastor of the Reformed Dutch churches of Shokan and Woodstock in the 1820s and 1830s, liked to explain the cause and effects of the American Revolution. Any grizzled Revolutionary veteran who heard Boyse's words soaring like Fourth of July rockets from the pulpit might very well have muttered, "The way I remember it, it warn't like that—not a bit." For in the Catskills, the Revolution stumbled along a confusing path. Some men struck their flints one week for the King and the next for the Revolution; they were alternately Whigs and Tories—these were the terms for the opposing sides which were in men's mouths as the Revolution got under way. That is why descendants of early settlers of the Catskills rummaging among ancient records in search of an ancestor who will entitle them to membership in the Daughters or Sons of the American Revolution sometimes come up with a forebear obliging enough to give them the right to membership not only in American patriotic organizations but also in those of men and women descended from Tories or Loyalists as they are called today. But few descendants of the Livingstons of Clermont are so fortunate. Their ancestors knew what they wanted as the rumblings of revolution grew louder, and they took steps to get it. That put them squarely among the Whigs.

In New York, large landlords like the Livingstons had good reason for being on the side of the Revolution. These men had long been aware that in order to be sure of keeping their grip on their lands they must resist Parliament and the King's ministers. Their motives were not altogether selfish, for they had a share in the confident spirit of independence which was growing strong in America, thanks to the colony's great distance from the mother country, to British mismanagement, and to the profusion of American natural resources. Opportunity was everywhere. All that was needed to seize it was freedom from interference from across the Atlantic. To the oppressed classes of American colonists—to New York tenant farmers, to Negroes, and to the Indians—opportunities were slight. But great landlords like the Livingstons fairly swam in a flood of opportunity which would surely rise higher as British bungling ceased. The landlords' ancestors had grabbed while the grabbing was good. As the Revolution approached, the task of the landlords was to hang onto the privileges which were theirs—to their vast tracts of land and to the structures of social standing and political power which rested on their acres.[2] The British Parliament was trying to impose taxes upon Americans without their consent. The Livingstons and other great landlords could look ahead as well as anyone. They could see that while the stamp and the tea taxes did not greatly harm them, these would inevitably lead to the birth of that fearful demon known as a general land tax. Such a tax, imposed on settled and unsettled land alike, would force landlords to sell. It would topple them from their position of privilege and change them into ordinary men.

For decades the New York landlords had shuddered at every mention of the land tax which found its way from the Houses of Parliament to the manors and estates of the Hudson Valley. The landlords led by the Livingstons were in a position of power in the Provincial Assembly; Livingstons were entrenched at the bar; they sat on the bench of the highest courts. Parliament viewed the power of the landlords with the gravest suspicion and was waiting for the right moment to turn their demon loose upon the landlords to ravage and slay. The landlords defended themselves with spirit. They became leaders in the opposition to every arbitrary action of Parliament or the King's ministers that might lead to an upsetting of the old system of land tenure in whose withered arms they had been nursed and caressed. Judge Livingston, an intellectual leader among the landlords, succeeded in convincing himself by a process of upper-class reasoning that what was good for the great New York landlords was good for America, and for the mother country as well.

If a member of the lower sort owned his own little farm, the judge reasoned, he would work no harder than was necessary to keep himself and his family barely alive. But if the man had a landlord to pay, why then he would be forced to work harder. This would produce a marketable surplus from the man's farm and this surplus when sent to market would stimulate trade. But if every member of the lower sort owned the acres he tilled, he would naturally indulge a "Habit of Idleness and Sloth." The American colonies would then become "a country scarce worth the Trouble of Defending, a Country of Indigence and Indolence, a Colony which does not at all answer the Purpose for which it was planted; which was to extend the Trade of it's mother Country."[3]

The lower sort could hardly be expected to go along with this brand of reasoning, and they didn't. In fact, to the poorer inhabitants of the city of New York the whole subject of systems of land tenure was a bore. New York was a thriving seaport; sailors and others who looked seaward rather than landward bustled in its streets and reeled home from its taverns. Its mechanics, too, were likely to work in ship-building, ship-supplying, or ship-connected trades. The ambition to own farms of their own animated few of them; city life with all its variety and excitement held them as if by a charm. They saw plenty of evidence every day of the luxury in which the better sort lived. They expressed their resentment in tavern and fireside grumbling and, when the opportunity offered, by rioting in the streets. The taxes laid upon Americans without their consent—especially the stamp tax and the tea tax—were not likely to become a serious additional burden on the poor, yet the poor rioted lustily in the streets of New York when clever members of the better sort pointed out to them the wickedness of these taxes. Before long, better sort and lower sort were making common cause against what could properly be called British tyranny.

On most Hudson River manors and large estates—at Clermont, at Livingston Manor, and in valleys hemmed in by the forested Catskills—the lower sort turned blank faces toward landlords who tried to persuade them to oppose Parliament and the King's ministers. The tenants knew little about these things. Most of them spoke only Dutch; news of the happenings of the great world filtered slowly and in distorted shape through the language barrier which set them off from English-speaking Americans. Sullenly they joined militia units at their landlord's urging and kept their thoughts to themselves.[4]

The great landlords of the Catskills were ardent Whigs except for the Verplancks who sat out the Revolution in New York without taking sides. The Livingstons, both of the manor and of Clermont, were in the forefront of the fight against Britain. Once it became apparent that war was coming, old Robert of Clermont turned all the energy he had shown in trying to settle the Catskills into cheering the Whig cause. He applauded every event that demonstrated Whig determination to resist parliamentary infringement of American liberties. The shots fired at Lexington and Concord in April of 1775 roused him to joyous excitement. An exaggerated tale of a vast disaster at Bunker Hill stunned the old man. He took to his bed and died. His last words were, "What news from Boston?"[5]

The judge had long shared in the leadership of the "Livingston party" of landlords which often dominated the Provincial Assembly with the "DeLancey party," composed largely of merchants friendly to King and Parliament, in opposition. He had vigorously opposed stamp tax and tea tax, and his Whig activity had made him something of a hero to the rioting mobs of New York. These same activities led his old friend, Royal Governor Tryon, to remove him from the bench of the Supreme Court of New York. The judge responded by building a powder mill at Clermont to supply the Whig forces. Then he followed his father in death.

He had stood upon the peak, toward which his whole life had pushed him, for a mere five months. For that length of time he had been landlord of Clermont and half a million acres in the Catskills. There had been no time to enjoy his position; the judge had spent his five months in struggling to maintain the system of land tenure that made it possible. He died, as he had lived, in a polite and gentlemanly way. He had been noted for the kindness and consideration he showed toward his social equals at all times, and he was widely mourned. At about the same time the judge's father-in-law, old Henry Beekman, died, and by this event thousands of acres of additional land were added to those managed from the Livingston house at Clermont. Three family deaths in rapid succession stunned the Livingstons and, as the Revolution moved into the stage from which there was no drawing back, they even seemed to falter in their eagerness to acquire and hold material things. With death at the door and Parliament baying at their heels, with their tenants avoiding their eyes, and with events on the American continent relentlessly pressing toward a bloody revolution, dark clouds must have brooded over the mansion at Clermont.

Across the Hudson in Ulster County the drums were beating and the fifes were squealing in behalf of the Whigs' cause. The Hardenberghs were in the very forefront of the activity, and most active of all was Colonel Johannis, son of the major who had given his name to the Great Patent. Thanks to the tracts of rich farmland which had come down to him from his grandfather, Jacob Rutsen, and thanks to the profits of family trade, the colonel was rich. Thanks to his father having linked the family name to a million and a half acres of land, his status was as high as was possible in Ulster. He had been a member of the Assembly for his county; he had been a power in the councils of the Reformed Dutch Church; for twenty years he had been colonel of the First Regiment of the Ulster Militia—this was a position of awesome dignity on the west bank of the Hudson. On the sixth of January 1775 (two weeks before Washington asked Lord Stirling to give him his lottery prizes), the colonel made it plain that he would put up with no nonsense from the British Government. On that day he presided over a meeting of "the most respectable freeholders" of Ulster. Small tenant farmers, the poor, Negroes, and Indians were not invited to attend. The freeholders resolved to support the actions of Congress in banning commercial intercourse with Britain until the mother country should come to terms. And they also took action which they hoped would indicate their detestation of the attempts being made by sympathizers with Britain to point out that the actions of a Congress were not likely to benefit the poor tenant farmers of New York.[6]

"A certain Pamphlet" addressed to the tenant farmers was produced by the chairman. It was entitled the "Free thoughts of the Resolves of the Congress etc." and was signed A. W. Farmer (A Westchester Farmer). This was a pen name of pro-British Samuel Seabury of Westchester who was later to become presiding bishop of the Episcopal Church in the United States. Seabury expressed his Tory ideas forcefully. The Ulster meeting heard the pamphlet read aloud. It was at once resolved that it "is replete with falsehoods, artfully calculated to impose upon the illiterate and unthinking . . . therefore, in detestation of such infamous publications . . ." that it be publicly burned. And so Seabury's pamphlet was solemnly destroyed by fire as those present looked on—with especial satisfaction, we may feel sure, if they were large landowners.

Colonel Hardenbergh had demonstrated his fitness for presiding over public meetings with skill; he had shown a talent for refuting argument by the simple process of burning it. He would have liked to go on to lead his regiment to glory in the dark days of war which were approaching. But, alas, he was nearing seventy. He was still vigorous—his bearing to the end of his days was haughty and soldierly—but he could not deny that he had reached the time of life when he could not expect to lead troops into battle. Late in 1775 he resigned after considerable pressure had been put upon him and saw his colonelcy become the object of an undignified scramble by aspiring Ulsterites.[7] Hardenbergh did not sulk; he immediately put his energy and influence to work for the Whig cause as a civilian. He was chosen a delegate to the Provincial Congress, and later he served as a member of the state of New York's Assembly.

Hardenbergh after Hardenbergh got into uniform—the uniform of officers, of course. Johannis Hardenbergh, Jr., of Swartekill, near present-day Rifton, became lieutenant colonel and then colonel of the Fourth Regiment of Ulster; his brother, the Reverend Jacob Rutsen Hardenbergh, fought for the Whig cause in his own way from the pulpit, using words instead of bullets. Family tradition boasts that he was so effective the British offered a reward for his capture and he slept with a loaded musket in bed beside him. Another Hardenbergh, Gerardus or Gross, became a captain. Later and long after the war was over, he was to leave his name in blood across the southern Catskills to bear witness to his pride of land. If there was military bustle in Ulster, a shocked stillness reigned across the Hudson at death-stricken Clermont. But before long, ambition began to stir once again in the new master of Clermont. The judge had left a remarkable eldest son who became sole heir to the vast holdings of lands accumulated over many years by his ancestors. The heir bore his father's name of Robert R.

Before his father died, Robert R. had been no more than a clever and promising young lawyer of New York. A graduate of King's College, now Columbia University, his quick mind and established social position made him popular among young men of the better sort. His ambition did not lie in legal or judicial advancement. He saw himself as an elegantly mannered, intellectually curious landed gentleman, an improver of agricultural methods, a benefactor of rural humanity, a kindly father to his poor tenants provided they knew their place—and kept it.

Events proved too much for Robert R.'s dream of benevolent rule over Clermont and his lands in the Catskills. The crises of 1774 and 1775 awakened him to the critical nature of the times, and he went off to Philadelphia as a delegate to the Continental Congress. He was now in a new position. No longer was he merely the prospective heir to one of the largest landed estates in New York. Although his mother was vigorously alive, he was, in effect, master of Clermont and all its appendages. His opinion was sought by the greatest men in the land and he was treated with deference and respect, for he had become one of the very best of the better sort.

The other large landholders among the Catskills hastened almost to a man to line up in the defense of English, or as they began to put it, American liberties. At this same time they kept sharp eyes on their lands and other properties upon which their position of privilege rested. War had come, some men were dying, others were getting rich, women and children were starving, yet the land, although scarred here and there by battle, would live on. The landlords were determined that it would emerge from the war held firmly in the right hands. Among the Catskills settlers, cabins were to be burned, fern spores and winged ash seeds were to invade cornfields; the whole region would become almost uninhabited for a time except for bands of Whig scouts or Tory raiding parties. Yet the slogan of the landlords throughout the war remained—as far as their lands were concerned—"business as usual."

In September 1775, Whig troops under the command of Benedict Arnold and General Richard Montgomery, the husband of the late Judge Livingston's daughter Janet, were plodding through the wilderness of upper New York with the aim of taking Quebec. Montgomery was to die heroically as his men were repulsed. At the same time, William Cockburn, the land agent of Robert R. Livingston, was plodding through the wilderness of the southeastern Hardenbergh Patent. Cockburn was bent, not on asserting determination to be free from arbitrary British rule, but to do what he could for his employer in determining patent boundaries. The southeastern line, long under dispute, had been surveyed and resurveyed. Now Cockburn hunted down old settlers and questioned them about the landmarks and place names of Lord Cornbury's time. Plagued by bad weather and the tendency of his horses to wander off in search of what scant pasture the wilderness afforded, Cockburn made his survey with care and intelligence. While Montgomery was dying and his employer was immersed in the events that were to lead to American independence, Cockburn conferred with the representatives of the owners of lands adjoining the Great Patent in Ulster County and he came to an agreement (unfortunately it proved to be only a temporary one) about their common boundaries.[8]

William Cockburn was the very man to keep the Hardenbergh Patent functioning along its traditional lines and to guard the interests of large landholders during the troubled times that lay ahead. Indeed, Cockburn saw life as, above all, a struggle by men to acquire and hang on to land. Land was in his blood, for he came of an old landed family of Duns in Berwickshire, Scotland. And land was his bread and butter, for since arriving in New York in the early 1760s he had earned his living as a land surveyor and a speculator in lands. Getting as much land as possible irretrievably recorded in the provincial records in his own name was his highest ambition. He took no interest in elevating his status. By birth he was entitled to membership in the better sort and that was good enough for him. Instead of marrying land in the usual way, he took as a wife, Catherine Trumpbour, a descendant of the Palatine refugees, and with her he settled down among her farming relatives at what is now known as Mount Marion in Ulster County. There, in the intervals of land work, he farmed with the help of eight Negro slaves on what is known to this day by old people as Cockburn's Hill.

The intensity of William Cockburn's feeling for land was not based on cold greed alone. That was present in large measure but, in addition, Cockburn was moved by a deep love of land for its own sake. This love found expression in the many maps of the Hardenbergh Patent which he made during the last third of the eighteenth century. On many of Cockburn's maps the Catskills are presented with an imagination and inventiveness that make earlier maps appear dry and dull.

Through 1776 Cockburn continued to survey among the Catskills. One of his clients, while the United States was declaring its independence, was John Burch, a prosperous New York tinsmith and japanner of violently Tory sentiments. Burch had bought a tract of six thousand acres of land along the East Branch of the Delaware—his lands are now covered by the Pepacton Reservoir—and there he installed half a dozen tenants with one William Cummins as his manager. When the Whigs of New York made life uncomfortable for Burch, he moved to Albany. There too he met with hostility. He fled to his refuge in the Catskills and stirred the whole upper Delaware Valley to give assistance to the King.

Early in 1777 General Burgoyne was threatening the Province of New York from the north and General Howe was in possession of a base for action in New York. That year Cockburn drew a seductive map for Whig Philip Livingston, the third lord of Livingston Manor, and for his brother-in-law Lord Stirling. The map showed the lands the two men owned along the eastern wall of the Catskills with the hamlet of Woodstock close by, looking very neat and proper indeed with its little houses strung out along the Sawkill. In one of those houses—the millhouse beside the Livingston sawmill—John Burch hastily stored many of his belongings. A mahogany bedstead and some barrels of tinsmithing and japanning tools were among them.[9]

When the state of New York came into being that year at Kingston, Cockburn got busy drawing a map of the new state which he hoped to have engraved and sold. But there was considerable competition for the honor of producing the first map of the state and Cockburn's map never saw print.[10]

The decisive year of the war for the Catskills and the Hudson Valley was 1777. It was in this year that the British plan for a joining of Burgoyne and Howe in the valley was defeated. Yet throughout this year of crisis William Cockburn worked on as usual taking orders from the Livingstons and Verplancks, from John Burch, and from many other landholding Whigs and Tories just as if the war had never begun. It was a difficult thing in those nervous days for a man to remain neutral. But Cockburn turned that trick. He did not serve in the Ulster militia, and he signed no pledge of allegiance to either King or Congress. Protected by his landholding clients, he went on his usual way making sure that, whatever might happen, the Catskill Mountains would remain in the hands of his employers. And from time to time, as payment for surveying services, Cockburn added to his own holdings among and around the mountains. He already claimed thousands of acres in the New Hampshire grants, not yet known as Vermont.[11]

The tenant farmers of the Catskills could not follow Cockburn in remaining uncommitted while the American Revolution raged. Pressures were put upon them from both sides to fight and die for King or Congress. And the tenants hesitated. The conduct of the Revolution in their own region was largely in the hands of their landlords, men whom most of them did not trust. Now and then earlier tenants on Hudson Valley estates had risen against the landlords. There were violent incidents in the early 1750s and a small-scale uprising in 1766. While Robert R. Livingston plunged ever more deeply into Whig activities which led to open war, his tenants heard reports of his doings with apprehension. Landlord Livingston had his own reasons for joining the opposition to King George. And wouldn't the King be grateful for any help even simple tenants might give against Livingston and his kind? And wasn't it likely that when the rebellion was put down, the King might confiscate the Livingston lands and distribute them among his friends, including loyal tenants?

At first all this was only rumor. Soon the rumor spread in more substantial form. It moved from clearing to clearing on Livingston Manor and at Clermont. It leaped the Hudson and made its way up the valley of the Esopus. It climbed the Pine Hill and followed the River Tweed to Pakatakan. The newly settled Scottish men and women around Stamford and Roxbury in the northwestern corner of the patent heard it; it moved up the Schoharie Valley; it traveled on the Delaware and reached the ears of Yankees, Jerseymen, and others living in what is now western Sullivan County. Could the rumors be trusted? If the King would reward his friends, men told each other, why then it would mean an end to the ancient European system of landholding which Dutch and English had imposed upon so much of the Hudson Valley and which was now being carried to the Catskills. As the tenants wondered in the spring of 1777, an answer seemed to come, this time not by rumor but from the mouths of agents of the King.

21

"Resolved to Stand by the King"

✤ A SHARP spring wind was busy in the valley of the upper Esopus on the one hundred eighty-eighth anniversary of April 23, 1777, the day when bits of the lands William Cockburn was guarding for their owners were offered as bait to catch soldiers for King George of England.

The Esopus, swollen with melted snow from the mountains above, raced seaward. Its surface was dotted with foamy rifts and seemed contorted with effort. Tall elms and sugar maples bowed before the wind; the shutters of the old summer boardinghouses at Mount Pleasant rattled and creaked. Mount Tremper and Mount Pleasant rising high on the opposite sides of the valley were helpless to check the wind which roared and sighed between them. Gusts of wind slapped the side of my car and made it hard for me to keep on the road that wound along the creek. In the lee of a wooded spur which flowed down from the mountains to the very edge of the road, I parked and studied my photocopy of John Cantine's survey and map of Jacob Longyear's farm. Cantine had made it in 1763, fourteen years before the King's agents passed close to this very spot.[1]

This was the place—there could be no doubt about that. When Cantine came here to make his survey, Jacob Longyear was already established and probably had the level lands along the Esopus cleared and planted. He may have begun to carve his farm from the wilderness as early as 1752.[2] Like most other first settlers on leased land in the Catskills, Longyear had not dickered with a landlord before choosing a place for his farm. He had simply gone into the woods and "squatted" on a place that took his fancy. Perhaps he had found an Indian clearing here, or perhaps the abandoned log hut of a trapper drew his attention to the place. Longyear had been a weaver in his native Germany, but by the time he reached the Esopus Valley he may have learned to judge land by the vegetation that grew upon it. The flats on which he settled are the kind of streamside land which was probably a *"beuke bosch,"*[3] as Dutch-speaking Americans of colonial days called a beechwood, and beechwoods were regarded as a sure sign that the land from which they rose would produce fine hay and the very best pasture. The steep mountain slopes that rose from the flats probably had a good number of oak trees whose acorns could be relied upon to fatten hogs, which would also cut down the rattlesnake population, for hogs eat rattlers greedily. Rattlesnakes abounded along the eastern side of the Catskills; they were believed to be attracted by oak trees and repelled by ash and beech.

In squatting on the land, Longyear was following an ancient European precedent. Squatters were a recognized group in England and on the continent; sometimes landlords encouraged them to live on parts of their land which might otherwise be useless to them. Squatters, or "borderers" as they were sometimes called, worked as extra hands at harvest and planting time, while their women often helped in manor house kitchens or laundries. In one part of England (Dartmoor) it was held that if a man began to build his shelter on "the waste" of a manor or large estate at sundown and by dawn the hovel was far enough advanced to have a door that could be closed and smoke visibly rising from its chimney, why then no power on earth could make the man move. He had what was called "keyhole tenure."[4] After twenty or more years of well-behaved squatting, a man might advance into the ranks of regular tenants or cottagers on a manor, for he would have by that time a few rights recognized by custom although not by law. In a similar way, squatters on Livingston lands and on those of other landlords in the Catskills sometimes became tenants under leases calling for the payment of rent and guaranteeing the tenant against being put off his land as long as he carried out his obligations.

It was not until 1768 or the "Eighth year of George III," as his lease agreement with Judge Livingston put it, that Jacob Longyear became a tenant farmer "in the Lothians."[5] A few other Livingston tenants had already been given leases that ran "forever," but Jacob was not so lucky. His lease ran during the lifetime of himself and his sons, Jacob Junior and Johannis. When the last of the three died the farm would revert to the landlord. The yearly rent was eighteen bushels of wheat and a fourteen-pound gammon, that is, a side of bacon. Most other Livingston tenants "for lives" paid their rents in wheat, hens, and a few days' labor. Longyear may have had a way with hogs and curing their meat. (Half a century ago, a descendant of his had a large hog farm nearby.) The Livingstons and their agents often tailored the terms of leases to suit the abilities and resources of tenants.

The orginal copies of Longyear's lease have been lost, but a sketchy summary of its terms precede a copy of Cantine's survey made in a notebook kept by William Cockburn. By comparison with leases that have survived, it seems safe to say that Longyear was under the same obligations as most other Livingston or Verplanck tenants. If there were white pine trees on his farm he would be forbidden to cut them, for this was the most valuable timber tree of the region. He could not cut oaks merely to use their bark in tanning. He must plant an orchard of a specified number of apple trees enclosed within a fence stout enough to be proof against his cattle and the wild deer, and he might be required to build a house of a certain size "with a cellar well laid up with stone." He would be forbidden to make a "browse pasture" by cutting down hardwood trees in order that his cattle might feed on the leaves or buds in the almost grassless wilderness.[6]

A tenant like Longyear had a right to sell his leasehold, but if he did he would have to pay his landlord part of the price he received, usually one sixth. If a farm went through several hands in quick succession, as sometimes happened, this might be very profitable for the landlord. The tenant by old custom had a right to the "improvements" he made; even squatters sometimes claimed and were given this right. In disputes, a jury of neighbors might be brought together to place a value on the improvements of a man who wanted to give up his "possession" or his lease or whom the landlord wanted to move away.[7]

For a man with no money first squatting and then signing a lease had one decided advantage. It made it possible for a man to build up a farm which could support him and his family with no more capital than his muscles and the willingness of the pioneer family. At first, game would supply meat, for deer, wild pigeons, and trout abounded in most valleys. Bears were plentiful and their warm skins became the pioneer's blankets. Clothing was often made of deerskin; buttons were whittled from birch or red cedar; shoes were Indian moccasins.[8] In fact, a pioneer like Jacob Longyear lived a life that was, at first, a good deal like that of the Indians who came and went through his clearing and with whom he was likely to be on friendly terms. Many pioneers in the Catskills were friendly enough to intermarry with the wandering Indians and today there is not a town in the region that is not proud of its old families with enough Indian blood to show plainly in their faces.

No one knows exactly why Jacob Longyear left Germany and came to this spot along the rushing Esopus. He may have had his imagination stirred by the sales talks of one of the "Newlanders,"[9] who were busy in the Germany of his day persuading poor people to sail for golden America. (The Newlanders were in the employ of ship owners.) He may have been lured by Cornelius Tiebout's promotional activities and, once arrived, decided to set up as a squatter, closer to the settlements than Tiebout's backwoods. But once settled on his farm, Longyear must have done fairly well, for he remained on this spot where four generations of his descendants were to follow him.

Somewhere near the roadside on which I parked that windy April day, old Jacob Longyear had built his little log house. It stood on a knoll high enough to offer safety from the flooding springtime Esopus. There was a spring nearby, and perhaps a bank of the kind of clay needed to daub the inside of a wooden chimney. I supposed that some of the old people whom I might find living in the well-kept white houses that formed the neat hamlet of Mount Pleasant could tell me just where the house had stood—the house to which a man named Jacob Middagh came so many years before on behalf of King George. The day I came to Mount Pleasant was a Friday, and I thought it might be better to come back the next day when people might be in a relaxed mood after the week's work was over and more willing to talk with a stranger. It was possible, I hoped, that some scraps of tradition lingered on in the neighborhood about what happened that long lost April 3 when a thrill of hope ran from farm to farm along the banks of the Esopus, when Livingston tenants and squatters alike were dazzled by the prospect of owning their own farms with no rent to pay to a landlord. All that was needed, it must have seemed to many a tenant listening to Jacob Middagh or his companion Lieutenant Jacob Rose, was a little daring, a trifling risk, and in a few weeks the grip of the great landlords on the Catskills would be broken. Young Jacob Longyear and his brother Andries were among the young men of the Esopus Valley who followed that hope, and in a few days heard themselves being sentenced to be hanged by their necks until they were dead. For it was to this and not to free land that the visits of Jacob Middagh and Lieutenant Rose were to lead.[10]

The next afternoon I was sitting on the porch of the tidy general store in Mount Pleasant deep in talk with Mrs. Hoyt, the wife of the proprietor. Across the road, a man and a boy were loading a pickup truck with boards and timbers from a building far advanced in the process of demolition. It had once been, so Mrs. Hoyt explained, the local station of the dying Ulster & Delaware Railroad. "I remember when forty summer boardinghouses sent their carriages to that station; trains went up and down all day taking boarders to hotels in the Catskills. That's the Cockburn House, the next house but one down the road." I asked if the owners of the house had been descendants of William Cockburn the surveyor and Mrs. Hoyt said, yes, Van Buren Cockburn had been the owner. The place had been started by his father, William Cockburn, around 1870. That wasn't the William Cockburn I meant, I explained. The first William had died in 1804; I'd seen his grave in the Mount Marion cemetery. I then asked Mrs. Hoyt about the Longyear boys of 1777. They were a little before her time, Mrs. Hoyt remarked dryly. But the old Longyear house, she could tell me where that had been. If I went down the road past the Cockburn House I'd see the spot at the sharp curve where the road heads toward the bank of the Esopus.

"Not that the original house is still there," Mrs. Hoyt warned. "The house that stands there now was built during the Civil War; the old one was torn down first. The new house was the finest in the whole neighborhood. Isaac W. Longyear built it. Doors two inches thick, doorknobs of mirror glass—everything that went into that house was the finest that could be bought, down to the last nail. It was all hauled up from the docks at Rondout by teams. About 1878 Isaac Longyear lost the place by foreclosure. It went to the Riseleys—that's my family. My brother lives there now."

No, Mrs. Hoyt said in answer to a question from me, she'd never heard of the young men of the neighborhood going off to fight for the King. She seemed to doubt what I said. Why, the Longyears were eligible to belong to the D.A.R. and things like that, she added. I said I didn't doubt it.

A few minutes later I was driving through Mount Pleasant. I parked near the sharp curve and stared at the fine house Isaac Longyear had built and lost. It was the kind of house a prosperous man of conservative tastes might have built in the late 1860s. Panels of cast-iron grillwork ornamented the front door; these were the last word on mansard-roofed houses of about 1870. But the steeply gabled roof was in the taste of the 1850s and the proportions of most of the house went back earlier. It had taken only a little more than a century for the Longyear family to climb from a log house in the wilderness to the modest elegance that I saw before me. At first they had been tenants; then they bought the land they tilled. Isaac had prospered for a time, operating one of the sawmills that chewed up the forests of the mountains along the Esopus Valley. The boom years of the Civil War paid for this house; the depression that followed took it away. More than a century earlier, Robert Livingston of Clermont had found a postwar slump almost as disagreeable.

The Mount Pleasant of 1965 had a deceptively peaceful air. The state of New York was expected to ruffle its quiet charm by forcing a highway through it in the near future. In 1777 the place could have had little charm

—the transition from wilderness to farmland was an untidy process which littered the landscape with unsightly debris and left men and women no time to care for the looks of things. Yet settlers in the Catskills and the people of the Mount Pleasant of 1965 had one thing very much in common. Both were filled with a simmering resentment against the state of New York. At the time of my visit, resentment was caused by the proposed highway, which turned out to be much less of a blight than expected. In 1777 as the new state was suffering the pangs of birth in Kingston—its birthday was April 20—the Longyears and other tenant-settlers resented the state because of the large share the Livingstons and other landlords had in its birth. They did not see how the state could be on their side or even give them what they regarded as justice. This feeling was born of more than half a century of resisting landlords.

Livingston Manor and Clermont across the Hudson had been from their beginnings places where all tenants did not take willingly to their subservient lot. The first tenants of both had been largely Germans— Palatines they were called because they were refugees from cold, war, and poverty in the Palatine along the Rhine River. First they fled to England, from there they were shipped to New York by Queen Anne's government with the understanding that after they had paid for their passage by carrying out a program of making tar and other naval stores for the Royal Navy, they would be given little farms of their own. The tar-making project was a failure for everyone concerned but one—for the Palatines, for Governor Hunter who sponsored it, for the government officials who tried to carry out a plan for making tar and pitch from varieties of pine trees which were not well adapted to the purpose. Only one man profited from the bungle—Robert Livingston of Livingston Manor, the father of Robert of Clermont. Livingston (the Palatines knew him as Lowenstein) sold the government land on which the Palatines camped. He was given contracts for supplying them with bread and beer, and he was appointed to help supervise the project. The Palatines soon learned that the tar and pitch making were doomed, but when they expressed resentment, soldiers appeared to stand over them as they worked. Briefly they rebelled—this was in 1711—and were talked out of resisting the authorities. When the project collapsed, Palatines spread out from the Hudson Valley to that of the Mohawk; some eventually found their way into the Catskills at Prattsville, and others headed for Pennsylvania. But many remained to become Robert Livingston's tenants. They were the human foundations of Livingston Manor and Clermont. The Palatines and their children, however, were never contented as tenants of the Livingstons. They had been promised forty-acre farms of their own back in 1710 and the promise had not been kept. In the 1750s and later in 1766 when Yankee land speculators questioned the title of Livingston Manor, the tenants joined in open rebellion. Both rebellions ended with the tenants in the same position as before, and their resentment simmered on.[11] All this was pointed out to British generals and the King's ministers as the American Revolution began.[12]

In London, high hopes were pinned on the resentful tenant farmers of the Hudson Valley. They could be trusted, it was believed, to rally to the King's cause and assist in overthrowing their Whig landlords. All they needed by way of bait was the promise of land free from rent and domination by landlords. In 1775 young Robert R. Livingston wrote that "many of our Tenants here . . . resolved to stand by the King as they called it, in hopes that if he succeeded they should have their Lands."[13]

Early in 1777, agents of the King were busy promising farms to tenants on Livingston Manor, at Clermont, and in the Catskills. They needed the tenants' help, for they proposed taking decisive action in the Hudson Valley. One British army was poised to move down from Canada, another up from New York, and a third from the fort at Niagara. The three would meet in the valley where an uprising of the tenants would have not only military but also propaganda value, for it would demonstrate that the revolution lacked popular support. In April of 1777 the Livingston tenants on the east bank of the Hudson were ready to rise up and smite their landlords. Across the river among the Catskills, other tenants were being urged not only to rise up against the landlords as the British approached but also to make their way to New York at once and there join the British Army.

The tenants, however, were not the only sympathizers with the Tory side in the mountains. In the northwestern corner of the Hardenbergh Patent, many Scottish families had just arrived. They had been driven from their homeland by the vanishing of small tenant holdings at the hands of landlords who wanted to convert their lands into sheep ranges or parks for shooting grouse or deer. The Scottish people knew nothing of America's quarrel with Parliament and so cared nothing about it. All they wanted was to settle down on the lands they had bought or rented and make new and happier homes for themselves. But these Scots were in no position to be neutral. To the west and northwest lay the vast region recently dominated by Sir William Johnson, and its people and its Iroquois Indians were largely on the King's side. To the east lay the Hudson Valley which in that spring of 1777 was in Whig hands with the exception of the city of New York. Pressure from both sides was applied to the

Scottish settlers. Many joined the King's forces; others left their clearings and retreated to the town of Catskill where they hoped to be allowed to remain neutral during the course of the rebellion.[14] But Whigs and secret Tory agents pushed and prodded and persuaded most into throwing in their lot with one side or the other.

Soon Tory recruiters appeared more frequently among the tenants of Dutch or German extraction in the Catskills. John Burch was actively enticing tenants in the western part of the Hardenbergh Patent and persuading many to join the King's forces. Throughout the mountains, Tory sympathies rose to a high pitch in the spring of 1777. As the new agents of the King went from door to door whispering their fine promises and dangling Livingston farms before tenants' eyes, they revived hopes which had never died out since the Hardenbergh Patent first cast its dark shadow over the Catskills.

22

Rose's Rangers

✿ RUMORS as well as British agents were darting in and around the Catskills in the late winter and early spring of 1777. Some of the inhabitants of Cochecton in what is now western Sullivan County listened to the rumors and sent out a cry for help. "There were a number of disaffected persons here to American liberty," they reported. "There is a plot hatching among them. . . . Our lives are on a very slippery foundation. . . ." The inhabitants were "at a great distance from help and in a wilderness . . ."[1] they complained. "I am more and more convinced that something is in agitation among the Tories,"[2] wrote young Robert R. Livingston from Clermont. The Convention which was the highest governing body of New York pending the setting up of the state government was meeting in Kingston within sight of the Catskills. A rumor that the Tories proposed to kidnap them and load them on a British man-of-war alarmed the delegates. Because they felt that the Continental Congress' articles of war adopted in 1775 were inadequate to deal with the Tory threat, they passed a resolution calling for the seizure and condemning to death of "enlisters for the King"[3] and spies.

Brigadier General George Clinton, soon to become the first governor of New York, was a levelheaded man. The rumors of Tory plots, which had many heads around him in a whirl, did not take his eye off the likelihood that the British would soon try to join their northern and southern armies in the Hudson Valley and by this act cut off all New England from the rest of the rebellious colonies. "I am sensible the Tories as usual intended to have executed some Wicked Plott this spring," he wrote to Robert R. Livingston, "but I believe it was nothing more than to embody in Parties according to the numbers willing to join" and to "march off & Join the Enemy plundering & disarming as many Whigs as they might be able on their Route."[4]

Wisely, General Clinton kept his eye on the British armies and pushed forward defenses against their approach, leaving the "Wicked Plott" to be handled through the usual channels. The plot was no more than an attempt to recruit men for the King among the tenant settlers of the Catskills and the Hudson Valley. It was this attempt that netted the two Longyear boys on the twenty-third of April, 1777.

In the earlier stages of the Revolution, efforts were made on both sides to sort out Whigs and Tories into two well-defined groups. Tory sympathizers behind the Whig lines were encouraged to go to the city of New York which the Tories held, and New York City Whigs were free to pick up as much of their property as they could and head up the Hudson into Whig country. This arrangement made matters easy for spies, distributors of "seditious utterances," recruiters for either side, and men bent on picking up easy money dealing with the enemy, especially in horses and beef cattle; such men were called "cowboys." By the spring of 1777, things had been tightened up. George Washington firmly opposed the continuous human flow between the lines which the sorting-out system made possible. But many in New York were profiting from the flow and favored continuing it. The tension that gripped the region threatened at any moment by massive British invasion settled the matter as far as it could be settled. Passes to enemy-held country became harder to get; strangers everywhere had to have convincing explanations of their presence if they were to keep out of crowded and dirty jails.[5]

Lieutenant Jacob Rose, or Roosa, the leader of the Wicked Plott, was merely a pawn in a confused and bungling British attempt to make capital of both tenant farmer discontent and the human flow between the lines. In April 1777, Rose was an officer in the King's American Regiment of Colonel Edmund Fanning of New York, a regiment which was actively recruiting men who were loyal to the King but who were living within the Whig lines. It was Rose's mission to bring in men from the Catskills.

Rose had not been an out-and-out Tory for long. He started his career in the Revolution on the Whig side and had been a captain in the Ulster regiment of which Johannis Hardenbergh of Swartekill was lieutenant colonel. But Rose's lukewarmness toward the Whig cause had been noticed. Among others, John Cantine, who had earlier made the survey of the Longyear farm, testified to it. Rose refused to obey orders and was court-martialed. The court's verdict was that he was to be cashiered and fined thirty pounds.[6] This was in February of 1777. Rose wasted no time but enlisted under Fanning. Before long he was back in his old haunts moving secretly by night—"there was not much danger of being Ketch[d] for the Torys had prepared Cellars a long the way which they stayᵈ in the Day Time"⁷ as another Tory put it. Rose's first trip to the Catskills yielded an encouraging number of recruits. One was Jacob Middagh who was a Livingston tenant on the East Branch of the Delaware below Pepacton. Rose's promises to Middagh were not kept, so Middagh afterward testified. He was told that he was under no compulsion to enlist, yet when he got to New York he found that "he could get no work and was obliged to enlist or starve."⁸ Rose had made him "a Promise of 5 Dollars Bounty and a Dollar to drink the King's Health but never received either." He had been promised a splendid uniform, but was offered instead no more than a "Shirt and Trowsers" which he spurned.

Jacob Rose was a tall and energetic man not overburdened with scruples. In spite of the way he had of failing to keep his promises, Middagh remained faithful to the lieutenant and accompanied him on his second recruiting drive among the Catskills. There he repeated to others the same promises with which Rose had lured him to New York. The most effective of these was the pledge that, following a victory for the King, every tenant farmer who supported him would receive a farm of his own—one hundred acres for himself and an additional fifty acres for each of his children.

This promise of land far exceeded the one authorized by the British Government. Fifty acres for each recruit and none extra for his children was all the British offered as a lure for "provincials" enlisting as common soldiers. Yet Rose may have made his promise in good faith. Later he testified that he had been told of it by "one Daniel McGuin, a Captain in Colo Fanning's regiment."⁹ McGuin had turned up in Ulster County immediately after Rose's court-martial and it was he who had persuaded Rose to join the British by making the same promises Rose was to use a few months later. McGuin, like all other officers in the loyalist regiments at the time, was under an obligation to bring in a certain number of recruits as part of the price of his commission. So, probably, was Jacob Rose. Colonel Fanning, who was the rich and influential son-in-law and secretary of Royal Governor Tryon, had been authorized to raise his regiment only after convincing the British authorities that he could raise the required number of loyalists with ease. But recruits came in slowly. Each officer applied pressure to those beneath him. Scruples were thrown aside and extravagant promises of land and cash bounties were made. Rose, Middagh, and the boys they lured from the Catskills were caught in this play.

The King was not alone in offering men land in return for their promise to enlist—the Whigs made similar promises. But here the Whigs were at a disadvantage. Most of the large American landowners were on their side. They were in fact the leaders of the Whig cause and could not offer the lands upon which the tenants lived, for these lands were vital to their landlords' privileged position. But the King's agents could. The Continental Congress in September 1776 offered land in return for enlistment. But the location of these lands was kept vague. Would they be on some far-off frontier or among the rocks and rattlesnakes of the New York mountaintops as yet ungranted by King or Congress? That seemed likely. What was as certain as anything could be in that uncertain time was that tenants of the Livingstons, the Van Rensselaers, and other great landlords would not be allowed to continue as owners of their own acres on the farms they had cleared and to which they were attached by a thousand emotional links. If the Whigs should win, their tenants would remain tenants or if they wished to claim a reward in land, they would have to leave home and begin the process of pioneering all over again far from friends and their familiar surroundings.

Lieutenant Rose and Private Middagh came to the Catskills knowing that they could make a far more attractive offer than the Whigs. And they found that their offer was arousing enthusiasm. By the time they reached the neighborhood of the Longyear farm at Mount Pleasant, they had a substantial band of recruits in tow. Three were from the Schoharie Valley, probably from the vicinity of Prattsville; others were sons of settlers along the East Branch of the Delaware. Their mission was succeeding, as old Robert Livingston might have put it, "like a snoeball."

On April 23, 1777, Andries Longyear, then in his early twenties, was still living with his parents on the little farm at Mount Pleasant, then known as part of Big or Great Shandaken. Jacob, Jr., the brother who was his elder by a few years, had taken up a farm of his own on Livingston land a short distance down and across the Esopus. Jacob, Jr., was married and had a young child. Jacobus Rose came to his door on that April day and turned loose his seductive tongue. ". . . by Rose's Purswasion," Jacob was to testify, "he went with him with an Intention of going to New York, and if he enlisted he was to have 100 Acres of Land for himself and 50 for his Child. That Rose informed him he should be Home again in a month's Time, for that the Country wou'd then be overrun [by the British forces]. . . ."[10]

While Rose was persuading Jacob, Jr., Middagh was working on Andries at his father's house. Middagh urged Andries "to [go] long with them to New York to the Regulars, for the Regulars would Come up this way Soon, and they would then . . . drive the Inhabitants before them and take their Estates from them. . . . His father Jacob Longyear did not prevent him from going with Rose to the Regulars; that he had a gun loaded with Powder and Ball. . . ."[11] So Andries testified at his court-martial.

Andries told too of how the Tory excitement spread through Big and Little Shandaken all the way to Shandaken Lake in Woodstock. "Peter Misener, a Neighbor of his, Said he would go alonge with him but his wife would not let him. . . . He heard that Christian Winner was gone [to] little Shandaken to get men . . . that Peter Winner, Hendrick Henning, Frederick Row at little Shandaken, Jacob Furlong and Wilhelmus Merkle at Great Shandaken were also friends to the King of great Britain."[12] All these men were Livingston tenants or squatters on Livingston lands. A year earlier, several had been persuaded to sign the articles of association by which they pledged themselves to support the Whig side of the argument. Now, in the mass excitement that gripped the neighborhood, they were coming out in the open as Tories.

Standing by the family fireside with his parents smiling approval and Middagh's little band of recruits from behind the mountains welcoming him share in their adventure, it did not take long for young Andries to decide to go to New York; his younger brother Christopher made up his mind to go too. Mrs. Longyear then put together three or four days' rations for the boys—Middagh assured her that would be enough to take them to British-held country. Before the men marched away, old Jacob gave Andries a gun and ammunition, and perhaps some last-minute wisdom as to the gun's use.

Middagh soon halted his men at the house of Jacobus Bush of Shokan. (Jacobus or Jacob was the son of Indian trader and mountain guide Henry Bush.) There, more recruits previously persuaded were waiting by agreement. Jacobus celebrated the occasion with drinks of rum all round and Middagh radiated optimism. The British Army would reach the Esopus Valley "as soon as the country wou'd afford grass for their horses,"[13] he assured his audience of tenant farmers. He urged Bush's sons to join the expedition—"all that would go with him he would make gentlemen of," he concluded. Tenant Wilhelmus Maracle [or Merkle] backed up Middagh with a powerful argument. He read aloud passages from his Bible in which nothing less than loyalty to good King George was plainly urged. Later on when he was thrown in the Kingston jail as a Tory, he was to regret this display of biblical scholarship.

Once the new recruits were assembled and Bush's son Peter had agreed to join, there was no time to be wasted. Middagh's men set out into the night to march through the woods to Marbletown. There Lieutenant Rose met them with his own recruits, including young Jacob Longyear, and Rose took over command. Schoolmaster Daniel Irvin wrote down the names of all the men and they marched out into the night across wearying fields and rivers and woods until, just before dawn, they laid down to rest in a barn in secluded Coxing Clove at the foot of the steep Shawangunk Mountains. All through the day they rested and when dusk came they climbed the Shawangunks and hid themselves under caves formed by projecting ledges—this was close to the place where the Lake Monhonk golf course would be laid out far in the future.

Up to this point it had been a rather lighthearted party that headed for New York. Rose and Middagh's cheerful predictions of an end to the war in a month or two had sounded reasonable enough. The prospect of seeing the city of New York with all its wonders and before long returning to the Catskills with the title deeds to their own farms in their hands had seduced their innocent minds. But as they huddled under the ledges of the Shawangunks, sober thoughts began tormenting them. From their mountaintop they could look back and, if the weather was fair, see the Catskills, among which they had lived their lives, standing blue and remote. Ahead lay the fertile valley of the Walkill, a valley in which the landlord-tenant system of the Catskills did not prevail. There almost every white man owned his own farm and his own black slaves, and almost every man was a fervent Whig.

A Tory messenger from the valley climbed to the mountaintop. The Whigs down below had learned of the approach of Rose's Rangers, he reported. They were sending out armed patrols to intercept them. But this news was not all that disturbed the cheerful confidence of the members of Rose's Rangers (the name they were to be remembered by in later years). The men had left the Catskills as a band of young mountain tenants of similar background and skills. By the time they hid out on the Shawangunks, new men had joined the party and given it a different character. There were a few escaped slaves who trusted the promises of Rose and Middagh that siding with the King would bring them freedom, and there were a number of young Tories from larger and more sophisticated settlements than any the Catskills could boast.

There was one man who did more than any other to lower the spirits of the band—he was Dr. Aussem, known as "the high-Dutch doctor"[14] because he was of German birth. Aussem had been practicing medicine in Rochester. He was arrested because of his outspoken Tory

DELAWARE LOTTERY.

For the Sale of L A N D S belonging to the EARL OF STIRLING.

The S C H E M E.

The *Scheme,* which advertised Lord Stirling's lottery, began boldly enough but made use of much fine and confusing print before it ended. (*Courtesy of the Historical Society of Pennsylvania.*)

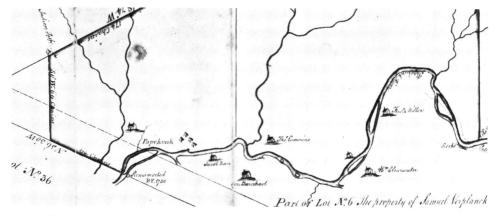

Here an old Indian trail, the apple orchard of Indian Henry Heckan, and the houses of settlers, most of whom joined the King's side, appear in a map drawn by William Cockburn for Tory John Burch in 1776. (*Courtesy of New York State Library.*)

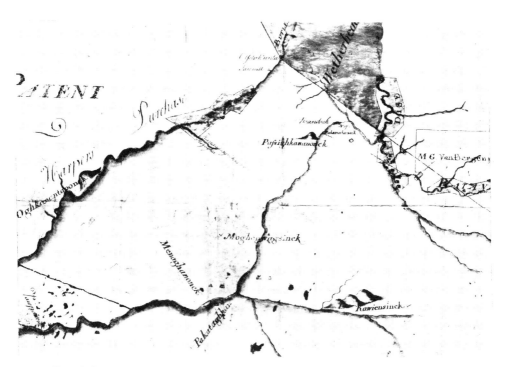

Detail from a map of the Hardenbergh Patent drawn in 1771 by surveyor William Cockburn. Here the lands claimed by General Bradstreet are shown lying between the two branches of the Delaware River. The Indian place names, Cockburn explains in another part of the map, were given to him by "John Paulin and Sapan, two Esopus Indians," through interpreter Thomas Nottingham. Kawiensinck is the Pine Hill of later times, Pakataghkan and Menaghenonck are in the Margaretville vicinity, Passighkawanonck is in Roxbury, and Otsthiunta is Utsayantha. The hamlet in the upper right is Schohariekill, now known as Prattsville. The original of the map is in the New York State Office of Surplus Real Property, Albany, N.Y.

Chancellor Robert R. Livingston. This portrait painted in Paris in 1804 by John Vanderlyn shows Livingston with one hand resting on the prospectus for the American Academy of Fine Arts which Livingston had helped establish the previous year. Visible to the right in the original painting is a bit of landscape which may be conventional but is likely to show the view from Clermont across the Hudson with the Catskill Mountains in the distance. (*Courtesy of the New-York Historical Society.*)

Left, the front door of the Longyear-Riseley house at Mount Pleasant. (*Author's photograph.*)

This earliest known view of a pioneer's clearing and cabin in the Neversink Valley once belonged to President Franklin D. Roosevelt. The sketch is signed P. Lodet. (*Courtesy of the Franklin D. Roosevelt Library, Hyde Park, N.Y.*)

Here the last Jacob Brink to practice as a witch doctor looks out from the pages of *Sylvester's History of Ulster County, New York.* (*Courtesy of New York State Library.*)

sympathies. In February he escaped from custody by crossing the thin ice of the Walkill, but the ice broke and his feet still hurt from the chill they received. The doctor had spent two months hiding out among the Shawangunks and had suffered greatly. Now he went from ledge to ledge on the mountain telling his tale, complaining about the unhappy state of his feet, and hinting broadly (when Rose and Middagh were out of earshot) that he'd had enough and was considering giving himself up to the Whig authorities.

To balance the high-Dutch doctor there was a "regular officer" in disguise who became a man of mystery and fascination to the simple young men from the Catskills. The officer was said to be carrying important messages from the army of General Burgoyne to that of Howe. He was "Blind with the left Eye . . . he had on a speckled Under Jacket, Brown Surtout Coat, a pair of Blew Wolling Stockings, and strings in his Shoes . . . he had a handkerchief in his hand. . . ."[15] The officer had come through Whig-held Albany disguised as a shoemaker with a bundle of leather lashed to his horse behind the saddle. His presence among Rose's Rangers added a touch of glamor and authority to their expedition and played a part in holding the expedition together as adversity began to strike.

Jacob Rose was well aware of the difficulties that lay in wait for him and had made careful arrangements to handle them. A succession of Tory guides was waiting to help his Rangers find their way to New York, and Tories had agreed to shelter him and his men and to feed them in their barns or houses. The first guide took over as the Rangers left the Shawangunks by night and came to the Walkill a little south of New Paltz. There a guide named Wouter Slouter (or Sluyter) was waiting. But soon an unexpected incident upset all Rose's plans. Two Whig patrols met and challenged them. One of Rose's men thoughtlessly fired his musket and slightly wounded one of the Whigs. Both were captured but released upon their solemn promise to say nothing of the encounter. They did not keep their promise. The wounded man—he was Lieutenant Terwilliger—ran to the nearest house and sent a man racing on horseback to the headquarters of the Revolutionary army at Newburgh. Soon exaggerated rumors of the size and strength of Rose's Rangers were being relayed everywhere throughout the region. Rose had a well-trained band of one hundred fifty-six well-armed men, some said. Determined militia units hastened to scour the countryside; Whigs everywhere were warned to be on the alert and to report any sign of the Rangers.

For two days Rose's Rangers struggled on through an increasingly hostile country. Sometimes they rested by day in the barns of unwilling men whom they threatened with violence if they did not do as they were told; at other times they had no choice but to hide behind brush fences until darkness came. Finally they reached Little Britain. There Lieutenant Rose and the one-eyed officer left their men and called upon Cadwallader Colden, Jr., who like his late father, John Bartram's friend, was of intensely Tory sympathies. Rose returned without the officer but with bad news. Colden insisted that the Whigs had cut off every possible way of escape. The band was trapped. Retreat to the Catskills with their friendly population was out of the question; advance toward New York had become impossible. There was only one thing to do—hide out in the Schunnemunk Mountains nearby and hope for the best.

Hardly had the Rangers reached the Schunnemunks when fifty Whig militiamen came upon them. Shots were exchanged and a number of Rose's men—some said five—were killed. Most of the Tories were captured; a few escaped but were soon picked up. At some time between the day spent on the Shawangunks and the end of the expedition, a number of recruits had quietly slipped away and headed for home. Among these was Christopher Longyear.

On April 30, just one week after he had left home with such high hopes, Jacob Longyear, Jr., Lieutenant Rose, Jacob Middagh, and most of the other recruits from the Catskills faced a court-martial at Fort Montgomery in the Hudson River Highlands. Andries Longyear and ten others were court-martialed on May 2 and during several days following. The outlook for the men as the proceedings began was not bright. The Whig forces were working frantically to fortify the Hudson Valley against momentarily expected attacks from the north and the south, and, with the help of the Indians lurking behind the Catskills, from the west. The tenants on Livingston Manor, preparing to support the British, were accumulating stocks of powder and lead, while false rumors that the British were about to arrive at any moment stirred both tenants and their masters daily. The lord of Livingston Manor barricaded himself in his manor house where he relieved his feelings by cursing his tenants and wishing that they might all be hanged and their children starved. It was far from a propitious time for tenants who had been recruited by Tory agents to go on trial for their lives before a court made up for the most part of landowning officers.

Three days before Middagh and Rose had begun their recruiting activities at Big Shandaken, the state of New York had come into being at Kingston. The captured men therefore might be judged guilty of treason against the duly constituted state even though many of them had not heard of its existence when they agreed to join Lieutenant Rose. But worst of all,

Rose's Rangers had fired upon and wounded a Whig soldier and had exchanged gunfire with the militiamen who captured them. They had not gone to join the British quietly and without violence. They had moved through Whig countryside as an armed band, firing upon those who opposed them, threatening to blow out the brains of men who hesitated to give them food, drink, or shelter on demand. This could not be regarded as anything but a very serious matter.

The testimony given at the court-martial at Fort Montgomery makes it plain that those on trial, even to once-bold Lieutenant Rose, were completely disheartened. Most spoke frankly and freely, and the recruits from the Catskills showed that they now believed that they had been deluded by false promises, that they had been caught, as a Tory who unwillingly gave them shelter during their march put it, "in a dismal snare."[16] With a few exceptions, all were found guilty and sentenced to be hanged. Mercy was recommended for seven of the men, including Andries Longyear, "in Consequence of their apparent Distress, open Confession and Promise of future Obedience to the Laws of the State of New York. . . ."[17]

The next day the sentences were confirmed by the Convention in Kingston. Those of three men who had aided Rose and his men were reversed. Robert R. Livingston abstained from voting on the cases of Jacob Longyear, Jr., and Jacobus Furlong, or Furlow, since both were his "tenants for lives" at Big Shandaken. He voted, however, on the cases of other mountain men who were squatting on his lands without the protection of proper leases, or who were close relatives of tenants of his. The condemned men were sent to Kingston and confined in the courthouse cellar or on board brigs at anchor in the Hudson. There they awaited carrying out of their sentences. While they waited, the Convention adopted a canny resolution. They resolved that all those condemned except for Rose and Jacob Middagh be pardoned but that these pardons be kept secret "during the discretion of the Convention, or Council of Safety, or Governor of this State. . . ."[18] As the Convention delegates expected, Whig recruiters talked with the young men and virtually all who were fit abandoned allegiance to King George and enlisted in the rebel army. On May 13, Rose and Middagh were hanged in Kingston. Many expected that they too would be pardoned at the last moment, but they were not. Their last words, in the Dutch tongue of their daily life, expressed penitence.

Jacob and Andries Longyear enlisted in the 5th Regiment of the New York Line on May 20 and were soon stationed at Fort Montgomery which, it was hoped, would help stem the imminent British invasion. On October 6 the fort was attacked and taken by the British. Jacob was made prisoner and sent to New York to be confined in a military prison. There he died, whether from wounds or disease we do not know.

Andries was reported missing in the action at the fort. That is the last time his name appeared in any record. Some say that he escaped and was seen many years later living in Albany; others have a less pleasant explanation for his sudden disappearance from human knowledge.

Chaplain Timothy Dwight of the Continental army—later better known as poet, traveler, and president of Yale College—visited the site of Fort Montgomery in the spring of 1778 and was saddened by what he saw. From a dank and scummy pool near the fort, he saw projecting parts of the corpses of men killed in the battle of the year before. An arm was raised as if calling for help from beneath the dismal pool.[19] It might, for all anyone knows, have been the arm of young Andries, for he may have been lured from the Catskills by a shining promise of land only to meet his fate in this pool.

Nineteen-year-old Christopher Longyear appears only once in the records of Rose's Rangers, when he was noted as one of the band who had given up and returned home before the capture in the Schunnemunks. Christopher was never arrested. In 1778 he became a soldier in the Whig army, as did his father and his brothers. Perhaps they did so out of resentment against the King and his agents, or perhaps they understood that, however hard it might seem at the time, their future and that of their family lay with the new nation—the United States of America.

In 1780 Christopher married Maria Conyes in Saugerties. Among the couple's children was a William C. Longyear, who in turn became the father of a baby named Isaac, who grew up to become the same Isaac Longyear who built and lost the fine white house in Mount Pleasant at which I stared that windy April day as the Esopus rushed by to merge with the Hudson and the sea.

23

War Divides the Catskills

✤ THE HANGING of Rose and Middagh chilled the souls of the King's men in the Hudson Valley and among the Catskills. But their ardor was revived some months later when a British fleet sailed up the Hudson and men under General Vaughan burned Kingston and the Livingston mansion of Clermont. Mysteriously, as it seemed to Tory sympathizers, the fleet did not continue up the Hudson to join Burgoyne's forces. Instead it returned to New York. Burgoyne was in trouble and quickly surrendered his defeated army at Saratoga. The British purpose of cutting the rebellious colonies in two had been thwarted thanks to the efforts of the Whig forces and the northern wilderness. Some of Burgoyne's German mercenaries deserted; singly or in small groups a few made their way up the Schoharie Valley to the Catskills.[1] There they melted into the population. Descendants of these Hessians, as they were called, are to be found scattered among the mountains to this day. Rose and Middagh had promised that the King's soldiers would soon come to the Catskills. They came indeed, but only in the form of these pitiful Hessians.

The Tory tenants of the Catskills were discouraged as 1777 came to its end, yet many continued to cherish a stubborn faith in good King George and a hope that once the war was over, he would give them their farms. The deeds of these men are still remembered and recited in the area.

Almost every neighborhood among the Catskills has an obliging old-timer who acts as custodian of the local Revolutionary lore. The old-timer has no tales to tell of great pitched battles, of George Washington's men marching to fight British redcoats to the music of fife and drum. The old-timer's talk is most likely to revolve instead around a single theme—the capture of the Whig settlers by local Tories and their Indian allies. For, during Revolutionary days and especially after 1777, the Catskill Mountains formed part of the broad belt of frontier which stretched all the way from

Maine to Georgia with advance posts as far west as Kentucky, Ohio, and Detroit. Throughout this belt the ever-present threat of Indian raids often became reality; cabins were burned, settlers lost their liberty and property and often their lives and scalps. Only the people of the towns and cities sparsely strung out along the Atlantic coast could feel free from fear of the "hell-hounds,"[2] as the Indians were called by the Whigs' good friend Lord Chatham.

Tales of the capture of whites by Indians had become an important part of America's stock of traditions long before the Revolution. Captain John Smith began it in 1624 with his tale of Pocahontas. The war multiplied such tales without making too much change in their classic form. After the celebration of the fiftieth anniversary of American Independence in 1826, survivors of Indian captivity in the region of the Catskills and elsewhere were reverently questioned and their stories were written down and printed. In this way the legends of Indian captivity among the Catskills received the form in which we know them today. This form has no room for subtle shadings—it is a thing of black and white. All its Indians and Tories are wicked, all its Whigs are models of virtue (an Indian who yields to a passing kindly impulse and saves a captive's life forms a necessary exception). In few of these legends as told in the Catskills is there any hint of the Indians' initial reluctance to become involved in the Revolution. There is no recognition of the parts played by Whig landowners and Tory tenants. All the doubts and ambiguities of Revolutionary days vanish in straightforward tales of struggles between good and evil.

In 1827 the patriotic fervor to which the celebration of 1826 had given birth stirred editor Charles G. DeWitt of Kingston to interview a man whom he described in his Sunday-best prose as "one of the spared monuments of a memorable era."[3] This human monument was an eighty-nine-year-old veteran of the the Revolution, by the name of Jeremiah Snyder, who in 1780 had been captured by an Indian raiding party.

It would have been hard for editor DeWitt to find a man better suited to playing the role of the hero of an Indian-captivity legend than Jeremiah. For he and the other members of the family to which he belonged were made of remarkably tough and resilient stuff. Jeremiah's father, Martin, came to America from Germany in 1726 with his wife Deamute and, before many years the two were established on a frontier farm in the shadow of the Catskills. There they labored in the fields and forests and at the same time reproduced with energy and efficiency. All of their fourteen children, except for one who died at twenty-two, lived to become hearty old men and women. The last reproductive effort of Martin and Deamute formed a fitting climax. When Deamute was forty-seven she produced twin boys. The thirteen children of the old couple inherited their parents' ability to reproduce, for they generated a grand total of ninety-eight children. And what is remarkable in an age when infant mortality was high, only four of these ninety-eight babies failed to reach mature years. What is even more remarkable is that of the living balance of ninety-two, exactly half were boys and half girls—so the Snyder family historian wrote with understandable pride more than a century ago.[4]

To eighteenth-century Americans, human reproduction had an economic motivation which it lacks today. Then a couple with a large brood were well on the way to becoming rich instead of poor. For in a society suffering from a chronic labor shortage, boys and girls of eight were productive farmworkers. And each child could be relied upon to give his parents ten years of free labor before he or she married, left the parental roof, and began producing his or her own family.

The Snyder boys and girls of Martin and Deamute's production left the home farm at the proper time and, married to the sons and daughters of their neighbors, sought fresh fields. Many of them, including Jeremiah and his brothers Zechariah and Abraham, settled along the base of the Catskills in what is now the northwestern part of the town of Saugerties. There they found broad and fertile flats waiting to yield amazingly large crops of wheat and corn to whoever would clear and till them. The flats are still there set in a bony framework of ridges running north and south to parallel the towering wall of the Catskills to the west. When freshly plowed their pinkish-red soil seems to glow with health and energy; when moistened by an afternoon shower it takes on the soft look of lavender velvet.

But in Jeremiah's day there was a catch—in fact, there were two catches. First of all, the land lay on the very rim of white civilization. It was exposed on the west to potentially hostile Indians and to forays by such mountain dwellers as rattlesnakes, bears, wolves, and corn-loving squirrels and raccoons. Then, and this was far more important, there was a good deal of controversy about the title to the land.

The Hardenbergh patentees had tried to claim it around 1726; much of it had been granted to men of the better sort who hoped to function as absentee landlords; the trustees of the Corporation of Kingston said a good deal of it was part of their commons on which their freeholders had rights to pasture cattle and cut wood or stone—or, if they chose, to request and receive leases of farmland.[5] In addition, the counties of Albany and Ulster both laid emphatic claim to the land and pushed the line dividing their jurisdiction back and forth by means of endless surveys and the piling up of affidavits from old residents. The exact location of the county line affected the title of lands claimed by such important people as Cadwallader Colden, Lord Stirling, Philip Livington, and others—that was why so much energy was expended in placing it where it would do the placer the most good.

The old Indian inhabitants were appealed to. In 1767 two Indians named Pieter Tap and Jan de Backer testified that the neighborhood of the fine agricultural lands had been within the hunting grounds of the Catskill and not of the Esopus Indians, and that whenever an Esopus Indian shot a deer across the line, he was obliged to share it half and half with the Catskill Indians, and vice versa. Pieter Tap and Jan de Backer were "sober and not drunk" when they testified, so Martin Van Bergen of Catskill swore.[6] Some believed that the county line followed the old Indian tribal division, which was the only reason why the Indians' traditions had importance.

Jeremiah and Abraham leased lands side by side in what is now Blue Mountain. Zechariah settled a little to the east near what is now known as Asbury. This was in the days when the debate about the county line was at its hottest. Both Albany and Ulster counties tried to collect taxes and exact military duty from the people in the Snyders' neighborhood, and rival landlords did their best to collect rents. A Kingston constable showed up one day to collect sixpence in taxes from a farmer named Hendrick Stroope. When the man refused to pay on the claim that he was paying taxes to Albany, the constable seized "a new pewter dish which cost the deponent Twelve shillings."[7] The next year the constable returned and demanded ninepence in Ulster taxes and when it was not paid "in the night time took a mare . . . worth Nine or Ten pound." The constable sold both the dish and the mare for much more than the taxes but refused to return the change.

It fell to Margaret Fiero, Zechariah's wife, to play an important role in the county-line dispute. When she was a girl living close to the present Ulster-Greene county line she had gone with her father, Valentine Fiero, to help rescue a cow which had become entangled in a swamp near a rock known from its shape as the Steene Herte or Stone Heart. This rock, Valentine believed, was on the true Ulster-Albany county line. In order to make sure that Margaret would remember the significance of the Steene Herte, Valentine—after he rescued the cow—gave his daughter a brisk spanking, once on the Albany side of the rock and again on the Ulster side. As he spanked, he pointed to cryptic inscriptions on the Steene Herte which, when properly interpreted, put the location of the county line beyond dispute.[8] The stimulation applied at once to her mind and her bottom made the smallest detail of her adventure at the Steene Herte vivid in Margaret's mind to the end of her days.

The long belt of good farmland that stretched along the eastern base of the Catskills became a stronghold of Tory sentiment as the Revolution began. The belt was settled almost entirely by descendants of the Palatine emigrants of 1710 and later years. These people were loyal to the King of England, some say, because of their gratitude to his predecessor, Queen Anne, who had sent the Palatines to America. But it is more likely that their uncertain position as tenant farmers in a debatable land and their isolation from the advanced currents of American thought by a language compounded of German, Dutch, and English poured their thoughts and feelings into a conservative mold. The Snyders' neighbors were, in the words of Jeremiah's wife, Catherina, "a cluster of envious and rigid Tories."[9] And as Catherina was later on to write Governor Clinton, Jeremiah's "Tory neighbors had pointed him out to sacrifice him and family, to satiate their vengeance upon him & to get him and son Prisoner in their Hands."

As rigid a Tory as any was Jeremiah's older brother Zechariah, but long before Jeremiah's capture was to be plotted, Zechariah had left with Margaret and their children for the Tory haven of Nova Scotia. Before that, he had formed a part of the Tory underground of his part of the country and had helped guide and shelter British agents like Jacob Rose who infiltrated the Whig lines in search of recruits or information or who carried messages from one British general to another. He was the only one of the ten Snyder brothers to be "a man for the King." Just why Zechariah swam against the strong family tide is obscure; all that seems certain is that he was unable to resist the social pressures of his Tory neighborhood.

Thanks to their unusual reproductive powers and their inherited physical stamina, the rest of the Snyder brothers had little to complain of in the way their Whig-dominated society treated them. All were doing well, some as farmers, or carpenters (the trade Jeremiah carried on in addition to farming), and one was a tanner. But brother Benjamin was the most successful. He had taken kindly to book learning, taught school, drew up wills and deeds for his neighbors, and became the owner and skipper of a sloop which traveled up and down the Hudson on trading ventures. During the Revolution he sold a sloop to the Continental forces to be used as a "fire-ship" intended to be set ablaze and sent into the midst of the British fleet on the Hudson. Benjamin and all but one of his brothers had broken out of the narrow world into which they had been born and had become part of the larger American society emerging as the war began.

Of all the brothers, Jeremiah was the most active in the Revolutionary cause. He was elected a militia lieutenant in the very first days of the war; in 1778 he was in command of the picket fort at Little Shandaken in the town of Woodstock. "The Company now Consists of Forty-one Privates, besides Serjeants & Corporals, and these I can not Suply with three Cartirages a peice."[10] So Snyder dolefully reported to General Clinton. Snyder's job was to patrol and protect the border from the picket fort to the Kaaterskill Clove, which put him into direct conflict with his Tory neighbors. These neighbors could not have regarded Jeremiah with friendly eyes, since he more than any other individual was responsible for thwarting their efforts on behalf of the King. And besides, by abandoning his old Palatine German friends for the English-speaking Whig world, he had proved what later generations would call "a traitor to his class." By 1780 it became possible for the Tories to deal with Jeremiah. Until then their resentment against him had merely simmered and sputtered. It was the entrance of most of the Indians of New York into the war on the side of the King that doomed Jeremiah Snyder to capture. In alliance with the Indians the Tories of the Blue Mountain neighborhood saw their chance to take care of Snyder, who by this time had advanced to the rank of captain.

Late in the summer of 1777 most of the Iroquois and many of the scattered Esopus Indians made up their minds to side with the British. Resentment at the way the colonists had treated them in land deals helped push them into alliance with the King. General Bradstreet, some of the Indians complained, had paid them for the lands they sold with nothing but promises; now the Whig authorities (many of whom were up to the elbows in land speculations) were preparing to grant these same lands all over again to members of their own crowd but without any additional payment to the Indians. All but a few of the Esopus Indians sprinkled thinly in and around the Catskills had already withdrawn to settlements such as Oghwagha and Coletien on the Susquehanna. There they joined other Indians and, under the guidance of New England missionaries, lived industrious and settled lives patterned on those of white farmers. For a while the remaining Indians of the Delaware Valley and the Catskills warned their white neighbors that trouble was coming, and they left for the Susquehanna with the explanation that they were afraid of the people of Esopus and Minisink.[11]

But soon the Indians of New York began talking and acting more aggressively—that was after Joseph Brant and his Iroquois braves paid them a visit. Brant was looked up to as a leader by New York Indians. He was a brother of Molly Brant who had lived with Sir William Johnson and borne his children. (The two were properly married on Sir William's death-bed in 1774.) Brant had been given a white man's education and had served as Sir William's confidential secretary. Now he was an officer in the British Army under Sir William's nephew, Colonel Guy Johnson. It was Brant's job to organize and direct Indian effort in New York toward win-ning the war for the King. Raids on settlements were carefully planned and carried out with the help of local Tories. A trail was laid out leading from the upper Susquehanna to the Delaware Valley and on over the Pine Hill to the Esopus country. It was expected that this trail would be used by Tory sympathizers who wanted to give expression to their resentment against the great Whig landlords of the Hudson Valley and the Catskills by joining the King's forces. Captured grain and cattle could be taken over it to feed the King's men; messengers between British officers and Tory agents might follow it; and it might also be used to pour Indian fighters into the Hudson Valley to join British regulars.

The Whigs fully realized the nature of the threat posed by the British and Indians behind the Catskills working in collaboration with the Tories within the mountains. They destroyed Oghwagha and Coletien. They built a number of forts which it was hoped would command the most direct routes across the mountains. One was at Great Shandaken, and another at Lackawack, both consisting of blockhouses surrounded by stockades. A number of new picket forts[12] were set up using existing houses around which log stockades had been built. At the same time, frontier families in the western parts of the Catskills were being urged to withdraw to the Hudson Valley, not only for their own safety but also to avoid having their crops seized to support British and Indian raiding parties. Many complied, but others remained either out of reluctance to leave the land around which their lives and hopes centered or because they hoped to remain neutral and sell their crops to the highest bidder. A few bold souls left but returned to plant or harvest, and some of them fell victims to Indian raiding parties.

George Washington was well aware of the uneasy nature of the bal-ancing of forces that prevailed in the Catskills. In 1778 he and his generals began making plans to knock out the Indian power behind the mountains, and in the summer of 1779 these plans were carried out. In a well-organized and boldly carried out expedition under Generals Sullivan and James Clin-ton, the flourishing Indian settlements of central New York and the Indians' stocks of food were destroyed and their land blighted. The Indian power was broken forever, but their spirit remained strong. In the spring of 1780 they launched several raids against the Catskills, one of which was to bag Jere-miah Snyder and his son Elias.

The Snyders had not been picked for capture merely at the urging of their Tory neighbors. It was British policy to encourage by every possible means the capturing of leaders among the Whigs. They offered payment for every Whig brought in to their headquarters at Fort Niagara, and the higher a Whig's military or political rank the greater was the reward paid upon his delivery. A Whig who could be persuaded to join the King's Army brought a handsome bonus to the Indian who captured him. Besides, plundering of the Whigs was allowed, and Whig scalps had a nice cash value.

Never had the rewards offered by the British seemed so glittering to New York Indians as they did in the cruel winter of 1779–80. All that winter the snow lay deep and the cold did not relent until the end of March—it was the most severe winter since that of 1740. Thousands of New York Indians who had lost their homes and their stocks of food to the Sullivan-Clinton Whigs huddled outside Fort Niagara where they lived on British bounty, and where many died from diseases caused by crowding and unaccustomed foods. Indian warriors could not wait until spring to seek revenge and profit from the hated Whigs. In February a few set out on snowshoes to begin raiding frontier clearings. On April 7 a raiding party struck Harpersfield near the northwest corner of the Hardenbergh Patent and carried off eleven Whigs who had ventured into the woods to make maple sugar. Rumors of widespread Indian activity reached the Catskills, and Whigs prodded their military leaders to get better protection for the frontier.

Captain Snyder must have known that the Indians were on the prowl that spring. Yet he probably felt safe enough on Saturday May 9 as he and eighteen-year-old Elias began plowing the cornfield that lay to the south of their house. As yet there had been no Indian raids in his vicinity, for the Catskills to the west were a formidable barrier and the country around the Snyder farm was fairly well settled. An Indian raid, if one were to take place, would most likely happen by night when the chance of success would be greater. It seemed safe enough for an unarmed man to do his plowing within sight of his own house. And besides, producing food was just as important as fighting Indians and Tories whether you looked at it from a personal or a patriotic point of view. The harvest of 1779 had not been bountiful, and the long hard winter had cut into stocks of food available for the Whig armies and for civilians. Generals were clamoring for grain and cattle, and prices of both were high. American militiamen, except in the greatest emergencies, were in the habit of taking time from military duties to plow, plant, and harvest. If they allowed their fields to lie idle, their whole war effort would be sure to bog down in famine and death.

What Captain Snyder did not realize as he hitched his horses to the plow that morning was the extent of Indian desperation. The Indians had begun to act as British allies in a halfhearted way, but after the destruction of their home country they were no longer halfhearted. They were ready to strike farther from their bases and to take greater risks in their search for revenge and British gold.

The first hint of danger did not come to the Snyders directly. It came when "the instinct of the horses then harnessed to the plow, denoted danger by wild and fearful looks,"[13] as editor DeWitt phrased it. Jeremiah and Elias looked around and saw three groups of Indians and Tories (with the Tories' faces painted in Indian-fashion) emerging from the woods which surrounded the field on three sides. "On the rear and on the right and left, they were completely beset by a ruthless foe. The manner and appearance of these frightful monsters indicated that their irruption was of an hostile nature. . . ."

Only in the direction of their house were there no enemies to be seen. The captain and Elias raced toward the door as the Indians "raised the savage yell." At this point three armed Tories appeared on the long ridge that rose behind the house. The last possibility of escape for Jeremiah and Elias was cut off. For, to fall back on editor DeWitt's words, the two Whigs were "completely environed." The Tory neighbors who were helping to surround them had a right to smile behind their painted disguises. A hated Whig leader was about to fall into their hands.

24

Captured by Indians

🌳 JEREMIAH and Elias had been working in different parts of the field. Each was quickly surrounded by a knot of Indians and Tories. An Indian named Hoornbeek seized Elias; another known as Runnip or John Renhope captured Jeremiah. At this a fierce squabble arose which came near costing Jeremiah his life and scalp. A custom among raiding Indians gave all rights in a prisoner and the reward he might bring to the man who first laid hands on him. Runnip had barely nosed out a fellow raider, "a villain of short stature and dark visage." Jeremiah was firmly in Runnip's possession but the villain of short stature did not accept the fact without a show of resentment. He suspected that Jeremiah had deliberately favored Runnip, an Esopus Indian whom he may very well have known before the war and from whom he may have expected kind treatment.[1] The short Indian swung his tomahawk at Jeremiah's head. The blow was a glancing one which merely sliced the scalp. Again the short one swung, but this time Runnip parried the blow. Another Indian tried to run Jeremiah through with his spear and Runnip turned the spear aside with his hand. Runnip may have been prompted by a kindly feeling toward Jeremiah, but it is just as likely that he was protecting his interest in a valuable piece of property. For the captain would bring far more cash from the British officers at Fort Niagara if he were delivered alive and complete than if only his dried scalp were presented.

Jeremiah's wife, Catherina, and Elias' six brothers and sisters watched in dismay from the house as their two men were taken prisoner. They fled into the woods behind the house and did their best to hide. Nearby Tory neighbors retreated in order to be out of range of the Snyders' cries for help. A few Whig neighbors had been tipped off in advance by a friendly local Indian known as Nachte John or Night John[2] that a raid would take place. These Whigs prudently hid their belongings and themselves.

The first step in a legendary Indian raid was taking prisoners; the second was looting the house. The Indians took maple sugar, pork, and other easily carried foods which might sustain them on the long trip to Niagara. They also grabbed papers, for the officers at Niagara were often very much interested in such things and sometimes paid well for them. Chests and cupboards were rummaged in a search for money, and good clothing was bundled up. When the Indians and Tories had taken what they wanted from the house and barn, they made ready to burn them down. Here Captain Snyder begged to be allowed to remove some of the family possessions spurned by the Indians, and the Indians gave permission. The British wanted the Indians to terrorize the Whig frontiersmen, yet their officers and Joseph Brant urged the Indians not to commit any more acts of cruelty than they had to. Often enough, legends of Indian captivities tell of Whig lives and property being spared even in the midst of bloodshed, scalping, looting, and burning. It was usually quarrels over the possession of loot or prisoners that gave birth to acts of cruelty.

While the Snyders hurried to save what they could, the Indians waited with growing impatience. They were eager to be off once their mission was accomplished and before the countryside could be aroused and militiamen sent in pursuit. They cut short the Snyders' salvage effort, and set their buildings ablaze. Then Indians, Tory allies, and prisoners set off toward the mountains.

And so the next stage of an Indian captivity of Revolutionary days began. In this case it was the long and sometimes grueling march through the forest toward the British headquarters at Fort Niagara many hundred miles away. As the march began, the youngest Snyder boy, Ephraim, who was nine years old and lame, was taken along by one of the disguised Tories. But he was soon released and sent back to join his mother.

At what seemed a safe distance from the scene of the raid, the whole party paused. The loot was repacked for greater convenience in carrying and the faces of the two captives were painted in accordance with Indian custom. The party headed toward the mountains in single file. William Van Bergen (he was the real or imitation Indian who had tried to spear Jeremiah) led the way as the "pilot" of this part of the expedition. Behind him came the prisoners. Elias was already suffering from sore feet. Jeremiah was allowed by the careless Indians to carry an ax he had snatched from the wreckage of his home. Before long the Indians and whites climbed one of the steep rock ridges that edge the fertile lands at the base of the Catskills. Jeremiah's ax got in his way as he tried to climb, and he handed it to Elias who was perched on the foothold above. Elias was seized by an impulse to put the ax to use by braining the pilot, who was climbing above him. With a shake of his head Jeremiah forbade so rash an act and took the ax back into his own hands again.

The most direct way to head toward Fort Niagara would have been by penetrating the Catskills through either Plattekill or Kaaterskill Clove. But the snow was still melting from the upper heights of the Catskills and the Plattekill and Kaaterskill were swollen and unruly as they tumbled toward the Hudson. The Indians crossed the Kaaterskill at the base of the mountain wall and then took to a trail which moved diagonally up South Mountain. They passed between North and South Lakes on their way to the headwaters of the Schoharie. That night the party camped somewhere in the present town of Hunter.

The Indians and Tories up to this point had been silent and hurried. They had rushed on without pausing to eat or rest. Now that they were beyond the point at which pursuit by Whigs was most likely, they relaxed and talked with their prisoners. During that first anxious day the Snyders had little clue as to what their fate might be. Would they be murdered once the Indians had taken them into the safety of the mountains? Would they reach an Indian settlement and there be made to run the gantlet by Indians eager to avenge the many wrongs visited on their people by the white race? Would they be tortured in the old Indian style before being put to death?

That night in the mountaintop camp Runnip explained that the prisoners were to be taken to Fort Niagara. There they would be delivered to the British and would then be prisoners of war who might be exchanged and returned home before very long. Jeremiah and Elias would be treated well, Runnip said in Dutch. Only if they tried to escape would they be shown no mercy. Some day, Runnip added, their situations might be reversed. He might become the prisoner and the Snyders the captors. For that reason if for no other, he would want to treat them well. Jeremiah and Elias knew that the rest of their family had not been harmed; the Indians had even seen them hiding in the woods near their burning house but had made no attempt to injure them. Catherina Snyder and her children were left destitute, it was true, yet there were plenty of relatives both of Catherina and of Jeremiah who could be trusted to help with food and shelter. The situation of the two captured Snyders began to seem somewhat less grim. That night each slept beside his captor to whom he was attached by a cord so that any attempt to escape might be quickly discovered.

The next day the future became even less grim for the Snyders, for then the Tory members of the raiding party took their share of the Snyder plunder and returned to their houses in the Blue Mountain neighborhood. They were among the "envious and rigid" Tory neighbors of whom Catherina was to write. The Snyders, like many other Indian captives of the Revolution, felt that they had more to fear from these resentful Tories than from the Indians. The leadership of the party was then taken over by Runnip, for he knew well the intricacies of the mountain country over which they were to make their way. On the first day under Runnip's leadership the party reached a cache of food which the Indians had previously prepared along the upper Schoharie. A stock of dried corn and peas had been stored in a hemlock tree on a platform raised about ten feet from the ground. Shelters of hemlock boughs and hemlock beds were made ready against the rain that had begun to fall. The Indians and their prisoners remained in their shelters until Tuesday morning when the sky cleared.

During this break in their toil, the Indians made up for lost meals by eating with abandon. "Nine hungry hogs" couldn't have eaten more than did the nine Indian captors, so Jeremiah was later to tell editor DeWitt. Runnip sat by the fire beside the dripping shelter and leisurely sorted the papers he had taken from the Snyder house. The little ones he tossed into the flames as valueless, for he could not read. He kept the larger ones including Jeremiah's commissions as lieutenant and captain in the Ulster militia. And Jeremiah must have watched with some satisfaction, for the little papers contained information about the defenses of the Catskills which the British officers at Fort Niagara would have been glad to see. The papers saved by Runnip in that mountaintop shelter were to have a curious fate. They passed from hand to hand and at last ended up in the British Museum where they are said to be still filed away.[3]

New York Indians traveled by water whenever possible as it was much easier than jogging along on foot. That was why Runnip's band took their prisoners over a roundabout route to reach Fort Niagara—they wanted to take advantage of every possible waterway. Water travel within the Catskills was out of the question, for the streams were too small and too broken by falls and rapids. But once the East Branch of the Delaware was reached after a day's journey from the cache in the hemlocks, then pleasant gliding down the swollen stream became possible. There was no canoe at hand, but that did not trouble the Indians. Among them was an aging tribesman known as Shank's Ben. He was a fearful figure to white eyes, being well over six feet tall and with a face disfigured by exploding gunpowder.[4] During the French and Indian War he had been an able frontier raider; now he was too far gone in years to lead a raiding party. Yet he went on the warpath as a humble member and put his skill to use whenever possible. It was old Shank's Ben who took charge of making a canoe. Jeremiah Snyder, a carpenter as well as a farmer, watched the canoe making with interest and gave a detailed report on it to Charles DeWitt. First, said Snyder, the bark was taken from an elm tree—the bark would slip easily in that month of June. The rough outside of the bark was cut away and the pliable remainder stretched over a framework of slender branches. The bark had been scraped thin at the bow and stern and this thin part was folded over to make tight joints fore and aft. A pulp of pounded elm bark was used to calk the craft, and it was ready to float away downstream with the aid of paddles made of split ash. The Indians and prisoners, carrying the packs each man had been assigned, took their places in the canoe. But at the end of three miles a more substantial canoe dug out of the trunk of a tree was sighted on the shore. It was the kind to which Esopus Indians were accustomed and it was without any obvious owner. The men and packs were shifted to the new canoe and the voyage downstream continued.

That day the eleven men covered some twenty-four miles in their canoe and by nightfall went ashore at "Middagh's Place" at the mouth of the Beaverkill. This was a clearing on the farm leased by John and Jacob Middagh in 1771 from Robert Livingston. By this time Jacob had been hanged along with Jacob Rose, and John had fled to Canada. The Indians found a cache of two bushels of musty corn on the Middagh place and the men, Indian and white, feasted on it as best they could. The next day Runnip's men left their canoe at the point of juncture of the East and West branches of the Delaware and took to the woods again on foot. Partly by way of the valleys of the Susquehanna, the Chemung, and the Genesee rivers, the Indians moved on toward Niagara. A canoe they put together from the bark of a chestnut tree gave them and their prisoners another taste of easy traveling—this was on the Susquehanna. All the time Jeremiah kept his eyes and ears open and absorbed details of Indian life and the Indians' wilderness ways.

The memory of an old man or woman is often an amazingly supple instrument for recapturing details of the distant past. It may falter when called upon to recall the precise location of a pair of spectacles or the first name of a next-door neighbor, but when it is required to supply crisp little details of the childhood or the high tide of adulthood of its owner, it can pour out its stored treasures with all the exuberance of a spring freshet. It was so with Jeremiah Snyder as he answered the questions of editor DeWitt. He recalled, almost as if he had eaten them the day before, the meals provided on his captive march. Besides the suppawn or cornmeal mush, and the boiled peas which accompanied it, there was salt pork taken from Jeremiah's own house. Later an elk was shot and eaten, and a deer caught and already chewed by wolves was gratefully consumed. The muskrats which the Indians caught and ate with pleasure were not for the Snyders. The food conditioning to which their society subjected them made muskrats taboo. Runnip fell ill of a fever and recovered after eating a boiled rattlesnake. Jeremiah was obviously impressed by this bit of wilderness medical wisdom. He was impressed, too, by the fact that while the Indians did not use salt, they carried some for the benefit of their prisoners.

All sorts of homely details of Indian ways floated to the surface of Jeremiah's consciousness as he talked with DeWitt. The Indian who had tried to spear him turned barber later, the old man recalled, and he shaved the captives twice a week with a European razor. His face and that of Elias were painted in Indian style and a stinging liquid was put into their eyes to give them the "fiery cast" suited to members—and prisoners—of an Indian war party. Most of the long trip passed in silence occasionally broken by bursts of speech in Dutch from Runnip who once confided to Jeremiah some of his plans for future raids on the frontiers of the Catskills.

Now and then Runnip's men met other wanderers in the forest, among whom were two Tory neighbors of the Snyders. One was eager for news of friends back home, but the other maintained a disdainful silence. In the Genesee country an attractive white woman married to an Indian was glad to talk with the Snyders. She was a captive of the days of the French and Indian War and had become reconciled to life as an Indian wife and mother. In crossing the trail of the Sullivan-Clinton expedition of the year before, the Snyders saw traces of that devastating event. Their Indian captors pointed out the graves of Whig soldiers killed by Indians, and a lonely horse rejoiced at seeing them. He had strayed from the Sullivan-Clinton forces and managed to survive the fearfully hard winter on his own.

The days of weary marching on aching feet and the alternation of overeating when food was available and starving when it was not neared an end as the war party came within sight of the stone walls of Fort Niagara. Runnip led the way through the straggling settlement of displaced Indians who had taken refuge outside the walls of the fort. When these Indians tried to make the prisoners run the gantlet, Runnip forbade it and guarded the Snyders into the safety—as it then seemed—of the fort.

25

Escape

✤ THE NARRATIVE of Jeremiah shows that once he and Elias had passed through an early stage of despair, they rallied and even managed to extract a good deal of enjoyment from their journey to Fort Niagara. To men of their day and to many of our own, there is a magic about the wilderness and the Indians who were once its masters. To watch the Indians finding their way to their objectives through mazes of trees and streams, to come to trust them to find food even when none is visible to a white man's eye, and to admire the skill with which they improvised tools and utensils from the raw materials of the woods helped many a captive look back on his weary march through the woods as something of an education.

The two Snyders could not have seen the walls of Fort Niagara appearing without apprehension mingled with relief. In war each side finds it to its advantage to magnify the hardships to be endured by those of their men who may be captured as this tends to discourage men from surrendering. Whigs and Tories alike had circulated rumors of the horrors of prison life among their enemies, and the Snyders could not have looked forward to exchanging their sunny wilderness existence for the squalor of a dark prison room. Once inside the fort they were subjected to an ordeal of questioning by British officers who hoped to extract—especially from Captain Jeremiah—useful information about the Whig plans and strength. Jeremiah told DeWitt that he had been properly evasive, yet in the clash of opposing intelligences which lay beneath the surface of such interrogations, he may have given away more than he realized.

The British officers in their imposing uniforms were not the only questioners to assail the captain. He and Elias were locked up in the fort's guardhouse. There they were visited by the man who was, of all the enemy, most hated and feared by the people of the Catskills. He was Joseph Brant.

Brant was tall and faced the world with a bold and confident air. When he questioned the Snyders, he was dressed in a mixture of British and Indian military haberdashery: a green British jacket with silver epaulets; a blue and red Indian blanket; beaded moccasins; and a European hat of black felt adorned with lace. But Jeremiah saw Brant as something very different from this elegant and intelligent straddler of two worlds. Among the Catskills and in all the region around, Brant's very name made people shudder and hasten to bar doors and windows, for he represented to these people all that was cruel in the Indian character. He was a killer of babies in their cradles, a scalper of white men and women; his was the cunning and ruthless mind which planned murderous raids on the frontiers of the Catskills. Some said that Brant had caused a small log fort to be built high in the Catskills on the southeastern slope of Round Top Mountain near the head of Plattekill Clove, but others claimed that the fort dated back to the French and Indian War.[1] From this observation post, they said, Brant could look out over the settlements lying beneath the Catskills and personally enjoy the burning, scalping, and looting of his warriors and their Tory friends. Nearly all this was nonsense born of the human complusion to oversimplify matters by wrapping such social evils as war in human garments—the scarecrows that result are easy to hate. Actually Brant had lost most of his Indian characteristics at Dr. Wheelock's school in New Hampshire at which he had been a prize student. He had all the desire to behave humanely which was taught in European culture—and was sometimes practiced. He urged his Indian warriors to avoid needless cruelty, yet it was his fate to become the embodiment in Whig eyes of all that was bloodthirsty and wicked.

It was the policy at Fort Niagara to make a try at enlisting all brisk young Whigs in the British forces. That was why when Brant questioned the Snyders he took pains to treat Elias gently. "You are young and I pity you," he said to Elias, and then, pointing a finger at Captain Jeremiah, "but for that old Villain I have no pity." But if Brant was harsh in his attitude toward Jeremiah, there were others at the fort who made up for it in kindness. An old neighbor of the Snyders, now a sergeant in the King's army, spoke pleasantly and gave the two prisoners hats to replace the ones snatched from their heads by some Indian squaws whom they had met on the Genesee Flats. Another visitor was a surprising one: Tory tinsmith John Burch, now driven out of his East Branch estate with the loss of his blooded horses, his curricles, his tinsmith's tools, his mahogany furniture, and all the other movables he had hastily sent from Albany. Burch had known and respected Jeremiah's successful sloop-sailing brother Benjamin, and for this reason he was kindness itself. Burch had been found unfit for active duty when he joined the British forces, which was why he was doing his best to help the King by serving as Indian storekeeper at Fort Niagara. It was his job to dole out supplies to His Majesty's Indian allies. As a little token of esteem for brother Benjamin, he sent a present of seven pounds of sugar and one pound of tea to the Snyders after they had been moved to the hold of a naval vessel on Lake Ontario. The Indians, it was safe to assume, would never miss this slight subtraction from the royal bounty intended for them. From their floating prison the Snyders were moved on to a more stable one at Montreal.

The fate of the prisoners taken by both Whigs and Tories during the Revolution was indeed hard. Captured men were crammed into tight and filthy quarters to which they were heartily welcomed by regiments of lice and bedbugs. Food was meager and often so revolting as to be past eating. During the winters there was scant or no provision for heating, and prison guards were often surly ruffians. Large numbers of potential fighting men were out of circulation in prisons, and this stimulated both sides to try to effect exchanges. But here formidable difficulties arose.

The British did not regard the Whig soldiers as the equals of their men—in conventional British eyes they were rebels and therefore traitors. That was why a basis for exchange was hard to arrive at. In the case of officers like Captain Jeremiah Snyder the situation was even more discouraging. George Washington very wisely insisted that one of his captains or majors who had been a butcher, a farmer, or a carpenter in private life be exchanged on an equal basis with their British opposite numbers—even when these were the sons of peers. The British could not swallow this leveling procedure and negotiations for exchanges of prisoners bogged down with each side charging the other with bad faith. As the numbers of prisoners increased, prison rooms which had been a tight fit for ten men managed to hold twenty and even forty.

Rumors of impending exchanges helped sustain the hopes of both prisoners and their families. In February 1781 a rumor of this sort came to the ears of Jeremiah's wife, Catherina, and prompted her to send an appeal to Governor Clinton, to present her "Distressed case before you."[2]

"Doubtless you have heard that my Husband Capt. Jeremiah Snyder and my son, were taken Captives by the Enemy in May last past, and burnt down my house and all my household goods, carreyed of or consumed in the flames, and now my children & self live upon the Benevolence of my good neighbors and relations which are good stanch whigs. . . ." Catherina asked that Jeremiah and Elias be included among the prisoners to be exchanged. A long list of friends added their signatures or marks to her own. But Catherina's petition had no effect.

As the crowding worsened and prisoners died or lay ill, an old military device was more and more often resorted to. Men were allowed limited freedom in return for their pledge or "parole" to make no attempt to escape. Such men took up residence—at their own expense—among the people living in the vicinity of their prisons. Many worked at their former trades or helped plant and harvest crops. So in the summer of 1782, Jeremiah and Elias Snyder gave their parole and were permitted to exchange the dirt and crowding of the great gray prison known as the Provost in Montreal for warm and clean farmhouse rooms nearby in St. Rosa on the Isle de Jesus. Jeremiah's skill as a carpenter now served him well and he was able to earn reasonably good wages building houses.

Life had become pleasanter for the two prisoners but it had not become pleasant enough—freedom to return home would be very much better. Talk of escape began to be indulged in as the paroled prisoners met on the Isle de Jesus. They had all given their solemn pledge not to escape, and yet, they wondered, if they could somehow manage to do so. The system of paroling prisoners of war had never worked well and it seldom worked less efficiently than it did during the Revolution. For it was founded in part on Old World ideas of personal honor which prevailed to some extent among the better sort. In America where members of the better sort were scarce, such notions had small currency. In New York, with its obsession with commerce and money-making, most men were guided by what they could get away with rather than by a code of personal honor. It was no wonder then that violations of parole were common during the days of the Revolution or that the men far from home among the French-speaking inhabitants of the Isle de Jesus should feel little compunction over violating their parole.

Yet there was another side, and a practical one, to the parole system. When a man violated his parole by making his escape, those remaining behind suffered. For their period of relative freedom came to an end, and they were thrown back in prison. In 1779 George Washington wrote that "A conduct of this kind, so ignominious to the individuals themselves, so dishonorable to their country and to the service in which they have been engaged, and so injurious to those gentlemen, who were associated with them in their misfortune, but preserved their honor, demands that every

measure be taken to deprive them of the benefit of their delin-
quency. . . ."³ Parole violators, Washington wrote, would be returned to
the enemy especially because their conduct was a factor in making the
exchange of prisoners so difficult.

When old Jeremiah told his tale to editor DeWitt in 1827, he felt
obliged to justify his violation of parole. Elias had been determined to
escape, he said. As for him, he had been unwilling, at first. He was
(although he did not bring up this point) the ranking officer of the group
and, therefore, responsible for holding the enlisted men with whom he
was in contact to observance of the military code. Finally, Elias, after much
pleading, had declared that whether his father approved and went with
him or not he would try to escape. His mind was made up. Here Jeremiah's
ethical scruples weakened.

It is easy enough to imagine old Jeremiah squirming a bit in his chair
as he tried to make his behavior understandable to editor DeWitt. Finally
he came out with what he regarded as the clincher. The parole agreement
was a two-way thing, and in his opinion the Tories had already violated it
thereby rendering it void. For when Sir John Johnson, colonel of the Royal
Greens, visited the Isle de Jesus in December 1781, the military authorities
of the place had insisted that the Snyders and their fellow parolees remain
within the houses in which they were quartered in order that Sir John
be spared the irritating sight of Whig prisoners going about at large. For
Sir John was among the most fiery of Tories. The state of New York
had attainted him and taken away the immense estates he had inherited
from Sir William. His regiment was engaged in harrying the Whig
frontiers and he was hated by the Whigs almost as deeply as was Joseph
Brant. In return, his fury at the sight of a Whig was said to be monumental.
For three days the Snyders had been obliged to keep out of Sir John's
sight. This, Jeremiah told DeWitt, constituted a violation of the parole
agreement, so thereafter he was free to escape if he chose.

The ethics behind Jeremiah's decision are still misty, but once the
decision to escape had been made, all mistiness was dispersed in a flurry
of guarded activity. Clothing and food had to be brought together without
arousing suspicion. The secret of the impending attempt to escape had to
be kept from fellow Whigs who were not to become members of the
little escaping club. Three compasses were bought. (The Whigs pretended
that they didn't know what they were and wanted them merely as curiosities.) Young Elias packed a treasured possession. It was one volume of
an English translation of the letters of the younger Pliny—a fellow prisoner
in the Provost had stolen both volumes somewhere and given them to the

Snyders. Pliny's polished and very literary letters were the only reading matter available to the Snyders during their imprisonment. Their information about Roman treatment of early Christians must have interested them more than the details of Roman provincial administration and upper-class life in which the letters abound.

The escape got off in fine style. It was the tenth of September and the night was dark and rainy. While the pious family with whom they were billeted were at evening prayers, the two Snyders left the house through a window and joined the three other men who were to be their fellow adventurers. One was a Connecticut Yankee, another a Pennsylvanian, and the third the Snyders' Catskill neighbor Anthony Abeel. Abeel and his father had been captured by an Indian-Tory band in much the same way as the Snyders, but a year later. The elder Abeel had been released and sent home because of his age.[4]

Montreal and the Isle de Jesus to the north are surrounded by broad bands of water, some of it tricky to navigate. The escaping men of the Isle de Jesus had to cross a great deal of this water in order to begin their march homeward. It was necessary, first of all, to find a boat. They found two small ones and lashed them together, then, using paddles they had brought with them, they set out on the most perilous part of their attempt. In spite of darkness, the rapids they had to struggle against, and the ever-present fear of pursuit, by dawn the five men had made good progress. They drew up their boats in a patch of tall grass where they hoped they would be concealed, and spent the day shivering in their wet clothes. Peeping cautiously through the grass that day, Jeremiah remembered, he had seen boats passing and even heard the voices of the boatmen. At dusk they put their boats in the water and paddled to Pointe au Tremble where they crossed the St. Lawrence and abandoned their crafts.

Safe on the homeward side of the great river, the Snyders had good reason to feel jubilant. There was one small tributary of the St. Lawrence still to cross—they did it in a borrowed canoe—and then only hundreds of miles of Tory country and savage wilderness would lie between them and their homes. They pushed ahead, sleeping as well as they could by day behind rocks and hedges and traveling through the night. Taking the most direct route was out of the question, for Ethan Allen and his associates in patriotism and land jobbery had declared the New Hampshire grants the independent nation of Vermont. Any Yorker setting foot on the soil of the new state would be treated harshly. The food supplies the men had started out with dwindled. They began living as well as they could on the country, and put to use their wood lore—learned perhaps from Runnip and his friends—and lived on leaves and roots such as that of the aralia known as spignet. Tracts of boggy wilderness snared them and tore their clothing and damaged their shoes. They were haggard and tattered when they emerged at the headwaters of the Connecticut River near Coos in New Hampshire. Settlers welcomed them and gave up their scanty stocks of food to the starving men. After days of nothing but wild roots they gorged on cornmeal pudding and moose pie. Soon military authority in the shape of a militia general gave the Snyders and their companions shoes and clothing, and what was just as important—identification papers. The escaped men were questioned closely about what they had observed in Canada. For although the war was nearing its end, a rumor that the British were preparing a massive invasion from the north was alarming many Americans. Because Jeremiah was an officer, he was given a horse on which to ride homeward. The rest of the party made their way on foot.

Jeremiah found that his farm was still there when he returned. A farm, before the bulldozer and atom bomb were invented, was a hard thing to destroy even in the madness of war. Today the shape of the farm to which Jeremiah brought back his reassembled family in 1782 is clearly visible lying across the undulating landscape at the foot of Plattekill Mountain. Hard wear has robbed the soil of its fertility and exposed the land's stony bones. On the field which was the scene of the Snyders' captivity, heaps of stones gathered together as the soil flowed away serve as monuments to the Snyders—and to the wastefulness of old-time American farming methods. The field is no longer part of the kind of farm Jeremiah Snyder knew; it is now one of the pastures of a riding school on which horse-lovers converge to spend weekends or vacations riding trails through the woods or taking lessons in advanced horsemanship. Jeremiah's stone-house, swollen by later frame additions, is in use as the school's headquarters, and visitors are taken on tours of its massive cellars to admire Jeremiah's workmanship in stone and to see the cool underground room where Catherina skimmed pans of milk and churned her cows' cream into butter.

Jeremiah and Elias do not lie with numerous other Snyders in the little cemetery in a pine grove near the house. For sometime in the 1790s, an exodus of Snyders took place from the neighborhood under Plattekill Mountain. Tory brother Zechariah had come back to his own farm from Nova Scotia but he soon left for New Jersey. In 1793, Elias married a neighbor's daughter and set up his own household, and Jeremiah took off for Rensselaerville in Albany County where he spent the rest of his life. Brother Abraham alone represents the eleven sons of Martin Snyder in the pine-shadowed cemetery on Jeremiah's former farm. There is no local tradition to explain why Jeremiah and most of his brothers left the Blue Mountain neighborhood. It may well be that the animosities roused by the tensions of the Revolution among the tenant farmers of the Catskills made him feel uncomfortable at his old stand. For in many parts of the Catskills, obscure old suspicions and hatreds lingered on for many years, setting neighbor against neighbor and brother against brother.

But while old Jeremiah Snyder left Blue Mountain he has not been forgotten on his old farm—or was not until recently. In a different form he is still there. The owners of the riding school have named one of their finest horses in his honor.[5] This Jeremiah Snyder of our own times sometimes crops the grass in the very field on which the Jeremiah of old and his son were captured. And sometimes he raises his head and looks westward—with apparent thoughtfulness—at the Catskills across which the Jeremiah of Revolutionary days was taken on his long journey to a British prison.

NOTE: Since the preceding three paragraphs were written, the old Snyder farm has changed hands. The house was burned and the old cellars disappeared under concrete. The horse named for Captain Snyder has left not even a memory in the neighborhood. The farm has ceased being a riding school. The little cemetery remains unchanged on the ridge above the house.

26

The Ghost of
General Bradstreet Walks

✤　　THE ENDING of the American Revolution sent a wave of human energy dashing against the Catskills. First to act upon the mountains were prewar settlers like Jeremiah Snyder who had been displaced by war and were eager to return to their clearings in the beech and hemlock forests. A few found their cabins unharmed except where bark roofs leaked or clay-and-stick chimneys had begun to come apart. Most stepped into their old clearings to see nothing more than a heap of blackened logs in the midst of a snarl of blackberry bushes where berry-loving bears fed in August and rattlesnakes lazily took the sun. Many returned settlers hastened to dig up the household and farm gear they had buried between the stumps of their fields when rumors of Indian raids passed from clearing to clearing and sent them flying to the settlements along the Hudson River. Some of the hiding places of frontier tools managed to escape finding, and thus gave rise to legends of buried treasures whose brass kettles and wooden ox yokes became transmuted in gullible minds to coined gold and silver.

As men, women, children, their oxen, and their dogs and cats came back to the Catskills, George Washington was chief man of the United States, and King George's reign was quickly becoming part of the fabulous past. Congress had already displaced Parliament, and the noble words of the Declaration of Independence had let the world know that a new nation had been born on the American continent—a nation with enlarged concepts of human freedom and dignity. Yet among the Catskills life went on very much as if King George still reigned. For the framers of the constitution under which the state of New York was governed were mostly rich and wellborn men who had not only a passion for enlarging human freedom but a desire to make sure that they themselves would continue to enjoy an enlarged freedom to own vast landed estates and profitable businesses, and to hold political and judicial offices. In order to exclude the poor from making their democratic notions felt, a man was not allowed to vote unless he owned a specified amount of property. Human slavery continued, and the Old World system of land tenure which had long prevailed in the Hudson Valley and among the Catskills was allowed to remain in effect much as it had under King George. No bill of rights was included in the state constitution to protect minorities and the poor. Chancellor Robert R. Livingston, who was the largest of all the landholders of the Catskills and who had played an important part in drawing up the state's constitution, always spoke of the document in terms of the greatest satisfaction. And well he might, for it effectively safeguarded his land interests and his privileged social position. But there was one thing the constitution could not do for the chancellor and his fellow proprietors of the Hardenbergh Patent—it could not lay the ghost of Major General John Bradstreet. And the general's ghost was once again abroad among the mountains.

All through the years of war the Bradstreet claim had lain dormant. And it might well have remained dormant forever had it not been for a very close friend of the general who revived it once the war had definitely ended. This good friend was General Philip Schuyler of Albany. Schuyler had been born into a family that ranked among the very first of the better sort by reason of its large landholdings and its relationships by blood or marriage to the other landholding families of New York. In his early twenties Schuyler had established a close tie with Bradstreet, serving first as his secretary and later as one of his officers. Bradstreet was known to his contemporaries as a man with a remarkable knack at picking up little profits on the side in the course of his military duties.[1] Schuyler became his partner in many of these enterprises, and the Bradstreet and Schuyler families came to live on terms of close and profitable intimacy. When Schuyler was in Europe in 1762, in part to take care of business matters for Bradstreet, Colonel Bradstreet, as he then was, took care of the construction of Schuyler's fine Georgian mansion, The Pastures. The building is now a museum and an unconscious monument to the close relations between two very acquisitive men.

Under Bradstreet's will, Mrs. Schuyler received the general's horses and carriage; her son John Bradstreet Schuyler received land; a large debt owed by Philip was canceled and he was named executor of the will. It was in his capacity as executor that he revived the Bradstreet claim to three hundred thousand acres of New York State land, including all the lands between the two branches of the Delaware.[2] Agatha Bradstreet, the general's daughter, and her husband, Charles John Evans, took over from Schuyler and vigorously pushed their claim. The battle that followed involved men and women on every level of New York State society, benefited countless members of the state bar, set lawyers and surveyors scurrying about the Catskills as never before to rummage among collections of old records and maps. For the big landholders in the Hardenbergh Patent were apprehensive, and Bradstreet's heirs, encouraged by General Schuyler's aid, were acting very cheerfully indeed.[3]

Among the settlers themselves there were fewer signs of the agitation which the revival of the Bradstreet claim had aroused in the better sort. Prewar settlers continued to return to the clearings created by their own hard work, and a scattering of new people moved in. But these people were likely to have the kind of recklessness that comes to those unburdened by material possessions. They were willing to take a chance on losing the scanty "improvements" they proposed making. There was no great risk involved if a man squatted at a promising location or signed a lease with Chancellor Livingston's agent, William Cockburn. If Cockburn rode into a squatter's clearing some day and brought up any nonsense about paying rent, all a man had to do was to vanish with his family, his kettle, his ax, and his ox. People poured into the Hardenbergh Patent in the 1780s and poured out again like water going in and out of a leaky millpond.[4] They paid little attention to the cloud that Judge Livingston had glimpsed hanging over the Catskills and that was now hanging lower than ever. Rumors of the preparations for the Bradstreet hearings were handed on from settler to settler but aroused little interest. The descendants of the old-time mountain people have a phrase they use to show that they are not easily diverted from their daily labor by irrelevancies. When they are told of any noisy going-on in the world outside the limits of the horizon line of their own valley, they are likely to say, "Well, that don't bother my time none."[5] As the preliminaries to the hearings of the Bradstreet claim went forward, the settlers remained quite unruffled. For the great Bradstreet claim hardly bothered their time at all. It was only the old-timers among them who were stirred by the controversy; they found themselves in demand as witnesses by agents for both sides. And they found it a very pleasant situation to be in.

The arguments of both Bradstreeters and Hardenberghers were based on Indian deeds, petitions to royal governors, old surveys and similar documents. But these were buttressed by testimony relating to place names—the names of the many branches of the upper Delaware River which carry off the water falling on the western Catskills to be delivered, after many turnings and tumblings, to Delaware Bay. Which one of the upper branches was the rightful northwestern boundary of the Hardenbergh Patent? Was it the West Branch rising in Lake Utsayantha, or the East Branch which was born in the narrow gorge north of Roxbury? Or was it the Bushkill which helped drain great Slide Mountain? Was it the Beaverkill or even the Neversink?

Each successive Indian deed and each petition to Lord Cornbury in the cradle days of the Great Patent had described the boundaries of the prospective patent in different terms. The confusion that was created seemed made to order to give the patent's proprietors license to expand their acreage almost at will. It may very well have been intended to do just that. They had only to follow the example of Robert Livingston, the great-grandfather of Chancellor Robert R. Old Robert had increased the lands upon which his manor was to be erected from a reasonably honest 2600 acres to 160,000 by a cunning manipulation of boundary lines. Jacob Rutsen and Johannis Hardenbergh had described the patent they were hoping for as "a small tract of vacant unimproved land"[6] and at first it probably was exactly that. But the patent's proprietors had pushed outward year after year, accumulating fresh Indian deeds to cover up their aggression as they went along. By the time the patent was divided in accordance with Ebeneezer Wooster's survey, it extended all the way to the West Branch of the Delaware River.

The original Indian deeds had given "the fish Creek River or kill to the northwest of the Marbletown bounds"[7] as one of the patent's boundaries. As the Bradstreet hearings got under way both in the 1770s and in 1785 and 1786, the central question became just which stream was meant by the "fish Creek River or kill." The Bradstreeters argued that it was the Neversink or at most the East Branch of the Delaware, then known as the Papakunk or Pepacton River. The Hardenberghers were clamorous in claiming the West Branch. A corollary to the main question arose. The patent issued by Queen Anne in 1708 had described the northwestern boundary in a new way—as "the fish Kill or River and so on to the head thereof." The corollary was, just where was the head of the Fish Kill?

The stakes of the dispute were high. For the Hardenberghers, they were nothing less than the soundness of their title to their entire patent. For the Bradstreeters, they were three hundred thousand acres of land. That was why both sides poured a vast amount of legal skill and effort into the contest. Back in the prewar days the same questions had been worked over. Then the problem of locating old records had been most important. Judge Livingston had sent an agent to the Oquaga Indians to get documents

which belonged in the public records but which were in the Indians'
possession. He got his records. Bradstreet's lawyers got wind of this triumph
and, since they had sought in vain for these records in the provincial
archives (they were the originals of Indian deeds), demanded to be allowed
to see them. Livingston had refused (as any lawyer would), until he was
ordered to show them by the governor's council. In the 1770s all obtainable
old records having a bearing on the title to the Hardenbergh Patent had
been unearthed and put on record. The governor and his council had
considered the evidence and then side-stepped making a decision. Now the
old documentary evidence was again brought forward to bolster the new
claim or to pile up weight against it. But all this took second place to the
endless wrangles over Indian place names. Indian names had come up in
the first hearing of the Bradstreet claim. Now they took on a vastly greater
importance.

From the earliest days of settlement, Indian place names had only one
overriding value in the Hudson Valley. They could be manipulated and
falsified and misinterpreted in order to enlarge royal grants of land whose
boundaries they defined. Few white men had any notion of how Indians
arrived at the names by which they referred to specific places in the Province of New York. The details of the structure and operation of Indian
society, the Indians' myths and their religious beliefs were of no interest to
the invading whites because no cash profit could be derived from studying
them. Only the Moravian missionaries with their notions of the brotherhood
of all men had taken an interest in the customs and language of the
Indians of New York. But because the Moravians treated the Indians with
love and respect, they were driven from the province as enemies to the
white man's way of life before they had time to set down in writing details
of the language and ways of living of the Algonkian Indians of the Hudson
Valley. That was why the prolonged wrangling over Indian place names,
which marked the Bradstreet hearings, was carried on in an atmosphere of
the murkiest kind of ignorance. Both Bradstreeters and Hardenberghers
assumed that Indians gave names to places in exactly the same way that
Europeans did. But this was far from being the fact.

The Indians never used the kind of place names we call proper names.
The names they applied to places were descriptive ones which might easily
change from time to time or be applied to a multitude of places.

One New Yorker very clearly understood the limitations of Indian
place names. He was Cadwallader Colden, who died in 1774. In 1732
Colden wrote an incisive report on the ways in which land was granted and
held in New York. The report had been addressed to incoming Governor

Cosby. Twenty years later Colden sadly noted that Cosby had never read it. Colden was as acquisitive as any man of his time, yet his acquisitiveness did not prevent him from using his first-rate mind in scientific explorations and speculations and in observing Indian customs with a keen eye. In his unread report Colden had set down the facts about Indian place names and the misuse of these names by whites. "There being no previous Survey to the Grants," wrote Colden, "their Boundaries are generally expressed with much uncertainty, By the Indian names of Brooks, Rivulets, Hills, Ponds, Falls of water etc. which were and are known to very few Christians, and which adds to this uncertainty is, that such names as are in these Grants taken to be the proper name of a Brook, Hill, or Fall of water etc. in the Indian language signifies only a Large Brook or broad Brook, or small Br^k, or high Hill, or only a Hill or fall of water in general, so that the Indians shew many places by the same name Brooks and Rivers have different names with the Indians, at different places and often change their names, they taking their names often from the abode of some Indian near the place where it is so called. This has given room to some to explain and enlarge their Grants according to their own inclinations by putting the names mentioned in their Grants in what place or part of the country they please, of which I can give some particular instances where the claims of some have increased many miles, in a few years, and this they commonly do, by taking some Indians, in a Publick manner, to shew such places as they name to them, and it is too well known that an Indian will shew any place by any name you please, for the small reward of a Blanket or a Bottle of Rum; and the names I observed, being common names in the Indian language, and not proper ones as they are understood to be in English, gives more room to these Frauds."[8]

Preparations for the postwar phase of the Bradstreet-Hardenbergh battle went forward in 1785 as if Colden's report had never been written. Warriors on both sides seemed to be spellbound into ignorance of the simple truths of Indian ways of naming places, and to assume that European ideas about place names had prevailed. More than a century earlier, men had ransacked the Catskills for their fabled veins of gold or silver. Now they rummaged among the mountains for old-timers who claimed to be experts at locating another kind of treasure—the names by which the Indians of old had referred to features of the Catskill landscape and especially to its streams. Tottering pioneers were tracked down in their clearings and their memories were judiciously stimulated by Bradstreet or Hardenbergh agents until floods of old Indian names tumbled from their lips before witnesses and were written down. Some were treated to trips to New York in order that they might give their testimony in person. Two rival groups of these backwoods witnesses once traveled down the Hudson on the same sloop and an angry dispute took place.

The shrewd Indian traders of the mountains also turned witnesses and made affidavits or were treated to trips to New York. Their testimony was in demand, for of all white men in the region, they were the closest to the Indians and they could speak the Indians' language.

27

A Telling of Fish Stories

✤ THE INDIAN TRADERS, no matter how well they knew their way around among the verbs and nouns of Indian dialects, were unable to agree. Half of them—the Bradstreet half—were convinced that the East Branch of the Delaware was the outermost limit of the Hardenbergh Patent. The Hardenbergh half were equally certain that the patent extended all the way to the West Branch. This was exactly what any sensible man might have expected. But in addition there were more substantial grounds for disagreement, for the Delaware is a river of contradiction and mystery.

The lower Delaware is an estuary which merges with Delaware Bay in so subtle a way that no man can say where the river ends and the bay begins. The upper part is even more confusing, for it is not composed of a single well-marked major channel with tributaries joining it in the usual way. Instead, a multitude of rambling streams flow together in ways that make it impossible for the human mind to arrange them in order of their importance. Today it is a simple matter for a man who lives within the watershed of the upper Delaware to argue that the Delaware begins at the source of almost any stream he chooses to name. The Beaverkill, the Willowemoc, the East and West branches, the Neversink, and a dozen ponds of the size of Lake Utsayantha or Mayham's—each of these has a fair amount of right to be considered as the source of the Delaware. Some practical people deny that the Delaware has any true source at all but say it begins as a co-operative venture in which many streams share. These people say that the Delaware proper begins at Hancock, once known as the Forks of the Delaware, because there the river is assembled from the waters of many streams collected and delivered by the East and West branches.[1]

It was easy enough for kindly Bradstreet or Hardenbergh agents to track down as many witnesses as they chose, each one of whom would be delighted to expound his own theory as to which stream was "the right Fishkill." Every stream in the western Catskills was in the running for the honor and each had its set of evidence. Every stream contained fish and therefore must have been referred to by the Dutch as a "Viskil," for the Dutch shared the Indians' leaning toward giving landscape features descriptive names which stemmed from their practical uses.[2]

"Peter Helm of Mamacoton in Ulster County aged fifty six years" was a typical witness who reminisced in an affidavit for the Bradstreet side.[3] Peter was well qualified. Not only had he been an Indian trader but his father, Michael, had traded with the Indians before him. (Michael had ended up by being killed and scalped by his customers.) Peter "spoke the Indian language from being a boy," and he swore that the "Weelewaugh-mack"—we know it today under the name of the Willowemoc, as a branch of the Beaverkill and not as the main stream—was a dividing line between the lands of the "Paupacton" and the Cochecton Indians who lived to the southeast of the river. The Indians "who frequented his Father's House" had told Peter that the Pepacton Indians owned the lands to the east of the Pepacton or East Branch. The lands between the two branches, the Indians said, belonged to the Mohawks and so were not included in any purchase of Johannis Hardenbergh and Company who dealt only with the Algonkian people. The West Branch, Peter stated, was known to the Indians as the Cookhouse Hacka Sepus. Here Peter adventured into etymology: "Cookhouse is in English an owl; Hacka, land; and Sepus, a river."

In Peter's opinion the Weelewaughwemack was larger than either the East or West branches and "always since his remembrance [it] carried its name amongst the native Indians to the junction of its waters with Paupacton Branch of the Delaware." Other witnesses agreed with Peter, if with many variations, but the Hardenberghers too had their innings. Their witnesses swore that they were skilled in the Indian language and that they had always been informed that the West Branch of the Delaware was the larger by far, that it was known to whites as the Fishkill and to the ancient Indians as the Lamas Sepos, which means the same thing, for Lamas is a corrupt form of Namas which is the Algonkian word for fish, and Sepos, or Sepus, means river. This name appears nowhere in the old records of the Catskills. It makes its first and only appearance in the testimony in the Bradstreet hearing, and a suspicious-minded person might have some reason for suspecting that it was manufactured for the occasion.

If contradictory versions of the names the Indians applied to the upper ramifications of the Delaware were plentiful, testimony in support of the right of the various streams to be called "the Fishkill" was overwhelming.

It was assumed by some that the stream in which the most fish had been caught in days of old had the best right to the name. All that seemed necessary to settle the tangled question in the case was to collect fish stories —told under oath—and let the best one win. The old-timers of the mountains settled down and let go.

Richard Jones swore that he had a "fishware" on the West Branch of the Delaware "near the Forks at Shehawken." He caught "quantities of Eils and Trout but no Bass not so much as one." However, said Jones, other owners of fishweirs below the Forks and up the East Branch did catch bass—"sea bass" as some called them. There was Ezekiel Samson of the East Branch—he caught "great quantities of Bass when at the same time none were to be found in the West Branch." At Papakunk, Jones added, the people took great quantities of shad in the spring—these were scarce in the West Branch. Joshua Pine, Jr., backed up Jones very nicely. He swore that he'd gone down the East Branch "with a cannoe" in 1784—that was the year of the big flood—and that the Pepacton people boasted to him, as he paused at their settlement, that they'd caught thirteen hundred shad at one haul of a net. Jones, Pine, and many others were Bradstreet witnesses; among those on the Hardenbergh side was Johannis Bevier, Jr. Johannis recalled having heard "two old Grayheaded Indians" talking with his father some forty years before, and he remembered that the Indians said that an extraordinary thing happened to the fish swimming up the Delaware. When the fish reached the Forks at Hancock, they divided into two groups. The big fish swam up the West Branch and the little fish chose the East Branch. Bevier said that the old Indians assured his father that in their language big fish were known as Mahak Lamas and that it was from this phrase that their name of Lamas Sepos was derived.

The Bradstreeters did their best to prove that not only people but fish regarded the East Branch or the Beaverkill as "the right fishkill." But they also offered something more appealing to the tastes of our time. It was what we might call "scientific evidence." This evidence was collected by Simon Metcalfe, the surveyor who had run the Line of Property on behalf of the Crown in 1768, and had long been a stanch upholder of the Bradstreet claims. Metcalfe carried out his scientific mission with impressive skill during the last days of August and the first days of September 1785. He set out from Lackawack with a party of six including himself and his son George. Jacob Chambers, an experienced woodsman, was his guide. Chambers was something of an authority on the southwestern Catskills. He told of having once led the search for a slave who had escaped to that part of the mountain region from an Ulster County farm. Chambers delivered the Metcalfe party safely to the Forks of the Delaware and there Metcalfe performed his scientific rites first in the West and then in the East Branch. First he measured the width of the streams, then he measured their depth "at equal distances with a staff marked for the purpose." Next he measured the velocity of the streams with a log and "fine line marked for that purpose." His son George held a stop watch as the log floated free for thirty seconds. Simon "minuted and wrote down" every fact and figure, George testified. Later, Metcalfe measured the other streams of the region, such as the Beaverkill and the Willowemoc, with equal care. And Metcalfe arrived at a not very surprising conclusion for so devoted a Bradstreet partisan. He found that the Beaverkill was the most copious stream of the lot, so he marked it as the true Fishkill on the map he submitted to the commissioners.

The Hardenberghers were not awed by Metcalfe's performance, for they had on their side William Cockburn who had been active in their behalf from the start of the proceedings. Cockburn had rounded up witnesses for his side, had testified about his surveying expeditions among the Catskills, and had put on record the results of conversations with Indians and Indian interpreters. In 1771 he had drawn his map of the patent on which he located, to the best possible Hardenbergh advantage, all the places that could be made to assume the Indian names mentioned in the deed Nisinos gave to Jacob Rutsen in 1706.[4] Now Cockburn duplicated Metcalfe's river-measuring efforts, if with considerably less scientific flair, and came to conclusions exactly the opposite of Metcalfe's.

It was not until 1786 that all the affidavits, the maps, and the copies of old deeds intended to support or cast doubt upon Bradstreet and Hardenbergh claims were ready and hearings could begin. It was a year of crisis for the United States. "I do not conceive we can exist long as a nation without having lodged some where a power, which will pervade the whole Union in as energetic a manner as the authority of the State governments extends over the several States," wrote George Washington in that year. He was expressing with his usual clarity of thought the widespread conviction that the Articles of Confederation under which the new nation lived were ineffective and that a stronger federal union with greater power was urgently needed. The large landholders of New York were enthusiastic over the prospect of greater federal power, for they feared that their state government might enact a land tax similar to the one the British Parliament had threatened in colonial days. The governor of New York was George Clinton, whose sympathies were not at all with the state aristocracy of landholders, and leading men in the legislature were considering the kind of land tax that might break up large holdings. The landholders were confident that a strong federal government could be counted upon to curb the leveling tendencies of Clinton and his following among New York lawmakers. Their state constitution safeguarded their privileged position, yet the administration of its provisions had fallen into the hands of a governor whom they had come to view with suspicion. These class and personal rivalries might have seemed destined to have a bearing on the Bradstreet claims when the legislature appointed the governor and half a dozen top officials of his administration as commissioners of the land office in May 1786. The commissioners at once proceeded to hold hearings on the Bradstreet case. Some of them were radical Whigs like Clinton; some were upholders of privilege; but all, even the governor, were personally involved in land speculations and were not eager to rock the boat they hoped would carry them to a port of large and easy profits. That may have been why all the place-name testimony, all the fish stories, the mountains of old deeds culled from the archives, and the arguments of the lawyers seemed to have played hardly any part at all in shaping the commissioners' decision.

In vain, too, were the learned arguments for the Bradstreet heirs of James Duane, Mayor of New York, and a past master of the intricacies posed by the conflicting and often dubious claims of members of the better sort to land granted by the Crown. Duane himself was the owner of a good percentage of New York State. The Hardenberghs were even better represented before the commissioners. Behind almost every phase of the preparation of their case could be glimpsed the tall and haughty figure of one of New York's most awesome men, Chancellor Robert R. Livingston. The Chancellor's legal skill and learning were great and he now placed them at the disposal of the united Hardenbergh proprietors of which distinguished body he was the leader. The notes of the Chancellor's arguments for his side have come down to our day. They are well organized and show that the Chancellor faced the weak spots in the Hardenbergh title boldly, and persuasively explained them away.[5] In his stately way he focused on an error Simon Metcalfe had made by confusing the Beaverkill and the Neversink. With effective deadpan humor he suggested that the Bradstreet heirs had been mistaken in supposing that their lands were in New York. Metcalfe, stated the Chancellor, had put most of them in Pennsylvania. The heirs should have taken their case to Pennsylvania's land office.

It is likely enough the Chancellor realized that the outcome of the hearings before the commissioners would be little affected by arguments however learned or eloquent. His brother Edward, who argued two points for the Hardenbergh side, may have taken the whole thing more seriously.[6]

Edward was twenty-two and freshly admitted to the bar. Everyone conceded his brilliance. In spite of a lank figure topped by an odd and quizzical face, he was a man of fashion and was already known as "Beau Ned." Edward must have been aware that among the commissioners before whom he was to speak were some of the state's most distinguished men. Here was the kind of chance that seldom comes to a twenty-two-year-old to show what he is made of. And young Edward made the most of the opportunity.

Earlier in the game, the Hardenbergh side had tried to fortify the various Indian deeds negotiated by Colonel Hardenbergh during the 1740s and 1750s by drawing up what purported to be a genealogy of the Indian families involved. Nisinos, who had given the original deeds back in 1706 and 1707, had been the son of "Dosto, an old Squa" who lived in the town of Rochester. The Mohawk Indians had presented Dosto with their lands between the branches of the Delaware. There Dosto's people set up their "hunting houses" and there they wandered freely without protest from anyone, so ran the Hardenbergh story. The Indians who had given deeds to Colonel Hardenbergh just before the partitions of 1749 and 1751 were direct descendants of Dosto and so had every right to sell the lands. All this rested on the flimsiest evidence. But equally flimsy was the evidence pasted together in support of Bradstreet's Indian deed, alleged to have been obtained from four Oquaga Indians seven days before the signing of the Fort Stanwix Treaty. Edward charged that the Indian deed submitted by the Bradstreet side was a fraud which had actually been drawn up after and not before the signing of the treaty. And the four Indians, he went on to say, had no right at all to sell any land to Bradstreet. The Oquaga Indians were not an old landowning tribe, but had been made up of remnants of various displaced Indians—Esopus, Mohawk, Oneida, and even Tuscarora. Edward orated sarcastically at the expense of the Bradstreet lawyer because of the use his side had made of the unfortunate Oquagas. Because the Bradstreet deed was signed, not by Mohawks but by Indians who "call themselves Aghquagos there was a necessity of some deduction from the Mohawks. This has been most ingeniously done, a tribe of Tuscaroras was conquered for the purpose & bro't from the southward, a treaty of marriage is set on foot with the Mohawks & Oneida squas—& their great-granddaughters are brought to bed of *Aghquagos* on the banks of the Delaware. . . ."

Edward had merely warmed up on the Oquaga Indians. He proceeded to do his best to dazzle the commissioners by going forward to attack the opposing lawyer on another front. ". . . nor are these the only wonders wrought by this man. Mountains rise at his command & rivers change not only their names but their courses, witness the *Mongape* which in days of yore ran evenly into the Delaware at Cashicton, on this mans approach [it] feels itself disturbed to its very source, it rises above the highest mountains & pours its rapid waters into the astonished Wilenawemack. . . ." Here young Edward was paying his respects to Jacob Chambers who had led his side into confusion when he misplaced the Mongaup River. But Chambers was behaving normally in relation to the Bradstreet case, for everyone concerned made his quota of geographical mistakes. Commissioners, lawyers, witnesses, Hardenbergh proprietors, and Bradstreet heirs wandered through the days of the hearings in a bewildering maze of shifting streams and mountains from which they were lucky to emerge at all.

With the evidence and the arguments on record, the commissioners went through the motions of considering the case and then gave the landholding world their decision. Fifty-two thousand acres between the West Branch and the Susquehanna (and so entirely outside the limits claimed by the Hardenbergh proprietors) was given to the Bradstreet heirs. The Hardenbergh Patent was left untouched and no decision was made about its validity. A twentieth-century lawyer, John D. Monroe, studied the surviving records of the case and characterized the decision as "a piece of pettifoggery."[7] That was probably an overharsh judgment, for the land office over which the commissioners presided was not a court of law but a government agency. Such bodies in 1786, as now, consider the pressures applied to them in arriving at decisions. The commissioners had obviously weighed the opposing pressure of the Bradstreet-Schuyler side and of the Livingstons, Verplancks, Desbrosses, and other members of the Hardenbergh proprietors and they responded with a decision that neither side was likely to take to court for a further battle.

By giving the Bradstreeters seventy thousand acres of land belonging to the public, which was not likely to complain about the loss, the Hardenbergh proprietors were allowed to remain in undisturbed possession of all the land they claimed. Judge Livingston's cloud still hung over the mountains, but the commissioners' decision had made it almost invisible for a while. General Bradstreet's foresight in using the shakiness of the title to the Hardenbergh Patent as a club by which to bludgeon the New York authorities into making a huge grant of land to himself and his heirs had been vindicated. The general's ghost could now cease troubling the Catskills.

The Hardenbergh proprietors rejoiced. Questioners of their right to the patent still yapped and barked at their heels. Their northern boundary was in serious question, and on the Rochester front the heirs of Cornelius Schoonmaker (one of the former trustees of the town) were making unpleasant sounds. Yet the patent had been given a kind of qualified endorsement by the commissioners of the land office. That was enough for the present. The jubilant proprietors at once set about pushing their advantage. They set surveyors to work cutting their valleys into farms and ferreting out sites for future sawmills and other manufacturing enterprises.

A few years later, Chancellor Livingston met English woolens manufacturer Henry Wansey and, in the course of conversation, Livingston told the wondering Britisher about the feverish speculation in land going on almost everywhere in the United States. A short time before, Livingston had been offered one hundred twenty thousand acres of land for two shillings per acre; a week later "when inclined to accept it, [he] found it had been sold at two shillings and sixpence, but that lately it had been disposed of at sixteen shillings an acre."[8]

The decision in the Bradstreet case allowed lands within the Hardenbergh Patent to share in a modest way in the general rise in land values, and landlords began asking somewhat higher rents from their tenants. But the hearings had other results. To those of a historical turn of mind, the evidence put on record offered an enormous amount of recorded detail about life among the Catskills in the eighteenth century. From the old affidavits, pioneers, Indians, and Indian traders still speak to us of the location of trails and roads and settlements as well as of place names and the luck of old-time fishermen. The Bradstreet case lured many an ancient Hardenbergh Patent skeleton out of its closet and set it to dancing in public for a moment. These skeletons gave rise to many puzzling questions in sharp legal minds. Had acting Attorney General May Bickley exceeded his authority in wording the grant to Hardenbergh and Company so as to include lands in Albany County when Lord Cornbury's instructions plainly confined him to Ulster? Had the juggling of the Albany-Ulster county line in 1765 by Cadwallader Colden and William Cockburn been a move in a murky scheme to cut the Hardenbergh Patent to size and so add acreage to lands owned by Colden and his friends to the north? Had the rivalry of Cornelis Cool and Hardenbergh and Company been the real thing, or was it a sham intended to cloak some sort of complicated scheme of collusion aimed at defrauding the Crown? All these and many similar questions rose in the minds of lawyers and landholders, filtered their way down through the many layers of New York society, and eventually lodged in the minds of the lower sort. There the old doubts about the solidity of the Hardenbergh Patent were awakened and fortified, and then half-forgotten. In this state the doubts smoldered quietly but were ready, when the proper wind blew, to burst into raging flames.

In the mind of one great landholder there seemed to be no doubt. He was Chancellor Robert R. Livingston who had inherited the optimism of his grandfather Robert of Clermont together with the old man's lands in the Hardenbergh Patent. Not for him was the skepticism of his citified father, the judge; he gloried as much in acting the part of an enlightened rural landlord as he did in playing a prominent part in guiding the destinies of the infant United States. No landlord of the Catskills did more than the Chancellor to attract settlers to the mountains, and no one did more to shore up the Old World method of land tenure which had so long dominated the Hardenbergh Patent.

28

"The Great Chancellor"

✣   THE CONSTITUTION of New York abolished all titles of nobility; so too did the Federal Constitution adopted in 1789. Yet one citizen of the United States managed until his death in 1813 to give the title he derived from his office the look of a badge of nobility—he was Chancellor Robert R. Livingston. His friend George Washington often referred to him simply as "the Chancellor"; his sisters called him "brother Chancellor"; to more distant relatives he was "cousin Chancellor." French friends knew him as "mon cher chancelier."[1]

Throughout the million and a half acres of the Hardenbergh Patent, Livingston was often spoken of as "the Chancellor." Old maps of the patent on which the lands owned by each man are marked with his name indicate Livingston's lands as those of "the Chancellor." "The Chancellor's mill," "the Chancellor's Bridge"—by such names were Livingston's possessions in the patent and at Clermont known. Records of the Livingston share in the Hardenbergh Patent abound in statements such as "The Chancellor forgives this man's back rent," or "The Chancellor has promised this man a farm on three lives." A Shandaken man asked for forgiveness of rent and additional land on the ground that he had nine children and a game leg. The Livingston agent granted the request and noted in the account book of the estate that this was "subject to the Chancellor's approbation."[2] The last lord of Livingston Manor, inflated with rage against his cousin the Chancellor in the course of a bitter family wrangle over the mill rights on the stream which divided the estates of the two men, could find no more promising way of hurting the pride of the master of Clermont than by referring to him derisively as "the Great Chancellor."[3] In 1783 the Chancellor resigned his post as Secretary of Foreign Affairs under the Articles of Confederation in order to be able to fight to retain his beloved chancellorship against a clique which wanted to snatch it away from him. He gave up the chancellorship in

1801 in order to become Minister to France—but "the Chancellor" he remained to the end of his days, as if the title were a hereditary one.

Seldom has a man appeared to fit his title as well as did Robert R. Livingston. The Court of Chancery over which he presided as chancellor was a relic of British Colonial rule. It struggled along in New York State until it was abolished in 1847 and its powers merged with those of the State's Supreme Court. Courts of Chancery were a peculiarly British institution, intended to supply remedies in cases to which the law did not apply. The British Lord Chancellor was often said to be "the keeper of the King's conscience."[4] His court was bound by concepts of equity as embodied in former Chancery decisions and not by British law, which had grown from ancient custom and acts of Parliament. In the days of Dutch rule, New York had no Court of Chancery, for such a court would have been incompatible with the Dutch system based as it was on Roman or civil law. But once the British took over, a Court of Chancery was created and ever after remained a prolific source of hostility between governor and Assembly. For the court had been established by the Crown without the consent of the Assembly, and its chancellor was the governor appointed by the Crown. In theory, at any rate, New York's chancellor functioned for the colony as keeper of the royal conscience and in complete independence of the colonists. That was why it was possible for inept governors—men of Lord Cornbury's caliber—to make decisions involving such Chancery matters as the division of lands or the profits of partnerships or the care and disposition of the belongings of propertied idiots, lunatics, and minors.

The New York Court of Chancery lumbered along through colonial days, viewed with scorn by Americans in whom the impulse toward freedom from cumbersome Old World trappings was growing, and the butt of jokes because of its slow pace and its whimsical and expensive habits. Yet, disliked as it was, the court certainly exhaled a curious sort of glamor derived from its royal and aristocratic connections. When the conservative and property-minded framers of New York's Constitution of 1777 made up their minds to retain the old court, they quickly chose Robert R. Livingston as its first chancellor. For, like the court, the Chancellor had aristocratic tastes, ancient lineage, and a veneration for property especially when it took the form of land. It was true that his excellent mind and legal acuteness often led him to take up advanced positions which made some regard him as a dangerous radical. The bouncy optimism of old Robert of Clermont welled up in him from time to time and led him into spells of enthusiasm for projects mechanical, agricultural, or political aimed at the simultaneous benefiting of his nation, his state, humanity, and himself. Yet no one could view the Chancellor's elegant and imposing figure and his arresting face from which beamed, at one and the same time, benevolence and a wry skepticism; no one could listen to his melodious voice pouring out classical allusions, daring figures of speech, statistics, and persuasive arguments without being struck with the conviction that the traditions of the Court of Chancery were safe in Livingston's hands.

The Chancellor was more than a mere chancellor—he was a power in many avenues of life in his state and nation. He led an active social life, and he experimented endlessly in efforts to improve American ways of living. Robert Fulton's steamboat was almost an obsession of his. He became Fulton's partner in the project and contributed many ideas which were not used and a great deal of money and energy which was. He persuaded the New York legislature, though its members laughed at the fantastic hope, to give him a monopoly of steamboat navigation in the state. In all this activity it was not surprising then that until fairly late in life he had little time to devote to the details of managing the family lands. Yet there is evidence that he was trained to look upon the care of the family acres as an important part of life. There was, for example, the case of Albartus Joy. In August 1772 when the future chancellor was a twenty-six-year-old New York lawyer, his father the judge wrote him from Clermont: "Albartus Joy a poor man who is one of my Tenants at Woodstock is sued in the County Court of Ulster by Johannis Schoonmaker. . . ."[5] Schoonmaker had rented a house to Joy and then turned him out and installed another tenant before the term of the lease was up but held Joy liable for the rent money. Schoonmaker owed Joy money for work but he apparently refused to pay. "Advise him what is proper to be done & [I] would not neglect it," the judge urged.

Clearly enough there was a paternalistic side to life on Livingston lands in the Catskills in which the Chancellor took part. A tenant in trouble might turn to his landlord for help, and, provided he observed the terms of his lease (or his agreement if he had no lease), and provided he did not expect any great expense in time or money to be borne by the landlord, he would receive help. In much the same way did Old World tenants on well-run estates turn to their landlords in difficult times. The Livingstons of Clermont carried on the ancient sense of interdependence of landlord and tenant passed on from feudal times, because unlike many other American landholders they did not value their lands primarily as objects for speculation but hoped to build up well-established estates peopled by industrious tenant-farmers and centered at great houses like the one at Clermont. And estates like this with the tenants paying all taxes might become a source of comfortable yearly profits to generation after generation of Livingstons and would steadily increase in value. Lands well removed from Clermont, such as those in present-day Sullivan County and the Stamford neighborhood in Delaware County, would do very nicely to speculate with. But the closer a farm came to Clermont the more Old World were the terms upon which it was held during the rule of the Chancellor.[6]

Old Robert of Clermont had regarded his lands in the Catskills with enthusiasm and had hoped for much from them. His son, the judge, put a great deal of effort into "trying to make something of the Patent" but his heart was never in the job. The judge had every incentive to make what he could of the patent for he was his father's only child and would inevitably inherit all the old man's property. But the judge and his wife had a brood of eleven children of whom the chancellor-to-be was the eldest. Under the rule of primogeniture, Clermont and the vast tract of land across the Hudson were claimed by the judge's eldest son. The judge had owned the lands for so short a time that he had not gotten round to mentioning them in his will. The rule of primogeniture still prevailed. Later, in 1786, the state would abolish it. It often happened that an eldest son, if he was generous by nature and if he was affectionate toward his brothers and sisters—and young Robert R. was both of these—would want to make some provision for the younger members of the family out of his inheritance as eldest son. That was why no one was surprised when the newly appointed chancellor decided to share part of the Hardenbergh Patent lands with his ten brothers and sisters. He made up his mind to give each of his three brothers about thirty thousand acres apiece, while twenty thousand would go to each sister. He would keep the balance of some quarter of a million acres for himself.[7] But the division was not carried out exactly as planned. One hundred non-Livingstons became sharers, in a modest way, in the Chancellor's inheritance.

The incident that sent these one hundred people trooping into the patent was the burning of Kingston by British troops under General Vaughan on October 16, 1777. The British burned not only Kingston but the old mansion of Clermont in which the judge's widow lived and the smaller, newer house nearby which was occupied by the Chancellor and, to the confusion of local historians, also named Clermont. The people of Kingston were in an uncomfortable fix as winter approached. They did their best to improvise lean-tos against the stone walls of their burned-out houses. And they were not slow in calling the attention of generous Whigs throughout the colonies to the plight into which their devotion to the Revolution had led them. Governor Clinton responded by favoring exemption from military duties for Ulster County masons and carpenters who would agree to work at moderate wages in that time of inflation. Contributions rolled in from as far away as Charleston, South Carolina.

It happened that Kingston's tragedy came at a time when the Chancellor had retired to Clermont after a period of energetic devotion to public affairs. He was by no means pleased with the way the Revolution was going, and he was especially concerned by the lack of gentlemen among the members of the state legislature gathered at Poughkeepsie. He found it irksome to work with these men because the majority of them were clearly no friends to the landed gentry. They were the kind who might be capable of even so ridiculous a piece of legislation as a general land tax. There was little Chancery business to be taken care of during the war years, so the Chancellor settled down for a while to the life of a country gentleman of innumerable acres. He and his mother strove to rebuild their Clermonts in spite of the high cost of labor and building materials; the determination of their tenants, most of whom were Tories, to withhold their rents; and the dampening effect on local Revolutionary ardor of the burning of Kingston.

The appeals of the people of Kingston touched the Chancellor, for the relations between Clermont and Kingston had long been close. Livingstons of both Clermont and the manor had done a great deal of business with Kingston, and their influence had some effect in softening the harsh commercial culture which had prevailed in the town ever since its foundation. Livingstons had encouraged the establishment of an academy at Kingston and had sent their children to study there. They felt an almost proprietary interest in the place; it was, after all, the principal business and cultural center of the region which they dominated.

Large New York landholders like the Livingstons were often troubled by a shortage of ready cash, which led them to pay some of their bills in acres. The Chancellor pondered the plight of Kingston and concluded he would aid the town's people with a gift of land. On March 1, 1778 he informed the trustees of Kingston of his intention in a letter breathing a fine spirit of eighteenth-century aristocratic condescension. "The inconvenience I daily experience from the destruction of my house, and the ravages of the enemy, serve only to increase my sympathy with the inhabitants of Kingston, and animate my desire, in proportion as they lessen my power, to contribute to their relief as liberally as I wish. My inattention to my private affairs for three years past and the disaffection of my tenants who had during this controversy very generally withheld their rents, put it out of my power to contribute, what might perhaps be of more immediate use to my distressed friends at Kingston. Yet, I flatter myself that my present proposal may meet with their approbation. . . ."[8] The Chancellor then offered the people of Kingston five thousand acres of the Hardenbergh Patent, the land to be located anywhere but in Woodstock, Shandaken, or any other place where a settlement had been made. The trustees were to bear the cost of a survey and they were to make their choice within three months.

It was a noble gift to the people of an afflicted city. The lands available, however, were on the frontier exposed to Indian and British forays, so their value lay in the future rather than in the present. The Kingston trustees summoned William Cockburn, who appeared carrying one of his handsome maps of the Hardenbergh Patent. The trustees studied the map and appointed a committee of two to scour the patent itself in search of a suitable location, and they engaged Cockburn to make the survey. It was not until 1782 that the five thousand acres were chosen, surveyed, and divided into fifty-acre lots. A few years later they were distributed among one hundred Kingston property owners who had lost houses or barns at the hands of the British. No part of the Chancellor's gift went to the city's poor or landless. Only a very few, if any, of the one hundred men settled on their lands in New Kingston, as the place came to be called. They sold out as soon as they could do so to advantage.

The descendants of the old settlers of the Catskills are grudging in any expressions of praise for the old mountain landlords. When a bridge crossing the Hudson from Rhinecliffe to Kingston was being built in the 1950s, it was proposed that it be named in honor of Chancellor Livingston whose Clermont lay close by. But old Hardenbergh Patent hands raised a clamorous shout of opposition to naming the bridge in honor of a man who had been the chief of the Old World landlords of the Catskills a century and a half earlier. The Chancellor's name was dropped and the bridge became simply the Kingston-Rhinecliffe Bridge.[9] In the same spirit, the generosity of the Chancellor in making his five-thousand-acre gift has become obscured by the ancient animosities of pioneer days. A stranger appearing among the the rolling hills and fertile valleys of New Kingston today may be surprised when he finds that a mention of the Chancellor's name evokes no enthusiasm and little interest. For if the Chancellor gave away his five thousand acres with any hope of earning the gratitude of New Kingston posterity, his hope was vain. Delaware County histories in treating of the gift give Livingston's first name as William (they confuse him with the eighteenth-century governor of New Jersey who admired the Moravians), and local historians descended from old Hardenbergh Patent settlers have been known to suggest that the Chancellor's motives were entirely selfish. He hoped to get back many times the value of his five thousand acres when the industry of its settlers would raise the value of his surrounding lands—

so these people say. It was the case of Cornelius Tiebout and the Moravians all over again.

The stranger who visits New Kingston today will find no statue of the Chancellor raised by the people who inhabit the dozen and a half pleasant white frame houses which form the center of the place. None of the three hollows that come together at the center bears his name, nor does any one of New Kingston's roads or streams. There is not even a bronze tablet intended to commemorate the Chancellor's generosity or shrewdness, whichever it may have been. Old Kingston, however, has been kinder to the Chancellor. Historians of that city usually speak of him in terms of admiration. In his own lifetime he felt the gratitude of Kingston's property owners in a most direct and heart-warming way. When the Chancellor visited Kingston in 1804, a public holiday was declared; a procession of enthusiastic citizens accompanied him through Kingston streets; and a public dinner was held in his honor to show appreciation of "the munificent gift he had given the trustees."

It was in the fall of 1779 that the land that was to become New Kingston was decided upon by the trustees. At the same time, the Chancellor turned over to his brothers and sisters their shares in his inheritance. Here again old tenant-landlord animosities have caused the Chancellor's motives to be questioned. And here too his hopes were probably not realized. Lawyer John D. Monroe—the man who found the decision in the Bradstreet case so unsatisfactory—was descended from Scottish ancestors who had settled on the Hardenbergh Patent. Monroe believed that the Chancellor deeded the lands within the patent to his brothers and sisters because he was obliged to by law. The grant of the Hardenbergh Patent, Monroe pointed out, stated plainly that the land was to be held "as of our Manor of East Greenwich in the County of Kent." In Kent the rule of primogeniture customarily gave way to the rule of gavelkind. This meant that property not otherwise disposed of by will did not go to a man's eldest son but was divided among all his sons. Monroe argued that because of the terms of its original grant the Kentish rule of gavelkind prevailed throughout the Hardenbergh Patent and bound the Chancellor in claiming his inheritance to share it with his brothers at least. What Monroe did not take into account was that nearly all Crown lands granted in England as well as America since the sixteenth century were to be held "in free socage as of our Manor of East Greenwich." The phrase was a formal one which had no effect at all on how the property was inherited and was intended to make it plain that the military service expected of those holding lands under the feudal form of tenure known as "knight service" was not required.[10] In deeding the lands to his brothers and sisters, the Chancellor stated that he was acting in accordance with what he believed were his father's wishes. There is no reason to question this explanation.

In many ways Chancellor Livingston was a contented prisoner of the past—he certainly was when it came to questions involving land. He may very well have hoped as he turned over parts of the Hardenbergh Patent to his brothers and sisters that they would settle down on their lands and that their descendants would live there far into the future. In his mind the future welfare of the United States was in danger unless the nation rested on a basis of "landed property to which the citizen is in some sort tied," the Chancellor wrote in 1803. This belief he shared with Thomas Jefferson and Jefferson's followers, but in the Chancellor's view the existence of landed estates like Clermont, rather than individually owned farms, was of the first importance for the national welfare. He gave to each of his brothers and sisters not only land but the opportunity of creating ten new Clermonts set among the Catskills, each with its Old World master or mistress and its diligent tenants. Such estates, in the Chancellor's view, would contribute to the national happiness and, by a fortunate coincidence, to the prosperity of the Livingstons. But strong currents in European and American life were carrying men and women away from the ancient faith in the virtues of land held in the form of large estates. In 1789 the outbreak of the French Revolution shocked conservatives and encouraged the poor everywhere. At the same time the Industrial Revolution set the minds of power-hungry men to turning from thoughts of acres to dreams of steam engines, water wheels, and whirring machinery. Cowed human machine tenders herded into smelly slums took the place in the minds of those yearning for quick wealth and higher status of respectful tenants laboring in fields and forests from dawn to dark and touching their caps respectfully whenever the master passed by. The Western world was changing. In this change the American Revolution had played its part. So too did the realization of the immensity of American resources of everything needed in a world which would soon be dominated less by landowners and more by the controllers of mines, factories, urban real estate, and pools of cheap man-power.

The first Robert Livingston was an intensely realistic man when it came to working out his ambitions. He scorned no method that might enable him to achieve dominance over his fellow humans. Engineering a dubious land grant, financing a privateer who teetered on the edge of out-right piracy, collecting little profits from deals made possible by his official position, exploiting the miserable Palatines to the limit of their endurance were all equally admirable means of reaching his goals. But by 1786 old Robert had been dead for sixty years. Although he had been the founder of the family fortune, he had become somewhat dim in the memories of most of his descendants. They preferred to recall ancestors like the Scottish Earls of Callendar from whom they claimed descent. They viewed themselves as aristocrats whose preferred place at the feast of life was as fixed and unarguable as the alternation of the seasons or the ebb and flow of the tides in the Hudson River. They were well aware that they lived in an age of Revolution, yet they were not free to exercise the kind of realism which, in the hands of old Robert, had made them rich and secure. Most of the Hudson River Livingstons kept informed of what was happening in France; many sympathized with the French peasants in their attempt to tear down a tyrannic aristocracy and king and build a better and more equitable world. They professed an enlightened belief in democracy and at the same time they never questioned their own right to aristocratic privilege. In their heads, radical French notions and medieval survivals jostled, but they found it a simple matter to harbor both as long as they could continue to be unmolested in their pleasant position on the banks of the Hudson.[11] A few inherited the unabashed acquisitiveness of old Robert and this led them into growling and sputtering conservatism. The Chancellor's brother John Robert and the third and last lord of Livingston Manor were among these. But most Livingstons faced the waning of the eighteenth century in what appears from our point of vantage to be a state of fearful confusion. Their self-interest demanded that they retreat into the past; their intelligent minds suggested a daring leap into the future.

In this state of conflict and led by the Chancellor himself, the Livingstons of Clermont got to work settling less fortunate men, women, and children upon their shares of the Hardenbergh Patent.

29

New Clearings and Settlers

❦ IF ALL the people then involved in settling the Catskills had lined up for inspection after the Bradstreet case was ended, they would have formed a line over a thousand people long.[1] And if they had lined up in accordance with their accepted social status, one end of the line would have been made up of the eleven Livingstons of Clermont plus additional Livingstons from the manor. Next to the Livingstons would stand another group of less than a hundred men and women all of whom had one reason or another for claiming membership in the club known as "The Better Sort." Their names would be well known and respected on the social and commercial upper levels of New York—Verplanck, Desbrosses, MacEvers, Ludlow, and the like. Most of these people had been given the kind of education that enabled them, when properly stimulated, to give off vocal emblems of their status in the shape of quotations from the Latin and British poets; they were well dressed, well fed, and had that air of being pleasantly at home in the world which comes so readily to those of privileged position.

Next in line would come another well-dressed and well-fed human assortment. These formed what might be called the better sort of the middling sort. Among them an alert observer could pick out the heirs of Cornelius Tiebout, Johannis Hardenbergh, and a half dozen other early Hardenbergh Patent proprietors. Many of this group would be hard to tell from members of the better sort until it became apparent that they were unable to come up with the poetical quotations which were a badge of club membership. Most of them worked hard at their occupations and schemed diligently to enlarge their fortunes to a size that would attract the greed of the better sort and lead to alliances by marriage. The human products of such marriages would be definitely better sort, and they would often be able to outquote older members of the club.

The kind of middle sorters who stood next in line were less well dressed. Many not only were unable to quote but even appeared to refined ears to have thick Dutch accents. They worked at useful but not elegant occupations. Among them were blacksmiths, tanners, and small farmers. They were the swarming posterity of men like Alderman Lewis and other early Hardenbergh Patent proprietors whose descendants had slipped a rung or two down the social ladder. These middle sorters were a cheerful group, sustained in difficult times by the possession of bits of paper or parchment which they had inherited from more prosperous ancestors: deeds to fragments of the Great Hardenbergh Patent. The middle sort people had one thing in common with those above them in the line all the way to the courtly person of the Chancellor himself. They too were proprietors of parts of the Hardenbergh Patent by virtue not of anything they had done but by reason of the speculative itches or the chicanery of ancestors. They were, in their own opinion, a decided cut above those who came just below them in line, the recently created small proprietors of patent lands who had usually acquired that dignity by purchase.

Smallest of the small proprietors were the fifty-acre citizens of Kingston who had been the beneficiaries of the Chancellor's largesse. They became unquestioned proprietors after the canny trustees of Kingston had decided to divide up the Chancellor's five-thousand-acre gift once the Bradstreet decision had made the expense indubitably worth while. These very Dutch-looking and very Dutch-accented citizens had every right to bring to an end the upper section of the line and give way to the very different kind of people who stood beside them and stretched all the way to the unfortunate Negroes who brought the line to an end. For from the proprietors downward the rest of the people in line owed their positions not to inherited ownership but to the fact that they were actual settlers and not pioneers by proxy engaged in doing their settling from a comfortable distance.

The actual settlers of the patent were an enormously mixed lot of people. Except for a few they had but one thing in common: they were very poor. Some spoke with a Scottish burr; others used Dutch for ordinary daily speech; some had a good many German phrases which had come down from Palatine parents or grandparents; the nasal tones of Connecticut or Massachusetts resounded in many valleys. Jerseymen and Long Islanders, each with the ways of speaking and behaving in which they had been reared, added to the new Babel in the Catskills. There were those among the actual settlers who looked upon the proprietors in a kindly way. These were the ones who owned their farms. Those who rented were likely to feel hostility toward the landlords. The squatters were most hostile of all. Beneath the bustle of settling—as giant trees crashed under the axes of pioneers and

landlords dreamed of becoming even richer through the efforts of others—
ran a current of hatred. It was the same current that had prompted Livingston Manor tenants to revolt in 1752 and in 1766; the same hatred for the rich
and powerful who kept poor men from the ownership of the New World
land which they watered with their sweat. The same current had played a
part in making Tories of Hudson Valley tenants. It had caused the soldiers
of the Livingston Manor regiment to disobey their officers and then to
break out in open revolt in 1777. The Revolution had been won; yet the
dark old current flowed beneath the quiet surface of life on Hudson Valley
manors and estates and found its way to the hollows of the Catskills.

The proprietors asked for nothing better than a rapid filling up of
their mountains with people, a multiplying of cows, horses, oxen, and sheep,
of sawmills, gristmills, and water-powered factories and shops, for all this
would inevitably raise the value of their lands. But how to accomplish this
without risking capital?—that was the question. Many absentee landlords
believed that if they sold up to one quarter of their holdings in fee simple to
buyers who would clear and build and farm, then the remainder would
increase in value by enough to more than offset the partial disadvantage of
selling. Landlords like the Chancellor often believed it would be to their
advantage to sell a few hundred acres at places destined to become trading
centers. In such spots, taverns, shops, and a church would appear close to
the landlord's mills, for water power was usually retained by landlords.[2]
Tenants would be attracted to the surrounding farmlands by the prospect
of living closer to some of the amenities of life. In this way Margaretville,
Woodstock, and many other mountain centers came into being in the 1760s
and expanded once the war was over.

Each center had a man who acted as agent or bailiff for the landlords
and was rewarded with a tract of farmland. These men often collected
rents and kept an eye out for timber thieves and squatters. They formed a
corps of landlord sympathizers who covered the Catskills. One of these
agents, Stephen Simmons of Windham, also acted as herdsman for the
Chancellor when he experimented with the Old World custom of summer
pasturing of stock and sheep among the mountains.[3] The Catskills in their
uncleared state, however, were the poorest pasture imaginable, and it was
not until a generation later that the custom took firm root. Through the
eighties, settlement moved on—but moved on slowly for a very good reason.
The years immediately following the end of the Revolution gave a brief
appearance of national prosperity, but the glow quickly faded and the
late eighties became a time of belt-tightening for most Americans. It was
not until the nineties that a speculative fever began to take hold of land-

owners and businessmen and turned hopes to the settlement of idle lands on a large scale. Connecticut farmers' young sons who had lingered on in their overcrowded paternal homes rather than face the uncertainties of the times on their own began crossing the New York State border in large numbers and hunted for land to till. At Clermont the Chancellor entered his rent roll in a large sheepskin-bound volume ornamented with one of the Livingston mottoes "Spero Meliora," meaning, "I hope for better things." This was all in the best English style. What was not was the instability revealed by most of the entries. It was nothing unusual for a farm to go through the hands of three or four tenants in a dozen years. The tenants were required at each change of leasehold to pay the Chancellor one sixth of the price they received for their lease and improvements, but more often than not they simply pocketed the money and lit out for distant parts. Many an account in the Chancellor's imposing book ends with the words "gone off." This meant that the tenant had vanished. Of the tenants who stuck it out, few paid their rent with anything like regularity, and most were years behind. Tenants and landlord were playing a game of wits in which each side tried to get the better of the other.

Although the laws carried over from the days of King George favored the landlords, invoking the law to eject a tenant who was behind in his rent or to catch up with a man who had "gone off" was expensive and time-consuming. The New York legislature pondered the difficulties of the landlords and came up with laws making collecting rents and ejecting delinquents simpler and cheaper[4]; yet tenants continued to play their game with considerable success. Many of the big landlords got together and employed William Cockburn to collect rents, defend the disputed boundaries, eject "intruders," and ferret out timber thieves.[5] Cockburn did his best but how could he cope with the defiant tenants scattered over the vast patent?

So, in a blundering, stumbling way, the land began to get settled. Squatters took possession of much of the best bottom land with no expectation of remaining to raise their families but merely to snatch a crop or two before selling their "rights" to some innocent newcomer who would then make the best bargain he could with the owner. Carelessness in clearing land was the rule. Many a fire set to clear girdled trees and dry logs or brush from a field escaped into the mountains and roared and hissed among the giant beeches, maples, and hemlocks for weeks before a heavy rain quenched its ardor. Timber thieves hunted out and carried off the best white pines. Surveyors for patent landholders took note of the destruction that was going on. "The timber much Destroyed by fire"[6] they often jotted down in their notebooks. Or "the best timber removed from this lot by thieves." The Old World landlords were not putting their mountains and valleys to efficient use at a time when the growing American nation needed what they had to offer. Other men stepped in and cleared fields and cut timber, even in violation of the law. For the arm of the law was not yet quite long enough to reach into the wilderness of the Catskills and catch every petty timber thief or nudge every squatter.[7]

If the landlords had their troubles, so, too, did the pioneers. A man felling the ancient trees of the Catskills took his life in his hands, and many a pioneer met his end when a great tree crashed down upon him. Benjamin Hine, the farmer-poet of Cairo, lamented one such tragedy in *The Uncertainty of Human Life, A Poem Written on the Death of John Loomis, Who was Casually Slain By the Fall of a Tree, April 21, 1796.*

> Boast not, frail man, of future days,
> Nor put thy trust in times to come;
> Behold tomorrow is not thine,
> Perhaps 'twill waft you to the tomb.

With this warning, Hine began his poem. He went on to tell of Loomis' death in these words:

> As usual when the morning smiled,
> He to his labour did repair,
> Thoughtless of death ere his return,
> As all his gay companions were.

> But, ah! that falling tree,
> By Heaven directed on his head:—
> One moment, lo, in health he stands,
> The next, he's numbered with the dead!

> With sore dismay the minds were filled,
> Of those who witnessed this event;
> Struck with surprise they stood aloof,
> The deathful object viewed intent.

> Fearful and trembling they beheld,
> Flow from his head the crimson stain;
> The tragic scene their strength subdued,
> And filled their hearts with grief and pain. . . .[8]

"Tomorrow is not thine" was true for many pioneers crushed beneath a falling tree or gashed by the edge of a slipping ax. It was true for pioneer women who died in childbirth and for babies who were swept away by threes and fours in "times of fever" and now lie beneath rough upended stones in many mountain valleys. Yet there was satisfaction and even joy in pioneering among the Catskills, for men and women have always rejoiced in struggling to tame nature and subdue the wilderness. "Possession men," tenant farmers, and freeholders alike took pleasure in the use of mind and muscle in the work of settlement. They were exalted too by the belief that they were carrying out a Divine command. For had not God said to Adam and Eve, "Be fruitful and multiply, and replenish the earth, and subdue it . . ."?[9]

Benjamin Hine told of a grim side of pioneer life. Another settler with a wholly different background celebrated one of its joys. He was Lewis Edson, Jr., a hymn and song writer and son of the Yankee Lewis Edson who wrote three of the best-known hymns of his time, "Lenox," "Bridgewater," and "Greenfield." The two Edsons settled on a tract of Desbrosses land lying near the head of Mink Hollow partly in Woodstock and partly in what is now the town of Hunter. The younger Edson traveled among the Catskills and in the surrounding country teaching singing schools, for singing filled an emotional need of pioneer life. He also operated a little sawmill, and there he made the boards from which were put together the packing cases in which glass was shipped from the glass factory located beside Woodstock's Sawkill and which came into being in 1809 not far from Edson's farm. The younger Edson wrote the music and words of many songs. In his notebook he jotted down an *Ode to the Forest* in which he praised—in the manner of the Roman poet Horace—the pleasures of frontier life in the Catskills:

> Let others tell of Cities and their Grandure
> Of swelling tides and beauties of the Ocean,
> Mine be the task to speak of humble stations,
> > In lonely forests.
>
> There nature's seen without a faulse disembler,
> There all is truth and harmonizing system,
> Hypocrisy ne'er shoes its hateful features,
> > In silent shadoes.
>
> Where shall a saint of Earth find safe retirement,
> But in the wild and vast extended forest,
> There all is simple and sincear, completely,
> > Without temptation.
>
> O, that I had a dwelling in the dessert,
> Where the false polish of the great ne'er enter'd,
> There would I rest secure from Earth's deceptions,
> > In contemplation.

O that the Lord would grant me this great blessing,
In shady groves, to walk with a kind partner,
There might we rest secure from Earth's temptation,
    And rise tow'[a]rds heaven

There whould our prayer ascend like morning incense,
Sweetly perfum'd by real devotion,
And gratitude should rise, when ev'ning shadoes
    Spread their dominion.[10]

In the fertile nooks and corners of the Catskills, in the high hollows carved into the mountainsides, beside the clear streams teeming with little trout, the work of subduing the earth went on. And on stump-littered fields surrounded by charred tree trunks, corn and wheat got planted, log cabins got built, and here and there a family prospered in a modest way. Other families quickly recognized that tomorrow would not be theirs if they remained among the rugged Catskills; they moved on to more promising frontiers leaving behind, often enough, unpaid debts and broken promises. Those who clung to their Catskill clearings, like men and women everywhere and in all ages, did not lead lives of clear-cut success or failure. They hoped one day and despaired the next. Sometimes they cursed the fate that had trapped them in narrow valleys owned by Old World landlords who continued to flourish under the Stars and Stripes. But at other times, and especially if the settlers were of Dutch or German origin, they cheerfully accepted their lot and made the best of it. Rich landlords and poor tenants, people upon whom life showered everything good, other people who received almost nothing during their brief stay on earth—such divisions were ancient and inevitable. So it had been in the Old World. So, it seemed, it was going to be in the new. A man could easily waste his life in railing against the rich, but he would do better to reserve his hatred for the Devil and for the witches of the Catskills. For against these evil beings a man could do something.

30

Dr. Brink Battles the Witches

🌳 IN THE EYES of the settlers pouring into the Catskills after the Revolution the great landowners of the region were powerful men. Yet the settlers knew another group of men who rivaled the landowners in power, though their power was of a very different kind. It did not rest on the possession of great tracts of land and on control of men sitting in the state legislature or on the bench. The power of these other men was of a subtle and secret kind: it held the witches of the region of the Catskills in uneasy subjection.

Men or women who knew how to deal with witchcraft and nullify malevolence were once known as "white witches." Locally they were called "witch doctors."[1] And the chief of all the witch doctors was Dr. Jacob Brink. In order to distinguish Brink from descendants of his who inherited a share in his power he came to be known as "the Old Doctor."[2] And by way of showing respect to the doctor and so winning his favor he was sometimes known as "Uncle Jacob," or as Dutch-speaking people put it, "Oom Jacob." It was possible for Dr. Brink to flourish as he did because nearly all the tenant-pioneers of the Catskills lived in an intellectual world that was as much a part of the past as the leases for three lives they signed. The pioneers accepted without too much question the official explanation of how there came to be ups and downs in life, and how it happened that some were born to misery and others to happiness, some to own land and others to lease it. All this was the result of a struggle between God who represented good and the Devil who had brought evil into a perfect world and was ever laboring to foil God's benevolence.

In our own day, underworld criminal organizations play a large and hidden part in American life. The witches of the Catskills, in an entirely unofficial way, once formed the dark underworld of the Catskills. Amateurs could not deal with the charms and spells of witches; to do this skilled witch doctors stood ready to aid the bewitched. But calling in the witch doctor was not as simple a procedure as it might seem. If a cow refused to give milk, if a previously vigorous man fell ill and seemed to be wasting away, if a child's growth became blocked, if money was lost, if butter refused to form in the churn, if household objects took to flying through the air apparently under their own power—in such cases a pioneer would usually try a prayer or two. And if the prayer didn't work, the pioneer would conclude that his trouble was beyond the help of heavenly officialdom. His thoughts would then turn toward the possibility that he was the victim of witchcraft and he would place his faith in the skill of Dr. Brink. But the witches of the region knew all about the doctor and were ever on the alert to keep appeals for help from reaching him. A messenger, no matter how fine the horse upon which he was mounted and no matter how well blazed the mountain trail he followed, was likely to get into trouble. His horse would come to a stop at a high fence or a cliff which seemed to materialize from nothing; the messenger would find himself tangled in a bottomless swamp; his horse would falter and stumble and perhaps break a leg. One sort of messenger usually got through to Dr. Brink: he was the kind who was a seventh son and therefore the possessor of mysterious strength against the wiles of witches. Jacob Bonesteel was a seventh son and so was in demand as a summoner of Dr. Brink. But even Bonesteel would reach the doctor's house in a state of near collapse with his horse so covered with lather that it could be scraped off with a stick. And it would not be until after the doctor had written a charm on a piece of paper and waved it in the air that the power of the witches would be sufficiently weakened to make it possible for Bonesteel to blurt out his message.[3]

"The whole country was full of witches," so Charles Dumond, an old Esopus Valley stagecoach driver, recalled more than half a century ago. Dumond was speaking of the mid-nineteenth century when the witches of the Catskills and the surrounding plains had not yet lost their power over men's minds, and the grandson of the Old Doctor, also named Jacob, had taken over the battle against the witches from Oom Jacob who died in 1843. Young Jacob died about 1888. He was a member of the Ulster County Board of Supervisors, a deacon of his church, and he fought the witches to the end.[4] His power, people whispered, descended to his son Theodore who was postmaster and storekeeper at Lake Katrine and who died in 1936. But Theodore Brink made light of his gift, for the days when witchcraft could dominate American minds was nearing its end.[5]

The heyday of the witches of the Catskills and their archenemy the Old Doctor was the half century following the end of the Revolution. In those days no old woman who lived alone and had the habit of muttering to herself was safe from being called a witch. Men, too, were believed to lay charms on their neighbors and their neighbors' cows, their pigs and horses, although male witches were less numerous than the female variety. Along the base of the eastern escarpment of the Catskills, witches abounded. They followed the windings of the Esopus Creek through the lowlands to deep within the mountains. They were especially numerous on the lands of the Chancellor and his ten brothers and sisters—and with good reason. For the witches of the Catskills were very much of the German school and were often descendants of the Palatines who settled the Livingston lands along the Hudson and later spread to Livingston lands in the Hardenbergh Patent. Germany was "the classic land of witchcraft."[6] There and in witch-conscious Britain lonely old women had little difficulty convincing themselves that they had promised the Devil their souls in return for a share of witchly power. Believing this and acting accordingly, they were able to draw attention to themselves and enjoy the fearful respect of their neighbors. For witchcraft always has two sources: one the desire of rejected human beings for acceptance and power; the other, the equally strong compulsion to face away from reality and see the world in simple terms with good and bad luck not the results of chance or skill but the effects of conscious effort by witches and wizards using mysterious powers over nature.

The witchcraft that flourished on Livingston lands was not entirely German in spirit; it had been altered by contact with the witch lore of the Dutch settlers. Holland had long showed great tolerance toward both religious sects and witches. The bloody persecutions of both sects and witches which once raged in Germany and also in Britain was less to the Dutch taste. When the Dutch reached the New World they brought their more tolerant attitudes with them which explains why there was no orgy of witch persecution in New York similar to the one that took place in Salem, Massachusetts, in 1692.[7] That was why Hudson Valley and Catskill Mountain witches were allowed to ply their trade in peace subject only to the traditional countermeasures of witch doctors such as those practiced by the Brink dynasty.

For a century, Brinks and witches fought it out among the Catskills. And while this lengthy battle earned no place in the history books, it resulted in the piling up of an enormous amount of folklore, much of which is still being repeated in the region of the Catskills. Much too has been collected and written down by such amateurs of witch lore as E. E. Gardner, C. G. Hine, Anita M. Smith, and Neva Shultis. The Old Doctor cuts an odd figure in the folklore, for he has been confused with his descendants and often transformed into an incredibly long-lived man who combines the best features of both himself and the younger Dr. Jacob. But thanks to the efforts of a skeptical and decidedly eccentric clergyman of long ago, the Old Doctor's character and methods have been captured and preserved. The Reverend William Boyse became the pioneer collector of Catskill Mountain witch and Brink lore. And what is more important, he met and talked with the Old Doctor and wrote an account of the interview.

The witch doctor whom Boyse knew in Woodstock between 1823 and 1837 was born in the southern part of what is now Saugerties, where the old Brink homestead still stands on land owned by Brinks ever since 1688. During the Revolution, refugees from the Esopus Valley—fourteen families of them according to family tradition—crowded into the Brink stone house. Among these families were the Longyears whose sons had joined Lieutenant Rose on his march to New York. In this way the boys' sister, Christina, may have met young militiaman Jacob Brink. The couple were married in 1780, and before long they were living near the elder Longyears in the Esopus Valley. After 1790 Jacob was active in local matters as commissioner of highways and later as assessor of the town of Woodstock, which then included the upper Esopus Valley.[8] Before very long he returned to the neighborhood of his birth and there built a house in which his descendant Hubert Brink lives today. He had begun his practice as a witch doctor about 1790; by 1832 he was enough of a local celebrity to be presented to Washington Irving in the course of Irving's tour of the valley his tales had made famous.

In 1840 William Boyse referred to the Old Doctor as an uneducated man "who professes to be master of witches, wizzards and all that sort of creatures"[9] and had an enormous practice as a witch doctor. "He has been sent for from all over the country far and near," Boyse wrote. "Ulster, Green, Albany, Rensalaer and Broome counties have been receiving his constant visits. He has a rod with which he whips the witches, and says he could whip them to death. He is generous, fair spoken, of agreeable manners, of good constitution, appearing about 80. He is believed to be able to take the fire out of burns, cure fever, stop the hemorrhage of the blood, heal breakings out in the flesh and skin; make a gun snap as often as he pleases, no matter how good well loaded and primed; in a word he is up to any complaint. He does it by blowing with his mouth, waving sticks; a little fresh butter is laid on if it is a sore. He also utters inwardly a certain form of words."

When Boyse came to Woodstock and Shokan he was amazed at two things. One was the speech of the people—he wrote that it was neither Dutch nor English but a strange mixture of both. He was amazed too at the extent to which ancient beliefs in witchcraft had hung on among the mountains into the age of realistic, democratic Andrew Jackson. Boyse knew a good deal about witchcraft. He had been born and reared in a Scottish settlement in South Carolina in which faith in witchcraft was strong. One of his neighbors, a Mrs. Hemigor, was said to be a witch. This lady once enchanted a man and then thumbed a ride on his horse to a lively witches' meeting, so the man testified. Boyse had been steeped in the whole complex broth of Scottish and Irish witch lore, and he learned a good deal of the fairy lore brought across the Atlantic. He was aware, for example, of the way fairies had of taking babies from their cradles and rearing them as their own. But all this appealing system of beliefs had succumbed in the course of Boyse's education at Moses Waddell's excellent school in South Carolina, at Transylvania College in Kentucky, and at the little divinity school operated in his own basement by the Reverend Dr. John M. Mason of New York.

If Boyse had been born two centuries earlier, he would surely have denounced the wickedness of witches from his pulpit and quoted the biblical injunction, "Thou shalt not suffer a witch to live."[10] But coming along when he did and with a mind and emotions directed by the prevailing forces of his time, he could not help regarding the whole structure of witchcraft as a vast and glittering bubble which clergymen had a duty to demolish as quickly as they could. Yet, as an educated man he had an obligation to be fair—and fair he was in reporting on the witches of the Catskills and their implacable enemy, Dr. Brink.

Whenever William Boyse stood before his congregation he knew he was facing men and women to whom witchcraft was a daily menace and to whom Dr. Brink was a stalwart hope. He argued against belief in witches and witchcraft—and after the service his congregation argued back. Even his deacons and elders tried to convince him of the reality of witchcraft and of Dr. Brink's power over witches by telling him tale after tale of strange local happenings. William Dubois, who was a member of his flock, told of how Dr. Brink had ferreted out a witch who was annoying him. When a woman of his household gave signs of being bewitched, Dubois sent for Dr. Brink.

"The Doctor told him [that is, Dubois] to make a throne in the house and put a piece of bread on it; then shut the door and allow no cat, nor any person besides his own family to come into the house. So he did. One day, the door being forgotten, in ran a black cat and quickly carried away the bread." The cat, of course, was the witch transformed into a cat, or else he was the witch's familiar spirit. Dr. Brink's charm was broken and Dubois again sought his advice.

"The Doctor told him to repeat the same process, and be more careful. So he did; but one afternoon a man named Coon, driving cows round the field, stopt and was going in the house. But W^m· was on the look out. But Coon stood some time in the yard, and when he got a chance, slipt in and lit his pipe, so the charm was broken again."

Up to this point the Old Doctor had been foiled. But word of Coon's guilt went from house to house around Woodstock and eventually, as Boyse put it, "Coon got paid for it." This happened one day when he went to the Woodstock mill. There a neighbor bluntly accused him of being a "wizzard." "Coon said 'it was no such thing.' Well, said the neighbor, a wizzard can't be drowned, nor go all under water. If you will go into the mill-dam, and go altogether under water, I will tell the people that you are not a wizzard, and they will let you alone. Coon said he would do it, so he stript off and in he plunged. The first trial—O, said the man, one of your hands was out. In Coon plunged again;—O, said the man, your head was not entirely under. In Coon plunged again; O, said the neighbor, your feet were not both all covered. So he kept Coon plunging and diving until he was nearly drowned. . . ." There was no doubt after that, that Coon was a wizzard. For the water ordeal he had undergone in a mild form is one of the oldest and most reliable of all tests of witches.

Many members of Boyse's congregation were troubled by witches who interfered with the production of milk and butter on their farms. "An elder said"—so Boyse reported—"one summer his wife could get no butter by churning, until he went and spoke to the Doctor. The Doctor told him to borrow a new horse-shoe, heat it red hot, and plunge it into the churn. This being done they got butter, the witch being burned took her departure." Boyse added to this account a rare instance of support for his own views on witchcraft among local people: "Some girls up in the mountains said 'if she had thrown in some boiling water, it would have been as good as the new red hot horseshoe. . . .'"

Jacob Bonesteel—perhaps the same Jacob who was a seventh son—told Boyse of a case which demonstrated how much more effective Dr. Brink's methods were than those of the officially recognized physicians. "A man by the name of Vredenbergh was getting logs in the woods, and cut his wrist with an axe. A regular physician was sent for immediately, he filled the wound with some stuff, but the only way he could stop the blood was [by] using clamps" on the patient's arm. "The moment the clamps were off the blood ran out in a constant stream. At last they sent 9 miles for Dr. Brink, when he came he took the stuff out of the wound, and when he had removed the clamps the blood went up to the ceiling. Then using his means, he stopped it immediately." What Brink's means were Boyse does not divulge but there are traditions still known to his descendants which tell of the Old Doctor's methods of stopping severe bleeding. He would write the words "afrat, farat, fracat" on a piece of paper and while waving the paper round over the wound, he would say, "Fra, wora, worato."[11] Or else the doctor would repeat this charm: "Blood go, blood stay, blood abide as the body of Christ abideth with the truth."[12] Some believed that these and similar charms were learned by the doctor from an ancient book of magic he owned[13]; others were convinced that they had come down to him by word of mouth. Mrs. Jane Buell, a Schoharie County relative of Dr. Brink, told E. E. Gardner how she had learned a moderate amount of witch doctoring: "Dr. Brink learned Kate, Kate learned Kimber, and Kimber learned me because I was a seventh daughter. But he didn't learn me everything."[14]

Finger Doctors,
Stick Doctors, and Prottle

☘ ONE SKILL Mrs. Buell apparently didn't learn from the Old Doctor was the one needed in order to heal at long distance. Unorthodox healers of our own century sometimes claim to possess this skill. It was an indispensable part of the equipment of every respectable witch doctor of the Catskills and was not used lightly but only when the pressure of other business made it impossible to visit the sufferer in person.

A man once called on one of the Doctors Brink to report that a horse of his was bleeding to death. The doctor sank into a spell of intense concentration from which he emerged to say, "Go home, the bleeding has stopped." And indeed it had.[1]

The Brinks had a good deal of competition in the long-distance-healing department—Dr. E. H. Benjamin gave them a hard run. Benjamin worked in a foundry at Oak Hill in the town of Durham where such objects as plows and stoves were made. Another product of the factory was an almost magical cabbage-cooking pot so constructed as to keep the odor of boiling cabbage from escaping and offending sensitive noses. After a patient told his woes to Benjamin, the doctor would lie down with his hands folded behind his head and go into a trance. In this condition he would diagnose and prescribe. Dr. Benjamin could treat a patient just as well if he never saw him but was furnished with a description or a lock of hair and his name.[2]

Dr. Bartholomew worked the northwest part of the Hardenbergh Patent from his base in Gilboa. Like all other witch doctors he treated beasts as well as men. When witches rode a horse by night and left him sweaty and exhausted by the time his owner entered the stable in the morning, Dr. Bartholomew would be called. Usually he cut a lock from the horse's mane, inserted it in a hole bored in a tree, plugged the hole while muttering incantations, and witches would never ride the horse again.[3]

Some competitors of the Brinks in the art of witch doctoring hovered on the line between white and black magic and were willing to do evil for a proper fee. There was one man among the Schoharie County foothills of the Catskills who specialized in a very nasty method of ridding people's houses and barns of rats. He was Dr. Moulter, and his way was to approach the rat-infested building by night, rap sharply on a corner of the building, repeat a charm, and order all rats within to leave the premises and go to the house of someone he named and against whom the doctor's employer had a grudge. And the rats, they said, would obey.[4]

Every hollow and crossroads among the Catskills has its tradition of the wonders wrought by the Doctors Brink, but none deal with any such capers as those of Dr. Moulter. The Brinks seem to have always been on the side of virtue; their magic never became black or even gray. That may have been why William Boyse once confronted the Old Doctor and asked him a very pertinent question: did he claim to cure people in the same way that Christ and his disciples did?

This was a tricky question for a man working in magic to handle. If he answered "yes" he would lay himself open to the charge of blasphemy, if he said "no" he would be likely to be thought to confess alliance with the Devil. The Old Doctor was sensibly evasive in his reply and pretended that he didn't understand what the minister meant. He added that all he could say was that his methods were "good."[5] And with this the people of the Catskills agreed. But there were dissenters from the general awed approval with which most people regarded the Brinks. Nathaniel Booth, an Ulster County businessman of literary leanings who had seen the Old Doctor operate, thought he was a good deal of a charlatan. "He cures by charms," Booth wrote in his diary. "His hands are kept in motion over the affected parts as if throwing off the disease and no application is used but fresh butter."[6] Booth estimated that one quarter of the doctor's income came from straightforward witch doctoring, the rest from laboring as what many people called a "finger doctor" or a "stick doctor."[7] Such practitioners claimed to cure by touch or by directing a current that flowed from their fingers, sometimes through a stick they held, to the part of the patient that hurt.

Booth was right in stressing the importance of the hands in the Brinks' attempts at healing. Brink descendants agree that the power of the two famous doctors was concentrated in the middle fingers of their right hands.[8] Some say they anointed this finger with unsalted butter before operating;

others claim that no unguent was used. A third group, among whom was the Old Doctor's grandson Hiram, spoke of an ointment called "prottle" composed of seven ingredients of which Brink had dreamed for three nights running.[9] Hiram and other descendants said their grandfather also used water garnered from the melting of the last snow of the season, or water taken from a running stream by scooping it up against the current.[10] Great-grandson Hubert Brink speaks of a hot needle being thrust through a raw egg—the egg represents the witch who had caused the malady. A number of people told of a cross made of fir twigs being a part of the doctor's medical armamentarium. He passed this cross over the ailing part several times while muttering what was believed to be the Lord's Prayer recited backward. Many believed that Dr. Brink also used truly religious observances to heal. He sometimes made the sign of the cross while seeing patients or he kept three candles burning while at work. These represented the Trinity. Once he cured a case of warts by crossing the back of a knife on each wart and then cutting a cross on the bark of a tree with the same knife. The warts disappeared within twenty-four hours; they had been communicated to the tree in accordance with an ancient magical law and the crosses had given a Christian flavor to the very pagan proceedings. At times the doctor would make the sign of the cross before a sufferer with the middle finger of his right hand while commanding the Devil to begone in the name of the Father, the Son, and the Holy Ghost. At other times he would work in complete silence and impose silence upon all members of the patient's household until after he had left the house. This was done in accordance with ancient teachings that if anyone spoke it might break the spells that were being woven.[11]

Throughout history witches have been thought to owe their powers to the help of evil spirits, and in Christian times, to the Devil. That was why old houses in the Esopus country often had door latches ornamented with crosses—these were charms to avert visits from witches who shared the Devil's fear of the Cross. A witch was thought to be lighter in weight than a Bible and often enough suspected witches were balanced against big family Bibles in an effort to test them. William Boyse reported a case of this sort which took place "back of Catskill" at the base of the mountains. There a very "amiable" family lived in peace until the lady of the house took it into her head to go away on a visit of several days. While she was away, witch-caused troubles arose among the cattle on the farm. When the lady returned, "her kind husband told her she should not come in the house—only the kitchen. He told her plainly that she was the one who had bewitched the cattle. The amiable woman was distracted and her husband was no better. At last they agreed to leave it to a confidential doctor who was in the neighborhood. The doctor, taking the hint, and sincerely wishing to make peace in the family, said he knew how to try whether she was a witch or not: 'The Bible is always heavier than a witch, we will try.' So in went the woman in one scale, and the Bible being placed in the other, was found to be much the lighter. But her husband was not satisfied, because it was an English Bible. He said if she was found heavier than a Dutch Bible, he would give it up. The doctor, being in some hurry, told him to get a Dutch Bible, and went his way." The doctor was probably Brink—Boyse does not give his name, nor does he give the outcome of the balancing act with the Bible. But it could have had only one result, for no grown human being is lighter than a Dutch family Bible with its binding of oak boards covered with leather, its ponderous brass clasps, and its wondrous copper engravings.[12]

The Brinks possessed the remarkable ability to take care of witches on the water as well as on land, and a number of instances of this versatility have been preserved. A witch once put a spell on all the boats using the Delaware and Hudson Canal on which many mountain men worked. The boats simply stopped and refused to respond to the pulling power of the mules on the towpath. Dr. Brink was called in when all other means of unsnarling canal traffic had failed. He knew the witch who had caused the tie-up and went to her house. The witch wasn't home but a skirt of hers was—it was flapping on the clothes line. The doctor got out his witch whip and put it to good use on the skirt. Soon the witch came running, for she had felt every stroke of the whip on her buttocks. Dr. Brink refused to stop whipping until the witch had released the canalboats.[13]

No witch-doctoring exploit on water of the first Doctor Brink is more memorable than his work on the *Martin Wynkoop,* once widely known as "the haunted sloop of the Hudson." The sloop was planned in 1820 by Abraham Hasbrouck of Rondout, a rich merchant and storekeeper. It was Hasbrouck's ambition to own the fastest sloop on the river, and he planned the *Wynkoop* with this in mind. But the keel had hardly been laid when trouble began. An old woman entered Hasbrouck's store and asked for a kind of snuff which he didn't have. The obliging storekeeper expressed regret and promised to get the snuff the woman wanted. But he did not keep his promise and when the old woman returned, he had to confess his failure. The woman, a gifted witch, thereupon in the strongest terms cursed the sloop Hasbrouck was building. From that time on nothing seemed to go well with the *Martin Wynkoop.* Men working on her were injured; work had to be ripped out and done over and over again as unsuspected flaws in materials were discovered. But finally the sloop was finished and ready for launching. Every timber that could possibly hold the sloop back was removed and the ways were liberally greased. But the *Martin Wynkoop* refused to budge from the stocks. No amount of effort, no trying of ingenious solutions offered by gray-haired Hudson River men had any effect. The sloop could not be launched.[14]

The inevitable next step was taken. Abraham Hasbrouck sent for Dr. Brink. The doctor stood beside the sloop and waved his hands in his usual way and he muttered incantations to nullify the witch's curse. The *Martin Wynkoop* responded with a rush as Brink's witch doctoring took effect. In fact, the sloop rushed down the ways so rapidly that the spectators thought she would be buried forever in the mud. But she floated well enough and work on completing her got under way. It would have been better, many people said, if the sloop had been wrecked in the launching, for she turned out to continue to carry with her wherever she went the curse of the snuff-taking old witch who had been deprived of her favorite brand by Hasbrouck's carelessness. On one of her early trips to New York, the sloop killed her owner's son—the man fell down the hold and broke his neck. She soon lost a valuable deckload and drowned her cook when she upset from no apparent cause. After that not a season passed when the *Martin Wynkoop* did not break an arm or a leg for some member of her crew. She ran foul of the sloop *Constitution* and nearly wrecked both; she dumped a load of hides worth nine thousand dollars; she sank while carrying a load of bluestone.

"She was always in trouble," so a reminiscing old-timer wrote in 1889 of the *Martin Wynkoop*—he wrote with feeling but with scant attention to grammar and punctuation. "She knew where every mud flat was between Kingston and New York. When she was lying alongside of the dock fastened you could hear her anchor run off the bow & the chain go out the men would turn out of their beds go on deck and could not see nothing or hear anything go to bed again they would hear a whole lot on deck getting up the sails go on deck everything would be quiet also hear men walking through the cabin at night. . . ."[15]

The *Martin Wynkoop* had been named for one of the ablest skippers on the Hudson. She was put under the command of a relative of Dr. Brink known on the river as "Brinkie." The Brink family had produced many noted rivermen, and one was cousin Andrew whom the Chancellor and Robert Fulton hired as skipper of the steamboat *Clermont.* Another was John who ran the ferry between Saugerties and Clermont. But all this and the power of Abraham Hasbrouck's wealth could not keep the

Martin Wynkoop from becoming a byword on the Hudson. Crewmen returning after a session in a riverfront tavern reported seeing the sloop aglow with lights, and hearing laughter coming from her decks. But when they reached the *Wynkoop* all was dark and soundless. Sometimes even stranger things would be seen aboard. One of the most unnerving appeared to mate Theodore Bush in the 1850s. Bush was "a very fancy man, he used to wear high standup collars. He got up one morning he went in the hole and their were two rats both of them were dressed up in his standup collars. . . ." Bush quickly sought a berth on another sloop, the old-timer of 1889 recalled. One mate was skeptical of the general belief that the *Martin Wynkoop* was haunted "to test the matter . . . [he] Smoked her out. But found nothing that ressembled spooks more than Rats which was 73 in no." Yet strange sights and sounds continued to plague the vessel.

The sloops of the Hudson were famous rivercraft. The early Dutch had designed them to meet Hudson River conditions and they busily plied the stream, carrying both freight and passengers, until the end of the nineteenth century. In them the China tea, tobacco, and molasses which were luxuries of early settlers came upriver to Rondout or Catskill to be hauled by ox or horsepower to log stores among the Catskills. They carried mountain maple to New York cabinetmakers, oak to shipbuilders, and white pine for housebuilders' use. They carried hides to and from mountain tanneries; they carried furs and deerskin and barrels of wild pigeons; they moved downstream heavily laden with great slabs of bluestone destined to serve as sidewalks in New York.

Hudson River sloops like the *Martin Wynkoop* were far from graceful except when under full sail. They were dumpy vessels of shallow draft, with a single mast and a fixed bowsprit. The larger ones were up to sixty to eighty feet in length with a beam of twenty or more. Often enough they were gaily painted as if to distract the eyes of spectators from their downright homely lines. Only when seen from a high peak by a traveler among the Hudson Highlands or the Catskills did they take on beauty. Then the sight of a hundred sloops scudding before the wind on a summer afternoon roused usually unimaginative men to rhapsody and homemade poetry. Their awkward lines were the price the sloops paid in return for workaday efficiency and ruggedness. They were rugged enough to win an occasional battle with such hazards of Hudson navigation as December ice. For it sometimes happened that a master of a sloop would decide to make one last trip upriver before the ice of December closed in, and then he might find himself in trouble. Captain Overbagh did just that when he

In this stereograph by E. and H. T. Anthony of New York, a traveler of the 1870s stands on the winding road that penetrates the Stony Clove. (*Photograph courtesy Catskill Public Library.*)

Below, as the Ulster and Delaware Turnpike pushed across the Catskills in 1802, settlements like this one at Big Shandaken expanded hopefully. (*Courtesy of New York State Library.*)

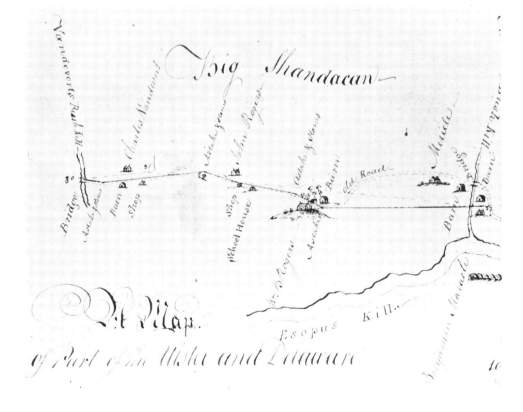

Left, High Peak and Roundtop were once favorite targets of sketchers of the Catskills. Here they are given highly imaginative forms on the right of this engraving from a sketch by J. Glennie, which appeared in *The Port Folio,* November 1813. (*Courtesy of the New-York Historical Society.*)

Below left, at almost every suitable waterfall, mills appeared as settlers moved in. This waterfall at Samsonville served a sawmill, a gristmill, and a clover-seed mill. (*Photograph by Harry Siemsen.*)

The new Catskill shows the effect of Yankee expansion in this sketch apparently intended to be engraved and published. (*Courtesy of the New-York Historical Society.*)

SKETCH of the TOWN of KAATS-KILL, HUDSON'S RIVER

This excavation into Overlook Mountain was probably dug before 1820 by searchers for coal who followed Dr. Mitchill. (*Author's photograph.*)

A summerhouse of Chinese inspiration commands a fine view of the Catskills from the Cruger's Island country seat of J. C. Cruger. The wood engraving is from a sketch by J. C. Woodward. Reproduced from the *Views of New York State* scrapbook. (*Courtesy of New York Public Library.*)

Bears delight in rolling in cool muddy spots called bear wallows. From *Harper's (New) Monthly Magazine*, May 1877.

Bear hunter Enos Brown of Shokan rests by his fireside, heads for the woods, and baits and sets a bear trap, all in engravings published in *Harper's (New) Monthly Magazine* for May 1877. Mrs. Brown was also a noted hunter.

"Rip Van Winkle in the Catskills." by A. D. O. Browere. The setting is true to the character of the higher levels of the mountains. (*Courtesy Shelburn Museum.*)

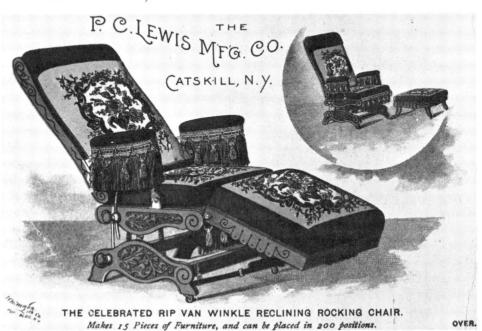

P. C. LEWIS MFG. CO.

THE

CATSKILL, N.Y.

THE CELEBRATED RIP VAN WINKLE RECLINING ROCKING CHAIR.
Makes 15 Pieces of Furniture, and can be placed in 200 positions.

OVER.

Chromolithographed advertisement of the 1890s for the Rip Van Winkle Reclining Rocker. (*Courtesy of the Greene County Historical Society.*)

made a mid-December voyage to Rondout from New York in 1835. Among many other kinds of goods, he was carrying raisins and rope, candles, nails, and soap consigned to Severyn Hasbrouck of Woodbourne in Sullivan County at whose store they would be sold to the settlers of the neighborhood. Captain Overbagh wrote Hasbrouck to explain the delay in delivery: "It has been a could and tuff time for us poor Boatmen—had to cut our way through Ice. . . ."[16]

Ice was a common enough obstacle to December sailing on the Hudson—but was it possible for a sloop to freeze fast in the river in midsummer? Yes, it was possible—but only if the sloop was the haunted and accursed *Martin Wynkoop*. For on a summer day the *Wynkoop* once stuck fast in the waters of the Hudson. And only by the skill of Old Doctor Jacob Brink was she released.

It happened just as the sloop was leaving Catskill. With a fine breeze blowing and the sun shining, the *Martin Wynkoop* simply stopped on the flowing Hudson. No forgotten ropes held her at Catskill; her anchor was up; she had not gone aground; she acted as if frozen fast. As on the day when Abraham Hasbrouck tried to launch her, she simply refused to budge. There could be only a single explanation—witches were at work on board and the curse of the old witch of Rondout had taken hold once more.

Dr. Brink arrived with his famous witch's whip in his hand. He was an old man and was nearing the end of his days on earth, but he knew exactly what to do and still had the vigor to do it. He methodically whipped the decks of the *Martin Wynkoop* from stem to stern. And as the crew members watched and listened in awe, they heard a succession of soft "plops"—these were the sounds the invisible witches made as they jumped overboard to avoid the terrible whip of Dr. Brink. As the last of the company of witches jumped, the sloop bounded forward, eager to be on her way.

Dr. Brink had rid the sloop of witches but he had not ended her troubles. The snuff-taking old witch died. So too did Abraham Hasbrouck; yet the curse remained alive and caused the *Martin Wynkoop* to be feared as an unlucky vessel. Captains came and went; crew members signed on and after a trip or two signed off; new owners lost money and hastily sold the sloop. At last, in 1889, she met her final misfortune when she went to the bottom of the North River off Brimstone Point on the Jersey shore with a load of bricks aboard. Her owners had just bought the sloop and this was her first trip for them. With tears in their eyes, they decided to make no attempt to salvage the sloop.[17]

The second Dr. Brink and the *Martin Wynkoop* died within about a year of each other and the old sloop was not replaced. The acceptance of the steamboat so enthusiastically pioneered by the Chancellor had made the sloops of the Hudson as obsolete as Indian dugout canoes. No member of the Brink family stepped forward to take up the task of witch doctoring which the second Dr. Jacob had laid down. Some felt the power stirring in their fingers but they knew that the witch population was gently declining. The future of a witch doctor, however gifted, seemed unpromising.

They say that the power over witches of the Brinks is still alive and may be used by future generations of the family should the activities of witches ever again become a menace to the people of the region of the Catskills. But others smile at the mention of such a possibility as if at the innocent speculations of a little child. For how could witches ever again infest the Catskills when the Devil from whom they derived their powers lies dead and buried in one of the mountains' cloves?

32

"When the Devil Was Romping in the Catskills"

✤   No PART of the Catskills did more to rouse awe and wonder in pioneer days than the rugged mountain passes known as "the cloves." The word "clove" comes from the old Dutch "kloove." It is similar in origin to the English "cleft" and means a gash or cut in the body of mother earth. The cloves furnished the easiest means of access to the interior of the mountains, yet using the cloves had its drawbacks. A pioneer picking his way up or down a clove must have felt as close to Hell as he was likely to get, at least in this life. For on each side, layer upon layer of rock formed treacherous walls on whose projecting ledges great boulders hung as if threatening to fall down and crush him and the wife, children, and oxen who were the companions of his journey to a new home. It was easy enough for a pioneering man who looked up at the narrow strip of sky overhead to think how quickly the rocky jaws on either side might close in and how he and all who were dear to him might be carried down in one great cosmic gulp to the very throne of the Devil. Such a thought might well have burst into the mind of a simple pioneer; something very like it had occurred even to the sophisticated brain of the great President Timothy Dwight of Yale, the same Dwight who had pondered the dreadful pool of death at Fort Putnam many years before. As Dwight stood in 1815 at the exact spot where John Bartram had once stood and looked out from the rim of the precipice above the Kaaterskill Falls into the dizzy gulf beneath, he noted that the dark and narrow bottom of the clove appeared to be "as it were, a solitary bye-path to the nether world"—that is, to Hell.[1]

One pioneer child is remembered for the question he asked as he traveled through the clove in the town of Roxbury which is now known as the Grand Gorge. Like the youthful Timothy Dwight, he had been taught back home in Connecticut that God was everywhere. As he looked around at the precipitous walls to which spruce and hemlock trees clung in contorted attitudes, doubts assailed him and he asked, "Mother, is God here, too?"[2] The mother gave the boy assurance that God was present even in this unlikely place. Yet she may have hesitated before she replied. For she must have known that the cloves were reputed to be haunts of the Devil. All the horror of mountains which was the ancient heritage of valley dwellers seemed to be concentrated in them, and there the Devil made an occasional personal appearance with all the proper accompaniments of smoke and flame.

To modern eyes the cloves of the Catskills have lost much of their former ability to shock and dismay. Quarrymen, lumbermen, and road builders have done their best to tame them. Tourists who pass through have been taught that the cloves are not the results of an angry slap of the divine hand or a mischievous swish of the Devil's tail but came about as water gnawed and tore and ice gouged during vast reaches of time in the earth's history, helped along by an occasional slow shiver of the planetary skin. The chill that clings to some cloves even on hot summer days does not suggest, to modern minds, the freezing chambers of hell but what practical men call "natural air conditioning." The rocky walls that shut in the traveler no longer bring to mind the yawning jaws of hell—they are more likely to summon an image of the soaring commercial temples that line Wall Street. For while the cloves have indeed greatly changed since pioneer days, the make-up of human minds and emotions has changed even more.

"Those were the days when the Devil was romping around in the Catskills," said a New Kingston old-timer as he told me traditions of the dawn of settlement among the mountains.[3] He spoke with a smile that showed plainly enough that while the Devil and his tricks are still well remembered in the Catskills, they are no longer taken with the seriousness that marked earlier generations.

"They used to say that for six days the Lord labored at creating this earth and on the seventh he threw stones at the Catskill Mountains."[4] In this way another smiling old-timer blamed the Lord for the stoniness of the mountain fields among which he had lived his long life.

Charley Herrick, who lived at the base of Overlook Mountain, had a different explanation. "The Lord hated to go to work making the Catskills," said Charley. "He didn't really want to make the Catskills at all because He knew what a lot of hell was going to be raised there someday. Well, the Lord kept putting it off. And by the time He had all the rest of the world made, He'd run out of dirt. All He had left was rock. So He made the Catskills out of that. Now don't go blaming the Lord, neighbor. He did the best He could with what He had. In His place you or I would have done the same."

"Some say it wasn't the Lord made the Catskills," Charley told me another time, "they say it was the Devil done it. The Devil was flying around in the sky with a big bag of rocks on his back. There was a little hole in the bag and it kept getting bigger. All of a sudden there was a rip like a clap of thunder, the bag busted right open and down fell all those rocks—and they became what we call the Catskill Mountains. It all goes to show what can happen when you don't mend a little hole in a bag in time."

Devil lore is still very much in circulation among the Catskills. And if the tales that are told are to be relied upon there can be no doubt that the Devil was once very active in the mountains. He appeared to pioneers as they worked their fields and there bargained for their souls. He left the prints of his feet upon the rocks. He strolled, he flew, he ran about the Catskills—he seems to have had a fondness for the region as intense as any ever fostered in our day by a chamber of commerce public relations man. And, above all, he was the good friend and adviser of the mountain witches, ever alert in prompting them to fresh acts of mischief and malevolence.

The strong attachment of the Devil to the Catskills is not surprising. It was once widely believed that the waste and uninhabited places of the earth were his favorite hunting grounds and lounging places. When the New World was being seized by white invaders, theologians hastened to warn that the Devil was master of the New World wilderness and that the native Indians were his willing servants and worshipers. The Reverend Cotton Mather, who once taught at Harvard College, expressed the belief that the discovery by Europeans of his American dominion had enraged the Devil and caused him to harass Christian settlers. "I believe that never were more satanic devices used for the unsettling of any people under the sun than what have been employed for the extirpation of the vine which God has here planted."[5] The vine, of course, was the Massachusetts colony of Englishmen. Mather attributed the 1692 outbreak of witchcraft in Salem to the work of an "army of devils" bent upon driving the Christian church from the continent. The explanation was welcome, for it helped ease the consciences of Europeans engaged in robbing the Indians.

The Dutch of New Amsterdam also quickly detected the presence of the Devil especially in unsettled places and among the Indians whom early Dutch reporters described as worshipers of the Devil. Dutch explorers had often seen Indians dancing on a high rocky platform above a cove of the Hudson River near the present city of Newburgh, and they named the place the Devil's Danskammer or dancing room. No early explorer, as far as is now known, set down a single bit of lore linking the Devil and the Catskills, but the abundant Catskill Mountain Devil lore which has come down to our own days makes it plain as a cloven hoof that the Devil has been long and intimately connected with the mountains that stand beside the river, and was probably impatiently waiting there for the first white settlers as they arrived.

The nature of the Catskills with their numerous rocks, their sudden floods and other obstacles to orderly farm life gave the Devil unusual opportunities in his quest for the possession of human souls. A man cursing at the stones which stopped his plow, or at the flood which washed away his crop of corn, wheat, or pumpkins would often enough see the Devil materializing from his very profanity. Anita M. Smith of Woodstock reports something of the sort happening to a farmer known as Petrus Stoll. When the Devil materialized before Petrus' eyes, he got right down to business and agreed to remove the stones from Petrus' fields for a year in return for his immortal soul. But Petrus was a cunning fellow; when the Devil returned and asked for the delivery of his soul, Petrus was ready. He tossed the Devil the soles of his shoes. The Devil knew that his agreement with Petrus had been a verbal one made without witnesses, and he probably suspected that no earthly or heavenly court would uphold his interpretation of the key word in the agreement. He vanished and was seen no more by Petrus.[6] But he freely appeared to others.

A Lewis Hollow old-timer named Riley once told me of a card-playing party which took place one Saturday night in a remote mountainside cabin. The players were absorbed in their game at one minute to midnight when one of them heard a faint noise outside and smelled a curious odor. All put down their cards and investigated. And at the threshold they beheld an immense black rooster who flapped his wings and crowed as midnight came near. The rooster was the Devil come a little too promptly to collect the souls of Sabbath-breaking card players. But thanks to the alertness of the men, the game had stopped just in time to save their souls from the flames of Hell. The Devil, who is often portrayed as a sporting loser in the lore of the Catskills, did not argue but flew off like a gentleman leaving behind a strong odor of brimstone and a few floating feathers of a re-markably intense black.

The Devil was powerful indeed among the Catskills and never was his power made more evident than when the mere writing down of his name wrenched a fine farm from the hands of the Chancellor himself. They say that a man had been offered a farm on the usual lease for three lives. He set down his own name, that of his son, and—the Devil's. The Chancellor shared in the religious skepticism of his time and his station in life; it is unlikely that he believed in the existence of the Devil; yet whether he believed that a lease with the Devil as tenant would be held by the courts to last forever or felt that it would be a good thing to have so ingenious a man as the prospective tenant on his lands, no one knows. But he took the remarkable step of selling the man his farm in fee simple, and so side-stepped the possibility of cosigning a document with the Devil's proxy.[7]

Sightings of the Devil were once even more common in the region of the Catskills than sightings of flying saucers were to become in a later era. But often the Devil would behave with subtlety and act invisibly either through a recognized witch or without revealing his identity. There was, by way of example, the mysterious case of the two brothers who were building a log cabin near Yankeetown Pond. They laid their first four courses of logs neatly and well and then went to sleep for the night in a shack they had run up nearby. But when they awoke they found their logs torn down and scattered. They laid their logs in place again. That night the brothers took turns sitting up to make sure the logs would stay where they belonged. They heard not a sound from the cabin all through that night. But when they looked at the cabin as the sun rose they saw that every log had been taken down again. The brothers stared at each other "and without a word, went into their shack and packed their things and left"—so Neva Shultis of Woodstock told the tale. Had the Devil himself been the cabin wrecker? No one has ever been sure. But no one was bold enough to build on that site again.[8]

The Devil made many appearances in many forms especially to lonely workers among the forests and in the cloves of the Catskills. One of the last to be recorded took place more than a century ago. The sighter was a member of the MacDaniel family of Shady. Woodsman MacDaniel had finished a hard day's work in the upper Sawkill Valley once known to William Cockburn as the Great Clove. He was trying to head for home with his oxen. But everything went wrong—it was as if something was preventing his oxen from moving on. Then just ahead of the oxen he saw the Devil. He tried profanity but realizing that this only encouraged the Devil, he fell on his knees and prayed. A fog descended on the Devil and when it dispersed, the Devil was gone and the oxen were free to proceed homeward.[9]

It could not have been long after the MacDaniel sighting that the Devil died—as far as the Catskills were concerned. Tangible evidence of his death has been shown to travelers for years now close beside the Stony Clove which had been a favorite haunt of the Devil ever since the first days of settlement.

The Kaaterskill Clove, the Plattekill Clove, and others, had their awe-inspiring features but early nineteenth-century travelers often saved up their fanciest figures of speech to describe the horrors of the Stony Clove. In the early 1840s Charles Lanman, a painter and writer who was soon to become Daniel Webster's secretary and a popular figure in Washington society, wrote of the Stony Clove: "It is the loneliest and most awful corner of the world that I have ever seen—none other, I fancy, could make a man feel more utterly desolate. It is a type of the valley of the shadow of death; in single file did we have to pass through it and in single file must we pass to the grave. . . ."[10]

The clove that Lanman visited was so narrow at one point that a single hesitant wagon track could barely be squeezed through a few years later. On one side mighty Hunter Mountain rose to some four thousand feet. On the other stood Mink or Plateau Mountain rich in ancient spruce and balsam fir trees, heavy with great sliding rocks, and treacherous with crumbling precipices. The clove's floor was almost as pinched as the one above the headwaters of Hollow Tree Brook where a man who wants to make the effort can stand today with one foot on West Kill Mountain and the other on a supporting ridge of Hunter Mountain so that he may boast ever afterward that he once stood on two mountains at the same time. Highway and railroad makers blasted and filled the Stony Clove, and there forest fires raged until the ancient horrors of the place were driven away. Tourists driving through the Stony Clove over the smooth surface of route 214 in mid-twentieth century wonder why their grandfathers wasted so much good emotion on the place. They may get some clue if they approach the clove from the north as a late afternoon thunderstorm is brewing among the mountains to the southwest. Then as the daylight dims they will see Hunter and Plateau mountains assume threatening postures, seem to grow in bulk, and move closer together. Lightning and thunder will be tossed back and forth from one mountain to the other. And it will not be hard for a man with a normal amount of imagination to put himself in the place of his ancestors and see the Stony Clove transformed into the very gates of Hell.

Several generations ago a vacationer among the romantic Catskills had only to pay his dime to be admitted to the Devil's Kitchen located at the head of Plattekill Clove. There a guide would show him great boulders deep in a gorge draped with ferns and alive with the tinkle and murmur of water. These boulders were the Devil's saucepans, his tea kettle, and other pieces of kitchenware. Ladders and stairways of wood led from one level to another. The guide would give details of the Devil's methods of cooking and point out his many ingenious household gadgets. In this way a generation of men and women who had been molded by nineteenth-century romantic thinking and feeling turned the old Devil-beliefs and Devil-fears of their ancestors into pleasant amusement. Vacationers were happy to pay their dimes to spend a half hour of mock horror among the Devil's pots and pans and to feel superior to the old-timers who had taken such things seriously.

Today the Devil's Kitchen is deserted. Its ladders and stairways have rotted away, and the kitchen utensils have long ago reverted to being simple boulders deposited by glacial power. The Devil's Pulpit which was once among the glories of the Stony Clove—it was an elevated ledge with a rude lectern—has also been forgotten. From it, so tourists of bygone times were told, the Devil had harangued his congregation of mountain witches and perhaps urged resistance to Dr. Brink. It has been many years since any summer boarder in blazer and boater has climbed into the pulpit and given his imitation of the Devil's platform manner.[11] Yet one stony object closely associated with the Devil still survives. Each summer it draws thousands of pilgrims. It is the Devil's Tombstone.

The Tombstone is a slab of sandstone almost six feet wide and perhaps seven feet high with a rudely rounded top. It was set on end many thousands of years ago by water and ice power and has much the look of a conventional tombstone of gigantic size. It stands within what is known officially as the Devil's Tombstone Camping Site of the New York State Department of Conservation. As far back as the 1860s the Tombstone was photographed for viewing in a parlor stereoscope. This earliest known photograph shows the stone with a mountain wagon and team beside it and some roughly dressed men cooking nearby. The men were probably fishermen—for the trout streams in the neighborhood were once famous, and Charles Lanman reported that he and his party caught seven hundred during their overnight stay.

There is unfortunately no inscription on the Tombstone giving the Devil's dates of birth and death and other pertinent information. But campers at the site are sometimes brought to rapt attention as they see a

slanting beam of late afternoon sunlight illuminating the face of the
Tombstone. Then for a few moments the rough surface of the stone seems
to pulse with meaning as ancient scratches and eroded pits appear to
arrange themselves into the symbols of a forgotten language which might
very well, could they be translated, give the world the details of the
Devil's death amid the scenic splendor of the Catskill Mountains. But
until a translator comes along, it will be necessary to take the Tombstone
and the great event it commemorates on faith.

33

"Propre Exertions"

🌿 WHILE WITCHES, the Devil, and Dr. Brink were supplying the pioneers of the Catskills with excitement and part of their explanation of the mysteries of human life, the eleven Livingstons of Clermont were carrying out plans for making the most of their shares of the old judge's vast domain in the Hardenbergh Patent. These Livingstons had a good many traits in common but each had his own personality and his or her own set of motives and prejudices. That is why the eleven Livingstons went about getting what they could from their Hardenbergh Patent lands in eleven different ways. Exactly how each one operated has been somewhat blurred by time, but enough of each outline remains visible to make it clear that the eleven Clermont influences left marks, and some of these marks still show upon the landscape and people of the Catskills.

The Chancellor as leader of the group and master of a quarter of a million acres in the patent had the most compelling reasons for putting his intelligence and energy to work at the task of raising his lands' value. He realized, as had his grandfather, that the timber of the mountains was likely to prove their greatest marketable product. Like his grandfather, the Chancellor did his best to prevent wasteful ways of clearing lands and harvesting timber, and the terms of his leases reflect this aim. During the 1790s and at the turn of the century he saw a good deal of a remarkable man named Frederick Augustus DeZeng, a former German baron who was the son of the chief forester of the King of Saxony. DeZeng had operated a sawmill in the Esopus Valley in the 1780s and looked at the trees of the Catskills with a knowing eye. He came from a part of the world in which modern forestry was being born; he was aware of the possibility that the Catskill Mountains' combination of water power, timber for fuel, and closeness to cheap transportation on the Hudson River could give birth to profitable industrial development. In 1802 he urged the

Chancellor to become his partner in setting up a glass factory in Woodstock. The Chancellor, then American minister to France, had many important things on his mind and declined to become involved or even to hunt for Flemish or French glass blowers for DeZeng's proposed glass factory. Inciting these skilled workers to emigrate was forbidden in Europe. The Chancellor was usually set ablaze by every hint of a new project, yet he was sensible enough to shy away from supplying illegal emigrants to DeZeng.[1]

The Chancellor was not at all reluctant, however, to work with DeZeng on other projects. The ex-baron shipped him a tierce of American hickory and butternuts which the Chancellor hoped to persuade French landowners to plant. He helped revive a failing road-building project in which the Chancellor was a prime mover—the road followed the course of the colonial one which had once made its bumpy way through the Esopus Valley and up steep Pine Hill and so on to the Susquehanna country. Soon the New York legislature chartered the road and authorized its managers to issue stock and collect tolls. The road, it was hoped, would challenge the very successful Susquehanna Turnpike which opened in 1801 and eventually ran from Salisbury in Connecticut through Catskill and on to Wattles Ferry on the Susquehanna. Two manor Livingstons were prominent stockholders. The road DeZeng promoted also began at the iron-mining town of Salisbury and ended at Wattles Ferry. But it reached its destination over lands belonging to most of the eleven Livingstons of Clermont, and passed through Kingston. It was first known as the Dutchess, Ulster and Delaware Turnpike—DUD for short. And a dud it proved for its stockholders. It quickly formed the habit of losing money year after year while performing a fine service for the Chancellor and the other Hardenbergh Patent landholders whose backwoods lands it made reachable and more valuable. Kingston men had begun the road which DeZeng carried to a rough completion. It was Kingston men who tried to push another road to the northwest.[2]

In 1783, with the Revolution barely ended, Kingston men became eager to help their town become a center of trade for the region of the Catskills. They sent out a group of "explorers"—so the Kingston trustees' records name them—to locate roads to the mountain backwoods, including the land the Chancellor had given them. A gang of some fifty local men was set to work building "the Schoharie Road"[3] which found its way through Woodstock's Mink Hollow to the valley of the Schoharie, on to the vicinity of Prattsville, and so westward. The "Widder Palling" sent a slave to help and several other Kingston slaveowners did likewise. The road followed the route marked by William Cockburn on a map dated 1773.[4] Over this road, settlers on Livingston, Hardenbergh, Desbrosses, and other lands traveled to and from their pitches in "Schohariekill," pausing for refreshment at the numerous taverns of Woodstock. Other prewar roads or trails were reopened and improved. One led away from Catskill over the route later followed by the Susquehanna Turnpike. In the late 1760s it had traversed the lands granted by King George to his old soldiers. Prewar roads into the wilds of Sullivan County were also reopened and ambitious new ones projected, all with the help of large landowners. Traders and traffickers who did business along the Hudson also lent an eager hand, for they understood that if they did not act to steer backwoods trade toward their own shops and wharves, the businessmen of rival Hudson Valley towns would. New towns were organized and they took over older roads and added new ones. The local politicians who dominated them were very often tools of the large landowners or of projectors of industries.

Small industries were springing into being at every accessible waterfall. Paint was made from red shale; barrel staves and headings were turned out; ingenious Yankees in the northeastern part of the mountains set up an amazing variety of manufactures many of them brought over bodily from Connecticut. The Yankee Bartons made sleigh and church bells in Purling; others fabricated clocks or made wagons and sleighs from the straight-grained oaks and ashes of the Catskills. Sawmills appeared like mushrooms after a late summer rain. Iron, brought over the new turnpike from Columbia County or Salisbury, became the basis of many industries. Ex-Baron DeZeng set up a forge in Woodstock and there processed pig iron with the help of charcoal and water-powered triphammers and converted it into tough bars for the use of blacksmiths.[5]

Almost a century after the Hardenbergh Patent had been devised, a sort of boom seized the area and surrounding lands. The boom had the usual accompaniments of speculation and a vast amount of sharp legal footwork aimed at taking advantage of slipshod early surveys or the incompetence or chicanery of ancient conveyancers and landowners. The northern line of the Hardenbergh Patent was surveyed three times and each time the results were different: Men who had settled there were kept in a perpetual state of anguish as the big landlords exchanged legal blows. Here and there a backwoods pettifogger uncovered a discrepancy in old surveys which encouraged him to claim a gore of land he believed to be public property. David Haynes built a house on such a gore in Sullivan County and fought a Livingston of Clermont over the title until he was beggared and the Livingston took possession.[6] William Cockburn was getting old but he kept busy ejecting the squatters who persisted in pouring into the patent. Cockburn found the task almost hopeless and squatters multiplied. Yet the price of the mountain lands rose substantially in the decade after 1790, sometimes from fifty cents an acre to three or even four dollars.[7] In 1802 DeZeng expressed what was going on very well in a letter to the Chancellor, who was far away from it all in Paris where he was beginning the negotiations that were to lead to the Louisiana Purchase.

"Nothing has been wanting to make the great *Patent flourish as propre Exertions* which thancks to fortune, are now visible . . . ,"[8] wrote DeZeng in his oddly accented English. He was right. "Propre Exertions" were being made all over the Catskills. By hard-working settlers, by hunters shooting bears or catching wild pigeons for the New York market, by gangs of lumbermen, by farmers, by surveyors and speculators and road builders. By rich and indolent landlords too when they signed papers authorizing the purchase of turnpike stock or additional lands among the mountains. Yankee peddlers made exertions when, with packs on their backs, they sought out isolated clearings to sell their treasures of needles, pins, and lace, before elections candidates' agents treated settlers in the backwoods to "Gammon & Bread."[9] In order to induce them to vote right, the witches and Dr. Brink redoubled their opposing efforts. Never before had human exertion reached so shrill a pitch in the region of the Catskills. The results began to become apparent as regiments of great hemlocks and beeches were slain, as smoke clouds rose from many a burning "follow," and joined together, at times, to form a great gray pall over the Catskills. They became apparent, too, as schoolhouses and little churches were noisily nailed together at muddy crossroads. Housewives worked at their spinning wheels and their smoky kitchen fires; children gathered berries under girdled trees and sometimes lost their lives in the course of this innocent pursuit when great branches fell upon them even on windless days.

The Catskills were doing no more than sharing in the march of Americans in the search for land which was a compulsion of the times. A mountain landlord had only to stretch forth his hand to catch settlers—if only temporary ones—for his lands. Even leases for three lives found takers, thanks to the gnawing land hunger of Americans.

The eleven Livingstons of Clermont did their share of exerting, and none of them exerted in more pleasant surroundings than the Chancellor. Comfortably installed at Clermont or at his town house at number 3 Broadway in the city of New York, he was waited upon by a staff of slaves headed by a dignified gray-haired butler. No American believed more firmly that all men were created equal; none lived amid surroundings that said more strongly that they were not.

At Clermont the Chancellor exerted in a fine house of French inspiration which he built in 1794. It was H-shaped—in one wing was his library of many thousands of books. In this library the business of the Court of Chancery was often carried on; here too his land agents came to discuss Hardenbergh Patent matters. At the southern end of the house was a conservatory. "In this greenhouse," wrote E. B. Livingston in 1910, "the dinner and supper tables were set on great occasions, the tables being so constructed that the largest and most ornamental of the plants rose from their center. Two head gardeners took charge of the greenhouse and gardens." A terrace between two wings of the house "was filled with orange, lemon and myrtle trees in summer." These exotic trees, of course, were in tubs. The furnishings of the house were elegant enough by American standards of the 1790s. When the Chancellor returned from his mission to France in 1804 he brought with him treasures to enrich Clermont. Treasures in the form of old tapestries, fine silver, and gilded or inlaid chairs and tables. These he had bought from French aristocrats impoverished by the social changes that had transformed their country. In later life, as a feminine relative recalled, "Cousin Chancellor would walk about among the young people relating the history of each piece of furniture or plate. The Chancellor was fond of riding, and was on horseback a great deal, but when he made calls he drove in a great gilded coach drawn by four horses. . . ."[10]

In order to maintain his style of living, the Chancellor's possessions among the Catskills were made to play their part. His grandfather had tied his patent lands to Clermont by means of a road from his Woodstock sawmill to the Hudson. The Chancellor made the tie stronger by buying land across the river at Saugerties, especially at the mouth of the Esopus Creek which drained much of his land in the mountains. His ingenious mind may have considered the possibility of floating pine and hemlock logs down the Esopus to the Hudson at Clermont. Some years later his son-in-law Robert L. Livingston was promoting a scheme to clear the creek of obstructions and use it to transport Livingston logs.[11] Timber in large quantities processed at his sawmills on the patent was hauled to the Chancellor's base at Saugerties by tenant labor and floated across the river to Clermont on days when wind and tide favored. The timber brought cash which enabled the democratic Chancellor to keep up his aristocratic way of life. In this way, great pine, oak, and tulip trees of the Catskills became transmuted into the French armchairs of Clermont, the mirrors in carved and gilded frames, and the sets of classic authors bound in tree calf ornamented with tooling in the taste of the French Empire.

Not only did the trees of the Catskills do their bits for the Chancellor's comfort, the very land itself sometimes turned into elements of the Clermont way of life. The plumbing, for example, was paid for in part by giving the plumber a wilderness farm far out on the western borders of the Chancellor's domain in the Catskills.[12] When agricultural improvements, or his very expensive experiments in making travel by steamboat a reality, demanded financial help, the Chancellor requested William Cockburn or Dr. Wilson, who succeeded Cockburn as bailiff, to put pressure on his tenants in the matter of back rents. The Chancellor was the kindest of men. Within reasonable limits he was able to sympathize with the struggles of his Hardenbergh Patent tenants. Only a need for money to enable him to pursue his visions of mechanical, political, or agricultural glory could persuade him to press his poor and struggling tenants. Outright sales of mountain lands at a safe distance from Clermont served to help extricate the Chancellor from the recurrent shortages of cash that plagued many a landed gentleman of his time who believed that it was his public duty to live well. The Chancellor was luckier than many other men of his class—he had a quarter-of-a-million-acre appendage to his home estate upon which he could draw for help on his rainy days.

The Chancellor's ten brothers and sisters also used their Catskill Mountain holdings as something for a rainy day. Brother John Robert was a businessman who had devoted the years of the Revolution to making as much money as possible from the conflict. When he came into his thirty-two thousand acres, much of it in Sullivan County, he leased as much as he could and sold what he had to when he needed capital. In 1808 he advertised fifty Sullivan County farms for lease for three lives. No rent was asked for the first three years; after that the rent would gradually rise until it stabilized at fifteen bushels of wheat per hundred acres. The tenant, of course, would pay all taxes. When John died in 1851 at the age of ninety-six he still owned nine thousand of the acres deeded to him by his brother the Chancellor in 1779.[13]

Sister Catherine's acres in the Catskills were put to use for very different ends. In 1793 Catherine married the Reverend Freeborn Garrettson, a zealous Methodist preacher who was to rise to the post of presiding elder of his church in New York. The marriage was a bit shocking to the older Livingstons for the Methodist Church appealed most powerfully to the lower sort who had been somewhat neglected by the staid Reformed and Anglican churches. Its converts praised the Lord in joyful shouts and sometimes fainted away in their meeting places from an overabundance of religious emotion. They believed in "conditional election" and "free will," doctrines which promised salvation to all who would repent and believe and not just to a select few. Catherine's mother was a woman of human warmth as well as business shrewdness. She accepted her new son-in-law and gave the young couple a farm adjoining Clermont. There they proceeded to build a Methodist church. The Reverend Freeborn then did his best to spread Methodism among the farmers of the Hudson Valley and the settlers of the Catskills. He worked diligently in co-operation with other pioneer New York Methodists and eventually saw the region dotted with little Methodist churches. Into this work went a share of the profits of his wife's Catskill Mountain lands.

Of all the eleven Livingstons of Clermont, the one who profited least from his mountain lands was Edward. He had gone far since the day he argued against the Bradstreet heirs in 1785. His fine mind and devotion to public affairs quickly made him a leader at the bar and in government. By 1803 when he was mayor of New York and federal attorney for the New York district, glory and disaster struck almost simultaneously. New York was being terrorized by an epidemic of yellow fever and the rich and wellborn were leaving the city for the refuge afforded by such rural sanctuaries as Greenwich Village. But Edward Livingston did his duty without flinching. He remained at his post and directed civic activities throughout the dreadful times, visiting the sick and in other ways not hesitating to expose himself to the disease. He became a popular hero.

But while Edward was doing his duty, a subordinate in his federal attorney's office was not. On the eve of the epidemic the man had embezzled more than forty-three thousand dollars of public money. Edward was responsible for the safety of the funds entrusted to his office, yet he might easily have escaped suffering for the embezzlement. But with the generosity that characterizes the aristocratic spirit at its best, he refused to evade responsibility and pledged all his landed wealth to make repayment with interest. And in this way, says Livingston family tradition, Edward lost his great landed estate in the Catskills. But the mortgage records of Ulster County suggest a different explanation. They show that the lands were mortgaged during the late 1790s when Edward was raising money to finance a political career in Washington where he was serving as a member of Congress. He mortgaged his mountain lands to two French businessmen named Lausett and Bouchard. The two eventually foreclosed their mortgages and became owners of Edward's Hardenbergh Patent holdings. Following his resignation as mayor, Edward left for Louisiana where he embarked on a new and successful career which was to raise him to the positions of United States Senator, Secretary of State, and Minister to France.

Others of the eleven clung to their lands with vigor and came to depend on the rents they yielded for income. Sister Janet was widowed when her husband General Richard Montgomery heroically fell in the course of the assault upon Quebec of 1775, and a widow she remained for the rest of her long life, devoting herself to cherishing the memory of Montgomery. "My General," she called him. When she was an old lady the sight of a silhouette of her General brought from her this touching if literary lamentation. "Hard was thy fate most amiable of men! But alas—how much more so, the lott of thy unhappy wife—condemned to live and live without thee, whilst cruel remembrance is continually comparing the past with the present, and imbittering the whole. . . ."

Mrs. Montgomery's income came from rents and occasional sales of her lands on both sides of the Hudson. This income was far from sending a steady flow of cash into the distinguished widow's bank account. On the Fourth of July, 1820 she wrote to one of her brothers who had expressed sympathy for her lonely lot: ". . . I am far better off than many. My debts are few, as my retired situation has enabled me to pay many off, and, in truth solitude is now becoming my wish. My farm supplies me with many things and is every year improving in beauty. My garden abounds in good fruit, and what more can an old woman require? If my rents were regularly paid, I should not want, but my poor tenants at Delaware have been pretty distressed by the grasshopper, which like Pharaoh's have devoured everything they had. [Their] cattle died by hundreds and they were reduced to take the thatching from their barn to feed them, notwithstanding one of my tenants lost twenty-six head. From these it were vain to hope or expect anything."[14] The lands of Mrs. Montgomery over which the grasshoppers swarmed were in Great Lot 40 in the present towns of Bovina and Middletown. They lay to the north and northeast of the Chancellor's gift to Kingston, in a great pastureland of soaring hills and fertile valleys.

Mrs. Montgomery had no desire to settle upon her lands in the Hardenbergh Patent. Their role in her life was merely to supply income. All her brothers and sisters agreed that life amid the cultural wastes of the Hardenbergh Patent would be far from pleasant. The winters in that region of high plateaus and dark valleys were long, and the snow came early and lingered in deep drifts until late April. The roads were good enough for the use of tenants and their oxen, but would have speedily jolted a Livingston carriage to pieces. There was no "society" except for that afforded by bears, wolves, and unlettered tenants. Livingstons had become used to living well. Their kind of living was not possible in the Catskills as the nineteenth century began. Perhaps in another generation or two it might be. Only one of the eleven Livingstons of Clermont made any attempt to settle on the lands deeded to them by the Chancellor. That was sister Gertrude, and her attempt when it came was to have a very interesting logic of its own. But before Gertrude and her husband, General Morgan Lewis, took up residence on their lands, a member of another Hardenbergh Patent family made a serious and successful try at settling down as a permanent resident on his share of the family lands. He was Isaac Hardenbergh, grandson of the old major.

34

Absentee and Resident Landlords

✣ ABOUT 1790 Isaac Hardenbergh appeared on his share of the family lands in the present town of Roxbury. He was in his mid-thirties and a great-grandson of the major. During the Revolution he had served under Jacob Rose or Roosa when that unfortunate man was a captain in the Whig forces. Once the title to his land in the northeast corner of Great Lot 19 was made reasonably secure by the decision in the Bradstreet case, Isaac proposed settling on it and making the care of it his lifework.

Unlike the Livingstons, the Hardenberghs had never managed to reach the upper level of New York society. They remained prosperous and comfortable people. With few exceptions their education was limited. They followed conservative Hudson Valley Dutch traditions in their way of life and seemed to have little desire to be thought of as fashionable. The Livingstons liked to dress in keeping with the latest fashions of London and Paris. Isaac, who possessed the tall and vigorous physique that marked the men of his family, wore the knee breeches and cocked hat of colonial days until he died in 1821. When Isaac came to Roxbury —which was then known as Beaverdam and formed part of the huge town of Woodstock—he had no craving to live as a manually idle and intellectually active country gentleman. He built and operated a sawmill and gristmill and kept a store in the basement of the fine stone house he built about 1806. It is this house that is now miscalled the Hardenbergh Manor House. And while a Livingston of his day would have arranged to have an obedient agent elected supervisor when Roxbury became a separate town, Isaac took the job himself. He sent down strong roots into the red soil of Roxbury and there his descendants lived until the death in 1933 of Agnes, the spinster granddaughter who was known locally as "the last of the Hardenberghs."[1]

As the patent became more thickly settled a number of nephews and grandsons of the Chancellor came to live on their Hardenbergh Patent lands, but in ways that were very unlike those of Isaac. They had suffered disappointments or difficulties in life and were retreating to their mountain lands, upon which they hoped to live in eighteenth-century style surrounded by their tenants. The dream could not come true; it was a dream that may have touched the Chancellor back in 1779 as he turned over shares of his father's estate in the Catskills to his brothers and sisters. He was giving them the chance to set up their own versions of Clermont among the mountains, each with its big house for the master and mistress and its humble cottages for the tenants, its little church and its mills. To an eighteenth-century mind there was no good reason why landed estates like these might not take root and endure for centuries and eventually become surrounded by the air of ancient and unchanging peace which appeared to the eyes of visiting Americans to hang over old English manors. The English manors were, in fact, awakening to the bitter class hostility that would lead to the reforms of the next generation, but the fact was hidden from better-sort Americans by a screen of Old World glamor.[2]

Robert Livingston Tillotson appeared in Sullivan County during the first half of the nineteenth century and proposed to settle down and become part of the land which had been deeded to his mother, the Chancellor's sister Maria. He was a lawyer and he married the daughter of Sullivan County Judge Gillespie and became surrogate. James E. Quinlan, the Sullivan County historian, wrote that Tillotson was "of a genial and pleasant humor—an aristocrat by birth, a man of the people at heart. Ever bubbling over with wit, he was yet chivalrous and punctilious, unfortunately he was of convivial inclinations . . . he was a duellist withal. . . ."[3] When the Civil War broke out, he joined the Union forces and died while serving with the Army of the Potomac.

About 1827 David Augustus Clarkson who had just married a granddaughter of the Chancellor proceeded to his wife's family lands near Lord's Pond in the town of Thompson in Sullivan County and there built a "fine stone mansion on a commanding site." Here, says Quinlan, "it was his intention to live like a lord of the manor among the tenants of his father-in-law, who were bound by their leases to deliver annually to the owner or his agents certain substantials and luxuries. But the tenants did not contribute enough for his support and to escape starvation he left the town, and to this day [1875] has been living in elegant idleness at Saugerties."[4] Clarkson lived at a time when a wife's property was at the disposition of her husband and he was one of a number of Livingstons-by-marriage who tried to set up manorlike estates on the old Hardenbergh Patent.

A Livingston by birth who made a try at the same thing was Dr. Edward Livingston, a physician son of the Chancellor's brother John Robert. The doctor's wife became insane not long after their marriage and Edward "buried himself in the woods" of his lands near what is known today in memory of his family as Livingston Manor in Sullivan County. He was generous to the poor and liberal in his gifts to the local churches. He took up drawing in 1840 and used the kind of sketchbook which befitted a Livingston of Clermont—its sides were of blue moiré and its back of tooled and gilded green morocco. He loaded this incongruous vehicle with records of Sullivan County scenery in the days of settlement. On its pages stump-filled hillsides were set down in pencil; so too were the haphazard log shelters of men and cattle; in every brook or pond, groups of logs were waiting for a flood to take them downstream where they would be made into rafts which would float down the Delaware to Philadelphia. The bleak and desolate landscapes which the doctor set down in meticulous detail—but without finishing a single drawing—well reflected the injured spirit that sent him to the backwoods in search of peace.[5]

Only one spot on all the vast Livingston holdings in the Hardenbergh Patent gave evidence of becoming anything like a little Clermont, and it still retains a good deal of the air that once hung over the estates elsewhere of the great absentee landlords of the Catskills. The continual resistance of tenants, the abolition of the rule of primogeniture, and the partial extension of democratic principles to the foggy realm of landowning, all made unlikely the duplication of Clermont among the Catskills. Yet on the far borders of the old Hardenbergh Patent, a few miles from Delhi in Delaware County, a Livingston estate of nearly two thousand acres came into being. Its name is Lake Delaware.

A stranger approaching Lake Delaware from the southeast over route 28 may sense a change in the landscape as he nears the side road leading to the hamlet of Bovina Center, the closest settlement to Lake Delaware. The stranger will have come to this part of the world through dairy-farming country. There pastures and cows are to be seen everywhere except on the highest hilltops from which an echo of the forest which once covered this region still faintly sounds. From the summits of those unforested hills, the stranger has had a good chance to become acquainted with the landscape of the western part of the Catskill foothills. He has probably stopped his car on an especially promising summit and been stirred by the rhythmic pattern of high hills and sweeping ridges which give the land a suggestion, on dark days, of a stormy sea. In the troughs of the waves he has caught sight of the white houses and the attendant red barns of the farmers who now own the lands—they were once the property of General Montgomery's widow. But as the road glides down into the town of Bovina a change seems to come over the landscape on the left. The barbed wire seen elsewhere gives way to neat rail fences; the rolling fields seem to be turning greener and more lush; a few buildings glimpsed from the highway are remarkably well kept.

Then something altogether unexpected happens—an imposing stone church appears amid a cluster of old trees to the left. A discreet notice board identifies it as the Episcopalian Church of St. James. It was built a generation or two ago of sandstone. Its style is not clear cut—although built all at one time, it mingles Norman and Gothic elements in the manner of European churches which have grown slowly through the centuries. A rectory and a parish house are loosely attached to the church by enclosed courtyards filled on bright middays with sunlight flickering through the surrounding maple trees. Similar churches are not uncommon in American suburbs where the rich congregate. Here in Bovina (the name is a tribute to the common cow to whose efforts the surrounding country owes its income) a church like this could not grow naturally out of the people and soil. How then did it come to this secluded valley far from the accepted haunts of the very rich?

The answer is hinted at by a modest private road which begins beside the church and leads up a gentle slope to a large white-pillared house which overlooks a lake of one hundred forty acres. The lake is edged by lawn and forest with only a neat boathouse to mar the integrity of its shoreline. This is Lake Delaware, the lovely center of an estate of nearly two thousand acres upon which are scattered stables and farm buildings and, hidden among stately old trees, the summer homes of a number of descendants of the Chancellor's sister Gertrude and her husband, Major General Morgan Lewis.

When the Chancellor deeded Gertrude her 19,400 acres on September 4, 1779, Gertrude was already married to ambitious young Colonel Lewis whose father, a New York tanner and furrier of Welsh origin, had given him a good start in life. In 1794 Lewis ordered his wife's tract of land surveyed and divided into farms upon which he settled tenants who paid their rents in bushels of wheat and labor.[6] With the help of their tenants he and his wife built the pillared house. Each summer the Lewises traveled across the Catskills on horseback to spend the hottest months of the year in their clapboard Greek temple beside the lake. Their motives in retreating to Lake Delaware have been hinted at by family traditions which dwell upon the amazing healthfulness of the place.[7] It was a charmed spot two thousand feet above the sea to which the deadly epidemics that gripped Atlantic coast towns in summer never dared venture. As the eighteenth century died and the nineteenth was born, rich Philadelphians, New Yorkers, and Charlestonians were building isolated rural sanctuaries where they hoped to escape the diseases of summer. The Lewises, whose sole link to the future was their daughter, Elizabeth, probably built their house far out in the Hardenbergh Patent in pursuit of this same hope. If so, the pursuit may have been worthwhile, for the general reached the age of ninety, while Elizabeth produced half a dozen children and died at eighty. The salutary air of the lake was less effective with Gertrude Lewis—she left this earth when a mere seventy-six.

General Lewis had many achievements to be proud of. He served as attorney general of his state and as the chief justice of its Supreme Court. He was elected governor and while in that office earnestly advocated a system of free public schools. During part of the War of 1812 he was in command of the United States forces on the Niagara frontier. Yet of all his achievements none seemed to give Lewis greater satisfaction than his alliance by marriage with the aristocratic Livingstons, for to tell the truth he was something of a snob. From a beginning amid the evil smells of the Swamp—the name of the tanners' district of New York in which his father worked and prospered—Lewis had climbed high. Thanks to an imposing presence and a genuine desire to do as well in whatever he undertook as his by no means outstanding abilities would permit, he had become thoroughly accepted by New York's better sort. At Lake Delaware he out-Livingstoned the Livingstons by creating the kind of landed estate that could have won the hearty approval of old Robert of Clermont. Lewis kept a tight rein on his tenants; at the same time he won their respect and loyalty by occasionally making the benevolent gestures customary among the more enlightened landlords of Europe in the Middle Ages.

When the War of 1812 broke out, many Lewis tenants or their sons enlisted and a number died while in service. Lewis instructed his land agent to forgive a year's rent for each campaign a tenant served. Later he announced that the agent would arrange to forgive all back rents of tenants who had been in military service and who were "actually resident on their farms." The back rents forgiven were estimated at $7402.63.[8]

Today the spacious old house at Lake Delaware suggests the sort of long and leisurely family occupancy that was the ideal of eighteenth-century New York landlords. The house has been greatly enlarged from its Lewis form, and its many additions quietly reflect a century and a half of changing taste. In the library are still to be found the rent-rolls of the days when the Lewis' daughter, Elizabeth, summered at the lake with her husband, Maturin Livingston, a descendant of a nephew of Robert the first lord of Livingston Manor. For to balance the erosive effects on large landholdings caused by the abolition of the rule of primogeniture, Livingstons had slipped into the habit of marrying one another and so keeping property in the family.

The paintings hanging on the walls within the temple at Lake Delaware tell a tale of the secure existence led by families like the Livingstons who have enjoyed the benefit of privileged position generation after generation. Dogs and horses of the past look down from the walls as dogs and horses of the present scamper or canter outside. Morgan Lewis in all his dignity ornaments a wall; so too do many of his descendants. His great-granddaughter Louisa is there, and her husband's likeness hangs in the hall. He was Elbridge Thomas Gerry, commodore of the New York Yacht Club and a kindly man who worked hard at establishing the Society for the Prevention of Cruelty to Children and to bring about the substitution of the electric chair for the hangman's noose in the belief that this would prove a kindlier method of killing people under law. The commodore was—as if all this weren't enough—a descendant of the Elbridge Gerry who had been James Madison's vice-president and whose name has found its way into the dictionaries as the verb "gerrymander,"[9] in tribute to Gerry's political skill. The descendants of the commodore and Louisa now own the Lake Delaware estate. The church at their gates owes its being to Gerry benevolence, and it would surely have delighted Judge Livingston had he been able to foresee it as he dreamed with pen in hand on Christmas Eve in 1766.

It is said that the old house at Lake Delaware is haunted by the spirit of Morgan Lewis.[10] If the old general and governor should descend the fine spiral staircase of native cherry wood he would find his gold-headed cane waiting for him in the broad hall amid a collection of silver-headed ones used by his Livingston descendants. If the Lewis ghost then proceeded, cane in hand, to inspect the shrunken remains of his almost twenty thousand acres he might well be puzzled. For in the governor's day his estate did more than symbolize his exalted status, it yielded a modest income. Clermont with its eighty farms out on lease in addition to those in the Hardenbergh Patent performed the same service for the Chancellor. The Lake Delaware estate of today has been shorn of its economic value; only its symbolic value remains. It is a notable example of the kind of pleasant and imposing style of life possible for the better sort of our own century.

Gertrude Livingston and the governor made only brief summer stays at Lake Delaware. They spent much of the rest of the year in the substantial house they built overlooking the Hudson River at Staatsburgh. From the Lewis place northward, a succession of Livingston and Livingston-related estates once adorned the riverbank and faced the Catskill Mountains. It was here that most of the Chancellor's brothers and sisters and their children chose to live. They spent much of the money from their lands among the Catskills on these Hudson River mansions and their surroundings. When these estates were at the peak of their glory they formed a remarkable feature of American life. But before they could reach that point a good deal was to happen. For one thing, a vast change began taking place in American attitudes toward the land upon which they lived. And a landlord who operated with much less finesse than the Livingstons and Morgan Lewis was murdered—by his own rebellious tenants. The landlord was known as Gross Hardenbergh.

35

"The Hardenbergh War"

✤ GERARDUS, JR., or Gradus, or Gross, Hardenbergh—he was known by both nicknames—was born in the old Jacob Rutsen house in Rosendale probably in the late spring of 1744. His Christian name was a hand-me-down from an uncle—his Albany great-grandfather had been known as Gerritt, sometimes used as a diminutive of Gerardus or Gerard. This economy in names was as common in the eighteenth century as it is today; then as now it gave a sense of the continuity of life and property and helped encourage family awareness and family pride. Young Gerardus came squalling into this world too late to catch more than a blurred glimpse of the grandfather from whom the great patent took its name and whom the baby was to grow to resemble in his obsessive passion for land.

The house in which Gerardus or Gross was born had long been the center of his family's efforts at defending the boundaries of the patent. It had begun its existence as a small building. Gross's father, known as Colonel Hardenbergh, enlarged it until, as Gross was growing up, it was among the great houses in its part of the world. There was nothing in the least showy about it. It was a heavy structure of Dutch inspiration ornamented outwardly with nothing at all but down-to-earth proportions, pleasant stone and shingle textures, and an air of unsophisticated simplicity. Within, it is said to have abounded in paneled fireplace walls and bed alcoves enclosed in the Dutch style by sliding doors. On July 5, 1911 a bolt of lightning ignited the old building and converted it to ashes. Some of the poor in the neighborhood felt that the lightning was not a matter of chance. It was a sign of divine displeasure with the family pride of the Hardenberghs, they assured each other.[1]

That family pride had reason to increase mightily as young Gross passed his boyhood in the old house in Rosendale. It was feeding on growing worldly prosperity and the emergence of the family, with all the prestige of the patent behind it, into undeniable prominence. Jacob Rutsen and two generations of Hardenberghs after him had piled up a snug fortune by "trading and trafficking" and by acquiring land. Early in the eighteenth century the charms of Jacob Rutsen's daughter had dazzled John Livingston, son of the lord of Livingston Manor. But the young woman had been judged not good enough for a Livingston of Livingston Manor, so John married a Massachusetts Winthrop instead. As the century moved along, the Rutsen-Hardenberghs, thanks to their prosperity and the superior status given to them by their lands, were able to become connected by marriage with a few patroon families across the Hudson. But in spite of this, the Hardenberghs lived on in rural simplicity. Not for them were patroon extravagances like trips to Europe, expensive education, or the wasting of time in frivolous letter writing to friends and relations. Their social lives were centered around the Reformed Church in whose affairs they took an active part. They played a cautious role in public affairs—the colonel was a long-time member of the New York Assembly where he kept an anxious eye on matters affecting the welfare of the class to which he belonged.

It was not the colonel but a sickly older brother of Gross who gave the family its mightiest boost into prominence. He was Jacob Rutsen Hardenbergh, D.D., S.T.D. The Reverend Jacob owed his eventually distinguished position not to the family obsession with the Hardenbergh Patent but to great natural abilities, religious zeal, and iron determination. His education was exceedingly meager, but with the help of a wise and well-educated wife, he overcame all obstacles to a successful career in the Reformed Dutch Church and became not only an outstanding clergyman but also first president of Queen's, now Rutgers, College. During the Revolution, George and Martha Washington spent some months as neighbors of Jacob and his wife in New Jersey and they must have become acquainted, for in June 1783 Martha Washington made a point of stopping to have breakfast with Jacob and Dinah, his wife, who were then living in the old house at Rosendale and tending to the spiritual needs of a group of Ulster congregations.[2] This visit was a great moment indeed for the Hardenbergh family.

Just what Gross thought of his sickly brother's rise to fame has not come down to us. The brothers were so different in physical constitution, in temperament, and in tastes that there is unlikely to have been much of a bond of sympathy between them. Gross was the baby of the family and he must have been an awkward baby brother for a revered church leader to possess. His size and physical vigor were impressive, but his emotional life was far from placid. In James Quinlan's words, Gross Hardenbergh became "a man of imperious and arbitrary temper, of convivial inclinations and habits."[3] While in his early twenties, Gross married Nancy Ryerson, a New Jersey girl, and the couple soon produced a brood of children—but here the normal phase of their lives ended. The habit of heavy drinking gained upon Gross; alcohol roused him to anger and suspicion. He quarreled with his wife, his father, and his children.

Family tradition gives Gross a heroic role in a frontier skirmish with the Indians during the Revolution, but the records do not bear this out.[4] His one moment of military prominence came when, under orders from his bungling colonel, he arrested a distinguished member of the Provincial Convention named Charles DeWitt and so brought down upon his head the anger of the Convention assembled in Kingston in May of 1777 and dealing at the time with the case of Jacob Rose and his rangers.[5]

"During Hardenbergh's military life," James E. Quinlan wrote in his *History of Sullivan County,* "he became more and more intemperate, and his existence ultimately [was] no better than a continued and unvarying debauch. His excesses nearly obscured whatever was at first humanitarian in his character, and inflamed all that was morose, impetuous and tyrannical in his disposition. It is related of him by men now [1871] yet living, that, when travelling through the country in his old age, he sometimes ordered the innkeeper at whose house he lodged to cover a table with candles and decanters of spiritous liquors, and taking his seat solitary and alone, at this somewhat rare festive board drink until his fiery and surly temper succumbed to insensibility."[6]

Gross had the right to look forward to the day when the death of his father would make him an owner of thousands of acres of land in the Hardenbergh Patent. But if he indulged any such hopes, he was to be very much disappointed. For, as James Quinlan put it, "In consequence of his wild and reckless ways, his high-toned father disinherited him, and willed what would otherwise have been devised to him to the heirs of Nancy Ryerson." Before 1800 the colonel and Nancy were both dead and so were several of the eleven children born to Gross and Nancy. "Consequently," Quinlan wrote, "the intention of Gerard's father was defeated. The dissipated son was the heir of his own deceased children. Thereafter he dominated over those who were in his power, and did not bend to his will, with remorseless vigor."[7]

In 1778 the old argument over the southeastern border of the patent seemed to have been settled and many ponderous documents testifying to the settlement were deposited in the office of the County Clerk of Ulster. Yet once the Revolution was out of the way, land-hungry men and lawyers wise in the intricacies of land began reviving old claims and calling the settlement into doubt. The heirs of Jochim Schoonmaker, for example, said that their ancestor who had been a trustee of the town of Rochester had never turned over his trust to a successor. Therefore, they claimed that a share of the common lands of Rochester belonged to them—and these lands extended into part of the Neversink Valley. The courts did not allow the claim, but a more serious one was put forward by Gross Hardenbergh.

Not long after the end of the Revolution, the heirs of Thomas Beekman began selling farms to pioneers in the Neversink Valley in the Woodbourne neighborhood where an earlier settlement going back to the 1750s had been abandoned during the war years. About 1802 Hardenbergh laid claim to part of these lands. He pursued his claim with such vigor and recklessness that he quickly became the terror of the Neversink Valley, a monstrous and dreadful figure to whom no wicked act seemed impossible. Around this man clustered all the ancient resentments to which the wrongdoings of the Hardenbergh patentees had given rise. He became a personification of greed on the part of rich absentee landlords who hoarded lands that might have supported poor people in reasonable comfort and security. He was seen as taking up the battle waged for so many years by his father and grandfather to expand the already immense patent obtained in the first place by dishonesty and sharp dealing.[8]

When a man is hated and feared, the emotions he arouses make it hard to untangle the facts and the fictions of his existence. It is likely enough that a good part of the wicked acts attributed to Gross Hardenbergh were simply transferred to him by people made irrational by hatred. Yet there is no doubt that the demon of land greed possessed Gross and caused him to ride up and down the Neversink Valley, threatening and blustering, and from time to time committing acts of cruelty and unreason. It was in 1802 that he first appeared to the settlers on the fertile flats along the river and told them bluntly either to leave or come to an agreement with him to pay rent. The settlers had been taken in by the Beekmans, Gross said; the lands the settlers thought they had bought weren't theirs. The deeds from the Beekman family they showed Gross were worthless.

Very quickly an ugly rumor went from log cabin to log cabin throughout the Neversink country. The Beekmans, descended from a fellow trustee of Jochim Schoonmaker, had a perfectly valid deed to their lands, the rumor went, but it had never been recorded. A member of the Beekman family had allowed a surveyor to borrow this deed and the faithless fellow had been persuaded to turn it over to one of Gross's sons, Dr. Benjamin Hardenbergh, a storekeeper and physician who was settled along the Neversink and was already showing signs of having inherited his father's love of liquor. The doctor recognized that the deed posed a threat to his father's claim and burned it.[9] Thus he wickedly destroyed the very cornerstone of the Beekman claim. A few of the settlers, faced with this kind of news, decided that it was useless to waste effort fighting a wicked and powerful Hardenbergh landlord and moved away to make fresh starts toward independence. A few accepted a deal offered by Gross. They exchanged their cleared valley farms for tracts of hilltop wilderness. This land was given in token payment for the improvements they had made, for even Gross Hardenbergh did not dare violate the old custom of paying a "possession man" for the clearings and the buildings with which he had raised the value of another's land. Other settlers decided to remain and fight it out. They and some of their descendants afterward called the struggle that followed the Hardenbergh War.

The "war" began in 1802 with threats and legal maneuvers. By 1806 it had reached a stage of open violence. That fall Gross fell upon the farm of James Bush and his three sons and seized all their crops including six hundred bushels of grain. He stored the grain in the local gristmill which he owned and which was located near his son Benjamin's house—both buildings were near the center of Woodbourne. The mill, a barn, and other adjoining buildings took fire and burned down. The fire was set by the people of the valley, who were "determined to wreak vengeance," as Quinlan wrote. A number of Gross's children had settled in the valley; now they became frightened and fled. Gross personally dispossessed the Bushes. He dragged Mrs. Bush from the house. She had given birth to a baby three days before, they said, and as Gross dragged her she held the baby in her arms. The wife of another settler was "dragged from her home by the hair of her head." A few days later she died. "During the next two years," Quinlan says, "outrage followed outrage. Hardenbergh became frantic; the blood of the pioneers was raised to a fever heat. Hardenbergh was looked upon as a public enemy, whose death would be a public blessing. . . . He feared neither man nor beast and had little respect for God or the devil."[10]

Fearless as Gross was, he knew better than to try to live on his lands. He retreated to Kingston and there he spent the last winter of his life as a boarder of Mrs. Maria Masten who lived in a big stone house on East Front Street. At intervals Gross sent Mrs. Masten's slave to Jonathan Hasbrouck's store on nearby Green Street for a pigtail of tobacco or for something with which to slake his perpetual thirst. Lisbon wine, Sicily wine, and rum were among the alcoholic treasures the boy carried back to Gross's quarters in the Masten house.[11] But just as important as the closeness of liquor supplies was the fact that Judge Lucas Elmendorf lived only a few minutes' walk away. The judge, who had recently served as a member of Congress, was the lawyer whom Gross had appointed to act as legal general in his campaign to defend what he conceived to be his hereditary rights to lands within the Hardenbergh Patent. And Elmendorf was just the man for the purpose. It is true that one observer of his career had noted that his mind "was not of the most compact and acute order." The judge was famous instead for the cloudiness and diffuseness of his public addresses and for his ability to obscure a simple subject in a veritable dust storm of words. Once he wrote a single sentence that filled almost two pages of legal paper and said virtually nothing. Yet Elmendorf was no fool— far from it.

Behind the verbal fog which hid Elmendorf's true self from the view of the undiscerning public lurked a mind of unparalleled acuteness when it came to grappling with land matters, especially when those matters concerned the Hardenbergh Patent. Ancient chicaneries and connivances, the mistakes of slipshod surveyors and the intentional errors of wily ones, the old unresolved boundary controversies which skulked behind every bush in the patent—all these were neatly arrayed on the spacious shelves of the judge's mind and formed parts of his stock in trade. He himself was a speculator in lands close to Gross's. He was to spend much of his life in trying unsuccessfully to promote a turnpike road which would lead directly from the city of Kingston to the "hemlock wilds" where his lands and those of Gross lay.

Old Judge Elmendorf was remembered longest not for his land speculations or his turnpike promotions but for the length of time he managed to keep a single land case before the courts. "The case ran backwards, and sideways through all the courts of the state for some fifty-two years," said the *Ulster Argus* of June 16, 1861. "Joseph Addison had been counsel in it; Aaron Burr tried his shrewd hand at it; Alexander Hamilton had argued it; John Sudam had given it a test; so too had Charles H. Ruggles.[12] . . ." The action had been begun in 1790; in 1843 a Chancery decree threatened to end it. Elmendorf hastened to Albany to move for reargument before Chancellor McCoun. While chatting with the opposing counsel at an inn—the two were about to take a friendly cup of tea together—a stroke of apoplexy ended Elmendorf's life and the suit at one decisive blow. Some years earlier, the judge, who was then surrogate of Ulster County, had presided over the settlement of Gross Hardenbergh's estate, a simple matter which required no more than twenty-seven years.

In the year 1808 however, Gross Hardenbergh was far from needing the services of a surrogate. He was very much alive and filled to the brim with determination to make life as unpleasant as possible for the hostile settlers on the banks of the Neversink. The previous winter, while in Kingston, Gross had prepared for the coming campaign not only by fortifying himself with alcohol but also by laying in supplies. He bought a new "Riding chair" or chaise to carry his two hundred fifty pounds of irascibility over highways. This was a light two-wheeled vehicle with a calash or folding top. Gross also bought a silver-mounted whip to go with the chair. He did not pay cash—in the manner of the land rich of his time and place, he used land as currency in all substantial transactions. His riding chair cost £44-0-0 and he paid for it with fifty-five acres of backwoods land.[13] He had a spencer made—this was a short jacket well adapted to wearing while on horseback, and a man would have to leave the comfort of his chaise when he came to the stump-filled and rutted roads of backwoods Ulster and take to horseback. That fall Gross came riding into the Neversink Valley on a perverse and willful horse. He announced to all who would listen that he "would raise more hell during the next seven years than had ever been seen on earth before."[14] The Neversink settlers had endured six years of the Hardenbergh War. They concluded that they'd had enough.

Death of a "Fat Old Buck"

✤ IF EVER there was a region well adapted to be the committing of an unsolvable murder, it was the Neversink Valley in the fall of 1808. There every man was a hunter and trapper and loaded guns were kept handy by men busy at farm tasks in case a deer or bear should wander near a field or barn. Hunting supplied a substantial part of each family's food. Furs and skins were often swapped for foodstuffs or clothing at backwoods stores. Almost every man prided himself on his skill as a marksman, and boys soon learned how to move through the forests without alarming animals by clumsy footwork—they were alert to wind directions which might carry their scent to the game they were stalking. When Gross Hardenbergh rode into the Neversink Valley on November 22, men with guns in their hands were said to be combing the woods for deer, and some, they said, were hunting for a very different sort of game.[1]

As Gross Hardenbergh traveled the valley he halted his plunging horse in front of a log cabin from time to time while he berated a settler who had not yielded to him. Lucas Elmendorf and his partner, John Sudam, were busy in Kingston drawing up more legal weapons—resistance, Gross made clear, was hopeless. A man named John Coney was living on land he had properly rented from Gross, yet he too was at fault. The chimney of the house he had built was not properly "topped." Gross told the man that unless the chimney was topped by the time he rode by again, Coney would be thrown out of his house. Coney, terrified, hastened to a neighbor named Jacob Sarr and got Sarr's promise to give a hand at finishing the chimney the next day.

That night Gross stayed with his son Herman who was living on a farm from which a settler named Peter Freer had been ejected a few years earlier. Shortly after dawn of the twenty-third, Gross mounted his horse and started up the valley to harry more tenants and probably to see how

Coney's chimney was coming along. Between seven and eight o'clock, several people heard shots coming from close to the river. At the time, Jacob Sarr was starting to help Coney with his chimney. When Sarr heard the shots he clapped his hands in glee and exclaimed, "A damned fat old buck has got it now!"[2]

It was Cornelius Sarr who found the buck. He was old Gross Hardenbergh and he was lying in the road beside the river, powerless to move or speak. People gathered quickly. Up the road one settler caught Gross's horse while others carried the wounded man into a nearby house which also did duty as a tavern. There Gross lingered until about three the following morning. Before he died he managed to speak a few surprising words. He said that his friends had warned him that some day that wild horse of his would throw him and kill him. "And now he has done it," said Gross.[3]

Not until after Gross died did anyone notice an odd hole in the shoulder of his coat and a wound no horse could have inflicted. Gross's friends made light of all this and proposed to bury the old man without benefit of an inquest. But an old-timer who had been a soldier and seen men die in battle declared that nothing in the world but a bullet could have caused Gross's death. After that, Dr. Ben Bevier was summoned and a coroner's jury was brought together to investigate the circumstances of the old landlord's death.

It had not taken long for news of Hardenbergh's death to race up and down the winding Neversink Valley. Hunters came in from the woods, farmers gave up husking corn, women left their kitchens—everyone hurried to the tavern beside the river where the body of the ruthless landlord lay.

Usually human beings show awe and sobriety in the presence of death, but the death of Gross Hardenbergh brought very different feelings to the Neversink Valley. There men and women gathered around Van Benschoten's tavern and openly celebrated the end of the landlord whom they hated with so much bitterness. They got drunk, they sang bawdy songs, and a local genius put together a rough ballad to commemorate the event—all that has survived are the words "They shot Gross Hardenbergh off of his horse."[4] Men streamed inside to take a reassuring look at the quiet body of the man who had thrown his energy against them. One settler who had been butchering that morning remarked as he stared at Gross's huge bulk laid out on a bed, "This is fatter pork than I killed today."[5] Witticisms took the place of conventional expressions of regret. "Gross has gone to hell to fee more lawyers," said a woman.

Dr. Benjamin Bevier who conducted the examination and the inquest was twenty-six years old; five years earlier he had graduated from the medical school at New York's Columbia College. Dr. Ben was smart as they came. He was not only a skilled physician, he was also a master at drawing up wills, deeds and contracts, especially when these documents had to do with land. He was, moreover, the land agent for the Tillotson family who had inherited a share in the Hardenbergh Patent from their Livingston ancestor.[6] With Dr. Bevier acting as coroner, assisted by Gross's son Dr. Benjamin Hardenbergh, the inquest was conducted with quiet skill and good judgment amid the tumult of a riotous holiday.

The course of the ball that had killed Gross was traced from its entrance in the shoulder to the spine. When Dr. Bevier discovered this he could explain part of the mystery surrounding the man's death. The ball had produced partial paralysis, which was why Gross had not heard the report of a gun. The sound made by the gun had traveled through the air less rapidly than the ball. By the time the sound waves set in motion by the firing of the gun reached old Gross's ears, he could not hear them, for the spinal injury had deafened him. So he died believing that his unruly horse and not his tenants had killed him.

With the medical aspect of the inquest out of the way, Dr. Bevier settled down to the difficult task of finding the murderers. Here he displayed those talents for ferreting out and organizing facts which helped lead a few years later to his appointment as County Judge of Ulster, an appointment he declined. But Bevier was facing a thorny situation. Most of the people in the vicinity hated Gross and some admitted upon questioning that they would have been glad to kill him had the chance turned up. Abijah Willey was one who said he didn't know who'd shot Gross but that he was sorry he hadn't done it himself, and added that Dr. Hardenbergh had offered him two hundred acres of land "to have his father put out of the way"—[7] so old-timers reminisced to James Quinlan in later years.

It became plain that the difficulty of the case was the endless numbers of possible suspects. Almost everybody in the valley, it seemed, wanted Gross "put out of the way." The morning of the shooting, men with guns in their hands had been wandering everywhere. The valley people, whatever their daily differences might have been, were united in one thing— they hated Gross Hardenbergh. And they would not betray any man who might have had a part in his murder.

On the hillside overlooking the spot at which Gross had fallen from his horse, evidence of an ambush was found. Several men had waited behind a tree and they had cut away some of the branches of a laurel bush in order to have an unobstructed view of the road with no twigs in the way to deflect a bullet. One man after another became a suspect, but what seemed to be evidence against each faded away as Neversink people refused to testify to anything except a profound ignorance of what had happened on November 23. One of the sons of the Mrs. Bush whom Gross was said to have dragged from her house by the hair was suspected; so too were John G. Van Benschoten, Jacob Maraquat, and David Canfield, but no one would testify against any of them. The case was finally closed, and the Hardenbergh War ended.

When the excitement died down, some of Gross's children settled again in the Neversink Valley. Most of them were reasonable people who soon reached compromises with the settlers over their land disagreements, and the settlers willingly smothered their old resentments for the sake of present peace. One of Gross's sons became extremely popular and was elected to the State Assembly from his district by an almost unanimous vote.

Dr. Benjamin Hardenbergh, however, found his father's old habit of excessive drinking gaining upon him. He wasted his inherited property, brought his children up badly, and lost whatever respect his neighbors may have once had for him. He came to form an instructive contrast with his virtuous and successful brother, the Honorable Herman, at a time when the first chirpings of the infant temperance movement were beginning to be heard in the land. Benjamin's old saddle horse, whose name was Pone, was said to have been the doctor's last and best friend. From time to time Benjamin slipped from Pone's saddle in a drunken daze and slept by the roadside. Then Pone would stand guard beside him until the doctor revived and pulled himself into the saddle once again.[8]

In the 1790s when Gross Hardenbergh had not yet come into possession of his Neversink Valley lands and while his son Benjamin was still no more than a promising young man, changes were beginning to take place in the way in which people saw the Catskill Mountains. John and William Bartram had been the first of all humans to look at the Catskills and their cargo of plant and animal life with an interest that had nothing at all to do with land speculation, lumbering, mining, or the acquisition of a farm upon which a simple man might hope to make a living. In 1793 another man came to the Catskills to climb and explore and to wonder at what he saw. No one like him had ever come to the Catskills before. He was the "Agent of the French Republic at New York" and his name was Peter DeLabigarre.

37

Liberty Cap

❧ IN THE CITY of New York of the early 1790s, "French manners, French customs, French cookery, French furniture, French fashions and the French language came into sudden vogue, and, for a season, New York seemed transformed into Paris," wrote Mary L. Booth in her history of the city of New York.[1] This explosion of interest in everything French was set off in part by the presence in the city of great numbers of French *émigrés* whose sympathies lay with the monarchy of Louis XVI and who were trying to escape the deepening revolution which was toppling Louis and the better sort of France from their comfortable niches in society. It was also given a decided push by widespread American enthusiasm for the French Revolution in its earlier stages. Many Americans saw the struggle going on in France as a reflection of their own war for independence so recently won with French help.

If the better-sort émigrés charmed New Yorkers into imitation by their sophisticated Old World manners and interests, any Frenchman who was linked to the newly proclaimed French Republic fascinated by his aura of revolutionary heroism. One Frenchman who lived in New York State after 1792 was lucky enough to possess both the cultivated mind and charm of the better sort Frenchman and a good share of revolutionary ardor. He was Pierre or Peter DeLabigarre. Just what DeLabigarre did in his official capacity as French agent remains obscure, but one unofficial activity of his became a matter of record. At eleven o'clock on the calm and clear morning of April 9, 1793, he made a memorable ascent of the Catskill Mountains. On July 26 of the same year, he returned. (The day was pleasant, the temperature 71 degrees, the barometer stood at 30 inches and the wind blew from the north.) This time DeLabigarre climbed what he mistakenly believed to be the highest summit of the Catskill and boldly gave it a new name—a name that honored the French Revolution.

"Excursions on our Blue Mountains" was the title of the account of DeLabigarre's two climbs which was published in the *Transactions* of New York's Society for the Promotion of Agriculture, Arts and Manufactures in 1794. The society's president was a good friend of the French Revolution and of DeLabigarre—he was Chancellor Robert R. Livingston. The mountain the French agent climbed on June 9, 1793 was Overlook, which stood directly across the Hudson from the Chancellor's mansion of Clermont almost as if it had been placed there by an understanding Providence in order to give the Chancellor the noblest possible climax to the view from his windows. The Chancellor himself had already climbed Overlook and measured its altitude by means of a mercury barometer. There is evidence that DeLabigarre had the benefit of the Chancellor's advice and experience before he undrtook his two excursions, and he may have made both from the base of Clermont. For he and the Chancellor had taken to one another at once and by the spring of 1793 they were firm friends. Before the 1790s ended, DeLabigarre was to help and encourage the Chancellor in many of the experiments aimed at improving human welfare which were perpetually on the fire at Clermont. He would pour out his quick enthusiasm and energy on behalf of a paper-making project, an early Livingston flutter in steamboats, silk-making, and hedge planting, while his copious writings for the *Transactions* of the Chancellor's society added to their sometimes pompous pages a touch of Gallic liveliness. The Chancellor, for his part, looked on with his famous benignity as DeLabigarre settled in the neighborhood, and began construction of a grandiose structure which overlooked the Hudson and the Catskills and was named the "Chateau de Tivoli." Beneath the walls of the chateau, DeLabigarre laid out a fine imaginary town and had his plan engraved on copper by his friend the émigré artist Charles Balthazar Julien Fevret de St. Memin. He married a daughter of the Beekmans and so became a connection by marriage of the Livingstons, and he plunged into speculations from which the Chancellor rescued him with loans. When DeLabigarre was thrown into the debtor's prison at Poughkeepsie, it was the Chancellor who bailed him out.[2]

All these tokens of close friendship were still in the future as DeLabigarre made his way up the buttresslike ridge which Overlook Mountain thrusts toward Clermont nine miles away. He was bringing to bear upon the Catskills all those late eighteenth-century French attributes which were earning him the devotion of the Chancellor. His lively imagination, his classical learning, his interest in food and drink, in natural history and in science, his faith in Jean-Jacques Rousseau's dictum that man living in close contact with nature is noble but that he is spoiled by the touch of civilization—all these came into play as DeLabigarre climbed from ledge to ledge and as he sat down later to write an account of his adventure.

From the summit of Overlook, DeLabigarre "had the pleasure of contemplating a most magnificent prospect all around the compass." In setting down his impressions of what he saw, he became the founder of a thriving minor industry of the Catskill Mountains: the writing for publication of descriptions of views from mountaintops.

"That large river, which I could hardly cross in half an hour appeared like a rivulet: a sloop was no more than a small canoe rigged with a blanket. What was become of those lands, places and buildings left in the morning? Was I able to perceive then any of those busy people riding on the roads or working in their fields? Could I distinguish the rich abode from the humble cottage? Could I hear the noise of a bustling world? No: the whole of it was confounded in the vast horizon before my eyes. . . ."

As DeLabigarre looked into infinity from Overlook, "elevated and noble ideas" rushed into his mind but he did not try to convey them to the readers of the *Transactions* as he felt inadequate to the task. As he struggled up the mountain, DeLabigarre had met no streams or springs at which he could quench his thirst. On the rocky buttress, when not far from the summit, he turned to the mountain's cool north side and found a bank of snow. He had prudently taken along a flask of brandy which he mixed with the snow. It "afforded me a delicious drinking, tenfold better than any ice cream," he commented. Inspired perhaps by his drink, DeLabigarre noticed that the south side of Overlook was "full of fox and winter grapes upon which I make no doubt, the bears make a pretty good vintage each fall. It confirms my former ideas on the possibility of cultivating the grape in this country with as much success as in Europe. . . . We may foresee the day when necessity with her iron rod, shall compel . . . Americans to cultivate the wild gifts of a rude but beautiful nature—then Madeira will give place to the Blue Mountain-claret."

From Overlook's top, DeLabigarre caught sight of two lakes which are known today as Cooper and Echo lakes. He plunged down the mountainside toward Echo Lake, "flying down" from ledge to ledge in a manner that reminded him (as it would any properly educated French gentleman of his time) of the attempt at artificial flight of "the rash and unfortunate Icarus." That night DeLabigarre and his companions camped out at the lake and tried to sleep on beds of hemlock boughs. But "I was awakened from time to time (for the sake of variety) by the howlings of wolves, wild cats, and bears: one of my men, though overcome with fatigue, and very sleepy, diverted me very much by his fears, keeping constantly in his hand a small hatchet, to defend himself against our surrounding musicians."

In the morning the party made its way to the northeast, noticing as they went along "a great many pidgeons, not in flocks, but in couples, building their nests in that undisturbed part of the world." DeLabigarre climbed a tree and glimpsed a lake to the north. It may have been a beaver pond or the millpond of a pioneer sawyer. As he moved down toward the Hudson Valley he found that the trees of what was probably Plattekill Clove were "thick, tall and a great deal larger than anywhere else. Enormous bodies rotting down afford nourishment to thousands of other young trees raising their proud heads to the clouds; the most stupid eye is forced to look with respectful awe at the eternal state of destruction and renovation which a Supreme Being has impressed to the wheeling turn of his works!" This last thought was familiar to men like DeLabigarre for it had furnished a central theme to Bernardin de St. Pierre's three-volume *Études de la Nature* published about nine years earlier and quickly read by every literate Frenchman.

DeLabigarre's second excursion among the Catskills was very different in spirit from the almost frolicsome one of April 9. This time DeLabigarre was accompanied by a man whom he describes only as "a natural philosopher," who was equipped with an instrument for measuring altitudes. It was a mercury barometer, an awkward gadget to carry through the tangled wilderness where a blow from a branch could break it and its mercury could be spilled should the philosopher who carried it—or his servant—take even a modest tumble. The excursion was what would before long be called a scientific field trip, though on a small scale and of hardly professional quality. Yet one of its objects was to give the mountains that soared above the valley settlements their first taste of scientific treatment since John Bartram's tentative beginnings so many years before.

Bartram had climbed to the vale of the two lakes through the untouched forest which covered the eastern escarpment of the Catskills. At best he had only the slender help of an old Indian trail, but by the time DeLabigarre followed Bartram, times had changed. The large landowners —various Livingstons, the Desbrosses, the Verplancks, and others—had been able to persuade the state legislature of 1790 to authorize building, at public expense, roads which would raise the value of their landholdings. These roads were to be laid out under the supervision of the commissioners of the land office.[3] One such road was planned to start at Catskill and proceed to what is now known as Palenville. From there it would wriggle its way up the face of the mountains, run between the two lakes, and continue down the valley of the Schoharie where scattered clusters of clearings broke the forest. The road followed the Indian trail used in 1780 by the captors of the Snyders. By 1793 the road was ready. It was a rough one, hardly a road at all in a modern sense. Yet it was good enough to serve science as represented by the DeLabigarre party and perhaps to save the natural philosopher's barometer a fatal knock.

To John and William Bartram, with their minds and eyes quickened by contact with the English phase of the romantic revolution, the vale of the two lakes had seemed to shimmer with a hint of the air of romance which was later on to be felt there by thousands of visitors. DeLabigarre approached the vale with improving, scientific, and romantic ideas mingled in his mind—he was panting to find wonders. The first wonder to appear was the very same rocky spring at which the Bartrams had quenched their thirst in 1753—the one that gushes from Moses' Rock. The rock, to De-Labigarre's imagination, assumed the appearance of part of a ruined fortification: the "front covered with a fine moss, represents a green carpet, and at the height of six feet, comes out of the rock a spout of water, three inches in diameter, as if Nature had intended to offer that refreshment to the thirsty traveller." The scene impressed the Frenchman as having the look of "a romantic situation." Here, the adjective "romantic," as applied to these mountains and which was to be so cruelly overused by future generations of writers about the Catskills, made its first appearance in print.

Moses' Rock was indeed a romantic wonder but a greater one lay ahead on the shores of North and South lakes. "We saw a kind of creeping plant adrift on the shore, unknown and undescribed: It is of a spungy nature, soft when in the water, and as hard as cork when dried; it looks very much like an old rope. Was such a thing found on Mount Ararat, a credulous Jew would directly take it to be some remains of the rigging of the ark of Noah. The plant is from one to two inches diameter, of a black color; and till it is better known, we are pleased to call it *the vegetable rope.*" The vegetable rope was not a plant unknown to botanical science and destined perhaps to immortalize its discoverer by bearing the name of DeLabiggaria; it was no more than part of one of the aquatic plants of the lakes —perhaps the yellow water lilies—which the muskrats whose lodges De-Labigarre observed may have set afloat as they nibbled the plants' starchy roots.

Like the Bartrams, DeLabigarre admired the Kaaterskill Falls. He found there a sign of a previous visit by the Chancellor in the form of the great man's "cypher" cut into the bark of a birch tree hanging over the precipice from which the Kaaterskill leaped "with such impetuosity, that the body of the water twisting itself into a spiral vortex, is in a great measure evaporated before it reaches the bottom of the precipice." The Bartrams could make no observations on any human inhabitants of the high interior plateau of the Catskills drained by the Kaaterskill, the Plattekill, and the Schoharie, for there were none. But by 1793 even the vicinity of the two lakes was attracting settlers. A log house already in ruins stood beside North Lake and gave the place something of the melancholy air that lingers around old and abandoned human habitations. Here, where "evergreens all around, add a very romantic appearance to the spot," DeLabigarre took shelter for the night in the log ruin. As he explained later, rocky roofs such as the one that had sheltered the Bartrams were not for him. "I would rather be exposed to any storm, than to trust my life to such [a] place—threatening ruin every moment" from the crumbling rocks above.

The next day DeLabigarre was delighted by a pair of young pioneers newly settled close by, probably at what is now Haines Falls. "We were welcomed with that cordial hospitality which seems peculiar to new settlers; our host, not above 20 years old, entertained us with particulars on the soil, temperature, and various subjects of agriculture, whilst his amiable consort, only fifteen years old, was preparing the dinner with a charming cheerfulness; the neatness of their log house and their manners, recalled to my mind the picture of the golden days: then I wished for a moment to be a Jupiter, in order to bestow on this young couple the reward formerly granted to Philemon and Baucis; but without having recourse to the fables of antiquity, let me express here my natural wish: May they never feel the bitter cares of a large society; may their present happiness never be disturbed by envious or ill-minded neighbors!" This incident is the best tradition of Jean-Jacques Rousseau and Bernardin de St. Pierre whose attitudes toward life and society played a part in giving form to the minds of the leaders of the French Revolution. The young couple represented to Revolutionist DeLabigarre innocent humanity uncorrupted by the poisons of society. Before long, that same day, he went on to give much more concrete expression to his revolutionary feelings, while at the same time accomplishing a scientific feat never before attempted. He climbed the mountain known as Round Top [today High Peak] and while his natural philosopher determined its altitude to be 3549 feet—only a little more than a hundred feet less than its modern measure—DeLabigarre gave the mountain a new name. He named it—with what ceremonies he did not say—Liberty Cap.

In 1793 liberty cap was a phrase surrounded by a mass of emotions. The liberty or Phrygian cap had been a symbol of freedom ever since the days of Greek and Roman power. The Sons of Liberty of the 1760s had adopted it as their own and almost every liberty pole they raised was crowned by a liberty cap. In 1789, as the French Revolution slowly began to gain momentum, a group of radical revolutionaries joined together in the Jacobin Club and took as their emblem a red liberty cap. (The American liberty cap had been blue.) As the Revolution increased in scope and violence, the red liberty cap became its accepted symbol. As DeLabigarre renamed Round Top, the Reign of Terror was under way in Paris and the liberty cap was being worn in the streets, in courtrooms, beside the guillotine, and at secret meetings of revolutionists.

From Clermont and indeed from much of the mid-Hudson Valley, High Peak is the highest object in sight, except for the sun and the moon, the stars and the high clouds. We know today that twenty Catskill summits rise higher than High Peak, but in 1793, and for many years after, no one suspected this. High Peak's position close to the great eastern wall of the mountains made it seem the indisputable chief among the Catskills. But this was not all that helped High Peak attract the attention of people in the valley it seemed to dominate. Its profile as seen emerging above the surrounding heights was arresting. It rose and fell in a bold curve which could not help suggesting to a man of 1793 who was aware of what was going on in the world—and especially if he looked at the mountain from Clermont— the upper part of a liberty cap. Agent DeLabigarre must have noticed this before he climbed the mountain to give it a name that would bring the triumph of the French Revolution into the minds of all who looked up at Liberty Cap as if at an immense sculptured monument placed there by nature herself.

Place names often bear useful witness to changing ideas and prejudices; sometimes they recall half-forgotten turning points in history. The mountain which DeLabigarre named Liberty Cap did not keep its new name for very long. Not that the French Revolution was not popular enough in 1793, especially among lower-sort Americans. When Citizen Genêt came to the United States as minister of the Revolutionary Republic (he landed on the very day DeLabigarre chose to climb Overlook), he was received with enthusiasm. Before long Genêt's use of his position to further revolutionary ends drew official disapproval and led to his recall. The revolution he had represented became less popular, especially with the propertied classes. However, the Antifederalist party with which the Chancellor was soon to become allied remained sympathetic toward the revolutionary aims of the

French people, which was why it was often called the "French party" in American politics.

High Peak was seldom called Liberty Cap as the nineteenth century came into being. DeLabigarre was not present to foster the use of the new name, for his plans for his town of Tivoli persisted in remaining in an unprofitable paper state and he followed Edward Livingston to Louisiana, where he died in 1806. As the years moved on, fewer and fewer people used his new name. Until the final decades of the century, the safe, conservative, unimaginative older name of Round Top would yield, in a confusing swap with its neighbor, to that of High Peak.[4] Revolutions, except for the American one, were no longer respectable. Americans, except for the Negroes, the Indians, and the laboring poor, were becoming very comfortable in their world, and they did not like to be reminded of the eruptions of violence which from time to time disturb society.

As early as the 1820s the Livingstons of Clermont of the Chancellor's generation, growing older and less daring, ceased calling the mountain that stood so nobly across the river from their estates Liberty Cap. Instead, they and their tenants knew it as Mrs. Montgomery's Cap, in honor of the Chancellor's sister and the widow's cap she wore until the end of her long days in memory of "my General."[5] This name, too, is now forgotten.

Agent DeLabigarre failed to change a summit of the Catskills into a memorial to the French Revolution, but he succeeded in another objective of his excursions among the Catskills, for he wrote his account and saw it in print. What he wrote about his trip for the Society for the Promotion of Agriculture, Arts and Manufactures was read by society members in New York. These were better-sort men, and professional men of standing. The *Transactions* of the society also circulated among like-minded Americans in other parts of the United States and copies made their way abroad, where they were read by European scientists, improvers, and natural history enthusiasts.

"Our Blue Mountains" was what DeLabigarre had called the Catskills. He tried by the use of "Our" to distinguish the mountains he had explored from the other Blue Mountains of the United States. He might have made the identity of the mountains he was writing about perfectly clear by calling them "the Catskills." But in his time the term "Catskills" was out of favor among those with pretensions to elegance. It smacked too much of the hearty, earthy Dutch days when it had been first used. Eighteenth-century descendants of the Dutch, it was true, had also called the Catskills both the "Blue Mountains" and the "Catskills." On one of the maps

William Cockburn drew in 1765, he tried to catch the rustic Dutch pronunciation by lettering "the Polue Mountains"[6] across their eastern flank.

Two years after the DeLabigarre account of the Catskills appeared, the
Society for the Promotion of Agriculture, Arts and Manufactures empowered their secretary to undertake an expedition which may very well
have been suggested in part by DeLabigarre's effort. The secretary, with
a corps of suitable assistants, was to undertake a survey of the rocky
heights that enclosed the Hudson Valley to the east and west. These included the Catskills. The secretary was as professional a scientist as the
United States had to offer in the 1790s—he made this plain when at the
outset of the report of his findings in the Catskills, he located the mountains
with considerable precision and named them with clarity.

"They are commonly known by the name of the *Blue Mountains,* on
account of a blueness or haze which they present to the eye when seen from
a distance. They are likewise called the Kaats-Kill Mountains, from a river
of that name which issues from them, and falls into the Hudson a little below Loonenburgh. They are considered, and perhaps with truth, the highest
land in the State of New-York; though by reason of their remoteness, not
visible by mariners arriving on the coast, are, however, to be seen from a
great distance inland."[7]

The secretary who wrote these words was a remarkable, even an
amazing, man. He was of Scottish descent and had been reared among the
Connecticut Yankee settlers of Long Island. He was Dr. Samuel Latham
Mitchill, "Professor of Chemistry, Agriculture and Other Arts Depending
thereon" at Columbia College. At his urging, the Catskill Mountains were
to take a long step forward toward becoming known as one of the romantic
regions of the world.

38

The Oracle of New York

✿ "OH BLESSED LAND! Oh ten times fortunate Americans could they but know and improve their natural and local advantages!" These were the words of Peter DeLabigarre, written in the course of a 1794 report to the Society for the Promotion of Agriculture, Arts and Manufactures, (later to be renamed the Society for the Promotion of the Useful Arts). The report dealt with silk-producing experiments in the Livingston country —Mrs. Montgomery alone had raised six thousand silkworms, said DeLabigarre. "Very few [of the worms] died in the course of their education,"[1] the Frenchman added with an unmistakable air of triumph. But educated silkworms, like educated humans, do not always go on to become productive workers, and silk making was never added to the tasks of Livingston tenants and slaves. The Chancellor and his friends in their Society for the Promotion of the Useful Arts quickly turned their attention to fresh means of improving their undeniable natural and local advantages.

When it came to such matters as making silk, paper, or wine, the society's members listened respectfully to DeLabigarre, for was he not a Frenchman and was not France a skillful maker of all three of these useful products? Silkworms having proved unco-operative, the members revived the ancient dream of becoming rich by means of the discovery and working of veins of the minerals still believed to be hidden away among the hills and mountains which hemmed in the Hudson Valley. And they entrusted the task of searching for minerals to a native son believed to be learned above all other Americans in such matters. He was Dr. Mitchill, and the mineral for which the doctor was instructed to pay particular attention was not gold or silver, but coal.

When old Cornelius Tiebout died in 1785, he left a legacy of hopes of mineral treasures on his lands in the Catskill Mountains. On the eve of the Revolution he had sold some of his lands in Woodstock, but he reserved all coal rights. His widow and the nephew who were his heirs continued to reserve such rights whenever they sold land on Overlook Mountain. They reserved, too, space for roads and buildings which might be needed in coal mining. All this was part of the early stages of the coal mania which would soon grip many American landowners. In England a coal mania had long been raging. There supplies of wood for use in making iron or glass or as fuel for home use had dwindled as the population grew and industries multiplied. This helped draw attention to the vast deposits of soft or bituminous coal that lay under many parts of England and Wales. Similar deposits of coal had been put to use far back in European history, but the British now found that their coal could be ignited and burned with ease by using methods not too different from those used in wood-burning fireplaces and charcoal-burning forges. In the America of late colonial days, firewood was becoming scarce in the vicinity of larger centers of population and industry, but explorers for coal usually found only hard, shiny anthracite—soft coal was imported from England. Anthracite has its own requirements for burning. Blacksmiths found that they could sometimes use it instead of the usual charcoal when they burned it in their forges where a forced draft was maintained by huge bellows. Pennsylvania gunsmiths occasionally used hard coal in making weapons for Revolutionary soldiers. But all efforts to work out a way of using anthracite as fuel for heating dwellings or in industry failed. The stuff was known as "stone coal"; people sometimes crushed it into small pieces and used it in place of the white gravel with which garden paths were surfaced and found that it gave a very odd effect indeed. The 1790s came and stone coal was still unsalable. Yet landowners continued to hope that at any moment a way of using the coal would be devised. In Virginia, soft coal deposits had been found and were being worked. The very first United States Congress came to the help of the infant venture and imposed a duty on British soft coal imported to Atlantic coast cities. This stimulated the search for coal of all sorts wherever hills or mountains rose close to cheap transportation by water.

The members of the Society for the Promotion of the Useful Arts knew very well that coal was helping transform England into a land of smoky manufacturing towns. Mine-owning landlords were prospering mightily; workers were being herded into dismal and brutalizing slums; their children were being set to work in factories the moment they ceased toddling. Most of the society's members were large landlords among the Catskills and other highlands along the Hudson. They had very compelling reasons for voting to send Dr. Mitchill "to examine mineralogically the banks of the Hudson and neighboring country," and to "inquire whether the country contained any considerable quantity of coal, within a reasonable carting distance from any landing on the river."[2] Rumors of finds such as Cornelius Tiebout had apparently made were afloat around the Catskills, and landowners had some right to hope that with a little luck and effort they might repeat the happy experience of their British counterparts.

But no similar dreams floated within the head of Samuel Latham Mitchill as he undertook the task of leading the society's expedition. He had his own reasons for being interested in coal: they were rooted in the urge to understand all aspects of the universe and to do his best to improve the lot of man as he gropes his way from birth to death on the surface of his native planet. In April of 1796 Dr. Mitchill wrote to his friend and admirer the Chancellor to tell of his most recent scientific enthusiasm. More than twenty years earlier it had been discovered that the air we breathe is a mixture of gases. One gas—the one we know as oxygen—supports life and combustion. Another known today as nitrogen doesn't, and was therefore viewed with suspicion and called "foul air." Dr. Mitchill as both a physician and a chemist had been on the lookout for a chemical substance that might be responsible for the summer epidemics which were slaughtering dwellers in American cities. He thought he had found it in nitrogen or "azote" as it was beginning to be called. Azote, reasoned Dr. Mitchill, formed in putrefying organic matter as "septic acid." When released into the air as a gas it could kill humans who inhaled it. He renamed the gas "septon."[3]

Septon might be conquered by two weapons, the doctor believed. The plants of our earth fed and prospered upon it. Therefore, when septon was released in the country where plants abounded it never had a chance to harm humans. But if it formed in the garbage-littered streets or in privies and backyards of cities where plants were scarce it became a fearful enemy of mankind. Septic acid could be neutralized by alkalis—a man might do worse than to sprinkle wood ashes, with their high alkali content, around his house during the hot August days when epidemics were breeding. But there was an even more promising method of fighting septon. The doctor had received reports which seemed to show that certain English families had become much healthier when they changed to heating their houses with coal instead of wood. Evidently the burning of coal released an alkali which neutralized the septon skulking in the air—at least so doctor Mitchill reasoned. If the air of American cities were to become dim with coal smoke, why then the epidemics of yellow fever and other warm

weather scourges might be conquered and the name of Mitchill might be
enrolled on the list of mankind's greatest benefactors.

Many a party of treasure hunters had climbed the Catskills before
1796, but none had been at all like the one headed that summer by Dr.
Mitchill. For Mitchill combined in a single individual the professional
improver, scientist, and romantic. He was a result of the enlargement of
human horizons that began in the late seventeenth century on a base
laid during the Renaissance and took on momentum during the eighteenth. If a pioneer had met Mitchill during his tour of the Catskills and
asked him what he was doing among the mountains, he would have been
overwhelmed by the cordiality and the completeness of his answer. For if
there was one activity the doctor loved above all others it was imparting
information. Whether a question dealt with geology, politics, medicine,
mineralogy, physics, chemistry, literature, languages, or the charms of
natural scenery, the doctor could be counted upon to gush facts, figures,
and theories with happy abandon. Upon request he would make a political
speech, write a poem, invent a word. He belonged to an age when a man
might still aspire to know everything—and no American aspired more
diligently than Dr. Mitchill.

Mitchill had every right to aspire. His curiosity was insatiable and
far-ranging, his mind was excellent; and he had the benefit of a fine
education at the University of Edinburgh. He had studied law, been
elected to the state legislature, and had joined scientific societies by the
dozen. He was only thirty-two when he climbed the Catskills but already
he was accepted as the "Oracle of New York." New York was proud of
"The Doctor" for it was by this title that Mitchill was best known. But
at the same time, it was amused by him. Philip Hone, Mayor of New
York and author of a well-known diary, was to conclude that the doctor,
learned and wise as he surely was, was "strangely deficient in that useful
commodity called common sense."[4] When he tried to change the name
of the United States to Fredonia, New Yorkers laughed. They laughed, too,
when Mitchill rewrote the Mother Goose rhymes in order that they might
instill "republican principles."[5] The doctor's imagination and his compulsion
to improve occasionally ran away with him, and now and then his habit
of heavy drinking affected his judgment. Yet something more important
lay beneath the surface of the amusement Mitchill aroused. New York
was a complacent commercial town in which Mitchill's combination of
scientific inquiry and romantic feeling was not taken seriously. What profit
could there be in studying inedible fish, useless weeds, or the pebbles
which lay everywhere? When had gazing at a distant view from a hilltop

ever put any money in a man's pockets? The doctor's mind was an awesome thing which sometimes produced practical results, yet there was something laughable about its owner's passion for childish and unprofitable things. Benjamin Franklin with his cool practical attitude was the kind of inquirer whom New Yorkers found very much to their taste. Dr. Mitchill dazzled them—and at the same time he puzzled them.

No one, as far as is now known, laughed as the doctor and his three or four fellow explorers climbed the Catskills in 1796. Coal was their primary target but they were impressively equipped to inquire into everything else that might stir their scientific curiosity. Like DeLabigarre's natural philosopher they carried a mercury barometer to determine altitudes; in addition they had flasks of ether and alcohol, plus a thermometer they expected to use in checking their barometer's findings. But there were no findings at all, for the barometer's mercury was soon spilled—a touch which must have pleased those who enjoyed the doctor in his aspect of a comic. A great deal of careful measuring and weighing was done; specimens of plants and rocks were collected to be studied later; and Dr. Mitchill set down the results of much acute observation. Although he took a special interest in fish, it was characteristic of his occasional whimsical ways that when he came to the two lakes and found them low and "uninviting" after a long drought, "he did not approach near enough to throw in a line."[6] So the doctor reported in a sketch of the *Mineralogical History of the State of New York* which he published in several parts in the *Medical Repository,* a pioneer journal of which he was a cofounder and editor.

Readers of the *Medical Repository* found the Catskills presented in its pages for the first time with very much the appearance the mountains would have to the eyes of the next three generations. There, by way of foundation, were the layered sandstones and shales of the mountains; there too were the varied plants which mantled the rocks. Shrewd speculations about the origin of the rocks and the dawning of an understanding of the relations between the plants and and their surroundings—these too foreshadowed nineteenth-century ways. But most nineteenth century of all were Mitchill's enthusiasic accounts of waterfalls and views.

No American of his time was better equipped than the doctor to persuade the world to begin seeing the Catskills as a region of romantic and scenic charm. His student days at Edinburgh had placed him squarely in the center of the current British passion for admiring rugged scenery and climbing to the tops of mountains. As young Mitchill studied medicine, the admiration of natural wonders was being organized with considerable skill into a kind of fashionable game. Back in John Bartram's day only the very rich or intellectuals with aesthetic leanings could be inspired by the new romantic way of seeing natural wonders. But by the 1790s any literate Briton with a reasonably good income might set out from home, instruction book in hand, and be delighted and thrilled by the kind of wild scenery from which his grandfather would have fled in horror. A rural parson named William Gilpin was turning out guidebooks in which he pointed to the exact spots from which a tourist to the lake district or other wonder regions might see famous combinations of mountains, water, and rocks to the best advantage. Gilpin classified views as correct or incorrect in accordance with the degree to which they complied with the paintings of such landscape masters as polished Virgilian Claude Lorraine or romantic Salvator Rosa. Many a tourist carried what he called a "Claude glass." This was a four-inch mirror that had a slightly convex surface and was backed with black foil. When a correct view was seen reflected in a Claude glass it appeared to be transformed into an oil painting of the most approved and expensive sort. Tourists without artistic ability but with correct taste could use their Claude glasses to turn scenery into temporary paintings.[7] Those fortunate enough to have had training and talent in sketching filled their sketchbooks with drawings in black and white or water color—drawing and painting of this kind had become a fashionable accomplishment. At the same time, professional British topographical artists were making detailed drawings of mountains, lakes, waterfalls, ivy-clad ruins, and desolate moors. These drawings were translated into engravings which sold merrily. Tourists in search of the romantic and picturesque were quoting lines from Thomson's *Seasons* or Dyer's *Grongar Hill*. Romantic feeling was in the British air and young Sam Mitchill breathed it deeply.

In company with other students, Mitchill had climbed Scottish mountains to pursue serious botanical and geological studies and to find pleasure in wild, rocky scenery and the distant views that carried a man into infinity and thrilled and humbled him with a sense of his relationship to the rest of the universe.[8] When he climbed the Catskills, Mitchill carried with him the romantic way of seeing nature he had acquired in Scotland. He described the waterfall we know as Haines Falls in romantic terms and did the same for the Kaaterskill Falls. He climbed Round Top and cleared away enough of the balsam fir trees crouched on its summit to open up a wide view across the Hudson Valley. He repeated this performance on High Peak. Mitchill described what he saw from these mountaintops in glowing terms. He compared the view from

Round Top—the High Peak of later years—to the one he had seen from the summit of Scotland's Ben Lomond. Of all the mountaintop views he'd seen, Mitchill wrote, only the one from Ben Lomond surpassed that from Round Top.

On February 7, 1798, Dr. Mitchill addressed a joint meeting of the members of the Society for the Promotion of Agriculture, Arts and Manufactures and both houses of the New York State legislature. He took care to prepare the landowners in the audience for a disappointment in regard to his search for coal. "It is to be regretted that, no discovery of importance, relative to this article, was made. . . . Nature which has bestowed upon us so many other favors, seems to have been sparing in regard to this."[9] The doctor went on to rub salt in the landowners' wounds by informing them that "A number of miners or persons skilled in the detection and working of metallic veins and ores, have, as I have been informed travelled extensively through the state from south to north in quest of those kinds of mineral treasures. Fortunately for our peace and happiness, no sources of gold and silver appear to have been detected. It is to be hoped our country contains none but those of productive labor and active industry."

When the report of the Mitchill expedition was finally published in the *Medical Repository* for 1799, its reference to coal in the Catskills was brief and discouraging indeed. The rocks of the Catskills, Mitchill wrote, "consist chiefly of a sand-stone (*lapis arenaceus*) which is grounded upon a slate of brittle and shivery texture (*schistus fragilis*), which when exposed to a high degree of heat, melts and gives evidence of bituminous quality (*schistus pinguis*)."[10] In these gloriously pedantic words the doctor disposed of coal in the Catskills. He had studied the thin veins of dark shale that many prospectors in the Catskills have taken for coal—they contain sparse relics of Devonian vegetation. This shale can be coaxed into giving off flames, but it is not coal. The public was not convinced. It smelled skulduggery in Mitchill's stark pronouncements about coal in the Catskills and for many years after believed that some sort of conspiracy involving the state government was afoot in order to prevent coal mining. The modern belief that the city of New York is involved in an elaborate attempt at preventing the use of oil beneath the Catskills is a robust present-day descendant of the rumors of Mitchill's time nicely adapted to the age of oil.

As the eighteenth century lay dying, the words "Catskill Mountains" were beginning to take on definite and exciting meanings. William Bartram's brief reference had placed a romantic picture of the Catskills in the minds of English and German poets. DeLabigarre, enthusiastic amateur that he was, had muddled the picture a bit by using the term "Blue Mountains." Now Dr. Mitchill came along with just the right proportions of scientific precision and romantic feeling to make the Catskill Mountains come to life in the consciousness of many human beings who had never seen them with their own eyes. For the doctor's report on the natural wonders of the Catskills made a decided impression wherever it was read. Count Volney reprinted it in his book on the United States published in Paris in 1803. James Mease of Philadelphia reprinted it as well as DeLabigarre's figures for altitudes in the Catskills in his pioneer book on American geography and geology of 1807. Yet awareness of the Catskills and their natural wonders was slow in spreading to the mass of Americans. By 1819, Henry E. Dwight, grandson of President Dwight of Yale, polled fifty of his cultivated New England friends and found that only one in ten had even heard of the Catskills.[11] But the seed had been planted and it was growing.

Historians of American science like to point out that Dr. Mitchill made no lasting contributions to man's knowledge of his world or his understanding of it. His theories were quickly discarded, his beloved septon was forgotten, coal smoke turned into a menace and not a blessing. All this is true enough, yet the doctor left his mark on his nation. His study of the lands along the Hudson and especially of the Catskills constituted the first scientific field trip to any region of the United States. And more than that, the doctor looked into the future and caught a vivid glimpse of what the Catskills would become in the course of the new century when tourists would climb its mountains and admire its natural wonders. He felt the suitability of the scenery of the Catskills as subjects for American landscape painters and recommended that these men paint Catskill waterfalls. Later, in 1813, Mitchill would end a long talk on American botanical writers by earnestly calling the attention of his audience (members of the New-York Historical Society) to the part that the beauty of the autumnal landscape of the United States might play in the art of landscape painting. "Our forests exhibit, during the season in which the leaves are preparing to fall, a spectacle of richness and gayety that all persons of observation admire, and which our artists might portray for the purpose of giving a national style and character to their landscapes."[12] By the time Mitchill died in 1832 (helped to the grave, some said, by his devotion to alcohol), the clearings he had made on the summits of Round Top and High Peak had been much enlarged and were lively each clear summer day with the admiring exclamations of tourists come to see the distant views which Mitchill and others had described. Near the two lakes a bustling summer hotel was in business. The waterfalls and autumnal coloring of the Catskills had been painted over and over again—they formed cornerstones of a school of painting born amid the Catskills and distinguished by the kind of "national style and character" Mitchill had foreseen.

In that same year of 1832, Henry E. Dwight also died after a distinguished career as educator and editor. If Dwight had taken a poll among his friends as a last service to humanity, he would have found the results of his poll of 1819 reversed. For by then the Catskills had long ceased to be no more than an unknown and neglected region of desolate wilderness pierced by narrow valleys in which tenant farmers lived in uneasy awe of absentee landlords and where hopes of mineral wealth flared up from time to time. It had become the very center of romantic feeling in the United States and the nation's favorite haunt of painters, writers, and amateurs of romantic feeling. The events of half a century had transformed the Catskills into a place of glamor and romantic charm. Men like the Bartrams, Peter DeLabigarre, and Dr. Mitchill began the process of transformation. It was taken up and pushed ahead with almost the relentless energy of a force of nature, and especially by a group of people whom the older settlers among the Catskills called "the Yankees."

39

Invasion by Yankees

✿ As THE FIRST Indians picked their way through the cloves of the Catskills several thousands of years ago, they met no opposition except from rocks, fallen trees, and grapevines. No human owners then claimed the Catskills. The deer, bears, and wolves were the mountains' most complex and advanced living things. Except when they were attacked or frightened, these creatures made no resistance to the strange two-legged mammals who had come to their part of the world. When Dutch- and German-speaking settlers pushed the Indians aside and took possession of their hunting grounds in the Catskills, they, too, met with little resistance. For by that time, the Indians had learned to fear the white man's military power and they had become enslaved by the charms of the rum, steel knives, and woolen blankets which formed parts of the white man's culture. But when the third invasion of the Catskills began— it was known as the Yankee invasion—signs of resistance appeared in every hollow and at every crossroads. Dutchmen rallied to protect their property and their way of life against the emigrants from Connecticut, Massachusetts, and Rhode Island whom they knew as Yankees. The Yankees brought with them new ways of thinking, new ways of feeling, and new ways of living. In addition they seemed to have a bottomless fund of energy and ambition; it was no wonder that they awakened fear and distrust among the older inhabitants of the Hudson Valley and the Catskills.

In 1798 George Washington cautiously observed to an English visitor that "the inhabitants of New-England are continually spreading themselves."[1] The Yankees of New England began spreading early in the eighteenth century, and continued to spread in trickles and torrents. Indeed, the human flow from New England has not yet ceased.

A large legacy of mutual distrust was already in existence when the

Yankee invasion of New York began in earnest. Years of bickering over common boundaries and land claims added to differences in language and customs had made Yankees and Yorkers look at each other with suspicious eyes. In 1776 one manor Livingston wrote to another to warn that "those Harpies who reside in or near Connecticut" would take all the advantage of a Yorker that "their great skill & dexterity in the art of deceiving might give them."[2] Other Livingstons had long shared these sentiments. The non-letter-writing part of the New York population founded a revealing folklore composed of tales of the evil doings of sharp Yankees come to live among the noble, trusting, and honest descendants of the early white settlers of New York. A shrewd little Yankee persuaded the hulking Dutch owner of a tavern at the base of the Catskills to make a bet with him. The Yankee claimed that he could swallow the tavern keeper. As the idlers of the neighborhood watched, the Yankee asked the tavern-keeper to lie down on a table and take off his shoes. The Yankee then bit the tavernkeeper's foot until the man jumped up and howled with pain. "Vot's dis?" he shouted. "Dis is not svallowing me!" "Lie down on the table and let me finish," the Yankee said. "You didn't think I was going to swallow you whole, did you?"[3] Another Yankee agreed to buy some cattle from a Dutchman, and he asked that the bargain be put in writing. The Dutchman refused for he was probably illiterate. "If you vant dis in writing you cannot be an honest man," he said. "I'll do no business with you."[4] They still tell of the Yankee trapper who found nothing but a single young coon in his traps one cold morning. He put the coon in his pocket and made for the Dutch settlement nearby. There he talked a Dutchman into trading an old hen for the coon. He traded his way through the settlement and when he came home his wife asked, "Well, Jonathan, what did you find in your traps in Mink Hollow this morning?" "Twenty pork chops, a dozen eggs, an ax, a bottle of wine, and a slab of bacon," Jonathan answered as he threw the lot down on the kitchen table, "and the cutest little coon you ever saw."[5] He pulled the wriggling creature from his pocket—in the course of a day's trading with the Dutch his coon had come back to him.

In all the folklore of the Yankee invasion of the Catskills there is no hint of the reasons why the New Englanders marched westward from their home country, yet those reasons were plain enough. Observant William Cobbett, the English farmer-editor-agitator, discovered the principal one when he met a Yankee in Pennsylvania in 1818. "Supped with a Connecticut farmer. . . ." he wrote. "He has *migrated*. His reasons are these; he has five sons, the eldest 19 years of age, and several daughters.

Connecticut is thickly settled. He has not means to buy farms for the sons there. He therefore goes and gets cheap land in Pennsylvania, his sons will assist him to clear it up, and thus they will have a farm each. To a man in such circumstances and 'born with an axe in one hand and gun in the other' the western countries are desirable. . . ."[6] In New England the available farmland was not adequate to take care of the increasing population. A farmer would not divide his land among half a dozen children, for then none of them could make a living. The farm went to one son, usually the eldest, and the younger sons headed west.

The Yankees who arrived in the Catskills were born with more than an ax in one hand and a gun in the other. They were born heirs to a tradition of far greater intellectual curiosity than the Hudson Valley Dutch —and most of them could read and write. As the Hudson Valley people began to place a higher value on literacy, the Yankees supplied them with schoolteachers. The Yankees asked questions wherever they went. They caught sight of endless ways of making a dollar—ways that had been invisible to the eyes of the complacent Dutch. They were easily stirred by new ways of looking at life, and to them a lively and imaginative man like Dr. Mitchill made a good deal of sense. Yankees coming to the Catskills were not usually attracted by lands to be had only on leases; they preferred to settle on lands they could hope to own outright. Wherever they settled they carried the New England style of life with them. In the town of Durham they built a Presbyterian church, set up stocks, a whipping post, and a library. In Windham, too, they voted "to erect a set of stocks near the meeting house on the Mountain" and resolved that "if any person suffer his or her dog to go to meeting he or she shall forfeit the sum of fifty cents for each and every offence."[7] With dogs barred from public worship and stocks standing ready to care for evildoers while little libraries of solid works of science, history, and literature sprang up wherever Yankees settled, New England ways took over in many parts of the Catskills. Even today and especially in a broad belt stretching from Catskill westward, strangers sometimes find it hard to believe that they are not in Vermont or New Hampshire. The Westkill of today, for instance, remains a charming New England hamlet of the kind settled early in the nineteenth century. When President Timothy Dwight of Yale revisited the Hudson Valley in 1804 and 1815, he found the houses "ordinary and ill-repaired"[8]; the roads were "disagreable," and the inhabitants lounging at taverns "rude in their appearance, and clownish in their manners." But when the president reached Durham, where a New England settlement had been made, everything changed. He found the land "thoroughly cleared, well-cultivated, and divided by good enclosures into beautiful farms. Indeed everything here wears the appearance of prosperity. . . ."[9] The reasons for the blossoming of Durham were not hard to find for a man as thoroughly prejudiced in favor of New England ways as Dwight. "Almost all the inhabitants are emigrants from Connecticut; and have preserved the habits of their own country, . . ." pontificated Timothy Dwight, who was known as the "Yankee Pope."

No settlement in all the region of the Catskills showed a more unmistakably Yankee face to the world than the new Catskill which began to rise close to the Hudson River about 1790. The older Dutch Catskill had been located farther inland in the midst of an abundance of fertile flatlands (it is now known as Leeds); the new Catskill aspired to become a port on the Hudson and to make its reputation as a trading center. In ambitious young Catskill, well-educated Yankee business and professional men settled. Benjamin Dwight, grandson of the great Timothy, sold drugs and practiced medicine; another Dwight dealt in hardware; and Henry Dwight, the educator-to-be, clerked in the store for a while. A newspaper was established in 1792, and soon Catskill men were publishing books and operating a paper mill. When paper-making experiments absorbed Chancellor Livingston's attention in the 1790s, it was to Major Pitkin's paper mill at Catskill that he sent obliging Peter DeLabigarre to coax the major's men into lending a hand in trying to make paper from an alga growing in the Hudson River.[10]

The new Catskill had grown from a small settlement of Dutchmen. Known in its day as Het Strand or the Landing, its rise to greater things came when Yankees from the city of Hudson across the river glimpsed the possibilities of the site. Hudson had been settled by a group of New Englanders, many of whom were seafaring men from Nantucket and Martha's Vineyard. They soon had a variety of industries in operation. Their ships made trading voyages along the eastern coast of the United States, to the West Indies, and even across the Atlantic, while their whalers and sealers left for lengthy cruises. In all this activity many Catskill Yankees shared. On their own they speculated in lands in and near the Hardenbergh Patent, they backed a great variety of industries hopefully set up along streams among the mountains. Sawmills, turning mills, barrel-stave and heading mills, clockmaking mills, ironworking projects, the Barton's bell factory—all these and more appeared in the Catskills as Yankee energy began transforming the region.

By any standards the Yankees of Catskill would have to be classed among the up-and-coming people of the world. Their up-and-comingness showed in almost everything they undertook. For instance, the manner in which they advertised must have confirmed older Dutch inhabitants in their opinion that Yankees were mad. The *Catskill Packet* of October 15, 1792 carried a fine example of novel Yankee advertising. It offers barrel staves to sell or buy in vigorous colloquial verse which cannot help reminding modern readers of the poetry Robert Browning was to write in later years to the delight and puzzlement of our grandparents. The advertisement begins:

> "Staves and Lumber Boys!
> Hallow! below, come on deck, I'll advertise
> To give four pounds, staves begin to rise;
> What's the price? three pounds ten—no more?
> Stand by I'll raise them up to four. . . ."

Commercial advantage was far from being the sole objective of the Yankees of the Catskills, as is revealed in their newspapers. For in their own little settlement on the Hudson and in those back in the Catskills, Yankee men and women felt the ebb and flow of the intellectual and aesthetic tides of their time. Like Dr. Mitchill, they mingled scientific and romantic curiosity and feeling. They wondered, as had John Bartram and Dr. Mitchill, how the Catskill Mountains had come into being and how they came to be clothed with plant and animal life. Never before had the inhabitants of the region felt so many questions rising in their minds as they looked at the Catskills; never had so many notions aimed at improving man's life stirred in so many local heads. How could the growing fascination with mountains and distant views, with the study of plants and animals and rocks be turned to account by clever businessmen? How could the settlement known as Catskill reach out toward the Catskill Mountains and convert them into the source of a new kind of profit? It was many years before a way was to be found. But, in the meanwhile, the Livingstons who lived on the east bank of the Hudson were calling attention to the romantic charm of the Catskills in a very effective way.

40

"Country Seats" and Mountain Views

✤ THE YANKEE businessmen of Catskill, shrewd and enterprising as they were, lagged a bit in aesthetic matters behind another assortment of human beings, the Livingstons of Clermont and Livingston Manor. These people were the first to feel the change taking place in the way men and women were beginning to see the Catskills. Before the Yankees of Catskill did more than explore possibilities, the Livingstons took action. They boldly seized the Catskills rising across the Hudson and set them to work as important elements of the landscaped settings of their houses.

Before the romantic movement changed the look of the world as seen through American eyes, a man chose the spot upon which to build his house after taking into account a number of very practical considerations. Closeness to roads or water, or to neighbors or to a mill, safety from storm and flood, the absence of screens behind which enemies might hide determined the locations of houses built in the Hudson Valley during the seventeenth and eighteenth centuries. But as the romantic movement took hold, this began to change. More and more people, especially if they belonged to the better sort, built upon sites that commanded sweeping views of distant fields, villages, and forests, of soaring mountains, of streams and lakes. The picture windows of modern suburban dwellings symbolize in a modest way this same desire to relate a house to the world of nature.

The first American Robert Livingston had placed his manor house on an elevation which commanded a view of the Hudson and the cultivated fields which slope toward the river. This was less in order to extract enjoyment from the charms of the Hudson River and the Catskill Mountains beyond, and more from a determination to keep a calculating eye on river traffic and slaves hoeing Livingston crops. As Livingstons multiplied on the east bank of the Hudson and the old Livingston lands were divided

up among them again and again, new houses rose up for Livingston occupancy, but each one was placed as the result of a different line of reasoning from the one that had guided the first Robert. The view to be had
from these houses became of the very first importance. A location that
would guarantee its owners a baking in the summer sun or a freezing in
the winter winds would have to be endured for the reward of a fashionable
"distant prospect" as much as possible like the ones enjoyed by the romantically minded nobility and gentry of Britain. And from the Livingston
country which stretched along many miles of the east bank of the river, a
variety of prospects meeting every requirement of the strictest British
connoisseurs was to be had. In fact, a man looking toward the Catskills
from the east bank could see a view the equal in almost every respect of
the already famous ones admired by so many British tourists to England's
Lake District. There was the Hudson, cut by its hilly shores into what
appeared to be a series of lakes; there at a proper distance stood the Catskills
rising in their "true character of bold and fearless grandeur"[1] from a
mixture of forest and meadows and fields. No part of the United States had
a more correct kind of romantic scenery to offer. The Livingstons took full
advantage of this gift dumped into their laps by a whim of the gods. They
appropriated the Catskills as a feature of their landscape and a source of
aesthetic pleasure to Livingstons and their guests. Horatio Gates Spafford
took note of all this when he compiled his gazetteer of New York in 1813.
The Catskills as seen from Clermont, he wrote, provided an "elegant
display of light and shade occasioned by their irregularity, their fine blue
color, the climbing of the mists up their sides, the intervention of the
clouds which cap their summits or shroud their sides only, with their
occasional reflections from the surface of the Hudson, succeeded by the
bursting terrors of their thundergusts, all combined from this point of view,
associate a mass of interesting, picturesque and sublime objects, no where
exceeded in this country."

Before long, twenty miles of the Hudson's east bank stretching from
Hyde Park to the city of Hudson were famous for their profusion of
elegant "country seats"[2] all looking out upon the Catskills and nearly all
belonging to Livingstons and their relations. The very names of the Livingston country seats suggest the kind of pleasant leisurely existence led by
those fortunate enough to inhabit them. Green Hill or The Pynes; Prospect
Hill; The Valley; Parndon, which so well "commands the River"; the
Chateau de Montgomery, later known as Montgomery Place; Rokeby,
which in the days when the Chancellor's sister Mrs. John Armstrong lived
there was known as La Bergerie; Callendar House, first known as Sunning

Hill; Wildercliff; Teviotdale; The Hill; Staatsburgh House; Richmond Hill; Glenburn; Talavera; Edgewater; The Hermitage—all these and more faced the Catskills from which they drew both aesthetic charm and part of their financial strength. At one period the Livingston admiration of French taste was reflected in the design of their houses, but soon they returned to British tradition or shared in the passion for things Greek which swept their nation. One result was Edgewater built in 1820 by John R. Livingston as a wedding present for his daughter Mrs. Lowndes. To this day it presents a ponderous Greek portico to the Catskills from the bank of the Hudson.

Horatio Spafford admired the way the Chancellor had blended art and nature at Clermont until it became "difficult to discriminate their respective beauties and boundaries."[3] He found old trees, shrubbery, extensive lawns, flowers, and the Catskill Mountains united as if in a glorious work of art. Other Livingstons had followed the lead of the Chancellor and enhanced the charms of their dwellings by achievements in landscape gardening unsurpassed in any other part of the United States. Miles of paths and roads wound through Livingston lands revealing vistas of the Hudson and the Catskills; and rustic benches sheltered by thatched roofs enabled strollers through Livingston parks to rest in comfort while admiring the view. Picturesque shelters were built encircling ancient trees, or to serve as boathouses on the river; waterfalls were "improved" in order to render them even more striking to the aesthetic eye. Tangles of trees, vines, and shrubs were planted to form "wildernesses" which imitated similar constructions of English landscape designers like those John Bartram had served. Trees were planted by the thousands—the favorite tree the Livingstons employed to frame their mountain and river views was the Robinia popularly known as the locust because the long seed pods which followed its lovely white flowers suggested the locust seeds on which John the Baptist was thought to have fed in the desert. After 1840, famous landscape designer A. J. Downing lent his talents to Hudson River estates, and although Downing was unenthusiastic about the locust tree, it continued to be planted.

Even before the beginning of the Revolution, locust trees had been planted at Clermont. Left to itself the tree does not venture north of Pennsylvania, but its feathery charm when young and its rugged nobility when aged led gardeners to plant it farther north where it appeared to thrive. The locust had practical value too: its wood resists decay and makes excellent fence posts, and it was in special demand during the eighteenth century for making treenails, the wooden pins used in attaching plank to ships' timbers. During the first decades of the nineteenth century, a locust-tree mania raged in the United States and England and planting these trees was believed to be the surest way of laying up wealth for the future. Mrs. Montgomery filled the pockets of her apron with locust seeds and planted them as she drove or walked about among the scenic wonders of her estate. Many of the trees the widow Montgomery planted have long survived her. Livingstons growing old left instructions that they be buried in coffins fashioned of the locust wood they believed to be virtually immune to decay.[4] Today Livingston-descended children, when they are old enough to understand, are taken to the east bank of the Hudson and shown the locust trees planted by their ancestors, and they marvel at certain very ancient, huge, and craggy ones. In one of these ruinous giants at Clermont, the children are assured, a cannon ball fired from one of General Vaughan's ships in 1777 is embedded to this day.[5]

Thanks to the lands and cash handed down to them, the Livingstons could afford to be hospitable on a grand scale. Visitors came and went in the Livingston country; many were rich, some were talented. Titled Europeans and eminent learned men, statesmen and gay young members of the British aristocracy, and the aristocracy being formed in the United States—all these visited Livingstons and were expected to admire their view of the Catskills. And admire it they did. When they left they carried with them memories of the mountains which added so much to the splendor of the Livingston way of life. They talked about the Catskills and so helped make the mountains known as objects of romantic beauty on both sides of the Atlantic.

In August of 1812 the Livingston view of the Catskills was being admired by a sensitive young man of social charm and aesthetic interests. His name was Washington Irving. Irving was twenty-nine but already famous for his rollicking Knickerbocker's *History of New York* published in 1809. He had spent two years traveling in Europe and storing away in his mind materials he would later work up into essays and tales. He was observant, a good listener, and hoped some day to build a literary career upon the success of Knickerbocker, but just how, he was not sure. In the meanwhile, he worked at whatever came to hand and kept his ears and eyes open as he enjoyed life among the rich and gifted who seemed to take pleasure in his company. Earlier in 1812, Irving finished revising *Knickerbocker's History* for a new edition. He then relaxed in a series of visits to the country homes of friends and in August became a guest for a week at the imposing country place of the Chancellor's brother John Robert Livingston at Barrytown. Here, as Irving wrote to his friend Henry Brevoort, he found himself "in complete fairyland." John Livingston's house was "spacious and elegant, with fine grounds around it," while the neighborhood was "gay and hospitable."[6] Irving delighted in the company of attractive young women of Livingston relationship and with them made excursions into the surrounding country where Livingston tenants dressed and farmed in much the same way as their German grandfathers had. He was invited to have dinner with old Mrs. Montgomery. Twice in that golden summer week he dined at the Chancellor's.

The Chancellor Livingston of Irving's visit was in his late sixties. He was aware that his strength was ebbing, and believed that death could not be far off. To the delight of his Methodist sister Mrs. Freeborn Garettson, the Chancellor took to spending solitary hours with his Bible (a book he had openly neglected in earlier life). For years he had been so deaf that his friends had to shout to make themselves understood; now his deafness took on the value of a welcome barrier between the Chancellor and earthly concerns. That spring he had seen his efforts to maintain the monopoly of steamboat travel, granted to him and Robert Fulton by the legislature at the insistence of Dr. Mitchill, upheld by the courts. This was the last material triumph of his busy and useful life. Once the monopoly appeared safe, the Chancellor began a retreat from earthly existence—that would culminate in death in February 1813. No longer was he interested in agriculture or mechanical improvement or politics; even the raising and improving of merino sheep which had been the profitable enthusiasm of his final years ceased to hold his attention. Like a man thoughtfully putting on his hat and coat in the hall of a house in which he has been a happy guest, the Chancellor was preparing to leave.

Ever since the critical infant days of the Revolution the chancellor had presided over the Catskills and determined much of what had happened there. Now others would have to take over this task. The Chancellor had made as sure as mortal man could that his lands among the mountains would continue to remain in Livingston hands. He had resisted pressures to sell and had maintained in their full anachronistic splendor the system of leases for three lives.[7] The two daughters, who were his only children, had been married off to relatives who bore the Livingston name. It was reasonable to expect that his grandchildren would take up the task of leading the Catskills in their struggle to remain secure within the Old World and the eighteenth century while the nineteenth flowed by. But all this was not to be.

No Livingston—and indeed no living human being—was to replace the old chancellor as the guiding spirit of the Catskills. His place would be taken by a creation of the imagination of the smart young man who had dinner at his house in August of 1812—a creation that came into the world some seven years later as a bearded old codger christened Rip Van Winkle. And as Rip Van Winkle made his presence felt among the mountains, the image of the aristocratic chancellor would fade away. No longer would people speak of the Chancellor's bridge or the Chancellor's mill or the Chancellor's road. Instead, they would begin to apply the magical name of Rip Van Winkle to features of the Catskill landscape and to many elements of its society.

Washington Irving had been exposed to the persuasive powers of the Catskills several times before that summer week of 1812. But never had he seen them under circumstances that appealed more strongly to his imaginative and dreamy nature. He had been set down in the Livingston "fairyland" in which Old World ways had survived transplantation to America. There tenants, unhampered by more than a smattering of literacy, dutifully tilled their masters' crops and handed down from generation to generation their rich lore of witches and supernatural happenings. Seen from the spacious houses of Livingstons, all this took on a rosier look than it would have had if Irving had been the guest of a simple tenant instead of a landlord, for the young writer was a good deal of a snob who made no secret of his sympathies with the privileged of this world and with old European ways. Looking across the Hudson, Irving saw the Catskills, and from no other place do these mountains appear more imposing or more seductive than from the estates of the Livingstons. Seen from the deck of a sloop on the Hudson (and Irving had seen them this way a number of times), they are likely to prove somewhat disappointing, for masses of highland intervene and detract from the mountains' bulk or break them into fragments. But from the Livingston country, the entire eastern wall of the Catskills with its higher peaks rising within the wall may be grasped in one delighted glance. The Hudson and the Livingston lawns and locusts furnish a splendid foreground; in the middle distance, fields and villages spread out over an irregular plain; white smoke rising from many village and farmhouse chimneys make the Catskills seem all the bluer and more mysterious by contrast.

Irving was the most amusing and charming of guests. But he was also an artist, and as he frolicked with his rich friends, he may well have absorbed an understanding of the Catskill Mountains which would, seven years later, help bring Rip Van Winkle to life. But while Irving stored impressions away in his retentive brain, the Yankee invaders of the Catskills were catching a glimpse of a means by which they might make a good thing of the newly romantic mountains. The scene of their operations was plainly visible to Irving as he gazed at the Catskills from the Livingston country. It was the break in the wall of the Catskills in which the two lakes lie and where a man can look out over the world from the edge of a rocky platform soon to become known as the Pine Orchard.

A Venture in Spruce Beer

✥ IN THE COURSE of a little lecture on the Catskills given to an English visitor to Clermont in 1794, the Chancellor remarked that he had recently bought 13,000 additional acres among the mountains for half a dollar per acre. This tract, the visitor reported, was "almost in a perfect state of nature"[1] with hardly any human settlers. It abounded instead in bears, wolves, wildcats, and other wilderness inhabitants. The fact was that while its coat of wilderness was shrinking from the Catskills, it was shrinking unevenly and the perfect state of nature the Englishman wrote of still prevailed over most of the region in spite of all efforts at settlement. It had prevailed in most of the vicinity of the two lakes and the Kaaterskill Falls, until the Schohariekill Road was opened after 1790. Then the ancient forests and the wild creatures who inhabited them were threatened and the integrity of the clear streams, the waterfalls, and the lakes of this part of the mountains was menaced. The two lakes of the Bartrams' shady vale and the Kaaterskill Falls were brought within easy striking distance of anyone who could puzzle out a way of making them yield a profit in cash at whatever cost to their romantic appeal or to the welfare of future generations of humans. In this way and in this part of the Catskills a state of tension began to be created between believers in two different ways of relating to the natural world. One group held that a man had a right to do anything he pleased in order to extract a profit for himself from trees and rocks and soil; the other saw values in their landscape which could not be expressed in dollars. As the shrinking of the wilderness proceeded some people became uneasy and wondered if the wasteful destruction of the American forests, often for a small and temporary profit, was worth the loss it brought in aesthetic values and in the diminished heritage to be handed down to new generations.

Across the Atlantic, Parson Gilpin in his own way was bewailing the destruction of British forests. "The picturesque eye," he wrote in his *Remarks on Forest Scenery*, ". . . is greatly hurt with the destruction of these sylvan scenes. Not that it delights in a continued forest; nor wishes to have the whole country covered with wood. It delights in the intermixture of wood and plain."[2] American romantic pilgrims agreed with the parson's views. They looked forward to a day when their land would be covered, like England, with an intermixture of woods and cultivated plains. They had no clear thoughts about the future of such scenic marvels as the Kaaterskill Falls and the mountain summits around, but innocently assumed that they would continue to exist much as they were to inspire and give pleasure to Americans of the future. They were pleased as the Schohariekill Road made its way up the mountainside toward the two lakes; similar roads in Britain had done much, over the previous half century, to stimulate interest in the landscape by making its most exciting features more easily reached.[3] The same result could be expected in the Catskills. But while romantics took to the new road with delight, so too did other men inspired by very different hopes. Some were speculators in land or agents of landlords bent on collecting rents from squatters along the Schoharie; some were ablaze with schemes for setting up industries beside waterfalls or for harvesting timber used for a variety of purposes. Many of the notions that had inspired Robert Livingston of Clermont when he began settling Woodstock now also inspired other men who took roads like the Schohariekill Road into the Catskills. At their direction, oars were made of white ash—in the winter of 1814–15, a man named Zadock Pratt was to ship a hundred thousand of them to New York.[4] Curly maple was cut for gunstocks and also for furniture. In 1790 Governor Clinton had some especially fine furniture made of this wood in order to direct attention to its silky beauty and perhaps help stop the flow of American dollars to the West Indies and Central America in return for mahogany. The stony soil of the Catskills, it was being said, produced the finest curly maple in the world. It produced, too, great black cherry trees from which mills high in the mountains sawed broad boards to be used in making tops for dining tables.[5] John Bartram had remarked on the great variety of trees that grew in the Catskills, and now that new roads were making them available, the trees were being sought out and put to use.

One man found an unusual way to use one of the kinds of trees which grew in the Catskills. He was John Ashley. Hardly had the Schohariekill Road been opened when Ashley was traveling it in order to set up on the shore of North Lake two log buildings in which he manufactured from the tips of the branches of spruce trees a substance known as the essence of spruce. This John Ashley was a man worth knowing, for he emerges from the old records seeming even yet to bounce and quiver with acquisitive energy and ingenuity. Of Yankee origin, he had come from the city of Hudson to serve as the town baker of Catskill. Years after Ashley was gone, old-timers recalled that he had advertised with a vigor worthy of more recent times. The signboard attached to his shop was actually bigger than the shop. On it were shown in natural colors monumental loaves of bread and giant barrels overflowing with crackers. Surmounting these appeals to the public appetite was a slogan reading, "May our County never want for Bread."[6] But baking could not absorb all of John Ashley's energy. He was ever on the alert for new ways of laying his hands on dollars. As a baker he supplied the people of Catskill with bread to eat. Sometime in the 1790s he proposed supplying them, as well as more distant Americans, with something to drink.

The tips of the spruce trees to be found beside North Lake were the raw materials of Ashley's method of quenching Americans' thirst. In Ashley's day, the artificially carbonated drinks daily consumed by millions in our time were yet unknown, although a beginning had been made by druggists who flavored, colored, and carbonated waters prescribed by physicians for those who could or would not visit spas where naturally carbonated waters were to be found. The place in life of the cola drinks, the ginger ales, and similar concoctions of our day was once filled very well indeed by a slightly alcoholic liquid known as spruce beer. People of all ages relished spruce beer but it was the especial favorite of children and adolescents. Old ladies and one-armed veterans often kept refreshment stands at which they offered spruce beer and gingerbread of their own brewing and baking. Such stands sprang up in cities on holidays and were a feature of summer resorts and of places to which people traveled to see natural wonders.[7]

Most spruce beer was made from the essence of spruce. To a small amount of the essence, water, sugar or molasses, and a little yeast were added. The mixture was allowed to ferment for a few days and was then bottled. John Ashley's plan was to settle on the shores of North Lake and there produce the essence of spruce which he could send down to the Hudson River over the new road. The log buildings were his headquarters, located close to the point at which the stream once known in his honor as Ashley's Brook enters the lake. For years the spruce trees bordering the lakes dwindled as Ashley's kettles boiled and bubbled. But by 1809 the project failed and Ashley was turning his attention to fresh paths to riches. An alum mine in the Kaaterskill Clove and a plaster mill near

Catskill had become the subjects of his dreams.[8] By that time a sawmill was at work deep within the Kaaterskill Clove; before long another sawmill would be set up a little below the outlet of South Lake and would interfere with the flow of water to the Kaaterskill Falls. Already a small part of the wilderness of the vicinity was giving way to clearings, burned-over fields, and unsightly mounds of dead branches, yet romantic pilgrims continued to come in an ever-increasing stream. For more and more Americans were eager to see the waterfalls, the lakes, and the mountaintop views of the Catskills.

At first the romantic movement had touched only members of the American better sort and a scattering of unusually sensitive and thoughtful people of other classes who were roused to observe and study plants and animals, rocks and soil, and to become aware of the existence within themselves of unconscious forces struggling to find their way through the rational veneer imposed by civilized society. By the end of the 1790s the romantic movement was trickling downward through the layers of the social order. Americans on many levels were beginning to show an interest in such romantic symbols as waterfalls, ruins, mountains, distant views, dark caves, and lakes set in the primeval wilderness. Among the Catskills the chief of all romantic symbols was the Kaaterskill Falls, but they owed a good part of their ability to bewitch Americans to another and greater natural marvel.

Hundreds of miles to the northwest of the lakes and the Kaaterskill Fall, the thunder of the chief of America's watery wonders, Niagara Falls, had been stimulating the imagination of travelers ever since 1683, when Father Hennepin published his eye-witness account of this "incredible Cataract or Waterfall which has no equal." At first Niagara impressed by its vastness and its overwhelming demonstration of power, but it soon began to acquire more subtle meanings. By 1700 it was possible for French engraver Sebastian Le Clerc to portray the prophet Elijah being borne aloft in his fiery chariot against the most glorious background imaginable—Niagara Falls. Soon British poets who felt impelled to deal with the sublime aspects of nature were sprinkling their stanzas with references to the great waterfall in the American wilderness. By 1778 so many travelers had visited the falls and described them in print that the author of Jonathan Carver's *Travels,* feeling that the subject had been overdone, decided "to omit a particular description" of them in his book published that year in London. By that time educated Europeans understood, with the help of Niagara Falls, that American scenery had an exciting character of its own. In 1791 William Bartram's book of travels persuasively alerted the world to the romantic charm of

Florida's scenery and living things; soon DeLabigarre and Dr. Mitchill, if with far less charm and effectiveness, performed a similar service for the scenery of the Catskills. American poets began turning out imitations of British topographical poetry in which they used American scenery, but with little of the understanding of its distinctive character shown by William Bartram. In 1802 the Catskills appeared in John D. M'Kinnon's *Descriptive Poems Containing Picturesque Views of the State of New York* as "the distant range/Of insulated mountains towering o'er Esopus plains in blue perspective vast."[9] M'Kinnon compared the Catskills to the Alps, paid dutiful tribute to Chancellor Livingston's Clermont, and then set down in shopworn poetic phrases a glimpse of the ever-changing Catskills seen as part of a great stage-set. ". . . approaching as we range the fragrant groves/And Clermont's halls, in elevation broad and sylvan/majesty, the mountains screen/The west, and shift, with varying lights and shades/Their grand imposing scenery. . . ."

Even as M'Kinnon penned his tribute to the Catskills, the chief natural wonders of his insulated mountains were in some danger from the efforts of Ashley and others. Yet in their eagerness to see these wonders, pilgrims resigned themselves to the growing disorder of the landscape in which the wonders were set. Another and very different group of Americans shared in this sad acceptance—they were the hunters and woodsmen who had long paid visits to the two lakes and their rugged surroundings.

For at least a thousand years before the first white hunter set foot on the shores of the lakes, Indian hunters had come and gone in the shady vale. They knew that a lake set in a wilderness attracts the kinds of living things whose flesh and skins are necessary to Indian existence. Indian eyes were sensitive to the ways of their forest neighbors, plant and animal. Every day Indians were made aware all over again that life and death are intertwined and that the life of each living thing is dependent on the lives of others. Nowhere did Indians see the patterns of life succeed more fully than at a wilderness lake. There the sunlight could pour down unhampered by leaves and branches and encourage life to thrive on the shore and in the water. Insects hovered thick in the sunlight and laid their eggs in the water. Many of the young who hatched out met their fate in the stomachs of the lake's fish, yet there were enough survivors to carry on their kind of teeming abundance. Frogs croaked on the lakeshore, deer drank or nibbled the low growth on the banks. Bears ate sun-ripened berries or overturned stones in search of damploving insects. They rolled, with many signs of pleasure, in the muddy "bear wallows" beside the lake. Beaver too were attracted to the place—their efforts at dam building sometimes raised the level of the lake. From time to

Edwardsville (now Hunter) as it looked in 1820. The New York Tannery,
run by Colonel Edwards, is on the right beside the Red Falls of the
Schohariekill which furnished it with power. Above the tannery are the
schoolhouse and church. A few tall trees, saved because they were not
hemlocks, tower awkwardly over the settlement. The painting is a copy
made many years ago from an original commissioned by Colonel Edwards.
(*Courtesy of Miss Dorothy Ingalls of Hunter, the owner of the painting.*)

Far right, barkpeelers at work among the Catskills. Reproduced from the *Illustrated News,* New York, May 17, 1853. (*Courtesy of New York State Library.*)

The mountain known as the Colonel's Chair is shown here towering above a lodge hall in the village of Hunter. (*Photo by Alex Viola.*)

Colonel Pratt at seventy-one leads a group of employees in an effort at repairing Prattsville road. (*Courtesy of New York State Library.*)

Benches cut from natural rock help pilgrims rest on the steep path that leads to the carvings on the face of Pratt's Rocks above. (*Photos by Alex Viola.*)

time beaver gave way to muskrats whose tunnels penetrated the beaver dams and helped them give way. And so the lake rose and fell over the centuries almost as if it it were slowly breathing.

Far away in Europe, sophisticated people had created a romantic cult of the wilderness nourished by travelers' tales of distant forests, deserts, and lonely lakes like those high in the Catskills. It sprang in large part from a growing suspicion that reason alone could not solve all human problems. Was it possible that the advanced civilization which prevailed in eighteenth-century Europe had brought evil as well as good to mankind? Would human beings lead happier and more satisfying lives if they threw off the artificialities of civilization and lived close to the eternal simplicities of nature? Many men and women caught in the swelling tide of romantic feeling answered "Yes." Peter DeLabigarre was among them, which was why when he saw the two lakes and the nearby pair of settlers they seemed to him to have materialized from the pages of the romantic authors he admired.

In America a different cult of the wilderness had developed among far less sophisticated people. They were members of the lower sort who had brought with them from Europe traditions of the saints and hermits, the outlaws and rebels who had sought safety or freedom from social pressures in dark European forests, or, like John the Baptist, in a desert. In the New World these people found a race of wilderness men in the Indians.[10] They hated the Indians and at the same time envied and admired them—from time to time a frontier dweller fled from the difficulties of his society and took to living among the Indians. Children captured by Indian war parties often refused to return to white civilization and chose to pass their lives among the Indians. White men sometimes chose to live alone in the wilderness as trappers and hunters. Some built little cabins; others wandered from place to place and found temporary homes in rock shelters like Bartram's Cave.

In the settlements that came to fringe the Catskills the influence of the wilderness was pervasive. And this wilderness clung to much of the Catskills, partly because of the Old World notions of absentee landlords, partly because most of the region was unsuited to farming, partly because as yet only a small number of its trees were worth cutting and hauling to the Hudson. As late as 1800 in the regions untouched by man, panthers, wolves, bears, and other wild creatures of whom the Chancellor had spoken throve and made raids by night on valley fields and pastures. Settlers kept rifles handy and often penetrated the mountains in search of bears or wolves who had made off with their lambs or little pigs. Many became half hunters and half farmers. Some found the charms of wilderness life so powerful that they neglected their crops and spent most of their time in the woods. Animal skins were salable, which made it possible for a man to rationalize his love for the wilderness by pointing to the profits of hunting.

In no place in all the region of the Catskills were the wilderness and the farming sides of life more thoroughly mixed than in the valley known as Kiskatom, which lay at the base of the Catskills directly below the two lakes. Formed of plains of deep and fertile soil framed in occasional rocky ridges, the valley was a continuation northeastward of the country in which Jeremiah Snyder lived. It took its name from the Indian word for the shagbark hickory trees which still stand tall and graceful on the borders of Kiskatom fields. There settlers came from the Palatine camps on the Hudson as early as the 1720s; they were joined by Dutchmen; and during the 1790s Yankees arrived. To all these people, the great mountainside which hung above their valley was a fact which could not be ignored. Hardest of all to ignore were the bears who lived there, especially near the lakes, and who were such frequent visitors to Kiskatom. It was not surprising that bear hunting became part of the life of almost every Kiskatom male, or that legends and traditions of bear hunting arose and were handed down with care. For the native black bear had become a symbol of the Catskill wilderness.

By the end of the first decade of the nineteenth century, the bear hunters of Kiskatom had a center about which to gather and tell of their exploits. This was the tavern kept by a prosperous Yankee named Merchant Lawrence. Hunting parties set out from Lawrence's and it was to Lawrence's that their members returned to refresh themselves after their battles with the wilderness. Botanists with their tin collecting-boxes stopped at Lawrence's before scaling the mountain and perhaps spending a night in Bartram's Cave. Romantic pilgrims, their heads filled with tags of English poetry, paused at Lawrence's before ascending to the wonders above, for Lawrence's had become accepted as the gateway to the wilderness and the romantic attractions of the Catskills.[11]

No stranger could visit Lawrence's without becoming aware that there the sense of the neighboring wilderness was strong and that at Lawrence's the black bear reigned as the spirit of the Catskills. Colonel Lawrence (he was Lieutenant Colonel of the 120th regiment of New York's militia) made a point of keeping several young bears on chains in an enclosure adjoining his tavern. The hollow trunks of large trees sunk into a sandy bank provided the bears with hibernating quarters. Visitors were shown the bears for a fee of three cents. Dishes of bear meat figured on the colonel's menu, and the high point of his year was New Year's Day when he served a supper of bear meat to which distinguished guests were invited. Throughout the year, bear tales were told and retold in Colonel Lawrence's barroom and in this way acquired polish and authority. Many of these tales have come down to our own day.

42

Bear Lore and Bear Day

When an older-timer in the Catskills settles down to reminiscing he seldom takes long before coming up with a bear story. And if he has a jug of hard cider handy to help the reminiscing process, his first story is likely to be a tall one. Charley Herrick used to tell a tale of a Platte Clove bee hunter who almost caught a bear instead of a bee.

The man and a neighbor had climbed a mountain to try to locate a bee tree with the aid of a bee box. This box is an ingenious little thing with a sliding lid. A bee is lured into the box with a bit of honey or other sweet and the lid is then pushed shut. When the bee is released he heads straight for his home tree. Several bees caught and freed in this way at different points give the hunter a good fix on the tree. The Platte Clove man had been told that a drop of the oil of anise would make a box irresistible to a bee. But his aim with the anise bottle was poor, and he succeeded in soaking the box and his jacket with anise and went up the mountain smelling like an old-fashioned German bakeshop at Christmas. He had reached a ledge where the bees were working on some early goldenrod when his neighbor startled him with a yell. "Look! That bear is going right for you," he shouted. And sure enough there was a big black bear heading toward the man with the bee box. The bear's tongue was hanging out and he was drooling. The man backed up until he stood at the brink of the ledge—below was a thirty-foot drop into the tops of some spiky oak trees. He didn't know what to do. It looked as if he'd have to choose between death by bear and death by collision with treetops.

Luckily, the neighbor happened to be a fast thinker. He knew that the outstanding thing about his friend was that he was the worst singer in all of Platte Clove. When he joined in the hymns at church, sensitive old ladies had been known to faint dead away. If kids or a peddler bothered him, all he had to do to make them clear out was to open his mouth and tackle a song. "Sing—that's your only chance," the neighbor advised from behind the rock where he'd sought safety from the bear. The Platte Clove man wet his lips and lit into "Nearer My God to Thee." The bear stopped. A shocked look came over his face, he turned round, gave a groan, and headed northward along the ledge. "And," said Charley, "where the bear went nobody knows. All I can say is that particular bear was never seen again in the Catskill Mountains—at least I never heard anybody tell of seeing him."[1]

A generation ago one of the strongest contenders for the honor of being chosen champion teller of tall tales about the bears of the Catskills was the same Judge Alphonso Trumpbour Clearwater who once saved archeologist Schrabisch from the claws of the law. The judge maintained that the bears were the best friends the people of the Catskills ever had—many a hunter lost among the mountains owed his life to a bear who courteously showed him the location of the nearest settlement. When the judge had a sufficiently able listener, he would hold him with his eye and tell one of his own adventures with the bears of the Peekamoose vicinity. Once upon a time he was picking huckleberries near Peekamoose Lake when a bear joined him and picked for a while on the other side of the same patch of bushes. But berries were scant and the bear soon gave up. He beckoned the judge to follow and led him over rocks and ridges to a spot unknown to the judge but in which huckleberries grew in magnificent size and plenty. The judge filled his bucket and then realized that he hadn't the slightest notion of where he was. But the bear seemed to understand. He led the judge back over the rocks and ridges to the exact place where the two had met. With a kindly wave of his paw he ambled off—and refused to accept any reward at all for his help. While his listener was still under the spell of his eloquence, Clearwater often added that one of the most remarkable ways in which bears helped humans was by their usefulness in preventing snakebite. He had never heard of a man being bitten by a Catskill rattler when a bear was around, and the judge even offered to make an affidavit to that effect.[2]

One of the best-known of tall bear tales goes back to colonial days. Its hero was an Indian hunter named Wancham. The story was set down more than a century ago by the Reverend Charles Rockwell of Kiskatom who had it from a native of Catskill named Peter Osterhout. Said Osterhout, "I have heard the story related by several aged persons who have no doubt of his [Wancham's] veracity. . . . While hunting in the Catskill Mountains he came upon the carcass of a deer, quite recently killed, as he supposed, by a panther, or a bear; so he hid himself behind a windfall nearby, and had not been there long when a large bear came up and began to make a meal out of the deer. A few minutes later, a large panther came also, and began to tear the carcass of the deer. This did not suit bruin, who claimed the deer as his spoil, and struck the panther, who jumped on the other side of the deer, when the bear followed him up and tried to hug him, but the panther soon (having doubtless leaped on the bear's back), ripped him open and killed him with his hind claws. The Indian, thinking that the game was now in his favor, fired and killed the panther; and thus he had a deer, a panther, and a bear, all in a pile, by a single shot of his gun."[3]

Wancham's tale has a strong resemblance to those of the renowned Baron Münchhausen. It was far from being the only bit of Catskill Mountain bear lore to have deep roots in the past, for the bears of the world from the days before history have been known to occupy human thoughts and rouse human emotions. A bear cult once girdled the northern world and had participants in Europe, Asia, and America. The oldest European constructions that may be described as altars were built perhaps seventy-five thousand years ago by bear cultists of what is now Switzerland. The purpose of these altars was to propitiate the spirits of the bears men slew for food and clothing.[4]

It was not only the physical strength of the bear and his usefulness to man that attracted human interest. The bear belonged to a group of mammals who have long been close to humans. Man's earliest non-human friends the dog and the bear have common ancestors not too far back as evolution goes, while the cat is a more distant cousin. The bear is capable of walking on his hind legs, and his feet rest on the ground very much as those of humans do. A skinned bear has a disturbingly human look. In the Catskills of the eighteenth and nineteenth centuries, an old half-buried sense of the closeness of man to other living things centered around the bear—especially on February 2. On that day the bears of the Catskills were believed to wake from their spell of hibernation and perform certain ritual actions which European bears had been believed to perform many centuries earlier. In Europe, as bears became less numerous, the common badger took his place as the hero of February 2. But in the Catskills, until well into the twentieth century, the day was celebrated as "Bear's Day." The Reverend Charles Rockwell, who had spent his early life as a chaplain in the United States Navy, came to Kiskatom about 1860 as pastor of the Reformed Dutch Church which stood across the road from the site of the old Colonel Lawrence tavern, and he became a convert to the local belief that the black bear acted out his important rite each year on February 2. Mr.

Rockwell set down the details of Bear's Day in his book *The Catskill Mountains,* which was published in 1867.[5]

"And now I come to a fact connected with the natural history of bears, of which I have never seen anything in books, but for the truth of which all the old hunters of the Catskill Mountains and the country around, and those connected with them, will solemnly vouch, as proved by their own personal observation, or the testament of those whose veracity cannot be impeached, and the truth of whose statements, no one who knew them well would ever question. And yet there may be those who would think it strange that an honest old Dutch dominie, of full size and mature age, should venture to tell as true what follows. My reply to such would be, that there always have been those in the world who doubt or deny the truth of what they themselves have never seen or known. A fool of this stripe, who said that he would not believe in what he had never seen, was very properly asked if he had ever seen his own back?

"What I here refer to is that the second day of February of each year is known as 'Bear's Day'; and that on that day bears wake from winter sleep, come forth from their dens, take a knowing observation of the weather for a few minutes, and then retire to their nests and finish their repose of some weeks or months,—it may be longer. It is further claimed that if the sky is clear, the sun shining so that they can see their shadows, and the weather cold, when they thus come forth, they sleep quietly on until about the first of April, thinking that cold weather will continue thus long. On the other hand, if the weather is mild and cloudy, they look for an early spring, and often leave their dens; or if the water from the melting snow above them penetrates the earth, so as to wet them in their dens, they seek some new resting-place and home.

"That bears do thus come forth from their dens the second day of February is known by the tracks made by them that day at the mouth of their winter quarters, as also by observing the habits of tame bears (which) come forth on Bear's Day, and after wisely observing the weather some five minutes, retire again to rest. As several tame bears have been kept by those whom I know well, men of Christian principle, and entirely reliable, and after a careful observation in some cases for two or three successive winters, thus come forth from their dens . . . I cannot therefore question or doubt the truth of the statement here advanced." Here Mr. Rockwell is referring in part to some of the bears kept at Lawrence's Inn and of which he had heard from the lips of the colonel's sons, one of whom was an elder of his church.

During the nineteenth century the wilderness of the Catskills in which the black bear was so much at home grew smaller and the bear population shrank. The woodchuck or groundhog pushed the bear from the February 2 limelight. The woodchuck is a creature of cleared fields and sunny meadows; he cannot thrive in the forests and among the rocks which are the bear's haunts. He is a marmot and so a close relative of the European badger whom the ancestors of settlers among the Catskills had honored on February 2. Today it is a rare old-timer among the Catskills who speaks of Bear's Day—the woodchuck (whom some call the "little bear") has triumphed. But in the infant years of the nineteenth century, the bear was the lord of the wild Catskills and woodchucks were still uncommon in a land where their way of life was only beginning to be made easy.[6]

Hunting bears was a favorite winter sport of strong men who trailed them along ledges high in the mountains. Some hunters made a business of sending bear meat down the Hudson to the city of New York where it was a staple in season in the markets. The bear's grease or oil was also readily sold—it was the favorite hairdressing of eighteenth- and early nineteenth-century men in both Europe and America. Europeans had first imported their bear's grease from Russia, but when American supplies became available the Russian bear took a back seat. So much sought after was bear's grease that substitutes were devised by unscrupulous men who claimed that use of the genuine article would cause hair to grow on the hands and produce other bearlike characteristics.

Tales of the adventures of the old bear hunters of the Catskills abound in every corner of the mountains.[7] They tell of brave men crawling into dens and entering hollow trees in pursuit of bears, of hand-to-hand fights with angry bears, of courageous bear dogs giving their lives to help their masters conquer bears. They tell, too, of bear trappers who constructed pens of heavy logs which a bear would enter, lured by the bait of a sheep's head or similar dainty, only to find a heavy door sliding shut behind him. James Quinlan set down the tale of a Sullivan County Frenchman named Samuel Mitteer who saved his daughter's life by tossing her into a bearless bear trap. He and the daughter, Quinlan says, were being pursued in the forest by a pack of wolves. The wolves were gaining by the moment when the desperate Frenchman remembered a nearby bear trap. He managed to reach it and thrust his daughter inside. He himself climbed a tree above the trap. And all that night and part of the next day the two waited for their rescuers while the frustrated wolves howled outside the stout log walls of the trap.[8] The story is a tall one for it does not ring true to wolf character.

Quinlan did his best to immortalize the bear hunters of the Catskills, as did the authors of various nineteenth-century accounts of Delaware and Ulster County history and tradition. But it was the Reverend Charles Rockwell whose tributes to the bear hunters of the region surrounding the two lakes entitle him to be remembered as the Homer of the settlement days of the Catskills. For he wrote with awed admiration of such old hunters as Connecticut-born Paul Peck, of "Uncle Frederick" Saxe and a number of other related Saxes—all of Palatine German descent. He also set down the deeds of Colonel Lawrence's sons and much bear lore which had been shaped in the old colonel's tavern beneath the bear-haunted mountain.

In the great years of the bear, young Merchant Lawrence came to the Schohariekill country high in the Catskills with his young Yankee wife. Born in Connecticut, he had been raised in the town of Northeast in Dutchess County, for like many a Yankee family, the Lawrences required two generations to make the jump from Connecticut to the Catskills. Mrs. Lawrence died a few days after giving birth to a son, and in 1794 the widower married, at the Katsbaan church, Sarah, daughter of rich Hezekiah Wynkoop of Saugerties. The Wynkoops were a Dutch-descended family, who had invested in lands stretching along the base of the Catskills—old Hezekiah and other members of his family owned a tract at what is now Palenville. On this land a sawmill stood and a gristmill soon followed. Merchant Lawrence bought some of this land from his in-laws in 1798; a few years later he was established to the north on the land upon which his famous tavern was to flourish. Partly by chance, partly by reason of his undoubted ability, Lawrence had reached what was to become for him a land of opportunity.[9]

Earlier, the building of the Schohariekill Road had promised for a while to bring prosperity to the owners of the high mountain lands over which it made its tortuous way. But the road had quickly aged and died leaving only a broken trail behind. When the success of the great Susquehanna Turnpike to the north led to an epidemic of "turnpike fever," Catskill Yankees and Dutchmen wondered if the old Schohariekill Road might not be worth reviving as a privately owned turnpike. Over such a road settlers would move. Later they would haul their butter or grain to Hudson River markets, paying a toll each time. The timber waiting to be cut along the Schohariekill would use the road, and it would provide a quicker route to the fertile lands along the upper reaches of the East Branch of the Delaware.

In 1805 the state legislature was asked to approve the road to be known as the Little Delaware Turnpike. Like the old Schohariekill Road it would pass between the two lakes. But its route up the side of the Catskills from the Hudson Valley would no longer swing southward to the mouth of the Kaaterskill Clove and then loop its way upward; it would turn a bit to the north and follow the deep wooded scar in the mountainside later to be known as Sleepy Hollow. This would take it past the very door of Merchant Lawrence's house. Turnpike fever was a disease that invited complications, some of which were very pleasant. Men who had advance information about the route of proposed turnpikes often bought up the land the turnpike would open to settlement and turn—or so it seemed to many a feverish speculator —to pure gold. As the Little Delaware Turnpike was being planned, those lands along its route which were not in the grip of large absentee landlords began to change hands. Knowing lawyers and politicians began to eye with decided interest even the rugged country surrounding the two lakes—and soon they took action.

43

Speculators in the Shady Vale

✤ MANY YEARS had passed since Lord Cornbury had granted the Hardenbergh Patent on behalf of his royal cousin, and many other royal governors had come and gone. George the First, George the Second, and George the Third reigned in succession—and the shady vale near the Kaaterskill Falls still remained the property of the Crown. Not of course because the Crown wanted it but simply because no one thought it was worth asking for. With the establishment of the United States, all crown lands became the property of the states within which they lay. The lakes and the mountaintop lands around them became the property of the people of the state of New York. It would have been easy enough for any speculator or politician to get possession of the lakes; it would even have been possible for a settler with the right connections and a little money to have had them transferred from the people to himself. But no one took the trouble, for the lands around the lakes seemed to be without a market value. John Ashley squatted beside North Lake and used the surrounding spruces without objection from the people. Timber thieves, once the Schohariekill Road was ready, picked out white pine trees and hauled them to the Hudson, and the people did not try to stop them. The land itself lay unwanted.

Shortly before 1805 a change began to take place. When Catskill men took over the crumbling and publicly owned Schohariekill Road to turn it into the privately owned Little Delaware Turnpike, they took a fresh look at the land along the road. Judge Caleb Benton of Catskill bought out John Ashley and became owner of North Lake.[1] William Cockburn, with his ardor for acquiring land unchilled by age, set afoot a complicated series of maneuvers by which a number of men, who asserted squatter's rights recognized by law to parts of the mountaintop, gave him powers of attorney to claim the lands on their behalf. In the fall of 1805 Cockburn's son James and his cousin Jacob Trumpbour, Jr., were empowered by the commissioners of the land office to survey the people's tract and to place a value on it. The two men found the lots containing the Kaaterskill Falls and the site of the great Catskill Mountain House of the future to be worth no more than twelve and one half cents per acre.[2] In 1809 much of the land was tranferred (in return for payment to the state of two-thirds of the value placed on it by surveyors Cockburn and Trumpbour) to old William's clients. And it came as no surprise that some of the choicest pieces went to William himself by way of payment for his efforts. But even after this, part of the people's lands on the mountaintop were still theirs because no one put in a claim for them. The unwanted lands were exactly those which would have the greatest future value: the lots containing the Kaaterskill Falls and the site of the Mountain House. For a few years longer they remained unwanted, but their Cinderella days soon came to an end.

As the Schohariekill Road gave way to the Little Delaware Turnpike, pilgrims in search of the romantic and picturesque continued to arrive in ever greater numbers to be thrilled by the sight of the lakes, the graceful double waterfall, and the mountaintop views. People in Albany and New York, hearing of the wonders of the mountaintop, assembled in parties, traveled the Hudson by sloop to Catskill, and hired horses to haul or carry them up the mountain. In 1810 Captain Alden Partridge of West Point began bringing parties of his cadets to the vicinity of the lakes. The cadets camped out, probably in Bartram's Cave, which continued to serve the traveling public as it had done for so long. As part of their field work in engineering, they measured the altitude of various points on the turnpike, of the lakes and the summits of the neighboring mountains.[3] Botanists and mineralogists also came in greater numbers to inspect the high world of the Catskills.

By 1813 the lakes and their nearby wonders made their first appearance as tourist attractions in any gazetteer or guide book. Horatio Gates Spafford reported that the view to be had from the point at which the Little Delaware Turnpike "crosses the Catsbergs" (this was Spafford's improvement on the name "Catskills") . . . attracts the notice of numerous parties in summer. The view from the mountains is inexpressibly grand, and well merits the attention of those who delight to contemplate the stupendous scenery of nature."[4] Spafford was referring to the view from the clifftop on which the Catskill Mountain House would one day stand. From the point of view of the stockholders in the Little Delaware Turnpike, the use of their road by tourists and pilgrims was gratifying enough, but it could not bring in the cash which a year-round stream of wagons laden with timber, firewood, butter, and wheat would produce at their tollgates. It soon became clear that the turnpike could not compete effectively with others which tapped much the same territory over less difficult routes. It had been stimulated into existence by the period of rising prices and frenzied speculation which were a by-product of war in Europe. When Congress passed the Embargo Act of 1807, a business slump followed and gave the hopes of the Little Delaware Turnpike promoters a bad blow from which they never recovered. Their road was planned to extend sixty miles to the East Branch of the Delaware River. Only fifteen miles were sketchily completed.

But while the turnpike stockholders groaned, Merchant Lawrence had reason to cheer. "Parties of pleasure" on their way to and from the wonders of the mountaintop above lodged at his inn in increasing numbers. The more adventurous, having eaten and drunk at Lawrence's, spent the night in the cave on the mountain and refreshed themselves at Lawrence's again on their way home. The less daring found the turnpike provided adventure enough for any man. When President Timothy Dwight used it in September 1815 he wrote that "Wagons, and at times even chaises, though it must be confessed with many a hard struggle, climb this ascent. We gained it partly on horseback, partly on foot. . . ."[5] Some travelers, warned in advance of the half-ruinous state of the turnpike, tried a roundabout route which led them up Kaaterskill Clove. They found this road even worse—certainly its accommodations for travelers were much inferior to Lawrence's. They consisted of the dwelling of a settler deep within the clove—one observer described it as "part log house, part hog pen—it was a hotel."[6]

In spite of the neglected state of the roads leading up the mountain, of the inroads being made on the wilderness, and of the presence of rattlesnakes and bears who seemed to be particularly numerous wherever the scenery was the finest, pilgrims were finding the charms of the Catskills irresistible. As in the Britain of a generation or two earlier, a number of natural wonders had been singled out for the admiration of devotees of the romantic and picturesque. Niagara Falls remained first on the list, but the attractions of the Catskills and the Hudson River probably came next. Certainly because of their convenient location they were drawing the largest numbers of pilgrims. When Robert Fulton and the chancellor began operating their steamboat on the Hudson in 1809, the river and the Catskills became all the easier to admire. Most early steamboat travelers were bent on business, but a growing number braved the hazards of the new means of traveling in order to enjoy their country's natural beauties. In Catskill, owners of inns and of horses and carriages for hire, guides to the mountains, and purveyors of meals and drink profited from the eager romantics who stepped ashore at their wharf. It was only a question of time before some quick-witted Yankee would realize that it would pay a man to take hold of the natural wonders of the mountains which were attracting so many people, and have them securely recorded in his name in the land records of county and state.

The man to whom this revelation came was a lawyer-politician-speculator named Elisha Williams.

In our times Elisha Williams is almost completely forgotten, but in his own day he was regarded as a very great man. Just how great he was thought to be is hinted at in Oliver Wendell Holmes' *Poet at the Breakfast Table* published in 1872. There Holmes tells of asking a searching question of a friend whom he describes as "A scholar and a writer of note; a pleasant old gentleman with the fresh cheek of an octogenarian Cupid." The friend was one of the absentee landlords of the Hardenbergh Patent, Gulian Crommelin Verplanck, a great-grandson of the Gulian Verplanck who had been the partner of Robert Livingston in buying a controlling interest in the patent back in the 1740s. He and his relatives owned many acres along the proposed route of the Little Delaware Turnpike as well as on the east bank of the Hudson River. His reputation as poet, wit, and politician was once considerable. He edited a handsomely illustrated edition of Shakespeare, and he served as a member of Congress. The question that Holmes asked this venerable being was, "Who, on the whole, seemed to you the most considerable personage you ever met?"[7]

Holmes tells of waiting for an answer. Would Verplanck choose "One of the great Ex-Presidents, whose names were known to all the world? Would it be the silver-tongued orator of Kentucky, or the 'God-like' champion of the Constitution. . . ." (The orator and the champion, of course, were Henry Clay and Daniel Webster.) But Verplanck's choice was none of these. It was Elisha Williams.

Williams was a hero to propertied men of his time because he was so plainly on their side. He was charming, intelligent, and able; his manners were polished and his voice was seductive. He was born poor but used his natural endowments and skills to such good effect that he died worth a quarter of a million dollars. Early in life Williams earned a reputation as a defender of poor clients accused of murder, but he soon turned to the defense of rich men engaged in squabbles over the ownership of real estate or other property. As a member of the state legislature, he thundered against allowing men who did not own property to vote. Once such men were allowed to vote, he said, the excesses of the French Revolution would be re-enacted on American soil, for political democracy always resulted in the overthrow of the propertied class. He saw nothing wrong in accepting a fee for helping put through the legislature of which he was a member a bill benefiting a private bank. His devotion to the rights of property was unflinching. As he prospered, Williams picked up bits of real estate from time to time. For a man in his position, with rich friends and inside knowledge of what was going on behind the scenes, speculation in land provided a sure road to fortune. Williams' major effort took place on the site of the town of Waterloo in Seneca County, New York. There he and a partner bought the land rights of a Revolutionary War veteran. They built houses and shops, mills and barns, an imposing mansion for Williams, and a hotel so large and elegant that it quickly became the wonder of the countryside. Williams did not settle down in Waterloo until late in life, he lived and practiced law in the city of Hudson within sight of the Catskill Mountains.[8]

In 1809 Williams was initiated by a former law student of his into the rewards and penalties attending speculation in mountain land. The former student, Amos Eaton, had bought, with speculative intent, five thousand acres a little to the north of Lawrence's tavern. Eaton was a Catskill lawyer and an agent for owners of hundreds of thousands of acres within the Hardenbergh Patent and adjoining it, but he chose a bad time to speculate on his own and on borrowed money at that. The slump in land values following passage of the Embargo Acts of 1807 and 1808 caught him unprepared. He struggled hard to cling to his acres, and in 1809 he was indicted on a charge of forgery in connection with a mortgage on part of them. Elisha Williams sprang to Eaton's defense and he was acquitted. But Eaton's troubles were only beginning.

Amos Eaton was a divided man. With half of himself he hammered his way toward reaching the major goal of his time and place; riches and economic power over his fellow humans. With the other half he listened to men like Dr. Mitchill and followed their example. As Eaton surveyed among the Catskills or served eviction papers on squatters or tenants, he observed with a loving eye the distant views, the great trees, the modest plants covering the ground and the rocks which pushed through the scanty earth cover on every side. He studied botany and mineralogy and in 1811 organized a botanical school and botanical garden in the town of Catskill—the first such attempt in the state except for the Elgin Gardens of his friend Dr. Hosack of New York. But as the school welcomed its first students, another charge of forgery was brought against Eaton. This time Elisha Williams was unwilling to defend him; he became counsel instead for the principal complainant against Eaton, rich Nathaniel Pendleton, a lawyer-speculator who had once been considered for appointment as Secretary of

State by George Washington. Eaton, this time, was convicted and sent to the state prison in Greenwich Village to serve a life term. In prison Eaton put his old land-speculating, land-managing ways behind him forever. He studied botany and other natural sciences and emerged a few years later under a pardon and with a warm recommendation from his faithful friend, Dr. Mitchill, to become one of the greatest teachers of the natural sciences of his time and a revered founding father of the Rensselaer Polytechnic Institute at Troy, New York.[9]

In 1812, as Amos Eaton was immersed in his studies in the state prison, Elisha Williams was up to the ears in something very different. His years of service on both sides of the Eaton case had put him very much in touch with the opportunities lying in wait among the Catskills for a man with capital and good connections. Williams could not have been unaware that the state-owned lands above Lawrence's tavern which contained the chief natural wonders of the Catskills were drawing increasing numbers of visitors who were building up a markert value for these wonders. He quietly went about getting these lands in his possession by acquiring the squatters' rights of two men—one of them was probably a dummy used because he could help put the grant through with a minimum of publicity. In April 1813 the commissioners of the land office granted to Williams the lots including the Kaaterskill Falls and the site of the mountain house-to-be.[10]

A shrewd speculator in land realizes that there is a time to act and a time to sit tight and wait while the efforts of others raise the value of his holdings. As each summer brought a growing number of pilgrims to Elisha Williams' natural wonders, Williams sat tight. In 1819 he was rewarded for his patience by an extraordinary stroke of luck. Rip Van Winkle was presented to the world and at once all the romantic feeling that had been hovering over the Catskills for a quarter of a century took on an almost tangible shape and centered on Elisha Williams' flyer in real estate.

44

Rip Van Winkle

❦ ANYONE who would like to see for himself how Washington Irving's "Rip Van Winkle" has changed the Catskills would do well to begin by reading the tale in which Rip was introduced to the world. This will present no difficulties, for the tale can be found almost everywhere. Since its first publication in New York in 1819, it has appeared in hundreds of editions and has been translated into French, Polish, German, Catalan, Yiddish, and more than a dozen other languages and dialects. It is available in elaborate illustrated editions printed on handmade paper, and can be found in editions so cheap that the paper visibly yellows and crumbles as the story is read. For the young there are editions rewritten in simplified language; for those who won't read anything else the story is available in shorthand, not only in the Gregg and Pitman varieties but also in Dewey's demotic.[1] Non-readers may absorb it via a phonograph record made by Lionel Barrymore, or in the musical terms into which it has been transferred in Ferde Grofe's *Hudson River Suite*. The learned will be glad to know that the little story has been analyzed and footnoted in scholarly journals. Numerous acting versions may be found in the libraries by drama lovers. The Library of Congress has a copy of the first film version, a few scenes acted for Thomas Edison's Vitascope, which was an infant form of the motion picture.

It is not surprising after all this that there are few inhabitants of the lands to which Western culture has been carried by infiltration, the wiles of traders, or the sword who have not heard how Rip Van Winkle went hunting with dog and gun among the Catskills after having been driven from home by his scolding wife; how Rip met some strange old-fashioned bowlers who may have been the spirits of Henry Hudson and his crewmen; how he drank from their flagons and then fell asleep to awaken twenty years later in a world which had forgotten him. All this has been part and parcel of European and American consciousness for almost a century and a half. But nowhere, as might be expected, has awareness of Rip been carried to such a feverish pitch as among the Catskills themselves.

The traveler eager to check this phenomenon might make a beginning by boarding one of the buses of Rip Van Winkle Tours, Inc., which run from New York City to the Sullivan County part of the Catskills region. Or he might drive along the east bank of the Hudson River and cross to the west bank over the Rip Van Winkle Bridge, having first had his medical and psychiatric needs taken care of at the nearby Rip Van Winkle Clinic. Once across the bridge the traveler will admire the words RIP VAN WINKLE spelled out in clipped privet bushes on a grassy bank, and he can then have his car's tank filled at the Rip Van Winkle Service Station. If he is hungry he may head for the Rip Van Winkle Restaurant and Motel. He will then be primed to take the Rip Van Winkle Trail into what has long been known as The Land of Rip Van Winkle. He will pass through the hamlet of Palenville where a sign reading PALENVILLE THE HOME OF RIP VAN WINKLE was erected some years back for the instruction of strangers. At Tannersville the traveler will see Lake Rip Van Winkle sparkling on his left, while Rip's Inn looms on his right. The Rip Van Winkle Bazaar (founded 1884) will attract his attention, and if he enters and inspects the wares for sale, he will discover that American industry has met its responsibilities by grinding out vast numbers of what are known in the trade as "Rip Van Winkles." These include Rip Van Winkle plates, Rip Van Winkle ashtrays, Rip Van Winkle vases, Rip Van Winkle statuettes, Rip Van Winkle postcards, Rip Van Winkle writing paper, and a host of other objects of glass, plastic, paper and wood.

A brief walk in the neighborhood of the Bazaar will turn up further signs of Rip's presence. Rip in his familiar aspect of a bearded old man leaning on a staff will be seen standing guard on a local lawn with the assistance of a pair of gnomelike retainers. In a miniature form, Rip will peer at the traveler from beneath a begonia leaf in the plant-filled window of an old cottage. As the traveler takes to his car again, the Rip Van Winkle Gas Station will come into view; so too will a sign informing him that the camp of the Rip Van Winkle Council of the Boy Scouts of America is located on a road branching to the right. The traveler will soon learn that no matter what part of the Catskills he visits, he will find that Rip Van Winkle has been there ahead of him. He may stumble upon a meeting of the Rip Van Winkle Stamp and Coin Club, or of the Rip Van Winkle Ski Council, or of the Rip Van Winkle Post of the Veterans of Foreign Wars. A roadside eating place will urge him to "TRY OUR RIP VAN WINKLE SPECIAL."

If he spends the night among the mountains he may very well sleep on a mattress made by the Van Winkle Bedding Company whose motto is EVEN RIP WOULD SLEEP BETTER ON A VAN WINKLE MATTRESS.

If the traveler following Rip's trail through the Catskills happens to be of antiquarian tastes and delves into the past of the region, he will find much of interest. Once upon a time, he will discover, Rip Van Winkle hotels abounded. They have since vanished and so too have a number of other curious nineteenth-century phenomena. One was the Kaaterskill Therapeutic Chair[2] made within the Kaaterskill Clove and often confused by the unwary with the genuine Rip Van Winkle Reclining Rocker which was a product of the town of Catskill. It was the claim of the makers of both that their chairs would do much to aid and comfort the afflicted or the merely tired. Something of the relaxing quality of the contents of the flagon from which Rip Van Winkle drank appeared to be inherent in both. According to its maker, the Reclining Rocker was "the most wonderful chair in the world."[3] It was capable of two hundred changes of position; by pulling here and pushing there, fifteen different pieces of furniture could be made from it. Those who enjoyed puzzling their friends would be sure to like it, for so ingeniously was it constructed that a viewer could not discover how the muscle power of the chair's occupant was applied in order to keep it moving. The secret of perpetual motion appeared to have been discovered among the Catskills. A Reclining Rocker was presented by its maker to Queen Victoria and another went to President Benjamin Harrison.[4] The rockers also became favorite gifts to those retiring from active life. The recipients could spend their remaining years happily changing from one to another of the rocker's two hundred possibilities while at the same time reading the pamphlet version of the "Tale of Rip Van Winkle" which came with the rocker at no extra cost. So old people might glide easily and smoothly from this world to the next; when sitting up became too great a task, they could lie down and continue to rock in that position as well as when in their sitting-up prime, or so the manufacturer assured the public. The optimistic manufacturer also let the public know that before long it would be possible for a man traveling by train to rock his way clear across the United States on a Rip Van Winkle Reclining Rocker. This hope unfortunately was never to be realized.[5] During the first decade of our own century, Rip lent his name to another product of a furniture factory when Dan Sully, well-known actor and producer of Woodstock, used the water power of the Sawkill to turn out a curious pair of products. One was what Sully called a "wireless telephone,"[6] the other was the "Rip Van Winkle Clock" which ticked away in an openwork case of a simple and attractive design inspired by the mission furniture so popular at the time.

Strangers following the spoor of Rip Van Winkle in the Catskills are often told by old-timers that "You should of come ten years ago when Rip's Retreat was goin', then you would of seen something, you could of shook the hand of Rip himself."

The Retreat was located on the windy pine-covered plateau to the east of North Lake. It aspired to become a kind of Disneyland-in-the-Catskills and at the same time a shrine honoring Rip Van Winkle. The Retreat offered food and drink, rides on an imitation railroad, a film version of the Tale of Rip Van Winkle, ladies in costume working at old-time crafts in houses which from a distance appeared to suggest the ones familiar to Rip during his early years. But best of all was the Retreat's presentation of Rip himself. Not of course, the Rip whom Irving had created, but an actor taking the part with skill and good humor enough to fool the young. Photographs of this living Rip may still be bought in the neighborhood of the Retreat. They show a keen-eyed bearded and benevolent man in an eighteenth-century costume, seated on a log and holding a musket in his hands. The Retreat was not the commercial success its promoters had hoped and it was eventually torn down by the New York Conservation Department which had never approved of its presence beside the lake.[7]

While Rip's Retreat, like many another shrine to a local guardian spirit has vanished, the true Rip has become established more firmly than ever in a wider consciousness. During the past half century, Rip has made many guest appearances in literature. He figured in the Dublin brothel scene of James Joyce's *Ulysses* when the cry of "Rip Van Winkle! Rip Van Winkle!" rang through the place and Rip appeared to Leopold Bloom "in tattered moccasins with a rusty fowling piece, tiptoeing, finger-tipping, his haggard, boney, bearded face peering through the diamond panes. . . ."[8] The American poet Hart Crane used Rip as one of the symbols with which he tried to build up "an image of man's anonymous creative power unifying past and present,"[9] as one critic put it. Side by side with his contributions to modern literature, Rip served the advertising profession as well. "Rip van Winkle had an aching back"—so one ad told newspaper readers during the 1960s. A few of the right sort of pills would take care of it, the readers were informed.

As the twentieth century passed its halfway mark, political speech writers showed full awareness of the possibilities of old Rip. In the presidential election campaign of 1964, both an editorial writer for England's *Manchester Guardian* and former President Harry Truman compared candidate Barry Goldwater to Rip Van Winkle, to enforce their opinion that Goldwater was dozing. In 1966 Governor Nelson Rockefeller of New York was charged with being "A Rip Van Winkle who wakes up only in election years."[10] The previous year those just too young to be allowed to vote used Rip in their own way—they were dancing to a brand new rock and roll tune called "Rip Van Winkle."

On November 5, 1961 Arthur Clarke writing for the New York *Times Magazine* suggested a new and startling future for Rip. The old codger, Clarke wrote, may be "the prototype of future astronauts." The distance to planets in other solar systems is so great, Clarke believed, that those traveling to them might have to be put to sleep for twenty years or even longer as they moved through space. To an active commercial mind of the sort which has permeated business enterprise among the Catskills with Rip Van Winkle, Clarke's thought suggests enticing vistas of profit.

Will the space platforms at which tourists of the future change from expresses to locals have stands at which Rip Van Winkle ashtrays will be sold? Will Rip's Retreat be reborn on an artificial asteroid complete with canned music and weaving and spinning ladies in appropriate costumes? And will space vehicles contain plastic images of Rip in his new aspect of guardian spirit not only of the Catskill Mountains but also of the mountains and valleys of endless space? If what has happened in the Catskills may serve as a guide, these things may well come to pass. Indeed, there is a hint that already Rip is making his first cautious entrance into the wonders of space.

In August 1965 a radio broadcast between one of the Gemini astronauts and the control center on earth entered millions of pairs of American ears. The astronaut was asked if he'd slept well. His answer came through spiced with static, yet understandable enough. He'd slept very well; in fact, in his opinion, his spacecraft would be just the place for Rip Van Winkle.

NOTE: Enterprises named for Rip Van Winkle come and go and some of those named in this chapter have now vanished. The most ambitious of all tributes to Rip faded away about 1970. It was the Rip Van Winkle Amphitheater, spectacularly placed on a mountainside for the purpose of housing an annual production of a musical version of Rip's story.

45

Washington Irving

🌲 RIP VAN WINKLE has been part of the Catskills for so long that he seems as native to the region as its singing streams, its layered gray rocks, its spruce and balsam-crowned summits. Yet for all that, Rip remains a man of mystery. His battered hat, his aged face and bony hands are as familiar to dwellers among the Catskills as their own front doors. What is mysterious about Rip is where he came from and how he found his way to the Catskills and became so essential an ingredient of the region's appeal.

Of one date in Rip's life there can be no doubt at all, for he first greeted the world in 1819 from the pages of *The Sketch Book of Geoffrey Crayon, Gent.* In this book Washington Irving presented Rip's tale as the work of pedantic old Diedrich Knickerbocker upon whom he had already fathered his Knickerbocker's *History of New York*. No one was taken in by Knickerbocker or by Geoffrey Crayon—both were obvious inventions—but many Americans, and especially those living in or near the Catskills, became convinced that Rip was a historical character and a true native of the Catskills. Whenever Irving was asked where Rip came from, he put the questioner off with a bit of the whimsy he handled so well. Throughout his life, whenever Rip was mentioned, he played a game of peekaboo with his public. But he occasionally dropped a sly little clue and the clues, when put together, lead to a partial solution of the mystery of Rip.

Even as a boy, Irving showed the qualities that would make him so persuasive a sponsor of Rip. The chilly virtues of his Presbyterian-deacon, hardware-dealing father gave him no easy model to follow. His affectionate mother and two much older brothers, who shared the interest in the arts then beginning to penetrate the solid commercial commitment of New York, gave direction to his young life. Washington Irving explored old books of travels, the works of Sterne and Addison, gothic novels, and every other kind of reading that allowed his imagination to escape from the rigidities of his father's world. He delighted in meeting odd people and he liked to roam among crumbling old houses, old trees, and fields and meadows mellowed by the labor of many generations.[1]

Irving was being formed at a time when few American writers and no painters had yet discovered America. In their contentment with following respectable British models, the personality of their own land remained invisible to them. Many Americans agreed with President John Adams that their nation was not ready for a flowering of the arts—there were too many important things to come first. Others, among them Thomas Jefferson, sensed the role of the artist as image maker for his people and tried hard to arouse a recognition of the great part which the arts might play in giving shape to American life. Irving's older brothers, William and Peter, had a foot in each camp. William, after a spell as a trader with the Indians, entered the family hardware business; Peter studied medicine. And both took to scribbling whenever the chance offered. In company with Washington and a few literary friends they wrote and published a little periodical called *Salmagundi,* in which they satirized, in eighteenth-century British fashion, the manners of their day. From this slender springboard, Washington Irving launched himself in 1809 into writing his Knickerbocker's *History of New York,* in which humor reminiscent of Laurence Sterne mingles with tall tales of the true American stamp. There had been nothing like it in America, although it may have owed something to the Reverend Samuel Peter's droll and waspish *History of Connecticut by a Gentleman of the Province* published in 1781. Knickerbocker's *History* took New York by storm and made Irving an American celebrity.

The book was the first American one to be read with widespread relish and approval in Europe. Walter Scott, who was then charming the English-speaking world with his romantic narrative verses, laughed at Knickerbocker's humorous passages until his sides ached.

In his Knickerbocker's *History,* Irving first gave expression in a crude way to obsessions that would later appear in a refined form in Rip Winkle and other tales of his *Sketch Book.* There were the sleepy Dutchman, the supernatural happenings, and the landscape enveloped in a seductive haze created by the lingering on of old ways and old hopes. There, too, were the sharp Yankee invaders who stirred the Dutch of New York from their somnolence. When Irving followed his book to Walter Scott's mock medieval mansion at Abbotsford in Scotland, his host opened up to him a whole new world of inspiration drawn from the writings of the German romantics who enthralled Scott and to whom Irving's Knickerbocker was already linked by unseen ties. Encouraged by Scott, Irving plunged into the study of German and German romantic literature and folklore. In the spring of 1818 he copied into a notebook a passage from Riesbach's *Travels Through Germany* which concerned a mountain near Salzburg in Bavaria within whose rocks the Emperor Charles the Great and his army were said to be condemned to be confined until doomsday. On a certain day of the year, "the spirit of the Emperor emerged at midnight from a cleft of the mountain from whence you hear a dull rumbling like distant thunder . . . from the cleft the stream precipitates itself with a loud noise and falls in a variety of cascades down the deep and narrow gully. . . ."[2] The sleeping spirits of Henry Hudson and his crew, the hollow rumbling of their bowling balls, the clove within the Catskills where Rip met the spirits— were all hinted at in Irving's notes from Riesbach.

At about the same time, a well-known German folktale found its way into Irving's mind. The tale told of a goatherd named Peter Klaus who followed his flock into a mountain cave and there acted as pin boy for a group of bowling strangers. Peter drank from the players' wine jug and fell asleep not to awaken until twenty years later.[3] He then made his way to his own village where he found himself forgotten until he came upon his daughter whom he persuaded to recognize him. As Irving absorbed tales like these, Rip Van Winkle moved closer and closer to taking form and emerging from the labyrinth of his mind. A crisis in the Irving family affairs set the stage for the shock needed to bring Rip to life.

Irving's brothers, William and Peter, had founded a hardware importing and exporting business in Liverpool. Through the kindness of his brothers, Washington was taken in as a silent partner with no particular duties. In the period of business depression after many years of war, the Irving firm ended in the dismal rites of bankruptcy. With his means of support gone, Washington Irving resolved to try to maintain himself by writing. But he found sustained writing difficult. Tortured by months of unproductive tension, he sought refuge with his sister and her husband, Henry Van Wart of Birmingham, whose cheerful house was alive with affection and gay with the voices of little nephews and nieces. Irving had taken up playing the flute; he made music for the Van Wart children, told them stories, and romped with them, but it was all in vain. The form of his *Sketch Book* had already come to him and he had written several sketches for it. But he was unable to go on. Then, on a lovely June evening, the months of sterility and struggle came to a dramatic end.

Henry Van Wart told in later years of how he had done all in his power to lure his brother-in-law from the desert in which he seemed to wander. Until that June evening no effort of Van Wart's had helped. Then,

as the two men went walking, Van Wart tried to cheer Irving by recalling the days when the two had played together as boys in the part of the
valley of the Pocantico River near Tarrytown, New York, known to them
as Sleepy Hollow. Sleepy Hollow was "the abode of the queerest characters
that were ever gathered together within the same space. Such quaint
Dutchmen, in speech, dress and habits, could not be found elsewhere in the
whole country."[4] As the two men talked of Sleepy Hollow, they smiled
and then laughed outright. Old memories crowded into their minds and
found release in eager words. Back in the Van Wart house, Irving "retired
to his room while it was yet dusk. He put pen to paper, and thoughts came
with a rush, faster than he could write them—all the faster, seemingly, for
being fettered so long by the ice of his mental despondency. . . ." Thus
Van Wart later described the events of that never-to-be-forgotten evening
when an intense burst of creative energy took hold of Irving and transformed bits and pieces shelved in his mind into Rip Van Winkle. As Irving
wrote that night, the Harz Mountains became the Catskills, the gorge from
which Charles the Great emerged by night was transformed into something
remarkably like the one beneath the Kaaterskill Falls as described by Dr.
Mitchill; Sleepy Hollow traveled upriver to nestle for a moment at the base
of the Catskills. The tensions between Yankees and Dutchmen of which
Irving had already treated in Knickerbocker now brought into being
Doolittle's Hotel in front of which the wondering Rip realized that he had
spent twenty years sleeping among the mountains. The old fellow, compounded of Peter Klaus, the quaint old Dutchmen of the Pocantico, and of
who knows how many observations of other living or fictional characters,
sprang into life and assumed his own personality and took his own place in
the world. The next morning it was a radiant Washington Irving who read
aloud at the Van Wart breakfast table the first version of the tale of Rip
Van Winkle. "It had all come back to him," he explained. "Sleepy Hollow
had awakened him from his long, dull, desponding slumber. . . ."

When Rip Van Winkle appeared in print in New York in 1819, Irving
took the trouble of adding a little note in which he explained, in the gently
humorous fashion that so well became him, that the tale was based on "a
little German superstition about the Emperor Frederick *der Rothbart,* and
the Khypphauser Mountain,"[5] which was the scene of Peter Klaus' long
sleep. Yet this open avowal of indebtedness was not enough to head off
charges of plagiarism. When Irving followed the smashing success of his
Sketch Book with the less successful *Bracebridge Hall* of 1822, he defended
himself somewhat sharply in the new book against the charges of picking
other men's literary pockets. "I find that the tale of Rip Van Winkle . . .

has been discovered by divers writers in magazines, to have been founded on a little German tradition, and the matter has been revealed to the world as if it were a foul instance of plagiarism marvellously brought to light. In a note which follows that tale, I had alluded to the superstition on which it is founded, and I thought a mere allusion was sufficient, as the tradition was so notorious as to be inserted in almost every collection of German legends. I had seen it myself in three . . . in fact I had considered popular tradition of the kind as fair foundations for authors of fiction to build upon. . . ."[6]

Irving was no more a plagiarist than Chaucer or Shakespeare, both of whom had dipped into the common stock of materials inherited from preceding generations and transformed what they chose into new creations. In the one moment of undoubted genius ever to be granted to him, Irving had done the same. Rip, whatever his antecedents, had never breathed until Irving gave him life that June night in Birmingham. Rip's story was old, but Rip himself was new.

Once he had made his statements of indebtedness to others, Irving ignored the charges of plagiarism which continued to be made from time to time. What he found a little harder to ignore was the American conviction that his Rip was a countryman of theirs whose story Irving had picked up during wanderings in the Hudson Valley and among the Catskills. The fact was that Irving had never set foot on any part of the Catskills when he wrote Rip's story. He had first seen the mountains as a boy in his teens when he traveled up the Hudson. Then, as he recalled late in life, an Indian trader (the trader was probably his literary brother William) had told him Indian legends of the Catskills, whether based on lore gathered among the Iroquois of the Mohawk Valley with whom William dealt or on his not inconsiderable imagination is hard to determine. In 1809 Washington Irving was once again exposed to the power of the Catskills. That was when, shaken by the death of his fiancée Matilda Hoffman, he retreated to the Kinderhook home of his friend Judge Van Ness and there completed his Knickerbocker's *History* with the distant Catskills running along the horizon like the waves of a sea in the sky. When he spent his week among the Livingstons of Clermont in 1812 he came closest of any time to the Catskills, especially to Overlook Mountain. He was then surrounded by the German-descended tenants of the Livingstons who may, for all anyone now knows, have had old German traditions of sleepers among the mountains still current among them.

Washington Irving inherited something of the shrewdness of his father the deacon. He soon realized that the belief that his Rip was a true American folk hero did him no harm. That was why he liked to surround Rip's origins—after his first frank explanation had been ignored—with the kind of whimsical mystery his readers had come to expect from him. He linked Rip even closer to the Catskills by writing about the mountains as "the fairy region of the Hudson"[7] filled with ancient legends and romance, and he told of listening to the Indian trader of his boyhood relating "marvellous legends" of the Catskills as the two lay on the deck of the sloop. Then as he watched the Catskills, "their ever-changing shapes and hues . . . appeared to realize the magical influences" of which the trader spoke. The Catskills at times "seemed to approach; at other times to recede; during the heat of the day they melted into a sultry haze; as the day declined they deepened in tone; their summits were brightened by the last rays of the sun, and later in the evening their whole outline was printed in deep purple against an amber sky. As I beheld them thus shifting continually before my eye, and listened to the marvellous legends of the trader, a host of fanciful notions concerning them was conjured into my brain, which have haunted it ever since."

A reader of passages like this might conclude that Irving was gracefully suggesting that the Catskills were indeed the haunt of Rip Van Winkle, for he had begun the tale of Rip with a similar tribute to the magical beauty of the mountains. But another reader might ruminate over the phrase "fanciful notions" and wonder if Irving meant that Rip was no more than one of Irving's especially fanciful thoughts. No one could be sure. The more Irving spoke and wrote on the subject, the more mystifying the whole thing became. But this did not prevent the Rip cult from taking root among the rocky ledges of the Catskills. Not long after the first publication of the tale, a reputed descendant of Rip was pushing drinks across a bar set up in "Rip's cottage" halfway up the side of North Mountain and skeptics were saying that the right of being Rip's descendants "was let with the establishment."[8] Soon the many settlements strung out along the base of the mountains were clamoring for the honor of having been Rip's home town. Old Catskill and new Catskill, Kingston and Stone Ridge in Ulster County were all in the running, especially after stage versions of Rip's tale began amusing Americans and Europeans.[9]

As Washington Irving became older and feebler, he looked on with amusement while Rip seemed to take an ever firmer grip on life and reality. The Catskill Mountains of Irving's lifetime had been the scene of arduous and often rewarding pioneering; there landlords and tenants had come into conflict as Old World notions met New World aims and ambitions; the Devil and his friends the witches had made merry in isolated hollows and on steep mountainsides; Gross Hardenbergh had been murdered; the Hardenbergh Patent had lumbered along and aroused the greed of new generations of speculators. But of all this Irving remained unaware. His Rip had become the unquestioned guardian spirit of the mountains.

Near the end of his life, Irving said his last word on the subject of Rip Van Winkle. Irving was then loaded with honors and beloved by thousands of men, women, and children throughout the world. He had well served his country as ambassador to Spain. He had written a long shelf of books—biographies, histories, and tales. His home of Sunnyside on the Hudson was a shrine to which reverent pilgrims came in an unceasing flow. But as his Rip grew in strength and power Irving lived in pain and bravely struggled to present his familiar genial face to the world. The strength of Rip Van Winkle was founded on the universal appeal of the seductive way in which he gave form to man's rueful contemplation of time, which is at once man's kindest friend and most merciless enemy. Time had once been kind to Irving; now it was destroying him. Yet even time could not dim the magic of Irving's whimsy, when the name of Rip Van Winkle was mentioned.

A boy who lived in the new Catskill wrote to Irving early in 1858 to report that he was puzzled as to whether Rip had lived in Catskill or in Kingston. The boy had been engaged in an argument on this subject with "a very old gentleman,"[10] and he appealed to Irving as the final authority on Rip Van Winkle. Irving's reply was a little masterpiece of humorous understatement.

"I can give you no other information concerning the localities of the story of Rip Van Winkle, than is to be gathered from the manuscript of Mr. Knickerbocker, published in the *Sketch Book*. Perhaps he left them purposely in doubt. I would advise you to defer to the opinion of the 'very old gentleman' with whom you say you had an argument on the subject. I think it probable he is as accurately informed as any one on the matter.

Respectfully, your obedient servant
Washington Irving."[11]

As Irving wrote these words he was well aware that Rip Van Winkle had long before passed out of his control. He had been taken over by the American people and forced, willy-nilly, to play the part of the kind of hero romantic Americans wanted.

Easy-going, shiftless Rip stood at the very opposite end of the scale from the acquisitive, aggressive, sharp-witted kind of American who was rising to the surface of the society of his time. Rip was without worldly ambition and did not try to struggle against the current of time as it hurried him along from birth to death. He lived in close contact with the earth, the sky, and the wind. He was on friendly terms not with the rich or powerful but with dogs and children and with the forested slopes and hollows of the Catskills. It was to these mountain sanctuaries that Rip fled with dog and gun whenever he was rebuffed by the hustling, materialistic society which so puzzled him but in which he was condemned to pass his life.

In the thousands of paintings and drawings of Rip produced during the nineteenth century, he is often shown seated high among the Catskills in the shade of a tree.[12] The trunk supports his back, the wind sings lullabies in the leaves above, and the old fellow falls into a pleasant doze and leaves the cares of the world behind.

But as Rip was being born, a lesser folk hero was taking form among the Catskills. To him a tree was no kindly natural parasol. If it was a hemlock tree, it was an enemy to be slain and despoiled without regard to the consequences to bystanders or future generations. This hero is known to this day in the town of Hunter in which he slew thousands of hemlock trees as "the man with the two story head."[13] He was Colonel William Edwards. His deeds are commemorated by the imposing mountain still known as the Colonel's Chair.

The Man with the Two-Story Head

🌲 THE PEOPLE of the Catskills have a normal amount of local pride. Yet there is one event in the past of their region of which they speak with mingled pride and shame. This is the struggle between men and hemlock trees which was begun in earnest by Colonel Edwards about 1816 and did not end until the hemlocks were completely routed during the 1870s. This struggle spread from the Catskills and followed the Appalachian Mountains into Pennsylvania, flowed westward over the Allegheny plateau, eventually reached Michigan, and went on to Wisconsin. It did not end until it reached the Pacific, where the eastern hemlock was unknown but where its western brother took its place and crashed down in defeat. It all began— after a series of preliminary skirmishes in New England—on the banks of the Catskills' Schohariekill in the town of Hunter. Yet the people of the Catskills take only a modest pride in this fact. They often speak of it in sober tones and with a shake of the head. One old fellow in Shandaken told me that the death and despoiling of the hemlocks had been a terrible thing, mostly because it was so wasteful. It was like shooting a beautiful bird for the sake of a single little feather in its tail and throwing the rest of the bird away. "People know better nowadays," said the old man. "Or do they?" he asked anxiously.[1]

Many writers about the struggle liken it to a war between pygmies and giants. Few men exceed six feet in height, and when their diameter reaches fifteen inches, they are dismayed. A hemlock tree, on the other hand, may soar one hundred and twenty-five feet into the air. As late as February 1867, newspapers announced that Lucius Pond of Jewett had cut down a "Leviathan of the Forest."[2] It was a hemlock four feet and nine inches in diameter. There are traditions of hemlocks six feet and more in diameter standing in the hemlock groves of the Catskills before 1816. By 1870, as A. W. Hoffman put it, "the prostrate trunks and branches of the hemlocks glistened white in the autumn sunlight, like the bleaching bones of some army of giants fallen in mighty combat upon the hillsides. And indeed the huge hemlocks had fallen in battle—the battle being carried on by Man, the ruthless destroyer of Nature, in his reckless and, as in this case, short-sighted scramble for wealth."[3] Hoffman, a Kingston newspaper editor, was writing long after profits from the slaughter of the hemlocks had ceased to flow into his town, and hence the vigor of his expression. He went on to explain that men had not cut hemlocks in order to clear land for farming, or to use their wood, for the market was oversupplied at the time with hemlock boards and timbers. All that was wanted was the bark that covered the lower part of the trunk. The rest, like the old man's bird with a single salable feather in its tail, was usually thrown away. The bark was valued for one reason: it was rich in tannin, a substance that could be used to convert hides into enduring and useful leather.

It would have been hard to find a man better suited to lead the attack on the hemlock giants of the Catskills than Colonel William Edwards. Descended from a long line of New England and New Jersey tanners, he was a grandson of the Reverend Jonathan Edwards who had been one of the greatest intellectual leaders of colonial days.[4] But what impressed most beholders was not Edward's ancestry, it was his resemblance to a giant in some old fairy tale. For he was six feet four inches tall and his frame was crowned by a head large enough to have seemed proportionate on the shoulders of a man twice his height. Children cried in fear when they first saw the colonel's head; grown people stared in disbelief and then stared again in complete disregard of good manners. One contemporary, Nathaniel Booth of Kingston, estimated that a half-bushel basket would have been too small to serve as a hat for the colonel. Those friendly toward the colonel said that his immense head was the result of an accidental bump received when at play in his boyhood. Those who didn't like the colonel said that he had played a once-popular game and had his big head to show for it. In the game, called "butting,"[5] two boys ran toward each other with lowered heads. The boy who emerged with the least damage was counted winner of the game, and young Edwards was a loser.

However the colonel came by his great head, there could be no doubt that within it an ingenious and efficient mind was at work. In April 1816, Colonel Edwards first came to the Catskills. At once he realized that here was a land of opportunity for a clever tanner. It was true enough that other tanners were already in business. There were at least twenty-five in Greene County and some forty in Delaware, with eleven more in Sullivan.[6] But all of them were doing business in a small way and using the traditional handicraft methods. These produced fine leather, but only after a year or more of much hard and disagreeable labor and the tying up of a disproportionate amount of capital. In New England, Edwards had lived in the midst of a revolution in manufacturing. Water and steam power were taking the place of human muscles in many industrial operations, and weaving, spinning, metalworking, and many other processes were yielding high profits to owners and managers, thanks to the use of new labor-saving methods and a higher degree of organization.

Edwards' quick mind grasped the ease with which the Catskills might become the scene of a new and far more profitable way of making leather. He could harness the strength of the mountain streams, take full advantage of the closeness of the cheap transportation supplied by the Hudson River, and use the recently discovered ways of cutting costs and speeding tanning time. But most important of all, he would hitch to the business of tanning the magic power of the large amounts of capital available to limited-liability stock companies. In 1811 the New York legislature had passed a law permitting the formation of such companies to engage in manufacture. But tanning had been excluded from the benefits of the act.[7] The small tanners of the state feared competition from large, heavily capitalized rivals and had exerted pressure to head off such a threat. Here was what looked like an unclimbable barrier to the kind of tannery the colonel wanted, but he was just the man to climb it.

William Edwards was skilled in every aspect of the tanner's trade. In addition, he had paid a fearful price for a thorough education in the ins and outs of corporation financing. As a boy of fourteen he had served his apprenticeship in the New Jersey tannery of his uncle Ogden, whose old-fashioned tannery was among the largest in all the United States. Later young Edwards tanned in Massachusetts. There he managed the Hampshire Leather Manufacturing Company capitalized at $100,000—this was the first incorporated tannery in the country.[8] Its owners were the rich leather merchants of Boston who were following an already old European precedent in financing establishments in which their product was made. In a similar fashion, Englishmen like Peter Collinson had put their profits to work in Lancashire textile mills.

Edwards was well aware of the many improvements in tanning which had been put into practice in Europe during the last quarter of the eighteenth century. He adopted many of these, sometimes added slight changes of his own, and held the American patent on one important European improvement.[9]

When the War of 1812 began, Colonel Edwards did his best to take advantage of the enormously increased demand for leather which war always brought in the days when horse harnesses and the military equipment of men made great use of leather. The Boston directors and stockholders of Edwards' company were fiercely opposed to the war with England, for it cut off profitable trade with Europe, but they were not averse to profiting from their own country's involvement in war. What they feared was a sudden ending to the war which might leave them with a large stock of expensive untanned hides and unsalable leather on their hands. As they sensed the approach of peace, they tried to restrain Colonel Edwards in his efforts at greater and greater expansion. They withheld the large sums of money due Edwards as his share of the profits, and they refused to supply him with raw hides. But all this could not hold back the colonel. He believed that he was on the brink of control of the leather markets of Boston and New York. He borrowed money from friends, from former partners, and from his large circle of relatives—the friends and relatives were put to good use in endorsing notes. The directors continued their grim squeeze on their superintendent until, still fighting and borrowing, he went down as the war ended. A tannery Edwards himself owned, as well as all the rest of his property, was seized and sold for the benefit of the stockholders of the Hampshire Leather Manufacturing Corporation. From standing on the verge of great wealth, he became penniless. And what was worse, he was saddled with an immense debt to friends and relatives whose dreams of wealth through association with the colonel now turned to bitter nightmares. With his friends and relatives sunk in despair, the colonel left Massachusetts and took refuge in New York.

Edwards had good friends in New York. With their encouragement his hopes began to revive, and his inventive mind began to awaken. He had observed that the traditional way of laying hides to soak in vats containing water and tanbark was wasteful in labor, for the hides had to be continually shifted in order to tan them evenly. Edwards proposed suspending the hides in a solution of tanbark instead. New York leather dealers offered to finance the experiment. It was to find a place to tan by suspension that Edwards first visited the Catskills.

When the New York legislature met in 1817, it had before it a bill sponsored by the colonel's cousin, Senator Ogden Edwards. The bill extended the provisions of the corporation act of 1811 to include tanners of morocco and other leather. Morocco leather is made from goatskins with tannin derived from sumac. Edwards had no intention of going into the morocco leather business—the phrase was used in the hope that it might quiet the fears of the state's small tanners. The bill was backed by a formidable list of men headed by Gideon Lee, whose business acumen when he was a young Massachusetts shoemaker had led Colonel Edwards to send him to New York to serve as his agent in selling leather and obtaining hides. Courteous, prepossessing Gideon Lee had quickly become a big man in the Swamp, the part of New York in which tanners and leather dealers had congregated ever since the beginnings of the city. The leather men of the Swamp were taking the lead in American tanning and currying (the finishing of leather after it is tanned). The Swamp men were powerful in state politics, yet their bill was not acted upon in Albany. Colonel Edwards' son, William W., known in later years as "the young colonel," was dispatched to Albany by the first steamer to sail up the Hudson that spring. Because of ice the steamer could get no farther than Athens, some thirty miles below Albany. Young Edwards drove up the valley toward Albany in an open wagon and arrived there at midnight, for every moment counted— the legislature was to adjourn in two weeks. Edwards lobbied diligently. A petition from the Yankee businessmen of Catskill helped his cause. He gained the support of Senator Martin Van Buren, but Senator Lucas Elmendorf of Ulster, who had represented Gross Hardenbergh, was opposed.[10] Elmendorf was aware that tanneries were far from popular as neighbors. The stink of decaying animal tissues radiated far around them; they polluted streams, lowered land values, destroyed forests, and left in their place a fantastic litter of trunks and branches which eventually resulted in fires that too often spread to the surrounding countryside. The stench of the tannery clung to their workers and made fastidious folks avoid them. The tannery mills in which bark was ground before being steeped sent up clouds of dust which made eyes smart and passersby cough and sneeze. The vats in which bark was steeped and hides soaked attracted small children who sometimes tumbled in and were drowned. In the city of New York, tanners were restricted to the Swamp; other towns and cities saw to it that tanners did business in prescribed districts where they would cause the least annoyance. Lucas Elmendorf would not agree to a measure that might result in an increase in the size and stench of tanneries, but Elmendorf was a reasonable man. He was persuaded to agree to a compromise. Incorporated tanneries would be permitted in Greene and Delaware counties but not in Ulster and Sullivan in which the Senator's land speculations centered and where most of his constituents lived.

With Elmendorf's help, the bill passed and became law. At once the New York Tannery was incorporated and its capital of sixty thousand dollars subscribed by five men of the Swamp plus another from Havana,

Cuba.[11] Edwards and the men of the Swamp had triumphed. Absentee stockholders were joining absentee landlords as shapers of the destinies of the Catskills. But it was a sad day for the small tanners of the mountains—and for the mountains' hemlock trees.

Tanners Versus Hemlocks

🌲 It is easy enough, even in this age when so many old ways are being swept out of the door, for a man to feel sympathy with trees when troubles overtake them. We no longer believe as our ancestors did that each tree has a spirit whose pardon must be asked before the tree may be cut down. Yet the painters, poets, and song writers still demonstrate how quickly trees may be accepted as symbols of our lasting sense of relationship to the other organisms with which we share this earth. In the Catskills the balsam fir is felt as reigning like a human king over windswept mountaintops. In many more sheltered places the hemlock has established a similar claim to respect.

When the Hardenbergh patentees took possession of their million and a half acres in 1708, most of these acres were covered by a mixed forest in which no single kind of tree had things altogether its own way.[1] Maples, oaks, beeches, balsam firs, spruces, hemlocks, and others struggled to get available food, water, and sunlight. Each kind of tree did its best to give rise to as many young ones as possible. For each living thing spends it energy in asserting itself and growing and expanding as completely as its inherited constitution and its circumstances will permit. In the Catskills, trees dominate the plant cover which keeps the mountains' thin soil from being wrenched away by frost, water, and gravity. Trees dominate because their genetic pattern makes it possible for them to soar above other green things and intercept much of the sunlight which would otherwise fall upon the leaves of grasses, ferns, and other earth-hugging plants. Temperature and moisture also favor the growth of trees in the Catskills, and in many places they favor one tree above all. That tree is the hemlock spruce or *Tsuga canadensis,* usually known simply as the hemlock.

In the green battle raging to this day among the plants of the Catskills, the hemlock has a few handicaps which keep it from taking possession of the entire region. It must have a great deal of water, yet its roots seldom find it possible to penetrate deep into the ground. Instead, hemlock roots are likely to form a thin mat which remains close to the surface where it will suffer in prolonged droughts. That is why hemlocks seldom do well on the dry and sunny slopes of the Catskills facing south and east. They flourish instead on the shady northern and western slopes and in moist and shadowed cloves and valleys. Often the hemlocks share living space with shaggy-barked yellow birches, with beeches and maples. But where conditions suit them especially well, they form dense groves from which they exclude almost every other green thing. Because of its shallow root system, a hemlock is easily tipped over by a push from the wind. Standing shoulder to shoulder in groves, they support one another as long as no break in their ranks occurs to give the wind a chance. In such groves, hemlocks are able to reach the greatest height and girth permitted by the rules of their being. There they send up tall and straight trunks from which all lower branches wither away when they are deprived of sunlight. It was groves like these, as well as his new way of tanning, that brought Colonel Edwards to the Catskills. A century earlier such groves would have meant little even to a tanner. But changes were taking place in American life that made hemlocks as attractive as the blasted trees on the cliffs of the Catskills had been to an earlier generation of men.

The tradition of making leather by soaking hides in solutions of tannin extracted from bark or other parts of plants stretches in a continuous line from the prehistoric inhabitants of Europe to Americans of today. Oak bark was the favorite source of tannin in Britain and western Europe. Willow, larch, and spruce also supplied tannin, especially in cooler climates and among mountains. The sole of a woman's shoe made in Roman times was dug up in Vandonissa in Switzerland some years ago and was found to have been converted from hide to leather with the aid of the bark of a member of the pine family, probably the Norway spruce.[2] This tree has enough points of resemblance to the American hemlock spruce to have suggested to early settlers its use as a source of tannin. There is no evidence that the settlers learned to tan with hemlock bark from the Indians who prepared the skins they used for clothing and moccasins by treating them with animal brains or smoke. These methods work well with the lightweight skins the Indians used, but they were not suited to the heavy cattle hides from which Europeans cut the thick soles of their shoes.

In the early years of American settlement, leather was far more generally used than it is today. Leather boots and shoes, leather breeches and skirts, leather saddles and harness, leather bookbindings and buckets, leather

stockings and hats, many other objects of leather were used daily. Soft deerskins prepared in the Indian way were popular for clothing and Indian moccasins were used; but as cattle increased and were slaughtered on white
men's farms, their hides were tanned by European methods in order to provide leather for boots, harness for horses, and other articles of European culture. In every settlement, shoemakers and harness makers tanned their own
stocks of leather. Some tanned for neighbors on shares and went on to become full-time tanners. In a few places where transportation by water was
available and tanbark was handy, a tanning industry began. Near Boston and
in New York's Swamp, hides shipped from the West Indies or South and
Central America were being tanned with oak bark long before 1700.[3] Soon
hemlock bark was finding its way to tanneries in the Boston area; later it was
shipped by sea from Maine. Hemlock bark gave a distinctive red-brown color
to leather. This color was not liked, at first, by people accustomed to the
warm brownish color imparted by oak tannage. Englishmen who saw the
first hemlock-tanned leather sent to Europe wondered what strange "red
Yankee tannin"[4] had been used, and dealers preferred selling the leather by
candlelight when its redness was less noticeable. Slowly the new kind of
leather made its way.

By the time the Yankees founded the city of Hudson in 1784, hemlock
tanning was a familiar story to them. At once they set up a tannery and
used hemlock bark peeled in the Catskills and the Helderbergs to the north
and carried across the Hudson River on flatboats.[5] Soon hemlock bark was
being shipped from Catskill wharves to the tanners in the Swamp, for by
then the oaks that had once grown so thickly in the New York vicinity were
beginning to show the strain. The time was approaching when someone
would wonder if it might not be worth his while to ship hides to the hemlock
woods rather than ship hemlock bark from the Catskills to the Swamp. The
new, more highly mechanized methods of tanning could easily be put into
practice in the Catskills. Thanks to the prevailing Old World ways of holding land, there were many square miles of forest still untouched. Where
land or "bark rights" could be bought, the price was low, for many settlers
were bypassing the Catskills and heading toward the well-advertised valleys of the Susquehanna and Genesee. Large quantities of pure water were
needed in tanning because muddy water made hides rot instead of becoming
leather, and the Catskills had clear streams everywhere. Lime was needed
to remove hair from hides—and at the base of the Catskills lay long limestone ridges.

It was Colonel Edwards and his friends of the Swamp who first
grasped the advantages of operating large tanneries in the Catskills, and it

was the colonel himself who led the way. The waste and destruction he left behind appal modern men. Yet there was something heroic in the colonel's struggle to overcome the obstacles that nature and society put in his way. Not only had he come to the Catskills laden with debt, but 1816, the year when Edwards explored the Catskills for a possible site for a tannery, was known as "the year without a summer."[6] Frost was felt every month in that year, and throughout northeastern America crops failed and men sank deep into debt. An air of gloom was spreading over the country and would culminate in the depression year of 1819. To make matters even worse, when masterful William Edwards explored the valley of the Schohariekill from what is now Prattsville to the stream's sources and found a tract of land on which hemlock trees stood thick enough to promise generations of support to a tanner, then buying the land appeared almost impossible. For like much other unsettled land in the Hardenbergh Patent, this tract of about two thousand five hundred acres in the present town of Hunter was surrounded by doubts and confusion. It took months even to find out who the owner was. When that important fact was ascertained, the colonel was almost as badly off as before. For the land had been deeded to Edward Livingston by the Chancellor in 1779. In 1795 Edward had mortgaged it to a French émigré who later returned to France, where he died. Investigation showed that the émigré had left his American affairs in the hands of two agents, Joseph Bouchaud of New York and Anthony Laussat of Philadelphia. Livingston was in arrears on his interest and the agents proposed foreclosing and then selling the land to the New York Tannery for two dollars per acre. The foreclosure took place, but when the land was duly offered for sale at auction at the Tontine Coffee House in New York, Bouchaud and Laussat, who had agreed to buy it in on behalf of the owners, bought all 23,000 acres for themselves at twenty-five cents per acre, much to the chagrin of the colonel who had agreed not to bid for his company. Finally, as a capstone to the whole structure of deceit and difficulty, the agents refused to part with the entire twenty-five hundred acre tract they had promised to the tannery; they would sell only half.[7] For now that word was getting around that a large piece of Hardenbergh Patent land had come out of its ancient prison and was on the market, buyers offered twice what the colonel was paying for the better parts of it.

In July 1817, construction of the New York Tannery got underway.[8] But first it had been necessary for the colonel to buy out squatters who had established themselves here and there on his twelve hundred acres. One had set up a sawmill at the Red Falls of the Schohariekill in Hunter, the exact spot upon which Edwards wanted to build his tannery. The man received a hundred-and-forty-acre tract elsewhere in return for his improvements. Even before title to the land was secure, gangs of carpenters and millwrights were brought to the Catskills from Massachusetts, and hemlocks from the surrounding groves were being felled and sawed at the mill taken over from the squatter. Soon the mill was torn down to make room for the tannery and another mill was built nearby. The settlement that arose around the Red Falls, soon known as Edwardsville, was indebted for its visible form to the hemlock trees which had so recently stood in almost unbroken ranks around it. For the first fallen trees were not wasted but were set to work to help carry the battle against their still-living brothers. Hemlock timber may not have been easy to sell at a profit because so much was available and because it could not match white pine in ease of working, in variety of uses, and in durability when exposed to the weather. Yet what material could serve better for fashioning a tanner's town in a hemlock forest? Large hemlock timbers were quickly being hewn; smaller ones were sawed by the up-and-down saw creaking and bumping at the mill. The buildings which rose were as thoroughly hemlock as the trees they had displaced. They had hemlock sills, hemlock joists, hemlock rafters. Their walls were covered outside with hemlock clapboards. Hemlock shingles kept their roofs tight; hemlock planks formed their floors, which were swept with hemlock brooms. Only the pins which kept snug the mortise and tenon joints of the houses and tannery buildings of Edwardsville were not of hemlock but of tough oak. Hemlock benches and tables served as furniture. A family lacking beds could make do, for a time, with heaps of fragrant hemlock boughs. Water was soon being carried from hillside springs in pipes bored from hemlock logs, and such pipes were still being made in the town almost a century later.[9]

In New England a good deal of hemlock lore had been formed and preserved. Now it was conveyed, in Yankee brains, to the Catskills. In 1672 John Josselyn had written that in New England hemlock bark "serves to dye Tawny; the Fishers Tan their Sails and Nets with it. . . ."[10] Yankees had learned medicinal uses of the hemlock from Indian friends—the inner bark boiled and beaten thin was sometimes applied to sores or burns. The tips of hemlock or spruce twigs taken in the form of a tea in winter vanquished the scurvy which often afflicted people existing on a diet of salt pork and corn meal. The very air in which the hemlock's graceful limbs swayed and danced was thought to have value in curing ailments. Before many years, people with lung trouble were coming to the "bark-peelings"[11] of the Catskills, for there the concentrated essence of hemlock was being released in full force as trees were stripped of their bark.

The heart of Edwardsville was the huge tannery set on the banks of the Schohariekill. From its four great brick chimneys, smoke and sparks poured as crackling fires warmed the contents of the long rows of vats. The building was three hundred feet long; in a few years it would grow to five hundred, and a two-hundred-foot auxiliary structure would come into being beside it. No building of anything like this size had yet been seen anywhere in all the region of the Catskills. Old squatters and hunters stared at it with open mouths. The colonel could boast—and he did—that his tannery was the most advanced in the United States, for all its operations were carried out efficiently under one roof. The water power of the Schohariekill had been enslaved to grind tanbark, to pump tanning liquors from one vat to another, and to run devices that gave finish to leather by rolling and beating. Beside the tannery stood clusters of dependent buildings: a blacksmith shop; an office and store; sheds for storing bark; rows of workers' cottages, each a miniature Yankee salt-box house. A large boardinghouse for single workers had been among the first of Edwardsville's buildings. Some years later a church and a Spartan little schoolhouse were added.

The method of tanning by suspension, which had encouraged the Swamp men to back the village amid the hemlocks, proved a failure. The colonel tried desperately to make it work, but it refused to carry out his hopes. The leather produced was uneven in quality. But that was not the worst—something known to tanners as "the gain"[12] was below normal. Leather and hides were sold by weight and a hide gained up to 20 or 30 per cent in weight during the tanning process. This difference was "the gain" and it formed a tanner's most substantial source of profit, for it belonged to him. Because tanning by suspension produced a disappointingly small gain, it was discarded and the older method was reverted to. The colonel had suffered a blow, but it did not discourage him and he went ahead with undiminished vigor.

The old colonel was known as a masterful man and he demonstrated that he deserved this reputation by acting as undisputed lord of Edwardsville, though for some years he did not own a single square foot. The records show that the place belonged to the men of the Swamp. Edwards and his son were merely its managers. It had been the old colonel's custom in his Massachusetts period to begin the day by having breakfast with his men, reading them a chapter of the Bible, and leading them in prayer. At Edwardsville a part of the loft where sides of finished leather were hung to dry was put to double use as a chapel. On Sundays, benches were set up and, surrounded by a drapery of leather cleansed of all odor of corruption by the tanning process and fragrant with the scent of hemlock, the old colonel himself often conducted services in true patriarchal style.

Few people questioned the depth or sincerity of Colonel Edwards' piety, yet this did not prevent ugly rumors about him from circulating. The device of incorporation was not yet generally understood. Many people who heard of the colonel lording it over Edwardsville supposed that he was its owner and that he had built it with capital withheld from his creditors in the course of a "profitable bankruptcy,"[13] from which he was discharged in 1818 in the city of New York. Such rumors increased in 1823 when the young colonel took sole title to the New York Tannery from its stockholders. He soon left for New York to become a partner in an importing firm. The old colonel continued to remain master of Edwardsville. His hides were now supplied by Jacob Lorillard of the Swamp. One of the colonel's sons was a clerk of Lorillard's in New York. Lorillard, the young colonel explained in later years, had supplied the money which enabled him to buy the tannery. The deal was a secret one never publicly recorded. Whatever the true ownership, the New York Tannery continued to thrive. Yet by 1825 competitors were giving it trouble. So much hemlock-tanned leather was coming to the Swamp from the Catskills that the price was starting to sink.

The profit to be made by large tanning ventures was so great that even a drop in leather prices did not discourage men from multiplying tanneries in the Catskills. In the Kaaterskill Clove, along the Sawkill, the Bataviakill, the Esopus—wherever pure water tumbled down mossy ledges and hemlock trees grew within reach of a road to the Hudson—new tanneries sprang into life, nourished by capital from the men of the Swamp. Travelers seeking romantic thrills among the Catskills soon met long lines of wagons laden with stinking hides destined for mountain tanneries. Flies buzzed around the wagons and tortured horses and oxen as well as men. Those who visited the Catskills in order to see its great primeval forests sometimes saw instead vast mountainsides and hollows covered with bleaching trunks which a long dry spell would convert into fire-blackened wastes. But that was only part of what an observant traveler might note. Trout were vanishing from many streams because the temperature of the water was raised too high for their comfort as the shading forests were ripped away.[14] The water became polluted with tannery wastes and ashes. As the mountain cover of matted roots and decaying leaves and branches burned out here and there, the very earth of the Catskills was migrating to the valleys and the sea below, transported by streams or slowly oozing down slopes. The great profits to be made in the leather trade had not only doomed the hemlock groves of the Catskills, but had also set off a bombardment directed at the soil, the air, and the water of the mountains. It was all ably planned and financed by the men of the Swamp. They were honored and respected in their society, and many were highly intelligent and cultured men. They were often benevolent toward the poor and considerate to their equals.

The old landlords of the Catskills began to take a back seat. The ownership of great tracts of land still remained an unimpeachable source of status, but the power of land was being challenged by the aggressive young vigor of shares in corporations. Some older Livingstons were reluctant to open their lands to the assault of the tanners or to regard tannery shares as an adequate substitute for deeds to land. Some carried over into the changing nineteenth century the old British concern for their timber whereby a British landowner of the old school would sell his timber only when in dire need and then it would be cut with care, with the poor of the parish often gathering to claim the "lop and chop,"[15] a right to small branches and chips which had sometimes been theirs from time immemorial. British Captain Basil Hall toured the Livingston estates on the east bank of the Hudson in 1827 and claimed to detect visible evidence of a decline in the glory of the Livingstons. He attributed it to the abolition of the rule of primogeniture, but it also owed a good deal to the decline in land values in the Hudson Valley and the Catskills because of the opening of the Erie Canal. The captain wrote—with considerable exaggeration—that everything Livingston "wore an air of premature and hopeless decay, the ancient manor houses were allowed to fall to pieces, the trees of the parks and pleasuregrounds were all untended; the rank grass was thickly matted along with weeds over the walks; and the old pictures were fast going to ruin under the joint influence of mould and indifference. . . ."[16]

Many Livingstons were continuing to live on their riverbank estates in leisured affluence. Yet they had glided past the crest of their power. Now they were becoming increasingly "land poor," and while their status remained high, their ability to influence the life of their time was diminishing. But as the Livingston luster faded, that of heroes like Colonel Edwards shone with a hard brilliance. Robert Livingston of Clermont had not included hemlock trees among those upon which he proposed founding a fortune in Woodstock back in the 1760s. Now this often despised tree (Jonathan Carver had called it "quite useless, and only an incumbrance to the ground")[17] was becoming the base of the colonel's fame. The colonel had taken sides in the green battle in the Catskills and had done it from motives of his own. But one effect was to give aid to the rivals of the hemlocks. These rivals were the grasses and low-growing plants, the oaks which thrive on dry and burned-over soil, the poplars and red-fruited cherries, the lusty magenta-flowered fireweed which delights in charred surroundings, the maples and birches and ash trees which the hemlocks had excluded from choice sites among the mountains.

By 1823 Colonel Edwards and the other tanlords who quickly followed him to the Catskills seemed to be replacing the vanishing hemlocks as the dominant organisms of the Catskills, for no other living things could rival them in power and influence. Edwards was spoken of with awe and respect. It was about this time, according to a granddaughter of his, that the mountain which hung with so regal an air above the smoke and smell of the New York Tannery was beginning to be called the Colonel's Chair. The uppermost ledges of the mountain when seen from the tannery formed the outline of a comfortable chair, from which the colonel may to this day be imagined directing the operations going on below.

The colonel had become a hero, yet not everyone was willing to bow down and do him homage. Nathaniel Booth of Kingston confided to his diary a dissenting opinion. The colonel, he wrote, was a grasping, over-reaching hypocrite. His Massachusetts creditors, too, spoke with bitterness of the colonel. Every now and then one of them brought suit against him in an effort to collect and to test the loosely drawn bankruptcy act behind which Edwards had taken shelter. Even in Edwardsville itself there were independent souls who braved the man with the two-story head. A tradition which still remains alive tells of how Richard Howk, "a large boned and powerful man,"[18] once braved the colonel's wrath. Howk was passing on the opposite side of Edwardsville's muddy main street from the tannery office when the colonel caught sight of him and commanded, "Howk, come over here." Howk looked at the intervening river of mud and asserted his manhood. "Colonel, I don't see that it's any farther from there to here than it is from here to there," he said. Colonel Edwards was the kind of man who never goes from here to there when he can persuade or compel another to go from there to here. He was single-minded in his devotion to business. He did not enter sympathetically into the lives of the men who worked under him, nor did he view the hemlock trees on which his success was founded as anything more than inanimate things to be used as he saw fit and then forgotten. Most of the other tanlords who followed Edwards into the Catskills were as thoroughly devoted to pursuing narrow goals of power and profit as he was. But there was one tanlord who was, in part at least, of a very different kind. He was Zadock Pratt of Prattsville. And Pratt had a kind of primitive respect for the hemlock trees he slaughtered. That may help explain why Pratt is still held in affectionate memory and it may also explain why he left pleasant signs of his presence which still endure among the Catskills.

48

Colonel Pratt of Prattsville

✤ ON WINTER WEEKENDS when the snow lies deep on the cold lands of the Catskills, thousands of people brave wind and storm to climb the mountain known as the Colonel's Chair. These people are not paying their respects to the memory of Colonel Edwards, and they climb sitting down, for they have come to the mountain to ski and do their climbing on a chair lift. If you mention William Edwards to the gay young people gathered in the Hunter Mountain ski lodge or in the barrooms of the village of Hunter below, you are likely to get a blank stare. For the skiers know the old tanlord only as "the colonel"—few have ever heard of William Edwards. Some of them sleep in the A-frame houses known as The Colonel's Chair Estates, and they may eat at a restaurant called The Colonel's Table. William Edwards, the man with the two-story head, has become transformed in their minds into a title without a man.

In Prattsville, some thirteen miles to the northwest, another tanlord once reigned. He was also a militia colonel, and, although born in New York, was of Yankee antecedents. He was Zadock Pratt. And today if you ask anyone you may meet on the streets of Prattsville who Zadock Pratt was, you will get a pleased smile and a torrent of enthusiastic anecdotes and information. Some will even call Pratt "old Zadock." Pratt slew more hemlock trees than Colonel Edwards; his tannery stank just as much as any other; the debris his men left on mountainsides gave rise to as many destructive forest fires as Colonel Edwards—yet he is remembered with affection and as a human being. Why is there so great a difference in the way the two tanners are held in remembrance? Was it because Pratt had a remarkable talent for getting favorable publicity while Edwards, the puzzling bankrupt, kept to the shadows through much of his life and dreaded publicity? This is part of the explanation. But it is by no means all. Pratt was as eager as Edwards to spend his enormous energy in a relentless search for profits and power over others. Yet his character had another side. This side of Zadock Pratt was beguilingly simple and even childlike and helped him become a folk hero. Pratt gloried like a ten-year-old in his physical strength and agility; he liked to boast of his feats of marksmanship; of jumping; of running; of horsemanship; and he purred loudly when he was praised. He was not conspicuously religious, yet when he dealt with hemlock trees he did it in something like a religious spirit. It was almost as if a hint of the spirit of his ancestors of the damp woods of northern Europe had come down to him and caused him to beg the pardon of a tree before he cut it down.

On the surface, Pratt's story conforms very closely to the standard legend, so beloved of older Americans, of success through hard work and self-denial. There were the poor but honest parents—his father was a struggling handicraft tanner. There was the instance of precocious industry—Pratt's first earnings came from picking and peddling wild huckleberries. There were the years of apprenticeship marked by long hours, devotion to duty, and the saving of a tiny bit of capital which was to become the nucleus around which great wealth would eventually gather. Pratt became a skillful saddler. He kept a country store and slept under the counter. By this and a myriad of similar economies, he hoped to increase his savings. At last he was able to enter into partnership with a brother in a small tannery in the Catskills. Shrewdly, he wound up the tannery just in time to avoid being ruined by the depression in tanning which followed the peace of 1815. In 1824, with fourteen thousand dollars in his pocket (derived partly from fur trading and the making of his hundred thousand ash oars), he drove a one-horse wagon to the hamlet then known as Schohariekill. He announced that he had come "to live *with* the local people and not *on* them."[1]

Pratt may have made his statement of purpose in order to assure the people of Schohariekill that he would not operate in the manner of William Edwards and suck the substance from his part of the Catskills primarily for the benefit of the rich men of the Swamp. It is likely, too, that he had something else in mind, for Schohariekill people had a very good reason to feel suspicious of tanners. Theirs was already an old settlement by the standards of the region; strangers had come from time to time among the descendants of the Palatine refugees who had settled there before the Revolution. Not long before Pratt's arrival two strangers set up a tannery at nearby Devasego Falls. By 1824 they were gone but they had left behind them debts and a wild tale of piracy on the high seas and of buried treasure.

The tale began on board a ship bound from Philadelphia to the West Indies on a trading voyage. It carried thirty-five thousand dollars in coin. This money, it was rumored, belonged to Stephen Girard, the Philadelphia financier. The presence of the cash proved too great a temptation to crew members, who killed the captain with an ax and the mate with an oar, and took command of the ship. They turned it around and headed for New York. The men landed on Coney Island, buried a chest of loot, and took off for the nearest tavern. There liquor opened their lips and the tales they told drew the attention of the police. Two of the sailors were taken and eventually hung on Bedloe's Island in New York harbor. The rest escaped. Two crewmen turned up in Schohariekill not long after with plenty of cash. They had been Philadelphia tanners and now took over the old tannery at Devasego Falls. The Swamp firm of Cunningham and McCormick supplied them with raw hides. After a year of operation the tannery burned down; the two tanners collected the insurance and vanished. Local suspicions had been mounting since the men first came to the Schohariekill Valley, and their disappearance touched off an investigation. It was concluded to the satisfaction of the people of Schohariekill at any rate that their vanished neighbors were "pirate tanners."[2] They had retrieved the treasure buried on Coney Island and used it to finance their tannery.

Zadock Pratt had little difficulty convincing Schohariekill people that he was no pirate tanner. He quickly bought a tract of land which had once belonged to the heirs of Johannis Hardenbergh's brother-in-law Alderman Leonard Lewis. It had passed into the hands of speculators, one of whom was Lucas Elmendorf; a more active one was Robert Dorlon, a Catskill lawyer. By November 17, 1824, Pratt's tannery dam was finished. Ice was forming in the Schohariekill, yet Pratt celebrated the completion of the dam by swimming its length.

The next spring Pratt began construction of his huge tannery building, and eighty-three days later the first hides were placed in its vats. Pratt knew that the settlement of Schohariekill had one decided disadvantage as a site for a tannery. It was located farther from the Hudson than any other large-scale tannery in the Catskills. That meant that transportation costs would be high. On the other hand, the growth of hemlocks that almost filled the valley from mountain crest to mountain crest was remarkably dense and far easier to harvest than in many places closer to the Hudson. But most favorable of all was Pratt's ability to keep a cool realistic eye on every aspect of his tannery's operations. He maintained remarkably detailed records of costs and at the same time kept his men satisfied with lives of hard work and small pay. Unlike many other tanners, Pratt proved able to resist the efforts of the Swamp to dominate him. He tanned hides for Gideon Lee, for Jonathan Thorne and Charles Leupp, who were among the biggest of the Swamp bigwigs, and yet he never yielded his independence to them. While most tannery settlements in the Catskills were shantytowns where buildings were run up hastily with no hope that they would last longer than the time it would take to use up the neighboring hemlocks, Zadock Pratt made his town one in which the lowliest worker could take pride.

An elegant pictorial map of Pratt's town, made to the colonel's order in 1835, preserves the appearance of the village at the height of its tannery prosperity.[8] At a discreet distance from the huge tannery stands Pratt's mansion with its two-story porch and its outbuildings. Ranging on either side along the village's main street stand the hundred houses Pratt built. They are mingled with the less pretentious one he found on his arrival in 1824, and have an air of simple refinement in their proportions and ornament. By means of such details as pilasters and sunburst gable windows, they share the classical taste of the 1820s. A covered wooden bridge 130 feet long crosses the Schohariekill. Pratt boasted that it was built in eleven days "without the use of ardent spirits"[4] while the snow lay three feet deep on the ground. The Albany *Argus* of July 10, 1839 was so completely carried away by its enthusiasm over the Pratt marvels that it claimed "the bridge is believed to be the longest bridge for a single arch in America" and that it was 224 feet long. A pair of circular fishponds are shown across the road from the Pratt mansion. They were stocked with the unstable combination of trout, sunfish, suckers, and bullheads. A man who could well be intended for Pratt himself is seen trying his luck in one. Pratt planted one thousand hickory, maple, and elm trees along the streets of his town—many of them appear on the map, and some are still alive. Two churches, one of the Reformed Dutch believers and the other of the Methodists, appear on the map. Later they were joined by an Episcopalian structure and a three-story school run by Dr. Wright; a little later a brick and verandahed academy was established, largely at Zadock Pratt's command. Small Pratt-financed industries began to appear—a woolens factory, another which produced oilcloth, two match factories, a rubber-goods factory, a chair- and cabinetmaking factory, a hatmaking establishment, machine shops and foundries.

For three years Pratt supplied rent-free quarters in which eccentric preacher-printer-daguerreotypist Levi L. Hill turned out Baptist religious publications and maintained a bookshop. But in 1850, when Hill startled the photographers of the world by announcing that he had invented a method of color photography, Pratt's realistic judgment of men led him to withhold endorsement of Hill's claim. Samuel F. B. Morse, president of the National Academy of Design and inventor of the telegraph, might visit Hill in his Westkill workshop and leave to hail him as one of the great geniuses of the age; senators and congressmen by the dozen might give Hill their enthusiastic approval, but Zadock Pratt realized that Hill's invention was either an attempt at fraud or the result of an honest mistake. No one knows to this day which it was.[5] Once Hill made his announcement, photographic studios were deserted as people everywhere waited to have their pictures taken when the Hillotype could come into use. Angry photographers besieged Hill in his Westkill parsonage and demanded that he either patent his process or admit that he hadn't any. It was characteristic of Zadock Pratt that at this point he lent Mr. Hill one of his watchdogs to protect him against the photographers, but he continued to keep his opinion of Hill's process a secret.

Once it was obvious that Colonel Pratt's tannery was a success, a bustling village came to life around it and people began predicting that unlike other tanning centers, Prattsville (for so Schohariekill had been renamed) had come to the Catskills to stay. Pratt himself shared in this belief and did all he could to make it come true. He liked to tell the world that by removing hemlock trees from his town he was performing an act not only profitable to himself but of lasting benefit to future generations of Prattsvilleans. He often said the "old tanners" claimed that when "hemlock land" was cleared of its trees and converted to pasture, the cows grazing upon it produced the finest butter in the world. It was equal to the famous Orange County butter which was so fine that the United States Navy would buy no other to place aboard its ships leaving for warm-water cruises. It was Pratt's hope that as tanning died out following the exhaustion of the supply of tanbark, Prattsville could live on as the center of a prosperous dairy-farming region. Such crops as hay and potatoes were raised and sold profitably closer to the Hudson, but to the farmers of a place as distant as Prattsville, transportation costs ruled these out as important cash crops. It cost half a cent to get a pound of butter to the Hudson by team as against fifty cents to move one hundred pounds of hay the same distance. Butter with its more concentrated value was the better crop, Pratt reasoned.[6] In order to demonstrate the advantages of butter production on hemlock land, Pratt set up a dairy farm at Prattsville across the Schohariekill from his tannery.

In all his business activities Pratt was a model to hold before the ambitious young men of America. His industry and determination, his attention to the smallest detail of his business, his early rising, his thrift—these made him the kind of hero whom Horatio Alger was to celebrate some years after Pratt's career was over. Yet Pratt could not help puzzling the businessmen who admired him, for it was clear to every observer that Pratt was decidedly odd. James Powers of the Greene County bar scorned Pratt as "almost illiterate."[7] A writer in Orson Fowler's *American Phrenological*

Journal for 1848, having studied Pratt's head, found that the great tanlord was "extravagantly organized. He is from these causes, consequently eccentric; each action and motion bears the impress of his mind, which makes him somewhat peculiar, isolated and detached from his species."[8] Whether a man believed in phrenology or not, he would have to conclude that never before had the Catskills known a man like Colonel Pratt—a man who cared for the look of the landscape he controlled and who took into consideration the effect of his actions upon future generations. Fellow tanners viewed Pratt with unbelieving eyes. For in a trade filled with secrecy about working methods, Pratt made public the minutest details of the way he ran his tannery; other tanners, without the payment of a cent, could learn and put to use the results of the Pratt shrewdness and energy. Then too there were the odd practical jokes Pratt liked to perpetrate. One Fourth of July he donned a fur coat, jumped into a sleigh, and drove into the Village of Catskill, to the amazement of the citizenry.[9] Was that any way for a rich tanner to behave? Pratt's love of military trappings led him into some curious byways of behavior. He liked to take to the field with his militiamen and the artillery under his command and blast down barns—for which he paid more than the full value to their owners. One historic day on the bridge at Windham, he re-enacted the battle of Lodi with fireworks. He liked more and more to boast of his feats of strength and skill. He competed with his men in jumping and—at the age of thirty-six—beat all comers in the running broad jump. When he set up a bank in a pillared little building by the side of his mansion house, Pratt puzzled bankers as much as he did tanners, for when a stranger asked for a loan, Pratt often brushed aside the applicant's proffers of collateral. Instead he studied the man's face and then asked to look at his hands. If the hands showed evidence of hard manual labor, the man got the loan—and Pratt boasted that no man who passed his hand-and-face test ever failed to repay the money advanced. Once when he met a deserving but broke young man, Pratt couldn't give him help because he hadn't a cent in his pockets. He picked up a flat stone from beside the road and with a rusty nail scratched a check on the stone. "Take that to my bank in Prattsville and they'll give you the money,"[10] the colonel said. And his cashier did. For he recognized the authentic Pratt touch.

Like many other men of limited education, Pratt saw a kind of magic in the printed word. When hard times struck the tanning business in the 1830s and the price of leather dropped, he reacted in his own way. He had a number of his favorite mottoes printed in letters of gold and distributed about Prattsville. "Be just, and fear not,"[11] "Honesty is the best policy," "Do well, and doubt not," were among the mottoes with which Pratt tried to battle economic turmoil. And his village weathered the storm better than most.

In his domestic life, too, Pratt puzzled orthodox thinkers. His first three wives died after relatively short experiences of married life. The fourth did not die—she got a divorce. In his late seventies, the colonel took his fifth bride. She was a mere twenty years old and an office employee of the trade paper of the leather industry, the *Shoe and Leather Reporter,* whose editor observed with pride that it was in his office that the final Mrs. Zadock Pratt had "acquired that amiability and flavor of The Swamp that made her attractive to the old tanner."[12]

"The Gem of the Catskills" was what Prattsville was called in the days when it was under the guidance of Zadock Pratt. For neatness and rural charm it was without a rival throughout the Hardenbergh Patent and beyond. It had no poor, Colonel Pratt liked to say. Its streets became well shaded as the trees planted by the old tanner came to maturity. Miles of sidewalks were laid down. People in mountain towns like Windham took notice and followed Pratt's example. Colonel Pratt was sent to Congress and there he labored to bring to the national scene the same kind of cheerful neatness, efficiency, and eccentricity he had made part of life in Prattsville. His passion for accurate record keeping led him to found the National Bureau of Statistics. He enthusiastically worked toward the planning of a transcontinental railroad. His admiration for George Washington gave him added zeal in pushing for the completion of the Washington Monument. When a group of mechanics proposed that a stone be built into the monument with an inscription praising Pratt himself, Pratt was pleased. But a storm of protest arose. Horace Greeley's New York *Tribune* which had opposed the construction of the monument anyway, sarcastically upheld the mechanics' proposal in the hope that it would lead to the plastering of the monument's sides with advertising for "quack merchandise"[13] to such an extent that the "awkward monstrosity" would be pulled down. What gave additional spice to the affair was that Pratt was president of the Mechanics Institute of New York, which had a hand in trying to maneuver the Pratt-praising stone into Washington's bosom.

For twenty years the hemlocks of the vicinity of Prattsville held out against the assaults of Pratt's barkpeelers. San Juan, Orinoco, and Laguira hides; Metamoros, Montevideo, and California hides; hides shipped from Buenos Aires, Rio Grande, and Honduras[14] made their way up the Hudson and were then carried by wagon from the wharves of Catskill to Pratt's tannery on the Schohariekill, to end as leather in the warehouses of the Swamp. As his hemlocks vanished, Pratt grew in wealth and power. And like many another man who has risen far above his fellows in worldly success, he was not satisfied. He craved further successes and an even higher position. It was then that Pratt entered Congress and took to delivering lectures at county fairs, at schools, and before audiences of workmen, farmers, and capitalists. He began taking keen pleasure in sitting for his portrait to painters, sculptors, and photographers—some said he looked like Henry Clay. Portraits of Pratt ornamented the periodicals in which laudatory accounts of his life and works appeared. When Freeman Hunt of the *Merchant's Magazine* compiled a book of biographical sketches intended to inspire young Americans to strive toward success, Zadock Pratt became Hunt's prime exhibit. Men like John Quincy Adams, Washington Irving, and Henry Clay took back seats in Hunt's book. Dr. Samuel Latham Mitchill, that other fine eccentric, had once published what he called his *Chronological Biography* in which he listed the most glorious achievements of his life. Pratt followed Mitchill's example and dictated his own story to a reporter for the *Shoe and Leather Reporter* and had it printed at his own expense in a number of editions. But all this was only a minor part of Pratt's effort to keep himself before the eyes of the world—even after death.

It is easy for a poor man, unused as he is to adulation, to believe without questioning that he is mortal and will some day disappear from the earth. But for a rich man it is much harder. And such men often try to achieve at least the shadow of immortality by arranging to have their names and perhaps their deeds and features live on in the minds of the humans of the future. Long ago, Egyptian and Persian monarchs ordered tombs hewn for themselves within rocky cliffs and saw to it that the tombs were ornamented with their own likenesses and a variety of symbols of their achievements. Zadock Pratt, too, so managed matters that his personality still broods over his former kingdom of Prattsville from the high cliffs which hang over the site of his tannery.

Just when Pratt decided to "let the rocks tell the story"[15] of his life is uncertain. But the notion probably did not enter his head until after a day in the 1840s when a wandering and penniless stonecutter or sculptor turned up in Prattsville and asked for help. The man was quickly set to work carving a likeness of Zadock Pratt on a large boulder at the entrance to his village. But the boulder happened not to be on Pratt land. It's owner, John Brandow, did not like Pratt. According to one contemporary, Brandow remarked that he did not want Pratt "to haunt him as he passed by,"[16] so he ordered the sculptor to pack up his tools and leave. It was then that Pratt set the man to carving what are known to this day as Pratt's Rocks. Not only did a bust of the great tanner emerge from the rocks but symbols of his deeds also took their places over a period of years to form a kind of biography in stone of Zadock Pratt. There is a bas-relief of his tannery building, and a strong arm with rolled-up sleeve symbolizes Pratt's belief that he succeeded "by hard knocks." There is a bust of his son George who was a Civil War casualty, as well as other carvings which record his children and his achievements as a congressman. And the hemlock tree is given its share of credit almost as if it had been a conscious partner in Pratt's career. The coat of arms Pratt adopted shows on the cliff—with a hemlock tree as a crest. A horse carved in bold relief pays tribute to the horses who hauled hemlock bark to the Pratt tannery, and a conventionalized hemlock stands beside him. Benches imaginatively hewn from outcroppings of rock along the steep path which leads from the highway to the cliff bear carvings of hemlocks. A statement cut beneath the relief of his tannery gives full credit to the hemlock for its share in the Pratt triumph. It reads "One million sides of sole leather tanned with hemlock bark, in twenty years, by Zadock Pratt." Other brags were edited with a chisel by order of Pratt's heirs who thought them unseemly—traces of the editorial work may still be seen on the Rocks.

Throughout his life Zadock Pratt liked to pay tribute to the hemlock tree. He liked to enlarge upon the usefulness of the tree's branches as beds for men spending a night in the wilderness; he liked to praise the value of hemlock timber and believed that a healing quality was imparted to the air permeated with the aromatic fragrance of hemlock. Today, thanks to the carvings on Pratt's Rocks, the old tanlord praises the hemlock from the grave.

A few years before Zadock Pratt settled amid the dense hemlock groves of what was to become Prattsville, another kind of evergreen tree was beginning to help bring fame and prosperity to another part of the Catskills. This evergreen was the pitch pine which grew on the top of a cliff on Elisha Williams' Catskill Mountain lands in an extremely picturesque way. The pitch pine is a very adaptable tree. It sometimes grows straight and tall in rich and sheltered lowlands but when its seedlings find themselves settled for life on sandy ridges or rocky ledges, they make the best of things by growing slowly into picturesquely gnarled forms. The pitch pine has given a distinctive character to New Jersey's Pine Barrens; it grows in noticeable uniformity on ridges close to the Atlantic coast, and a stand in Branford, Connecticut, has long been known as the Pine Orchard. Sometime before 1820, travelers to Elisha Williams' clifftop began calling it by the same name, and which Pine Orchard was named first is uncertain. Both were distinguished by dwarfed pitch pines growing in almost regular formation.

As the Catskills' Pine Orchard drew more and more visitors, many of its pines were cut down in order to extend even further its enormous view. In 1823 more trees vanished to make room for a large hotel building known at first as the House on the Pine Orchard and in later years as the Catskill Mountain House. The number of pines that died to make room for the hotel was minute compared with that of the hemlocks felled to give wealth and fame to Zadock Pratt, but their sacrifice opened the way to an extraordinary passage in the history of the Catskills.

Meanwhile, the conversion of the cliffs above his town into a sculptured memorial grew. Pratt set a stonecutter to work carving a burial place for himself deep within the rocks. But the stone proved resistant as the workman penetrated a few feet inside and only a niche resembling a sentry box remains. A child once asked if this was a telephone booth of the ancient Indian inhabitants of the land, and his error is understandable. Foiled by the hardness of the rock, some say, Pratt ordered a splendid coffin of hemlock wood for himself. Such coffins play a part in the folklore of the Catskills. It was a matter of common observation that a piece of green and knotty hemlock thrown on a fire would react like a bunch of firecrackers. Men often ended their traditional brags with the words, "And when I die let me be buried in a hemlock coffin so I'll go through hell snapping."[17] Pratt's coffin never had a chance to startle the residents of hell. For a flood carried it off from the shop in which it was being made and it was never seen again.[18] When Pratt died he was buried in a way that must have seemed to some the fulfillment of a prophecy. In 1853 romantic novelist and poet Mrs. Ann Sophia Stephens had praised Pratt and his works in a long poem titled *The Tanner and the Hemlock*. Mrs. Stephens wrote:

> So the Tanner loves that stout old tree,
> With its great trunk looming there,
> And its light leaves dancing joyously,
> As they sing in the mountain air

And she ended the poem with these words:

> For well he knows that the hemlock bough
> Will weep o'er his honored tomb.[19]

There is no evidence that hemlock boughs wept over Pratt's grave in the Prattsville Cemetery but they certainly surrounded it and waved above it. Hemlock hedges still surround it and hemlock trees clipped into geometric shapes ornament the cemetery and help keep it green throughout the year.

The "Yankee Palace"

✤ IN THE YEAR 1819 when Rip Van Winkle made his bow to the public, Elisha Williams was no longer sitting tight on his mountaintop near the lakes. He was beginning to cash in on his speculation. Ten miles to the west, Colonel Edwards' tannery was chewing up the hemlock groves of the upper Schochariekill Valley, and Zadock Pratt was doing the same near his Lexington base. In the Kaaterskill Clove, not two miles from Williams' lands, a sawmill had been busy since shortly after 1800. There Palen's tannery was at work—the Palens had been small Catskill tanners who were now backed on a large scale by Gideon Lee. A grandson of Colonel Edwards was to write that as the hemlocks began to disappear about this time, "the glory of the mountains had departed forever."[1] There was truth in the statement, yet another kind of glory was about to descend on the Catskills and make its first landing on Elisha Williams' mountaintop.

Williams' mountaintop was not greatly affected in 1819 by the destruction launched by the tanlords. Thanks to the failure of the Little Delaware Turnpike, his lands were a bit off the beaten track for heavy traffic. The lands were too high and too thin of soil to bear the kind of crop of hemlocks that would attract the tanners' barkpeelers. They remained a sanctuary for romantics who obligingly overlooked the stumpy clearings here and there and the occasional log cabins of squatters.[2] Yet the pressure of tanning was being felt even there and may have helped set up a sawmill at Parmenter's Pond a little above the brink of the Kaaterskill Falls. All this did not discourage romantic pilgrims. By 1819—and probably some time earlier—an effort was being made to cater to the needs of these people.

On Williams' Pine Orchard, two Yankees named Hiram Comfort and Joseph Bigelow had set up a refreshment stand for the romantic pilgrims and also for hunters and travelers on business. About this time North Lake was stocked with pickerel in order to attract fishermen. Before long, Bigelow and Comfort (who was a carpenter) used rough hemlock boards from the nearby sawmill to add to their stand and provide a few bunks in which travelers might spend the night.[3]

From time to time Elisha Williams sold parts of his lands on the mountaintop but he never relaxed his grip on the seven-acre tract known as the Pine Orchard. Williams was a man of the world, a familiar figure at resorts favored by the rich and the fashionable, and he was especially well known at the hotels of Saratoga Springs. It seems possible that he realized that his seven acres of clifftop had a future as a site for a new kind of hotel. But Williams was content to turn over any aspirations of this kind to another man. This man was James Powers of Catskill who, like Amos Eaton, had been a student in Williams' law office. As a lawyer, Powers often profited by representing absentee landlords and tanlords of the Hardenbergh Patent and using his talents in matters involving the perennial disputes over boundaries in the Catskills. In private life his attitude toward the mountains had another side—he seemed to have had a genuine love of the mountains for their own sake. On summer evenings it was Powers' custom to drive from his Catskill office to Merchant Lawrence's tavern and fish for trout in the clear streams which leaped down the mountains to Kiskatom. He would sleep overnight at Lawrence's and return to Catskill the following morning refreshed by a night spent close to untamed nature. Powers was also among the guests whom Colonel Lawrence invited to his New Year's Day feast of bear meat. His interest in the Catskills extended to their historic background. Late in life Powers liked to recall that when he was a student in Elisha Williams' office and lived in the great man's household, Joseph Brant, the same man who had been the terror of the Catskills in Revolutionary days, was sometimes brought to dinner by his friend John McKinstry, landlord of the King of Prussia Inn in the city of Hudson. Brant was living in Canada on lands granted to him by the Crown. He dressed and behaved like a white man, Powers remembered, yet he was easily persuaded to carry the members of the Williams' household back to the colonial past by performing Indian dances and telling tales of his Indian youth.[4]

By the summer of 1822, Powers was in command of the seven acres of the Pine Orchard, evidently under an agreement to buy out Williams. That summer a sixty-foot-long addition was built to the barroom and bunkhouse of Comfort and Bigelow. The purpose of the addition became evident early in September when a group of Hudson Valley men, congressmen, judges, editors, and lawyers sent out to people "of the first respectability"[5] an invitation to a "Rural Ball" to be held "at the Pine Orchard, on the Catskill Mountains" on September 18. James Powers was the chief sponsor. The Rural Ball was the first such social event to be held high among the Catskills—but it was more than that. It was an attempt by Powers to test the ability of the Pine Orchard to attract people and to lay the foundation for the formation of a corporation to exploit the appeal of the place.

In every imaginable way the ball was an immense success. The weather itself did its best. The eighteenth was "one of those clear and beautiful autumnal days that seem to diffuse life and gladness everywhere; the mountain scenery was in the fullness of its pride. . . ."[6] reported the Catskill *Recorder,* whose editor, Edwin Croswell, was among the ball's sponsors. The ballroom was lighted by candles; its walls were draped with fragrant boughs of balsam fir. Fiddlers played as the guests danced until two in the morning, and refreshments were served by Comfort and Bigelow, who were in charge of the affair. Then the men retired to the upstairs room where they slept in "bins" partitioned off on the floor. The ladies had better accommodations; they slept in an adjoining structure "fitted up upon the principle of steamboat berths,"[7] an observer of the next summer recalled. Indulging in what may have been the first pun inspired by the place, he added that the ladies slept "like Niobe, all in *tiers.*" The next morning the guests visited and admired the Kaaterskill Falls, and in the afternoon they assembled at Merchant Lawrence's where they were "promptly provided with an excellent dinner" before leaving for home.

Powers and his Yankee friends of Catskill hesitated no longer. Within a few months the Pine Orchard was conveyed from Williams to Powers and an application was drawn up asking the state legislature to charter a corporation to be known as the Catskill Mountain Association and to authorize it to build "a large and commodious hotel"[8] on the Pine Orchard and to take over and operate the part of the old Little Delaware Turnpike which linked the Pine Orchard and its neighborhood to Lawrence's Inn. The following March the legislature granted the charter. Powers became the Association's president; Caleb Day, a law partner of his, was secretary. One of the incorporators was James Pierce, a talented amateur in natural history whose observations on the wolves of the Catskills would one day be quoted by Charles Darwin in his *Origin of Species.*[9] Another was John T. Thompson, noted throughout his state as a horticulturist. Judge Caleb Benton, who had a finger in every pie that promised a profit, was also one of the group—it was in his garden that some of the sessions of Amos Eaton's ill-fated Catskill Botanical School were to have been held. Another was Catskill editor Edwin Croswell, who was soon to move on to a post of great authority as editor of the Albany *Argus.*

The incorporators formed an unusual group to be drawn from any small American town. They were businessmen, yet they were sensitive to the rising romantic tide and took an interest in the plants, the rocks, and the soil of the natural world. Most had come to Catskill from the Hudson Valley's Yankee capital of Hudson. The old rulers of the Catskills—the Hardenbergh Patent landlords and their Dutch-descended allies—were not represented among them. These new men were bringing new faces and new ideas into the Catskills, and were showing a daring in putting the mountains to use which contrasted strongly with the cautious conservatism of the old landlords and the reckless waste of the tanlords. No one could deny the boldness of their enterprise. To set a large hotel on top of a mountain was an unheard-of thing, a startling thing. In Europe mountain climbers often took shelter in the huts built by mountain shepherds or herdsmen for use on their high summer pastures—such structures were called "shielings" in Britain. Here and there where a dangerous mountain pass was often used by pilgrims and traders, religious orders established themselves and took in travelers. The hospice of St. Bernard in Switzerland was the best-known example. Swiss health resorts like Leukerbad had simple inns. But to build a hotel on a mountain to which people might go for amusement or relaxation was quite another thing. Yet to men sensitive to the forces shaping life in their time, building a summer hotel on a mountain close to a number of natural wonders would fill a need that was growing almost from day to day.

By 1823 summer resorts for Americans were already an old story. Resorts like these had their beginnings early in the eighteenth century when planters from the West Indies, the Carolinas, and Virginia sailed north each June to flee the summer fevers and intense heat of their own parts of the world and to escape the thinning effect on the blood which uninterrupted residence in hot countries was thought to produce. With these people came royal governors and judges who left their sweating deputies to carry on while they themselves enjoyed the delights of their favorite resort, sea-swept Newport in Rhode Island, where so many Old World amusements and so many pleasant ways of passing time were to be had. Newport was soon known as the "American Bath" after the ancient British resort to which men and women went to drink the medicinal waters, to bathe, to gamble, and to enjoy a lively social whirl, for European resorts from the days of the Romans combined gaiety with therapy.[10] Rich city dwellers soon joined the planters. Philadelphians were prominent among them since their city by summer was not only hot but subject to recurrent epidemics of fever. Other summer resorts arose here and there. Pennsylvania's Yellow Springs with its fine piazzaed inn was a Philadelphia favorite in colonial days; Bristol in New Jersey drew many New Yorkers bent on curing physical ailments or jaded spirits. (Among the Hardenbergh Patent landlords who turned up at Bristol were the Verplancks.) Chancellor Livingston favored Lebanon in New Jersey. Throughout the colonies a number of springs were discovered, each said to have healing virtues and each, it was rumored, an ancient haunt of ailing Indians. At such resorts accommodations were primitive at first: tents or log shanties provided shelter, and visitors cooked at a communal fire. Virginia abounded in springs; Connecticut had its very popular Stafford Springs; New York had Lebanon and, later, Saratoga and Ballston. Many of these springs became fashionable resorts with comfortable lodging houses. After 1800, hotels appeared and it was around these hotels with their Negro musicians, their dancing, their horse racing, and their gay social life that summer resort activities came to center. A standard hotel soon evolved: it was of three stories and boasted a long pillared portico or piazza on which guests sat and chatted or took their daily walk on rainy days—so many laps being equal to a mile. It was a hotel like these which James Powers planned to build on the high clifftop in the Catskills.

In 1807 a writer in *Salmagundi,* the publication to which Washington Irving and his brothers were contributors, gave a satirical, yet informative picture of summer life at Ballston Springs, then far more popular than nearby Saratoga. Ballston had once been "a charming, humdrum careless place of resort, where everyone was at his ease . . . when lo! all on a sudden Style made its baneful appearance . . ." and "now, the worthy, fashionable, dashing, good-for-nothing people of every state, who had rather suffer the martyrdom of a crowd than endure the monotony of their own homes, and the stupid company of their own thoughts, flock to the Springs. . . ."[11] But the Ballston Springs were lacking in what was coming to be an important ingredient of summer resort life—they had no romantic scenery.

"After breakfast," sneered *Salmagundi,* "everyone chooses his amusement:—some take a ride into the pine woods, and enjoy the varied and romantic scenery of burnt trees, post and rail fences, pine flats, potato patches, and log huts, others scramble up the surrounding sand-hills, that look like the abodes of a gigantic race of ants:—and then—come down again; others who are romantic, and sundry young ladies insist on being so whenever they visit the springs, or go anywhere in the country, stroll along the borders of a little swampy brook . . . watching the little tadpoles as they frolic . . . and listening to the inspiring melody of the harmonious frogs that croak upon its borders. . . ."

Newport was amply blessed with romantic natural surroundings. Part of the eighteenth-century appeal of the old Belgian resort of Spa (which gave a generic name to all inland watering places) was its location high among the wild and craggy Ardennes. In New Jersey, a spring located at an elevation of about one thousand feet on Schooley's Mountain became popular and gave rise to a hotel. By 1823 hotels were appearing close to a variety of natural wonders. There was one of the usual three stories and with the usual piazza beside Niagara Falls. A "coffee house" was in business on the shores of Lake George. A hotel was being built at Trenton Falls near Utica, New York. Medicinal waters and sea bathing had made the reputations of many resorts. Now romantic scenery was beginning its vogue.

James Powers made no claim to having healing springs on the Pine Orchard. Instead he rested his claim to "salubrity" on the coolness of the elevation and its freedom from fever. Mountain air took the place of the waters of the usual summer resort. Romantic surroundings became the chief bid of the Pine Orchard for public support. The Kaaterskill Falls, the two lakes lying in apparent contradiction of the laws of nature almost on the edge of a cliff high on a mountain, and the vast and all-encompassing view were romantic assets unlike those possessed by any other resort. It was on them that Powers and his Yankee associates rested their hopes as construction began.

Through the summer of 1823, the combined barroom and office of Comfort and Bigelow, with the new dance hall and the dormitories, continued to thrive, but under the management of Helmus Van Bergen, proprietor of the Greene County Hotel in Catskill. Beside these now outdated buildings the new hotel was rising. Carpenters banged away all that summer, woodsmen felled giant hemlocks on the mountain and hewed them into timbers. The trowels of masons and bricklayers clinked. Oxen and horses strained up the mountainside hauling glass, lime, window and door trim, and a host of other materials destined to be woven into the fabric of the hotel building. The mill at Parmenter's Pond worked at capacity as its up-and-down saw turned out the rough boards and planks needed for the structure.[12]

Down below, the Dutchmen of the Hudson Valley looked up from their fields and saw the frame of the hotel being raised on the Pine Orchard. (The Association bought a barrel of rum to help fuel the raising.)[13] The Dutchmen—skeptical as they always were of Yankee projects—soon dubbed the hotel the "Yankee Palace,"[14] and some predicted that the first stiff breeze would blow it all the way to Connecticut where it belonged.

The Dutchmen were not the only humans to look up from the Hudson Valley at the hotel and wonder that summer of 1823. The Hudson River had become one of the greatest American arteries of travel and commerce. Thousands of passengers on steamships and sloops stared at the mountains over which Rip Van Winkle had thrown a veil of romance. Their eyes dwelt upon the building rising on the Pine Orchard and they examined it through shiny brass telescopes. Livingstons and other fashionables who gave the east bank of the river such a reputation for elegance followed the progress of the hotel from amid the Warwick vases and potted lemon trees of their gardens and, it may be, laid bets on the date of its completion.

James Powers and his friends had done a shrewd thing. By building their hotel on the Pine Orchard—and as close to the edge of the cliff as they dared go—they had made the building its own most glorious advertisement. The advertising and promotional methods of their day were crude enough by modern standards, but the managers of the Catskill Mountain Association had shown sophistication in placing their hotel in so conspicuous a place in defiance of tradition, wind, and snow. A man would be able to look out from the windows of the hotel at infinity. But the inhabitants of the earthly prelude to that infinity would be able to look back at the hotel. And they would stare and wonder and speculate and would be unable to rest until they had climbed the mountain and experienced the new wonder for themselves.

50

"This Olympic Retreat"

❧   "The trade of advertising is now so near to perfection, that it is not easy to propose any improvement,"[1] wrote Dr. Samuel Johnson in 1758. Yet improvements insisted on appearing. By the time the House on the Pine Orchard was being built, the trade had long since exposed the hollowness of the great doctor's pronouncement and had ventured into vast tracts of fresh territory. Proprietors of American resorts aimed at attracting the traveling and summering public, for example, were in such hot competition that ingenuity was stimulated and new ways of putting their wares before the public were evolved. James Powers and his associates knew that the public had come to believe they might be safe from summer epidemics at higher altitudes than those of the older resorts. It became their business to make the most of their 2200 plus feet[2] above sea level. The altitude of the hotel was the greatest known in either Europe or America for any establishment of its kind. DeLabigarre's natural philosopher had found the height of the two lakes to be the merest trifle over 2000 feet. Captain Partridge and his cadets raised these figures a bit and the result of their measurements had been well circulated. Their 2200 plus feet was an accurate altitude for the Pine Orchard, but 3000 would be much better. The management of the House could not raise the height of their clifftop by even the most strenuous exertions; instead, they painlessly raised its altitude in their publicity material. Most of the nineteenth-century makers of gazetteers and guidebooks accepted Partridge rather than Powers. Yet the Hotel on the Pine Orchard stuck to its 3000 feet until late in the nineteenth century, when publicity makers for competing hotels revealed the cheat and the correct figure was reluctantly accepted.[3] Even today the Powers' figure has its adherents. Most authoritative among them is the state of New York, which set up a historic marker on the Pine Orchard early in 1967 and gave the elevation of the spot as 3000 feet.

Dr. Johnson had remarked that paid advertisements had become so commonplace that they were but "negligently perused." The trick, of course, was to resort to invisible advertising, and here Powers proved himself a master. He placed no advertisements in the newspapers, but began with what we must assume was simply an extraordinary by-product of the talk, instigated by Powers, of the wonders of the Pine Orchard. In February 1823, the venture on the Pine Orchard became the beneficiary of one of the finest pieces of promotional writing to ornament the nineteenth century. It appeared in a two-volume novel (and an indisputably great one at that), *The Pioneers* by James Fenimore Cooper.

Cooper did not make either the Pine Orchard or the Kaaterskill Falls the scene of any episode in *The Pioneers*. But he interpolated an account of both in his book, apparently as an afterthought. He described with enthusiasm the natural wonders within easy striking distance of the House on the Pine Orchard, not as they were in 1823 but as he supposed them to have been in the 1790s. This patch of eloquence is put into the mouth of Cooper's hero, old Natty Bumppo, also known as Leatherstocking. And it is superbly done. For Cooper, first of all American writers after William Bartram, fully grasped the character of the American landscape. And he rose to the best that was in him when he described it. Even today, Cooper's tribute to the Pine Orchard and the Kaaterskill Falls conveys an exciting sense of the American wilderness, and the tribute gains an added romantic value by its use of the history of the region of the Catskills.

It didn't matter that Natty's descriptive effort slowed up the action of the novel or that it was by no means consistent with Natty's character. Readers of 1823 felt themselves being fairly picked up and impelled toward the Catskills by Cooper's prose. And when these readers arrived at the Pine Orchard they found themselves in something of a pickle. For so many others had felt the force of Cooper's best seller that the Pine Orchard was not able to accommodate all the pilgrims in comfort. As the new hotel rose, the old buildings beside it continued to serve the public as best they could under the management of Helmus Van Bergen and his wife. But the Van Bergens, obliging and eager to please as they were, could not hope to care for all comers. Many a night found men and women sleeping under the stars or in Bartram's cave. Some who arrived in style but "not in time for a bin in the garret or a soft plank in the dining room,"[4] used their carriages as "sleeping apartments." These vehicles were "scattered about grotesquely enough" on the Pine Orchard, as a visitor of that summer recalled in later years.

The hotel struggling into being on the Pine Orchard in the summer of

1823 symbolized a change taking place in the look of the Catskills. Earlier romantic visitors to the mountains had seen them through the eyes of European painters and poets. The Catskills had appeared to these people to be provincial cousins of the old World's romantic and picturesque marvels made familiar in engravings and put into words by Gilpin and Wordsworth. Now, as the new House on the Pine Orchard rose, it was becoming apparent that the building and the Catskill Mountains around it were no blurred copies of European models, but things with a distinctively American character in which New and Old World elements were excitingly mingled. No visitor of 1823 caught this new look of the Catskills better than a distinguished man who arrived late in August with the plump quarto volume in which he kept his diary.[5] He was DeWitt Clinton, former mayor of the city of New York and former governor of the state. Clinton had been a pupil of Dr. Mitchill's. He coveted fame as a natural scientist, a classical scholar, and an improver. He was sensitive to the romantic tides of his day.

When Clinton entered the rude ballroom on the Pine Orchard, he was moved by the beauty of its balsam fir drapery. As if remembering his literary leanings, he quoted John Milton. The improver in him then took over and he expanded upon the medicinal uses of the tree. At both Lawrence's Inn, where he paused on his journey to the Pine Orchard, and in the ballroom, he studied the albums which lay open on tables for the use of guests who wished to record their emotions or pay tribute to the scenery of the Catskills—albums like these had long been in use at European resorts. With all the condescension of an English milord traveling on the continent, he expressed scorn at the "stale comments and insipid attempts at wit" he found there and quoted Sir John Denham to express his contempt for them. But when a record of the killing of a rattlesnake caught his eye in the Lawrence album, Clinton swelled with patriotic pride and jotted down rattlesnake lore with a very American enthusiasm.

The cliff on which the hotel was being built reminded Clinton of the Tarpeian Rock at Rome. From its edge he admired the rising sun in the manner of tourists on Switzerland's Rigi-Kulm, and he reflected upon the sublimity of nature "in this Olympic retreat." But he also thought of "Leatherjacket" for he had recently read *The Pioneers,* and indulged in a long reverie in which bears, wolves, wildcats, buffalo, and grizzly bears were mingled. Henry Hudson came into his mind, and so did the greatly wronged Indian inhabitants of the land. When he gazed at the Kaaterskill Falls he was reminded of Roman amphitheaters and quoted both Ennius and Lucretius. At once he became an American again and jotted down the information, probably gained from his guide, that "during the Revolutionary

War the Tories congregated near this place and built houses for habitation and depots for plunder. . . ." He then suggested the construction of "a spiral and covered staircase . . . on the plan of that near the Niagara cataract," to make the descent to the base of the Falls possible "even to the aged and the invalid." Clinton had only recently recovered from a broken leg (he still walked with a limp) and the struggle with the steep trail beside the Falls had taxed his strength and aroused his improver's ardor.

Although Clinton's diary was never printed, it did much to draw public attention to the Catskill Mountain House. For Clinton's friend Horatio Gates Spafford borrowed the diary and filled two columns of the new edition of his gazetteer of New York with information from it about the plans and scenic assets of the Catskill Mountain Association. He accepted without question all Clinton's statistics—even his statement that the elevation of the House on the Pine Orchard was about three thousand feet. In this way Powers' try at raising the elevation of his project found its way into a respected reference book whose authority few questioned.

DeWitt Clinton wrote in his diary that Powers had "infused his enterprising, intelligent and energetic spirit" into all aspects of the Catskill Mountain Association's activities. But President Powers was not only able, he was also lucky and, more important, he was skillful in making the most of such diverse pieces of luck as Natty Bumppo's soliloquy upon the Pine Orchard—and the decision of the Supreme Court of the United States in the famous case of Gibbons *vs.* Ogden. It was this decision, written by Chief Justice John Marshall, which ended the Livingston monopoly of travel by steamboat on the Hudson founded by the Chancellor. While it lasted, travel had been expensive and boats relatively small and simple in their accommodations. Fares had been high. But with the monopoly broken and fierce competition ruling the river, fares sank. An Albanian could reach the wharf at Catskill Landing for "a dollar and all found." Sometimes a dollar or a dollar and a half would carry a New Yorker all the way to Albany. Competing owners built ever faster and more luxurious boats. A trip on the Hudson soon became a favorite amusement for people of almost all social classes and incomes.[6] The House on the Pine Orchard had been brought closer to heaven by Powers' skill in publicity. Now it was moved closer to the rest of the world by a decision of the Supreme Court.

As the House opened for the season of 1824, Powers saw to it that newspaper editors and reporters came to the place in platoons and left with enthusiasm for its aesthetic and material attractions. Some were presented with cases of Madeira as they stepped ashore at Catskill[7] and this made life at the Pine Orchard appear even rosier to their eyes. The New-York

Statesman's man had a plausible explanation for the high spirits in which one editorial party enjoyed the Pine Orchard. He wrote that "The inspiration rising from the sublime, beautiful, and picturesque scenery around, from good company, good music, good wine, and a hundred other good things, produced an elevation of mind far above the cloud-capt heights of these hills. Who would think of meeting with champaign [sic] in these wild and romantic regions, the home of the bear and the panther?"[8] So elevated did the mind of another editor become that when he caught sight of a bear ambling beside North Lake, he gave chase and tried to catch the bear with his naked hands. Both bear and editor escaped.

One party of newspapermen lured to the Pine Orchard included Major Mordecai Manuel Noah, an extraordinary man who played a large part in the life of his day as editor, Tammany Hall sachem, sheriff, and leader of New York's Jewish community. He became the first of his religion known to have been entertained at a resort hotel in the Catskills.[9] Another editor with a military title was Colonel William Leete Stone, a native of Ulster County who had lived and edited in the city of Hudson. Stone wrote a lengthy report on the Pine Orchard for his New-York *Commercial Advertiser* and it served for generations as a huge quarry from which managers of the hotel could cut complimentary paragraphs to use whenever needed. The criticisms Stone also made were omitted from future reprintings of his account, but they shed some useful light on the cradle days of the resort industry among the Catskills. The Association had underestimated the appeal of their hotel, Stone implied. Not enough "lodging rooms had been provided to accommodate all who wanted them,"[10] and two-thirds of the seekers for lodging had to be turned away. But this was being corrected. A wing containing additional bedrooms would be added at each end of the main body of the hotel before another summer season came.

Less easy to remedy was a little circumstance which Stone found detracted from the romantic appeal of the Kaaterskill Falls. To him the sawmill above the Falls sounded an ominous and graspingly commercial note in what was billed as a wilderness paradise in which nature reigned unchallenged. Powers and his friends could not help knowing that the efforts of tanlords and lumbermen were threatening the existence of the wilderness setting which was among the greatest glories of the Pine Orchard. The Association's charter permitted it to buy adjoining land without limit to protect its investment, and it allowed the Association to own and operate the road from Lawrence's—a road upon which pilgrim-patrons would not be subjected to the ordeal of passing wagonloads of noisome hides. The Association's directors tolerated the sawmill at Parmenter's Pond because it was a necessity if their hotel were to be built without extravagant cost. But they had quickly added to their original seven and one-tenth acres and bought the two lakes and much of the surrounding forest. Yet in a rainless summer, admirers of the Falls often found that the demands of the sawmill above kept the water, which would normally be leaping down the great precipice, locked up in Parmenter's Pond.

Colonel Stone was the first to criticize in print this eclipse of the Falls' freedom and to report on the curious compromise which had been worked out in a way that accommodated the opposing demands of romance and private gain.

Stone reported that the canny sawmiller had taken to working in a profitable part-time partnership with the manager of the Falls who was established in a "chanty" at the Falls' brink. After tourists had descended to the foot of the first leap, the manager and the miller opened the gates of the millpond. The reconstituted Falls then tumbled down in all their glory. The manager, by prearrangement, lowered a basket from his chanty containing the materials for a picnic, often including champagne. He capped the proceedings by firing a "swivel" or small cannon which sent an ear-shattering echo bouncing back and forth among the surrounding heights. When the tourists climbed up to the chanty they would be greeted with outstretched hands by the manager and the sawmiller, both eager to receive rewards for their parts in the show. Was a wonder of nature still a wonder when it could be turned on for a fee? Stone was the first of many generations of Americans to stand at the Kaaterskill Falls and ponder this interesting question.[11]

In spite of the confusion which reigned on the Pine Orchard during the summer of 1824, it was apparent enough to all concerned that they had a success on their hands. As promising as any development was the acceptance of the Pine Orchard and the Kaaterskill Falls as stops on the American grand tour. In eighteenth-century England the term grand tour had first been applied to the leisurely journey from place to place on the continent of Europe which young British aristocrats made upon leaving Oxford or Cambridge, usually with a tutor to point out the historic or cultural values of famous sights. Later the term was widened to include the kind of continental jaunt becoming popular among moneyed Britishers of all sorts. In 1824 Colonel Stone set down the itinerary of an American grand tour as he understood it. He included Schooley's Mountain, the valleys of the Hudson and Connecticut rivers, Lebanon and Saratoga springs, Niagara Falls, and "climbing the stupendous and lofty cliffs of the Catskills."[12]

That same summer young Englishmen began visiting the Pine Orchard and its adjacent wonders as part of an extension of their own traditional grand tour. An early instance was recorded by a reverent and observant American guest at the House on the Pine Orchard when he spied a "young, fair-haired, well-looking man, in a plain cotton suit, a sort of pepper-and-salt mixture, with gaiters on his feet, and a white beaver on his head." The well-looking man was getting his first glimpse of the view from the rocky platform in front of the hotel.[13] "He appeared to be in a perfect ecstacy at the *coup d'oeil,*" the American reported. The man was soon joined by two companions, similarly dressed, one of whom used what was probably a Claude glass to help him enjoy the view. As "the scene burst upon their eyes," the three gave "a hearty cheer together, with boyish glee . . . how grand! How splendid! they cried." The men were the future Lords Wharncliffe and Taunton, and the future Earl of Derby who was to rise through many important posts to the dignity of Prime Minister.

The next summer a friend of the earl-to-be followed him to the Pine Orchard and the Kaaterskill Falls. He was Daniel Webster. The year before, Webster had won one of his greatest court victories when he represented the anti-monopolists in Gibbons *vs.* Ogden. Included in Webster's party when it arrived at the Pine Orchard was Supreme Court Justice Joseph Story, who had concurred in John Marshall's decision in the case. The two men with their wives and a friend had set forth, following the delivery of Webster's first Bunker Hill oration, to make a tour of watery wonders. They admired the Connecticut River and the springs at Lebanon. At Albany they embarked, with an odd kind of appropriateness, on the steamboat *Chancellor Livingston* and arrived at Catskill to enjoy the view from the Pine Orchard and the sight of the Kaaterskill Falls before going on to admire more tumbling water at Trenton and Niagara Falls—and to consume less innocent fluids while they admired.[14]

The arrival on the Pine Orchard of more and more distinguished visitors gave outward evidence that the place was taking a firm grip on the American imagination and purse. Powers felt encouraged to enlarge and expand the hotel which had been leased to New York hotelman C. H. Webb. Stockholders were urged to pay up their subscriptions, for the venture was as yet far from showing a profit and Webb was slow in paying his modest rent. The Catskill Bank (in which the directors of the Catskill Mountain Association were heavily interested) lent them twelve thousand dollars on a mortgage on their real estate and chattels.[15] The enlargement of the hotel building went ahead. The Association, with James Powers at the helm, had weathered its first period of trial. It had become sufficiently firmly established on its dizzy cliff to be able to borrow money. It was becoming a center around which wilderness lovers, devotees of the romantic and the picturesque, and admirers of distant prospects could gather. It had impressive literary associations. All around, the tanners were at their destructive work, and from time to time great fires swept toward the Pine Orchard. Yet the House stood firm and proclaimed by its very existence the arrival in the Catskills of romance.

In the fall of 1825 a powerful addition to the forces of romance arrived. Irving and Cooper had given the mountains an air of glamor by means of words. The new arrival proceeded to deal with the Catskills not only with written words but also with brush strokes. He was a landscape painter named Thomas Cole.

Picturesque Views of the Catskills

✤ THOMAS COLE was far from being the first man to look at the Catskills with a painter's eye and try to set down what he saw and felt on the
flat surface of paper or canvas. From the beginnings of the white man's
intrusion into the Catskills, a succession of men had made drawings and
paintings of the mountains and had thus preserved a record of how the
mountains appeared to them in the light of their varied desires, training,
and skills.[1]

First of all surviving representations of the Catskills to be set down
were those drawn by the surveyors who made maps for great landowners.
These men drew the mountains in accordance with old conventions of
European map making. When Augustine Graham drew his crude map of
1706 for Cornelis Cool and the other men of Hurley, he portrayed part of the
wall of the Catskills facing the southeast as a series of overlapping scales.
The result is not unlike a child's drawing of a dragon who might be imagined to guard the yet unborn Hardenbergh Patent for its absentee owners-
to-be. Ebeneezer Wooster's maps made a naïve appeal to the imagination,
but it was not until the 1760s when William Cockburn began studying the
Catskills that the mountains were mapped with conscious art. Even before
Cockburn was born, however, the Catskills had found their way into art
by a most respectable route—that of oil painting.

By 1725 the growing prosperity of Hudson Valley landowners and
merchants led them to think it fitting to their station in life to have their
portraits painted. These portraits often used as background standard
properties borrowed from European court paintings of the day and known
to American painters through engravings. Men, women, and children were
posed against noble columns, lush draperies, well-kept lawns, and glimpses
of distant mountains. But sometimes a less snobbish painter formed his
backgrounds of actual American landscapes. The seventeenth-century

Dutch settlers of the Hudson Valley were born into a culture of which landscape painting formed a part; etchings of Dutch fields, skies, trees, and buildings were sold cheaply in their native Holland, where they might be found even in humble homes. Something of this interest in landscape managed to get into an occasional portrait. A fine example is that of Pau de Wandelaer which is in the Albany Institute of History and Art. Another is the 1742 portrait of eight-year-old Cornelius D. Wynkoop posed at full length beside a pair of gamecocks with what tradition and the modern eye both accept as the valley of the Esopus Creek with the Catskills rising beyond. The painting was on loan until 1978 to the Senate House Museum in Kingston, New York.

The acknowledged masterpiece among early portrayals of the Catskills resulted from combining, in the 1730s, the two kinds of portrait painting. One sought to give elegance to sitters; the other tried to tie them to their familiar landscape setting. The painting is known as the **Van Bergen Overmantel**, and it hangs in the galleries of the New York Historical Association at Cooperstown, New York. It shows the Catskills' eastern wall stretched out at full length under a warm gray sky to serve as background to an amusing tableau. Beneath the mountains stand the members of the family of Marten Van Bergen of Old Catskill. The painter has given the father and mother and their children the costumes and attitudes of the subjects of the fashionable or "Patroon" portraits of the day. Around them are the family possessions as if in a pictorial inventory of their property. There is the Van Bergen haystack, the substantial farmhouse, the cows, the sheep, the horses and wagons. An Indian stalks by followed by his wife with a baby on her back; a Negro slave girl approaches a cow; a horseman supplies comic relief by taking a tumble on the road which passes the house. And above it the Catskills, brooding in all their wilderness mystery, make an impressive entrance into the world of art.[2]

By the 1760s the Catskills were being sketched and painted not for local consumption but to bring them within reach of the European hunger for romantic scenery. Shortly before 1760, Thomas Pownall, who was governor of Massachusetts, made sketches of American scenery from which a series of engravings, including the earliest known of the Catskills, was made and published in London. Pownall was what was known in England as "a man of taste." Like many other Englishmen of taste he carried a sketchbook with him on his travels. He was among the first Europeans to sense the novel character of American scenery. Pownall's American sketches were taken in hand by Paul Sandby, an eminent British topographical artist and water colorist. Sandby made six water colors from the sketches, and then made engravings from his water colors. His "View in Hudson's River of Pakepsy and the Catts-Kill Mountains. . . . Sketched on the Spot by Governor Pownal . . ." presents the Catskills in a new way. They have few of the characteristics of an eroded tableland so plainly visible to modern eyes. Instead they rise to peaky summits very much like those of British mountains, even if the Hudson from which they seem to rise is American enough in the clearings which break its wooded banks and in the rivercraft which ply its surface. The view remained the standard one for many years and formed European notions of the Catskills' appearance.[3]

Not long after the end of the American Revolution, the Catskills were interesting the painters who were coming from England and the Continent to try their luck in the new nation. In 1792 or 1793 a man known only as P. Lodet[4] sat down to sketch in a pioneer's clearing along the Neversink Creek near the spot at which Gross Hardenbergh was to die some fifteen years later. Lodet's sketch was once owned by President Franklin D. Roosevelt and is now in the Franklin D. Roosevelt Library at Hyde Park. Other European painters followed Lodet (he was either Swiss or French) and sketched along the Hudson River. In 1802 the first native American painter traveled the Hudson with sketchbook in hand. He was John Vanderlyn, born in Kingston, and the grandson of talented Kingston portrait painter Dr. Peter Vanderlyn. Young Vanderlyn had studied art in Paris as a protégé of Aaron Burr. He returned to the United States in 1802 to make sketches for a series of engravings of American scenery.[5] He sketched the Hudson Highlands, West Point, and other points along the river, but the only sketches to reach the goal of engravings were of Niagara Falls. They were presented to the public at a Fourth of July party given by Chancellor Livingston in Paris. The Chancellor, a patron of the arts, had been a prime mover in setting up the American Academy of Fine Arts of which his brother Edward was president. His daughter Margaret had a talent for drawing, and took lessons from Alexander and Archibald Robertson, two Scottish émigrés who conducted an art school in New York. By the 1790s amateurs like Miss Livingston and professionals like the Robertsons were sketching the estates that looked upon the Catskills from the Hudson's east bank. The mountains were supplying the kind of background so much admired in Europe, but no painter was yet entering the Catskills to paint its waterfalls, its far-ranging views, or its worn and broken rocks.

The Livingstons' American Academy paid young painters like John Vanderlyn to collect plaster casts of acknowledged masterpieces of ancient

This crude yet informative view of the Catskill Mountain House appeared in the *Rural Repository,* Hudson, N.Y., 1828. (*Courtesy of New York State Library.*)

The Van Bergen overmantel, the earliest known view of the Catskills.
(*Courtesy of the New York Historical Association, Cooperstown, N.Y.*)

Left, the oldest known engraving to show the Catskills is titled "A View in Hudson's River of Pakepsy & the Catts-Kill Mountains-from Sopus Island in Hudson's River, Sketch'd on the SPOT by his Excellency Governor Pownal, Painted and Engraved by Paul Sandby." The engraving was one of a group published in London in 1761 as "Six remarkable Views" of American scenery. The Catskills as shown here have lost much of their true character and become Europeanized. (*Courtesy of the New-York Historical Society.*)

Right, Thomas Cole. The portrait is by Cole's friend Asher B. Durand. (*Courtesy of the Berkshire Museum, Pittsfield, Mass.*)

Below, this pencil sketch titled "Lake of the Dead Trees" appears to be one of those made by Thomas Cole on his sketching trip to the Catskills in 1825. Its straightforward realism is in marked contrast to the romantic paintings Cole made from it in his studio. It was these paintings which established Cole as a major figure in American art. The sketch was made from the point at which the overflow of North Lake enters South Lake. (*Courtesy of the Detroit Institute of Arts.*)

"Sunny Morning on the Hudson" is an excellent example of Cole's
mature manner. It shows the Hudson River as seen from the neigh-

borhood of High Peak. (*In the Karolik Collection, Museum of Fine Arts, Boston.*)

The tannery chimney at Claryville in Sullivan County. (*Author's photograph.*)

This tracing was made in 1910 from a view of Prattsville drawn in 1835. The covered bridge and the roadside inn with sheds across the road for the shelter of horses and vehicles is typical of the days of heavy horse and drover use of main mountain roads. (*Greene County Clerk's Office.*)

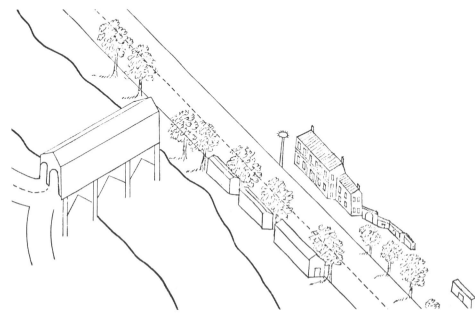

European sculpture and encouraged Americans to make copies of the works of the Old Masters. In their concern with the respectable art of the past, they remained unaware that a fresh and vital current was heading toward American art. Fostered by the romantic movement, the European interest in landscape was finding expression in paintings and drawings that went far beyond the pedestrian efforts of the older topographical artists. These works made little appeal to reason and aesthetic theory but instead stirred hidden layers of consciousness and awakened emotions of kinship with nature in all her moods. The romantic movement was beginning to transform European notions of the place in life of painting.

During the 1790s and the early 1800s the British public was being offered volume after volume of views of landscapes and ancient buildings presented by a newly improved method which Paul Sandby termed "aquatinta." No method of reproduction ever devised up to that time was the equal of the aquatint in conveying the romantic appeal of ruined abbeys, of moody skies from which a single ray of sunlight slanted down to illuminate a thatched cottage or an ancient castle. In aquatints, when at their best, rich meadows, distant prospects, and mist-shrouded mountains took on romantic overtones. The aquatint did much to prepare a wide public for accepting the work of the romantic landscape painters who were struggling toward the light in Britain.

By 1795 an English aquatint man named Parkyns arrived in New York and announced that he was about to prepare a series of aquatints of American views to be accompanied by descriptive text and a map, which would enable American amateurs of the romantic and picturesque to find their way to the actual spots to be depicted. Parkyns appeared to be hoping to deal with American scenery somewhat as Gilpin had done in Britain.[6] Parkyns' venture failed, for few Americans were ready to see their own land as a fit subject for art. The kind of intensely conservative feeling about art that animated the founders of the American Academy was widespread. But slowly a change began to take place. In 1816 DeWitt Clinton, who was then president of the Academy, must have made the Academy members purse their lips in doubt as he asked, "Can there be a country in the world better calculated than ours to exercise and to exalt the imagination—to call into activity the creative power of the mind, and to afford just views of the beautiful, the wonderful and the sublime? Here nature has conducted her operations on a magnificent scale; extensive and elevated mountains, lakes of oceanic size, rivers of prodigious magnitude, cataracts unequalled for volume of water, and boundless forests filled with wild beasts and savage men and covered with the tall oak and the aspiring pine. . . ."[7] Clinton urged American painters to deal with American subjects.

Three years later, Americans were indeed turning their eyes to the wonders of their country which Clinton, like Dr. Mitchill before him, had pointed out. Those with an interest in the arts were beginning to lose something of their devotion to plaster casts and copies of Raphael and Poussin. Washington Irving's *Sketch Book* and especially his "Legend of Sleepy Hollow" and "Rip Van Winkle" abounded in alluring little prose vignettes of American scenes. Soon a series of aquatints of American scenes was at last launched. It was published in 1820 under the title of *Picturesque Views of American Scenery*. Both the painter of the water colors from which the prints were made and the aquatint man were émigrés from England. The series was not completed for lack of public support, yet it made history, for in some of its plates the wonder of the American wilderness was hinted at for the first time, and the romantic approach to American painting was foreshadowed. A few years later a splendid aquatint series called *The Hudson River Portfolio* was delighting American leaders of taste. In it the Catskills were shown as they appeared from the city of Hudson. Like the *Picturesque Views,* the *Portfolio* was the work of Britons and its plates were colored by hand. But both helped open the eyes of American collectors, patrons of art, and young painters to new possibilities which might combine art, romantic feeling, and national pride.[8]

In Philadelphia a young leather currier and painter named Thomas Doughty had been employed to color plates of *Picturesque Views*. Doughty, helped along perhaps by his association with the transplanted version of British topographical painting exemplified by the *Views,* announced that he was giving up working with leather and would try to earn his living as a landscape painter. He sketched widely and by 1823 was exhibiting a painting of Niagara Falls and a Hudson River scene at the Pennsylvania Academy. By this time Doughty had found a patron, Robert Gilmor, Jr., a rich Baltimore businessman and collector of paintings. Gilmor encouraged Doughty to paint straightforward American scenes with the kind of piling up of detail which marked both of the recent aquatint series.[9] About 1820 someone, possibly Doughty, was employed by Colonel Edwards to paint a view of his tannery village along the Schohariekill. The painting is known at present only through an enthusiastic but crude copy made about 1880 to hang in a country store close to the site of the old Edwards tannery.

Doughty's landscapes attracted a good deal of favorable comment, but no one was more deeply stirred by them when they were exhibited in Philadelphia than Thomas Cole. Already Cole had made a beginning at drawing and painting landscapes. Now when he saw what Doughty and others had accomplished he felt discouraged and wondered if he could ever do as well.

52

Thomas Cole, Painter-Romantic

❧ ANYONE familiar with the vigorous promotional efforts of James Powers and his associates of the Catskill Mountain Association might be pardoned for wondering if Thomas Cole came to the Catskills at Powers' urging to paint pictures of the Association's scenic attractions. But there is no evidence—no presently visible evidence at any rate—that the Association had anything at all to do with the sketching trip Cole made to the Hudson Valley and the Catskills in 1825. He made the trip as the protégé of George W. Bruen,[1] a rich New York dealer in China tea. Bruen, like Robert Gilmor and many other American businessmen, was finding patronage of the arts, and especially the encouragement of American landscape painters, not only pleasant but useful as a symbol of elevated social status. European princes and the aristocrats of Greek and Roman society had patronized artists of all sorts to public applause. American businessmen, as they came more and more to great wealth and power, followed this example. And as they helped men like Doughty and Cole, or subscribed to the *Hudson River Portfolio,* they could glow with patriotic pride, for they were contributing to the praise of the beauty of their own nation.

George W. Bruen was a small-time patron of the arts. Even before Bruen had bought a landscape of Cole's (he saw it on display in the window of a shop), a greater patron had heard of Cole's work and had bought one of his landscapes. This patron was Robert Gilmor. Gilmor heartily encouraged Cole by paying him the same price for his work as he paid Doughty—it was fifty dollars.[2] So as Cole reached the Catskills in the early fall of 1825, he was, like Doughty, being subsidized on a sketching trip. Like Doughty, he was now of interest to collectors. Two years earlier he had stood in awe and humility before Doughty's landscapes and those of English-born Thomas Birch. Now he had some right to hope that he might soon stand beside Doughty as his equal.

The route over which Cole had found his way to the Catskills was filled with struggle and romantic incidents. He began life in a grim Lancashire mill town where his father found it impossible to change from the old handicraft methods of his woolens factory to the new mechanized ones. Some fifty miles away, and in the utmost imaginable contrast to the Cole family's surroundings, lay the beautiful Lake District where the poet William Wordsworth was giving expression in enduring verse to his feelings toward the mountains, the waterfalls, the lakes, and the simple people among whom he had settled. The Coles were a cultured family with the keen interest in poetry, painting, and music which the triumph of the romantic movement had made part of British life. There is no tradition that his parents ever took young Thomas on a pilgrimage to the Lake District. He was twenty-four before he found a lake district of his own in the shady vale near the Pine Orchard and its bustling hotel.

Even as a boy, Thomas Cole showed a decided inclination to draw and paint. That was why, after a brief experience of school in the ancient city of Chester, he became apprenticed to an engraver of blocks from which the charming floral and geometric calicoes of the day were printed. But this commitment to semiartistic labor did nothing to check Cole's sensibility. In company with a favorite sister he visited such romantic spots as old manor houses and landscaped parks of the gentry and there expressed his reaction by playing his flute while his sister sang. Such attempts at sending one art to the aid of another were usual among Britons of romantic leanings.[3] For to them the barriers that had kept the various arts from trespassing upon each other's territories were crumbling. But Cole's days of sharing, however mildly, in British romanticism were soon to end. His father was caught up in the wave of enthusiasm for emigrating to the American Midwest which swept his part of England during the years of business depression following the end of the Napoleonic Wars. The Coles did not find Ohio or western Pennsylvania to be the earthly paradise of which they dreamed and there the elder Cole repeated his British failures in a series of attempts at handicraft manufacturing of wallpaper, floor coverings of painted cloth, and other unrecorded ventures. Thomas helped his father or worked as a designer or engraver in Philadelphia. He aspired to become a portrait painter, but turned to landscapes, and it was then that he was so overwhelmed by the paintings of Doughty and Birch. Early in 1825 the elder Cole moved to New York to test yet another manufacturing hope. Thomas exchanged his cramped Philadelphia garret for an even smaller one on Greenwich Street in New

York. By that time Thomas Cole was thoroughly committed to the life of a
painter. In Philadelphia he had painted decorative canvases and portraits;
he had painted on the backs of chairs and on the sides of bellows. Yet
during this time of struggle to keep alive, his interest in landscape painting
had grown ever stronger and more compelling. It was at this point that
George W. Bruen sent him on the sketching trip which was to change the
direction of Cole's life and alter the look of the Catskills in the eyes of
Americans. Cole sketched that fall in the Hudson and Mohawk valleys, but
a good many painters had preceded him there. It was not until he reached
the still almost unpainted Catskills that he caught fire. To the end of his days
he was to protest that, although he had traveled widely and painted in
many places, the Catskills held first place in his heart.[4]

With Cole's discovery of the Catskill Mountains, the vale of the two
lakes and its vicinity became the scene of a remarkable romantic drama.
Irving had dealt with the Catskills in a mood of urbane detachment;
Cooper had devoted only a few pages to them. But Cole passionately
identified himself with the Catskills.[5] William Wordsworth believed that a
poet should have a strong tie with a particular region of the earth, prefer-
ably the one in which he was born. European painters of the early nineteenth century often dealt with a single region or a narrow range of natural
phenomena. England's John Constable was the son of a Suffolk wind
and water miller. He painted mossy old mills and waterside meadows
rich with moisture, and delighted in great windy skies with scudding
clouds. Joseph M. W. Turner began as a meticulous topographical artist.
Later he saw the world in terms of light, of luminous mists, of the glowing
sunlit spray of waves or waterfalls, of tangles of dewy leaves and stones
reflecting the colors of the rainbow. In Prussia, Caspar David Friedrich
painted along the shores of the Baltic. He used enigmatic figures, showing
only their backs to the observer as they pondered the mysteries of life and
nature. In 1825, as Cole headed for the Catskills, Samuel Palmer was
arriving in Shoreham in Sussex. There he lived for years and worked up
into his romantic visions the old churchyards, the bending fruit trees, and
the fields heavy with harvest.

Like all these painters, young Cole was what has since been sometimes
known as a "romantic realist."[6] He saw the natural world with remarkable
clarity and intensity and could give its meanest details universal significance once they had been transformed by his romantic sensibility.
William Blake, the romantic poet-painter, expressed this sensibility with
unforgettable force when he wrote:

> . . . To see a World in a Grain of Sand,
> And a Heaven in a Wild Flower
> Hold infinity in the palm of your hand
> And Eternity in an hour.[7]

In the fall of 1825 Thomas Cole first saw the whole world in the trees, the rocks, the waterfalls, and the mountains of the Catskills. It was then that they became to him what the Lake District was to Wordsworth. It didn't matter that their wilderness poetry was interrupted by burned-over fields, by snarls of dying branches, by clattering sawmills, and by the stinking wagons of tanners. It didn't matter that a huge hotel disfigured—to Cole's way of feeling—the clifftop from which a man might almost hold infinity in his hand. Cole overlooked these blemishes as a man overlooks the blemishes on the face of his beloved. He saw the Catskills fresh, as he might have said, from the hand of their Creator with all their beauty unsullied by thoughtless men.

Once he was back in his Greenwich Street garret, Cole used his sketches in four paintings, three of which dealt with the Catskills. Again a shop window became his exhibition gallery and again his paintings were noticed, not by ordinary citizens who wanted nothing more than something to relieve the blankness of a parlor wall, but by three men eminent in the world of American art. It is likely enough that word of Bruen's and Gilmor's interest in the young Englishman had come to their ears. The men were William Dunlap; engraver Asher B. Durand, who was soon to become a landscape painter; and the awesome John Trumbull, dean of American painters. Trumbull's amazement at Cole's work echoes down the years to our own time. "This youth has done what I have all my life attempted in vain!" Trumbull exclaimed.[8]

These first Catskill Mountain landscapes of Thomas Cole owed much to the usual manner of British topographical artists of the preceding generation. They were dry and unimaginative in color, with the paint laid on in a meticulous manner, almost as if the painter were engaged in taking a census of all the leaves and twigs in sight. Yet through all these inadequacies, Cole's romantic emotions made themselves felt. For there was far more in these landscapes than literal transcription of scenes. There was something in them that touched the emotions of Americans. When Cole was an English boy of five, William Wordsworth had written:

> There was a time when meadow, grove and stream,
> The earth and every common sight,
> To me did seem
> Apparelled in celestial light. . . .[9]

A similar celestial light shone from Cole's paintings and carried be-holders back to the days of their childhood when the glory of the natural world first made itself known through their innocent and eager eyes. And at the same time the landscapes had so unmistakably American a flavor that they made an observer feel a new pride in being an American.

William Dunlap showed his purchase to rich Philip Hone, former mayor of New York. The painting showed South Lake and some of the dead trees that stood on its shores probably as a result of a rise in the waters caused by a man-made dam. Hone offered Dunlap fifty dollars for the painting, which was double what Dunlap had paid.[10] And such were the necessities of theatrical and artistic existence in that day that Dunlap felt compelled to accept. At once remorse tormented him. He should turn over his profit to the poor young painter who had actually earned it, his conscience told him. But that Dunlap did not do. Instead he addressed a letter in praise of Cole to the editor of the New-York *Evening Post*. He told of Cole's early struggles, and of the privations he had suffered in his garret studios. He told of his trip up the Hudson and to the Catskills and finally of Cole's discovery by three fellow artists. The letter appeared on November 22, 1825. Dunlap signed it "American." At once Cole became the talk of New York. The tale of his success following years of struggle in order to interpret the American landscape endowed him with the air of an American hero. His link with the Catskills was recognized and he took his place beside Rip Van Winkle as an embodiment of a new and exciting aspect of the mountains.

Early in the summer of 1826 Cole was settled in a studio in the house of Mr. Bellamy of Catskill. There he was painting industriously from sketches made on his frequent trips into the mountains. And he was also writing prose sketches and verses inspired by the days and nights he spent wandering among the Catskills in a state of romantic exhilaration. In a notebook he entitled *Catskilleana,* and probably intended to be published, Cole wrote a tale called "The Bewilderment." It deals with an adventurous night in the mountains and foreshadows the mood of tales Edgar Allen Poe was soon to write. The hero, lost in a dark cave, says: "I felt a wild and vivid pleasure as I advanced. I shouted—sung—whistled for the very horror of the thing."[11]

In the pages of *Catskilleana* there are no tourists or tanners. But Cole turns settlers in isolated valleys into figures of romance which would have inspired Wordsworth. He quotes one settler speaking of pioneer days: "There were few of us then and we loved one another, and helped one an-other; but it is not so now."[12] In the paintings Cole produced that summer of 1826, it is easy enough to catch a similar nostalgia for a golden age when the wilderness of the Catskills was almost unbroken by man and only wandering Indians visited the two lakes. As Cole sketched, painted, or wrote that summer of 1826, he received encouraging letters from Robert Gilmor. Cole's use of dead trees in his views of South Lake struck Gilmor as excellent, and he advised the young painter to take as his model, Salvator Rosa, the baroque precursor of European romantic painting, for Salvator had used dead trees to notable advantage. Cole protested when Gilmor wrote that figures would give "character and spirit to solitariness itself . . . an Indian hunter judiciously introduced (even in shadow behind a tree, with a *catching* red light on a *red* plume or a mantle, with his rifle levelled and one or two deer crossing an open space, would not defeat your object, but rather assist the idea of solitude. . . .")[13] Before long, Cole was accepting Gilmor's suggestions and Indians and deer were becoming minor features in his paintings.

Robert Gilmor had visited the House on the Pine Orchard before 1826. He commissioned Cole to paint the establishment as it first appeared to a traveler on the road leading upward from Merchant Lawrence's (by this time Cole had replaced Doughty in Gilmor's esteem), but Cole refused. He saw the Catskills as a romantic wilderness and not as a goal for tourists. Gilmor took this rebuff in good spirit and accepted another painting which was guiltless of any hint of the House.[14] A year or two later Cole had a change of heart and painted the House from the exact spot Gilmor had specified. Through the late 1820s Cole's painting grew in breadth and boldness and his color became less somber. His landscapes of the Catskills, the White Mountains, and the Adirondacks sold almost as fast as he could turn them out. Under the influence of success Cole's ambitions soared. He painted dramatic biblical subjects and followed Doughty in trying his hand at paintings based on scenes from Cooper's novels. Meanwhile, he longed to visit Europe and study the works of the Old Masters. In 1829 a loan from Gilmor made this possible.

When Cole returned to the Catskills in the summer of 1833, he once again painted the mountains among which he had roamed eight years before. But the romantic delirium which had once held Cole in its grip had run its course. Cole painted the Catskills with ever greater skill and understanding. He protested over and over that the Catskills held the first place in his heart. But he was no longer an ardent and shy young romantic—he had become accepted as the leading painter of the United States and he was taking this position very seriously indeed.

53

"Public Confidence Is Shaken"

✤ THE CATSKILL MOUNTAINS to which Thomas Cole returned in 1833 were about to enter a decade and a half of tumult and change. During these years the Catskill Mountain House twice stood on the verge of extinction; the water wheels of the mountain tanneries sometimes stopped turning; and the idle barkpeelers and tannery teamsters found other work or starved. And finally the tenant farmers of the Hardenbergh Patent armed themselves and rose up in anger against their absentee landlords. The causes that brought about the fifteen years of turmoil were complex. But what set all these causes into motion was the pair of business and financial collapses that followed the orgy of speculation in the twenties and the early thirties.

It was late in 1833 that the first storm broke. As Philip Hone wrote on the last day of that year, "The change is melancholy and has fallen upon us so suddenly that men feel the blow and know not whence it comes. Public confidence is shaken, personal property has no fixed value, and *sauve qui peut* is the maxim of the day. . . ."[1]

Readers of books, magazines, and newspapers had every reason to feel confident that the Catskill Mountain House would weather the storm. For the House and the natural wonders around it were being lavishly praised, both at home and in Europe, even without prodding from James Powers. In 1828 a magazine of considerable literary reputation, the *Atlantic Souvenir*, had lauded the place and printed an engraving from Thomas Doughty's drawing of the Kaaterskill Falls. In 1826 the first dramatization of "Rip Van Winkle" made its debut in Albany, and by 1830 Londoners were being treated to another stage version of the tale of Rip. In 1830 the Mountain House itself was lugged bodily onto the stage in New York in a farce titled *A Tour of Niagara* written and staged by William Dunlap. The feature of the farce was its scenery. A panorama showing the banks of the Hudson was unrolled throughout one scene set on a Hudson River steamer; the Mountain House itself supplied the backdrop of another scene in which Rip Van Winkle figured; the Kaaterskill Falls with old Natty Bumppo as commentator gave interest to still another.[2] As if all this were not enough to boost the morale of the stockholders in the Catskill Mountain Association, poet William Cullen Bryant now chimed in and strengthened the image of the romantic wilderness of the Catskills already formed by Irving, Cooper, and Cole.

In the first of a proposed series to be edited by Bryant and called *The American Landscape,* the Catskills, both in plates by engraver-painter Asher B. Durand and in Bryant's text, are given a prominent place. Bryant wrote, "The traveller as he looks from the shore of the [Hudson] River to the broad woody sides of this mighty mountain range, turns his eye from a scene rich in cultivation, populous with human beings, and ringing with the sounds of human toil, to one of primeval forest as perfect as when the prow of the first European navigator divided the virgin waters of the Hudson— a wide sylvan wilderness, an asylum for noxious animals, which have been chased from the cultivated regions, the wild cat, the catamount, the wolf and the bear, and a haunt of birds that love not the company of man. . . ."[3]

Of the House on the Pine Orchard, Bryant had this to say: "For my own part, however, I am not sure that it does not heighten the effect of the scene when viewed from below, to know, that on that little point, scarce visible from the heart of the mountain, the beautiful and the gay are met and the sounds of mirth and music arise, while for leagues around the mountain torrents are dashing, and the eagle is uttering his shriek, unheard by human ears."[4]

Bryant's prestige was great among American romantics and nature lovers. In 1821 the final version of his *Thanatopsis* had appeared. It was a poem of truly Wordsworthian insight and majesty. Other poems followed and added to Bryant's position of authority among American cultural heroes. When this great man wrote that the Catskills formed an unbroken wilderness—well, that settled that. Pilgrims en route to the Mountain House might hold their noses as tanners' wagons passed by or rub their eyes when the smoke of forest fires made the mountain air thick and biting, yet they could console themselves by reflecting that they were in the midst of what the best authorities certified to be a wilderness Garden of Eden into which only the famous Mountain House intruded.

By 1833 the mere mention of the Catskills or the Mountain House was enough to bring a rush of pleasing romantic images into the minds of sensitive people. That summer, Frances Anne Kemble, the famous young English actress, set down some of these images in heated prose. As she caught her first glimpse of the Catskills from a Hudson River steamer, a fellow passenger told her "long stories like fairy tales, of caverns lately discovered in the bosom of these mountains, of pits black and fathomless, of subterranean lakes in gloomy chambers of the earth, and tumbling waters which fall down in the dark. . . ."[5]

"How I should like to go there," Miss Kemble exclaimed. "Oh, who will lead me into the secret parts of the earth, who will guide me to the deep hiding places, where spirits are. . . . ?" Thomas Cole had used similar images in his tale "The Bewilderment"; they show how neatly European mountain romanticism was being transferred to the Catskills. But not all writers gave the Catskills unstinted praise. Some, and these were usually Englishmen, found a little room for improvement. And their very criticism had a value to the directors of the Catskill Mountain Association because it showed the region in a cool and realistic light that did something to correct the extravagant comments of writers like Miss Kemble. When Henry Tudor, Esq., barrister of London, visited the Mountain House he found much to praise and a little to blame. "The House," Tudor wrote, "is one of the *choses à voir* in passing along the Hudson, which the tourist, whether of American or European paternity, neglects not to see. Latterly indeed, it has become, during three of the summer months, quite a place of fashionable resort, in consequence of the superior accommodations furnished by a handsome and spacious hotel lately erected there by a joint-stock company, and where the double advantage is enjoyed of a fresh and pure air during sultry weather, and of a magnificent prospect."[6]

Whatever may have been Tudor's skill as a barrister, as a writer he had an eccentric charm. And he never displayed this charm to better effect than when he told of his expedition to the Kaaterskill Falls. "Here," he wrote, "I first tasted the sweets of a corduroy road. This is composed of whole trees of which the leaves and branches have been divested, placed side by side, in a transverse direction, without the interstices being filled up so as to form something approaching to an even surface. The effect of such a turnpike, you may easily fancy, without much effort of imagination. We were jerked, and bounced, and tumbled about in a most unphilosophical manner, receiving withal sundry contusions, and undergoing the risk of various dislocations; and I believe, on balancing the account of profit and loss, after our return to the hotel to breakfast, beautiful and romantic as were, I confess, the falls and the scenery around them—setting off our bruises against the landscape, and our exhausted patience against the rocks and cascades—we found we had gained but little interest, in this instance, on our capital stock."[7]

If Henry Tudor had closely questioned the directors of the Catskill Mountain Association he might have learned that they were worse off than he was—they were getting no interest at all on their capital stock. For behind the façade of glitter and glamor their hotel presented to the public, skulked the specter of failure. Their venture had never showed a profit in dollars; its bills were often paid slowly; its notes went to protest with alarming regularity; it had fallen behind on its interest payments to the Catskill Bank. The Mountain House had succeeded as a romantic shrine, but even in the flush years before 1833 it had failed as a business venture.

The location of the Mountain House on its lofty cliff was among its greatest attractions but it was also a major drawback when it came to making the project pay. For every bottle of wine and every roast of beef enjoyed by guests, the hotel paid a tax to the Catskill Mountains in the shape of added transportation costs. The horses and oxen that hauled guests and supplies up the steep mountain road could not be expected to live long under the strain. A curve on the road is still known as Dead Ox Curve because an ox collapsed and died at that point. Tough and wiry horses known as "mountain horses" were used but they too often gave their lives in order that the Mountain House guests might eat and drink well. For in order to remain in business the Mountain House had to compete in material attractions with the many other summer resorts springing up among other mountains, at spas, and on the seashore.

As the thirties began, the Mountain House directors had a new source of uneasiness. From the days of Comfort and Bigelow, and probably even earlier, the sale of liquor had been a substantial source of income on the Pine Orchard. Now it was being threatened by the rise of the temperance movement. A Greene County Temperance Society was formed. In 1832 it claimed that one of every seventeen inhabitants of the village of Catskill was a habitual drunkard and that three hundred others were fast advancing toward that state by their growing devotion to the bottle. They claimed that all local crime and poverty were caused by drinking and that were the sale of alcoholic beverages to be prohibited, the county jail and its poorhouse could be closed and the taxpayers saved a vast sum. To many Catskill citizens the Mountain House with its busy bar and its hordes of sophisticated strangers began to seem one of the local "fountains of sin . . . pouring forth rivers of pollution and death upon the community. . . ."[8] One third of the inhabitants of the village of Catskill signed the pledge. Eight Catskill men who had been engaged "in the traffic in ardent spirits" turned to other means of making a living. But the directors of the Mountain House held firm, for without the income from liquor they would surely have had to abandon their already shaky venture.

While the first crest of temperance enthusiasm was racing over the Catskills in 1832, a bizarre ally was rushing to the aid of the Mountain House. It was the first American epidemic of Asiatic cholera. People in the Catskills took steps to combat the disease. In the town of Bethel in Sullivan County, a board of health was organized and plans were made to care for possible cholera victims.[9] In Woodstock the Reverend William Boyse led his flock in prayers aimed at sending the epidemic back to its birthplace. In jubilation Boyse told of his success: "The prayers of the church are heard. The Asiatic cholera is back away to the region of terror whence it emerged. Where is Asia? Whence is this dire pestilence?"[10]

The cholera did not invade the Catskills and as this became known, every inn and farmhouse among the mountains had its share of apprehensive city people. The Mountain House was crowded and because cholera was not known to have afflicted its guests, it gained vastly in reputation. During a later epidemic it was sometimes said of a locality that it was "as free from miasma as the Mountain House itself."[11] But even with the help of the epidemic the Mountain House management found the going hard as the season of 1833 opened. They announced a revised scale of charges. Board would be lowered to $10 per week. Erastus Beach, who operated the stage from Catskill, reduced his charge for the trip to the Pine Orchard from $1.25 to $1.00.[12] In spite of these bargain rates and a change of managers, the Mountain House went on losing money. It closed for the season that September on a dismal note: the new manager resigned. For some months the fate of the Mountain House was in doubt. That fall the dark economic storm that so disturbed Philip Hone made the future of the Mountain House appear even more doubtful. In the spring of 1834 the directors of the Catskill Bank took a step they had considered for some time—they foreclosed the mortgage they held on the Mountain House property and its chattels. The real estate was advertised for sale at public action on August 11. The furnishings would be sold on May 1.[13]

The listing of the Mountain House chattels in the advertisements of the sale seemed by their businesslike phrasing to laugh at the bright hopes that had led James Powers and his friends to set their House upon the Pine Orchard ten years before. "70 sacking bottoms for bedsteads, 70 sacking bottoms for cots, 24 settees, 6 wooden settees, 150 Windsor chairs, 53 screw bedsteads, 18 common bedsteads, 35 rose blankets, 100 marseilles quilts, one silver tea urn, 13 castors"—so the list began. Even the presence of "3 dozen fancy gilt chairs," "one piano forte," and "two billiard tables" could not keep the sale from sounding like thousands of others marking the failures of less ambitious projects which lacked the romantic and idealistic motivations that had urged on the directors of the Catskill Mountain Association.[14]

Behind the scenes the directors continued to struggle. The sales were postponed again and again. And even with the threat of death by public auction hanging over it, the Mountain House opened late in June with John Cuyler of Catskill hastily installed as manager. During 1834 a short-lived upturn in business activity encouraged many Americans in the belief that their economic woes had come to an end. The directors of the Mountain Association may have shared this belief, for they made the sacrifices needed to keep their venture alive as a thing of gaiety and glamor in the eyes of the public, and a source of sleepless nights and harried days to its investors. For the moment, at least, the Catskill Mountain House was saved.

In Edwardsville, a few miles west of the Mountain House, the colonel with the two-story head was arriving at a decision of his own during 1833 and 1834. Was this a good time to call it quits as far as the tanning business was concerned? And was it a good time to take final and irrevocable action to call off the pack of creditors who continued to pester him in spite of his bankruptcy and in spite of the passing of so many years since his Massachusetts failure? Edwards consulted his lawyer, James Powers of Catskill, and Powers agreed to work out a way of solving Edwards' problem.

54

Tanlords, Turnpikes, and Railroads

✤ IN 1833 the tanneries of the Catskills as well as the Mountain House felt the effect of the blow that struck the national economy. Earlier the price of leather had sometimes varied; now it fell sharply and decisively. Handicraft tanneries that had survived shut down and soon the large Swamp-dominated tanneries were in trouble. Smith and Schultz of the Swamp were building a large tannery near Margaretville but by September of 1833 they were offering it for sale. Other large-scale tanneries went on the market or closed down. Tanner Solomon Carnright of Shandaken tried to dispose of a one-quarter interest in his tannery. The place was full of leather and twelve hundred cords of tanbark stood ready for use. But with the price of leather sinking, buyers were slow in coming forward.[1]

An old-timer recalled in 1902 that all the tanneries he had once known in the Esopus Valley had met their ends by fire. "They were presumably well insured. . . . This is an economic way of ending the life of such manufactories,"[2] the old-timer added. In 1833 what amounted to an epidemic of tannery fires hit the Catskills. Many of the buildings that burned were not insured at all. Carelessness of the sort that afflicts every enterprise that isn't doing well was often the root cause. Tanneries were firetraps even when they were new and well kept. The dust that was a by-product of grinding tanbark lay thick on tannery floors and beams, and was fearfully flammable stuff. Smoking in tanneries was forbidden. Gilbert Palen had so intense a fear of fire that when he left the Kaaterskill Clove in 1831 to set up a tannery at Fallsburgh in Sullivan County, he forbade smoking even while his tannery was being built. The builder's men defied Palen's prohibition and when he tried to enforce the rule by flourishing a pistol, the men knocked him down. The trial of Palen's assailants in 1833 drew widespread attention and, in that year of raw nerves, sharpened hostility between tanners and their workers. The assailants were found guilty.[3] And Palen's caution paid off, for his tannery was one of the few in the region that did not end in flames. It stayed in business under Palen's strict fire rules for forty years.

As the price of leather continued to slide lower, many ineffectual proposals were made to check the decline. Worried men wrote to their local papers suggesting that the tanners of the Catskills unite to check falling prices, but just how this might be accomplished no one could suggest.[4] The operators of the haunted sloop *Martin Wynkoop* and the *Trumpbour,* "the largest and best sloops on the North River," announced that they would carry hides from New York to Catskill for only one cent per hide. Some tanners tried to take advantage of the fact that oak-tanned leather was still preferred to that tanned with hemlock bark. Especially in the southeastern parts of the mountains where oak trees abounded, Swamp-financed tanners turned from using hemlock and produced oak-tanned leather. At Ellenville, Abraham Schultz began making what was called "Union leather" with a mixture of 90 per cent hemlock and 10 per cent oak bark.[5]

A temporary flush of prosperity came to the United States with 1834, but the flush did not extend to the tanning industry. Colonel William Edwards reached the decision to which he had long been impelled both by his conscience and pressures exerted by his old creditors and the tanning slump. He authorized James Powers to draw up a plan whereby he would turn over his possessions to his creditors. His old debts, he stated, "were no longer payable under the statutes of limitations of New York and Massachusetts."[6] Yet "whereas it is impossible from [his] advanced age and natural infirmities . . . and the present unprosperous condition of the tanning business in which he has been engaged that he will be able to add to his property . . ." and "from a sense of moral obligation (although absolved from all legal obligation) . . ." he had concluded upon dividing his property among his creditors.

The old colonel's property listed by James Powers was by no means adequate to pay off his creditors in full, even with interest from 1815 omitted from the reckoning. A house and farm in Edwardsville, horses, a one-hundred-dollar interest in Edwardsville's parsonage, farm tools and household gear, a share in an insurance policy, a few saddles and stoves, a hundred shares of turnpike stock . . . Skepticism as to the old colonel's motives was widespread, especially when it appeared that his property was to be sold to his own sons and at a time when values in tannery towns were fantastically low. Years passed before James Powers completed the sale and division, and many were of the opinion that the day of reckoning would never come. But come it did and the colonel retired to live with a son in

Brooklyn in an atmosphere of the utmost comfort and piety. His creditors made the best of a settlement of something like twenty-five cents on the dollar. The amount of the indebtedness that had haunted Edwards ever since his Massachusetts failure was $93,114.31.

Colonel Edwards had made his settlement with the understanding that he would never again be gainfully employed. For the almost twenty years of life that remained to him he studiously abstained from all remunerative work. In 1852 he died at the age of eighty-two. His children believed that his abstention from gainful work for so many years had been the death of the old man. And perhaps they were right. For the colonel was no Rip Van Winkle who could take a twenty-year doze in his stride.

By the early 1840s the United States was emerging from the long slump which had begun in 1833 and reached its lowest valley in 1837. While old Colonel Edwards prayed and studied his Bible in Brooklyn, the New York Tannery was doing well under the management of young Colonel Edwards, in whose name the tannery stock had been held for more than fifteen years. The young colonel was trying to sell the tannery and before too many years he would succeed, but while he managed it, he managed it well. He made a "bark road" through the awesome Stony Clove and so was able to fell the hemlock forests of the long valley running southward to what is now Phoenicia. The Clove had been so narrow and so choked with great masses of fallen rock that people had laughed when the young colonel proposed building his road. But the road was built and one man recalled that, "I have seen ten to twenty of his [Edwards] teams come home at night in Winter with full loads of hemlock bark, two cords each, drawn through the notch. . . ."[7] By this time the hemlocks closer to Edwardsville were gone, but by using those beyond the notch, the New York Tannery was rejuvenated. By 1849 it was tanning 26,000 hides per year and it was predicted that the Edwards tannery would outlast all others in the upper Catskills.[8]

Tanner Zadock Pratt, when he used up the Prattsville hemlocks, tanned elsewhere in partnership with a number of other men. He tanned in Windham and in Samsonville in Ulster County, where his partner was Henry A. Samson, who was to become a general. Other tanners who had been active in the Greene County part of the Catskills moved southward and some left the state for the hemlock forests of northern Pennsylvania. The war with Mexico of 1846 gave a powerful impetus to tanning and it raised profits high enough to attract new capital and energy. Under its influence none of the Catskills' large stands of hemlock was safe. Even the Livingstons, who had once looked askance at the reckless slaughter launched in the Catskills

by early tanners, now began to sell bark rights and land to tannery operators. And so some dense groves of hemlock around which the tanning flood
had flowed now met their doom.

Tannery workers were not well paid and their work was unpleasant
and often dangerous, which was why many of them were recent immigrants
from Ireland, Germany, and elsewhere. Some of the oldest Roman Catholic
churches among the Catskills were founded to serve Irish barkpeelers and
tannery workers. The Church of St. Mary of the Mountain in Hunter was
organized by 1840. The German Catholic church of Fallsburgh was organized about 1860 by German tanners.[9] David Friedman, who was a Ger-
man-Jewish immigrant, worked in the Edwards tannery during the 1840s;
later he was a respected dry-goods dealer in Saugerties and for a while the
owner of a small tannery there. For the tanneries, while they brought death
to the Catskills' hemlocks and to many of their workers crushed beneath
falling trees or rolling logs, also gave fresh opportunity to some. Most tannery workers followed their bosses to Pennsylvania and then moved westward. But a good many remained to farm the soil of narrow hollows whose
hemlocks they had helped destroy. Irish-born John William Mackay is said
to have worked as a Shandaken barkpeeler while in his teens; later he became a Nevada mining magnate. Dennis Hylan, who worked for the New
York Tannery, settled in the vicinity where some of his descendants still
live; one of them, John F. Hylan, went to New York and became the city's
mayor.[10]

The outbreak of the Civil War, with its immense demand for leather,
brought the tanners of the Catskills their last great opportunity and gave a
final blow to the mountains' famous groves of hemlock. In Sullivan County,
tanneries multiplied. James Quinlan said that the Civil War was fought on
boots made of Sullivan County leather. In Shandaken, hemlock trees had
grown in amazing abundance—the very name of the place is derived from
the Algonkian Indian words for hemlock. There throughout the war, James
A. Simpson tanned hides sent up from the Swamp to his Phoenix Tannery
which gave its name to the hamlet of Phoenicia. In 1843 he and a partner
from Woodstock had taken over an older Shandaken tannery and were, in
good time, to take advantage of both the Mexican and Civil War leather
booms.[11]

During the expansive years of the 1820s, many new turnpikes had
been planned in order to make stands of hemlock trees as well as tracts of
absentee-owned land at a distance from the Hudson more easily reached.[12]
But through the years of hard times that followed 1833, many turnpikes
were neglected or partly abandoned. And the tanneries that had the most

expensive methods of moving their hides from and to the Hudson were likely to be the first to shut down. By the 1830s Sullivan County tanners and those in the southeastern part of the Hardenbergh Patent had a decided advantage over those elsewhere in the Catskills, for ever since 1828 they had been able to ship their hides and the ground tanbark they supplied to the Swamp tanneries over the Delaware and Hudson Canal. The canal had been built in order to provide a cheap method of carrying coal from the mines of northern Pennsylvania to the tidewater Hudson at Rondout; for anthracite coal, widely used to heat houses by the 1820s, had at last become worth mining and selling. The canal also carried passengers and a great variety of goods.

Another and much longer canal to the north was playing a part in discouraging tanners in the northern Catskills. The Erie Canal was opened for traffic in 1826 after more than a generation of hoping, planning, and working. It brought many good results to the people of the state of New York, but to many who lived among the Catskills, the Erie Canal was a disaster. It greatly lowered freight charges on goods brought from the west and so increased competition with the farm products, the leather, and other manufactures of the Catskills. It dealt a body blow to the Susquehanna Turnpike which had enjoyed a fantastic success since 1800. Emigrants bound westward poured over the turnpike by the thousand. Wagonloads of butter, hay, hides and leather, firewood, castings made in mountain mills, planks, wood turnings, oars, and a host of other products all rolled over the turnpike to the Hudson River. But with the opening of the Erie Canal the flush days of the Susquehanna Turnpike came to an end, though it continued in business on a reduced scale, and the large and comfortable roadside inns entertained travelers night after night. (One of these inns has been transported to the Farmer's Museum at Cooperstown, New York, where it may be seen furnished as it was in the days of the turnpike's glory.)

As the Erie Canal was in its planning stage, Catskill men had urged that their town become its terminus on the Hudson. The canal, they claimed, could hug the northeastern base of the Catskill Mountains. The men were disappointed when their plan was rejected but they did not give up. A new means of transporting goods had come into the world and was being talked about in Catskill and elsewhere—it was the railroad. As early as 1825 an Atlantic and Mississippi railroad which would cut through the hemlock wealth of Sullivan County was being discussed. It would use horsepower and not steam, for "animal power may be considered the natural power of the country,"[13] so its managers sagely observed. That same year the Catskill men (one of them was Orrin Day, president of the prosperous Tanners'

Bank) proposed building the Canajoharie & Catskill Railroad to restore the business lost by the town to the Erie Canal. Unlike canals and rivers, it could function the year round. It would use horsepower at first but as traffic increased might turn to steam. After many delays part of the railroad was built and for about two years it carried passengers and miscellaneous freights as well as hides and leather for tanneries in the northeastern Catskills. The collapse of a bridge in 1840 wrecked most of its rolling stock and put it out of business forever.[14]

Elsewhere in the Catskills other short railroads were hopefully projected by mountain tanners eager to find an economical way of tapping still untouched hemlock groves. Early in 1837, Asa Bigelow of Malden on the Hudson planned one to run from his town through Woodstock and Mount Tremper to Shandaken. There were tanneries all along the route and their proprietors enthusiastically supported the road until the worsening of the American economy later that year put an end to this and many similar schemes.[15]

Months before the Erie Canal was opened in October 1825, landowners and businessmen in the region of the Catskills and the parts of New York that bordered Pennsylvania were demanding that the state finance railroads which would make up to them for the help given by the state-financed Erie Canal to the central and western parts of New York. Lucas Elmendorf was an especially conspicuous battler on behalf of landowners and speculators of the Catskills. The pressures put on the legislature succeeded, and by 1851 the dream of an Atlantic and Mississippi railroad had given way to the reality of the New York & Erie running between Piermont, New Jersey, and Elmira, New York. It followed the western bank of the Delaware instead of piercing the heart of Sullivan County. The road opened with impressive ceremonies. President Millard Fillmore rode on the first train, and old Daniel Webster, seated in a rocking chair lashed to a flat car (he didn't want to miss any of the fine scenery), whizzed across the countryside, aided, they say, by an occasional dose of his favorite medicine, an old remedy known as whiskey.[16] The New York & Erie opened up to exploitation huge stands of still untouched hemlocks which were to fall by the thousands during the Civil War years.

Railroad hopes were not alone in the minds of tanners and landowners of the Catskills as the New York & Erie was planned and built. New highways were constructed during the 1840s and 1850s and old ones were improved. By the end of 1850 one of the Catskills' oldest roads was largely rebuilt to meet the needs of the tanners. William Cockburn had first showed this road on a map in 1765—it was the one leading up the Esopus Valley and over the Pine Hill into what was to become Delaware County. In 1802 Frederick Augustus DeZeng rebuilt it on behalf of Chancellor Livingston and other great landlords, and it then became the Ulster and Delaware Turnpike. The turnpike, in its new incarnation, was floored with heavy hemlock planks—a dream of salvation by plank roads was then cheering many Americans. Until the Civil War leather bonanza ended, the road held up well. Then, as its planks rotted and were not replaced, it became a stimulus to profanity unrivaled in the entire region of the Catskills. But in its heyday during the 1850s and 1860s, the smooth plank road was one of the wonders of its part of the Catskills. During the 1890s, Abram W. Hoffman, the Kingston editor, recalled that at one time it had not been unusual to see fifty teams following closely behind each other on the plank road. Seven tanneries in Shandaken and five across the Pine Hill in Delaware County used the road. Shandaken tannery teamsters took three days to make the round trip to and from the Rondout wharves with loads of finished leather or "vile smelling hides."[17] Hoffman remembered the many inns and taverns that had lined the road to comfort and care for the teamsters who passed their doors in such great numbers. He remembered the names of some of these inns: "The Hog's Back, the Stratton Place, Garrison's, Kline's, Slosson's, Terry's . . ." Farmers taking produce to market stopped at the inns. So too did drovers with their cattle, hogs, sheep or turkeys, all headed for market under their own power. While the drovers rested in the inns, their animals ate and dozed in the capacious sheds attached to every roadside inn and the turkeys roosted through the night in neighboring trees. A turkey drover, one old-timer recalled, had to use good timing, for as dusk approached, his birds would make for the trees whether there was an inn for their master conveniently close or not. Stagecoaches thundered along the old plank road. So too did horsemen carrying the United States mail. Peddlers urged on their old horses. Surveyors and land speculators came and went. At the height of the tanning days, the road was a thing of romance as well as use to the people who lived in the part of the Hardenbergh Patent through which it passed.

Seventy years ago, reminiscences of old-time stagecoach drivers were being printed in newspapers circulating among the Catskills. One printed in the Pine Hill *Sentinel* on October 30, 1906, conveys in rough yet vigorous verses much of the romance of Ulster and Delaware stagecoach days. It begins:

How dear to my mind are the old coaching days,
With eight months of wheeling and the other four with sleighs,
When the crack of the long whip created a commotion,

And the four big prancing horses were set in speedy motion.
How we rocked, how we rolled over hill, and over dale
So that when we reached a stopping place the passengers looked pale.
For along the banks and dugways, at a fearful pace we went
So a two or three inch diversion, to 'Davy Jones locker' might be sent.
Yet the 'jehu' was a trusty man who knew his horses well
And to handle gracefully, caused his breast with pride to swell.
So from Hudson to the Delaware, a full day was spent,
In a thorough braced stage coach, as thro a mountain country went. . . .

The verses go on for many more lines filled with detail of stagecoach operation and personalities.

Once the Civil War came to an end, the tanneries of the Catskills began vanishing. Some lingered on through the 1870s and a few to the end of the century, but the postwar railroad-building boom came too late to affect them. By then the great hemlock groves of the Catskills were gone and steam power was taking the place of water power in industry. Old-timers remember that after the Ulster & Delaware Railroad worked its way from Kingston to Oneonta in the 1870s, it hauled tanbark from outside the Catskills to a few diehard tanneries which could no longer produce their own. But these tanneries, too, soon faded away and the heart of the tanning industry moved from the Atlantic coast to the Midwest.

Wherever groves of giant hemlocks once stood in the Catskills, signs of the tanning days can still be seen—in eroded hillsides, in decay-resistant bits of charcoal often buried deep in the soil, in the presence of immigrant European plants such as oxeye daisies, Queen Anne's lace, European grasses and clovers which long ago seized parts of the living space once held by hemlocks. Memorials to the old tanlords are plentiful, not only in the names of tanners' towns such as Prattsville, Palenville, and Samsonville, in Pratt's Rocks and the Colonel's Chair, but also in once-utilitarian stone structures to which time has given something of the air of consciously created memorial towers. These are the tall and massive tannery chimneys which still stand here and there. One at Claryville keeps alive the memory of three tanners named Cook, Bushnell, and Reynolds who came here in 1848. A similar chimney which once served the Liberty Falls Sole Leather tannery of Isaac Horton is now irreverently used as a TV tower.

The humble tannery workers also have their memorials in stone. Climbers of many mountainsides among the Catskills often wonder at the almost endless stone walls crisscrossing the forested slopes. They see, too, great mounds of rocks carefully raised under century-old oak or maple trees. And often they wonder at columns of stones raised higher than a man upon flat boulder bases. Some climbers return to the world below with tales of having discovered ancient Indian enclosures and ruined temples near which they saw stone columns marking the burial places of Indian chiefs and princesses. What they have seen are often enough memorials to the tannery workers who tilled little farms from which the hemlocks had been cleared. The soil on these farms was at first rich with humus. But every rainfall carried off a burden of soil from the tilled fields and exposed a crop of stone. The stones were gathered into heaps—the smaller ones by the children of the family—and later were hauled in stoneboats to be worked into walls. The mounds and columns are no more than surplus stones heaped up so as to occupy a small as possible part of the fields.

The lore and legends of tanning days are dying out in the mountains. Sometimes a tanner's knife or the tool used in peeling bark (it was called a spud) comes up for sale at an auction. And often enough, unless there is a collector of old tools present, no one knows what it is. A few old people still tell of having seen, rotting in the woods, the log bunkhouses in which barkpeelers lived. Or they offer, should their lumbago ever desert them, to guide inquirers to a place in the mountains where a pile of hemlock bark was never collected and is visible as a mossy heap among the ferns—one such pile is said to remain high on Panther Mountain.

Local historians of a generation or two ago sometimes set down bits of the lore of tanning days and so kept them from extinction. They told of how tanner Simpson of Phoenicia tried to cure himself of lung trouble by sitting over one of the vats in which his tanbark was steeped. Every day he inhaled the hemlock vapor until he became well again—he had tanned his lungs. Old-time local historians also hint at the roughness and toughness of tannery days. One tells of the heavy drinking of "rum, cherry brandy and cider" which prevailed—at times rum cost only twenty-five cents per gallon. Men drinking during their off hours in a roadside inn would sometimes fight on the barroom's sanded floor, "a dozen men in one grand knock-down fight in the manner of an old-styled 'ring-wrastle.'"[18]

Seventy years ago Abram W. Hoffman recorded the reminiscenses of several barkpeelers. One told of working in the Big Indian Valley when he was only thirteen years old. He lived in a log hut 16 by 20 feet in size. "There were two beds, a fireplace, a small stove, some benches and a table in the one room downstairs. Above there was a loft where the men slept on the floor. There was a ladder alongside the chimney leading upstairs, and right under that ladder there was a big black bear chained. I tell you my eyes stuck right out when I saw that bear, for I had come down from Prattsville, where there was a village. There was an old woman cooking and smoking a pipe over the kettles. In that house lived the owner and his wife, six children, four workmen, the bear, and a couple of dogs."[19] It isn't likely that a similar aggregation of living things will ever be found under one roof in the Catskills again, for their tannery days are over for all time.

"Accommodations of the First Character"

❧ MANY DESCENDANTS of the Dutch and German settlers of the Hudson Valley must have smiled smugly in 1833 as their predictions of disaster for the Yankee Palace seemed about to come true. But their smiles were premature. The Palace continued to feed and shelter guests as usual to the end of the season. By 1834 the upswing in the economic cycle came to the aid of the directors of the Association. The same upswing—brief as it was to be—set off a renewed national orgy of speculation, especially in western lands. British capital poured into the United States to finance new railroads and canals as well as flutters in land.

The landlords of the Hardenbergh Patent could not use their lands as an admission fee to the orgy. The success of the Erie Canal which lowered the value of their mountain acres made them unattractive to speculators.[1] Many mountain people were leaving for western New York and for Illinois, Michigan, and Indiana. "Westward Ho! is the order of the day,"[2] one Ulster County man wrote. In March 1835, David Brown, a former Sullivan County man, wrote to his old friend Severyn Hasbrouck, who was postmaster and storekeeper at Woodbourne, of his enthusiasm about the advantages of the West. Brown had settled in Lockport on the Erie Canal and he was thinking of moving farther west. "From what I can learn of the western country," Brown wrote, referring to Illinois, "I think it far before Sullivan County. I am well persuaded a farmer in this country can live much easier and with much less labor than he can where you live but I suppose you eastern fellows think when you get out in this country you are clear out of the world but if they would come out here they would think they were just getting among folks . . . and I dont know but it is as healthy here as it is in Sullivan County. . . ."[3]

Young and adventurous people like David Brown took off for the West but more cautious men and women hesitated, and a good number concluded to stay where they were. After all, life among the Catskills had certain advantages even to a small tenant farmer. The rights of estover in the commons of the old landholdings continued to be available to most tenants—they could cut firewood, stone, or timber for their own use whenever they needed it. Many made maple sugar each spring on the commons. The small water-powered industries scattered among the mountains could give a farmer a small cash income if he was willing to do teaming or woodcutting or charcoal burning for part of the year. His sons might peel bark for tanneries or trap fur-bearing animals. The butter his wife made had a ready market at the Hudson River wharves. Trout still abounded in those mountain streams uncontaminated by tanneries, and during the 1830s a man could catch hundreds of them in an afternoon. In the winter when fresh meat was hard to come by, the humblest mountain family might feast on venison or "deer meat" as they called it. For deer were more numerous than in the mountains' wilderness days; they increased as they fed on the brush which sprang up on recently cleared land.

In the winter, deer might be killed by a method known as "crusting." Sometimes an icy crust formed on the snow and became strong enough to support the weight of a dog or of a man on snowshoes but not of a deer. Under these conditions, reported a newspaper writer of January 1834, "rifles are needless, as the deer when overtaken make no resistance. Their legs are lacerated by the ice. . . . Whole droves are sometimes caught and their throats cut."[4] In December of 1833 the snow covering the Catskills crusted. Then there began "a season of carnival with the famished wolves, the curs and their masters. . . . One individual in a single week killed upwards of forty [deer] without firing a gun. In the town of Windham one of the largest bucks ever seen in that vicinity was killed unresisting by a boy who clambered on his back and cut his throat. He was described as being a "patriarch of the forest with hair almost white with age and antlers like an old-fashioned armchair."

Many mountain people disapproved of crusting. But the practice continued because it supplied food and the money which venison and deer hides brought. In the same way the slaughter of wild pigeons was a feature of mountain life during those years when the beautiful but almost helpless pigeons arrived in immense numbers. The Big Indian and Neversink valleys were known for the quantities of pigeons who fluttered down in early spring to nest and gathered to eat beechnuts by fall. 1840 was remembered as a "great pigeon season"[5] and so was 1860 when the

Neversink Valley was said to have been "literally alive with them [the pigeons]; they cover an area of some nine miles by about two in width, up and down the valley." Squabs were taken from their nests and their necks wrung, older birds were trapped and shot and clubbed. Ira Beadle of Oliverea recalls hearing his father describe pigeon netting. The net with sticks supporting it was rigged above a spot where beechnuts lay thick. The netters hidden nearby pulled cords attached to the sticks and so let down the net on the feeding birds. Squabs were shipped in bulk on Hudson River craft with ice used to keep them in edible condition until they reached New York markets.[6] Older birds were shipped alive in crates. By 1871 John Burroughs could write in his *Wake Robin* that the huge flocks of pigeons which had once bent down the trees of the Big Indian and Neversink countries had dwindled to "a few pairs" of nesting birds.[7] In 1902 regional newspapers reported claims of sightings of a few pigeons—after that there was silence. One of the wonders of life on the American continent had come to an end and with it a supporter of human life among the Catskills.

There was still another advantage to living in the Catskills which grew instead of declining. This advantage was not of great economic importance in the 1830s, yet it was destined to grow year by year and would eventually become the Catskills' dominant source of income. This was the profit to be made by entertaining the people drawn to the Catskills by the ever-increasing reputation of the region as a place of romance, a place where city dwellers might find relaxation close to nature and as a hunting and fishing ground.

Even before the tale of Rip Van Winkle's adventures while hunting in the Catskills brought the region to the notice of the world, parties of hunters and fishermen had begun to arrive. Many of these sportsmen were touched by romantic feeling and became interested observers of waterfalls and other scenic wonders. They hunted or fished in such wild spots as the Stony Clove and marveled at the Clove's caves in which ice often remained the year round. They jumped up and down on the mat of vegetation afloat as an island on the little Clove Lake, later to be known as Devil's Lake.[8] They fished the Esopus and the Delaware, the Willowemoc, the Sawkill and the Beaverkill. Men like these hired local farmers as guides, and spent nights as lodgers in mountain farmhouses or in native hunters' cabins.

Early settlers in the more traveled valleys among the mountains had often functioned as innkeepers in a small way and some, like Merchant Lawrence, went on, if their locations were favorable, to stress the innkeeping side of their personalities and to become well-known among the fishermen and hunters who came from New York City, Albany, and other urban places. In 1819 William Darby of New York reported that he'd been told that it was an easy matter to obtain a night's lodging almost anywhere in the Catskills in the humble homes of its settlers.[9] By the 1830s Milo Barber's inn close to the Esopus in Shandaken was becoming a favorite of trout fishermen. By the 1840s a writer for the Catskill *Democrat* praised the place and said that "any quantity of trout may be taken by those skilled in that delightful recreation" in the Esopus Creek near Barber's, while enjoying "accommodations of the first character, every attention being paid by the obliging Mr. Barber and his attentive lady. . . . The scenery of the neighborhood is of the most romantic kind."[10]

By the 1830s the fine streams and lakes of Sullivan County were well known to fishermen. In 1832 Charles Fenno Hoffman, who was then beginning a brief but notable career as poet, editor, and novelist, told of watching a six-pound trout being taken from Sullivan County's White Lake. Not long after, a boardinghouse was built at the lake for summer visitors. More and more often the Catskills were mentioned in newspapers, magazines, and books as an excellent and conveniently located paradise for hunters and fishermen. The painters who were attracted to the Catskills by Thomas Cole's success took to traveling the mountains with a paintbrush in one hand and a trout rod in the other. Landscape painter Asher B. Durand was painting and fishing from bases in local inns and farmhouses by the 1840s, and he was often accompanied by students who might acquire painting and fishing skills simultaneously. No painter-fisherman was more enthusiastic about the Catskills than Henry Inman, the fashionable portrait painter who delighted in working on Sullivan County fishing scenes. Upon Inman's death in 1846 it was written that "in trout fishing especially he excelled. . . . A more ardent, accomplished or delightful disciple old Isaac Walton never had. In throwing a fly or spinning a mirror, he had few equals. . . . Hunting and shooting came in second and third."[11]

The air of romance that had given glamor to the vicinity of the Pine Orchard and the two lakes was beginning to spread by the 1830s to the rest of the Catskills. Paintings of the Delaware and the Esopus as well as of the two lakes and the Kaaterskill Falls were appearing in exhibitions. In Sullivan County a young lawyer named Alfred B. Street was writing poems which invite comparison, because of their loving recital of the natural beauties of the region and their glamorizing of pioneer days, with the landscapes of Thomas Cole.

The spreading of romance and a love of the wilderness was reflected in the changes taking place in the old frontier inns—Barber's was not the only one to change. In Roxbury the town's oldest inn, set up in a small way in 1798, grew by the 1840s into the romantically named Hendrick Hudson House. Years earlier it had been a noted haunt of trout fishermen. As time went on the inn became more elegant, and by 1846 it was even featuring baths. The management could boast of "a fine fall of pure mountain water within view of the hotel, where you can resort and have a bath which far surpasses any shower bath. . . ."[12] The inn went through a series of progressively more sophisticated incarnations until it succumbed to the bulldozers of a highway building project in 1965. In Woodstock the presence of two glass factories and a tannery as well as a position on a road leading into the heart of the mountains had prompted the opening of several inns where urban fishermen and hunters and city dwellers eager for a breath of country air or safety from an epidemic were rubbing shoulders by the 1830s with local patrons or those traveling on business.

Just before the storm of 1833 struck, Woodstock became the scene of an attempt to set up a rival to the Catskill Mountain House. This was the first of a long series of such efforts. Its site was to be a plateau high on Overlook Mountain, then known only as South Peak or Woodstock Mountain. The site had many parallels with that of the Catskill Mountain House. It commanded a magnificent panoramic view which many later connoisseurs in such matters were to rank well above that from the Pine Orchard in variety and extent. Nearby was a lake known as Schue's Pond. The Plattekill Clove was not too far away for its waterfalls to become possible attractions for guests at the proposed hotel.

In the hopeful days preceding the crash of 1833, James Booth of Woodstock had hacked a trail passable on foot or on horseback to the site of his venture in hotelkeeping. There he had built what he called "a temporary Mountain House"[13] which he proposed expanding into a large structure he hoped might appeal to the same people who were finding the Catskill Mountain House so attractive. In the newspaper publicity attending Booth's disclosure of his plans, he showed very plainly that he understood the sources of the appeal the Catskills were making to the urban public. He wrote that at his hotel, "secure from dust and the noises and perplexities of city life, the artist, the merchant, the traveller and all others may find a refreshing retreat from the rays of a summer sun, abounding with scenery, hunting and fishing grounds in its vicinity, for the amusement alike of the sportsman, the poet, and the philosopher." James Booth's syntax may have been shaky but his meaning was clear. He made it even clearer on July 4, 1833. On that day he played host at dinner in his temporary Mountain House to a group of well-heeled men, many of whom were from Saugerties. It was Booth's hope that these men who had ascended the mountain on horseback over his trail would agree to finance a magnificent "Summer Mansion" on the mountain a little above "the prominence which is celebrated by the fishermen on the North River, for its resemblance, as they imagine, to a *minister's face."* (The prominence is still known by that name.)

The upper slopes and summit of Overlook had changed but little since Peter DeLabigarre described the mountain in 1793. Its lower parts had been denuded of their forests by tanners and glassmakers; the tanners had taken oak and hemlock bark from the southeastern slope, and the glassmakers had used the hardwoods of the northern and western slopes. But the summit was still well covered, largely with spruce and balsam fir trees. Booth's guests that Fourth of July were favorably impressed with the site. One wrote that "if there is anything between heaven and earth that can regale the romantic imagination, it is here. . . ." After enjoying the view over the Hudson Valley, as seen through the "salubrious and elastic air" which enveloped Overlook, the guests proceeded to amuse themselves in a way becoming quite customary in the Catskills. The slow retreat of the last ice sheet to cover the Catskills had left many large boulders stranded on the mountains' higher ledges. These were dislodged sometimes after several days' preparatory work and sent careening down the mountainside, leaving behind a battered trail of wreckage. Booth's guests sent several rocks rolling "from the lofty pinnacle which precipitated themselves almost to the mountain's base." Then they "returned home, highly gratified and inspired with admiration in the scene which we have enjoyed of tracing nature up to nature's God." Hardly had Booth made his appeal to the men he hoped would back him when the economic storm of 1833 broke. The old Catskill Mountain House survived the storm. But James Booth's did not.

Elsewhere in the United States a drift toward summer living among mountains and on the seashore was gaining momentum, and during the speculative years of 1835 and 1836 it gathered speed. Romantic scenery was being exploited by men willing to invest substantial sums to give the public what it seemed to want. At Saratoga, New Lebanon, Niagara Falls, Lake George, Trenton Falls, and other attractions, summer hotels were enlarged. The population and wealth of the United States were increasing amazingly; speculators were counting on an even more rapid future growth and were borrowing heavily from the days to come. Canal and railroad building schemes blossomed anew. In 1837 the boom collapsed, prices fell, and soon some state governments repudiated their bonds while Europeans bitterly resolved to invest no more in the United States. As the public felt the pinch, summer tourist activity slowed down. Once again the Catskill Mountain House was in trouble. Once again payments on its mortgage fell behind. The Catskill Bank took action to protect its investment. During 1838 foreclosure proceedings began and on January 1, 1839, a writ of execution was in the county sheriff's hands, empowering him to sell the Mountain House and its belongings at auction.[14]

As in 1834, the sale did not take place. It was a time of universal distress. The financial and business center of New York was half deserted. Nearly every businessman was insolvent. Yet few were forced into bankruptcy, for their assets would bring hardly anything at public sale and creditors preferred waiting for better times. Properties like the Catskill Mountain House which had a long record of losing money were simply unsalable at any price. The hotel opened for business late in June as it had for so many years. But now a new and able man was in charge as lessee. He was lean and lively Charles L. Beach, born of Yankee parents in a log house in what is now the town of Jewett. Beach was the son of Erastus Beach, who had had a monopoly to operate the stages linking the Mountain House with the steamboat landing at Catskill. Charles, like his father, was a stagecoach man, but his operations were on a far larger scale. In later years Beach liked to say that at the height of his success in the stagecoach business in the Hudson and Mohawk valleys, his stages ran a total of three thousand miles daily; in a week they traveled the equivalent of the circumference of the earth.[15] By 1839 Beach was so solidly rich that even the financial troubles of the time left him unaffected. From 1839 until 1846 the Catskill Mountain Association retained title while the hotel was operated under Beach's guidance, although not always under his direct management. On March 22, 1845, the hotel and its contents were put up at auction (the economic climate of the nation had improved by that time) and the property was "struck off and sold"[16] to Beach for only $5000. During the fifteen-month period that followed, the Association had the right to recover the property by paying off the Catskill Bank. This was not done and by the end of June 1846, the Mountain House became Beach's property. Even before his title became absolute, Beach had begun to transform the hotel and to set it on the path to a new and more glorious future.

Editor and social reformer Horace Greeley had sensed something of the shortcomings of the old Mountain House on his visit of July 3, 1843—

the hotel that year was under Beach's personal management. "Although nearly everything but milk and mountain berries must be hauled up from Catskill and New-York, his [Beach's] table would do honor to a hotel in the City, and the arrangements for the comfort of visitors are well-designed and ample, though the house itself about as inconvenient as possible, its windows port holes, its kitchen at one end while its dining room is at the other. . . ."[17] Attached to the hotel, Greeley noted, were four hundred acres of land which fed two cows and produced nothing additional except huckleberries. Much of the inconvenience of the hotel stemmed from its odd proportions. It was 140 feet long and much of it was only 24 feet wide—this enabled the building to present the largest possible front to travelers on the Hudson and to give as many patrons as possible a chance at the famous view from the "port holes" of their rooms. But it made operation more expensive since it added to the distances servants had to travel on their duties. Guests, too, had much walking to do within the hotel, for they entered at one end of the long building.

The old hotel had been a normal specimen of the "spa architecture" of its day adapted, with some awkward results, to an unusual site. Under Charles L. Beach's rule it became an outstanding triumph of the American phase of Greek Revival which had begun in England during the late 1760s with the publication of Stuart and Revett's *Antiquities of Athens* and blossomed in the United States after the late 1820s, in part under the influence of Byron's romantic poetry and the struggle of the Greek people for independence. In his authoritative survey called *Greek Revival Architecture in America,* Talbot Hamlin wrote that under Charles L. Beach the hotel "was brought up to date by substituting for the old slim columns a one-storey porch of thirteen square piers, which in turn supports an upper porch two stories high, of thirteen Greek Corinthian columns more squat than the normal proportions and crowned with the rich capitals of the Choragic Monument of Lysikrates."[18] Hamlin added that the building had "a certain superb daring, a true sense of scale and proportion, an almost breathtaking quality in its long horizontals and its sweeping colonnade crowning the precipitous cliff. It is a perfect expression of the joining of two great enthusiasms, for Greece and for nature; a wedding, unexpectedly successful, of Stuart and Revett with the Hudson River School painters."

Behind the noble new face the hotel now showed to the world, many practical improvements had been made by the end of June 1846. The old entrance was done away with and a new central one under a handsome Corinthian porch was built in the rear of the hotel. New furniture was

installed and suites of rooms were prepared, some of which had rooms
for servants attached. Guests no longer saw the view through "port holes"
but through plate-glass windows. A writer in the *Catskill Democrat* of
June 24 exclaimed that Beach had so "beautified" the hotel "that those
who have heretofore been visitors to this delightful spot would hardly
know it." Yet prudent Mr. Beach had not tried to outdo the Saratoga or
metropolitan hotels in elegance of furnishings. "The house is plainly,
though neatly furnished," wrote a correspondent of the Albany *Argus* of
August 14, 1846.

One feature of the new Mountain House would surely have been
familiar to old habitués of the place. This was the custom of bringing the
outdoors within by lining the walls of public rooms with balsam fir trees
and boughs and sending spirals of hemlock and laurel climbing up pillars.
Similar decorations were familiar in other resort hotels, but nowhere were
they used more lavishly than at both the old and the new Catskill Mountain
Houses. The fragrance of the balsam fir continued under Charles Beach to
pervade the hotel on the Pine Orchard as it moved into more than thirty
years of successful life.

The new Mountain House was kept as spick and span as a well-run
ship. Formerly when visitors penciled their names on the sides of the
building, no one had been very much disturbed. But Charles L. Beach
put an end to that. He forbade any name writing anywhere in the
building and established a scale of penalties. If a man wrote his name on
one of the Corinthian pillars he would have to bear the cost of repainting
the entire pillar, which would come to fifteen dollars. Those who scratched
their names on windowpanes with their diamonds would have to pay the
cost of replacing the glass.

While guests slept, a corps of invisible cleaning women with mops,
pails, and brooms restored the public rooms to their customary brilliance.
"Has Mr. Beach in his pay a troup of little 'mountain men' the hobgoblins
of legend, who in the weird hours of night silently do the sweeping and
dusting, the scrubbing and polishing?"[19] asked a reporter after almost
forty years of Beach management. Outside the gleaming walls of the
hotel the effects of the Beach touch and the Beach expenditure were
obvious. The old Association had never added to its landholdings of
something under four hundred acres bought during the first few years of
its existence. But soon Beach began taking advantage of every opportunity
to add to the hotel's surrounding lands. He bought "the whole riverside
[of the Hudson at Catskill] and the top of the mountain." "I am occasion-

ally asked to sell timber for spars," he reminisced in 1881, "but I reply that my price is $1000 per tree. My affection for this place is great and I wish to see the natural beauty of the mountain preserved for the enjoyment of the people."

In 1846 Beach did something quite different for the enjoyment of his guests. Up to that time rates had been somewhat elastic. An Englishman with a title and a prosperous air would be sized up and made to pay extra for his social exaltation. An obviously rich American expected to pay a little more for a room than a less important individual. The newly rich often took this as a deserved tribute and would have felt hurt if this kind of gouging were omitted. But Beach did away with all that as far as he could. A definite scale of prices was established so that people planning to visit the Mountain House could know in advance what it would cost. The price of each room was the same for an earl, a Hudson Valley landed gentleman, or a clerk who had scrimped for a year in order to enjoy a day or two at the Mountain House.

Long before 1839, James Powers had faded from his position of energetic leadership of the Catskill Mountain Association. His imagination and understanding of the romantic needs of the public had done much to establish that hotel and to give it the wide—even international—reputation upon which Beach could build. But by the 1830s qualities not possessed by Powers were needed if the hotel was ever to become a financial success. The kind of strict attention to detail, the scrupulous neatness, the ability to organize details of transportation and supply into an economical and efficient system while at the same time giving an outward effect of lavishness and carefree elegance were highly developed in Charles L. Beach. If any American could make a financial success of a temple of romance and nature worship, it was Beach.

As Charles L. Beach achieved his ambition to become sole owner of the Catskill Mountain House, the Great Hardenbergh Patent which stretched away mile after mile to the south and west was in an uproar. The ancient hostilities between landlords and tenants had erupted and were leading to armed conflict. The whole Hardenbergh Patent was talking about one such incident which had taken place in Woodstock just a few days before Beach bought the hotel at the sheriff's sale of March 22.

Thanks to the fact that the Pine Orchard was not included in the Hardenbergh Patent, Charles L. Beach could stand aside in safety from the nearby tumult. It was quite otherwise with Hardenbergh Patent landlords. Once again the titles to their mountain lands were being called in question. And never before had their tenants showed so great a determination to force reforms in the patent's prevailing system of land tenure and even to drag into the open the whole sordid tale of the patent's original granting.

56

Sheepskin Masks and Calico Gowns

✤ THE SAME "hard times" that pushed the Catskill Mountain House to the brink of ruin helped rouse the tenant farmers of the Hardenbergh Patent into rebelling against their absentee landlords in what came to be known as the Anti-rent War of 1839–45. The war, which was no war at all but a mere armed rebellion, was not born among the Catskills. It began in the valleys of the Helderbergs, the rugged hills which keep the Catskills company to the north. Then it crept step by step toward the Catskills.

Early in 1839 news of strange happenings in the Helderbergs found its way to farmhouses on the Hardenbergh Patent. Thousands of Helderberg farmers shared with their brethren of the Catskills the distinction of holding their acres as tenants of great landlords. Now the grievances of tenants like these were coming to a boil. Late in January the landlord of the Helderbergs and other adjoining regions had died. He was Stephen Van Rensselaer, owner of what had once been the manor of Rensselaerwyck. And rich and powerful Van Rensselaer had at least one thing in common with his poor tenants: like them he had been squeezed by the economic collapse of the thirties. His will disclosed that he was in debt to the tune of about $400,000, for he had been first a hopeful player and then a loser in the game of land speculation which helped bring about the troubles of the times.[1]

By an odd stroke of fate, Van Rensselaer's tenants owed him almost exactly $400,000 in back rents. Van Rensselaer had been an indulgent landlord who found it distasteful to press a poor tenant for his rent. He was also aware that it was to his advantage to have tenants who didn't pay rather than no tenants at all, and that an abandoned farm quickly lost most of its value. Under the provisions of Van Rensselaer's will, his heirs were given an uncomfortable choice. They must pay his debts from the proceeds of the back rents or they must pay them from the estate in which they shared. The heirs responded as might have been expected from people of their background. They took advantage of the laws which favored landlords and set about trying to collect the old rents.

What followed made enough noise to be plainly heard even in the most secluded valley of the Catskills. It came from the thud of horses' hoofs carrying sheriffs with eviction notices in their pockets, the tramp of militiamen trying to support the sheriffs, the crackling of fires over which kettles of tar were being heated in preparation for the tarring and feathering of sheriffs, the rolling phrases of orators addressing meetings of tenants who were uniting in their refusal to pay back rents until after the validity of their landlords' titles had been examined in court. Hardenbergh Patent tenants listened eagerly when they were told of Anti-rent leaders asking government officials why a tenant should pay rent to a landlord with a shaky title under a system that shackled a farmer's energy and initiative and was contrary to accepted American ideas. In Albany, politicians, who hoped to rise high with the help of Anti-rent support, coaxed and wheedled and applied pressure on their fellows and made whispered deals. Men of inherited money and position pounded their mahogany tables and denounced all Anti-rent sympathizers as levelers who were out to destroy civilization. Many clergymen declared from their pulpits that refusal to pay rent was an act of rebellion not only against landlords but against God who had created rich and poor and expected both classes to be satisfied with what He had done. Rich worshipers nodded in agreement: they were satisfied with their lot in life, why could not the poor show an equally pious acceptance of theirs? Young Van Rensselaer tenants meeting at crossroads taverns muttered threats against landlords and their agents, and as whiskey warmed them their threats grew louder. All this was heard and pondered by the tenant farmers of the Catskills.

During the late summer and early fall of 1839, the Anti-rent argument grew ever louder and more shrill. Election Day was coming and there was good reason to hope that when the votes were counted many Anti-rent supporters would be found to have been elected to the legislature. During earlier peaks of tenant discontent, only men who owned property could vote; the convention that changed the State Constitution in 1821 had given the vote to nearly all adult white males. This meant that in 1839 it was possible for tenant farmers to express their discontent at the polls. And this was what they did.[2]

James Powers of the Greene County bar and the Catskill Mountain House had represented the people of the Hardenbergh Patent in the state senate during the session of 1839. Powers was the agent of "purse-proud and aristocratic landlords"[3] of the patent, so an opponent charged. Thanks to the manipulations of politicians greedy for Anti-rent support as well as to the efforts of the voters, Powers vanished from the senate. His place was taken by dashing, Yankee-born Erastus Root, the shining hero of Hardenbergh Patent radicals. In the eyes of the rich and wellborn, General Root wore horns and a tail for he was a foe of all special privilege and a battler for such dreadful innovations as the abolition of capital punishment and human slavery and the widest possible extension of the franchise—he even favored equal rights for women. Although Root was an avowed skeptic in religion, the voters returned him to office year after year. His popularity survived even a long-remembered incident that took place beside the stove in the Delhi shop in which Deacon Abner Thurber made and sold "Castor, Rorum, Felt and Children's Fancy Hats" as well as "Ladies Beavers." The argument had turned upon the divinity of Christ. "I tell you, Deacon," the general said, "the man you call Christ was neither more nor less than the illegitimate son of a Galilean peasant girl."[4]

In the election of 1839, so many other friends of the tenants were elected with Root that it seemed for a while that control of the state senate would pass from the hands of landlords and their representatives although the Assembly remained under tight landlord control.

The Van Rensselaer heirs were taken aback by this development and hastily put added pressure on their tenants to pay up at once. But their tenants were now in too confident a mood to knuckle under. They defied the sheriffs and militiamen sent into the Helderbergs. Armed conflict on a substantial scale seemed imminent. Then Governor Seward brought reason to bear on the problem. He offered to withdraw the militiamen sent from Albany and to urge the legislature to make sweeping reforms in the Old World system of land tenure, if the tenants would cease resistance. The tenants laid down their arms and dispersed, for they trusted the governor.

The new legislature met on January 7, 1840, and the members heard Governor Seward demand that they change the old system of leaseholds. The members sat until May 14, when they adjourned without having accomplished anything to bring the old leasehold system into accordance with the ideals and aspirations of the increasingly democratic society which seemed to be emerging in the United States. The legislatures of 1841, of 1842, of 1843 and of 1844 did no more. For the great landlords and their moneyed allies still dominated the legislature. They were also supported in their struggle to maintain the old order by many citizens who had fallen under the spell of romantic writers and liked to think that the vestiges of Old World ways surviving on the great New York landholdings gave their state a minor substitute for the ruined castles and titled families they had met in the poems and novels of Sir Walter Scott and the tales of Washington Irving.

The ballot had not solved the tenants' problems, yet there was something else working in their favor—that was the spirit of the times. For they lived in what is often called the Age of Revolution when respect for authority was weakening, when daring notions were coming into mens' minds and when the poor and oppressed in many countries were rising in revolt. The American Revolution and the far more revolutionary one in the France of 1789 had given hope to the downtrodden and the merely dissatisfied. Everywhere men were promoting new forms of government, new religions, new philosophies, new social structures. European intellectuals founded Utopian colonies on the banks of the Ohio and Wabash; geologists and other scientists were casting doubt upon the literal accuracy of the biblical account of the creation. In Britain and in the United States prophets arose to predict the imminent end of the world. (Vermont-born William Miller gave the world until 1843 to wind up its affairs before the final judgment day.) In Europe the ideas that were to find expression in the Communist Manifesto of 1848 were stirring in the minds of Karl Marx and Friedrich Engels. It was an age of change and tumult when men with urges to reshape society were dashing here and there in a search for converts. It is no wonder then that what had begun as a local refusal to pay rents to landlords under a system that did not have general public support in the United States soon became the object of attempts to steer it into the mainstream of the revolutionary activity of the time.

Two outstanding Anti-rent leaders were deep in revolutionary theory and action. One was Dr. Smith Boughton of the Van Rensselaer's East Manor, who in 1837 had gone to Canada to fight on the side of the French Canadians in the short-lived Papineau Rebellion. The other was Thomas Ainge Devyr, who had fled to the United States after the failure of a Chartist uprising in Newcastle, England, in 1837. Devyr had been a leader in the Chartists' struggle to bring to the poor of Britain a share in the benefits of the Industrial Revolution and a measure of political power. These two men did much to mold Anti-rent feeling into a strong organization, for they had zeal wedded to professional competence and experience. Yet they found the tenants wavering in their desire to hitch their little wagons to a larger one. They wanted an end to perpetual leases and not a second American Revolution. By comparison with the tortured slum dwellers whom Devyr had led in England, they were well off and might soon be even better off. For Erastus Root assured the tenants of the Catskills that

General Bradstreet had been right in asserting that the title to the Harden-bergh Patent was invalid. The patent rightfully belonged to the state of New York. And the state might grant it to those very men who were now its tenants. Then the descendants of the original patentees who were dancing and feasting and admiring the view at the Catskill Mountain House would be ejected and each tenant would become lord of his own acres. On the Livingston and Van Rensselaer manors similar hopes diminished revolutionary ardor.

As the legislature dawdled year after year, the Anti-rent organizations managed to surmount internal dissensions and external blows and become tighter and stronger. By the spring of 1844 their leaders judged the time ripe for bringing into the fold the tenants of the Catskills who, up to this time, had stood to one side, helping only by their votes and spoken encouragement. Organizers called "lecturers" were dispatched to Delaware and Ulster counties where they held enthusiastic meetings with General Root's blessing, first at Andes and Pine Hill, and later at many other places. Under the guidance of the lecturers, local Anti-rent organizations were formed with members bound by a secret oath to refuse to pay their rents.[5]

It was the younger tenants who rushed most eagerly to take the oath. Older men joined up too but were seldom as active in Anti-rent work. Moses Earle, "a grave and discreet individual,"[6] as a friendly newspaper reporter called him later, was among the patriarchs of the Anti-renters, for he was sixty-three. Earle took the oath but he did not join the mystic brotherhood of the "Calico Indians."[7] That was for young and adventurous men.

The outward shell of one Calico Indian has survived the attacks of time and has come down to our own day. It is on display in a glass case in the Senate House Museum in Kingston. A stranger might suppose it to be the kind of thing some mountain boy might bring home from a trip to the ends of the earth on one of the Hudson River whaling ships of a century and a half ago to prove to his friends that he had indeed been among strange and primitive people. It is an animal-like mask made of sheepskin, shaped to pull over the head like a cap, and ornamented with a false nose, tufts of hair, a few feathers, and some scraps of once-shining tin. Beside it hangs the gown worn with the mask—it is of flowered calico and has a red vest over it.

Outfits similar to this one go far back in man's history. They have been used in many parts of the world in religious, fertility, and healing rites. Men wearing masks and gowns like these easily escape their own identities and imagine themselves to become the gods or animals they are impersonating.[8] Behind this mask in the glass case a young tenant farmer of the Catskills might once have felt himself freed from the restraints of his own culture as he played at being a wronged Indian on the warpath against his oppressors.

Masks and gowns were for the young and strong, yet the Anti-rent movement provided other means of binding all Anti-rent believers into a disciplined army. Anti-rent lyrics were adapted to old and well-loved tunes and sung at meetings and in the fields where men worked with plow or scythe. Some of these new songs told of "feudal lords" grinding their tenants; others narrated incidents involving the discomfiture of writ-serving sheriffs like Bill Snyder:

> The moon was shining silver bright;
> The sheriff came in the dead of night;
> High on a hill sat an Indian true,
> And on his horn this blast he blew—
>   Keep out of the way—big Bill Snyder—
>   We'll tar your coat and feather your hide, Sir![9]

The horn blown by the Calico Indian in the ballad was the traditional tin dinner horn of New York farms which had been put to use in the Helderbergs to warn of the approach of sheriffs. As Anti-rent organization proceeded in the Catskills, dinner horns ceased being blown for their usual purpose. They sounded from house to house up valleys and across hills only when men like Undersheriff Osman Steele sought to harry tenants.

And as 1844 moved along another sound imported from the Helderbergs was heard. It was the shouted, chanted, or whispered Anti-rent slogan: "Down with the rent!"[10] Tenants used it whenever two of them met; they tested strangers by demanding that they repeat it: they roared it in the halls in which they gathered. The slogan floated on banners raised high on liberty poles set up in tiny hamlets, and it was crudely lettered on the sides of barns and corncribs. Seldom has an effort at rebellion had so simple and effective a slogan. By the summer of 1844, "Down with the rent" was echoing in every Catskill valley on which the land collectors of Lord Cornbury's time had laid their acquisitive hands.

On the last day of February 1845, the dinner horns sounded with shrill urgency near Cooper Lake (formerly known as Shandaken Lake) in the town of Woodstock. An employee of the agent of Chancellor Livingston's grandsons was approaching to make a bold assertion of a landlord's rights. A tenant had cut some logs, whether on the commons or on his own leased land has not been recorded, and the Livingston agent had sent John Lasher of Woodstock to seize the logs as rightfully belonging to the landlord. Quickly about fifteen young tenants transformed themselves into Calico Indians and hastened to the spot where Lasher with two helpers and a yoke of oxen was about to make off with the logs. A brief struggle took place. Lasher fought back with a handspike but was overpowered. His oxen took fright and tumbled down a cliff. Lasher was tarred and feathered and then released.[11] For the first time the Calico Indians had taken violent action among the Catskills. The reaction was quick in coming.

By February 1845, the Anti-renters and the adherents of the landlords had reached a deadlock. In spite of the vigorous efforts of Anti-rent leaders to pressure the legislature into action, nothing had been accomplished to remove the root cause of tenant discontent. The spreading of the Calico Indian organization to the Catskills had produced a large body of determined young men itching for action. The previous December, two men had died on Van Rensselaer lands in incidents growing out of tenant-landlord conflicts in which masked and gowned Calico Indians had taken part. Dr. Boughton had been arrested and was awaiting trial in the jail at Hudson. When the legislature met in January, it dealt with the situation, not by coming to grips with the essentials of the problem, but by passing a law which imposed heavy penalties on men meeting in disguise. In mid-February, Undersheriff Osman Steele had arrested Calico Indian Daniel Squires of Roxbury and lodged him in the Delhi jail in what seemed to be an attempt to test the new law. When Lasher received his coat of tar and feathers beside Cooper Lake, an even better test case seemed in the making. Ulster officialdom took speedy action to bring the Calico Indians who had attacked Lasher to trial. But first they had to catch their Indians, and that proved no simple matter.

Sheriff's posses and bodies of militiamen invaded Woodstock, preceded by the blasts of tin horns blown from every farmhouse window. There were Kingston men, Saugerties men, and the militia unit known as the Hurley Greens resplendent in uniforms of green and silver lace with ostrich plumes bobbing on their hats. They captured a few suspected Indians and the Indians vanished mysteriously from their custody. They plodded on through the slushy March snow to the derisive music of tin horns only to find every man they suspected flown. They glimpsed a few Indians, "looking more like cats than men"[12] as one posse member put it, climbing the mountains which surround Cooper Lake. In a swamp they captured a cache of gowns and masks—the outfit in the Senate House Museum was probably among them. But only a few of the men who had tarred and feathered Lasher were immediately arrested. Their leader, Asa Bishop, whose Indian name was Black Hawk, remained in hiding in Delaware County until September. Twenty-eight Calico Indians were indicted by the Ulster grand jury that spring and their trial was set for October. But most of them were still at large.

In Kingston, practical people took what advantage they could of the excitement in Ulster County. Because calico continued in great demand, E. Dubois advertised that his were "rich and rare, some vieing with the rainbow hue. . . ."[13] Another Kingston merchant hinted that he would accept the money of both sides with equal pleasure, "Ye up-renters, down-renters, one and all/Do come in and give Eaman first a call,"[14] he rhymed. An amateur Kingston theatrical group ran up a topical play titled *The Calico Indian War*. It was "performed in character with sheepskin faces, calicoes and all." The Ulster *Republican* reported that it was received with "unbounded applause."[15] That summer a showboat named *The Temple of the Muses* moved up the Hudson and moored off various towns. One of the plays it presented was timely indeed, *The Rent Day,* a melodrama dealing with the sorrows of the English counterparts of the tenant farmers of New York.

The Temple of the Muses had more than the timeliness of its wares to offer: it was billed in valley papers as the coolest spot around. And that meant something in 1845, for that spring and summer were the hottest and driest within living memory. Newspaper subscribers among the Catskills read that spring of fires raging in dry cities, and they also read of Ulster and Delaware tenants holding meetings to disclaim any intention of using violence and to deplore the acts of the hot-headed Calico Indians who had dealt so harshly with John Lasher. They read that Old School Baptist elder Hezekiah Pettit of Lexington urged that the landlords' titles be "examined in court." He asked, "Why will not our rulers open the way for us to test them?"[16] They could read between the lines that the Reverend Levi L. Hill of nearby Westkill saw things differently. He was resigning to become pastor of a Saugerties church after preaching an "up-rent" sermon which antagonized his flock.[17] By July many newspapers were printing daily lists of those killed by the heat of American cities. And they reported that Governor Silas Wright had permitted Dr. Boughton to be released on bail: a mistrial had resulted when he came to court that spring and he would be tried again in September.

Newspaper correspondents in many parts of the United States reported corn wilting and pastures turning brown; fierce thunderstorms sometimes brought a little rain only to be followed by dry winds which sucked up all the rain. From Delaware County came reports of arrest after arrest of Calico Indians by Undersheriff Steele—that March an attempt by Indians to kidnap the undersheriff had come close to succeeding.

Many of those who could afford it that summer took refuge from the heat and the difficult times at resorts like the Catskill Mountain House. There the thermometer never rose above 79 degrees, so manager William Scobie boasted. The guide to the Kaaterskill Falls told visitors that never in his sixteen years on the job had the water been so low. Yet such was the power of visitors' quarters that they could still persuade the captive falls to trickle if not to gush. Although times continued to be hard, eighty guests (its capacity was one hundred), found the Mountain House "a truly grateful spot"[18] at the height of the season.

While rich people idled at the Catskill Mountain House, the tenant farmers of the Hardenbergh Patent sweated out that hot summer. Men like Moses Earle watched their pastures fading and the grass they hoped to convert to hay cease growing. They heard endless tales of the doings of Undersheriff Osman Steele, who was untiring in his efforts to fill the county jail with Calico Indians, many of whom were still in their teens. All around Moses Earle resentment against Steele quivered in the hot summer air. Earle's town of Andes and the adjoining one of Bovina were centers of Calico Indian activity in the Hardenbergh Patent. Many of their young men had been arrested by Steele, and among them were relatives of Earle's hired girl, Perthena Davis. And Perthena was thoroughly on the side of her relatives and against the landlords.

57

Moses Earle Withholds His Rent

🌴 IN THE SUMMER of 1793, Moses Earle was a lad of eleven, and Perthena Davis was yet unborn. That was the summer when Peter De-Labigarre tried to crown the Catskills with the liberty cap of the French Revolution. It was also the summer when a surveyor hired by Gulian Verplanck, the rich New York banker, began to prepare for settlement what would become Moses Earle's farm on the Dingle Hill Road in the town of Andes. The surveyor was Jehu Burr of Connecticut's Fairfield County. He climbed the Dingle Hill Road of the future with his instruments and helpers to divide the wilderness he found there into farms which, his employer hoped, would soon be stripped of their forest coats and be converted by tenants into fine fields and pastures.[1]

It was not the first time that the descendants of old Gulian Verplanck, who had been Robert Livingston's partner in buying into the Hardenbergh Patent, had sought to prepare their wilderness lands for settlement. Old Gulian, the father of the Gulian of 1793, had died in 1751 in possession of 280,000 acres of the patent as well as much land elsewhere. In the early 1770s young Gulian, his older brother Samuel, and their brothers-in-law Charles MacEvers and Gabriel Ludlow had commissioned William Cockburn to survey their shares of old Gulian's holdings in the Hardenbergh Patent and to divide the land into farms. But Cockburn never got as far westward as what was to become Moses Earle's farm—the uncertainties of the Bradstreet suit and the beginning of the American Revolution brought Cockburn to a halt. Only one little settlement resulted. It briefly bore the name of Verplancksburg and straggled along the East Branch of the Delaware opposite the lands of Tory John Burch, whom most of the Verplancksburg tenants followed into the British Army and eventual exile in Canada.

By 1793 survey and settlement once again seemed desirable. The prices of land and goods were rising sharply in the boom of the '90s. Gulian Verplanck was in the optimistic, energetic prime of life. He and his wife had four daughters and one son. The youngest was baby Charlotte Delancey who was fated to become the landlord of Moses Earle and his neighbors.

Upon Charlotte's birth, Verplanck, as if aware that his family was now complete, made a will in which he divided his lands among his children, with his wife to retain a life interest. Then he proceeded to take action in order to make his lands produce the utmost in income and status first for himself and then for his offspring. A survey and a division into farms formed the first step of this project.

An essential part of Jehu Burr's job for Gulian Verplanck was keeping a field book in which he recorded his surveys and described each farm he laid out so that his employer might form an estimate of its value. Burr wrote of what was to become Moses Earle's farm with enthusiasm. The part he numbered Lot 45 was "a very good lot being situate in a very pleasant Valley a very good proportion of Arible land, the Timber is Beach, Maple, Basswood etc. Well watered by a branch of Trimper-kill, so called, and a number of small Streams and Springs."[2] Of the land adjoining which would also be farmed by Earle (it formed part of Lot 46), Burr wrote that the land "was somewhat rough and uneven containing Deer Mountain, so called, but on the western side thereof some fine land. . . ." On this lot Burr noticed some "deer licks"—these were places where salt or other minerals attractive to deer were found on the surface. Licks like these were of value to settlers for they promised many a venison dinner during the lean years of early settlement.

By 1845 the promise that Jehu Burr had seen on the slopes rising eastward from the banks of the Trimper-kill seemed to have been fulfilled. The valley held a string of farms each with its patchwork of fields, pastures, and woodlots on the hillsides above, and each with a small farmhouse and a barn framed of substantial timber. The town of Andes in which the valley lay was more prosperous than most others on the Hardenbergh Patent for it had become one of the leading butter-making towns of the state—its butter was believed equal in quality to famous Goshen or Orange County butter. And butter had become the town's chief cash crop. Butter money paid its farmers' taxes; butter money paid for subscriptions to Horace Greeley's New York *Tribune;* butter money would make possible before long the rise of an academy known as the Andes Collegiate Institution. And it was butter money that made it possible for farmers like Moses Earle to pay their rent—with commendable promptness until 1844—to Miss Charlotte Delancey Verplanck of New York.[3]

By 1845 Miss Verplanck was a spinster of fifty-four. She spent her time visiting her married sisters and relatives, such as her distinguished cousin Gulian Crommelin Verplanck. She became what many unmarried ladies of her age and station settled down to be: a professional aunt with a kindly interest in nephews and nieces toward whom, thanks to her landed and other possessions, she could behave with generosity.[4] And the lands that came to her after her mother's death in 1818 were substantial. There were isolated farms and forests; there were blocks of farms; and there were farms strung out in river valleys like the pearls of a necklace. One Hardenbergh Patent tract embraced Dingle Hill which, two miles from the winding valley of the Tremperkill, rises in bold slopes to over 2800 feet. The Moses Earle farm lay near the beginning of the road that climbed toward the hill from the valley.

There is no evidence that Miss Verplanck ever set foot on her farms in the Hardenbergh Patent, nor did she deal directly with her tenants except on a few rare occasions. It would have been thought unseemly for a rich spinster to care for her rented property. Miss Verplanck did not have to look far for an agent to manage her farms: she found him in her brother-in-law William Allen who had wasted in speculations the money that came to him with Miss Verplanck's sister Maria Cornelia and was in need of a job. Later William's son John took over, and in 1845 he was Miss Verplanck's sole land agent in the Catskills. It was John Allen who came to Delaware County from his home in the prosperous Hudson River port of Rondout during the hot summer of 1845 to ignite the fuse that would set off a fatal explosion of resentment beside the Dingle Hill Road. John began by obtaining a warrant of distress under which the sheriff of Delaware County was obliged to sell at auction enough of the livestock of Moses Earle to pay—with costs added—the rent of thirty-two dollars per year which Earle had withheld ever since the recruiting drive of the Anti-renters had struck the Hardenbergh Patent. The sale was set for July 29.

The sale, as John Allen and his aunt Miss Verplanck viewed it, was a fiasco. As at other similar sales Sheriff Greene More had conducted that year, there was not a single bid. Calico Indians assembled at each sale with guns tucked under their gowns. They made it plain that if a single cow or calf was declared sold, they would immediately shoot and kill it. The tenant who owned it would be reimbursed from a fund formed by a tax of two cents per acre on each tenant's land. The landlord, of course, would get nothing. When the Earle sale produced no bids, it was postponed to August 7. And soon it became apparent that the sale on August 7 would be no ordinary one, for landlord supporters and tenants were planning to confront each other in force that day beside the Dingle Hill Road. And the landlords and their adherents had good reason to look forward to the sale with pleasure. For Moses Earle was a confirmed shilly-shallyer in his devotion to the Anti-rent cause. He had strongly hinted by recent actions that on the day of the sale he would pay the sixty-four dollars in rent he owed Miss Verplanck. But if the landlords entertained hopes of an easy victory on August 7, they were overlooking the power of militant Anti-renter Perthena Davis. They may not have been aware that in Perthena's resolute hands Moses Earle became as plastic as the contents of a firkin of Delaware County butter on a summer day.

The tale of Earle's life up to August 7, 1845, forms as unlikely a prelude as can be imagined to what was to happen. It presents Earle as a cautious, property-loving, hard-working man of conservative leanings—just the kind of man who would be likely to defy the demand of Calico Indian neighbors that he violate the new law against "resisting process" by refusing to pay his rent. Moses' father, Jonathan Earle, had come to the Tremperkill Valley from Smith's Clove in Orange County about 1790 bringing his son with him. By the late 1820s Moses was farming on his own on Miss Verplanck's land in the "very pleasant Valley." His farm had been settled and at least partly cleared as far back as 1804 by Samuel Davis, a member of a family which swarmed like bees in the vicinity. When he took over the farm Moses was married to Sarah Washburn, a local woman who was twelve years his senior. The couple had one daughter who died young—it was after this event that the Earles took Perthena Davis into their household, Perthena's brother Henry helped Moses with the farm work. As Moses prospered he took part in town affairs. In 1828 he was elected assessor. He was roadmaster for his neighborhood and during the early 1830s served as poormaster of Andes.[5]

It was while he was poormaster that Earle moved a step upward in his community by joining a hybrid class of Hardenbergh Patent tenants— he became a landowner as well as a tenant. Unlike his neighbors, Earle did not pay his rent to the Allens as they made their rounds of Miss Verplanck's share of the patent; he paid in New York and apparently directly to Miss Verplanck. In 1833 Miss Verplanck sold Poormaster Earle, for a trifle more than one dollar per acre, one hundred acres of Lot 46 which rose above his rented farm. He now had a farm of 260 acres.[6] The sale was carried through on behalf of Miss Verplanck by Charles Hathaway of Delhi who was to become a leader of "Up-rent" power in the county. As the Anti-rent movement began dominating the lives of the tenants of the Hardenbergh Patent, Moses Earle was comfortably placed on the declining

side of life. He was sixty-four years old; his wife was seventy-six. Perthena
Davis, at a mere thirty-six, had established herself as a dominant force on
the Earle farm. And Perthena was a scrapper by inheritance. Her grandfather had fought in the American Revolution, her father in the War of 1812.
When the Anti-rent organization came to the patent, they found eager converts in Perthena and her many young relatives. And Perthena was in a fine
position to put old Moses Earle back on the Anti-rent track whenever he
tumbled off, for she was the butter-making queen of his household.

"Every housewife [in Delaware County] is, or wants to be, a famous
butter-maker,"[7] wrote essayist John Burroughs, who was himself a product
of the Hardenbergh Patent's butter region. Butter-making was women's
work. It was the women who skimmed the cream from the milk and
churned the cream and worked and packed the butter. They endlessly
scrubbed and scoured to keep the whitewashed dairy house or basement
dairy room spotless and odorless. Each morning they hung a glittering
array of milk pans beside the dairy-house door to sweeten in the sun. The
Earle farm had at least thirty-three such pans.[8]

In the early days of settlement before forests gave way to pastures and
before hillside springs had been captured and set to racing through pen-
stocks to chill and cleanse dairy houses, the men of the western part of the
patent had been the economic lords of their families. It was they who
brought home money dangerously earned by floating rafts of timber down
the Delaware, or by raising grain and converting it into whiskey, or by leaving home at intervals to cut wood or peel bark or drive teams for mountain
tanneries. But by 1845 the frontier disorderliness of their land was vanishing
and the men's role was changing. Cows grazed on high sunlit pastures; wild
strawberries, freed from imprisonment in the forest, ripened there in June
and filled the whole land with their fragrance. And as the land changed, so
did its people. Women were aware that their skill in butter-making was
now a key factor in bringing a cash income into the family. They knew
that their position in every farm household in the butter region was high.
Evidence of this came when they were permitted to join the Anti-rent
organizations and to take the Anti-rent oaths. It was a little step forward
in the liberation of women which had begun with the French Revolution.
Perthena Davis, hired girl though she was, knew the strength of her
position.

As August 7 approached, Moses Earle appeared to most observers to
be standing firm in his decision to withhold his rent. But there is evidence
that behind the scenes he was trying to wriggle out of a situation in which
he felt extremely uncomfortable. He wrote to Sheriff Greene More to

promise to pay his rent in cash on the day of the sale. And he asked two of his Anti-rent neighbors to bid for his cattle and so enable him to save face should the sale take place in spite of his promise to the sheriff.

August 7 dawned sunny and warm. On Moses Earle's farm life went on much as usual, for farm routine must follow the path determined by the seasons and sun. Perthena Davis and Sarah Earle busied themselves with the care of milk and butter. Moses set his farmhands to work cutting the grass of the lower meadows near the Tremperkill Road. But in one particular, life on the Earle farm was very different indeed. Since before dawn, Calico Indians had been converging on the place and concealing themselves in the woods above the house where a cache of arms had already been established.

At about ten that morning the sheriff arrived aboard a one-horse wagon. He was accompanied by lawyer Peter P. Wright of Delhi, the legal representative of Miss Verplanck and John Allen. The sheriff showed Moses the letter in which he had agreed to pay his rent and Earle acknowledged its genuineness. He added that since writing the letter he had changed his mind and would not pay the rent after all. "You'll have to make the rent out of the property," he added. He and the sheriff argued the matter for a while and Earle once again underwent a change of mind. He entered his house and came out with a pocketbook in his hand—it contained the sixty-four dollars of his rent money. At that Perthena Davis emerged from the wings and took the center of the stage for a single dramatic moment. She asked Moses what he was up to and when he replied that he intended to pay his rent, Perthena seized the pocketbook and thrust it into the bosom of her dress. She then denounced Moses for backsliding. Moses quietly turned to the sheriff and remarked that he wasn't going to pay his rent after all. Perthena vanished with the pocketbook very much in her possession.

Sometime that morning the two neighbors whom he had asked to bid on his cattle approached Earle, who told them that the local Calico Indian leader, Daniel Northrop, had sent word to him from the woods to indicate that he did not approve of the proposed deal. The neighbors, Justice of the Peace Richard Morse and Scotch-born Colin Campbell, said that in that case they would not bid. Moses Earle, after all his scheming to prevent a confrontation on his farm, now knew that his efforts had failed. The sale was scheduled to begin at one o'clock, and there was nothing Earle could do to stop it.

58

Death on the Dingle Hill Road

❧ A DAY OR TWO before his sale was scheduled to take place, Moses Earle had slaughtered several sheep picked from his flock, obviously intending to feed the multitude of Calico Indians he expected to gather for the sale. Over two hundred Indians turned up and waited hungrily in Earle's woods as noon of August 7 approached. Perthena Davis and Mrs. Earle fed the Indians by adding potatoes and bread and butter to the fresh mutton and sending the meal to the men in the woods. When the Indians had finished eating they donned their masks and gowns and drew up in military formation on the open space between Earle's barn and the road. Their leader was young Warren Scudder of Roxbury, an arresting figure in a black military cap, a close-fitting red mask, and a striped calico gown. He waved a bright sword as he marshaled his men.

When the Indians had taken their positions, Moses Earle emerged from his house in the role of gracious host. He carried a bucket of whiskey which he handed to a man at one end of the formation. The man drank and handed the bucket to the next man and so the bucket was passed along the formation with each man drinking as well as he could without taking off his mask. Whiskey drinking, in spite of temperance agitation, was still a necessary part of almost every masculine gathering on the Hardenbergh Patent, and the sheriff and lawyer Wright waited until the ceremony was completed. Then Wright strode along the line of Indians, peering at each man in an effort to identify him. Warren Scudder stopped the lawyer with his sword and a heated argument followed. Tension grew. Wright and Scudder displayed pistols. Then a diversion headed off conflict. A blast on a tin horn announced the arrival of Undersheriff Osman Steele.

Just what part Steele was expected to play on Moses Earle's farm that day is still far from clear—perhaps he himself was not certain of his role. Had he come to earn the sixty-four dollars owed by Moses Earle by bidding on his cattle? Some swore that Miss Verplanck through her agent John Allen had made this deal with him. Others swore that Sheriff More had forbidden Steele to come to the sale unless with an armed posse of forty men to help keep peace. Steele usually arrived at sales like Earle's in a cloud of red dust kicked up by the horses of his posse, but this time he came alone except for a constable named Erastus Edgerton. The two men had stopped to refresh themselves and the fine gray horses they were riding at the Andes tavern. There they keyed their nerves for what might lie ahead by drinking whiskey. Tavernkeeper Huntley warned Steele that if he went on, his life would be in danger from the Calico Indians. Steele replied with a bit of bravado that would be long remembered: "Lead can't penetrate Steele," he said.

As soon as Steele arrived, Sheriff More got down to the business of the day. With the help of a few bystanders he drove the cattle to be sold from the nearby pasture toward the barway which gave access to the Dingle Hill Road, where the sheriff intended to hold the sale. At this, Anti-rent leader William Brisbane protested. He argued that the cattle could be sold under law only on Earle's property and not on the public highway and pointed out that the official notice posted on Earle's barn gave Earle's "premises" as the place of sale.

Brisbane was a persuasive and intelligent Scotchman and his protest was not brushed aside. While the Calico Indians sweated under their gowns and masks, the sheriff and lawyer Wright examined the notice on the side of the barn and debated the point Brisbane had raised. The Scotchman had the law on his side, as the sheriff and Wright must have been well aware. For although ever since the state of New York had come into being the rights of landlords and tenants had been the subject of endless and often complicated and confusing legislation, it was clear enough that property could not be seized and sold on a public highway for failure to pay rent. At the same time the sheriff and Wright had their reasons for not wanting the sale to take place on the open space in front of the Earle barn. For that space was filled with two hundred menacing Calico Indians armed and filled with a fierce eagerness to prevent Miss Verplanck's rent from being collected. Brisbane and Scudder assured the sheriff and Miss Verplanck's lawyer that if they held the sale in the midst of the Calico Indians they would not be harmed. But these assurances were not accepted. With his hat in one hand and his cane in the other, lawyer Wright clambered over the bars to lead an attempt to drive the cattle to the highway.[1] Steele and Edgerton followed Wright's lead—they jumped their grays over the bars. Edgerton called on all present to assist him. He drew a pistol and waved it, threatening to shoot anyone who tried to prevent him from driving the cattle to the barway. All that morning, tension had been growing. Now Constable Edgerton's words released it in a burst of gunfire.

No Anti-rent leaders had ever suggested that their men shoot sheriffs or landlords' agents. Their Calico Indians were armed in order that they might intimidate writ servers and rent collectors, shoot cattle when sold, and halt mounted men by shooting their horses. That morning, for example, a detachment of Indians had been stationed by Warren Scudder at the foot of the Dingle Hill Road with instructions to halt Steele and the members of the large posse he was expected to bring by shooting their horses if necessary. As Edgerton flourished his pistol and, as many testified, fired a first shot, the Calico Indians raised their rifles and fired at the two gray horses. From somewhere among the Calico Indians, two or more rifles were raised and aimed from behind sheepskin masks, not at the two grays, but at Osman Steele. The horses and Steele fell to the ground mortally wounded. The hatred Steele had aroused by his harrying of tenants, abetted perhaps by Moses Earle's whiskey, the shelter of a mask, and the pitiless heat, had taken the form of deliberate murder.

The Calico Indians did not disperse but lingered on the spot as if uncertain what to do. Steele was carried into the Earle house and laid on a bed. A doctor who was present did what he could for him but it was apparent that Steele could not live long. Sarah Earle wrung her hands in misery; lawyer Wright sat beside the wounded man and cried. Sheriff More told Steele that if Edgerton hadn't been so rash the Calico Indians wouldn't have fired. When Steele caught the eye of Moses Earle he said, "Old man, if you had paid your rent there would have been none of this. I wouldn't have been shot."[2]

Moses Earle was no longer a wobbler—at least for the rest of that day—in his adherence to the Anti-rent cause. "I have paid rent long enough," he told Steele. "Until I know what I pay it for, I shall pay no more if I can help it. If they will show me their title, I will pay every cent of the rent, but if they mean to bully me out of it I will not pay if it costs forty lives."

Steele died at about quarter after eight that evening. While Mrs. Steele sobbed over her husband's body, Moses Earle gave an odd sort of comfort to Dr. Ebenezer Steele, the dead man's uncle. He said that Steele "was created for the very course he had taken. He was ordained to die that way. . . . I can assure you the Almighty makes no mistakes." All this was in line with the belief in predestination which was having a vogue on the Hardenbergh Patent at the time. But when taken in connection with his

belligerent remarks of a few hours earlier they helped weave a net of suspicion around Moses Earle and to plant in many suggestible minds the
notion that Earle was the master schemer in a conspiracy which had killed
one man and might yet claim many more.

As it became apparent that Steele would not survive his wounds, a
good deal of their confidence oozed away from the Calico Indians and the
previously sustaining apparatus of masks, gowns, the slogan, and the songs
began to lose their magic. The Indians dispersed in an apprehensive mood.
Many went into hiding and some left the state. At the same time, fear took
possession of large numbers of propertied men and women and gave birth
to dreadful fantasies. Steele's death had been no more than a first step in a
widespread revolt of the poor not unlike those which had been tormenting
the rich of Europe. Before long the rich might be pried out of their niches
in society by the envious poor and all law and order would be at an end.
An air of crisis soon hung over the state of New York.

Mounted bodies of Delaware lawmen rounded up all the Calico
Indians they could lay hands on, even those who could not be connected in
any way with the tragedy on Moses Earle's farm. The slogan of "Down
with the rent!" was no longer heard on the Hardenbergh Patent. Instead,
the triumphant friends of the old system were shouting "law and order!"

The grand jury sat in Delhi and called in hordes of witnesses. Many
were former Calico Indians now willing to testify that their jailed comrades had taken the Anti-rent oath, bought calico, or paid dues to the Anti-
rent organization. Among the witnesses were Perthena Davis and Sarah
Earle, for it was hoped that their activity in preparing food for the Calico
Indians on August 7 might be presented in court as part of the evidence of a
well-planned conspiracy to murder in which Moses Earle was a central
figure. As the grand jury worked late into the hot August nights, men who
had recently been shouting "Down with the rent" were doing some hard
thinking. The shooting of Osman Steele had doused Calico Indian enthusiasm and shocked many Anti-rent sympathizers into doubt and confusion.
Meetings held in towns all over the Anti-rent country passed resolutions
denouncing the shooting of Steele. Masks and calico gowns were burned or
packed away in attics as relics of the past. At the same time, the hopes of the
landlords soared, thanks to the law of January 25, 1845, for the shooting of
Osman Steele had given them what seemed to be an opportunity to crush
the Anti-rent movement forever.

The law did a good deal more than merely prohibit the gatherings
of disguised men. It made it possible for judges to condemn to death on the

gallows every disguised man who was present at a gathering at which a human being was killed. It was not necessary to prove that these men fired a shot or helped or encouraged anyone else to fire: their mere presence in the crowd was enough. More than two hundred men, most of them in their late teens or early twenties, had watched through their masks as Steele was shot, and every one of them now became a candidate for the rope.

Back in 1766, William Prendergast had been sentenced to death for his part in leading the Anti-rent riots on Livingston Manor. The judge had recommended clemency and Prendergast was pardoned, but the great landlords of New York had been pleased by the speed with which the news of Prendergast's sentence had quieted Anti-rent protests—if only for a while. Now the grandsons of the landlords of 1766 clamored and pressured and persuaded behind the scenes; they demanded the swift and severe avenging of the death of Osman Steele. But times had changed. In 1766 it had been a relatively simple matter to get Prendergast convicted on a charge of treason. Then the courts, the members of the bar, and the legislature had been under the thumb of rich landowners and merchants, and the poor could express their feelings only through narrow and tortuous channels. By 1845 the white, male portion of the people had won the right to vote and no prosecuting attorney or judge could avoid taking this fact into account. The voters were watching as preparations for indictments and trials went on in Delhi, and if the voters exerted their united strength they might wreck the careers of officials who displeased them. The Anti-rent forces were discouraged—but they remained organized.

The landlords made vigorous efforts to woo public opinion. Newspaper editors wrote daily in the landlords' defense and demanded the most extreme punishment permitted under law for the killers of Steele and for all Calico Indians. Clergymen preached Anti-rent sermons; politicians denounced Anti-rentism in all its forms. The landlords themselves took their case directly to the public by means of statements and advertisements in the newspapers.[3] They offered their lands for sale to their tenants, but those who investigated found the terms of sale far from attractive.

By August 27, Anti-rent activity had come to a complete halt in Delaware County. It was then that Governor Silas Wright proclaimed the county "in a state of insurrection" and imposed martial law. In his proclamation he expressed abhorrence of disguises and assured the tenants that God could recognize the faces behind their masks. He advised tenants to seek a solution of their problems by mutual agreements with their landlords, and advised the landlords to be kind and generous. The effect of the proclamation was immediate. As three hundred militiamen poured into

Delhi at the Governor's order and placed cannon loaded with nails and ball in positions commanding the principal streets, the rumors of the existence of a widespread conspiracy took on fresh life. Householders armed themselves, and in the words of the reporter for the Albany *Evening Journal* of September 1, "Every house became a fort and every window a port hole." The atmosphere of crisis thickened; indictments proceeded in wholesale lots from the grand jury room. The soldiers sent to Delhi found little to occupy their time, and some were set to work with axes building ample log annexes to the Delhi jail for the accommodation of the prisoners rounded up by the sheriff and his men as, day after day, they scoured the western part of the Hardenbergh Patent. By the time the grand jury had ended its work, more than two hundred men were under indictment—one hundred of them for the murder of Osman Steele.

The first to go on trail for murder was bearded twenty-one-year-old John Van Steenbergh, and the last was imaginative, romantically inclined Edward O'Connor. Both pleaded not guilty. No evidence was presented to suggest that either man had taken part in Steele's killing beyond such testimony as that Van Steenbergh had expressed the opinion that Steele had gotten what he deserved and that O'Connor had asked another Calico Indian for a ramrod to use in reloading his rifle. Both men were found guilty of murder. The other tenants who came to trial for murder were persuaded to plead guilty to manslaughter in order to avoid a possible sentence of death. Among these was Moses Earle.

Immediately after Steele's murder, newspaper editors, landlords' agents, and up-renters in general began directing a large share of public anger at Steele's murder against Moses Earle. It was Earle who had started it all by refusing to pay his rent; it was on Earle's farm that Steele had been shot; it was in Earle's house that he had died. In a movement of young and often idealistic men, Earle was an oddity, a childless old man "of large property,"[4] as some said, a former poormaster and assessor. The public did not know of Perthena Davis' power over old Moses. They found it very odd indeed that an old man bearing all the outward marks of conservatism should have become a central figure in the Anti-rent War. People puzzled over what Earle's motives might have been. They asked themselves what strange motivations might have caused him to cast his lot among the leaders of a movement which could promise him so little discernible profit. And many concluded that those motives must have been very evil indeed.

Hardly had Earle been thrown in the Delhi jail when his wife paid up his back rents in an obvious effort at bettering the old man's postion. It was then rumored that Miss Verplanck had given the rent money to Steele's widow. When Edward O'Connor came to trial, Earle was brought into court as a witness for the prosecution. Dr. Ebenezer Steele questioned Earle's competence as a witness, in part because of what the doctor described as his "lack of religious belief."[5] But Earle was sworn in as a witness and then proceeded to deny everything. He didn't know how many Indians had come to his farm on the day of the sale; he didn't speak to the Indians; he didn't "deliver up my property to them. . . . I had no conversation with them, or they with me."

Once Earle reached the jail he was cut off from the influence of Perthena Davis and abandoned his Anti-rent stand completely. In one of the affidavits he made he stated that he had wanted to pay his rent but had "been overruled by others." He went on to complain that he could not prepare his defense properly because he was deprived while in jail of the "counsel, aid and advice of said hired girl, Perthena Davis."[6] He first pleaded not guilty to the charge of murder which had been brought against him. On the morning of October 3 he changed this plea to one of guilty of manslaughter, having "feloniously, wilfully and of his malice aforethought killed and murdered Osman N. Steele."[7]

Everyone concerned in the trial knew perfectly well that Earle had not killed Osman Steele. They knew too that he could not possibly have been convicted under the act of January 25, 1845, for he was not present at his sale in disguise or carrying arms. But newspapers and landlords clamored for the conviction of "that prince of brutes,"[8] Moses Earle. Attorney general John Van Buren had just triumphantly prosecuted Dr. Boughton in his second trial at Hudson and had just heard Boughton convicted. At once he rushed to Delhi to work for the conviction of Moses Earle. Van Buren felt confident that he could persuade the jury to find Earle guilty of murder. Judge Amasa Parker, who presided over the Delhi Anti-rent trials, and Judge Ruggles of Ulster doubted that he could. On the eve of his trial, pressures were applied to old Moses. It was then that he agreed to plead guilty to manslaughter and so enable Van Buren to get a conviction if only on a lesser charge. Part of what appears to have been a deal was Earle's signing of a promissory note for $187 in payment for the gray horse of Osman Steele which had been shot at his sale.[9]

When those convicted in the Anti-rent trials came up for sentencing, Van Steenbergh and O'Connor heard Judge Parker condemn them to death by hanging. Moses Earle was the next to stand up. He begged the judge to be lenient to him. But the judge was not: he gave Earle the maximum sentence allowed by law in the case of a man found guilty of manslaughter, which was imprisonment for life in the state prison. About sixty other Anti-renters were given sentences ranging from terms in prison to fines, though some of the sentences were suspended. An air of gloom came over the courtroom as the convicted men received their sentences. Some of the men gave way to tears; others showed despair in their faces and attitudes. Only Edward O'Connor breathed defiance to the end. He turned to the spectators in the courtroom and said, "Remember, my friends, I die an innocent man!"

The convicted men and all Anti-renters had good reason for feeling despair. The results of the trials in Hudson, Delhi, and Kingston, where the Calico Indians who had tarred and feathered John Lasher were being tried, had unhappy results for the Anti-rent cause. During the summer of 1845, many once fervent Anti-renters had recanted. Enthusiasm for hitching the tenant farmers' cause of reform in land tenure to the broader ones inspiring European revolutionaries died out entirely. Yet the determination to end the old system of land tenure in New York State remained alive and vigorous even as Moses Earle and the others sentenced to prison terms were taken by wagon to Catskill on their journey to Clinton Prison in Dannemora. Van Steenbergh and O'Connor remained behind in Delhi, for it was there that they were to be hanged.

As preparations for the hanging went forward, preparations of a very different kind were underway throughout the state. In November an election would be held. The voters would have a chance to call a constitutional convention which would consider many reforms, that of land tenure among others. They would have a chance to send new representatives to the legislature. On Election Day the constitutional convention was overwhelmingly authorized and more Anti-rent men than ever were elected to the legislature. As the news of the election results reached the Anti-rent counties, bonfires were lighted. Tin horns were brought out of hiding and blown in triumph. Hope was returning to the tenant farmers of New York.

59

End of the Anti-rent War

✢ THE TENANT FARMERS of the Catskills waited expectantly to see what would happen when the Albany politicians digested the results of the election of the fall of 1845. Already the people of all the Anti-rent counties had left no doubt about what they wanted. They had answered the legal violence available to their landlords with illegal violence of their own which had ended in the death of Osman Steele. They had endlessly debated the question of what was to be done about the state's antiquated laws dealing with land tenure. Through their representatives they had discussed the subject in the state legislature, in barrooms, in hayfields, in the woods as hemlock trees fell to the axes of barkpeelers, in churches, and in schoolhouses. And at last the people had spoken with unmistakable meaning through the ballot. Would the politicians understand? And would they take action at last to give the people what they wanted?

The answer began to trickle in on November 22, 1845. On that day Governor Young, who had defeated Silas Wright with strong Anti-rent support, commuted the sentences of Van Steenbergh and O'Connor to life imprisonment—the day set for the two men's execution was only a week off. The following January, Young urged the legislature to take up the question of reform in the state's system of land tenure. Later in that year of 1846, the Constitutional Convention authorized by the voters met. Among other reforms it abolished further perpetual leases of agricultural land (leases in force were allowed to run on). It did away with the "quarter sales" which enabled landlords to collect a part of the purchase price whenever a tenant sold his leasehold. The legislature took action too. It ended a landlord's right to seize and sell a tenant's movable property in order to pay back rents—it was the exercise of this right more than anything else that had paved the way to Steele's murder. Still, Anti-rent members of the legislature, Anti-rent editors, and leaders of Anti-rent associations continued to push for a thorough investigation of the original land grants upon which the state's landlords rested their claims to special privilege. With this heavy club poised over their heads, landlords and their representatives in government showed a greater disposition to compromise.

The great landlords' control of the legislature was shaken; their favored position was weakened under the new constitution; they could not go on doing business as usual. Some did their best to cling to what was left of the old order. Among these was James Powers' valued client, John Hunter of Hunter's Island in Long Island Sound. Hunter had married Elizabeth Desbrosses, whose father James had left to her a vast number of Hardenbergh Patent acres he had inherited from his uncle Elias, the rich distiller. As Miss Elizabeth entered the marriage market, rumor endowed her with two million acres in the Hardenbergh Patent, for by then the size of the patent was already being exaggerated. Thanks to his wife's lands, Hunter became one of the greatest of the Hardenbergh Patent landlords. He did not manage the lands himself. James Powers and surveyor John Kiersted of Saugerties did that for him while Hunter enjoyed existence on his island with its terraced formal gardens, its Palladian mansion, and its collection of European works of art assembled by an agent who rummaged for such treasures in the wreckage of rich old families ruined by the French Revolution and the Napoleonic Wars.

James Powers had been a stout supporter of the landlords of the Hardenbergh Patent until the end of the Anti-rent War. By that time he was ailing—after 1846 he signed his name with a shaky hand on the register of the Catskill Mountain House. Yet Powers was still agile enough to bend before the new breeze blowing across his state. By posing as a tenant's friend he got himself elected a delegate to the Constitutional Convention of 1846. Political opponents charged that the tenants on the lands Powers managed for John Hunter were afraid to vote against him and that even tenants under the voting age voted for Powers the politician lest failure to do so would be held against them by Powers the land agent.

Once the reforms of 1846 had been approved by the voters, Powers applied to John Hunter for instructions. And Hunter, who like Powers was feeling the weight of his years, responded in a spirit of bitterness toward his tenants. "I have not been in any way instrumental in bringing about the state of things which exists," he wrote. "No father was more indulgent than I was or wished less to separate from his children than I did from my tenants—if we are separated, and by force of law, separated, it has been their own act, not mine."[1] Hunter insisted on every cent of back rent due him under law. Other landlords might forgive the back rents which had so cruelly piled up during the difficult thirties—but not John Hunter. "The farms are mine," he told Powers. He would not sell nor would he enter into the leases for twelve years which were now the longest permitted for farm land—not until all back rents were paid up.

Other and especially younger landlords took the changes of 1846 with a better grace. They recognized that with leases for lives and perpetual leases outlawed and with the competition from western lands likely to keep the value of their own low, it might be wise to sell while they could. And tenants flushed with their recent triumphs were eager to buy. No Hardenbergh Patent landlords divested themselves of their inherited lands more quickly than two of the Chancellor's grandsons, Eugene Augustus and Montgomery Livingston, who owned immense tracts in Woodstock, Olive, and Shandaken. Both lived by summer on the Clermont estate (Montgomery lived in the old Chancellor's house), but the lust for land which had burned so strongly among their ancestors flickered feebly in Eugene and Montgomery. They were among the Hardenbergh Patent landlords who had offered to sell to their tenants even before the death of Osman Steele. And apparently they had made their offers seriously, for they at once began discussing terms with tenants, and by 1846 many pages of the deed books of the County Clerk of Ulster were needed to record sales to former tenants. Back rents were apparently forgiven, for they are not mentioned in the deeds. And the prices paid the two Livingstons were reasonable—they sold each farm for a sum which when invested at 5 per cent would produce the same annual income as the farm's former rent.

Many Hardenbergh Patent tenants hesitated to buy from their landlords even at fair prices. These were the men who placed faith in the traditions which held that the title to the patent was invalid because of the trickery that had marked its granting. They remembered that Generals John Bradstreet and Erastus Root and many other respected men had proclaimed that the patent's title was invalid. If a tenant waited just a little longer, wasn't it possible that he might eventually receive his farm from the state and without payment?

In Albany, Anti-rent leaders encouraged the hopes of hesitating tenants by pushing harder than ever for a court test of the titles to the old land grants. At the same time Governor Young was weighing the possibilities for gaining voter support opened by the recent Anti-rent successes. In February 1847, and only after a vigorous prodding from Anti-renters, Young had made good on one of his campaign promises by pardoning the men sentenced at the trials of 1845. The return home of the pardoned men had much of the look of a triumphal procession. When those headed for the western part of the Hardenbergh Patent reached Prattsville they were heartily welcomed by Zadock Pratt himself—the old tanner had always been a stanch upholder of the Anti-rent cause. Pratt treated the men to a fine dinner and provided four horses and a wagon in which they rode the rest of the way while brass bands played, tin horns blew, and bonfires blazed.

It was not until 1848 that relentless pressure on the state legislature induced members to authorize the state's attorney general to bring suits[2] to test the validity of what were known as "the manorial titles." The news of this step stirred a ripple of excitement through the Hardenbergh Patent. In Andes, Middletown, and elsewhere, mass meetings were called by "the tenantry of the Hardenbergh Patent," and the tenants passed resolutions offering to help press the suit the attorney general was said to have instituted against the landlords of their patent. The tenants meeting at Andes in the spring of 1849 called themselves "the friends of Equal Rights."[3] They petitioned the attorney general asking him "to stay the collection of rents" until the suits were decided.

As the attorney general's suits dragged on, Hardenbergh Patent tenants did not quietly await the outcome. When John Kiersted stopped overnight in the Neversink Valley while on his way to attend a trial in Monticello, his wagon was carried off and burned and his horse was stolen. "Mr. Kiersted's offense is that he is agent for the Hunter estate. He has recovered his horse," said the Rondout *Courier* of October 19, 1849. Elsewhere on the patent and on other old New York land grants, similar incidents showed that Anti-rent emotions were still very much alive. And in many places Anti-renters were encouraged to revive old claims involving boundaries and to try to make these bases for claiming ownership of the lands they occupied. Sheriff Neal Benson of Sullivan County had been a leader in his county's Anti-rent association. In 1849 he assumed the town of Rochester's claim to something like thirty thousand acres of land held by Livingstons ever since the attempt of William Cockburn to settle an old boundary dispute while the Revolution raged. Benson maintained that the recorded agreement between Chancellor Livingston and other patent landlords and the Rochester trustees, in which their common boundary was agreed upon, was invalid and that his purchase of the Rochester rights made him and the other tenants of the lands their owners.

The Benson claim resulted in a law suit once famous as "the Livingston heirs case."[4] After vast amounts of testimony about old surveys had been submitted, the case was decided on appeal in June 1859, in favor of the Livingston heirs. The attorney general's suits moved along, comparatively speaking, at a lively clip. The lower courts found that the great landlords' titles were indeed invalid. This decision was based on the discovery by "black letter lawyers" that when the land grants were made by colonial governors, they were made in violation of an English statute of 1290 known from its opening words as "quia emptores." In 1853 the Court of Appeals reversed this decision in part because it was not consistent with an act, often called a "quieting act," passed by the legislature in 1830. As far back as within Lord Cornbury's lifetime, such acts had been passed by New York's Assembly at the insistence of large landholders. Their objective was to confirm doubtful titles to land, and the act of 1830 provided that if the title to a tract of land had not been contested in court for a period of forty years, it became unassailable. And while titles to the "manorial grants" had been the subject of countless petitions and protests, their tenants had never been able to summon the money or influence needed to bring their grievances before the courts. Ironically enough, the tenants' attempt at upsetting their landlords' titles resulted only in putting the titles beyond further question for all time.

From the beginning of the Hardenbergh Patent the region had been a profitable hunting ground for the lawyers who played parts in causing and then unsnarling the patent's ambiguities. May Bickley, of course, became the prince of them all when he represented both sides in the original granting and was rewarded with a one-eighth share of the patent. None of the later lawyers who worked the patent equalled Bickley's record, but it was not for lack of trying. Lawyers had been prominent on both sides during the Anti-rent War; when the war ended, the new conditions provided glorious opportunities for legal profit. There were new laws to be tested in court and speculative enterprises which depended on legal sharpness to make them succeed. For example, there was the purchase by Walter Church of the rights to immense tracts of land from the discouraged Van Rensselaer heirs. Church, like John Hunter, insisted on his rights, harried tenants for back rents, and pursued them through the courts with tenacity. Nothing like this happened on the Hardenbergh Patent, for there most landlords sold much of their land to tenants, grumbling as they did it, but selling just the same.

By 1863, the year when Moses Earle died, Anti-rent excitement had greatly lessened although it was not to disappear for many years. Many tenants continued to pay their rents to their old landlords or the landlords' heirs under leases which predated the constitution of 1846. Moses Earle was one of these rent payers to the last day of his life. Once he was pardoned he returned to his old farm and there, if the figures he gave the census taker of 1850 are to be credited, he continued to prosper with Perthena

Davis still serving as butter-making hired girl. During the fifties Sarah
Earle died and Perthena left to keep house and make butter for one of her
brothers. Moses died alone in the house in which Osman Steele had died,
wearing a red nightcap and attended by a dog named Bruce and a squad of
cats.[5]

By the year of Perthena Davis' death at eighty-two (she died in 1893
of complications from a broken hip), many old Hardenbergh Patent perpetual leases were still in force. For a perpetual lease will run on forever
unless it is brought to an end by the failure of a tenant to pay his rent or by
the purchase by the tenant of the land he has rented. In that case landlord
and tenant coincide in one person and the lease expires.

Every now and then over the years a buyer of land which formed part
of the Hardenbergh Patent is told by the lawyer he has employed to search
the title, that before the sale can be consummated a little encumbrance must
be removed. For the seller-to-be holds his land under an ancient lease which
must be brought to an end if the buyer is to hold his land on the terms customary in our own day. One of the most curious of such cases was that of
Jason Clum of Clum Hill in the town of Hunter. Ever since August 1,
1802, the possessors of Clum's farm had paid an annual rent of $14.69, first
to James Desbrosses, then to John Hunter, then to Hunter's heirs and then
after 1879 to surveyor Isaac Showers to whom the heirs sold out for $.69½
per acre the 7000-acre remnant of Hunter's holdings in the town of Hunter
(the town was by then named for its old landlord). Much of this land was
cutover bark land and rocky hilltops. By 1910 Isaac Showers' son and heir
Cyrus was receiving the rent.[6]

In 1910 a man named Welles Bosworth appeared on the Clum farm
and—after Clum's perpetual lease had been "taken up"—bought part
of the farm, a hilltop with a broad view of the upper Schohariekill Valley.[7]
Bosworth was a distinguished man, the trusted architect of John D. Rockefeller and the Rockefellers' adviser on matters related to all the arts. Later
he was to be responsible for such Rockefeller-financed projects as the restoration of Rheims cathedral and the royal palace at Versailles. In 1910
Bosworth was looking for a site upon which he might build a summer home
of his own modeled on the country houses he had observed overlooking
panoramas of sea or valley in Greece.

Jason Clum in his own way was every bit as distinguished as Bosworth.
For he was a living survival of the old school of Hardenbergh Patent tenants. In 1810 Clum would have gone unnoticed; by 1910 he had become
conspicuous. Some who knew Clum described him as mean and irasci-
ble; others said he was proud and independent. He could not read or write.

He chewed tobacco, and the colossal brown Bennington spittoon into which he spat his juice is still in the possession of his descendants. Jason Clum struggled against the changes he saw taking place all around him. When his wife had electricity brought into his house, he smashed the light bulbs. When he was informed on one of his visits to Tannersville with horse and wagon that he must carry a lighted lantern on the wagon when he drove by night, he hastened to the security of his hilltop never to leave it again.[8]

Here and there on the parts of the Hardenbergh Patent where old land-lords like John Hunter had struggled to cling to their acres, men like Jason Clum could linger on. But elsewhere, once the sales to tenants which followed the reforms of 1846 had been made, the old way of life receded leaving only traces not always easy to detect. Marius Schoonmaker, the Kingston law-yer and historian, was an excellent observer of what happened on the lands relinquished to tenants by landlords like Eugene Augustus and Montgom-ery Livingston. He wrote that before 1846, on the Livingston lands in Wood-stock, Shandaken, and Olive, "all the interest of the inhabitants centered in the present, to make the most out of the land they could, and with as little expense as possible. Their want of, care for, and interest in the future was shown by their dilapidated houses and out-buildings, their common and temporary fences. Paints and paint brushes were apparently almost un-known in that locality. The tenant's interest was in the uncertain contin-uance of life; the landlord's upon reversion in death [here Schoonmaker was writing of leases for lives]. The whole face of the country told the sad story.[9]

"The inhabitants eventually rebelled against such tenures, and the re-bellion ended in their abolition. What a change in that country between *then* and *now!* Thrift and prosperity now put forth their blooming and smiling faces in every direction; comfortable, pleasant and indeed luxuri-ant homes can be seen on every hand tempting the denizen weary of city life to come annually for a season to enjoy their comforts." Schoonmaker was right in suggesting that the ending of the old system of land tenure helped clear the way for a flow of summer visitors similar to the guests at the Mountain House to many parts of the Hardenbergh Patent. The court decisions which put the patent's original title beyond dispute also played a part, for they made possible large investments in accommodations for summer people, and in means of moving them to and from the patent. But these investments were not to become visible until the 1870s. Through the middle years of the nineteenth century, mountain trees promised greater opportunities for profit than city people.

Made of Wood

✤ WHEN PERMANENT settlers arrived in the Catskills, the mountains' trees began to move out. Before human beings became part of the society of living things which surrounds and covers the Catskills, trees rarely left the mountains. Each tree struggled to live and reproduce on its birthplace and, if it escaped fire, wind, competition from its fellows, and insect and fungus attack, it lived out its destined span of life and died. Then its body would be taken apart by bacteria, fungi, and flying and wriggling things, and it would be returned to the earth to become the building material of new bodies. Indians had carried away parts of trees: the gum of the balsam fir for medicine or to calk canoes, maple syrup to sweeten their diet; or bits of wood well adapted to one purpose or another. But this had caused no visible change in the Catskills' forests. Nor had John Bartram's gathering of seeds and seedlings for his British landscape-gardening customers. But when the first settlers and their sawmills appeared, things began to change. The trees cut to make way for fields and pastures were reduced to ashes which could be sold or traded and sent from the Catskills to be put to many industrial uses. Sawmills picked out white pines, oaks, and cherry trees which the Hudson River and the Atlantic Ocean could carry far from their birthplaces as boards, planks, and timbers.

Once the Revolution ended, settlers and sawmillers sent vast numbers of trees flying from the Catskills in bits and pieces. Bark went to the tanners of Hudson and the Swamp. A bewildering variety of objects made of native wood soon began streaming to the lowlands, and eventually to every continent on the globe. Even the low plants which grew beneath the trees were examined to find parts which might be sent away—the roots of the ginseng, for instance, were gathered and sent in large quantities to the drug dealers of China. Only one tree left the Catskills intact as to trunk, roots, and branches—this was the balsam fir. The charming young of the balsam firs were kidnaped among the mountains and set to work ornamenting the grounds of prosperous Hudson Valley and New York people. In September 1788, for example, Elias Hasbrouck, the first supervisor of the newly organized town of Woodstock, received an order from a Kingston merchant for two young balsam firs to be delivered well packed in wooden boxes. Hasbrouck had just settled on land in Mink Hollow leased from James Desbrosses. He promised to deliver the trees quickly although as he wrote, he was "mitey busy in my new land."[1] Later young balsam firs left the Catskills by the hundreds and were being planted in rows by nurserymen in the city of New York to await sale. By 1835 the young balsam firs were so much depleted in the neighborhood of the Catskill Mountain House that when Michael Floy, Jr., son of a New York nurseryman, was sent there to dig some he reported that the trees had become so scarce he could find none. A few weeks later when Floy was back home he reported receiving a shipment by sloop of two hundred of the trees, gathered by others in some part of the Catskills not too close to the Mountain House.[2]

Few trees left the Catskills in so dashing a way as the white pines of the southwestern part of the mountains. Their trunks, fastened together in huge rafts, raced down the Delaware on the crests of spring or summer freshets and reached a market in such river ports as Trenton, Easton, or Philadelphia. Often rafts bore "top loads" of oak timbers for Philadelphia shipbuilders, of cherry for the frames of schoolboys' slates, of stone slabs for Philadelphia sidewalks, of charcoal, whiskey, or butter produced on Delaware or Sullivan county farms. It is not surprising that rafting on the Delaware acquired a folklore of its own and gave rise to its heroes. Of these the first was Daniel Skinner, a Connecticut Yankee, who came to the vicinity of Cochecton about 1760 in pursuit of part of the lands to which his state claimed title by virtue of old land grants which ran from the Atlantic Ocean westward to just where no one could be sure.

Skinner became a prosperous landowner and speculator, but he lives in legend for another reason: he is believed to have been the first man to guide a raft down the Delaware. Until Skinner died in 1801, he was known as the Admiral of the Delaware. And as long as the old man lived, every youngster who wanted to become a Delaware raftsman had first to present the Admiral with a bottle of wine. If his ambitions led him to aspire to the dignity of a steersman he had to give the admiral two bottles. For some time, only riverside dwellers of the Delaware banks below the point of junction of the East and West branches of the river at what is now Hancock had to fee the admiral. But as the demand for white pine logs and timber increased, raftsmen grew more venturesome and then the pines growing along the West and East branches began to fall and the admiral began drawing his wine from a wider area.[3] One well-known "rafting ground"[4] or "banking ground" was a little above Margaretville. It was to places like this that logs cut by winter were drawn over the snow and made into small rafts known as "colts." When spring freshets came, the colts were floated downriver and when they reached the main stream of the Delaware, the colts were assembled into large rafts often about one hundred and twenty feet long and thirty feet wide. One giant raft of 1870 reached a length of two hundred and one feet and a width of seventy-five feet. It had eight oars fore and aft, and a crew of eight. It carried a deckload of hardwood planks—hardwood, being less buoyant than the softwoods, could not raft on its own.[5]

Sailing down the rushing Delaware on a raft was often dangerous but it was more often a delightful adventure. In the later years of rafting, raftsmen often took friends and family along and, as John Burroughs would write, made "a jollification all the way to Trenton or Philadelphia."[6] The Delaware's eddies—the pools of still water which occurred here and there —were lined with taverns at which Delaware "water dogs" might revel when in the mood and indulge in fist fights. When the goal was reached and the raft's lumber or logs sold, there was the roundabout return trip home to be faced, for the upper Delaware was a one-way stream. Raftsmen carrying coils of ropes and the big augers they used in making their rafts became familiar figures on stagecoaches between Philadelphia and New York and on steamboats sailing up the Hudson. Passengers on the Concord coaches which sped westward from Newburgh, Kingston, and Catskill shared space with returning raftsmen after the freshets had sent thousands of rafts down the Delaware in each peak year of the rafting period.[7]

Rafting was all very well for the parts of the southern Catskills where salable timber grew and where suitable tributary streams were ready to convey colts to deeper and wider water. People of other parts of the Catskills looked on with envy as the rafting country profited by its combination of pine trees and the adaptability of the Delaware to rafting. By the 1830s tanners within easy reach of the Delaware could hope for a double profit, for as pines were picked from the forests of northeastern United States, the hemlock they cut for bark came to be more and more in demand for lumber. And the tanners' barkpeelers, who could work only from mid-May to early August when the bark peeled easily, found seasonal work in the rafting industry and so could make something like a year's wages in the Catskills.

Wherever among the mountains a fairly strong stream flowed and obstacles were not too great, men dreamed of raising money to remove rocks and rapids and so make the streams capable of floating logs or rafts. It was this kind of dreaming that led Chancellor Livingston's son-in-law Robert L. Livingston to propose clearing the Esopus so that the pines and hemlocks of the central Catskills might be sent to Kingston and there shipped on a proposed railroad to Hudson River wharves. (The presence of many busy mills near the mouth of the Esopus made rafting logs all the way to the Hudson impossible.) Landowners along the Neversink, which flows into the Delaware at Port Jervis, had plenty of fine pine and hemlock trees but because of the many obstructions in the river could not take to rafting. In 1811 the state legislature obligingly advanced $10,000 to be used in clearing the Neversink. For two years, rocks were removed and wooden aprons were built to make possible passage over waterfalls. The first raft to try the Neversink was wrecked. So too was the second—it was broken into bits by the river and two of its crewmen were drowned.[8] After that there was no further talk of rafting on the Neversink.

The arrival of railroads and the depletion of the Catskills' reserves of pines and hemlocks brought both tanning and rafting to an end. But the forests—if their soil was not disturbed by the plow or grazing cattle—did not stand still. The gaps left by the loss of great pines and hemlocks began to be filled almost as soon as the treetops touched the earth. And they were not filled with a new generation of pines and hemlocks, for the young seedlings of these trees do not thrive under the sun which beats down on a clearing. Instead, a mixture of grasses, trees, shrubs, and lowlier plants made their bids for life in the clearings, and in the struggle that followed it was usually hardwoods such as birch, ash, maple, and oak that won out and came to form dense stands of straight, tall trees.

It was in the northern Catskills at Hunter and in the Kaaterskill Clove that the cutting of hemlock groves for the tanlords had begun. There the new hardwood forests first reached a size useful for firewood or for making charcoal. Hardwoods like these were beginning, in the 1830s, to have another and a very promising use when processed by the skill of craftsmen and the power of mountain streams. As the United States grew in wealth and population, household furniture made of native hardwoods came into ever greater demand, and the craftsmen of the Catskills responded. Earlier, furniture had been made in and around the Catskills by time-honored handicraft methods. Dutch models were often followed, with variations, by men working in the Hudson River trading towns, and their products found their way into the homes of the more prosperous settlers among the mountains. When the Yankees marched into the Catskills they brought with them their own furniture-making skills and designs. One of these Yankees was Zephaniah Chase of the island of Martha's Vineyard, where Chase had combined furniture making with sailing on whaling voyages. By the fall of 1787 he was settled in Jewett, where he farmed and made or mended furniture and a great variety of wooden objects. A candlestand, sets of six "strip-backed chairs,"[9] shingles, coffins, a "Great Chair," and a cherry table were among the sales of furniture Chase listed in his account book. He also mended sleds, tools, and spinning wheels.

Craftsmen like Zephaniah Chase worked in many parts of the Catskills making furniture, bowls and spoons, butter paddles, barrels, firkins and boxes, and a long list of other things fashioned of native wood. But this tradition of handicraft work by part-time farmers was doomed. Colonel Edwards was not the only Yankee to bring factory methods in using forest products into the Catskills. The manufacture of such things as wooden clocks, wooden shaving boxes, and kitchen gadgets got underway beside waterfalls. By 1835, furniture making, with the use of waterpower and factory methods, made its beginnings in the town of Hunter close to the Edwards tannery. Its owner, Samuel Chichester who had helped build the Catskill Mountain House,[10] employed forty men and made chairs with cane and wooden seats. Twenty years later, "chair factories" like Chichester's were numerous wherever tanning had encouraged the growth of young hardwoods or left roads leading to older stands of maple, ash, beech, and birch. By 1857 the Edwards tannery was abandoned—there was no longer sufficient hemlock bark within reach to keep it going. Then a bedstead factory, established nearby some years before, moved into one end of the main tannery building. A maker of ash rims for the sieves necessary in every kitchen took over the other end. Before many years, furniture and woodenware making had displaced tanning as the economic base of life in Hunter. And the products were being sold in an ever-widening circle spreading out from the Catskills. By 1843 the "therapeutic chair" which was the ancestor of the Rip Van Winkle chair of the future was in lively production in the Kaaterskill Clove. The water, which delighted visitors as the Kaaterskill Falls went down the mountains, turned the wheel of the therapeutic chair factory to such good effect that the "highly ornamental"[11] chair created something of a sensation when it was exhibited at one of the fairs of the American Institute. Near this chair factory, and using the same stream, stood a paper factory. Both occupied the site of an earlier tanning settlement.

Many German-born immigrants came to the Catskills and worked at furniture making. One was George Fromer, who set up a factory in Hunter in 1846 and made "a fine grade of chairs for the New York trade."[12] In 1855 Fromer employed twelve men and twelve women. He paid the men $26 per month and the women only $6.50 because the women worked at home in the intervals of household duties, putting cane seats in frames which would later become parts of finished chairs. Fromer was making eight hundred dozen chairs per year by 1855, and their wholesale value was a modest $7400. At the same time Baldwin and company employing six men, were annually turning the posts of twelve hundred bedsteads on their water-powered lathes. By the late 1860s woodworking factories had greatly increased in size, number, and volume of production. Some were "stock factories" which made parts to be shipped far and wide to furniture makers large and small. Others turned porch pillars and balusters, wooden bowls, policemen's billies, belaying pins, wooden legs, rolling pins, the little covered wooden boxes in which druggists dispensed ointments. Some small handicraft "turning mills" like that of the Vosburgh brothers in Woodstock would turn anything at all to order.[13] Once the Civil War had ended, woodworking factories among the Catskills were sending the hardwood trees of the mountains to South and Central America, the West Indies, and Europe in vast quantities. The export trade in cane-seated chairs and in rocking cradles became so important that it dominated the industry and influenced design. Because shipping rates by sea were based on volume rather than weight, chairs had to be so designed and so packed as to occupy the smallest possible space in the boxes in which they were shipped in dozen lots. Years of refinement and experimentation brought these packing boxes down to a length of about forty-two inches, and a width and depth of twenty inches. The chairs were first assembled, painted or varnished, and then knocked down before being packed.[14]

Samuel Chichester's son Lemuel brought chair- and cradlemaking in the Catskills to its peak of volume in the factory he built in Chichester a few miles north of Phoenicia, where 3600 chairs and 900 rocking cradles per week were sometimes turned out.[15] In the Shandaken Valley only a few miles from Chichester, Hiram Whitney, who claimed to be a grandson of Eli Whitney, the inventor of the cotton gin, was also making chairs on a large scale. In Hunter, chairs, bedsteads, washstands, chests of drawers, and other articles of household use continued to be made, with part of the production going to the Catskill Mountain House and other local establishments for summer hospitality. Graining and painted ornament were widely used. In Chichester in 1874, chairs and cradles for export to Central and South America were being "decorated in such gaudy colors as will make the dusky natives of the south yell with delight when they gaze upon their

The Greek Revival facade grafted on the old Catskill Moun-
tain House after Charles L. Beach took charge.

Above, a leather mask used during the Anti-rent War. (*Senate House Museum, Kingston, N.Y.*)

Right, "The Inhuman Anti-rent Murder," a lithograph drawn and published by political cartoonist H. R. Robinson while Anti-rent War excitement was at its height. (*Courtesy of the Cannon Free Library, Delhi, N.Y.*)

ONE GOOD TURN DESERVES ANOTHER

V & S

Left, a turning-mill letterhead demonstrates with whimsy how the work was done. (*Courtesy of Craig Vosburgh, Shady, N.Y.*)

Below left, the Laurel House as it looked before its 1882 enlargement.

This detail from a composite panorama of the Catskills drawn and published about 1880 by H. Schile gives an imaginative view of an Ulster and Delaware train crossing the mountain barrier at Pine Hill while trackside charcoal kilns belch smoke.

Above, the dining room at the Overlook Mountain House in 1871. The waiters were students at Lincoln University in Pennsylvania. From a stereograph taken by "Lewis of Kingston."

Left, the briefly fashionable Tremper House at Phoenicia relied on its closeness to a railroad station to make up for the lack of a spectacular view from its piazzas. From a wood engraving in *A Catskill Souvenir*, 1879.

By 1936 when this photograph of U&D engine no. 34 was taken on the line's Catskill Mountain and Stony Clove branch, the U&D had passed its hopeful days. Photograph by Frederick Bonte, New York. (*Courtesy of the Greene County Historical Society.*)

In this wood engraving from a drawing by Catskills' Colonel B. B. G. Stone, an old-fashioned Beach carriage carries the passengers and luggage to the Catskill Mountain House above. From *Lippincott's Magazine*, September 1879. (*Courtesy of New York State Library.*)

beauties, . . ." said the Kingston *Freeman* of June 23. Some of the chairs were painted carmine and were "figured with gold."[16] For use in the United States, the Chichester factory emphasized sober "slat-bottomed camp chairs" used in the lecture rooms and theaters for which they also made settees or benches. By 1874 their three water-powered turbines were being helped out by a steam engine.

The making of barrel staves and headings for assembling elsewhere had long been a mountain industry. By the middle years of the nineteenth century, factory methods had taken over and stave and heading mills stood on almost every stream among the mountains that provided enough water power. Sawmills making boards, planks, and joists (larger timbers continued to be hewn by hand) were located on similar streams wherever stands of usable trees stood conveniently close. These sawmills shut down when winter ice gathered on their water wheels or when streams dried up in summer. They were often ramshackle affairs—the census takers of 1855 valued few at more than two hundred dollars—but they were numerous. In 1855, eighteen water-powered sawmills were listed as being at work in two of Hunter's three election districts. As the tanning period ended, sawmillers turned to working up the many spruce, hardwoods, and pines found in difficult places among the precipices of the Catskills. As late as 1902 a white-pine mast seventy feet long was cut in the town of Woodstock and sold to a Rondout shipyard.

Water-powered up-and-down saws like the ones used in Chancellor Livingston's busy mill at Yankeetown Pond in Woodstock were not altogether discarded in favor of the more efficient circular saws and steam until well inside the twentieth century. By then all reason for locating sawmills on the banks of streams had vanished, yet many mills went on doing business in their old locations as if mesmerized by the music of running water into defying floods and economic handicaps. Little settlements with stores and churches had grown up around some sawmills and factories, and many a hamlet in the Catskills owes its location to a now-forgotten sawmill or chair factory taking advantage of what was once a "fine mill seat."

The flight of the trees from the Catskills accelerated as factory methods became established. But not all old handicrafts gave in at once to the factory age. A few, like the making of "hoop poles" from which barrel hoops were fashioned, held out almost to the end of the nineteenth century. Machinery for making the staves and headings for barrels had been invented and was in use beside many Catskill streams, but no one had been able to devise a way of making by machinery the wooden hoops which held barrels together. That was why, year after year, thousands of men of the Catskills made hoop poles by splitting and shaving two-inch saplings of the hardwoods that sprang up on lands recently cut over by the tanners' men. The saplings were usually cut in early fall and were sometimes sunk in "hoop pole ponds" to keep them from drying out before they could be worked up. Winter was the hoop-pole-making time and then here and there among the Catskillls hoop-pole shanties which had been vacant all summer came to life and their huge stone fireplaces blazed with the debris that resulted from splitting and shaving saplings into flexible bands which could be converted into stout hoops at the barrel factory. The sapling was held in a wooden horse and split with a draw knife—it took time for a man to acquire the skill and speed necessary if he was to make a living shaving hoops. Some turned out a thousand hoops in a single day; a few did even better than that. The finished hoops could be traded at valley stores for tobacco, whiskey, and food, and were used almost like currency in many transactions.[17]

The men who shaved hoops were often eccentrics who preferred a lonely life, but many were farmers or other workers who took to hoop shaving in the season when their usual work was dull. The "shingle weavers" of the Catskills, like the hoop shavers, were made up of hermits and farmers who followed their craft seasonally. White pine and hemlock were the usual woods from which shingles were split by the use of a tool called a froe. (Pine shingles outlasted those of hemlock almost two to one and so brought a higher price.) By the eighteen-nineties, shingle weaving and hoop-pole shaving were both dying out. A machine for sawing barrel hoops from wood, and the development of a metal hoop doomed hoop-pole shaving, while shingle-making machinery came into the Catskills and made splitting shingles by hand a losing game.

But during the time that shingle weaving and hoop-pole shaving were at their height, a newly discovered use for the young balsam firs of the Catskills sent up to two hundred thousand of these trees hastening from the Catskills each November and December. During the 1830s and 1840s Christmas trees had come into American homes. At first no organized attempt at supplying the trees was undertaken—they were cut in nearby woodlots or brought into towns to order by farmers. By 1851 the fragrant balsam fir with its cross-tipped branches was elbowing out all others as America's favorite Christmas tree. That year, Mark Carr of the town of Hunter wondered if the demand for young balsam firs might not be turned to account. Following years of good seed production the trees grew like weeds in the pastures of the high "cold lands" of Hunter and had to be cleared out at intervals to keep them from dispossessing the grass. They swarmed up the surrounding mountains to their summits, but it was in pastures and at the edges of clearings that they reached the symmetrical form which raised the hopes of "the jolly woodsman,"[18] Mark Carr. Carr's friends and his wife laughed at the notion of shipping Christmas trees from the Catskills to the city of New York. But Mark Carr was not discouraged. With the help of his sons he cut two wagonloads of the trees, hitched his oxen to the wagons, and hauled the trees to the Hudson River at Catskill where they were loaded on a steamboat for New York. There Carr rented space on the corner of Vesey and Greenwich streets. And there he sold his trees with a speed and at a price that amazed him. The Christmas-tree business in New York had begun.

For years after that, Hudson River steamboats making their last trips of each season sailed to New York laden with balsam fir and spruce trees, their boughs bent back so that they might be tied into convenient bundles. Christmas-tree cutting and the gathering of other "Christmas greens" moved westward, northward, and southward from the town of Hunter. Carloads of balsam firs were being shipped to New York from northern Sullivan County over the New York, Ontario & Western by the 1870s; soon the opening of the Ulster & Delaware Railroad spurred cutting of balsam firs on the mountainsides near its tracks. It became obvious after a while that the flight of young balsam fir trees from the Catskills would some day go beyond the ability of their elders to replace them, but few showed concern about it. Mountain people seldom took the trees into their own homes. They usually set them up only in their churches where the trees became the centers of community Christmas celebrations. In Prattsville, Zadock Pratt, as might have been expected, was among the first mountain people to bring a Christmas tree into his house. The tree, of course, was a hemlock, and Pratt invited his neighbors in to admire it and to receive the presents with which its branches were laden.

As young balsam fir and spruce trees left the Catskills, millions of even younger trees left the mountains in disguise. They had been transformed into wool and mutton. The uncritical appetites of sheep make them remarkably effective as deforesting machines—of all domestic animals only goats nibble more widely or cut closer to the earth. Chancellor Livingston's enthusiasm for sheep-growing had helped turn the attention of mountain people to sheep. Later the opening of the West to sheep-growing made it seem unlikely that the Catskills would ever become one great treeless sheep pasture, as some had predicted. Yet large flocks of sheep continued to graze and many a high hill or mountaintop became an open sheep pasture where seedling trees had no chance at all for life. In early fall in years when the crops of beech and acorns were abundant, men went from house to house and from farm to farm in the Hudson Valley collecting great numbers of hogs whom they took, at so much per head, to the Catskill forests and the fattening food spread on the earth. The acorn or beechnut pork which trotted back to the valley, leaving the trees behind, was highly esteemed.

In spite of the departure of millions upon millions of trees from the Catskills, the region remained predominantly tree country as the first century of American independence approached. Each fall, wind, water, gravity, and the efforts of animals scattered prodigious quantities of the seeds of the mountains' mature trees. And a good proportion of the seeds did well. For just as some parts of the world are desert country or grass country, so the Catskills are tree country in which trees are given unusual advantages over other living things. From the earliest days of settlement the Catskills trees had been cut and burned, peeled and sawed and shredded and sent out into the world in a hundred disguises. Yet trees had continued to spring up and prosper among the mountains. There the temperature range and the abundant rainfall caused by the Catskills position on the leeward edge of the great Allegheny plateau helped mightily in encouraging the growth of trees. The roughness of the land kept enough old seed trees from the ax to replace those which fell or burned and to cover abandoned farmland quickly with thrifty young trees.

By the 1870s two principal ways of making a living were open to the people of the Catskills. They could work in the industries based on their dwindling, yet still extensive forests, or they could care for summer visitors. In either case most of them would do some farming, make maple sugar, trap, fish and hunt, or gather ginseng root to help support their families. The heart of the summer-visitor district continued to be the Catskill Mountain House with the widely scattered turnpike and fishermen's inns getting a modest share of the business. But summer visitors were increasing year by year, and by 1870 there were many signs to show that the entire region of the Catskills was on the verge of becoming one great summer playground. The identification in many minds of the old Mountain House area as being the Catskill Mountains was nearing its end.

61

Overlook Joins
the Romantic Catskills

❦ WHEN CHARLES L. BEACH took possession of the Catskill Mountain House in 1846, the threat of rival summer hotels among the Catskills was already growing. Even then the reforms in methods of land tenure which seemed likely to follow the end of the Anti-rent War were dissipating the doubt that had hovered for so long over the Great Hardenbergh Patent. The patent's mountaintops and waterfalls, its trout streams and views into infinity would soon be open to attract tourists like those who came to the Pine Orchard. Only difficulties of transportation held back the appearance of summer hotels on Overlook, High Point, or other elevations on the top of the eastern wall of the Catskills.

James Booth had failed in his attempt to build a hotel on Overlook Mountain, but as Charles L. Beach rebuilt the old Catskill Mountain House, Overlook was being praised in a way that might very well foreshadow the appearance of a rival establishment on the mountain. Charles Lanman, the young landscape painter and travel writer led the chorus of praise. Lanman was among Thomas Cole's greatest admirers and seemed to be trying to give Overlook—then known as South Peak—a glow of romance equal to the one created by Irving, Cooper, and Cole, which had done so much to make the Pine Orchard famous.

During the years of the Anti-rent War, Lanman and a number of painting and writing friends made their headquarters at the "Dutch farmhouse" of Levi Myer near the foot of the Plattekill Clove. The war did not interest Lanman—he was having a love affair with Overlook Mountain. He sketched the mountain and he wrote of it: "Like a cornerstone, it stands at the junction of the northern and western ranges of the Catskills, and as its huge form looms up against the evening sky, it inspires one with awe, as if it were the ruler of the world; yet I have learned to love it as a friend. Its name, its image, and every tree, and shrub and vine, which springs from its rocky bosom, can never be forgotten. I have reflected upon it when reposing in the noonday sunshine, or enveloped in clouds, when holding communion with the most holy night, when trembling under the influence of a thunderstorm, or encircled by a rainbow. It has filled my soul with images of sublimity, and made me feel the omnipotence of God."[1]

In his *Letters of a Landscape Painter,* which was published in 1845, and in magazine articles, Lanman devoted many pages to enthusiastic accounts of climbing Overlook and fishing in the streams which furrowed its sides. He wrote of the beauty of Schue's Lake which lay not far from Overlook's summit, of the strange horror of the mountain's rattlesnake dens, of exploring romantic Yager's Cave. He told of the "Bear Bank," so called, said Lanman, because bears were in the habit of sunning themselves there. As effective as any of Lanman's bits of Overlook lore was his tale of how what he called the Eagle's Cliff got its name. Long ago an eagle had snatched and carried to the clifftop an Indian baby. The mother made her way to the cliff, but she was too late. With the mangled body of her dead baby in her arms she leaped to her death "in the abyss below."[2]

Lanman described with passion and in his fanciest prose a night spent on the moonlit summit of Overlook. He was familiar with the many waterfalls and other scenic wonders so much admired by Mountain House guests in the Kaaterskill Clove, and now he presented the Plattekill Clove as equally romantic and picturesque.

The clove, he wrote, "abounds in waterfalls of surpassing beauty, varying from ten to a hundred and fifty feet in height, whose rocks are green with the moss of centuries, and whose brows are ever wreathed with the most exquisite of vines and flowers. There's the Double Leap, with its almost fathomless pool, containing a hermit trout that has laughed at the angler's skill for a score of years; the Mountain Spirit, haunted by the disembodied spirit of an Indian girl, who lost her life there while pursuing a phantom of the brain. . . ."[3] Lanman went on to list other Plattekill Clove wonders, "The Black Chasm, the Gray Chasm and the Devil's Chamber" among them. No one had ever written as he did about parts of the Catskills not included in the neighborhood of the Mountain House. And no one before Lanman had dealt with the simple inhabitants of the Catskills in so sympathetic a way. In Europe, the people who lived the year round in regions sought by pilgrims in quest of the romantic and picturesque had become the objects of almost as many admiring glances as waterfalls, mountaintops, or lakes. The Catskills had for picturesque human interest only Rip Van Winkle who was fictional, and Leather-stocking whose relationship was of the slightest. Thomas Cole, first of all, had given the living people of the mountains a touch of romantic interest. Now Lanman carried this process much farther. He wrote, for example, of visits to sugar camps at the base of Overlook and told of attending a "sugar bee." He reported that "everybody is invited, old men and their wives, young men and maidens; . . . the principal recreation is dancing to the music of a fiddle . . . a most sumptuous and exceedingly miscellaneous feast is spread before the multitude . . . that an abundance of maple sugar is met with on these occasions will be readily imagined, and we may add that, in those districts where temperance societies are unpopular, the sugar is taken considerably adulterated in whiskey."[4] Lanman wrote much of his favorite guide, Peter Hummel, who was, like Levi Myer, a descendant of one of the Palatine families which had helped populate the eastern Catskills. Hummel became one of the first of the native woodsmen to be closely associated in the minds of tourists with the Catskills; he combined the best features of Rip and Leatherstocking.

"Hummel was born in a little hut at the foot of South Peak," Lanman wrote, "is twenty-seven years of age, and has never been to school a day in his life, or in his travels further away from his home than fifteen miles. He was *educated* for a bark-gatherer, his father and several brothers being engaged in the business; but Peter is averse to commonplace labor, to anything, in fact, that will bring in money . . . he is probably one of the most perfect specimens of a hunter now living; and very few, I imagine, could have survived the dangers to which he has exposed himself. He seems to be one of those iron mortals that cannot die with age and infirmity,—or be killed by man, rock or water; he must be shivered by a stroke of lightning. Although one of the wildest of God's creatures, Peter Hummel is as amiable and kindhearted a man as ever lived. He is an original wit withal and shrewd and very laughable are many of his speeches, and his stories are the cream of romance and genuine mountain poetry."[5]

One day Lanman took Hummel and another fisherman's guide (probably the one known as White Yankee) to the Catskill Mountain House. He wrote that "I met a few acquaintances there, to whom I introduced my comrades, and in a short time each one of them was spinning a mountain legend to a crowd of astonished and delighted listeners. In due time I ushered them into the dining room where was enacted a scene which can be better imagined than described. A Chinese in Victoria's drawing-room would not be more completely out of his element, or be the cause of heartier laughter, than were these men among the soup, ice-cream, and silver forks of the 'Yankee Palace,' as the house has been christened by the Dutch under the mountains."[6]

Lanman's zealous promotion of South Peak drew the attention of other writers and painters to the mountain. One painter who probably climbed the mountain after hearing Lanman's praises was Thomas Cole. In August 1846, Cole and a large party of friends, including two poetic clergymen, set out by wagon from Catskill and slept that night in a "wigwam" which they built of balsam fir boughs close to the top of South Peak. The members of the party sang hymns and prayed and one of them, poet-clergyman Louis L. Noble, did "an Indian dance" by the campfire. Cole slept in his brown monk's robe and awoke to the song of birds. He wrote a charming and lighthearted account of the trip and concluded with the heretical statement that the view from the Overlook was "far finer" than that from the Pine Orchard.[7]

By 1846 Cole's lighthearted creative days were over. Since his return to the Catskills in 1839 he had painted many landscapes of which Catskill mountain scenery was the subject, but more and more often these landscapes were painted to order. They took second place in Cole's affections to the series of allegorical subjects like his *Voyage of Life* and to the religious paintings which occupied most of his time. When in Italy, Cole had certainly known of the German religious painters of the Nazarene group who lived and worked in an abandoned monastery near Rome. Like the Nazarenes, Cole took to praying before painting. His closest friends became admiring clergymen who encouraged him to attempt grandiose religious works far beyond his skill. Worn down by the struggle to do something which was impossible for him, Cole retreated from life and seemed to his friends to be convinced that he had not long to live. In October 1847 Cole paid what seemed to be a formal final visit to the Catskills he had helped make famous and which in return had given him his most enduring satisfactions as a painter. Cole had painted landscapes in the White Mountains, the Adirondacks, in England, France, and Italy. But until the last two years of his life he had never ventured outside the part of the Catskills easily reached by Mountain House guests. Now he chose for his final visit not the Pine Orchard or the Kaaterskill Falls or the summit of one of the mountains close to the two lakes, but the top of Overlook Mountain. When Cole's minister, the Reverend Louis L. Noble, came to write his parishioner's biography, he treated Cole's farewell to the Hudson River and the Catskills from the Overlook Cliff with reverence. "From this dizzy crag Cole took a long and silent look up and down the beloved valley of the Hudson. He had gazed upon it, from other points unnumbered times, alone and with companions . . . it had filled his heart for years. This was his last look. A few hundred feet below, by a rivulet, expanding into a small, glassy pool, bordered with moss, and roofed with the gay foliage of the month, he took his final mountain repast, a sandwich and an apple, seasoning a quiet hour with his usual pleasantry. . . ."[8] A few months later Cole died.

When Noble's biography appeared it contained accounts of Cole's two visits to the summit of Overlook Mountain. But because Noble referred to the mountain only as South Peak, most readers took it for granted that he meant High Peak which rises to the southwest of the Pine Orchard. Many an admirer of Cole, having read Noble's book, climbed High Peak and there enjoyed the excitement of standing on the exact spot from which he supposed his hero to have taken his last look at the Catskills and the Hudson. Cole's own account, in which he called the mountain The Overlook, remained locked up in a volume of his journal preserved by his descendants in his old house in Catskill.

Even without Cole's help, the tide of public interest was showing signs of flowing southward from the old Mountain House. For the first time, Overlook Mountain was capturing more pages in print than the Pine Orchard and its stock of natural wonders. This could not have been very pleasing to Charles L. Beach. But what must have given Beach something of a shock was the departure for Overlook Mountain of his popular manager, William Scobie. Scobie had been a well-known Saratoga hotelman with an excellent following. In 1845 he leased the plateau on Overlook with the copious spring and the unexcelled view of the Hudson Valley on one side and range after range of wild Catskills on the other. He proposed carrying out James Booth's old dream of building a Summer Mansion there. Perhaps it was the combination of Scobie's plan and the beginning of the intensive publicizing of Overlook Mountain (and the two may well have been related) that caused a booklet titled *The Scenery of the Catskill Mountains* to go on sale at Beach's Mountain House in the summer of 1846. The booklet's compiler was the Reverend Dr. David Murdoch, an able and eloquent native of Scotland who had come to Catskill's Reformed Dutch Church after a stay of some years in Canada. Murdoch functioned as a sort of staff preacher at the Mountain House and conducted services there when more eminent visiting clergymen were not available.

In Murdoch's booklet the praises lavished by many writers on the Pine Orchard and its hotel and the romanticizing words of Irving, Bryant, and Cooper were all conveniently brought together to make a forcible appeal to the summer-traveling public. There was not a word, of course, about Overlook Mountain or the many inns scattered throughout the region which were the favorites of serious trout fishermen. Murdoch seemed to assume that only the Beach Hotel and its surroundings were included in the Catskill Mountains.

In 1861 eccentric Dr. Murdoch died after a somewhat stormy departure from Catskill and nine years of conflict with members of the Elmira church over which he presided. That same year saw the publication of one of the greatest boons to the Catskill Mountain House to appear in many years: *The Dutch Dominie of the Catskills.* It was Dr. Murdoch's loosely written novel of Revolutionary days in the northeastern Catskills. Murdoch made every locality familiar to Mountain House visitors the scene of a lively meeting between, among many others, Tories, Indians named Shandaagen and Kiskataam, an upper-class Englishman masquerading as the Hermit of the Hollow, complete with crystal ball and an ancient book of magic, slaves with African fetishes, brave Whigs, a highborn English lady, and numerous Dutch-speaking old-timers. Confusing as the book's plot certainly was, it made lively reading and did much to uphold the Pine Orchard's claim to be the only part of the Catskills worth a summer-tourist's time. But in spite of all the efforts of Charles L. Beach and his adherents, that claim was becoming hard to maintain.

The growth of population and its increasing concentration in the cities of the United States, plus the more comfortable living conditions and incomes of large classes of white people made at least a few summer weeks in the country more and more a part of American life. And where could the prosperous people of New York and other cities of the mid-Atlantic region find more glamorous and conveniently reached summer recreation than in the fabled Catskills around which so many romantic associations had come to cluster? But only one glittering bit of the Catskills could be reached without an undue amount of jolting over ill-kept turnpikes and hazardous windings over steep mountain roads. That bit was the Pine Orchard and its immediate surroundings. Trout fishermen and hunters from New York might rough it in the inns of the Esopus Valley, the East Branch, and Sullivan County's Beaverkill and Willowemoc. But most Americans preferred the comfort of the Mountain House. Until railroads could penetrate the Catskills, there could be no substantial spreading of the Pine Orchard's glamor to the rest of the region. And the railroads were slow in arriving.

62

Great Days for
the Catskill Mountain House

✤   THE YEARS BETWEEN 1846 and 1871, when the first railroad penetrated deep into the Catskills, were the most prosperous and glamorous in all the long history of the Catskill Mountain House. Over and over at the height of the season in August, cots were set up in halls and odd corners to take care of the overflow of guests. From time to time Charles L. Beach enlarged his hotel. But he could not keep up with the demand. In 1862 Matthew Vassar, the Poughkeepsie brewer who was to found a college, traveled to the Mountain House one August day only to report finding a hundred and fifty people ahead of him. Some had been waiting three days for rooms.[1] At times like this, men and women camped out in neighboring barns, sheds, and farmhouses.

By 1852 this kind of crowding encouraged Peter Schutt, who had been a lowland innkeeper, and his son Jacob L. to add keeping boarders and lodgers to their management of the Kaaterskill Falls. Their Laurel House had a decided charm. It remained open until after winter arrived and then guests, among whom were many famous painters and writers, liked to sit by the huge open fireplace in the Laurel House office or beside the Franklin stove in the parlor and listen to Jacob Schutt's tales of perils suffered while hunting in the wilderness. They called the younger Schutt "Shakespeare Schutt" because of his resemblance to the William Shakespeare of the Chandos portrait.[2] The Schutts advertised their willingness to act as hosts and guides to winter visitors to the wondrous "ice castles" which often formed around their Kaaterskill Falls and which were the subject of a romantic poem by William Cullen Bryant, which had been included in the *Scenery of the Catskill Mountains*. During the '50s and '60s, many farmers who lived reasonably close to the Pine Orchard turned part-time boardinghouse keepers. They were able to offer enticingly low rates and a simple rural atmosphere. They fed guests the milk, meat, fruits, and vegetables produced on their own farms. Charles L. Beach did not see the Laurel House or the other smaller boardinghouses as threats to his own hotel. They appealed to less prosperous people than his patrons and to the out-of-season trade. And neighboring summer boarders added to the Beach income when they came to his house to admire the view and to have a few drinks in his bar or a meal in his dining room.

The success of the Catskill Mountain House and its satellite boarding-houses meant much to the businessmen of Catskill. Supplies for the Mountain House were bought in Catskill and Catskill men and women found work in Beach's House, as some called the place. Prospective guests on the mountaintop landed from Hudson River steamboats at Catskill and spent money there while waiting. The businessmen of other Hudson River towns within easy distance of the Catskills looked on with envy as their Catskill rivals reflected Beach's success. In Kingston especially, the talk of building a summer hotel on Overlook Mountain, or Woodstock Mountain or Point as it was often being called, grew louder and louder. In 1855 Nicholas Elmendorf, a Kingston steamboat man, raised the hopes of his fellow townsmen by proposing to take the lead in building a mountain house, which, many in Kingston said, would out-shine Charles Beach's because of its higher elevation and its remarkable view. And that view was indeed far more glorious than the one that had helped to make the fortune of the Catskill Mountain House. To the east lay the towns and farms of the Hudson Valley; to the southeast the Shandaken Mountains rose; to the west and northwest the mountains with the wildest and boldest profiles of all the Catskills gave an almost Alpine air to the scene. Compared with this view, the Pine Orchard's was bland indeed. But even with the view from the Overlook on his side in a day when views were the most powerful of allies for a hotel projector, Elmendorf could not raise the capital to make his plan a reality.[3] The transportation and supply difficulties of the Overlook site caused capital to shrink in horror from the mountain.

By 1857 Kingston hopes were revived after the Elmendorf fiasco. It was announced that a summer hotel would be built on Overlook Mountain by a man who had the authentic golden touch. He was Robert Living-ston Pell, a descendant of the manor Livingstons, the Duanes, the Pells of Pelham Manor in Westchester County, and of numerous other better sort families of colonial days. But Pell was not content to rest on his genealogi-cal laurels. He graduated from Harvard and made the Grand Tour of

Europe. He collected copies of masterpieces of Italian painting, and some of these copies were put together to ornament the ceilings of his residence on the banks of the Hudson a few miles below Kingston. The house was described by an admiring contemporary as "Greek without and Roman within."[4] Around this monument to leisured culture lay the productive and landscaped acres of Pelham Farm, which was among the wonders of its day because of its orchards, its vineyards, its fishponds, its wharves from which Pelham Farm apples were shipped to Europe and some even to China. It had its own cider mill, its distillery, its hothouses and grape houses. Pell was proud of the prizes he had won at agricultural exhibitions with such exotic crops as Hudson Valley cotton and tobacco. It was true enough that as Pell took hold of Overlook, the mountain remained as far away as ever from a Hudson River landing—much farther than the Catskill Mountain House. It was also true that there was no road climbing up Overlook and help from public funds and turnpike investors, such as had played so important a part in sending a road up the wall of the Catskills to the Pine Orchard, was not to be thought of. But Pell was a hero who was expected to accomplish wonders. How could he fail when he turned his attention to building a Mountain House on Overlook Mountain—or Pell's Mountain as some were already calling it? But fail he did.

When the economic slump of 1857–58 struck, it made no exception in favor of Robert Livingston Pell—in fact, it hit him hard. He joined James Booth, William Scobie, and Nicholas Elmendorf as disappointed Overlook dreamers. The name Pell's Mountain was hastily discarded. Once again the Catskill Mountain House was without any sign of a rival in all the region of the Catskills. Over and over the hotel had teetered on the edge of collapse and each time it had been saved. It had weathered not only economic storms, threats from Overlook, and competition from other summer resort regions but had also repeatedly defied fire and lightning. On Thursday June 30, 1850, for example, lightning struck the hotel. It "passed down the conductor near the Porter's room"—"it passed up to the shelves lined with brass and iron candlesticks" (one of these was handed to each guest as he retired in the evening)—it "left its imprint upon twenty to thirty of them, welding two together, then passed up the bell wires into the office"[5]—and stunned the clerk. The clerk was otherwise uninjured and no damage resulted to anything but the candlesticks. Not long afterward the hotel roof sprouted dozens of lightning rods, each about five feet long, until the building looked like a pincushion.

More than once, fires which devoured the debris of clearing, lumbering, and barkpeeling on the mountaintop swept close to the Mountain House and threatened to destroy it. In August 1854 such a fire, although at a safe distance from the Mountain House, gave rise to a pall of smoke which seemed to have swallowed up the entire range of the Catskills. The New York *Herald* reported that the Mountain House had been totally destroyed. Other newspapers copied the report. But when a heavy rain checked the fire, the Mountain House emerged from the smoke clouds as sound as ever.

The Greene County *Whig* of Catskill reflected the fear of competition to their Mountain House which was disturbing Catskill businessmen when it said that the report of the end of the hotel was "undoubtedly the work of some evil-minded person, performed with a view of injuring it. . . ."[6] Some readers probably interpreted this suggestion as hinting at dirty work from the direction of Overlook Mountain. Others took it as a jab at the New York *Herald*'s editor, James Gordon Bennett, who had a way of blackmailing businessmen into advertising by printing unfavorable rumors about them.

Storms tore at the Mountain House, and floods often ripped out sections of its turnpike, yet it survived and flourished. Rattlesnakes appeared under the very feet of sauntering Mountain House patrons, yet they never injured anyone. Although the hotel vicinity abounded in dangerous precipices, no one ever tumbled down to his death or even serious injury. In 1850 Charles B. Foster of Utica slipped over the brink of the lower Kaaterskill Falls and fell eighty feet to the rocks below. The doctor who was summoned patched Foster as best he could and before long his patient was well. In 1868 another victim of a fall did not do as well. He was Vite, a dog, who had been trained to jump when his master whistled. When the master gave a "thoughtless signal to 'jump,'" while standing at the brink of the falls, the dog jumped to his death on the rocks below. The master commissioned a Catskill stonecutter to inscribe a rock with a tribute to the dog—and the inscription honoring "Vite, the Bayard of dogs"[7] may still be seen. The turnpike road over which Mountain House guests ascended and descended by thousands each year in carriages was admittedly dangerous. But no serious accident was ever reported to have occurred. And if one had taken place, Charles L. Beach would surely have done his best to minimize it. He knew that a few widespread reports of injury to his guests from rattlesnakes, fire, lightning, or carriage accidents would have done irreparable damage to his business. In its early years, many timid folks had been afraid to risk a visit to the Mountain House. By the fifties and sixties fears like these were vanishing. The Catskill Mountain House appeared to be under the special care of providence.

The triumph of the romantic movement had given religious associations to many features of the landscape and to none more generously than to mountaintops. The Pine orchard in James Powers' time had taken on something of the feeling of holy ground. After 1846 the hotel became a kind of temple with Charles L. Beach functioning well as high priest. In ancient Greece and Rome, temples had often been built in the midst of carefully created hilltop wildernesses known as sacred landscapes. To cultivated eyes the original Catskill Mountain House had more than a hint of the look of a mountain villa of the kind pictured in the frescoes unearthed at Pompei and Herculaneum.[8] But after Charles L. Beach endowed the building with its new pillared façade it became definitely templelike. Visitors who set down their emotions in writing continued to deal with the "spiritual" aspect of the Pine Orchard and its hotel. In 1858 Professor C. C. Bennett descended to the lowland to declare, "I have seen and heard unutterable things in the mountains—visions and voices—forms of mighty and bewildering magnificence beyond mortal ken. . . ."[9] In 1860 the New York *Christian Inquirer* found a stay at the Pine Orchard to bring about "a purification of sense and spirit conjointly. We feel less sinful than when the arms of dame earth hug us closely to her heart and smother us in her thick breath."[10]

Rich worshipers, fashionable worshipers, worshipers who were both rich and fashionable, owners of old money and owners of new money all came to the Catskill Mountain House. And Charles Beach showed the conservatism of a true temple custodian by keeping ritual and surroundings unchanged. He did not pander to newly rich guests by installing furniture and draperies of the latest styles. Nor did he try to match the elegance of his Corinthian portico with a similar elegance in interior design. Public rooms and private rooms, corridors and kitchens were squeezed in behind the portico in the most confusing fashion, for it was the portico facing the Hudson that mattered most. Service at the Catskill Mountain House religiously adhered to the manner of an earlier day. In 1854 Nathaniel Booth of Kingston gave a graphic account of the quaint old way of serving dinner that prevailed on the Pine Orchard.

At the sound of the three o'clock bell, guests hastened to the dining room. There "ladies and gentlemen indiscriminately seat themselves on each side of the long tables" to eat a meal Booth found to be "formal, prosaic and endless." The waiters, said Booth, "were mere automatons, they moved, marched and counter marched, twisted and turned, by certain snaps executed by the fingers of an important-looking chap wearing a white apron, at the head of the room—tramp, tramp, the measured tread like a corps of village militia, bring arms in the shape of dishes. . . ." The waiters advanced "in file on each side of the table—snap—down go the dishes with a crash—snap—they come again and again and again until the better part of two hours are gone. . . ."[11] The performance was a triumph of well-organized mass feeding of humans such as had once prevailed at the three-o'clock "ordinaries" of large inns in Britain and America.

On sunny days the duty of Charles Beach's guests was plain. It had been given ritual form by more than a generation of observance. Just before dawn the sunrise gong sounded or a servant rapped at the guest's door and called out "Sun rising, sir!" At this the guest hastily clothed himself and made for the platform or clifftop in front of the hotel to watch the sun rising from behind the New England hills to the east. Later there was the drive between the two lakes to the Kaaterskill Falls. If the guest's thirst for the sight of falling water was still unsatisfied he could go on to impressive Haines Falls, to which Dr. Mitchill had tried in vain to give his own name, but which instead bore that of a family of pioneer settlers. There all the apparatus of civilization was to be found. A refreshment stand, steps of wood and stone to make descent to the falls' base easier, and even a pond above with a custodian to receive visitors' money as a reward for turning on the falls. Lower down the Kaaterskill Clove a succession of smaller but charming waterfalls had been given names and turned into attractions for those eager to indulge in further adventures with falling water—even amid the clove's wreckage of dying tanneries.

At the Mountain House a bear cub or two was to be found in a cage or on a chain and "Old Thorpe, the bear hunter," was in attendance to tell tales of his hunting exploits. Some guests strolled on the shores of the two lakes—for a while one bore the more elegant name of Sylvan Lake. Or they took the advice of painter-writer T. Addison Richards who wrote in the July 1854 number of *Harper's New Monthly Magazine:* "You may enter one of the skiffs which skim the waters, and mingle your voice in happy carol with the murmur of the breeze, which never fails to play with the bright image cast by tree and rock and sail on the pellucid bosom of the lake . . . occasionally glancing at the fly which you have cast upon the waters to lure the wary trout." The lakes were continually being stocked with pickerel, black bass, and trout—the trout did not do as well as the pickerel, and serious trout men scorned the lakes.

More and more young and active people climbed Round Top or High Point and spent the night on these summits in shelters made of balsam fir boughs. As the years moved on, the climbers less frequently amused themselves by pushing great boulders over the edges of cliffs and enjoying the destruction of trees thereby.[12] The supply of suitable boulders near the Mountain House was dwindling and the once-popular sport of boulder pushing was dying out. And, until the arrival and departure of another ice age, these playthings would not be renewed. Other guests followed footpaths which led to many points of interest. Among these were rocks which seemed to willing eyes to mimic the shapes of such objects as helmets and ruined castles. By the 1870s, profiles of George Washington and other famous men were being admired. So too were such rock animals as whales and alligators, and later a sphinx joined their company. The emotions of romantic visitors were stirred by the sight of a rock apparently struggling to look like a man-made object or a living thing—rocks like these hinted at mysteries in the relationship of the animate and inanimate parts of the universe.[13]

Most guests spent only one or two nights at the Mountain House. That gave them enough time to perform the prescribed rites at the Kaaterskill Falls and the Pine Orchard clifftop and to experience the physical and spiritual benefits of the pure mountain air before dashing off to the gaming tables, race track, and fashion parade of Saratoga. But if a guest arrived on one of the rainy or foggy days not unusual in August, he would find the mountain air a disappointment. He could not see the sights but would have to make do with the amusements available within the dripping walls of the Mountain House. And these amusements were far from being either numerous or exciting. A piano was provided but until the mid-seventies, when a two-man orchestra appeared, members of the hotel staff doubled as musicians and played with varying results for Saturday-night dances. On Sunday mornings, Protestant religious services were conducted in the red-and-black-carpeted parlor by visiting clergymen who were paid in room and board. When word of the presence of an eminent clergyman got around, guests from the Laurel House and boarding-houses in Haines Falls and Tannersville turned up on Sunday morning and were made welcome.

Beyond the provision of two billiard tables (the same two listed in the inventory of 1833), Bibles and hymnbooks, and an abundant supply of copies of *The Scenery,* there was little additional effort to help guests pass the time pleasantly on days when fate made the natural wonders unreachable in comfort. Nathaniel Booth's account of how he spent a rainy and foggy Sunday at the Mountain House in 1857 makes its point with admirable brevity. An excellent sermon did nothing to dispel the fog—in fact after the sermon, the fog increased. Dinner provided distraction but once that was over the fog grew even thicker. The fog, Booth wrote, "drives through the passages—the verandah is deserted—coats are buttoned to the chin—the twice-read papers are again perused—no use—ennui reigns supreme. Nothing is left to sustain existence but a nap—we ascend the reeking stairs from which the damp is falling in drops—tumble on the beds—just begin to dream of shower baths—Niagara—or the great deluge when ding! dong! supper is ready."[14]

One thing that guests could and did do on rainy days was to look at each other. And this could be very interesting, for many famous, eccentric, and glamorous people were to be seen at the hotel. One guest reported to the Pittsburgh *Gazette* that he had observed "a score of sallow wayfarers from South America, Cuba, Mexico, and other tropical climes—I was amused in observing the national listlessness and indolence with which they vamoosed around. But by nightfall the mountain air had begun to operate upon even them, and the way they broke for the supper table, when the bell rang, and the way they went at the warm biscuits, the preserves, the toast and kindred trifles, was really cheering. . . ."[15] There were often Livingstons of Livingston Manor and Clermont and members of other old landholding families, whom people on the way up—especially if they had marriageable daughters—contrived to lure into conversation. There were famous painters, writers, statesmen, and bishops. Edwin Forrest, the great actor, was a guest just before the papers made his divorce news. In 1852 Forrest, Madame Marietta Alboni, the illustrious operatic contralto, and naughty and talented Lola Montez "and suite the latter consisting of a poodle-dog and a monkey"[16] were all to be seen at the Mountain House at about the same time. Local eccentrics found the Mountain House an irresistible target and they often served to brighten a dull day. Among them was Henry Backus, "the Saugerties Bard, a Cosmopolitan, A Travelling Minstrel," as he was inscribed on the hotel register. Backus sang songs he composed and sold printed copies of them to guests. He put together a Mountain House ballad in 1856. Years later local people remembered some of the ballad's lines: "C. L. Beach mine host of the mountain house/Polite and debonair/For the guests who call at this retreat/Ev'ry luxury will prepare/Spruce-colored gents and ladies/your orders will obey/. . . . The genteel clerk of the mountain house/Plays on the violin/The Polka, Hornpipe, Schottish, Waltz./A caution to all sin. . . ."[17]

Odd characters and offbeat achievers from far away also showed up at the Mountain House and helped amuse those who might otherwise have succumbed to ennui. One was D. V. Martin, the vegetable wherryman, as he was called. The wherryman had come all the way to the wharf at Catskill in his little wherry. Guests wondered "how so small a craft and so apparently ill-constructed to bear the buffets of the ocean waves, could safely be brought from Boston to New York."[18]

During rainy and foggy summers the Mountain House business inevitably fell off. Yet there were a few faithful groups of customers who arrived rain or shine. Most faithful of all were the southerners. These people were rising to new heights of prosperity as their slave-based, cotton-centered economy expanded, and many spent their summers in Newport.

From their base in Newport some traveled for a change to the Catskill Mountain House and then on to Saratoga, Trenton Falls, and Niagara. But a few families and especially those from the Carolinas settled down at the Mountain House for weeks each year to enjoy its cool air— even when that air was also damp and thick with August fogs. Philadelphia and Baltimore families also fled from the intense summer heat of their cities and made long stays at the Mountain House.

Toward the end of 1860 South Carolina became the first of the southern states to secede from the Union. The following April the Civil War began with the bombardment of Fort Sumter. That summer the names of the prominent southern families whose members had for so long been valued guests of the Catskill Mountain House did not appear on its register. But the loss was hardly felt. For as always, if war brought death to some, it brought riches to others. New names and new faces began to appear on the Pine Orchard, beside the two lakes, and at the Kaaterskill Falls. New fortunes born of war began to pay bills to Mr. Charles L. Beach. By the summer of 1866 the rush of guests became so great that Mr. Beach decided to "put up an addition to the already immense Mountain House," said the Catskill *Recorder and Democrat* of January 4, 1867. The sound of carpenters' hammers echoing through the guestless hotel in the dead of that winter announced that the old Mountain House which had already survived so many blows had also survived the Civil War and emerged from the war's waste and slaughter stronger and healthier than ever.

Had Charles L. Beach been able to look into the future, he would have felt uneasy at the sight of a young guest who came more and more often to the Pine Orchard in the late sixties and through the seventies. The guest was George Harding, the son of a Philadelphia newspaper publisher. Harding had first visited the Catskill Mountain House in 1849. That same year he became a member of the Pennsylvania bar and quickly embarked on an immensely successful career. Not for Harding was the involvement with land, politics, and commerce which had proved profitable to previous generations of lawyers. He was a man of his time. And that time was the expanding, machinery-loving nineteenth century with its mushrooming corporations founded upon the great advances being made by scientists and technicians. Railroads, bridges, Professor Morse's electric telegraph, Mr. McCormick's reaper which was having so remarkable an effect on American agriculture—the legal complications of these were the cornerstones of the fortune young Mr. Harding was running up. He had an unusual gift for absorbing a technical subject and then appearing in court to be master of its most intricate convolution. He was determined and he was resourceful. By the early 1880s Harding would be established in the Catskills as a rival to Charles L. Beach. In the public mind he would symbolize great changes which were radically altering the character of summer life in the Catskills. He would be known to many as "the magician of the mountains."[19] But as the 1860s ended, Charles L. Beach greeted Harding each summer with an especial warmth. For the rich Philadelphia lawyer was spending money at the Catskill Mountain House with delightful abandon. He was, in fact, Beach's star boarder.

63

Railroads

✤ By the time the first southern visitors began straggling back to the Catskill Mountain House in the late 1860s, the hotel possessed an unusual distinction. Other great American summer resorts were then easily reached by railroad, but the one on the Pine Orchard held railroads at a distance and seemed to cherish its aloofness from the mechanical wonders of the mid-nineteenth century. In 1859 British traveler Charles MacKay had observed that "in England hotels are conducted in a style suitable to the days of the solitary horsemen, gigs and mailcoach . . . but in America the hotels and railroads grew together, and have been made to fit into each other. . . ."[1] Ever since 1852 it had been possible for travelers to leave the cars of the Hudson River Railroad opposite the village of Catskill, take a Beach-owned ferry across the river, and then transfer to a Beach stagecoach for the rest of the trip to the Pine Orchard. But this seemed to be as close as Charles L. Beach wanted to get to a railroad. His hotel had been born in the days of the solitary horseman and was unwilling to emerge into a new world of steam, rails, and smoke.

Mr. Beach had good reasons for guarding the image of the Pine Orchard as a romantic outpost of civilization set in a wilderness. The spell of the romantic movement was still strong enough to fill his establishment with readers of Irving, Cooper, and Bryant, and admirers of Thomas Cole. Many of these people regarded railroads as uncouth destroyers of romantic charm. They valued the temple on the Pine Orchard because it preserved the atmosphere of the high tide of the romantic triumph. Yet they must have known that the Pine Orchard could not remain forever apart from the railroad age. For everywhere in the Western world, schemes for new railroads were bringing pretty visions of profit to speculators and the disposers of hoards of capital, who would not forever respect the sanctity of the Pine Orchard.

During the 1850s and 1860s great and daring improvements in railroad design and construction had been made, and in Switzerland and the United States men were planning railroads that could climb mountains far higher than the Catskills. In 1869 the first railroad spanned the United States from coast to coast. That same year a cog railroad lifted its first batch of apprehensive tourists to the summit of Mount Washington in New Hampshire's White Mountains. At the same time plans for new railroads which had been laid aside during the Civil War were being brought out, dusted off, and dangled before the eyes of the investing public. The Midland Railroad, later to become known as the New York, Ontario & Western Railway, was being pushed through Sullivan County fed in large part by capital subscribed by the county's tanners, who were eager to finish off Sullivan's remaining groves of virgin hemlocks.[2] A road known at first as the Rondout & Oswego (it would be renamed the New York, Kingston & Syracuse and later, the Ulster & Delaware) was moving forward from Kingston toward its original objective of Lake Ontario by way of the Esopus Valley and Pine Hill. The Wallkill Valley Railroad was slowly and jerkily crawling from its beginning at a junction with the Erie in Orange County toward Albany. Charles L. Beach stood aside from all this activity. He and his father before him had been stage coachmen and a stage coachman he remained.

As late as August 1879, a writer for *Lippincott's Magazine* hinted at Charles L. Beach's feelings toward railroads: "Let not the Catskills be made more accessible; they are accessible enough. We want no more railroads, no improved means of transportation to transform pleasure-paths and byways into highways. The old lumbering stagecoach was the vehicle best suited to mountain roads."[3] For many years the Catskill Mountain House had been a showpiece of the romantic movement; now it was defending its position against the assaults of an age that valued speed, efficiency, and comfort more than the Catskills' veil of romance. The businessmen of Catskill began earnestly talking railroad, for their prosperity depended upon a flow through their village of visitors to the mountains,[4] but Mr. Beach did not listen even as railroads approached closer and closer to his temple.

Of all the railroads being born amid the railroad fever of the late 1860s and the 1870s, the one that most clearly threatened the Catskill sphere of influence was the Rondout & Oswego. And the Kingston and Rondout capitalists, the tanners along its route, and landowners large and small who were promoting it were well aware of this. In 1866 the *Argus* newspaper of Kingston had said that Catskill had had its chance to become a railroad center when it built the Catskill & Canajoharie in 1835, but it had "foolishly rejected" the chance. "Kingston now has her opportunity. Will she embrace it?"[5] the *Argus* had asked as opposition to the road found expression from an influential group headed by Civil War General George H. Sharpe, and Delaware and Hudson Canal lawyer Jacob Hardenbergh. A descendant of old Major Hardenbergh, he was soon to become a state senator. These men claimed that the Rondout & Oswego would destroy Kingston's prosperity as a terminus of the highways which crossed the Catskills and over which teamsters drew leather, hay, Delaware butter, and many other products of the region. Besides, it will "strike ruinously at our wagon-makers, our blacksmiths, our harness makers, our flour and feed establishments, our merchants and dealers generally."[6] The place of all this would be taken by "a single iron horse speeding past us to the depot on the Hudson." And, argued Sharpe and Hardenbergh, while the road was to be privately owned it was "backed by no private aid worthy of note." Nearly all the money needed to construct it was to be subscribed by the public.

The protests of Sharpe and Hardenbergh were drowned out by the chorus of approval that rose all along the line of the proposed road. Lobbyists got busy in Albany, Hudson River steamboat magnate Thomas Cornell of Rondout, Dr. Orson M. Allaben of Margaretville (an Anti-rent champion now grown rich and respectable), Charles Hathaway of Delhi, who had been a doughty fighter for the rights of the absentee landlords whom he served as agent—these and a host of others joined in cajoling and reasoning, pressuring and intimidating in the interests of building the Rondout & Oswego. The legislature authorized building the new road. And it also passed an act that permitted towns along the proposed route to issue bonds whose proceeds would be used to buy stock in the Rondout & Oswego. Landowners hastened to donate land for the railroad right of way. For the argument that by doing so they would greatly profit from the increase in value of their remaining land seemed incontrovertible. People began talking of chipping in to build stations that might shed architectural luster on their towns. Under the guidance of President Thomas Cornell, the Rondout & Oswego Railroad moved up the Esopus Valley toward one of the most formidable obstacles on its proposed line—the Pine Hill.

Many problems had to be solved by the planners of the Rondout & Oswego. The road would follow the Esopus Creek for many miles, and the creek was an untrustworthy fellow traveler. One day it would be a gentle rustic beauty smiling shyly at admiring fishermen; the next day—thanks to one of the heavy rainstorms characteristic of the Catskills—it might become an angry giant and destroy houses, barns, soil, and railroad tracks in its valley. One dweller along the lower Esopus used to say that the flooding creek had brought him all the materials and contents of his house and barn except for an anvil for his blacksmith shop—and he was expecting that on the next flood.[7]

Although a good many mountain people said that no railroad could ever climb the steep Pine Hill, the Rondout & Oswego engineers assured the road's directors that they could send the tracks up the hill in a series of exciting curves. But agitation for piercing the hill with a tunnel grew louder. The legislature was asked to appropriate half a million dollars to provide the R. & O. with a tunnel. Lobbyists for the road fluttered about the capitol, the legislature authorized the grant—but Governor Hoffman vetoed it. The Rondout & Oswego engineers were not dismayed: they pushed their tracks up the hill's steep eastern side and then moved down into Delaware County.

Even before the rails of the R. & O. had done more than touch the feet of the Catskills and long before the road was officially open for business, freight was carried. The first train carried dry hides to an Esopus Valley tannery on its outward trip and brought down a cargo of Delaware County butter. Open cars began hauling lumber from forests of the southern Catskills which had been untouched up to then, thanks to transportation difficulties. On May 2, 1870 the first scheduled passenger train puffed into West Hurley. A little later that year it reached the station named Longyear's in honor of that rich and respected citizen, Isaac W. Longyear, who was a director of the road and whose newly built house looked out upon its tracks. Two years later, on November 21, 1872, the first train puffed and whistled its way to Stamford, but, rejoicing over this event was muted. For the Rondout & Oswego was in serious trouble.

As the railroad had pushed its way across the Catskills, the United States was experiencing an extraordinary orgy of corruption. In New York, Boss William Marcy Tweed, having established looting of the city on a secure basis, was moving to Albany where he bought favors from legislators of both parties with as much ease as if he were buying cheap cigars. Tweed often worked with a shrewd little man named Jay Gould who had been born on a Delaware County farm from which, by 1872, the whistle of the Rondout & Oswego could be clearly heard. Gould had written a history of his county, had become a surveyor, a partner of Zadock Pratt in a Pennsylvania tannery, and a leather dealer in the Swamp. Then he turned his attention to railroads. Already Cornelius Vanderbilt had showed that it was possible for a man with no concern for the public welfare to enrich himself at the expense of the holders of railroad stocks and bonds. After some preliminary looting of railroads in a small way, Jay Gould tackled Vanderbilt and the two battled for control of the Erie.

Citizens of the towns that had been bonded for a total of well over a million dollars to build the R. & O. followed the adventures of Tweed and Gould in their newspapers with anxiety. The directors of their own road remained tight-lipped and the manager parried questions. But it was apparent that an attempt was being made by "railroad pirates"[8] to seize their "peoples' railroad." Thomas Cornell was ousted from the presidency of the R. & O. and his place was taken by General Sharpe—the very same man who had vehemently opposed building the line on the ground that it would ruin the teaming business. Wild rumors circulated in the Catskills. Down went the stock of New York, Kingston & Syracuse (by now this was the name of the Rondout & Oswego.) Two months before the first train pulled into Stamford, the Kingston *Daily Freeman* charged that "seven out of the ten directors own only one share each."[9] In 1872 General Sharpe had transferred "the people's railroad to a set of sharpers," the *Freeman* declared. These men "make a business of gobbling up railroads and . . . haven't a dollar's interest in the locality."

In 1869 the Gould-Vanderbilt struggle for control of the Erie led through illegal stock manipulation to physical violence by hired thugs. All along the line of the New York, Kingston & Syracuse people asked if a similar fate was not in the making for their own railroad. Before long they had an answer. By the fall of 1873 workers on the N.Y., K. & S. were leaving because their wages had not been paid, the trains and roadbeds were deteriorating, the railroad stock was sinking ever lower, until, in the words of the *Freeman,* "it was not worth a copper."[10] The directors of the road remained mum and the public took this as evidence that the road was in very bad shape indeed. As a national financial panic signaled its approach, Director Isaac W. Longyear was having money trouble. He vanished from the board of the railroad and the name of the station honoring him was changed to Mount Pleasant.

By September 1873 the illusion of prosperity created by wartime inflation and postwar speculation fever ended with a bang. Banks and great business houses suspended payments, and idle workers walked the streets of every city in a fruitless quest for work. The past few years had produced a succession of shocking scandals, some involving men close to President Grant. Boss Tweed had been exposed and put on trial for his many misdeeds. That fall railroads throughout the country gave obvious signs of ill health. In October the Hudson River line laid off four hundred men because of a drop in freight shipments. In November, Palen and Company, the big Sullivan County tanners, went into bankruptcy after forty years of prosperity—they were heavy investors in the New York, Oswego & Midland Railway which seemed headed for collapse. Near the end of November, Tweed was sentenced to imprisonment for twelve years. As the onetime boss moped in his cell a few days later, a court-appointed receiver tried to take possession of the offices of the N.Y., K. & S. The manager refused to admit him. The receiver returned with a band of fifteen or twenty armed men. Manager Litchfield and his aides met them boldly— they were armed with bits of heavy railroad gear and one of them flourished a pistol.[11] After a few blows were exchanged and a few men injured, the receiver took possession. It was all in the true Jay Gould style.

For a year and a half reorganization went on, and on June 15, 1875 the road emerged with its Oswego & Syracuse ambitions forgotten. It bore the more modest name of the Ulster & Delaware. The president was once again Thomas Cornell, who was also president of the Wallkill Valley Railroad. Cornell was becoming the big man of his region. When he won the battle for the Ulster & Delaware, men who had never met him liked to refer to him as "Tommy" Cornell, while others called him, as some do to this day, the Jay Gould of the U. & D. His success made Cornell admired even by the taxpayers who had to swallow hard to stomach the heavy losses their towns had incurred by issuing bonds to build his road.

All through its years of trial, the trains of the little railroad had kept moving. Up the Catskills from Kingston and down to Stamford. Up the mountains from Stamford and down to Kingston. Up and down, up and down, day after day with only minor interruptions. It is not surprising that under its new name of the Ulster & Delaware the line was given the nickname of the Up & Down.[12] During the tense days of December 1873, many had said that the road was ruined, that it had been a sham from the beginning and that its right of way would now return to pasture and wood lot, cornfield and swamps. What these people did not grasp was the extent to which the Up & Down had become an indispensable part of the life of the region. It had brought in new people and new ideas. Even through the black winter of 1873–74 it continued to send its trains up and down while the poor of American cities rioted.

Almost from the day its first passenger train made the run to West Hurley, the U. & D. started converting the towns along its line to summer-boarding centers. On August 12, 1873 the Kingston *Freeman* took note of the fact: "It is astonishing to see the number of city people who are spending the summer along the line of the N.Y., K. & S. R.R., not only is Delaware County flooded, Pine Hill and Shandaken are filled to overflowing, but even lower down in the town of Olive, boarders are spending their vacations. Shokan has a large number of these folks, most of them are young ladies in moderate circumstances who came into the country to spend their short vacations climbing the mountains, picking berries, and drinking fresh milk. Their board bills are very much less than if they remained in the city."

The *Freeman* reporter was a good observer but he had not noted a fact of great future significance. This was that many of the boarders brought to the Catskills by the U. & D. were immigrants from German-speaking countries. They did not share in the Puritanical approach toward life which muffled all Sunday sounds but those of sermons and hymns at places like the Catskill Mountain House. They liked to sing jolly songs together when the impulse struck them; they felt no compunction about speaking to strangers who sat near them in the cars of the U. & D.; they made more noise and dressed more gaily when on vacation than those reared in the Puritan traditions of England and the United States.[13] Most of these new boarders were Protestants; many were Roman Catholics; a rapidly increasing number were Jewish; but all of them shared the Continental way of enjoying life. Boardinghouses along the U. & D. found it profitable to woo German-speaking people, and by the late seventies some were advertising that they preferred German guests or that their houses were favorite resorts of Germans.[14] Most of these places welcomed all German-speaking people whether of Protestant, Roman Catholic, or Jewish religious beliefs. But a few foreshadowed future developments by becoming known as Protestant or Catholic or Jewish houses. No one was turned away from these boardinghouses because of his religion—the segregation was at first voluntary. It was simply an expression of the old desire of human beings to surround themselves with people sharing their own ways of enjoying life, their own ideals, and their own irrational notions.

Some railroad promoters of the 1830s had dreamed of sending a branch (or even the main line) of the New York, Erie & Buffalo up the Esopus Valley by way of Phoenicia and through the Stony Clove and so down the valley of the Schoharie to that of the Mohawk. Many dreamed, too, of a line leading to the very base of Overlook Mountain in Woodstock. The Stony Clove branch would penetrate the sphere of influence of the businessmen of Catskill by its back door; the Overlook line would give a summer hotel on Overlook a decisive advantage over the Catskill Mountain House. Once the Rondout & Oswego came into being, hopes like these revived.

Although railroads were threatening to surround him, Charles L. Beach seemed undisturbed. His hotel was doing well and he seemed confident that it would do just as well for the younger Beaches to whom he would some day entrust it. As railroads moved toward him, he showed his confidence by adding greatly to the hotel lands by buying many bordering farms and tracts of rocky woodland. He began showing great pride in his long association with the Pine Orchard and liked nothing better than to sit in an armchair placed on the clifftop in front of his hotel, high hat pushed back on his head, and eyes fixed on the landscape below. From this little throne, Beach would tell the guests who gathered round the story of his Mountain House. He would not mention Elisha Williams, or Comfort and Bigelow, or James Powers, or John Ashley and his extract of spruce. He would say nothing of the struggle for survival of the hotel during the 1830s. Instead he would spin a tale as romantic in its own way as that of Rip Van Winkle. The tale began with the discovery in 1819 by Beach's father, Erastus, of the wonders of the Pine Orchard, then wrapped in an unbroken wilderness, of his dream that year of a great hotel to be built on the spot, of how the hotel materialized and how old Erastus had watched it move onward from success to success until his son Charles L. took over its ownership and management. Like all well-established institutions, the Catskill Mountain House had evolved its own mythology.[15]

In 1870 Charles L. Beach was sixty-two years old. Most men of his age and social class were grandfathers at that age, but Beach was not. His oldest child, daughter Mary A., was seventeen; son George H. was thirteen; son Charles was fifteen. Should Charles L. be suddenly called from this earth, his sons would be too young to pick up where he left off and keep the Mountain House on its glorious old path until they in turn would relinquish control to Beaches yet unborn. Major Johannis Hardenbergh and the Livingstons had hoped to make a bid for immortality by founding landed families; in 1870 Charles L. Beach apparently translated a similar ambition into late nineteenth-century terms. He set up a corporation to take over the Mountain House and ensure continuous control and operation of the family business by Beaches. By the thirteenth of March, 1871, the Catskill Mountain House Company had been set up, with a majority of its five hundred shares controlled by Charles L. Beach. Its president was S. Sherwood Day, long-time president of the Tanner's National Bank of Catskill, of which Charles L. Beach had been a trustee ever since its founding in 1831 as an adjunct to the booming tanning industry of the Catskills.[16] Day, an old friend of Beach, was a cautious and prudent man who exemplified all the bankerly virtues. Hardly had Charles L. Beach agreed to hand over the Catskill

Mountain House to the new company in return for a payment in cash of $20,000, when the first direct challenge to the old Mountain House was boldly laid down by a competing hotel. On June 15, 1871, the first Overlook Mountain House opened for business. It was made possible by the closeness of the West Hurley station of the Rondout & Oswego—a nine-mile trip by stage would take guests from the station to the new Mountain House. The much-talked-about branch to the base of Overlook had not been built. But that would come before long, some said, and then Mr. Beach's establishment would have to take second place, or so the new hotel's promoters assured each other.

.

64

The Overlook Mountain House

🌲 FROM THE DAY James Booth first thought of building a hotel on Over-look, ill luck had haunted every promoter of a hotel on the mountain. Booth and William Scobie had failed completely. To the amazement of everyone, rich Robert Livingston Pell had become insolvent, and then one of his sons died and the other committed suicide in his grief. In 1869 Isaac N. Secor of New York and New Rochelle assumed the Overlook dream. Secor was a healthy and vigorous man—suddenly he died.

By February of 1870 a corporation had been formed to take up where Secor left off. The largest stockholder was William Brinkerhoff, the owner of a Woodstock hotel favored by summer boarders which had developed step by step from a simple inn dating from about 1790. Another was Assemblyman Charles H. Krack, an adventurous native of Germany who had a summer home in Woodstock.[1] Krack had commanded a troop of cavalrymen sent from New York to cow Anti-renters during the trial in Hudson of Big Thunder, and he had managed hotels but owed his prosperity to his ownership of a floating bathhouse on New York's East River. The remaining stockholders were local men, all of whom obviously hoped to profit not only from their stock dividends but also from contracts for building and operating the hotel. They included a butcher, a grocer, dealers in lumber, paint, and hardware. New Englander George Mead, who was already operating a small summer boardinghouse in the Wide Clove halfway to Overlook's top, also bought stock. His place would inevitably be used as a refreshment stop for horses and guests bound for the Mountain House above.

A modest shelter of some sort had stood on the site of the hotel-to-be for years.[2] There hunters and fishermen headed for Schue's Lake had spent the night. And there parties of sports of another sort had gathered to carouse far from the disapproving eyes of friends and neighbors. By midsummer of 1870, designer and builder Lewis B. Van Wagonen of Kingston had the construction of the new hotel well along. A barn Van Wagonen built served as a bunkhouse for workmen and visitors. A stall in the building was set to work as a barroom so that those who climbed the mountain to check on Van Wagonen's progress could find a liquid reward. Every visitor compared the view from the Overlook Cliff with that from the Pine Orchard and most—even those who had not sharpened their senses and improved their judgment in the barn—pronounced the Overlook view far better than Mr. Beach's.[3]

Early in the spring of 1871, John E. Lasher leased the hotel. Mr. Lasher had made a name for himself as the manager of Rondout's finest hotel, the Mansion House.[4] Now he flooded the Hudson Valley with press releases —and rumors—extolling his new venture. The building would be up-to-the-minute in appearance and equipment. It would boast a mansard or French roof similar to those so much admired on the newest and most fashionable hotels at Saratoga. It would be lighted by gas and would have an electric telegraph. Instead of the long dining tables still used by Mr. Beach, the Overlook Mountain House would have small round tables with some square ones which could be put together to accommodate large parties. Each table would be assigned a waiter who would hand each guest a printed menu and assist him in making his choice. One communication to the press hopefully claimed that Charles L. Beach had been driven into panic by the prospect of so splendid a rival and had offered the backers of the Overlook Mountain House double the amount of their investment if they would abandon their venture, but the backers had refused.[5]

The Overlook Mountain House opened in as inauspicious a fashion as could well be imagined. When the fog shrouding the hotel occasionally lifted, no one could say much in praise of the building. It was thoroughly unsuited to its mountaintop location, for it was no more than an enlarged version of the kind of small-town dwelling that bankers and businessmen were building in many parts of the country, and it made no appeal at all to the imagination. Drops of liquefied fog dripped from the hotel ceiling on opening day; the electric telegraph refused to work; much of the hotel was still unfinished. It was of some comfort to Mr. Lasher to learn that Charles L. Beach's hotel was swallowed up in the same fog and that his guest list was small. Business picked up later that summer, but not enough to make the new hotel the smashing success its backers had hoped for. The strongest possible measure was taken to focus public attention on the Overlook Mountain House and its charms. It was announced that President Grant had been persuaded to visit the place.[6] The Catskill Mountain House management liked to boast of the illustrious people who had been their guests—talented people, socially prominent people, people distinguished by the possession of vast amounts of money. But no President of the United States had ever traveled to the Pine Orchard—not, at least, while in office.

General Grant was fond of visiting American summer resorts and there were few of any importance he had skipped. In 1869 he had been among the first to ascend Mount Washington over its new cog railway. This expression of confidence did much to encourage others to make the trip. The season of 1871 ended; so did that of 1872; the hotel on Overlook opened in June 1873 and still President Grant had not arrived. By that time life at the Overlook Mountain House had settled down into a pattern similar to that of the Catskill Mountain House, but with features of its own. There were shooting and croquet matches, dances, shadow pantomimes, and other entertainments gotten up by the guests. The hotel pianist, Professor A. Lee Van Buren of Kingston, not only played on the excellent parlor piano but also gave music lessons and composed the *Overlook Hotel Waltz*. There were famous and eccentric visitors to stare at. And solitary singers, choruses, amateur musical clubs, one-man bands, and trained-bear impresarios sought out the hotel and did their acts for guests' applause or for their small change. DePuy Davis, who worked as a Kingston bartender in his more conventional moments, amazed with feats of high and broad jumping. Although most of the boulders in the Pine Orchard vicinity had been used up and Charles L. Beach discouraged the sport of boulder pushing, many promising ones were still perched on Overlook's clifftops. In the summer of 1872 boulder pushing was one of the two principal amusements at the Overlook Mountain House, said the Kingston *Daily Freeman* of August 6— the other favorite amusement was looking at the scenery. The *Freeman* told of one huge boulder cutting "a swath as it rolled down as if a bolt from Jove's hand had swept through the forest." But not all clifftop boulders were pushed. Those that bore some resemblance to people, animals, or pieces of furniture, or that aroused thoughts of historical or mythological events were often spared. In this way Hannibal's Rock (it apparently commemorated Hannibal's crossing of the Alps in 218 B.C.), the Turtle Rock, the Pulpit Rock, and many others survived for the admiration of strolling hotel guests. A rocky Poet's Bench, a Lover's Retreat, and a Devil's Kitchen furnished amusement to visitors of varied tastes. In 1851 the publication of Nathaniel Hawthorne's tale of "The Great Stone Face" had stimulated a search for human profiles at many summer resorts, and the Duke of Wellington was found lurking among the rocks of Overlook. Most talked about of all Overlook sources of amusement was the mountaintop air, which was extravagantly praised for its purity and its exhilarating qualities. One waggish newspaperman even proposed bottling the air and selling it as *Overlook Oxy-Gin.*[7] But some guests breathed the air from the most serious of motives.

The Overlook Mountain House stood at the highest elevation of any mountain hotel in the state, which was why it quickly attracted people who hoped that its pure and balsam-scented air might cure their hay fever or tuberculosis. Back in the 1860s, lung sufferers had favored the farm boardinghouses of Pine Hill, but now they pinned their hopes on the Overlook Mountain House. In good weather they sat in shawled and blanketed rows on the hotel piazzas, where they coughed and traded remedies. Some who had tried the air of Switzerland stated that Overlook's air was even better. Talk like this, when added to the somewhat alpine look of the hotel site, led to much comparison of the place to similar establishments in Switzerland. In fact, throughout the life of the Overlook Mountain House, its guests liked to play at being in Switzerland. More than ten years after the hotel opened, a reporter for the New York *Times* watched with amusement the antics of "pedestrians in picturesque costumes, carrying long walking poles tipped with iron. Many of these make believe they are in the Alps (thus saving the expense of an ocean journey) and a noble Saint Bernard dog, who answers to the name of *Rex* is gentlemanly enough to assist in the illusion. . . ."[8]

Some vigorous guests made the Overlook House their headquarters and from there walked and climbed in all directions—sometimes they walked to the Catskill Mountain House for breakfast and returned to Overlook in time for dinner. The surroundings of the old Mountain House had become a timeworn tale, while those of the new Overlook Mountain House were fresh and filled with a sense of wilderness. Rock-climbers dared the perils of the Minister's Face and its rattlesnakes; energetic young men dipped into the upper Sawkill Valley and scrambled up steep Indian Head, returning flushed and triumphant to the envy of the lung patients still sitting on the hotel piazzas. In July 1875, George Ripley commented on these walkers and climbers in a dispatch to the New York *Tribune*. Ripley had once presided over the famous experiment in communal living at Brook Farm in Concord, Massachusetts; now he was the *Tribune*'s literary editor and an Overlook enthusiast. "The climate is simply delicious," Ripley wrote, ". . . everybody speaks of an exhilaration which makes wine an impertinence. . . ." He praised the hotel's food and service and then paid his respects to its climbers and walkers: "The infatuated persons who cultivate a passion for mountain scrambles may have a chance to break their necks at any moment in paths as steep and perilous as the Mauvais Pas at Chamonix."[9]

Hardly had Ripley expressed these feelings when it was announced that at long last President Grant was about to make good on his promise to visit the Overlook Mountain House. During the last days of July 1873, Grant left his summer White House at Long Branch, New Jersey, and proceeded in a triumphal tour to Kingston. There he was met by his friend General Sharpe, who was the local Republican boss whom Grant, a few months before, had rewarded with the very desirable post of surveyor of customs of the Port of New York. The two, accompanied by Grant's secretary, General Babcock, and a cabinet member or two, boarded a special train of the New York, Kingston & Syracuse on the first leg of their journey to the Overlook. At every step along the way there were cheers and crowds and brass bands. Similar enthusiasm greeted the President at the Overlook Mountain House which was draped with flowers and greenery in his honor. When Grant left the next day, manager Lasher had good reason for feeling immensely encouraged, for everything seemed to have gone very well indeed. For one thing, Grant, who was possibly the least musical of all the men who have occupied the White House, had stoically endured band after band, chorus after chorus, soloist after soloist at the Lasher Mountain House. He gave obvious signs of boredom only when the famous Hutchinson Family of singers led a chorus of one hundred voices in singing "America" on the very summit of Overlook.[10] Hardly had the last note of his entertainment on Overlook died away when ugly stories of Grant's behavior there began to be whispered—and shouted.

When Grant promised to visit Overlook, he was at the height of his national popularity. By the time he kept his promise, the many scandals in his administration had made him the target of bitter personal attacks. Reformers in his own party were planning to deny him renomination to the presidency. Before becoming President, Grant had been a heavy drinker; after his election he was careful to drink only in moderation. Yet as his hero's halo began to lose its shine, he was accused of being a habitual drunkard even while in the White House, and he had become drunk, people said, while aboard the *Chauncey Vibbard* which took him up the Hudson. When General Sharpe met him, said the Rhinebeck *Gazette,* he warned the President that if he drank any more he "wouldn't be fit to be seen." Traditions in the vicinity of Overlook Mountain maintain to this day that Grant disregarded Sharpe's advice and emptied bottle after bottle as he sped toward the summit of Overlook Mountain behind relays of fast horses.

When he reached the hotel, according to one Woodstock old-timer, "They had to pour him in bed."[11]

By 1873 the organized American temperance movement was forty years old and gaining strength. To many people the Overlook Mountain House where Grant was believed to have had his drunken orgy became a haunt of evil to be avoided at all costs. But that was not the only piece of bad luck to strike the place. On September 18 the financial panic of 1873 began with the failure of Jay Cooke & Company. A few months later the affairs of the N.Y., K. & S. R.R. reached their unhappy crisis and the road seemed headed for extinction. The next summer the Overlook Mountain House opened for business. It staggered through that summer of 1874 losing money every day as the national income and prices slid downward. That summer, people were reading a booklet called *The Traditions of the Overlook Mountain*—a tongue-in-cheek collection of mock Indian lore of Overlook whose author was lawyer-educator-pamphleteer Dexter A. Hawkins. But readers of the *Traditions* did not feel impelled to flock to Lasher's hotel. Nor was the public attracted in droves when a group of musical amateurs gave a "grand matinee concert"[12] on the very summit of the mountain. The program included Richard Wagner's Tannhauser Overture and Pilgrims Chorus, plus a reading of the Declaration of Independence, and the serving of sparkling Catawba. The hopes of the backers of the hotel sagged when the place closed that fall. Many did not expect to see the hotel open again. But on April 1, 1875, manager Lasher left the mountaintop to try to raise enough money in Kingston to enable him to keep the hotel going for one more season. In another year the hard times might be over and then rich men and women might flock to his establishment.

While Lasher was away, one of his children noticed dark smoke pouring from one of the hotel chimneys and being carried away by a brisk wind. He told a workman on the place about it. But the workman laughed. He knew that it was April Fool's Day and he was too smart to be taken in by so transparent a dodge. Another workman responded to the child with similar sophistication. By the time anyone took the child's alarm seriously, what had been a minor chimney fire had become a raging blaze. The hotel burned to its foundations.[13]

What Charles L. Beach said when he heard of the disaster has not been recorded. It is likely that he expressed polite regret. But he could not have helped experiencing a sense of relief. Once again his was the only first-class hotel in the Catskills. Old guests who had been seduced by Mr. Lasher's talk of a higher elevation, purer air, and a finer view now began returning to the Pine Orchard. But any relief Beach might have felt could not last long. Change was in the air, and the old Mountain House was about to be pushed and pulled and prodded in an attempt to force it to change with the times.

Nowhere was change more apparent than in the city of New York. There speculators in real estate were piling up large fortunes and at the same time leaving ugly marks on the face of their city. Immigrants from Europe and upstate farm boys and girls in search of opportunity were crowding into the cities and were being packed into ever-expanding slums. By summer the slums sizzled in the intense heat and gave off an atmosphere which penetrated almost every nook of the city. For years the rich had been fleeing from New York in July and August, and many had built summer homes on the banks of the Hudson. Summer hotels had sprung up on the river—a well-known one was Cozzens at West Point. In 1869 a Hudson River hotel, the Prospect Park, had risen in the village of Catskill. Like the Catskill Mountain House, it presented a large and imposing front to travelers on the river. The hotel was slow in becoming established but by the mid-seventies it was raiding the guest list of the Mountain House. At the same time the Ulster & Delaware Railroad was hard at work carrying growing numbers of the poor and the near-poor from the slums and near-slums of New York to the summer delights of the cheap boarding-houses along the railroad's line. This flow of unfashionables to the mountains was wearing down the reputation of the Catskills as a haunt of those who occupied the upper roosts in American society. Urban newspapers were devoting columns to doings at Newport, Saratoga, and Long Branch for every line of chitchat about the Catskills. Social climbers were finding the old Mountain House a little less attractive, for German and Irish accents were competing more often with those of old family Bostonians and descendants of Hardenbergh Patent landlords. Yet, thanks to its difficulty of access, even in the railroad age and its maintenance of old customs such as the rigid "English Sunday," many rich and distinguished persons remained loyal to the Pine Orchard. They tended to find it a comforting refuge from the aggressive new ways which were disturbing to people getting through life on old money and shuddering at every threat to their security.

The Overlook Mountain House had died in 1875—but it refused to stay dead. So many people came to view the remains that a "refreshment saloon" was set up beside the corpse to comfort mourners. A demand for the hotel's resurrection was soon heard. On June 25, 1878 a new hotel was standing on the foundations of the old one and was welcoming its first guests on a day of fog and wind. Its owners were the Kiersted brothers of Saugerties, sons of the Hunter family's surveyor and land agent, John Kiersted, Sr. They had made their money in Hardenbergh Patent land speculation and in tanning. Their hotel was largely a Saugerties show, and it became the symbol of a Saugerties bid for dominance of the Catskills' summer-visitor business.[14] Saugerties labor went into the building and staffing of the hotel. It was hoped, at first, that guests would leave river steamers at Saugerties' Long Dock and take stagecoaches for Overlook. Later, if all went well, a railroad would take the place of the stagecoaches.[15] Then Saugerties might become known as the Gateway to the Catskills and Kingston and the village of Catskill would dwindle in wealth and power.

The manager of the new Overlook Mountain House was Colonel James Smith of Poughkeepsie, said by some to be related to the family that produced "Trade" and "Mark" Smith of cough drop fame. In the opinion of many, the colonel worked under a heavy handicap. The town of Woodstock in which his hotel was located was seething with prohibition activity. Tavern after tavern had been closed down by crusading ladies and clergymen, and in the spring of 1879 the sale of liquor was prohibited throughout the town. Intoxicated by their success, local people were eyeing tobacco, coffee, and tea with prohibiting intent, while some were abstaining from salt, pepper, and pickles on moral grounds. Colonel Smith accepted his new assignment in good spirit—and made it plain that he intended to comply with local wishes. He provided no bar but he permitted guests to bring their own supply of liquor when they arrived and to consume it on the premises. Anyone who ran short might buy all he required from members of the hotel staff who were glad to act as bootleggers. Colonel Smith liked to boast that his temperance hotel was the kind of place to which a careful father might send his young daughter in full confidence that she would return home with her morals uncorrupted. On this basis the new Overlook Mountain House seemed—for a while—to be prospering. A playground was provided for the children of guests. The dining room was staffed by young ladies described as "buxom, rosy and amiable farmer's daughters and school teachers."[16] The English Sunday so much dreaded by continental Europeans was strictly enforced.

The guests who thronged to the new hotel on Overlook in the summer of 1878 were aware that the previous summer had marked an important turning point in the history of American summer resorts. That year Judge Henry Hilton, who was managing the very fashionable Grand Union Hotel at Saratoga Springs for the estate of department store magnate A. T. Stewart, refused accommodations to Jewish banker Joseph Seligman. The two men had clashed before over political and business matters, but Seligman's exclusion was not altogether the result of personal animosity. It reflected a growing cleavage among Americans over the position and the rights of Jews in their society. The Hilton-Seligman dispute brought to light the existence in the Catskills of a trend toward dividing the mountains' boardinghouses and hotels into separate Christian and Jewish establishments.

When American newspapers denounced Judge Hilton for his exclusion of Seligman, the judge protested that he did not mean to exclude all Jews but only what he called "a certain class of Jews"[17] or "Seligman Jews." But keepers of some other summer resort hotels and boardinghouses, including a few in the Catskills, began making it clear that they intended to refuse rooms to all Jews. A dispatch sent from the Catskill Mountain House as the Hilton-Seligman storm broke hints strongly at how Charles L. Beach felt about the matter. "There is none of the shoddy aristocracy here," the dispatch read. "New England furnishes more than her usual proportion of appreciated guests. . . ."[18] It was noted that there were a few "Germans" at the hotel, but they were described as being "lovers of fine scenery." Obviously Mr. Beach was not excluding Jews but he was suggesting that they stay away and allow him to continue on his Protestant romantic course. On August 11 the Catskill *Examiner* sprang to the defense of Jews and said, "In the limits of our village we have a number of these descendants of Solomon and if we have observed rightly a better class of visitors could not be desired."[19]

During the summer of 1878 a reporter for the New York *Herald* arrived on the Pine Orchard loaded with embarrassing questions. He had been told that promoters of cog railroads like the one on Mount Washington had more than once approached Charles L. Beach with schemes for sending a similar railroad up the Catskills and directly to the Beach hotel. When the reporter questioned one of Beach's sons, the young man was evasive. Old Beach himself would only say that such a railroad "would bring a great many people here who wouldn't be desirable and whom I wouldn't care to have."[20] Beach's undesirables included the poor and the near-poor of the sort who used the Ulster & Delaware. But he probably also had in mind Jews whose cultural complex had no room for such features as observance of the English Sunday or the particular brand of reverence for nature which was of major importance on the Pine Orchard.

Jews had long touched the life of the Catskills. The Hardenbergh Patent Memoranda in the Clermont account book of the Livingstons may have mentioned the first Jew to settle down among the Catskills; in 1773 a man identified only as "Jacob the Jew" leased some Livingston land, apparently in Woodstock.

Early in the nineteenth century, Jewish peddlers were roaming the Catskills with their packs. In 1837, that year of economic collapse, a colony of Jews established a settlement at a place they named Sholam in the town of Wawarsing which borders the Hardenbergh Patent. The settlers hoped to farm, although they brought with them evidence of a prosperous town background in the form of fine furniture, paintings, and gilded mirrors. The tract bought by the Jews was unsuited to farming, and they turned to such industries as making quill pens and fur caps. They bought used clothing in New York, cleaned and mended it, and peddled it in the countryside. The synagogue they built at Sholam was the first in all the region.[21]

The failure of the colony of Sholam and the closing of its synagogue left the region without a center around which Jewish life might thrive. Peddlers continued to follow the mountain roads and trails, and many arranged their itineraries to make it possible to spend their Sabbath at a "pedlar's boardinghouse" in the city of Hudson. There they were given the kind of food required by their religion and traditions and there they could observe their Sabbath ritual.[22]

In the summer of 1879 Austin Corbin announced that he would bar all Jews from his Manhattan Beach Hotel at Coney Island and that he would exclude them from the beach he also controlled. The step went considerably beyond the one taken by Judge Hilton and was headlined in such newspapers as the Saugerties *Evening Post* as a blow in "The War Against the Jews."[23] In the Catskills, Jews were turned away that summer from a growing number of smaller boardinghouses. But the names of people of Jewish background appeared on the registers of the Overlook and Catskill Mountain houses. These visitors were not encouraged to come, but they were not being excluded.

As Corbin's actions and the vigorous attempts of New York Jews to fight back were making headlines, the people of the Catskills were taking sides. Many opposed excluding Jews from mountain hotels and boardinghouses as a matter of principle, but others yielded to the pressure applied by old customers who threatened to leave unless Jews were turned away. At every resort center in the Catskills, tension increased. Guests observed their fellows with a new sort of attention and gave exaggerated importance to cultural traits differing from their own. The old tendency of human beings when formed in groups to exalt and defend their own ways of life at the expense of all others, took on new, vigorous life. A scattering of Jewish guests at the Catskill Mountain House throughout its history had aroused no opposition. But the arrival of ever larger numbers in the late 1870s was quite another story. The old hatred of Jews fostered by the medieval church now found new converts in mountain people who argued that by excluding Jews who desecrated their Sunday by playing cards or croquet, or cast aspersions on the normal Christian diet by refusing certain foods, they were defending their religion as had the martyrs of old. At a majority of boardinghouses Christians and Jews mingled on tolerant terms but it became obvious that serious trouble was on the way.

Charles L. Beach made no public statements on the subject which was causing so much talk throughout the nation. But his actions made it plain that he had decided to continue on his familiar course: he would operate the Mountain House as he had always done and would make no concessions to the changing times. He would pin his hopes on the power of the past. It was hardly surprising that when the New York *Herald* man wrote of the Pine Orchard and its master in 1878 he found "Rip Van Winkleism" to be "rampant." Nor was it surprising that before long it was being hinted that not only did Mr. Beach resemble Rip Van Winkle but that as he passed his seventieth year and his beard whitened, he had actually *become* Rip Van Winkle.

65

Rivals Challenge
the Catskill Mountain House

✤ ALL THROUGH THE 1870s, George H. and young Charles Beach moved toward manhood while their father managed the Catskill Mountain House with his usual skill and careful attention to detail. The boys' older cousin, Charles A. Beach, owned and managed the half-century-old stage line which carried guests from the landing at Catskill to the Pine Orchard. Unmarried Charles A. lived with Charles L. Beach as a member of his household. Thanks to a strong family feeling and the organization of the Mountain House Company, there was reason to hope that in spite of the railroad menace, old Mr. Beach would be able to hand on his hotel to the next generation for endless years of smooth operation. But change was on the way, and the final years of Charles L. Beach were filled with struggle and doubt.

The hard times following the panic of 1873 checked but did not end the multiplication and growth of American summer resorts in many mountain regions, at the seashore, and beside springs with claims to medicinal virtues. Railroads were making the wonders of the American West accessible, and the Yosemite and Yellowstone were displacing such sights as the Kaaterskill Falls and the view from the Pine Orchard as goals for European and American tourists. The Adirondack Mountains had "sprung into sudden and universal fame and favoritism," as John D. Bachelder said in his *Popular Resorts and how to reach them* of 1875. Wilderness lovers were finding the Adirondacks as appealing as the Catskills had been to their grandparents. By 1879 a spurt of economic recovery gave a boost to the building of endless new resort hotels equipped with the comforts and gadgets which were becoming important elements of American life. Many older resort hotels were being modernized to meet the demands of guests for gas lighting, flush toilets, supper rooms, and elegant furnishings, but the Catskill Mountain House resolutely continued on a course consecrated by tradition and given support by its rich mythology. There guests willingly groped their way along the hotel's endless corridors by the light of candles, and ate at the traditional long tables. They accepted as an unalterable rule of life among the mountains that if a guest were late for a meal—even if he were a millionaire—he would have to go hungry. Few dared to ask for a dish not placed on their tables by Mr. Beach's corps of waiters. If they did, they would receive the chilly refusal such presumption deserved. Other large and small resort hotels also hesitated to take the plunge into modern times and paid for their hesitation with bankruptcy. But thanks to its great fame and its noble traditions, the Catskill Mountain House was able to remain successfully in the past as the world moved on. It began to take on the charming air of a temple-museum devoted to preserving the ritual and color of the days when American romantic sensibilities were first being awakened at the touch of Irving and Cooper. It continued to be run well and to make older guests feel comfortable and well cared for. The absence of more than a few of the Catholics, Germans, Irish, and Jews who made Americans of older stock feel uneasy and resentful gave older guests a sense of security. Younger people found the old temple on the mountain quaint and amusing. On August 1, 1881 a young reporter for the New York *Times* captured the feeling of the place in pungent fashion.

Although the *Times* man had arrived at what he supposed to be a reasonably early hour on a Saturday night, he was warned to be quiet because "most of our guests are going to bed and don't care to see strangers around." The reporter tiptoed through the hushed public rooms and came upon a sign tacked to a post—it told of the time and room of Protestant religious services to be held in the morning. The reporter explored further and discovered two billiard tables "of the style in use when Capt. J. Smith and Pocahontas had their little love affair." The tables were the very ones listed in the inventory of 1834. The reporter and his companion were then sent off to bed with a single short candle end stuck in a heavy iron candlestick. When they protested, they were graciously allowed a second candle end.

Every now and then a young and brash guest complained to Mr. Beach about his hotel's combination of high rates and old-fashioned service. And Mr. Beach had a pleasant and whimsical answer ready—an answer which might have brought an approving smile from the creator of Rip Van Winkle. "How can you complain about your room and board?" Mr. Beach would ask. "You don't pay a cent for either. I charge only for the mountain air [sometimes it was for the view]. I throw in your room and board free."[1]

Before the change-bearing year of 1879, Mr. Beach's bit of whimsy served him well. He had been sufficiently confident in the power of his location and its natural and cultural attractions to pay little heed to what was going on along the line of the Ulster & Delaware Railroad. There he saw without concern old turnpike inns changing from putting up only team-sters, drovers, and trout fishermen to bulging in July and August with cheer-ful summer boarders. He could not help knowing that many farmers of the old Hardenbergh Patent were thinking of themselves less and less as farm-ers and more and more as proprietors of summer boardinghouses which they hoped would grow and grow until no one could say at what Moun-tain House-like greatness they might not arrive. Old Mr. Beach heard of the Shady Lawns, the Twin Maples, the Broadview Houses, and the Cold Brook Farms appearing in all parts of the Catskills. He saw the hayfields which had once swept up to their parlor windows giving way to lawns and flower beds. He realized that hammocks by the hundreds were swaying where cows had grazed a year or two earlier, that here and there a pigsty had retreated behind a hotel barn to make way for a croquet ground. He knew, too, that many a boardinghouse owner, by means of prodigious straining after economy, could offer room and board of a sort for as little as four or five dollars per week. But how could such meager establishments pose any threat at all to his Mountain House? When hotels and boardinghouses in-creased in Beach's own vicinity—at Haines Falls, Tannersville, Hunter, and Windham—Beach was not at all disturbed. He seemed to regard these places as no more than modest satellites revolving around the glorious sun which shone from his Pine Orchard. They did not detract from his splendor—they magnified it. But in 1879 all this began to change.

It was in 1879 that the Kiersted brothers enlarged their Overlook Mountain House until it could hold almost as many guests as the one on the Pine Orchard. Smaller but very modern hotels burst out here and there among the Catskills. These new hotels scorned the archaic sim-plicities of the old Mountain House and went in for elegance in black wal-nut furniture, tasseled curtains, and flowered carpets. Palenville's Winchelsea had materialized in 1878 from the drawing boards of Nicholas and Hal-cott, the smart Albany architects. It did so well that soon a large "cottage addition" was run up in what a contemporary described as "a combination of Swiss and Gothic styles. . . ."[2] It was painted "granite gray, trimmed in olive green, window caps, white." In Margaretville, in Stamford, and in many other resort centers among the Catskills, similar fashionable splendors beckoned to summer visitors.

In June 1879 the first true "railroad hotel" challenged Charles L.

Beach from the entrance to the winding valley that leads northward to the
Stony Clove and the upper Schoharie Valley from the Phoenicia station of
the Ulster & Delaware. The new Tremper House fitted into the railroad age like a hand in a well-worn glove—it was located within a few minutes walk of a railroad station. And even greater railroad advantages were to
come. For Thomas Cornell had made definite plans for a branch of his U.
& D. to take off from within sight of the boarders on the Tremper piazzas and enter the territory of Charles L. Beach through the Stony Clove.
Tremper guests might soon be able to glide to the wonders of the Pine Orchard and the Kaaterskill Falls in greater ease and comfort than Charles
L. Beach's own boarders. Architecturally the new hotel was not in the same
ornate league as the many new hotels springing up in Saratoga Springs,
Long Branch, Manhattan Beach, and similar resorts. At first its white clapboard bulk appealed to ornament lovers only with its portico and piazzas,
though a year or two later a pair of French-roofed towers helped when
they burst through its roof. But the hotel's site made it imposing. Unlike the
Catskill Mountain House and the hotel on Overlook, the Tremper House
was not set on a mountaintop but on a plateau with a noble mountain forming a background—ease and cheapness of access had triumphed over the excitement of a distant view. The mountain was the Timothy Berg, now
renamed Mount Tremper in honor of the hotel's manager, Major Jacob
H. Tremper, Jr., of Kingston. Hudson River steamboat Captain William
C. Romer of Romer and Tremper, who owned the hotel, was immortalized
when another nearby mountain was given his name. Shandakenites, in
whose town the hotel was located, were not at all pleased at this appropriat-
ing of their landscape by Kingston men, especially when they learned that
the Tremper House would sell liquor even though Shandaken was on the
verge of going dry. Supplies, employees, and materials for the hotel
arrived by rail from Kingston, so local people saw little prospect of
profit for themselves from this liquor-dispensing giant set down in their
midst.

As if to mollify local resentment, the Tremper management invited
a platoon of well-known clergymen, members of the Brooklyn Ministerial
Association, to arrive on its opening day. Controversial Henry Ward
Beecher, none too triumphantly cleared a few years before of a charge of
adultery with a member of his flock, was the speaker of the occasion. From a
position halfway up the grand staircase which rose from the hotel's oblong
"Rotunda," Beecher charmed a large audience with his usual wit and
eloquence. He predicted a prosperous future for the vicinity as a summer
resort and asked God to bless the Tremper House. The place had sound

practical reasons for expecting to be blessed for it had many novel attractions, such as elevators for passengers and baggage, steam heat, bathrooms,
and even a resident physician. Dr. H. R. Winter was an ardent fisherman
who often prescribed a course of trout fishing for businessmen wearied in
the pursuit of dollars and for urban clergymen worn out by the care of a
large parish, and he was as ready with advice on trout flies and rods as he
was with pills and powders. In addition, Winter contributed little essays on
trout fishing to mountain guidebooks which began in 1879 to include
information on what they were beginning to call the southern and western
Catskills. The Tremper House provided a trout pond on its grounds to
which Dr. Winter's feebler patients might stagger in order to gain strength
for more distant efforts at therapeutic angling.[3]

As rich and distinguished guests came and went at the Tremper House
through its first season, they moved in an atmosphere of expansive
rumor. People close to Thomas Cornell were planning an Ulster & Delaware Railroad hotel even larger and more glamorous than the Tremper
House. It would be located on a mountaintop with a superb view and at the
same time beside a railroad station and would be larger and far more luxurious than Beach's old Mountain House. All sorts of railroad schemes were
being talked about, the most spectacular being a railroad designed by
Brooklyn civil engineer George Hussey which would climb the Catskills on
tracks laid on wooden stilts.[4] It would begin in Saugerties and enter Charles
L. Beach's domain by its side door, probably at Haines Falls at the head of
the Kaaterskill Clove. That summer, gangs of Italian laborers began setting
up camps and swinging picks near the Tremper House. They were clearing the way for Thomas Cornell's Stony Clove and Catskill Mountain
branch of the Ulster & Delaware. Mr. Beach had apparently won his battle
to keep a cog railroad from invading his Rip Van Winkle realm, but he was
now being outflanked.

That August, as *Lippincott's Magazine* offered its readers a defense of
the old lumbering stagecoaches of the Catskills, Charles L. Beach and his
friends in the village of Catskill were deep in defensive railroad plans.
They were considering building a line that would strike out from Catskill
toward Cairo at the northeastern corner of the great wall, head southward
along the wall's base to a Mountain House station close to the site of Merchant Lawrence's tavern, and then go on to a conclusion at Palenville.[5] Guests
at the Mountain House, the Laurel House, and others on the mountaintop would continue to rely on horsepower to get them up the mountain wall,
for no cog railroad would be permitted to scar the Beach domain. While
what would become the Catskill Mountain Railroad was being discussed, the

railroad-on-stilts plan failed to attract capital and died. Beach and his friends responded by hesitating and dawdling over their own railroad scheme.

Railroads and new hotels were not alone in applying pressure to force change from the Pine Orchard's atmosphere of "Rip Van Winkleism rampant" which the New York *Herald* man had sensed on the Pine Orchard in 1878. An older and much simpler means of getting about on the earth's surface was also playing a part. In the summer of 1862 Arnold Guyot, professor of geology at Princeton College, had begun exploring the Catskills, and he returned summer after summer. In the pivotal summer of 1879 it was being rumored that Guyot's feats of walking and climbing were about to produce a concrete printed result which would focus public attention on the upper Esopus Valley and give that valley and its surrounding mountains a share of the glamor that had hung for so long over the vale of the twin lakes, the Kaaterskill Falls, and the Pine Orchard alone.

66

Professor Guyot
Measures the Mountains

❧ THE EARLIEST EXPLORERS of the Catskills were not enthusiastic walkers. Even the first Indian visitors to the mountain region preferred traveling by canoe—they walked with amazing skill, but only when transportation by water was impossible. The early white explorers, surveyors like the Woosters and botanists like the Bartrams, traveled as much as possible on horseback, the way respectable eighteenth-century people got around. Walking was for the poor, for vagabonds, for children too young to know better. Much of the region of the Catskills was inhospitable to horses, for it lacked grass on which they might feed. In many of the forested parts of eastern North America, occasional grassy "openings" provided a dining place here and there for horses. But such openings were not too frequent among the Catskills. In 1762 Robert Livingston of Clermont wrote of one "on the great Hill"[1] within an English mile of his sawmill at Woodstock. He described it well—there was "no underwood upon it but here and there a tree." By the time Dr. Mitchill came to the Catskills it was possible for a gentleman to walk without risking a loss of status. The romantic revolution had raised walking into a respectable sort of adventure if tackled in the right spirit. William Wordsworth was soon composing much of his poetry while walking in his Lake District, while before him Jean Jacques Rousseau had praised the value of walking to creative minds. Botanists and other nature lovers had found that it is the walker and not the rider who comes into the most intimate and understanding contact with many of the marvels of nature which remain invisible to a horseman or a man rolling along in his carriage. It is the walker whose senses take in the largest possible share of the world around him—the dewdrops fringing a wild strawberry leaf, the texture of an insect wing, the smell of sun-warmed earth, the shadow cast by a fern frond. A walker can hardly escape feeling that he has established personal contact with the natural world. And the rhythm of his footsteps helps organize the thousands of impressions crowding in upon him into a feeling of kinship with all living things. It was in this spirit that Thomas Cole had walked among the Catskills during his brief period of romantic intoxication, and in this spirit young Cole painted and wrote.

By Cole's time, walking tours of such European regions as the Harz Mountains were popular among German students and romantic intellectuals, while Britons walked in ever larger numbers in the Lake District and elsewhere. In the United States walkers and climbers were soon radiating from the Catskill Mountain House. Every summer, walkers of Charles Lanman's sort might be met on the Catskills' eastern wall and as far west as the Stony Clove. Occasionally a group of college students in charge of a tutor might come along.[2] These people aided hunters, surveyors, and fishermen in beating the trails leading to many mountaintops and waterfalls by the middle of the nineteenth century. By then shelters of evergreen boughs stood on the higher summits and were used and repaired by party after party.

In 1844 the greatest of American walkers came to the Catskills—he was Henry David Thoreau. Unfortunately, Thoreau left no easily identified sign of his brief walking tour in the Catskills. The volume of his journal in which he recorded the tour—probably in considerable detail—has vanished. A few paragraphs which found their way into later journal entries, a letter or two, and a comment by William Ellery Channing, his companion in the Catskills, are all we have to tell us that Thoreau once walked Catskill trails. It is not much, yet it is enough to be worth bringing together if only because Thoreau's trip to the Catskills resulted in a memorable passage in his *Walden*—a passage in which the Catskills are not once mentioned.

In the spring of 1844 Thoreau's friend Isaac Hecker, who became the founder of the Paulist Fathers, invited Thoreau to join him on a trip to Europe. Instead, Thoreau chose to walk "to the Catskill Mountains, over the principal mountains of this state (Massachusetts) subsisting mainly on bread and berries and slumbering on mountaintops."[3] As he reached the summit of one of his Massachusetts mountains, Greylock near Williamstown, he wrote that he had caught a glimpse of "the summits of new and yet higher mountains, the Catskills, by which I might hope to climb to heaven again, and had set my compass for a fair lake in the southwest. . . ."[4] This was South Lake which a number of friends, including Horace Greeley had recently visited. At the railroad station in Pittsfield, Thoreau met, by arrangement, William Ellery Channing, the poet-nephew and namesake of the great Unitarian divine. Channing was shocked by Thoreau's ragged clothing and his dusty unshaven face. The two set out for the Hudson River. They crossed on a steamer—it was probably on this crossing, as Channing recalled, that, "after a 'hem' or two, the passenger who stood next inquired in good faith: 'come, now, can't you lend me a chaw of 'baccy?' "[5] For Thoreau in his battered walking togs had been mistaken, as he stood at the steamer's prow admiring the moonlight on the Catskills, for a member of the crew.

Just how Channing and Thoreau made their way up the mountain from the landing at Catskill is not known. They probably walked by moonlight, for such walks had great charm for Thoreau. What we do know is that the two men lodged that night at a "mountain house," but not at *the* Mountain House. Their little mountain house was the one Ira and Mary Scribner were in the process of building near Ira's sawmill a short distance above the brink of the Kaaterskill Falls. Ira and his father, Silas, before him had operated the sawmill; in 1823 Silas had bought the millsite and a large tract surrounding it from Elisha Williams. Both father and son were noteworthy people. For it was they who turned on and off the waters of the Kaaterskill Falls for the pleasure of tourists and for their own profit, though, before long, the Schutts of the Laurel House built a dam closer to the falls and took personal charge of domesticating the stream. As Channing and Thoreau turned up, the Scribners were enlarging their house, probably with a view to taking care of summer visitors, for before long the place became a boardinghouse known as the Glen Mary in honor of Mrs. Scribner.

In July 1844 Thoreau's mind was busy with his project of building a cabin beside Walden Pond. That may help explain why the half-finished Scribner house and nearby South Lake made so strong an impression on him. They may have taken on in his mind something of the magical air which envelops cherished projects before they come into reality. On the first day he spent in his own house on Walden Pond the next summer, Thoreau's thoughts turned to the Catskills. He wrote in his journal, "Yesterday I came here to live. My house makes me think of some mountain houses I have seen, which seemed to have a fresher auroral atmosphere about them, as I fancy of the halls of Olympus. I lodged at the house of a saw-miller last summer, on the Caatskill Mountains, high up as Pine Orchard, in the blueberry and raspberry region, where the quiet and cleanliness and coolness seemed to be all one—which had their ambrosial character. He was the miller of the Kaaterskill Falls. They were a clean and wholesome family, inside and out, like their house. The latter was not plastered, only lathed, and the inner doors were not hung. The house seemed high-placed, airy and perfumed, fit to entertain a travelling god. It was so high, indeed, that all the music, the broken strains, the waifs and accompaniments of tunes, that swept over the ridge of the Catskills, passed through its aisles. Could not man be man in such an abode? And would he ever find out this groveling life? It was the very light and atmosphere in which the works of Grecian art were composed and in which they rest. . . ."[6]

In the first manuscript version of *Walden*, the book Thoreau wrote while living beside the pond, he rephrased what he had written in his journal about the sawmiller and his house and added two sentences about South Lake. Walden Pond, he said, "reminded me of a tarn high up on the side of a mountain, and the whole region where I lived seemed more elevated than it actually was. The pond was like a mountain lake I had seen in the grey of the morning draped with mist, suspended in low weather from the dead willows and bare firs that stood here and there in the water. . . ."[7]

In the final published version of *Walden*, Thoreau cut all mention of the Catskills from his passage dealing with the sawmiller and his house. And so the Catskills made their way quietly and in disguise into a literary triumph greater and far more relevant to our own times than *Rip Van Winkle* or *The Pioneers*.

Today the sawmiller's house which so stimulated Thoreau's imagination is gone—bulldozed into oblivion, except for a part of its foundations, in order to make room for a parking lot for the New York State Conservation Department. But Thoreau's passion for walking remains alive and active, for that passion was not the isolated eccentricity of one man but an important part of a broad surge. In 1850 and 1851 Thoreau's entries in his journals praised walking with eloquence and understanding. Like Wordsworth he found that walking stirred his mind and imagination: "How vain it is to sit down to write when you have not stood up to live! Methinks that the moment my legs begin to move, my thoughts begin to flow. . . ."[8] Thoreau walked by moonlight, as the sun set, in cold and in heat. He liked to walk without a definite purpose and to allow nature to guide him and penetrate him. In 1836 Ralph Waldo Emerson in his great essay on Nature wrote of the "wild delight" a man attuned to nature could feel: "In the woods, too, a man casts off his years, as a snake his slough, and at what period soever of life, is always a child. In the woods, is perpetual youth." Emerson said that the people of his day saw "God and nature at second-hand through the ideas and experiences of previous generations." He urged that each man establish "an original relation" to the universe of which he forms a part. By the light of his powerful genius, Thoreau walked his way to his own original relation.

In 1856 Walt Whitman celebrated walking in his *Poem of the Road—*

later called *A Song of the Open Road*. By 1861 walking was acquiring charm for Americans who had little interest in acquiring an original relation to anything but found that walking had a sporting value. That year a young man named Edward Payson Weston walked from Boston to Washington to watch Abraham Lincoln inaugurated as President. He was a bit late in arriving, but Lincoln congratulated him anyway. Early the next year Thoreau died. In June of the same year the *Atlantic Monthly* printed his essay "On Walking" which had been put together from his journal entries and lectures of the early 1850s. Once the Civil War had ended, walkers with staffs in their hands and knapsacks on their backs became familiar sights along the eastern wall of the Catskills—each was seeking his own original relation. At the same time, in England and the United States, walking as a sport gained new converts. In 1867 Weston walked from Maine to Chicago in a little less than twenty-six days and became a minor hero. The betting world discovered walking and so it became of intense personal and financial interest to many Americans who would otherwise have continued to find it a bore. By the mid-seventies a "walking mania" was being reported by newspapers and New York *Times* editorials were praising walking.

In the same summer that Thoreau's "Walking" appeared in the *Atlantic,* a new kind of walking enthusiast came to the Catskills for the first time. He combined in one vigorous fifty-five-year-old body the walker for pleasure and the walker for scientific inquiry. No walker among the Catskills ever had a more powerful effect on the region or did more to upset long-established beliefs. And no walker before or since climbed more mountains in the Catskills, crawled along more ledges, or visited more hollows. For Arnold Guyot was making a study of the entire Appalachian chain, with particular emphasis on the Catskills. Even before his map and report on the Catskills appeared in 1879 and 1880, the Ulster & Delaware Railroad, the Catskill Mountain House, and the boardinghouse keepers and landowners of the region were stirred into action by his findings. For Guyot made some astonishing discoveries which caused the world to see the Catskills in a new way.

Arnold Henry Guyot was born in Switzerland and planned to be a clergyman, but the enthusiasm for the natural sciences that prevailed among his fellow students in Switzerland and Germany made him feel doubts. Perhaps he also felt the influence of men like De Saussure who had climbed and botanized and studied the rocks and water of the Alps back in the 1780s and 1790s. Certainly he was given direction by one of his teachers, the eminent geographer Karl Ritter, who handed on to Guyot his passion for relating geography to history and culture. In 1848 Guyot followed his friend Louis Agassiz to the United States, where Agassiz became an illustrious professor of zoology at Harvard College while Guyot settled down to teach physical geography at Princeton. He wrote successful textbooks, helped lay a foundation for the U. S. Weather Bureau, and battled against Darwin's theory of evolution until late in life when he became a convert. But nothing Guyot did seems to have given him more satisfaction than his summer walks and climbs among the mountains which roughly parallel the Atlantic coast.

When he first came to the Catskills, Guyot came as a prisoner of a number of long-accepted beliefs. One was that the mountain we know as High Peak was the very highest of all summits in the Catskills. Another was that the vicinity of the Pine Orchard, the twin lakes, and the Kaaterskill Falls comprised the heart of the Catskills; the confusing jumble of mountains lying to the west and southwest were not only lower but were without any special interest. The early explorations and measurements of DeLabigarre, Dr. Mitchill, and Captain Alden Partridge and his West Point cadets had helped enforce the impression of High Peak's supremacy which seemed so obvious to any traveler on the Hudson River. And the presence of the busy Catskill Mountain House on the Pine Orchard had given the clifftop a secure status as the center of interest in the Catskills.

It did not take Guyot very long to find that High Peak's reputation as the highest of the Catskills was undeserved: before he was through Guyot placed it a mere twenty-third in the hierarchy of Catskill summits. As Guyot studied and measured the northeastern parts of the Catskills, he first concluded that Black Top was the highest. In August 1871 one of his assistants, Henry Kimball, whom Guyot described as "the most indefatigable and skillful mountain climber of the Catskills,"[9] guided him up Hunter Mountain. And Guyot changed his mind. Hunter and not Black Top was the King of the Catskills, he concluded.

The next summer Guyot climbed Slide Mountain, some twenty miles to the southwest of Hunter. And when he came down he made no secret of his belief that not only did the Shandaken Mountains have every right to be known as part of the Catskills but that Slide was the highest mountain in the entire region. And in addition Slide and its companion mountains surpassed anything the Pine Orchard had to offer in wilderness charm. They were every bit as wild as the Adirondacks. It is not surprising that such heretical opinions were received—especially by Charles L. Beach and the businessmen of Catskill—with open disbelief. It was soon known that Guyot had determined the elevation of the Pine Orchard to be 2225 feet.

But Mr. Beach defiantly continued to advertise it as 3000. In order to account for the failure of earlier observers to understand the true rank of the Catskills' summits and to include the Shandakens in the region of the Catskills, some resorted to the easy explanation of the existence of a plot to conceal evidence.

Henry Kimball had first begun climbing the Catskills near the Mountain House in 1847. After his climbs with Guyot he wrote that the attractions of the Pine Orchard and Overlook were splendid enough but they formed only a very small part of the charms of the Catskills. When he first walked and climbed among the mountains, Kimball asserted, "the Beaches held practical possession of every point of interest on the Catskills. . . ."[10] They also controlled the stagecoaches which carried visitors to the mountains and they used their power in an effort to confine visitors to their own little corner. "In those days," Kimball stated "the Beaches suborned the poets, artists (except Cole), tourists, Bohemians of the press, the scribbling clergy, and deadheads generally to laud only the Pine Orchard, North Mountain, South Mountain, Cauterskill Falls and the Twin Lakes." Kimball admitted that Washington Irving had been a great writer but he charged that Irving had been "too indolent to acquaint himself with the flowers born to blush unseen in the unexplored regions of the Catskills."

It was true enough that Charles L. Beach and his predecessors on the Pine Orchard had confined their promotional efforts to praising the attractions easily available to guests at their establishment, for it was very much to their advantage as businessmen to persuade the public to accept their small part of what we know as the region of the Catskills as the whole. Charles Lanman had extended the romantic Catskills southward to Overlook Mountain to the accompaniment of disapproving stares from the old Mountain House. Then, thanks to the efforts of the Ulster & Delaware Railroad promoters and to Arnold Guyot, summer people became aware of a large and more varied region of the Catskill Mountains which extended from southern Schoharie County to the borders of Sullivan County. Late in 1879 this new region of the Catskills was first presented in the form of Guyot's map. By the following summer Guyot's study of the region appeared in the *American Journal of Science*. At once the new and enlarged region was generally accepted. Writers of guidebooks to the Catskills hastened to revise their works to include accounts of the attractions of the Esopus Valley and the valley of the East Branch of the Delaware. Slide Mountain and its companions were given lavish praise. Guyot's map was sold with the guidebook of one of his assistants, Samuel E. Rusk, while the publishers of others ran off copies. A region of the Catskills exactly like the one we know today had come into being in all but one detail: no part of Sullivan County was yet included.

The quick acceptance of Guyot's new Catskills was not due to the accuracy of his measuring and mapping alone, although that delighted walkers and climbers. Guyot also helped by clearing up many old confusions about place names. He was the first to set down in print a system of names for all summits of any importance among the Catskills. He divided the mountains into chains and ranges to which he gave appropriate names making it easier for summer boarders to grasp the complexities of the Catskills' topography. Guyot found that many mountains had no discoverable names. Then as now, people living beneath a mountain usually referred to it as "the mountain" almost as if no other mountain existed. To these unnamed mountains Guyot gave appropriate names, often those of early neighboring settlers or inspired by some physical characteristic of the mountain. Where other resources failed, Guyot inexpensively rewarded his amateur assistants by naming mountains for them. In this way Kimball and Rusk mountains were named. A summit adjoining Slide Mountain appeared for the first time on any map as Mount Cornell in honor of the U. & D.'s president. A Georgia mountain higher than any in the Catskills already bore Guyot's own name but this did not prevent the many friends he made while exploring the Catskills from trying to rename Hunter Mountain in his honor. In 1877 the Mount Guyot Lodge of a temperance organization known as the Good Templars was formed in Hunter. The lodge promptly expired and no more was heard of Mount Guyot. But Guyot's Hill in the Shawangunks, close to the point at which Captain Rose and his men crossed the range, still does its modest best to honor the professor.

In his effort to clear up confusions among the Catskills, Guyot did away with many names that duplicated others. Thus Roundtop at the head of Drybrook became Doubletop, and the neighboring South Mountain became Graham Mountain. Guyot accepted all well-established place names, rejecting only some of the "fanciful names so much in vogue." After Guyot had determined Slide Mountain to be the highest in the Catskills, local summer people felt that the name was not dignified enough for the King of the Catskills. They tried to impose the name of Thunderhead or Lion Mountain—but Guyot would have none of this prettying up and stuck to the old name derived from a conspicuous rock slide which had tumbled down the mountainside about 1830. However, he gave one mountain near Roxbury the fanciful name of Ontiora which he mistakenly believed to be "the old Indian name of the region." Here and there he gave well-defined minor summits such names as Strawberry Knob or Sister Knob. The term "knob" was not previously in use in the Catskills—Guyot may well have picked it up in the course of his work in the southern Appalachians where it abounds.

Most debatable of all Guyot's efforts was his bold transposing of the names of High Peak and Round Top which rise close together on the eastern wall of the mountains between the Kaaterskill and Plattekill cloves. The mountain Peter DeLabigarre had tried to rename Liberty Cap in 1793 was known in his day as Round Top—it was closer to the Hudson than its companion which was then known as High Peak. Both mountains' original names described them well. Roundtop had a rounded summit; High Peak was peakier, as seen from the Hudson Valley, than most of the Catskills. But after it became known that High Peak was lower than Round-top there was some dissatisfaction with the two names. Guyot's solution was to switch names, making them more accurate as far as altitudes go and less accurate in suggesting their forms. Guyot's switch was generally accepted and is still in force in spite of an occasional attempt to upset it.

Inevitably there was some grumbling at Professor Guyot's tinkering with the Catskills and especially at the enlargement of the region of the Catskills to which his map and scientific report gave such an air of authority. If Charles L. Beach felt that Guyot's expansion of the Catskills threatened to dilute the splendor of his own realm and threaten the prosperity of his hotel, he had good reason. But he had even better reason to feel threatened in the summer of 1880 when his star boarder, George Harding, came to his hotel as usual—and left determined, they said, never to return again.

67

The Fried Chicken War Declared

✤   THE FEW living people who remember George Harding describe him as a frail white-bearded man who always carried a handkerchief with something held in one corner by a knot. (It was the medicine the old man took when he felt heart trouble approaching.) But in July 1880 Harding was a tall, well-proportioned man abounding in health, personal charm, good spirits, and the millions his profession had brought him. When he first came to the Catskill Mountain House in the late 1840s it was to stop briefly before hurrying on to other stations on the American grand tour. By the seventies he was no longer spending the month of July at Saratoga as had been his habit, but was settling down for that month at the Mountain House. There Harding was a dominating figure accepted as the hotel's social leader, especially by the rich Philadelphians who continued to flock to the Catskills each summer. By 1877 Harding's conspicuous position at the Mountain House was being commented on in newspapers. The Catskill *Recorder* of August 17 said that "a gentleman from Philadelphia is the life of the house"; the next year the *Recorder* identified the gentleman as George Harding. It told with admiration of how Harding brought his own horses and carriages to the Mountain House and had his own "beautiful boat for the use of his family on North Lake."[1] The *Recorder* told too of how tireless George Harding was in devising amusements for his friends.

When George Harding arrived at the Mountain House early in July 1880 he was accompanied by his ailing wife and his ailing daughter. Daughter Emily was on a strict diet which excluded red meat and relied instead on chicken. Harding must have been well aware of how the Mountain House dining room was run—that guests were expected to eat what was set on their table and to ask for nothing more. Other hotels might have their supper rooms and their kitchens staffed to prepare whatever a guest might want whenever he might want it. But not the Catskill Mountain House, where the old-fashioned ordinary reigned in all its anachronistic rigidity. It is likely that Harding felt Charles L. Beach would make an exception in his favor, for one day he asked a waiter to bring some fried chicken for Emily. The waiter replied that fried chicken wasn't being served at that meal. When Harding insisted, the waiter hunted out Mr. Beach and Beach backed up his waiter.

Harding protested. Beach remained unyielding. Harding persisted in his demand for fried chicken and Beach resorted to a bit of sarcasm. If Harding didn't like the way the Mountain House was being run, why didn't he build the kind of hotel he wanted? There are a few bits of evidence to suggest that Beach and Harding had clashed before—perhaps Beach resented the position Harding had made for himself at the hotel. But this was the last time the two stubborn men were to clash on Beach property. Harding looked thoughtful and then quietly said that he might think about Beach's suggestion.[2]

It did not take George Harding long to make up his mind about his next step. He decided to build a hotel that would dwarf Beach's Mountain House by its size and eclipse it by its modernity. In this way, according to the most plausible of many versions, what was called the Fried Chicken War began.

At once, word of the Beach-Harding struggle traveled from town to town among the Catskills and to every trading center along the Hudson River. People lined up—those from the village of Catskill and the vicinity of the Mountain House on one side; Kingston people and dwellers along the Ulster & Delaware on the other. Fervent Beachites portrayed George Harding as a malevolent associate of "Grab-all Cornell"[3] motivated by nothing at all but a passion for crushing Beach and destroying the prosperity of Catskill. Hardingites saw Beach as a greedy and arrogant reincarnation of Rip Van Winkle who was determined to keep the modern world from penetrating the Catskills. Never since the days of Major Johannis Hardenbergh had so many fantastic tales come into being in and around the Catskills. The rivalry between Harding and Beach came to symbolize the changes taking place. The expansion of railroads, the multiplication of hotels, the change from the old simplicities to the comforts and sophistication of the final two decades of the nineteenth century— all became reduced to two men squabbling over a fried chicken.

Like most very rich men, Harding was used to having his own way and having it quickly. Once he had decided to build a hotel as close as he could get to Beach's Mountain House, he was all impatience to see it completed and in operation. All great struggles have their poets and the Fried Chicken War was no exception. A verse found scrawled on a wall of a building a little below South Lake suggests Harding's impetuous haste. It goes: "Far yonder on South Mountain stands/The structure built by Harding's hands./The cock that crew defied him twice;/I'll build a hotel in a trice!/Then up the towering Catskills went,/To build a hotel he was bent,/He bought the lands stretched far and near/which then belonged to John Scribner."[4] The poet erred in at least one respect. It was Ira Scribner, Henry Thoreau's old host at the Kaaterskill Falls, and not his son John who sold to Harding the lands extending eastward from the old sawmill and taking in a fine plateau on South Mountain a mere mile as the chicken flutters from the old Mountain House. It was on this plateau with its sweeping view of the Hudson Valley that Harding planned to build an immense hotel to which he could welcome the first guests by the final week of June 1881. Beachites laughed as word of Harding's hope reached them. The Philadelphia lawyer might know a lot about patents but he didn't know how cruelly the winds blew on South Mountain or how early the snow came or how late in the spring it lingered. There was not even a proper road to the site of the proposed hotel.

In Philadelphia, architect S. D. Button got to work on plans for the hotel as men, oxen, and horses began preparing the site. By October the plans were completed and twenty men in Lampman's steam-powered carpenter shop in Catskill received the word to go ahead and rush a vast amount of work for the hotel. Doors and windows, baseboards and elaborate trim, cornices and staircases, brackets and tall pillars were soon taking form. A clue to the scale of Harding's hopes lay in the fact that Button's first plans called for five hundred and fifty windows. That October, mountain sawmills worked overtime turning out joists and studs for Harding, and gangs of old-timers hewed and mortised great trees into timbers fit to withstand the gales of South Mountain as sills and plates.[5]

Accounts of the physical appearance of the new mountain house-to-be circulated and brought cheer to the hearts of loyal Hardingites. The building would be four stories tall and three hundred twenty-four feet long, with another three hundred feet of length to be added at the close of its first season. The building would have almost everything—a pillared portico surmounted by a pediment, acres of piazzas, gas and electric light, walnut and ash trim, steam heat, a barbershop, smoking rooms, open fireplaces, an elevator, modern plumbing—some rooms would even have private baths. The furnishings would be elaborate and all in the style of naïve elegance inspired in American brains by the writings of the late

Sir Charles Eastlake, the eminent British authority on interior decoration whose book on the subject was having an extraordinary success in the United States. The whole building would be topped off by tower after French-roofed tower. It would be reached, at least pending the completion of Cornell's railroad spur, by a road to be sent zigzagging up the side of precipitous South Mountain from Palenville at the foot of the Kaaterskill Clove—a road so daring in its conception and engineering that it could stand comparison (the Bishop of Albany stated) with the greatest achievements of world-famous Swiss road builders.

The scope of Harding's plans, especially when revealed at a time of economic expansion, was much exaggerated. Harding became known as the man who was spending $2,000,000 for a fried chicken but the actual cost of his hotel when finally completed was closer to $250,000. It was being said that a new era of huge luxury hotels was being ushered into the Catskills by Harding. Every mountaintop along the Ulster and Delaware was explored by prospective builders of such hotels. Old-time tanners like James Simpson of Phoenicia, now that a shortage of bark had closed their tanneries, were working out routes to the tops of mountains such as the Wittenberg from which their efforts had stripped the forests, and were trying to raise enough capital to go into the summer hotel business. Jacob Tremper, Jr., of the Tremper House enlarged his hotel until it could hold two hundred and fifty guests.

Rumors of the impending arrival of a colossal railroad hotel which might outshine anything else in the Catskills grew louder and louder. The hotel would be located near the point at which Monka Hill and the Pine Hill come together. In design and quality of accommodations it would rival the best any American summer resort had to offer. At the same time in Catskill, Margaretville, and many other places, boardinghouses and hotels were enlarged and given symbols of elegance in the form of French-roofed towers and bracketed piazzas. In Stamford, Dr. S. E. Churchill's Churchill Hall was about to become one of the gayest and most profitable hotels in the region. With all this going on, it was no wonder that it was being widely predicted that before long every mountain in the Catskills would be topped by its own hotel until the region, to Americans at least, would take on the look of the *schloss* country along the Rhine.

During the winter of 1880–81 even the weather seemed to favor the expansive and speculative mood gripping Americans as they climbed at last out of the depression into which they had tumbled in 1873. The winter was very mild and spring came early in 1881. At once the sounds of hotel construction echoed among the Catskills. And nowhere did these sounds draw more eager listeners than at the plateau on South Mountain where George Harding was weaving clapboards, shingles, nails, and timbers into his hotel. Hundreds of carpenters and other workmen gathered to assemble the mounds of materials accumulating on South Mountain. Such workmen were scarce, for agents for other booming resort regions—especially those on the Atlantic coast—were combing the Catskills and the Hudson Valley for them. Harding's men realized their scarcity and struck for higher wages. Harding drew the applause of local employers by firing the leaders of the strikers—and construction went on. Widespread stealing of building materials was then rumored, for the workmen were raising their own wages in this time-honored way. Harding did little to discourage stealing—it was cheaper to wink at it than to pay higher wages.

When drunkenness on the job caused comment among the temperance and prohibition believers in the town of Hunter in which Harding's hotel was rising, Harding took quick action. He could not afford to antagonize Hunter people, for he would have to go to them to get the liquor license he was determined to have. And Harding was aware that he might have trouble getting his license. Hunter was the wettest town in all the Catskills, with over a dozen "grog shops," yet there too the movement to refuse liquor licenses was gaining strength with each year. On August 29, 1879, Henry Kimball had paused in his walking and climbing among the Catskills long enough to write to the Kingston *Daily Freeman* that "the moral virtues of these hills are very marked. . . ." Kimball went on to list some of the towns that had displayed moral virtue by withholding liquor licenses. Windham was the leader among them—and the town was becoming widely known as a quiet family summer resort with no large hotels. In Pine Hill, Kimball wrote, there had been five grog shops and "then the women took the matter in hand and cleaned out the place teetotally. . . ." And in Woodstock that spring the voters had dried up the town at the polls. Since 1868 Hunter had had an anti-liquor organization whose leaders were women and employers who may have been rich in moral virtues but who surely felt annoyed at the diminished profits resulting from employees who tippled while at work and became damaged in brawls at the roadside taverns where, as one old-timer put it, "all hell busted loose on Saturday night after the men were paid off."

George Harding did not dream of building the kind of hotel where, as at the Overlook Mountain House, drinking would be done on the sly. A hotel like that could never meet the competition of the old Mountain House. Harding wanted to have a glittering bar and an extremely well-stocked wine cellar. And he was not a successful lawyer for nothing. He knew how to handle people in order to get what he wanted. When scandalized voices began spreading—and greatly exaggerating—the news that workers on his hotel were getting drunk on the job, Harding took decisive action. He had his drunks arrested and thrown into the county jail. And even better, he put pressure on nearby tavern owners to observe the law by closing down on Sundays.[6] Local employers had nodded in approval when Harding fired his striking workers, now those who were prohibition leaders nodded again and began to wonder if Harding mightn't be the sort of man who would use a liquor license wisely. It was obvious by this time that he had no intention of selling drinks to the poor. When Harding made his application for a license to Hunter's Board of Excise, it was granted. It was good, of course, for one year only.

In the meanwhile the construction of the Hotel Kaaterskill (for so Emily Harding had named it in the spring of 1881) went ahead. By mid-May several hundred reasonably sober men were working on the job and hiding bundles of shingles and crates of plumbing fixtures behind rocks and bushes, to be called for after dark.[7] The new road from Palenville was ascending South Mountain; in Saugerties citizens were holding mass meetings to promote the construction of a good highway from Palenville to their steamboat wharf and so persuade George Harding to make Saugerties and not Catskill or Kingston his base on the Hudson River. At the same time Cornell's railroad branch was moving ever closer to the Hotel Kaaterskill, and the Catskill Mountain Railroad, with Charles L. Beach as its first president, was at last pushing on from the steamboat wharf at Catskill to the foot of the mountains beneath the Pine Orchard.

It was rumored that Harding had offered to help finance the Catskill Mountain Railroad and that his offer had been haughtily rejected by the Beach clan. It was being said, and with much better evidence, that Harding had then agreed to recommend Cornell's road to his guests for a period of five years. But for the moment he seemed to be neutral in the rivalry of trading towns. Part of the materials for his hotel were unloaded from river steamers at Catskill and part at the dock in Malden in the town of Saugerties. Local railroads played no part in the building of the hotel—neither the Beach nor the Cornell line were yet completed.

Early in May it was being said that Harding had set June 20 as the opening day of the Hotel Kaaterskill. Extra men were hired to speed the work. Many—especially in Catskill—said that Harding would never make it. But in Saugerties people radiated confidence. One of them estimated that the guests at the Kaaterskill would spend close to a quarter of a million dollars at the hotel that summer. If Harding used the dock at Malden or the

Long Dock in Saugerties, then a good bit of that quarter of a million would end up in Saugerties pockets. Saugerties gave Harding its enthusiastic support. On June 14 the Saugerties *Post* stated that four hundred and twenty-five men were at work getting the hotel ready to receive guests on the twenty-seventh. And these men "won't disappoint Mr. Harding," the *Post* assured its readers "and don't you forget it."

68

The Fried Chicken War Won

✤ JUNE 26 dawned as usual on South Mountain but it found the Hotel Kaaterskill still far from being ready to open the next day. Lumber, bags of plaster, paint cans, and sawdust lay everywhere. Crates of glasses, of cups, plates, and saucers were unopened. The grounds around the building had become a muddy battleground as men, horses, and oxen came, labored, and went. The machinery for producing the electric arc lights which were expected to make the exterior of the building glow by night like a fallen star was still in its crates inside the storehouse built for Harding on the Hudson River dock at Malden. Last minute decisions had to be made. The hotel would have to open on schedule even if that meant opening without benefit of the electric light and a number of other cherished attractions. All through the twenty-sixth and all through the following night, hundreds of men worked at the hotel in a prodigious outpouring of energy. Carpenters and cleaning women slaved inside the building. Outside, nurserymen's wagons arrived laden with potted foliage plants such as Centaureas and Achyranthes, while others bore geraniums in dazzling bloom. A corps of gardeners, among them Peter Troy who had been a gardener for the Earl of Waterford in his native Ireland, prepared the hotel's surroundings for planting. Hollows were filled with anything that came handy—boards, bricks, lead pipes, and assorted rubbish. Over all this a thin layer of soil was spread, the soil was tamped down, sod was put in place, paths were graveled, ornamental plants were set in geometrical beds.[1] And behold, as the sun rose on the twenty-seventh, the Hotel Kaaterskill was ready to receive its first guests.

The steamer *Catskill* moved in triumph up the Hudson that day to the booming of cannon and the music of bands. She was under charter to George Harding, and her cargo was precious, for the ship was loaded with more than two hundred newspapermen who could reasonably be expected to show gratitude for the junket in printed words. Opening day, according to the newspapermen, was an unqualified success, marred only by the failure of Charles L. Beach and his sons to show a neighborly spirit of rejoicing. Many of the opening day guests made their way to the old Mountain House, and one of them, editor Flynn of the Bordentown, New Jersey *Register,* stated that old Charles L. Beach "showed unmistakable discourtesy to such of the excursionists as visited his premises. He thereby proved that he did not know how to keep a hotel."[2]

That night travelers on the Hudson looked up expectantly at the new hotel which had joined the Overlook and the old Mountain House on top of the great wall of the Catskills. They saw that the Kaaterskill far outshone its rivals and told each other that they were seeing the new wonder, the electric light in action. These people, of course, were mistaken. It was merely the blaze of the gas-burning chandeliers hanging in the Kaaterskill's great Rotunda that was dazzling thousands of pairs of eyes in the Hudson Valley that memorable night—the electric light would appear a little later. But it was plain enough that even without the help of the electric light George Harding had won the first skirmish of the Fried Chicken War. He had opened his hotel on schedule.

The Kaaterskill was not the only new mountain hotel to crash into public awareness in 1881 and the next two years. During those years of soaring hopes, the hotel building mania which had begun in the late seventies reached its climax. First to follow the Kaaterskill was the Grand Hotel—it opened for business with a "grand opening ball" on July 1, 1881.

Those Beachites who saw George Harding as a monster felt their suspicions were confirmed when the Grand Hotel appeared close to the Ulster & Delaware station high on Monka Hill, for it was obvious to them that Thomas Cornell and Harding were in an alliance to run down and destroy Charles L. Beach. And the Grand was indeed a formidable competitor to both the Mountain House and the Hotel Kaaterskill. An eighth of a mile long, it was an architectural copy of Coney Island's generously towered and piazzaed Oriental Hotel, an establishment of such elegance that it was a favorite of blue-blooded Bostonians. The Grand made a novel bid for patronage among mountain houses through its extravagant praise for the waters of its Diamond Spring. Day and night the water gushed from a marble fountain in the hotel Rotunda. "It is specifically recommended by eminent physicians to have a fresh supply from the spring served to each room before breakfast,"[3] the Grand's management advertised. While the waters of Saratoga were loaded with a variety of helpful minerals, those of the Diamond Spring relied upon their "almost absolute purity" to comfort kidneys and to urge digestive organs to perform their functions without protest. The same water also washed vegetables in the hotel kitchen and flushed the hotel toilets. The water of the twin lakes and the Kaaterskill Falls had done much for the old Mountain House; now the Diamond Spring was expected to perform a similar service for the Grand.

Like the Catskill and Overlook Mountain houses, the Grand Hotel had a magnificent view from its piazzas. But while Mr. Beach's guests had little more than a view of the Hudson Valley, and those at the Overlook a view that was half valley and half mountains, the Grand could boast that its view was almost 100 per cent mountains—and of the highest mountains in all the Catskills at that. By way of contrast it offered a patch of the sweeping pastures of Delaware County on the extreme right; and as if to make Slide and its companions appear even more massive, trains of the Ulster & Delaware climbed the Pine Hill's famous horseshoe curve within sight of the Grand's guests. The curve was so sharp that mountain people sometimes assured credulous summer boarders that if a man in the caboose chose the right moment he could shake hands with the engineer in his cab.[4] Depth in historic time was given to the scene by the presence within sight of the Grand's piazzas of several stumps of the pine trees which had given the hill below its name—some were four and five feet in diameter. The trees themselves had been riven into shingles by pioneer settlers and timber thieves (in this form even a giant pine could be profitably carried through the forests to market).[5]

From its earliest days the religious associations of the old Mountain House had made it a favorite resort of the fashionable Protestant clergymen who did much to set the tone of the polite society of their time. The services some of these men conducted on Mr. Beach's Pine Orchard seemed to verge dangerously upon a sort of nature worship, but to most participants they conveyed a sense of the kind of closeness of man to the rest of the natural world which marked the romantic movement. Sermons at the Mountain House were often based on biblical texts containing the word "mountain" or "mountains." A favorite was "he took them up into a mountain apart," Matthew 17:1. The Overlook Mountain House closely followed Mr. Beach's lead in Sunday observances, and sermons preached there were sometimes enthusiastically commented upon in Hudson Valley newspapers. When the more worldly Hotel Kaaterskill came into being, it laid a lessened stress on sermons and the rites and observances of the English Sunday. But at the Grand Hotel, in its opening years, the Mountain House kind of Sunday was very much part of hotel life. And some of

Mr. Charles L. Beach's heaviest ecclesiastical guns deserted his hotel for the Grand. Among them was the Reverend Theodore Ledyard Cuyler, D.D.

No one had ever more effectively captured the spirit of a Pine Orchard Sunday than Dr. Cuyler did in his "A Sabbath on the Catskills," reprinted in the 1864 edition of the *Scenery of the Catskills*. There the doctor told of worshipers beginning the day's observances by standing on the clifftop wrapped in shawls and blankets to watch with reverence as the sun rose. He told of pious people strolling with books in their hands "into the thickets toward South Mountain" while waiting to plunge into singing hymns, listening to sermons, and joining in prayers in the hotel parlors. A few guests, it was true, actually drove to the Kaaterskill Falls on Sunday, Dr. Cuyler reported, but nine-tenths of the guests shared in the "Sabbath arrangements of our Sabbath-observing host," Mr. Beach. The hotel was indeed, to use Cuyler's words, "a sanctuary on the Lord's day."

Charles L. Beach could not have watched with pleasure as Dr. Cuyler took off for the Grand Hotel with its modern plumbing, its gaslights, its frequent conventions of religious organizations, and its weekday air of cheerful late nineteenth-century materialism. He must have been even less pleased when Dr. Cuyler, the author of countless magazine articles and nineteen books, turned his literary talents to praising the Grand and disparaging the Catskill Mountain House to which he had so long been faithful. The Grand, Cuyler wrote, was located in the very "heart" or "core" of the Catskills whereas Mr. Beach's establishment stood on the edge or fringe of the Catskills and therefore, he implied, it barely qualified for inclusion in the mountain region.[6] Others amplified this thought in a way that would some day help bring northern Sullivan County within the boundaries of the romantic Catskills. They claimed that the vicinity of the Grand Hotel and Slide Mountain was surrounded by a mountain buffer zone some twenty-five miles in depth and extending deep into Sullivan. The air that patrons of the Grand breathed was the product of this zone and was therefore pure mountain stuff. But it was quite otherwise with the air breathed by guests at the old hotel on the Pine Orchard. These unfortunate people lacked a buffer zone; they were compelled to inhale air that all too often had drifted in from the Hudson Valley and was repulsively thick with the smoke and dust of human habitations.

Like Dr. Cuyler, Dr. Howard Crosby had been among the clerical deserters from the Pine Orchard. He was minister of a fashionable Presbyterian church in New York, an author and biblical scholar, professor of Greek, and the founder and guiding spirit of New York's Society for the

Prevention of Crime, which mildly harried the gamblers and prostitutes of its time. Dr. Crosby was soon praising the Grand in print and, what was even more important, he was giving Slide and the neighboring mountains which rose so nobly before the eyes of sitters on the Grand's piazza, a high standing among hikers and climbers. Crosby had been a frail child, and he believed that walking and climbing in pure mountain air had strengthened him and made possible his many achievements. Accompanied by clerical and academic associates and friends, he furiously climbed every mountain within sight of the Grand's piazzas, disdaining hunters' trails and plunging with passion into labyrinths of tumbled boulders and almost impenetrable blowdowns.[7] When Crosby and his learned friends became lost, which happened every once in a while, and when they were rescued by some mountaineer who could read and write only with difficulty, mountain people chuckled. But many summer boarders, inspired by Dr. Crosby as well as by Professor Guyot, left the piazzas of the Grand and neighboring boardinghouses for the summits of Slide, Panther, Cornell, and the Wittenberg. Others who preferred the air of barrooms to that of mountaintops found the Grand to have a singular charm. The hotel had been built on the line that divided two towns and two counties—its site was part of the tract deeded by Chancellor Livingston to his sister Alida. When Shandaken refused a liquor license, the barroom was merely moved into Middletown at the other end of the vast building. When Middletown prohibitionists grew hostile, the barroom traveled back to a now-wet Shandaken. The sliding barroom of the Grand proved one of its greatest attractions. The hotel office was also a wanderer, for tax reductions could be induced by shifting the office from one town or county to another.[8]

By the early 1880s, summer life among the Catskills had acquired two major centers. One was the Catskill Mountain House-Hotel Kaaterskill vicinity, the other the Grand Hotel-Slide Mountain area. A third was in the making at Stamford. The Grand area, nourished by the Ulster & Delaware Railroad, the work of Arnold Guyot, and the efforts of the hotel's staff of clerical supporters, was growing and expanding mightily. The hamlet of Pine Hill beneath the Grand acquired a concentration of clerical talent unmatched anywhere in the region as eminent clergymen made it their summer headquarters. In 1880, while the Grand Hotel existed only on paper, Dr. J. Glentworth Butler had begun buying up land between the hotelsite and the hamlet of Pine Hill with speculative intent. A very successful physician and the publisher of a five-volume work of biblical exposition written by his father, he poured his profits into the building of summer homes. Dr. Crosby and other clergymen of similar rank, college professors, and college presidents were soon adding the benefit of their summer presence to Pine Hill beneath the Grand.

The owners of small hotels and boardinghouses in Pine Hill took the cue provided by the Grand's Diamond Spring promotion and labeled their resort the Saratoga of the Catskills, a title also to be claimed by Stamford. Pine Hill was blessed with a number of fine springs which supplied water similar in quality to that of the Diamond Spring. A pump house and a great spa hotel-sanatorium were talked of. Meanwhile, the water of the Crystal Spring was bottled and sent by the carload to New York City. Eventually the Grand Hotel, controlled and managed by Thomas Cornell's half-brother and his nephew, issued a handsome advertising booklet which gave much space to praise of the hotel by clergymen. This was the Grand's answer to Charles L. Beach's reprintings of his *Scenery of the Catskill Mountains.*

The Grand and the Kaaterskill were one-year-old infants when the Laurel House joined the company of large Catskill Mountain hotels claiming the right to be called first class. For the nearly forty years of its existence the Laurel House had been content to play the part of a dutiful poor cousin to the Catskill Mountain House, but now, as the old Mountain House seemed to be staggering, the Laurel took on the look of still another rival. The hotel had begun as a small boardinghouse in 1852. In 1860 it tripled its number of rooms and from time to time after that it had been further enlarged. Then in 1882 it opened for the season in a new and astonishing dress. Mr. Button, the architect of the Hotel Kaaterskill, had provided the Laurel with long three-story porticos which gave the hotel a little of the look of a smaller version of Harding's. But Mr. Button designed only one observation tower for the Laurel: a central one covered by a many-gabled roof. The capacity of the Laurel was enlarged to two hundred and fifty.

Stamford had been denied a role as a leading summer-boarding center by the absence of a good water supply. In 1883 the pipes of a water company began to gush, and that same year ambitious Dr. Churchill emerged as master of Churchill Hall and the leader of his town's drive toward summer resort fame. Along the Esopus, Lament's Hotel, long known as a good turnpike inn, was reborn as a Queen Anne-style summer hotel. It had been a typical white-painted inn of its class with the capacious upstairs and downstairs verandahs and Greek Revival air of most inns of its kind among the Catskills. But by 1883 all that was becoming part of a musty past. The new Lament House earned widespread admiration for its many gables and its color scheme of old gold, terra cotta, and Indian red. Moreover, it hired a new chef who appealed to admirers of the rich and powerful because he had once cooked for the younger James Gordon Bennett on board his yacht.

In 1883 the Catskills' hotel-building mania came to an end as the spell of pleasant economic weather which had prevailed since 1879 gave way to chill and fog. During the next few years guests came to the Catskills in fewer numbers and weaker hotels and boardinghouses suffered keenly. The Overlook Mountain House had been doing well, but by 1883 its owners were said to be considering an offer by George Harding to buy them out and use their place as a picnic ground and observation point for his own guests—it would be connected with the Hotel Kaaterskill by a railroad. The Laurel House was finding its brave new dress a burden as it entered upon a period of decline. In 1884 playwright Steele MacKaye chose the half-deserted Overlook Mountain House as a quiet retreat in which he tried in vain to turn out a new play to follow his immensely successful melodrama *Hazel Kirke,* but by then the hotel had been struck an economic blow from which it would never recover.

At the height of the season during the mid-eighties, the Grand Hotel and Churchill Hall were filled—but only for a few weeks. The Kaaterskill too lost money—it needed an average of six hundred guests to pay the expenses of keeping it open. George Harding could afford to endure a few years of loss and he could take comfort in the knowledge that, during these years of trial and anguish for Catskill Mountain hotelkeepers, he was emerging not only as the victor in the Fried Chicken War but also as the proprietor of the most elegant, the most fashionable, the most talked-about hotel in all the Catskills.

69

"The Mixed and Undesirable Element"

❦ IN EUROPE the popularity of resorts for health and pleasure often dated from royal visits. Mythical King Bladud, who did much for Bath, was said to have visited the place long before the Roman conquest. In 1733 Royal Princesses Amelia and Caroline took the waters of an obscure spa at Islington; the nobility and gentry followed their example and the place had a joyful spurt of popularity. When George III showed early symptoms of the irrationality that would later increase, he became convinced that all he needed was a visit to a little known spa called Cheltenham. The King burst upon Cheltenham riding one of the elated crests of his malady. He roused respectable citizens before dawn with a demand to be shown the sights, and chatted in friendly manner with astonished subjects whom he met on the streets while his attendants were at their wit's ends to control the royal sufferer's passion for galloping, dashing, fraternizing, and chattering. It might have been thought that the King's delight in Cheltenham would have made sober people avoid the place. Not so. Following the royal visit of 1788, Cheltenham became famous and popular. A few years earlier the presence of the Prince of Wales had made the fortunes of Brighton.

American resorts of the early days of the republic could not fall back upon royalty when business was dull. They had to make do with what was available under the Stars and Stripes. Presidents took the place of royalty as prime boosters of resort business—President Grant's visit to the Overlook Mountain House was a fine example. The very rich, senators, generals, judges, and members of what some were kind enough to call the aristocracy of talent—poets, painters and even actors and musicians—all did their best to play the parts usually assigned at European resorts to the nobility and gentry. The Catskill Mountain House had entertained a constant stream of such celebrities ever since 1823—only Presidents had held back. Charles L. Beach had not been at all modest in letting the public know of the great names adorning his register. But as the 1880s came, it was George Harding's turn to boast.

Hardly had the Hotel Kaaterskill opened when Harding's publicity men began sending out the names of the great guests whom their employer had bagged. Railroad presidents, bishops, diplomats, cabinet members, titled foreigners, reigning beauties of what was coming to be called "society," and literary heroes were used as live bait to lure the part of the general public which could afford to pay the Kaaterskill's high daily rate of $4.50 for room and meals. Metropolitan newspapers now printed chitchat about life at the Kaaterskill, the Grand, the Tremper House, and Churchill Hall right beside bits of froth from Newport, Saratoga, and Long Branch. They reported in 1882 that young Oscar Wilde chose to deliver his aesthetic lectures only at the Tremper House and the Kaaterskill Hotel. Wilde praised the Catskills' scenery but shocked older hotel proprietors by stating that their "mountain houses are always built in the wrong spots. The top of a mountain is no place for a mountain house. . . . it should be put in the valley, there the picturesque and the beautiful is ever before you. . . ."[1] Wilde explained that "a stately tree" when seen from a mountaintop becomes reduced to a mere spot of green, and argued that the distance of most of the charms of nature from mountaintops deprived them of all charm. And besides, "one soon tires of the view before him" when one stands on top of a mountain.

The next season, ex-President Grant took Wilde's place as the Kaaterskill's chief attraction. He was driven from the hotel to the Catskill Mountain House to admire its view, and remained for an hour of handshaking. He was very much impressed by the favorite view of Kaaterskill guests—the one to be seen from Inspiration Point near the hotel. Grant stared deep down into the Kaaterskill Clove and let his eyes follow the clove's opposite wall, up, up, up its forest-clad precipices to the summits of High Peak and Round Top. He amused local people by calling the clove "the canyon."[2] In 1884, President Chester A. Arthur gave the Catskills the closest thing to a royal visit the mountains ever experienced when he spent a week at the Kaaterskill. During his stay, Arthur was driven to the Overlook Mountain House over the fine scenic road which had linked the hotel to Platte Clove ever since 1879. He visited Hunter, transacted official business at the Kaaterskill, and so gave the place some right to be called a summer White House. The President and his daughter Nellie strolled to the old Mountain House to take in the view. One evening at the Kaaterskill, those eminent lawyers George Harding and General Sharpe staged a mock trial in the case of Charles Dickens' Bardell *vs.* Pickwick. Arthur sat on the Kaaterskill's piazza in the dusk surrounded by girls who entertained him by playing guitars and singing. He laughed heartily one day as he watched a "novel fire escape exhibition"—bellboys and other daring young hirelings of Harding were shot through a canvas tube from a third-story window. On Sunday, George Harding took the President to see the Haines Falls, which were owned by Charles W. Haines, proprietor of the Haines Falls House and a man of such strong religious feeling that he was known as "Christian Charley." But Haines, according to tradition still repeated in the neighborhood, refused to turn on his Falls on Sunday, "not even for the President of the United States,"[3] he declared. If Arthur wanted to see the Falls, Haines told him, he'd be glad to turn them on—on Monday.

Eighteen eighty-five brought rumors of a return visit from General Grant to the Kaaterskill. That summer the general was dying of cancer at Mount MacGregor near Saratoga. In April, during a brief period of improved health, Grant had accepted General Sharpe's suggestion that he try the pure air of the Kaaterskill. George Harding offered the ex-President and his family free quarters and board at his hotel, and a suite of nine rooms and four baths was reserved for Grant's use in August.[4] As the rooms were being made ready, word came that Grant was failing and then that he had died—just one week before he was expected at the Kaaterskill. After Grant's burial in his tomb on New York's Riverside Drive, the steamer *Kaaterskill* and then the *Catskill* sadly blew their whistles in tribute as they passed by. Other steamers followed their example and, for a while, the whistled tribute became a custom of the Hudson River.

The Kaaterskill shared some of its great names with other hotels among the Catskills. Jay Gould and his children visited there, but they also showed a fondness for the Grand. More than once guests at the Grand stared in fascination as old Mr. Gould tackled his dinner in the hotel dining room, his dark eyes fixed less on his soup than on the stock market quotations rushed from the hotel telegraph to his table. On the siding below the Grand, Gould's private railroad car, the Atalanta, waited for him. Guests were told that the car was seventy feet long and weighed 78,000 pounds. When President Arthur was at the Kaaterskill, the manager of the Grand angled for a presidential visit. Arthur seemed interested, then shied away. But the Grand could always boast of its clergymen, while the Tremper went in for rich Central and South Americans, as did the Ackerley House at Margaretville. Churchill Hall guests were similar to those at the Grand but usually with less money—they were the sort who could take the refusal of their host to serve "ardent spirits" in their stride.

Hunters and hikers high among the Catskills often spent nights in shelters fashioned wastefully from the lower bark of old spruce trees. This photograph was made about 1890. (*Geroldseck-Schadle Collection.*)

The millpond above the Kaaterskill Falls, used by Henry Thoreau's host, Ira Scribner. From a stereograph of the 1870s. (*Courtesy of the Greene County Historical Society.*)

The Grand Hotel from a
12 x 16 inch photograph taken,
as the hotel was being rushed to
completion, by "Lewis, photo,
Kingston, New York."

The Hotel Kaaterskill photographed from the road winding down to Palenville during its early years. (*Courtesy of Haines Falls Public Library.*)

Ornate Churchill Hall, Stamford, as it looked during the 1890s. (*Author's collection.*)

This earliest known engraving of Slide Mountain is from *A Catskill Souvenir,* 1879.

Henry Ward Beecher graced Churchill Hall's opening day in 1883, climbed halfway up its grand staircase, and spoke much as he had at the Tremper House opening but with his material neatly adapted to Dr. Churchill's needs.

The Catskill Mountain House, too, had its share of famous names. But it must have been the realization that he was outclassed in this department by George Harding that helped cause Charles L. Beach to retreat into reticence. The Catskill *Examiner,* which remained loyal to Beach interests through thick and thin, gave up its custom of printing lists of Mountain House guests, nor did it reveal the names of those who were enjoying the Hotel Kaaterskill's hospitality. Thus local people could not compare the two rivals. When the Kaaterskill had an especially famous guest, the *Examiner* sometimes ignored his presence but printed a pert little item intended to emphasize the superiority of guests at Beach's mountain house. On July 26, 1889, the *Examiner* proclaimed that the house on the Pine Orchard "receives the patronage of the very best class of people, who can appreciate the beauty of its surroundings." An elegant stable with a hundred fast horses, corsages for the ladies sent up from New York by train, a steamboat named the *Gussie Paige* on South Lake, a chef whose salary exceeded that of the bishop of Pennsylvania—all these vulgarities might be good enough for Mr. Harding's people. But the Beach's guests had far nobler sources of satisfaction—the *Examiner*'s item delicately suggested.

In 1886 essayist Charles Dudley Warner gave the public his impressions of American summer resorts in a lightly fictionalized volume titled *Their Pilgrimage.* One of Warner's characters, a veteran of resort life, says that "the Old Mountain House standing upon the ledge of rock . . . has somewhat lost its importance since the vast Catskill region has come to the knowledge of the world. A generation ago it was the center of attraction, and it was understood that going to the Catskills was going there. . . ." The character mused over "the vanity of human nature and the transitoriness of fashion," and dissolved into a spasm of nostalgia when he saw the ancient haircloth chairs and sofas in the parlor, the hymnbooks, the familiar melodeon, and the "Bible Society edition of the Scriptures."

By the mid-1880s Charles L. Beach had turned over all but one of his shares in the Catskill Mountain House Company to his sons. But he still maintained a firm grip on policy for the hotel. He advertised rarely and then only in a spare and formal manner. This restraint made it possible for him to pick and choose among applicants for rooms and board and weed out those whom he regarded as undesirable and who were forming an ever-increasing percentage of visitors to the Catskills. The observance of the English Sunday, the emphasis on distant views—in spite of the remarks of young upstarts like Mr. Wilde—the admiration of falling water, these were among the bonds which held Beach guests together in a snobbish little society of their own as the world around them turned its attention to quite different matters. New guests came on the recommendation of old ones—thus maintaining the continuity of life at the old Mountain House.

Earlier visitors had felt at once the temple character of the house on the Pine Orchard. Now more and more of their successors detected the museum quality of the place. Charles Dudley Warner was among them. He tells of old Mr. Beach—probably seated, as was his custom, on his clifftop —denouncing the vandal excursionists who marred his exhibit with their initials or picked the fragrant pink trumpets of the native azaleas which bloomed in June at the edge of the surrounding forest of spruce, balsam fir, and oaks all dwarfed and picturesquely gnarled by exposure to wind and frost. Mr. Beach clung to the kind of landscaping favored by John Bartram's British subscribers. Other hotels in the Catskills were vying in the quantities of bedding out plants which they consumed each year. Star-shaped, lyre-shaped beds, crescent beds surrounded the hotels of Mr. Beach's rivals, each stuffed to bursting with plants grown in lowland greenhouses and set out in their maturity each June. Hotel names spelled out in gray-green leaves against a background of dusty red and hotel monograms placed on a sloping bank delighted the public. Charles L. Beach maintained only an austere strip of grass to mediate between the forest and his shining house, and it was no smooth suburban lawn but one with the rich texture of an upland pasture.

Sensitive excursionists lowered their voices and walked on tiptoes after they read the placards prominently displayed by Mr. Beach: "The owner cheerfully submits to all necessary use of the premises but will not permit any unnecessary use, or the exercise of a depraved use or vandalism. . . ."[5] Vulgar excursionists took pleasure in disobeying the signs when they could, much as they ignored the "Please do not touch" warnings in the museums of their time.

Vandal excursionists and undesirables were not the largest threat to the Catskill Mountain House during the 1880s. Harsh economic necessities were working against the Beach domain; even the magic of white paint and scrubbing brushes could not hide the fact that the Beaches were losing money. They had been forced to go into the railroad business, and now their railroad was threatening to destroy them.

When the Catskill Mountain Railroad was organized in 1880, the Beaches became its largest investors. Charles L. Beach became the line's president, his nephew, Charles A., began grooming himself for the post of the road's general superintendent. The Beaches hoped that the Catskill Mountain Railroad, in co-operation with the horse-drawn stagecoaches which climbed the mountain from the railroad stations, would ensure their control of the transportation of summer travelers from the steamboats and railroads of the Hudson Valley to the top of the mountain wall and deep into the great plateau that lay beyond. But this was not a realistic hope—only an all-rail line linking the river and the mountaintop might do. And even this was no sure thing because the country traversed by such a road was unlikely to provide the kind of substantial freight shipments needed to keep a railroad in good health. And old Mr. Beach, true romantic that he was, stubbornly opposed scarring his mountainside with a railroad. He had made his concessions to the times—he would go no further.

The first train of the Catskill Mountain Railroad reached the base of the mountain in 1882, just in time to suffer from the dull years that were approaching. In 1885 a group of investors forced the line into court, foreclosure of mortgages, and reorganization. For some time, Alfred Van Santvoord, powerful head of the Hudson River Day Line, had been acquiring stock in the Catskill Mountain Railroad. Now he became its president. Charles L. Beach stepped backward into the post of vice-president. That same year the Catskill Mountain House was mortgaged to the Tanner's Bank for $55,000—the mortgage protected a series of loans made to the hotel company over a period of years.

On December 29, 1885, the new board of directors voted on an important matter. Should they co-operate with a newly formed company which had as its purpose sending a cable railroad straight up the Catskills' great wall from near their Mountain House station to the Pine Orchard itself? Alfred Van Santvoord was involved in the proposed Otis Elevating Railroad, which would form a superb attraction for passengers on his steamers. The directors voted to yield. Charles L. Beach voted with them.[6] He could no longer afford to protect his mountain against hacking and scarring by railroad builders which he had opposed for so long.

The first plans of the Otis called for a kind of railroad already in use in Switzerland. It would have two cars operating, somewhat like those of many indoor elevators, at the two ends of a cable—as one car rose the other would descend. The descending car needed to be heavier than the rising one unless steam or electric power were used. The Swiss railroad had a supply of water available close to the top of its line, and water was pumped into a compartment of the descending car. When the water-weighted car reached the base station, the water was dumped. At the same time, the car above invoked the force of gravity by filling its own water compartment.

W. H. Ritter, who was the master planner of the proposed railroad, had visited the Catskill Mountain House every summer for twenty-four years. He was very familiar with the natural attractions of the place and knew that North and South lakes played a vital part in giving the Beach domain its romantic charm. But Mr. Ritter knew something else. He knew that two lakes set high on a mountain and close to an almost sheer drop of about a thousand feet were a potential source of power. They could easily be made to serve the purposes of the age of the machine by filling the water compartments of the proposed railway. No longer need the twin lakes slumber in romantic idleness; the ingenuity of an inventive age had made it possible for them to be harnessed and set to do work that might pay profits in cash to investors.

The original plan of the Otis Elevating Railroad was never carried out. For six years a set of the plans dozed in the office of the Greene County Clerk. And while the plans dozed, the Catskill Mountain House experienced a brief flare-up of its former glory. The year 1889 brought a modest revival of prosperity to the Catskill Mountains' summer-boarding industry and the old Mountain House had its best season in several years. A distinguished visitor that year was popular poet Will Carleton, best known today for his *Over the Hill to the Poorhouse*. On August 7 a far more distinguished guest arrived—Civil War hero General William Tecumseh Sherman.[7]

Sherman's visit was given intensive publicity by the Mountain House management and many admirers crowded into the hotel. Sherman went on to Stamford, where he surprised the public by bypassing the pretentious Churchill Hall and putting up at the lesser-known Bancroft House. The fact was that the general was a modest man who disliked the atmosphere of large and elegant hotels; he preferred smaller and quieter places to the kind run by George Harding and Dr. Churchill. Moreover, he was not at all well and this increased his desire for quiet.

Old-timers of today still tell anecdotes of Sherman's stay at the venerable Mountain House, of his kindness to children and autograph hunters, and of his lack of pretension. But they have nothing to say of another event of the same summer, one of far greater significance. On May 7, 1889, the New York *Times* took notice of a rumor that had appeared in many other New York newspapers and that dealt with what the *Times* called "the anti-Hebrew crusade" recently launched in the Catskills. Some said that most of the hotel and boardinghouse keepers of the Catskills had joined in "a combine" to exclude Jews. The *Times* reported that the story was greatly exaggerated—only the boardinghouse and hotel owners of Pine Hill were joining in a pledge to refuse rooms to Jews. New York Jews were aroused, said the *Times,* were circulating petitions of protest, and had gained the support of prominent Christian clergymen.

In Pine Hill that year, people speculated as to whether the anti-Hebrew crusade would succeed, and there was a good deal of difference of opinion. And some, as might be expected, tried to devise means of turning the agitation to account. On May 15 a traveling tuner of boardinghouse pianos advertised in the Pine Hill *Sentinel* in these words: "Jews or Gentiles? No matter which, they will appreciate it more than a little to find that instrument in order when they arrive. James Warswick, the piano tuner from New York, who tuned with such remarkable success in the place last season, will be in Pine Hill next week."

The rumor was indeed exaggerated, yet the anti-Hebrew crusade was real enough. Boardinghouse men in all parts of the Catskills were printing the phrase "No Hebrews need apply" on their advertising circulars, and similar statements were appearing on placards hung on mountain porches. The Cornells added a "Special Notice" to their Grand Hotel circular that year. It began: "In order to exclude the mixed and undesirable element, who are at times found in summer hotels, it is our intention to be very strict in making engagements. Each applicant will be required if not personally known to give references. . . ." Charles L. Beach was already using a similar method of excluding those he didn't want from his hotel.

In 1888 it was being said that half the summer travelers over the Ulster & Delaware were Jewish.[8] Many were recent immigrants who had fled from persecution in Russia and in many parts of eastern Europe. They had found refuge in the already crowded slums of New York where many lived very much as they had in ghettos across the Atlantic. It did not take these people long to learn about the summer advantages of the Catskills, but when they asked for rooms and board in mountain resorts they found that this land of freedom was not quite as free as they had been led to think.

Catskill Mountain people usually belonged to the more rigid Protestant sects such as Methodists or Old School Baptists, whose churches stood at every crossroad. The more liberal denominations, such as the Episcopalian and Reformed Dutch, had fewer adherents. Methodist preachers had long denounced the keeping of summer boarders as a snare of the devil. Some of them said that many men and women who were good Christians at home came to the Catskills for "an ethical vacation"[9] during which they desecrated the Sabbath, played cards, drank liquor, committed adultery, and contaminated local young people. Methodist district meetings of the 1880s often took up the question of the evils of summer boardinghouse keeping and issued indictments of the practice. Even before the arrival of the Jews, many a mountain boardinghouse keeper wondered if he were not doomed to pay with an eternity of the torments of hell for the briefly enjoyed profits extracted from his sinful boarders. His sense of guilt deepened as Jews arrived in larger and larger and more and more confident groups. The Catskill Mountain House had set an example for lesser establishments in its combination of strict Protestant Sunday observance with a religious "appreciation of fine scenery." The newcomers could hardly be expected to join in the Sunday observance; the admiration of distant views and falling water formed part of the culture of few Jewish boarders when they first came to the Catskills, and in addition, anti-Semitism was growing to monstrous proportions throughout the Western world. Other groups with differing ways—Roman Catholics of Irish origins and Christian Germans— had established strong beachheads in the mountains and had been able to set up resort centers of their own, while a boardinghouse restricted to black Americans was said to have maintained itself for a while at Hunter-field.[10] But attempts to establish boardinghouses or hotels at which Jewish ways and religious observances would rule met with strong local opposi-tion. By 1889 at least one such boardinghouse had managed to make a be-ginning and to survive: that of Simon Epstein at Saxton midway between Kiskatom and Jeremiah Snyder's former farm. And it was at Epstein's that the anti-Hebrew crusade of 1889 found expression in an outburst of violence.

The Kingston *Daily Freeman* was first to tell the story. Pine Hill people could read a reprinting of it in their *Sentinel* of August 7. "Ruffians Raid a Boarding House," the story was headlined. It went on to report that "on Saturday night men calling themselves 'Yellowstone Cowboys' . . . armed with bowie knives, revolvers and horse pistols, entered the boarding-house of one Epstein, a Hebrew at Saxton, where there are 60 boarders. The men brandished their weapons and demanded supper. The boarders fled. After about an hour's possession of the house the gang left. . . ."

The following morning five men returned. One was armed not only with a small revolver but also with brass knuckles; another carried "a dirk knife which opened by touching a spring." The local police had been alerted the previous evening and were watching the boardinghouse. The men were arrested, quickly tried, and sentenced to fines and terms in the

Albany penitentiary. There was no further violence in the anti-Hebrew crusade.

As the summer of 1889 approached its end, many hotel and boarding-house keepers found that they were losing money by excluding Jews and subsequently admitted all humans who could pay their bills; others continued to refuse rooms to Jews. Yet a divide had been passed that summer: it had been demonstrated that an open anti-Hebrew crusade would not work. In 1893 Simon Epstein moved up the Catskills to Hunter where he operated the Grandview House, the forerunner of many Jewish hotels and boardinghouse resorts in the Hunter-Tannersville vicinity.[11] He was prominent among those leading the establishment in the Catskills of a summer culture very different from that embodied by the old Catskill Mountain House, which Charles L. Beach was struggling to maintain. Before long the popular image of the Catskills would owe much to the persistent, never discouraged efforts of men like Epstein. But as the 1880s came to their end, the older summer Catskills were showing amazing vitality, and nothing demonstrated that vitality more clearly than the prevalence in the mountains of legend pirates.

70

Legend Pirates

❧ LEGEND PIRACY is an old trade. The value of legends in giving people pride in themselves and their culture and in persuading neighbors to have a good opinion of them has made conscious and unconscious piracy of legends flourish in all the many varieties of human society. The fact that legends had a cash value to resort operators of the nineteenth century helped put their piracy on a more calculated and businesslike basis. By the 1870s, Irving's tale of Rip Van Winkle had become accepted as the most effective of all the "legends of the Catskills," so the capture of Rip became the objective of many a piratical foray.

Washington Irving had been vague in giving a definite location to Rip Van Winkle's home town and the scene of his mountain adventure. This helped keep alive the theory that Rip had actually slept not in the Catskills' Sleepy Hollow but at the foot of the Kaaterskill Falls. When actor Joseph Jefferson, with the help of Irish-born playwright Dion Boucicault, turned out his very successful dramatic version of the tale of Rip, he gave the impression that Rip had lived in Palenville and had slept somewhere up the Kaaterskill Clove on a slope of South Mountain and not in the Beach's Sleepy Hollow below the Pine Orchard. George Harding made the most of all this. He reprinted the tale of Rip in his hotel publication *The Kaaterskill* in so confident a manner that innocent guests assumed that Rip was an old retainer of Harding's establishment. In 1884 the New York, Buffalo and West Shore Railroad, in a promotional book for their "summer excursions," presented both the Beach and the Harding claims and sensibly allowed their readers to make their choice. At the same time a third true site of Rip's sleep was discovered by Postmaster Joseph Smith of Big Indian—it was on his own land close to the base of Slide Mountain. When a Rip Van Winkle Hotel corporation offered to buy the land, Smith refused on the curious plea that the place "was too sacred to be profaned by summer boarders."[1] The picturesque Queen Anne-style Rip Van Winkle Hotel was built anyway, but in Pine Hill. In later years the Smith discovery stimulated members of the Van Winkle family of Stone Ridge near the lowland Esopus to claim Rip as an ancestor and Smith's land as the site of his sleep. During the 1930s fruitgrower Howard Van Winkle of Stone Ridge aroused wide interest when he repeated the claim—with some pretty embellishments—on a national radio program.[2]

In 1884 the backers of the Overlook Mountain House Company rejoiced at a daring act of legend piracy. That year Mrs. A. E. P. Searing, wife of the secretary of the company, presented in a very handsome format a work titled *The Land of Rip Van Winkle.* Here for the first time the mantle of Rip was sufficiently enlarged to cover most of the parts of the Catskills included in Professor Guyot's mountain region. Mrs. Searing pieced together bits of old legends in order to form new ones better adapted to the current shape of the romantic Catskills and the needs of its hotels. She gave Kaaterskill Clove a legend that combined the story of Captain Kidd with a very popular one long current in Old Catskill some eight miles to the north of the clove. William Salisbury, a member of a rich local family, had actually been charged in 1762 with the murder of a servant girl named Anna Dorothea Swarts. By way of punishment for some real or fancied fault, Salisbury tied the girl to the tail of his horse with a cord, and then in the words of the old parchment presentment in the library of the Greene County Historical Society, "did beat and force and compel the said Horse So Swiftly to Run that the Horse aforesaid the aforesaid Anna Dorothea Swarts upon her Body did Strike of which the said Anna Dorothea Swarts then and there Instantly died. . . ." The grand jury did not find a true bill in Rex *vs.* Salisbury and the man went free. But by the time the Catskill Mountain House was entertaining its first guests, Colonel William Stone could report an ending to the case far better suited to the romantic air of the Catskills. Salisbury had been tried, Stone said, and was sentenced to be hanged—but not until he reached the age of ninety-nine. Until then he was to wear a halter by day and night. And when Salisbury died as a very old man, a silken halter was indeed found round his neck, though a modern folklore scholar suggested that the halter was a folk device for warding off rheumatism.[3] In Mrs. Searing's version the tragedy took place in the Kaaterskill Clove; the girl was a Spanish beauty and Captain Kidd's bride; the murderer was a villain named Ballridge who found and abducted Mrs. Kidd as he searched the Clove for the captain's buried treasure. Never have visitors to the Catskills been treated to a richer or less digestible concoction of popular romantic ingredients.

When Mrs. Searing dealt with Overlook Mountain she did her duty to her husband's company by giving Echo Lake an ancient Indian legend of her own manufacture. It involved an Iroquois brave, an Indian maiden, and vampires. The lake needed such a legend for it had become an important asset to the Overlook Mountain House Company and its "Overlook Park" advertised that it comprised three thousand acres. Guides rowed guests out on the lake and blew horns in order "to obtain the echo"; a "refreshment saloon" was in business on the shore.

No direct try at pirating the tale of Rip Van Winkle and setting him down on the side of Overlook appeared in *The Land Of Rip Van Winkle*. But the book contains the statement that it was on Overlook that the spirits of Henry Hudson and his men were believed by "early Dutch settlers to have kept vigil over his loved river." These spirits had been referred to by Irving in a way that linked them closely to the scene of Rip's great adventure—any Overlook guest could follow Mrs. Searing's hint to a very pleasing conclusion. When Mrs. Searing reprinted the Catskill Mountain episode from Cooper's *The Pioneers*, she prefaced it with the flat statement that it was on the cliff near the Overlook Mountain House that Natty Bumppo had stood when he looked out over "all creation." No bolder act of legend piracy graced the 1880s. And it was moderately successful, for many people to this day regard the summit of Overlook Mountain as the favorite haunt of Natty Bumppo and the stage of his great Catskill Mountain scene.[4]

The Indian associations, true and fictional, of the Catskill Mountain House inspired promoters of other hotels and resort centers to honest imitation, so that a thriving legend-manufacturing and -improving, industry arose. As Dr. S. E. Churchill applied his skill and energy to converting Stamford to a major summer resort, the town's legend producers worked up the very popular *Legend of Utsayantha* into usable form. The legend had its birth in 1872 when the *Yale Literary Magazine* printed a well-made poem by student Eugene A. Bouton, a native of the Stamford area. Bouton's Utsayantha was an Indian girl who loved a white man and bore him a child which her angry father drowned. The girl then committed suicide by plunging into Lake Utsayantha. The formula was an attractive one to nineteenth-century readers of popular fiction and verse. More recently Elder Arnold H. Bellows of the Old School Baptist Church gave it wide circulation in his Hiawatha-like *The Legend of Utsayantha*.

During the early 1880s the grave of "Princess Utsayantha" was discovered in a convenient spot high on Mount Utsayantha which rises above Stamford. A stone was placed on the grave and flowers were soon decorating it. On the mountaintop an observation tower erected by private enterprise formed a decided tourist attraction—it was staffed by genuine imported Indians who made and sold beadwork and objects of leather and wood. The spirits of Utsayantha, her lover, and her cruel father revealed themselves at a seance in the city of Rochester. The white lover appeared in a dream to a guest at a Stamford hotel and pointed out the location of a treasure beside Lake Utsayantha; however, the treasure could not be found. In 1884 Professor E. C. Phelps of Brooklyn composed a musical tribute called "An American Legend," which was performed in New York under the direction of Theodore Thomas. Thomas Peaslee, a well-known singing teacher of local birth, wrote an operetta "from the spiritualist angle." A Southerner named McDevitt built a fine summer hotel on a spur of Mount Utsayantha. It burned down before it could open but not before local wits could name it the McMountain House. The legend, the tower, and the grave of Princess Utsayantha were taken under the protection of the Stamford town fathers and her story thrived for several decades in an official form.[5]

Proprietors of summer hotels and boardinghouses outside of Stamford watched with envy the Princess' rise to a fame which threatened for a while to eclipse even that of Rip Van Winkle. And rival Indian "legends" resembling that of Utsayantha took form elsewhere. In Roxbury, the painted figure of a man with his gun and dog amused summer visitors from a cliff high over the town of Roxbury—it is believed today to commemorate the attempt of a farmer to escape the invasion of potato bugs by planting his potatoes in the field just beneath the cliff and so, he hoped, above the beetles' normal range. As the farmer planted, his son painted the figure on the cliff. It is quite possible that the figure represents a forgotten attempt at legend piracy, for the White Man could well be meant to be Rip Van Winkle. In the early 1890s a Roxbury booster insisted that the White Man was an unprincipled usurper who had taken over the space upon which "Princess Devasego" had once painted a memorial to her lover. The lover (an Indian this time) had been shot by white men, and the Princess had painted his portrait on the cliff in his own blood. The tale did not catch on and the White Man still stands above Roxbury while the descendants of the potato bugs which may or may not have inspired his creation in the late 1870s are still hard at work in Roxbury fields, however high on the town's mountainsides. Princess Devasego is forgotten.[6]

From the earliest years of the Ulster & Delaware Railroad, the country along its route had been ransacked for scraps of Indian associations which might be worked up into bait for summer visitors. Every American summer resort of any consequence had its stock of such attractions, and the more sentimental, the greater their pulling power. The Big Indian Valley which joins that of the Esopus about thirty miles from the Hudson, had an Indian association which was genuine beyond question. The valley had once been part of Edward Livingston's share of the Catskill Mountains. William Cockburn referred in surveys made as early as 1786 to "the flatt at the Big Indian, below Misner's improvement."[7] There Gerret Constable of Hurley proposed settling. On August 28, 1862, the *Recorder and Democrat* of Catskill printed one of the oldest known versions of the legend of the Big Indian. It was told by the Reverend J. R. Hoag of Windham upon his return from fishing for trout "above Wey's tannery" near where the "Big Indian Creek" joined the Esopus. Mr. Hoag wrote of "a monster of a red man who prowled the neighboring mountains" in Revolutionary days and now and then swooped down on the settlements to kill and burn "the inoffensive inhabitants." When the Big Indian killed "a beautiful little girl," an "old settler grasped his death-weapon and notified his family that he would never return until himself or Big Indian was slain." He shot the Indian as he sat beside his campfire and buried him "in a pine bower" at the spot known ever since as Big Indian. The legend had some obvious elements of fact and it well reflected the fears and hatreds of Revolutionary days. But was it the kind of thing to set city people packing their carpetbags and heading for the Catskills? The passenger agent of the Ulster & Delaware thought not. It was he, they say, who stimulated the development of an improved version of the legend.[8] In this railroad version, the Big Indian is loved by the wife of a white man, and carries her off to his valley. There the husband finds the couple and shoots the Indian, who crawls into a great hollow pine tree to die. The improved version has been subjected to further embroidery and is among those still current in our own day.

In one respect the hotel and boardinghouse keepers of the Up-and-Down part of the Catskills had a positive advantage when it came to genuine romantic legends. Their country had been the scene of stirring incidents in the Anti-rent War—the Pine Orchard had not. Many a proprietor of a small boardinghouse could tell guests of his father's adventures in the war, of how he had hidden out in a cave still to be seen above the pasture while the sheriff's men scoured the valley for him. He might even startle young ladies by capering into his parlor wearing an Anti-rent War mask brought down from the attic. In Pine Hill's liveliest resort days, legends of the Anti-rent War especially delighted summer people. In the August 23, 1902, issue of the Pine Hill *Sentinel,* summer resident Herbert

N. Casson, a professional writer, expressed feelings which had been intensifying ever since the infant days of the Up-and-Down when he said: "Nothing more romantic ever occurred in the Scotch Highlands or the Swiss Alps than the struggle made by the first settlers against the land monopolists who claimed to be owners of the land. Many a regiment of deputy sheriffs was driven back to New York by the heroic men who claimed their farms by right of settlement and cultivation, and not because an English king had signed his name to a parchment. . . . How like the circling red cross of the Scottish Highlands, the watch fire flashing from peak to peak and flaming on Belle Ayre, Rose Mountain and the Summit [the site of the Grand Hotel]. How the long-blown horns echoing down the valleys called the farmers to arms!" Casson expressed the hope that an American Sir Walter Scott would appear, "to make vivid with his imagination" the stirring events of the Anti-rent War. In Woodstock, boarders were shown a roadside stone called "the Tory stone." Every year men and boys treated the stone to a coat of tar and feathers to keep alive the memory of the old hostility of local people toward the Up-renters or Tories as some called them.[9]

Summer boarders who showed fascination with the Catskills' lore and legends were treated to tales of treasure buried naturally or artificially and they were sometimes encouraged to try their luck with pick and shovel at spots where "lost mines" were rumored to have once been discovered and unaccountably lost again. George Mead could relate a fine treasure tale to guests at his Mountain Home in Woodstock's Wide Clove. In 1874 a party of serious treasure hunters had made his boardinghouse their base. They were following up "an old Indian legend that there is a gold mine in the Catskills."[10] The major part of the party's equipment consisted of "a boy medium, who has an enchanted stone, which he looks through to discover hidden treasure." The medium claimed to have seen gold near Mead's. His employers dug as the boy gazed through his stone and directed the work. But somehow gold was never found. The men paid their bill at Mead's and left still talking hopefully of organizing a stock company to work the mine they couldn't find.

Tales of treasure hidden during the Revolutionary War abounded everywhere among the mountains and delighted thousands of summer people. Near Yankeetown in Woodstock, boarders were shown a curious pyramid of stones laid up with surprising regularity—local farmers said that their fathers and grandfathers had said that the pyramid held the clue to the location of a Revolutionary treasure. During the 1930s a silver spoon and a silver snuffbox engraved with a Masonic emblem were dug up on a

Woodstock farm where a "box of silver and a pitcher of gold"[11] had long been rumored to have been hidden, which suggests that there was at least a little substance to the old tales of buried treasures in the Catskills.

Even more attractive to summer people than listening to lore and legends was meeting mountain people who embodied the romantic spirit of the Catskills. Of these the bear hunters continued to be the most highly valued. No summer boardinghouse or hotel was properly in business without a few caged bears and its resident or neighboring bear hunter who carried on traditions already old when Merchant Lawrence's inn was a center of the Catskills' bear cult. A few bear hunters capitalized on their attractiveness by setting up as boardinghouse keepers on their own—a famous one was Barney Butts of Windham. Albert Post was often called the champion bear hunter of Greene County: by 1894 he had done in fifty-nine bears. Charles Eckert of West Shokan had done even better—he was telling summer visitors that he had killed one bear for each of his sixty-four years. In Lake Hill three generations of Howlands were mighty bear men and tellers of bear tales.[12] Traver Hollow had its Enos Brown— he and his wife, also a hunter of note, had come to the Hollow to cook and otherwise keep house for a troop of barkpeelers. They remained to become summer boarder attractions. But the Browns and other bear hunters had much effective competition for boarders' attention. For the Catskills were remarkably rich in hermits and other eccentrics who made an irresistible appeal to vacationers. Rich Americans had never taken to keeping salaried hermits to ornament their estates as had some of John Bartram's patrons, but American hermits did reasonably well by going into business on their own.

From the earliest days of settlement, the Catskills had been a nursery for offbeat humans who took refuge from the world in cabins in lonely hollows or in rock shelters abandoned by the Indian hunters. The old squatting tradition lived on, while the persistence of large forests made it possible for people tucked away on someone else's land to make a sort of living shaving hoop poles, gathering ginseng and other healing plants, carving scoops, hunting, trapping, and sometimes entertaining summer people by a display of eccentricities. Some of these people took over abandoned lumbermen's or barkpeelers' cabins and here and there formed little backwoods communities of their own. Such groups were found in Sullivan County and summer boarders were warned to leave them alone because their ways were strange indeed. They were said to be in the habit of swapping wives, and one man was reported to have given a dozen wooden scoops of his own making as boot in such a trade.

The admiration of people who lived close to nature that Peter DeLabigarre had shown in 1793 was common among summer people and they liked nothing better than to come upon a genuine hermit or, better still, a whole family of hermits. In April 1878, such a family turned up in Shandaken and drew comment from even the sedate Kingston *Daily Freeman*. The family had "scarcely any more shelter than afforded by the forest trees, the *Freeman* said. "They never labor or purchase food of any kind, subsisting wholly upon acorns, nuts, herbs, fish and animals which abound in that locality and what they can procure by foraging. They have repeatedly refused offers of assistance, and express the desire to continue living their wild life."

Every hamlet among the Catskills had its own share of romantic eccentrics. The Slide Mountain hermit, whose name was Heroy, was said to have buried a horde of cash near his shack, and when the old fellow wasn't looking, boarders dug for the money. A female hermit named Lucy Slater Lobdell once lived in a cave along Basket Brook. Lucy, a dead shot with her hunting rifle, shared her cave with another lady to whom she was married.[13] The Reverend James Beecher, half-brother of Henry Ward Beecher, was known as the Hermit of Beecher's Lake. He lived in semi-seclusion with his wife and an adopted daughter. Religious eccentrics added their own sort of charm to the Catskills. Ira Krom of Big Indian was one of them. Ira had been told by the Lord in a vision that if he fasted for forty days he would be able to walk on water and perform miracles. At the end of his fast Ira tried in vain to walk on the surface of a Big Indian brook. Again he had a vision and this time the Lord advised an additional fast of fifteen days. But before the fifteen days were over, Ira was dead.[14] In Sullivan County a man named Decker announced that he was God Almighty. But when he proceeded to act accordingly, Decker was "sent away." No work of fiction dealing with the Catskills during the height of its summer-boarding period could hope for success without at least one hermit. George W. Owen's *The Leech Club or the Mysteries of the Catskills* of 1874 dealt with political corruption of the Boss Tweed era, and its hermit was an Indian returned to the mountain home of his ancestors. DeWitt Clinton Overbaugh's *The Hermit of the Catskills* of 1900 in which the Hardenberghs of Revolutionary days were among the chief characters, made much of a luxuriously furnished cave on High Point or Shokan Mountain, which included a Masonic temple visited by George Washington.

One of the most popular non-fictional "hermits of the Catskills" was Boots Van Steenbergh. His contribution to the pleasure of summer people was his own kind of satire. He tramped from boardinghouse to boarding-house and sang parodies of operatic airs in his powerful voice, making what sounded—unless you listened carefully—like political speeches. Boots declaimed poetry in which familiar phrases added up to nonsense, "One cent, two cents, shinplasters up to the stars/Rise my soul shake off thy fear/ The Saratoga Springs they stand,/the seashore of this barren land . . ." so one of Boots's poems is still remembered to have begun. When Oscar Wilde came to the Catskills, Boots hoisted his many-colored "aesthetic umbrella" and toured the mountains in Wilde's wake, giving a parody of Wilde's talks to audiences of boarders. He liked to rattle off popular slogans—with variations. When he declaimed John A. Dix's famous, "If any man tears down the American flag, shoot him on the spot," Boots made it come out: "If any man shoots, tear down the American flag on the spot." When Boots was young, like many other eccentrics he liked to wear vast numbers of buttons; in later life he fashioned bits of rags and hand-me-down clothing into hilarious parodies of military uniforms. The house he built for himself at Flatbush near Saugerties anticipated a recent phase of art. Abstract sculptures made of odds and ends of boards rose from the roof. Inscriptions in what seemed like a dead language and in a variety of colors were lettered wherever there was space. Wires coiled round and round the building. Pennants made of strips of newspapers rustled and fluttered. Boots had a favorite phrase by which he explained himself to the summer people. He would place his hand on his belly and say, "Inside I make sense, outside I make nonsense." Many a boarder thought-fully pondered that phrase and wondered if bearded, wild-eyed old Boots hadn't managed to catch a glimpse of a layer of reality hidden from the eyes of those who passed as sane.[15]

The taste for hermits and other eccentrics could not help but stimulate the supply. Many a mountain man cultivated his pecularities of speech and behavior and set up as a goal for pilgrimages by summer people. Rowland Bell who lived close to High Point was a fine example. "Rowl" and his wife Becky lived in a log cabin of their own making. Barefooted Rowl was a master of old-fashioned fiddling. He played "Money Musk" and "The Devil's Dream" while his wife kept him company on castanets. When boarders demanded an encore, Rowl would explain that he suffered from a kind of rheumatism of his fingers that made further playing im-possible. There was only one cure for his ailment, Rowl would explain, and that was money. At this Rowl would pass his battered old hat and the boarders, smiling at the old fellow's shrewdness, would send coins jingling into the hat. Then Rowl would perform the music with which he fiddled the rattlesnakes out of their den on a nearby mountain each spring. As the snakes woke from their winter sleep to Rowl's fiddling, they would wriggle out into the sunshine only to be shot with the very Colt revolver Rowl would hold up for the boarders' admiration. Rowl "tried out" the snakes and used the oil he obtained in treating the aches and pains of his neighbors. But if a neighbor came down with "fever and aguer," Rowl would cut a lock of his patient's hair and—while reciting appropriate charms—insert the hair in a hole in an ancient chestnut tree that stood down the road. The patient would be cured at once and the tree would shiver and shake as the ailment was communicated to it.[16]

Boarders often questioned mountain eccentrics about the meanings and origins of the Catskills' place names and the eccentrics were happy to oblige with explanations which made up for whatever they might lack in accuracy with picturesqueness and romantic appeal. In this way the confusion of place names in the Catskills was abetted. And the confusion is deep indeed.

Place-Name Puzzles

✣   FROM THE TIME the first Europeans sailed up the river later called the Hudson, the question of what to name the Catskills began causing confusion. In 1609, Henry Hudson's mate Robert Juet referred to the mountains as "other mountains which lie from the river's side." In this way Juet distinguished the Catskills from the Highlands of the Hudson which rose steeply from the riverbanks. In 1655, the Visscher map of New Netherland showed what was to become the state of New York in the greatest detail attempted up to that time, and it designated what are plainly meant for the Catskills, which were called "Hooge Landt van Esopus,"[1] the Highlands of Esopus. To the north of the Hooge Landt lies what seems to be a valley called the "Landt van Kats Kill." Above this, more mountains are sketched in but are not given a name. They are evidently meant for the northern Catskills which were apparently confused with the Helderbergs. The Visscher map has decided value in helping clear up the mystery of how the Catskills got their name, for it illustrates one stage in a process by which many American river names came to be given to other geographic features—including mountains. To early explorers the rivers they traveled were of the very first importance and so were often given names while other landscape features continued nameless. Later the river names emerged from the water and made themselves at home on the land. The Allegheny River lent its name to the Allegheny Mountains; the Mississippi River eventually gave a name to a state.

The word "Esopus" is a Europeanized form of an Algonkian word for a brook or small stream. Dutch settlers applied it to the stream that rises in the Catskills and enters the Hudson at what became Saugerties.[2] The settlers transferred the name to the Indians who lived on its banks and then to the land along the river. On the Visscher map the name is shown trying to take possession of the stream's mountain birthplace. On the same map another stream appears to the north—this was the Catskill. The name "Catskill" was in common use by the 1640s by Fort Orange and Rensselaerwyck people who took an interest in the promising flatlands lying about ten miles from the junction with the Hudson of the placid stream already known to the Dutch as the Catskill.[3] It did not take long for the Indians who lived on the stream's banks to become known as the Catskill Indians or for the rich flatlands of what is known today as Leeds to be called Catskill.

In 1659 a phrase in a letter written by the directors of the Dutch West India Company to Governor Peter Stuyvesant suggested that the "mountains which lie from the river" were not going to become known as the Esopus Highlands but as the Catskill Mountains. That happened when the directors placed the site of the hopes for mineral wealth of Gerrit Jansen Kuyper and Abel de Wolf as "near the Esopus Kil in and about the high Catskil Mountains." In 1686 the tributary of the Hudson which rises near what is now known as Haines Falls, and at the outlet of South Lake, made its first official appearance as the "Kaaterskill."[4] By then the days of Dutch rule were over. New Netherlands had become New York; Fort Orange was Albany; the North or Mauritius River bore the name of its British explorer, Henry Hudson; the South River of Dutch times honored British Lord Delaware.

By the time the Hardenbergh Patent was granted in 1708, Dutch place names were still in common use throughout the province but some were having a hard time. The Catskills were being called, especially by British officials, the "Blue Mountains,"[5] the Kaaterskill was Cartwright's Kill—here a British family name was yoked with the Dutch "kill" which had long before broadened its original meaning of an inlet or channel of the sea and included streams of almost all sorts except the largest.

Catskill Mountains or Blue Mountains—which would it be? Land records appeared to lean toward the Blue Mountains or Hills but cautious people liked to use both names in order to avoid any possibility of error. When Henry Beekman and Gilbert Livingston petitioned for a grant of land at the base of the mountains in 1719, they described the land they wanted as "lying under ye Blew hills, commonly called the Katts Kill hills." William Cockburn wrote of "the Great Mountains, commonly called the Blue Hills." Variations of the two phrases were common in the records of the eighteenth century. John Bartram remained faithful to the "Katskill Mountains," but Peter Kalm, the eminent Swedish botanist who visited him in 1750, always used the name of the "Blue Mountains." Livingstons who followed British ways liked to speak of the Blue Mountains. When Henry G.

Livingston of Tivoli advertised his country seat for sale in 1798, he praised the place as having "a beautiful view of the Blue Mountains."

Once Washington Irving's tales had added romance to the name Catskill Mountains and the Catskill Mountain House had spread the name even farther abroad, the Blue Mountains began fading away, but James Booth's attempt to name his venture in hotel building the Woodstock Blue Mountain House showed how long the British-favored name persisted. It lingers to this day only in the hamlet of Blue Mountain which includes what was once Jeremiah Snyder's farm. Late eighteenth-century church records call the neighborhood "Blauw Berg" or "Blauwbergen," an apparent translation into Dutch of what may have been originally an English name.

The name Blue Mountain inevitably led into perplexities, for there was a confusion of Blue Mountains in North America. The mountains "which the English call the Blue Mountains . . . extend in one continuous chain from north to south, or from Canada to Carolina,"[6] wrote Peter Kalm in his report on his conversations with John Bartram. What we know as the Appalachian system had been referred to as the Blue Mountains for more than a century before Kalm's visit. The origin of the name was simple enough. The mountains were densely covered with vegetation and so appeared green by summer, but this color seen through even a slightly hazy atmosphere became an intense blue. Where ranges of mountains broke through the rule of green and showed their bones, this was taken into account; the rocky summits of the White Mountains had suggested their name as early as 1623. The Shawangunks were sometimes called the "Crystal Mountains" in tribute to their gleaming conglomerate walls.

Shortly after 1800 dissatisfaction with the usual name of the Catskills was growing stronger. Ordinary people who spoke it every day were perfectly satisfied with the name—until Washington Irving spoke up, it was those with intellectual and literary pretensions who found fault with it. In his 1813 gazetteer of New York, Horatio Gates Spafford summed up a good deal of current feeling: the name "Catskill" positively infuriated him. Spafford did not understand the reasonableness of the process by which the name of a river is transferred to a nearby mountain. He believed that the "cat" in Catskill referred to the American wildcat—"wilde kat" in Dutch. And Spafford seems to have had no very high opinion of cats of any sort. He sputtered that the name "Catskill Mountains" is a "contemptible name when applied to a chain of mountains." He urged legislative action to clean up the disorderly litter of place names resulting from the occupation of the land by Indian, Dutch, German, and British settlers. "It is a common feature of Dutch and German population in this country to multiply the distinctions of places by local names; and a Township of 10 miles square, inhabited by those people, will probably have 10 times as many names to designate parts of its area, as it would if inhabited by English Americans,"[7] Spafford complained. He suggested as a good name for the Catskills the Catsbergs. His friend Samuel Jones, first comptroller of New York and a man learned in the law of real property as well as a bold explorer of ancient black letter law, spoke up in opposition. The name "Catsbergs" was a linguistic contradiction, he argued, for the first syllable was English, the second Dutch. Smith suggested instead "Kaatsbergs" which—in his opinion—was Dutch from beginning to end. The new name, in a great variety of spellings, came into wide use. Many believed that it had been the old Dutch name of the mountains. Novelist Charles Fenno Hoffman liked it, as did editor William Leete Stone. Henry Rowe Schoolcraft wrote of it with approval in 1844, although he preferred his own invention of "Ontiora."[8] Before the end of the nineteenth century a large hotel called "The Katzberg" was doing business in Hunter, and the name was being used in guidebooks. But ordinary citizens persisted in speaking and writing "The Catskills." The "Katzbergs" died away during the early years of the twentieth century, and were forgotten.

When Emily Harding chose the name "Kaaterskill" for George Harding's new hotel, she opened the way to a standardizing of its spelling and pronunciation—it is most often pronounced as if spelled "Cotterskill." Before Emily made her choice the name had been the subject of countless variations and arguments. In old official documents and land records it was the Caderskill, the Katerskill, the Caterix Kill, the Kauterskill, the Katterskill, and a dozen others. First of all men to set down in print a theory of the name's meaning was Horatio Spafford. Spafford stated—and here at least he was on firm ground—that the Dutch word for a domestic she cat was "kat," that for a tomcat was "kater." Thus, Spafford said, "Kaaterskill" meant "Tom-cat's-creek," "Catskill" meant "she-cat's-creek" and "Catskill Mountains" to Spafford's undisguised horror, meant "she-cat's-creek-mountains."[9] Spafford's etymologies were generally accepted. Washington Irving himself did not question them, especially because they were believed to be backed up by the kind of local traditions Irving loved and that were given authority by former New York Attorney General Egbert Benson in an address to the New York Historical Society in 1816.[10]

In spite of all the efforts of Spafford, Benson, and their successors, both the name "Catskills" and "Kaaterskill" have never been given convincing explanations. There is no evidence at all that the banks of the Catskill were ever infested by wildcats. Attempts to connect the name with totemic animals of the Indians met failure when it developed that the wildcat was not a local totemic animal, and the suggestion that Dutch explorers mistook the wolf, which was a local totem, for a cat is a bit lame. Wassenaer's *Historisch Verhael* of 1626–28 mentions a Mohican chief named Cat, but there is no evidence that Cat ever lived on the banks of the Catskill, although other Mohicans certainly did. In his book of American travels published in 1799, the Duc de la Rouchefoucauld Liancourt reported that he'd been told while visiting Catskill that the old name of the place was Katsketed and that this was an Indian word meaning fortification. Liancourt expressed doubt that this was a fact. Yet it might have had a germ of truth. Dutchmen called the Indians' stockades "kasteels," and such a stockade stood on the banks of the Catskill when early white settlers arrived. Albert Carnoy, a Belgian authority on the place names of his country, states that "Kat" is a common syllable in place names and that it usually has nothing to do with cats but with parts of fortifications such as glacis (outwardly sloping surfaces), or of small forts, dikes, or earthworks.[11] Place names involving "kat" which occur in Holland are likely to have had a similar origin.

No expert toponymologist (a student of place names) has ever used his talents to clear up the place-name problems of the Catskills. But amateurs have followed Spafford and Benson in large numbers and each has developed his favorite theory as to the origin of the name "Catskills." Some have assured us, but without any evidence, that the name was bestowed to honor Jacob Cats, poet, Keeper of the Great Seal of the Netherlands, and a shrewd speculator in lands reclaimed from the sea. No one has yet delved into the seaman's slang of the seventeenth century and found the beginnings of the mountains' name there—but that may not be far off. For "cat" or "kat" to old-time seamen of northern Europe could mean a kind of ship or a part of a ship's equipment. A ship named *The Cat* sailed up the Hudson just before the name "Catskill" first appeared. To an amateur place-name theorizer of any imagination at all, the fact that many riverside New Netherlands names were given by seamen might lead into yet untouched regions of speculation involving ships anchored at the mouth of the Catskill and the little island at that point which, on a misty morning, might be taken for the kind of ship known as a cat.

Still another region in which a speculating place-name buff might wander is that of the games the Hudson Valley Indians played. A favorite was a rough, fast game in which long-handled rackets and a ball of stuffed deerskin were used—the French of Canada named the game lacrosse. Early Dutch explorers found a level court upon which local Indians played the game in the present town of Saugerties at a place they called Katsbaan or Kaatsban. In Dutch and Flemish "kaats" means "tennis" or a number of other games played with racket and ball, while "baan" means a place or court. There is no evidence that the Indians who lived along the stream known as the Catskill had a tennis court of their own and that from this the mountains came to be called the "tennis creek mountains," but at least there is no evidence to the contrary. And that should be enough for those place-name enthusiasts who share Horatio Gates Spafford's dislike of cats.

In spite of the expenditure of a great amount of speculative energy on searching for its origin, the name "Kaaterskill" remains just as obscure as "Catskill." As the Catskills grew into a busy summer resort region, the tomcat theory of the name's beginnings was found not glamorous enough and a more attractive origin was sought. There were those who found it in "cataract"; they reasoned that the first Dutchmen to see the stream had been impressed by its waterfalls or cataracts and had called it the "Cataract-kill." It is an unlikely theory, for the word "cataract" did not form a part of a seventeenth-century Dutchman's everyday vocabulary but is a "book-word" and of Greek origin. The New Netherlands Dutch phrase for a stream made up of falls and rapids was "fontein kil"; a slowly moving lowland stream was a "platte kil"; the two names occur over and over on old maps and are still in use. Indian words more or less resembling "Kaaterskill" have been mulled over, but here as in so many other cases of the region's place names, convincing evidence of Indian origin is lacking.[12]

Once the 1880s had come and the summer-boarding business was booming, pressures to improve upon the place names of the Catskills grew more and more insistent. Origins, whether Indian or Dutch, became of secondary importance. Finding the kind of name that might attract summer refugees from the nation's big cities was the object of the game. As early as 1853, Snyder's Hollow began giving way to Woodland Valley; later, Sawkill Head became Mount Guardian. In the course of the mid-nineteenth-century enthusiasm for Indian names, a Sullivan County lake long known as East Pond or Pleasant Lake was renamed Kiamesha Lake, said to have been an old Indian term meaning "clear water."[13] The new name did not quickly catch on, and it was not until the 1890s that it pushed Pleasant Lake aside. At about the same time, Liberty Falls, which apparently owed its name to the anti-British emotions of 1803, acquired a new name much more to the taste of boarders—it was Ferndale. By 1880, Shue's Pond or Lake had joined the ranks of the Echo lakes which were becoming essential parts of all mountain resorts. But Judge Clearwater, who much later on befriended archeologist Schrabisch, held out for Schue's Lake, which he innocently derived not from the old local woodsman named Schue whom it seems to commemorate but from the Dutch "schoon" which means "beautiful."[14] Monkey Hill upon which the Grand Hotel stood was soon officially named Monka Hill. Friends of the Grand explained that the name was a corruption of "Murky Hill," given, they said, because the hill's great elevation caused it to be surrounded at times with great swirls of romantic mists. Local people derive the curious name from a whimsical version of the name of a family which lived on the hill. What the name was is uncertain but all agree that it began with "M." Nearby Rose Mountain had been named for the family which contributed its first pioneer farmers, but summer people were told that the name celebrated the wild roses that bloomed there in June. Beaverkills had once been common in all parts of the Catskills—the name described a stream with abundant colonies of beaver. There were so many Beaverkills that summer people were confused, and some of the Beaverkills were weeded out. Much earlier Beaverdam along the East Branch of the Delaware had become Roxbury. Now Beaverkill Mountain, divided between Woodstock and Hurley, took on the then popular name of Ohayo Mountain—the name in varied spellings had been taken from Indian dialects and meant a stream.

Few hosts of summer boarders were more alert to the value of attractive names than George Harding. He was delighted when his daughter Emily suggested Kaaterskill as a name for his hotel, for it was one with considerable magic. Before long Harding was working the name for all it was worth. He was advertising not only the Kaaterskill Hotel but Kaaterskill Lake, Kaaterskill Mountain, Kaaterskill Park, and Kaaterskill Clove. Under this bombardment of Kaaterskills it was only to be expected that many people supposed that the name was a more correct form of "Catskill." Harding formed plans for improving existing names of mountains to the music of bands and the rolling sentences of orators. For a time he went along with an older attempt to change the name of High Peak to Kaaterskill High Peak, but then he thought up something better. He proposed to a convention of Republican politicians meeting at his hotel in the late 1880s that High Peak be renamed Mount Lincoln in honor of the great Republican President and that its companion—the old High Peak and present Round Top—be named Mount Stanton in honor of Lincoln's Secretary of War. Both Lincoln and Stanton had been legal associates of Harding. Harding did not own High Peak but that did not matter. He would buy it and re-erect on its summit the dismantled Pennsylvania building of the 1876 Philadelphia Centennial. He would build a road to the summit so that his guests might be driven there for picnics, and better still, he would run a cog railroad up Mount Lincoln. The mountain's renaming day would be honored by the presence of Abraham Lincoln's son Robert and by Mrs. U. S. Grant. It would be one of the most memorable days ever to be celebrated among the Catskills. The scheme sputtered out and Harding returned to plugging the very sensible Kaaterskill High Peak.[15] An attempt was made to call the southern part of the Catskills the Livingston Hills in tribute to its onetime owners, but the name did not have appeal to mountain people with traditions of Livingston landlords and their leases for three lives. The name was quickly dropped.[16] Livingston Manor in Sullivan County eventually commemorated the family although, of course, it had never formed a part of their manor. Here and there many names of old landlords survived because of the glamor their remembered wealth and power conferred upon the landscape. The town of Hunter remained; so too did Denning, named in 1849 for a landowning Verplanck relation. The name Hardenburgh bestowed in 1859 for the old major had its own romantic charm although officially misspelled and given to a very small and impoverished town destitute, they said, of even those minimal aids to proper existence: a general store and a saloon. Hardenburgh managed to achieve its own sort of local fame: because of its remoteness and poor roads its election returns were often a week late in reaching the Ulster county seat of Kingston. The "Hardenburgh vote" and that of neighboring Denning was awaited eagerly after a close election for it might decide the winner. Under these circumstances it was rumored that the Hardenburgh vote was subject to a more than ordinary amount of tampering.

The changing names of natural and governmental features of the Catskills reflected change in ways of working and in ways of thinking and feeling. A fresh set of names which came to the mountains during the height of the summer-boarding era indicated that boarders were sharing the summer mountains with a new class of people. When names like Onteora Park, Elka Park, and Fleischmanns were first printed on maps and in guidebooks, the public was notified that the summer cottage had arrived in the Catskills and with it a different kind of summer life. Large hotels like the Kaaterskill, the Grand, and the Catskill Mountain House began losing much of their charm to the rich, the wellborn, and those engaged in the sport of social climbing. Elsewhere in the United States, "cottage colonies" were nurturing the feelings of superiority of many groups of Americans. By a route of its own, the summer cottage came to the Catskills and left an enduring mark on the mountains' people and their landscape.

72

Lotus Land

❦ I WAS CALLING one summer afternoon on the stately eighty-year-old lady who presided over a huge gray shingle-sided house on a steep hillside in Onteora Park. The room in which we sat was furnished much as it must have been in the days of the park's cheerful youth: a few pieces of good antique furniture; others showing the influence of the cattail and bamboo aestheticism of the late 1880s; a good but worn oriental rug on the floor; a gold-framed landscape of the Hudson River school type hanging on a pine-boarded wall; a spray of dried bittersweet clinging nearby. The newel post of the stairway was of yellow birch with its bark still in place. When I admired the yellow birch newel post, its owner corrected me: "*We* don't call that yellow birch!" she said, "we call it 'golden birch.'" This led to a botanical discussion and the lady said that a book in her late husband's library would clear an obscure point. As I bounded up the stairway in search of the book, my hostess called out a warning: "Watch out when you turn right up there," she said, "there's a big hole in the floor. We think squirrels made it a few years ago, or maybe it was chipmunks."

Later that day I called on an elderly lawyer in a nearby hamlet. We talked first about the Hardenbergh Patent, of which Onteora Park occupies parts of Great Lots 24 and 25. These lots had been partitioned in 1749 to Robert Livingston and Gulian Verplanck, and the buyers of the share of Benjamin Faneuil. The lawyer had begun his practice only half a century ago—by that time the patent could have had little practical interest to an ambitious young lawyer—and he spoke of Major Hardenbergh, Robert Livingston, and the patent in much the same dreamy, half-believing way that an old Roman of the first decades of our era must have used when referring to Romulus and Remus and the wolf which suckled them on the hills of what was to become Rome. When we talked about the parks, the old man's words turned crisp and incisive. "Yes," he said, "the old parks are still here in the town of Hunter—Onteora, Twilight, Elka, Sunset, and Santa Cruz —but things have changed. The people who founded the parks were rich. When they died they left their children quite well off. Now it's grandchildren and even great-grandchildren who own the cottages in the parks. And the money has been divided up so many times that there's not much left. Some of the descendants of the founders are doing well in the world, but others aren't. They hang on to their cottages even when they can't afford to care for them. Some of them have never learned to do remunerative work—they get along on little quarterly or semiannual payments. When the money comes in they pay their bills. In between some of them have a hard time."

I remarked that it was in much the same way that descendants of the grantees of the Hardenbergh Patent had clung to their subdivided shares two centuries ago and found comfort and hope in the bits of parchment symbolizing their possession of a bit of the earth's surface. The lawyer nodded with the grave respect with which lawyers greet references to the now profitless but still venerated past, and said that having a rich grandfather can be a bad thing.

Francis B. Thurber, the rich New York wholesale grocer, and his talented sister, Mrs. Candace Wheeler, the founders of Onteora Park, shared a reasonably poor grandfather and a succession of ancestors going back to the first years of the European invasion and settling of New England. During the summer of 1883, as Mrs. Wheeler remembered it many years later she and her brother left an Ulster & Delaware railroad car at the Phoenicia station, hired a one-horse wagon, and drove northward through the Stony Clove on a journey of exploration.[1] They discovered the tract of farm and mountain land which would grow into Onteora Park. But they were searching at first for no more than a site for a summer home.

Like the Goulds, the Thurbers were natives of the region of the Catskills—they had been brought up on the borderland of the Hardenbergh Patent in Delhi. They were children of the very Deacon Abner Thurber to whom General Erastus Root had spoken his shocking words as the Antirent War simmered. Little Candace Thurber had heard them as she lay quietly in a chair beside the deacon's stove, and she remembered to the end of her days her father's angry but barren threat to have the general indicted for blasphemy. She remembered, too, the excitement of the Anti-rent War, the marching and disguised men, the songs they sang and the feverish days of the Delhi murder trials.

Francis Thurber owed something of his business success to the Philadelphia Centennial Exposition of 1876. There he had exhibited a monster cheese which helped spread his fame among the cheese-minded. In 1881 he had charmed coffee lovers by writing his *Coffee from Plantation to Cup*. By then Thurber was among the leading wholesale grocers of the country, and a few years later his annual sales were estimated at fifteen million dollars.[2]

Like her brother, Candace Thurber Wheeler also owed a debt to the Centennial Exposition. In her case it was an exhibition at Philadelphia of needlework which helped give a new direction to her life. The exhibition was that of London's Kensington School of Art Needlework. The school had been established to help "decayed gentlewomen" earn a living through applying the ideas about craftsmanship of William Morris and others who were rebelling against the uglier aspects of the machine age. Before long Mrs. Wheeler was helping found a Society of Decorative Arts in New York whose object was to encourage the sort of needlework exhibited by the Kensington School, but without requiring its makers to show visible signs of decay. Soon Mrs. Wheeler found an even more promising field for her developing talents in organizing activity in the crafts: she joined in founding a group known as the Associated Artists. Louis Comfort Tiffany, later famous for his Favrile glass, was the group's prime mover. Mrs. Wheeler was in charge of designing embroideries, wallpaper, textiles, and greeting cards. Her work attracted much favorable attention and sold well. When aesthetic evangelist Oscar Wilde visited the United States in 1882, he dropped in uninvited at Mrs. Wheeler's studio, took a cup of tea, and expressed approval of what he saw.[3]

Before 1883 Candace Wheeler and her brother had liked to stay at the old Catskill Mountain House, where the spirits of Thomas Cole, James Fenimore Cooper, Washington Irving, and William Cullen Bryant walked the long corridors and could easily be glimpsed—at least by culturally aware Americans—gazing out from the edge of the Pine Orchard toward the Thurber homeland of New England. To people like Candace Wheeler and her brother there was still magic in the Mountain House, and they hoped in the summer of 1883 to find some nearby spot to which a part of that magic might be transferred. They found the spot on Widow Parker's farm on the Eastkill Valley Road near Tannersville. Not only did the hilltop they discovered command a splendid view but also the farm of which it formed part had been the base for sketching expeditions of Asher Durand and Thomas Cole and other revered landscape painters. Mrs. Wheeler sat down on the hilltop and read a poem from John Greenleaf Whittier's newly published *Tent on the Beach*. Her brother strode downhill to call on the widow. When he returned it was to announce that he had persuaded

Mrs. Parker to sell him the hilltop. Candace read aloud to her brother a few lines: "They rested there, escaped awhile/From cares that wear the life away,/To eat the lotus of the Nile/And drink the poppies of Cathay. . . ." The two agreed to name their hilltop Lotus Land.

By 1887 Lotus Land had expanded far beyond the limits of its original hilltop. Some seven hundred acres had been added and friends of the two dwellers in Lotus Land were being invited to buy parts of the tract and build summer homes. An imposing history of Greene County published in 1884 had informed Candace Wheeler that the original Indian name of the Catskills had been Ontiora or Onteora; the new cottage colony was called Onteora Park. To hold and manage it, a corporation called the Catskill Mountain Camp and Cottage Company was formed in the city of New York. In recognition of the part railroads would play in the development of the park, old Thomas Cornell and his heir-to-be, Samuel D. Coykendall, were placed on the board of directors.[4]

Onteora Park was no isolated phenomenon. When railroads first demonstrated their ability to carry country dwellers to daily city jobs, suburban real estate developments followed. Some pretentious ones were called this or that "park"—Llewellyn Park in New Jersey dates from 1853. The opening on June 7, 1886, of Tuxedo Park some eighty miles to the south of Lotus Land stimulated the development of many other parks for summer dwellers, Onteora among them.

Each park had its own character. Tuxedo was formed by a group of members of very rich and very well-established American families. Their money had come from business activity, but now the myths that sustain some successful businessmen were failing them and they aimed at setting up an aristocracy resembling, as closely as possible, that of England. Riding, coaching, and other expensive outdoor sports favored by the British were popular. Architect Bruce Price gave an English tint to the park's houses, its clubhouse and other buildings. English antique furniture was imported to add to the air of upper-class English exclusiveness which—it was hoped—would pervade the park.

While Tuxedo Park people were very rich, those of Onteora were merely rich. The lavishness of Tuxedo was beyond their means and, besides, the myths which powered Candace Wheeler and her brother drew their strength not from membership in a self-created aristocracy but from sensitivity to the arts and to nature. Mrs. Wheeler had many friends who were active in the arts and who were welcomed to Lotus Land and soon to Onteora Park. Performances of chamber music, the reading aloud of poetry, amateur theatricals, sketching from nature, and observing the ways of birds, bears, and bees—all these became central parts of life at Onteora Park. The closeness of the Catskill Mountain House with its many ties to the arts and to the appreciation of natural beauty soon made the creation of an Artists' Rock, chiseled with the names of five leaders of the Hudson River school of landscape painting, seem altogether fitting. The first houses to be built at Lotus Land eloquently expressed the myths of their builders. On November 2, 1889, the *Examiner* of Catskill described Francis Thurber's cottage as "most artistic. It is built of solid logs, with the bark peeled off, which shine like silver in the sun. Inside . . . the walls are of logs too, covered with skins and rugs and wasps' nests and wildflowers and everything that is mountainous, beautiful and unconventional." The *Examiner* took note of "a big music room" where "impromptu concerts" were given, for Mrs. Francis Thurber was a patroness of music who encouraged composers like Anton Dvorak.

By the 1890s Onteora Park was the scene of doings that amazed the surrounding mountain people. Characteristic of the park was the dedication —for it could hardly be called the housewarming—of the studio of Mrs. Wheeler's painter-daughter Dora. A candle was lighted directly from the sun through the medium of a magnifying glass and from this a blaze in the fireplace was started. An "acolyte swinging a censer,"[5] "libations of wine and oil," "a priest of the Sun in flowing robes covered with the signs of the zodiac," and "four beautiful virgins of the Sun" all played appropriate parts in the ritual. On other ceremonial occasions, processions that resembled Keats' *Ode to a Grecian Urn* come to life might be seen winding across fields once plowed by the Widow Parker's late husband, Daniel. One afternoon a yoke of oxen wreathed with daisies and wild roses led off at the dedication of a new road. They were guided "by a man in a long smock with girdle and scarf of green," and drew "a wainful of children dressed as woodland gods, tossing daisies and field flowers as they went along." Gnomes and a Roman centurion on horseback followed; next came a Roman emperor and his empress riding in a phaeton. A "bevy of maidens in pale flower-tinted frocks carrying sheaves of blooming grasses" brought the procession to its conclusion.

Taking part in cultural activities like these were many accepted figures in the American world of the arts: Richard Watson Gilder, editor of the respected *Century Magazine;* Brander Matthews, professor of English at Columbia University "and perhaps the last of the gentlemanly school of critics and essayists in America."[6] Almost as gentlemanly was Onteora's Lawrence Hutton, author of many volumes of theatrical and literary chitchat. Fashionable portrait painter Carroll Beckwith represented the art of painting and gave lessons in his studio picturesquely placed on a rocky ledge; later, John Alexander, president of the National Academy of Design and a portrait painter and stage designer, spent his summers at Onteora Park. More robust tenants were also welcomed, once they had received public acceptance. Mark Twain spent the summer of 1890 at Onteora, and while he did not find the park's atmosphere favorable for serious work, he delighted Onteoreans who assembled outside his cottage in the dusk to hear him read aloud with his customary skill.

Other parks came to the Catskills—an outstanding one was Twilight Park, an invention of sanitary engineer Charles F. Wingate and named for a New York club in which he was active. Wingate, attending an engineers' meeting at the Hotel Kaaterskill in 1887, went to Haines Falls and there "was given the unique experience of seeing a waterfall 'turned on' by human hands."[7] He was captivated by a nearby sheep pasture from which he looked down the Kaaterskill Clove to the broad valley and New England mountains beyond. Wingate offered to buy the pasture but the owner proved reluctant to sell—and for a surprising reason. He was C. W. Haines, proprietor of the Haines Falls House, the boarding establishment operated on perhaps the strictest Christian and temperance principles of any in the Catskills. Haines was among those who had deplored the arrival in his town of the Hotel Kaaterskill with its sophisticated patrons and its huge stock of wines and liquors. Each year men like Haines opposed renewing the Kaaterskill's liquor license and worked to dry up the town. If tales current in the Catskills to this day are to be trusted, George Harding fought back, even bribing voters and putting pressure on members of the state legislature to persuade them to alter the eastern boundary of Hunter in order to put his hotel inside the more obliging town of Catskill.[8] A compromise was arrived at between Haines and Wingate. The sheep pasture was leased to Wingate's newly formed Twilight Park Association and a bond of one thousand dollars was posted—the bond would be forfeited the moment a drop of intoxicating liquor was sold in the old sheep pasture. That winter, construction of the first cottages in the park was begun, and soon the park was thriving.

During the 1890s, park after park was projected. Many were catchpenny real estate selling devices which soon fell apart. Some, like Elka Park, were decided successes. Like Twilight Park, Elka Park owed its name to a New York club—in this case the German-American Liederkranz. "Elka" was composed of the initial letters of the two words which were joined to from Liederkranz—a German name for a choral society. Lawyer Paul Goepel was the initiator of Elka Park, and he soon attracted to the colony many men and women prominent in the Christian German-American society of New York. A clubhouse, substantial cottages, and a conspicuous memorial tower were built close to the spot at which the old colonial road emerged from the head of Woodstock's Mink Hollow to push on to the valley of the Schohariekill.

It was not by accident that the rush to create parks among the Catskills came as the "anti-Hebrew crusade" of the late 1880s and early 1890s reached a peak. As late as 1953, Burgess Howard of Tannersville reminisced that the founders of Onteora Park had "represented America at its best."[9] By that Howard meant that the park people were descended from early waves of European emigrants to America and that their culture was essentially that of the Protestant early nineteenth-century United States. Other parks—except for Elka—were summer refuges for people of similar background and with similar fears of contamination by the cultures being brought to the United States by Roman Catholics from Ireland and by Jews from eastern and central Europe. It was the Jewish visitors to the Catskills who gathered in most of the largest hotels and overflowed to smaller boardinghouses who aroused the keenest fear. While Charles L. Beach was trying to preserve the past at his Mountain House, the backers of most parks aimed their projects toward the same goal. In order to make exclusion of unwanted humans easier, the parks adopted the form of associations or clubs, for such organizations were permitted by state law to pick and choose among applicants for membership.[10]

By the mid-1880s, living outside the parks, the hotels, and boardinghouses in a cottage of one's own was becoming especially popular, among people whose style of life did not conform to the usual American standards. In 1883 when the Chinese minister decided to spend the summer in the Catskills, he rented a house in Catskill and brought his staff and servants there. Then both summer and mountain people were delighted at the sight of the minister and his retinue being driven to see the sights of the Catskills in a superb landau gleaming with silver trimmings and aglow with the rich oriental silks worn by the minister and his staff. Or they might encounter a pig-tailed cook scouring the farms and markets of Greene County for suckling pigs or fat ducks for His Excellency's table. And a boarder who attended the Greene County fair on the right afternoon might be lucky enough to see the minister following a spirited baseball game with what appeared—to Western eyes at least—to be understanding and enjoyment.[11]

By the year of the Chinese minister's arrival, a number of very rich people were planning to build summer homes of their own among the

Catskills. Some of these people, like the Fleischmanns, were Jewish, or, like the Goulds, thought to be Jewish, and they felt unwelcome or uncomfortable at the parks and the big hotels.

First of the very rich to become conspicuous independent householders were the Fleischmanns, who were of Hungarian Jewish origin. In 1883, as Francis Thurber and his sister were buying their Lotus Land, Charles F. Fleischmann, the well-known Cincinnati yeast and distilling magnate, was buying sixty acres near the Ulster & Delaware Railroad station then known as Griffin's Corners. Before many years, Fleischmann influence changed the station's name to one that some said honored the family and others claimed advertised their brand of yeast. Senator Fleischmann—he was an Ohio state senator—and a group of relatives proceeded to transform their part of Griffin's Corners into a summer settlement in which American and central European elements were mingled. The buildings, of which the senator's was often called "Schloss Fleischmann," abounded in porches, turrets, and terraces, and were painted in what were described at the time as "tasty colors." Within, a luxury unheard of in the Catskills awed visitors. The Pine Hill *Sentinel's* reporter told on August 1, 1887, of seeing impressive works of art and "costly rugs," and noted that "carved and expensive furniture gives an air of ease and refinement." Senator Fleischmann's huge outdoor "swimming bath" was filled with pure spring water artificially heated to a comfortable temperature. Nearby was a trout pond guarded by a gamekeeper installed in a tower; a deer park; a riding academy; and the most elegant baseball park in all the region. All this gave the Fleischmann domain glamor in the eyes of Catskill mountain people and their summer boarders. The Griffin's Corner Band, supplied with new uniforms and instruments by Fleischmann generosity, played at the railroad station as Fleischmanns arrived in their private railroad cars from their yachts anchored in the mouth of the Rondout. The band also played at the baseball games which brought "country sports and summer sports" from all over the Catskills. Famous professionals played on the Fleischmann team under assumed names. Max and Julius Fleischmann played too. (Julius was mayor of Cincinnati.) The band helped when the Fleischmanns put on an "exhibition of Equestrianism" at which Fleischmanns in person, wearing blue-and-white costumes, entertained the public by riding standing up, by changing horses, and by performing many other equestrian feats. Moreover, Mayor Fleischmann won the admiration of mountain fishermen, who resented the increasing severity of the state's game laws, when he was arrested for fishing illegally and was said to have responded by knocking down the arresting officer.[12]

By 1890 the Fleischmanns were sharing the attention of millionaire admirers among the Catskills with a neighboring family, the Goulds. Old Jay Gould was among the most thoroughly disliked men of his time, not so much for his relentless pursuit of money without regard to the welfare of his fellow humans as because he had managed to become the country's richest man in spite of being, as most Americans whispered, a Jew. His children found themselves thwarted when they tried to become accepted by the upper level of the Christian society of their day, and Jay himself had been blackballed when he tried to join New York's topmost clubs. The younger Goulds set about building up a firm base for future social conquests by putting emphasis, as old English landed families did, on the land from which their ancestors had sprung. They enlarged and improved the old Gould house on Roxbury's main street and built a park behind it rising from the banks of the Delaware's East Branch. Helen Gould soon became known as the Lady Bountiful of Roxbury to whom those in trouble might come for help. Elderly Gould servants were sent to Roxbury to live on pensions or to conduct small businesses, and these people gave rise to a Gould-dependent layer of Roxbury society which endures to this day. But it was George J. Gould, the oldest son of Jay, who took the first bold step toward the status of a rich landed family of the Catskills for his family. This happened in the late 1880s when he bought from Ulster & Delaware president, Thomas Cornell, Furlough Lake and the lands surrounding it. (The lake's name was an improvement upon that of an old local family, the Furlows.)

On the lake shore Gould built one of those elaborate log structures by which millionaires of his day were expressing a relationship to the wilderness and the American past and which also owed something to the hermitages and "bark temples" of eighteenth-century British romantics. The porch pillars were formed of logs chosen for the perversity of their curves and the oddity of their bumps. Around Gould's "palace of logs," as the Kingston *Freeman* called the main building, gamekeepers' lodges, kennels for Russian wolfhounds and other sporting dogs, and breeding pens for pheasants stood in a clearing on an estate of thousands of acres. A well-fenced game preserve held deer and elk—the latter illegally captured in the west by Gould agents. Very quickly young Gould acquired an image similar to that of a British country gentleman of vast means, and it was not long before local people accepted Gould as the great man of their corner of the world and easily yielded to Gould whims. When the master of Furlough Lodge became alarmed by a smallpox scare, he sent his personal physician from New York to the lodge with instructions to vaccinate everybody within infecting distance of his estate. Eighty-nine people submitted without a single recorded protest.[13] The Gould private railroad car, the *Atalanta,* sped toward Furlough Lodge; the Gould yacht lay at anchor at Rondout; special trains carried Gould servants, horses, and dogs to the station of Arkville from Gould's estate of Georgian Court at Lakewood, New Jersey. All this was regarded with awe and respect. But something even more awesome was to be brought to the Catskills by Gould millions.

In 1892 old Jay Gould died. Newspapers commented that his will gave not a penny for any public or charitable purpose; instead, it tied up his fortune in a way that seemed to show a desire to keep the money together even at the cost of tearing his family apart. The family lawsuits which followed entertained the public on both sides of the Atlantic and enriched lawyers for two generations. But before settling down to spend their lives in legal conflict, the Gould heirs agreed on one thing. They would set down in Roxbury an elegant stone church rich in Tiffany stained glass, thick red carpets, and carved oak as a memorial to their parents. The architect they chose was an eminent one, Henry J. Hardenbergh, a direct descendant of Major Johannis. Once the church was completed it became one of the most popular sights of the Catskills; summer boarders making pilgrimages to it found that as they gazed they could bask in the glow of the Gould millions without spending a single cent. Today, with the Gould fortune largely dissipated in lawyer's fees, social climbing, and gay living, the church attracts fewer summer pilgrims. But more and more pilgrims come to the shrine of another Roxbury boy who was a schoolmate of Jay Gould and who, like the Goulds, returned to the place of his family origins as a summer resident.

In the heyday of the parks they had no more welcome native-born visitor than gentle, bearded nature essayist John Burroughs. Burroughs visited all the parks of any standing but seemed especially devoted to Onteora, where he was an honored guest at the 1894 dedication of the Artists' Rock. Burroughs was so park-minded that he often considered founding a park of his own but in 1908 he established a summer home known as Woodchuck Lodge in Roxbury. In her book of memoirs, Candace Wheeler suggested the place which Burroughs filled as a visible symbol of what the Catskills had come to mean to people of her sort. Mrs. Wheeler wrote that Burroughs "loved Onteora. . . . He was and is so essentially a part of the high clear oversight of the region, and of air sharpened by height, and of vastness of space. The very obligation of simplicity which exists when nature is in the ascendant and man on a lower plane made him what he is—as clear and pure as the morning. When he came to us at Onteora he was like another of the family, which, indeed was incomplete without him. . . ."[14]

As a boy on the side of Old Clump Mountain in Roxbury, Burroughs, like Candace Wheeler, had stared at the masks worn by Calico Indian neighbors. He had worked hard on the farm put together bit by bit from the wilderness of the Hardenbergh Patent by his Yankee-descended father. But Burroughs had found time even as a boy in a stern Old School Baptist family to take pleasure in wondering at the ways of birds and other creatures. He had felt even then some sense of the oneness of the natural world—a oneness he was to express with charm and persuasiveness in his later writings. By the 1860s, Burroughs' first nature essays were appearing in magazines. His first volume of such essays, *Wake Robin,* appeared in 1872 and alerted many Americans to the fascination of the world of birds. It contained two essays dealing with nature among the Catskills. Burroughs' *Locusts and Wild Honey* of 1879 contained more essays springing from the Catskills.

When he read this book, Kingston poet-businessman Henry Abbey was among those who understood at once that the Catskills had found a new artist who would change and enhance the old image of the mountains formed by Irving, Cooper, and Thomas Cole. "Our streams and mountains have a meaning that they did not have before he [Burroughs] wrote of them,"[15] said Abbey. As Burroughs climbed and walked, camped and fished among the Catskills, he wrote essay after essay. And these essays still have the power to let us see the Catskills through Burroughs' understanding eyes. He shows us a region of splashing brooks, of balsam fragrant mountain tops, of enclaves of primitive wilderness, of mossy barkpeelers' cabins standing in isolated clearings amid new growth of blackberry bushes and poplar. He wrote of boating down the East Branch of the Delaware, of climbing Slide Mountain, of catching trout, of watching warblers flitting in and out of leafy branches, of shingle-weavers and hoop-pole shavers and of farm families in remote hollows carrying on the traditions of their past.

As the years went by, Burroughs wove an ever deeper spell over the Catskills by the magic of his prose. In Burroughs, the old romantic attitude toward nature gave way to one better suited to the temper of his time. He observed nature through the cool and keen eyes of a poet, willing to accept the world as he found it and eager to make the best of it. He did not deny the cruelty and hostility that often face the individuals who make up the earth's living population but, like his master Ralph

Waldo Emerson, he had faith in the essential goodness of life. The belief in predestination of his Old School Baptist forebears became transformed in Burroughs' mind into the kind of serene acceptance of life to which he gave expression in his very popular poem *Waiting*. It opened with these lines: "Serene, I fold my hands and wait,/Nor care for wind nor tide nor sea;/I rave no more gainst time or fate/For lo! my own shall come to me."[16] But John Burroughs did not spend his life sitting with folded hands. He could fight valiantly for his beliefs or on behalf of his friends. Burroughs was among the first Americans to understand the greatness of the poetry of his friend Walt Whitman. Year after year while the literary lions of America roared savagely at Whitman, Burroughs defended both his poetry and his character with unfailing vigor.

It was the serene, bird-watching aspect of John Burroughs that appealed to the park people and made them overlook his championing of what they regarded as the indecent and vulgar poetry of Whitman. Burroughs was deeply rooted in the earlier agricultural America out of which the myths of respectable moneyed Americans grew, and his battling on behalf of Whitman was forgiven as a mere personal oddity. During the 1880s, Burroughs' nature essays began to be read in American schools; by the mid-nineties, people were coming to the Catskills to experience the world to which Burroughs had imparted a new kind of glamor. But most visitors to the Catskills of these years had never heard of Burroughs or read his books—they lived in cultural worlds in which bird watching and reading about nature had little interest. Some of these visitors spoke with Irish brogues; many spoke Yiddish. They were recent immigrants, their energies absorbed by the struggle for economic betterment, and the Old World culture into which they had been born still retained a grip upon their minds and emotions. As they poured into the summer Catskills, their cultures left marks upon the mountains, and the mountains' older culture modified theirs. The children and grandchildren of these people would read Burroughs and watch birds with all the enthusiasm of the park people, but the time for that had not yet come.

By the 1890s, cheaper and speedier means of reaching the resort centers of the Catskills encouraged the non-park kind of visitors to arrive in ever greater numbers, and they came most eagerly to escape the summer heat of New York's crowded tenements. The Otis Elevating Railroad brought thousands of them up the Catskills each summer. It had become a reality in 1892 and was powered, not by the waters of the lakes, but by a stationary steam engine.

The gain of summer boarders turned out to be a loss to Charles L.

Beach and his sons. The "Otis" cars were filled for only a short period each year when nights in the city of New York were at their hottest. The rest of the year the line usually lost money. Charles L. Beach's son George recalled in later years that "when we had only stagecoaches running up the mountain we made so much money we didn't know where to put it. But once the Otis was built we knew what to do with our money—we fed it to the Otis."[17]

The Stony Clove & Catskill Mountain offshoot of the competing Ulster & Delaware met the challenge of the Otis by "broad gauging" its tracks, and then parlor cars ran from Weehawken and Philadelphia directly to the stations for the Hotel Kaaterskill and the Mountain House. By 1890 the U. & D. had speeded up service and the boardinghouse keepers of Tannersville and Hunter were prospering. It was then that Simon Epstein moved up from Saxton and began operation of the Grandview House in Hunter, the first large "Jewish boardinghouse" to appear in the high Catskills—many others quickly followed. They provided food and an atmosphere in which people of Jewish cultural background felt at home. These boardinghouses were by no means all alike, for each catered to people of one or the other of the many subdivisions of Jewish life. The Hotel Kaaterskill and the Grand now admitted Jews without argument, while the Catskill Mountain House still did its best to keep them out—but without entire success.

Once the S.C. & C.M. R.R. had been broad gauged, the directors of the Otis were faced with even stiffer competition and even larger losses. The Otis could never hope to carry much freight, could not operate the year round, and with its mountaintop terminus at the Mountain House it could not tap the profits of summer-bulging Tannersville and Hunter. That was why a group of backers of the Otis promoted the construction of a new railroad which would make "a connection at the Summit [station] of Otis to Haines Falls, the Parks, Tannersville and other points,"[18] as they told the directors of the Catskill Mountain Railroad. What freight business they'd had, had been "entirely cut off" when the S.C. & C.M. R.R. had been broad gauged. The new road, called the Catskill & Tannersville, was built and its deficiencies were guaranteed by the parent company, the Catskill Mountain Railroad.

The 1890s had been a period of financial uncertainty when American railroads throughout the country were faltering or failing. As the decade neared its end, many railroads rallied but the awkward combination of the C.M. R.R., the Otis, and the C. & T. sank ever deeper into financial mire. In 1899 the Otis had its back to the wall and was forced into court and reorganization. In February of that year the directors of the Catskill Mountain Railroad agreed to take over operation of both the Otis and the C. & T.

In April 1899, Charles L. Beach celebrated his ninetieth birthday. It could not have been too happy an occasion. Old Mr. Beach had seen the fading away of his dream of preserving the picturesque and romantic past at his hotel. He had hated railroads and had become a central figure in railroad building and operation. He had done his best to keep the people he regarded as undesirable away from the Catskills. Now, except for the parks, the undesirables were everywhere. Beach had not gone willingly into participation in the new order coming to the Catskills but he had been compelled to recognize its presence and to do his best to live with it.

By 1885 the shape of the Catskills' new order was clearly visible even to the slow eyes of officialdom. That year Inspector Charles F. Carpenter studied the Catskills and wrote a lengthy report on what he saw for a recently created agency called the New York State Forest Commission. The inspector stated that once upon a time, before the arrival of railroads, the "Old Catskill Mountain House had been sought out by the aristocracy of New York and Baltimore."[19] The rest of the region, said Carpenter, was then known only to fishermen, farmers, and woodcutters. But a great change had taken place. The entire region had become "the natural picnic ground of the vast population of New York and vicinity."

Year by year the number of picnickers grew, and each summer the Catskills were alive with their efforts to amuse themselves. Never has any mountain region on this earth been the scene of so concentrated an effort to provide summer amusement. And that amusement effort took a great variety of forms—some traditional, others new and somewhat bizarre.

73

The Pleasures of Summer Life

❧ EVEN BEFORE the Otis Elevating Railroad began scaling the eastern wall of the Catskills, mountain people were telling each other that the glory of the Catskills' big hotels was fading. Only a few years earlier these hotels had been the pride of the mountains; all through July and August they had been filled to capacity with fashionable and gay people; now even at the height of summer, half the rooms at the Catskill Mountain House, the Kaaterskill, the Grand, and the Overlook Mountain House remained empty. In March 1890 the Laurel House was sold by the Greene County sheriff in foreclosure proceedings,[1] and that same year the Catskill Mountain House was again mortgaged to a Catskill bank. By then the Tremper House was faltering, and in 1891 its owners considered giving up, but a new manager took over and the hotel struggled on with four-fifths of its space empty. In 1893 a bruising nationwide depression struck business, finance, and industry. The Catskills' big hotels shuddered, and that year the long-suffering Overlook Mountain House failed to open. But all this did not mean that summer visitors were deserting the Catskills—far from it.

Richard Lionel DeLisser explained what was happening in his *Picturesque Catskills* of 1894. "Some of the best and wealthiest people of New York, Brooklyn and Philadelphia" were building or renting cottages in the "country paradise" of the various parks, where they might "determine who shall and who shall not be admitted within their precincts." Less fortunate humans were filling the smaller boardinghouses. "The days of the great hotels may have gone by," DeLisser wrote, "but people are coming here just the same, and they will go where they can get the best for their money." And nowhere within easy striking distance of New York and Philadelphia, DeLisser hinted, could summer people do better with a limited amount of money. It was not surprising that small boardinghouses increased in number, in variety and in liveliness. It was true that some bravely carried on old traditions and observed Sunday with all the Mountain House strictness; at such places the proprietor often locked the house doors at ten or eleven each evening and forbade dancing and playing cards at any time. Both whiskey and the bulky Sunday newspapers to which urban Americans were becoming addicted were contraband at these houses and had to be smuggled in and consumed in secret. After 1892 a "newspaper train" reached the mountains early on Sunday mornings (it reached the Kaaterskill by eight) and left fat bundles at each station. Once Sunday reading in mountain boarding establishments had run heavily to the deeds of Abraham, Job, and the disciples; now scandals in high society and the details of the most recent instance of corruption in building municipal sewers were taking their place.[2]

A new and more worldly spirit was coming to the boardinghouses of the Catskills, pushing old ways aside. Boarders wore less solemn clothing, laughed more often, were less likely to quote from the Bible to express their pleasure at the sight of a waterfall or a distant view. The Germans who penetrated the Catskills over the tracks of the Ulster & Delaware in the early 1870s had brought an open enjoyment of life into the mountains; now a similar kind of enjoyment was everywhere.

On summer evenings, music and the laughter of dancers floated out from boardinghouse parlors and from outdoor dancing platforms lighted by the stars and Japanese lanterns. In Pine Hill, Tannersville, and Woodstock, old people awoke and grumbled as wagonloads of hayriders creaked by, horns blowing, bells ringing, girls squealing, and young men giving off sounds that local people likened to the braying of jackasses. Bats residing in old barns heard something new, for now the voices of city boarders were mingled with those of farmers at the barn dances which mountain people held in August. There local fiddlers overcame the obstacles of work-worn hands and a day spent in the harvest field to produce stirring music, while old-timers told boarders sitting on heaps of new hay of the great old days of mountain barn dances when fiddlers and dancers alike kept in action around the clock until all hands collapsed from exhaustion. Once bands of gypsies had come to the mountains in the fall to match wits with local horse-trading farmers; now they also came in summer when their women might detect a future husband in a young lady boarder's palm or a million dollars in that of her male companion. For the pleasure of boarders, Indians returned to the Catskills. They came from Canada and northern New York to make and sell baskets and beadwork over Main Street shops, and one group operated a

"bazaar" at the Laurel House. Trained European bears and their masters
trudged from hamlet to hamlet to perform on village greens or boardinghouse lawns, and, according to boardinghouse wits, heard local bears growl
from their cages at this "invasion of cheap foreign labor." Mounted men in
Indian and western costumes galloped through the streets of boarding
centers arousing interest in medicine shows to be put on after sunset.
There cures for whatever might ail man or beast might be bought, as
might potions guaranteed to step up sexual power. Monkeys and organ
grinders came and went and collected their tributes of pennies; so did
weight lifters, high jumpers, and the little German bands which tooted
and sawed before passing a hat.

As at all other pleasure resorts in man's history, professional gamblers
wandered about on the prowl for victims. One such expert was said to
have taken four thousand dollars from a boarder named Clark in a poker
game which floated from village to village in the late 1880s. When last
heard from, Clark was making his way back to his job in New York on
foot. Slot machines invaded the Catskills during the late nineties and did
business in "refreshment saloons" and many other places. When it was
rumored that Anthony Comstock of the New York Society for the Suppression of Vice was coming to the Catskills, a mountain editor warned
farmers to put pantalettes on their chickens. But Comstock ignored bare-
legged chickens and instead smashed a number of slot machines with a
sledge hammer before going on to Stamford where he gave a hand with
setting up a Presbyterian church bazaar. Boarders who preferred losing
their money at race tracks were given every opportunity, for horses ran
not only at the mountains' county fairs but at many private tracks such as
the well-known one at Tannersville.

The appearance on the market of photographic film and simpler cam-
eras made amateur photography a favorite passion of summer boarders,
and some proprietors of boarding places, bazaars, and refreshment saloons
supplied darkrooms. Professional photographers drove their horse-drawn
"photographic cars" from valley to valley leaving behind a flutter of paper
images of buildings and notable scenes as well as a vast number of
tintypes of boarders in solemn, loving, or comic poses. Traveling theatrical
troupes came to village halls, and ventriloquists, glass blowers and magi-
cians performed there as well as in hotel parlors. Churches tempted
boarders not only with frequent weekly prayer meetings but also with
concerts by well-known singers such as the Hampton Quartette and the
Gilbert family singers who sang their southern Negro songs for fifteen
consecutive summers in the mountains. Master Ralph Bingham, once

famous as a "boy orator," favored mountain churches when displaying his skill, though by the nineties he was having a hard time remaining sufficiently boyish to justify his title.

The walking mania of the 1870s gave way to that of the 1880s and 1890s—to most able-bodied boarders walking and climbing formed an indispensable part of a summer stay in the Catskills. Each hotel and boardinghouse had its favorite walks and climbs. Observation towers appeared on popular summits to provide improved views. Boarders left behind their initials to commemorate their conquest of this or that summit. Chancellor Livingston had been satisfied with carving his initials on a tree trunk; boarders of the eighties and nineties carried tools up mountains and cut their initials deeply into rock. The all-time champion initial leaver may have been J. H. Austin of Clifton, Staten Island. On August 1, 1885, the *Examiner* of Catskill reported that eighty-five-year-old Austin had just made his sixtieth annual trip to the Catskills and had cut his initials and the date on "one of the highest spots." He had marked every one of his climbs since 1825 in the same way. Kaaterskill guests favored climbing High Peak and Round Top; so too did the cottagers of Twilight Park who had their own walking organization which jocosely offered "degrees in Pedistry." A fine crop of guides sprang up, many of whom were excellent woodsmen who laid out and maintained the trails they used. James Dutcher, who kept a boardinghouse at Big Indian and served as the hamlet's postmaster, was among the best-known of all mountain guides and the guardian spirit of Slide Mountain. Dutcher began leading groups of boarders up Slide in the late 1870s. He camped out overnight with his parties, told them tales of the Catskills and of bear hunts as he sat beside the campfire, and then, returning to his Panther Mountain House, he presided over one of his famous trout dinners, for many smaller mountain boardinghouses followed similar establishments in Switzerland in emphasizing local trout as a table treat. Barefoot boys also turned guides, and some found that by building small fires at certain spots at the bases of cliffs they could send smoke through hidden crevices to emerge on a mountaintop. The boys led boarders, at so much a head, to see their newly discovered "volcanoes."[3] The goal of many a walk was a "profile rock" or a ledge from which a succession of ridges and summits might be made out to resemble the profile of a man lying on his back—these were called Old Men of the Mountains and fanciful Indian legends were devised to explain them.

When rainy weather put a halt to walking, a boarder's attention was likely to be fixed more intently on the pleasures of the dining table;

complaints of the shortcomings of food grew in proportion to the length and intensity of rain. Then, except at the strictest establishments, novel reading flourished and so too did a diversity of parties: phantom parties at which guests dressed as ghosts; potato parties; bean-bag parties; cake-walks; Mother Goose parties; soap-bubble parties; and Kate Greenaway parties at which guests were required to dress in the manner of the characters in Miss Greenaway's popular illustrations; card parties (euchre was a favorite game); and fancy-dress parties. At one of these held at the Hotel Katzberg in Hunter, a lady dressed as the Goddess of Liberty in a costume composed of American flags. At the same party, another lady wore nothing visible but pages of the New York *Tribune* stitched together. Charades and *tableaux vivant* were popular. At a Catskill Mountain House tableaux of 1889, the changeable weather of the season was honored when a young lady appeared with an umbrella in her right hand and a sunshade in her left—and looked in bewilderment from one to the other. Sometimes the guests at one boardinghouse entertained those at another, as in August of 1889 the boarders at Palenville's genteel "Pleasant View" gave a reception followed by a dance and a banquet for guests at the equally genteel "Mountain View House." On occasions like these, ladies displayed their finest plumage and details of what they wore were often given to the public in regional newspapers. At the Pleasant View party, for example, "Mrs. Aiken wore a gown of black silk and lace, diamonds; Mrs. Hamilton pongee with diamonds; Mrs. Kelly navy blue moire; Mrs. Wilson, blue India silk with Irish point, diamonds. . . ."

The high point of many a boarder's stay in the Catskills came when he set forth on a day's excursion to a larger and more expensive house than his own. On that day the boarder leaped over the walls of custom and habit which surrounded him and came into close touch with a more expansive and glittering way of life. The Kaaterskill, the Catskill Mountain House, and the Grand were the choicest goals for these excursions. From its very beginnings the Catskill Mountain House had valued the income it derived from trippers, and once the hotel began to decline, it welcomed trippers with an even broader smile. During their optimistic early years, the Kaaterskill, the Grand, the Overlook, and the Tremper had been none too hospitable to the surreyloads of trippers from lesser houses who came to stare at their elegant public rooms and their rich guests. Trippers complained that "intellectual young ladies"[4] on the Kaaterskill's staff gave them chilly looks and charged them ten cents for a glass of South Lake water—at the old Mountain House good spring water was free although the whiskey was not.

By the mid-1890s all the Catskills' big hotels were co-operating with railroads in organizing "cheap excursions" which would bring paying men and women into their dining rooms and bars. Excursions over the lines of the Ulster & Delaware and Stony Clove & Catskill Mountain railroads originated in Stamford and Rondout and picked up boarders at way stations. The Otis offered a fifty-cent round trip to excursionists, who would get "Mr. Beach's famous dinner" for an extra dollar. At the old Mountain House the trippers usually outnumbered the regular guests. They surrounded Charles L. Beach as he sat in his usual clifftop station and listened to him expounding the view and denouncing the tripper-vandals who continued to desecrate his temple-museum. Social climbers in his audience would listen eagerly as the old man pointed out the great Hudson River estates visible below, many of which now belonged to millionaires with such new names as Astor and Vanderbilt while others still remained in the Livingston name.

From the very beginning of their trip, excursionists on the Ulster & Delaware would become aware that they were close to fame and millions. For it was over these very tracks that the private cars of the Gerrys, the Goulds, and the Fleischmanns traveled, and if they looked sharp, the boarders might be lucky enough to catch a glimpse of one of the "tally-hos" of the New York Coaching Club speeding a load of millionaires over a trackside road heading toward Lake Delaware. Once arrived at the big hotels the hunt for millionaires and famous men and women was on in earnest.

No longer were these people to be found in the abundance of earlier years, but a diligent hunter could always be sure of at least a few. They were most easily bagged at the Kaaterskill, where excursionists and boarders might also gape at millionaires' mates laden with trophies of their husbands' triumphs in the fields of finance, pork packing, or railroad juggling. In 1884 an agent of the Kingston *Freeman* told of observing a lady eating in the Kaaterskill's dining room although handicapped with the weight of eight rings on one hand—several were mounted with diamonds. Diamonds, emeralds, and rubies ornamented her ears. When the lady walked out into the sunshine the agent noted that she glittered "like the Kaaterskill's electric lights." Similar ladies were on display—if in smaller numbers—through the nineties. The choicest game to be found at the Mountain House were representatives of old money, or of respectable old southern families who had not been able to shake the Mountain House habit even as the place became less and less fashionable. Moreover, the inhabitants of the exclusive parks emerged from time to time from behind their high stone walls and fences to have dinner at one or the other of the large hotels and might then be visually captured by an excursionist.

No excursionist with good observing power could fail to notice that the big hotels differed from his own little boardinghouse in more than the wealth and social standing of its guests: the percentage of male guests at such places was far greater than at his own. Many city men who supported their families on modest wages or salaries sent their wives and children to the Catskills so they might benefit from the pure cool mountain air while they worked at their jobs as usual, for the vacation with pay had not yet been made part of American life.

An anonymous amateur statistician estimated in the Pine Hill *Sentinel* of August 21, 1889, that there were then "over one thousand husbandless wives" in the town and noted that each Saturday two hundred husbands arrived from New York on what were called "husband trains." These men returned to New York on Monday morning. This lack of balance between the sexes had easily predictable results. Farm boys and single boarders fell into dalliance with married women, and many a divorce suit was based on evidence gathered in the Catskills. In the summer of 1888, for example, a New York man accompanied by his lawyer appeared by night at a Margaretville hotel at which his wife was spending the summer. The lawyer was an enthusiastic amateur photographer and carried what was known as a "dectective camera." After much tiptoeing in corridors and trying of doorknobs the two men burst into a room in which the wife lay asleep in bed beside her husband's best friend. The lawyer touched off a blaze of flash powder. The resulting picture stirred much local pride, for it was believed to be the first such effort ever submitted in evidence in a New York divorce suit. The Catskills' summer shortage of men rose to an all-time high in the late 1890s when the Spanish-American War drained off manpower. Then what the newspapers called an acute "beau famine" raged. One Tannersville hotel with a capacity of two hundred harbored no more than seventy-five women, one man and a boy—as one paper reported. Proprietors of hotels like this were rumored to be offering free accommodations to young and single men.

As a boarder's stay in the Catskills neared its end, he was likely to look with increasing interest at the displays of souvenirs to be seen in almost every crossroads store. There were silver or plated souvenir spoons with views of the big hotels; Rip Van Winkle spoons; as the nineties moved along, German china marked "Souvenir of Pine Hill" or of Haines Falls or some other resort; lapel pins bearing the names of smaller hotels; mounted photographs of hotels and waterfalls; stereoscopic views of the

Catskills' scenic attractions; Indian baskets and beadwork. But as popular as anything else were objects advertised as having been made "of native wood with native skill." The smaller mountain furniture-making shops urged chairs, tables, cradles, or chests of drawers upon boarders. One shop in the town of Prattsville took orders each summer for their dashing Directoire-styled sofas of curly maple which would be made and delivered in the winter. Turning shops abounded—few hamlets were without one or two—and many of them converted during the eighties and nineties to making souvenirs for the boarder trade. Wooden napkin rings and cuff links, round boxes for holding jewelry, bowls, vases, rolling pins, and lazy Susans, and many more objects were turned of the hardwoods of the Catskills. An American version of the European alpenstock was bought early in a boarder's stay. These "mountain sticks" were usually made of ash, but cherry, black walnut, and other woods were added for ornamental effect. A blue bow was tied on and they were ready to help a boarder climb Slide or High Peak. Some turners went from boardinghouse to boardinghouse peddling wagonloads of their wares made the previous winter, but many boarders enjoyed watching their wooden souvenirs being made to order in dusty, shaving-littered shops.

A valued souvenir was a pillow filled with balsam fir needles—not only would it bring back memories of the high ledges of the Catskills, but also its fragrance was believed to be soothing to a sore throat or aching chest. The mountains' bazaar Indians sold these pillows, but cautious people who preferred to be sure of getting the real thing returned from expeditions to High Peak, the Wittenberg, or Slide laden with balsam fir boughs. These they spread on their boardinghouse barn floor to dry. Then on a rainy day the needles could be stripped and ladies sitting in gossipy comfort on the house verandah might stitch and fill and take home their own imprisoned bit of the Catskill wilderness.

At the first touch of September coolness, boarders fled from the Catskills as from a sinking ship. The herds of fifty or a hundred cows which had arrived in June from Delaware farms to supply milk to the Mountain House and Kaaterskill guests also made their way home again. Farmers who had carted the swill and table scraps from the hotels to feed to their hogs now put the hogs on a more fattening diet in preparation for the November slaughtering which would supply hickory-smoked hams, bacon, and slabs of salt pork to fill the stomachs of another summerful of boarders. There was much fall work to be done: adding another verandah; repainting the slant-roofed upstairs rooms in the pale pinks, blues, and greens which were favored; mending tears in the parlor sofa; shipping barrels of potatoes, apples, or butternuts to boarders who had ordered them; writing letters in an attempt to track down boarders who had skipped out before dawn of a summer day without paying their bills.

With the chilly days of early December the Catskills seemed to roll back year after year, generation after generation. Except for the evidence of the gaunt-looking boardinghouses and hotels standing amid leafless trees, the boarder fever of the summer seemed no more than a dream. Farmers easily reverted to the ways of the past. With gun and dog they tracked foxes along the mountains' ledges; their boys brought out rusty traps and made ready for a winter campaign against muskrats, skunks, and mink. As mountain families drove to church or store through the frosty air they noticed a marked change in the people they passed. The newly immigrated Germans and eastern European Jews were now almost totally absent, as were the slickly dressed dudes and the fashionably dressed "summer girls." That made one element of the population all the more conspicuous— these were the poverty-stricken Irish quarryworkers whose disturbing presence had been masked by the cheerful crowds and bustle of summer. Now with winter unemployment upon them, the quarrymen stood in clusters at corners and talked, or gathered inside taverns from which they emerged from time to time to settle an argument with their fists or to make the surrounding mountains ring with their shouts as they chased a wandering pig.

Boardinghouse keepers looked askance at the quarrymen and the quarries in which they worked, for many believed that quarries and quarrymen were destroying the charm of the Catskills. And, given enough time—say a century or so—they might destroy the Catskills altogether. Quarries could be seen in every hamlet and on a thousand mountainsides. A man couldn't escape the sight of quarries and quarrymen—not even if he climbed to the very top of Slide Mountain.

Bluestone Quarries

❧   DURING THE HEIGHT of Catskills' bluestone-and-boarding period an interesting addition was made to the stock of lore that tries to explain the granting of the Hardenbergh Patent, and it grew out of a popular amusement of boarders. At the same time it can be used to illuminate an important aspect of bluestone quarrying and its devastating effect on the landscape. The bit of lore came from the boarders' delight in climbing Slide Mountain. It places Major Johannis Hardenbergh and the Indian Nisinos on top of Slide Mountain shortly before 1708. The two were admiring the view in the manner of proper nineteenth-century summer boarders. With a wave of an arm, Nisinos indicated the whole expanse of mountains and valleys which surrounds Slide. "All this is yours, my friend," said Nisinos, "I'm giving it all to you."[1] And in this way the extent of the patent was determined.

To a boarder standing on top of the rickety observation tower which had appeared on Slide's summit during the 1870s, the tale of Hardenbergh and Nisinos seemed plausible enough. All the mountainous parts of the patent were in plain view even if most of the valleys were hidden by the mountains enclosing them. In spite of all the destruction of plant life which had taken place, the mountains were still green by summer. Deciduous trees had taken the place of most of the evergreens, and burned-over slopes had quickly become clothed with low-growing plants. A few checkerboards of fields, a tiny cluster of buildings here and there, the Grand Hotel on Monka Hill—only these broke the summer green of the Catskills. To the eyes of a boarder the Catskills would have much the same look as in the days of Hardenbergh and Nisinos had the two found a tower rising above the view-concealing balsam firs of Slide's top just before 1708, or if they had climbed to the top of the balsam firs and managed to look around. Yet in one significant respect the view from Slide had changed: it was somewhat darker and bluer because there was more smoke and dust in the air.

By the 1880s thousands of wood- and coal-burning stoves had displaced the few Indian campfires once widely scattered in the Catskills' valleys. The smoke of industry rose from most valleys, for sawmills and wood-using factories were turning from clean water power to smokily burning wood or coal. Acid factories which converted wood into alcohol, acetic acid, and other products with industrial uses oozed clouds of waste gases into the air of Sullivan and Delaware counties. All along the lines of the mountains' railroads and in nearby hollows, the kilns in which charcoal was made contributed their fumes to the air. (Their product was shipped by rail from the mountains to go into the making of a high grade of iron.) The upper Esopus Valley was so rich in these kilns that it was sometimes called the "charcoal fields of the Catskills."[2] The locomotives of mountain railroads added their quotas of smoke and prompted the production of even more as they pulled endless carloads of firewood to the brickyards of the Hudson Valley. From the tower of Slide on a clear day, dozens of brickyards could easily be seen belching smoke.

To all but a few, the smoke and dust they saw from the tower formed an encouraging sight. It was a symbol of what Americans liked to call "progress," by which they meant an increase in cash, comfort, and material well-being. Only a few saw it as something disturbing—a symbol of the grab-and-run looting of the American continent which had been ac- celerating ever since the land had been snatched from the Indians. It was almost as if this were a conquered province from which the conquerors would flee once they had squeezed it dry of its almost fabulous riches.

Smoke was the chief symbol of progress but it was not the only one visible to a watcher perched on the swaying balsam-pole tower on Slide. On a rainless day the watcher could make out certain streaks and clouds of dust which had a special significance of their own: the clouds marked the locations of bluestone quarries, and the streaks marked the roads over which the quarried stone was hauled for shipment to railroad stations or to Hudson River stoneyards and wharves.

Today an observant walker among the Catskills can look up from many valleys and make out the ruins of old quarries on the slopes above. Each one, even though completely smothered in vegetation by summer, can be picked out easily enough by anyone who knows one kind of tree from another. For white birch and butternut trees seem to delight in marking the quarries by taking root and thriving in the loose masses of waste stone that have accumulated around them. In late fall after a light snow a maze

74

of ghostly old roads becomes visible from the valley; it was over these often perilous tracks that bluestone moved down from the mountainsides. Today hardly a single one of the many hundred quarries that were once worked among the Catskills is still in business, though a similar but more easily quarried stone is still being produced to the west and southwest of the mountains.

The beginnings of the bluestone quarries which were to raise so much dust were disarming enough. For thousands of years the kind of hard and durable stone that can be worked without too much effort into smooth-faced slabs for building and paving has been valued by human beings. Early settlers at the eastern base of the Catskills found a hard, blue-gray stone like this breaking through the earth and forming long parallel ledges which often alternated with bands of soft, red shale. Later on, geologists traced these ledges to Upper Devonian days some two hundred million years ago. They found that at higher elevations among the Catskills the bluish sandstones turned gray, green, or pinkish and lost something of their hardness and strength. Once discovered, bluestone quickly became intimately connected with the lives of the Catskills' pioneers.[3] When one of them died, it was a slab of bluestone, usually picked from a plowed field and rudely trimmed, that served as a headstone. Many of these stones were unmarked but as time went on more and more were lettered and traditional verses were added. The stone of Harriet Winner (Winne) who died in 1810 at the age of twenty-one still stands in the Zena cemetery in the town of Woodstock. The verse goes:

> Behold me now. As you pass
> by. As you am now. So ons was I
> As I am now. So must you be.
> Prepare for death to foll
> ow me.

In the same graveyard Henry Short who died in 1815 offers a bit of pious advice from his bluestone tombstone:

> Come all my friends go
> home dry up your Tiers
> For I must lie here till
> Christ appears.

As pioneer days faded away, the old bluestone gravemarkers took on a crude old-fashioned look and mountain people became easy marks for the sales talks of Yankee agents for fashionable white marble stones. Then the old bluestones were uprooted and displaced by marble ones. What to do with the old stones puzzled some but it came to be generally agreed that they had lost their sacred character and might be put to any mundane use. Many—turned face down, of course—served as paving stones or steps at front or back doors, and some kept feet from being muddied as water was drawn from wells. As the craft of bluestone-working acquired refinement, smooth rectangular slabs were laid down around houses and cellars were handsomely paved. Circular pieces of bluestone covered crocks of pickles and sauerkraut in those cellars or a row of these "potlids," as they were called, leaned idly against cellar walls waiting for the moment when they would be needed. Chimneys and fireplaces of early houses were of bluestone with an especially handsome piece serving as a hearthstone. The cellar walls were of bluestone, usually picked from fields but sometimes taken from a nearby ledge. An occasional builder set slabs of stone in the inner surface of a cellar wall to project a foot or less and so serve as shelves. Chimneys were topped by a slab of stone set on four small corner pieces. These were intended to check the downdrafts common in hilly and mountainous country—William Wordsworth commented on similar devices in his Lake District. Stone walls divided fields and pastures and served a double purpose. They disposed of the stones which appeared as soil washed ever thinner and they kept cattle in their proper places. A memorable stone wall was the one that Henry Davis of Woodstock agreed to build for his landlord, the Chancellor's mother, Margaret: he promised in his lease of 1791 to build a good wall to enclose his farm of forty acres and in this way he proposed to pay his first four years' rent.[4]

For building the smokehouses in which they would hang their hams and bacon in clouds of hickory smoke, pioneers turned to bluestone; even an occasional dwelling house was fashioned of the stone. A notable one was that built in Woodstock traditionally in 1799 for Judge Jonathan Hasbrouck who was said to be the richest man in Ulster County. It is likely that Hasbrouck used the house as a refuge from the summer epidemics which harassed Hudson Valley people. What is certain is that the stone of which the house was built was cut in a nearby quarry.

Growing skill in working bluestone led to the making of stone troughs from which hogs ate their meals and of bowls to hold salt for the cows in pastures. Small stone bowls held water in chicken yards, while dogs and cats sometimes fed from bluestone bowls set beside kitchen doors. By Civil War days bluestone hitching posts stood in front of prosperous houses, and near them were bluestone horse blocks or carriage steps in a variety of designs. A common one took the form of a stone table with four legs and a top with a step or two to make ascent easier when ladies stepped into a wagon or carriage. At soapmaking time a square of bluestone lying near the kitchen door was put to use. A pattern of incised lines decorated its surface. The lines were the channels through which water ran into a container after leaching through a cask of ashes placed on the stone. The amber-colored liquid which resulted was the lye necessary to convert fats into soap. Beside every blacksmith shop lay a larger and thicker square of bluestone with a hole in its center. It was used to hold wagon wheels as red-hot iron tires were being fitted to their rims.

The days of working bluestone as a craft contributing only to local comfort and convenience and giving an outlet for the creative energies of individuals began coming to an end about 1830. During the thirties, bluestone quarrying as an organized industry took its first tentative steps.[5] By then the same growth of urban population and wealth that helped send travelers to the Catskill Mountain House was spurring city dwellers to demand such refinements as better-paved streets and sidewalks—and there was no better sidewalk material than what New Yorkers were soon calling North River bluestone. The economic difficulties of the thirties which threatened to smash the Catskill Mountain House and the surrounding tanneries kept the new bluestone industry from growing rapidly. But as an economic change for the better came during the 1840s, wagonloads of bluestone flagging for the sidewalks of New York and many other cities traveled to the Hudson River trading towns in convoys of a dozen or more. The stone was put on board sloops and sent sailing down the river.

From small quarries in Quarryville in the town of Saugerties, from quarries in the Hurley Woods which had once been the subject of a dicker between Cornelis Cool and the Hardenbergh patentees, from Jockey Hill, from the banks of the lower Sawkill, and from Moray Hill where grind-stones are said to have been cut in the 1820s at what is still known as the Graystone Ledge—from all these quarries and more, flagging stone and stone for steps and curbing moved toward the trading towns. There it passed into the temporary possession of big stone dealers. At first these men were of Yankee background, but before long some were Irishmen who had drifted to the United States during the hard times that followed the peace of 1815 and the even harder times that resulted from the potato-crop failures of the early 1820s. The stone dealers by late in the 1840s were acquiring tidy little fleets of sloops and were expanding the stoneyards in which skilled stonecutters worked over the roughly cut slabs brought in from the quarries and gave them the high degree of finish customers now required.

Albany may have been the first city to lay down bluestone sidewalks—

before 1830 the stone was being quarried from the northern end of the formation that runs from near Albany to Pike County in Pennsylvania. In colonial days New Yorkers had used planks, bricks, and stone cut on Manhattan Island, plus New Jersey sandstone to pave sidewalks. In March 1735, "Curious fine flat purple Stones"[6] had been advertised in the New-York *Gazette* as suitable for a variety of uses including pavements—it was a kind of slate quarried in Hyde Park in Dutchess County and carried by sloop to New York. But once bluestone invaded New York and conquered some opposition, it pushed all competing sidewalk materials aside and its use spread to other cities and towns. By 1850 sloops laden with bluestone flagging were leaving the wharves of Hudson Valley trading towns not only for New York but also for Boston, Philadelphia, Baltimore, Charleston, and other cities up and down the Atlantic coast. Before the end of the century, sidewalks of North River bluestone were echoing under the feet of people in San Francisco, Milwaukee, St. Louis, and Havana, Cuba. And the stone deserved its popularity. It was hard and long-lasting, it dried out quickly after a shower, and it did not become slippery with wear as some other stones did. In response to the demand, stone dealers continued to enlarge their yards and installed steam engines to power the cutting and planing machinery that was taking the place of human skill and muscle. Only in years of economic weakness did they retreat.[7]

With the arrival of the Ulster & Delaware Railroad in the Catskills, some older quarries distant from the railroad tracks were abandoned and new ones convenient to railroad transportation were opened. Phoenicia, Margaretville, Roxbury, and many points between had thriving quarries and trackside stoneyards. Summer boarders could look out from their railroad carriages and see stonecutters working in yards at almost every station. The men wore derby hats to protect their heads against flying spalls and they spat tobacco juice to clear their mouths of stone dust. At Phoenicia the boarders smiled at the sight of a young bear chained to a post in the stoneyard and looking up with interest at passing trains.

Stone dealers grew more and more prosperous and pushed aside more and more of the small part-time quarry operators with one or two employees who had been the rule in the early days of the industry. They took advantage of the railroads of Sullivan County and of the Delaware and Hudson Canal to open busy quarries in western Ulster and Sullivan counties. They were big men whose names were spoken with awe throughout the region of the Catskills. Among them were Fitch Brothers, Burhans and Brainard, Bigelow, Sweeney, Noone, and the Booth

Brothers. (Nathaniel Booth who wrote so revealingly of the sloop *Martin Wynkoop* and the Catskill Mountain House was a partner in this firm.) John Maxwell of Saugerties was another big bluestone trader. He was the son of an Irish-born veteran of the Peninsular Wars who, when he came to the United States, first found work as the keeper of the tollgate on the turnpike road that led up the Kaaterskill Clove to the tanneries beyond.[8]

As competitive corporations in any industry grow in size and profits, they usually try hard to find new outlets and uses for their products, and it was so with the giants of the bluestone trade. The use of the stone for the water tables and sills and lintels of brick buildings increased mightily; architects specified bluestone for buildings which attracted attention, such as the showy W. H. Vanderbilt house on Fifth Avenue in New York and the handsome Tiffany house on Madison Avenue. Architect and arbiter of taste Stanford White liked to use bluestone—he knew the stone's background well, for he often passed through the North River bluestone country on his way to vacations at Mead's Mountain House in Woodstock. A floor paved with what were called black and white squares of marble came to rely on a fine-grained dark bluestone for its "black" squares while, on a less elegant level, sewer heads and basement steps in cities were likely to be of bluestone.

The bluestone industry saw changes almost from year to year. Power became concentrated in fewer and fewer hands as machinery came into ever greater use, and, after the slaughter of the Civil War made workmen scarce and their wages high, sloops gave way to two-masted schooners which required fewer hands to work them. It had become customary in the stone industry for each man to sit down with his employer in April and strike a bargain for his own wages and working conditions.[9] But labor began to organize in the favorable Civil War days and after that strikes interrupted quarry and stoneyard operation from time to time, and these strikes grew more frequent as the nineteenth century moved along.

If the stoneyard owners were at the top of the bluestone pyramid, the men who took the stone from the quarries were obviously at the bottom. Theirs was not an easy or a safe job. Broken limbs, smashed hands, blindness, dust-caused lung disease, and other calamities were frequent. The first possibility of accident came when a promising ledge of stone was to be stripped of its "top"—this was the earth and broken stone above the "block" of usable stone. The top was removed by blowing it off with blasting powder, which sometimes exploded prematurely with fatal results. Once the block was exposed, wedges were inserted along one of the horizontal seams known as "lifts." A man drove in each wedge with a sledge hammer as the foreman kept the blows falling in unison. Sometimes the stone crumbled above the wedges, and sometimes the lift cracked into many unsalable pieces. But if all went well, the entire lift bounded by the north and south trending "side seams" and the east and west "headers" rose in one piece, which was occasionally as large as sixty by twenty feet. The next step was to cut the lift into rectangles. To do this it was necessary first to drill a series of holes along each proposed line of division. One man held the kind of drill known as a "jumper" while another struck the drill with a heavy sledge hammer.[10] A favorite quarry tale tells of a young man looking up from his jumper to observe that the man swinging the sledge above him was cross-eyed. "Which eye are you striking by?" he asked. "Both," said the man with the sledge. "Then, by God, you can hold your own jumper," exclaimed the young man.

Holding a jumper was the work of new hands in a quarry, which usually meant that they were newly arrived Irishmen—so newly arrived sometimes that they passed through the immigration station at New York's Castle Garden on a Monday and found themselves holding a jumper in the Hurley Woods or Jockey Hill on Tuesday. Irish quarrymen like these left their mark upon the Catskills—and it was a mark worth looking for.

75

Quarrymen and Quarry Lore

❧ IN THE SUMMER OF 1850 old established people in the North River bluestone country were turning uneasily in their beds at night and walking the public streets by day with timid alertness. The Saugerties *Telegraph* of September 7 explained why. Rowdyism was rampant, said the *Telegraph*. And the rowdyism "was committed by Irishmen, mostly." These Irishmen usually worked in the bluestone quarries. "It is characteristic of that people when they get intoxicated" they "cannot get along without fighting," the *Telegraph* stated. And the paper must have been something of an authority on fighting for its proprietor was "General" Samuel S. Hommel who had led the Saugerties detachment of militiamen into Woodstock in the Anti-rent War comedy of 1846.

The *Telegraph* went on to pay a crooked compliment to the Irish and to their pastor, the Reverend Mr. Gilligan. The quarry Irish deserve great ·credit for their attendance at the funerals of their people, said the *Telegraph;* their example might well be followed by other classes· of the local population. But once a funeral was over and Mr. Gilligan had left, the "solemnities" "gave way to debaucheries." And fighting inevitably followed. The *Telegraph* proposed taking action. The next time an Irish funeral turned into a fight it would print the names of the combatants. On September 14 the *Telegraph* devoted almost an entire column to a blow-by-blow account of the funeral of John McCormick in which two battlers named Burke and Lynch were starred. On October 19 the *Telegraph* told of a fight between a Mrs. Ham and a Mrs. Rourke "at the quarries"—a chamber pot was used as one of the weapons and Mrs. Rourke was arrested.

On November 23 the *Telegraph* reported a "Riot at Rhinebeck": several hundred Irish workers engaged in pushing the tracks of the Hudson River Railroad onward toward Albany had fought a battle with Con-

naughtmen on one side and "far-downers" on the other. On December 14
the readers of the *Telegraph* were given the details of an argument over a
debt owed to quarryman Laverty by quarryman Tracy. Before the fight
was over Laverty had bitten off the end of Tracy's nose. By the year of the
Laverty-Tracy fight, many Americans had formed underground organizations to combat what they saw as a threat to their own welfare posed by
the immigrant Irish and their Roman Catholic Church. During the 1830s
anti-Irish riots had taken place in Boston and Philadelphia, but then the anti-
Irish movement died down. It flared up with the arrival after 1846 of a
torrent of Irish immigrants driven from their own land by a succession of
total failures of the potato crop. Secret "native American" societies throve
in the North River bluestone country and elsewhere. Local politicians
like Solomon S. Hommel were quick to take advantage of this promising
source of support—it would soon sweep many a man into office and
would almost carry Hommel into the position of Ulster's County Clerk.

Seldom has any group of people arriving in a foreign land to begin a
new life brought with it so many traits and customs that aroused hostility.
In the first place, the Irish immigrants' brand of Christianity appeared to
many Protestants to be an especially sneaky device for destroying their
society. The immigrants were talkative, imaginative, and given to the
open expression of emotion. On Sundays they attended mass and then fearfully shocked their Protestant neighbors by dancing, singing, and drinking
in their little "shebeen shops,"[1] as the *Telegraph* referred to their taverns.

Long years of British misrule had shaped the Irish character into one in
which a profound distrust of government, the ability to endure hardship
without losing a love of life, and a fierce will to survive until Ireland
should be free were all mingled. The Irish drank heavily in order to escape
their miseries, if only for a while. Split by shrewd British policies into opposing groups, they made "faction fighting" with fists and shillelaghs almost
a part of their daily lives. "What, ten o'clock in the morning and not a blow
struck yet!" is a remark sometimes attributed to an Irish grandma and
sometimes to a policeman.

The Irish came among the sober descendants of the pioneers of the
North River bluestone country as an explosion of vitality which could not
be ignored. Those who settled down in American cities took over blocks
or wards and there had to lead lives different in many ways from the ones
they had known in Ireland. But the quarry Irish living in little rural settlements clustered around the quarries could carry on much as they had done
in the old country. Newly arrived young men usually lived in boardinghouses set beside the great slopes of waste stone or "tailings" which rose

beside every quarry. James Butler, a second-generation Irish quarryworker, described one of these houses in Stony Hollow as he saw it one spring morning in 1868. "What a miserable looking place that boarding house is," Butler wrote. "The walls were never lathed or plastered and the chinks and holes in them were in some places ¼ of an inch wide. . . . There were 4 or 5 men seated around the stove with short [clay] pipes black with use and age stuck in their mouths. There was a table on which the remains of the men's breakfast yet laid, this table was composed of pine boards. . . . There were three women all young looking and two of them rather handsome. The youngest named Conroy is a green horn was fetched from Castle Garden yesterday as I looked at her innocent but not unhandsome face I felt sorry to see her situated in such a place. One of the other women was the Boarding master's wife. The other sat by the stove holding a baby, a rough looking character who looked as if she was 'the right woman in the right place.' "[2]

Married men and their families became squatters and ran up hemlock-board shanties close to the quarries and often on their employer's land. There, as in Ireland, the family pig, the family chickens, and the family potato patch were important parts of life. Many of the shanties were not unlike that of a Concord railroad worker which Henry Thoreau vividly described in the first chapter of *Walden* and which he bought, took apart, and used in making his own cottage at Walden Pond. Some quarrymen realized that with prudent management they might do something that was impossible back in Ireland: they might own their own bit of land. One quarryworker found a tiny gore of unclaimed land which had resulted from an imperfect survey at a corner of the lands Robert Livingston of Clermont had taken title to in a swap with Cornelius Tiebout. It was high on the side of Overlook Mountain in a quarry settlement still remembered by a few old-timers as the Irish Village. The man had bought a small but well-framed house in a valley settlement known then as Toodlelum and now as Veteran. He waited for a fine snowy winter day and had the house hauled up Overlook by oxen and set down on his gore.[3] And there it still stands.

No longer standing is a nearby pioneer log cabin taken over by an Irishman and used as a shebeen. Across the road a wooden dance floor was built in a grove of pine trees; it became the center of Irish Village life on summer evenings and drew crowds from other quarry settlements. A quarryman named Patrick Keegan did well in the Irish Village and is remembered with wonder. He eventually saved enough to buy the old Lewis house and farm at the head of Lewis Hollow in which the Village was located. The steeply tilted soil had worn thin after three-quarters of a century of farming, but the house was big enough to hold the Keegan's fifteen children who slept in rows upstairs, the boys at one end of the single room, and the girls at the other. Keegan was a man of prodigious energy and determination. He is said to have been seen plowing his fields by moonlight after a hard day's work in the neighboring California quarries. When a blizzard tore the roof off of his barn, he brought the family cow into the house where she chewed her cud beside the kitchen stove. Up the brook which ran past his house Keegan operated a little part-time quarry of his own. There he cut slabs of flagging to take to valley stores where he could trade them for food for his family—in the North River bluestone country, flagging had almost the status of an official currency and slabs of it might be seen any day leaning against the walls of crossroads stores while waiting to be hauled to the Hudson River stoneyards. Sometimes Keegan worked his quarry at night by the glow of stable lanterns held by his older children. When the brook interfered with work on a promising block of stone, Keegan put together a flume of hemlock boards to carry the stream above his head. And so, old-timers say, he became the first man to quarry bluestone under water.[4]

Life in the Irish Village and in other quarry settlements combined familiar old country ways with new ones. James Butler tells of a greenhorn arriving in a quarry and asking for a job. He had been a stonecutter in a well-known Irish quarry, he explained, and knew the business well. As the older hands looked on, he was set to work on a piece of stone. But he made a botch of it because American bluestone was different from the stone he was used to and insisted that a cutter handle it according to its own requirements.

Most immigrant quarrymen were soon enrolled as voters by Democratic party workers, yet they retained a decided loyalty to Ireland. Periodicals devoted to promoting Irish freedom circulated among them. Young James Butler, walking to work at a quarry one lovely May morning, was reminded by bird voices of a snatch of an Irish song: "The birds ever singing merrily/Hopping from tree to tree/And the song they sang was old Ireland free."[5] Butler wrote in his diary that "my thoughts dwelt long and deep," as he listened to the birds, on the efforts being made to liberate Ireland.

No feature of life in the quarry settlements was more striking than the presence of that wonder of the Western world, the rattlesnake. And these snakes seemed to thrive on the very mountainsides where bluestone could most readily be quarried. Old-timers in the Catskills used to say that,

"St. Patrick drove the bedbugs, the potato bugs and the rattlesnakes out of Ireland—and they all come over here."[6] It was true that there were no snakes in Ireland and that the quarry Irish, potatoes, rattlesnakes, and the bedbugs which move in with the poor tended to gather together in the bluestone country. Before long the Irish had added much to the already rich rattlesnake lore of the Catskills. It was said that Irish Villagers used to toss a few rattlers in a barrel and then head it up. When the children became restless all they had to do was to strike the barrel with a stick and they had as fine a rattle as a youngster could wish. At the base of Overlook, the Lown brothers combined quarrying with making and selling remedies for the physical ills of man and beast. Irish Villagers bought the Lowns' skunk grease for treating their children's colds, and quarrymen swore that nothing would heal a smashed finger more quickly than the rattlesnake oil made by the Lowns from snakes slain at the den on the Minister's Face. They bought snakeskin hatbands to ward off sunstroke and wore belts of rattlesnake skin to prevent the cold and wet of the quarries from giving them rheumatism. They learned to live without fear of the rattlers who turned up at their shanty doors in midsummer. "A rattler is like a bottle of whiskey—you leave it alone and it'll leave you alone,"[7] they used to say.

By the early 1880s the Grand Hotel, the Overlook Mountain House, the Tremper House, and lesser establishments were competing for business with old Mr. Beach's Mountain House—and all were in a kind of race for survival with the bluestone quarries which were threatening to destroy the landscape charm of the Catskills. Boarders grumbled at the ugly quarry scars on mountainsides. They noticed with displeasure a conspicuous quarry erupting even before 1880 near the Catskill Mountain House and a short walk from romantic Moses Rock, and saw quarry after quarry breaking into other mountain forests. Quarries began to threaten the Tremper House from its flanks, while others were unpleasantly visible to boarders approaching the Overlook Mountain House from the Ulster & Delaware station at West Hurley. A stroller on top of Overlook did not have to go many minutes from his hotel porch to hear the songs of wind and birds mingling harshly with the bang and clatter and human shouts of a quarry. In all parts of the mountains, boarders never knew when their surreys or tallyhoes might meet a ponderous stone wagon driven by a cursing teamster in the cloud of dust raised by its horses' hoofs and its wheels. In Kingston, proceedings in the County Court House paused when a succession of bluestone wagons passed by on their way to the great stoneyards of Wilbur; judges, lawyers, plaintiffs and defendants coughed as they resumed their efforts in the dusty air.

Most people accepted the ugliness of the quarries with the same calm their parents and grandparents had shown when faced with the destruction of forests during the tannery days of the Catskills. If some were in a position to get rich by offending the aesthetic sensibilities of others, or by damaging the air they breathed, or by assaulting their ears with unpleasant noise—well, they had every right to do it. Many continued to believe that God had planned the world in this way and that complaining was rank impiety. But a few mountain people resisted. A report of the New York State geologists for 1902 tells that some landowners refused to permit bluestone quarrying on their property because "they feared it would spoil the beauty of the mountains."[8]

The tanlords of the Catskills had not closed up shop because of any clamor by boarders or by lovers of natural beauty; they vanished when the tanbark they required was used up. And it was not a desire to preserve the beauty of the mountains that brought difficulties to the bluestone dealers of the trading towns—it was a cold industrial fact. Two stone-using industries powered by Irish muscle had arisen in and around the Catskills—both went down to defeat together at the hands of a villain named Portland cement. One of the industries was that based on bluestone; the other was based on a kind of clay-bearing limestone found near the old homestead of Jacob Rutsen and Major Johannis Hardenbergh—it could be burned and ground into what became famous as Rosendale cement. The valuable qualities of the formation of limestone accessible near Rosendale and northeastward through Rondout became known in the course of digging for the Ulster and Delaware Canal. At first cement was made from it for use in the canal construction, but by the late 1820s it was manufactured for general sale at Rosendale on lands owned by that keen scenter-out of possible opportunity, Lucas Elmendorf. The Rosendale cement had a few drawbacks but these were usually balanced by virtues. It set slowly but it also set well under water. And it was cheaper than the Portland cement of its day, though that had the advantage of being stronger than its Rosendale rival. Improvements in the quality and manufacturing methods of Portland cement were coming thick and fast by the 1880s. Thomas Cornell's son-in-law, Samuel D. Coykendall, had come to control much of the Rosendale cement industry, and he financed expensive experiments to make Portland cement at Rosendale.[9] Portland cement was not made of a single sort of rock as was the Rosendale kind. Its quality and cheapness depended on finding the right mixture of rocks and clays or shales. Coykendall's experiments failed and in so doing ensured the collapse of both the bluestone and the Rosendale cement industries. Bluestone sidewalks gave way to concrete ones and the Rosendale mines and kilns stood empty. Irish villages and New Dublins came to wear a look of dejection as men and women deserted them and searched for work elsewhere. Those who remained behind were likely to have lungs diseased from overlong breathing of bluestone or cement dust and did not have the energy to move on.

Even before the collapse of the bluestone and cement industries, two new ways by which human beings might relate to the Catskills had begun to affect the mountains. One grew out of the need of city dwellers for increased amounts of water, not only for drinking and bathing but also for fighting fires and flushing toilets. The other way—and this one was more important—grew out of the realization that some of the sad remnants of the magnificent forests which had once covered so much of the land would reward Americans if they were to be preserved from destruction. Forests like these had stirred romantics because they reflected in their wildness the untamed forces that lurk beneath the surface of civilized life. Now they appealed for another reason: their fate seemed to be intertwined with that of prosperous businesses and industries. Certain forests had acquired a value quite apart from the value of their trees at the sawmill, and that value could be expressed in dollars and cents.

76

Commissioner Cox
Climbs Slide Mountain

✤ IT IS HARDLY SURPRISING that when some people think of Slide Mountain they break into sentimental smiles. For the story of Slide belongs to one of the most appealing of all families of stories. Slide is a mountain which rose from obscurity to fame, from rags to riches, suggesting a combination of Cinderella, the Sleeping Beauty, and the heroes of Horatio Alger's books. For a once obscure and even unnamed mountain to become King of the Catskills is the kind of success story that encourages even the least of human beings to smile and feel that he, too, may someday find his most unlikely dream come true.

Apart from all this, Slide has many other and better reasons for fame. One of them is that it played a part in an almost revolutionary event of the mid-1880s. It was then that much of the land once cunningly separated from the Crown by the Hardenbergh patentees was returned to the Crown's successor, the State of New York. The state held and still holds the land in order to protect it against just the kind of shortsighted use the patentees had in mind and to make certain that it will benefit all the people of the state and not a few at the expense of millions of others.

On June 11, 1886, official rites were celebrated on Slide to mark the beginning of the new way of using the Catskills. The central figure in the rites was the Honorable Townsend Cox, one of the three newly appointed forest commissioners of the state of New York. On a fine July morning eighty-four years after Commissioner Cox's visit, I climbed Slide, following as closely as I could in Cox's footsteps. No one had ever paid tribute to the man and to the climb that first drew the attention of Catskill Mountain people to the fact that a new era was opening for the Catskills, and I felt that both deserved commemoration.

I had climbed Slide many times but never before on a day like this—a day when the air was so clear that it seemed hardly to exist and mountains miles away seemed to have moved almost within jumping distance. It had rained fiercely and copiously a day earlier; the world still seemed newly washed and cleansed of its impurities. Encouraged by the rain, the spring near the beginning of the official trail up Slide gushed and gurgled into its roughly fashioned wooden trough; here and there puddles stood on the trail, each with its varied company of little winged beings hovering above it intent on mating and other matters of importance. As I left home that morning I had picked a few ripe raspberries in my garden one thousand feet above sea level; now I noticed that along the trail at well over two thousand feet wild raspberries were still small and green and that a few blossoms still dawdled on to summon bumblebees now that the chill of night had left their joints. I did not follow the New York Conservation Department's well-kept trail up the mountain—it had not been in existence in Commissioner Cox's day. Instead, I turned left a short distance past the watering trough and followed the neglected trail that old Jim Dutcher had laid out soon after Arnold Guyot had found that Slide was the highest of the Catskills. The trail turned this way and that to take advantage of picturesque bits of rock which would be sure to delight the boarders whom Dutcher guided, and it passed through dense beds of ferns and clumps of raspberry bushes. In a patch of sun beside one of these clumps I saw a young blacksnake enjoying the morning warmth—he did not stir as I passed him.

This was the very trail used by Commissioner Cox in 1886. He and his party had climbed up the same series of stone steps which had been put in place by Dutcher in order to make the ascent easier for lady hikers. Higher and higher the trail led. Soon an occasional balsam fir tree appeared among the twisted yellow birches. More and more leaves of the striped oxalis filled spaces between decaying logs and boulders, their green leaves punctuated by anemonelike blossoms. At last a few late blossoms of the dwarf cornel stood side by side with the oxalis flowers, a sure sign that I was nearing the point near the summit at which the Dutcher trail and the newer official one coincided. Suddenly the two trails met.

Balsam firs now stood along the broad official trail sometimes packed as closely as humans along a Fourth of July parade route—gaunt skeletons of elderly trees killed by a dry spell of a few years back, vigorous young trees, and little ones less than a foot high helping to saturate the air with their sun-released fragrance. The trail moved gently upward over stretches of exposed bedrock alternating more and more often with patches of white

sand and pebbles formed by the breaking down of the conglomeratic sandstone which forms much of the capstone of the Catskills.

The top of Slide is long and broad and sometimes seems to a hiker
as if it would never come to an end. But at last it does, and in a sort of
magical illusion like nothing else to be seen among the Catskills. The
upward angle of the path lessens, the path levels, it leads on over white
pebbles between what appear for a while to be sand dunes sprinkled with
the kind of low bushes able to survive the rigors of the rocky coastline
which seems to lie just ahead. Beyond that line, of course, are the blue
waves of the sea coming in from a distant and blurred horizon. For a
moment the illusion holds, then it crumbles as we realize that it is
impossible to be on a mountaintop and a seacoast at the same time. The
waves resolve themselves into a combination of the great artificial lake
known as the Ashokan Reservoir and long lines of hills and mountains.
The rocky coastline becomes the topmost ledge of Slide's abrupt eastern
face, cleared for almost a century of the thicket of balsam firs it once bore.

In June 1886, Commissioner Cox had climbed to the top of Slide
accompanied by a party of officials. I was climbing in 1970, alone. I walked
to one of the log shelters the New York Conservation Department maintains
on Slide's broad summit and chatted with a man and a boy camping out in
one of them. They spoke of having been roused the night before by a
porcupine and a raccoon, and asked the names of some of the mountains
visible from Slide's top. After that contact with humanity, I felt better
able to imagine the commissioner and his attendants standing close to where
I stood but on top of one of the many towers that had been raised on
Slide in a never entirely successful effort to provide a satisfying view in all
directions from a single spot.

I did not know much about the commissioner other than that he had
been a New York businessman and City Commissioner of Charities and
Correction. I visualized him as of medium height, rather plump, and
with a squarish, overpurposeful face. But here I was guessing and probably
letting my prejudices against politicians affect my imagination. But if Cox's
appearance was a mystery, why he came to Slide and what he did there
were plain enough, for his visit had been given ample publicity and newspaper reporters had accompanied him and written stories to let the public
know exactly what the commissioner did and said on Slide. He had come
to make an official inspection of that part of the recently created State
Forest Preserve which lay among the Catskills. Mountain people first
heard of the commissioner's impending visit when the Kingston *Leader*
of June 9 told them that on Monday the seventh at half-past two o'clock,

"four men on horseback, dressed in rough mountain clothes, left Kingston." The men were all high Ulster County officeholders, and they proposed joining Commissioner Cox and a group of state officials at the Big Indian station of the Ulster & Delaware Railroad. They were well mounted— Judge A. B. Parker, who would run for President of the United States against Theodore Roosevelt in 1904, bestrode "a buckskin mustang," while another official rode "a yellow Mexican with a brindle eye." The party rode through Woodstock to the Corner now known as the hamlet of Mount Tremper and so up the Esopus Valley to Big Indian, pausing along the way to tell town dignitaries of their important mission. At Big Indian more county officials were waiting with the editor of the *Leader* and a reporter for the New York *Times*. The whole party piled into two wagons and were driven to the point on the banks of the West Branch of the Neversink Creek at which the trail up Slide began.

The ascent of Slide by the commissioner and his party was far more difficult than might have been expected. The Dutcher trail was in deplorable condition. The erosion caused by spring rains and melting snow had not been repaired, trees felled across the trail by a recent storm had not been removed, and it required twice the usual hour and a half for the commissioner and his party to make the climb. All this was understandable enough to mountain people of 1886. Commissioner Cox was a Democrat who served under Governor David B. Hill, the Democratic boss of New York State. Hill was known for his presidential ambitions, his awesome ability at squeezing political advantage from the most unlikely situations, and his skill in holding together a political party which threatened every moment to fly apart. That was why Commissioner Cox's retinue was composed entirely of working Democrats who would be grateful to the governor for this chance to be seen taking part in an important public event. It was probably why, when it came to choosing a guide, Republican Jim Dutcher, who had laid out and maintained the only trail up Slide and was known as the very incarnate spirit of the mountain, was passed over in favor of hotel man C. C. Winne, a Democrat with a large and devoted following.[1] And it is also apparently why Dutcher had not made the slightest attempt to clear the trail up which the commissioner and his fellow Democrats had to struggle.

Once on top of the tower on the summit, the commissioner pronounced the view to be every bit as fine as anything to be seen in the Adirondacks. He commented, apparently with surprise, at the small amount of fire damage to be seen. On the way down he paused to point out one of the many places which still kept its original thick forest carpet of mosses and decaying vegetation. He picked up a handful and, as he squeezed water from it, explained that this was a good example of the usefulness to man of forests such as that covering most of Slide—their spongy floors held water and released it slowly to replenish rivers and check floods. After spending the night in a simple farmhouse near the base of Slide and sampling the maple syrup, trout, and buckwheat cakes of the vicinity, Commissioner Cox discussed his trip to Slide and its neighborhood with the reporters. The state-owned lands on Slide and in its vicinity were important to the people of the state of New York, he said, because of the rivers to which they helped give birth. Rains falling on Slide might find their way into the West Branch of the Neversink and so by way of the Delaware River to the sea. Rains falling a bit farther north would rush down the Esopus to the Hudson and on to New York Bay. Greene County water—and the state also held lands in Greene as part of its Forest Preserve—might go down the Kaaterskill to the Hudson or take the Schohariekill and flow by a roundabout route to the Hudson, serving on the way to replenish the Erie Canal.[2]

For many years there had been animated discussion in many parts of New York State of setting apart much of the Adirondacks as a Forest Preserve to be kept as untouched wilderness or perhaps used for growing timber. The discussion had often been heated and angry, for powerful financial, industrial, and commercial interests were involved and had come into direct conflict with the hopes of men and women who had no personal interest in the Adirondacks but wanted them guarded for the benefit of future generations. Until the year before Commissioner Cox's visit, no one had urged in public that the Catskills be joined with the Adirondacks to form a Forest Preserve. The inclusion of the Catskills, to which Cox's visit drew widespread public attention, was not the result of the arguments of artists or other idealistic people, of summer boardinghouse and hotel keepers, or of trout fishermen, all of whom had reasons for wanting the Catskills' forests preserved. The Catskills became part of the Forest Preserve because of human motivations as devious as those which prompted the granting of the Hardenbergh Patent in 1708. In 1879 and 1881 the political leaders of Ulster County had successfully urged upon the state legislature actions that soon threatened to cost the people of Ulster dearly. It was in order to prevent this threat from being realized that the Catskills became—almost surreptitiously—a part of the Forest Preserve.

77

The Catskill Forest Preserve

✣ IN 1849, Arnold Guyot published a book called *Earth and Man* which dealt with the ways in which the earth's mountains, plains, rivers, and seas had affected the human race. In 1864 a friend of Guyot's, the brilliant Vermonter, George Perkins Marsh, published his *Man and Nature* which reversed Guyot's direction and dealt with the ways in which man had affected the earth—and these did not make pleasant reading. The book had an immediate effect both in the United States and in Europe. It marked the beginning for Americans of an understanding of what later came to be called ecology. Once Marsh spoke out, many thoughtful Americans wondered if their policy of looting the continent they had snatched from its Indian owners was as sensible as they had once believed. In his 1823 opinion in the case of Johnson *vs.* McIntosh, Chief Justice Marshall had encouraged the belief that the conquering and robbing of the American Indians by European invaders was justified because the Indians were not making a good use of the land but were keeping it in wilderness. Now at least some Americans realized that by slaughtering the American wilderness and mistreating soil and water they had been behaving like thoughtless and poverty-stricken heirs who have come into possession of limited bank deposits which they were spending in such a spectacular way that everyone believed them to be enormously rich. But they were merely hastening the day when their deposits would be exhausted and they would be poor once again.

As a boy in Vermont, Marsh had seen forests vanish wastefully down the throats of sawmills, and newly cleared hillside farms give good crops for a few years and then send their topsoil down into the valley to choke rivers and form swamps. Later, when he traveled in the Near and Middle East, he had seen lonely deserts which had taken the place of great cities and of fertile valleys once capable of supporting thousands of human beings. In a flash of illumination, Marsh related what he had seen in Vermont to what he was seeing on the sites of vanished Eastern cities and farms, and he understood that unless the looting of the soil and water of the United States were checked, his nation, too, might become as incapable of supporting human life as much of the East. He wrote *Man and Nature* as a warning to the people of the United States.

The distant ancestors of Marsh and other Americans had once understood that all living things of their earth and the rocks, air, and water were interrelated. They had given expression to this understanding, which is common to all people who live close to the soil, by a system of magical and religious observances. Later, romanticism renewed the sense of kinship of man with all other living and non-living things and gave it expression in the arts and in the study of the natural world. The cult of the noble savage and of the wilderness arose even as most Americans regarded Indians and trees as their natural enemies and as they devoted much of their energy to destroying them and then looting the soil in which tree roots had spread. The novels of James Fenimore Cooper, George P. Morris' sentimental and popular "Woodman Spare That Tree," the paintings of the Hudson River school, and many other indications of concern with the ravaging of the American landscape began having an effect by the 1840s. In that decade James Cullen Bryant suggested that New York City create green parks in order to help city dwellers keep in touch with the world of nature, and painter George Catlin proposed that the federal government establish national parks.[1] By the early 1850s Henry Thoreau was proposing that mountaintops and other areas of interest and value to the growing body of American nature lovers be publicly owned as democratic successors to the great parks of European royalty. During the 1860s work on New York's Central Park was proceeding, and in 1864, as Marsh's book appeared, social worker Charles Loring Brace wrote an editorial in the New York *Times* to suggest that the Adirondack Mountains were "fitted to make a Central Park for the world."[2]

New York City businessmen, aroused by Marsh's warnings, began to give some thought to Brace's suggestion. Their city owed much of its prosperity to its fine harbor and its position at the mouth of the navigable Hudson leading on through the Erie Canal to the west. What if Marsh's fears were to prove justified and if their harbor were to be choked with silt brought down from the Adirondacks as lumbermen bent only on immediate private profit ripped away the mountains' protective coat of trees? What if the streams feeding the Erie Canal were to fail as the mountains among which they were born lost their forests and ceased helping to maintain a more nearly regular flow of water from their sides?

The businessmen of New York and those who profited from traffic on the Erie Canal began joining forces in a small way with other groups urging that the Adirondack forests be protected. Some of these groups were moved by aesthetic considerations; others wanted hunting and fishing preserved; still others followed Verplanck Colvin who began a private survey of the Adirondacks in 1865 and in 1868 urged "the creation of an Adirondack Park or timber preserve, under the charge of a forest warden and deputies."[3] Colvin was in sympathy with a group that wanted the Adirondacks protected in order to ensure a timber supply for future generations. Of all the groups the only one with power to put effective pressure on the state legislature, which alone had the power to create a park or preserve, were the businessmen of New York. Their chief opponents were upstate lumbermen, land speculators, and railroad promoters—and these men also wielded power over the legislature.

In the early years of discussion of the setting up of a Forest Preserve, the Catskills were not mentioned. And while the Catskills stood aside from the argument, the battle to protect the Adirondacks continued.[4] In 1872 the protectionists were heartened when the national Congress set up the Yellowstone National Park at the urging of those who believed that great natural wonders should belong to all the people. Because the Yellowstone was not yet reachable by railroad, no powerful interests had been able to devise ways by which it might be turned to private profit, which made its conversion into a park possible. That same year the New York legislature was prevailed upon to create a State Park Commission charged with the duty of reporting on the proposed Adirondack state park, and Verplanck Colvin became the commission's secretary. His private survey of the mountains was now sponsored and financed by the state. The commission's report made in 1873 favored the creation of "the projected forest park." But the legislature did nothing to carry out the commission's recommendations—the pressures applied by those who profited from the destruction of the Adirondacks' forests were too strong to be overcome by the none-too-well organized opposition. For ten years the report rested in its pigeonhole, emerging now and then for a brief flutter.

During the late seventies the same spurt of building that had placed so many hotels on summits and in valleys of the Catskills sent the price of lumber soaring and set lumbermen to attacking the Adirondacks' forests with renewed vigor. By 1882 editorials in New York newspapers and in sportsmen's magazines were urging the public to get together to "save the

Adirondacks" from the conquering lumbermen. The editorials increased in number in 1883 when attempts to open up the Yellowstone Park to private exploitation closely followed the arrival of a railroad and seemed likely to succeed and furnish an example to raiders of the Adirondacks. The public responded, especially the New York City businessmen who felt their profits would suffer from a stripping away of the Adirondacks' forests. In 1884 mass "Save the Adirondacks" meetings were sponsored by a group of New York businessmen's organizations including the Board of Trade and Transportation, the Mercantile Exchange, the Maritime Exchange, the Anti-monopoly League, real estate associations, the Produce and Stock Exchange, and the Wine, Spirits and Distillers' Exchange. The meetings were enthusiastic and well attended. Former Secretary of the Interior Carl Schurz was applauded when he stated that the "Adirondack forests must be protected"[5]: if not, the Erie Canal would become unnavigable and the Mohawk Valley and much of the rest of the state "a barren waste." Schurz was listened to with respect, for it was he who had presided over the creation of the Yellowstone National Park. Another speaker was Francis Thurber, fresh from his Lotus Land in the Catskills. The state legislature soon reeled under the pressures being applied from all sides. Hunters and fishermen, lovers of wilderness scenery, lumber barons with huge bank accounts, followers of Wordsworth, Emerson, and Henry Thoreau, waterfall fanciers, advocates of scientific tree growing and lumbering—all made their ideas and hopes known. Some proposed hitching the saving of the Adirondack forests to a state college of forestry, to a museum, to the use of all state-owned land in all parts of New York for growing trees to ensure a good supply of timber for the future. When it became apparent that the phrase "Adirondack Park" had a frivolous sound to upstate and rural ears, advocates of the park began calling it the Forest Preserve.

Both houses of the state legislature first responded to the pressures by appointing a variety of committees; the committees reported; their reports were filed; and more committees appeared and in turn reported. In January 1885 the committee of committees reported—its chairman was the greatest American authority on trees of his day, Charles Sprague Sargent, Professor of Arboriculture at Harvard and long-time director of the great Arnold Arboretum.

Professor Sargent and his committee visited the Catskills and concluded that they were not suited for inclusion in the Forest Preserve. They had been so thoroughly ransacked by lumbermen and barkpeelers that their "merchantable timber"[6] was gone. Fire had "more than once swept the

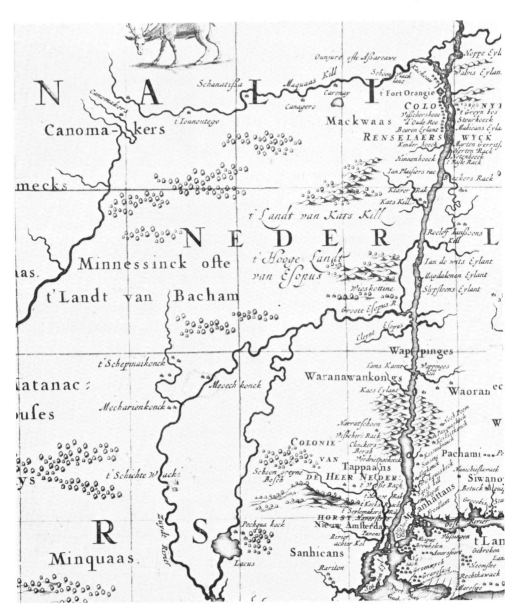

Detail from the Visscher map of New Netherlands, 1655. Here the Catskills are shown in a way that reflects confusion about their character and name. (*Courtesy of Rare-Book Room, New York Public Library.*)

Right, looking up the line of the Otis Elevating Railroad from its station at the base of the mountain. Early twentieth-century photograph by Davis of Catskill. (*Courtesy of Mabel Parker Smith.*)

Below, the elaborate Twilight Park Inn shown as it looked shortly before it was destroyed by fire in the 1920s. (*Courtesy of Greene County Historical Society.*)

Below right, observation towers like this one on the Wittenberg were often lashed together from spruce and balsam fir poles. (*Geroldseck-Schadle Collection.*)

Walking in the Mountains.

ARE you a lover of this art, and do you know the pleasures of this recreation? If not the mountains are the place to learn how to enjoy walking?

FREE AND EASY.

There are fashions and airs of pedestrians as in dressing, and not one lady in ten practices it correctly for health or true pleasure. There is the swaggering air, the erect gait, the contented tread of aristocracy, the quiet pace, the shuffling step, the stoop or the halt pace—and few walk correctly.

The toes should point out; keep the head erect, the shoulders carried back, the chest well expanded, and let the feet move in graceful curves, using "the Alpine staff" for support. One fault of most ladies walking easily is tight shoes and close, unfitting garments.

Few women give their feet the necessary backward spring for carrying the body lightly and evenly forward. Nearly all walk on their heels and in a deliberate manner, as if they knew it and were glad of it. Others stride on flat footed and heavy, with noses in the air and hands clinched as if they meant business, or

TEN MILE GAIT.

SWEET SIXTEEN.

step unevenly as if avoiding imaginary obstacles, or carry their heads forward, their steps loose and shuffling, and not a few have that walk peculiar to affected women of taking a step and turning the head one way, and going another way. But perhaps the most ungraceful walker is the woman who turns her toes in and lets her feet fall with a slouchy, flip-flap motion. Unless the foot is really deformed, this horrible habit can be controlled by walking slowly and with care.

THE STOOP GAIT.

Students have a walk characteristic of their profession. They amble along in a day dream, forgotten in the absorption of some beautiful fancy, their heads lowered, eyes fastened on the ground, or looking dreamily into space, the inevitable book or portfolio under their arms.

You can always tell a real swell girl by her walk. She goes along so swimmingly and yet doesn't seem conscious of it. She is so light and yet so firm, and there is so much elasticity in her step.

It is easy to tell the girl who has just returned from abroad. Her skirts quite short, she holds an umbrella with airy grace, and her two little feet, (with no more spring than if they were made of wood), peep in and out as she walks.

Among various groups of hurrying girls some carry themselves with dignity and ease, though walking fast; but, as a rule, they surrender grace to speed and get over the ground on their heels, the shoulders strained forward in the effort to walk against time. For this reason most of them swing their arms or their elbows.

With women devotees the fashion of walking is much the same.

Woman's disposition has been judged by her palm, face, dress, voice, etc., and why not by her walk, what is more characteristic?

Our special artist W. D. Nichols, of *Outing*, sketched some of these gaits of ladies during his visit to the Columbian last summer.

OUR BLOOMER.

Walking was a major activity of summer boarders in the nineteenth-century Catskills. These instructions in the art appeared in Sylvanus Lyon's *Outing in the Catskills*, N.Y., 1889. The booklet was published to attract patrons to the Columbian Hotel in Cairo in which author Lyon had an interest.

Summer boarders climb
Blackhead Mountain. From
*Frank Leslie's Illustrated
Newspaper,* September 1, 1877.

Below, summer boarders
explore an abandoned
barkpeeler's cabin in
Woodland Valley.
(*Geroldseck-Schadle
Collection.*)

Every fall, after their boarders left, mountain men went hunting. Sometimes, as in this case, they took city people along. (*Geroldseck-Schadle Collection.*)

Even in isolated hollows mountain people dressed up on Sunday and if there was nothing more exciting to do could always lean against the pasture fence. Photograph of early 1890s. (*Author's collection.*)

A bluestone quarry of the early twentieth century. Painted from memory and old photographs by folk painter Marie Siemsen of Sawkill. (*Courtesy of Marie Siemsen.*)

Hauling bluestone to market. (*Photograph from Harry Siemsen, Sawkill.*)

entire region," the Professor wrote, "destroying the reproductive powers of the forest as originally composed and ruining the thin soil covering the hills." Sargent did not regard protecting the Catskills as of "much general importance." Nor did he believe that the Catskills' streams deserved protection because, in his opinion, they were "of local influence only." Yet when the Forest Preserve bill became law, there were the Catskills safely inside.

What had happened forms as fine an example as anyone could wish of the way human beings have of sometimes doing the right thing for the wrong reason. All the details will never be known but it is plain that a deal had been made by which lands in the Catskills owned by the County of Ulster and lying on and near Slide Mountain were turned over to the state as part of the Forest Preserve in return for the forgiveness of a tax indebtedness by the county of about forty thousand dollars. The indebtedness started to be built up in 1879 when Ulster was included by act of legislature in a group of counties that became the owners of lands for which no acceptable bids were received at the tax sales held from time to time, though ordinarily such lands would go to the state. And there was a great deal of such land in Ulster. Tanners and lumbermen and charcoal burners were in the habit of buying mountain lands, taking what trees they wanted, and then abandoning them, which made good sense from a private point of view but bad sense for the public. When taxes remained unpaid for a stipulated period, the lands came up at tax sales. Lawyers and politicians and their hangers-on were frequent buyers. Because tax titles had certain disadvantages which weighed more heavily against the poor than the rich, few ordinary citizens were buyers at tax sales. The lands most easily sold were those suitable for the hunting and fishing preserves being built up in the Catskills around 1880 by rich New Yorkers. These preserves were resented by mountain people who found themselves forbidden to fish or hunt on land they and their ancestors had roamed at will ever since the days when they formed parts of the commons of the holdings of the Livingstons and other Hardenbergh Patent landlords. Armed guards patrolled the preserves and sometimes arrested local citizens for trespassing.[7] The burned-over or cutover county lands were open to the public but they were not good hunting or fishing country. Old-timers and young alike grumbled at being refused the right to hunt and fish which had been theirs from the first settlement of the Catskills. Year after year the county-owned lands were increasing, and were left unprotected against fire or depredation, for the county had named no official to care for them and they existed in a legal limbo. With years of taxes still unpaid to the state, the county would not even have a good title to them until the back taxes were cleared away.

In 1708, Major Johannis Hardenbergh had been a key mover in the successful attempt to separate a million and a half acres of the Catskills from the British crown. Now, as about fifty thousand of those acres went back to the state of New York, there was a kind of appropriateness in the fact that a central figure in the process was a descendant of the major. He was bearded bachelor Cornelius A. C. Hardenbergh, supervisor of the town of Shawangunk and at times chairman of Ulster's Board of Supervisors. Supervisor Hardenbergh was widely known for his views on money and taxes. He was in favor of money but not in favor of paying taxes. During the early days of the Civil War he had been a wheelwright, but when his shop became subject to a wartime tax, he closed it rather than pay. He then announced that he did not favor losing a single life or spending a single penny to free the slaves. When he vigorously opposed a tax meant to supply money for bonding his town for railroad purposes, admiring fellow citizens elected him supervisor on the Democratic ticket.[8] As a member of the County Board of Supervisors he quietly played a part in the maneuvers that had led to the acquiring of tax-sale lands by the county; after that he supported the reluctance of his board to pay to the state the back and current taxes on their rapidly increasing mountain lands. When the comptroller of the state billed the board for taxes, Hardenbergh was ready with objections. He was appointed a committee of one to visit Albany and discuss the matter with Comptroller Chapin. Hardenbergh returned to report no progress but that the comptroller had informed him that of all the sixty-four counties in the state, Ulster was the sole tax delinquent. The comptroller went to the courts and obtained an order requiring Ulster to pay up.[9]

By the time Hardenbergh faced Comptroller Chapin, the news of Ulster's tax difficulties was spread abroad—the New York *Times* made its comment on November 24, 1884—and Supervisor Hardenbergh was on the verge of leaving his post on the Ulster Board of Supervisors, for his sound views on money and taxes had elected him a member of the State Assembly. There Hardenbergh lost no time in offering legislation designed to correct "illegal, unequal or erroneous assessments" for tax purposes; he also took part with his Republican Ulster colleague G. D. B. Hasbrouck in a complex series of deals, compromises, and trades which were going on as the legislature buckled down to the task of putting together a bill to create a State Forest Preserve. The businessmen of New York with their horrified vision of a choked harbor, a weed-grown business district, and a dry Erie Canal had prevailed. In March 1885, Cornelius Hardenbergh introduced a bill that forbade the state to sell a single acre of its lands in the Catskills. On April 20 the acts of 1879 and 1881 under which Ulster County had become possessed of its mountain lands were repealed and the lands passed in due time to the state. On May 15 the bill creating the Forest Preserve and providing for its administration and protection became law. The Ulster politicians had triumphantly gotten off the hook. Instead of having to face their constituents as bunglers who had saddled their county with a debt of forty thousand dollars, they had become heroes of a battle to save the Catskills. And it must have been a source of great satisfaction to Assemblyman Hardenbergh that under a provision of the new law, the state now would pay taxes every year on its lands in the Catskills to Ulster towns.

To pass an act is one thing, but to put it into operation is quite another. The upstate lumbermen, railroad promoters, land speculators, and bankers who had opposed the law were not disheartened. Their allies in the legislature had yielded to the protectionists; now they were prepared to be equally yielding toward the anti-protectionists. Members were appointed to the Forest Commission who were secret partners in schemes for acquiring state timberlands in the Adirondacks; at least one was frankly in the lumber business. The state openly sold or traded parts of its forest lands and permitted cutting of timber on lands it retained. In 1893 the legislature legalized the kind of flouting of the Forest Preserve Act that had been going on ever since 1885. It passed a law giving the Forest Commission authority to approve the alienation of its forest lands and the cutting of the most commercially valuable timber.[10] It seemed, for a moment, that the end of the Forest Preserve was in sight.

The members of the legislature were not prepared for the cry of outrage which rose all over the state and especially in the city of New York. There the business organizations that had originally sponsored the Forest Preserve engaged in a second struggle to save the Adirondacks. As before 1885, the New York Board of Trade and Transportation, the Chamber of Commerce, and many other groups took the lead. This time they hit upon a masterly piece of strategy. A State Constitutional Convention was scheduled for 1894; the businessmen would bypass the hopelessly corrupt legislature and make the convention their battleground. They sponsored an addition to the constitution that would not only require the lands of the Forest Preserve "to be forever kept as wild forest lands," but would also specifically forbid the abuses of the previous nine years. Thereafter the Forest Preserve was directly under the protection of the constitution, and neither the legislature nor the governor could connive at evasions. The constitutional protection could be altered only by amendments approved at the polls by the people.[11] This has proved an awkward arrangement. Yet it left—and still leaves—less opportunity for private raids on the Preserve than any other arrangement known to our society.

Once the Catskills came under the protection of the State Constitution, most mountain people accepted the new Forest Preserve as a good thing. The presence of state-owned and protected land to climb and hike in stimulated the summer-boarding business. The fear of being trapped in a forest-surrounded hotel by a forest fire lessened as patchwork fire fighting by towns was buttressed by the state's regional approach to this regional problem.

In no way did the creation of the Catskill Forest Preserve arouse greater approval among mountain and summer people than by its efforts toward increasing the supply of game fish and mammals. During the 1870s the state was already supplying trout for use in restocking the state's streams. By the time the Forest Preserve became a fact, nearly all the Catskills' streams were recovering from the pollution of tannery days, and primeval and second-growth forest protecting their headwaters made them cool enough to furnish a good environment for trout. The legislature had been liberal in its appropriations for growing and distributing young trout and the trout were being used to stock even private streams and lakes. Mountain people did not like to see the trout placed in the streams controlled by private fishing clubs or New York City people rich enough to have private preserves of their own and expressed their resentment by poaching.[12]

With the help of the State's Forest Commission, deer were brought back to the Catskills. Once deer had been especially numerous on the brushland which separated fields and pastures from the inhospitable forest. But by the beginning of the 1880s intense hunting and a growing human population had made a glimpse of a deer an event to be talked about for months. In 1887 the state legislature authorized the Forest Commission to set up a deer park along the headwaters of the west branch of the Neversink, close to the foot of Slide Mountain. Two hundred acres were enclosed within a ten-foot-high fence, and the deer confined there soon multiplied. Young people who had never seen a deer visited the park on Sundays and goggled at these wonders. By 1895 the herd had grown so large that ninety-five deer were released.[13] These deer were small because of the artificiality of their upbringing, yet they were healthy and vigorous and before long their descendants were thoroughly at home among the mountains. Farmers sometimes complained that the deer fraternized with their cattle and taught them to jump over fences or destroyed crops. But most mountain people and the summer boarders heartily welcomed the returning deer.

A new era was beginning for the Catskills. As second growth trees on state-owned land reached marketable size, they remained to protect the Catskills' streams and soil instead of being cut and so beginning a new cycle of fire, stream pollution, and erosion. Mountaintops were available for hikers, climbers, and campers. Fishermen and hunters were welcomed. Opposition to public ownership continued and from time to time attempts were made to turn over parts of the mountains to people who hoped to use them for private profit without regard to the public welfare. But by the late 1890s the Forest Preserve was inspiring confidence in its ability to survive all attempts to destroy it; land was being added in both the Catskills and the Adirondacks; and better fire-control measures were being taken. Still some mountain people were filled with hostility toward the Preserve. They objected to the state's refusal to allow them to burn off mountainsides in order to improve the huckleberry crop and they resented the increasingly strict enforcement of game laws. These people grumbled more than ever during the 1890s when rumors began spreading around the southern Catskills that the mountains were in danger from a new source. A corporation called the Ramapo Water Company was moving into the mountains. Its agents were going from farm to farm in the Esopus Valley and that of Woodstock's Beaverkill. They were buying options on land and stream rights in what looked like an attempt to monopolize the water of the Catskills. In 1885 Professor Sargent had stated that the streams of the Catskills had only a "local influence." Now he was about to be proved wrong.

78

The Ashokan Reservoir Is Built

✤   In 1861 the trustees of Kingston began looking toward the Catskills in the hope of finding a good source of water for their growing
village. In that year a committee appointed by the trustees reported that
Kingston's water supply was far from adequate.[1] The Committee stated
that once the village had been known for the large numbers of its people
who reached an advanced age, but this was no longer true. A poor water
supply was breeding disease and shortening lives. In addition water was
not available when fire broke out; a better supply was urgently needed.
The members of the committee did not recommend the conveniently
placed Esopus Creek as a source because they found it to be badly
contaminated by the tanneries which were devouring the hemlock forests
along the creek's upper waters. Woodstock's Sawkill seemed more promising: its headwaters were free from contamination. A quarter of a century
after the committee made its report, the Esopus tanneries had disappeared
with the hemlock forests. The stream's water had become less evil in smell
and taste and Kingston considered building a reservoir at Bishop's Falls on
the Esopus. There the bedrock was strong enough to support a big dam.[2]
For years a gristmill had stood beside the falls—it had been operated by a
famous blind miller named Bishop. The miller was said to be able to do
almost anything a sighted man could do. Local people, wondering at his
remarkable adaptation to blindness, said that Jake Bishop could even tell
the color of a horse by touching it. Bishop's Falls had long been a favorite
goal for summer boarders who liked to watch the water tumbling down the
walls of the rocky amphitheater beside the romantic-looking old mill where
blind Jake Bishop had once gone about his work with confident steps. As
the boarders exclaimed at the loveliness of the falls and as the trustees of
Kingston dawdled over the project of damming the Esopus at that spot,
engineers of a somewhat secretive corporation, the Ramapo Water Com-

pany,[3] stepped in and seized the falls. Kingston had to be satisfied with a monopoly of the waters of Woodstock's Sawkill, Mink Hollow Brook, and Cooper's Lake.

The city of New York had grown in wealth and population during the last quarter of the nineteenth century. As the century approached its end, it became plain that what had once been suburbs of the city—places like Brooklyn, the Bronx, and Staten Island—had become for all practical purposes parts of one immense city, and in 1898 the boroughs officially did become parts of the city of New York. This made certain problems glaringly apparent. One was that the water supply of the consolidated city was a leaky patchwork of reservoirs, wells, and streams which could no longer be relied upon to take care of New York's needs. The men behind the Ramapo Water Company had been aware for some time that this moment of understanding would soon come and they had taken steps to profit by it. For years they had been assembling options on water rights. At first on New Jersey's Ramapo River. Later they fanned out into Connecticut, Rockland, Dutchess and Orange counties in New York. In 1899 they sent their men to invade the Catskills in search of all the water rights they could find, and soon they were buying options in Sullivan and Delaware counties. When New York City officials began considered planning a better supply of water they found themselves blocked wherever they looked by the Ramapo men. Ramapo made a proposition to the city: they would supply it with excellent water in virtually unlimited quantities—for a price.[4]

As in the days of the fight to save the Adirondacks, New York business organizations took up the battle to save New York City from exploitation by men bent only upon private profit. A vast number of hearings, angry disputes, legal arguments and behind-the-scenes dealing followed before the battle was won and New York was free to have a publicly owned and operated water system using the Catskills' Esopus and Schoharie creeks and their tributaries. In the spring of 1905 the state legislature created state and municipal water commissions—over the vehement objections of Kingston's Judge A. T. Clearwater. On November 25 of that year the State Water Commission held the first of a series of public hearings at Kingston as a preliminary to buying land and rights and constructing two reservoirs with a combined watershed of 571 square miles, one on the Esopus and the other—to be built later—on the Schohariekill near Prattsville. This second reservoir would empty into the first by means of a tunnel bored through the underlying rocks of the Catskills. An aqueduct would convey the water ninety-two miles to the New York City line.

The hearing room was packed to capacity as Judge Clearwater took the lead in opposing construction of the Ashokan Reservoir. The legislative act under which the hearings were being held was unconstitutional, he argued. In addition the reservoir would constitute a perpetual menace to the towns and cities located downstream, for the Esopus Creek in flood was a murderous tyrant which no amount of engineering skill could domesticate. The judge battled fiercely for he was representing not only his favorite client, the Ulster & Delaware Railroad, but also a troop of banks, business houses, large landowners, and business organizations. His client Samuel Coykendall spoke in person on behalf of his railroad which lay in the path of the proposed reservoir. By 1925 the reservoir would prove inadequate, he stated, so why not build a reservoir to take advantage of the far greater watersheds of the Adirondacks? Such a plan had been under discussion for more than a quarter of a century and corporations had been formed to promote it. The people of the Catskills did not want a New York City reservoir; their boardinghouse keepers would lose half a million a year in profits should the Ashokan Reservoir be built, Coykendall said— boarders would be frightened off by the thousands of rough men brought in to work with picks and shovels.[5] The people of the Catskills would be saved from disaster only by the building of an Adirondack water supply for New York.

All arguments were in vain. The State Water Supply Commission decided in favor of the city of New York. The anger and resentment sputtering in and around the Catskills became a roar of protest. The city of New York now had the right under law to buy the land their ancestors had cleared from farmers and to force rural shopkeepers to find other employment. It was like the days of the Livingstons and the other old landlords all over again. "It is such acts as this that caused the Antirent War seventy years ago,"[6] the Kingston *Freeman* asserted. Unless New York City behaved with greater respect for the rights of mountain people, a "People's Rights War" might follow, so the Pine Hill *Sentinel* hinted on April 14, 1906.

The lawyers of Kingston reacted to the decision of the Water Commission with elation. To this day elderly Kingston people sometimes refer to the years of construction of the Ashokan Reservoir as "the time they shook the plum tree." They call the Esopus Valley "plum tree land." Never since the greatest days of the Hardenbergh Patent had such profits been squeezed out of the Catskills and into lawyers' pockets as during the years between 1906 and 1915 when the reservoir was completed and began sending water to the city of New York. But few citizens of the lands to be covered by the reservoir shared the lawyers' elation—not at first. When they protested against building the reservoir they saw themselves caricatured in New York newspapers as uncouth bumpkins. Later they were subjected to the rudeness of surveyors who invaded their fields, cut down trees, and made gaps in their pasture fences as they prepared part of the Esopus Valley for conversion into a lake. Hidden hostility toward the New Yorkers who had been their summer boarders now came into the open. New York people, it was said, were arrogant Sabbath-breaking and ignorant barbarians who believed that the people north of their city line existed only for the convenience or profit of New York.[7]

As the size and scope of the proposed reservoir and its watershed became known, apprehension increased. Two fleets of battleships could do battle on the reservoir. If all the water in the proposed reservoir should join that in all New York's other reservoirs and descend upon the city at once, New York would be flooded under two hundred and fifty feet of water and everyone there would be drowned—and a good thing too, thought many an upstater. Bishop's Falls would disappear behind the longest dam of its kind then existing anywhere in the world. The inhabitants not only of farms but also of seven hamlets would be forced to flee. They would be joined by the bodies of almost three thousand people who had been quietly awaiting the judgment day in thirty-two Esopus Valley cemeteries, for New York's almost twenty-four square miles of the Esopus Valley would be scraped clean of every vestige of its former inhabitants and their works before fastidious New Yorkers would drink the Ashokan Reservoir's water.[8]

Resentment reached a peak early in 1906. And then it quickly faded. People who had taken out the Anti-rent War masks and gowns of their grandparents and were thoughtfully examining them for moth damage now put them away, got out pen and paper, and wrote to their lawyers requesting appointments on urgent business. For the example set by lawyers and politicians was rousing hopeful interest in landowners, large and small. If the plum tree could be shaken for lawyers and politicians, why not—in a smaller way of course—for lesser folks? For a share of the proceeds, the mountain lawyers and those of the trading towns would be glad to help outsmart New York by assisting clients in getting more for their property than it was worth. And the local lawyers were shrewd enough in land matters—they had not been sharpening their teeth on the Hardenbergh Patent for more than five generations for nothing. Optimism soared. On June 9, 1906, the Pine Hill *Sentinel* quoted an editorial in the Kingston *Daily Freeman* predicting that "next New Year's Day will

see every man in Ulster County free of debt and with money jingling in
his pockets."

Until the last claims and lawsuits were settled a quarter of a century
later, the bank accounts of local lawyers swelled into unbecoming corpulence.
And lawyers' efforts had a pleasant side effect, which was to amuse newspaper readers clear across the country and even amid the frosts of Alaska.
The case of scrappy seventy-year-old Mrs. Emma Cudney did much to
cheer thousands of Americans. Mrs. Cudney had a "ginseng plantation"
on her little farm and claimed that her ginseng was enormously valuable.
Under the skillful direction of her lawyer, Judge Clearwater, the Cudney
case went on appeal from court to court, piling up wagonloads of testimony
as to the cash value of ginseng in "the China treaty ports" and to the
Chinese faith in its value as an aphrodisiac and cure for almost any ailment.
A claim of Saugerties manufacturers clustered on the banks of the Esopus
had no sex interest, but it had what was almost as good; it involved millions.
The manufacturers estimated the damage done to their prospects by the
building of the reservoir at three million dollars and they threatened if
their demands were not met to get an injunction just as the reservoir was
about to begin sending water to New York. In this way they would dry
up the city.[9]

The owners of the farmlands bought for the reservoir and its surrounding protective border were well paid by the standards of the time—
they received an average of $485 per acre. Claimants and litigants outside
the reservoir proper did not do as well. Among the unfortunates for whom
the plum tree did not shake were the Saugerties manufacturers and a very
determined lady named Cecelia E. Wentworth. For years the doings of
Mrs. Wentworth, her husband, and their onetime friend and neighbor,
famous sculptor J. Q. A. Ward, had lightened many a dull day for the
people of the Catskills and their summer boarders. Mrs. Wentworth was
known locally as "one of the most noted artists of the world,"[10] her husband was a rich businessman; their fourteen-hundred-acre estate at the foot
of Peekamoose Mountain served as both a hunting and fishing preserve
and an artist's retreat—as Mrs. Wentworth worked at her easel her husband
doggedly pursued poachers. The Wentworths and the Wards were the
chief movers in founding the Peekamoose Fishing Club located on lovely
Peekamoose Lake. When Mrs. Wentworth discovered that a little spring on
a cliff above the lake possessed what seemed to be miraculous curative
powers, she built a chapel on the spot and invited kindly, scholarly
Michael A. Corrigan, Archbishop of New York, to consecrate it. Protestant
Mr. Ward was shocked at the prospect of seeing secluded Peekamoose Lake

becoming "an American Lourdes"[11] with daily deputations of hopeful pilgrims and with the steep mountainside which plunges so romantically down to Peekamoose Lake decorated with avalanches of discarded crutches. He called together his supporters at the club and had them elect him president of the organization. Wentworth assembled his forces and was also elected president. Sculptor Ward then appealed to the courts for relief. The case entertained readers of metropolitan newspapers for years. Local statisticians estimated that it required the abilities of thirty-two lawyers to keep the case alive for a combined fee in the vicinity of $100,-000.

The Peekamoose Fishing Club case was hardly over with the club's dissolution by order of the court, when Mrs. Wentworth crashed through again as a public entertainer. J. Q. A. Ward at seventy-seven kept out of the act—he had just been married to a very young woman. The construction of the Ashokan Reservoir had lessened the value of the Wentworth estate by $20,000, Mrs. Wentworth claimed as she filed suit against the city of New York. The stores at which she bought her groceries were being demolished; the post office she used had disappeared; the church at which she worshiped and which had been built with her own money was being spirited away. Mountain people did not express much sympathy for the Wentworths and her suit faded from public attention.

From the time the first shovelful of earth was disturbed as construction began, believers in the tradition that the Catskills were a great storehouse of mineral wealth were on the alert. Many a rumor of rich strikes was solemnly repeated and then disproved. But at least one rumor lived long enough to result in the filing of a claim to mineral rights with the State government in Albany. Mr. William H. Burhans had observed with interest the building of a new railroad siding in Kingston for the Ulster & Delaware which was profiting enormously from Ashokan Reservoir business. The rock used for ballast caught Burhans' attention; he examined it and concluded that it contained gold, silver, lead, zinc, and copper. The rock had obviously migrated, but from where? Burhans traced it to a rock cut being made to accommodate the rerouted Ulster & Delaware tracks on the northern edge of the reservoir. He filed a claim which covered both the Kingston siding and the new cut.[12] The claim was never worked. How could it be, old-timers asked, when working it met with a veto from both the rich city of New York and the rich Ulster & Delaware Railroad?

As lawyers, litigants, amateur prospectors, and construction workers kept busy, some people remained skeptical about the Ashokan project which they called the "Esopus Folly."[13] It was being hinted that politicians had started the whole thing for unworthy motives of their own. It was predicted that even if the great hole in the ground should be completed it would be no more than a dry, weed-grown emptiness serving only as a monument in reverse to the human capacity for error and corruption.

But step by step the mountains of engineers' blueprints for the Esopus Folly were translated into such realities as vast excavations, footings for dams and dikes, demolished trees and buildings, blasted rocks, quarters for the workers who would man picks and shovels, horse-drawn wagons, earth scoops and steam shovels. A schoolhouse appeared for workers' children and was also used for evening classes in English for Italian, Polish and Lithuanian laborers who were taught American patriotic songs which they sang for visitors while slowly waving American flags in unison.[14] A police station cared for weekend drunks and the fatalities that occurred in the course of arguments often arising in the taverns and whorehouses which appeared in response to the arrival of the construction workers but outside the bounds of their project. Reservoir officials liked to boast in their public relations releases that not only was their project one of the greatest engineering feats of all time but also that it had been carried out with a sympathetic understanding of the human beings involved, an attitude in keeping with the reforming spirit of the times. It was true that the quarters of many "better class" workers were not at all like the miserable shacks in which Italian laborers had lived while working on the railbeds of the Catskills during the 1870s and 1880s. They were neat and new and clean, if somewhat barracky; an infirmary with doctors and nurses stood ready and the wages paid were good. Never before had unskilled workers been so well treated in the Catskills.

But the unskilled foreign-born and native black men who did the rough and dirty work on the project fared less well. Although New York officials discouraged the padrone system which had been the cause of many evils, it was used by many contractors at Ashokan. Workers lived in slumlike conditions to which some responded with much publicized violence. Local citizens shuddered, double-locked their doors and spoke of a "reign of terror"[15] as having come to the Catskills.

The Italians were joined by Irishmen from the dying bluestone settlements. Some cut stone for walls and for dam-facing in quarries soon to be buried under the waters of the reservoir. Other workers poured in from the mountains and the Hudson Valley as the plum tree spread its less juicy fruits far and wide. On September 9, 1913, the gates in the dams were closed so that water could begin to accumulate in the reservoir's two basins. The weather had been dry, springs and streams were low, and those who mocked the great plan as the Esopus Folly smiled smugly. They spread a rumor that the bottom of the reservoir had proved so porous that millions of dollars worth of a new and still secret compound would have to be used to calk the leaky basins. But as water rose behind the dam such rumors ceased.

On June 19, 1914, all the steam whistles used in the construction effort blew for a solid hour to proclaim that work on all the dams and dikes which were the reservoir's major engineering feats were completed except for the facing and finishing of the upper parts. By then Bishop's Falls were well under water, which stood ninety feet deep nearby, even though dry weather had continued.

Before the closing of the gates in 1913, the engineers had built a scow which they expected to float on the waters as they accumulated and which would be used in the job of facing the upper parts of the dams with stone. When the scow floated at last on the rising waters, the engineers paid their respects in song to believers in the Esopus Folly. Ever since their Ashokan job began, the engineers, in accordance with a custom of their profession, had run up new words to popular tunes to commemorate notable events. Now they sang:

Oh Noah built himself an ark, the dear old Christian soul,
Put all his family aboard and left, his neighbors in a hole.
As Noah pushed out in the stream, with all his kith and kin,
The neighbors stood up on the bank, and merrily said to him,

Chorus

Go to hell then, go to hell then and now
With your damned old scow
Cause it ain't gonna rain anyhow
It ain't gonna rain anyhow

Oh Noah got down on his knees and prayed that they would drown,
That the Lord in his almighty wrath would destroy the whole
    damned town
The animals kicked up a fuss, that would have raised your hair
And there was wafted on the breeze, this most ungodly air,

Chorus

For forty days and forty nights, the rain it did pour down,
The water stood 3000 feet o'er every hill and town
Old Noah walked around the ark, looked through a window pane,
Said now where are those poor damn fools who said it wouldn't rain?

Chorus

Gone to hell then, gone to hell then and now
While we right now are floating around on this damned old scow.[16] . . .

When water from the Esopus Valley began entering New York in 1915, not even the most hardened skeptic could deny that the Ashokan Reservoir was admirably accomplishing the end for which it had been planned. Work on the Schoharie Reservoir and the Shandaken Tunnel began at once. Later other Catskill streams were dammed and sent gurgling to New York. The Rondout was dammed at Lackawack. The Neversink and finally the East Branch of the Delaware were also dammed. As each project reached its first stage, the same sequence of events followed among mountain people. First the sense of shock at the thought of having to leave their homes; then the merging of the images of old-time landlords and New York City politicians; then the invocation of the spirits of the Anti-rent warriors; then the realization that, after all, there might be money in it; finally the retaining of lawyers to fight for every possible penny.

Once the Catskills had passed through their half century of pushing, gouging, blasting, and digging, for water-supply purposes, they had a different look. Gone were many of the old mill-centered valley hamlets with their verandahed inns and low open-fronted blacksmith shops; mill wheels vanished by the dozen; so too did time-stained covered bridges. The sites of Indian camps and of the orchard of Henry Hecken sank forever under water. Many families descended from Catskills' pioneers were dispersed by the thirst of the city of New York and their names are no longer heard among the Catskills. When the lakes that filled the valleys aged a little, they reflected the surrounding mountains with a charm that made some travelers think of England's Lake District. There the city of Manchester had annoyed tourists by putting to work and rudely enlarging an existing lake, Thirlmere, as a source of water. The absence of indications of longtime human activity on the shores of the Ashokan and other new lakes gave them a curiously aseptic and official character. After each reservoir was built, driving around it on the new roads provided by the bounty of the city of New York became a favorite Sunday treat. But before long this ceased to amuse or interest with its initial intensity. Only the great cluster of fountains which aerated the water before it left for New York continued to keep its appeal. Once tourists like Daniel Webster came to the Catskills to watch water tumbling down for a fee in a wilderness setting. Now tourists come to see water being thrown upward in a way that suggests, not the vanishing American wilderness, but the great fountains that once formed part of the settings of the palaces of European monarchs.

As the immense construction jobs intended to supply New York with water brought change to the Catskills, another influence was at work to bring another kind of change. Like the valley of the Esopus, the valley in which Woodstock lay was being invaded by outsiders. These outsiders felt the attraction of the Catskills not for such humdrum purposes as to supply water to a city but to serve as the base for what its leaders hoped might become an experiment that would help bring about a new and better way of life than any ever known on our planet.

Ralph Radcliffe Whitehead

✿   In 1861 Americans with an interest in the arts were reading a new book by clergyman-poet Louis L. Noble called *A Voyage . . . with Church the Artist*. It told of the adventures of Thomas Cole's pupil Frederick E. Church as he painted in Labrador with Noble as his companion. One sentence in the book puzzled many readers; it described a coastal path which "wound among rocky notches and grassy chasms, and led out to dizzy 'over-looks' and 'short-offs.'"[1] Neither of the two nouns Noble placed within quotation marks were to be found in any dictionary, and it was many years later that the great Oxford English Dictionary cited this sentence as marking the first known use in print of "over-look," soon to become "overlook," as a noun. The verb, of course, was an old one which meant to look down from an elevation, to bewitch, or to fail to notice. Washington Irving had used the verb in the first of these senses in his *Rip Van Winkle*.

Only one class of readers would have found Noble's two nouns perfectly understandable—those who lived in Woodstock beneath the massive mountain they sometimes called the Overlook and within sight of the long ridge which runs down from close to the summit of the mountain and over the Minister's Face. This ridge was known to Woodstock people as the "short-off," either because it projects deep into the valley and so seems to cut short the long eastward wall of the Catskills or because the Minister's Face cuts short the flow of the ridge. "Short-off" has failed to become an accepted part of the English language—though it is still born by a North Carolina mountain—but "overlook" in the old Woodstock sense of a high place with a view has given rise to endless Overlook roads, drives and streets, Overlook parks, and Overlook hospitals, to Overlook Rock Creek in the city of Washington, and to many another feature of the American landscape. Before Thomas Cole and Louis Noble climbed

Overlook Mountain in 1846 neither had ever heard of "over-looks" or "short-offs," but it is probable that Noble learned to use both nouns on his trip to Woodstock where both seem to have originated.

It is not every small town that contributes a new noun to the English language—even fewer small towns see their own names, after two centuries of use, taking on new and vital meanings. Yet this happened to Woodstock. By the 1960s its name was being heard around the world whenever there was talk of the young people who were rejecting the values of their society, substituting other drugs for alcohol and tobacco, and exalting the human values being ground into the earth by the tyranny of money and machines. Many of these young people called themselves members of "the Woodstock nation." The name did not acquire its new meaning by accident. A foundation for it was laid in Woodstock in 1902—a foundation composed of ideas and materials that grew out of the English aspect of a rebellion against the evils visited upon the land and its people by the triumph of the Industrial Revolution.

The rebellion was set in motion by the dissatisfaction many English people felt as their country acquired a pall of smoky air, as their once sparkling rivers carried human and industrial wastes to the sea, as many of their people were condemned to live in filthy slums, as children once past the toddling phase were set to work long hours tending machinery in textile mills. Were the cheapness and uniformity of machine-made goods made possible by the Industrial Revolution worth the cost in human lives and misery and in the defilement of air, water, and the landscape? There were some who thought not. Many of these doubters were not poor or oppressed. They lived in comfort on profits made possible by steam-powered industry; some were moved to struggle against the prevailing system by the love of their fellow men of which they had read in the New Testament; others were uneasy under the weight of the guilt that burdened them whenever they reflected upon the fact that they were living in luxury at the expense of the less fortunate people whose enslavement to factories made their comfort possible. Writer Thomas Carlyle spoke up eloquently against the machine culture during the revolution-breeding 1840s. Among those whom he inspired was a younger man named John Ruskin. The influence of Ruskin was decisive in what happened in 1902 at Woodstock in the Catskills.

John Ruskin was the only child of a rich, religious, and art-loving London sherry merchant and his evangelical wife. As a child he traveled widely with his parents in search of picturesque old castles, lovely scenery, and collections of works of art. While yet a student at Oxford, Ruskin began writing his *Modern Painters*. Intended at first as a defense of the landscape paintings of J. M. W. Turner, it expanded into many brilliantly written volumes of theory, analysis of all sorts of paintings and of the forms of rocks, vegetation, and clouds—plus attempts to find moral purpose in the arts. Ruskin became famous and added to his fame by writing many more books on architecture and the arts. And then, as his position in English life seemed secure, a change came over him. By 1860 his involvement with aesthetics had made him feel deeply the visual ugliness of industrial England and the monstrous disfigurement industry brought to the lives of the slum-dwelling poor. Soon Ruskin's aesthetic motives for attacking the established order gave way to a deep concern for the welfare of his fellow humans. Then Ruskin lectured and wrote tirelessly to bring about social reform and began describing himself as a Socialist. In 1870 he was appointed Slade Professor of Art at Oxford, where his lectures were immensely popular among idealistic young men who looked upon him as a prophet and hero. Among the young students whose minds and emotions were set ablaze by Ruskin was a shy, sandy-haired Yorkshireman who came to Oxford's Balliol College in 1873—he was Ralph Radcliffe White-head, the founder-to-be of the new Woodstock born in 1902.[2]

By 1873 both the streak of irrationality and the emotional turmoil that had run together through John Ruskin's life were growing broader and deeper. He had been married, but the marriage was annulled on the ground of Ruskin's impotence. He had fallen in love with an Irish school-girl thirty years his junior, and when Rose La Touche died, Ruskin saw the landscape of England darken and the blue of the sky quite literally fade to gray. His lectures grew less coherent and more cryptic, but they shone with an even greater verbal and emotional radiance. Ralph Whitehead, at first an admirer, quickly became a follower and a friend of the tall professor with the disconcertingly blue eyes. He realized that his own favorable position in life and his family background could make it possible for him to carry out some of the social reforms his master had outlined.

Whitehead was born in 1854 in the town of Saddleworth in the West Riding of Yorkshire. For generations the Whiteheads of West Riding and their kinsmen the Radcliffes had played a part in making the West Riding into a center of felt and woolens making. By the 1840s eleven Whiteheads owned woolens mills along the river Tame and its tributaries, and they were prosperous enough to build a fine new church closer to the Royal George Mills of the Whitehead Brothers than ancient St. Chad's with its many memorials of Whiteheads and Radcliffes of the past.[3]

By the year of Ralph Whitehead's birth, Saddleworth had been converted from a green valley watered by the clear river Tame to a grim and grimy factory town. Against a background of smoke, soot, and child labor, young Ralph Whitehead spent his boyhood in a conventional upper-class manner. As he lived at Beech Hill, described by local historian Joseph Bradbury as an "elegant stone mansion," he learned to ride, shoot, and fish. (The Whiteheads maintained a shooting box on the moors which brood above the valley of the Tame.) This pleasant life was interrupted at midnight on May 10, 1864, by an appalling tragedy. The great factory chimney of the Royal George Mills, after having given repeated warnings that it stood on inadequate foundations, crashed to earth and killed eleven human beings including Whitehead workers Henry and Anne Jeffry and seven of their children. Such accidents were not uncommon in industrial towns, and the Saddleworth tragedy sent a brief shiver down British backs and was then forgotten.[4] But it may well have helped stir in Ralph Whitehead's eleven-year-old consciousness a distrust of industrial might and power which would some day flare up at the sound of John Ruskin's voice.

When the proper time came, Ralph Whitehead was sent off to Harrow, one of the public schools that existed to give shape and polish to the young males of Britain's power-holding classes. From Harrow he went on to Balliol College—and his meeting with John Ruskin. At Balliol, Ruskin's influence awakened in Whitehead a passion for arts and social reform, while another man gave him an abiding love of classical music. This man was the Reverend Sir Frederick Arthur Gore Ousely, Bart., Oxford's Professor of Music. He possessed not only a splendid inherited fortune and refined musical taste and skill but also absolute pitch—at the age of five the future baronet exclaimed, "Only think, papa blows his nose on G." The love of classical chamber music Whitehead acquired at Oxford remained with him to the end. He carried it across the Atlantic to the Catskills' Woodstock and there it thrived and has continued to thrive to the present day. More immediate in its effect on Whitehead was John Ruskin's determination to put an end to the factory system. Under Ruskin's influence Whitehead came to a decision. When his time of ownership came, he would convert the family factories, which made woolens and felt in the valley of the Tame, into co-operative enterprises[5] where contented workers would make beautifully designed and colored textiles amid charming and healthful surroundings. All the factory chimneys would harmlessly follow the chimney of the Royal George Mills to the ground as steam power was relinquished and the air above the Tame turned clean once again.

When elder Whiteheads heard of this plan they were shocked. A quarrel followed and young Whitehead left home and college for Paris. There he worked for a year as a carpenter's helper, and he often said that this was the happiest year of his life. The quarrel was patched up and a somewhat chastened Whitehead returned to Balliol where his admiration for Ruskin continued unabated. He left in 1880 with the degree of Master of Arts, then seemed to waver for a while on the road that was to take him to Woodstock. He returned to Saddleworth and there served as a justice of the peace—a position reserved then as now for the safely conservative. He left Saddleworth for Surrey, then left Surrey for the continent of Europe. His life there gave rise to a mingling of fact, fancy, and ill-founded assumptions. He bought and restored a castle in Styria, where he shut himself up with a learned German professor who guided the excursions of his wide-ranging mind. He lived a fashionable and gay life in an Italian palazzo, designed an extraordinary garden in Avignon, married a princess, a duchess, an American, a barmaid, a ballet dancer. He didn't marry at all, he was divorced—all these bits of gossip would some day be repeated in Woodstock.[6]

What seems most likely is that during the 1880s Whitehead passed through a period of indecision with spells of study alternating with years of yielding to the temptation to enjoy life in the many ways possible to a man who had become both rich and independent as his elders died. The stimulation of association with John Ruskin was no longer possible, for Ruskin had given up the Slade Professorship on the plea of ill health, soon ceased writing and lecturing, and sank into the confused world of mental fog in which he lived to the end of his days. When Ralph Whitehead first came to Oxford, Ruskin was embodying his ideas on social reform in a plan for an organization to be known as St. George's Company or Guild. The guild made a lasting impression on young Whitehead and when he came to Woodstock in 1902, the plans he had formed for the colony he was about to establish owed more to Ruskin's guild than to any other single source.

St. George's Guild evolved in Ruskin's mind from simple beginnings into a complex organization with an almost feudal social structure. Contributors to the fund which would maintain the guild would govern it—these people would not necessarily be the ones who lived and worked on the farmland upon which guild workers would be settled and where they would work the earth by hand or with animal power, make their own clothing, houses, and objects of household use. The natural forces of wind and water might be used to make objects less well made by hand but steam power would be absolutely forbidden in order to avoid further pollution of air and water and damage to the green things of the earth. "Companions" of the guild would be required to sign a credo which began with a statement of trust in the goodness of God and went on with: "I trust in the nobleness of human nature, in the majesty of its faculties, the fullness of its mercy, and the joy of its love. . . . And I will strive to love my neighbor as myself, and, even when I cannot, will act as if I did. . . . I will not kill or hurt any living creature needlessly, nor destroy any beautiful thing; but will . . . guard and protect all natural beauty, upon the earth. . . ."[7]

Ruskin had come to feel apologetic about his possession of wealth in a suffering and poverty-filled world, so he poured money into the guild and urged his richer admirers to do likewise. But the admirers found it impossible to give so painful a proof of devotion to their master and his ideals. The guild faltered, changed its course, and finally fell into a doze. Its one tangible achievement was the Ruskin Museum at Sheffield, founded and endowed by Ruskin as part of the educational program of the guild— Ruskin himself gave the museum fine collections of works of art and examples of such natural objects as shells and crystals.

St. George's Guild was a failure by the usual standards, yet it was successful as an influence upon a new generation of protesters against the cruelties and inequities of Western society. As Ruskin stared wearily by the hour from his Lake District home across Coniston Water at the mountain known as the Old Man, his ideas were mingling in young minds with the more vigorous ones of Karl Marx and other social innovators to produce an upsurge in Socialist organizing and propagandizing. By 1891 the air was fairly crackling with schemes for social reform, and books that sketched out ideal societies were being widely read. That year, while living in Florence from whose old laws Ruskin had drawn some of the rules of his Guild of St. George, Whitehead ceased hesitating and made a contribution to the literature of social reform. His contribution outlined the plans he would some day try to put into practice at Woodstock.

The Search for Woodstock

✥ IN 1888 the very popular *Looking Backward* of New England's Edward Bellamy had appeared. The book dealt in fictional form with life at the end of the twentieth century when machine culture had peacefully turned away from devotion to private profit and existed for social usefulness alone. Soon Theodore Hertzska's *Freiland* was finding many readers— it described an ideal community imagined as existing in Central Africa. At about the same time a friend of Ralph Whitehead was publishing serially in a Socialist periodical he edited an extraordinarily appealing look into the future which appeared in book form in 1892 as *News from Nowhere*. The author, William Morris, was one of the most energetic and creative men of his time. And Morris was second only to John Ruskin as a lifelong influence upon Ralph Whitehead and the colony he was to found in the Catskills.

Like Whitehead and Ruskin, Morris was an Oxford graduate of ample means. While still a student he revealed a talent for poetry and it was as a poet that he first became known. Later he began using his great gift for design. Chintzes, cotton and woolen materials, tapestries, rugs, wall decorations, church windows, and carvings all began to give scope to Morris' inventiveness and to prepare the way for important aspects of twentieth-century design. Like Ruskin, Morris was appalled by the ugliness of life which accompanied the Industrial Revolution and, like Ruskin, he found hope in Socialism. But while Ruskin relied for reform on an appeal to the conscience of the upper classes, Morris—having studied Karl Marx's *Das Kapital* with care—came to believe that nothing short of a revolution by workers could shake off the misery of the poor. While continuing to design, to work with his hands at many crafts, to write volume after volume of poetry and prose, and to establish and operate the Kelmscott Press, Morris plunged into Socialist activity. His sturdy blue-coated figure appeared on hundreds of platforms from which he appealed with simple eloquence for support of Socialism. He contributed money to the Socialist cause, and took part in demonstrations. On Bloody Sunday of 1887 he was arrested by the police who had mortally wounded one member of a large group demonstrating peacefully in Trafalgar Square. He was released when the police realized that they had captured, not an impoverished victim of oppression, but a rich and famous Englishman.

In his *News,* Morris envisioned a happy and just twenty-first-century society following the triumph of the predicted revolution of 1952. The land had been healed after the assaults of the Industrial Revolution, smoky factory chimneys were gone, the air was clear and unpolluted, rivers ran unburdened by filth to the sea. Work was no longer an unpleasant task imposed upon the poor by the rich but a pleasure eagerly sought after, for thanks to an efficient social system there was sometimes not enough work to go around. Beautifully made objects for daily use were to be had in shops without payment, for money had been abolished and co-operation had become the rule. Old and unnatural restraints on sexual activity had faded away and freer and happier relations between men and women had resulted. All this was presented in the seductive style of which Morris was master. Readers felt themselves entering a lovely dream world where they were penetrated by a gentle word-induced euphoria with more than a little resemblance to that produced by opium.

When Ralph Whitehead wrote out his scheme for an ideal community in an essay called "Work," he adopted much of Ruskin's system of social classes. Like Ruskin he planned to have a man of literary skills choose the books for his community and a musician choose the music; like Ruskin he planned to finance the community by a tax of 10 per cent on the incomes of the richer members. But Whitehead followed Morris in emphasizing the role of work in the crafts. While Ruskin's guild had been primarily agricultural, Whitehead's centered around the arts and crafts.

Whitehead pointedly rejected the Morris and Ruskin attitude of looking backward for a social model. The Guild of St. George was largely based on medieval models; the world Morris described in *News* as set in the twenty-first century had many characteristics he mistakenly believed to be medieval. He credited the Middle Ages with a cleanliness, a brightness, and a cheeriness that they did not in fact possess. Even the broad belts with silver filigree buckles, the gold chains and other ornaments that the characters in *News* wore strongly suggest the late Middle Ages. But the ideal community which Whitehead described in "Work" had no room for this kind of antiquarianism. Whitehead wrote: "Let us no longer look to the past and try to live amid a world of beauty which we half galvanize into life from the Renaissance or the Middle Ages or the East. . . . We must live in the future, not in the past. . . . Not in vain sentimental longing for the simple happy times which we imagine to have been when the world was young, but in confidence that the golden age lies ahead of us. . . ."[1]

Under the influence of a new hero, the American poet Walt Whitman, Whitehead had substituted the kind of golden age of the future spelled out in Whitman's unconventional verses for the golden age of the past to which men like Ruskin and Morris dreamed of returning. While Whitehead was a student at Oxford, Whitman had dawned upon a small group of cultured young Englishmen as not only one of the greatest of all poets but as a social prophet as well. By 1891 Whitehead was strongly hinting that he planned to bring the community he outlined in "Work" into existence in the America to which Whitman had given glamor, although his master John Ruskin detested both the United States and Walt Whitman. Whitehead was probably helped toward this decision when he met and became engaged to a young American woman who shared his interest in the arts, music, and social reform—she was Jane Byrd McCall of Philadelphia.

"Work" first reached the public in print in 1892 as part of a collection of Whitehead's essays printed in a handsome format by the Chiswick Press under the title *Grass of the Desert*. The book ended with a tribute to Walt Whitman and a lengthy quotation from his *Passage to India*. In this indisputably great poem, Whitman saw the machine culture of the nineteenth century and the lore and religions of all our planet's people uniting at the bidding of the arts to form a world in which "nature and man shall be disjoin'd and diffused no more. . . ." The final lines of the quotation used by Whitehead have the force of a passionate declaration of purpose. They are,

> Sail forth—steer for the deep waters only!
> Reckless, O soul, exploring, I with thee, and thou with me:
> For we are bound where mariner has not yet dared to go,
> And we will risk the ship, ourselves and all.[2]

During the year of publication of *Grass of the Desert,* Whitehead sailed for the deep waters of the United States and marriage to Jane McCall. And then—for a while—he seemed to lay aside his plans for founding an arts and crafts colony. In 1893 the Chiswick Press printed his edition of Dante's *Vita Nuova*—its notes were intended to make this thirteenth-century classic accessible to readers of modern Italian. Next Whitehead bought two hundred lovely acres overlooking the Pacific in the part of Santa Barbara, California, known as Montecito. There he built a house of Mediterranean antecedents. It surpassed in elegance and sophistication anything seen up to that time in its part of the world. Santa Barbarans stared in awe at the gardens at Arcady, for so Whitehead had named his estate. At first glance most of the gardens seemed untouched efforts of nature. But a closer look often revealed that the master of Arcady had created a landscape design of extreme subtlety.[3] Among the many visitors to Arcady who were positively enchanted by the carefully planned landscape was one who would soon come closest of all Americans to Whitehead—he was a young writer and social worker named Hervey White. In 1922 White used the grounds of Arcady as settings for many scenes in a novel called *Man Overboard,* which dealt with the relationships of a group of feminists installed at Arcady. White described the "lawn of native grasses, unmown and sprinkled in with flowers introduced with such modest art . . . as to yield the effect of [a] natural bloom-strewn meadow. . . . Great boulders heaved their smooth backs here and there, while the receding slope of [the] hill-top gave so unobtrusively into the wide terraces of the [formal] garden" that the entire setting seemed centuries old. Olive orchards and vineyards blended into the landscape, a lone palm tree rose against the Pacific "shimmering away into tints of lost horizons."[4] Visitors were all the more impressed when they learned that Whitehead spent two hours each day working with his own hands at making the gardens—he believed that this amount of hearty manual work was necessary to a sound and healthy life.

As he was bringing his garden to the perfection he insisted upon, Whitehead was also deep in a number of activities intended to improve the quality of life in his corner of the world. As if to carry on from where John Ruskin had left off, Whitehead wrote and issued the first two pamphlets of what he apparently hoped would become a series much in the manner of Ruskin's *Fors Clavigera.* The running title of the series was *Arrows of the Dawn,* which was obviously suggested by Ruskin's two volumes of collected letters to the press to which he had given the title of *Arrows of the Chace.* The first pamphlet dealt lucidly and with supporting statistics with the problem of unemployment from a Socialist point of view and found the cause of the large number of unemployed in the stagnant year of 1895 not in an imagined reluctance of the poor to work but in the irrational structure of American society. As a remedy, Whitehead urged public works when needed, with those who refused to work being sent to corrective centers where they would be taught handicrafts.

The second number of Whitehead's proposed series was called *The Lesson of Hellas*. It was linked to a campaign by which Whitehead hoped to bring to the children of Santa Barbara something of his own great sensitivity to music, design, painting, and honest craftsmanship. In *The Lesson,* Whitehead held up the example of the vision of ancient Greece he had learned to see at Balliol College under Ruskin's guidance. He explained his belief that children who had been exposed to the best in the arts would "hardly be very coarse in their daily lives."[5] As the pamphlet appeared, Whitehead was trying to introduce manual training into the schools of Santa Barbara. He had formed and financed a small orchestra which played for the children. He obtained permission to maintain classes in woodworking and other handicrafts in a charming schoolhouse which he built at Arcady. But all this made little headway. The school system resisted his efforts, and his pamphlets remained unread. Repulsed in one direction, Whitehead began turning back to thoughts of establishing an arts and crafts colony of his own. Before long, dreaming gave way to action—that was after Whitehead met another arts and crafts colony dreamer, Hervey White.

Although he was in his forties when he first met Hervey White, Whitehead had managed to hang on to much of the fervent idealism and hostility to the established order that had fired him in his years at Balliol College. He was of medium height and weight, gray-eyed, and marked to normal American eyes by a very British reserve. To these eyes he appeared hesitant—almost apologetic. Yet those who breached his reserve found him to be charming in manner and awesome in his learning in the fields of the arts, economics, and literature. Among these was Charlotte Perkins Gilman, leading theoretician of the movement for equal rights for women, poet, lecturer, and author of *Women and Economics*. After he had heard Mrs. Gilman lecturing in New York, Whitehead had sought her out and warmly congratulated her. Earlier Mrs. Gilman had come to know and respect Hervey White as they worked at a settlement house in a part of Chicago known as Little Hell, where the two had collaborated on a play which never reached the stage. When White completed a novel, Mrs. Gilman introduced him to her own Boston publishers. She applauded when White organized a small group to make furniture by hand, and she was sympathetic when the group fell apart after having made only one piece, a settee for a doctor's office. She encouraged White in his increasing interest in founding a colony where the arts and crafts and a free way of life might flourish and she seized every opportunity to help him. That was why when she met Ralph Whitehead for the second time—this was at Summer Brook, a Socialist colony in the Adirondacks—she realized that the two men had much more in common than a syllable of their names, and she resolved to bring them together. She dashed off a note to White, then working as a librarian in Chicago, "I am sending you a Yankeeized Englishman who is to spend a few days in Chicago. His name is Whitehead. Be nice to him, you may find him interesting."[6]

Whitehead's reason for visiting Chicago was to pursue one of the many brief enthusiasms that marked his life—he proposed to investigate some mediums for the Society for Psychical Research. The mediums proved disappointing—not so Mr. White. He had, as many people were noticing, a positive genius for friendship. And besides, no man whom Whitehead had met in the United States could have more fully realized Walt Whitman's American of the future. Hervey White was warm and intelligent, cheerful and generous, quick in gaining the affection and respect of others. He loved music, art, and the theater. Like Whitman, he found it perfectly natural to act as nurse to sick friends, and like Whitman he had a homosexual tendency which gave added warmth to his friendships and colored his Socialist beliefs. The incidents of his life before he met Whitehead all worked together to cast him in the role of the kind of Whitman hero who would appeal to a man who had been formed in the rebellious Whitman-admiring atmosphere which began seeping into Oxford in the late 1870s. White's birth in a small Iowa town, his years of growth in a sod farmhouse set on the bleak Kansas plains, his fiddling at square dances, his pleasure in acting as cook for the farm crew, his friendships with people of all sorts as he studied at the University of Kansas, the adventurous year he spent as a geologist member of an all-male scientific expedition to a little known part of Mexico—all these suggested the kind of "comrades" who people *Leaves of Grass*. But there was another side to White's personality and it was one that gave him much in common with Whitehead. Harvard College at which he spent two years played a part in White's life similar to that which Balliol College had played in Whitehead's. There White had found John Ruskin's thinking in high favor with many of his professors. A course in Applied Ethics made Ruskin's *Fors Clavigera*, which dealt in large part with his Guild of St. George, required reading. Charles Eliot Norton and Charles Herbert Moore, under whom White studied the history of the fine arts, were Ruskin's closest American friends and followers. A year of travel in Europe on a budget of less than fifty cents a day followed graduation from Harvard. And it was not surprising that White spent much of his time in Italy admiring the paintings and buildings given approval by

Ruskin and studied a few years earlier by Ralph Whitehead. White had already picked up some skill in Spanish, now he learned to read and speak Italian although with nothing like the fluency of Whitehead.[7]

While at Harvard, Hervey White had committed himself to a career as a writer, but in order to give concrete form to his socialistic and humanitarian convictions, he turned to social service. In Chicago, Jane Addams had already made Hull House famous as the leading American settlement house. It had been inspired in part by the work in the slums of London of Ralph Whitehead's fellow student at Balliol, Arnold Toynbee. At Hull House, White, while supporting himself by a variety of jobs, wrote steadily, staged plays, organized musical events and worked with boys clubs. He then moved on to Little Hell and his friendship with Mrs. Gilman or "Sister Charlotte" as he called her. By the time he met Ralph Whitehead his novel *Differences* was soon to be published, and highly praised, and Sister Charlotte was telling everyone who would listen that charming, bearded Hervey White was the most promising of all young American writers.

The first meeting of the two men was followed by many others over the course of the next few years. Whitehead met Hervey White's Chicago friends, craftsmen, social workers, Socialists of all shades of belief, painters, psychologists, and professors, many of whom later turned up in Woodstock. Visiting at Arcady, White swung more and more into the rich Englishman's orbit. He was twelve years Whitehead's junior, and at Arcady he came to know other younger men to whom Whitehead was a patron. Behind his back these men called their patron "Papa Whitehead."[8] They respected his youthful idealism and his constant faith that a better future lay ahead for the human race, but they also saw him as a dilettante who would easily drop his protégés or projects when they lost the excitement of novelty and ceased to amuse him. It is likely enough that Whitehead was well aware of the mixed feelings with which he was regarded. Hervey White sometimes said that Whitehead was like a character out of a novel by Henry James. He was unusually sensitive to the currents of feeling which flowed back and forth among the people around him, and he had a quick eye for the ironies, the self-delusions, and the contradictions that form so large a part of the pattern of human behavior. "I like you," he once said to Hervey White in a moment of merciless self-analysis, "because while you understand me, and in no way approve of me, you never tell me of your disapproval or make criticisms."[9]

By 1901 Whitehead gave evidence of moving slowly toward founding his arts and crafts colony. Without letting Hervey White know what he was doing, he hired Bolton Coit Brown, professor of art at Leland Stanford

University and a dealer in Japanese prints, as furniture designer for the colony-to-be.[10] Brown had never designed furniture but he brimmed over with self-confidence at all times and was prepared to design any quantity of furniture whatever at a moment's notice.

For some months White and Brown eyed each other with the wariness of rivals as they joined in a search for a site for the proposed colony. Brown saw the search as a first step toward realizing a burning ambition of his—he was eager to become head of the great American art school he dreamed of persuading Whitehead to found. Hervey White continued to expect that once Whitehead founded his colony he would soon become bored with it. And then, White hoped, he and his friends might take over.

If Whitehead was aware of the secret ambitions of his helpers—and it would have been strange if he weren't—he gave no sign but continued to be his usual kindly, courteous self. Then, thanks to a fresh development, the search that was to end at Woodstock went ahead with positive urgency.

Woodstock Found

✤ THE FIRST few years of planning, discussing, and dreaming of his arts and crafts colony were probably the pleasantest years of Ralph Whitehead's life. He was associating daily at lovely Arcady with the people he liked best, creative and idealistic young men of Hervey White's kind. Every once in a while there was a trip to inspect a possible site, and there was a good deal of visiting and studying other colonies, whether based on the arts and crafts or Socialism in its many forms. Whitehead was a man who loved to linger over a dream, in which he felt more secure than among the chilly realities of actual life, and he needed a sharp prod to push him out of his dreams into action. A prod of this kind was applied shortly before the spring of 1902. The tongues of Santa Barbara people were then busy with a tale—whether true or fancied—of Whitehead's involvement with a glamorous and eccentric local woman. Mrs. Whitehead had naturally taken this hard. But a reconciliation was arrived at, and one of its conditions was said to have been the prompt creation of the long-delayed colony at a good distance from the tongues of Santa Barbara.[1]

In the spring of 1902, Whitehead, White, and Brown set out to find a definite site for their colony. The first two headed for Virginia and the Carolinas, while Brown made for New York State. As the three started out they had a number of requirements in mind. First of all, the spot they were looking for must be among mountains and it must have outstanding scenic charm. John Ruskin had described the sort of place in the fourth and fifth books of his *Modern Painters*. There he had written that for him "mountains are the beginning and end of all natural scenery." He had said: "Rocks and hills such as are good for the vine associated with arable ground form the noblest and best ground given to man. In these districts only, art of the highest kind seems possible."[2] The bleakness of very high elevations had a chilling effect on art and life, Ruskin believed, while seacosts were enervating, but at a level of something like fifteen hundred feet on a "slope of meadows, orchards and cornfields"—there man's mightiest creative energies could be released.

Scenic beauty and the proper elevation alone were not enough. Sister Charlotte could point out another essential after she had visited Ruskin, Tennessee, one of the many colonies that sprang into brief life in the course of the upsurge of arts and crafts enthusiasm of the 1890s. She observed that already the human members were moving out and rats—they appeared to be friendly rats—were moving in. The colony had been "sublimely planned, devotedly joined," but it had quickly been revealed as one of the "high-minded idiocies"[3] of the time because it ignored the "necessity for a legitimate local economic base and relationship." It had been placed too far from the cities whose people might buy its products, and it had no relationship at all to the people of the surrounding country, Mrs. Gilman wrote in her autobiography.

Left to himself, Whitehead might have produced another Ruskin, Tennessee, for he seemed to be strongly attracted by isolated spots far from any possible markets for the furniture and other products he hoped to make. He favored Asheville, North Carolina, which had been a summer resort for fashionable Southerners ever since 1830. Its climate and scenery would have delighted even John Ruskin. Nearby, forestry-minded George Vanderbilt had brought into being Biltmore, a colossal French château set on 125,000 acres. Upper-class horsey and golfy Americans and even a rival arts and crafts colony were already converging on the vicinity. White and Brown, however, vetoed Asheville and pointed out the necessity for locating within an easy distance of the population center of the eastern coast. They told Whitehead that of all possible locations the one that most nearly filled their requirements—and Ruskin's—was somewhere in the Catskills. But Whitehead would have none of the Catskills. He had once spent some time there at one of the big hotels, probably the Kaaterskill. And he had not enjoyed the experience. "I won't go to the Catskills," he asserted. "They are full of Jews."[4]

Bolton Brown was not only an aggressive and self-confident man, he was also extremely persuasive. He left for the Catskills—if without Whitehead's blessing at least with his permission. When he was an old man Brown liked to talk about his adventures among the Catskills in the spring of 1902. Dressed in his roughest mountain-climbing togs and equipped with the newly issued U. S. Geological Survey maps, Brown left no mountain or valley uninspected. "I scrambled over summits so wild it seemed no man or even animal could ever have been there. Some were flat table rock, covered everywhere with dry grey dead moss a foot thick, the same grey moss hanging in sad festoons from all the branches of the few stunted spruce trees that barely survived. I am an old hand at mountain work, having served my apprenticeship in the wildest of the California Sierras, but for sheer savage impenetrability and utter laboriousness some of these Catskill trips really capped my experience. . . ."[5]

After three weeks of exploration Brown emerged near the crest of a ridge of Overlook at the point where Mead's Mountain House stands. He stared down almost in disbelief. Then as Brown wrote shortly before his death in 1936: "Like Balboa . . . I . . . first saw my South Sea. South indeed it was and wide and almost as blue as the sea, that extraordinarily beautiful view, amazing in extent. . . ." Brown walked along the road that led toward the view and "came upon an old man with a white beard doing something . . . in an apple orchard—all the trees in full blossom. . . ." He asked the man the name of "the earthly paradise" stretched out below and the man replied, "That is Woodstock."

Before many weeks had passed, Whitehead and White stood at Mead's with Brown and were moved by the same view. Whitehead had come to Woodstock reluctantly, "determined to be disagreeable,"[6] as White recalled in 1937, for his dislike of the Catskills had "positively increased." The three men walked that clear, sunny day along the upper pasture of the farm that lay to their right and sat down on the grass. The view of mingled fields, pastures and woodland, the distant Hudson River, the hills and mountains that edged the river's valley and the southern Catskills to the right began to work their magic on Whitehead. All this, he could not help realizing, was exactly the landscape setting John Ruskin had prescribed as essential for good work and a good life. It was true that the flanks of Overlook boasted no vineyards but they were obviously well suited to that purpose. Indeed, though Whitehead did not know it, more than a century earlier Peter DeLabigarre had observed with pleasure the robust growth of native grapevines which twisted their way toward the treetop sunlight of these very slopes.

As the three men sat on the short pasture grass and talked, Ralph Whitehead's strong anti-Catskills obsessions began to wilt. Then Bolton Brown was able to speak up persuasively. Brown was a thorough man and had informed himself in advance of the attractions of the surroundings of the mountainside farms he had discovered. He had already pointed out to Whitehead and White the ruins of the old glass factory in the valley to the north of Mead's—these ruins that had made an impression on Thomas Cole in 1846. The three men had hailed the ruins as "a good omen for our craft intentions."[7] A ruined glass factory was by no means all that Bolton Brown was prepared to bring to bear on Whitehead. The state of New York, as he had found in his days of exploration, owned and protected much of the Catskills, so the piratical raids on the landscape that were robbing America of its once noble beauty were less likely here than in regions open without hindrance to individual and corporate greed.

The vicinity, Brown had discovered, abounded in charms of many sorts. For example, just below Mead's a rustic Episcopalian chapel, although recently built, gave a romantic, almost Old World air, to the neighborhood. If you passed the chapel and climbed Overlook—its summit could be reached by a vigorous man in an hour or so—then you would face what so many connoisseurs characterized as the most beautiful view in all the eastern United States. Traditions of visits by great painters and other artists clustered almost visibly about the now neglected hotel on Overlook: Mead's too could—and did—boast of many artist and writer guests.

By the most extraordinary stroke of luck, the "earthly paradise" of Woodstock in the valley below was no tired and ramshackle agglomeration of wooden boxes in which the rural poor allowed life to slip drearily from their grasp. Instead it was a cheerful, well-kept hamlet. Its streets were lined with thrifty sugar-maple trees, and most of its women were so passionately devoted to cleanliness and neatness that the radiance of their kitchens positively awed newcomers. There were a dozen other features of Woodstock which the inquisitive Mr. Brown had investigated and upon which he could report. For example, he had learned that in case of illness among arts and crafts colonists they would not have to rely upon some gnarled old medical practitioner who had learned his trade by holding his predecessor's horse and rolling his pills. Woodstock, in its Dr. Downer, had an able and devoted young physician who was a graduate of one of the country's greatest medical schools. For another, there was at least some indication that Woodstock people might be less rigid in their attitudes than might be expected of the people of so small and isolated a town. Ever since the 1870s, circus and theater people had lived in the town's Mink Hollow. Woodstock was especially proud of actor Dan Sully. In a day when the Methodist Church set its face dourly against dancing, card playing, the Pope, and play acting, Woodstock Methodists had cheerfully allowed Sully, a Roman Catholic, to rehearse his plays in their church hall.

And finally—and this was of positively crucial importance—Woodstock was entirely without Jewish landowners, Jewish shopkeepers, and Jewish boardinghouses. "Every requirement Mr. Whitehead had insisted upon was met here; . . . he would be ashamed of himself forever if he did not buy . . ."[8] wrote Hervey White in his *Autobiography*.

As the three men talked in the pasture, Whitehead hesitated, raised objections, and hesitated again. Rather suddenly he made up his mind. His words were not of the eloquent sort suited to cutting in marble or casting in bronze. They were: "Well, all right, let's have it here."[9]

Whitehead at once retreated to Arcady leaving his two employees to buy the seven contiguous farms they had agreed upon. But first he pledged Brown and White to put off inquiries as to their motives with cloudy generalities lest local knowledge that an arts and crafts colony was planned should result in a rise in the price of land. As Brown and White reasoned, cajoled, and took advantage of weak spots in the defenses of the seven farm owners—only one of whom had the slightest desire to sell— speculation about what the two were up to flourished. They planned to build an immense mountain house that would eclipse even the Kaaterskill and Mr. Beach's establishment; they were intent on a monster chicken farm; a mysterious Englishman was behind the scheme. He was an emissary of the Pope come to convert local Methodists to Catholicism.[10] Gold had at last been discovered on Overlook and would soon be mined, or was the old dream of mining coal about to come true? Color was given to this last by the fact that an extension of what had long been known as the Coal Mine Ledge ran across the upper part of the seven farms which formed part of old Great Lot 26 and had once belonged to coal enthusiast Cornelius Tiebout.

Woodstock people felt that they might understand Bolton Brown— after all, he was himself a native of upstate New York. But his companion, smiling, curly-haired Mr. White, was a puzzler. He wore a flaming red Windsor tie to advertise his Socialist convictions; he also wore tight knee-length bicycle pants; and instead of settling like Brown in one of the excellent farm boardinghouses in which Woodstock abounded, he chose to take up residence in a disused Lutheran church where he slept on straw heaped up in a pew. He was soon sharing the discomforts of the church with two friends. One was handsome Swedish-born Carl Eric Lindin, a painter-poet who had been responsible for some mural paintings at Hull House. The other was a small, bearded and mustached veteran of the Dutch side of the recent Boer War, and he was clad in the remains of a tropical military uniform. As Mrs. Bolton Brown would write, Captain Van der Loo was "one of those purely fictional characters who now and then occur in real life"[11]—romantic and heroic legends crystallized about him. Van der Loo took not the slightest interest in the arts and crafts but was bent on worldly success. Yet he was a friend of White's so he and Lindin joined Brown and White on Whitehead's payroll.

By the first week of August, considerable progress had been made on getting options on the seven farms. By that time word of Ralph Whitehead's intentions had leaked out and was being reported in Ulster County newspapers.[12] By mid-September the farms were all safely in Whitehead's possession and construction of the buildings of the colony, planned in detail, was ready to begin.

Like many men of unimpressive physique, Brown believed that he appeared to advantage on horseback. With his hair carefully combed to cover his bald spot, he mounted a fiery horse named Billy and proceeded to round up all available local carpenters, masons, teamsters, and diggers of holes in the ground, and he commandeered the entire production of all the sawmills in the vicinity. Nineteen hundred and two was a very warm and rainy year when leaves expanded, roses doubled in size, and cabbages swelled to enthusiastic dimensions. Even in May the weather had affected the landscape and given Woodstock an almost English lushness as if on purpose to charm Whitehead. But as fall days came and the rains refused to cease, Brown's workmen pleaded fear of rheumatism as a reason for quitting work. But Brown was not to be stopped. He planned to cover the site of each building with a tarpaulin to serve as a temporary roof, and it was only when he learned that the weight of these temporary roofs would make their use impossible that he gave up. Instead he bought all the local stocks of raincoats and boots, issued them to his men, and sent them back to their stations. When his overly high-spirited horse threw and killed a worker who had ventured to mount him, anti-Brown feeling rose high—but construction went on.

Late in the fall of 1902, Whitehead returned to Woodstock and looked over the situation. He found that excellent progress had been made. He also found that Brown's place in the colony was threatening to eclipse his own. Brown was building a fine enough frame house for Whitehead but he was also building a thirteen-room stone house for himself conveniently placed in relation to the art school that Brown had told friends he would be heading for the rest of his life. Whitehead firmly changed Brown's house from stone to frame, and he assigned Hervey White, who had been in charge of building roads up the steep mountainside, to take charge of much of the building.[13]

Through the early days of their dream of the arts and crafts colony, White and Brown had felt some sense of being partners in the enterprise. Now Whitehead made it plain that they were mere employees. The colony would be his and his alone. Just as John Ruskin had been "Master" and even "Dictator" of the Guild of St. George, so Whitehead would be the unchallenged ruler of his colony in the Catskills. As if to emphasize all this he gave the colony a very personal name made up of syllables of the middle names of his wife and himself: Byrdcliffe. As Byrdcliffe's visual symbol he chose his own personal symbol, the old Florentine version of the fleur-de-lis he had used on the title page of *Grass of the Desert,* where it was combined with the colophon of the book's designer, Walter Crane.

The spirit of Walt Whitman left Byrdcliffe; that of John Ruskin now took possession.

The "Art Village" of Byrdcliffe

🌱 EARLY IN 1903, Whitehead, his wife, and their two sons took up residence at White Pines, their Byrdcliffe house. The house and the other Byrdcliffe buildings promised well: they were clean and simple in design, honestly built and grouped not for show but with their functions clearly in mind. They conformed to the arts and crafts feeling of the time, showed Swiss elements thought to be appropriate to a mountainside, and also owed something to the new spirit becoming apparent in the work of some young California architects. Whitehead himself was responsible for most of the design, for which Bolton Brown had made working drawings in a drafting room he set up in a Woodstock barn.[1]

But the buildings were only buildings until Ralph Whitehead, with great energy and skill, threw himself into the task of bringing them to life as parts of a functioning arts and crafts colony. The master of Byrdcliffe spent lavishly in order to provide his workshops with the best of equipment for wood and metalworkers, potters, weavers, and other craftsmen. He installed his own fine library with his collection of reproductions of the work of Old Masters and the Pre-Raphaelite painters in a room adjoining the studio which would house the Byrdcliffe Summer School of Art. Local tradition credits Whitehead with spending more than half a million dollars on the buildings and equipment of Byrdcliffe up to the time the colony began to function.

Bolton Brown had devoted much care to designing and building the studio for the art school, and now he saw himself taking a back seat in its operation. Tall Herman Dudley Murphy, a well-known landscape painter, became the school's leading teacher, and would also teach the craft of frame making. Brown was relegated to the position Whitehead referred to as "drawing master." The school's prospectus praised the beauty of the Woodstock landscape, emphasized Whitehead's association with Ruskin and Morris, and promised that eventually the school, set in the "art village" of Byrdcliffe, would offer year-round instruction in drawing and painting from the human model. It explained that the art village had been set on a tract of twelve hundred acres in order "to protect it against undesirable neighbors, to guard against land speculators and prevent the destruction or vulgarization of the landscape."[2]

As students and craftsmen assembled at Byrdcliffe in June, the future of the experiment seemed bright. To many young people the kind of beautiful future sketched by William Morris in his *News from Nowhere* seemed to be moving closer through the efforts of the kind, rich, cultured, ever-helpful master of Byrdcliffe. Thirty years later, Carl Eric Lindin set down in words his memories of "many foolish and marvellous days in the early life of the Byrdcliff colony . . . the birds sang as if the earth had just then been newly created. And the Byrdcliffers sang too, and danced and made love to each other, just like the birds. Later the summer came on— with wonderful warm summer nights, when fireflies danced over dew-laden meadows, and when we gathered in bands and climbed the Overlook, in search of adventure and romance; singing as we went, through the blue-green, moonlit night. . . ."[3]

On three nights of each week the students danced in their studio-schoolroom. In the late afternoon Mr. and Mrs. Whitehead liked to assemble the students on the beautiful terrace before White Pines and lead them in rustic English dances. Sometimes Mrs. Whitehead with a companion or two might be seen descending to the fields and meadows below carrying a bowl of non-alcoholic mead for the refreshment of haymakers. Wearing the floating veils she favored, she offered to dance and sing for the embarrassed farmhands. She smiled approval when students wore consciously rustic corduroys and denims. All this seemed to strengthen the air of happy make-believe which shimmered in the air of Byrdcliffe.

Whitehead himself flowed with optimism that first summer. He wrote an account of Byrdcliffe and the ideas and aims behind it which was published as "A Plea for Manual Labor" in *Handicraft,* the organ of the American arts and crafts movement. In his "Plea," Whitehead brought up to date and further Americanized the thoughts he had expressed in his essay "Work" of 1891. He continued to praise Walt Whitman and wrote with approval of thinkers like his friend John Dewey. He criticized the American greed for material possessions, urged a more relaxed way of life, and spoke up strongly in favor of an increased interest in enjoying the beauty of the natural world. He wrote that "the healthy love of beauty depends on the strength and sanity of the sub-conscious faculties of the human mind; in the possession of what has been called by some of the Orientals 'Nirvana,' by the early Christians 'the peace of God'; on a certain harmony between man the microcosm and the Kosmos."[4] The picture of Byrdcliffe that emerges from the "Plea" is a charming one which shows a group of intelligent and creative people voluntarily associating to set an example of rational and beautiful living for the rest of the world to follow. But nowhere in the "Plea" did Whitehead tell of the rigid hierarchical structure of the Byrdcliffe experiment. Bolton Brown and Hervey were sharply aware of it, and later Brown wrote. "Whitehead was all for 'democracy' in theory; but down in his British sub-conscious, class consciousness was an influential ghost of medieval arrangements—in scales with steps up and steps down and a central court. . . . The idea implied something like a benign reign over gracious and grateful dependents. But in twentieth-century America this ideal found no suitable atmosphere."[5]

Students, craftsmen, and visitors to Byrdcliffe were so thoroughly enchanted by the physical beauty of the place and its surroundings and by the speed and efficiency with which its major crafts projects got under way that they did not realize at first that all this was under the rule of a man who was pleased when he was referred to as the "Dictator" of Byrdcliffe. Byrdcliffe people did as they were told, danced when they were told to dance, worked when they were told to work, and climbed Overlook only with the approval of the Dictator. The eminent sociologists, psychologists, educators, and other visitors with an eye on the future were favorably impressed—at first—by what they found at Byrdcliffe. They were especially interested in the apparently thriving furniture-making project upon which the economic well-being of the colony would depend. Not only was the furniture outstandingly well made but also most of it had the kind of local base of which arts and crafts enthusiasts approved. In the 1850s John Ruskin had urged that "British Flora" be used as sources of the carved ornament in the University Museum then being built at Oxford. He believed that craft objects should use natural forms for ornament, and the stonecutting O'Shea brothers had used ferns growing in the vicinity as models for capitals in the museum. Now Byrdcliffe furniture made use for ornament of the plant population of the Catskills and usually depended not on imported cabinetmaking woods but on maple, oak, and ash trees which had grown and been seasoned in the Catskills. Design of chests, tables, and chairs was of a sturdy arts and crafts simplicity which owed much to William Morris. Much of the furniture was ornamented with shallow and often hand-colored carvings of wild flowers, foliage, and fruits of the Catskills or the irises and lilies growing in the Whiteheads' lovely hillside garden—these two flowers had long ago given rise in Europe to the Byrdcliffe symbol of the fleur-de-lis.[6]

The furniture began with sketches and working drawings by two talented and attractive young women who had recently graduated from Brooklyn's Pratt Institute of Design: Zulma Steele and Edna Walker. Miss Steele was proud of the fact that she had strong ancestral ties with the Catskills, for she was descended from the largest of the Hardenbergh Patent's landlords and the founder of Woodstock, Robert Livingston of Clermont. Whitehead worked very closely with the two girls—very closely indeed, local rumor said, with lovely and elegant Miss Steele. Under Whitehead's direction the two made careful water-color studies from life of mountain laurel, pink azalea, dogwood, chestnut and apple blossoms, and other flowering plants growing on the Byrdcliffe property. In the fall they drew brightly colored autumn leaves and especially woodbine vines whose frost-reddened leaves contrasted handsomely with clusters of the vine's blue berries. From their studies the girls made graceful designs, so true to nature that they would have drawn admiring remarks from even John Ruskin. If the designs for furniture and its ornament won the approval of the Master of Byrdcliffe, they were handed over for execution to the foreman of Byrdcliffe's woodworking shop. And the foreman, like the furniture, demonstrated Whitehead's desire to give his crafts a local base. He was no imported aesthete but Woodstock's Fordyce Herrick, an heir to the fine traditions of working with wood which had long flourished among the forested Catskills. Herrick had been foreman of the carpenters who put up the buildings of Byrdcliffe and had remained to supervise the making of furniture.

The carving required was done during Byrdcliffe's first and second summers by a Norwegian-born craftsman named Erlenson. Signor Giovanni Battista Troccoli, who taught crafts in the Byrdcliffe art school, supervised the carving. Some of the drawer pulls and other hardware needed were designed and made at the Byrdcliffe Forge—subject, of course, to the Master's approval—by a shy and very gifted young Pratt graduate named Edward J. Thatcher. Finally a light stain or clear finish was applied and the carvings were colored by Miss Steele or Miss Walker; sometimes the two painted delicate mountain landscapes, flowers, or foliage on the uncarved panels of large pieces of furniture.

Byrdcliffe furniture-making had a companion craft which Whitehead hoped would make a large place for itself in the life of the art village—this was the production of color prints. In his "Plea" Whitehead had announced that Byrdcliffe would carry on "the truly democratic art of color-printing, by which work in colors of really artistic worth may be made accessible to those who cannot afford to buy easel-pictures."[7] At that time there was much interest in color-printing of this sort. The Ipswich Prints of Arthur W. Dow of the Pratt Institute were being widely admired, and Dow sent many of his most promising students to Byrdcliffe. Efforts at producing a series of Byrdcliffe prints took several directions. One series was of somewhat oriental inspiration. It was keyed to the Byrdcliffe furniture, made use of the local flora, and the prints were signed with a mark showing two "byrds" flying past a "cliffe." More striking were prints made in 1904 by the well-known painter Birge Harrison, who used rice paste and pastels to create some simple yet charming local landscapes distinguished by their clean and happy color.

Byrdcliffe's first summer season ended on an ambiguous note. The colony appeared to be thriving. It had bustled with activity that summer; craftsmen and craftswomen had set up pottery-making, weaving, and other craft projects; and the furniture- and printmaking ventures had seemed to promise well. But at the same time, many students had made up their minds not to return to the art school for the next season, many craftsmen departed for good, Herman Dudley Murphy resigned from the school— and Bolton Brown was fired by the Master. The failures to return, the resignations, and Brown's dismissal were all rooted in the lack of individual freedom that pervaded Byrdcliffe.

Bolton Brown had seen with ever-deepening gloom the dissipation of his dream of heading the colony's art school, and he protested to Whitehead at his diminished part in Byrdcliffe life. Whitehead told him only that he "mistook his position."[8] He dismissed Brown, but generous in money matters as always, softened the blow by making Brown a handsome present. When Brown asked whether Whitehead would object if he settled nearby but outside the Byrdcliffe boundaries, Whitehead replied that he would not and added with characteristic kindness that he didn't know any man who "wouldn't be glad to have you settle in the neighborhood."[9] At this, Brown bought a tract of some thirty acres in the neighborhood known as Rock City and built a house with a studio set by itself in the woods. Brown, the explorer, had discovered Woodstock for the arts and crafts. Now Brown, the dismissed employee, set an example that many would follow in the years to come and that would make Woodstock and not Byrdcliffe into the lively and vigorous art colony it was destined to be.

Like Brown, Hervey White had chafed under a sense of having been assigned a less satisfying role at Byrdcliffe than he had hoped for. He and his friend Lindin were given the tasks of running the farm and recruiting people for Byrdcliffe. To help in recruiting, they had converted an old farmhouse on the Byrdcliffe property into a sort of clubhouse they named the Lark's Nest. White wrote letters to his many friends urging them to come for visits. Many varied people did—some distinguished, others not, but all had one thing in common: a strong drive toward activity in the arts and social reform. Whitehead met the Lark's Nest guests and if he liked them, invited them to settle as Byrdcliffe tenants. If he liked them very much, he would offer to sell them land for building in one of the "ridings" into which he had divided Byrdcliffe in memory of his native Yorkshire.

As fall approached in 1903, Hervey White felt that the skepticism regarding Whitehead's ability to run an arts and crafts colony that he and his friends had expressed at Arcady in the late 1890s was now justified. And he realized that his plan of eventually buying out Whitehead would have to be discarded. When he came to write his *Autobiography,* White explained: "To be sure we had anticipated all this from the beginning . . . but we said we will get a start, keep it going, and when our rich man is tired of his plaything we will be able to get together and buy him out. But here he had blocked all our plans by the extravagance and wealth of his purchases; seven farms, thirteen hundred acres, thirty buildings expensively equipped and furnished, water piped a mile down the mountain and leads branching off to every structure, baths, toilets, every luxury save electricity and motor cars—he was antagonistic to those. It required a fortune to keep the place going to say nothing of buying him out. But we liked and still believed in our idea, we liked Woodstock and the valley that it occupied. We determined to stay and start again. Lindin would buy the church we had lived in and on which I still had an option. I would find a farm and build simple shops, we would hang on in Byrdcliffe a year longer, gain time to look about and make decisions."[10]

Even before he first met Ralph Whitehead, Hervey White had dreamed of founding a colony whose people would follow the example of Walt Whitman more closely than that of John Ruskin. The colony would have no master or dictator but would be based on an easy and democratic association of individuals who wanted to live their lives as fully and as completely as possible in defiance, if need be, of the rules and regulations of the money and machine culture which surrounded them. Some years earlier White had given his dream colony a name, the Maverick.

During White's Kansas boyhood he had known a canyon near the Saline River. A wild sorrel stallion with a white mane lived there and had evaded all attempts at capture. The stallion was known as the Maverick, a term used in the West to designate an unbranded animal. Later, when White visited a Colorado co-operative farm on which his sister lived, he was shown another canyon with a curiously similar tradition—here the canyon itself was known as The Maverick. White told his sister that, "If I ever get a place of my own I will call it The Maverick, and it will be like a maverick, belonging to no one, but also to whoever can get it."[11]

During Byrdcliffe's second summer, that of 1904, Hervey White's Maverick took a long step toward realization. Trivial events often precipitate changes long in the making, and in this case it was a dispute over a few quarts of milk.

The Maverick Secessionists

✤ IN JUNE 1904, Hervey White turned over his option to buy the old Lutheran church to Carl Eric Lindin who at once bought it and settled in. Lindin's good looks and the effectiveness of his reading aloud of poetry had thrilled young lady guests at the Lark's Nest, who now mourned as Lindin withdrew from Byrdcliffe life. But Lindin's departure seemed to many to be balanced, for a short time, by the arrival of a new and distinguished head of the Byrdcliffe School of Art. He was Birge Harrison, landscape painter, writer of travel sketches, friend of popular writer Robert Louis Stevenson, and a man who had lived not only in the most famous French artists' colonies but also among the Indians of America's southwest. Harrison's relations with art students were marked by kindness and thoughtfulness; his manners were polished without being stiff; and he radiated warmth and goodwill.

As Harrison took up his duties, a fresh crop of young people was entering the enchanted world of Byrdcliffe. Among them was Bertha Thompson who was to become a distinguished craftswoman in metals and a Byrdcliffe resident throughout her long and productive working life. In 1933 Miss Thompson looked back on her first Byrdcliffe summer and expressed the hopefulness that filled many young students: "Those glorious summer days of 1904 will long be remembered by those of us who were there. . . . With all the enthusiasm of youth we planned extravagantly for the future. All things seemed possible and time limitless. We worked and played with untroubled minds and carefree hearts. . . ."[1]

As the summer moved along, Ralph Whitehead was far from being carefree or untroubled. He had found that while presiding over the making of Byrdcliffe furniture was fun, selling it was quite another matter. The cost of production was extremely high and those who could afford to buy it were not ordinary people but those rich, aesthetically alert souls who were turning from buying arts and crafts productions to *art nouveau* with its sweeping elongated curves, abstracted and not copied from natural forms. Art nouveau owed something to William Morris' innovative textile and wallpaper designs of the 1870s. But set beside art nouveau furniture, that made at Byrdcliffe looked a bit prim and old-fashioned. Put on the market twenty years earlier it would have aroused great interest. But by 1904 it did not excitingly foreshadow the future: it pointed—if with grace and charm—to the past. Whitehead's expectation of seeing his colony become self-supporting through the sale of its furniture now seemed certain to be disappointed. The making of furniture would have to be given up and reliance placed on less ambitious crafts such as pottery and weaving.[2] As this prospect stared Whitehead in the face, he received a blow from another source.

Birge Harrison let him know that he had not found teaching at Byrdcliffe as satisfying as he had hoped and would not return for another season. Like Bolton Brown and Lindin, he had found the charm of Woodstock hard to resist. He proposed buying land and building a house in Woodstock, but on the borders of Byrdcliffe.

The strain of finding himself involved in a long-cherished project that was giving so many clear signs of not doing well began to have its effect on Whitehead and to show in his actions. For a time he had paid bills in the careless manner of an English milord making the Grand Tour and being cheated at every turn without deigning to notice it. During the summer of 1904 the Master of Byrdcliffe took to scrutinizing bills with care and to questioning many items. Favorite targets for questioning were bills presented by Captain Van der Loo, whom Whitehead had put in charge of transportation. The captain moved people and goods back and forth by carriage and wagon. Whitehead began displaying an unfamiliar irritability and on one hot August evening he lost his temper with Van der Loo and Hervey White.[3]

The summer of 1904 had none of the warm, moist luxuriance of that of 1902. As in the year of Sheriff Steele's murder, rain clouds performed reluctantly, and seldom made it necessary to postpone sketching trips or pilgrimages to the summit of Overlook Mountain to watch the sun or the moon rise. By late July, pasture grass was sparse and brown; by August the herd of thirty Byrdcliffe cows was giving less milk than usual. Farm manager, Hervey White, and transportation man, Fritz Van der Loo, met the situation in what seemed to them to be the only fair way. They scaled down the number of quarts of milk delivered daily to the Viletta where students boarded, to the households of painters and craftsmen—and to White Pines. At this last, Whitehead exploded. If his farm managers could not supply him with the milk his family needed, then, he said, he would hire other managers who could. White and Van der Loo quietly resigned. There was no frank and open discussion of the disagreement—that was not Whitehead's way. On the surface, relations appeared as cordial as ever as White slowly cut his ties with Byrdcliffe. He had a reason for not hurrying. During the thirty-eight years of his life, he had never felt the urge to get married. Now he did, and to a Byrdcliffe girl. "Vivian had a wild sort of beauty," White wrote, "that drew attention wherever she went. I was breathless the first time I saw her and my mind was made up on the instant."[4]

Vivian Bevans had come from Chicago to Byrdcliffe to work in the color-printing venture, and she was almost young enough to have been Hervey's daughter. The two expected to marry and leave Byrdcliffe together once the summer season was over. White now felt a new sense of responsibility. He planned to move to New York and get a job while he waited for a chance to join with Van der Loo in establishing his Maverick. He soon had the chance. After a winter of doing odd jobs of writing— friends in publishing had come to his aid—White found a farm he liked. It was three miles southeast of Byrdcliffe, just over the Woodstock line in the adjoining town of Hurley. It lay in what was known to lawyers as part of the Hurley patentees' woods, the tract that had been conveyed to Cornelis Cool and his associates as part of the complex deal which had resulted in the Hardenbergh Patent. Once White decided to buy, friends helped. A Philadelphia woman who had been a schoolmate of Mrs. White-head gave him five hundred dollars. An older friend, the botanist on the Mexican expedition of many years earlier, lent another five hundred to cover Van der Loo's share of the purchase, while a third five hundred was left as a mortgage.[5] Van der Loo sailed for China at once, where he did very well as agent for a British line of patent medicines. He played no further part in the creation of White's Maverick.

Byrdcliffe had begun with all the power of willing wealth behind it. Now the Maverick was about to demonstrate the power of poverty when yoked to a spirit of sharing. Byrdcliffe had taken pains to make it known that it was no community. In *A Plea,* Whitehead had explained his belief that communities had always failed because the family and not the community was "the basis of Anglo-Saxon life."[6] The Maverick, like Byrd-cliffe, was privately owned yet it functioned as a community in which good and ill were shared and in which its owner-manager often lived in the smallest cabin on the place, called Six by Eight because of its dimensions in feet. Those who could afford to pay rent for one of the cabins which began appearing the first Maverick summer, did so; those who couldn't, didn't. For many years a bowl stood on Hervey White's table holding odds and ends of small change, and any Mavericker who needed a little money was welcome to help himself.[7] Predatory people inevitably turned up, but in time they were weeded out. Still, anyone with a wish to work at anything worth while and a willingness to live close to the heartbeat of the earth, was welcome. Hervey White liked to say that he believed in "giving every fellow his chance."[8] His colony, like the stallion with the white mane, "belonged to no one and at the same time to whoever could get it."

During its first summer the pattern of life "on the Maverick"—this became the usual phrase—was established. The colony expanded in size and vitality year after year. But only the dedication and vigor of Hervey White enabled it to remain alive in a society that viewed it with suspicion. Finding the money to pay its bills was no easy task. Hervey, as he was known to his tenants and neighbors, sold milk and eggs, taught school in nearby West Hurley, and served as a nurse under the direction of Woodstock's beloved Dr. Downer. In the winter he sometimes went to New York where he worked as a substitute teacher or at some other job—one winter he was assistant to his friend John Quincy Adams who was secretary to the city's Fine Arts Commission.

Money was not Hervey's only problem. During the first three years of the Maverick's struggle for existence, he had deep personal conflicts to endure. By the time his young wife had borne him two sons, it became clear that marriage was not for Hervey and that his attitude toward his own sex, which had for so long been expressing itself in warm friendships, could no longer be denied.[9] His wife drifted away with the couple's sons and eventually remarried. Hervey did not see his sons again until they were grown men. Once the separation became final, Hervey gave the Maverick a greater share of his energy. True to his training in social service, he tried to involve the neighboring farmers in his project and to make it serve the whole countryside as a means of awakening an interest in music, the arts, and the crafts.[10] In this he was not successful except in earning the friendship and goodwill of his neighbors who could not help contrasting his democratic warmth with the glacial upper-class reserve of Ralph Whitehead.

During the Maverick's second summer, a new and powerful force came to Woodstock and gave a different direction to the changes in Woodstock life which had begun in 1902. It was the summer school of the Art Students League of New York.

The Byrdcliffe school began to weaken once Birge Harrison abandoned it. In 1906 the Art Students League moved in to take its place, not in Byrdcliffe, but in the hamlet of Woodstock. Through the summer of 1905 Birge Harrison had taught at a summer school with which the League was experimenting in Lyme, Connecticut. When the school proved unsuccessful there, John F. Carlson, a promising young League student who had been a scholarship student at Byrdcliffe in 1904, suggested moving it to Woodstock, and to Woodstock it was moved. Once he had overcome his feelings of disloyalty to Ralph Whitehead, Harrison was persuaded to be the new school's teacher[11] while Leonard Ochtman taught at Byrdcliffe.

The people of Woodstock were now faced with a disturbing phenomenon set in a former livery stable and undertaking shop in the very heart of their hamlet. They had accepted the oddities of Byrdcliffe without too much straining. After all, its proprietor had that most effective of all passports to admiration, his wealth. The Maverick was still too small to have made much impression. And besides, like Byrdcliffe, it formed an enclave apart from the center of Woodstock life. But the young men and women who arrived to study at the Art Students League had a startling effect on Woodstock eyes and Woodstock minds. They were not only lively and irreverent towards their elders, but they were also heirs to the tradition of Bohemianism which had expanded after the French Revolution among young French painters and writers and had crossed the Atlantic to make itself at home in little colonies in a few American cities. Walt Whitman had been a leader among American Bohemians as his poetry expressed the Bohemian zest for living, its scorn of cramping conventions, and its faith that some day a new and more just social order would prevail on earth. Primitive French Bohemians had adopted beards and long hair as outward signs of their separateness. Eventually these and the eccentricities of dress accompanying them were taken over by conventional people and so lost their value as symbols. The art students who came to Woodstock in 1906 did not wear beards or long hair; instead, some went in for shaven heads or short hair cut in patterns such as stripes or checkerboards. Paint-streaked trousers became their most conspicuous symbol. It was about 1912 that beards returned, accompanied this time by berets.[12]

Most of the students gloried in their poverty. Some slept in fields or woods under sheets of oilcloth. Barns became favorite Woodstock shelters. A corner of a barn with a heap of hay for a mattress could be rented for thirty-five cents per week, and an additional twenty-five cents would entitle a student to a bowl of milk at each milking time.[13]

The art students' unconventional ways puzzled Woodstockers and antagonized many, and they were further antagonized early in August of 1906 when the League figured in an outburst of national laughter. Anthony Comstock had raided the League's New York building, seized thousands of copies of its publications, and arrested its secretary. The publications, Comstock swore, contained obscene pictures—some of them were nudes by students who had come to Woodstock for the summer. Most newspapers reflected urban opinion and treated the incident as a joke. But among the Catskills, Comstock was forgiven for having smashed local slot machines. And when he spent his vacation as usual in Stamford that summer, he was regarded as a good deal of a cultural hero. The students, however, took a very different view of Comstock. They covered the walls of the League studios with caricatures of their enemy and hung him in effigy from the windows of the League building in New York. When the case came up for trial that fall, students crammed into the courtroom and made drawings furiously amid hearty laughter. For many years, even after his case against the League ended in defeat for Comstock, he remained the favorite butt of League wits and the symbol of all that they most disliked in their society.[14]

Woodstock people did not share in the students' view of Comstock. Their horizons were limited; their lives remained centered on what they regarded as the old and sound verities expounded from local pulpits and hallowed by their ancestors' acceptance. To have a branch of an art school which Mr. Comstock swore in court was a hotbed of obscenity enter their town and settle there to stay was no laughing matter. Art and obscenity became inseparably associated in many Woodstock minds. Rumors of unspeakable goings-on among "the artists" flew about the town. When a few men's shirts were ripped in a burst of horseplay at an Art Students League dance, sheriffs were summoned from Kingston to punish this case of "nude dancing." Righteous citizens peeped among the bushes along the Sawkill which flowed through Woodstock, hoping to detect instances of "nude bathing." Some Woodstock people reacted in a more kindly way toward the artists, and sometimes closer contact broke down prejudices—as in the case of Rosie Magee. Mrs. Magee was the wife of a bluestone-quarry teamster. She ran an artists' boardinghouse in Rock City and came to be widely and affectionately known because she acted as a kindly substitute mother for many a lonely or discouraged student.[15]

By 1912 Woodstock had been divided as never before in its history. The art students looked up at staid old Byrdcliffe with smiles and nicknamed it "Boredstiffe."[16] Ralph Whitehead looked down from Byrdcliffe in wonder and horror at what was going on in the valley below. He saw studio after studio being built for students who had succumbed to the charm of Woodstock and proposed to spend their lives there. He remained faithful to John Ruskin and to his Renaissance and Pre-Raphaelite gods. The paintings being produced in Woodstock appeared to him to be decadent. When Whitehead looked toward the Maverick it was with chilly eyes. Once he had called Hervey White by the affectionate nickname of "Niccolo," but now he avoided speaking of him and, when he had to mention him, called him "Mr. White." Potters, metalworkers, and weavers continued to work at Byrdcliffe, and painters sometimes gave lessons there. But rich art-loving business people also settled in Whitehead's ridings and moved its atmosphere closer to that of Onteora Park. Private musical performances continued to be a feature of Byrdcliffe life—for a time emphasis was on old music played on recorders, the viola da gamba, and Mr. Whitehead's clavichord. John Burroughs was a visitor and sometimes Whitehead, having yielded to the motorcar, drove to Woodchuck Lodge in Roxbury to pay his respect to the Sage of the Catskills at his summer home.

Once Whitehead had been sorrowfully convinced that he himself had no talent at all for working in the arts and crafts. But after 1904 he discovered that he was wrong. He took up weaving and making pottery with creditable results, and Mrs. Whitehead joined him in working at these crafts. The two made vases of great refinement, and Whitehead's work as a potter eventually earned him listing among the "masters" of the American Society of Arts and Crafts. Byrdcliffe had not fulfilled the hopes he had once had for it. But it provided him with a pleasant and in many ways satisfying existence. Almost to the end of his life he worked as a craftsman for several hours a day and when he left home to travel, strangers regarded him with puzzled interest, for they saw a reserved-looking man in middle life absorbed in weaving a silk scarf on a little lap loom.

While Byrdcliffe shrank in stature as an arts and crafts colony, the hamlet of Woodstock, thanks to the presence of the Art Students League, became ever more important as an "art colony." The school had begun with twenty-nine students; by 1912 it had two hundred. Birge Harrison was not far from the truth when he called it "the principal landscape school of the world."[17] The Maverick stood somewhat aside from both Byrdcliffe and Woodstock. As yet it attracted no painters or craftsmen but filled its cabins each summer with musicians, a few writers, and a good many offbeat thinkers, such as radical lawyer Clarence Darrow, economist and sociologist Thorstein Veblen who was shocking proper people with his theory of "conspicuous consumption" and the unconventionality of his own sex life, and leaders in organized labor and the feminist movement. The mood on the Maverick was one of confidence as the colony expanded rapidly. In 1906 a printing press had been set up with Lindin's help, and it filled a deep need for Hervey. His career as a promising novelist had been checked by the bankruptcy of his publishers; now he proposed printing his own work and the work of others. In the fall of 1911 he founded a little literary magazine, *The Wild Hawk*.

In 1915 the Maverick and the Woodstock art colony began visibly joining forces. The previous year Hervey had organized a concert given by his tenant-musicians in the Woodstock Firemen's Hall for the benefit of Belgian refugees from the German invasion—most of his musicians were of Belgian origin. The musicians were naturally angered by the invasion, as were most Americans. Woodstock people crowded the Firemen's Hall to hear the concert. Townspeople, Maverick people, artists and art students, even Byrdcliffe people, sat side by side on the hard benches of the hall. The concert demonstrated one thing beyond all doubt. It was possible for the people of Woodstock, divided as they were, to co-operate when a sufficiently strong motive drew them together. The next spring Hervey put Woodstock co-operation to another test. This time the motive was to pay for a communal well on the Maverick.

From its beginning the cabins on the Maverick got along without such refinements as running water and flush toilets. It was not that Hervey felt such things to be wicked or immoral, but that he believed they were relatively unimportant and could easily be done without. Increased population on the Maverick, however, strained the few dug wells beyond their capacity and it became necessary to have a new well drilled. Day after day that winter the drill bit ever deeper into the bedrock of the Catskills—at a cost of three dollars per foot—one hundred feet, two hundred, three hundred, four hundred, five hundred feet. At five hundred forty-four feet, drilling stopped when a modest vein of water was struck. The well driller, long since converted from a stranger to a friend of Hervey's, agreed to wait for his money—twenty years if necessary—if payments were made from time to time. But how to raise the money for these payments? Hervey decided that when the moon was full the next August he would stage a rollicking, money-raising festival in which his friends on all levels of Woodstock life would be asked to co-operate.

The friends responded eagerly and helped plan a festival which ended up by having a good deal of a Russian flavor. The long struggles of the Russian people against the tyrannical government of their czars had aroused great American sympathy and had helped to attract Russians to the United States and to make their arts popular. (The Russian Revolution of 1917 with its chilling effect on Americans was still two years in the future.) The Maverick's Russian singer, Madame Narodny, volunteered. She had a "soul-thrilling voice" like those "of the women in Dostoyevsky's novels,"[18] Hervey proclaimed. A young and lovely American dancer just back from study in Russia also volunteered. The artists of Woodstock, almost to a man, got to work on painting scenery and immense banners and making decorations for the booths which would house a variety of sideshows. Hervey's farmer neighbors helped turn an old bluestone quarry into an amphitheater with rude seats and a stage. Craftsman Edward Thatcher, who had once been the pride of Byrdcliffe but had by now set up on his own, provided lights improvised from the headlights of a junked car. The dancer's rich mother, as her contribution, consulted astrologer Evangeline Adams, who picked upon Friday of the week of the full moon as most favorable. That Friday it rained with passion. The festival was postponed to the following day.

Hervey had printed a thousand advertising circulars and sent them throughout the Catskills. In response, people poured in from Pine Hill, Tannersville, Onteora Park, and many other resort centers as well as from the Hudson Valley trading towns. Most wore picturesque costumes— gypsies, pirates, shipwrecked sailors, princesses, and peasant girls swarmed over the Maverick. All the scheduled performances were received with enthusiasm. The afternoon concert by fourteen members of the Metropolitan Opera Orchestra, who were paid the full union scale, was applauded wildly. The picnic suppers of hundreds of groups gathered about campfires in a grassy clearing, the evening musical and dramatic performances, the white goat with her horns painted blue who assumed striking poses on the tops of rocks—all were smashing successes. As the festival ended, a body of young admirers seized Hervey and carried him on their shoulders to the stage as a hero. Hervey managed a few words of thanks and then in the elation of the moment announced that he had that day determined to carry out a plan that had haunted him ever since he had come to the Maverick. The next summer he would build a woodland concert hall where the best of chamber music would be performed each summer Sunday afternoon, for an admission fee of fifty cents per concert. At this the audience cheered fervently. Hervey then asked those who would like to subscribe to the concerts to send him the money for the first season's tickets. Again there were cheers. Everyone concerned agreed that the first of the Maverick Festivals was an immense success. Yet in one way it hadn't succeeded. When the receipts were counted, it became apparent that expenses had been barely covered and that there was no money left over for the well or for the promised concert hall. But Hervey was not discouraged. There would be future festivals—and what was more important, he had discovered that it was possible to carry out big projects without any money of his own at all.

When Hervey first arrived in Woodstock, it was as a quite conventional sort of Socialist with a red tie. After a while the red tie was discarded and so too were many of Hervey's earlier convictions. He had substituted for them a Whitmanlike faith in the value of warm personal relationships and of freedom from social restraints grown obsolete with time. He found that a man who expected no reward in money for himself might accomplish wonders without having a penny of his own if only he had plenty of friends and was willing to borrow from the capitalist world parts of its notions about credit. A sawmill owner who was a friend of Hervey's agreed to furnish lumber for what was first called a "music chapel" and to wait for payment from the proceeds of future concerts and rent from the musicians' cabins. Farmer neighbors who could afford to wait for their wages agreed to do so. Hervey designed his chapel himself, using as a model the community houses of villages on the Fiji Islands. Drawing upon recollections of a rather dubious theory of acoustics picked up in a college physics class, he planned his chapel in multiples of two numbers only. The frame of unpeeled logs was assembled on the ground and was raised in the old-fashioned way, bent by bent. When the unseasoned roofing boards were nailed on they proved too heavy for the frame, which threatened to buckle. Hervey put to practical use the lectures on Gothic architecture he had heard from Charles Herbert Moore at Harvard and improvised flying buttresses to distribute the weight. The building is still standing after more than half a century.[19]

Thanks to the excellence of the musicians whom Hervey had assembled on the Maverick and thanks to the remarkably good acoustics of his hall, The Maverick Sunday Concert drew satisfactory audiences from the beginning. A little of Hervey's indebtedness could be paid off and more would be paid from future festivals and concerts. But what pleased Hervey as much as anything else was the presence at his first concert of an unexpected music lover: Ralph Radcliffe Whitehead, who now descended from Byrdcliffe and took his seat in the hall with a group of friends. After ten years of refusing to recognize Hervey, he spoke to him once more, but this time with what White described as "formal courtesy."[20] After that he and Hervey resumed their friendship, though in a far less intimate way. Hervey liked to say afterward that his Maverick concerts had their roots in Byrdcliffe, that it was from Whitehead he learned to love chamber music.

The appearance of Whitehead at the Maverick concerts might serve as a symbol of what was happening among the painters, writers, musicians, craftsmen, and unorthodox thinkers who were gathering in growing numbers in the valley beneath Overlook Mountain. Byrdcliffe, the Maverick, and the painters centered around the Summer School of the Art Students League were moving closer together and joining forces to produce a new Woodstock to which all three groups contributed—but which would be different from all three.

The Woodstock Art Colony
Comes of Age

✤ BY THE EARLY 1920s the Woodstock art colonists had become self-conscious enough to have developed a respectable mythology of their own. Just as Thomas Cole was revered in Catskill for having claimed the vicinity of the Catskill Mountain House for art, so Woodstock's three discoverers of 1902 were enshrined as founding fathers of the art colony. The mythology of the Catskill Mountain House had gone back to the Indians for added authority, and Woodstock people of about 1920 were repeating bits of "Indian lore" which seemed to give their town a mystical basis for its character. It was being said that the ancient Indian inhabitants of the region had believed that Woodstock's Overlook Mountain exerted a magnetic force which drew human beings toward it and made it hard for them to leave.[1] The Indians, like all other people who did not use iron, are not known to have had any lore about magnetic mountains, yet the belief was valid enough as an expression of the charm Woodstock was exerting on those young people who were seeking for a favorable place in which they might throw off irrational restraints of their society. It was buttressed by another bit of lore which held that the Indians had felt strange emanations from the earth at the very spot where the art colony would flourish. In June 1970 the Woodstock *Aquarian* put the belief in this way: "Woodstock, a town, but more a name that symbolizes a state of consciousness . . . the town, nestled in a valley surrounded by the lush forestry [sic] of the legendary Catskill Mountains . . . this valley rumored, by the Indians who lived here many moons ago, to be haunted by strange spirits, a sacred kind of place. . . ." Woodstock sculptor Alfeo Faggi claimed that when he first arrived in the colony shortly after 1920, he felt stimulating vibrations from the earth. They were of precisely the same sort,

Faggi insisted, as those he had felt in Rome, Paris, his native Florence, and a handful of other centers of creativity in the arts.[2]

As art colony members explored their town's past they came upon all sorts of materials which appeared to strengthen Woodstock's claim to having a curious bent toward creativity. Even the plants of the town, some said, had shown a creative urge. In the late 1920s a monument was erected to honor the Jonathan apple which is a world-famous native of Woodstock. It appeared a little after 1800 in the orchard that Livingston tenant Philip Rick had planted in accordance with the terms of his lease. The Jonathan apple made its way round the world and became a leading variety in Japan, Korea, Italy, France, New Zealand, and Australia.[3] And that was not all. A Woodstock farmer grew a new sort of plum named, in his honor, the Van Bunschoten; it was yellow and much favored for canning. A Woodstock clergyman named Tuthill developed a new kind of sweet corn once popular in the vicinity. Much later a delver among old records of the Hardenbergh Patent's Great Lot 25 found that in the mid-1790s William Cockburn had noted the surveying and leasing to a man named John Chapman of a farm at the entrance to Mink Hollow. Chapman cleared a few of his wooded acres and then vanished. The farm was eventually re-entered upon by an agent of its owner.[4] What is interesting about this is that the true name of that American hero Johnny Appleseed was John Chapman and that the years of his life during which the Woodstock John Chapman was clearing his land in Mink Hollow form a blank in the known record of Johnny Appleseed as he made his way from Massachusetts to Pennsylvania. Were the two John Chapmans the same? As yet it has neither been proved nor disproved.

As John Chapman disappeared from Woodstock, a father and son, both named Lewis Edson, were clearing a nearby farm. (They were the Edsons mentioned in an earlier chapter as composers and singing-school teachers.) Eventually the Edsons were rediscovered as Woodstock composer Henry Cowell used themes of the elder Edson in hymns and fuguing tunes of his own which were played in the Maverick Concert Hall. The Edsons then gave Woodstock musicians a valued sense of continuity in the musical life of their town. More recently, Woodstock painters also acquired a figure from the past to whom they could look for the material of myth: he was Montgomery Livingston. Livingston and his brother, Eugene, were the last Livingston landlords of the town of Woodstock. Montgomery was a landscape painter of sufficient standing in his day to become an Associate of the National Academy of Design.[5] Until his early death in 1855, he lived and worked in the Clermont of his grandfather, the

Chancellor. He painted in the Catskills, the White Mountains, and the Alps. A miniature portrait of Montgomery still preserved by his brother's descendants suggests that if he were to have walked down Woodstock's Tinker Street during the late 1960s he would have seemed very much part of the scene. For he favored the look and manners of the French Bohemians of his day: his hair hung to his shoulders, a blond beard ornamented his chin, and his eyes looked out upon the world with a message of peace and goodwill.

Fortunately for the success of Woodstock mythmaking, the town had an impressive topographical feature to serve as a center around which myth and legend might accumulate—this was Overlook Mountain. The mountain's conspicuous position, jutting out as it does from the rest of the Catskills, and its bold contours made it a striking object even when seen from afar. It is not surprising then that Overlook became the most often-painted of all the Catskill Mountains and probably of all American mountains from the day of the master of the Van Bergen overmantel to the present. Governor Pownall had sketched it as he sailed up the Hudson in the 1760s; Thomas Cole had seen it daily from his Catskill studio; Frederick E. Church had often sketched it from the windows and balconies of his Persian-American palace of Olana; Hervey White's teacher, Charles Herbert Moore, had sketched it in 1869.[6] Once landscape painters came to Byrdcliffe and spread over much of the rest of Woodstock they seized upon Overlook not only as a model but as a symbol of their colony. So often was Overlook painted and in so many manners during two centuries and more that it would be an easy matter to paraphrase the Japanese printmaker Hokusai and bring together "Thirty-six Views of Overlook" which could be by thirty-six different painters working from 1732 to the present. The views would form an outline of American landscape painting, proceeding logically enough until it reached the work done by Woodstock painters about 1912. Then a mixture of excitement and confusion would become obvious, reflecting turmoil in the art colony.

The first painters to reach Byrdcliffe in 1903 had worked in a manner influenced by the Barbizon painters of France and by the Impressionists who followed them, and students at the Art Students League painted in a similar fashion. Then, in 1911, a young man named Konrad Cramer arrived from Munich, Germany, bringing news of the rise there of a fresh and exciting way of seeing and painting the visible world. The next year brought Andrew Dasburg back from Paris where he had acquired a missionary enthusiasm for the paintings of the Postimpressionists, and especially for Cézanne.[7] By the time the famous Armory Show of 1913

awakened Americans to the birth of what was called "modern art," many
Woodstock painters were already deeply immersed in it. The older painters
stuck to their guns and joined Ralph Whitehead in denouncing the new
spirit as decadent—old friends sometimes ceased speaking after hotly de-
bating the value of modern art. Bolton Brown had been the painter-
pioneer of Rock City; now he saw the neighborhood becoming a seedbed
of revolution. Brown had painted, dealt in prints, made pottery, and raised
squabs for the market in Rock City. Later he would teach lithography at
his new home in Zena. But when modern art invaded Rock City, Brown
viewed it as an enemy. As he walked each morning from his house to
the Woodstock post office, he passed Rosie Magee's where revolutionary
notions positively swirled in the air. Brown walked with head high and
eyes fixed straight ahead lest he make contaminating contact with the
Rock City rebels.

Overlook now began to appear on canvas as seen in the reflected
light of Paul Cézanne, and it was also being translated into planes and
angles of Cubism. Birge Harrison and John F. Carlson, who taught together
at the Art Students League, resisted the new revelations in painting and
the number of students who worked under them in Woodstock fields and
meadows diminished. Woodstock was taking the bit in its teeth and was
intent on plunging into the future. It had rejected the Old World aspects
of Whitehead's Byrdcliffe, and now it was rejecting with equal vigor painting the Woodstock "moods of nature" which Harrison and Carlson loved.
The meadows through which pearly brooks wound by moonlight, the
brief October glory of maples, Overlook seen through an opalescent haze—
these subjects were losing their power to stimulate many young Woodstock painters who were bent on experimentation. Their experiments led
for many into the group of painters dubbed by important art critics
the Woodstock school.[8] Included in the school were such diverse men as
Eugene Speicher, Henry Lee McFee, Henry Mattson, and Judson Smith.
In 1922, Harry Gottlieb settled on the Maverick as its first resident painter
and was joined by Arnold and Lucille Blanch, ceramist Carl Walters, and
sculptor John Flannagan. The Maverick painters were soon popularly
placed in the Woodstock school, and by the end of the 1920s the school
was being described as the most daring and advanced in the United
States. Their work had little in common except for a derivation from Post-
impressionism, and a somewhat romantic approach in dealing with their
favorite subjects: the Woodstock landscape and Woodstock people. Not
since the days of the Hudson River school had the Catskills made so strong
an impression on American art. Woodstock's mountains and streams, its

red barns and weatherworn farmers and their wives became widely known. Woodstock painters, such as George Bellows, who stood apart in the public consciousness from the school also used local subjects.

The young people of the Woodstock art colony became known as experimenters in art, but they experimented with more than that. To them Byrdcliffe came to seem ever more staid and proper, but they were in rebellion in their own fashion against the same money and machine culture which Ralph Whitehead, Ruskin, and Morris had found to be destroying many of the most desirable human values. They experimented with means of expressing their rebelliousness in many ways: they expressed it not only in their work but also in unconventional dress, and in a freedom of thought and language which shocked old Woodstockers. Their women followed the lead of the prominent workers for equal rights for women who had been part of Woodstock life ever since Charlotte Perkins Gilman spent the summer of 1903 at Byrdcliffe. These women had few or no children, for they recognized that their society made rearing children into responsible and happy adults extremely difficult, and many poured their energies instead into working in the arts and crafts or supporting protests against social injustice.

What was happening among the artists of Woodstock reflected in a concentrated way a period of deep social change on a national scale. By 1920 the stiffly starched collar was beginning to disappear from the necks of young males, and with it went a good deal of stiff and starched behavior. The Bohemian way of life was seeping into many levels of society. In urban art colonies like New York's Greenwich Village and in similar colonies in Chicago, Minneapolis, and Boston, Woodstock was being talked about more and more and with growing enthusiasm. It was being said that here was a remarkable small town set in the midst of beautiful mountain scenery—a town that actually welcomed artists, writers, musicians, and people with unconventional ways.[9] Not that the town's older residents approved of the newcomers—not at all. But they found them an irresistible source of profit. Once the new kind of people began flocking to Woodstock, property values rose, and men thrown out of work by the closing of the bluestone quarries or the decline of farming could get work at good wages. Farmers learned that if they put a large window in the north wall of an outbuilding, however ramshackle, they could rent it as a studio, and artists began displacing chickens, sheep, and cows as tenants. Shopkeeping and the control of churches and politics remained in the familiar local hands; most of the new people seemed bored with all three. They were willing to provide the town with a healthy economic base as long as they were permitted to live in their own way with a minimum of interference. Older Woodstock people stifled their disapproval and usually treated "the artists," as they called all the newcomers whether they painted or not, with polite consideration lest they scare them off. But a strong current of dislike flowed steadily beneath the surface and erupted from time to time in displays of open hostility. The artists for their part usually regarded "the natives" with amused condescension.

Hervey White did not share in this attitude. He continued to hope to find common ground upon which Maverick people, Byrdcliffe people, the artists brought to the town by the League, and the natives might meet and co-operate for their mutual benefit. In 1918 he had printed at the Maverick Press a novel of his own which dealt with Woodstock hostilities. The central character of *The Prodigal Father* is a young minister who grows in understanding through association with the artists in projects for improving the music and the visual quality of his church. Another older and very bigoted minister denounces "the wickedness and debauchery of these idolatrous artists, who are corrupting, not only themselves, which is an unimportant matter as they are but fuel for the flames of God's wrath at best, but they are corrupting the pure lives of these simple villagers and turning them into gamblers and harlots."[10] The novel was much discussed in Woodstock but it did nothing to quiet local conflicts.

The Prodigal Father was a somewhat naïve effort at healing the sharp division in Woodstock life which had followed the intrusion of the arts and crafts and social reform into the conservative, well-organized kind of society developed during the years after Robert Livingston had set up his sawmill in 1762. The book gave vivid expression to an aspect of Woodstock mythology which would grow in importance in the future and which crystallized around the clash of two main groups of Woodstock people, each with a different vision of what constitutes a good life and each with its own set of prejudices and irrationalities.

By 1920 artist pilgrims often stood on the very spot from which Bolton Brown had caught his first exhilarating glimpse of Woodstock and looked down on the valley with delight. They saw a landscape which did not look quite the same as it had in 1902. The new Ashokan Reservoir in the middle distance added charm, but the growth of brush along marginal Woodstock fields and pastures deprived the landscape of some of its former appearance of being well cared for and even loved. The ragged, rejected look of a few parts of Woodstock was a result of the substitution of the cultivation of artists for that of corn, apples, and hay. Yet the view from near Mead's was very nearly as appealing as it had been in 1902. The valley still seemed so quiet and peaceful that it was hard to believe its people were divided and in conflict with visions of a happier and freer future filling one set of minds and hope for a return to a golden pre-Byrdcliffe past occupying others.

85

Tourists, Artists, and Townsmen

🌲 TWENTY-FIVE YEARS after Bolton Brown had looked down from the Wide Clove at Mead's on his South Sea, the art colony of Woodstock was growing like a healthy child in a loving family. Nothing seemed able to check its momentum, not even the closing in 1923 of the Art Students League, the school that had done so much to nourish the art colony in its days of infancy. It closed when the kind of out-of-doors landscape painting it taught ceased to be fashionable among the knowing, and it did not reopen until 1946. Meantime, half a dozen private art schools filled the gap.

As the art colony grew, a Woodstock Chamber of Commerce was born and did its best to increase the flow of spending tourists. Soon Woodstock was rivaling the Kaaterskill Falls as a tourist attraction. While few visitors attended the Maverick concerts which continued to thrive without their help, some entered the art gallery to observe examples of artistic nudity and were pleased at being able to recognize Overlook Mountain and other features of the Catskills hanging on the walls beside nudes and more baffling efforts. Many tourists came to Woodstock to attend the Maverick festivals which gained in splendor each year and each year became more and more bacchanalian revels with bootlegged mountain apple-jack, in that era of Prohibition, doing its share to raise the spirits of celebrants.[1] The reputation of Woodstock for sexual freedom brought unwed couples to the doors of the boardinghouse-keeping members of the Chamber of Commerce in pleasing volume.

From all the mountain resort centers and the trading towns, taxi-drivers brought parties of visitors eager to see the wonders of Woodstock. The drivers had taken the place of the old-timers with their horse-drawn surries and were regarded as experts on the eccentricities and nudities of Woodstock. Their tales of naked women popping out from behind bushes encouraged patrons to keep their eyes open, and if they happened to pass Hervey White, they looked with horror at his Russian blouse, for after 1917 just such a garment was worn by the Bolsheviks in newspaper cartoons who leered at the American public while carrying bombs with sputtering fuses. The drivers would point out the restaurant Hervey had built on the Maverick. It was called The Intelligencia—a name with revolutionary implications. For a time the place was run by a well-known Greenwich Village anarchist named Hippolyte Havel, who sometimes muttered "bourgeois pigs" as he waited on tourists.[2] Nearby, as Havel muttered, the beginning of Woodstock's greatest tourist attraction of the future was taking shape, however unintentionally. The dramatic spectacles presented at the Maverick festivals had been applauded with fervor, and this had stimulated Hervey White to write plays of his own. In July 1923 an offshot of the once famous Ben Greet players presented Shakespeare's *As You Like It* and *Midsummer Night's Dream* in the appropriately wooded setting of the Maverick festival's amphitheater. By the following year a Maverick Theater had been built; it matched the Concert Hall in its very effective log-and-slab construction. The theater's first director, Dudley Digges, explained in the July 5 number of Woodstock's *Hue and Cry* that he did not see the Maverick Theater as aimed at the tourist trade; "The venture is altogether in the nature of a holiday in the woods"[3] for the cast, and would present "plays of artistic distinction before an audience of distinguished artists." This relaxed approach did not quite jibe with Hervey White's plans for the theater: he wanted it to stress experiment and to present, not familiar plays, but new and untried ones, including his own. Almost at once the theater ran into difficulties, but it set in motion a frenzy of theater activity elsewhere in Woodstock. In 1925 the old studio of the Byrdcliffe Summer School of Art, with a stage added, became the Phoenix Theater and there excellent plays were presented by Ben Webster, a young architect of Byrdcliffe background who had turned to the theater in New York some years earlier. In Woodstock itself, a barn, which had once served the well-known Riseley farm and boardinghouse, had become a theater, and at one point during the 1920s, six theater ventures were said to be in competition for tourist dollars. Experimental, classic, and avant-garde plays bored tourists or made them feel uneasy, but they were soothed and reassured by Woodstock productions of Broadway successes starring familiar Broadway names.[4]

Tourists were soothed and reassured as well by a few other attractions of Woodstock. Among these was the new Woodstock Country Club and its golf course where prosperous members of the Woodstock school might be seen sporting, not in the nude, but in baggy plus fours of the latest cut. Golf was still considered an amusement of the rich, so here was evidence that not all artists were bad. More venturesome summer boarders left their automobiles or taxis and paraded up and down Woodstock's Tinker Street to observe what many called "the freaks." There was no telling what a parader might see: a lady wearing men's trousers and smoking a cigar; a stout former ballerina clad in a pink turban and flowing orange robes; a couple walking hand in hand—his hair powdered with gold, hers with silver. Artists could usually be picked out because in a day when every respectable male considered himself half-naked if he ventured hatless out of doors, Woodstock artists seldom wore conventional hats.[5] At a time when the adult human foot was regarded as an obscene object, artists—male and female—often wore sandals which exposed their toes to the gaze of strangers. Paraders had to be on guard against pamphleteers for a variety of causes. Tall, bearded poet William Benignus, for example, might catch the eye of a tourist and then deftly hypnotize him into buying a copy of his *Stories of the Catskills*. The paper-covered book had almost nothing to say about the Catskills but it did convey the information that its author was "A Sun Child," and that "Sunchildren are always young and happy. Music is in their hearts which are ever alight by the Star of Pure Joy. The souls of Sunchildren are woven from sunrays."[6] Music was also in the heart and a smile was always on the face of Woodstock's Jaache Schwamb, known as "the Play Boy." Schwamb believed in allowing life to penetrate and suffuse him: "This opening of heart and letting the Light enter has been the experience which has made of life one glad sweet song," Schwamb wrote in the *Woodstock Weekly* of December 26, 1924. He was accounting there for his ability to derive intense enjoyment from all forms of art, from the most conservative to the most adventurous, but he applied the same method to all aspects of life.

Visitors arriving on a Saturday morning would see the famous Market Fair in progress on the Village Green. Here Woodstock-made craft objects in metal, fiber, and wood were on sale, as were cut flowers and vegetables. The women who presided over the Fair's colorful booths were often the wives of artists or were themselves active in the arts. They wore—and sold—attractive long dresses which suggested Kate Greenaway's illustrations and Central European peasant garb and were known as "Woodstock dresses." "The effect of Woodstock on the morning of the Market Fair is as bright and glowing as anything this side of Czechoslovakia on the one hand and Hollywood on the other," said a writer in the New York *Times Magazine* of August 25, 1929. Visitors who wanted to learn the story of Woodstock's past might buy a copy of expatriate Englishman Richard LeGallienne's beguiling *Essay on Woodstock,* published by the newly born Woodstock Artists Association and illustrated with reproductions of the work of Woodstock painters, sculptors, and craftsmen. If it was the future that interested a visitor, he might consult the colony's resident astrologer—the first to practice this ancient profession among the Catskills. And if he were determined to get the greatest possible bang out of the present, he could attend a Maverick festival. There artists, tourists, and young villagers mingled joyously in the moonlight with all thought of their hostilities forgotten for the moment. The festivals had appeal for everyone. They featured impressive spectacles—a great pirate ship afloat on a simulated ocean, the ancient Carthage of Flaubert's *Salammbo,* the feast of King Nebuchadnezzer, Rip Van Winkle awakening from his twenty years' sleep to find himself in Woodstock surrounded by artists. Featured too were Graeco-Roman wrestlers, George Barrère playing his famous golden flute in blackface, nude and seminude performers, and music in endless variety. Usually the festival show was held together by a script of Hervey's. Such talented Woodstock men as Rusell Wright, Hunt Diedrich, and Robert Winthrop Chanler, that imaginative and hedonistic descendant of both John Jacob Astor and Robert Livingston, worked week after week to create stage sets while the women of the art colony cut and stitched costumes. The festival ended at dawn as the last of the dancers in the concert hall gave up. Hervey White presided over the revels dressed as the god Pan and with vine leaves wreathing his head, which was why he was called the "Pan of the Catskills."[7]

Until 1921 the festivals had been celebrated in their original bluestone quarry setting. But the previous summer a production of poetess Edna St. Vincent Millay's war-condemning play *Aria da Capo* had drawn such a large audience as to strain the capacity of the quarry beyond its limits. As the Millay sisters and their friends of the Provincetown Players, James Light and Charles Ellis, acted out the play on a stage crammed with spectators, the orchestra was bombarded with rocks dislodged by members of the audience perched on the top of the quarry walls. The next year a new and larger outdoor theater was built. And this, too, was filled through the 1920s as the full moon of August glowed over the Catskills.

The Maverick festivals welcomed all comers, Jews and Christians, non-believers, blacks, whites, people who spoke English and people who didn't. But in Woodstock people whose appearance led them to be taken for Jews often reported that they were not treated with courtesy in shops and that they were the last to be served in the many little restaurants springing up. In August 1924 an agent of the expanding Ku Klux Klan arrived in Woodstock to organize local prejudices, especially against Jews, into a conventional form. A fiery cross was burned and local businessmen were signed up as members and issued white robes. The organizer collected substantial initiation fees and vanished. The Woodstock chapter of the Ku Klux Klan vanished too, but the misunderstandings and hostilities that had led to its appearance remained. Even Hervey White, though among the most tolerant Americans of his time, was affected by the fear of a Jewish capture of Woodstock which held many of his friends in its grip. In his long narrative poem called *Tinker Tom,* written in the early 1920s though Hervey did not print it until 1930, he gives evidence of a narrowing of his sympathies and a sharpening of many of his prejudices. On page 6, he refers to

> . . . the invasion of Belgium by the Germans, us, by Jews,
> Which is the worse, I leave you free to choose.

The absence of Jews which had made it possible for Byrdcliffe to appear in Woodstock in 1902 was not an accident. While many resort centers in the Catskills had given up their earlier attempts to exclude Jews, Woodstock, Windham, Stamford, Onteora, and several other parks and towns had succeeded. None of the painters, craftsmen, or students of the early years of Byrdcliffe had been Jewish—the first Jew to whom Ralph Whitehead is known to have rented a house at Byrdcliffe was the brilliant economist and publicist Walter Weyl. In 1908, when Weyl married Bertha Poole, a worker at Hull House, Clarence Darrow influenced the couple to go to Woodstock to spend their honeymoon. There to their surprise they met an old friend of Weyl's days as a graduate student at the University of Pennsylvania: Martin Schutze, professor of German literature at the University of Chicago. Schutze was a close friend of Ralph Whitehead and this plus Weyl's high degree of charm helped persuade Whitehead to rent the Weyls a house and after a year or two even to offer to sell them land for building at Byrdcliffe. But Weyl preferred buying a lonely farm on Ohayo Mountain across the Woodstock Valley from Byrdcliffe and high above the Maverick. There he worked on the books which were to make him known to a wide public—*The New Democracy* was one of them. Weyl became a force in Theodore Roosevelt's Progressive party. And when the party went down to defeat in 1912, Weyl joined with a group of others in founding and editing the *New Republic,* long an influential weekly. Until his death in 1921, Weyl remained fascinated by Woodstock with its opportunities for a freer life, its submerged and open hostilities between groups, its mixing into new patterns of people with varied cultural and ethnic backgrounds. Like Hervey White, Weyl sensed the town's importance as a portent of the future.[8]

On the surface, at least, the determination of Woodstock landowners and businessmen to keep out Jews was becoming ineffective by the mid-1920s. Weyl had been the forerunner of many Jewish students, writers, painters, craftsmen, and musicians to settle in the colony and find life there good. Jewish summer boarders also became more numerous. About 1915 the Overlook Mountain House, after many years of struggle to remain alive, was sold to Morris Newgold of New York. One summer Newgold turned the hotel into a resort for a club of young women members of the predominately Jewish Ladies Garment Workers Union of New York. When the old hotel burned in 1924, Newgold aroused strong anti-Semitic symptoms in Woodstock by announcing plans to build a larger and more modern structure, which many assumed would be the kind of all-Jewish hotel the Catskill Mountain House and many other large hotels in the region were becoming.[9] Construction was well under way when the virtual collapse of the American economy which began in 1929 and equalled the one of 1837 which had so strongly affected the future of the Catskill Mountain House brought an end to the era of mountaintop hotels among the Catskills.

Nineteen twenty-nine brought an end not only to any reasonable hopes for a rebirth of the Overlook Mountain House but also to the first phase of Woodstock's career as an art colony. In October 1928, seventy-five-year-old Ralph Whitehead had invited his friends to White Pines to a party celebrating the departure for South America of his oldest son, Ralph, Jr. Among those invited was Hervey White—this was the first time since the summer of 1904 that White had been a guest at White Pines. The ship on which young Whitehead sailed was the *Vestris*. The *Vestris* foundered in the Caribbean and Whitehead was among those lost. His father was deeply shaken. In February 1929 he died in a Santa Barbara hospital. His obituary in the New York *Times* stated that "the arts and crafts settlement that he established at Woodstock is known as a remarkable community that bears the impress of the refinement and idealism of its founder."[10]

Whitehead's refinement and idealism had certainly left their marks upon Woodstock—but so, too, had many other influences. American Bohemianism, the Hull House kind of approach to social problems, the patronage of rich people who settled in Woodstock because they enjoyed the company of artists and strayers from the path of convention, conflict between artists and older Woodstock people with their ambivalent feelings toward the young and the new and the lively aspects of their world. The natural scenery and the geographical location of Woodstock along with the town's traditions and history had helped make Woodstock into a rallying cry for the young and rebellious.

Ralph Whitehead remained apart from the Woodstock villagers in death as he had in life. It was true that he had always responded to appeals for contributions for local projects and that he had been a leader in founding the Woodstock Club with its dual purpose of providing Woodstock with a library and relieving the burdens of the poor. Yet Whitehead had kept his distance. His ashes were eventually placed in what was called the Artists' Cemetery and not in that used by the older Woodstock people. The cemetery neatly symbolized the separation of artists and villagers. Some say that the first of the Woodstock artists to die had been refused space in the Woodstock Cemetery on the ground that his life had been Sabbath-breaking and otherwise immoral; others say that the artist's family believed that they were too important to lie forever among the ordinary folks of Woodstock, so the Artists' Cemetery was organized around the solitary grave of a promising young man who had been killed in an automobile accident within sight of the old one but at a higher elevation and with a much better view of Overlook Mountain. A lovely relief of the Mother and Child in the manner of Della Robbia was brought down from Byrdcliffe to mark Whitehead's grave. This very relief had nourished Woodstock people of 1902 in the belief that Whitehead was a secret agent of the Pope.

86

Woodstock Rebels

THE DESCENT of Ralph Whitehead from Byrdcliffe to the Artists' Cemetery caused no noticeable change in the life of the art colony. The founder of Byrdcliffe had long ago passed in most minds from effective life into legend. Another event that took place a little more than a year after Whitehead died had a far greater impact on the art colony. This was the ending of the Maverick festivals. The festivals ended for two reasons. The chief one was that the depression of the 1930s made festival celebrants reluctant or unable to spend money. It was also said that the rowdiness of outsiders snuffing the spicy air of the Maverick made policing the festival grounds impossible, but this difficulty could have been overcome had the festivals continued profitable. The ending of the festivals marked the ending of the Maverick's period of growth. It was largely festival money that had built the more than thirty cottages, the theater, and the concert hall. Festival money had made it possible for Hervey to allow penniless young people to live rent-free and had helped them pay their grocery bills. With the festivals over and with Hervey White entering the ranks of the elderly at sixty-five, no more cottages were built, for it took all the cash and energy available to keep the old ones in a modest degree of repair. Yet the cottages continued to function as homes and studios of painters, writers, musicians, and a few craftsmen and more and more of the cottages were made habitable through the winter by the efforts of their tenants. As in the past, many of the tenants who couldn't pay rent, didn't.[1]

For years the Maverick Press with Hervey as director and printer had been a central feature of Maverick life. There Hervey had printed many of his own novels, poems, and plays. As a job printer he printed booklets, pamphlets, and other ephemera. He continued to publish *The Wild Hawk* until 1918, when it turned into the *Plowshare,* an interesting periodical with covers of wood and linoleum cuts in color by Woodstock artists. In

the *Plowshare* as in *The Wild Hawk,* illustrations and translations by Carl
Eric Lindin were frequent, as were examples of Hervey's own work. The
Plowshare died in 1920: in 1923 Hervey printed a lively summer weekly
devoted to art colony doings and named the *Hue and Cry.* It ran inter-
mittently under various editors for many years, but was often printed in
Kingston. As the festivals died, so too did much of Hervey's interest in
printing, and the last of his books was printed in 1935.

As he grew older, Hervey liked to refer to himself as a Yankee or
as "the old Puritan,"[2] and to mention that he was a descendant of
Peregrine White born on the *Mayflower* at anchor off New England in 1620.
Between 1927 and 1929 he printed three little books in which he turned back
to his childhood and youth and his Mexican adventure; they are *Childhood
Fancies, Boy's Vision,* and *Youth's Worship.* Readers who penetrate their
low-keyed manner will find that they give an absorbing picture of Mid-
western life in their day and shed light on the formation of Hervey's
personality. The appearance of the three books heralded the beginning of
the retreat by Hervey from the intense activity of his middle years. The
Maverick concerts alone of all the attractions which had given the Maverick
its glamor remained alive and thriving. The theater lingered on but it had
proved a disappointment to Hervey. Producing the kind of new and experimental plays he favored turned out—in the absence of a kindly angel
—to be rather more expensive than he had expected. The one play of his
own which was produced, *The Blizzard,* did not arouse enough enthusiasm
to encourage the succession of Maverick Theater lessees to stage any more.
Some summers the theater stood dark and empty. The theater groups which
leased it found it possible to remain reasonably solvent only by falling
back on Broadway hits which could fill the small theater with audiences
drawn from the trading towns and resorts of the Catskills. And even more
disappointing was the pressure which the theater exerted on the Maverick
itself. Theater lessees urged Hervey to bring electricity, running water, and
other refinements to the Maverick and sometimes they tried to install "improvements" on their own.[3] Hervey resisted all this with a determination
that surprised many people. He knew that the Maverick could maintain its
easy, communal spirit only for so long as it offered living at a minimum of
expense and comfort. Once it became more expensive and comfortable it
would have to change its character. When the theater people proposed
improvements, Hervey first told them that he couldn't authorize any
changes without the consent of his partner, Captain Van der Loo. And
where was the captain? Well, Hervey would say, he was somewhere in
China busily promoting Dr. Jayne's remedies; with luck an answer from

him might come along in six months. If the improvers insisted after that, Hervey sometimes lost his temper and denounced them in strong words as would-be wreckers of the Maverick.

During the mid-1930s the theater was being managed by a young man who had much to recommend him in Hervey's eyes. He was Robert Elwyn, a descendant of the innkeeping Elwyns who had been part of Woodstock life ever since the 1790s when one of them had acted as local agent for Chancellor Livingston. Under Elwyn the theater drew large audiences but its plays did not meet Hervey's taste for the experimental. A dispute inevitably followed, which is said to have centered around Elwyn's refusal to stage a play of Hervey's in which the entire cast performed on roller skates. Elwyn left the Maverick and built the handsome— and much larger—Woodstock Playhouse which has functioned with varying fortunes ever since and has been among Woodstock's most reliable tourist attractions. It was not until after Hervey's death that his theater briefly took on the character he dreamed of, when a group known as the Loft Players acted there under the direction of Jose Quintero and went on to establish a pioneer off-Broadway theater in New York which became famous as the Circle in the Square.[4]

In 1935, Hervey White turned over his press to a group of young people who were disciples of both White and writer D. H. Lawrence. They printed a literary and propagandist publication named *The Phoenix* and at the same time worked toward reviving handicrafts on the Maverick. Many of their ideals and objectives as expressed in the pages of the *Phoenix* would have met with the approval of John Ruskin, William Morris, and Ralph Whitehead. In the number of *The Phoenix* for Spring 1939, editor James P. Cooney pledged allegiance to "the complete renunciation of machines and mechanized modes of life; the unequivocal condemnation of Industrial forms of society, whether they be of Capitalist (with all its varying shades of Democratic, Liberal, Conservative, Technocratic etc.), Marxian Communist, Fascist, or Nazi variety; and the unswerving determination to serve under none of these degrading, deathly states, but to break away in small communities, in small precursors of a resurection [sic] and renascence of mankind through a return to the dignity and purity and religiousness of a mode of life rooted in agriculture and the handicrafts."[5] On another page of *The Phoenix,* Cooney wrote of his determination to establish "ourselves in a commune through tilling the earth, hunting, fishing and handicrafts." The Maverick group hoped eventually to move their commune to a part of South America where industrial society was unheard of.

There was an important difference between the Maverick idealists and the other social reformers who had preceded them to Woodstock. While Ralph Whitehead, Hervey White, and their earlier followers were by no means conventional in their attitude toward sex, they usually followed the reticence and caution of their society when they spoke or wrote on the subject, so it is not easy to know just what their convictions were. The new Maverick people followed D. H. Lawrence in giving sex a far more open and central part in life than White or Whitehead had ever dreamed possible; the sexual revolution outlined in William Morris' *News from Nowhere* was anemic indeed set beside that advocated by Lawrence and his disciples. As might have been expected, rumors of odd sexual goings-on with *The Phoenix* people circulated in Woodstock among both artists and townspeople. One man was said to have had several wives; another had no wife at all but when he felt the need of a mate, stood in the Maverick woods and bellowed like a bull—and a mate would arrive.[6] *The Phoenix* people did not believe in war, and as World War II began they opposed it and lost many of the subscribers to their publication. When the United States entered the war, some of their people were drafted and their commune collapsed. But they had brought to Woodstock a significant kind of rebellion against Western society which stood part way between that of Byrdcliffe and the Maverick and a new and more drastic rebellion which was to erupt in Woodstock during the 1960s.

While *The Phoenix* group struggled to establish their commune on the Maverick, Hervey White lived in relaxed co-operative fashion with a group of six to eight young Maverick men. In his youth he had been cook for a similar group on the Kansas plains; now he became a cook and housekeeper once again and sometimes called the Maverick "the ranch." Throughout his life as a writer he had been proud of the fact that he had not "sold out,"[7] had never written to order but had written as he pleased. In 1937 he accepted an advance of a thousand dollars from a New York publisher in return for his autobiography. He hastily tossed the book together, and the result was an informative but often confused narrative which was never published. But the money Hervey received helped make possible the final idealistic venture of his life, and so placated his Yankee conscience. He dreamed of creating a sort of winter Maverick on a tract of land he bought at St. Mary's, Georgia, close to the Florida border, where a Passion Play would be given each year at Easter time. He wrote the play and brought together as singers and actors hundreds of the black people of the vicinity. The play was given at least once, with the ruined walls of an ancient church as background.[8] On the night of

Ground cover made up of dwarf cornel, oxalis montana, ferns, and young balsam firs covers much of the spongy floor which Commissioner Cox pointed out on Slide Mountain. (*Author's photograph.*)

An elegantly dressed fisherman of about eighty years ago relaxes beside a pasture trout brook in the southern Catskills. Photographer unknown. (*Author's collection.*)

The Ashokan Reservoir with the
southern Catskills rising to the west.
(*Photograph by Alex Viola.*)

The fountains which mingle air with water to improve the water's quality draw thousands of tourists each year to the Ashokan Reservoir. (*Photograph by Alex Viola.*)

Ralph Radcliffe Whitehead of Byrdcliffe in an early twentieth-century photograph. Photographer unknown. (*Courtesy of Peter Whitehead.*)

Below, White Pines, built in 1902–03 as Ralph Whitehead's Byrdcliffe residence. (*Photograph by Roger Vandermark.*)

October 20, 1944, just before Hervey was to leave the Maverick for St. Mary's, he died in his sleep in the cabin he called Six by Eight.

In his autobiography Hervey White said that he had been a failure and so too had Ralph Whitehead and Bolton Brown. Of all those active in founding the art colony, only Birge Harrison had been a success for he had brought to Woodstock the Art Students League, and the League, in turn, had brought the young painters who became known as members of the Woodstock school and as the central figures of the art colony. There was some truth in this overly harsh judgment. The heart of the art colony after leaving Byrdcliffe and dallying for a while first at the Art Students League and then at the Maverick had become securely fixed in the population center of the town of Woodstock.

By the year of Hervey's death, the Woodstock school of painters was being mentioned with amused condescension by art critics, for it had fallen very much out of fashion. The 1930s had brought a federal art project and a craft school to Woodstock, and both helped move painters and craftsmen toward reflecting something of the social awakening of the decade. But in its turn, this too faded away. By 1944 abstract expressionism was seizing hold of the imaginations of Woodstock painters and they were soon floating and merging with this strongest current in contemporary art. They lost the regional distinctiveness which had marked the work of the Woodstock school, though a few members of the school, such as Eugene Speicher and Henry Mattson, stubbornly hung on and refused to yield to the force of the new current.

Hervey White's funeral ceremonies were held in the "music chapel" over which he had for so long presided like a priest. The expenses of burial in the Artists' Cemetery were borne by friends, for Hervey had died as he had lived, without benefit of cash. The tattered remnants of the men and women who had rejoiced at Byrdcliffe more than forty years earlier were present in the hall decked with gay autumn leaves, where they heard old Professor Martin Schutze read a few of Hervey's poems and one of his own. Then they went out into a Woodstock they now found it harder than ever to understand. It sizzled with a new kind of energy and a new kind of human being. Commercial artists, magazine illustrators, comic-strip people, advertising and radio professionals, rich people who enjoyed the company of artists, manufacturers of clothing and other articles requiring designers had converged upon Woodstock and were setting the pace for the art colony's life. Studios and dwellings were growing larger and more elaborate; tiled baths were taking the place of privies; and each summer the number of large, chic parties defied enumeration. Jews had by now won an uncontested place in Woodstock except in a few old and shaky boardinghouses which still refused to admit them. The sons of the men and women who had detected archeologist Schrabisch preparing machine-gun emplacements overlooking Woodstock for Kaiser William's armies in 1917 had equated all artists with invading Jews; their grandsons discovered, as the Cold War of the 1940s waxed in fury, that all artists were communists. In the late 1940s these people burned a fiery cross to warn the artist-communists that their plot to guide Russian armies in an attack upon Woodstock had been unmasked.

By the 1950s a more pragmatic attack was under way. Industry was finding it profitable to move out of the traffic-clogged and garbage-littered cities it had helped create into the sun and green of the countryside. The pressure of the legislative lobbies of the automobile industry was causing more and more tax money to be spent in building highways leading from city to city and into hitherto almost inaccessible country places. As industry moved up the Hudson Valley and even into Woodstock, workers' housing was quickly and cheaply run up on the flood plains of creeks and rivers. Woodstock with the theater, concert hall, and other attractions which were by-products of the art colony became the favorite dormitory for young engineers and administrators employed nearby. Experts in town planning predicted that this trend would accelerate and that Woodstock would before long become a residential suburb of the city of Kingston. Speculative builders and the local politicians who were their allies shared this view, and one builder was widely quoted as having said: "We don't need the artists any longer, we can do much better without them." Then, just as Woodstock seemed safe for industry, a new group of rebels came into the picture and threw the town into confusion and turmoil. The new rebels were known as "the hippies."

The people of the Catskills had long had a way of naming even minor conflicts "wars." There was the Anti-rent War, the Fried Chicken War, the Trout War when poachers and owners of game preserves struggled over fishing rights, the Railroad War when Thomas Cornell and the Beach family were locked in conflict, the Paint Rag War when cows, with fatal results, swallowed paint rags discarded in Woodstock pastures by landscape painters of about 1912. It is likely, then, that local historians of the future will know the struggle that followed the arrival in Woodstock of the people called hippies as the Anti-hippie War. And this war was surely the most bizarre ever to be waged among the Catskills. Most of its incidents of conflict happened in Woodstock, but its most memorable episode took place many miles away in the Sullivan County part of the Hardenbergh Patent.

Summer Boarders Come to Sullivan

❦   THE GUSTY opening years of the twentieth century swept many things and people out of the Catskills and swept in many new ones. The arrival of Woodstock's art colony and of the Ashokan Reservoir were only two of the features changing the look of the mountains as the new century began. In addition, a fresh mix of people was being stirred up in the summer resorts of Sullivan County and that county was on the verge of being accepted as part of the legendary Catskills from which it had for so long stood aside. And as the century began, a new human mixture was also bubbling on the piazzas and in the corridors of the Catskill Mountain House whose proprietor had fought ever since the late 1870s to keep the past alive on the Pine Orchard.

Never has the beginning of a new century of the Christian era been welcomed with anything like the hope and enthusiasm Americans showed on the evening of December 31, 1899. But it is doubtful if ninety-two-year-old Charles L. Beach of the Catskill Mountain House displayed a spirit of rejoicing that memorable evening. For he was aware that a sad turning point for him had arrived at the Catskill Mountain House and the other summer resorts of the Catskills. During 1899 he had given up his battle against the "undesirables" who had for so long besieged his hotel and had handed over complete control of the hotel to his two sons, who were initiating a series of changes completed by the time Bolton Brown stared down in wonder at Woodstock in May 1902. As the Catskill Mountain House opened for the summer season of 1902, its familiar candles and oil lamps had been displaced by seven hundred electric light bulbs; plumbers had installed flush toilets to banish the rows of privies which had stood for so long in back of the hotel; tennis courts and a golf course had been built; conventional lawns and even flower beds had crept close to the hotel.[1]

Until late in the summer of 1902, Charles L. Beach continued to expound the fine points of the view from the Pine Orchard as he sat in his armchair on the clifftop in front of the hotel. But by night a powerful electric searchlight's beam roamed over the Hudson Valley from the Pine Orchard and commented in its own twentieth-century way on points of interest. It "dueled"[2] with the searchlights of Hudson River steamboats, and awakened valley people by entering their windows. That October, Charles L. Beach died. By then the new Catskill Mountain House appeared to be a success. It accepted all white comers—even Jews—without protest.[3] It was in lively competition once again with other American summer resorts, and once again it widely advertised its attractions. The long tables and table d'hôte meals had vanished from its dining room; small tables and printed menus were now the rule.

As at the Hotel Kaaterskill, the Laurel House, the Grand, and the Tremper House, the guest list of the Catskill Mountain House had become what was often called "mixed." Most of its guests had one thing in common: they were rich or tried to seem so—they had to be one or the other to pay the hotel's high midseason rates of four to five dollars per day at a time when board and room in small hotels in nearby Tannersville and Haines Falls might be had for six or eight dollars per week with the best room in the house fetching twelve. Small boardinghouses which did not waste money on advertising and skimped on food and blankets fell even below the six-dollar level. The registers of the Mountain House for 1902 and the years following show a large number of names of Germans and German Jews as well as of Irish families. All these people had been in the United States long enough to win out in the race for money which was the national obsession. For those less fortunate but still well above the poverty level there were establishments in Tannersville, Hunter, and Haines Falls which would admit them. Many boardinghouses continued to refuse to accept Jews, but a growing number, especially in Tannersville, were operated by Jews and emphasized Jewish observances. Leopold Bieber of Tannersville's Cold Spring House openly advertised that his was a kosher establishment; his accommodations were good and his rates relatively high.[4]

Members of the materially successful old American families who had once favored the Catskill Mountain House now abandoned it; they were unwilling to lend the grace of their presence to a mixed hotel. On August 7, 1889, in the midst of the anti-Hebrew crusade, the Kingston *Argus* had given its readers an account of what was happening at Long Branch, the first of American summer resorts to go mixed and accept Jews. There the "reign of English reserve in public," which marked American resorts of the fashionable world, was gone; a remarkable degree of gaiety and even jollity had taken its place with "such romping and fun on the beach at bath hour, and such unaffected and noisy laughter on the hotel piazzas. . . ." A similar shift to jollity became apparent at the Mountain House as the twentieth century arrived. But English reserve still prevailed at the many "no Hebrews taken" boardinghouses nearby. Guests at these places watched with pained faces as those at the mixed or Jewish places played cards or croquet on Sunday or laughed with unconcealed enjoyment of life, even in the presence of the Kaaterskill Falls or the view from the Pine Orchard. By the beginning of the twentieth century so many German Jews were enjoying summer life in Tannersville that they were able to organize reformed Congregation Anshi Hashoran, and before long they built a clapboard-and-shingled synagogue, the first to rise in the region since the ill-fated Sholam venture of 1837. Before many years American-born Jews of German background with their relaxed attitude toward religion were greatly outnumbered in Tannersville by newer Jewish immigrants from Russia and eastern Europe who clung to strict religious observances. The synagogue passed into the control and ownership of the stricter sect.[5]

By the time the transformation of the Catskill Mountain House got under way, it was widely, if erroneously, believed among American Christians that the Catskills had become an almost exclusively Jewish summer resort (Ralph Whitehead had shared this belief before he came to Woodstock). On August 26, 1899, the Pine Hill *Sentinel* reported the opinions on the subject of octogenarian Albert G. Nichols. Sixty-five years before, Mr. Nichols had helped make surveys for the Ulster and Delaware Turnpike; now he retraveled his old route and expressed astonishment at what he saw. Said Nichols: "Now I am quite seriously impressed that on these hills the Jerusalem of America is to be built, a type or emblem of the ancient city in Palestine. . . . That ancient people who, in the reign of Solomon were the greatest people on earth, now humbled and wandering over the whole world and whose heart and love are bound up in love of ancient Jerusalem . . . seem to be drawing, providentially or otherwise, to this locality."

Nichols was referring in his poetic way to the vicinity of Pine Hill. But it was not there but in the Sullivan County part of the Grand Hotel's buffer zone that the great American summer Jerusalem rose to flourish for a time and then to begin to merge with the prevailing culture of the United States. Sullivan County in 1902 was a summer resort area which had developed independently of the Catskills to the north. After 1872 the county experienced the beginnings of a boom similar to that following the progress of the Ulster & Delaware Railroad up the Esopus Valley, across the Pine Hill, and into Delaware County. The boom owed much to the New York & Oswego Midland Railroad, later renamed the New York Ontario & Western Railway. This road had been jerry-built with the welfare of its promoters always in mind and that of the public too often ignored. Its trestles and ties were of hemlock, the cheapest and least durable wood available for the purpose and its roadbed was shoddily put together from whatever stone or gravel was handy. Its route was inefficiently planned and abounded in odd zigs and zags. It was made to sell to investors of a speculative turn of mind and not to be used. In July 1873 the road was forced into bankruptcy and receivership; it was overhauled by the receivers and in 1879 was sold to a group of New York investors who soon merged the road, for a while, with the West Shore Railway. By 1890 the opening of a branch leading to the coal fields of Scranton led to a reasonably secure and profitable coal-hauling period.[6] But as the receivers took over in 1873, the prospects for profit were bleak indeed. Their line ran through sparsely settled country with little industry to be depended upon for heavy freight shipments; the carrying of milk and butter, which would one day become worth while, was only in its infancy. But the "Midland," as it was at first called, had one resource the receivers proceeded to make the most of: it had much that was attractive to summer boarders. While plagued by a shortage of money, by strikes, and by courtroom struggles, the managers of the Midland set about building up an image of Sullivan County that would look attractive to prospective summer people. They probably had a hand in the appearance in the appendix to the 1874 edition of Appleton's popular *Hand-Book of American Travel* of a fervent tribute to the charm of Sullivan County.

Leaving Ellenville in Ulster County, "which of late summers has become, on account of its secluded beauty and its excellent society, much in vogue with New Yorkers," said the *Hand-Book,* "the traveller soon finds himself in the secluded mountain-fastnesses of Sullivan County, abounding not only in sport for the huntsman and the angler, but in famous summer resorts hitherto considered accessible only to the favored few." And this snob appeal was not all—the scenery of the mountainous part of northern Sullivan was so glorious that this region might "be not inaptly" called "The Yosemite of the East" (the wonders of Yosemite being then very much in the public consciousness).

Sullivan County, of course, was not to be compared with the Yosemite

—except in railroad publicity. Yet it had a multitude of charms of its own to dazzle summer travelers. The county's poet laureate, shy, small Alfred B. Street, talented as he was, had never been able to give Sullivan anything equal to Rip Van Winkle. But as the railroad linked the county to New York, James E. Quinlan published his long-delayed *History of Sullivan County,* a book that pleased old-timers and summer people alike with its wealth of enchanting Sullivan County traditions and lore. It brought together for the first time in reachable printed form the proud Hardenbergh Patent landlords, Indian-killer Tom Quick, murdered Gross Hardenbergh, pioneer and Revolutionary heroes, and the bold Delaware River raftsmen.

But more than lore and tradition were needed to draw summer boarders to Sullivan. The Catskill Mountain House had relied heavily at first not only on Rip Van Winkle but also on the appeal of the romantic natural wonders to be enjoyed nearby. Sullivan County had nothing very impressive of this kind, yet it did have an unusually rich combination of rural charm and untouched natural scenery. Its first boarders had been the fishermen and hunters who had come from New York City before the 1820s and who had slept and eaten in turnpike inns or at farmhouses. By 1872 both the inns and the farmhouses had greatly increased in number and the raw frontier look of the county had given way, in the more fertile valleys at least, to one of settled peace. Inviting lakes, ponds, and trout streams were scattered in profusion—there were so many that the tanneries had been able to pollute only a few. Well-tended fields and meadows clothed the lower hillsides; above them groves of maple trees served as farm wood lots and sap bushes and supplied shade to adventuring boarders. From the tops of rocky ledges the boarders could look out on broad views by no means equal to the ones to be seen from the Pine Orchard or the Overlook Cliff, yet with their own characteristic beauty. Periods of rain and fog were less frequent in Sullivan than in the resort centers of the high Catskills, and because the elevation of boardinghouses was from one to two thousand feet, days were not overly hot, and pleasant sunshine and cool breezes were usual. By the 1870s many farmhouse-boarding regions had grown up within a day's travel of New York, and once easy rail transportation became available, the many attractions of Sullivan singled it out for rapid growth. Ever since 1873 the Ulster & Delaware Railroad to the north had been printing and distributing booklets in which it praised the scenery and boardinghouses along its route. In 1878 the Midland began producing an annual booklet soon called *Summer Homes;* the railroad's successor, usually known as the O. & W., continued the practice for many years.

In response to the promotional efforts of the railway managers, summer boarders began crowding the county's hotels and boardinghouses. Then more and more farmers with able-bodied wives and daughters transformed themselves into proprietors. Lakeside and riverside hotels arose and tantalized city folks with displays of white paint and breezy piazzas. Owners of dilapidated turnpike inns scrubbed and hammered as they dreamed of sharing in the profits of the summer-boarding trade. The hopeful activity along the tracks of the Midland was very much like that taking place in the towns of the high Catskills served by the Ulster & Delaware. As in the U. & D.'s territory, most Sullivan boardinghouses and hotels had a Protestant character. But some made their appeal to Roman Catholics, to the rising class of New York Irish policemen and politicians. The growing number of German houses gave shelter to the earliest Jewish boarders to be drawn to Sullivan. Before long Jews were turning up at non-German houses too and finding that they were not always welcome. In the 1880 edition of *Summer Homes,* J. B. Nichols of Liberty Falls, now known as Ferndale, let the world know that he "wants no Jews." Others discouraged Jewish applicants by less open means. But the anti-Hebrew crusade of 1889 found no organized support in Sullivan.

Sullivan could not hope to match the appeal given to the high Catskills by its generations of fashionable and famous visitors. That was why, when the hotel-building boom of the late 70s and early 80s struck, it produced nothing to compare in splendor with the Hotel Kaaterskill, the Grand, the reborn Laurel House, or Churchill Hall. Fashion and fame had touched Sullivan resorts so lightly that Baedeker's Guide to the United States of 1893 didn't even mention Sullivan resorts, although it devoted almost seven pages of fine print and a map in colors to the Catskills stretching from just south of the Esopus Valley to beyond the Schoharie and on to the Pine Orchard. But Baedeker's editor overlooked one part of Sullivan that had some claim to the aura of wealth and fashion his readers craved. This was the northernmost part of the county which included the valleys of the Beaverkill, the Neversink, and the Willowemoc. These streams had become the goals of trout fishermen who scorned all less noble methods of taking trout than by using artificial flies. Generations of mountain people had taken trout by any means that came handy: by netting; by using worms as bait; by "fishing with a sledgehammer" (which meant stunning fish by hammering on the ledges beneath which they rested). By the final decades of the nineteenth century, fly fishing had acquired high value as a symbol of upper-class leisure such as flourished among England's noble classes so much admired by socially climbing Americans. And the Beaverkill, the Willowemoc, and the Neversink became classic trout water. There one of the greatest of American anglers, Theodore Gordon, created his famous trout flies, and there a few rich sportsmen set up fishing preserves and clubs. Illustrious writer-fishermen like the Reverend Dr. Henry Van Dyke and Edward Ringwood Hewitt paid high tribute in words to the quality of Sullivan's trout streams even as John Burroughs did the same for the nearby Ulster streams which splashed down the sides of Slide Mountain. The O. & W. helped by stocking Sullivan streams with trout and by running fishermen's and hunters' special trains.

Fishing—and especially trout fishing—had long done much to draw summer people to all parts of Sullivan. The claim that the largest American trout ever hooked had been a native of White Lake did much to give the spot an early start as a summer resort.[7] But White Lake was far from the railroad line which began bringing boarders to Sullivan in 1872. By the early 1890s a spurt of building larger and more elaborate hotels than any yet known to Sullivan was cheering the people of the towns conveniently strung out along the railroad tracks, and not even the depressed years between 1893 and 1897 could bring the spurt to a halt. The village of Liberty was booming as the Wawonda took shape—it was Sullivan's largest and most ambitious summer hotel. The O. & W. had taken part in the building boom by giving specially low rates to builders, or even by carrying lumber and other materials free. The Wawonda benefited notably from this policy.[8]

On what was known as Coaching Day, Liberty overflowed with thousands of cheerful people. The passion for horses and for driving on the part of inhabitants of more fashionable resorts had made Coaching Days important events in American summer life. Liberty and some other Sullivan resort towns adopted the custom, but lacking the smart and expensive turnouts of the summer haunts of the very rich, Liberty evolved a popular Coaching Day on which family and farm horses and everyday rigs were decorated with flowers and colored paper to parade through the village. Sullivan resorts in which life centered on lakes had their Regatta Days on which rowboats and canoes were decorated in the manner of Liberty's horses. By the 1890s Sullivan County had come to have a cheerful summer life much like that of other New York State resorts but with charms of its own. The county's future as a middle-class, predominantly Protestant resort seemed bright. It seemed all the brighter when Sullivan people looked across their eastern border at nearby resorts like the Lake Mohonk Mountain House high on the Shawangunks. There fashionable and rich people of a quiet and decidedly unmixed sort gathered in the kind of atmosphere Charles L. Beach had tried so hard to maintain at his own Mountain House. There Sunday was observed under the guidance of the hotel's Quaker owners in all its old-fashioned solemnity. Might the example of Lake Mohonk spread into Sullivan County and bring success to the Wawonda and the other Sullivan hotels with aspirations toward a fashionable future? To some it seemed possible. And then as hope soared, an unexpected event signaled the approach of trouble.

From the incubation days of the Hardenbergh Patent, the Catskills had lain very much at the mercies of the city of New York. It was in New York that most of the patentees lived. There Lord Cornbury had caroused and paraded in woman's dress. There Surveyor General Augustine Graham had flourished and, according to Lord Bellomont, had roused the people at night by breaking windows in fits of alcoholic exuberance. There the Livingstons had maintained businesses and elegant town houses, and there the leather dealers of the Swamp had presided over the adventurous Yankees who slew hemlock trees and tanned hides at their bidding. New York was the prime market for the mountains' timber and bluestone, and it was the chief source of the boarders who invaded the Catskills each summer and retreated each fall leaving behind satisfying amounts of cash.

During the early 1890s fear was rising in the city of New York. The city's death rate was going up and was already higher than that of such Old World cities as London, Paris, and Berlin. And the New York death rate from tuberculosis, or consumption as it was usually called, was very disturbing, for it was far higher than in any other American city or town. New York's Board of Health was composed of do-nothing politicians. The public protested and there were resignations and reappointments. In 1894 the new Board of Health put into effect a series of regulations adopted late in the previous year and based on a new understanding of the causes of tuberculosis. Physicians were required to report their tubercular patients; who were to be isolated in special hospitals; spitting in public was forbidden; circulars describing the symptoms of the disease were printed in English, German, Hebrew, and Italian and were distributed in the New York slums and especially in those crowded sections known from their high tubercular death rate as "lung blocks."[9]

Prominent among those New Yorkers who were following the actions of the Board of Health as it drew up its new rules late in 1893 was one

of New York's best known and most skillful diagnosticians of lung diseases, Dr. Alfred L. Loomis. Loomis was well aware that the Board of Health's plans were unlikely to be carried out in any degree of completeness, and he knew that the city's isolation hospital on North Brothers Island was utterly inadequate to accommodate the thousands of penniless tubercular patients who would have no other place to go under the new rules. Loomis planned to raise funds to build a dispensary for treating the tubercular in New York and a rural sanatorium at which incipient cases might receive the benefits of the new and promising methods of treatment then making a great stir in the medical world. But even before the rules of the Board of Health were printed, and had sent a shiver of fear down the backs of New Yorkers, Dr. Loomis died. Fortunately, he left many friends among New York's rich and powerful. Banker J. P. Morgan, who had been first Loomis's patient and then a close friend, was chief among the millionaires who served as pallbearers at Loomis's funeral and was a leader among those who at once resolved to carry out the plans the doctor had made for founding a dispensary and a sanatorium.[10] In making gifts to charities, Morgan was usually brusque and offhand as if eager to get the unpleasant task over quickly, but he showed a kind of softness when asked to help people with tuberculosis. His first wife had contracted tuberculosis during their engagement, and characteristically Morgan had insisted on marriage even though his reluctant bride had to be held up during the ceremony. She died three months later. This searing experience may help explain why Morgan contributed an amount estimated by his son-in-law Herbert L. Satterlee as half a million dollars to the Loomis Memorial Sanatorium and personally acted as its banker for many years.[11]

In accordance with Dr. Loomis' wishes, the sanatorium was built near Liberty in the heart of Sullivan County's resort section. The designers of the buildings were two of the favorite society architects of their day, so it was not surprising that the buildings they evolved after consultation with the Memorial's governing board of socially prominent New York women and physicians had more the feeling of a millionaire's country residence than of a charitable institution. Sullivan County boarders and owners of hotels and boardinghouses were delighted as they watched the elegant buildings taking shape, and were also pleased at what seemed to be a sincere tribute to the healthfulness of their county's climate. But by the time the twentieth century arrived and settled down to stay, they were no longer delighted or pleased—in fact they wished that the Loomis Memorial Sanatorium had been built a thousand miles away.

Memorial to Dr. Loomis

✤ FROM THE VERY BEGINNING of the Catskills' fame as a summer resort, people with sick lungs had been coming to the mountains in search of help. Many early nineteenth-century doctors advised lung patients who could afford it to try a change of scene and especially recommended long sea voyages in mild weather or trips through the country on horseback. Some doctors advised against mountain travel for they believed that a shift to a higher elevation might precipitate a worsening of lung trouble. But old traditions approved of mountains and made much of the value of breathing the air of evergreen forests, which were often found among mountains.[1] During the Catskills' tanning years the saturation of the air of many valleys with the fragrance of hemlock sap, needles, and bark attracted sufferers from tuberculosis. Here and there a pioneer tenant farmer settled among the Catskills in the hope that the mountain air would cure his lung troubles. According to traditions in the town of Hunter, the first Clum to settle on Clum Hill came there from Columbia County to escape tuberculosis. The air of the hill agreed with him so well that he lived a long and active life and fathered three sets of children by three successive wives.[2] Tanner Simpson's cure after he breathed the aroma of his tan vats encouraged a few more people with lung disease to seek out the Catskills. And even more came after new and promising European ideas about tuberculosis crossed the Atlantic during the 1860s.

About 1850, German botanist Hermann Brehmer became convinced that traveling among the Himalayas had cured him of tuberculosis. He became a physician and in 1859 founded the world's first open-air sanatorium for tubercular patients; it was set among the pine woods of the Woldenberg Mountains in Silesia. Other similar institutions soon followed and evolved a regimen which stressed breathing fresh unconfined air in both summer and winter, good food, rest, and an amount of exercise proportioned to the individual's ability. The aim of the open-air treatment was to build up the patient's strength and power of resistance in the hope that a natural cure would follow.[3]

It did not take long for what was happening among the Woldenberg Mountains, and very soon in Switzerland, to have its effect on the Catskills. By 1870 men and women with diseased lungs were turning up at almost every boardinghouse and hotel among the mountains—the Overlook Mountain House in its early seasons took on almost the feeling of a sanatorium. Among Overlook's lung patients was Mrs. William Lawton, wife of an ambitious Kingston lawyer. In the letters she wrote to her husband and children, Mrs. Lawton gave a detailed picture of the life of a tubercular patient at a hotel in the Catskills. She had spent the summer of 1870 at Pine Hill, where she rode and played croquet for exercise, and took cod liver oil and a daily salt bath. By the time she moved on to Overlook for the next summer, she had lost ground and had given up the salt baths and the attempt at regular exercise. Then she put emphasis on taking pills, syrups, and troches, and anxiously avoided getting chilled, for this would worsen her "very troublesome" cough.[4] When chilly and foggy days confined Mrs. Lawton to her room, friends and members of the hotel staff rallied to her aid. Cheerful curtains were hung at her window; and a staff member tried to comfort her with a glass of claret. Mrs. Lawton was not used to drinking wine; she wrote her husband that the claret tasted like "inky water." One day she had nine visitors in her room. "People here are so kind to me," she wrote to her husband more than once. Kindness to sufferers from tuberculosis was not unusual in the Catskills during the 1870s. But the time when kindness to these people might be relied upon was running out. It came to an end when Robert Koch in 1882 isolated the germ that causes the disease and the significance of this feat slowly penetrated the public consciousness.

It had long been recognized that pulmonary tuberculosis could be communicated from one person to another; now it was plain why. As patients talked and coughed and spat, they broadcast germs. And given favorable conditions, these germs could infect other people who had not acquired immunity. The open-air treatment of tuberculosis lessened the multiplication and spread of germs, especially when patients spend the winter at the high, cool, sunny, and isolated elevations Dr. Brehmer and his disciple, Dr. Peter Dettweiler, approved of. By 1880 Dettweiler had designed a reclining chair, similar in principle to the Kaaterskill Therapeutic Chair of the early 1840s, which made resting irresistibly pleasant. He also designed the pocket sputum flask which quickly became an indispensable part of patients' equipment.

By 1875 an intensive hunt was on for places to which Americans afflicted with tuberculosis might go in pursuit of health. Minnesota, South Carolina, Santa Barbara, California, and Suffern, New York—these and many others were boosted as having proper conditions for the natural healing of diseased lungs. By the mid-1880s, Dr. William B. Wood had invented his "pneumatic box"; when a patient was sealed inside and the air was rarified to the right point, he might have all the advantage of the air of any mountain on the globe that Dr. Wood thought might be helpful. When the doctor took to spending his summers at Onteora Park in the Catskills, he set up the box on his lawn and there gave treatments to many Onteora celebrities, including actress Maude Adams who became famous in *Peter Pan* and *The Little Minister*.[5]

In the 1880s various parts of the Catskills were being considered and approved by eminent doctors as resorts for the tubercular. A son of Sullivan, Dr. Daniel Bennett St. John Roosa, was recommending his native county and especially the country around Liberty. And Dr. Roosa's word carried weight. He was a leading ear and throat specialist of New York, took a keen interest in the effect of climate on human ills, and was head of New York's Post Graduate Medical School and a prolific writer for professional journals. Roosa urged the merits of Sullivan upon his friend Dr. Loomis, and Loomis listened. In the early 1870s, Loomis had sent lung patients to the neighborhood of Massena on the St. Lawrence River; in 1876 he sent his first patient to Saranac Lake. There the patient met a fellow sufferer who soon became a friend of Loomis. He was Dr. Edward Livingston Trudeau. And in 1884 Dr. Trudeau made Saranac Lake famous as the site of the first and most influential of all American open-air sanatoriums modeled on those of Brehmer and Dettweiler.

Dr. Loomis shared in the American love of the wilderness; whenever he could snatch a vacation, he liked nothing better than to camp and fish in the Adirondacks. During the early 1880s the campaign to save the Adirondacks found him an eager and helpful recruit, and he testified to the value of the forested Adirondacks as what many were calling a "natural sanatorium"[6] in which the ailing might be healed. Loomis gave much valuable help to Trudeau as he struggled to establish his sanatorium and Mrs. Loomis contributed a cottage for patients to the cluster growing at Saranac under Trudeau's able direction. But as the death rate from tuberculosis rose in the city of New York, Loomis realized that the distance from the city of the Trudeau Sanatorium made it unlikely that the place could ever effectively care for the tubercular poor of New York's lung blocks, and unless these people were isolated and treated, no one in New York, however rich and powerful, would be safe from the disease that was among the chief killers of its day. It was considerations like this which caused Dr. Loomis to yield to Dr. Roosa's arguments in favor of steering tuberculosis patients to the lovely and healthful country centered on the village of Liberty. To the west of the village the land swelled in fields and pastures to the summit of a series of long and massive ridges known to early settlers as *The* Blue Mountain; the ridges reached a height of about 2300 feet. Someone found that if you drew a straight line on a map of the state from the city of New York to Lake Erie, the ridges to the west and northwest of the village of Liberty would be the highest land encountered. In 1873 James E. Quinlan wrote of a spot on the ridges known as Sumac Point that there "the air is seldom at rest. In sultry weather when Aeolus is idle in other places, the refreshing breeze and the grateful zephyr are found here. This has given birth to the popular error that, after leaving Lake Erie, the wind does not touch *terra firma* until it reaches Sumac Point.[7]

The land chosen as a site for the Loomis Memorial Sanatorium lay just beneath the crest of a sunny, windy ridge close to Sumac Point. It formed part of a tract known as Brodhead's three-thousand-acre lot, which had been among those included in the share in the Great Patent deeded to old Major Johannis Hardenbergh's son-in-law, Charles Brodhead. Even today the site has an exhilarating, almost intoxicating character. The contours of the surrounding world seem designed on a grand and noble scale with small stands of woodland interspersed with great sweeps of clear-cut slopes. To the south and southwest the site faces a rich and deep view over lowlands extending far, far into the blue distance. By winter it is bathed in dry and brilliant sunshine. A building placed on the ridge would have the quality Henry Thoreau had discovered in the sawmiller's house above the Kaaterskill Falls: it would be "high-placed, airy and perfumed, fit to entertain a travelling god." It would have been hard to find a more promising location for the memorial to Dr. Loomis. Work on the project began early in 1896.

Sullivan resort proprietors had hoped to attract the rich and fashionable; now they did just that if for only one day. That day was November 20, 1896, dedication day of the new Loomis Sanatorium. A special train of the O. & W. brought one hundred and fifty New York people of money, fashion, and eminence in medicine and the church to Liberty. (J. P. Morgan was not among them, for his self-image was that of a cultured Anglo-American gentleman who believed in keeping his benefactions if not secret at least devoid of the least suspicion of public display.) But even without Morgan, Sullivan County had never before played host to so glittering a group. Presiding over the ceremonies was the appropriate figure of Episcopalian bishop Henry Codman Potter.[8] No churchman of his day better exemplified clerical awakening to an awareness of the inequities of industrial society than did Potter. He spoke up bravely against New York's municipal corruption, and he shocked many New Yorkers by spending the summer of 1895 working in a little church mission on Stanton Street, a neighborhood called the most criminal, poverty-stricken, and tubercular in the entire city of New York. The Episcopalian Church's leading layman, J. P. Morgan, regarded the bishop with respect and responded generously to his requests for funds to relieve the miseries of the poor—without, of course, disturbing the existing social structure.

The Loomis Sanatorium, well financed, well built, and well dedicated, was caring for about forty carefully selected patients with incipient tuberculosis by the end of 1896. The members of its governing board hoped eventually to treat one hundred and fifty. But the effect of the sanatorium on the county in which it was located was far greater than the number of its patients would suggest. At the end of its first year of operation, the sanatorium released some optimistic figures. Ninety per cent of its patients had showed improvement; 10 per cent no longer had any discoverable tuberculosis bacilli in their bodies; four patients had been discharged with their disease arrested.[9] A rush of people with tuberculosis to Sullivan County was on. And the publicity men for the O. & W. did their best to speed the rush.

In the earliest issues of *Summer Homes,* the Midland managers had said of Sullivan County that "its comparative dryness and uniformity of temperature and the resinous perfume of the pines, hemlocks and cedars, make it a desirable region, at least in the summer and early autumn for persons afflicted with pulmonary or rheumatic diseases."[10] *Summer Homes* for 1889 went much farther. It offered several pages of praise of the Liberty vicinity for its year-round value in treating tuberculosis and printed many testimonials from physicians who had sent patients there. And once the Loomis Sanatorium was established, the railway produced an annual booklet called *Winter Homes* intended to increase the influx of the tubercular to Sullivan County. The railway offered special low rates to tubercular patients, and launched a newspaper advertising campaign in which the value of Sullivan County in combatting tuberculosis was extolled. The railway's efforts were successful.

In a glowing account of the Loomis Sanatorium in the New York

Times of January 27, 1897, those not eligible to enter the sanatorium or not wishing to were told that Liberty abounded in hotels at which they might stay, for the rush of the tubercular to Sullivan County was now aimed at hotels and boardinghouses of all kinds. Many of the people who came to Sullivan were not in the early stages of the disease which was being so successfully treated at Loomis, but had reached the more advanced stage at which the despondency of the newly ill was succeeded by what doctors called *spes phthisica,* the irrational hope of recovery which often sent sufferers dashing from one doctor and health resort to another, from taking one newly advertised pharmaceutical "cure" to one even more recently advertised. The 1899 edition of *Baedeker's Guide to the United States* recognized what was happening in Sullivan when it mentioned Liberty for the first time but only as a summer and winter health resort notable for "the well-known Loomis Sanatorium for cases of incipient consumption." Baedeker said nothing of Sullivan's claims as a lively summer resort for healthy humans.

When boarders came to Liberty and surrounding hamlets to enjoy a quiet and relaxing vacation, many were aghast at what they found. Tubercular men and women walked the streets or sat on boardinghouse piazzas, coughing and spitting in their sputum flasks. With their flushed cheeks, their emaciated bodies, and their unnaturally bright, seemingly enlarged eyes, the tubercular patients appeared a disquieting race apart. Boarders who had come back year after year to the same house sometimes found the familiar place converted into a sanatorium with the blankets of its patients flapping in the sun from windows and piazza railings.[11] The sprinkling of fashionables who had once stayed at the Wawonda hastily departed; Ye Lancashire Inn, a rival bidder for the fashionable trade, eventually gave up the battle and became a sanatorium. Boardinghouse keepers developed a skilled eye in detecting tubercular symptoms and turned away applicants with suspicious coughs. Sometimes a rumor that a fellow boarder had tuberculosis would creep through a house and cause all the boarders to leave in a frightened stampede. Now and then a tuberculosis sufferer who had managed to remain undetected would die. The proprietor of his house would then smuggle the body to the local undertaker in the dead of night and tell inquirers no more than that the missing boarder had found it necessary to leave.[12] If the truth leaked out, the proprietor might have had to choose between going out of business and converting to a sanatorium.

What was happening in Liberty and its vicinity brought uneasiness to many Sullivan resort hamlets as yet free from tubercular patients. There was no telling when a rumor of an almost miraculous cure might rouse a wave of mass *spes phthisica* which might send crowds of lung sufferers into their midst. In Liberty itself the village Board of Health took action late in 1901, when it barred all tubercular patients from within their village limits. But the ordinance proved hard to enforce and the tubercular flood continued.

The people of Sullivan County were neither more nor less sympathetic and helpful than other groups toward fellow humans who were stricken with serious illness. But they formed part of a society in which the protection of property was regarded as far more important than showing kindness toward suffering strangers. A few Sullivan people saw the invasion of their county by tubercular people as a chance to be of help to others. But the majority saw it as a threat not only to their own health and the health of their families but also as a menace to the property they owned and to that which they were scheming to accumulate in the future. In situations like this a scapegoat usually appears and the O. & W. filled this role very neatly, for it had done its best to channel as many tubercular people as possible to Sullivan. The O. & W. was especially well suited to the role of scapegoat because Sullivan people knew that its rival to the north, the Ulster & Delaware, had done everything within its power to discourage tubercular sufferers from coming to the territory it dominated. In 1904, as the anti-tubercular hostility of Sullivan people rose to a historic height, the Ulster & Delaware took open and spectacular action to prevent the menace from spreading to their own area. The action centered around what had once been that promising and briefly fashionable hotel, the Tremper House.

The Tremper House, after years of adversity, had become The Nordrach Milk and Rest Cure—most of its patients had ailments such as heart disease which were not infectious. But as faith in the open-air treatment of tuberculosis set hundreds of sanatoriums in many hilly and mountainous parts of the United States, the Nordrach's managers decided to join the march, and the town board of Shandaken was persuaded to give its blessing. At once, S. D. Coykendall, president of the Ulster & Delaware, and Judge A. T. Clearwater, the road's energetic counsel, descended upon the assembled supervisors of Ulster County in white-hot anger. They wasted no time in speaking of the benefits believed to be brought to tubercular thousands by the open-air treatment, but got right to the pith of the matter and phrased their arguments in terms the supervisors understood: dollars and cents. The U. & D. had spent a million dollars luring summer boarders to the Catskills, they declared; ten thousand boarders came to Pine Hill each summer; houses had been built there which cost as much as thirty thousand dollars. If a tuberculosis sanatorium were to spring up in Phoenicia, it would constitute "a crime to humanity"; it would cause "a blight in the entire valley"; property there would not be worth "ten cents on the dollar." Without mentioning Sullivan County's experience, Coykendall stated that "wherever such sanatoriums are founded a blight follows," as the Pine Hill *Sentinel* reported on November 19, 1904. Shandaken's town board quailed before the wrath of Coykendall and the judge. They rescinded their approval of the proposed sanatorium and ordered all mention of their error to be expunged from the town records.

Coykendall's railroad had not always opposed tubercular passengers— far from it. In 1891 the U. & D. had welcomed them in the first of a series of handsome annual booklets aimed at urging city dwellers of all sorts to rush to the Catskills each summer over the lines of the U. & D. At first the Catskills were referred to as "a Great Summer Sanatorium"[13]; the mountain air was said to be "inimical to pulmonary affections"; and Dr. Howard Crosby was worked hard as an example of the power of the Catskills' air. He had come to the mountains after having been told that one of his lungs was "gone," and that he had only a year to live. By returning each summer to Pine Hill and furiously climbing and hiking he had been restored to "robust vigor." All this was in the 1891 edition of *The Catskills*. But as the vogue for open-air sanatoriums developed, the U. & D. policy-makers did their best to discourage any from invading their territory. Their copywriters eliminated all mention of "pulmonary affections"; they deleted Dr. Crosby and substituted for him "the nomadic gypsy tribe" whose continual change of air and scene seemed to keep its members in "robust health and vigor"; and the Catskills were no longer referred to as a "summer sanatorium." The copywriters of the U. & D. now used their skill in presenting the Catskills as no more than a place of "relaxation, recreation and absolute rest . . . uncontaminated by the dregs of city civilization" but abounding instead in lovely scenery and romantic legends. At the same time the promotional specialists of the O. & W. were wooing tubercular business with a vigor that eventually brought heated protests from Sullivan people. And the O. & W. responded to the protests. It deleted references to tuberculosis from *Summer Homes* and gave up publishing *Winter Homes* after 1906. In 1905 the city of New York, which had recorded 8512 deaths from tuberculosis the previous year, bought nine farms in Sullivan's neighboring Orange County and established its own open-air tuberculosis sanatorium. By that time similar sanatoriums were being set up in many parts of the United States and the pressure on

Sullivan began to ease. It revived in the 1920s as a by-product of the first World War, when veterans with lung troubles often caused by inhaling poison gas were sent by the federal government to recuperate in the pure air of the Liberty vicinity. No hospitals were built for these men—they were housed and cared for on a contract basis by local people in existing boardinghouses or in quarters built to meet their requirements. The men were referred to as "contracts" and the term is still in local use when speaking of the survivors who settled down for life in Liberty.

Sullivan continued to attract lung people until close to the middle of the twentieth century when the successful use of streptomycin and other drugs and, some say, a lessening in the virulence of the tuberculosis bacillus, made the open-air treatment virtually obsolete. The Loomis Sanatorium was sold to rich publisher Bernarr McFadden, remembered by Liberty people as a "health nut."[14] McFadden used the place as one of his projects for restoring lost health and vigor by means of such exercises as walking and by a vegetarian diet. McFadden left the Liberty scene eventually and the main sanatorium building became the first general hospital to serve Liberty and its surroundings. The conversion of the sanatorium into a hospital marked the end of the massive invasion of Sullivan County by sufferers from tuberculosis, and visitors to the county ceased giving Liberty a wide berth from fear of contagion.

As the tubercular flood was nearing its crest during the early years of the twentieth century, however, the number of Jewish patients and summer boarders had been increasing at a rapid pace in Sullivan County. By the time the army of tuberculosis victims had begun deserting the county, Jewish visitors and year-round residents were taking their place as both topics of conversation and important factors in the county's life.

From the Ghetto to the Catskills

✤ IN THE LATE SUMMER of 1899, many people living in the valley of
Sandbergh Creek in eastern Sullivan County were talking apprehensively
among themselves and were "seeking legal advice," according to the
Ellenville *Journal* of September 1. And these people had a valid reason
for apprehension. The concentration of summer hotels and boardinghouses
in their valley had resulted in the pollution of the creek once known for
its purity and for the excellence of its trout fishing. Now the stream stank
and its trout had fled. The Sandbergh and many other streams of the
resort centers of the Catskills and its surrounding region had been turned
into "mere sewage channels," the *Journal* reported. The increase in the
number of summer boarders and the introduction of running water and
flush toilets had produced more liquid wastes than the soil could easily
absorb, and much of it was run directly into streams into which tin cans,
paper, and old mattresses were tossed to be carried off by high water.
The situation was especially noticeable below two hamlets which were
rapidly expanding their summer population: Mountaindale, formerly known
as Sandbergh; and Centreville, soon to become better known as Woodridge. The pollution of the stream that drained the two hamlets became the
subject of heated discussion because of a certain change taking place in
both Mountaindale and Centreville: both were increasingly attractive to
the recent Jewish immigrants who lived in New York's Lower East Side
or ghetto. The protest against stream pollution was sincere, but it was
given added muscle by the hostility of many of the older valley people to
the proliferation of Jewish boardinghouses which brought with them a
way of life conspicuously different from that of the older houses.

The valley of the Sandbergh was appropriate enough as the door
through which a new kind of summer boarder could enter what would
soon be known as part of the Catskill Mountains. An Indian trail had once

followed the banks of the Sandbergh to the Neversink Valley where it joined another trail heading southward to the point at which the Neversink and the Delaware joined forces. The Sandbergh or Sand Hill from which the creek took its name was a familiar landmark to early explorers and land speculators, for it was a conspicuous accumulation of sand and gravel which had resulted from the sorting action of water as the ice sheets of a distant past melted. The Sandbergh was an important point on the perimeter of the Hardenbergh Patent: generations of surveyors had inspected it because it marked a corner of the grant. Most of the upper part of the Sandbergh Valley lay in Great Lot I, which had been partitioned in 1749 to John, the son of Thomas Wenham. Later it had been bought by the speculating group which included Cornelius Tiebout of New York. The "good road" which Tiebout and his partners held out none too honestly in June 1752 to attract German settlers may have led up the Sandbergh Valley, and it is likely that this was the route by which the Moravian explorers penetrated the patent later the next year.[1] Certainly many of the early settlers of what became Sullivan County moved up the Sandbergh Valley, and later the Midland Railroad chose the valley for its entry into the county. By 1890, recently arrived Jews from eastern Europe were turning up as boarders in the Sandbergh Valley, and by the end of the decade they were pouring into the valley in large numbers.

Just when the first boardinghouse catering to Jews from eastern Europe and Russia appeared in the Sandbergh Valley is uncertain. Such establishments did not advertise in English-language publications—many of their patrons did not as yet speak, and most did not read, English. The operators of Jewish houses often did not buy property but leased it and leases like these seldom leave any trace in land records. What is beyond doubt is that in 1899 the O. & W.'s *Summer Homes* carried its first listings of two boardinghouses operated for Jews only and that both were in the valley of the Sandbergh. One advertised "Hebrews taken only"; the other assured the public that it observed "Jewish faith and customs throughout." The following year the High View Farm of Mountaindale proclaimed that it would accept a good class of Hebrews only," a phrase meant to describe the prosperous Americanized German and Sephardic Jews who were the first of their religion to become numerous as summer boarders in and around the Catskills. The phrase was aimed at excluding the newer wave of Jewish immigrants who still clung to most of the ways of the Old World ghettos. Similar indications of attempts at segregation were visible in the Schoharie Valley resort towns of Hunter and Tannersville and in Pine Hill. The newer boarders were not required by any law of the

United States to concentrate in ghettos, yet economic and cultural forces compelled them to create a New York ghetto which had much in common with its Old World ancestors, though it had a hopeful spirit of its own. The culture of the new immigrants was too different and their numbers were too great for them to be able to plunge directly into American life without the kind of halfway stations the ghetto and its Sullivan County outpost could provide.

By the 1890s New York's ghetto had become one of the chief wonders of the city. It was among the liveliest, noisiest, busiest, and most densely populated places on earth. It fairly exploded with energy and ambition for material, artistic, and intellectual success. Pushcarts elbowed each other along the entire length of some streets. By night, flaring oil lamps lit up their displays of a thousand kinds of goods from pins and buttons to overcoats, from live chickens to eyeglasses. Gesticulating housewives bargained in vigorous Yiddish with equally vocal and histrionic vendors. Pullers-in stationed at the doors of clothing shops seized visitors to the ghetto by their arms and virtually dragged them inside to be converted into customers. The signs of dozens of struggling little synagogues hung from upper stories of buildings, and bearded, black-clad old men learned in Talmudic law made their way with difficulty through unbelievable concentrations in the streets of playing, singing, shouting, running children. Yiddish theaters prospered, as did coffee houses which served as meeting places and arenas for dispute among conservative people and those many younger ones who had turned to belief in socialism.[2] "The scene bristled, at every step, with the signs and sounds, immitigable and unmistakable of a Jewry that had burst all bounds,"[3] wrote novelist Henry James when he came back to New York like an elegant Rip Van Winkle after an absence of more than twenty years in Europe. James recognized in his somewhat lordly manner that he was seeing a new fact of American life that forecast changes in the American culture he had up to this point taken for granted. These changes were already beginning and they were becoming visible in Sullivan County.

Many kinds of human beings had come to the Hardenbergh Patent and each kind had experienced difficulties with its predecessors. The Indians had first welcomed and then tried to repulse the earliest white land speculators, surveyors, and settlers. The first settlers of German, Dutch, and English backgrounds had viewed the Yankee invaders with profound mistrust. The mixed population which grew out of intermarriage between Yankees and earlier people tolerated summer boarders because they were sources of profit. But they usually remained aloof from the boarding population even as friendships and marriages between the two groups grew more and more frequent. German Jews had not at first aroused hostility because their ways did not seem too different from those of other summer people. But when the people of New York's ghetto discovered the resorts which had come into being on the old Hardenbergh Patent, older patent people were not at all happy. The anti-Semitism of the time and hostility to those with different ways had affected them. But equally important was that they read unpleasant things in their newspapers about the ghetto from which the new summer boarders had come.

The picturesque and romantic side of ghetto life had been given much attention in the newspapers of the 1880s and 1890s. And so too had the fact that the 11th Police Precinct of New York, which coincided with most of the ghetto, was regarded as the most corrupt in all the city of New York. Jewish immigrants had pushed the Irish immigrants who had preceded them northward and had taken possession of the ghetto. But corrupt Irish politicians and policemen, with the backing of the Democratic party's Tammany Hall, had retained control of the precinct. It became an outstanding example of the kind of profit-sharing alliance between criminals and officials which has been all too common a feature of urban life in the United States. In the precinct, burglars and confidence men flourished under the benign eye of the law; pimps and prostitutes did business with an openness that profoundly shocked people used to seeing such things carried on in secrecy; traffickers in stolen goods found the air of the eleventh congenial; "Mother" Mandelbaum operated as a fence behind the front of a modest notions shop—and had a national reputation and clientele.[4]

Each fall during the late 1880s, Dr. Howard Crosby returned to New York fortified by breathing the pure air of Pine Hill to direct the New York Society for the Prevention of Crime in its program of revealing the depths of depravity of New York and particularly of the ghetto. After Crosby's death in 1891, the Reverend Charles Parkhurst took over, and three years later the Lexow Committee of the New York state legislature was making headlines with lurid details of crime and corruption in the 11th Precinct. Little improvement followed. When Frank Moss, the counselor of the Society for the Prevention of Crime, published his three-volume *The Great Metropolis* in 1897, he headed his chapter on the ghetto with these words: "New Israel: A Modern School of Crime."

When the Yankees first began pushing into the Catskills, they found they were regarded as sharp, dishonest, and unbearably aggressive. The Yankees for their part looked upon the older Dutch and German inhabitants as slow, dull-witted, and without ambition or enterprise. About 1900 it was the turn of the Jews bursting the bounds of the ghetto to come into contact with Hardenbergh Patent hostility. Like the Yankees before them, the Jews were not discouraged. They persisted in moving into the region and in sending their roots deep into the rocky soil. A few places such as Onteora, Elka, and Twilight parks remained, and still remain, forbidden ground to them. But in Sullivan County they surmounted all obstacles, became large landowners, and evolved a way of life that would have national impact.

At first the Jews born in Russia and eastern Europe arrived only as boarders escaping the fierce summer heat and unhealthiness of the ghetto. Many worked in sweatshops crammed into their owners' flats. There men, women, and children worked at cutting tables, sewing machines, and pressing boards, and slept in rows on the floor or, on hot summer nights, on the roof. Tuberculosis and other diseases throve in the lung blocks of the ghetto. Many ailing Jews were sent by relatives or by the mutual welfare societies or labor unions to which they belonged to try to recover— or to die—in the healthy air of Sullivan, an area easily and cheaply reached by train. The demand for rooms and board acceptable to Orthodox Jews soon exceeded the supply. Then boardinghouses catering to Jewish customs and serving Jewish food began appearing. By 1900 enough of them were in business in the Sandbergh Valley to attract attention. That same year a powerful boost was given to the flow of Jews toward Sullivan County and the adjoining part of Ulster when the Jewish Agricultural Society was formed with the financial backing of two organizations which had come into being to help refugees from savage persecution in Russia and eastern Europe. One was the Jewish Colonization Association; the other was the Baron de Hirsch Fund. Until his death in 1896, Baron de Hirsch, an enormously rich international banker, had worked tirelessly to help Jewish refugees emigrate to and establish themselves in new countries. In 1891 he financed the purchase of five thousand acres on the edge of the Pine Barrens at Woodbine in New Jersey, where a Jewish farming community was set up. Upon his death in 1896, much of his fortune went into the Baron de Hirsch Fund which carried on his philanthropic work and furnished much of the money which enabled the Jewish Agricultural Society to help refugees who had congregated in the New York ghetto.[5]

Helping American Jews to leave their ghettos and to settle on the land had long been a dream of American Jewish leaders. In the early 1820s, Mordecai Manuel Noah had planned a colony on Grand Island in the Niagara River. There, Noah hoped, Jewish settlers would combine farming with working in industries powered by the river's waterfalls. The project—and a later one at Sholam—did not succeed. Yet the dream persisted and led to many further attempts. The Sullivan County project quickly became so successful that it set Hardenbergh Patent tongues to wagging even faster than they had at the height of the Yankee invasion. By 1906 factual newspaper accounts of what was happening helped quiet the wildest rumors. The explanation of the Port Jervis *Gazette* as reprinted in the Ellenville *Journal* of August 10 was balanced and detailed. Since 1900, the paper reported, 1200 farms had been sold to Jews—the farms lay in a ten-mile strip embracing parts of the valleys of the Sandbergh and the Neversink and part of Ulster County near Ellenville. "Nearly everyone of the purchased farm houses is used as a summer boarding house and much of the produce of the land is consumed on the place by the boarders . . . the presence of these people [the Jewish boarders and farmers] does much to put money in circulation . . . and keeps up the price of poultry, eggs and vegetables. Their coming has enabled many a poor farmer to get rid of land from which he could not get a living. . . ." Jewish real estate dealers had risen up and were doing a profitable and lively business settling their people on the land. So many Jews were traveling by the trains of the Ontario & Western that the line's stock was rising in price. The Jews have "not come to spy out the land and see if it flows with milk and honey. They know it does and they have come to stay and bear their share in the payment of taxes. They are as a rule law abiding people and will make good citizens . . . at the present time their methods are much criticized, but every year there will be an improvement in this regard."

Both criticism and improvement continued as more and more Jews poured into Sullivan County. There were cases of cruel harassment, there were fist fights, there was much concealed hostility.[6] Many Hardenbergh Patent old-timers agreed with the doubts put into blunt words by Frank Moss in *The American Metropolis*, where he expressed the belief that the ghetto people formed "a danger, a detriment, a drag to our City's progress."[7] Moss wondered if as these people were fused "into the mass of American citizenship" they might not crack the "smelting pot" in which fusion would take place. "The rotten police administrators that have been given to New Israel have demoralized adults and children," Moss wrote, but he saw some hope in the increase in ghetto literacy which the public schools were producing and in the rise of participation in politics which resulted from "a feeling of responsibility among the better elements of this dense population."

On his visit to the New York ghetto, Henry James had penetrated far deeper than Frank Moss had. He felt the vitality and what he called the "intensity" of the ghetto Jews with a sensitivity unmatched by any other American of his day. He realized beyond all doubt that the ghetto people would not emerge from Frank Moss's "smelting pot," as neat copies of nineteenth-century Americans of proper Anglo-Saxon, Protestant background, but that they would evolve into something quite different. James foresaw too that the Jews of the ghetto would help give a new shape to American life. What that shape would be James admitted he could not guess.[8] But if he had been able to visit Sullivan County a year or two before his death in 1916, he would surely have seen the outlines of the new shape. And that shape evolved with the help of something James saw both as a potential menace to the quality of life and as giving a new dimension to aesthetic sensibility—the automobile.[9]

90

Automobiles Conquer the Mountains

✾ THE LAST THIRTY YEARS of the nineteenth century had seen railroads invading the Catskills, bringing in new kinds of summer people, speeding up the pace of life, booming trackside villages, and condemning settlements they by-passed (such as Prattsville) to economic stagnation. But the triumph of the railroads would not endure forever. During the first thirty years of the twentieth century, the automobile would help topple the railroads from their position of power and would make its own influence felt in every aspect of mountain life. In fact, as the automobile gained in strength, the railroads of the Catskills weakened and finally died.

On September 14, 1895, the Pine Hill *Sentinel* printed a significant item that was going the rounds: "A dry goods firm in New York has imported a horseless carriage to be used as an experiment in delivering packages, but the invention can hardly be said to have been introduced here. It has crossed from France to England, however, and is coming into general use there. . . ." The *Sentinel* pointed out that "a New Jersey inventor is said to have devised a horseless carriage that runs faster than the French vehicle." Actually many American inventors were tinkering with motor vehicles modeled on those of Europe. In 1895 only four automobiles were registered in the United States; by 1899 there were 3200, mostly of native manufacture; and in 1900 there were 8000.[1] One of these 8000 that summer conquered what many regarded as the most difficult road of the Catskills, the one that snaked its way up the precipitous sides of the Plattekill Clove. The vehicle was a seven and one-half horsepower Locomobile with a steam engine which had been designed by the bearded and derby-hatted Stanley twins of Stanley Steamer fame, and it was driven up the clove by Augustus J. Philips of Kingston, assisted by Captain W. W. Webb of the United States Navy.[2]

After Philips and Webb had steamed their way up the Plattekill

Clove Road and other difficult mountain roads had been conquered by other automobilists, many people in and around the Catskills recognized that the horseless carriage was not a passing fad. "The various forms of the new vehicle generally called the automobile are steadily coming into vogue and it need occasion no surprise to the traveller on the highway to meet one of these anywhere at any time," remarked the Ellenville *Journal* on July 5, 1901. By that time enterprising people were talking of the possibility of running "motor stages" to link towns bypassed by the railroads to railroad stations; a Monticello and White Lake to Fallsburgh line was being rumored. By the next year local newspapers were reporting that gypsies were concocting motor-powered vans. Old-timers in Willow, in the town of Woodstock, tell how a woman in their hamlet behaved at her first sighting of an automobile. She had been picking beans in a roadside garden with the help of her children when the first automobile to travel her road rattled by. The woman hid her children among the bean vines and threw herself face down on the earth. She explained afterward that she was afraid that her children would be kidnaped by gypsies.[3] But gypsies were in a decided minority among early users of automobiles, most of whom were either millionaires or sport-minded people of substantial incomes. After 1900 the Catskills' summer millionaires began arriving less often by private railroad car and more often by automobile. (Their horses and human servants were sent ahead by rail.) The Goulds and Fleischmanns were notable automobile enthusiasts, and rich residents of Onteora, Elka, Twilight, and other parks were not prevented from buying automobiles by the steep and ill-kept roads leading up to what Greene County people call "the mountaintop" on which most parks were located.

It seemed for a time that the automobile was destined to become a powerful dividing force between rich and poor. The Catskills' people, like those in many other places through which the automobiles of the rich paraded, were angry when their horses bolted as an automobile filled with gay and well-dressed people approached. Indeed, mountain people were often injured as their terrified horses ran out of control. Automobilists digging their vehicles out of soft spots, which bore the weight of horses and wagons without difficulty, left gaping holes in roads and impeded horse-drawn traffic. In March 1906, Woodrow Wilson, then president of Princeton University, expressed the feeling of many Americans when he said that "nothing has spread socialistic feeling in this country more than the automobile. . . . To the countryman they [the automobilists] are a picture of the arrogance of wealth, with all its independence and carelessness,"[4] Wilson added. But even as Wilson spoke, the situation was changing.

In the fall of 1903, Pine Hill people lost much of their hostility to the automobile and even saw their village becoming a prosperous center of activity which, they hoped, would attract rich people to the vicinity. This optimism was caused by the choice of Pine Hill as a station for that year's American Endurance Run of the newly formed National Association of Automobile Manufacturers. The Runs of the two previous years had taken contestants through Albany and on to Buffalo, but the poor condition of roads west of Albany had caused the route between New York and Buffalo to be swung southward and through Pine Hill, which an improved highway built by state money was tying to the Hudson Valley.

The Pine Hill *Sentinel* and many other publications reported the Run in great detail. After careful advance preparation, thirty-four contesting automobiles straggled into Pine Hill in a drizzling rain during the afternoon of October 7. They had left that morning from Weehawken opposite the city of New York and were bound for Pittsburgh, 827 miles from the starting point. The goggled and dustered drivers and passengers ate and slept at Pine Hill hotels that night and filled the tanks of their automobiles from a cache of gasoline at the general store of Geroldseck and Co. The next morning the automobiles left Pine Hill under the eyes of a large and admiring gathering of local people. That day five of the cars had trouble making the Pine Hill; twenty failed to get up Palmer's Hill at Andes without calling upon neighboring farmers and their horses for help; and only six managed to reach their immediate goal of Binghamton on the night of the ninth. As the contestants passed out of the Catskills, they left behind a kindlier feeling toward automobiles. Thanks to advance warning to horse owners, not a single horse had bolted and injured either his driver or his rig, and not a single car had blown up or toppled over a cliff. Instead, the thirty-four automobiles of the endurance contest had brought money, newspaper reporters, and a day of entertainment to Pine Hill.[5]

By 1913, 1,194,262 automobiles were raising the dust of American highways. One of them was registered in the unexpected name of the Catskills' beloved nature essayist, John Burroughs. Manufacturer Henry Ford had been captivated by the flavor of the rural American past in many of Burroughs' essays, and in consultation with his advertising department, Ford presented Burroughs with an automobile.[6] It turned out to be a shrewd move. Automobiles were ceasing to be playthings of the rich and the young and beginning to be thought of as necessities of life. The sight of Burroughs at the age of seventy-six, his white beard buffeted by the wind, bouncing in his black Ford over the rough roads radiating from his summer quarters at Woodchuck Lodge in Roxbury reassured many people who had had their doubts about horseless carriages. Burroughs' enthusiasm about his Ford was well publicized. Henry Ford and inventor Thomas A. Edison visited Burroughs at Woodchuck Lodge and the three rode out together. Like many of Burroughs' other passengers, the two squirmed as the essayist took a hand from the wheel and turned in his seat to point out a bird or a mountain. Because Ford was becoming a good deal of an American folk hero, his association with Burroughs delighted the people of the Catskills. From time to time a rumor circulated among them that Ford was planning to build a summer home on their mountains in order to be near his friend.

Burroughs' conversion to an automobilist was all the more remarkable because the roads of the Catskills were notably ill-adapted to the automobile. In order to reach the mountaintop or the "Heart of the Catskills," as its promoters called it, it was necessary to climb—and that was something that very often brought early automobiles to a banging, boiling halt. Once an automobilist managed to reach the mountaintop he had a new set of woes to face. There the old turnpike roads of the days of the great landlords and tanlords had survived in exasperating numbers. The roads were badly maintained and frequent stops to pay tolls were annoying and expensive. Many grim accidents began to give the Kaaterskill Clove Road, through which most automobiles climbed to the mountaintop, a bad name, while the profanity of automobilists echoed at every tollgate. It was obvious by 1912 that the highways of the Catskills would have to come to terms with the age of the automobile if their hotel and boardinghouse keepers were to remain in business. Already the Otis Elevating Railway and its two sister lines, like so many other narrow-gauge independent railroads, were faltering under the attack of the automobile.

Suitable pressures were applied to the state legislature and the state was persuaded to take over the Kaaterskill Clove Road and to rebuild it. By 1913, eighty brawny convicts were working on the road under the direction of armed guards. The men lived in barracks within the lower clove.[7] By 1918 the new road was completed, and that year the Otis, the Catskill Mountain Railway, and the Catskill & Tannersville ran their last trains. Optimistic Morris Newgold, the final operator of the Overlook Mountain House, dickered with the Otis people in the hope of buying their line, taking it apart, and reassembling it on Overlook to make the hotel at last accessible by rail, but the plan fell through. By then the turnpike roads of the mountaintop had passed into public ownership and maintenance. Soon motorbuses were wheezing and groaning their way up the

Kaaterskill Clove Road carrying summer boarders from the steamboat dock or the West Shore Railway station at Catskill. But even in its new form, the steep, twisting clove road proved almost as hard on automobiles and buses as its predecessor had been on horses. A public garage—the first in the mountaintop region—appeared at the head of the clove and did a brisk business in rescuing motorists and supplying hired cars and chauffeurs to summer boarders.

As the Kaaterskill Clove road was completed and the convicts returned to their cells, the last of Charles L. Beach's two sons died. The management of the Catskill Mountain House passed to an able son-in-law, John K. Van Wagonen, who struggled to keep the hotel in business against ever-increasing odds. In 1924 the Hotel Kaaterskill, then a Jewish resort, roared skyward in flames. It was not thought worthwhile to make any attempt at rebuilding. Although the Ulster & Delaware's Catskill Mountain & Stony Clove branch continued to run, the line drew fewer and fewer passengers, for the once bustling Jewish summer hotels of Tannersville and Hunter were losing out to resorts more easily reached by automobile. Pine Hill, into which Jewish boarders had long been pouring, began a process of decline, as did many other once-thriving centers of summer life along the main line of the Ulster & Delaware. Stamford, which had successfully fought against boarders from the Lower East Side, shared in the decline.

The white-haired owner of the last kosher hotel in the Tannersville-Hunter area likes to say that he can remember the day in the early 1920s when one hundred hotels and boardinghouses in his vicinity served kosher food. Then seven kosher butchers were at work in Tannersville. "Today there is only one and he works part time, at that. We were in competition with the resorts of Sullivan County," says the hotelman, "and the Sullivan people won out. They had certain advantages on their side. Of course we had Rip Van Winkle—he was the big thing here once. But that wasn't enough."[8] (A Yiddish translation of the Tale of Rip Van Winkle had been published in New York shortly after 1920. But it had no noticeable effect on the declining fortunes of the higher Catskills.) And neither did the inauguration about the same time of Ye Olde Rip Van Winkle Line, Inc., which provided direct passage from New York in buses that sometimes proceeded so slowly as to justify their corporation's name. The hotelman sometimes says that a big blow was delivered to Tannersville and Hunter resorts when President Franklin D. Roosevelt closed the banks in the banking crisis of 1933, for after that, hard-pressed local banks foreclosed mortgages on hotels and boardinghouses and refused to make further loans.

Other Tannersville people take a more sinister view of the part played in the decline of their resort business by the Bank Holiday of 1933. Their part of the Catskills was one of sound conservative Republicans who opposed the New Deal, they say. But in Sullivan, liberal Democrats were rising to power, which was why Sullivan hotels had no trouble getting bank loans while Greene County hotels did. Behind this bit of folklore lies an inescapable fact: as the Jewish resorts of the high Catskills lost ground, those of Sullivan gained. More and more boarders were arriving in Sullivan in their own automobiles or in hired ones called hacks driven by men known as hackers. The trip from New York was beset by hostile rural constables and confused by badly marked and bumpy roads. Yet unlike the approach to the older resorts in the upper Catskills, the route had no hazardous clove roads to deal with and took less time than a drive to Tannersville or Pine Hill. As automobiles increased in numbers, so did the boarders headed for Sullivan County.

The bursting of bounds Henry James had observed on New York's Lower East Side in 1904 and 1905 had greatly accelerated by 1920. The ghetto environment had proved to be one of the most stimulating ever known. A sprinkling of people of dozens of national origins lived among the Jewish immigrants, while the district bordered on Chinese, Italian, Greek, Syrian, and Irish neighborhoods. To the north lay the rich and fashionable part of New York with its millionaires' mansions, its luxurious hotels, its elegant carriages and automobiles. There Jewish millionaires' brownstone palaces might be admired from the public sidewalk, and their owners were encouraging products of earlier waves of immigration. Within the ghetto, attendance in the public schools was compulsory for both boys and girls. (Traditional Jewish schooling was for boys alone.) Settlement houses with classes in English, housekeeping, music, dancing, and many other subjects speeded the awakening to American possibilities. They helped release in the young a determination to fight their way to positions in American life as doctors and lawyers, businessmen on a grand scale, teachers and scholars. It seemed almost as if all the energy and ambition repressed for so long in European ghettos had been hoarded up and was now being spent with lavish enthusiasm.

Many prospering Jewish immigrants and their children expressed their rise in the social scale by moving out of the ghetto—over the new Williamsburgh Bridge to Brooklyn, up the new subway to the Bronx, to cities and towns within a reasonable distance of New York where a doctor, a dentist, or a clothing store or restaurant was needed and where prejudice against Jews was not strong. Each summer a vacation in what

was known as "the mountains" or "the Catskills" grew in importance as
a symbol of emergence from the ranks of the grossly un-Americanized. For
years "the mountains" included Tannersville, Hunter, and Pine Hill, but
as the tide of summer travel set in ever more strongly toward Sullivan, the
resort part of that county alone came to be accepted as "the mountains."
This completed the process, long in the making, by which the Hardenbergh
Patent lands lying within Sullivan County were joined in many millions
of minds to the Catskills. Dr. Cuyler had given the process a notable
boost. Inspector Carpenter had helped in 1886 when he put all Sullivan
clear to its southern border inside the "Catskill region." By 1900 an
occasional Sullivan hotel owner was cautiously advertising that his place
was located in the Catskills,[9] and by the 1920s, Jewish Tannersville and
Hunter hotel people were angrily charging their Sullivan counterparts with
having "stolen" the name which had done so much to give distinction to
their vicinity alone. When they spoke of the boarders who were flocking
by bus and hack to Sullivan, they often called them "low class" Jews. The
division of the Jews who came to the Catskills into "high class," meaning
of pre-1880 origin, and "low class" of post-1880 Russian and eastern
European origin, was much discussed whenever a spurt of anti-Semitic
feeling rose among the Catskills. The two phrases were in daily use during
the outburst of anti-Semitism which marked the early 1920s and brought
Ku Klux Klan organizers to Woodstock and elsewhere among the Catskills.

During the First World War, the theory that the conflict had been
caused by the machinations of an international conspiracy of Jews gave
birth to organizations supporting this point of view both in Europe and
the United States. Prominent among the leaders of this new anti-Semitism
was John Burroughs' friend Henry Ford.[10] Ford's anti-Semitic Dearborn
Independent had many readers among the Catskills and did much to
excite mountain people; at the same time anti-Catholic publications were
also circulating among them, but with less effect.

The outburst of war-born anti-Semitism joined with the reckless
multiplication of automobiles combined to intensify the pattern of segregation that had long before been imposed on the Catskills. The topography of the region with its mountain barriers favored the division of
people into groups living in isolation from each other. The partition among
the landlords of 1749, the rivalries of the trading towns, the ambitions of
turnpike promoters, the coming of railroads—all these had worked toward
dividing the mountain people instead of uniting them and giving them a
sense of a common past and a common destiny. In some ways the
automobile proved a uniter but often it only increased division, for it

required roads suited to its frailties and these were not evenly distributed through the mountains. Moreover, the automobile made it easier for summer people of like origins, tastes, and prejudices to gather together and dominate their own little corners of the Catskills. With the help of the automobile, people were more than ever sifted and sorted into groups of various sizes and degrees of departure from the standard American ways of living. The Jewish centers of Tannersville and Hunter took on the air of Brooklyn or Bronx neighborhoods and could not easily spread out for they were surrounded by a ring of parks in which a genteel yet unrelenting anti-Semitism held sway. Beyond the parks, colonies of Irish, Italians, Armenians, Methodists, or of Brooklyn Protestants took shape. Later, Ukrainians built a lovely timber church as the central point of a colony of their people, while a variety of little-known Protestant sects each gave its own flavor to a selected spot among the mountains. The Jews who came to the Catskills from the Lower East Side liked to board at houses operated by their own countrymen, so Russian or Polish or Hungarian Jewish groups of boardinghouses arose. Occupations tended to segregate still further: there were houses favored by garmentworkers, cigarmakers, or members of one of the large unions making their way toward power.

Once Sullivan County was widely accepted as a part of the Catskills and once the automobile had come into general use, the center of Jewish-summer-boarding concentration swung to the southwest and bypassed Pine Hill. For many years Pine Hill and Tannersville and Hunter had been rivals in the race to become what old Mr. Nichols had named the New Jerusalem. There had been much to give Pine Hill an advantage in the race. While Tannersville and Hunter were cramped by the surrounding parks, no such barrier to expansion existed at Pine Hill and nearby Fleischmanns. Both were also helped by the fact that they had a good deal of community spirit, which the mountaintop resorts conspicuously lacked. "There is a high wall between us and the park people," says a New York doctor who has followed his Jewish parents and grandparents as a summer resident of Tannersville. The existence of this wall made any co-operation in community activities between park and non-park people out of the question. But in Pine Hill and Fleischmanns co-operation did take place. Prosperous summer people presented their villages with libraries as memorials to members of their families. The Fleischmann family did much to brighten their village—their baseball park was an outstanding example. In 1903, when Stamford was in the grip of a campaign to exclude Jews, the Reverend G. S. Davis of Pine Hill had preached a sermon in which he pointed out the good qualities of Jews and expressed condemnation of the Stamford campaign.[11] Pine Hill Christians did not object to the establishment of a Jewish school for boys in their midst, and the Weingart Institute seems to have been an excellent one in which Pine Hillites of all sorts took pride. When the huge Grand Hotel came under Jewish management, there was only a moderate amount of public alarm among Pine Hill Christians, among whom the failure of their anti-Hebrew crusade of 1889 had given rise to a sometimes grumbling tolerance of people whose ways differed from theirs but to whom they were linked by geographical facts and a common economic interest. Yet all this was not enough to give Pine Hill the distinction of becoming the New Jerusalem of the Catskills.

In the valley of the Sandbergh and in the adjoining part of the Neversink Valley, the Catskills' true New Jerusalem was growing in size and strength and vigor. It was extending southward to Monticello and to White Lake, near which the Moravians had hoped to settle in 1752, and it was pushing on through Liberty to Livingston Manor, to which unhappy Dr. Edward Livingston had retreated many years before. Fewer and fewer boarders came over the lines of the O. & W., as it declined the road came to be called the Old and Weary. At last, in 1957, trains of the O. & W. ceased running. By then, pressure from Sullivan resort owners and politicians, combined with the work of the powerful lobbies maintained by the automobile industry, resulted in the construction of improved highways leading from New York to Sullivan—highways far better than those leading to the resorts of the high Catskills—though they were isolated in many places from the natural world by walls of billboards loudly praising the county's hotels and bungalow colonies. They were crowded with automobiles and buses carrying guests, with trucks hauling hotel supplies, and—most important of all—with the entertainers upon whose efforts so much of the success of Sullivan resorts depended. For by the 1950s, Sullivan resort operators rarely mentioned fine scenery or pure air in their advertisements or even hinted at their county's wealth of romantic legends. Instead they rested their hopes for profit squarely on entertainment and, most effectively of all, on "Broadway entertainment."

91

The Borscht Belt

✡ EVERY SIZABLE GROUP of immigrants has left its mark upon the American brand of the English language as German, African, Irish, Spanish, and Dutch words and phrases were added to American speech. By the 1920s the presence of millions of Jewish immigrants was being reflected in the acceptance by many Americans of such words as "kosher," "kibitzer," "schlemiel." In the city of New York the phrase "Borscht Belt" was coming into use as a new name for a group of summer resorts within an easy day's journey from New York's Lower East Side. The Belt included resorts favored by Jews in Pennsylvania's Pocono Mountains, in parts of New England's Berkshires, and in some of the more accessible areas of the Adirondacks. But the Borscht Belt's capital lay in Sullivan County.

Borscht is a soup to which a red color is given by the use of beets. It was invented in Russia where it was a favorite of Jewish families. When the people of the Lower East Side of New York took to setting up summer colonies of their own, they carried their borscht kettles along and the soup soon added color and flavor to the tables of every hotel or boardinghouse in which Jews gathered, where it was usually served with sour cream and boiled potatoes. The big, popular Flagler House served borscht, as did the dozens of rival but lesser hotels that lined the highway going through the Neversink Valley from the century-old stone bridge which marked the road to Woodridge and Mountaindale. Borscht was served at the huge hotel the Grossinger family had built on the outskirts of Liberty and which grew until it absorbed even the old Nichols farm with its anti-Semitic memories. Borscht was served at the bustling hotels of Lake Kiamesha, Monticello, White Lake, and Livingston Manor. It was a feature of life at the bungalow colonies clustered thick on Sullivan hillsides, and especially on those in the Woodridge-Mountaindale neighborhood. It was a staple in Sullivan's many lakeside camps in which young people gathered, sang around campfires, listened to the tales of local old-timers, danced, made love, hiked, played games, and hammed or stammered their way through parts in amateur stage performances.

Borscht was by no means the only liquid to play a part in the transformation of much of Sullivan County, for alcohol was seeping into Jewish resorts and having some unexpected effects. Jewish culture had gotten along through the centuries with very little help from alcohol, but as prohibition arrived, many Jews were adopting friendly American attitudes toward alcohol as part of their Americanization process. Outstanding New York bootleggers came to Sullivan to supply summer people with liquor and to linger at hotels. And because these bootleggers were closely associated with the underworld of organized crime, evidences of their activity appeared in the form of bodies of executed mobsters found in Sullivan lakes which had up to then known nothing more shocking than an occasional suicide. To this day Sullivan people say that many undiscovered bodies wired to concrete blocks or scrap metal still lie on the bottoms of their lakes as invisible memorials to the prohibition era.[1] Actually, Sullivan was not the only part of the Catskills to attract prohibition era gangsters. "Legs" Diamond operated and hid out from his enemies in Cairo in the northern part of the region.

Luckily it was borscht and not alcohol that became a convenient symbol of the Jewish-American culture making itself very much at home in Sullivan County and elsewhere in the Belt. By the 1920s the Flagler and Grossinger's were outstanding among the Belt's big hotels, and the Flagler was leading the way toward a fresh outward look for hotels of its kind. Earlier summer hotels throughout the Catskills had been content with coats of white-painted clapboards, but in 1907 the Twilight Inn at Haines Falls hinted at the future when it was originally designed as a stucco-and-mock-half-timbered Swiss chalet of enormous size and great visual charm—as finally built it was stucco-less. White-painted clapboards had been good enough for the old Flagler House in Fallsburg founded by a granddaughter of the Sullivan County tanning family from which it took its name. The Flaglers were descendants of Palatines sent to the Hudson Valley by Queen Anne in 1709. The house was bought about 1908 by two former door-to-door peddlers named Fleischer and Morganstern.[2] By 1920 the partners had built the New Flagler not in the old white-paint-and-clapboard tradition but of warm-tinted stucco. Its walls were topped by parapets and false gables in a mild version of Spanish-baroque taste which was becoming the smart thing in apartment houses and hotels in California,

Florida winter resorts, and in Brooklyn and the Bronx. Daylight poured into the public rooms of the New Flagler through a modification of arched French windows familiar to Americans in pictures of Louis XIV's palace at Versailles and, closer to home, in the sun rooms attached to the mansions of early twentieth-century American millionaires.

Many other Sullivan hotels and boardinghouses followed the New Flagler's lead and a period of furious stuccomania arrived. The burning of the Twilight Inn in 1926 with the loss of more than twenty lives probably encouraged the flood of Sullivan stucco. Owners of elderly Sullivan hotels often masked them with stucco, which had the advantage of giving a deceptively "fireproof" as well as an elegant look at moderate cost. Some hotels turned "Tudor"—Grossinger's adopted a cream-and-mock-half-timbered dress. And it was not only in their outward appearance that Sullivan's hotels were changing. The guests inside approached life in ways that differed considerably from those of visitors to the Catskills of Rip Van Winkle, Thomas Cole, and William Cullen Bryant.

Pilgrims to the old Catskill Mountain House and its satellite hotels and boardinghouses had been strongly drawn to the Catskills by the mountains' reputation for legend and romantic scenery, but legends and romantic scenery were dwindling in their appeal to the 1920s, which found deeper meaning in Sinclair Lewis' *Main Street* and Theodore Dreiser's *An American Tragedy* than in Washington Irving's genteel-seeming creations. The people who came thronging to Sullivan County resorts from the Lower East Side and then from Brooklyn and the Bronx were of urban background; they cared little for the wonders of nature and such sports as watching birds or waterfalls did not thrill them. They were accustomed to finding the sources of life's significance in other human beings, in members of their families, in their friends, in the ever-changing drama of the crowded ghetto streets. Of all publicly shared aspects of their culture, the one that stirred them most deeply was the Yiddish Theater. Poverty-stricken sweatshop workers went to the theater and mothers took their babies there. The theater's actors traveled with retinues of admirers and hangers-on and were heroes to the ghetto's girls. Organizations sometimes bought all seats for performances in the ghetto's many Yiddish theaters, resold them to their members, and so are said to have originated the institution known as the theater party. Many a stage-struck ghetto boy spurned the attractions of a future as a doctor, a lawyer, or a millionaire clothing manufacturer to set his sights on a career in the theater. Without this shaping of Lower East Side, Brooklyn, and Bronx human beings toward theatrical ambitions, the world of entertainment on the stage, on film, on radio, and in television of our century might have been very different—and the Catskills might not have made one of their most massive contributions to the changing culture of the United States.

The Yiddish Theater is a comparatively modern institution, having had its beginning in Bucharest, Roumania, in 1876. Stage representations were held by the rabbinate to be forbidden by Jewish Law, and the Yiddish Theater arrived as a by-product of the reforming spirit among the Jews of eastern Europe. By 1883 the theater had spread to Russia where it was outlawed by the government. Many Jewish actors and playwrights then came to New York, where they carried their theater to the greatest heights it was ever to achieve and created a public which demanded theatrical entertainment.

As big hotels crowded along the highways of Sullivan County, competition stimulated new means of attracting customers. In more innocent earlier days, Sullivan's summer hotels had relied upon plenty of good food and the opportunity for young women and men to meet on a less constricted basis than that which prevailed at home. They drew social climbers who knew that it was easier to make contact with the upper levels of their society at summer resorts than anywhere else. They appealed to tired and ailing people eager for fresh clean air and sunshine. But as the New Flagler first shone in its stucco glory, all this was no longer enough. Social directors were being hired to organize the waking hours of guests into an endless series of group activities and to provide acceptable stage entertainment. When all else failed to amuse, the social director, also known as the "toomler"[3] (the word derives via Yiddish from the German "tummler" which means, among other things, a tumbler or dancer) played the clown, fell down flights of stairs, bungled fully dressed into pools and otherwise brought laughter from his flock. Amateur acting continued to be part of planned activity, but by the 1920s professional players and theaters developed out of the Sullivan world of relentless hotel competition. In 1928 the Flagler built a fine theater seating about fifteen hundred, and its stage design and equipment would have been sophisticated enough for Broadway. At this and other theaters in Sullivan a great variety of stage entertainment was provided.

The conscious provision of entertainment for summer boarders did not originate in Sullivan County, but had long formed part of life at resorts in Europe and America. The Annex of the Hotel Kaaterskill of 1883 had a very large theater or concert hall where, one summer during the 1880s, to give one example, Leslie Gossin and his New York Theater Company gave a number of plays which they repeated at the Grand

Hotel. Violinists, pianists, singers, and lecturers also went from hotel to hotel, often working for no more than their room and board. The Kaaterskill gave working and living space in one of its towers to a landscape and portrait painter named David John Gue, whose studio was a source of refined distraction to hotel guests on rainy days. The Catskill Mountain House countered by displaying for sale landscapes on mountain themes painted on weathered old roofing shingles by an anonymous genius rumored to be a famous New York painter or critic. Captain Gillet, a Civil War hero who managed the Grand in the late 1880s, organized the hotel's chambermaids into a "broom brigade." He drilled the girls into such perfection that guests were astonished and delighted as they watched the brigade performing the manual of arms with true military smartness. The brooms used were sold to guests at auction in order to raise money for the girls' dashing uniforms, and the broom used by a particularly attractive girl once brought seventeen dollars.

Even before the days of social directors at Sullivan hotels, the Jewish resorts of Tannersville, Hunter, and Pine Hill were providing entertainment of a kind within the limits of the traditions of their guests. Jewish comedians who had pleased audiences on the Lower East Side sometimes performed. A high point in entertainment in Hunter came when the famous actor Boris Thomashevsky and his company gave Yiddish plays in the open air on the grounds of a hotel. (This is said to have happened about 1905.)[4] But once Sullivan resorts came of age, they outdid anything ever before provided for the entertainment of the summer boarders of the Catskills.

"Entertainment" as understood in the Borscht Belt had a broad range of meanings. Toomlers and the students and other promising young men on the staffs of summer hotels were expected to exert themselves to make the lot of the less attractive female guests more enjoyable, for, as at earlier hotels, females outnumbered males. They danced with the ladies, made love to them on demand, and sang duets with them; they played tennis, canoed, swam, and otherwise did their best for the less fortunate girls— all of which was as much a part of their jobs as anything else. So too was mollifying boarders who complained about the shortcomings of plumbing or the hardness of mattresses. In his autobiography, *Act One,* successful playwright Moss Hart gave classic expression to the loathing for the human race that the "mingling" part of his duties could inspire in a sensitive toomler who found himself becoming a cog in a machine designed to exploit human weakness for profit.[5] And Hart knew what he was writing about. He had been toomler of the Flagler and was once known as King of the Borscht Circuit, the entertainment aspect of the Belt.

Borscht Belt entertainment was tailor-made for its audiences. These audiences were composed of many elements of Jewish-American society. There were the elderly couples, sent to "the mountains" for the summer by prospering sons in a gesture that gave the sons a neat boost in status; there were stenographers and clothing-industry girls who saved all year to be able to afford two weeks at hotels like the Flagler, the Concord or Grossinger's where they hoped to lure a rich manufacturer or lawyer to the altar. Young men who were doing well as doctors, lawyers, or businessmen and could afford it took their wives to the more expensive Sullivan hotels as a visible proclamation of success. There they could meet richer, older men who might help them in their careers, and also they encountered aggressive young people on the make sexually or in business and learned to spot and avoid the bungalow people who crashed the big hotels at every opportunity as part of their endless obsession with moving upward.

In order to please as large a proportion of their lighthearted, vacationing people as possible, resort managers entertained with a minimum of serious drama and put emphasis on the earthy acts familiar to patrons of the vaudeville circuit and of the burlesque houses which supplied sexual titillation and broad comedy in the rowdier sections of many cities. Singers of popular songs, bands of dance musicians, and comedians with "big names" entertained in the elaborate night clubs which were attached to every hotel of any consequence and which replaced the detached "casinos" where nightly revelry had taken place in simpler days. Club entertainers found the Borscht Circuit an excellent proving ground for talents which might be put to more profitable future use on a national scale in the movies, on radio, in urban night clubs, and, when the time came, on television. Many a million-dollar career sprang from small beginnings on the Borscht Circuit. Toomlers sometimes rose to become heads of important Hollywood film-making corporations—Dore Schary of the Flagler and Don Hartman of Grossinger's made this spectacular leap. Among the many entertainers who rose to the top of the entertainment industry from Borscht beginnings (usually they first performed the ritual act of changing their names to more easily pronounceable ones suggesting Anglo-American origin) were Danny Kaye, Jerry Lewis, Tony Curtis, Milton Berle, Red Buttons. Some well-known opera singers, such as Jan Peerce and Robert Merrill,[6] were also Borscht alumni.

By the 1930s the Borscht Belt magnates recognized the value of commercial sports as entertainment for their guests, and boxers' training camps were set up at the larger hotels. A generation or two earlier, men of Irish background had dominated boxing. British-born Bob Fitzsimmons, who won the world's heavyweight title from "Gentleman Jim" Corbett in 1897, sometimes visited those Sullivan hotels favored by the New York politicians, policemen, and sporting characters. In 1900 Kid Wilson set up his training quarters at Ortman's roadhouse near the Centreville station of the O. & W.[7] Eventually sons of Jewish immigrants became well-known fighters and fight managers, and these heroes were often seen and admired at Sullivan hotels. In 1933, Barney Ross, who soon became welterweight champion, set up his training camp at Grossinger's at the expense of the house, and his punctilious observance of Jewish ritual brought approval from paying guests. Max Baer, too, trained at Grossinger's, and later, Sonny Liston trained at The Pines in South Fallsburgh. By 1971 Joe Frazier had trained for seven fights at the elegant Concord Hotel, where hard-boiled sportswriters sat gingerly on the edges of gilded chairs as they watched him working out. Boxing, important as it was, was not the only big-time and big-money sport used to entertain guests at Sullivan hotels. A change in the names of many of them showed the extent to which interest in a variety of sports had seized upon Sullivan's summer boarders, and the term "country club" began to be heard among them.

The country club was very much an American invention. As residential parks appeared during the 1880s and 1890s, so did country clubs at which prosperous white Christian Americans and their families might enjoy social life, golf, swimming, tennis, riding, and other sports in surroundings of rural exclusiveness. In the eyes of those excluded, these sometimes very dreary clubs throbbed with a happy, healthy, and altogether desirable sort of existence set well above that of the average American. In his *Plea for Manual Work* of 1902, Ralph Whitehead had written of "the fine qualities" of "the Anglo-Saxon race." Anglo-Saxons, he claimed, were "physically saner and pleasanter to look upon, owing to their constant round of outdoor sports, and to their use of the tub." During the first quarter of the twentieth century, country clubs became conspicuous shrines of the sort of snobbery Whitehead had expressed. It was only to be expected in a commercial nation that a great variety of imitation country clubs should arise and cater to social aspirants, and that Sullivan hotels and farm boardinghouses should scrap their stationery, repaint their signs, and be reborn as "country clubs." The Sullivan country clubs vied with each other in the size and quality of the tennis courts, the golf courses, and the stables of horses provided for the entertainment of guests. Once swimming in streams and lakes had been good enough for boarders. But soon concrete swimming pools of ever-larger size dotted the Sullivan landscape; then the pools moved indoors and were heated for year-round use. "Health clubs," beauty salons, and batteries of sun lamps of the most advanced design clustered around the pools until they threatened to rival even the fabled baths of imperial Rome. Every possible outdoor sport was brought under cover to avoid interference from sun, wind, and rain—Borscht Circuit audiences laughed appreciatively when their comedians told them that the Concord was building indoor mountains for their guests to climb when it rained. When snow-making machinery was added to the list of triumphs of Western technology, skiing was added to the Borscht Circuit's many sports. For years, skiing had been a Christians-only activity centered at the very anti-Semitic Lake Placid Club in the Adirondack country. Big names in baseball, basketball, skating, golf, and other sports were induced to turn up at Sullivan hotels and to give instruction in their specialties.[8] An elaborate harness-racing track called the Monticello Raceway—as yet still functioning in the open air—became an important source of entertainment to sedentary guests at Sullivan hotels. And when the racing season of 1970 ended, the Raceway staged snowmobile contests on its track.

By the 1960s, Borscht Belt hotels and farm boardinghouses had moved a long way from the simple Jewish establishments of Sullivan's earlier days when playing cards under a spreading maple tree had supplied entertainment enough for older Jewish boarders while younger ones had been delighted with the pleasures of the neighborhood swimming hole. Veterans of the forced migration from Europe which began about 1880 and was checked by federal restrictions of the early 1920s were dropping out of life. Their places were being taken by children and grandchildren who had absorbed much of the older American culture with astonishing facility and had modified that culture in ways probably more evident in Sullivan County than anywhere else in the country. The rise to power of Adolph Hitler set in motion a new wave of Jewish immigrants, and many of them quickly discovered the summer resorts of the Catskill Mountains, which they found reminiscent of the resorts they had known and loved in mountainous parts of Germany and Austria.[9] Many of these refugees were well-educated professional and academic people who exerted some pressure toward raising the standards of Borscht Belt entertainment and encouraged sports such as skating and skiing. The younger refugees, packs on their backs, hiked on the trails which the New York Conservation Department maintained among the higher Catskills, and because Rip Van Winkle had so many points of resemblance to folk heroes of the mountains of eastern Europe, the refugees gladly accepted the old fellow. Those refugees with an interest in the arts were often drawn to Woodstock, where they supported the Maverick concerts, the art galleries, and the theater. They did much to keep the town alive as an art colony through a difficult period. Others brought new life to Pine Hill, Tannersville, and Fleischmanns to which their presence gave a temporarily continental air. Some stayed at the Catskill Mountain House in its last seasons when the old hotel, shorn of its once huge park, its frame wracked by a century of storms, operated as a kosher establishment. It was bought by the state and burned to the ground by the Conservation Department in 1963.[10]

By the middle years of the twentieth century, people of Russian and eastern European Jewish background had become accepted as important elements in the life of many towns among the Catskills. Nowhere in the region did more of these people play leading parts in local activities than in Sullivan County. There Jews were prominent not only in business, hotelkeeping, in the practice of law, medicine, and dentistry, and in farming, but some also held positions of political power. Jewish police chiefs, supervisors, and other town and village officials were numerous. "Bucky" Mintz represented the district which included Sullivan in the State Assembly, which was itself a direct descendant of the colonial one in which Major Johannis Hardenbergh's father-in-law, Jacob Rutsen, had sat in 1693 and 1694. At the same time, many hotels and boardinghouses of Sullivan relaxed their strict adherence to Jewish dietary law. The Laurels Country Club on Sackett Lake launched a verbal tempest when it openly advertised that it would serve the forbidden delicacy known as lobster. Other Jewish hotels stuck to tradition, and a leader in orthodoxy was the Pioneer across the county line near Ellenville. The Pioneer, as comedian Joey Adams wrote in his lively and entertaining *The Borscht Belt,* was so very orthodox that "even most Jews won't go there"[11] and Christian help had to be hired to enable the place to stay in business on the Sabbath when Orthodox Jews are forbidden to labor. But more and more Sullivan hotels found that Christian guests were arriving in profitable numbers and that some sort of compromise had to be worked out. The bigger hotels lured meetings and conventions of business, professional, and political groups, and many a Christian returned to Sullivan after having first felt the county's charm as a delegate to a convention.

So far out had Sullivan resorts moved into the stream of American life that after the 1920s no non-Jewish politician of state or national stature could feel that he had campaigned properly if he failed to shake hands and smile at Sullivan hotels and add his testimony to the excellence of borscht, bagels, and blintzes.

Some of the hotels, even as they swelled to enormous size made a point of clinging to their former images of warm, friendly, family-run places. Outstanding among these is Grossinger's. Ever since its beginning as a small farm boardinghouse, Grossinger's has welcomed its guests with a friendliness and geniality which has made it world famous—as famous in the twentieth century as the Catskill Mountain House was at the height of its glory in the nineteenth. Some Sullivan hotels, growing larger, have chosen to try for a more sophisticated air, the leader among these being the Concord, which the restless energy of Russian-born, hair-tonic millionaire Henry Winarick had shaped through frame, stucco, and half-timber phases into a shining modern building differing little in outward appearance at least from many others with which global American drive has encircled our planet. Its architect was Morris Lapidus, famous for his sumptuous Miami hotels.

Sullivan County publicity workers, as their hotels became ever more sophisticated, discouraged the use of the phrase "Borscht Belt." They explained that the phrase no longer suited the character of the county's hotels, boardinghouses, country clubs, motels, and bungalow colonies.[12] And to a considerable extent the publicity men were right. Strict Jewish resorts continued in business—Woodridge developed a colony of Hasidic Jews and a Conservative rabbinical school. But many aspects of Sullivan life showed clearly that a merger of Jewish and the older American culture was taking place there as on the national scene. Sullivan people had helped to create this merger largely by the part they played in the growth of the entertainment business.

In the early summer of 1969, the officers of a well-financed corporation known as Woodstock Ventures came to Sullivan County and proposed presenting that August what they called at first the *Woodstock Music and Art Fair, an Aquarian Exposition*—an event which very soon became famous as the Woodstock festival. The promoters of the festival had first planned to hold it in or close to Woodstock and then in Wallkill in Ulster County. They had met with opposition and difficulty in both places. They found opposition in Sullivan, too. But there they also found understanding on the part of powerful Sullivan forces which shared the promoters' involvement in the entertainment business. The festival seemed to promise to these people a way of helping Sullivan lose its by now officially rejected Borscht Belt image and of substituting a shinier new one.

Dairyman Max Yasgur agreed to rent his 600-acre farm in the town of Bethel as a site for the festival. As word of what Yasgur had done spread through Bethel, descendants of old Hardenbergh Patent families braced themselves for trouble. But the trouble when it came took a form and reached a size they did not expect.

92

The Woodstock Festival Planned

✤ IT IS EASY for a stranger visiting almost any part of the Catskills to meet men and women who have close family ties with all aspects of the region's past. Mountains everywhere are likely to be conservative places to which change comes slowly and where the past clings desperately to life and where people, especially older people like those in whom the Catskills abound, cling for comfort to the past. It is sometimes said that the chief industry of the quieter parts of the Catskills is local history. Strangers often get this impression as they listen to reminiscing descendants of Calico Indians, real Indians, of tannery workers and Irish quarrymen, and of tenants of Livingstons, Hunters, Verplancks, and other old landlords. Men and women descended from Major Johannis Hardenbergh continue to live here and there among the mountains. If a stranger were to stop at the Bethel Post Office and general store and ask how to find the scene of the Woodstock festival of 1969, he might be speaking to Postmaster Richard C. Joyner, who is one of Major Hardenbergh's descendants. Joyner and his neighbors survived the festival by what many of them believe to have been the personal intervention in their favor by God. For three days most of them lived in fear, cut off from the rest of their world by a restless sea of 400,000 young people; the air they breathed was thick with the fumes of the automobiles which choked every highway for miles around in one of the most unusual traffic jams on record. Some Bethel citizens responded with kindness to the people they described as "bewildered and pathetic children."[1] But many locked their doors and closed their windows tightly in order to preserve both their lives and their supply of uncontaminated pre-festival air. Once the festival was over, Bethel would express its opinion by throwing out the town supervisor who had approved of it and electing in his place an outspoken anti-festival man. In Bethel's days of trial, Postmaster Joyner earned a special niche in his town's history when the strain

Walter Goltz of the Art Student's League in Woodstock teaches landscape painting at the base of Overlook Mountain about 1910. (*Photograph by Sam Wiley.*)

Hervey White greeting
early arrivals at a
Maverick festival of
about 1920. (*Courtesy of
Mrs. Stephen Gitnick.*)

Tree houses built for a
Maverick festival of the 1920s.
(*Photograph by Stowall
Studios, Woodstock, courtesy
Walter Peters.*)

Charles L. Beach looking out at his magnificent view from the Pine Orchard. The time is about 1890, photographer unknown. (*Courtesy of the Greene County Historical Society.*)

MANSION HOUSE,

J. D. Sherwood,

Proprietor.

A Fine Summer Resort!

Good Living & Liberal Charges.

Jeffersonville, N. Y.

ALSO DEALER IN

Country Produce!

Flour, Feed, &c.

An early Sullivan County hotel advertised for summer boarders in Hamilton Child's *Gazetteer and Business Directory of Sullivan County,* Syracuse, N.Y., 1872.

The first car to conquer Overlook Mountain reached the top about 1904. Behind it is the caretaker's cottage close to the Overlook Mountain House. Photographer unknown. (*Courtesy Will Hutty.*)

The Concord shares top billing with
Grossinger's among Sullivan County's
many luxurious hotels. The modern
white buildings crown a hilltop beside
Kiamesha Lake.

Grossinger's has grown from modest
beginnings to becoming a world-famous
hotel. Years ago the mention of the Catskill
Mountains immediately brought thoughts
of the great Catskill Mountain House on
the Pine Orchard into most American
minds. Now a similar mention suggests
Grossinger's in Sullivan County.

Scenes which combine mountain, forest, and water appeal carry the old romantic charm of the Catskills into our own century. Today mountain people and conservation-minded people outside the region are uniting to protect this kind of landscape beauty against shortsighted exploitation. (*Courtesy of New York State Department of Commerce.*)

of the festival days and the period of preparation preceding it caused him to lose twenty pounds.

If an inquiring stranger had primed himself on local history before he came to Bethel, he would realize that as he looked out from the post office's Greek Revival portico and past its gas pump he would be seeing a landscape that had once been part of the Hardenbergh share of the Great Patent. By about 1800 it had come into the possession of an unlikely developer, rich bachelor John K. Beekman of New York, known after he and John Jacob Astor bought New York's finest theater, the Park, as Theater Jack. Beekman was also known as the owner of one of the finest wine cellars of his time. Unfortunately, his powers of digestion faded prematurely, and when he could no longer drink his wine he took satisfaction in becoming a grim wine miser who refused even a sip to his relatives and friends. After Beekman's death in 1843, his nephew, J. Beekman Finlay, inherited his money, his Sullivan lands, his summer retreat at Saratoga Springs, and the Beekman bottles. Finlay lost little time in pulling corks at a clip that made him one of the most popular hosts of his day.[2]

While Theater Jack was young and still able to enjoy his wine, he put a good deal of cash and energy into bringing settlers to his lands in Sullivan. Not long after 1800 he installed an agent at White Lake. The agent built a sawmill, started a settlement, and encouraged the floating of white pine logs down the Delaware. As bad relations between the United States and Britain worsened and cut off trade, a mill for making linen thread, formerly imported from Ireland, joined the sawmill. In 1818 the Reverend William Boyse, after preaching in the unfinished White Lake church, wrote to his fiancée that this was "a pretty wild part of the country, you would say it is a perfect wilderness."[3] Yet settlement was proceeding well, and as farms were cleared they were revealing a land of fine rolling ridges, of swamps in which wild creatures found shelter, and of streams, lakes, and ponds cool and clear enough to encourage trout to multiply.

A road takes off northward a little to the west of the Bethel Post Office and leads over the first right turn, to the scene of the Woodstock Festival. It crosses the northern line of the Hardenbergh Great Lot 16, passes out of Beekman's theater of operation, and enters "Wenham's Great Lot I." Near and a little to the south of the point where the Moravian explorers came to inspect the land offered them in 1752 by Cornelius Tiebout on behalf of the Lot's group of owners, the road crosses a strip partitioned to Robert Livingston and one to the north which went to

William Alexander, the Lord Stirling who advertised half of it as a prize (worth eight shillings per acre) in his lottery of 1772–74. In this neighborhood so rich in memories of a past in which Moravian idealism and love of fellow men and of peace struggled long ago with the devious commercialism of Tiebout, the Woodstock festival, after much fluttering and several false descents, at last came to earth.

To many Woodstock citizens the use of the name of their town for a festival held sixty miles away in Bethel seemed unreasonable and confusing. But to others the name had a respectable amount of logic behind it. Ever since the arrival of Ralph Whitehead in 1902, Woodstock had been known as a place that attracted people who looked hopefully to the future and were determined to live not as convention demanded but as they chose. Even earlier Woodstock had shown a power to fascinate people from outside. A century ago, the Reverend Henry Hedges Prout recalled that when he was a boy in what is now the town of Windham, people from there used to travel through the Stony Clove to visit the Woodstock Valley where the town's glass factories stood. The glassmakers were free-living, picturesque people who put on a good show as they worked beside their glowing furnaces. Wrote Prout: "People used to go from this place [to Woodstock] to see the curiosities, and see them blow glass, and bring home [glass] canes and glass pitchers. . . ."[4] After 1902 even more people came to Woodstock to see curiosities of another sort.

Ralph Whitehead brought to Byrdcliffe two convictions that would be shared by the young people who came to Woodstock in growing numbers in the three decades after the end of the Second World War: he believed in peace and in folk music. In 1902 Mrs. Whitehead had published a book of folk songs intended for children, and in 1912 Ralph Whitehead, with some help from Professor Martin Schutze, published *Folk Songs of Eastern Europe.* The book contained folk tunes to which Whitehead had written new lyrics—one of which, called *The Czar Has Gone to War,* might have been sung to applause at any peace rally of the 1960s with the Pentagon or the President substituted for the Czar. During the 1930s, Leadbelly visited Woodstock friends; by the late 1940s folk singer Pete Seeger was spending much time in Woodstock; and many other folk singers were soon settling in the town. Joan Baez became the center of much youthful enthusiasm, and so did Peter, Paul, and Mary. The 1960s brought an increase in Woodstock interest in folk and rock music. Bob Dylan made Woodstock his home base when he moved into one of the largest Byrdcliffe houses. But when his fans pursued him, he moved on and bought the isolated house built many years before by Walter Weyl. (It still retained much of its hundred and fifty acres of farmland to serve as a buffer.) As Dylan settled in Woodstock, more and more young people from the most remote parts of the country hitchhiked to see their idol who now gave the town an almost supernatural glamor in their eyes. Dylan lived apart in romantic mountaintop seclusion, his privacy guarded by Woodstock constables, so worshipers could do no more than breathe the air of his town, but to many that was enough.

As Woodstock became an ever livelier center for young enthusiasts for the various kinds of popular music, the town's first recording studio was built. There was talk of organizing a festival based on rock music but also including all the arts that flourished in the town. A number of ambitious plans and a few beginnings were made. At the same time, older Woodstock people looked on with amazement as they saw the town seem on the verge of being taken over by young people who had thrown overboard many of the most cherished elements of the culture of their parents. Communes were organized and a few head shops appeared to sell the kind of clothing and personal adornments in high fashion among the rebellious young. These shops took the place of more sedate establishments. Crafts, as practiced by young recruits to the town, achieved an importance they hadn't had since the early days of Byrdcliffe. So many people from all over the region came to Woodstock no longer "to see the artists" but "to see the hippies" or the "flower children" that traffic jams became weekend commonplaces. The visitors saw long-haired people holding guitars and sitting on the steps of shops, talking, watching the passing scene, or merely displaying the latest word in beads, leather coats, or granny eyeglasses often enclosing nothing more helpful than window glass. They saw girls parading the sidewalks in their grandmothers' trailing-skirted gowns and hats ornamented with ostrich plumes. Lucky visitors might even see a constable nabbing a shirtless young man, for ever since the 1930s, town ordinances had regulated the amount of human epidermis that might be offered to the public eye.

As hippies and flower children both genuine and imitation flowed into Woodstock, the town was acquiring attractions for more conventional people. The Turnau Opera Players in 1956 took over the handsome Byrdcliffe building in which Bolton Brown had hoped to preside as director of the art school. There they gave sparkling and meticulously produced performances in a setting as romantic as that on the estate of some aristocratic eighteenth-century European patron of the arts.[5] Byrdcliffe, under the guidance of Ralph Whitehead's younger son, Peter, continued to supply working and living space for many people active in the arts. The Whitehead colony, like Woodstock down below, had never ceased attracting painters, craftsmen, writers, and musicians, as well as those who merely enjoyed life among artists. Like the rest of Woodstock it had experienced spells of languor and neglect, yet it had never lost the involvement with the arts and crafts of its infant days. Actually, during the 1950s and 1960s, Brydcliffe had something of a rebirth and Bob Dylan's presence, temporary though it was, revived its charm for the young.

Across the valley and a little over the Hurley line, an additional charm came to Woodstock and symbolized a local increase of creative activity. There sculptor Clarence Schmidt used discarded bits and pieces of the machine culture of his time as raw material for a prodigious work of pop art. Chrome-plated parts of deceased automobiles, refrigerators, and other images of demigods from the pantheon of the mid-twentieth century; broken mirrors, tin foil, discarded bottles, artificial flowers, and hundreds of other machine-made artifacts came together under Schmidt's guiding imagination to form an enchanted temple rich in aesthetic values for our time. The temple rose from a quarry from which bluestone had once gone to form sidewalks for New York, and in the quarry hollow beneath the temple, passages wound in entrail-like curves, their walls furnished with little shrines made of junk garnished with broken mirrors which reflected the faces of visitors and so made them become part of the work of art they were seeing.

By the 1960s Byrdcliffe was old enough and conservative enough not to send shivers down official backs. But Clarence Schmidt's junk temple —this at first was something very different and even threatening to those who held local political and economic power. Schmidt sometimes assured nervous visitors that he was merely an incarnation of Rip Van Winkle. And indeed he might well have been, with his white hair and beard, his scorn for the accepted though irrational approach to life of his society, and his determination to live his own life in his own way and to do what he felt the need of doing. Once seen as Rip Van Winkle, Schmidt was somewhat less disturbing to official emotions, and when he and his castle appeared on television, in national magazines, and in a film—and especially after his temple burned down—he lost much of his power to cause fear. The wide publicity he received made him almost part of the Establishment.[6]

But the throngs of bewhiskered, beaded, and marijuana-scented young people who thronged the holiest true shrine of Woodstock, its business center, produced shivers enough to frighten even the bravest of officials and holders of economic power. These men hoped for large profits from their speculations in land and businesses, and founded their hopes on the expectation—valid enough up to the mid-1950s—that Woodstock would soon be converted into an industrial suburb with mass-produced houses crowded into the valleys and rising ever higher on the surrounding hills and mountainsides. Now these hopes seemed threatened by young people in open rebellion against the accepted American culture.[7] As in the early years of Hardenbergh Patent settlement, land became a focus of struggle. Landowners strove to derive the utmost profit from their acres, but young people, who wanted no more than land to live on, poured into the town in search of what their underground newspapers called "free land." They often set up as squatters in fields and meadows, planted gardens, and roamed the woods in search of wild foods. They spent little cash in local shops and none at all in taverns. Predatory people bent on sexual adventure or money profits came among them. So too did police agents in various levels of government, who were suitably disguised with long hair, musical instruments, and some skill in using the hippie dialect. This infiltration resulted in much confusion and made it easy for officialdom to rally public support for a campaign using every possible weapon to drive away the rebellious young. The police made false arrests, clubbed men and women standing quietly on the village green, and maintained a continuous program of petty harassment. The Anti-hippie War was openly declared. The town board passed ordinances curbing the right of citizens to camp, to wander freely in fields and woods, and to assemble peacefully, in accordance with an old Woodstock custom, on the village green. The town's official newspaper campaigned vigorously against what it called "the undesirable element."[8] On its front page the paper printed weekly lists of arrests of young people, often on charges of drug possession or trespassing, but also for more bizarre reasons, as in the case of one young man who was reported seized on a charge of playing a flute while sitting in a tree. In the spring of 1969, a "meditation center" inspired, according to Michael Green, one of its founders, by the "Karma vibrations of American Indian tribal consciousness,"[9] was created on a part of the State Forest Preserve in Woodstock. It was looted and burned by local men encouraged by the hostile official attitude. A high point in the Anti-hippie War seemed to have been reached and the odds seemed for a while to favor the official side.

The Woodstock Nation

🌲 THE POLITICIANS and businessmen who were battling to drive all hippies from Woodstock were not wicked men. They were often kind and thoughtful toward friends and members of their families. But like the old Hardenbergh Patent landlords and the original patentees, they had been trained by their society to regard the accumulation of property and power over others as the chief goals of life. The hippies threatened these sacred goals, therefore they had to be driven from the town. Just as Samuel Coykendall and Judge Clearwater had felt justified in fighting against the establishment in Phoenicia of a sanatorium for tubercular patients because it might lower property values, so Woodstock officials felt that they were true to their trust in waging the Anti-hippie War in defense of property. Local clergymen and moneyed people usually backed the officials. But an exception was Father William Francis, who had given new life to the chapel below Mead's now known as the Church of Christ on the Mount. Father Francis came to be called, from his understanding of rebellious young people, "the hippie priest." Another notable exception was Woodstock's leading industrialist, J. Constant Van Rijn, the founder of an electronics-related industry called Rotron. Van Rijn had done much to help Woodstock keep its art-colony character against the assaults of industries like his own. Now he expressed sympathy for the hippies and their goals of peace and love. In spite of all the money, men, and equipment that officialdom threw into the Anti-hippie War, the hippie forces gained ground and dug in to stay. During the 1940s many young people had avoided Woodstock in the belief that it had lost its meaning; now other young people came in numbers that strained the town's ability to absorb them.

By the summer of 1968, a series of small weekend folk and rock events known as the Woodstock Soundouts were doing well just over the border in Saugerties, where performers, promoters, and audience would be safe from Woodstock police. The Soundouts attracted much attention from would-be promoters of the kind of large Woodstock festival that was being talked about, and in many ways the Soundouts served as scale models for the big event to come.[1] Elsewhere in the country, youthful enthusiasm for rock festivals was rushing toward a climax. In Woodstock a group of young promoters discussed holding a festival in officially hostile Woodstock or on its borders but they realized that this was impossible. The progress of suburbanization had made such strides that the town had few of the un-wooded plains and gently rolling hillsides a large outdoor festival would need. The promoters left Woodstock bearing with them their project's name, the Woodstock Music and Art Fair, and found both land and official permission in the town of Wallkill in southern Ulster. But after they had done considerable work on their site, the permission was withdrawn. By that time the festival was already a box-office success, for in response to an ex-tremely skillful advertising campaign, fifty thousand tickets had been sold.[2] The promoters had baited their trap lavishly with the combined appeals of peace, astrology, clean uncontaminated air, adornment in silver, leather, and beads, the prospect of camping out, and workshops for making music, pottery, or poetry. And above all they offered a list of the biggest names of 1969 in folk, protest, and rock music—Joan Baez, Creedence Clearwater Revival, Jefferson Airplane, Janis Joplin, The Who, and Joe Cocker were among them, while Ravi Shankar added oriental appeal. The visual symbol of the festival for the Woodstock Fair's "Aquarian Exposition" was a dove of peace sitting on the neck of a guitar. Never had any appeal to the rebellious young managed to offer so artful a bag of lures.

The festival, which had aroused the hopes and collected the cash of so many, had to go on. Its promoters once again packed their belongings, including the name, and this time headed for Sullivan County. There, plenty of open farmland suited to festival purposes was available just outside the big resort centers, and there officialdom proved far more sympathetic than in Ulster. The entertainment business and its big names had brought prosperity to Sullivan, and the proposed festival obviously had many features in common with the attractions which were drawing so many thousands each year to Sullivan resorts. And besides, influential Sullivan people were often sons or grandsons of immigrants to the Lower East Side. They had done well in the existing American society, yet retained much of the emphasis on human values and change in ways of living and feeling their

Socialist grandfathers had debated in East Side coffee houses. There was inevitably some objection by conservative Sullivan people but they were quickly overruled.

Once preparations started on the Yasgur farm in mid-July, word of the festival's rebirth spread throughout the nation by advertising, word of mouth, and in a flood of radio commercials on programs featuring rock and folk music. In thousands of American homes, parents argued with children bent on attending the festival, which seemed to the children to sum up the goals of peace and of freedom in a world based on love which in their minds would replace the devotion to money and physical comfort of their elders. Some wrung consent from still anguished parents; others left home without it. In late-model sport cars, in hired trucks, in oil-burning heaps, in imported vans, by bus and trailer, in rusty or Day Gloed pick-ups, in old hearses set to serving the living, on motorcycles and bicycles, on foot and by thumb power, the rebellious young of America began converging with glowing eyes and happy hearts on Bethel. Bethel in Hebrew means a holy or consecrated spot. The Bethel in Sullivan County acquired additional sanctity from the fact that it had also, by a miracle of modern advertising and promotion, become a temporary incarnation of Woodstock with its long history of struggle toward a better, nobler, and freer way of life.

Transforming a part of Bethel into a three-day Woodstock festival advertised to begin on August 15 was far from easy. Stands for performers, lighting towers, and an amplifying system of enormous power had to be installed. Fences and the trailer headquarters for the festival staff, wells, toilets and water pipes, camping sites, paths and roads had to be brought to the corn and alfalfa fields of Max Yasgur's farm. Obstacle after obstacle was conquered, side-stepped, or jumped over as preparations for the festival went ahead. No one took seriously a threat rising from what some of its citizens were now calling "the real Woodstock."[3] There officials were mumbling about going to the courts to apply for an injunction to prevent the festival promoters from using the name of Woodstock. The threats were naïve—Woodstock itself had borrowed its name. There are more than seventy Woodstocks scattered around the English-speaking parts of the world, and there had long been a hamlet called Woodstock in neighboring Greene County. All derive their names from the ancient Woodstock in Oxfordshire long famous for its associations with Fair Rosamond of the legendary maze, with Queen Elizabeth, the Duke of Marlborough and Sir Winston Churchill, as well as for its manufacturers of jewelry steel and fine gloves.[4] Now a new, and to elderly eyes an evil, glamor was added to the respectable old name, but it would be shared to some extent by all the Woodstocks of the world.

On Thursday, August 14, thousands of cheerful young people were waiting in the New York Port Authority Bus Terminal. Signs guiding them to their buses had by then dropped all reference to a "Music and Art Fair" or an "Aquarian Exposition" and read "Woodstock Festival, Bethel, N.Y. Load Here." For young Americans had overruled the promoters and given the festival the name by which it would go down in history. As the buses leaving every fifteen minutes came within twenty miles of the festival grounds, they joined a massive traffic jam. During long intervals when no vehicle moved, festival-goers sat on the hoods of cars or at the bases of roadside billboards, talked, and shared their stocks of food or marijuana. There was none of the vocal hostility toward fellow victims that often marks traffic jams. Even older and more conventional people bound for nothing more startling than a weekend at a Sullivan hotel or a bet at the Monticello Raceway and now caught in the jam shared in the pervasive feeling of good-humored tolerance. Summer boarders stood on piazzas or in front of their roadside hotels and returned the peace sign given with uplifted fingers by the traffic-jammed young people. Elderly Hasidic Jews in black hats and coats smiled and waved. Farmers smiled too as they allowed strange young people to drink from their wells. The day seemed to have come when the lion and the lamb were about to lie down in peace together. Even policemen seemed to have lost their hostility and turned into pleasant human beings. But some thought they detected frightened or even hateful eyes looking out from smiling roadside faces.

Many abandoned their vehicles and walked the final miles to Max Yasgur's farm. There they found the same mixture of confusion and the same sense of good humor and brotherhood they had encountered on the highway. And they were amazed by the number of people who had come together to form the three-day Woodstock. Acres of people, miles of people, people growing like corn on hillsides and like hay in the valleys, people forming a thick undergrowth in farm wood lots, people sitting in trees like birds. One man, thinking back to the Sunday school lessons of his childhood, wondered, as the sight first burst upon him, if the end of the world had not come. And he had good reason. All the people who had ever lived on this earth seemed to have risen from their graves—looking, of course, as they had in their teens and twenties—and hastened to Woodstock at the blast of a cosmic rock trumpet. Their costumes represented all times and places from the days of the cavemen to the present, from the South Seas to the pueblos of America's Southwest. The Woodstock people wore leather vests, embroidered headbands, India-print and tied-and-dyed robes and shirts, floppy hats, beards, Afro haircuts, and beads of a thousand shapes and colors. They could easily be imagined to have come to this sacred place to celebrate the final Judgment Day when God would right all wrongs and usher in an eternity of peace and love.

Certainly in the minds of many of its celebrants, the festival was indeed a judgment day, if of a less literal sort than that described in the Sunday schools. By their mere presence in such overpowering numbers, in one spot on the earth's surface, the rebellious young were passing judgment on the society that was striving to mold them into forms of which they did not approve. They were passing judgment on the cult of money, machines, and war, on the repression of normal human emotion, and on the hypocrisy of those of their elders who denounced marijuana and LSD while swigging bourbon and smoking cigarettes. The sense of what they called "community" kept the festival people in high and confident spirits. Rain fell and turned the Yasgur farm into a giant mud pie. Mud-bespattered hippies danced and sang or stood around their tribal fires and exulted in being members of what would soon be called "the Woodstock nation." Rain might soak their clothes but it could not dampen their ardor. Helicopters, bringing in bands, singers, additional doctors, and ferrying out the wounded, drowned the music, but the audience accepted the roar of the helicopters as the voice of a new musical instrument added to the rest. Thousands never got near enough to the stage to see or hear the big-name performers, and many realized that they had been brought together by the power of skillful advertising, but that didn't matter. A few thousands were discouraged by rain, mud, and general confusion and left for home, but the rest drew strength to stay from the fact that they were there—that they were helping their own generation to make its most ringing declaration of its belief in peace and love. Never again would the hippie generation rise to so glorious a peak. The sense of brotherhood and the mutual helpfulness, which had first appeared on the highways leading to Bethel and had caught up even non-hippie and older people, intensified on the festival grounds. Free food and free water were supplied by Sullivan neighbors. In nearby Monticello the ladies of the Jewish Community Center made thirty thousand sandwiches, which were distributed free by the sisters of the Convent of St. Thomas.

As the festival took on its destined shape, the promoters adapted their ambitions to realities. When the chain-link fences that enclosed the space reserved for paying guests broke down under human pressure, they ceased collecting admission charges and declared the festival free. When concessionaires charged more for food than festival-goers were willing to pay, the official loudspeakers blared out the location of commune people like the Hog Farmers, who were handing out a delicious whole-wheat porridge with raisins—for nothing—and who wore orange armbands with a symbol of a hog sitting on the neck of a guitar. Free entertainment appeared for those out of earshot of the great stage. It might be nothing more than a structure of tree trunks with hay-covered platforms for sitting on. Or an amateur singer or guitar player performing in a circle of friends, or a flock of chickens within a wire fence brought there by someone merely to be looked at. Seated on flat stones suspended by ropes were silent and motionless disciples of Meher Baba, the Avatar, who were testifying to their faith as thousands watched. The arts and crafts exhibitions were present but did not live up to the advance billing, at least not in numbers. Behind the scenes the members of the promotional group wrangled and the group came undone. Their hope for profit was not from the festival itself but from the film that was being made with the people as unpaid actors, and from the record of the performances, both of which seemed sure to be successful if the interest aroused by the festival was any indication.

Back in 1789, surveyor John Cox, Jr., had made a sketch map of the line separating Great Lots 1 and 16 and had marked the vicinity of the Woodstock festival-to-be as a "very good ridge."[5] And all through the days of settlement and the long period of farming that followed, the ridge had fitted Cox's description. There was nothing good to the eye about the scene that emerged as the festival people vanished and the ravaged landscape they left behind became starkly visible. But very quickly the discarded papers, plastics, and cans littering Max Yasgur's fields and woods were removed and the landscape began returning to its normal pastoral condition. It was no longer Woodstock but once more a mere part of the town of Bethel. Hundreds of thousands of pairs of human feet had crushed and mangled millions of low plants, sent thousands of mice and squirrels fleeing in panic, and destroyed earthworms and smaller earth-livers by the billions. The festival celebrants had polluted the air with the smoke of campfires, the exhaust of internal-combustion engines, and the burning breath of marijuana and hashish. But the soil of the festival site would slowly win back its ability to foster life, and to the eye at least, the festival which had swept over the landscape left few traces that were visible a year later. Once again the Catskills had demonstrated their ability to take punishment and to survive. It was a good omen for a future in which assaults against the integrity of the region will be many and bold.

What of the Catskills' Future?

In 1969, as a by-product of the Woodstock festival, institutional advertising for resorts in the Sullivan County part of the Catskills took a new turn. Ever since the days of James Powers and his associates in the Yankee Palace, those advertising the Catskills had drawn upon a rich variety of themes. Natural wonders and romantic legends; Irving's "Rip Van Winkle" and Cooper's "Natty Bumppo"; the scenery painted by Thomas Cole and those artists who came after him; the region's pure air and water and its freedom from yellow fever, cholera, and malaria; its summer coolness in the days before air conditioning or even electric fans; Broadway entertainment—all these had been called upon singly or in varied combinations to bring paying customers to the Catskills' resorts. Workers on Sullivan County's Publicity Commission had observed with astonishment the free publicity given the Woodstock festival, and at once they took up the old theme of pure air and water and a wealth of natural surroundings, adapted it to post-festival conditions, and deftly hitched it to the festival image still fascinating millions of people.

When the festival participants arrived in the Catskills, said the Commission's ad in the New York *Times Magazine* of October 26, 1969, "They saw that it [the Catskills] had lakes hiding in the woods. That they could stand knee-deep in crystal streams and have a waterfall rain down upon them. Or try to catch fish with their bare hands. They saw what it was like to camp out in the woods." The ad continued on a less romantic note to assert that the Catskills offered great opportunities for outdoor sports and that "its luxurious hotels complement the simplicity of nature. . . ."

Since 1969 the Commission has further embellished the theme of an unspoiled natural environment and it has renamed the Sullivan end of the region of the Catskills, The Kaaterskills. The new name is claimed, though without any foundation in fact, to have been the one used for local streams by old Dutch settlers. It has one decided value, which is that it helps separate the county from its former Borscht Belt image with its suggestions of Broadway entertainment and crowded hotels and bungalow colonies. At the same time it allows individuals to advertise their resorts in any way they please. This approach capitalizes effectively on the mid-twentieth-century aspect of the long wave of protest against the pollution of our environment by aggressive industrial society—a protest that was among the forces that made the Woodstock festival a success. The romantic involvement with nature shared by festival celebrants had much in common with that first put in words for the Catskills in 1794 by revolutionist Peter DeLabigarre. Since 1969 it has sent young people who attended the festival, and many who didn't but wish they had, hitchhiking their way toward a renewed contact with nature in all parts of the Catskills. With heavy packs on their backs they tramp the trails maintained by the New York Conservation Department (now in tribute to recent developments renamed the Department of Environmental Conservation). These people know little of the Catskills' past and of the series of struggles that enabled them to keep remnants of their wilderness character. They have never heard of Major Johannis Hardenbergh and his obsession with landownership. But many know of a landless and temporary Hardenbergh. She was Sojourner Truth, born a slave of Colonel Johannis Hardenbergh and known until she was sold to another family as Isabelle Hardenbergh or Hardenbergh's Belle. Sojourner Truth became a powerful agitator for abolition of slavery and for women's rights and a mighty walker in pursuit of the reforms she advocated.[1]

As more and more people turn to immersing themselves romantically in a natural environment and as others try to escape the hazards of urban life by taking to the woods and fields, the Catskills' forests, mountaintops, and streams are threatened as never before. Young people with backpacks, bird watchers, hikers for sport, and troops of Boy Scouts are all on the increase. Each fall, hunters crowd many valleys and wooded slopes and blaze away at deer and bears and sometimes at each other. Many of these people have well-developed ecological consciences and do not leave litter or destroy plant or animal life needlessly. But others leave behind trails of paper, cellophane, bottles, cans, and hacked tree trunks. Some clear temporary campsites even in such irreplaceable treasures as the bit of virgin spruce forest that clings to part of Cornell Mountain. As the growing passion for getting close to nature combines with the promotional efforts of manufacturers of camping and hiking equipment, the Catskills' trails are showing the effects. Each year thousands of pairs of feet cut into popular trails such as the one that leads to the base of the Kaaterskill Falls and make it easy for rain water to wash away soil and undercut trees and rocks. The reawakening of Americans to the importance of personal contact with the world of nature is an encouraging development, but new ways of relating to nature must become accepted on our crowded earth if areas of natural beauty and usefulness like the Catskills are not to be destroyed.

The most urgent threat to the Catskills comes not from hikers and campers but from a group of people who are carrying on into our own time the motivations of the old land speculators of the Hardenbergh Patent. As American cities become less and less satisfying places to live, as their air grows less healthful and their streets dirtier and more crime-ridden, many of those who can afford it dream of buying land in the Catskills on which to build small weekend or summer homes, while some set trailers beside streams or on hilltops commanding distant views. Speculators are hoarding much land at higher elevations and at the heads of little-known valleys, for jeeps and snowmobiles have now made land like this reachable the year round. Much wooded land, especially in north-eastern Sullivan and adjoining parts of Ulster, is still owned by rich individuals or clubs and used as hunting and fishing preserves, but such land is likely to be thrown on the market as taxes on "unimproved land" rise.[2] Then it will join the rush toward division into ever-smaller plots for sale to refugees from New York and its crowded dependencies. Owners of old family farms are finding it easier and more profitable to sell to speculators or to subdivide and unload bit by bit on weekend and summer people than to go on farming. The incursion on so much of the region's fertile valleys by reservoirs and broad highways has gone far to reduce the appeal of farming.

Once again, as at so many times in the past, pressures from outside are forcing change upon the Catskills and bringing in new people, new ways of relating to land, and a new crisis. Once again the people living among the Catskills are playing a passive role and are floundering as they try to adjust to a new way of life.[3] One feature of the Catskills remains on the side of those who would like to see the mountains escape the disorderly chaos that has become the rule wherever Americans (except for the rich) settle. That feature is the Catskill Forest Preserve. And as land values go up, it is toward the preserve that speculators are looking, and they are exerting pressures to break it up.

Many people recognize that the Forest Preserve lies at the very heart of the Catskills' success in maintaining and improving the freedom from widespread pollution and disorderly speculative land use that has given the region its appeal to city people of our time. Skeptics point out that the managers of the Forest Preserve have departed widely from their constitutional duty of keeping the Catskills forever wild: sometimes they have acted on their own; at others, with the approval of the voters.

Organized hunters and fishermen have long been among the stanchest upholders of the Forest Preserve and have been rewarded by seeing the Forest Preserve managers devote much time and money to providing them with game and making capturing it as easy as possible. As manufacturing and selling hunting and fishing equipment became a powerful industry, well-financed lobbies appeared in all state capitals to urge legislative action to stimulate sales. When snowmobiles came on the market, their makers propagandized and lobbied to open the Forest Preserve to them. Earlier, skiing emerged from its restricted infant phase to give rise to an industry able to pressure governmental agencies and to build up a market for its products by active efforts at molding public thinking. The state responded by constructing and operating a ski center on Belleayre Mountain. As camping equipment crossbred with the automobile to produce mobile camps offering almost every comfort of an urban apartment, the Forest Preserve managers altered their modest trail- and campsite program to provide facilities for mechanized camping at North Lake. There, within sight of the ledge from beneath which the campfire of John and William Bartram flickered in 1753, within a short walk of the site of the Catskill Mountain House, on the very spot where John Ashley set up his spruce-beer venture and Peter DeLabigarre spent a night in a ruined log cabin, campers now indulge in the competitive displays of costly equipment we have been taught to value so highly. Ample precedent had been established for yielding when snowmobile manufacturers began to exert pressure during the 1960s, and they were provided with snowmobile trails in the preserve. It seems reasonable to suppose that as newer gadgets come on the market, for use in moving human beings quickly on the earth and in the air, their makers will be able to bring about their welcome to the preserve. A process like this, continued for a few decades, cannot help reducing the Catskills to the state of slovenly disorder that marks so much of the American landscape. Already owners of ski centers have shockingly scarred the Catskills by sweeping away forests and dynamiting cliffs and ledges in order to provide more and better skiing terrain. Pressures are unrelenting for building new and broader highways leading to commercial recreational attractions—some of the highways being promoted would seriously compromise the integrity of scenic values like those of the Kaaterskill Clove. Yet there is some reason for hope.

The Catskills have taken much punishment in the past from land speculators, absentee landlords, tanlords, quarrymen, charcoal makers, and others. After each assault the mountains have had enough vitality left to bounce back and become covered again with healthy living things. The Catskills bungled their way into the protection of the Constitution as part of the State Forest Preserve. Now there are signs that they may be bungling their way toward joining the devastated regions of America in which market values have been allowed to override all others. At the same time, Americans—and especially young Americans—have shown an awakening unmatched anywhere else on earth to the necessity of defending their environment against further deterioration. Ninety years ago people of many kinds joined in battling to save the Adirondacks. The people of our own generation, if they make the effort, may still save the Catskills.

Postscript:
Eleven Years Later

🌲 DURING THE YEARS since I tried to peer into the future of the Catskills, in the preceding chapter, many other people have made similar attempts; people who lived in the region, others who lived outside of it and still others whose experience of the Catskills was confined to the summer months. Many of those who took a look ahead and then set down what they saw on paper were recipients of grants from public or private generosity. Their reports, when they achieved printed form, had such plainspoken titles as *The Catskills of Tomorrow* or *The Future of the Catskills.* Of course there were less articulate and unfunded futurists. These sometimes stood up at public meetings and shouted, "The future of the Catskills? The Catskills, as I see it, are headed straight for Hell."

What lay behind this concern for the future of the Catskills? It might have been that people were aware of what happened when Rip Van Winkle awoke after his twenty year sleep and found himself plunged into a strange new world for which he was unprepared. They wanted to cushion themselves against what they saw coming. That might have been the reason. But it wasn't.

The reason was that the people of the Catskills and some outside who had an interest in this mountain region were responding to a worldwide concern for the future of the planetary environment. They were responding on a regional level in an awareness that the Catskills had a distinct personality which had long been recognized by the outside world and which was woven into the economic life of the region.

For the Catskills, the 1970s became a time of self-examination, of collecting and analyzing statistics, and of much thought and discussion by government and the private sector. Finally, it was a time for the formulation and presentation of plans which, it was hoped, might guide the Catskills into a future consistent with its past and well adapted to its present physical, social and economic needs. This unprecedented burst of self-examination was given urgency by the appearance of many visible threats to the well-being of the region. The sense of urgency has been building since shortly after the end of the Second World War. It became obvious then that the former economic base of the Catskills was weakening. The once numerous farm boardinghouses were going out of business as the vacationing and recreational habits of the public changed under the impact of technological and social innovations. Many small summer hotels too were calling it quits. It was true, especially in Sullivan County, that some large resort hotels were doing very well indeed, but there were also lesser resorts and many camps and bungalow colonies which were receding from the peak they had reached in pre-War years. Farming was declining and so too was the business of the general stores of the region's many small hamlets.

In the 1950s many industries were finding it profitable to move from urban centers to rural surroundings. So, it happened that a kind of irregular ring of industries grew around the Catskills region. An International Business Machines (IBM) plant located in the town of Ulster. In Sidney, Binghampton, Albany, and other places industries could then give jobs to people who lived in the mountains and drove back and forth to their work daily. A few industries penetrated the mountains and set up in Woodstock, Olive, Roxbury, Stamford and Durham.

Welcome as industrial employment was, it could not make up for the jobs lost as the older ways of making a living diminished. By the early 1970s most employed people in the Catskills were working for government agencies. The rise of central school systems with their elaborate facilities and large staffs, the increased activity of the Department of Environmental Conservation in response to greater public use of the Forest Preserve, and the expanded list of services expected from town and county governments all worked together to form a changed employment pattern. And this change had visible effects on the landscape.

Well kept fields, pastures, fences and stone walls were less frequently seen. In the place of land cultivated for over a century appeared a succession of plant societies leading through a brush and sapling stage to a return to forest. Owners of hotels and boardinghouses saw this change in the local landscape as less of a threat than the narrowness and bumpiness of the roads leading to their establishments. Earlier patrons of mountain hotels and boardinghouses had arrived by bus or in hired cars. Now, they used their own automobiles and so it seemed logical to suppose that were roads to be widened and given smoother surfaces, summer boarders who had drifted away might drift back. So, resort people exerted pressure on those in political power to rescue them from dwindling incomes by improving roads. Commuters to nearby industries joined in the effort as did parents of the school children who were now making their way to and from school not on foot, but by bus.

The new roads were accompanied by a considerable expenditure of public money. Many did away with the curves and adaptations of the old roads to the shape of the land, detracting greatly from the scenic routes which had once charmed summer visitors. The new roads often altered the direction and character of mountain streams, did away with little falls, pools and rapids, and made some streams approach the banality of neat ditches. They lessened the appeal of streams not only for humans but for trout. The new roads were not easily cared for as they were attacked by the powerful natural forces of a mountainous region. And they did not bring back the rush of summer people of former years. They were plowed, sanded and salted in the winter for the benefit of industrial commuters and for another group which began in the early 1950s to contribute in moderation to the economic revival of a few parts of the Catskills. This group was composed of skiers who were considerably less interested in the landscape than they were in the speed with which they achieved their sporting objectives.

Skiing had begun to be an economic force and a changer of the landscape after the late 1940s when the state opened its skiing center at Belleayre Mountain. The success of the center, which was widely conspicuous as a clear cut area on the mountain, stimulated the widening of Route 28, which led from the New York Thruway to Belleayre. Soon the route, in some stretches, took on a new look. Distinctions between the little hamlets which had once lined it were blurred. Parts of Route 28 became lined with a disorderly accumulation of shops, filling stations, billboards and old car lots which mark heavily used highways throughout the country. With Belleayre a success, earlier skiing entrepreneurs were encouraged to try again, but not always with success. The Hunter Mountain Ski Center, however, after a period of difficulty, established itself well on a site overlooking the valley where Colonel Edwards had made leather. Its attempt to expand into the surrounding State lands was defeated by the voters when the proposition was put on the ballot as required by law. The fact that the State owned the summits and upper slopes of most mountains among the Catskills that were suited to skiing restricted the proliferation of skiing ventures and caused criticism among skiing enthusiasts and entrepreneurs. In 1980 a private skiing club at Windham was opened to the public. Windham then lost much of its peacefulness and attracted tourist shops, eating places, and other marks of a town to which outsiders come in pursuit of pleasure.

In order to put the ski facilities at Hunter Mountain to profitable summer use, a mammoth week long German Alps Festival was staged based on
the well known annual Beer Festival at Munich. By the mid-1970s the
festival was offering the patrons, who arrived in tens of thousands, more
than a hundred kinds of beer, ethnic foods, dancing and bands innumerable.
It was followed by a National Polka Festival in which more than fifty Polish
bands competed and where Polish dancing, food and costumes were part of
the scene. Both of these events had an appropriateness in the Catskills with
their ethnic diversity. This diversity, once looked upon with some scorn, was
becoming a source of pride and profit by the 1970s. It was now said that
if a vacationer put his mind to it he might enjoy a dinner of a different
ethnic flavor every day of his two week stay in the mountains.

If a man who was bent on bettering Rip Van Winkle's record in the
long distance sleeping category had dozed off in 1940 and awakened in
1980, he would have seen astonishing changes. If this man were aware of
the role of buildings as barometers of social change, he would have observed buildings that reflected those in the homelands of the region's ethnic
groups—German, Lithuanian, Ukranian, Spanish and so on. He might well
have been shocked to see that the once great Catskill Mountain hotels—
the Catskill Mountain House, the Grand and the Laurel House, had been
torn down or burned. He would have noticed smaller hotels and boardinghouses standing empty and uncared for while they awaited collapse or
destruction by vandals. Near the new ski centers the awakened sleeper
would have seen large new structures put there for the sleeping, eating and
merry-making convenience of skiers. He would have seen too that nearby,
especially in Hunter, older summer resort buildings had been made over
into housing for skiers. If Rip's successor had made inquiries at the Kaaterskill Falls, he would have learned that following the burning of the Laurel
House in 1966, a village of tents had come together close to the hotel site.
The village had expanded under the influence of the passion for getting
close to the earth which formed part of the body of beliefs of the Woodstock Nation people. There were deaths by tumbling over the Falls' brink.
The village became surrounded with litter and the debris of trees cut for
fuel. The State finally stepped in and abolished the village. The newly
awakened viewer of the Catskill scene would surely have been puzzled at
the clusters of trailers and A-frame dwellings which by 1980 had taken
over many a cow pasture. He would have been amazed too by the sight
of the huge hotels of Sullivan County which had grown by gobbling up
the smaller ones. He might have been reassured in this changing architectural picture by noting that many of the old parks, such as Onteora, Twi-

light and a few others, still clung to their distinctive buildings in the teeth of pressures to tear down and build up again.

Finally, the awakened sleeper, aware of the part the arts had played in the Catskills, might have looked for architectural signs of life in the tradition of arts and crafts. He would have found them in abundance in Woodstock where the colony's studios and shops had greatly increased, where the Gallery of the Artist's Association was still functioning as was the Maverick Concert Hall. He might have seen recording studios and night clubs giving evidence that popular music was doing well in the colony side by side with classical chamber music.

Elsewhere in the Catskills signs of expanding activity in the arts would have made themselves visible in a variety of ways: In an occasional church taken over by an artist or craftsman; in the revision of Mountaindale, in Sullivan County, into an art colony; in dance; theater; and musical ventures in Catskill, Lexington, Palenville and other places.

One change in the use of buildings which could only have struck the ex-sleeper as extraordinary was caused by the shifting of religious ideas and observances. By 1980 many young people had acquired a taste for religious beliefs and practices very different from those of their parents and grandparents. In the Catskills, groups of believers in Oriental or other exotic cults had reprieved older, sometimes decaying buildings and modified them for new lives in the service of their beliefs.

In Sullivan County the Sinanada Yoga believers, the Dai Batsu Zendo, Hare Krishna and the Emissaries of the Divine Light all bought former resorts. Still others found buyers among painters, operators of movie theaters, sculptors and musicians.

The recycling of old boardinghouses, churches and other buildings for uses more in keeping with the emotional needs of a new generation was only one among many related signs of change. Church bells ceased ringing in some valleys of the Catskills. Young people meditated instead of attending weekly prayer meetings, Buddhist chants floated out from buildings which had once known only the singing of hymns or the laughter of summer boarders. Monks of Oriental birth shopped in local stores to the delight of local business people who were less pleased when they discovered that the monks' real property was as eligible for exemption from taxation as Christian or Jewish church property.

Nowhere in the Catskills did this kind of exemption from taxation ignite so vigorous a social conflagration as in the little, thinly populated town of Hardenburgh. There, fishing and hunting clubs of prosperous outsiders had paid substantial taxes ever since they were founded in the final decades of the nineteenth century. The population of Hardenburgh slid downward as its farm and lumber resources became played out. Then the outsiders' taxes went up as town officials strove to meet the town's bills on a diminishing income. By the early 1970s, club members were feeling pinched, especially as the recession of the time arrived. They were willing to sell to the kind of tax exempt groups which were eager to find quarters in the Catskills. Enough sold to remove an important source of tax money from the assessment rolls. This meant that the average, native Hardenburgher would have to pay higher taxes to make up for the loss. More than half the Hardenburghers reacted in a way that made the news around the country. They joined a west coast mail order church which ordained them ministers and as exempt from taxation as any Buddhist or other clergy person. A vast amount of controversy in and out of court followed. Some proposed that the Town of Hardenburgh go out of business with its territory divided among its neighbors. And in other towns in the region the appearance of a man with a clerical collar or an Oriental cast of countenance as a candidate for buying an old former hotel or clubhouse gave rise to apprehension that their town might suffer the same tragic and, at the same time, comic fate as Hardenburgh.

While the different appearances and uses of buildings in the Catskills show many ways in which the life of the region has changed, there are other changes which have left less obvious signs. One is the growth in awareness of the necessity of taking action to prevent the degeneration of the environment. This awareness had been growing in the United States for more than a century and it reached a peak in the Catskills during the 1970s. John Burroughs had stirred mountain dwellers and tourists into a sense of the close relationship between the land and its people. In 1960 the publication of Rachel Carson's *Silent Spring* deepened this sense. The people of the Woodstock Nation shared in the consciousness of crisis aroused by Miss Carson and supported by experts in many scientific disciplines. Many of the Woodstock Festival attendants had discovered the appeal of the Catskills and were finding their way to the region. They expressed a concern for the need of a greater closeness to nature by wearing leather and other "natural" non-mass produced garments, by backpacking on mountain trails, by "bushwhacking" over trailless areas, by eating what they believed to be natural foods. Some went into the woods and tried, without success, to live on only what nature supplied in the way of roots, berries, leaves and bark. They lived in the woods in tents and some expressed their admiration of the western Indians' way of life, by setting up tipis in the

Catskills. They avoided public or commercial campgrounds and preferred putting up a shelter at a spot where, as far as they could make out, no one had ever camped before.

Other groups of people with a concern for the environment expressed it in other ways. They began working together to collect information about the Catskills to form a base on which they might agitate for laws aimed at protecting the integrity of land, air, water and living things. They sought to bring about the protection of those parts of the Caskills which retained a wilderness character and at the same time, to explore means of helping the inhabitants of the region earn better and more dependable livings.

In order to further these aims, two groups were organized. One, made up of faculty members of the New York State Agricultural and Technical Institute at Delhi, proposed making studies of soil, water and living things of the region—they were known as the Catskill Consortium. The other came to be known as the Catskill Center for Conservation and Development. The Center, besides sponsoring studies, proposed exerting influence on governmental thinking in order to clear the way for a land use plan and agency for the Catskills. Plant geneticist Sherret S. Chase became the first president of the Center. The short-lived Catskill Consortium and the Catskill Center for Conservation and Development were stimulated into existence in part by the activity of environmentalists in other areas of New York State. These activities were among the effects of a growing national awareness of the need to defend the American environment.

In the Hudson Valley in 1966 the plans of the regional power monopoly to build a pumped-up storage plant at scenic Storm King Mountain had roused strong opposition and resulted in court battles which focused public attention on the danger to the environment of allowing a narrow approach to the use of natural resources to overshadow all others. A number of organizations for protecting the ecological, scenic and cultural values of the Hudson were formed. In 1966 the State created the Hudson Valley Commission with the avowed aim of protecting the river and its valley.

In 1968 the State announced the establishment of a Temporary Study Commission on the Future of the Adirondacks. The Commission would have unexpected side effects on the Catskills. The Commission's work aroused a mixture of approval and hostility among Adirondack people with large landowners generally favoring it and the less wealthy in opposition. Concerns with protecting the Adirondack environment, with heading off the proposed creation of a federal Adirondack Park, with fears of a loss of local control, and with an unwillingness to go along with anything so

strongly backed by the Rockefeller family, which was also a power in the
Hudson Valley Commission, had their effect on the minds of Catskill Mountain people as the Catskill Center was born.

The Center commissioned Sheafe Satterthwaite of the Center for Environmental Studies at Williams College to make a study of the Catskills
which might serve as a guide to their efforts. The study was completed
in the fall of 1969. It was the first attempt to look at the Catskills in a
regional way from an environmentalist point of view with all the various
aspects of the Catskills taken into account. While all the Satterthwaite
recommendations were not carried out, many were. Among these was the
push to create a State commission for the Catskills—a commission which
would study the region in depth, find acceptance for its character as a
region with a special value not only to its inhabitants but to the country as
a whole, and lead to the emergence of a regional board which would guide
change in accordance with the newly developed environmental consciousness of America. The report recognized the difficulties ahead—the frag-
mentation of the Catskills people along economic, political and cultural
lines.

In 1970, Dr. Chase wrote to Governor Nelson Rockefeller and suggested the creation of a temporary commission to study the Catskills. The
Governor and the legislature approved the idea and nine commissioners
were appointed by the Governor and legislative leaders. All were Republicans and lawyers were the largest occupational category represented. It
was not until 1973 that the appropriation of funds for the Commission
made it possible for it to begin work at headquarters at the Rexmere, a
former resort hotel in Stamford in the Catskills.

The work of the Commission, at a cost of nearly a million dollars,
brought to the Catskills a concentrated scrutiny such as the region had
never known before. Never had so many people examined so many aspects
of the Catskills' physical, governmental, economic and social life. Never had
so many people been interviewed and questionnaired. Never had so many
old animosities been stirred up. Never had so many people found expression
in defense of their new environmental consciousness, or their old prejudices,
or their eagerness to profit personally by the changes that were taking place.
And never had so much information, statistics and opinion about the Catskills been presented to the public in print and at meetings.

The Commission employed experts from outside the region or on its
borders to make technical reports on all relevant aspects. From time to time
the Commission's director, Albert Hall, a career man in fish and wildlife
management, made progress reports to the press, and the Commission

eventually issued preliminary reports. These made it evident that the Commission was not having an easy time. It was quite simple to collect information but it was another thing to arrive at conclusions and make recommendations for the future of a region so filled with conflicting jurisdictions, economic groups, eager speculators and developers, and conservatives who wanted nothing to do with new ideas.

The Catskill Center tried hard to help the Commission. Because it was able to get grants it commissioned graduate students at Yale, Pennsylvania and Boston Universities to make independent studies of a variety of subjects dealing with the Catskills. The reports which resulted were added to those commissioned by the Study Commission to help it form a solid core of detail on which it might base its own report. In addition the Center published a series of guides to its own thinking about means by which the Catskills' future might be safeguarded. It stressed the wisdom of creating a regional commission for the Catskills which might coordinate planning by county and local agencies in accordance with the environmental thinking which had been finding its way into State and national legislation. It urged planning action by town agencies, but if these were not undertaken it recommended that county and a proposed regional commission should act. Because so many features and needs of the region like streams, highways, means of transportation and air quality are regional rather than local in their implications, these would best be handled regionally.

The Catskill Center, like the Commission, did much to arouse thought and discussion about the region's future hazards and future welfare. It held meetings at which authorities on many phases of the region spoke and answered questions. It issued press releases and publications dealing with the problems facing the people of the Catskills. Yet like the Study Commission it touched only a few segments of the complex and varied society of mountain people. Neither the Center nor the Commission was able to bring about a substantial agreement as to the best means of assuring a good future to the Catskills and its people. Many of those people related both the Commission and the Center to the approach that had marked the Adirondack Study Commission's report and conclusions. They ignored the fact that the Adirondack Commission's mandate restricted it to the thinly populated Adirondack State Park, while the Catskill Commissioners dealt with a varied and far more populous region extending over more than eight counties with most of it outside the blue line of the Catskill State Park. Inevitably, any plan for the Catskills' future would have to give more power to local government bodies.

The Commission for the Catskills issued a final report in 1975. Their analysis of the region's problems was excellent, yet their recommendations for dealing with them were vague. They asked that their term be extended for two years more so that they could draw up a detailed land use plan. The extension was not granted and the Commission died. Strong pressures from resort and development interests largely in Sullivan County had been a major force in its death.

Governor Hugh Carey, who took office in January, 1975, asked the Department of Environmental Conservation to set up a non-funded Task Force within its own department and call upon other state agencies for help when needed in forming the land use plan and drawing up a bill to be introduced in the legislature aimed at creating a regional land use agency for the Catskills. The foes of a regional approach mobilized; it was a time of recession and the bill did not pass. The long and often heated struggle to recognize the Catskills as a distinctive region and to provide means of guiding the region into an environmentally sound future was brought to a halt.

The failure of the land use bill to become law did not cause the problems of the Catskills to go away. Yet, the efforts of the Commission and the Catskill Center to inform the people of the region about the problems of a deteriorating environment, high unemployment and conflicting jurisdictions helped make an influential segment of the mountains' people aware that there were possibilities for dealing with these problems.

As the Commission members were being appointed, few towns or counties in the Catskills had planning officials and those that had them did not often enforce their own ordinances. Therefore, the increasing suburbanization of the region with strip development along major highways and a decline in the quality of the old town centers with their shops, churches and schools was allowed to detract from the rural appeal of the region. New people coming to the region did not like to settle in a town center. Even those with strong environmental consciences preferred building amid the rural landscape, and so contributed to the further loss of its rural character. Once people with a concern for their environment had stood by helplessly as they saw suburbanization creeping over the Catskills. Now they realized that if they protested, town and county officials would often listen. This was especially the case as continuing unemployment sent many out of the region and drew others in to settle for the summer or year round, on land vacated by the emigrants. The new people, with incomes derived from outside the Catskills were more often shaped in their attitude toward the land by the surge of environmental commitment which had been a feature of the 1960s. Many were eager to prevent further degradation of the Catskills.

Through the 1970s and the early 1980s many threats to the future well-being of the Catskills provoked the emergence of varied groups of concerned mountain people whose protests were often effective. One threat which began in the 1960s and continued into the 1980s was the view of the Catskills as a major source of electric power for New York and other cities. As the controversy over the Storm King electric project was erupting in the Hudson Valley, similar plants were being planned for the Catskills. The Power Authority of the State of New York (known as PASNY), began constructing their plant at Breakabeen in the Schoharie Valley, and planned others for Prattsville and its vicinity. The Breakabeen project involved the destruction of some of the finest agricultural land in the state as well as archeological sites; the plan for high power transmission lines radiating from it and stalking across the landscape caused vigorous protest from the Greene County Board of Supervisors, as well as from the Catskill Center. Both saw the project as having a destructive effect on the Catskills visual charm and so on its tourist industry. Labor unions and unemployed mountain people favored the projects in the belief that they would supply jobs for a while at any rate. PASNY also proposed building nuclear energy plants in Cementon, Lloyd and Red Hook in the Mid-Hudson Valley. These possibilities too were the objects of protestors. In 1969 the State legislature had passed an act requiring statements of the effect on the environment of projects which might pose a threat to the well-being of the land, water, air, living beings and people. This gave the protestors a useful tool which was used to fight PASNY's plans to place power plants in and around the Catskills. It was found that the pumped-up storage plants seemed likely to cause turbidity and a raised temperature when their waters were released in the Esopus Creek via the Shandaken tunnel under the mountains. This stirred fishermen to opposition. Trout fishing was a major asset to the economy of the Catskills and the Esopus was a major trout stream. Sportsmen's organizations were then agitating for a separation of the management of fish and game from the Department of Environment Conservation on the ground that the Department's recently acquired duties to protect the environment were causing it to grow slack in such tasks as stocking trout streams. These organizations now joined in the battle to head off the proposed power explosion.

It had been recognized in the reports of the Temporary Commission to Study the Catskills and by the Catskill Center and the Department of

Environmental Conservation that retaining the features that made the Catskills attractive to tourists—their rural landscape, trout streams, lakes and waterfalls, mountaintops with their wide views—was vital to the restoration to health of the Catskills' economy. So, those who sought to defend their economic assets joined environmentally-minded people. When bills to permit casino gambling in the Catskills were being formulated in Albany (after the first legal gambling casino in Atlantic City, New Jersey, had prospered), environmentalists, with the Catskill Center playing a conspicuous part, opposed gambling casinos in the Catskills. Owners of the large Sullivan County hotels strongly favored the casinos. They testified to the effect that the old rural image of the Catskills was no longer valid and that a more modern one was needed for the region's economic salvation. Protestant church members lined up in opposing casino gambling .

Neither the gambling issue nor that of building power plants for urban centers has been finally settled in this year 1982. But various groups have united in opposition to proposals and actions which seemed likely to have harmful effects on the region while making short term profits for a few. The struggle to safeguard the Catskills which had begun to move ahead in the late 1960s was demonstrating that it had an educational effect and was giving many of the region's people an ability to look ahead and assess the effect of present policies and actions on the future. During these years the awakened concern for the land on which they lived resulted in the concerted effort of its inhabitants to improve and protect the aspects of life which gave their region its distinctive appeal and character.

In 1974 the Catskill Center took over the Old Mill at East Meredith to ensure its continuance as an industrial museum. For more than a century the mill had been using water, steam and electric power to make a great variety of products from flour and cattle feed to turned objects and other wooden articles; it had also functioned as a local store. Over the years an extraordinary collection of equipment had accumulated in the rambling, picturesque structure. The Old Mill now promises to become an important center for telling the story of many aspects of the Catskills' industrial history to a wide public. In the early 1960s an attempt to preserve the Thomas Cole house and studio at Catskill as a museum devoted to the work of the Hudson River School of painters had failed. Later the house came on the market again. The Hudson River Arts Consortium tried in vain to raise funds to preserve the house. It alerted the Catskill Center, which soon bought the buildings and grounds and set in motion a series of events which resulted in the property finding its way into the possession of a not-for-profit organization which will make it a center for the display and study of the work of the Hudson River school of painters. The Mill and the Cole property were placed on the National Register of Historic Places. So, too, through the efforts of Woodstock residents, was the cluster of mountainside arts and crafts buildings known as Byrdcliffe where the town's art colony had begun. The Yeomans House in Delhi which forms part of an outstanding nineteenth century civic center also went on the register, following a campaign to save the building. In Stamford the huge Rexmere House, one of the few survivors of the Catskills' great hotel boom now appears on the National Register. So did other structures in the region as a realization of the importance of historic preservation spread over the Catskills.

Buildings can be eloquent interpreters and symbols of the character and history of the past of a place. The land, water and living things speak with equal authority and expressiveness on the Catskills' traditional appeal. So, miles of the upper part of the West Branch of the Delaware River came to be federally protected under the Scenic and Wild Rivers Act. The Basha Kill came under the protection of the State and negotiations were begun to guarantee that the deep rocky gorge of the Neversink would be protected as far as possible. At the head of Plattekill Clove, long one of the scenic wonders of the Catskills, a large tract of land was donated by its owners to the Catskill Center to be protected and used as an interpretative center for the mountain landscape and the painters who made it so well known round the world. The center also provided protection of the 3,600-acre Beaverkill Conservation area.

During the 1970s, books and magazine articles dealing with the Catskills, proliferated as never before. The Catskill Center sponsored a splendid photographic picture book of the region, one on its architecture, a guide to an understanding of wetlands, and a well thought out and executed map of the region. A good regional magazine was published but did not survive the economic upheavals of the 1970s. Yet, the attempt had been made and is likely to be revived. The Center sponsored a trail guide to the Catskills. At Prattsville an interpretative center was set up at the base of Colonel Zadock Pratt's sculptured rocks so that tourists and local people alike might learn their history and meaning. With financial help from the Temporary Commission to Study the Catskills and the O'Connor Fund of Oneonta, the Center sponsored a half hour film devoted to stressing the need for common action to preserve the quality of regional life.

A good number of young painters now work at the sites where Hudson River School painters once sketched—they feel that they are working in their own ways to celebrate the landscape of the Catskills. The ethnic festivals at Hunter and elsewhere have added country music, a Celtic and an

American Indian Festival to the German and Polish events which have grown in breadth and size. In High Woods at the base of the Catskills thousands are attracted each year to Harvey Fite's Opus 40, a striking sculptured landscape created from an old bluestone quarry and its mounds of waste stone. On the Esopus Creek below Phoenicia white water racing has become a popular sport and tubing (floating downstream on an oversized inner tube) has soared in popularity. Trout fishing now draws more fishermen than ever.

In many parts of the Catskills buildings of regional historic value have been placed on the National Register; The Thomas Cole house and studio at Catskill have been guaranteed a safe and useful future; the Old Mill Museum at East Meredith has surmounted many problems to become a fine center for understanding nineteenth century industries of the Catskills; local historical societies among the Catskills have grown in number and in the range of their activities in interpreting the region. If efforts like these which marked the late 1970s and early 1980s—are carried forward it may well be that the old magic of the Catskills will survive. Yet that magic faces threats.

All these signs of a growing regional consciousness are encouraging to those who value the Catskills. But there is a dark side to the picture. Economic necessity continues to force farmers to sell out and subdividers to move in. Developments are planned to surround lakes which environmentalists believe should be open to the public in part at least. Chain stores, motels and other enterprises owned by outsiders appear in the region, bringing with them the same standard architecture and standardized services which they provide everywhere else. Low employment causes many to welcome them even though many new commercial ventures deals a damaging blow to regional values they cherish.

In recent years it has become widely recognized that the economic development of a region and the preservation of its natural resources and cultural values must proceed harmoniously if the region is to achieve long range prosperity. That is why every new proposal for projects that are promoted as sure to bring economic benefit becomes the subject of debate—and usually heated debate. Among such projects during the 1970s and early 1980s were lakeside housing ventures which would build up to a thousand small summer dwellings of campers beside some quiet lake without due regard for the sanitation, traffic and other inevitable problems. A proposal by the nationwide Marriott Corporation to make over the borders of Lake Minnewaska on the edge of the Catskills into a site for a shiny conference center with accompanying condominiums triggered the usual economic benefit versus protection of the environment debate. A debate that was central to the welfare of the Catskills erupted after the abandonment of freight service on the Ulster and Delaware Railroad (passenger service had ended in 1954). This marked the death of the once thriving rail system which was remembered as a vital element in the bustling, joyous heyday of summer boarding. To many the railroad had become a symbol of better days that could stir emotion. Besides, the line seemed essential to hopes for farm and industrial prosperity.

A committee put together by the Catskill Center tried to work out means by which the railroad might be saved from threatened abandonment and become once more a viable rail line hauling both passengers and freight and eventually tourists. Many problems developed as the committee negotiated with the line's owner, the Pennsylvania Railroad, with state officials, and industries which liked to ship their products by rail. The committee kept the railroad from destruction while its future could be considered. Changes in the ways in which Americans amused themselves also brought the railroad into heated debate.

Americans of the kind who had once found amusement in visiting the spot where Rip Van Winkle was said to have slept were thronging by the 1960s to such sophisticated commercial wonders as Disneyland in California, Walt Disney's World in Florida, and The World's Fair in New York, among many others. European vacations became economically feasible for an increasing number of Americans. Rip's Village beside North Lake had been an unsuccessful attempt at profiting from this change in taste; the Catskill Mountain Game Farm at Lawrenceville is one that does well. In the mid-1970s a plan developed for taking over the Ulster and Delaware and using it as the central element in an amusement venture featuring a railroad theme park on the Kingston Flats with trains to carry tourists up the line, perhaps as far as Pine Hill. The Ulster County legislature bought the Ulster part of the line; grants made possible much promotional effort. The proposal, however, encountered opposition from environmentalists and from those who saw it as a Disneyfication of the Catskills without due regard for the region's color and character. Local efforts succeeded in using part of the line in connection with white water racing and tubing on the Esopus Creek. But the future of the old railroad is still in some doubt.

There are likely to be many similar proposals by disposers of outside capital intended to exploit the Catskills' traditions and attractive physical assets in ways that are consistent with present day methods of profitably supplying mass amusements. And they will often find opposition from those regional people who have been educated by the environmental conflicts of the 1970s. Out of future conflicts balanced solutions can grow which will give thoughtful consideration to both economic and environmental needs.

Today, the defeat of the plans of the 1970s for a tightening of regional awareness and the creation of a regional land use plan have left the Catskills vulnerable to assaults on the assets and values which more and more of its people cherish.

In 1971 I ended *The Catskills From Wilderness to Woodstock* with a statement of my confidence that the region will surmount its problems and retain the distinctiveness and power to enchant which have made it a place of glamor to people around the world.

I still feel that confidence. And I believe that the logic of events will eventually bring to the Catskills a land use plan that will safeguard the future of its so closely intertwined people, wild life, water, air, land and traditions.

Notes

1. Told to me by Charles Herrick, Woodstock during the 1940s. The same thought was expressed in a more sophisticated form by Woodstock lawyer Martin Comeau when he suggested on July 22, 1954 that a recent instance of "political backwardness" of mountain people might reflect their relatively brief experience of democratic ways.

2. For a few of many comments on the blue of the Catskills, see Horatio Gates Spafford, *A Gazetteer of the State of New-York* . . . , Albany, 1813, p. 164; *Yearbook*, Dutchess County Historical Society, vol. 17 (1942), pp. 86–88; "No wonder the Catskills look so blue after what they've been through," said a Dutchess man to me after a discussion of the granting of the Hardenbergh Patent; "All those born within the shadow of the Catskills are a little mad," is a Catskill saying reported to me by Mabel Parker Smith, Historian of Greene County; A. J. Downing in *Rural Essays,* New York, 1853, p. 196, writes of the blue "fantasies of the color-genii" of the Catskills.

3. Told to me by Daniel Revzan, Woodstock, June 7, 1961.

4. George Dangerfield, *Chancellor Robert R. Livingston of New York, 1746–1813,* New York, 1960, p. 309.

5. Lockwood Bow, The Hunter-Desbrosses and Allied Families of New York City and Hunter's Island . . . , New York, 1945, typescript in the New York Public Library, —here the Hunter way of life is suggested; for the Verplanck way, see W. E. Ver Planck, *The History of Abraham Isaacse Ver Planck and His Descendants in America,* Fishkill Landing, New York, 1892.

6. Washington Irving, *Spanish Papers and Other Miscellanies,* Pierre M. Irving, ed., 2 vols., New York, 1866, vol. 2, p. 484.

7. Ibid., p. 481.

8. Told to me by Charles Herrick.

9. James E. Quinlan, *History of Sullivan County,* Liberty, New York, 1873, republished 1965, South Fallsburgh, New York, p. 209.

10. Told to me by Ralph M. Lord, Tannersville.

11. From "Ten Days in a Tannery," unpublished typescript of humorous poem by C.F.C., given to me by Ralph M. Lord.

12. Told to me during the 1920s by Gross Freer of New Paltz.

13. The bounds given here correspond with those in T. Morris Longstreth, *The Catskills,* New York, 1921, pp. 44–45. For a more recent and different view, see *Geography of New York State,* John H. Thompson, ed., Syracuse, 1966, pp. 32–33, 373.

14. The phrase "maturely dissected" is used in J. L. Rich, *Glacial Geology of the Catskills,* Albany, 1935, p. 12.

15. Told to me by Mrs. Elizabeth Wyman, Woodstock.

16. *History of Greene County, New York, with Biographical Sketches of its Prominent Men,* New York, 1884, p. 324.

17. The traditions given here have been widely printed. See Edward T. Corwin, *A Manual of the Reformed Church in America,* 4th ed., New York, 1902, pp. 513–14; Margaret Van Kleeck Gillmore, "Hardenbergh Foundations in American History," in *Journal of American History,* vol. VII, no. 1 (January, February, March, 1913), pp. 829–33; interesting variants sometimes appeared in regional newspapers as in the Ellenville *Journal,* April 19, 1901.

18. Hardenbergh fact and fantasy were separated in "The Hardenbergh or the 'Great' Patent," in *Olde Ulster,* vol. VI, no. 5 (May 1910), pp. 129–36. The Hardenbergh genealogy was put on a sound basis in W. J. Hoffman, "An Armory of American Families" in *New York Genealogical and Biographical Record,* Vol. LXX, nos. 3 and 4, pp. 253–58, 337–42.

Chapter 2

1. Kingston *Daily Freeman,* September 20, 24, 1917.

2. Ibid., September 24.

3. William A. Ritchie, New York State Archeologist, in conversation.

4. William E. West, Woodstock.

5. Of help here was William A. Ritchie, "The Indian in His Environment," in the *New York State Conservationist,* vol. 10, no. 3 (December-January 1955–56), pp. 23–27, and Ritchie, *Indian History of New York State,* New York State Museum and Science Service, Part III, 1950.

6. "The Third Voyage of Master Henry Hudson" by Robert Juet, in *Narratives of New Netherland, 1609–1664,* J. Franklin Jameson, ed., New York, 1909, p. 21.

7. E. M. Ruttenber, *History of the Indian Tribes of Hudson's River,* Albany, New York, 1872, pp. 93–96.

Chapter 3

1. Jameson, ed., *Narratives,* pp. 25, 26–27.

2. Georg Agricola, *De Re Metallica,* trans. Herbert and Lou Henry Hoover, New York, 1950, p. 38.

3. Gustave Anjou, *Ulster County, N.Y., Probate Records in the Office of the Surrogate, and in the County Clerk's Office at Kingston, N.Y.,* 2 vols., New York, 1906, vol. 1, p. 28.

4. Agricola, *De Re,* 38–41.

5. Ibid., 36–37.

6. *Documents Relating to the Colonial History of the State of New York,* E. B. O'Callaghan and B. Fernow, eds., 15 vols., Albany, 1849–81, vol. 2 (new series), 1881, p. 100; N. B. Sylvester, *History of Ulster County, New York, with Illustrations and Biographical Sketches of Its Prominent Men and Pioneers,* Philadelphia, 1880, Part I, p. 22; Timothy Dwight, *Travels in New England and New York,* 4 vols., New Haven, 1821–22, vol. 4, p. 17.

7. Henry W. Longfellow, *Poetical Works,* 6 vols., Boston and New York, 1906, vol. I, pp. 408, 412–13.

8. I have relied for this episode on John Romeyn Brodhead, *History of the State of New York, First Period, 1609–1664,* 2nd ed., New York, 1859; the story has been

printed many times and in many forms as in John Ogilby, *America: Being a Description of the New World . . .* London, 1671, pp. 170–71.

9. Rev. David Murdoch, D.D., *The Royalist's Daughter or, the Dutch Dominie of the Catskills,* Philadelphia, 1865, pp. 92–93. This book is a novel but contains much which, like this incident, rings true to local traditions and is currently being repeated as such.

CHAPTER 4

1. Warren G. Sherwood, *History of the Town of Lloyd,* Poughkeepsie, 1953, Emelyn Elizabeth Gardner, *Folklore from the Schoharie Hills,* Ann Arbor, 1937, pp. 13–14. James Pierce, "A Memoir on the Catskill Mountains," in *American Journal of Science,* vol. 6 (new series), 1823, p. 96—here flames are reported seen in the Catskills "generated in beds of coal or sulpheret of iron."

2. Brodhead, *New York, 1609–1664,* p. 531.

3. *Documents Relating,* vol. 2 (new series), p. 99.

4. Ibid., p. 100.

5. *Documents Relating,* vol. 2 (old series), 1858, p. 63.

6. Ms. map of Great Lot 19, Hardenbergh Patent, n.d., Cockburn Papers, New York State Library; An excerpt from Cosby's will, Cockburn Papers, 10:10, puts the mines in Rochester where the Governor also had land interests.

7. Sir William Johnson, *Papers,* J. Sullivan, A. C. Flick, and A. W. Hamilton, eds., 14 vols., Albany (1921–65) vol. 6, pp. 737–38.

8. Much has been written about the mining explorations and operations of Dutch days. In 1750 Swedish botanist Peter Kalm reported traditions of Spanish miners and played with the notion of Norse miners, *The America of 1750, Peter Kalm's Travels in North America,* trans. and ed., Adolph B. Benson, 2 vols., New York, 1966, vol. 1, pp. 202–03. Quinlan, *Sullivan County,* pp. 378–88, brings together much interesting material; "The Old Mine Road" in *Olde Ulster,* vol. 3 (February 1907), pp. 35–41, seems to rely on Quinlan; the classic on the subject is Charles G. Hines, *The Old Mine Road,* republished from the original 1909 edition, with an informative introduction by Henry Charlton Beck, New Brunswick, 1963.

9. Carroll Simpson, Phoenicia, in conversation.

10. Earl Bennett, Chichester, in conversation.

CHAPTER 5

1. John B. Brebner, *The Explorers of North America, 1492–1806,* Garden City, 1955, pp. 117–18.

2. Marius Schoonmaker, *History of Kingston, New York, from Its Early Settlement to 1820,* New York, 1888, pp. 5–20; *History, Greene County,* 1884, pp. 86–97.

3. For a brief overall view of Indian-white misunderstandings, see Alvin M. Josephy, *Indian Heritage,* New York, 1968, pp. 3–9; for a sympathetic local view, see Augustus H. Van Buren, *A History of Ulster County Under the Dominion of the Dutch,* Kingston, 1923, pp. 5–14 and passim.

4. Kenneth Scott and Charles E. Baker, "Renewals of Governor Nicolls' Treaty of 1665," in *New-York Historical Society Quarterly,* vol. 37, (July 1955), pp. 251–72.

5. Quoted by Schoonmaker, *History of Kingston,* p. 52.

6. Sylvester, *History of Ulster County,* Part 1, pp. 37–44, 49–60, 65–66 and passim, narrates in a simple fashion the story of the expulsion of the Indians from the lowlands beneath the eastern Catskills; Scott and Baker cite many sources for the expulsion.

7. Earlier, those holding land under the Dutch West India Company were required to obtain conveyances from the "Lords Sachems of New Netherland," see "New Project of Freedoms and Exemptions" in *Documents Relating,* vol. 1, 1856, p. 99.

8. Dangerfield, *Chancellor R. R. Livingston,* p. 12.

9. Myrtle Hardenbergh Miller, *The Hardenbergh Family,* New York, 1958, pp. 16–19. William J. Hoffman, loc. cit., pp. 337–38.

10. "The Leisler Tragedy," in *Olde Ulster,* vol. 2, no. 10 (October 1906), pp. 292–94; genealogy of Colonel Jacob Rutsen in *Olde Ulster,* vol. 8, no. 4 (April 1912), pp. 111–18; "The Hardenbergh House at Rosendale," in *Olde Ulster,* vol. 5, no. 2 (February 1909).

11. Mrs. Anna Grant, *Memoirs of an American Lady,* Albany, 1876, has an excellent account from first-hand observation of the eighteenth-century Indian traders of New York, pp. 62–72.

12. New York State Library, *Calendar of Council Minutes,* 1668–1783, Albany, 1902, vol. 8, p. 312, records the reading of Hardenbergh's petition for this land; a petition preserved in New York Colonial Mss., Indorsed Land Papers, 1642–1803, 63 vols., New York State Library, vol. 4, p. 24, deals with a petition for land, possibly the same made in March 1701.

13. Petition of Cornelis Cool, Indorsed Land Papers, New York State Library, vol. 4, p. 26.

CHAPTER 6

1. William Spenser, High Woods.

2. For Cornbury's cruise of 1702 see *Memorial History of New York,* James Grant Wilson, ed., 4 vols., New York, 1892–93, vol. 2, p. 64; Charles Worthen Spencer, "The Cornbury Legend," in *Proceedings, New York Historical Association,* vol. 13, 1914, p. 311.

3. Ibid., p. 313.

4. Reminiscences of Janet Montgomery, in *Yearbook,* Dutchess County Historical Society, vol. 15, 1930, pp. 61–62.

5. Spencer, op. cit., p. 310.

6. "Leisler Tragedy," loc. cit., pp. 292–93.

7. Marjorie Hope Nicolson, *Mountain Gloom and Mountain Glory,* Ithaca, 1959, pp. 1–33 and passim.

CHAPTER 7

1. Petition of Cornelis Cool, Indorsed Land Papers, New York State Library, vol. 4, p. 26.

2. The *Calendar of Council Minutes,* vol. 9, p. 481, shows that the survey was authorized, October 4, 1704; it was made October 10, 1706, Indorsed Land Papers, vol. 4, p. 97; the survey was returned to the governor, June 18, 1707, with a map, Indorsed Land Papers, vol. 4, p. 98.

3. Ibid., p. 77.

4. A copy of the deed is in the Senate House Museum Library, Kingston.

5. Indorsed Land Papers, vol. 4, p. 115.

6. Ibid., p. 88.

7. Indorsed Land Papers, vol. 40, p. 126 (3).

8. Book of Patents, 1664–1786, 17 vols., New York Secretary of State's Office, vol. 7, p. 363; the deed from the Hardenbergh patentees to the Cool group, Ulster County Deed Book AA, p. 447; the warrant for the patent confirming the deal, Indorsed Land Papers, vol. 4, pp. 156–57.

9. The restrictions on land grants in force in 1708 will be found in convenient form in *Documents Relating,* vol. 5, pp. 21–26.

10. Book of Patents, vol. 7, p. 363.

11. Edward G. West, Allaben, New York.

12. Abstracts of the instruments by which Lurting and Rokeby conveyed their shares in the Patent to Wenham and Bickley are in Indorsed Land Papers, vol. 40, p. 129.

13. *Colonial Laws of New York from the Year 1664 to the Revolution,* 5 vols., Albany, 1894–96, vol. 1, pp. 633–36.

14. Ibid., pp. 712–13.

15. Copy of a Journal kept in the Service of Hardenbergh & Company, October 24 to November 1, 1742, Ancient Manuscripts, file 1857, Dutchess County Clerk's Office, Poughkeepsie; letter Robert Livingston to Robert R. Livingston, March 1, 1762, in Robert R. Livingston Papers, Box 1, Ms. Room, New-York Historical Society.

CHAPTER 8

1. Hardenbergh's rise in status is outlined in Miller, *Hardenbergh Family,* p. 25.

2. Alexander Hamilton, *Gentleman's Progress,* ed., Carl Bridenbaugh, Chapel Hill, 1948, p. 77.

3. As in the Ms. Minutes of the Court of Sessions of Common Pleas of Ulster County, March 1711–September 1720, New York State Library, entry for September 2, 1712.

4. An abstract of Hardenbergh's will was printed in New-York Historical Society *Collections,* New York, 1895. Abstracts of Wills, 1744–53, *Liber* 16, p. 339.

5. Caroline Evelyn More and Irma Mae Griffin, The *History of the Town of Roxbury,* Walton, New York, 1953, p. 264.

6. Gillmore, *Hardenbergh Foundations,* loc. cit., was illustrated by photographs of the ruins of Castle Hardenberg in Germany and the "picturesque village of Nörten" beneath. Frederick S. Dellenbaugh, "The Hardenberghs" in *Proceedings of the Ulster County Historical Society, 1933–1934,* Kingston, n.d., pp. 60–85, mingles fact and fantasy and devotes pp. 62–64 to the princely Von Hardenbergs; Quinlan, Sullivan County, pp. 202–4 states that Hardenbergh patentees aspired to live on their lands as "patroons and barons." The nineteenth-century likening of the Hudson River to the Rhine, especially after castellated mansions began to spring up on the river's banks and the spreading of a Germanic haze to the Catskills, helped nourish Hardenbergh fantasies, comparable to those enjoyed by many other American families of the late nineteenth and early twentieth centuries.

7. Miller, *Hardenbergh Family,* p. 30—here the patent is characterized as a "truly royal domain." Most of the material in this paragraph was obtained in conversation with descendants of Major Hardenbergh.

8. More and Griffin, *History of Roxbury,* pp. 263–74.

9. Mrs. Sadie Hardenbergh, Hasbrouck, New York, in conversation.

10. Martin Comeau, Woodstock, tells me of a belief that the Patent became two million acres instead of two thousand "by mistake."

CHAPTER 9

1. Charles Worthen Spencer, "The Land System of Colonial New York," *Proceedings of the New York Historical Association,* vol. 16, 1917, pp. 150–64; Irving Mark, *Agrarian Conflicts in Colonial New York,* Port Washington, 1965, pp. 13–17; Dangerfield, op. cit., pp. 16–17.

2. Cadwallader Colden, "The State of Lands in the Province of New York, in

1732," in *The Documentary History of the State of New-York,* 4 vols., Albany, vol. 1, p. 384.

3. Deed Book BB, Ulster County Clerk's Office, p. 465.

4. *Documents Relating,* vol. 5, pp. 110–12, contains criticism of Cornbury grants; see ibid., pp. 54–55, for instructions given to Cornbury's successor about granting land, see also ibid., pp. 161–62, 180.

5. New-York Historical Society *Collections,* 1895, Abstracts of Wills, 1708–28, Liber 9, p. 36.

6. Indorsed Land Papers, vol. 8, p. 71. On October 23, May Bickley petitioned that the survey be made on behalf of "Hardenbrook & Comp.," the same day Surveyor General Cadwallader Colden was authorized to make it.

7. Ms. Advertisement, October 20, 1727, in Kingston Papers, CV 10181-17, New York State Library.

8. Cockburn Papers, New York State Library, 5:90.

9. This document, dated September 27, 1726, is in the Senate House Museum Library, Kingston.

10. *Documents Relating,* vol. 5 (old series), p. 357.

11. Conveyance from Hardenbergh patentees to James Graham, September 6, 1729, exemplified copy in Indorsed Land Papers, vol. 40, p. 126 (17).

12. See a listing of Fauconnier lands made by a descendant, no. 38.189.29, Library of the Museum of the City of New York. The wedding gift is said to have never been "acknowledged or recorded," according to this Ms.

13. Cockburn Papers, 5:90 and 5:94—these are memoranda made about 1785.

14. Ulster County Deed Book BB, p. 380. A deed of March 1714/15 mentions, "Doesto an Esopus Indian woman and one of the Sachimeets of sd. Indians in the county of Ulster, and Awarawat and Octperawim, her two sons and Asuchtwichtoga, her Daughter, lawful owners of several tracts of land in the county of Ulster."

15. Letter, William Johnson to Col. John Bradstreet, May 17, 1760, in *Olde Ulster,* vol. 3, p. 324, November 1907.

16. Petition of the Sachems or Chiefs of the Schoharie Mohawk Indians in behalf of them and their Castles, ca. 1734, in Indorsed Land Papers, vol. 11, p. 106.

17. Ms. Journal kept in service of Hardenbergh & Company, Ancient Manuscripts, File 1857, Dutchess County Clerk's Office.

18. Miller, *Hardenbergh Family,* p. 27, takes note of the belief that the Major's signature indicates "nobility" and states that his knighthood has not been proved.

CHAPTER 10

1. I have relied for Robert Livingston's youth on Edwin Brockholst Livingston, *The Livingstons of Livingston Manor,* New York, 1910; my source for the Indian story is Julia Delafield, *Biographies of Francis and Morgan Lewis,* 2 vols., New York, 1877, vol. 1, p. 122.

2. E. B. Livingston, *The Livingstons,* p. 145; both Claremont, N.H., and the New York City neighborhood known as Claremont traditionally owe their name to the English Claremont. For an estimate of the importance of the English Claremont on landscape design see Christopher Hussey, *English Gardens and Landscapes, 1700–1750,* New York, 1967, p. 39; for an account of the many associations which made the name popular, see "Claremont Park," in *Country Life,* London, vol. 10, no. 258 (December 14, 1901).

3. Letter, Robert Livingston to Robert R. Livingston, March 1762, Robert R. Livingston Papers, New-York Historical Society.

4. Copy of affidavit of Henry Bush, September 15, 1785, Indorsed Land Papers, vol. 40, p. 128 (4–5).

5. The conveyances of the interests in the Hardenbergh Patent of William Nottingham, Peter Fauconnier, and Augustine Graham to Robert Livingston and Gulian Verplanck are recorded in Deed Book DD, various dates in 1741 and 1742, Ulster County Clerk's Office. May Bickley's interest was conveyed to Robert Livingston alone on November 18, 1741.

6. *Calendar of Historical Manuscripts in the office of the secretary of state, Albany, N.Y.,* ed. E. B. O'Callaghan, Albany, 1865–66, pp. 538–39.

7. The arbitration agreement is recorded in Deed Book EE, p. 302, Ulster County Clerk's Office.

8. Two Indian deeds covering different parts of the Patent were filed in Deed Book EE, pp. 61–64, Ulster County Clerk's Office.

9. Ibid., p. 130.

10. Letter, Robert Livingston to Robert R. Livingston, March 1, 1762, Robert R. Livingston Papers, New-York Historical Society.

CHAPTER 11

1. Just when this survey began is not clear. A statement by General John Bradstreet, May 4, 1769, puts the beginning "in or about the year 1740"; see Sir William Johnson, *Papers,* vol. 6, p. 735.

2. For traditional evidence of hostility of Indians to surveyors on the borders of the Hardenbergh Patent, see L. Cote, "Folklore of Orange and Sullivan Counties," in H. W. Thompson Archive, New York Historical Association Library, Cooperstown, New York.

3. Statement by Gen. John Bradstreet in Johnson *Papers,* vol. 6, p. 736.

4. See note 9, Chapter 10.

5. Johnson, op. cit., vol. 6, p. 737.

6. Affidavit, William Cuddeback, January 21, 1771, in Indorsed Land Papers, vol. 28, p. 71.

7. Declaration of Esopus Indians, ca. 1769, in Johnson *Papers,* vol. 6, p. 739.

8. Affidavits, January 1771 of Pieter Kuykendal, Indian trader, and William Cuddebeck in Indorsed Land Papers, vol. 28, p. 71.

9. Years of controversy over the location of the Hardenbergh Patent's western boundary has put on record much confusing testimony as to just what happened during Henry Wooster's survey. I have been unable to find any contemporary documentary material on Henry's survey. Ebeneezer's resulted in a map and field notes which I have used here and in succeeding chapters. I worked from a photographic copy supplied by the New York Conservation Department and examined originals belonging to the New-York Historical Society and the New York State Library.

10. Declaration of the Esopus Indians, Johnson *Papers,* vol. 6, p. 739.

11. Petition of the sachems or chiefs of the Schoharie Mohawk Indians, Indorsed Land Papers, vol. 11, p. 106.

12. Affidavit, Petrus P. Low, Indorsed Land Papers, vol. 40, p. 128.

13. Ibid.

14. Affidavit, Petrus Dumond, December 29, 1785, Indorsed Land Papers, vol. 40, pp. 128 (19–20)—here Dumond reports a conversation with Henry Bush.

15. Quotations in this and preceding paragraph from notes on the Wooster map of the Patent belonging to the New York Conservation Department.

16. I have used the copy of the deed, dated May 1, 1751, in the Senate House

Museum Library, Kingston. For more information and an opinion on this enlargement of the Patent see, John D. Monroe, *Chapters in the History of Delaware County, New York,* Delaware Historical Association, 1949, p. 26.

17. Exemplified copy of the partition agreement, Cockburn Papers, 5:74.

18. Copy of unsigned letter to surveyor Cornelis Hornbeck (of Rochester), probably from Henry Beekman, dated New York, February 22, 1749/50. See Sylvester, *History of Ulster County,* Part 2, p. 21, for a letter from Beekman to the Rochester trustees which seems to have followed this one.

Chapter 12

1. For the purchase and partition of the Wenham share in the Patent, I relied largely on the Mss. relating to the estate of Philip Livingston, New-York Historical Society.

2. Agreement to sell lands formerly in the Wenham share, dated June 3, 1752, in Misc. Mss., Hardenbergh Patent, New-York Historical Society; see also draft of letter, William Alexander to Israel Pemberton, Jr., October 26, 1751, in Alexander Papers, New-York Historical Society.

3. For this chapter I have used John W. Jordan, Proposed Moravian Settlement in Ulster County in *Olde Ulster,* vol. 7, (1911), pp. 297–306, 329–35, 360–66. This account is reprinted from *The Moravian,* September 16 and 23, 1896. The reference to settlers of 1752 is in *Olde Ulster,* vol. 7, pp. 305, 361.

4. For Cornelius Tiebout see Francis V. Morrell, *The Ancestry and Posterity of Cornelius Henry Tiebout of Brooklyn,* New York, 1909 and the Ms. notes on Tiebout in Dr. John E. Stillwell, "Documents and Papers Relating to New Jersey and Long Island (1650–1850)," in New-York Historical Society. Tiebout's offer to Bishop Spangenberg will be found in *Olde Ulster,* vol. 7, pp. 298–99.

5. Ibid.

6. Quoted from *Ecclesiastical Records, State of New York,* 7 vols., Albany, 1901–16, vol. 5, pp. 3332–33.

7. *Olde Ulster,* vol. 7, p. 302.

8. Abstracts from the reports of Moravian explorers Lawatsch, Rice, and Loesch on their inspection of the lands offered between May 4 and May 14, 1753, are in *Olde Ulster,* vol. 7, pp. 303–6.

9. Ibid., p. 305.

10. Ibid., for Count Zinzendorf's plans for Zauchenthal and for the preparation of deeds, pp. 330–33.

11. Ibid., p. 335.

12. Letter, Robert Livingston to Robert R. Livingston, May 1, 1762, Robert R. Livingston Papers, Box 1, New-York Historical Society.

13. *Olde Ulster,* vol. 7, p. 365.

Chapter 13

1. *Travels of John Bartram,* Dover Publications, New York, n.d., p. 224, this book was first published, Philadelphia, 1791.

2. Petition of Johannes Hardenberg (sic), February 4, 1707–8, Indorsed Land Papers, vol. 5, p. 112.

3. For popular eighteenth-century enthusiasm for the study of nature, see Charles Singer, *A Short History of Scientific Ideas to 1900,* Oxford, 1959, pp. 380–81.

4. For biographical sketch of Collinson, see *Dictionary of National Biography,* 22 vols. + supplements, London, 1938. Excellent details of Collinson's relations with

John Bartram are numerous in Josephine Herbst, *New Green World, John Bartram and the Early Naturalists,* New York, 1954, pp. 7, 45ff. and passim.

5. Quoted by Nan Fairbrother, *Men and Gardens,* New York, 1956, p. 213.

6. *A Selection of the Letters of Horace Walpole,* W. S. Lewis, ed., New York and London, 1926, p. 13.

7. *The Sloane Herbarium,* J. E. Dandy, ed., British Museum, 1958, p. 89.

8. William Darlington, *Memorials of John Bartram and Humphrey Marshall,* Philadelphia, 1849, p. 145.

9. Ibid., Letter, Collinson–Bartram, February 25, 1740–41, pp. 139–41.

10. Ibid., Letter, Collinson–Bartram, September 1, 1741, pp. 144–46.

11. Ibid., Letter, Bartram–Collinson, September 6, 1742, pp. 160–61.

12. *Cadwallader Colden Papers,* in New-York Historical Society Collections, New York, 1920, vol. 3, p. 6.

13. Herbst, op. cit., p. 66.

CHAPTER 14

1. Rogers McVaugh, *Flora of the Columbia County Area, New York,* Albany, 1958, pp. 382–83.

2. For the density of balsam-fir growth on Catskill mountaintops in 1796, I have followed Samuel Latham Mitchill, "A Sketch of the Mineralogical History of the State of New York," in *Medical Repository,* New York, vol. 1, 3d ed., 1804, pp. 300–1; for lying and sitting on the treetops, see Walton Van Loan, *Van Loan's Catskill Mountain Guide,* New York, 1887, p. 82.

3. Henry E. Dwight, "Account of the Kaatskill Mountains," in *American Journal of Science,* vol. 2, 1820, p. 25.

4. For European adoption of Indian plant lore, I have used John Josselyn, Gent., *New-England's Rarities Discovered,* Edward Tuckerman, ed., Boston, 1865, pp. 8ff. and passim.

5. Told to me by Ralph M. Lord. The notation "oil trees hereabouts from whence is taken the oil of balsam" appears near Pine Hill on a map of 1765 and probably refers to balsam fir. The map is "A Map of the Division Line between the Countys of ALBANY and ULSTER from the Mouth of the Sawyers Creek"—the survey and map were made by William Cockburn; the map is in the Print Room, New-York Historical Society.

6. Dwight, op. cit., p. 25.

7. For Christmas trees, see Chapter 60.

8. *John and William Bartram's America,* Helen Gere Cruickshank, ed., New York, 1961, p. 73.

9. Herbst, op. cit., p. 106.

10. Darlington, op. cit., Letter, Collinson–Bartram, July 3, 1742, pp. 157–58.

11. "A Journey to ye Cats kill Mountains with billy 1753," Ms. in collections of Historical Society of Pennsylvania, 9 unnumbered pages.

CHAPTER 15

(Except where otherwise noted this chapter is based on John Bartram's "Journey to ye Cats kill Mountains . . .")

1. Because Colden owned a share in lands adjoining the Hardenbergh Patent's northwestern boundaries and had surveyed and helped shift boundary lines, he knew the part of the Catskills toward which the Bartrams were riding. See Letter, David Cox–William Alexander, April 14, 1767, in Alexander Papers, New-York Historical

Society, for a hint as to Colden's involvement with the Hardenbergh Patent's northern boundary.

2. Darlington, op. cit., Letter, Collinson–Bartram, February 3, 1741/42, pp. 147–50.

3. Ibid., Letter, Collinson–Bartram, March 3, 1741/42, pp. 150–53.

4. Ibid., Letter, Bartram–Collinson, July 6, 1742, pp. 158–59.

5. Ibid.

6. William Gilpin, *Observations on . . . the Mountains and Lakes of Cumberland and Westmoreland,* London, 1808, p. 119.

7. Darlington, op. cit., Letter, Collinson–Bartram, March 3, 1741/42, pp. 150–53.

8. F. A. Michaux, *The North American Sylva,* trans. with notes by J. Jay Smith, 3 vols., 1850, vol. 3, p. 111, "after 15 or 20 years of its existence, the balsam fir loses its lower branches, has a sickly hue, and should then be dismissed from the pleasure grounds," Smith comments.

9. "A Visit to the Catskills," in *The Atlantic Souvenir,* 1828, p. 280.

10. Mary E. Woolley, "The Development of the Love of Romantic Scenery in America," in *American Historical Review,* vol. 3, no. 1 (October 1897), pp. 56–66, traces the rise of American interest in natural scenery and distant views. See also Hans Huth, *Nature and the American,* Berkeley, 1957, pp. 1–53 and passim.

CHAPTER 16

1. Letter, Robert R. Livingston to Robert Livingston, July 20, 1760, Robert R. Livingston Papers, New-York Historical Society.

2. Quinlan, op. cit., p. 209. See Dangerfield, *Chancellor Robert R. Livingston,* p. 425, for land agent Dr. William Wilson's characterization of the Patent as "the most abominable place on the face of God's creation."

3. Letter, Robert R. Livingston to Robert Livingston, February 2, 1762, New-York Historical Society for the phrase "the lower sort of People."

4. Schoonmaker, *History of Kingston,* pp. 126–44; Benjamin M. Brink, *The Early History of Saugerties,* 1600–1825, *Kingston,* 1902, pp. 60–66.

5. Schoonmaker, op. cit., p. 137, quotes a letter of 1757 which tells of militiamen "ranging the woods and guarding the frontiers."

6. Letter, Robert R. Livingston to Robert Livingston, March 17, 1762, Robert R. Livingston Papers, New-York Historical Society, "If you would consent to raise a little money on the Great Patent it would enable us to do what we please. . . ."

7. Letter, Robert R. Livingston to Robert Livingston, April 12, 1766, Robert R. Livingston Papers, New-York Historical Society.

8. Letter, Robert Livingston to Robert R. Livingston, May 1, 1762, Robert R. Livingston Papers, New-York Historical Society.

9. Robert Livingston's plans for the Patent are considered critically in letter, Robert R. Livingston to Robert Livingston, April 12, 1766, Robert R. Livingston Papers, New-York Historical Society.

10. Receipt, tenant Barent Lewis from John Brink acknowledging delivery of "bords" to landing opposite Clermont for Mrs. [Margaret] Livingston, dated September 11 and October 13, 1795, Robert R. Livingston Papers, New-York Historical Society (uncatalogued): Lease, Margaret Livingston and Henry Davis, Ulster County Clerk's Office, Liber 18, pp. 17ff.

11. For the use of "Township" in the sense of a settlement, see letter, Robert R. Livingston to Robert Livingston, July 6, 1763, Robert R. Livingston Papers, New-York Historical Society; for the difficulties of potential buyers of Hardenbergh Patent land, see letter, William Gallagher to Robert Livingston, January 30, 1769, in Robert R. Livingston Collection (uncatalogued Mss.) New-York Historical Society; for a pro-

posed Irish settlement see letter, Robert R. Livingston to Robert Livingston, June 7, 1764, Robert R. Livingston Papers, New-York Historical Society.

12. Letter, Robert Livingston to Robert R. Livingston, April 17, 1762, Robert R. Livingston Papers, New-York Historical Society.

13. Sergeant Abram Post had been in charge of a party of scouts on the Ulster County frontier in the mountains during 1757; see Brink, op. cit., p. 65.

14. The letter is among the Robert R. Livingston Papers, New-York Historical Society.

CHAPTER 17

1. Letter, Robert R. Livingston to Robert Livingston, April 12, 1766, Robert R. Livingston Papers, New-York Historical Society, "it is high time for us both to look forward to a future State. . . ."

2. Great Patent Memoranda in Clermont Account Book, New-York Historical Society; William Cockburn's account book of Hardenbergh Patent leases of Livingston lands, Cockburn Papers, 15:5, New York State Library; both have references to land "in the Lothians"; a Ms. map of the Hardenbergh Patent, Cockburn Papers, 5:29, shows the Patent divided into the various Lothians.

3. Claim of R. R. Livingston and others, Indorsed Land Papers, vol. 40, p. 137.

4. Told to me in conversation, February 22, 1965, by Martin Ecker, aged 90, West Shokan.

5. Letter, Robert Livingston to Robert R. Livingston, April 17, 1762, Robert R. Livingston Papers, New-York Historical Society.

6. Letter, Robert Livingston to Robert R. Livingston, March 1, 1762, Robert R. Livingston Papers, New-York Historical Society.

7. Ibid.

8. These roads appear on William Cockburn's Map of the Division Line between the countys of ALBANY and ULSTER. . . . 1765, Print Room, New-York Historical Society. Many details of landlord-tenant relations during the 1760s and 1770s are in the Great Patent Memoranda in the Clermont Account Book and in many of the Robert Livingston-Robert R. Livingston letters, all in New-York Historical Society.

9. Letter, Robert R. Livingston to Robert Livingston, June 15, 1764, Robert R. Livingston Papers, New-York Historical Society.

10. Ibid.

11. For a good account of the "Levellers" uprising see, Irving Mark, *Agrarian Conflicts* . . . , pp. 131–63; for a strong expression of opposition to "the mob" of tenants, see letter, Robert R. Livingston to Robert Livingston (of Livingston Manor, not of Clermont), May 14, 1766, Franklin D. Roosevelt Library, Hyde Park.

12. Letter, Robert R. Livingston to Robert Livingston, April 12, 1766, Robert R. Livingston Papers, New-York Historical Society. The quotations and paraphrases in the next four paragraphs are from the same source.

13. I have not been able positively to identify the C— family.

14. Letter, Robert R. Livingston to Robert Livingston, of Livingston Manor, May 14, 1766, Franklin D. Roosevelt Library, Hyde Park.

15. E. B. Livingston, *The Livingstons*, pp. 144–48.

CHAPTER 18

1. Matthew, 6:19.

2. For a biographical sketch of Bradstreet see, *Documents Relating,* vol. 8, p. 379;

Don R. Gerlach's *Philip Schuyler and the American Revolution, 1733–77*, New York, 1964, contains much scattered material about Bradstreet but nothing about his Hardenbergh Patent land hopes.

3. Indorsed Land Papers, vol. 17, pp. 323–542 and elsewhere, give a running history of the grants to reduced officers and men of the late 1760s and early 1770s.

4. Traditions about Dies are brought together in *History of Greene County,* New York, 1884, pp. 88–89. Dies may have been the officer mentioned here and there in Sir William Johnson, *Papers,* and the ironmonger who did business at the sign of the Golden Key in Hanover Square, New York, before 1754.

5. The Dies road appears on a number of Ms. colonial maps, among them the Benzel map, 1767, Indorsed Land Papers, vol. 63, p. 162. The road is mentioned as having been made by John "Dyer" in Richard Smith, *Tour of Four Great Rivers* (1769), Francis W. Halsey, ed., New York, 1906, pp. 12–13. For a Livingston reference to the road, see letter, Robert R. Livingston to Robert Livingston, April 12, 1766, Robert R. Livingston Papers, New-York Historical Society. The use of the road by Morris and the Duchess is mentioned in Smith, *Tour,* pp. 13–14.

6. Charles W. E. Chapin, "The Property Line of 1768," in *Magazine of American History,* vol. 17 (January 1887), pp. 49–57.

7. Letter, John Bradstreet to Gov. William Tryon, December 27, 1771, New York State Library.

8. Petition, Robert Leake and others, March 19, 1771, Indorsed Land Papers, vol. 28, p. 115.

9. Sir William Johnson *Papers,* vol. 6, p. 739.

10. Quoted in John D. Monroe, *Chapters in the History of Delaware County, New York,* Delaware County Historical Society, 1949, pp. 23–24.

11. Ibid.

12. *Documents Relating,* vol. 8, pp. 410–13.

13. A copy of Bradstreet's will is in the Indorsed Land Papers, vol. 40, p. 124.

CHAPTER 19

1. Broadside headed "SCHEME" in the Library of the Historical Society of Pennsylvania.

2. George Clinton, *Public Papers,* Hugh Hastings and J. A. Holden, eds., 10 vols., Albany, 1899–1914, vol. 7, footnote pp. vi–vii.

3. Since this chapter was written, the appearance of Alan Chester Valentine, *Lord Stirling,* New York, 1969, has superseded the earlier printed sources which I have used here. I refer the reader to Valentine's study and will cite only direct quotations from other sources for the Stirling lottery.

4. François Jean de Beauvoir, Marquis de Chastellux, *Travels in North America,* Chapel Hill, 1963, p. 106.

5. For New York laws aimed at preventing private lotteries see, *Laws of the Colony of New York,* Albany, 1894–96, vol. 2, pp. 61–62 (1721), vol. 5, p. 351 (1772), vol. 4, p. 639 (1774). For the Royal anti-lottery proclamation, see *Calendar of Historical Manuscripts in the Office of the Secretary of State,* E. B. O'Callaghan, ed., 2 vols., Albany, 1865–66, vol. 1, December 1, 1773.

6. "Head of Delaware" was sometimes used as the name of the source of the small stream which flows into Lake Utsayantha from a point about two miles to the north, sometimes the lake itself was so called. J. D. Monroe, *Chapters in the History of Delaware County, New York,* 1949, p. 26, calls the phrase as used elsewhere "a fraudulent device" for extending the bounds of the Hardenbergh Patent.

7. Statement of the appraisers, Alexander Papers, Box 1, New-York Historical Society.

8. *Laws of the Colony* . . . vol. 4, p. 351.

9. Letter, Alexander Small to Lord Stirling, September 2, 1772. Alexander Papers, Box 1, New-York Historical Society.

10. Letter, U. Scott to Lord Stirling, May 28, 1772, Alexander Papers, Box 1, New-York Historical Society.

11. J. Brett Langstaff, *Dr. Bard of Hyde Park,* New York, 1942, p. 108.

12. Draft of letter from Stirling, or on his behalf, to Hugh Wallace, March 21, 1774, Box 1, Alexander Papers, New-York Historical Society—here Washington is said to have received tickets.

13. I have revised here to include material on the progress of the Stirling lottery from *Valentine,* op. cit., pp. 130–36.

14. George Washington's letter quoted from *Writings of George Washington,* J. C. Fitzpatrick, ed., 39 vols., Washington, D.C., 1931–44, vol. 2, pp. 264–65.

CHAPTER 20

1. *Writings of William Boyse, A Year of Jubilee,* New York, 1840, p. 426.

2. Irving Mark, *Agrarian Conflicts in Colonial New York, 1711–1775,* Port Washington, 1965, pp. 89–92 and passim.

3. Quoted from Beverly McAnear, "Mr. Robert R. Livingston's Reasons Against a Land Tax," in *Journal of Political Economy,* vol. 48, no. 1 (February 1940).

4. See Staughton Lynd, "The Tenant Rising at Livingston Manor, May 1777" in *New-York Historical Society Quarterly,* vol. 48, no. 2 (April 1964), pp. 163–77—Lynd mentions the "sullen Toryism of the manor tenants."

5. Quoted by Dangerfield, *Chancellor Livingston,* p. 63.

6. Schoonmaker, *History of Kingston,* p. 164.

7. *New York in the Revolution,* Berthold Fernow, ed., Albany, 1887, pp. 297–98.

8. The boundary agreement of 1776–78 is recorded in Deed Book 22, pp. 447–49, Ulster County Clerk's Office; a map is filed with the agreement. The draft of a field book of a Cockburn survey of the boundary in question made in 1775 is among the Cockburn Papers, New York State Library, 5:83.

9. For the versions of Burch's Revolutionary activities given by Burch and his associates, see *Ontario Bureau of Archives, Second Report,* 2 vols. Ottawa, 1905, vol. 2, pp. 992–94, 1000. For Whig versions see George Clinton, *Public Papers,* vol. 3, pp. 504–7 and passim.

10. The slipcover of Cockburn's map of the state is in Cockburn Papers, uncatalogued; the whereabouts of the map, if it was ever drawn, is unknown.

11. Irving Mark, *Agrarian Conflicts . . . ,* pp. 21, 22, 171, 183.

CHAPTER 21

1. William Cockburn's lease and survey book of Livingston lands in the Hardenbergh Patent, Cockburn Papers, 15:5, New York State Library.

2. Louise Hasbrouck Zimm, Ulster County in *Southeastern New York,* Zimm, Corning, Emsley, and Jewell, eds., 3 vols., New York, 1946, vol. 1, pp. 209–10; Edmund J. Longyear, *The Longyear Family,* New Haven, 1942, p. 1.

3. "Beuke Bosch" and its English equivalent are used in Julia Delafield, *Biographies of Francis Lewis and Morgan Lewis,* vol. 2, p. 4. The phrase becomes "Buccobush" on a William Cockburn map of Great Lot 26, Hardenbergh Patent, in Print Room, New-York Historical Society.

4. George Lawrence Gomme, *The Village Community,* New York, 1890, pp. 128–29.

5. The terms of the Longyear lease are summarized in William Cockburn's lease and survey book, Cockburn Papers, 15:5, New York State Library.

6. For a typical lease of Livingston tenants on Great Lot 8 and adjoining lands, see Margaret Livingston-Henry Davis lease, May 1, 1794, Deed Book 18, Ulster County Clerk's Office. Here the tenant is forbidden among other things, to "fall any tree or trees . . . for the browsing of cattle."

7. A lease agreement on a printed form and for three lives between Margaret Livingston and Peter Short, Jr., dated May 1, has two endorsements which show how leaseholds were sometimes transferred. In 1803 the Short farm was sold for $250 and in 1809 for $350—one-sixth of these sums went to the owner. The lease is among the uncatalogued Mss., Robert R. Livingston Papers, New-York Historical Society. The Cockburn lease and survey book, New York State Library records the valuing of the improvements of John and James Dingwall of New Stamford by two neighbors and the leasing of the farm to James Grant with the proviso that if the Dingwalls should return and demand the farm back, they might have it if they paid Grant for whatever improvements he might make. The Dingwalls were unlikely to return—they had joined the King's army during the Revolution and eventually settled in Canada.

8. Neva Shultis, *From Sunset to Cock's Crow,* Woodstock, 1957, p. 30.

9. Marcus Lee Hansen, *The Atlantic Migration,* 1607–1860, New York, 1961, p. 51.

10. For sources of this paragraph, see notes to Chapt. 22.

11. For Palatine emigrants, see W. A. Knittle, *Early Eighteenth-Century Palatine Emigration,* Philadelphia, 1937, pp. 111–204.

12. Mark, op. cit., pp. 13–14.

13. Lynd, "Tenant Rising . . . ," loc. cit., p. 167.

14. For the problems of one group of neutral Scottish settlers stranded in Catskill, see Clinton, *Public Papers,* vol. 6, pp. 856–58; "being poor and strangers, we declined having any hand or concern in the War," they declared in a petition to Gov. Clinton, May 12, 1781.

CHAPTER 22

1. *Journals of the Provincial Congress, Provincial Convention . . . of the State of New York* (1775–77), 2 vols., Albany, 1842, vol. 2, p. 709.

2. Clinton, *Papers,* vol. 1, p. 709.

3. *Journals of the Provincial Congress,* vol. 2, p. 437.

4. Letter, n.d., George Clinton to Robert R. Livingston in Clinton, *Papers,* vol. 1, pp. 710–12.

5. The air of tension and suspicion which reigned in and around the Catskills at this time is strongly reflected in the entries for the first eight months of 1777 in *Journals of the Provincial Congress,* vol. 2, and in the Clinton, *Papers,* vol. 1, pp. 693–94, 716–18 and passim.

6. Clinton, *Papers,* vol. 1, pp. 613–14.

7. *Calendar of Historical Manuscripts Relating to the War of the Revolution,* 2 vols., Albany, 1868, vol. 2, p. 72.

8. Clinton, *Papers,* vol. 1.

9. Ibid., p. 754.

10. Ibid., p. 756.

11. Ibid., p. 768.

12. Ibid., p. 168.

13. *Calendar . . . Manuscripts . . . Revolution,* vol. 2, pp. 128–29.

14. Clinton, *Papers*, vol. 1, p. 780.

15. Ibid., p. 169.

16. *Calendar . . . Manuscripts . . . Revolution*, vol. 2, p. 135.

17. Clinton, *Papers*, vol. 1, p. 782.

18. *Journals of the Provincial Congress*, vol. 2, p. 928.

19. Timothy Dwight, *Travels in New England and New York*, ed. B. M. Miller, 4 vols., Cambridge, 1969, vol. 3, p. 305.

CHAPTER 23

1. A Hessian soldier named Julius Egger became a matter of legal controversy when as a childless, unmarried old man, two towns sought to disown responsibility for his support. One result was that much of his life story was set down in writing and his leasing of a farm in the Hardenbergh Patent became a matter of some importance, James Powers Papers, Box 3, folder 17, New York State Library.

2. Basil Williams, *Life of William Pitt*, 2 vols., London, 1913, vol. 2, p. 322. The phrase was used by Pitt in a famous extemporaneous speech and has been variously recorded.

3. "The Captivity of Capt. Jeremiah Snyder and His Son Elias Snyder of Saugerties, Ulster County, New York. During the Revolutionary War," in *Ulster Sentinel*, January 31, February 7, February 14, February 21, February 27, March 7, 1827. The DeWitt account was reprinted in the Kingston *Democratic Journal*, November 19 and 26, 1845 and in Saugerties *Telegraph*, January 25 and February 1. DeWitt's version formed the base for many later retellings—two notable ones are on pages 73–99 of Charles Rockwell, *The Catskill Mountains*, New York, 1867, and B. M. Brink, *Early History of Saugerties*, Kingston, 1902, pp. 168–90.

4. "The Lineage of the Snyder Family," in *Olde Ulster*, vol. 1, p. 29; Kingston Freeman, July 4, 1874.

5. There is little in print on the boundary disputes between Albany County, Ulster County, and the Hardenbergh patentees incited by owners eager to extend their boundaries.

6. Affidavit, Martin Van Bergen, September 3, 1767, Ms. 6812, New York State Library.

7. Affidavit, Hendrick Stroope, August 20, 1767, Ms. 6813, New York State Library.

8. Quoted by Brink, op. cit., pp. 99–101.

9. Letter, Catherina Snyder to George Clinton, February 23, 1781, in Clinton, *Papers*, vol. 6, p. 654.

10. Letter, Jeremiah Snyder to George Clinton, October 15, 1778, in Clinton, *Papers*, vol. 4, pp. 164–65.

11. *American Archives . . . A Documentary History of . . . the North American Colonies*, Peter Force, ed., 5th Series, 3 vols., Washington, D.C., 1837–53, vol. 3, pp. 214–15; *Cal. New York Hist. Ms.*, vol. 2, pp. 93–94.

12. Anita Smith, *Woodstock, History and Hearsay*, Saugerties, 1959, pp. 7–8.

13. This and other quotations in this story of the Snyder captivity, unless otherwise noted, are from editor DeWitt's account.

CHAPTER 24

1. DeWitt refers to "the celebrated Runnip" and writes in his installment of February 14 that "Runnip, though an Indian, had one or two manly traits."

2. Brink, *Saugerties*, pp. 83–84.

3. Ibid., pp. 171–72.

4. Shanks Ben figures in many tales of frontier conflict, see Quinlan, *Sullivan County*, pp. 317–20, 395–96. See also Indorsed Land Papers, vol. 40, p. 150, for statement of Shanks Ben and Jacob Haken about a meeting with General Bradstreet.

CHAPTER 25

1. Local traditions of Brant as a "braggart-fiend" are presented in *History of Greene County*, 1884, p. 81. For a more balanced view see Quinlan, op. cit., 304–14 and passim; the location of the "fort" is shown on Arnold Guyot's map of the Catskills, 1879. In 1823, DeWitt Clinton recorded in his Diary, now in the New-York Historical Society, local traditions of some sort of Indian base which may have been the fort of Revolutionary days.

2. Petition of Catherina Snyder, Clinton, *Papers,* vol. 4, p. 654.

3. *Correspondence and Journals of Samuel Blachley Webb,* ed. W. C. Ford, 3 vols., New York, 1893, vol. 2, pp. 198–99.

4. The Abeel captivity of 1781 was given its generally accepted form on pp. 68–73 of Charles Rockwell's *Catskill Mountains.* See Rockwell, op. cit., for the story of the captivity and escape of Peter Short and Peter Miller of Woodstock, fellow-prisoners of the Snyders in Canada; Anita M. Smith, op. cit., pp. 10–11, gives a version of the Short and Miller captivity, which is current among the men's descendants. Two other captivity narratives of the Catskills deserve mention. One is the gory Schermerhorn narrative first set down by Josiah Priest in his *The Low Dutch Prisoners,* Albany, 1839; the other is the story of the Bush children in *Olde Ulster,* vol. 2, pp. 264–68. The three Bush boys were captured in Shokan, adopted by Indian families, and found and brought home after they had become accustomed to Indian ways.

5. Told to me by William Rodie formerly of the Blue Mountain Riding School.

CHAPTER 26

1. The General's "power and consequence might be said to increase with the disasters of the country; his department was a very lucrative one, and enabled him first, greatly to enrich himself, and, in the process of time, his friend Philip Schuyler," wrote Mrs. Anne Grant in her *Memoirs of an American Lady,* of 1808, republished, Albany, 1876.

2. The memorial of the Bradstreet heirs asking for the lands formerly petitioned for by General Bradstreet is in Indorsed Land Papers, vol. 40, p. 139.

3. The Livingstons displayed the utmost confidence in the Hardenbergh side of the struggle. When an agent of the General approached Judge Robert R. Livingston with an offer of compromise, the Judge wrote, "I could not help smiling and told him that it would never do." Letter, March 18, 1771, Robert R. Livingston to Robert Livingston, Robert R. Livingston Papers, New-York Historical Society.

4. Many entries in the Woodstock Account Book of the Livingstons of Clermont indicate the instability of tenants of the 1790s; William Cockburn's lease and survey book offers the same kind of evidence for the 1780s.

5. The phrase was in daily use among the Catskills fifty years ago but it is rarely heard today.

6. Petition, Johannes Hardenberg (sic), June 16, 1706, Indorsed Land Papers, vol. 4, p. 91.

7. Deed from Nisinos, March 13, 1706/07, Indorsed Land Papers, vol. 4, p. 92.

8. Cadwallader Colden, "The State of Lands in the Province of New York in 1732," in *Documentary History of New-York,* E. B. O'Callaghan, ed., 4 vols., Albany, 1849–51, vol. 1, p. 383.

CHAPTER 27

1. See Rudolph Ruedemann, "Development of Drainage of Catskills," in *American Journal of Science,* 5th Series, vol. 23, no. 136 (April 1932), pp. 337–94 for maps and theories of the development of the Delaware and other drainage systems of the Catskills.

2. "The Dutch were practical in their naming," writes George R. Stewart in *Names on the Land,* New York, 1945, p. 70.

3. The quotations from the affidavits submitted in the Bradstreet hearings, which I have used in this chapter, are easily located in the Indorsed Land Papers vol. XL where they are grouped at page 128, with the names of witnesses given at the beginning of each affidavit.

4. The map of the Hardenbergh Patent made by William Cockburn in 1771 is on file in the New York State Bureau of Surplus Real Property, Alfred E. Smith Office Building, Albany.

5. Notes of Arguments Urged by the Chancellor to show it is impossible that the Mahackamack or Neversink can be the Fish Kill, Indorsed Land Papers, vol. 41, p. 12(10).

6. Argument for Hardenbergh Patent Proprietors by Edward Livingston, Indorsed Land Papers, vols. 41, p. .

7. Monroe, *Delaware,* p. 24. Here the evidence and decision in the Bradstreet case are analyzed; the documents involved are in Indorsed Land Papers, vols. 40 and 41. The grant was known as the Evans Patent in honor of Agatha Bradstreet's husband, Charles John Evans.

8. Henry Wansey, *An Excursion to the United States of North America in the Summer of 1794,* Salisbury, 1796, pp. 80–81.

CHAPTER 28

1. The phrases frequently occur in Livingston biographies and letters. Some are quoted here from Dangerfield, *Chancellor Livingston,* pp. 123, 138.

2. The Chancellor's Bridge is shown on a map of Cockburn's Patent by Jacob Thompson, May 1796, Cockburn Papers, New York State Library, 3:10–6.

3. Quoted by Dangerfield, op. cit., p. 216.

4. William M. Geldart, *Elements of English Law,* 4th ed., Oxford, 1951, p. 27.

5. Letter, Robert R. Livingston, Sr., to Robert R. Livingston, Jr., August 5, 1772. Robert R. Livingston Papers, New-York Historical Society.

6. The terms of leases in R. R. Livingston Great Patent Account Book, Middletown, New York, for lands in Delaware County are much less like those prevailing at Clermont than those recorded in the Woodstock Account Book, both books in New-York Historical Society. Many letters in the Robert R. Livingston Papers in the same library show that outright sale of land in the Hardenbergh Patent was usually more frequent as distance from Clermont increased.

7. The Chancellor's conveyances of lands in the Patent to his brothers and sisters are recorded in Ulster County Deed Book 18, pp. 354–58.

8. Quoted by Sylvester, *Ulster County,* Part 1, p. 196, where details of the Chancellor's gift are given; see also Monroe, *Some Chapters,* pp. 21–22.

9. Told me by William G. West, Allaben, New York.

10. Monroe, *Delaware County,* p. 21; E. P. Cheney, "The Manor of East Greenwich," in *American Historical Review,* New York, vol. 11 (1906), pp. 29–35.

11. For the Chancellor's acceptance of the French Revolution, see Dangerfield,

Chancellor Livingston, pp. 264–66; for his liking for the French people, see 321–22; for a good brief view of the ambivalence which the Chancellor shared with other Livingston landlords, see p. 6.

CHAPTER 29

1. Population figures from the *U. S. Census, 1790, Heads of Families, New York,* Washington, D.C., 1907, and the statement of 1785, that there were five hundred owners of the Hardenbergh Patent, helped me arrive at this estimate, Indorsed Land Papers, vol. 40, p. 137.

2. When John Hebener leased a farm in Woodstock, February 16, 1733, a millsite and four acres surrounding it were reserved; June 1, 1784, the Chancellor leased the Woodstock gristmill (on what is today known as the Tannery Brook) and the adjoining farm to John McKenzie for an annual rent of forty bushels of wheat to be paid "at the Riverside"; by 1789 the Chancellor had sold the McKenzie gristmill and farm to Isaac Davis of Rhinebeck for £200, see William Cockburn lease and survey book, 15:5, Cockburn Papers, New York State Library, and Bruno Louis Zimm, "A Chain of Woodstock Land Titles," in *Publications of the Woodstock Historical Society,* no. 5, August 1931, pp. 9–27.

3. *History of Greene County,* 1884, p. 393.

4. An Act concerning Distresses, passed February 21, 1788, in Greenleaf's *Laws of New-York,* 3 vols., New York, 1798, vol. 2, pp. 63-73.

5. Agreement by William Cockburn to act as agent for a group of landowners, January 16, 1795, Cockburn Papers, Box 5, 22–23, New York State Library.

6. This quotation from Field Book of Survey for John Burch, 1776, Cockburn Papers, Box 5, 25, New York State Library.

7. Timber stealing was a continuing activity. Land agent Ebeneezer Foote resorted to newspaper advertising to check it, see Delaware *Gazette,* June 15, 1820. Here Foote warns against "cutting down or carrying off any Pine, Hemlock, Cherry or other Timber."

8. Benjamin Hine, *Miscellaneous Poetry or the Farmer's Muse,* New York, 1835, pp. 52–56.

9. Genesis, 1:28.

10. Quoted in Irving Lowens, "The Musical Edsons of Shady" in *Bulletin of the New York Public Library,* vol. 65, no. 4 (April 1961), p. 247.

CHAPTER 30

1. Both names were in use in England, in *Country Life,* vol. 10, no. 251 (October 26, 1901), a correspondent reports the death of a male "old 'white witch' or witch doctor" at Ilminster in Somersetshire. In and around the Catskills, the term "white witch" was rarely used. When Washington Irving visited Ulster County in 1833, he noted in his journal the phrase "witch doctor" as if it were in common use, see *The Journals of Washington Irving, from July 1815 to July 1842,* eds. W. P. Trent and G. S. Hellman, 3 vols., Boston, 1919, vol. 3, p. 190.

2. Edmund J. Longyear, *The Descendants of Jacob Longyear,* Los Angeles, 1942, pp. 9–10.

3. "Hurley Witches," unsigned account from notes of talks with Charles Dumond, stage driver, typescript, folder 2685, document 4036, Senate House Museum Library.

4. N. B. Sylvester, *History of Ulster County,* Part 2, facing p. 377.

5. Told to me by Hubert Brink, August 28, 1966.

6. Quoted by H. C. Lea, *Materials for a History of Witchcraft,* 3 vols., New York, 1957, vol. 3, p. 1231.

7. Ibid., vol. 2, pp. 1217–28, for sources for witch persecution in the Netherlands. The Ms. New York Council Minutes, vol. 3, pp. 150–51, records a rare instance of a charge of witchcraft being brought against someone living within sight of the Catskills—this was on May 22, 1673. I quote this from L. H. Zimm, "Edward Whitaker's Wife," in *New York Gen. and Biog. Record,* vol. 70, no. 2 (April 1939), p. 114. In 1748, Robert R. Livingston, not yet a judge but being considered for a judgeship, wrote in a Ms. titled "A charge to a Grand Jury," "If, upon enquiry, you find any people have been dealing with ye Devil, in that uncoman (sic) way [witchcraft] I blieve you'l not fail to Present them." The Charge is dated 1748, and is in the Robert R. Livingston Papers, New-York Historical Society.

8. Woodstock Town Clerk's Minute Book, 1787–1804, in office of Town Clerk, Shandaken.

9. The quotations used here and in the rest of the Chapter, unless otherwise noted, are from *The Writings of William Boyse, A Year of Jubilee,* New York, 1840, pp. 559–62.

10. Exodus, 22:18.

11. Told to me by Harry Siemsen, Sawkill.

12. Told to me by Hubert Brink, Lake Katrine.

13. E. E. Gardner, *Folklore from the Schoharie Hills,* Ann Arbor, 1937, p. 53.

14. Ibid., p. 47.

CHAPTER 31

1. Told to me by Hubert Brink, Lake Katrine.

2. Gardner, *Folklore Schoharie Hills,* p. 51.

3. Ibid., p. 51–52.

4. Jeptha R. Simms, *History of Schoharie County,* 2 vols., Albany, 1845, vol. 2, p. 164.

5. Boyse, *Writings, Year of Jubilee,* p. 559.

6. Ms. Diary of Nathaniel Booth, 44–97: 2 vols., Senate House Museum Library, vol. 2, pp. 89–94, 161.

7. For Dr. Brink as a "stick doctor," see Mary H. Skeel, "Stick Doctoring," in Notes and Queries," in *Journal of American Folklore Society,* vol. 4 (1891); sometimes as in the Hurley Witches Ms. used earlier, Brink is called a "finger doctor."

8. Told to me by Hubert Brink.

9. Gardner, op. cit.

10. Anita M. Smith, *Woodstock, History and Hearsay,* 1959, p. 114.

11. Most details in this paragraph from Gardner, *Folklore Schoharie Hills,* pp. 53–54.

12. Boyse, op. cit., p. 561.

13. Anita M. Smith, "Hearsay and History," in *New York History,* vol. 17, no. 1 (January 1936), p. 67.

14. I have based the version of the story of the *Martin Wynkoop* given here on the Ms. Diary of Nathaniel Booth (see note 6, chapter 31). The same story in simpler form was told me by Hubert Brink and by Louise Hasbrouck Zimm, Woodstock, but neither identified the sloop.

15. This and the next quotation from an unsigned and penciled note, not in Nathaniel Booth's hand, inserted in the second volume of his diary with a rough sketch of the sloop.

16. Letter, Overbaugh to Severyn Hasbrouk, in New York Historical Society.

17. The note inserted in the Booth Diary.

CHAPTER 32

1. Timothy Dwight, *Travels in New England and New York* (*1796–1815*), 4 vols., New Haven, 1821–22, vol. 4, p. 177.

2. Told to me in 1964 by a Roxbury woman who said she had seen the anecdote in print.

3. Told me by Frank Russell, New Kingston.

4. Reported to me by my son, Christopher Evers.

5. Quoted in *Library of American Literature,* eds. E. C. Stedman and E. M. Hutchinson, 10 vols., New York, 1888, vol. 2, p. 114.

6. Anita M. Smith, *Woodstock,* p. 69.

7. Ibid., p. 7.

8. Neva Shultis, *From Sunset to Cock's Crow,* Woodstock, 1957, pp. 5–6.

9. Told to me by Martin MacDaniel, Shady, New York.

10. Charles Lanman, *Adventures Among the Wilds of North America,* 2 vols., Philadelphia, 1856, vol. 1, pp. 181–82.

11. See *History of Greene County,* 1884, p. 83, for account of Devil's Pulpit and an "Indian Maiden's Cliff" in the Stony Clove.

CHAPTER 33

1. For a biographical sketch of DeZeng, see *New York Genealogical and Biographical Record,* vol. 2 (1871), p. 52. My source for DeZeng's glassmaking proposal is Letter, F. A. DeZeng to Robert R. Livingston, April 8, 1802, Robert R. Livingston Papers, New-York Historical Society.

2. For a brief account of these projects based on entries in the Minute Books of the trustees of Kingston, see L. H. Zimm, Ulster County in *Southeastern New York,* vol. 1, pp. 74–75. The Field Books for the Ulster and Delaware Turnpike are in New York State Library.

3. A list of men "imployed upon the rode to Schohary kill by the Marchents of Kingston," dated November 16, 1784, is in the Senate House Museum Library, folder 3036, document 4259.

4. The map of "the Northerly part of the Great or Hardenbergh's Patent," was made for Ludlow and McEvers and is in the museum of the Ulster County Historical Society, Marbletown.

5. There is much scattered information about the early industries of the northern Catskills in *History of Greene County,* 1884. For the DeZeng forge, see Letter, F. A. DeZeng to Robert R. Livingston, November 30, 1802, Robert R. Livingston Papers, New-York Historical Society; persistent tradition tells of a forge in the Dry Brook Valley at which "bayonets and cutlasses" were made for the use of Revolutionary soldiers. The Pine Hill *Sentinel* of August 8, 1891, reprinted an account of the forge at Furlough Lake in a story about George Gould's estate in the New York *World.* The forge is mentioned and the site pictured in R. Lionel De Lisser, *Picturesque Ulster,* Kingston, published in parts, 1896–1905, pp. 170–71.

6. Quinlan, *Sullivan County,* 1884, p. 539.

7. Quoted by Allen Nevins, *American Social History as Recorded by British Travellers,* New York, 1928, pp. 21–22; William Strickland, Ms. Diary, Chapter 10, pp. 219–20, New-York Historical Society.

8. Letter, F. A. DeZeng to Robert R. Livingston, April 8, 1802, Robert R. Livingston Papers, New-York Historical Society.

9. Quoted by L. H. Zimm, "Captain Elias Hasbrouck, 1741–91," in *Publications* of the Woodstock Historical Society, no. 16, September 1951, p. 31.

10. E. B. Livingston, *The Livingstons*, 1910, pp. 481, 482.

11. For R. L. Livingston's scheme of 1833, see *Ulster Republican*, June 12 and 16, 1833; see also Thomas F. Gordon, *Gazetteer of New York*, New York, 1836, p. 742.

12. Dangerfield, Chancellor Livingston, p. 282.

13. Quinlan, op. cit., p. 498n.

14. Quoted by John Ross Delafield, "Montgomery Place," in *New York History*, vol. 20, no. 4 (October 1939), p. 450.

CHAPTER 34

1. More and Griffin, *History of Roxbury*, pp. 264–72; the phrase quoted was used in conversation by J. B. Merwin, Grand Gorge; a collection of Isaac Hardenbergh's papers are in the New York State Library.

2. Old World glamor was persuasively conveyed to Americans in the English tales in Washington Irving's *Sketch Book* and *Bracebridge Hall*.

3. Quinlan, Sullivan County, pp. 134–35.

4. Ibid., p. 539.

5. Ibid., p. 497. *Collections of the New-York Historical Society, 1941; National Academy of Design Exhibition Record, 1826–60*, 2 vols., New York, 1943, vol. 1, pp. 296–98, lists Dr. Livingston as exhibiting between 1838 and 1852; I own the sketchbook mentioned.

6. Copy of abstract of title to Lake Delaware estate given me by the estate manager Thomas Wallis; the estate rent roll is preserved in the library of the Elbridge T. Gerry house.

7. Delafield, *Biographies of Francis Lewis and Morgan Lewis*, vol. 2, p. 125.

8. Ibid., pp. 120–21.

9. Dictionary of American Biography, Allen Johnson and Dumas Malone, eds., 22 vols., New York, 1928–44, vol. 7, pp. 227–28.

10. Reported to me May 22, 1965, by Mrs. Elbridge T. Gerry—Mrs. Gerry had not seen the ghost.

CHAPTER 35

1. For a description and pictures of the Hardenbergh-Rutsen house (later the Cornell house), see Margaret Van Kleeck Gillmore, Hardenbergh Foundations in American History in *Journal of American History*, vol. 7, no. 1, (January, February, March 1913), pp. 829–33; the bit of lore about the burning of the house was told to me in my boyhood by Mrs. Charles Wood of Tilson.

2. For Jacob Rutsen Hardenbergh, see Corwin. *Manual of the Reformed Church*, ed. of 1902, pp. 511–14, and Miller, *Hardenbergh Family*, pp. 90–94.

3. Quinlan, *Sullivan County*, p. 231; see also Miller, *Hardenbergh Family*, p. 134.

4. There is confusion as to which Hardenbergh led the fight against Indian attackers of Wawarsing in August 1781, but there is no evidence that it was Gross. Quinlan, op. cit., p. 231 n., slightly misquotes Ruttenber, *Indian Tribes*, pp. 284–85, in a way that makes Gross seem to be the hero, and Hardenbergh family historians have followed this lead. In the very full version given in Abraham G. Bevier, *The Indians; or Narratives of Massacres*, 1846, the leader is Capt. J. L. Hardenbergh.

5. Schoonmaker, Kingston, pp. 263–64. Schoonmaker's account is based on the many mentions in the *Journals of the Provincial Congress, Journal of the Council of Safety*, vol. 1, pp. 906–44.

6. Quinlan, op. cit., p. 231.

7. Ibid., 231–36; because William Cockburn had much to do with the lands

bequeathed to Nancy Ryerson's children, a copy of Col. Johannes Hardenbergh's will and many surveys and other land papers are included in the Cockburn Papers, esp. Boxes 4 and 5.

8. Quinlan, op. cit., 230–31, for both Schoonmaker and Beekman claims.

9. Ibid., p. 232.

10. Quotations here from Quinlan, op. cit., pp. 233–34.

11. Jonathan Hasbrouck's bill to "Gerard Hardenbergh, his estate" is in file box 19, Surrogate's Office, Ulster County Building, Kingston.

12."Judge Elmendorf and the Lucas Turnpike," in *Olde Ulster,* vol. 9 (May 1913), p. 147.

13. Jonathan Hasbrouck's bill, cited earlier.

14. Quinlan, op. cit., p. 254.

CHAPTER 36

1. Woodbourne people whom I questioned emphasized that men with rifles in their hands were everywhere on the morning of November 22.

2. Quinlan, *Sullivan County,* p. 236. In this and the preceding chapter I have followed Quinlan's version and noted direct quotations and other sources. Quinlan's version is believed to be accurate by the Woodbourne people I questioned. A Mr. Misner told me that because of Quinlan's frankness about the shooting and the events leading up to it, powerful Hardenberghs had tried to prevent the publication of Quinlan's book back in 1873 and, when they failed in that, rammed a bill through the State legislature forbidding any future reprintings. No such law exists and the book was reprinted without protest in 1965.

3. Quinlan, op. cit., p. 235.

4. R. L. De Lisser, *Picturesque Ulster,* pp. 244–45.

5. Quinlan, op. cit., p. 235.

6. For a portrait and biographical sketch of Dr. Bevier, see Sylvester, *Ulster County,* Part 1, pp. 135–36.

7. Quinlan, op. cit., p. 235.

8. Ibid., p. 344 n.

CHAPTER 37

(This chapter is largely based on Peter DeLabigarre, "Excursions on Our Blue Mountains," in *Transactions of the Society for the Promotion of Agriculture, Arts and Manufactures,* vol. 1, part 2, 1794, pp. 128–39. All quotations unless otherwise identified are from DeLabigarre.

1. Mary L. Booth, *History of the City of New York,* 2 vols., New York, 1867, vol. 2, pp. 608–9.

2. For biographical account of DeLabigarre see Helen Wilkinson Reynolds, Peter DeLabigarre, in *Year Book, Dutchess County Historical Society,* Poughkeepsie, 1928, pp. 45–60.

3. *Laws of the State of New-York,* 3 vols., Greenleaf edition, New York, 1798, vol. 2, Chapter 53, section 1, passed April 6, 1790.

4. See Rockwell, *Catskill Mountains,* p. 182, for an 1867 use of the name Liberty Cap. Thomas Cole noted in his journals, for 1834, New York State Library, that High Peak and Roundtop sometimes exchanged names. The change became permanent on the Arnold Guyot map of 1879.

5. Letter, Mrs. Montgomery to unnamed correspondent, April 17, no year. Franklin D. Roosevelt Library, Hyde Park. Delafield, *Biographies,* vol. 1, p. 217 mentions "Mrs. Montgomery's Cap" as in use by "the country people."

6. The map is among the Cockburn Papers, 10:163.

7. S. L. Mitchill, "A Sketch of the Mineralogical History of the State of New York," in *Medical Repository*, New York, vol. 1, 3d edition, 1804, p. 295.

CHAPTER 38

1. Peter DeLabigarre, "Mr. DeLabigarre on Silk Worms," in *Transactions Society for the Promotion of Agriculture, Arts and Manufactures*, vol. 1, part 2, 1794, pp. 172–97.

2. S. L. Mitchill, "Address to the Agricultural Society and Both Houses of the legislature," February 7, 1798, in *Transactions Society for the Promotion of Agriculture, Arts and Manufactures*, p. 205

3. Ibid., February 7, 1798, in *Transactions Society for the Promotion of Agriculture, Arts and Manufactures*, vol. 1, part 3, 1798, pp. 44–58.

4. Philip Hone, *Diary*, Allan Nevins, ed., 2 vols., New York, 1927, vol. 1, p. 46.

5. J. W. Francis, *Old New York . . .* , New York, 1865, pp. 87–96.

6. Mitchill, "A Sketch," loc. cit., p. 298.

7. Christopher Hussey, *The Picturesque*, London and New York, 1927, pp. 48, 107.

8. William Dunlap, *Diary*, in *New-York Historical Society Collections*, New York, 1930, vol. 1, pp. 1–10.

9. Mitchill, "Address," loc. cit., pp. 205–6.

10. Mitchill, "A Sketch," loc. cit., p. 296.

11. Henry E. Dwight, "Account of the Kaatskill Mountains," in *American Journal of Science*, vol. 2 (1820), pp. 11–12.

12. S. L. Mitchill, "Writings on American Botany," in *New-York Historical Society Collections*, New York, 1814, vol. 2, p. 215.

CHAPTER 39

1. *American Social History as Recorded by British Travellers*, Allan Nevins, ed., New York, 1923, p. 33.

2. Letter, Robert R. Livingston to Robert Livingston, June 4, 1776, Livingston-Redmond Papers, Box 4, Franklin D. Roosevelt Library, Hyde Park.

3. John W. Barber and Henry Howe, *Historical Collections of the State of New York*, New York, 1841, p. 187.

4. Alonzo F. Selleck, *Recollections of an Itinerant Life*, New York, 1886, p. 156.

5. Overheard in a Woodstock tavern, 1955.

6. William Cobbett, *Journal of a Year's Residence in the United States*, London, 1818, pp. 37–38.

7. J. V. V. Vedder, ed., *History of Greene County*, vol. 1, 1651–1800 (no more published), Catskill, 1927, p. 120.

8. Timothy Dwight, *Travels*, vol. 4, p. 11.

9. Ibid.

10. R. R. Livingston, "A New Discovery Relative to the Art of Manufacturing Paper," in *Transactions Society for the Promotion of Agriculture, Arts and Manufactures*, vol. 1, part 4, pp. 354–57.

CHAPTER 40

1. Spafford, *Gazetteer*, 1813, p. 164.

2. See "Country-seats on Hudson's River" in *Year Book of Dutchess County Historical Society*, vol. 20 (1935), p. 60.

3. Spafford, op. cit., p. 164.

4. James H. Smith, *General History of Duchess* (sic) *County from 1609 to 1876 Inclusive*, Pawling, 1877, p. 259; *New York Genealogical and Biographical Record*, vol. 71, no. 3 (July 1940), p. 227.

5. Told to me by Nicholas Dederick, once gardener to Mrs. John Henry Livingston who was the last of the family name to live at Clermont.

6. *Life and Letters of Washington Irving*, P. M. Irving, ed., New York, 1864, vol. 1, pp. 283–84.

7. See Dangerfield, *Chancellor Livingston*, p. 5–6, for a glimpse of the Chancellor as a captive of the past.

CHAPTER 41

1. William Strickland, Journal, *New-York Historical Society*, part 10, p. 219.

2. William Gilpin, *Remarks on Forest Scenery*, 2 vols., 3d edition, London, 1808, vol. 1, pp. 306–7.

3. Hussey, *The Picturesque*, pp. 100–1, "The perception of the sublime in nature increased in direct ratio to the number of turnpike acts." This was in the Lake District during the eighteenth century.

4. Zadock Pratt, *Chronological Biography of the Hon. Zadock Pratt of Prattsville, New York*, New York, 1868, p. 5.

5. Richard Wynkoop, *The Wynkoop Genealogy*, New York, 3d edition, 1904, p. 86; S. L. Mitchill, "A Sketch," loc. cit., p. 297.

6. James D. Pinckney, *Reminiscences of Catskill. Local Sketches* (Binder's title, *Sketches of Catskill*), Catskill, 1868, p. 43.

7. Charles H. Haswell, *Reminiscences of New York by an Octogenarian (1816 to 1860)*, New York, 1896, p. 58; Pinckney, *Reminiscences*, p. 30; Rev. Clark Brown, "A Topographical Description of Catskill, in the State of New-York, 1803," in *Transactions of the Massachusetts Historical Society*, 1804, vol. 9, p. 114. The spruce used was *picea mariana*, the black spruce which favors moist locations.

8. "Town of Hunter, Catskill Mountains," a typed copy from an unknown source in Library of the Greene County Historical Society, ca. 1815; map of unappropriated lands by James Cockburn and Jacob Trumpbour in Bureau of Surplus Real Property, Albany.

9. John D. M'Kinnon, *Descriptive Poems*, New York, 1802, p. 11.

10. See Paul Shepard, *Man in the Landscape*, New York, 1967, pp. 179–189.

11. Among the botanists who climbed the mountain above Lawrence's was eccentric C. S. Rafinesque who lived at Clermont in 1817 as tutor and drawing master to the Chancellor's grandchildren. Rafinesque found "the mts. Kiskanon or Catsberg . . . rich in boreal and Canada plants etc. . . . ," this in Rafinesque, "A Life of Travels," reprinted in *Chronica Botanica*, vol. 8, no. 2 (1944), p. 331.

CHAPTER 42

1. Told to me by Charles Herrick.

2. Undated clipping of editorial in *Ulster County Press*, given to me by Helen Simmons, Woodstock.

3. Rockwell, *Catskill Mountains*, p. 141.

4. A. Irving Hallowell, Bear Ceremonialism in the Northern Hemisphere, in *American Anthropologist*, n.s., vol. 28, 1926, esp. pp. 26–33.

5. Quotations in the next three paragraphs from Rockwell, op. cit., pp. 134–35.

6. By 1890 the woodchuck was beginning to take over. On February 8 of that year the Catskill *Examiner* cautiously reported that "Sunday was Candlemas Day,

the time when the bear or the ground hog or both come out of their holes or dens. . . ."

7. Much bear lore of the Catskills has been collected by folklorists as in Harold W. Thompson, "Tales of the Catskill Bear Hunters," in *New York Folklore,* Summer, 1949, pp. 128–33.

8. Quinlan, *Sullivan County,* pp. 352–53.

9. Among the sources used for Merchant Lawrence were, Wynkoop, *Wynkoop Genealogy,* p. 92; "The Wynkoop Cemetery," Saugerties, New York, in New York Genealogical and Biographical Record, vol. 67, no. 4 (October 1936), p. 347; the assessment roll for Greene County, 1813, in the Library of the Greene County Historical Society. The unknown author of the Ms. "Town of Hunter, Catskill Mountains," cited in the notes to Chapter 21, mentions stopping at the Lawrence inn.

CHAPTER 43

1. The conveyance of the two lots to which Ashley had squatter's rights was recorded in Book of Patents, no. 26, pp. 305–6, Office of the Secretary of State, Albany. His period of squatting is noted in Field Book no. 22, Survey near Catskill, 1805, p. 29, in Secretary of State's Office, Albany.

2. The Field Book cited above, p. 130.

3. Lieut. A. Partridge, "Barometric Altitudes of Catskill Mountains, November 19, 1810," in United States Military Philosophical Society, Minutes and Records, 1802–13, New-York Historical Society.

4. Spafford, *Gazetteer,* 1813, p. 330.

5. Dwight, *Travels,* vol. 4, p. 176.

6. The survey of Lot no. 1 in Field Book 22, cited above, tells that "A Road from Scharry kill to West Camp on Hudson's River . . . passes through this lot." This road which climbed up- the Kaaterskill Clove joined the road authorized by the legislature in 1790 on the mountaintop. The quotation about the "inn" is from "Town of Hunter, Catskill Mountains," Greene County Historical Society.

7. O. W. Holmes, *The Poet at the Breakfast Table,* Boston and New York, 1904, pp. 330–31.

8. For biographical material on Elisha Williams, see Chester Alden, *Courts and Lawyers of New York,* 3 vols., New York and Chicago, 1925, vol. 3, pp. 1048–49; Franklin Ellis, *History of Columbia County, New York,* 1878, pp. 83–85; see also Dictionary of American Biography.

9. The most detailed treatment of Amos Eaton is Ethel M. McAllister, *Amos Eaton,* Philadelphia, 1941. An exhaustive bibliography is included.

10. Land Office Minutes, vol. 5, 1812–17, Secretary of State's Office, Albany, vol. 5, p. 89; I have found only very scanty mention in local records of Robert Davis and William Shaw, the two squatters whose rights became the base of much of Elisha Williams' grant.

CHAPTER 44

1. S. T. Williams and M. A. Edge, *A Bibliography of the Writings of Washington Irving,* New York, 1936, pp. 125–41.

2. A good description of the chair appeared in the Catskill *Messenger,* November 4, 1843. It was made by Johnston, Adams, and Moore and was exhibited in 1843 at the fair of the American Institute in New York.

3. Quoted from advertising leaflet in the Library of the Greene County Historical Society.

4. The *Examiner,* September 28, November 2, 1889.

5. Ibid., November 9, 1889. Rights to the chair were given to the Harris Palatial Car Co. of Boston.

6. Letterhead of Dan Sully in my collection of Woodstock materials.

7. Harold Hargreave, former owner of Rip's Retreat, in conversation.

8. James Joyce, *Ulysses,* New York, 1946, pp. 529–30.

9. *Oxford Companion to American Literature,* 3d ed., 1956, p. 165.

10. The charge was made by Democratic candidate Frank O'Connor, reported on radio station WCBS, New York, October 1, 1966.

CHAPTER 45

1. See Stanley T. Williams, *Life of Washington Irving,* 2 vols., New York, 1935, for a critical and biographical study of Irving.

2. Quoted by Walter A. Reichart, *Washington Irving and Germany,* Ann Arbor, 1957, p. 23.

3. Washington Irving's indebtedness to Peter Klaus has been pointed out at intervals ever since 1822. Reichart, op. cit, esp. pp. 26–31, handles the subject thoroughly. For a less charitable view than Reichart's, see Williams, op. cit., pp. 182–85 —here Irving's imitation is seen as "slavish."

4. Elihu Burritt, birthplace of Rip Van Winkle, in *Packard's Monthly,* vol. 1, (1869), pp. 332–34.

5. Reichart, op. cit., pp. 25–26.

6. Ibid.

7. Irving, "The Catskill Mountains," in *Spanish Papers,* 1866, vol. 2, pp. 481–83.

8. W.B.D. in the New-York *Mirror,* vol. 12, May 24, 1834, p. 370; the anonymous author of "A Visit to the Catskills" in *The Atlantic Souvenir,* 1828, took pains to deny that the host at Rip's Cottage, or inn, was in fact a descendant.

9. For the stage history of the play, see William Winter, *The Life and Art of Joseph Jefferson,* New York, 1894, esp. pp. 174–84, 203–10. The most popular version of the play was written by Jefferson and Dion Boucicault. This was published in its final form as *Rip Van Winkle as Played by Joseph Jefferson,* New York, 1896.

10. *Life and Letters of Washington Irving,* Pierre M. Irving, ed., vol. 3, pp. 53–54.

11. Ibid.

12. Rip became a favorite subject of nineteenth-century American painters, illustrators, and sculptors, among them John Quidor, Asher B. Durand, Henry Inman, F. O. C. Darley, and John Rogers. Thomas Cole as early as 1825 made a drawing of Rip and the bowlers—it is in the collection of the Albany Institute of Art and History, Albany.

13. Miss Helen Ham and Miss Dorothy Ingalls of the Village of Hunter tell me that the phrase was once in common use in their vicinity.

CHAPTER 46

1. I did not get the man's name—I came upon him as he was mending a roadside fence in the town of Andes.

2. Catskill *Recorder and Democrat,* February 22, 1867.

3. A. W. Hoffman, "The Passing of the Hemlock," in De Lisser, *Picturesque Ulster,* p. 185.

4. Edwards' family background is given in *Timothy and Rhoda Ogden Edwards of Stockbridge, Mass.,* compiled by W. H. Edwards, Cincinnati, 1903, pp. 25–27 and passim.

5. Nathaniel Booth, Diary, vol. 1 (entry for August 22, 1844); see *History of*

Greene County, 1884, pp. 335–36, for a version which has the butting an accidental collision with an Indian boy.

6. Tench Coxe, *A Statement of the Arts and Manufactures of the United States for 1810*, Philadelphia, 1814, p. 351.

7. Chapt. 67, 34th Session, March 22, 1811. The manufacturers listed were allowed to incorporate but others—including tanners—were required to petition for special acts of incorporation.

8. *One Hundred Years of American Commerce*, Chauncey M. DePew, ed., New York, 1895, p. 495.

9. Peter C. Welsh, *Tanning in the United States to 1850*, Washington, D.C., 1964, pp. 31–32.

10. Frank W. Norcross, *A History of the Swamp*, New York, 1901, pp. 51–53.

11. Ibid., p. 52.

CHAPTER 47

1. Robert P. McIntosh, "The Forest Cover of the Catskill Mountain Region," in *Midland Naturalist*, vol. 68, no. 2, esp. pp. 420–22.

2. A. Gansser, "Early History of Tanning," in *Ciba Review*, vol. 6 (August 1950), p. 2948.

3. Edgar M. Hoover, *Locative Theory and the Shoe and Leather Industry*, Cambridge, 1937, pp. 125–38; Welsh, *Tanning*, 1–36. Both authors give good accounts of early American tanning and Welsh has a good bibliography of sources for tanning in the United States.

4. Zadock Pratt, *Chronological Biography of the Hon. Zadock Pratt of Prattsville*, N.Y., New York, 1868, p. 30; Norcross, *A History of the Swamp*, p. 163.

5. Franklin Ellis, *History of Columbia County*, Philadelphia, 1878, pp. 165–66.

6. A scrapbook labeled no. 5 in Library of Greene County Historical Society contains a clipping dated "Catskill, June 24, 1918," which give traditions of the summerless year; Edwards, William, *Memoirs of Col. William Edwards . . . with notes and additions by W. W. Edwards and W. H. Edwards*, privately printed, Washington, 1897, p. 77.

7. Ibid., pp. 71–73, 76–77; Deed Book E-2, Greene County Clerk's Office, p. 67.

8. Edwards, *Memoirs*, pp. 77–80.

9. Ibid., pp. 78–79.

10. John Josselyn, Gent., *New-England's Rarities Discovered*, 1672, reprinted Boston, 1865, p. 118.

11. "Bark peelings" were areas from which bark was being removed or had been removed. John Burroughs used the phrase, as in his *Wake Robin*, Riverby edition, Boston and New York, 1904, p. 44.

12. For mentions of "the gain" see "The Prattsville Tannery" in *Hunt's Merchant's Magazine*, vol. 17, no. 2 (August 1847), p. 161; Norcross, *History of the Swamp*, p. 54, "The only property the tanner held in the leather was the gain."

13. *History of Greene County*, 1884, p. 335.

14. J. A. Richards, "The Catskills," in *Harper's New Monthly Magazine*, vol. 9, no. 1 (July 1854), p. 153.

15. Gilbert White, *Natural History of Selborne*, London, 1870, p. 36.

16. Basil Hall, *Travels in the United States in the Years 1827 and 1828*, 3 vols., London, 1833, pp. 456–57.

17. Jonathan Carver, *Three Years Travels Through the Interior Parts of North America*, Philadelphia, 1792, p. 258.

18. Quoted in *Old Times Corner*, G. Chadwick, ed., Catskill, 1932.

CHAPTER 48

1. Zadock Pratt, *Chronological Biography*, New York, 1868, p. 8.

2. Oliver Pilat and Jo Ransom, *Sodom by the Sea, An Affectionate History of Coney Island*, Garden City, 1941, pp. 1–5; *History of Greene County*, 1884, p. 386.

3. A tracing is on file in the Greene County Clerk's Office.

4. Pratt, *Chronological Biography*, New York, 1868, p. 11.

5. For Hill's own version of his life and his inventions, see L. L. Hill, *A Treatise on Heliochromy*, New York, 1856, pp. 1–37 and passim.

6. Zadock Pratt, "The Dairy Farming Region of Greene and Orange Counties, New York, With Some Account of the Writer," in *United States Patent Office Report, Agriculture*, Washington, D.C., 1861, p. 414. (Like much else that appeared under Pratt's name, this appears to have been written by someone else.)

7. The charge was made during election campaigns and was repeated in 1846 by the anti-Pratt, Catskill *Messenger*. It has proved persistent and found a place in *Brass Buttons and Leather Boots*, published in 1963 by the Sullivan County Civil War Centennial Commission, p. 41. There Pratt is described as "a tanner, business-man, and Congressman, though illiterate. . . ."

8. Zadock Pratt (phrenological analysis) in *American Phrenological Journal and Miscellany*, vol. 10 (1848), pp. 137–48.

9. F. A. Gallt, *Dear Old Greene County*, Catskill, 1915, p. 148.

10. William Hunt, *The American Biographical Sketch Book, New York*, 1848, p. 28.

11. Pratt, *Chronological Biography*, New York, 1868, p. 12.

12. Norcross, op. cit., p. 1–6.

13. New York *Tribune*, July 24, August 2, 1854.

14. The origin of hides tanned at Prattsville are given in "The Prattsville Tannery," loc. cit., p. 162.

15. The phrase in this form was repeated to me by several Prattsville residents. The Stamford *Mirror* reprints a letter to the Kingston *Freeman* written by a man who had interviewed the *Mirror*'s editor S. B. Champion on the subject of the Rocks. Champion had lived in Prattsville as the Rocks were first carved—he quoted Pratt as saying, "The rocks must tell the story." A good account of the Rocks is Frederick F. Purdy, "The Talking Rocks," in *Four Track News*, col. 9, no. 1 (July 1905), pp. 24–25; a good recent account is Mike Wales, "A Stone Cutter's Art Still Lives in the Catskills," in *Living in Capitaland* (a supplement to the Albany *Times-Union*), December 18, 1966.

16. Stamford *Mirror*, August 30, 1887.

17. Gross Freer, New Paltz, in conversation, 1920s. The Catskill *Recorder*, August 9, 1907, tells that Capt. Peter B. Haines of Haines Falls gave "positive instructions that, when he died, he should be placed in a coffin of 1½ inch hemlock planks in the rough, so that, if he landed in hell, he could make it as hot as any devil in the hottest corner. . . ."

18. Many traditions of Pratt's life and burial have been brought together in admiring fashion in Stuart Close, M.D., "Zadock Pratt—A Personality," in *The Quarterly Journal of the New York Historical Association*, vol. 12, no. 2 (April 1931), pp. 141–48.

19. *Illustrated News*, New York, May 7, 1853.

CHAPTER 49

1. Edwards, *Memoirs*, p. 99.

2. Horatio Gates Spafford, *Gazetteer*, New York, 1813. Spafford writes, pp. 10 and

330, that the view from the vicinity of the clifftop soon to be called the Pine Orchard "is inexpressibly grand," that the view "attracts the notice of numerous parties in summer," and that "this immense curiosity" may be enjoyed by even an indolent man "at the expense of his horse." The Pine Orchard, wrote Basil Hall in *Travels*, vol. 1, p. 95, "had long been a place of resort of picnic parties from New York and Albany, even when the worthy citizens had to find their way up and down the river in sailing boats." Hall referred to the days before the first hotel was built.

3. Rockwell, *Catskill Mountains*, p. 355, tells of a "rude building or shanty" preceding the hotel; the editor of the Rondout *Courier*, August 31, 1849, recalled "a series of hemlock shanties." The Albany *Argus*, October 11, 1822, states that "Messers Bigelow and Comfort" were "the proprietors of the establishment." A writer in the New-York *Mirror*, August 30, 1833, tells of studying a sketch of the buildings which stood on the Pine Orchard before 1823—he goes on to say that "Colonel Lawrence's house was now first abandoned for the shanty on the mountain." The pickerel are mentioned in DeWitt Clinton, Ms. Diary, New-York Historical Society.

4. Rockwell, op. cit., p. 104.

5. The Catskill *Recorder*, December 27, 1907, printed the invitation from a copy by a descendant of a guest—I have found no original example.

6. Albany *Argus*, October 11, 1822, reprinted from the Catskill *Recorder*.

7. New-York *Mirror*, August 31, 1833. All quotations in this paragraph except the first are from the same source.

8. Laws of New-York, 46th Session, Chapt. 84, passed March 24, 1823.

9. Fred Somkin, "James Pierce's Catskill Wolves: A Forgotten New Yorker's Contribution to Darwin," typescript in Library of Greene County Historical Society.

10. Carl Bridenbaugh, "Colonial Newport as a Summer Resort," in *Rhode Island Historical Society Collections*, vol. 26, no. I, pp. 1–23; Bridenbaugh, "Baths and Watering Places of Colonial America," in *William and Mary Quarterly*, 3d series, vol. 3, no. 2, pp. 151–81.

11. *Salmagundi*, no. 16, October 15, 1807. Quotations from 3d edition, New York, 1820, pp. 406, 413.

12. Catskill Mountain Association, Treasurer's Account Book, 1823–86, esp. entries 1823–26, New York State Library, furnished information on the construction of the hotel.

13. Ibid., entry for December 29, 1823.

14. Charles Lanman, *Letters of a Landscape Painter*, Boston, 1845, p. 10, "The 'Yankee Palace' as the house has been christened by the Dutch under the mountains." The phrase was used in my boyhood by Charles Wood who spoke of the expectation of valley people that the hotel would blow away.

CHAPTER 50

1. *The Works of Samuel Johnson, LL.D.*, 9 vols., Oxford, 1825, vol. 4, p. 269.

2. United States Geological Service Contour Map, Kaaterskill New York Sheet, edition of 1946.

3. Arnold Guyot's figure for the elevation of the Mountain House was published in his "On the Physical Structure and Hypsometry of the Catskill Mountain Region"; in *American Journal of Science*, 3d series, no. 19, January–June, 1880, p. 449.

4. New-York *Mirror*, August 30, 1833.

5. The entries in the Clinton Diary used here and in the next four paragraphs are those in the Ms. diary, *New-York Historical Society*, for August 23–24, 1823.

6. Carl Carmer, *The Hudson*, 1968, pp. 158–63.

7. W. L. Stone, "Ten Days in the Country," New York *Commercial Advertiser,* August 26, 1824. In his installment of August 31, Stone writes, "The steward came puffing up with a box marked Madeira no. 1 for the editors about to visit the mountain, with the compliments of (we will not say what Company . . .), not a goblet was quaffed unmindful of the Company. . . ."

8. Albany *Argus,* July 21, 1824 (reprinted from the New York *Statesman*).

9. W. L. Stone, "Ten Days," loc. cit., September 3, 1824. Here Major Noah is mentioned as "Major N—."

10. Stone, loc. cit., September 3, 1824.

11. Ibid.

12. Stone, "Ten Days," loc. cit., September 25, 1824; advice for "all those who intend to make what is now called the 'Grand Tour'" [of the United States.]

13. Pine Mountain House in New-York *Mirror,* August 31, 1833; all quotations in this paragraph are from this source.

14. William Wetmore Story, *The Life and Letters of Joseph Story,* 2 vols., London, 1851, vol. 1, pp. 449–55. See Henry James, *William Wetmore Story and His Friends,* 2 vols., New York, 1903, vol. 1, p. 36, for a comment on Justice Story's letters about the excursion as "a subtly suggestive document."

15. Mortgage Book 1, pp. 79–80, Greene County Clerk's Office.

Chapter 51

1. In 1679 the Labadist missionary Jasper Danckers made a rough sketch of the Catskills as seen from the Hudson River; see James and Jameson, eds., *The Journal of Jasper Danckers,* 1679–80, New York, 1913, p. 219.

2. Kristin Linde Gibbons, *The Van Bergen Overmantel,* an M.A. thesis, 1966 State University of New York College at Oneonta, Cooperstown Graduate Program, is a good study of the overmantel.

3. For Pownall see John A. Schultz, Thomas Pownall, *British Defender of American Liberty,* Glendale, Calif., see also Dictionary of National Biography and Dictionary of American Biography. None of these sources deals with Pownall's interest in the arts and the landscape. For Pownall's understanding of the American landscape I have relied on his, *A Topographical Description of such Parts of North America as are contained in the (annexed) Map of the Middle British Colonies etc. in North America,* London, 1776, p. 9 and passim.

4. I have been unable to find any information about Lodet beyond that given here.

5. A sketchbook which I own and which Vanderlyn used in Paris in 1799 and later in the United States contains the sketches of Hudson River scenery referred to.

6. James Harrison and G. Parkyns advertised proposed views of American scenery "in Aquatinta," in 1795 and 1796; see *The Arts and Crafts in New York, 1777–1799,* Rita S. Gottesman, comp., New York, 1954, pp. 47–49.

7. Thomas S. Cummings, *Historic Annals of the National Academy of Design,* 1865, pp. 11–17.

8. Richard J. Koke, "John Hill, Master of Aquatint," in *New-York Historical Society Quarterly,* vol. 43, no. 1, p. 82. Here Koke writes that "some of the untamed wilderness scenes were there depicted in stormy and melancholy moods foreshadowing the romantics of the Hudson River School."

9. Anna W. Rutledge, Robert Gilmor, Jr., Baltimore Collector, in Journal of the *Walters Art Gallery,* vol. 12, 1949, pp. 19–39.

CHAPTER 52

1. Louis L. Noble, *The Course of Empire, Voyage of Life and Other Pictures, by Thomas Cole, N.A.,* New York, 1853, pp. 56–57.

2. Letter, Cole to Gilmor, July 2, 1825, in Noble, op. cit., p. 92.

3. Letter of S. T. Coleridge quoted in John Livingston Lowes, *The Road to Xanadu,* New York, 1959, p. 195. Here Coleridge tells of observing two young men who were visiting Denbigh Castle, "I will play my flute here," said one, "it will have a romantic effect." This happened during the 1790s—by the 1820s Cole was playing his flute beside waterfalls and on mountaintops in the Catskills.

4. For Thomas Cole's life before 1834, I have followed the earliest published account of substance. It is in William Dunlap, *History of the Arts of Design in the United States,* New York, 1834, republished, Boston, 1918, 3 vols., vol. 3, pp. 139–59 and passim. I have also used Louis L. Noble, op. cit., pp. 15–59. Noble, it should be borne in mind, does not always quote exactly from the Cole Ms. he used.

5. Kenneth LaBudde, *The Mind of Thomas Cole, a Doctoral Dissertation,* University of Minnesota, 1954, Chapt. 4. LaBudde writes that during the late 1820s, Cole "saw natural facts as manifestations of meaning beyond the natural world . . . Cole often responded to nature with the simple admiration of a lover. . . ."

6. For a discussion of "romantic realism" and "romantic idealism," see James T. Flexner, *That Wilder Image,* Boston, 1962, pp. 11–14.

7. *Auguries of Innocence,* in *Poetical Works of William Blake,* ed. John Sampson, Oxford, 1905, p. 288.

8. Dunlap, op. cit., vol. 3, p. 149. Trumbull's remark is differently quoted by other of Cole's contemporaries.

9. Ode: *Intimations of Immortality from Recollections of Early Childhood,* William Wordsworth, *Poetical Works,* Henry Reed, ed., Philadelphia, 1860, pp. 470–72.

10. Dunlap, op. cit., vol. 3, pp 149–50.

11. *Catskilleana* is among the Cole Ms., New York State Library. The quotation is from Louis L. Noble, *The Course of Empire, Voyage of Life and Other Pictures by Thomas Cole, N.A.,* New York, 1853, p. 77.

12. Ibid., p. 67.

13. Typed copy of letter from Robert Gilmor, Jr., to Thomas Cole, December 13, 1826, among the notes of E. Parker Lesley, Jr., for an incompleted dissertation (Princeton), vol. 1, p. 64. In the same letter Gilmor suggests that Cole paint "real American" scenes. In another letter among the Lesley notes, Gilmor urges Cole to read William Gilpin who wrote in his *Remarks on Forest Scenery,* vol. 1, p. 14, that "the *blasted tree* has often a fine effect" and recommended "the *withered top* and *curtailed trunk*" as painted by Salvator Rosa. The Lesley notes are in New-York Historical Society.

14. Letter, Gilmor to Cole, August 1, 1826. Copy among Lesley notes, New-York Historical Society.

CHAPTER 53

1. Philip Hone, *Diary,* New York, 1927, vol. 1, p. 108.

2. The play was published in New York, 1830, as *A Trip to Niagara, or, A Traveller in America, A Farce in Three Acts,* pp. 27–39 are concerned with the Catskills.

3. W. C. Bryant, *The American Landscape,* New York, 1830, p. 9.

4. Ibid.

5. Frances A. Kemble, *Journal of Frances Anne Butler*, 2 vols., Philadelphia, 1835, vol. 2, pp. 172–73.

6. Henry Tudor, *Narrative of a Tour in North America*, London, 1834, pp. 145–46.

7. Ibid.

8. "Facts showing the Evils resulting from the use of Intoxicating Liquors, reported to the Catskill Temperance Society, February 26, 1833, in Sixth Report of the American Temperance Society," pp. 107–11. Reprinted in *Permanent Temperance Documents of the American Temperance Society*, Boston, 1835.

9. Quinlan, *Sullivan County*, p. 135.

10. William Boyse, *Writings*, p. 553.

11. Ulster *Republican*, September 6, 1843.

12. Catskill *Recorder*, July 4, 1833.

13. Catskill *Messenger*, May 1, 1834, advertisement of foreclosure of real property and chattels under mortgage of 1826. Postponements were advertised from time to time and ceased in October.

14. Ibid.

CHAPTER 54

1. The Smith and Schultz tannery was advertised for sale in the Catskill *Recorder*, September 12, 1833; the Carnright tannery on April 25.

2. The *Argus* (Kingston), July 30, 1902.

3. The inflammability of tanneries is explained in Edwards, *Memoirs*, pp. 99–100; the Palen fight was widely reported; see the Catskill *Recorder*, June 13, 1833, for an account reprinted from the Sullivan *County Herald*, May 30.

4. In the Catskill *Recorder*, "Tanner" urges concerted action to check falling prices.

5. The advertisement of sloop operators is in the Catskill *Recorder*, May 9, 1833; the year when union leather was first made has been variously given; Frank W. Norcross, *A History of the Swamp*, pp. 91–92 makes it 1833.

6. The indenture by which Col. Edwards made his assignment to creditors is on file in Deed Book 5, pp. 252–58, Greene County Clerk's Office. I have used this document with its listings of figures, names, and assets as the source for the Edwards settlement.

7. "The Catskills Seventy Years Ago" in the Catskill *Recorder*, August 9, 1907.

8. The Rondout *Courier*, January 18, 1850.

9. Mabel Parker Smith, *Greene County, New York, A Short History*, Catskill, 1968, p. 15; Hamilton Child, *Gazetteer . . . of Sullivan County*, Syracuse, New York, 1872, p. 141.

10. Told me by Ralph M. Lord. Tannersville.

11. Simpson manuscripts, owned by A. G. Simpson, Phoenicia.

12. "The Building of Plank Roads" in *Olde Ulster*, vol. 8, no. 10 (October 1912), pp. 289–97; "Judge Elmendorf and the Lucas Turnpike," in *Olde Ulster*, vol. 9, no. 5 (May 1913), pp. 142–43.

13. Quinlan, *Sullivan County*, p. 666.

14. See William F. Helmer, *Rip Van Winkle Railroads*, Howell-North books, Berkeley, 1970, pp. 12–35, for a detailed history of the C&C.

15. For the Malden Railroad I have used "Plank Roads" in *Olde Ulster*, vol. 8, no. 10, p. 292; the Kingston, New York & Erie line appears on the map of Ulster County in David H. Burr, Atlas of New York, revised ed., Ithaca, 1839. All three lines are listed among projected railroads in J. H. French, *Gazetteer of the State of New York*, Syracuse, 1860, pp. 76–79.

16. Stewart Holbrook, *The Story of American Railroads*, New York, 1947, p. 62.

17. A. W. Hoffman, "The Passing of the Hemlock," in *Picturesque Ulster,* Kingston, 1896, p. 189; the inns are mentioned, ibid., p. 190.

18. *History of Greene County,* 1884, p. 329.

19. Hoffman, loc. cit., p. 191.

CHAPTER 55

1. Ellis, Frost, Syrett, and Carman, *A Short History of the State of New York,* Ithaca, 1959, p. 188.

2. Letter, E.H.B. to Severyn Hasbrouck, March 2, 1836, in author's possession.

3. David Brown to Severyn Hasbrouck, March 3, 1835, in author's possession.

4. Catskill *Recorder,* January 30, 1834.

5. Catskill *Examiner,* March 31, April 21, and May 5, 1860.

6. Charlton Ogburn, Jr., "The Passing of the Passenger Pigeon," in *American Heritage,* vol. 12, no. 4 (June 1961), p. 90. The best local account of the pigeon is W. T. Brent, "Wild Pigeons," in *Picturesque Ulster,* pp. 164–65.

7. John Burroughs, *Wake Robin,* Boston, 1904, p. 174.

8. The island first appears in print in Henry E. Dwight, "Account of the Kaatskill Mountains," in *American Journal of Science,* vol. 2, 1820, p. 23; here Dwight tells of a man who jumped too hard and was saved from slipping through into the water.

9. William Darby, *A Tour from the City of New York to Detroit in the Michigan Territory,* New York, 1819, p. 33.

10. Catskill *Democrat,* May 29, 1844; the fish story which begins the next paragraph is from a note by the Reverend J. B. Williams, p. 107, Hamilton Child, *Gazetteer . . . Sullivan County,* 1872. Here Hoffman's report is put in 1832. Williams states that "the largest trout in the world" were once found in White Lake.

11. *Catalogue of Works by the late Henry Inman,* in art room, New York Public Library; the quotation I have used first appeared in the *Spirit of the Times,* a lively publication founded in 1831.

12. Ulster *Republican,* September 2, 1846.

13. My source for the Woodstock Blue Mountain House here and in the next paragraph is the Ulster *Republican,* July 10, 1833.

14. Mortgage books, Liber 39, p. 278. Greene County Clerk's Office.

15. Interview with Charles L. Beach, Catskill *Recorder,* July 22, 1881.

16. Mortgage books, loc. cit.

17. Horace Greeley, "A Visit to the Catskill Mountains," Catskill *Recorder,* July 15, 1843 (reprinted from New York *Tribune*).

18. Talbot Hamlin, *Greek Revival Architecture in America,* New York, 1964, pp. 261–62.

19. Interview with Charles L. Beach, loc. cit.

CHAPTER 56

(In this chapter I have most often followed Henry Christman, *Tin Horns and Calico,* New York, 1961. Where I have used other sources I have noted them.)

1. For the Van Rensselaer view, see Killian Van Rensselaer, "The Van Rensselaers of Rensselaerwyck" in *New-York Historical Society Quarterly,* vol. 29, no. 1, pp. 17–38. Here the author states that in Stephen's day, the Van Rensselaer income came from "the Lumber District in North Albany. For years it was the largest lumber distribution point in the east and the income and profits it supplied supported the family, not rents wrung from reluctant tenants."

2. Ellis and others, *Short History . . . New York,* pp. 146–48; Elisha Williams and Stephen Van Rensselaer were among convention delegates who struggled against change; Erastus Root with his Hardenbergh Patent constituency was a leader on the reforming side.

3. Editorial in Catskill *Democrat,* April 22, 1846.

4. Candace Wheeler, *Yesterdays in a Busy Life,* New York, 1918, p. 41; in his own day and later, Root was often likened to the extremists of the French Revolution; "Root would have graced the Mountain thirty years before in France" wrote D. R. Fox in A. C. Flick, ed., *History of New York,* vol. 6, p. 17.

5. The *Democratic Journal* of Kingston, July 24, 1844, reported an Anti-Rent meeting at "Pine Hill Clove" with 300 disguised men amid the 5000 present. An examination of the titles to "lease lands" was demanded.

6. Quoted in Christman, op. cit., p. 206, from the New York *Herald.*

7. The disguised Anti-Renters called themselves "Indians"—the phrase "Calico Indians" was first applied in derision by their opponents. The Ulster *Republican,* June 4, 1845, put the phrase in both quotation marks and italics to indicate its recent and colloquial character.

8. The Welshmen known as the Rebecca Rioters of 1842–43 dressed like women and rode horses; like the Calico Indians the Rebeccas were divided into familylike groups. The participants in the Boston Tea Party of 1773 of course had dressed like Indians; see E. J. Hobsbawm, *Social Bandits and Primitive Rebels,* Glencoe, Ill., 1959, esp. Chapt. 9 ("Ritual in Social Movements").

9. Christman, op. cit., pp. 336–37; see pp. 331–53 for a good selection of Anti-Rent songs.

10. The phrase "Down with the rent!" was in use among the Helderbergs by 1840; by 1845 the tenants' uprising was being called the "Down-Rent War"; see the *Democratic Journal,* March 19, 1845. "Down-Rent War" is still used by old mountain people in preference to "Anti-Rent War."

11. This episode was reported in detail in the Albany *Argus,* March 10, 11, 13, 15, and 17, 1845, and in the Ulster *Republican,* March 12 and 19.

12. Albany *Argus,* March 17, 1845.

13. Ulster *Republican,* July 23, 1845.

14. Ibid., April 16.

15. Ibid., April 9.

16. Catskill *Democrat,* May 12, 1845.

17. L. L. Hill, "Treatise on Heliochromy," New York, 1856, pp. 10–11. Hill's sermon "plainly exposed the whole system of *disguises* and the hypocrisy of those professors of religion who countenanced the practice. . . ." Hill explained.

18. Albany *Argus,* August 22, 1845.

CHAPTER 57

1. Field books, Hardenbergh Patents (sic), Great lots 35, 37, 39, lot 46, in Delaware County Clerk's Office.

2. Field book, lot no. 45, Delaware County Clerk's Office.

3. For buttermaking in *Delaware County, New York, History of the Century, 1797–1897,* David Murray, ed., Delhi, 1898, pp. 108–10; for Andes prosperity, see p. 284.

4. For the background of Miss Verplanck and her father, I have used W. E. Verplanck, *The History of Abraham Isaac Ver Planck and His Male Descendants in America,* Fishkill Landing, 1892, pp. 162–67; Moses Earle is the subject of an

informative chapter, which I have used, in John D. Monroe, *The Anti-Rent War in Delaware County, New York,* privately printed, 1940, pp. 97–109.

5. Town Clerk's Minute Book, Town Clerk's Office, Andes, New York.

6. Deed book M, p. 222, Delaware County Clerk's Office.

7. John Burroughs, *Signs and Seasons,* Boston and New York, 1904, p. 250.

8. Inventory of Moses Earle's chattels, October 25, 1848, in File Box J, Delaware County Surrogate's Office.

CHAPTER 58

1. Wright's version of the events of August 7 will be found on pp. 40–44, "The People *v.* Van Steenburgh," in Amasa J. Parker, *Decisions in Criminal Cases,* Albany, 1855.

2. This quotation and those in the next two paragraphs from Christman, *Tin Horns . . . ,* pp. 193–94.

3. A letter signed "A leaseholder," Albany *Argus,* October 4, 1845, presents the case for Morgan Lewis, who died in 1844, and for other Hardenbergh Patent landlords; the Kingston *Democratic Journal,* May 19, 1845, praises large landowners of New York for their "liberal policy"; an advertisement in the Albany *Argus,* August 18, 1845, offers Hunter, Overing, Verplanck, Armstrong, and Livingston farms for sale.

4. Delaware *Gazette,* October 8, 1845.

5. Both quotations in this paragraph from Ibid., October 15.

6. J. D. Monroe, *Anti-Rent War in Delaware County, New York,* p. 99.

7. Oyer and Terminer minutes, Supreme Court Minutes, no. 2, September term, 1845, p. 105, in Delaware County Building.

8. Albany *Evening Journal,* August 15, 1845.

9. John D. Monroe, *Anti-Rent War,* pp. 101–2. Earle's trial was widely reported. I have used the account in the Albany *Argus,* October 6, 1845.

CHAPTER 59

1. Letter, John Hunter to James Powers and John Kiersted, March 31, 1847, Durham Center Museum.

2. David M. Ellis, *Landlords and Tenants in the Mohawk-Hudson Region,* Ithaca, 1956, gives a well-documented view of the attempts to invalidate landlords' titles after the end of the Anti-rent War.

3. Quotations in this paragraph from the Rondout *Courier,* May 25, 1849, reprinted from the Albany *Freeholder;* the *Courier,* August 17, 1849.

4. Hunt and Wife *v.* Johnson et al., 19 New York Reports, 279; A. C. Niven, "A Chapter of Anti-Rent History," in *Albany Law Journal,* vol. 24 (1881), p. 127.

5. Monroe, *Anti-Rent War,* p. 107; 1850 census records, Delaware County Clerk's Office; death records in Andes Town Clerk's Office.

6. Rent roll of John Hunter's lands kept by John Kiersted, pp. 44–45, in Durham Center Museum.

7. Greene County Deed book 196, p. 205; Ralph M. Lord in conversation.

8. Mary B. Mullett, "He Sits on the Top of a Hill and Lets the Rest of the World Go by," in *American* magazine, vol. 104, no. 1, pp. 56–57, 124, 126–27—this is an admiring account of Jason Clum. I have relied too on conversations with Ralph M. Lord who knew Clum.

9. The quotations in this and the following paragraph from Schoonmaker, *History of Kingston,* pp. 100–1.

CHAPTER 60

1. Letter, Elias Hasbrouck to Peter Van Gaasbeeck, September 23, 1788, folder 2908, document 428, Van Gaasbeeck Papers, Senate House Museum Library.

2. *Diary of Michael Floy, Jr.,* R. A. E. Brooks, ed., New Haven, 1941, p. 183.

3. For Daniel Skinner I have relied on Quinlan, *Sullivan County,* pp. 186–92. Skinner's claim was to lands on the West Bank of the Delaware but he and his associates also settled on the East Bank. "A Traverse of the Delaware River from the 7th to the 5th Monument" by surveyor John Cox, Cockburn Papers, New York State Library, 5:129, shows the advanced state of settlement along this part of the Delaware in 1790.

4. The phrases quoted here are all used in Leslie C. Wood, *Rafting on the Delaware,* Livingston Manor, 1934.

5. William Heidt, Jr., and Charles T. Curtis, *History of Rafting on the Delaware,* Port Jervis, n.p., under caption, "The Largest Raft."

6. John Burroughs, Pepacton, 1904, p. 30.

7. Heidt and Curtis, op. cit., "Raft Men Returning."

8. Wood, op. cit., pp. 127–28.

9. Zephaniah Chase account book, 1785–1804 (catalogued Greene County, residents, 10542), New York State Library.

10. Sylvester, *Ulster County,* 1880, Part 2, p. 313.

11. The Catskill *Messenger,* November 4, 1843, reprinted from the New York *Commercial Advertiser.* The chair is described as the "chef d'oeuvre" of its manufacturers, Johnston, Adams, and Moore.

12. Town of Hunter, "Reminiscenses of Willis Baldwin," typescript 46 pp. in Library of the Greene County Historical Society, dated January 1930. The details of Fromer's operations which follow are based on the original sheets of the New York State Census of 1855 for the Town of Hunter, Greene County Clerk's Office.

13. A great variety of wooden objects made among the Catskills are mentioned in the report of Inspector Charles F. Carpenter in the *Second Annual Report of the* [New York State] *Forest Commission,* Albany, 1887, pp. 120–23, 131–42 and passim.

14. Baldwin, *Reminiscenses . . . ,* p. 42 and passim.

15. Sylvester, *Ulster County,* 1880, Part 2, p. 15.

16. Quotations and figures here are from the Kingston *Freeman,* June 23, 1874.

17. H. A. Haring, *Our Catskill Mountains,* New York, 1931, pp. 106–17; De Lisser, *Picturesque Ulster,* pp. 167–68; John Burroughs, *Signs and Seasons,* p. 248.

18. Quoted in Catskill *Examiner,* January 11, 1879, from New York *Tribune;* Daniel J. Foley, *Christmas Trees,* New York, 1960, p. 159. Foley uses the New York *Tribune* source.

CHAPTER 61

1. Charles Lanman, *Letters of a Landscape Painter,* Boston, 1845, pp. 36–37.

2. Ibid., pp. 39–42.

3. Ibid., p. 49.

4. Charles Lanman, *Adventures among the Wilds of North America,* 2 vols., Philadelphia, 1856, vol. 2, pp. 225–27.

5. Lanman, *Letters,* pp. 3–4.

6. Ibid.

7. Journal 6, Thomas Cole Papers, New York State Library; L. L. Noble, Cole's biographer edited Cole's account of his visit to South Peak; he published it as

"A Visit to South Peak by the late Thomas Cole," in *The Literary World*, New York, January 13, 1849; finally a still further edited version appeared on pp. 370–72 of Noble's *Course of Empire*, New York, 1853.

8. Noble, *Course of Empire*, pp. 399–400.

CHAPTER 62

1. Henry N. MacCracken; *Blithe Dutchess*, New York, 1958, p. 232.

2. The Catskill *Examiner*, July 3, 1858; in a letter dated July 3, 1825, Justice Joseph Story writes of "a small, rude house of entertainment, erected on the brow of the precipice which overlooks the falls." W. W. Story, *Life and Letters of Joseph Story*, vol. 1, p. 452. The Laurel House came into being nearby, its "palmy days were . . . back in the fifties," said a writer in the Catskill *Examiner*, November 23, 1889.

3. Letter signed "W" in the Kingston *Journal*, August 22, 1855, praises the "rare and magnificent prospect" from Overlook; the Greene County *Whig*, August 29, 1857, refers to Nicholas Elmendorf's failure in what seems to be a reprint from the Rondout *Courier*.

4. "An Afternoon with Robert L. Pell," in the Catskill *Examiner*, August 28, 1858. This laudatory account had a long life; it was first published in the Newark, N.J., *Daily Advertiser* and was used after Pell had gone under a cloud, in Hamilton Child's *Gazetteer of Ulster County, New York*, Syracuse, 1871.

5. Kingston *Journal*, July 3, 1850.

6. Greene County *Whig*, September 2, 1859.

7. George T. Strong, *Diary*, Allan Nevins and M. Y. Thomas, eds., 4 vols., New York, 1852, vol. 4, p. 292. A register of the Catskill Mountain House in the Library of the Greene County Historical Society shows Strong to have been a guest with his son, June 16–20, 1870.

8. Georgina Masson, *Italian Gardens*, New York, n.d., pp. 33–39.

9. The Catskill *Examiner*, December 18, 1858.

10. Reprinted in the Catskill *Examiner*, October 6, 1860.

11. Nathaniel Booth, Ms. Diary, vol. 2, entry for August 16, 1857.

12. A notable episode of boulder-pushing was described in Raymond H. Torrey, "Dr. John Torrey in the Catskills," in *Torreya*, vol. 32, no. 1, pp. 1–2. In July 1844, Dr. Torrey, the well-known botanist, and his party interrupted their studies of the flora of the region while they undermined a boulder of ten or fifteen feet in diameter and sent it crashing from the summit of Roundtop.

13. See Alf Evers, "The Old Men of the Mountains, A Tour of Romantic Catskill Imagery," in the *New York State Conservationist*, April–May 1960, pp. 16–19.

14. Booth, Diary, entry for August 16, 1857.

15. The Catskill *Messenger*, July 21, 1849, reprinted from Pittsburgh *Gazette*.

16. Greene County *Whig*, September 18, 1852.

17. Newspaper clipping, n.d., in a scrapbook titled *In Old Catskill*, vol. 2, Library of Greene County Historical Society. The ballad is stated to have been printed June 30, 1856.

18. Catskill *Examiner*, September 8, 1860.

19. *History of Greene County*, 1884, p. 324.

CHAPTER 63

1. Charles Mackay, *Life and Liberty in America*, New York, 1859, p. 30.

2. For the history of the New York, Ontario & Western Railway, see William F. Helmer, "O & W, The long life and slow death of the New York, Ontario & Western Railway," Howell-North, Berkeley, 1959.

3. Catskill and the Catskill Region, in *Lippincott's Magazine,* vol. 24, no. 9, pp. 279–80.

4. Throughout the 1870s regional newspapers advocated a railroad from Catskill westward; on September 14, 1877, the Catskill *Recorder* asked, ". . . when will the wise heads of Catskill awake from their Rip Van Winkle lethargy and see the necessity of a railroad through these regions . . . ?" The Saugerties *Evening Post,* August 8, 1879, carried a reprinting of a story from the Poughkeepsie *Eagle,* of August 7, outlining plans for a line to begin at Catskill and to end at "the piazza of the Mountain House."

5. The Kingston *Argus,* July 11, reprinted from the Margaretville *Utilitarian.*

6. The Kingston *Argus,* July 4, 1866.

7. The bit about the anvil has been repeated to me in various forms by a number of oldtimers. It achieved an appearance in print in "How the Town Was Located," by J.A.M., in the Kingston *Daily Leader,* May 28, 1902.

8. My notes are not clear as to when this and the following phrase quoted were used, except that it was between September 1872, and the end of 1873. Also used during this period by the Kingston *Freeman* were "the forty thieves" and the "Rogue's Quartette."

9. Kingston *Daily Freeman,* September 27, 1872.

10. Kingston *Daily Freeman,* November 29, 1873; the opposition Kingston *Argus* also criticized the railroad management—on January 21, 1874, it stated that "this railroad as a robbing machine has no equal."

11. Kingston *Daily Freeman,* November 29, 1873. For a different version of the brawl see the biographical sketch of Elisha M. Brigham, the receiver, in *Commemorative Biographical Record of Ulster County,* New York, Chicago, 1896, p. 39.

12. Today service on the U. & D. has been ended, but the line is still called the Up & Down because as Stanley Shultis of Bearsville tells me, the freight train in its last years went "up one day and down the next."

13. Alice Hyneman Rhine, "Race Prejudice at Summer Resorts," in *The Forum,* vol. 3 (July 1887), pp. 527–28.

14. Walton Van Loan, *Van Loan's Catskill Mountain Guide,* 1882, p. 100.

15. "Charles L. Beach . . . has spent seventy summers on the mountain" reported the Kingston *Daily Leader,* October 11, 1892; on June 29, 1880, the Stamford *Mirror* stated that the Beach's Mountain House had been under the same management ever since its beginnings in 1823—similar statements in other newspapers and books show a wide popular acceptance of the Beach Mountain House mythology which began to flourish as the hotel's fortunes declined during the 1870s.

16. Deed book 80, pp. 397–403, Greene County Clerk's Office.

CHAPTER 64

1. Krack was assemblyman for the district; for his career see H. H. Boone and Theodore P. Cooke, *Life Sketches,* Albany, 1870, pp. 257–58.

2. Martin MacDaniel, born about 1881, describes the structure as a small "ordinary house," standing in his father's time.

3. The building of the hotel was reported in considerable detail by regional newspapers. See the Kingston *Argus,* August 17, 1870, for one account.

4. John E. Lasher's biography and portrait are on p. 476, *Commemorative Biographical Record of Ulster County,* 1896.

5. Kingston *Press,* December 1, 1870.

6. Grant had been visiting his friend William E. Dinsmore at The Locusts in Staatsburgh on the Hudson, when he saw the new hotel on Overlook in the distance

and expressed a wish to visit the place—General Sharpe of Kingston was a fellow-guest of Dinsmore's and had an interest of some kind in the hotel; see Kingston *Press*, July 27, 1871.

7. Letter from Overlook, signed "Don Peppe" in Kingston *Press*, July 13, 1871.

8. Clipping from New York *Times*, August 11 (no year), in Sanford scrapbook, local-history room, Churchill Library, Stamford, New York.

9. Reprinted in the Kingston *Daily Freeman*, July 28, 1875.

10. Newburgh *Daily Journal*, July 13, 1873, reprinted from the Rondout *Courier* of the same day. Grant's stay on Overlook was widely reported and the details of his musical entertainment varied.

11. J. M. Longendyke, Woodstock, in conversation, May 27, 1961.

12. Kingston *Freeman*, August 10, 1874.

13. A running story of the fire went out from the telegraph instrument in Edgar Snyder's general store in Woodstock. On April 2, the Kingston *Daily Freeman* published a graphic account followed over the next few weeks by additional details.

14. The building and opening of the new hotel was covered with especial zeal by Saugerties *Daily Post*, December 1877–July 1878. Kingston and Catskill papers showed a proper restraint. The Kingston *Argus* reported the opening of the hotel in its issue of July 3, 1878, and stated then that manager James Smith aspired to maintaining "a high-toned moral atmosphere."

15. The construction of a spur from the U. & D. station at West Hurley also continued to be discussed; see the Kingston *Argus*, September 11, 1878.

16. The Kingston *Journal*, August 7, 1878, reprinted from the New York *Herald*.

17. New York *Times*, July 19, 1877. The *Times* covered the Seligman-Hilton incident during June and July, 1877.

18. The Catskill *Recorder*, June 29, 1877.

19. I have found no newspaper in the region to have upheld the exclusion of Jews from hotels and boardinghouses.

20. New York *Herald*, July 16, 1878.

21. "Jewish Colony at Sholam, Ulster County" in *Olde Ulster*, vol. 8, no. 6 (June 1912), pp. 161–67; Gabriel Davidson, *Our Jewish Farmers*, New York, 1934, Supplement, pp. 196–204.

22. Dr. Bernard Kahn, Tannersville, in conversation.

23. Saugerties *Evening Post*, July 24 and 28, 1879.

CHAPTER 65

1. Told to me by Ralph M. Lord and others.

2. The Catskill *Recorder*, June 24, 1881.

3. I have relied on newspaper stories of the first season of the Tremper House, on the Poughkeepsie *Daily Eagle*, June 16 and 21, 1879; The Kingston *Daily Freeman*, June 9 and August 4, and the New York *Daily Graphic*'s illustrated story of June 16.

4. The Kingston *Argus*, May 7, 1879; Kingston *Daily Freeman*, May 3, 1879; Saugerties *Evening Post*, May 5, 1879.

5. Plans for the railroad were often mentioned in regional newspapers during 1877 and 1878; see the Kingston *Argus*, May 16, 1877, for one instance.

CHAPTER 66

1. Letter, Robert Livingston to Robert R. Livingston, March 1, 1762, Robert R. Livingston Papers, New-York Historical Society.

2. Letter, signed "Pedes," New York *Times,* May 26, 1874, recalls a boyhood walking tour of the Catskills with several companions and a tutor.

3. Letter, Henry Thoreau to Isaac Hecker in *The Correspondence of Henry D. Thoreau,* Walter Harding and Carl Bode, eds., New York, 1958, p. 155.

4. Henry D. Thoreau, *A Week on the Concord and Merrimack Rivers,* 9th ed., Boston, 1867, p. 202.

5. Walter Harding, *The Days of Henry Thoreau,* New York, 1965, p. 172; William Ellery Channing, *Thoreau, the Poet-Naturalist,* Boston, 1902, pp. 138–39.

6. *Journals of Henry D. Thoreau,* Bradford Torrey and Francis H. Allen, eds., Boston, 1906, reprinted New York, 1949, vol. 1., pp. 361–62.

7. J. Lyndon Shanley, *The Making of Walden,* Chicago, 1957, pp. 138–39.

8. Henry D. Thoreau, "Walking," in *Atlantic Monthly,* vol. 9, no. 56, June 1862, pp. 657–74.

9. Arnold Guyot, "On the Physical Structure and Hypsometry of the Catskill Mountain Region," in *American Journal of Science,* 3d series, vol. 19, no. 114 (June 1880).

10. Story signed "H.K." reprinted in the Kingston *Daily Freeman,* August 31, 1874, from the Brooklyn *Eagle.*

Chapter 67

1. The Catskill *Recorder,* July 19, 1878.

2. Many versions of the Beach-Harding collision have found their way into print and remain in oral tradition. Mabel Parker Smith, "$1,500,000 Hotel Built for Spite," Catskill *Examiner-Record,* June 24, 1952, is a lively statement of one version; Mrs. Smith's "In the 80's They all Came to the Mountain House," Catskill *Examiner-Record,* April 16, 1953, contains additional material on the relations of the two hotels from a Catskill point of view; for a version acceptable to the people of Saugerties and Kingston, see "How Harding Came to Build the Kauterskill Hotel," in the Saugerties *Evening Post,* May 12, 1881.

3. The epithet was first used, as far as I know, in the Catskill *Recorder,* August 31, 1877.

4. M. P. Smith, "1,500,000 Hotel . . ." loc. cit.; the verse is here attributed to Ezra Cornwall.

5. I have based this treatment of the building of the Hotel Kaaterskill on newspaper material published between August 1880 and the summer of 1881; because Catskill businessmen feared that the new hotel would bring them no profits, their town's newspapers printed little about the progress of Harding's building. An exception was a fact-and-figure-filled story (apparently supplied by Harding) in the *Recorder,* December 3, 1880. Saugerties papers covered the story with gusto.

6. Saugerties *Evening Post,* May 14, 1881.

7. There is much lore about the stealing of building materials from Harding which is still being repeated; among those who spoke of this to me were Mabel Parker Smith and Miss Eva Trumpbour of Palenville. See, Francis Overbaugh, *The Hotel Kaaterskill,* privately printed, ca. 1968, n.p., 4th page of text.

Chapter 68

1. Here I am much indebted to a conversation, May 10, 1968, with Miss Eva Trumpbour, aged 82, of Palenville. Miss Trumpbour's father was employed by George Harding as a superintendent during the construction of the hotel and afterward.

2. Reprinted in the Saugerties *Evening Post,* July 12, 1881. Much of the detail I have used in this chapter appeared in the Saugerties *Evening Post* during June and July 1881.

3. *New Grand Hotel, Catskill Mountains,* advertising booklet, 1887, p. 9.

4. Told to me by Melvin Mayes, Pine Hill.

5. Rev. J. C. Cornish, *Reminiscenses of Pine Hill,* published in installments in the Pine Hill *Sentinel.* Mr. Cornish gives the figure I have used in his installment of September 29, 1906, but quotes the Reverend Amos N. Molyneaux as saying that his father, who had lived nearby, put the pines' height at 200 feet and their diameter at 10 feet.

6. Rev. T. L. Cuyler contributed to the promotional booklets issued by the Grand Hotel. For the 1887 booklet, a piece he had written for the New York *Evangelist* was used under the heading, "The Heart of the Catskills." In the same booklet the Reverend Dr. Howard Crosby wrote that those who knew only the vicinity of the Catskill Mountain House had "only a meager idea" of the Catskills "grandeur and beauty." On p. 11 it was claimed that since the Grand was "surrounded by a wilderness of peaks," pure air rushed at it from all directions.

7. Crosby's climbs were often reported in local newspapers and Dr. Cuyler wrote in the Grand's promotional booklet for 1888 that "there is not a single mountain within a dozen miles [of the Grand] whose summit his [Crosby's] bootheels are not familiar with."

8. The Grand's movable bar room has become firmly fixed in oral tradition. Among Pine Hill people who told me of it was Charles Griffin. On April 30, 1898, the Pine Hill *Sentinel* reported that the manager of the Grand had moved the hotel office into Delaware County to get a tax advantage.

CHAPTER 69

1. The Catskill *Examiner,* October 21, 1882. Wilde's visit to the Catskills was amply covered by the regional newspapers if not always in a friendly spirit; see Catskill *Recorder,* August 25 and September 8, and the Saugerties *Evening Post,* August 8 and 23; Wilde's manner, said the *Post,* suggested "a fancy bartender mixing a drink."

2. Kingston *Daily Freeman,* August 2–10, 1883.

3. The anecdote of President Arthur and Christian Charley was told to me, October 2, 1969, by Mabel Parker Smith. The presidential visit was covered by the New York *Times,* August 2–16, 1883, and by the Kingston *Daily Freeman* and other regional newspapers.

4. "Extensive preparations are being made at the Kaaterskill for the reception of General Grant and family . . . on August 1," reported the Catskill *Examiner,* July 11, 1885. The Kingston *Argus,* May 6 of the same year, had told of Grant's acceptance of George Harding's invitation for a month's stay.

5. Charles Dudley Warner, "Their Pilgrimage," New York, 1826, p. 60.

6. For information on the Catskill Mountain Railroad (after July 1886, renamed the Catskill Mountain Railway), I have studied the Minute Books, Board of Directors of the Catskill Mountain Railway in the Library of the Greene County Historical Society. Beach's vote in favor of the Otis is recorded in vol. 2, p. 11. I have also used stories of the railroad's difficulties which appeared in New York and regional newspapers.

7. Sherman's visit to the Catskill Mountain House is the subject of a newspaper story by Mabel Parker Smith, "Sherman Won Atlanta, Near Surrender to Female Pen Brigade at Mountain House," in Greene County *Examiner-Record,* April 23, 1953.

8. Saugerties *Evening Post,* July 28, 1888.

9. "City Folk Corrupt Country People," in Pine Hill *Sentinel,* April 29, 1905. Here the subject is vigorously discussed by the Reverend Frank L. Wilson, presiding elder of the New York Conference of the Methodist Church. The Saugerties *Evening Post,*

July 18, 1881, defends boarders against the aspersions of presiding elder King of the New York Conference.

10. At Ferndale in Sullivan County, "William Harden (colored)" advertised for summer boarders in *Summer Homes,* published by the New York, Ontario & Western Railway, New York, 1900.

11. In 1893 Epstein bought a small piece of land in Hunter; Deed book 133, p. 12, Greene County Clerk's Office.

CHAPTER 70

1. Pine Hill *Sentinel,* January 6, 1886, and June 5, 1897.

2. Told to me by Harry Siemsen.

3. W. L. Stone, "Ten Days in the Country," in New York *Commercial Advertiser,* September 3, 1824. This is the earliest appearance in print of the story which I have seen. A good study of the tale is Charles A. Huguenin, "Condemned to the Noose," in New York *Folklore Quarterly,* vol. 16, no. 3, pp. 187–96; here Huguenin suggests a solution to the mystery.

4. The association of Natty Bumppo with Overlook Mountain has been accepted in Judge A. T. Clearwater's *History of Ulster County,* Kingston, 1907, H. A. Haring, *Our Catskill Mountains,* New York, 1931, and R. L. De Lisser, *Picturesque Ulster,* Kingston, 1896.

5. I owe much about the Utsayantha legend to Stamford's town historian, Mrs. Leo De Silva, who permitted me to study her notes on the subject. I also used the notebooks of former Stamford historian, Don Macpherson, esp. vol. 3, in the local history room of the Churchill Memorial Library, Stamford.

6. Roxbury town historian, Irma Mae Griffin, was my principal informant on the White Man; I also used More and Griffin, *History of the Town of Roxbury,* Walton, 1953, pp. 101–2; the Princess Devasego story appeared in the Pine Hill *Sentinel,* September 17, 1890, reprinted from the Roxbury *Times.*

7. William Cockburn's lease and survey book, Cockburn Papers, 15:5, New York State Library.

8. The charge was made in the Stamford *Mirror,* August 30, 1877. The Poughkeepsie *Eagle,* July 19, 1873, had published an unromantic version which had the Big Indian a drunk and a thief.

9. R. L. De Lisser, op. cit., pp. 247–48, tells of the first tarring and feathering of the stone, long since removed when the road was widened.

10. Kingston *Freeman,* June 1, 1874.

11. Told to me by Wilna Hervey who had it from Gene Shultis, the former owner of her farm on the Cooper Lake Road.

12. Howland bear lore is brought together in M. S. Forde, "Lore of the Catskills," in the Harold W. Thompson Archive, Library of the New York Historical Association.

13. Mrs. Lobdell was the subject of many newspaper stories. An informative one is, "The Story of Two Women Who Insisted They Were Man and Wife," in the Stamford *Mirror,* June 23, 1885.

14. Pine Hill *Sentinel,* November 18, 1893.

15. From the late 1850s until his death in 1898 and even later, paragraphs about Boots's eccentricities amused newspaper readers in the Hudson Valley and occasionally elsewhere in the United States. A fictional account of Boots's love for Jenny Lind and its sad results was written by a reporter for the New York *Sun,* July 22, 1878, and became widely believed. The speech I quote was written down from a recitation by Harry D. Carle of Flatbush, taped by Harry Siemsen. The parody of the flag

quotation is taken from the Saugerties *Daily Post,* May 9, 1878. The sentence quoted near the end of the paragraph was repeated to me with gestures by a Kingston oldtimer; in somewhat varied form it appeared in the Saugerties *Daily Post,* May 9, 1878.

16. I am indebted to Squire Elwyn Davis of West Shokan for much material about Rowl Bell. Of help was a story titled, "A Trip to High Point," in the Kingston *Daily Freeman,* August 7, 1873.

CHAPTER 71

1. For background on the Visscher map, see *Narrative and Critical History of America,* Justin Winsor, ed., 8 vols., Boston, 1884–89, vol. 4, pp. 437–38.

2. George R. Stewart, under "Esopus" in American Place-Names, New York, 1970.

3. The name was used in 1637 in the log of the ship *Rensselaerwyck,* see *The Van Rensselaer Bowier Manuscripts,* Albany, 1908, p. 376.

4. The name occurs in the grant of land to William Loveridge, Jr., February 8, 1686, description quoted in J. V. V. Vedder, *History of Greene County,* 1651–1800, vol. 1 (no more published), Catskill, 1927, p. 43.

5. Early uses of "Blue Mountains" as applied to the Catskills are listed in H.W.R. (Helen Wilkinson Reynolds), "I Will Lift up Mine Eyes to the Hills," in *Yearbook, Dutchess County Historical Society,* vol. 17, 1942, pp. 86–88.

6. *The America of 1750, Peter Kalm's Travels in North America,* rev. and ed., Adolph B. Benson, 2 vols., New York, 1946, vol. 2, p. 65; in vol. 2, on p. 617, Kalm writes of "the Catskills Mountains which are also called the Blue Mountains."

7. Spafford, *Gazetteer,* 1813, p. 9.

8. Henry Rowe Schoolcraft, "Comments, Philological and Historical on the Aboriginal Names and Geographical Terminology of the State of New York," Part I, in Proc. New-York Historical Society, 1845, pp. 37–38.

9. Spafford, op. cit., pp. 78–79.

10. Egbert Benson, *Memoir Read before the Historical Society of the State of New York,* 31 December, 1816 . . . , New York, 1817.

11. Albert Carnoy, *Dictionnaire Etymologique du Noms des Communes de Belgique,* Louvain, 1939, Première partie, A–K, p. 303.

12. E. M. Ruttenber, Indian Names of the Valley of Hudson's River . . . supplement to *Proc. New York Hist. Assn.,* n.p., 1906, espouses the cataract theory, Mrs. J. V. V. Vedder, *History of Greene County,* 1927, favors Jacob Kats as inspiring the name; Captain Andrew S. Hickey in, *The Story of Kingston,* Kingston, 1952, states that the name Catskill resulted from the combining of cat, meaning steep and kill, meaning stream; Gouverneur Morris, in a letter of December 20, 1800, may have been the first to set down in writing the wild-cat theory; see DeWitt Clinton, *Memoir of David Hosack,* New York, 1829. W. M. Beauchamp, *Aboriginal Place Names of New York,* Albany, 1907, brings together Indian names which may have been corrupted into Kaaterskill.

13. Quinlan, *Sullivan County,* p. 618.

14. *History of the Valley of the Hudson, River of Destiny,* Nelson Greene, ed., 5 vols., Chicago, 1931, vol. 2, p. 921. Here E. M. Ruttenber is quoted as the source of this folk etymology.

15. The Catskill *Examiner,* August 17, 1889, tells of a group of Republican politicians climbing High Peak and planting "a banner . . . reading Lincoln" on the summit. As far as I know the new name was not used.

16. Henry Kimball wrote of the "Shandaken or Livingston Hills" in the Kingston *Argus,* September 2, 1874. The southwestern part of the Catskills lying in Ulster

County was sometimes called the Pine Mountains; J. H. Mather, *Geography of New York*, New York, 1847, p. 296, writes that the "Pine Mountains or Kaatsbergs" bound Greene County on the southwest; John Burroughs wrote of the Pine Mountains, *Wake Robin*, p. 171. But Mather, p. 182, had called these mountains the Blue Mountains which "enter the county [Ulster] from Sullivan County and spread over its westward section mingling in the northern part with the Catskill range."

CHAPTER 72

1. Mrs. Wheeler's account of the beginnings of Onteora Park is given on pp. 268–323 of her *Yesterdays in a Busy Life*, New York, 1918. Eventually Mrs. Wheeler's dominant position and the accuracy of her recollections came to be questioned by some of the Park people—see p. 322, *Yesterdays,* for Mrs. Wheeler's feelings toward these people. Burgess Howard in "Onteora Road Ramblings; Atop the Catskill Mountains," in the Greene County *Examiner-Record*, September 3, 1953, gives a story of the discovery of Onteora Park which differs from Mrs. Wheeler's.

2. Pine Hill *Sentinel*, October 31, 1891. Bankruptcy overtook Thurber in 1901 as the center of the wholesale grocery trade moved to Chicago and many New York grocers proved unable to adapt.

3. Wheeler, op. cit., 209–67. A decorating job on which Mrs. Wheeler worked with Tiffany and Lockwood de Forest in 1881 may still be seen by the public in the Mark Twain house, Hartford, Conn.

4. In 1890 the company changed its place of business from New York to Onteora Park; in 1903 it sold its lands to the Onteora Land Co.

5. This quotation and the five which follow are in Wheeler, op. cit., pp. 268–323.

6. Quoted from *Oxford Companion to American Literature*, 3d ed., 1956, p. 471.

7. John A. MacGahan, *The Twilight Portfolio*, Twilight Park, 1942. I have relied in several places on this compilation of Twilight Park material.

8. Ralph M. Lord and Miss Eva Trumpbour in conversation.

9. Burgess Howard, *Onteora Road Ramblings,* loc. cit.

10. Book of Incorporations, Greene County Clerk's office, vol. 2, p. 208.

11. I have used here items about the Chinese Minister from the Catskill *Examiner*, June 29–October 12, 1889.

12. Pine Hill *Sentinel,* May 20, 1899. I have used many items about the Fleischmann family from the Pine Hill *Sentinel,* 1887–1904. *Cincinnati, Queen City of the West,* G. M. Roe, ed., Cincinnati, 1895, esp. pp. 74–76, supplied information on Fleischmann background, so did Clara Longworth de Chambrun, *Cincinnati, The Story of the Queen City,* New York, 1939, pp. 314–15. I benefited greatly from a conversation of January 13, 1969, with 80-year-old John Kelly, for many years Postmaster of Fleischmanns. Protest against changing the name of Griffin's Corners was made in New York's not very respectable *Town Topics* and was reprinted July 23, 1892, from the Kingston *Daily Freeman* abbreviated reprint, by the Pine Hill *Sentinel.*

13. Pine Hill *Sentinel,* June 6, 1903. Gould activities became a favorite topic of many regional newspapers.

14. Wheeler, *Yesterdays,* pp. 202–3.

15. Kingston *Daily Freeman,* May 19, 1879.

16. The poem is printed on p. 5 of *The Light of Day,* vol. II of the Riverby edition of Burroughs' works.

17. Told to me by Elmer Pelham formerly of Haines Falls.

18. Minute books, Board of Directors, CMRY, vol. 2, pp. 63–67. I have used this volume as a source for much of this and the next paragraph.

19. Charles F. Carpenter, "The Catskill Preserve," in Second Annual Report of the Forest Commision of the State of New York, April 13, 1887, Albany, 1887, pp. 115–16.

CHAPTER 73

1. The Pine Hill *Sentinel,* March 26, 1890, reported the sale as taking place on March 19. The purchaser was Jacob Fromer of Tannersville. Fromer paid $7000 subject to a decree in foreclosure of $29,765.23. Mr. Schutt, the former owner of the Laurel House, became a desk clerk at the Catskill Mountain House.

2. The picture of summer life in the Catskills given in this chapter has been put together from hundreds of items printed in regional and New York newspapers. I have given sources of direct quotations and of information not derived from newspapers.

3. Griffin Herrick of Woodstock told me during the 1950s that as a boy he had acted as guide to a manufactured volcano on Overlook.

4. Pine Hill *Sentinel,* August 11, 1886, and September 3, 1890.

CHAPTER 74

1. Reported to me by E. C. Elmendorf of Coeymans in a letter of March 7, 1966.

2. Kingston *Daily Freeman,* July 21, 1879.

3. For the handicraft period of bluestone working, see Alf Evers, "Bluestone Lore and Bluestone Men," in *New York Folklore Quarterly,* vol. 18 (1962), pp. 86–107.

4. Lease, Margaret Livingston-Henry Davis in Deed Book 18, pp. 17–19, Ulster County Clerk's Office.

5. The *Annual Reports* of the New York State Geologists, 1890–1912, furnished much material on the geological and economic sides of bluestone quarrying. Especially useful were Frank L. Nason, "Economic Geology of Ulster County, 1893," and N. H. Darton, "A Preliminary Report on the Geology of Ulster County"—both are in the *Forty-seventh Annual Report of the State Museum,* Albany, 1894. Later reports tell of the changes and the eventual decline of the bluestone industry. Also useful were James B. Gordon, "The Bluestone Industry of New York," in *Stone,* vol. 19, no. 2 (July 1899), pp. 113–31, and Leon Barritt, "Hudson River Bluestone," in N. B. Sylvester, *History of Ulster County,* 1880, pp. 61–62.

6. *Arts and Crafts in New York,* 1726–76, R. S. Gottesman, comp., New York, 1938, p. 186.

7. Newspapers in Kingston, Saugerties, and Catskill carried many stories on a variety of aspects of bluestone quarrying between the 1850s and the end of the nineteenth century; I have used these stories freely here and elsewhere in this chapter.

8. Biographical sketches based on information furnished by the subjects appeared in local mug books published after 1880. The *Commemorative and Biographical Record, Ulster County,* 1896, is rich in this kind of material dealing with bluestone entrepreneurs. I have used this material with proper caution.

9. James Butler, *Diary,* No. 2, March 29, 1868–September 19, 1870, Ms. belonging to the author, pp. 9–10.

10. Here I have used A. W. Hoffman, "Ulster County Bluestone," in R. L. De Lisser, *Picturesque Ulster,* Kingston, 1896, pp. 119–22, and Charles E. Foote, "Bluestone," in *History of Ulster County.* A. T. Clearwater, ed., Kingston, 1907, pp. 541–44. The story about the cross-eyed quarryman was told to me by Cy Keegan formerly of Lewis Hollow, Woodstock. The story in a different version appeared in Anita M. Smith, *Woodstock, History and Hearsay,* Saugerties, 1959, p. 102.

Chapter 75

1. Saugerties *Telegraph*, April 5, 1851.
2. James Butler, Ms. *Diary*, pp. 44–45.
3. Told to me by Walter Kruesi, a former owner of the house.
4. Told to me by Cy Keegan and his sister, Mrs. Hayes.
5. Butler, *Diary*, p. 91.
6. I heard the saying in my boyhood in lowland Ulster. Later Charles Herrick of Woodstock repeated it to me.
7. This saying as well as much of the lore in this paragraph from Alf Evers, "Rattlesnake Lore of the Catskills" in *New York Folklore Quarterly*, vol. 7, no. 2 (Summer, 1951), pp. 108–15.
8. From notes on the report made by Harry and Marie Siemsen.
9. N. B. Sylvester, *History of Ulster County*, Part 2, pp. 240–45. Here is a detailed account of the Rosendale cement industry from a local point of view. Coykendall's experiments are referred to hopefully in Frank L. Nason, "Economic Geology of Ulster County," in *47th Report, New York State Museum*, Albany, 1894, p. 578.

Chapter 76

1. In 1880 Dutcher was named Slide Mountain Postmaster by Republican President Rutherford B. Hayes; Dutcher's summer boarders valued the Slide Mountain cancellation available on the premises. Winne, while not an officeholder, had considerable influence behind the scenes; his obituary appeared in the Pine Hill *Sentinel*, May 8, 1897.
2. New York *Times*, June 12, 1886; Kingston *Daily Freeman*, June 11, 1886; Kingston *Daily Leader*, June 14, 1886.

Chapter 77

1. Hans Huth, *Nature and the American*, Berkeley, 1948, pp. 30–53, and passim.
2. *History of the State of New York*, A. C. Flick, ed., 1931–37, vol. 10, p. 273.
3. Quoted in Norman J. Van Valkenburgh, *The Adirondack Forest Preserve: A Chronology*, unpublished typescript, 1968, p. 23.
4. I have depended on four principal sources for the struggle to "save the Adirondacks." They are *Adirondack Bibliography*, Adirondack Mountain Club, 1958, pp. 58ff.; Alfred L. Donaldson, *History of the Adirondacks*, 2 vols., New York, 1921, vol. 2, pp. 164–79, and passim; the many stories printed in the New York *Times* and Van Valkenburgh's *Adirondack Forest Preserve*.
5. New York *Times*, April 10, 1884.
6. Report of the Forestry Commission, published as *State of New York, no. 63, In Assembly, January 23, 1885*, Albany, 1886, pp. 14–15.
7. Among the cases of poaching which aroused interest throughout the Catskills was that in which rich New Yorker Clarence M. Roof pursued two sons of chair manufacturer Hiram Whitney of Shandaken, and picturesque backwoodsman John Bill Rogers from court to court for years; see the Pine Hill *Sentinel*, July 30, 1890, for a reprint of the New York *World*'s account of the case at the midpoint of its career. The *Sentinel*, November 6, 1897, printed its own story of the Roof-Beadle case; Ira Beadle of Big Indian informed me of the fine points of this case in which his father was defendant.
8. For a biographical sketch of C. A. J. Hardenbergh, see N. B. Sylvester, *Ulster County*, 1880, Part 2, p. 169.

9. The Kingston *Argus,* November 11, 1885.

10. Van Valkenburgh, *Adirondack Forest Preserve,* pp. 55–56.

11. Ibid., pp. 58–59.

12. Owners of game preserves did little to encourage respect for law; they frequently violated the state game laws themselves. On July 16, 1891, to cite but one example, the Saugerties *Weekly Post* reported the conviction of rich game preserver Josiah Wentworth and famous sculptor J. Q. A. Ward on charges of fishing out of season.

13. The *Annual Reports* of the New York State Forest Commission, 1888–97, give the history of the Slide Mountain Deer Park. Regional newspapers reflected reader interest by printing many Deer Park items; see Pine Hill *Sentinel,* September 14, 1895, for one instance.

CHAPTER 78

1. The report was authorized August 7; it was published in the Kingston *Democratic Journal,* August 21, 1861.

2. Report of Committee on New Water Supply, City of Kingston, New York (1893), Senate House Museum Library.

3. I believe this company was an offshoot of the Ramapo Improvement Company which had tried without success to sell the city of New York a water supply in 1884. The water was to be from Rockland and Orange counties, New York, with the Catskills available should they become necessary. See, *Ramapo Improvement Co., Proposal to the Sinking Fund Commission for a Supplementary Supply of Water for the City of New York, N.Y.,* 1884. A copy is in the Science Division of the New York Public Library.

4. *A General Description of the Catskill Water Supply, Board of Water Supply of the City of New York,* New York, 1940, p. 3; John H. Freeman, *Digest of a Report upon New York City's Water Supply,* New York, March 31, 1900; Lazarus White, The Catskill Water Supply of New York City, New York, 1913, pp. 15–17; see also New York *Times,* April 18, 1899; a detailed report on the Ramapo Company's activities and plans appeared in the Pine Hill *Sentinel,* July 1, 1899, as well as in many other regional and New York newspapers at about the same time.

5. Pine Hill *Sentinel,* December 2, 1905. Coykendall's suggestion that New York turn to the Adirondacks for water formed part of a revival of a plan which had been around for a quarter of a century. For a good outline of the Adirondack proposal, see J. T. Thomas, *Report no. 2 on a Water Supply for New York and other cities of the Hudson Valley,* New York, 1884.

6. Quoted in the Pine Hill *Sentinel,* April 14, 1906.

7. A cartoon in the New York *World,* December 3, portrayed the lawyers for the people of the Esopus Valley as "Reubens of the first water," stated the Pine Hill *Sentinel,* December 9, 1905. City officials had aroused anger by statements like that attributed in the *Sentinel* of March 4, 1905, to New York corporation counsel Delaney who was reported to have said "rural communities must be sacrificed to the needs of a great city."

8. Figures given here are from *General Description of the Catskill Water Supply,* 1940.

9. Among many newspapers reporting the Cudney case was the Pine Hill *Sentinel,* March 28, 1914; on April 25 of the same year the *Sentinel* told of the case of the Saugerties manufacturers.

10. Pine Hill *Sentinel,* July 26, 1913.

11. Kingston *Weekly Freeman,* August 17, 1899.

12. Pine Hill *Sentinel,* May 10, 1913.

13. The phrase was often used by the New York *World* which consistently opposed constructing the Ashokan Reservoir; see the *World,* February 21, 1906.

14. Here I have used conversations with old people in the Reservoir vicinity, among them Squire Elwyn Davis, West Shokan, and John Saxe, West Hurley; I also used "Wonder City of the Catskills," reprinted in the Pine Hill *Sentinel,* September 19, 1908, from the New York *World.* The *Sentinel,* December 12, 1908, reprinted the New York *World*'s story of IWW agent S. A. Stodel's report of bad treatment of Ashokan workers.

15. "Sergeants Carmody and Ocker, The Catskill Reign of Terror," in Ulster County *Townsman,* September 28, October 5, and October 12, 1967. "Ten thousand men, mostly unskilled, and a wild and desperate lot, suddenly dumped into an un-policed district can work a lot of havoc—They did."—so the reminiscences of these former Ashokan Reservoir policemen begin.

16. *Board of Water Supply, Esopus Division, Songs, High Falls, New York,* 1911.

CHAPTER 79

1. Louis L. Noble, *A Voyage to the Arctic Seas in Search of Icebergs, with Church, the Artist,* New York, 1861, p. 57.

2. For dates, places, and education in Whitehead's life I have relied here and elsewhere on Alumni Oxoniensis, Joseph Foster, ed., Oxford, 1888; The Balliol College Register, 2nd ed., Sir Ivo Elliott, ed., Oxford, 1934, and Who's Who in America, 1924–25, Chicago, 1925.

3. *The Parish Registers of St. Chads,* John Radcliffe, ed., Saddleworth, Uppermill, 1891; and Joseph Bradbury, *Saddleworth Sketches,* Saddleworth, 1871, helped provide family background; George Dodd, *The Textile Manufactures of Great Britain,* 6 vols., 1844–46, vol. 2, pp. 121–22 and passim, lists Saddleworth woolen manufacturers by name.

4. The *Times,* London, May 12, 1864.

5. Ralph Radcliffe-Whitehead, *Grass of the Desert,* London, 1892, p. 61.

6. Hervey White, "Ralph Radcliffe Whitehead," in *Publications of the Woodstock Historical Society,* no. 10, July 1933, pp. 19–20.

7. John Ruskin, *Fors Clavigera,* vol. 28 of Library Edition of Ruskin's Works, A. T. Cook and A. Wedderburn, eds., 39 vols., London, 1903–12, Letter LVIII, pp. 418–19.

CHAPTER 80

1. Whitehead, *Grass of the Desert,* p. 71.

2. Walt Whitman, *Leaves of Grass, with Autobiography,* Philadelphia, 1900, p. 354.

3. Hervey White, "Ralph Radcliffe Whitehead," in *Publications of the Woodstock Historical Society,* no. 10, pp. 21–22.

4. Hervey White, "Man Overboard," Maverick Press, 1922, pp. 5–6, 12–13.

5. Quoted in Anita M. Smith, *Woodstock, History and Hearsay,* Saugerties, 1959, p. 41.

6. White, "Ralph Radcliffe Whitehead," loc. cit., p. 14.

7. Here I have used the typed copy of Hervey White's unpublished autobiography lent me by the Iowa Authors Collection, University of Iowa Libraries.

8. Ibid., p. 125.

9. White, "Ralph Radcliffe Whitehead," loc. cit., pp. 25–26.

10. White, autobiography, p. 145. For a biographical sketch of Brown, see Carl Eric Lindin, "Bolton Brown," in *Publications of the Woodstock Historical Society,* no. 13, August–September 1937, pp. 15–17.

CHAPTER 81

1. Allen Staley, *Byrdcliffe and the Maverick,* a Master's Thesis, Yale School of Fine Arts, 195 p.

2. John Ruskin, *Modern Painters,* vol. 7, Library Edition of Ruskin's Works, pp. 175–79.

3. Charlotte Perkins Gilman, *The Living of Charlotte Perkins Gilman,* New York, 1935, p. 252.

4. Bolton Brown, "Early Days at Woodstock," in *Publications of the Woodstock Historical Society,* no. 13, August–September 1937, p. 4. Brown and White disagreed in their accounts of the beginnings of the art colony at Woodstock but they agreed on Whitehead's anti-Semitism. Hervey White was very outspoken on this subject in "Woodstock, 1902 . . . Enter the Art Immigrants," n.p., a Ms. in the collection of the Woodstock Historical Society.

5. This and the other quotations in this paragraph are from Brown, "Early Days at Woodstock," loc. cit., p. 13.

6. White, "Woodstock, 1902 . . . Enter the Art Immigrants."

7. Ibid. In a conversation with me shortly before his death, Hervey White spoke of Brown's "thoroughness" in investigating Woodstock.

8. White, autobiography, p. 151.

9. Brown, "Early Days at Woodstock," loc. cit., p. 6.

10. White, autobiography, p. 152.

11. Lucy Brown, "The First Summer in Byrdcliffe," in *Publications of the Woodstock Historical Society,* no. 2, August 1930, p. 16.

12. The Kingston *Argus,* August 6, 1902, reprinted a report from the Kingston *Daily Freeman.*

13. White, autobiography, pp. 152–55. Brown's story of the building of Byrdcliffe is quite different; see his "Early Days at Woodstock," loc. cit., pp. 10–11.

CHAPTER 82

1. Peter Whitehead, Ralph R. Whitehead's son, tells me his father was responsible for the design of the Byrdcliffe buildings; in his "Early Days at Woodstock," p. 10, Bolton Brown strongly implies that he and not Whitehead was the designer.

2. "Byrdcliffe Summer Art School" (1903). A copy of this four-page prospectus is in the New York Public Library.

3. Carl Eric Lindin, "The Woodstock Landscape," in *Publications of the Woodstock Historical Society,* no. 7, July 1932, p. 18.

4. Ralph Radcliffe-Whitehead, "A Plea for Manual Work," in *Handicraft,* vol. 2, no. 3 (June 1903), p. 66.

5. Brown, "Early Days at Woodstock," loc. cit., p. 13.

6. Much very handsome furniture made at Byrdcliffe, 1903–04, is still in use at White Pines.

7. Whitehead, "A Plea . . ." loc. cit., p. 73

8. Brown, "Early Days at Woodstock," loc. cit., p. 13.

9. Ibid., p. 14.

10. White, autobiography, pp. 161–62.

11. Ibid., p. 115.

CHAPTER 83

1. Bertha Thompson, "The Craftsmen of Byrdcliffe," in *Publications of the Woodstock Historical Society,* no. 10, July 1933, pp. 10–11.

2. Ibid., pp. 9, 12.

3. White, autobiography, pp. 167–68.

4. Ibid., p. 169.

5. Ibid., p. 170–71. Deed book 423, p. 328, Ulster County Clerk's Office.

6. Whitehead, "A Plea . . ." in *Handicraft,* vol. 2, no. 3, p. 70.

7. Henry Morton Robinson, "Hervey White and Woodstock," in *Proceedings of the Ulster County Historical Society,* 1945–46, Kingston, ca. 1946, pp. 24, 28.

8. Hervey White used this phrase and the one quoted in the next sentence in conversations with me during 1943 and 1944. See A. M. Smith, *Woodstock, History and Hearsay,* Saugerties, 1959, p. 67.

9. The reticence about sex which prevailed during Hervey's lifetime kept open references to his homosexuality from appearing in print and from being mentioned in his autobiography.

10. Hervey White, "Art and the Community, an Outline of a Scheme of Co-operation between Artists and Farmers," in *The Wild Hawk,* vol. 5, no. 5, (March 1916, n.p.).

11. John F. Carlson, "The Art Students League of New York in Woodstock," in *Publications of the Woodstock Historical Society,* no. 9, September 1932, pp. 11–18. This otherwise excellent account is marred by some errors especially in dates.

12. Told to me in conversation, March 26, 1956, by painter Edward L. Chase who came to Woodstock as an Art Students League student about 1906; "We hated the natives and they hated us," said Chase. The natives "slept with their neighbor's wives but thought we were immoral," said Chase.

13. E. L. Chase and Sam Wiley who arrived in Woodstock not long after Chase.

14. Comstock's raid and what followed were reported in detail by many newspapers; see esp. the New York *Times,* August 3–4, 1906.

15. For recollections of "nude dancing" I am indebted to E. L. Chase; nude bathing was the subject of "Snooperism," in *The Hue and Cry,* Woodstock, August 30, 1929, p. 10.

16. *The Pochade,* Woodstock, vol. I, no. 1 (August 1912).

17. Ibid.

18. White, autobiography, p. 203; the story of the Maverick Festivals given here is based in large part on White, autobiography, esp. pp. 207–10.

19. Ibid., pp. 214–16; "Birth of the Maverick Concert Hall," in *The Hue and Cry,* September 1, 1933, p. 12.

20. White, autobiography, p. 168.

CHAPTER 84

1. A. M. Smith, *Woodstock, History and Hearsay,* p. 4.

2. Told to me by Alfeo Faggi in several conversations during the late 1940s.

3. Alf Evers, "We Call It the Rickey," in *New York Folklore Quarterly,* vol. 15, no. 1 (Spring, 1959), pp. 36–47.

4. Hardenbergh Patent, Great Lots nos. 25, 41, 53. Lands of James Desbrosses, Misc. Field Book. Cockburn Papers, 6:30, New York State Library.

5. National Academy of Design Exhibition Record, 1826–60, in *Collections of the New-York Historical Society,* 2 vols., 1941, vol. I, published 1943, pp. 296–98; here many of Dr. Edward Livingston's paintings are listed with dates of exhibition.

6. Two of Church's sketches which show Overlook as seen from Olana were reproduced in *Art in New York, New York World's Fair,* 1964 as plates 30 and 31.

7. Frank Schoonmaker, "A Note on Woodstock," in *The Arts,* vol. 12, no. 4 (October 1927), pp. 227–28; critic Virgil Barker wrote in *The Arts,* vol. 4, no. 5 (November 1923), "The Woodstock painters . . . really have something in common beyond geographical location. As to what that something is, it is hardly possible to be more definite than to call it a spirit of adventurousness. . . ."

8. Two approaches to painting which were "mutually antagonistic" had developed in Woodstock, wrote R. L. Duffus in "An Eden of Artists Fights a Serpent," in New York *Times Magazine,* August 25, 1929. The serpent was the possibility that the town might become fashionable among non-artists.

9. Hervey White, *The Prodigal Father, A Novel of Woodstock (and the World),* published as a serial in *The Plowshare,* beginning vol. 7, no. 4, March 1918, n.p.

10. Hervey White, *The Prodigal Father,* . . . loc. cit.

CHAPTER 85

1. Hard cider, whiskey, and rum had been the favorite alcoholic drinks of nineteenth-century Woodstock; the artists liked hard cider but when Prohibition arrived in 1920, they turned to applejack produced in local stills. Illicit "apple" continued to be made and drunk even after Prohibition came to an end in 1933.

2. White, Autobiography, pp. 220–22; for Havel's background I have used Albert Parry, *Garrets and Pretenders,* New York, 1960, pp. 270–71, 289, 347.

3. Dudley Digges, "The Maverick Theatre," in *The Hue and Cry,* vol. 2, no. 2, July 5, 1924.

4. Hervey White, "The Maverick Theatre," in *The Hue and Cry Annual,* vol. 3, nos. 10 and 11, 1925. Here White expressed his aims for the theater, ". . . we like experiment, even failure; the doing of the thing rather than the thing done; but if the 'thing done' comes along, we accept it and are grateful according to its value."; editorial, "Broadway Actors in Broadway Plays," in *The Hue and Cry,* vol. 7, no. 5, July 27, 1929, also expresses the conflict between experimental and standard theater which continued to be part of Woodstock life.

5. The standard costume of Woodstock artists is described in F. Gardner Clough, *Woodstock, Proem and Essay,* privately printed, 1923. The studied simplicity noted by Clough had come to the valley from Byrdcliffe; the kind of costume which pleased tourists was usually of Maverick origin.

6. William Benignus, *Stories of the Catskills, Songs and Lays,* privately printed, 1919.

7. Hervey White "suggests the God Pan in a pink blouse and workmen's trousers" wrote Richard LeGallienne in *Woodstock, An Essay,* Woodstock, 1923, p. 17.

8. For Weyl in Woodstock I have used *Walter Weyl, An Appreciation,* privately printed, 1922; especially useful was the chapter by Martin Schutze, titled, "As I knew him in Woodstock," pp. 54–83.

9. The irregular method of building the new Overlook Mountain House, largely of secondhand materials, helped make the structure a target for humorous and mildly anti-Semitic stories in Woodstock publications. See, "Overnook (sic) Hotel Opens," in *The Hue and Cry,* vol. 2, no. 6, June 30, 1933.

10. New York *Times,* February 24, 1929.

CHAPTER 86

1. Henry Morton Robinson, "Hervey White and Woodstock," in Proceedings of the Ulster County Historical Society, 1945–46, Kingston, ca. 1946, pp. 28–29.

2. Although White presided over what many regarded as Bacchanalian festivities on The Maverick, his self-image remained that of a proper descendant of his Puritan New England ancestors. Hedonistic Robert Armstrong Chanler, White wrote on p. 238 of his autobiography, admired him as "the old Puritan whose will he could not bend."

3. A. M. Smith, *Woodstock, History and Hearsay*, pp. 62–64. Miss Smith gives a disapproving view of Hervey's management of the Maverick Theatre.

4. Ibid., p. 64.

5. Editorial in *The Phoenix, An Augur*, vol. 2, no. 1 (Spring, 1939), pp. 120, 128.

6. Smith, op. cit., p. 66–67.

7. "I have never sold out but I have had offers," Hervey wrote on p. 183 of his autobiography.

8. An undated newspaper clipping from the Ulster County *Press*, ca. 1940, given to me by Harriet and Elsie Goddard, Woodstock, quotes Hervey's report, by letter to a friend, of the staging of the Passion Play.

CHAPTER 87

1. My sources for this view of the change in Mountain House policy are newspaper reports and advertisements. On April 20, 1901 the Pine Hill *Sentinel* reported the installation of electric lights. A 1902 advertising leaflet in the Library of the Greene County Historical Society mentions electric lights, tennis, and golf. In 1901 the hotel resumed conspicuous advertising on the resort pages of the New York *Times*. The earliest printed menu of the Mountain House which I have found is in the Library of the Greene County Historical Society—it is dated July 14, 1901.

2. The searchlight began to operate in 1901. For its effectiveness, see Roland Van Zandt, *The Catskill Mountain House*, New Brunswick, 1966, p. 274.

3. A study of the registers of the Mountain House shows a very sharp upward turn in names suggesting Jewish background by 1902. The registers used were one volume covering 1839–52 belonging to Harold Hargreave, Hurley; and three volumes, covering 1853–69, 1902–13, and 1915–16, all belonging to the Greene County Historical Society. There is probably some significance in the fact that those registers, which appear to have vanished, cover the hotel's less prosperous periods.

4. Bieber began advertising as a kosher establishment in the Ulster & Delaware's *The Catskill Mountains*, after 1900—I have used the edition of 1903.

5. I am indebted to Joseph Warm of Tannersville, a member of congregation Anshi Hashoran, for this information.

6. Here I have used William F. Helmer, *O & W, The long life and slow death of the New York, Ontario and Western Railway*, Howell-North, Berkeley, 1959.

7. Hamilton Child, *Gazetteer and Business Directory of Sullivan County, New York, for 1872–73*, Syracuse, 1872, p. 107; Quinlan, *Sullivan County*, 1873, p. 490, writes that "for many years these streams [of northern Sullivan] have been the favorite resorts of artists and men of wealth and refinement" Sullivan lakes had first attracted fishermen, as lake fishing declined in quality the county's streams became more attractive.

8. Manville Wakefield, *To the Mountains by Rail*, Grahamsville, New York, 1970, pp. 222, 224–25.

9. The story was covered by New York newspapers; see New York *Times*, April 27, 1894.

10. Dr. Loomis' obituary with a list of pallbearers, New York *Times*, January 24, 1895; organization of dispensary and sanatorium, New York *Times*, May 5, 1895.

11. Herbert L. Satterlee, *J. Pierpont Morgan, An Intimate Portrait*, New York, 1939, p. 300.

Chapter 88

1. Selman A. Waksman, *The Conquest of Tuberculosis*, Berkeley and Los Angeles, 1964, p. 70. Dr. Loomis published a paper on "Evergreen Forests as a Therapeutic Agent in Pulmonary Phthisis" in *Transactions of the American Climatological Association*, Philadelphia, 1887, vol. 4, pp. 109–20.

2. J. V. V. Vedder, *History of Greene County*, 1651–1800, vol. 1, p. 96.

3. Waksman, op. cit., pp. 63–64.

4. The quotations used here are taken from eleven letters, Fannie Louise Lawton to William and George Lawton, 1869–72. Some letters are undated. The letters belong to the author.

5. Dr. Wood tried to head off rather than cure lung ailments with his box. Phyllis Robbins, *Maude Adams, An Intimate Portrait*, New York, 1956, pp. 220–21, gives a firsthand view of Dr. Wood's treatments.

6. A biographical sketch of Dr. Loomis is in *History of Medicine in New York*, James J. Walsh, ed., 5 vols., New York, 1919, vol. 5, pp. 25–26.

7. Quinlan, *Sullivan County*, p. 339.

8. New York *Times*, November 21, 1896.

9. Ibid., January 27, 1897.

10. *Summer Homes*, published by New York, O & W Ry., 1880, p. 7.

11. Told to me in conversation by Dewey Borden, Liberty. See also Wakefield, *To the Mountains . . .* , pp. 240–45.

12. Harold Jaedeker Taub, *Waldorf-in-the-Catskills, The Grossinger Legend*, New York, 1952, pp. 38–45.

13. *The Catskills*, published by the Ulster & Delaware Railroad, 1903, pp. 13–14.

14. Dewey Borden, in conversation.

Chapter 89

1. The report of the explorers, *Olde Ulster*, vol. 7, no. 10, p. 303, strongly suggests that they entered what is now Sullivan County through the Sandbergh Valley over the road of 1752.

2. Hutchins Hapgood, *The Spirit of the Ghetto*, with Drawings from Life by Jacob Epstein, new edition—Preface and Notes by Harry Golden, New York, 1965 (first published, New York, 1902).

3. Henry James, *The American Scene*, Bloomington and London, 1968, p. 131.

4. Frank Moss, *The American Metropolis, from Knickerbocker Days to the Present Time*, 3 vols., New York, 1897, vol. 3, pp. 54–60, 154–71, 220–40.

5. Here I have relied on Gabriel Davidson, *Our Jewish Farmers*, New York, 1943; Davidson's supplement, pp. 194–204, gives a good account of Jewish rural-colonization schemes in the northeastern part of the United States. For Sullivan County colonization, I used Davidson, pp. 85–86; for the Baron de Hirsch Fund, pp. 10–12. Mrs. Ben Miller and David S. Roher, *Ellenville's Early Jewish Families*, Ellenville, 1959, contains much which bears on Jewish beginnings in Sullivan.

6. Wakefield, *To the Mountains by Rail*, pp. 81–82.

7. F. Moss, op. cit., vol. 3, p. 220.

8. Henry James, op. cit., pp. 116–39.

9. *The Letters of Henry James*, selected and edited by Percy Lubbock, 2 vols., New York, 1920, vol. 2, p. 71. Here James writes that, "The motor car is a magical marvel—discretely and honorably used. . . ."; on p. 86, James implies that the motor car, when properly used, gives "a huge extension of life, of experience, and consciousness. But I thank my stars that I'm too poor to have one."

Chapter 90

1. Encyclopedia Britannica, 14th ed., 1930, under Motor-car.

2. Letter, Augustus J. Philips to Kingston *Daily Freeman,* August 13, 1906, recalling drive up Platte Clove "about 8 years ago"; *Southeastern New York,* vol. I, p. 78, quotes news story of Philips' purchase of a steamer in 1900.

3. Told to me by Grenville Quick, Willow, New York.

4. Quoted in Mark Sullivan, *Our Times, The United States,* 1900–25, 6 vols., New York, 1926–36, vol. 3, p. 431.

5. The *Sentinel's* weekly reports began August 22 and ended October 31. The rules of the contest were reprinted from *Automobile Topics* on September 19.

6. Clifton Johnson, *John Burroughs Talks, His Reminiscences and Comments,* Boston and New York, 1922, pp. 325–26, 333.

7. John A. Gallt, *Dear Old Greene County,* Catskill, 1915, pp. 94–97.

8. Joseph Warm in conversation.

9. *Summer Homes,* 1900, p. 130. Here the White Sulphur Springs House advertises its therapeutic spring and fine location "among the hills of the southern Catskill (sic)." More usual were claims like that of Cohen and Feltman of Liberty's Hotel Monitor to a view which included "the distant Catskills," ibid., p. 118.

10. Ford's anti-Semitic activities are summarized in Roger Burlingame, *Henry Ford, A Great Life in Brief,* New York, 1957, pp. 103–4; they are given much more detailed treatment in Keith Sward, *The Legend of Henry Ford,* New York, 1948, pp. 151–60.

11. Pine Hill *Sentinel,* June 27, 1903.

Chapter 91

1. Wakefield, *To the Mountains by Rail,* pp. 187–91.

2. Joey Adams with Henry Tobias, *The Borscht Belt,* New York, 1966, p. 17.

3. Ibid., pp. 40–58.

4. Told to me by Joseph Warm.

5. Moss Hart, *Act One,* pp. 136–59, 233–35; Adams and Tobias, op. cit., pp. 113–15.

6. Adams and Tobias have missed few big Borscht Belt names; they bring together many on pp. 3–15, others passim.

7. Pine Hill *Sentinel,* September 22, 1900.

8. Adams and Tobias, op. cit., have reported these and many other details of mid-twentieth-century devices for amusing guests in a chapter entitled "From Borscht to Champagne," pp. 199–214.

9. Among many who have commented to me on the refugees liking for the Catskills are John Kelly, Fleischmanns, and Joseph Warm, Tannersville.

10. For a moving treatment of the struggle to save the old Mountain House, see Roland Van Zandt, *The Catskill Mountain House,* New Brunswick, 1966, pp. 310–40.

11. Adams and Tobias, op. cit., p. 170.

12. Homer Millard, formerly Director of the Sullivan County Publicity and Development Committee.

Chapter 92

1. Mrs. Richard C. Joyner, Bethel.

2. Philip Hone, *Diary,* 1828–51, Allan Nevins, ed., 2 vols., New York, 1927, vol. 2, pp. 754–55.

3. William Boyse, *The Writings of William Boyse,* New York, 1839, p. 311; Quinlan, *Sullivan County,* pp. 117–21, tells of Beekman's settlement at White Lake.

4. Rev. Henry Hedges Prout, *Old Times in Windham,* Cornwallville, New York, 1970, p. 71

5. During the 1950s, the Woodstock Festival Committee was formed to promote attendance at Woodstock art, music, dramatic, and craft events—it published a series of annual booklets, 1959–70.

6. Among many published accounts of Schmidt and his creation are David L. Goodrich, "Miracle on a Mountain," in the *Saturday Evening Post,* vol. 257 (September 12, 1964), pp. 23–26ff.

7. The New York *Times,* July 9, 1969, carried a story about Woodstock fear of change threatened by "unsavory characters."

8. Column, "Between Me and the Lampost" in Ulster County *Townsman,* April 17, 1969.

9. Ellen Jacob, "Meditation Center Burns," ibid., July 10, 1969.

CHAPTER 93

1. Among the newspaper reports of the Sound-Outs which I have used are, "Hippie Festival Upstate is Cool. . . ." New York *Times,* September 4, 1967. For the arrest of one of the Sound-Out's promoters, I used "Woodstock Man Arrested on Nuisance Count," in the Kingston *Freeman,* September 7, 1967; for a later account of the series of Sound-Outs, I used, "Sound Out or Freak Out," in the Woodstock *Record-Press,* September 11, 1968. Here the possibility was raised that the events might be "subversive backed."

2. My principal source from this point to the end of the chapter has been the reports of the Festival carried in the New York *Times,* June 27–November 21. I also questioned many participants in the Festival and a sampling of Monticello and Bethel residents.

3. The *Woodstock Festival* booklet, 1970, uses the phrase in the first paragraph of a section headed "Woodstock, a Name Usurped?"

4. Official Guide to the Borough of Woodstock, with a note by the Rt. Hon. Winston S. Churchill, C.H., M.P.; Oxford, 1951.

5. This map and another similar one, dated 10 September, 1801 are among the uncatalogued RRLP in the New-York Historical Society Library.

CHAPTER 94

1. For a modern view of Sojourner Truth, see Jacqueline Bernard, *Journey Toward Freedom,* New York, 1967; for a contemporary white view, see Harriet Beecher Stowe, "Sojourner Truth, The Libyan Sibyl," in the *Atlantic Monthly* (April 1863), reprinted in *Olde Ulster,* vol. 10, No. 10 (October 1914), pp. 289–303.

2. "The greatest threat to the Catskills today lies in the inflating value and increasing cost of holding private lands," wrote Sherret S. Chase in, "The Catskills of New York, Past, Present, Potential," in *American Forests,* vol. 73, no. 8 (August 1967), p. 46.

3. I have been helped in forming views of the Catskills' future expressed here by conversations with Dr. Sherret S. Chase, president of the Catskill Center for Conservation and Development, and with Sheafe Satterthwaite of the Center for Environmental Studies, Williamstown, Mass., and with Edward G. West, former Superintendent of Land Acquisition for the New York State Conservation Department. I have found common ground with all three but have not entirely agreed with them on the Catskills' problems and their possible solutions.

A Select Bibliography

(The printed and manuscript materials listed have been chosen from those cited in the notes because I believe they have especial value for anyone wishing additional information on the Catskills.)

PRINTED MAPS

Catskill Map, published by the New York State Conservation Department, Albany, 1957. This map revised from earlier editions going back to 1899, shows patent and lot lines as well as subdivisions often as small as an individual farm. State-owned lands are indicated.

Topographic Maps, U. S. Geological Survey, Washington, D.C., 1892–1967. The earlier editions show buildings and roads which often no longer exist; contour lines help in determining elevations.

Original maps used will be noted below under Public Records and Manuscripts.

THESES AND DISSERTATIONS

Gibbons, Kirstin Linde, *The Van Bergen Overmantel,* M.A. Thesis, 1966, State University of New York College at Oneonta, Cooperstown Graduate Program.

La Budde, Kenneth J., *The Mind of Thomas Cole,* Ph.D. Dissertation, University of Minnesota, 1954, University Microfilms, Ann Arbor.

Staley, Allen, *Byrdcliffe and the Maverick,* M.A. Thesis, Yale School of Fine Arts, 1960, New Haven, Conn.

PUBLIC RECORDS

Albany, Delaware, Greene, Sullivan, and Ulster County Clerks' Offices; Deed and Mortgage books, Incorporation Records. Maps placed on record are in separate volumes but many can be found in the earlier Deed Books.

Albany, Delaware, Greene, and Ulster County Surrogates Records, wills and probate records.

New York Colonial Manuscripts, Indorsed Land Papers, 1642–1803, 63 vols., many maps included, New York State Library. These manuscripts were indispensable in tracing the granting of the Hardenbergh Patent: they are often the original documents involved in making land grants, with official action noted on backs, hence "Indorsed." Much material relating to the Bradstreet claim is here.

New York State Census Records. These are the original sheets filed by census takers in the Delaware and Greene County Clerks' Offices. The 1855 census was useful in supplying data about industries.

Woodstock Town Clerk's Minute Book, 1787–1804, in possession of Town Clerk of Shandaken. Since the town of Woodstock as organized in 1787 included much of the Catskills to the west and north of the present town lines, this book was very helpful.

Inaccessible to me as I worked on *The Catskills* were the early records of Ulster County formerly stored in the basement of the County Clerk's Office. These records were turned over by the Board of Supervisors of Ulster, in a bizarre instance of official bungling, to the Paul Klapper Memorial Library, Queens College, Flushing. They are now in dead storage, with microfilms available at the Klapper Library and print-outs on file in the Ulster County Clerk's Office. These records contain much that bears on the early history of the Catskills.

MANUSCRIPTS AND MANUSCRIPT COLLECTIONS

Alexander, William, Papers; 5 vols., New-York Historical Society.

Bartram, John; "Journey to ye Cats Kill Mountains with Billy 1753"; 9 pp., Pennsylvania Historical Society.

Booth, Nathaniel, Diary, 1844–57, 2 vols., Senate House Museum Library, Kingston.

Bow, Lockwood, *The Hunter-Debrosses and Allied Families . . .* , New York, 1945, typescript, New York Public Library.

Butler, James; Diary no. 2, March 29, 1868–September 19, 1870. *Diary of a bluestone quarryman,* in author's possession.

Catskill Mountain Association, Treasurer's Account Book. Covers building and furnishing of first Catskill Mountain House, 1823–43; a few later and less interesting entries to 1886.

Catskill Mountain House, Registers, I vol., 1839–52, belonging to Harold Hargreave, Hurley, New York, 3 vols., 1853–69, 1902–13, and 1915–16 in Library of Greene County Historical Society.

Catskill Mountain Railway, Minute Books of Board of Directors, 1880–1915, 2 vols., Library of Greene County Historical Society.

Chase, Zephaniah, Account Book, 1785–1804. Furniture-making and other accounts of a Martha's Vineyard man who moved to the Catskills, New York State Library.

Clinton, DeWitt, Diary, 1803–28, 10 vols., New-York Historical Society.

Cockburn Papers, 1749–1850, 18 boxes. A very informative series of the surveys, field books, maps, letters, etc., of a surveyor, land agent, and speculator in the Hardenbergh Patent and elsewhere, New York State Library.

Cole, Thomas, Papers, ca. 1820–48, notebooks, letters, poems, essays, and a few sketches. Microfilms are in the New-York Historical Society Library. The originals which I used are in the New York State Library.

Livingston, Robert R., Collection, an immense and rich collection of some 21,000 items many of which are as yet uncatalogued. Letters, land papers, and account books tell of Livingston land activities among the Catskills. The maps can be found in the 43 boxes of uncatalogued materials, New-York Historical Society.

Town of Hunter, a typed copy from an unknown source in the Library of the Greene County Historical Society; believed to have been written ca. 1815. It sheds light on the Kaaterskill Clove and the mountains to the north before they had become well known to the outside world.

United States Military Philosophical Society, Minutes and Records, 1802–13, 4 vols. Includes Capt. Alden Partridge's measurements of Catskill elevations. New-York Historical Society.

White, Hervey, *Autobiography,* typescript of unpublished Ms., 1937, in Iowa Authors Collection, University of Iowa Libraries.

Printed Primary Sources

American Archives . . . A Documentary History . . . of the North American Colonies, 4th series, 6 vols. (March 7, 1774 to August 21, 1776), 5th series, 3 vols., May 3, 1776 to December 31, 1776; Washington, D.C., 1837–53.

Board of Water Supply of the City of New York, A General Description of the Catskill Water Supply, New York, 1940.

Clinton, George, *Public Papers,* Hugh Hastings and J. A. Holden, eds., 10 vols., Albany, 1899–1914. Valuable for American Revolution in Catskills.

Colonial Laws of New York from the Year 1664 to the Revolution, 5 vols., Albany, 1894–96.

Documentary History of the State of New York, E. B. O'Callaghan, ed., 4 vols., Albany, 1849–51.

Documents Relating to the Colonial History of the State of New York, E. B. O'Callaghan and B. Fernow, eds., 15 vols., Albany, 1849–81.

Grant, Mrs. Anne, *Memoirs of an American Lady with Sketches of Manners and Scenes in America* . . . first published, London, 1808; reprinted, Albany, 1876.

Johnson, Sir William, *Papers,* James Sullivan, A. C. Flick and M. W. Hamilton, eds., 15 vols., Albany, 1921–65.

Journals of the Provincial Congress, Provincial Convention of the State of New York . . . 1775–77, 2 vols., Albany, 1842.

Laws of the State of New York, W. P. Van Ness and John Woodworth, eds., 2 vols., Albany, 1813.

Narratives of New Netherland, 1609–64, J. Franklin Jameson, ed., New York, 1909.

New York State Forest Commission (after 1895 the Fisheries, Game, and Forest Commission), *Annual Reports,* Albany, 1888–97.

New York State Library, *Calendar of Council Minutes,* 1668–1783, Albany, 1902.

New York State, Secretary of, *Calendar of Historical Manuscripts in the Office of the Secretary of State,* E. B. O'Callaghan, ed., 2 vols., Albany, 1865–66.

Ramapo Improvement Company, *Proposal to the Sinking Fund Commission for a Supplementary Supply of Water for the City of New York,* New York, 1884.

Scheme of Lord Stirling's Lottery, a broadside, Philadelphia, in Pennsylvania Historical Society.

Smith, Richard, *A Tour of Four Great Rivers* (1769), Francis W. Halsey, ed., New York, 1906.

United States Census, 1790, Heads of Families, New York State, Washington, D.C., 1907.

Werner, E. A., *A Civil List and Constitutional History of the Colony and State,* Albany, 1888.

Local Books and Other Printed Materials

Adams, Joey, with Henry Tobias, *The Borscht Belt,* New York, 1966.

Brink, Benjamin Myer, *The Early History of Saugerties,* Kingston, 1902.

Brass Buttons and Leather Boots, prepared and published by the Sullivan County Civil War Commission, 1963.

Brown, the Reverend Clark, "A Topographical Description of Catskill," in the *Transactions of the Massachusetts Historical Society,* vol. 9, 1804, pp. 11–20.

Burroughs, John, *In the Catskills,* New York, 1911.

The Catskill Mountains, The Most Picturesque Mountain Region on the Globe, Ulster and Delaware Railroad, Rondout, various editions, 1891–1913.

"Catskill and the Catskill Region," in *Lippincott's Magazine,* vol. 24 (August and September 1879).

Chase, Sherret S., "The Catskills of New York, Past, Present and Potential," in *American Forests,* vol. 73, no. 8, p. 46 (August 1967).

Child, Hamilton, *A Gazetteer and Business Directory of Sullivan County for 1872–73,* Syracuse, 1872.

——, *A Gazetteer and Business Directory of Ulster County, New York, for 1871–72,* Syracuse, 1871.

Christman, Henry, *Tin Horns and Calico,* first published 1945, republished 1961.

Darton, H. N., "A Preliminary Report on the Geology of Ulster County," in the *Forty-seventh Annual Report of the State Museum,* Albany, 1894.

DeLabigarre, Peter, "Excursions on Our Blue Mountains," in *Transactions of the Society for Promoting Agriculture, Arts and Manufacturing in the State of New York,* vol. I, Part 2, 1794.

Delaware County, New York, A History of the Century 1797–1897, David Murray, ed., Delhi, New York, 1898.

DeLisser, R. Lionel, *Picturesque Catskills,* Northampton, Massachusetts, 1894.

——, *Picturesque Ulster* published in parts, Kingston, New York, 1896–1905.

Dwight, Henry, "Account of the Kaatskill Mountains" in *American Journal of Science,* vol. 2, 1820.

Gallt, J. A., *Dear Old Greene County,* Catskill, 1915.

Gould, Jay, *History of Delaware County and the Border Wars of New York . . . ,* Roxbury, 1856.

Greene County Historical Society, Publications, vol. I, *The "Old Times" Corner,* George H. Chadwick and Mr. J. V. V. Vedder, eds., Catskill, 1932, republished from the Catskill *Examiner.*

Guyot, Arnold, "On the Physical Structure and Hypsometry of the Catskill Mountain Region," in *American Journal of Science,* 3d series, vol. 19, no. 114 (June 1880).

Hanover, Crane, *Guide to Trout Fishing in the Catskill Mountains,* Outdoor Publications, Ithaca, New York, 1968.

Haring, H. A. *Our Catskill Mountains,* New York, 1931.

Helmer, William F., *O & W, The long life and slow death of the New York, Ontario & Western Railway,* Howell-North, Berkeley, 1959.

——, *Rip Van Winkle Railroads,* Howell-North, Berkeley, 1970.

History of Greene County, New York with Biographical Sketches of Its Prominent Men, New York, 1884.

History of Ulster County, A. T. Clearwater, ed., Kingston, 1907.

Hoffman, A. W., "The Passing of the Hemlock," in R. L. DeLisser, *Picturesque Ulster,* Kingston, 1896–1905.

Longstreth, Morris, *The Catskills,* New York, 1918.

McIntosh, Robert P., "The Forest Cover of the Catskill Mountain Region, New York as indicated by Land Survey Records," in *American Midland Naturalist,* vol. 68, no. 2 (October 1962).

McIntosh and Hurley, "The Spruce-fir Forests of the Catskill Mountains," in *Ecology,* vol. 45, no. 2 (Spring, 1964).

MacGahan, John A., *The Twilight Portfolio,* Twilight Park, 1942

Mack, Arthur C., *Enjoying the Catskills,* New York, 1950. Included are good panoramic views which make it easy for hikers to identify mountains.

Monroe, John D., *The Anti-Rent War in Delaware County, New York . . .* privately printed, 1940.

——, *Chapters in the History of Delaware County, New York,* published by Delaware Historical Association, 1949.

More, Caroline E., and Irma Mae Griffin, *The History of the Town of Roxbury,* Walton, New York, 1953.

Mulholland, W. D., *Catskill Trails,* State of New York, Conservation Department, Albany; various editions, the one used here, 1966.

Nason, Frank L., "Economic Geology of Ulster County, 1893," in *Forty-seventh Annual Report of the State Museum,* Albany, 1894.

Olde Ulster, Benjamin M. Brink, ed., 10 vols., published monthly, 1905–14; the many articles on local history unsigned and undocumented yet usually reliable.

Pierce, James, "A Memoir on the Catskill Mountains . . ." in *American Journal of Science,* vol. 6 (new series), 1823.

Pinckney, James D., *Reminiscences of Catskill, Local Sketches,* Catskill, 1868.

Pratt, Zadock, "The Dairy Farm Region of Greene and Orange Counties, New York, with some account of the Writer," in *United States Patent Office Report, Agriculture,* Washington, D.C., 1861. Written for Pratt, not by him.

———, "The Prattsville Tannery" in *Hunt's Merchant's Magazine,* vol. 17, no. 2 (August 1847). Like the preceding not actually written by Pratt.

Prout, Rev. Henry Hedges, *Old Times in Windham,* first published serially in Windham *Journal,* February 18, 1869 to March 31, 1870, republished as a book, Cornwallville, New York, 1970.

Quinlan, James E., *History of Sullivan County,* Liberty, New York, 1873, reprinted, South Fallsburgh, New York, 1965.

Rich, J. L., *Glacial Geology of the Catskills,* Albany, 1935.

Richards, T. Addison, "The Catskills," in *Harper's New Monthly Magazine,* no. 50, vol. 9 (July 1854).

Rockwell, Rev. Charles, *The Catskill Mountains and the Region Around,* New York, 1867, reprinted, Cornwallville, 1973.

Schoonmaker, Marius, *History of Kingston, New York, from Its Early Settlement to 1820,* New York, 1888.

Shultis, Neva, *From Sunset to Cock's Crow,* Woodstock, 1957.

Smith, Anita M., *Woodstock, History and Hearsay,* Saugerties, 1959.

Smith, Mabel Parker, *A Short History of Greene County,* Catskill, 1968.

Summer Homes Among the Mountains on the New York, Ontario & Western Railway (title varies), New York, Ontario & Western Railway, New York, 1878–1915.

Sylvester, Nathaniel B., *History of Ulster County, New York, with Illustrations and Biographical Sketches of Its Prominent Men and Pioneers,* Philadelphia, 1880.

Taub, Harold Jaedeker, *Waldorf-in-the-Catskills, The Grossinger Legend,* New York, 1952.

Thompson, Harold W., "Tales of the Catskill Bear Hunters in New York," *New York Folklore Quarterly,* Summer, 1949, pp. 128–33.

Van Buren, Augustus H., *A History of Ulster County Under the Dominion of the Dutch,* Kingston, 1923.

Van Loan, Walton, *Van Loan's Catskill Mountain Guide with Bird's-eye View, Maps,* etc., New York and Catskill, various editions, 1879–1915.

Van Zandt, Roland, "The Catskill Mountain House," New Brunswick, 1966.

Vedder, Jessie Van Vechten, ed., *History of Greene County,* vol. I, 1651–1800 (no more published), Catskill, 1927.

Wakefield, Manville, *To the Mountains by Rail,* Grahamsville, New York, 1970.

Wood, Leslie C., *Rafting on the Delaware,* Livingston Manor, 1934.

Woodstock Historical Society, *Publications,* nos. 1 to 17, Woodstock, 1930–54.

Zimm, Louise Hasbrouck, "Ulster County," in vol. I, *Southeastern New York,* 3 vols., New York, 1946.

NEWSPAPERS

Albany *Argus;* Albany *Evening Journal,* New York State Library.

Catskill *Examiner;* Catskill *Messenger;* Catskill *Recorder,* Greene County Historical Society.

Delaware *Gazette;* Cannon Free Library, Delhi, New York.

Greene County *Whig;* Greene County Historical Society.

Kingston *Daily Freeman;* Kingston *Daily Leader;* Kingston *Democratic Journal;* Kingston *Press;* all on microfilm in Kingston Area Library.

New York Statesman; New York *Tribune;* Newspaper Division New York Public Library.

New York *Times,* microfilm edition, New York State Library.

Pine Hill *Sentinel,* office Ulster County Community College.

Poughkeepsie *Eagle,* Adriance Memorial Library, Poughkeepsie.

Saugerties *Daily Post,* Sumner Hall, Saugerties.

Saugerties *Telegraph,* Saugerties Public Library.

Stamford *Mirror,* Churchill Memorial Library, Stamford, New York.

Rondout *Courier,* Senate House Museum Library, Kingston.

Ulster *Republican,* Kingston Area Library.

Ulster *Sentinel,* Senate House Museum Library.

Index

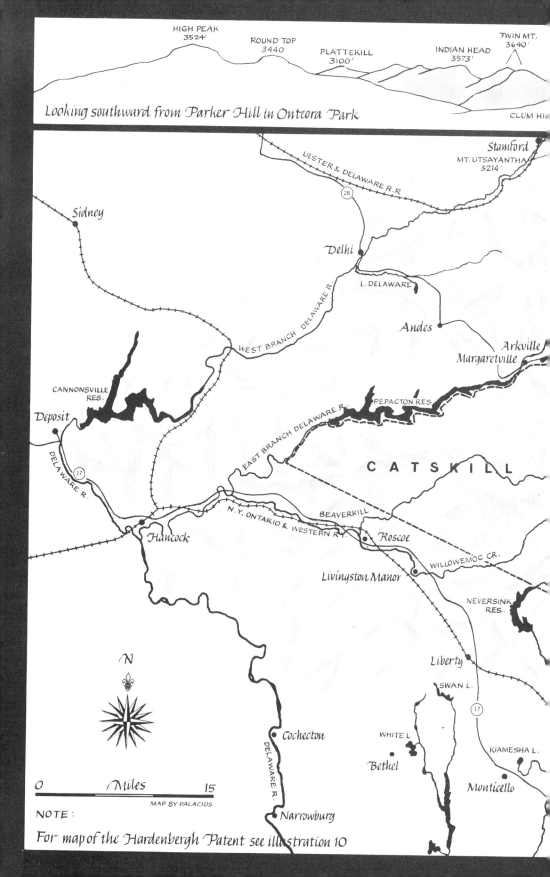

Looking southward from Parker Hill in Onteora Park

HIGH PEAK
3524'

ROUND TOP
3440'

PLATTEKILL
3100'

INDIAN HEAD
3573'

TWIN MT.
3640'

CLUM HI

Stamford

MT. UTSAYANTHA
3214'

ULSTER & DELAWARE R.R

28

Sidney

Delhi

L. DELAWARE

Andes

Arkville
Margaretville

WEST BRANCH DELAWARE R.

CANNONSVILLE
RES.

Deposit

PEPACTON RES.

EAST BRANCH DELAWARE R.

C A T S K I L L

DELAWARE R.

17

BEAVERKILL

N.Y. ONTARIO & WESTERN R.Y.

Roscoe

Hancock

WILLOWEMOC CR.

Livingston Manor

NEVERSINK
RES.

N

Liberty

SWAN L.

17

Cochecton

WHITE L.

KIAMESHA L.

DELAWARE R.

Bethel

0   Miles   15

MAP BY PALACIOS

Monticello

NOTE:

Narrowburg

For map of the Hardenbergh Patent see illustration 10